Radi Doncheva

INTERNET AND WORLD WIDE WEB

HOW TO PROGRAM

Deitel & Deitel
Books and Cyber Classrooms
published by
Prentice Hall

Visual Studio® Series
Getting Started with Microsoft® Visual C++™ 6
with an Introduction to MFC
Visual Basic® 6 How to Program
Getting Started with Microsoft® Visual J++® 1.1

How to Program Series
Internet and World Wide Web How to Program
Java™ How to Program, 3/E
C How to Program, 2/E
C++ How to Program, 2/E
Visual Basic® 6 How to Program

Multimedia Cyber Classroom Series
Internet and World Wide Web Multimedia Cyber Classroom
Java™ Multimedia Cyber Classroom, 3/E
C & C++ Multimedia Cyber Classroom, 2/E
Visual Basic® 6 Multimedia Cyber Classroom

The Complete Training Course Series
The Complete Internet and World Wide Web Training Course
The Complete Java™ Training Course, 3/E
The Complete C++ Training Course, 2/E
The Complete Visual Basic® 6 Training Course

For continuing updates on Prentice Hall and Deitel & Associates, Inc. publications visit the Prentice Hall web site

http//www.prenhall.com/deitel

To communicate with the authors, send email to:

deitel@deitel.com

For information on corporate on-site seminars and public seminars offered by Deitel & Associates, Inc. worldwide, visit:

http://www.deitel.com

INTERNET AND WORLD WIDE WEB
HOW TO PROGRAM

H. M. Deitel
Deitel & Associates, Inc.

P. J. Deitel
Deitel & Associates, Inc.

T. R. Nieto
Deitel & Associates, Inc.

PRENTICE HALL, Upper Saddle River, New Jersey 07458

Acquisitions Editor: ***Petra J. Recter***
Production Editor: ***Camille Trentacoste***
Chapter Opener, Icon and Cover Designer: ***Tamara Newnam Cavallo***
Art Director and Interior Designer: ***Heather Scott***
Buyer: ***Pat Brown***
Editorial Assistant: ***Sarah Burrows***

A Pearson Education Company
Upper Saddle River, New Jersey 07458

Printed in the United States of America

10 9 8 7 6 5 4 3 2 1

ISBN 0-13-016143-8

Prentice-Hall International (UK) Limited, London
Prentice-Hall of Australia Pty. Limited, Sydney
Prentice-Hall Canada Inc., Toronto
Prentice-Hall Hispanoamericana, S.A., Mexico
Prentice-Hall of India Private Limited, New Delhi
Prentice-Hall of Japan, Inc., Tokyo
Prentice-Hall Singapore Pte. Ltd., Singapore
Editora Prentice-Hall do Brasil, Ltda., Rio de Janeiro

TO

Dr. James Gips
Professor of Computer Science, Boston College

For the thousands of students who have benefited from your unswerving commitment to excellence in teaching.

For the hundreds of faculty and academic administrators who have the deepest respect and appreciation for your integrity and your colleagueship.

For the people with multiple disabilities and their families whose lives have been profoundly improved by your academic research.

Sincerely,

Harvey, Barbara, Paul and Abbey Deitel
Tem Nieto

Contents

Illustrations

2 Introduction to Internet Explorer 5 and the World Wide Web

3 Introduction to HyperText Markup Language 4 (HTML 4)

4 Intermediate HTML 4

5 Paint Shop Pro

11 JavaScript/JScript: Functions

12 JavaScript/JScript: Arrays

15 Dynamic HTML: Object Model and Collections

16 Dynamic HTML: Event Model

17 Dynamic HTML: Filters and Transitions

18 Dynamic HTML: Data Binding with Tabular Data Control

19 Dynamic HTML: Structured Graphics ActiveX Control

20 Dynamic HTML: Path, Sequencer and Sprite ActiveX Controls

21 Multimedia: Audio, Video, Speech Synthesis and Recognition

22 Dynamic HTML: Client-Side Scripting with VBScript

23 Electronic Commerce and Security

26 Active Server Pages (ASP)

Preface

Live in fragments no longer. Only connect.
Edward Morgan Forster

Welcome to the exciting world of Internet and World Wide Web programming. This book is by an old guy and two young guys. The old guy (HMD; Massachusetts Institute of Technology 1967) has been programming and/or teaching programming for 38 years. The two young guys (PJD; MIT 1991 and TRN; MIT 1992) have each been programming and/or teaching programming for 18 years. The old guy programs and teaches from experience; the young guys do so from an inexhaustible reserve of energy. The old guy wants clarity; the young guys want performance. The old guy seeks elegance and beauty; the young guys want results. We got together to produce a book we hope you will find informative, challenging and entertaining.

The Internet and the World Wide Web are evolving rapidly, if not explosively. This creates tremendous challenges for us as authors, for our publisher—Prentice Hall, for instructors, and for students and professional people.

The World Wide Web now increases the prominence of the Internet in information systems, strategic planning and implementation. Organizations want to integrate the Internet "seamlessly" into their information systems.

Why We Wrote *Internet and World Wide Web How to Program*

Dr. Harvey M. Deitel taught introductory programming courses in universities for 20 years with an emphasis on developing clearly written, well-designed programs. Much of what is taught in these courses is the basic principles of programming with an emphasis on the effective use of control structures and functionalization. We present these topics in *Internet and World Wide Web How to Program* exactly the way HMD has done in his university courses. Our experience has been that students handle the material in the early chapters on control structures and functions in about the same manner as they handle introductory Pascal or C courses. There is one noticeable difference though: students are highly motivated by the fact that they are learning three leading-edge scripting languages (JavaScript, VBScript and Perl) and a leading-edge programming paradigm (object-based programming) that will be immediately useful to them as they leave the university environment for a world in which the Internet and the World Wide Web have a massive new prominence.

Our goal was clear: to produce a textbook for introductory university-level courses in computer programming for students with little or no programming experience while offering the depth and the rigorous treatment of theory and practice demanded by traditional, upper-level programming courses and satisfying professionals' needs. To meet this goal, we produced a comprehensive book that patiently teaches the principles of control structures, object-based programming and various markup languages (HTML, Dynamic HTML and XML) and scripting languages (JavaScript, VBScript and Perl). After mastering the material in this book, students will be well prepared to take advantage of the Internet and the Web as they take upper-level programming courses and enter industry.

Internet and World Wide Web How to Program is the fifth book in the Deitel/Prentice Hall How to Program series. It is distinguished by its focus on Web-based application development (emphasized in our server-side treatment). We wrote it fresh on the heels of Java How to Program: Third Edition.

We have emphasized color throughout the book. Almost from the start, the World Wide Web has been a colorful, multimedia-intensive medium. It appeals to both our visual and auditory senses. Someday it may even appeal to our senses of touch, taste and smell as well! We suggested to our publisher, Prentice Hall, that they should publish this book in color. The use of color in this book is crucial to understanding and appreciating scores of the book's programs. We hope it helps you develop more appealing Web-based applications.

Many books about the Web concentrate on developing attractive Web pages. We certainly discuss that subject intensely. However, the key focus of this book is really Web-based applications development. Our audiences want to build real-world, industrial-strength, Web-based applications. These audiences care about good looking Web pages. But they also care about client/server systems, databases, distributed computing, etc.

Many books about the Web are reference manuals with exhaustive listings of features. That is not our style. We concentrate on creating real applications. We provide the live-code examples on the CD accompanying this book so that you can run the applications, and see and hear for yourself the multimedia outputs. You can interact with our game programs and art programs.

The Web is an artist's paradise. Your creativity is your only limitation. But the Web contains so many tools and mechanisms to leverage your abilities that even if you are not artistically inclined, you can still create stunning outputs. Our goal is to help you master these tools and mechanisms so that you can maximize your creativity and development abilities. Not only will the Web help you increase your productivity, but it will also open up to you whole new areas of expertise that you never thought you had.

We are excited about the enormous range of possibilities the Internet and the Web offer. We have worked hard to create hundreds of useful live-code examples to help you master Internet and Web programming quickly and effectively. All of the code examples are on the accompanying disk and are available for free download from our Web site:

http://www.deitel.com/

Dynamic HTML is a means of adding "dynamic content" to World-Wide-Web pages. Instead of Web pages with only text and static graphics, Web pages "come alive" with audios, videos, animations, interactivity, and three-dimensional imaging. Dynamic HTML's features are precisely what businesses and organizations need to meet today's information processing requirements. So we immediately viewed Dynamic HTML as having the potential to become one of the world's key general-purpose programming languages.

People want to communicate. People need to communicate. Sure, they have been communicating since the dawn of civilization, but computer communications have been mostly limited to digits, alphabetic characters and special characters. The next major wave in communications is surely multimedia. People want to transmit pictures and they want those pictures to be in color. They want to transmit voices, sounds and audio clips. They want to transmit full-motion color video. And at some point, they will insist on three-dimensional, moving-image transmission. Our current flat, two-dimensional televisions will eventually be replaced with three-dimensional versions that turn our living rooms into "theaters-in-the-round." Actors will perform their roles as if we were watching live theater. Our living rooms will be turned into miniature sports stadiums. Our business offices will enable video conferencing among colleagues half a world apart as if they were sitting around one conference table. The possibilities are intriguing and the Internet is sure to play a key role in making many of these possibilities become reality.

There have been predictions that the Internet will eventually replace the telephone system. Why stop there? It could also replace radio and television as we know them today. It's not hard to imagine the Internet and the World Wide Web replacing the newspaper with completely electronic news media. Many newspapers and magazines already offer Web-based versions, some fee based and some free. Increased bandwidth is making it possible to stream audio and video over the Web. Companies and even individuals already run their own Web-based radio and television stations. Just a few decades ago, there were only a few television stations. Today, standard cable boxes accommodate about 100 stations. In a few more years, we will have access to thousands of stations broadcasting over the Web worldwide. This textbook you are reading may someday appear in a museum alongside radios, TVs and newspapers in an "early media of ancient civilization" exhibit.

One exciting possibility is that people with disabilities will be able to take advantage of computing and communications through the Internet and especially through the Web. In this regard, the World Wide Web Consortium (W3C) is pursuing its *Web Accessibility Initiative*. Information about the Web Accessibility Initiative is available at

`http://www.w3.org/WAI/`

The goal of the WAI is to transform the Web into a medium in which all people, are able to access and use the technology and information available.

Teaching Approach

Internet and World Wide Web How to Program contains a rich collection of examples, exercises, and projects drawn from many fields to provide the student with a chance to solve interesting real-world problems. The book concentrates on the principles of good software engineering and stresses program clarity. We avoid arcane terminology and syntax specifications in favor of teaching by example. The book is written by educators who spend most of their time teaching edge-of-the-practice topics in industry classrooms worldwide. The text emphasizes good pedagogy.

Live-Code Teaching Approach

The book is loaded with hundreds of live-code examples. This is the focus of the way we teach and write about programming, and the focus of each of our multimedia *Cyber Classrooms* as well. Each new concept is presented in the context of a complete, working program immediately followed by one or more windows showing the program's input/output dialog. We call this style of teaching and writing our ***live-code approach***. *We use the language to teach the language.* Reading these programs is much like entering and running them on a computer.

Internet and World Wide Web How to Program "jumps right in" with HTML programming from Chapter 3, then rapidly proceeds with programming in JavaScript, Microsoft's Dynamic HTML, VBScript, Perl and XML. Students really want to "cut to the chase." There is great stuff to be done in all these languages so let's get right to it! Web programming is not trivial by any means, but it's fun and students can see immediate results. Students can get graphical, animated, multimedia-based, audio-intensive, database-intensive, network-based programs running quickly through "reusable components." They can implement impressive projects. They can be much more creative and productive in a one- or two-semester course than is possible in introductory courses taught in conventional programming languages such as C, C++, Visual Basic and Java.

World Wide Web Access

All of the code for *Internet and World Wide Web How to Program* (and our other publications) is on the Internet free for download at the Deitel & Associates, Inc. Web site

`http://www.deitel.com/`

Please download all the code then run each program as you read the text. Make changes to the code examples and immediately see the effects of those changes. It's a great way to learn programming by doing programming. [*Note:* You must respect the fact that this is copyrighted material. Feel free to use it as you study, but you may not republish any portion of it in any form without explicit permission from Prentice Hall and the authors.]

Objectives

Each chapter begins with a statement of *Objectives.* This tells the student what to expect and gives the student an opportunity, after reading the chapter, to determine if he or she has met these objectives. It is a confidence builder and a source of positive reinforcement.

Quotations

The learning objectives are followed by quotations. Some are humorous, some are philosophical, and some offer interesting insights. Our students enjoy relating the quotations to the chapter material. Many of the quotations are worth a "second look" *after* you read each chapter.

Outline

The chapter *Outline* helps the student approach the material in top-down fashion. This, too, helps students anticipate what is to come and set a comfortable and effective learning pace.

10,889 Lines of Code in 202 Example Programs (with Program Outputs)

We present features in the context of complete, working programs. This is the focus of our teaching and our writing. We call it our "live-code" approach. Each program is followed by the outputs produced when the document is rendered and its scripts are executed. This enables the student to confirm that the programs run as expected. Reading the book carefully is much like entering and running these programs on a computer. The programs range from just a few lines of code to substantial examples with several hundred lines of code. Students should download all the code for the book from our Web site and run each program while studying that program in the text. The programs are available at **`http://www.deitel.com/`**.

499 Illustrations/Figures

An abundance of charts, line drawings and program outputs is included. The discussion of control structures, for example, features carefully drawn flowcharts. [*Note:* We do not teach flowcharting as a program development tool, but we do use a brief, flowchart-oriented presentation to specify the precise operation of JavaScript's control structures.]

367 Programming Tips

We have included programming tips to help students focus on important aspects of program development. We highlight hundreds of these tips in the form of *Good Programming Practices*, *Common Programming Errors*, *Testing and Debugging Tips, Performance Tips*, *Portability Tips*, *Software Engineering Observations* and *Look-and-Feel Observations.* These tips and practices represent the best we have gleaned from a combined seven decades of programming and teaching experience. One of our students—a mathematics major—told us that she feels this approach is like the highlighting of axioms, theorems, and corollaries in mathematics books; it provides a foundation on which to build good software.

77 Good Programming Practices

When we teach introductory courses, we state that the "buzzword" of each course is "clarity," and we highlight as *Good Programming Practices* techniques for writing programs that are clearer, more understandable, more debuggable, and more maintainable.

95 Common Programming Errors

Students learning a language tend to make certain errors frequently. Focusing the students' attention on these *Common Programming Errors* helps students avoid making the same errors. It also helps reduce the long lines outside instructors' offices during office hours!

30 Testing and Debugging Tips

When we first designed this "tip type," we thought we would use it strictly to describe how to test and debug programs. In fact, many of the tips simply describe aspects of markup languages and scripting languages that reduce the likelihood of introducing "bugs" in the first place and thus simplify the testing and debugging process for programs.

36 Performance Tips

In our experience, teaching students to write clear and understandable programs is by far the most important goal for a first programming course. But students want to write the programs that run the fastest, use the least memory, require the smallest number of keystrokes, or dazzle in other nifty ways. Students really care about performance. They want to know what they can do to "turbo charge" their programs. So we have included many *Performance Tips* that highlight opportunities for improving program performance.

25 Portability Tips

Some programmers assume that if they implement a Web application, the application will automatically be "perfectly" portable across all browsers. Unfortunately, this is not always the case. We include *Portability Tips* to help students write portable code, and also to provide insights on how complex an issue portability truly is.

87 Software Engineering Observations

The *Software Engineering Observations* highlight architectural and design issues that affect the construction of software systems, especially large-scale systems. Much of what the student learns here will be useful in upper-level courses and in industry as the student begins to work with large, complex real-world systems.

17 Look-and-Feel Observations

We provide *Look-and-Feel Observations* to highlight graphical user interface conventions. These observations help students design their own graphical user interfaces to conform with industry norms.

Summary (1111 Summary bullets)

Each chapter ends with additional pedagogical devices. We present a thorough, bullet-list-style *Summary* of the chapter. On average, there are 38 summary bullets per chapter. This helps the students review and reinforce key concepts.

Terminology (2445 Terms)

We include in a *Terminology* section an alphabetized list of the important terms defined in the chapter—again, further reinforcement. On average, there are 84 terms per chapter.

Summary of Tips, Practices and Errors

For ease of reference, we collect at the back of each chapter the *Good Programming Practices, Common Programming Errors, Testing and Debugging Tips, Performance Tips, Portability Tips, Software Engineering Observations* and *Look-and-Feel Observations*.

498 Self-Review Exercises and Answers (Count Includes Separate Parts)

Extensive self-review exercises and answers are included for self-study. This gives the student a chance to build confidence with the material and prepare for the regular exercises. Students should attempt all the self-review exercises and check their answers.

590 Exercises (Solutions in Instructor's Manual; Count Includes Separate Parts)

Each chapter concludes with a substantial set of exercises including simple recall of important terminology and concepts; writing individual statements; writing small portions of methods and classes; writing complete methods, classes, applets and applications; and writing major term projects. The large number of exercises across a wide variety of areas enables instructors to tailor their courses to the unique needs of their audiences and to vary course assignments each semester. Instructors can use these exercises to form homework assignments, short quizzes and major examinations. The solutions for most of the exercises are included in the *Instructor's Manual* and on the disks *available only to instructors* through their Prentice-Hall representatives. [*Note:* **Please do not write to us requesting the instructor's manual. Distribution of this publication is strictly limited to college professors teaching from the book. Instructors may obtain the solutions manual only from their regular Prentice Hall representatives. We regret that we cannot provide the solutions to professionals.]** Solutions to approximately half of the exercises are included on the *Internet and World Wide Web Multimedia Cyber Classroom* CD (available in bookstores and computer stores; please see the last few pages of this book or visit our Web site at **`http://www.deitel.com/`** for ordering instructions).

Approximately 5800 Index Entries (with approximately 8000 Page References)
We have included an extensive *Index* at the back of the book. This helps the student find any term or concept by keyword. The *Index* is useful to people reading the book for the first time and is especially useful to practicing programmers who use the book as a reference. Each of the terms in the *Terminology* sections appears in the *Index* (along with many more index items from each chapter). Students can use the *Index* in conjunction with the *Terminology* sections to be sure they have covered the key material of each chapter.

"Double Indexing" of All Live-Code Examples and Exercises
Internet and World Wide Web How to Program has 202 live-code examples and 590 exercises (including parts). Many of the exercises are challenging problems or projects requiring substantial effort. We have "double indexed" each of the live-code examples and most of the more challenging projects. For every source-code program in the book, we took the file name and indexed it both alphabetically and as a subindex item under "Examples." This makes it easier to find examples using particular features. The more substantial exercises, such as "Maze Generator and Walker," are indexed both alphabetically (in this case under "M") and as subindex items under "Exercises."

Bibliography
An extensive bibliography of books, articles and online documentation is included to encourage further reading.

Tour of the Book

As we write this, there exist few formal university courses dedicated solely to programming for the Internet and the World Wide Web. This book is our view of an Internet and World Wide Web programming course—we felt that writing a book on this subject would prompt faculty to teach these topics.

We welcome any feedback you may have about how to improve this book for future editions. In addition, please let us know if you have Netscape-specific requirements that we might be able to help with so that you may effectively use the book in your classes.

The student should have two key projects in mind while reading through this book, namely: Developing a personal Web site using simple HTML markup and JavaScript coding, and developing a complete client/server, database-intensive Web-based application using techniques taught throughout this book.

The following brief walk-through discusses the exciting technologies covered in the book. Chapter 1 contains a more detailed walk-through.

In Chapter 1 we present some historical information about computers and computer programming, as well as introductory information about the Internet and the World Wide

Web. In Chapter 2, we introduce Microsoft's powerful Internet Explorer 5 (IE5) browser and several of its included programs such as Chat, NetMeeting and Outlook Express (included on the CD for both the professional and academic markets).

Chapters 3 and 4 present HTML 4 from the introductory through intermediate levels. We introduce the basics of creating Web pages in HTML using a technique we call the *live-code approach.* Every concept is presented in the context of a complete working HTML/JavaScript/Dynamic HTML document (or Web page) that is immediately followed by the screen output produced when that HTML document is rendered by Internet Explorer 5. By the end of Chapter 4, students will be creating substantial, visually appealing Web sites.

Chapter 5 is an introduction to Jasc Software's Paint Shop Pro 5 (a 30-day evaluation copy of the software is included on the CD). Great Web pages often come alive with rich graphics and multimedia. This chapter explains how to use many of Paint Shop Pro's powerful graphics capabilities to create images that can add pizzazz to Web pages.

In Chapter 6, we introduce Microsoft FrontPage Express—a simple WYSIWYG HTML editor that allows you to create Web pages quickly and easily.

Chapter 7 is an Introduction to Microsoft Visual InterDev 6, a heavy-duty, industrial-strength integrated development environment for developing Internet and World-Wide-Web based applications. In this chapter, we discuss the basics of the InterDev environment. In later chapters of the book, you can use InterDev with various server-side technologies such as Active Server Pages to quickly build powerful Web-based applications. [*Note:* Although Chapter 7 is the only chapter of this book that uses Visual InterDev, you can (optionally) choose to use InterDev throughout the book. Readers not interested in using InterDev should simply skip Chapter 7.]

Chapters 8 through 13 introduce programming and scripting for nonprogrammers. We use JavaScript to introduce programming, control structures, functions, event handling, arrays and objects (object-based programming). We then use the features of JavaScript in Chapters 14 through 21 to demonstrate dynamic manipulation of We page contents. JavaScript enables us to present fundamental computer-science concepts at the same depth as other programming languages (such as C, C++, Java and Visual Basic), but in the exciting context of the Internet and World Wide Web.

[*Note:* JavaScript was created by Netscape. Microsoft's version is called JScript. The languages are close. Netscape, Microsoft and other companies are cooperating with the European Computer Manufacturer's Association (ECMA) to produce a universal, client-side scripting language, the current version of which is referred to as ECMA-262. JavaScript and JScript each conform to this standard. We tested the JavaScript programs in Chapters 8 through 12. Each of these programs works in the latest Netscape and Microsoft browsers.]

In Chapters 14 through 20 we teach Dynamic HTML. In these chapters we cover Cascading Style Sheets (CSS), the DHTML object model and collections, the event model, filters and transitions, data binding with the Tabular Data Control, and four ActiveX controls useful for enhancing your page's visual appeal—the Structured Graphics Control, Sprite Control, Sequencer Control, and Path Control. Dynamic HTML is stunning! In these chapters, students will turn their Web sites into dynamic masterpieces. From sorting data on the client side to applying dynamic light filters to images, Dynamic HTML is a truly powerful way to add glitz, glimmer and animation in a way that minimizes the load on your servers and the Internet to your Web pages.

Chapter 21, "Multimedia", is a delight! We focus on the explosion of audio, video and speech technology appearing on the Web. Students will learn how to add sound and video to their Web pages. They learn how to add animated characters which handle both speech synthesis and voice recognition with Microsoft Agent. This chapter demonstrates how to incorporate streaming audio, specifically for the *RealNetworks RealPlayer* into a Web page. We also demonstrate an example of embedding VRML, the three-dimensional Virtual Reality Modeling Language.

In Chapter 22, we assume the reader is now familiar with the principles of programming and scripting (from studying and using JavaScript in Chapters 8 through 21), so we present Microsoft's *VBScript* condensed into a single chapter. VBScript is a peer scripting language to JavaScript. It is a subset of Visual Basic. It can certainly be used for client-side scripting, but because it is a Microsoft-specific technology you would probably use it for client-side supporting only on Microsoft Intranet-based applications. VBScript has become the de facto standard for writing server-side *Active Server Pages (ASP),* which we discuss in detail in Chapter 26. Because we need to discuss VBScript before ASP, we have chosen to include this chapter as the last in our discussion of client-side scripting (so in this book you see VBScript being used for both client-side, and server-side scripting).

Chapter 23, "Electronic Commerce and Security," is a unique chapter for an introductory programming textbook. The Web has caused a complete rethinking of the way systems should most effectively be designed and implemented. E-Commerce is hot! Businesses are reinventing themselves online, incorporating Internet and Web technology into existing systems and new information systems design. The trade publications are abuzz with e-commerce. This chapter discusses the fundamentals of conducting business on the Internet and the Web. Our goal is to give students an understanding of how important this topic is now and how it will continue to be important as they pursue their careers. We present a number of case studies, with the key goal of highlighting the common core of technologies needed to implement e-commerce systems. We emphasize the importance of Internet and Web technology, database technology, security technology and others. Then in the remainder of the server-side programming chapters, we put many of these technologies to work in constructing actual multi-tiered, client/server, database-intensive Web-based systems.

In Chapter 24, we present several major Web servers in use today. We focus on setting up Microsoft's Personal Web Server (PWS) as a simple server with which students can begin to grasp the complexities involved in running a Web site. Three other Web servers—Microsoft's Internet Information Server (IIS), the W3C's Java-based Jigsaw Server and Apache (the most widely used server on the Web today)—are presented later in that chapter, with overviews and directions should the student desire to move past the limited functionality and configurability of Personal Web Server. ***[Note: Although we mention these server software packages in our book, our organization does not provide support for them.]***

A common topic among all three server technologies is the ability to interact with databases. Databases are crucial to any intensive e-commerce application—maintaining customer lists, product lists, user names and passwords. To that effect, our book offers discussions of a variety of database technologies. In Chapter 17, we cover Microsoft's Tabular Data Control (TDC), which uses an ActiveX control to sort and filter data directly on the client side. Chapter 25 is devoted exclusively to database topics, including an introduction to the Structured Query Language (SQL), the de facto language for querying databases), a discussion of ActiveX Data Objects (ADO), Open Database Connectivity (ODBC) and Remote Data Services (RDS), which complements the TDC by allowing the client effect state changes in the server-side database. The chapters devoted to ASP, Perl, and Java Servlets all cover implementing database access smoothly into your Web-based applications.

In Chapter 26 we discuss Microsoft's Active Server Pages (ASP), the first of the three most popular server-side software development paradigms the book presents. Active Server Pages can be programmed in a variety of languages—by far the most popular of these is Microsoft's VBScript which we discuss thoroughly in Chapter 22. In a typical *multitiered Web-based application*, there is a *top-tier* containing the code that interacts directly with the user. This tier, called the *client*, is usually the browser (such as IE5) rendering a Web-page and executing scripting commands. These commands can be implemented in a variety of languages, but JavaScript has become the de facto standard universal *client-side scripting language*. Microsoft offers its version of JavaScript which is called *JScript*. We have tried to use only the common portions of these languages for the client-side scripting code in the book. The *bottom tier* is the database containing the organization's information. The *middle tier*, called the *server*, contains the *business logic*. Active Server Pages is Microsoft's technology for implementing middle-tier business logic. This a crucial chapter for those readers who will want to implement substantial Web-based applications.

Chapter 27 presents a nice introduction to CGI and Perl, including many real-world, live-code examples and discussions, including demonstrations of some of the most recent features of each of these technologies. As an example, we use Perl's *regular expressions* and file I/O capabilities to construct a simple search engine.

Chapter 28 covers one of the hottest new technologies—XML. XML is a language for creating new markup languages. The possible uses for XML are endless. Chess fans might want to transmit marked-up chess moves—in this chapter we do just that, using JavaScript to interpret XML markup into moving images of chess pieces across a board in an HTML Web page!

In Chapter 29 we discuss Java servlets, a third popular way of building the server side of Web-based applications (the other two are ASP and Perl/CGI). This chapter is included as a "bonus section" for the portion of our audience that is familiar with Java.

Internet and World Wide Web How to Program Companion CD

The CD-ROM at the end of this book contains Microsoft's Internet Explorer 5 and Personal Web Server 4, JASC Software's Paint Shop Pro 5 (30-day evaluation version) and Adobe Acrobat Reader 4. The CD also contains the book's examples and an HTML Web page with links to the Deitel & Associates, Inc. Web site, the Prentice Hall Web site and the many Web sites listed in the Web resources sections of several chapters. If you have access to the Internet, this Web page can be loaded into your World Wide Web browser to give you quick access to all the resources.

For complete CD-ROM installation instructions, use your browser to read the file **`WELCOME.HTM`** on the CD. We will be putting additional information on our Web site: **`http://www.deitel.com/`**. We do not provide support for the software application programs. However, if you have technical questions about the installation of the CD, please email **`media.support@pearsoned.com`**. A timely response will be returned to you.

Internet and World Wide Web Programming Multimedia Cyber Classroom and The Complete Internet and World Wide Web Programming Training Course

We have prepared an interactive, CD-ROM-based, software version of *Internet and World Wide Web How to Program* called the *Internet and World Wide Web Programming Multimedia Cyber Classroom.* It is loaded with features for learning and reference. The *Cyber Classroom* is wrapped with the textbook at a discount in *The Complete Internet and World Wide Web Programming Training Course.* If you already have the book and would like to purchase the *Internet and World Wide Web Programming Multimedia Cyber Classroom* separately, please call 1-800-811-0912 and ask for ISBN# 0-13-016842-4.

The CD has an introduction with the authors overviewing the *Cyber Classroom*'s features. The 202 live-code example programs in the textbook truly "come alive" in the *Cyber Classroom.* If you are viewing a program and want to execute it, simply click on the lightning bolt icon and the program will run. You will immediately see—and hear for the audio-based multimedia programs—the program's outputs. If you want to modify a program and see and hear the effects of your changes, simply click the floppy-disk icon that causes the source code to be "lifted off" the CD and "dropped into" one of your own directories so that you can edit the text, recompile the program and try out your new version. Click the speaker icon for an audio that talks about the program and "walks you through" the code.

The *Cyber Classroom* also provides navigational aids including extensive hyperlinking. The Web browser remembers in a "history list" recent sections you have visited and allows you to move forward or backward through them. The thousands of index entries are hyperlinked to their text occurrences. You can key in a term using the "Search" feature and the *Cyber Classroom* will locate occurrences of that term throughout the text. The *Table of Contents* entries are "hot," so clicking a chapter name takes you to that chapter.

Students like the hundreds of solved problems from the textbook that are included with the *Cyber Classroom.* Studying and running these extra programs is a great way for students to enhance their learning experience.

Students and professional users of our *Cyber Classrooms* tell us they like the interactivity and that the *Cyber Classroom* is an effective reference because of the extensive hyperlinking and other navigational features. We recently had an email from a person who said that he lives "in the boonies" and cannot take a live course at a university, so the *Cyber Classroom* was a nice solution to his educational needs.

Professors tell us that their students enjoy using the *Cyber Classroom*, spend more time on the course and master more of the material than in textbook-only courses. Also, the *Cyber Classroom* helps shrink lines outside professors' offices during office hours. We have also published the *C++ Multimedia Cyber Classroom (2/e),* the *Visual Basic 6 Multimedia Cyber Classroom* and the *Java 2 Multimedia Cyber Classroom (3/e).*

Acknowledgments

One of the great pleasures of writing a textbook is acknowledging the efforts of the many people whose names may not appear on the cover, but whose hard work, cooperation, friendship and understanding were crucial to the production of the book.

Barbara Deitel managed the preparation of the manuscript and coordinated with Prentice Hall the production of the book. Barbara's efforts are by far the most painstaking of what we do to develop books. She has infinite patience. She handled the endless details involved in publishing the four-color text book; the instructor's manual and the 650-megabyte CD *Cyber Classroom.* She used FrameMaker page-layout software to prepare the book. Barbara mastered this complex software package and did a marvelous job giving the book its clean style. She spent long hours researching the quotes at the beginning of each chapter. Barbara prepared the *Table of Contents*, the *List of Illustrations* and every one of the approximately 8000 page references in the index. She did all this in parallel with handling her extensive financial and administrative responsibilities at Deitel & Associates, Inc.

Abbey Deitel—a graduate of Carnegie Mellon University's industrial management program—Chief Operating Officer of Deitel & Associates, Inc., co-authored Chapter 23, "Electronic Commerce and Security," and suggested the title for the book.

We would like to thank Paul Brandano, Jacob Ellis and David Gusovsky—participants in our Deitel & Associates, Inc. *College Internship Program.* Paul Brandano, a senior in Marketing at Boston College's Carroll School of Management—co-authored Chapter 23, "Electronic Commerce and Security." Jacob Ellis, entering his freshman year at University of Pennsylvania, co-authored to Chapters 2, 3, 4, 6 and 7. David Gusovsky, a freshman in Computer Science at the University of California at Berkeley, co-authored Chapters 2 through 7, Chapters 14 through 20 and contributed to Chapters 21 and 27. David also reviewed several other chapters of the book.

[*Note:* The Deitel & Associates, Inc. *College Internship Program* offers a limited number of salaried positions to Boston-area college students majoring in Computer Science, Information Technology, Marketing or English. Students work at our corporate headquarters in Sudbury, Massachusetts full-time in the summers and part-time during the academic year. Full-time positions are available to college graduates. For more information about this competitive program, please contact Abbey Deitel at **deitel@deitel.com** and check our Web site, **http://www.deitel.com/**.]

Eric Natale, an employee of Eggrock Partners, co-authored Chapter 24, "Servers." Robin Trudel, an independent consultant, co-authored Chapter 26, "Active Server Pages." Ted Lin, a junior in Computer Science at Carnegie Mellon University, co-authored Chapter 28, "XML." Chris Poirier, a senior at the University of Rhode Island, co-authored Chapter 27, "CGI and Perl." Dave Moore, a junior in Computer Science at the University of Illinois Urbana-Champaign, worked on the RDS material in Chapter 25.

Roger Lederman, a freshman at Brown University, researched Web resources for most of the chapters of the book. Josh Deitel collected Web resources for Chapter 21, "Multimedia."

Allegra Pollock, a senior in English at Boston College, and Kate Steinbuhler, a senior in English and Communications at Boston College, reviewed and edited Chapter 23, "Electronic Commerce and Security."

We are fortunate to have been able to work on this project with the talented and dedicated team of publishing professionals at Prentice Hall. We especially appreciate the extraordinary efforts of our computer science editor, Petra Recter, her assistant Sarah Burrows and their boss—our mentor in publishing—Marcia Horton, Editor-in-Chief of Prentice-Hall's Engineering and Computer Science Division. Camille Trentacoste did a marvelous job as production manager.

The *Internet and World Wide Web Programming Multimedia Cyber Classroom* was developed in parallel with *Internet and World Wide Web How to Program.* We sincerely appreciate the "new media" insight, savvy and technical expertise of our editor Karen McLean. She did a remarkable job bringing the *Internet and World Wide Web Programming Multimedia Cyber Classroom* to publication under a tight schedule.

We owe special thanks to the creativity of Tamara Newnam Cavallo (**smart_art@earthlink.net**) who did the art work for our programming tips icons and the cover. She created the delightful creature who shares with you the book's programming tips.

We sincerely appreciate the efforts of our reviewers:

Kamaljit Bath (Microsoft)
Sunand Bhattacharya (ITT Technical Schools)
Jason Bronfeld (Bristol-Myers Squibb Company)
Bob DuCharme (XML Author)
Jonathan Earl (Technical Training and Consulting)
Jim Gips (Boston College)
Jesse Glick (NetBeans)
Jesse Heines (University of Massachusetts, Lowell)
Shelly Heller (George Washington University)
Peter Jones (Sun Microsystems)
David Kershaw (Art Technology)
Ryan Kuykendall (Amazon)
Hunt LaCascia (Engenius, Inc.)
Yves Lafon (W3C)
Daniel LaLiberte (W3C/Mosaic/NASA)
Wen Liu (ITT)
Marc Loy, (Java Consultant/Cyber Classroom)
Dan Lynch (CyberCash)
Massimo Marchiori (W3C)
Simon North (XML Author)
Ashish Prakash (IBM)
Rama Roberts (Sun Microsystems)
Arie Schlessinger (Columbia University)
Deb Shapiro (Computer Learning Centers)
MG Sriram (GoMo Technologies)
Sumanth Sukumar, (IBM Transarc Labs [HTTP / AFS & DCE DFS])
Scott Tilley (University of California, Riverside)
William Vaughn (Microsoft)
Michael Wallent (Microsoft)
Susan Warren (Microsoft)
Stephen Wynne (IBM Transarc Labs/Carnegie Mellon University)

Under an impossibly tight time schedule, they scrutinized every aspect of the text and made countless suggestions for improving the accuracy and completeness of the presentation.

We would sincerely appreciate your comments, criticisms, corrections and suggestions for improving the text. Please address all correspondence to our email address:

deitel@deitel.com

We will respond immediately. Well, that's it for now. Welcome to the exciting world of Internet and World Wide Web programming. We hope you enjoy this look at leading-edge computer applications development. Good luck!

Dr. Harvey M. Deitel
Paul J. Deitel
Tem R. Nieto

About the Authors

Dr. Harvey M. Deitel, CEO of Deitel & Associates, Inc., has 38 years experience in the computing field including extensive industry and academic experience. He is one of the world's leading computer science instructors and seminar presenters. Dr. Deitel earned B.S. and M.S. degrees from the Massachusetts Institute of Technology and a Ph.D. from Boston University. He worked on the pioneering virtual memory operating systems projects at IBM and MIT that developed techniques widely implemented today in systems like UNIX and Windows NT. He has 20 years of college teaching experience including earning tenure and serving as the Chairman of the Computer Science Department at Boston College before founding Deitel & Associates, Inc. with Paul J. Deitel. He is author or co-author of several dozen books and multimedia packages and is currently writing many more. With translations published in Japanese, Russian, Spanish, Basic Chinese, Advanced Chinese, Korean, French, Polish and Portuguese, Dr. Deitel's texts have earned international recognition. Dr. Deitel has delivered professional seminars internationally to major corporations, government organizations and various branches of the military.

Paul J. Deitel, Executive Vice President of Deitel & Associates, Inc., is a graduate of the Massachusetts Institute of Technology's Sloan School of Management where he studied Information Technology. Through Deitel & Associates, Inc. he has delivered Java, C and C++ courses for industry clients including Compaq, Digital Equipment Corporation, Sun Microsystems, Rogue Wave Software, Computervision, Stratus, Fidelity, Cambridge Technology Partners, Open Environment Corporation, One Wave, Hyperion Software, Lucent Technologies, Adra Systems, Entergy, CableData Systems, NASA at the Kennedy Space Center, the National Severe Storm Laboratory, White Sands Missile Range, IBM and many others. He has lectured on C++ and Java for the Boston Chapter of the Association for Computing Machinery. He has taught satellite-based Java courses through a cooperative venture of Deitel & Associates, Inc., Prentice Hall and the Technology Education Network. He is the co-author of sixteen books and multimedia packages with Harvey Deitel and is currently writing many more.

Tem R. Nieto, Principal Instructor with Deitel & Associates, Inc., is a graduate of the Massachusetts Institute of Technology where he studied engineering and computing. Through Deitel & Associates, Inc. he has delivered courses for industry clients including Sun Microsystems, Digital Equipment Corporation, Compaq, EMC, Stratus, Fidelity, Art Technology, Progress Software, Toys "R" Us, Operational Support Facility of the National Oceanographic and Atmospheric Administration, Jet Propulsion Laboratory, Nynex, Motorola, Federal Reserve Bank of Chicago, Banyan, Schlumberger, University of Notre Dame, NASA, various military installations and many others. He has co-authored five books and multimedia packages with the Deitels and contributed to several others.

The Deitels are co-authors of the best-selling introductory college computer-science programming language textbooks, *C How to Program: Second Edition*, *C++ How to Pro-*

gram: Second Edition, Java How to Program: Third Edition and *Visual Basic 6 How to Program (co-authored with Tem R. Nieto)*. The Deitels are also co-authors of the *C & C++ Multimedia Cyber Classroom: Second Edition*—Prentice Hall's first multimedia-based textbook, the *Java 2 Multimedia Cyber Classroom: Third Edition,* the *Visual Basic 6 Multimedia Cyber Classroom* co-authored with their colleague Tem R. Nieto and the *Internet and World Wide Web Programming Multimedia Cyber Classroom*. The Deitels are also co-authors of *The Complete C++ Training Course: Second Edition*, The *Complete Visual Basic 6 Training Course, The Complete Java 2 Training Course: Third Edition and The Complete Internet and World Wide Web Programming Training Course*—these products each contain the corresponding *How to Program Series* textbook and the corresponding *Multimedia Cyber Classroom*.

About Deitel & Associates, Inc.

Deitel & Associates, Inc. is an internationally recognized corporate training and publishing organization specializing in programming languages, Internet/World Wide Web technology and object technology education. Deitel & Associates, Inc. is a member of the World Wide Web Consortium. The company provides courses on Java, C++, Visual Basic, C, Internet and World Wide Web programming, and Object Technology. The principals of Deitel & Associates, Inc. are Dr. Harvey M. Deitel and Paul J. Deitel. The company's clients include some of the world's largest computer companies, government agencies, branches of the military and business organizations. Through its publishing partnership with Prentice Hall, Deitel & Associates, Inc. publishes leading-edge programming textbooks, professional books, interactive CD-ROM-based multimedia *Cyber Classrooms*, satellite courses and World Wide Web courses. Deitel & Associates, Inc. and the authors can be reached via email at

deitel@deitel.com

To learn more about Deitel & Associates, Inc., its publications, public seminar schedule and worldwide corporate on-site curriculum, see the last few pages of this book and visit:

http://www.deitel.com/

Deitel & Associates, Inc. has competitive opportunities in its College Internship Program for students in the Boston area. For information, please contact Abbey Deitel at **deitel@deitel.com**.

Individuals wishing to purchase Deitel books and multimedia packages can do so through

http://www.deitel.com/

Bulk orders by corporations and academic institutions should be placed directly with Prentice Hall—see the last few pages of this book for worldwide ordering details.

INTERNET AND WORLD WIDE WEB
HOW TO PROGRAM

1

Introduction to Computers and the Internet

Objectives

- To understand basic computer science concepts.
- To become familiar with different types of programming languages.
- To understand the evolution of the Internet and the World Wide Web.
- To understand the roles JavaScript, VBScript and Perl play in developing distributed client/server applications for the Internet and the World Wide Web.
- To preview the remaining chapters of the book.

Our life is frittered away by detail … Simplify, simplify.
Henry Thoreau

High thoughts must have high language.
Aristophanes

The chief merit of language is clearness.
Galen

My object all sublime
I shall achieve in time.
W. S. Gilbert

He had a wonderful talent for packing thought close, and rendering it portable.
Thomas Babington Macaulay

Egad, I think the interpreter is the hardest to be understood of the two!
Richard Brinsley Sheridan

Outline

1.1 Introduction

Welcome to Internet and World Wide Web programming! We have worked hard to create what we hope will be an informative, entertaining and challenging learning experience for you. As you read this book, you may want to refer to our Web site

```
http://www.deitel.com/
```

for updates and additional information on each subject.

The technologies you will learn in this book are fun to use for novices while simultaneously being appropriate for experienced professionals building substantial information systems. *Internet and World Wide Web How to Program* is designed to be an effective learning tool for each of these audiences. How can one book appeal to both groups? The answer is that the common core of the book emphasizes achieving program *clarity* through the proven techniques of *structured programming* and *object-based programming*. Non-programmers will learn programming the right way from the beginning. We have attempted to write in a clear and straightforward manner. The book is abundantly illustrated.

Perhaps most important, the book presents hundreds of working programs and shows the outputs produced when those programs are run on a computer. We present all concepts in the context of complete working programs. We call this the *live-code approach.* These examples are available from three locations—they are on the CD-ROM inside the back cover of this book, they may be downloaded from our Web site **`http://www.deitel.com`** and they are available on our interactive CD-ROM product, the *Internet and World Wide Web Programming Multimedia Cyber Classroom*. The *Cyber Classroom*'s features and ordering information appear in the last few pages of this book. The *Cyber Classroom* also contains answers to approximately half the exercises in this book, including short answers, small programs and many full projects. If you purchased our boxed product *The Complete Internet and World Wide Web Programming Training Course*, you already have the *Cyber Classroom*.

The early chapters introduce the fundamentals of computers, the Internet and the World Wide Web. We show how to use software packages for creating graphics, attractive Web pages and powerful Web-based applications. We present a carefully paced introduction to computer programming with the popular JavaScript programming language. In this book, we will often refer to "programming" as *scripting* for reasons that will soon become clear. Novices will find that the material in these chapters presents a solid foundation for the deeper treatment of scripting in JavaScript, VBScript and Perl in the later chapters. Experienced programmers will read the early chapters quickly and find that the treatment of scripting in the later chapters is rigorous and challenging.

Most people are familiar with the exciting things computers do. Using this textbook, you will learn how to command computers to do those things. It is *software* (i.e., the instructions you write to command the computer to perform *actions* and make *decisions*) that controls computers (often referred to as *hardware*), and JavaScript is one of today's most popular software development languages for developing Web-based applications.

Computer use is increasing in almost every field of endeavor. In an era of steadily rising costs, computing costs have been decreasing dramatically because of the rapid developments in both hardware and software technology. Computers that might have filled large rooms and cost millions of dollars just two decades ago can now be inscribed on the surfaces of silicon chips smaller than a fingernail, costing perhaps a few dollars each. Ironically, silicon is one of the most abundant materials on earth—it is an ingredient in common sand. Silicon chip technology has made computing so economical that hundreds of millions of general-purpose computers are in use worldwide helping people in business, industry, government, and in their personal lives. That number could easily double in a few years.

This book will challenge you for several reasons. Your peers over the last few years probably learned C, C++ or Java as their first computer programming language. Indeed, the Advanced Placement Examination that is administered to high-school students wishing to earn college credit in computer programming is now based on C++ (switched recently from Pascal, a programming language widely used at the college level for two decades). Until recently, students in introductory programming courses learned only the programming methodology called *structured programming.* You will learn *both* structured programming and the exciting newer methodology called *object-based programming.* After this you will be well-prepared to study the C++ and Java programming languages and learn the even more powerful programming methodology of *object-oriented programming.* We believe that object orientation is the key programming methodology as we begin the new millennium. You will work with many *objects* in this course.

Today's users want applications with graphical user interfaces (GUIs). They want applications that use the multimedia capabilities of graphics, images, animation, audio and video. They want applications that can run on the Internet and the World Wide Web, and communicate with other applications. They want to move away from older file-processing techniques to newer database technologies. They want applications that are not limited to the desktop or even to some local computer network, but that can integrate Internet, World Wide Web components and remote databases as well. And programmers want all these benefits in a truly portable manner so that applications will run without modification on a variety of *platforms* (i.e., different types of computers running different operating systems).

In this book we present a number of powerful software technologies that will enable you to build these kinds of systems. The first part of the book (through Chapter 22) concentrates on using technologies such as HTML (HyperText Markup Language), JavaScript, Dynamic HTML and VBScript to build the portions of Web-based applications that reside on the so-called *client side,* i.e., the portions of applications that typically run on Web browsers such as Netscape's Communicator or Microsoft's Internet Explorer. [*Caution:* Some of the material we discuss in this portion of the book is portable to both of these browsers and some runs only on Microsoft's Internet Explorer 5.] The second part of the book (through Chapter 29) concentrates on using technologies such as Web servers, database, Active Server Pages, Perl/CGI, XML and Java Servlets to build the other major portion of Web-based applications, the so-called *server side*, i.e., the portions of applications that typically run on "heavy-duty" computer systems on which company Web sites reside. Each of these terms will be introduced in this chapter and carefully explained throughout the book. Readers who master the technologies in this book will be able to build substantial Web-based, client/server, database-intensive, "multi-tier" applications. We begin with a discussion of computer hardware and software fundamentals.

1.2 What is a Computer?

A *computer* is a device capable of performing computations and making logical decisions at speeds millions, and even billions, of times faster than human beings can. For example, many of today's personal computers can perform hundreds of millions of additions per second. A person operating a desk calculator might require a lifetime to complete the same number of calculations a powerful personal computer can perform in one second. (Points to ponder: How would you know whether the person added the numbers correctly? How would you know whether the computer added the numbers correctly?) Today, the world's fastest *supercomputers* can perform hundreds of billions of additions per second, and computers that perform a trillion instructions per second are already functioning in research laboratories!

Computers process *data* under the control of sets of instructions called *computer programs.* These computer programs guide the computer through orderly sets of actions specified by people called *computer programmers.*

The various devices (such as the keyboard, screen, disks, memory and processing units) that comprise a computer system are referred to as *hardware.* Regardless of differences in physical appearance, virtually every computer may be envisioned as being divided into six *logical units* or sections. These are:

1. *Input unit.* This is the "receiving" section of the computer. It obtains information (data and computer programs) from various *input devices* and places this information at the disposal of the other units so that the information may be processed. Most information is entered into computers today through typewriter-like keyboards, "mouse" devices and disks. In the future, most information will be entered by speaking to computers, by electronically scanning images, and by video recording.
2. *Output unit.* This is the "shipping" section of the computer. It takes information processed by the computer and places it on various *output devices* to make the information available for use outside the computer. Information output from computers is displayed on screens, printed on paper, played through audio speakers, magnetically recorded on disks and tapes, or used to control other devices.
3. *Memory unit.* This is the rapid access, relatively low-capacity "warehouse" section of the computer. It retains information that has been entered through the input unit so that the information may be made immediately available for processing when it is needed. The memory unit also retains information that has already been processed until that information can be placed on output devices by the output unit. The memory unit is often called either *memory, primary memory* or *random access memory (RAM).*
4. *Arithmetic and logic unit (ALU).* This is the "manufacturing" section of the computer. It is responsible for performing calculations such as addition, subtraction, multiplication and division. It contains the decision mechanisms that allow the computer, for example, to compare two items from the memory unit to determine whether or not they are equal.
5. *Central processing unit (CPU).* This is the "administrative" section of the computer. It is the computer's coordinator and is responsible for supervising the operation of the other sections. The CPU tells the input unit when information should be read into the memory unit, tells the ALU when information from the memory unit should be utilized in calculations and tells the output unit when to send information from the memory unit to certain output devices.
6. *Secondary storage unit.* This is the long-term, high-capacity "warehousing" section of the computer. Programs or data not being used by the other units are normally placed on secondary storage devices (such as disks) until they are needed, possibly hours, days, months or even years later. Information in secondary storage takes longer to access than information in primary memory. The cost per unit of secondary storage is much less than the cost per unit of primary memory.

1.3 Types of Programming Languages

The computer programs that run on a computer are referred to as *software*. Programmers write the instructions that comprise software in various programming languages, some directly understandable by the computer and others that require intermediate translation steps. Hundreds of computer languages are in use today. These may be divided into three general types:

1. Machine languages
2. Assembly languages
3. High-level languages

Any computer can directly understand only its own *machine language.* Machine language is the "natural language" of a particular computer. It is defined by the hardware design of that computer. Machine languages generally consist of strings of numbers (ultimately reduced to 1s and 0s) that instruct computers to perform their most elementary operations one at a time. Machine languages are *machine dependent* (i.e., a particular machine language can be used on only one type of computer). Machine languages are cumbersome for humans, as can be seen by the following section of a machine-language program that adds overtime pay to base pay and stores the result in gross pay.

```
+1300042774
+1400593419
+1200274027
```

As computers became more popular, it became apparent that machine-language programming was simply too slow and tedious for most programmers. Instead of using the strings of numbers that computers could directly understand, programmers began using English-like abbreviations to represent the elementary operations of the computer. These English-like abbreviations formed the basis of *assembly languages. Translator programs* called *assemblers* were developed to convert assembly-language programs to machine language at computer speeds. The following section of an assembly-language program also adds overtime pay to base pay and stores the result in gross pay, but more clearly than its machine-language equivalent.

```
LOAD BASEPAY
ADD OVERPAY
STORE GROSSPAY
```

Although such code is clearer to humans, it is incomprehensible to computers until translated to machine language.

Computer usage increased rapidly with the advent of assembly languages, but programming in these still required many instructions to accomplish even the simplest tasks. To speed the programming process, *high-level languages* were developed in which single statements could be written to accomplish substantial tasks. The translator programs that convert high-level language programs into machine language are called *compilers.* High-level languages allow programmers to write instructions that look almost like everyday English and contain commonly used mathematical notations. A payroll program written in a high-level language might contain a statement such as:

```
grossPay = basePay + overTimePay
```

Obviously, high-level languages are more desirable from the programmer's standpoint than either machine languages or assembly languages. C, C++, Visual Basic® and Java™ are among the most powerful and most widely used high-level programming languages.

The process of compiling a high-level language program into machine language can take a considerable amount of computer time. *Interpreter* programs were developed to execute high-level language programs directly without the need for compiling those programs into machine language. Although compiled programs execute much faster than interpreted programs, interpreters are popular in program-development environments in which programs are recompiled frequently as new features are added and errors are corrected. Once a program is developed, a compiled version can be produced to run most efficiently. In this book we study three key programming languages, namely, JavaScript, VBScript and Perl. Each of these so-called *scripting languages* is processed by interpreters. You will see that interpreters have played an especially important part in helping scripting languages achieve their goal of portability across a great variety of platforms.

1.4 Other High-Level Languages

Hundreds of high-level languages have been developed, but only a few have achieved broad acceptance. *Fortran* (FORmula TRANslator) was developed by IBM Corporation between 1954 and 1957 to be used for scientific and engineering applications that require complex mathematical computations. Fortran is still widely used.

COBOL (COmmon Business Oriented Language) was developed in 1959 by a group of computer manufacturers and government and industrial computer users. COBOL is used primarily for commercial applications that require precise and efficient manipulation of large amounts of data. Today, about half of all business software is still programmed in COBOL. Approximately one million people are actively writing COBOL programs.

Pascal was designed at about the same time as C. It was created by Professor Nicklaus Wirth and was intended for academic use. We say more about Pascal in the next section.

Basic was developed in 1965 at Dartmouth University as a simple language to help novices become comfortable with programming. Bill Gates implemented Basic on several early personal computers. Today, *Microsoft*—the company Bill Gates created—is the world's leading software development organization, Gates has become—by far—the world's richest person and Microsoft has been included in the list of prestigious stocks that form the Dow Jones Industrials–from which the Dow Jones Industrial Average is calculated.

1.5 Structured Programming

During the 1960s, many large software development efforts encountered severe difficulties. Software schedules were typically late, costs greatly exceeded budgets, and the finished products were unreliable. People began to realize that software development was a far more complex activity than they had imagined. Research activity in the 1960s resulted in the evolution of *structured programming*—a disciplined approach to writing programs that are clearer than unstructured programs, easier to test and debug, and easier to modify. Chapters 9 and 10 discuss the principles of structured programming.

One of the more tangible results of this research was the development of the Pascal programming language by Nicklaus Wirth in 1971. Pascal, named after the seventeenth-century mathematician and philosopher Blaise Pascal, was designed for teaching structured programming in academic environments and rapidly became the preferred programming language in most universities.

The Ada programming language was developed under the sponsorship of the United States Department of Defense (DOD) during the 1970s and early 1980s. Hundreds of separate languages were being used to produce DOD's massive command-and-control software systems. DOD wanted a single language that would fulfill most of its needs. Pascal was chosen as a base, but the final Ada language is quite different from Pascal. The language was named after Lady Ada Lovelace, daughter of the poet Lord Byron. Lady Lovelace is generally credited with writing the world's first computer program in the early 1800s (for the Analytical Engine mechanical computing device designed by Charles Babbage). One important capability of Ada is called *multitasking;* this allows programmers to specify that many activities are to occur in parallel. Other widely used high-level languages such as C and C++ generally allow programs to perform only one activity at a time. Java, through a technique called *multithreading*, also enables programmers to write programs with parallel activities.

1.6 History of the Internet

In the late 1960s, one of the authors (HMD) was a graduate student at MIT. His research at MIT's Project Mac (now the Laboratory for Computer Science—the home of the World Wide Web Consortium) was funded by ARPA—the Advanced Research Projects Agency of the Department of Defense. ARPA sponsored a conference at which several dozen ARPA-funded graduate students were brought together at the University of Illinois at Urbana-Champaign to meet and share ideas. During this conference, ARPA rolled out the blueprints for networking the main computer systems of about a dozen ARPA-funded universities and research institutions. They were to be connected with communications lines operating at a then-stunning 56KB (i.e., 56,000 bits per second), this at a time when most people (of the few who could) were connecting over telephone lines to computers at a rate of 110 bits per second. HMD vividly recalls the excitement at that conference. Researchers at Harvard talked about communication with the Univac 1108 "supercomputer" across the country at the University of Utah to handle calculations related to their computer graphics research. Many other intriguing possibilities were raised. Academic research was about to take a giant leap forward. Shortly after this conference, ARPA proceeded to implement what quickly became called the *ARPAnet*, the grandparent of today's *Internet.*

Things worked out differently from what was originally planned. Rather than the primary benefit being that researchers could share each other's computers, it rapidly became clear that simply enabling the researchers to communicate quickly and easily among themselves via what became known as *electronic mail* (*e-mail*, for short) was to be the key benefit of the ARPAnet. This is true even today on the Internet with e-mail facilitating communications of all kinds among millions of people worldwide.

One of ARPA's primary goals for the network was to allow multiple users to send and receive information at the same time over the same communications paths (such as phone lines). The network operated with a technique called *packet switching* in which digital data was sent in small packages called *packets*. The packets contained data, address information, error-control information and sequencing information. The address information was used to route the packets of data to their destination. The sequencing information was used to help reassemble the packets (which—because of complex routing mechanisms—could actually arrive out of order) into their original order for presentation to the recipient. Packets of many people were intermixed on the same lines. This packet-switching technique greatly reduced transmission costs compared to the cost of dedicated communications lines.

The network was designed to operate without centralized control. This meant that if a portion of the network should fail, the remaining working portions would still be able to route packets from senders to receivers over alternate paths.

The protocols for communicating over the ARPAnet became known as *TCP—the Transmission Control Protocol*. TCP ensured that messages were properly routed from sender to receiver and that those messages arrived intact.

In parallel with the early evolution of the Internet, organizations worldwide were implementing their own networks for both intra-organization (i.e., within the organization) and inter-organization (i.e., between organizations) communication. A huge variety of networking hardware and software appeared. One challenge was to get these to intercommunicate. ARPA accomplished this with the development of *IP*—the *Internetworking Protocol*), truly creating a "network of networks," the current architecture of the Internet. The combined set of protocols is now commonly called *TCP/IP*.

Initially, use of the Internet was limited to universities and research institutions; then the military became a big user. Eventually, the government decided to allow access to the Internet for commercial purposes. Initially there was resentment among the research and military communities—it was felt that response times would become poor as "the net" became saturated with so many users.

In fact, the exact opposite has occurred. Businesses rapidly realized that they could tune their operations and offer new and better services to their clients, so they started spending vasts amounts of money to develop and enhance the Internet. This generated fierce competition among the communications carriers and hardware and software suppliers to meet this demand. The result is that *bandwidth* (i.e., the information carrying capacity) on the Internet has increased tremendously and costs have plummeted. It is widely believed that the Internet has played a significant role in the economic prosperity that the United States and many other industrialized nations have enjoyed in the 1990s and are likely to continue enjoying for many years.

1.7 Personal Computing

In 1977, Apple Computer popularized the phenomenon of *personal computing*. Initially, it was a hobbyist's dream. Computers became economical enough for people to buy for their own personal use. In 1981, IBM, the world's largest computer vendor, introduced the *IBM Personal Computer*, making, personal computing legitimate in business, industry and government organizations.

But these computers were "stand-alone" units—people did their work on their own machines and then transported disks back and forth to share information (this was called "sneakernet"). Although early personal computers were not powerful enough to timeshare several users, these machines could be linked together in computer networks, sometimes over telephone lines and sometimes in *local area networks (LANs)* within an organization. This led to the phenomenon of *distributed computing,* in which an organization's computing, instead of being performed strictly at some central computer installation, is distributed over networks to the sites at which the bulk of the work of the organization is performed. Personal computers were powerful enough to handle the computing requirements of individual users, and to handle the basic communications tasks of passing information back and forth electronically.

Today's most powerful personal computers are as powerful as the million dollar machines of just two decades ago. The most powerful desktop machines—called *workstations*—provide individual users with enormous capabilities. Information is easily shared across computer networks where some computers called *servers* offer a common store of programs and data that may be used by *client* computers distributed throughout the network, hence the term *client/server computing.* Today's popular operating systems such as UNIX, OS/2, MacOS, Windows, Windows NT and Linux provide the kinds of capabilities discussed in this section.

1.8 History of the World Wide Web

The *World Wide Web* allows computer users to locate and view multimedia-based documents (i.e., documents with text, graphics, animations, audios and/or videos) on almost any subject. Even though the Internet was developed more than three decades ago, the introduction of the *World Wide Web* was a relatively recent event. In 1990, *Tim Berners-Lee* of CERN (the European Laboratory for Particle Physics) developed the World Wide Web and several communication protocols that form the backbone of the World Wide Web.

The Internet and the World Wide Web will surely be listed among the most important and profound creations of humankind. In the past, most computer applications ran on "stand-alone" computers, i.e., computers that were not connected to one another. Today's applications can be written to communicate among the world's hundreds of millions of computers. The Internet mixes computing and communications technologies. It makes our work easier. It makes information instantly and conveniently accessible worldwide. It makes it possible for individuals and small businesses to get worldwide exposure. It is changing the nature of the way business is done. People can search for the best prices on virtually any product or service. Special-interest communities can stay in touch with one another. Researchers can be made instantly aware of the latest breakthroughs worldwide.

Internet and World Wide Web How to Program presents programming techniques that allow applications to use the Internet and the World Wide Web to interact with other applications and with databases. These capabilities allow programmers to develop the kinds of enterprise-level, distributed applications so popular in industry today. Applications can be written to execute on any computer platform, yielding major savings in systems development time and reduced costs. If you have been hearing a great deal about the Internet and World Wide Web lately, and if you are interested in developing applications to run over the Internet and the Web, then learning the software-development techniques discussed in this book may be the key to challenging and rewarding career opportunities for you.

1.9 Hardware Trends

The Internet community thrives on the continuing stream of dramatic improvements in hardware, software and communications technologies. Every year, people generally expect to pay at least a little more for most products and services. The exact opposite has been the case in the computer and communications fields, especially with regard to the hardware costs of supporting these technologies. For many decades, and with no change in the foreseeable future, hardware costs have fallen rapidly, if not precipitously. This is a phenomenon of technology, another driving force powering the current economic boom. Every year or two, the capacities of computers, especially the amount of *memory* they have in which to execute programs, *secondary memory* (such as disk storage) they have to hold programs and data over the longer term, and processor speeds—the speed at which computers execute their programs (i.e., do their work)—each tend to approximately double. The same has been true in the communications field with costs plummeting, especially in recent years with the enormous demand for communications bandwidth attracting tremendous competition. We know of no other fields in which technology moves so quickly and costs fall so rapidly.

When computer use exploded in the sixties and seventies, there was talk of huge improvements in human productivity that computing and communications would bring about. But these improvements did not materialize. Organizations were spending vast sums on computers and certainly employing them effectively, but without the productivity gains that had been expected. It was the invention of microprocessor chip technology and its wide deployment in the late 1970s and 1980s that laid the groundwork for the productivity improvements of the 1990s that have been so crucial to economic prosperity.

1.10 The Key Software Trend: Object Technology

One of the authors, HMD, remembers the great frustration that was felt in the 1960s by software development organizations, especially those developing large-scale projects. During his undergraduate years, HMD had the privilege of working summers at a leading computer vendor on the teams developing time-sharing, virtually memory operating systems. The was a great experience for a college student. But in the summer of 1967 reality set in when the company "decommitted" from producing as a commercial product the particular system that hundreds of people had been working on for many years. It was difficult to get this software right. Software is "complex stuff."

Hardware costs have been declining dramatically in recent years, to the point that personal computers have become a commodity. Unfortunately, software development costs have been rising steadily as programmers develop ever more powerful and complex applications, without being able to significantly improve the underlying technologies of software development. In this book you will learn proven software development methods that can reduce software development costs—top-down stepwise refinement, functionalization and especially object-based programming.

There is a revolution brewing in the software community. Building software quickly, correctly and economically remains an elusive goal, and this at a time when demands for new and more powerful software are soaring. *Objects* are essentially reusable software *components* that model items in the real world. Software developers are discovering that using a modular, object-oriented design and implementation approach can make software development groups much more productive than is possible with previous popular programming techniques such as structured programming. Object-oriented programs are often easier to understand, correct and modify.

Improvements to software technology did start to appear with the benefits of so-called *structured programming* (and the related disciplines of *structured systems analysis and design)* being realized in the 1970s. But it was not until the technology of object-oriented programming became widely used in the 1980s, and especially widely used in the 1990s, that software developers finally felt they had the tools they needed to make major strides in the software development process.

Actually, object technology dates back at least to the mid 1960s. The C++ programming language developed at AT&T by Bjarne Stroustrup in the early 1980s, is based on two languages—C which was initially developed at AT&T to implement the Unix operating system in the early 1970s, and Simula 67—a simulation programming language developed in Europe and released in 1967. C++ absorbed the capabilities of C and added Simula's capabilities for creating and manipulating objects. Neither C nor C++ was ever intended for wide use beyond the research laboratories at AT&T. But grass-roots support rapidly developed for each.

What are objects and why are they "magic." Actually, object technology is a packaging scheme that helps us create meaningful software units. These are large and highly focussed on particular applications areas. There are date objects, time objects, paycheck objects, invoice objects, audio objects, video objects, file objects, record objects and so on. In fact, any noun can be represented as an object.

We live in a world of objects. Just look around you. There are cars, and planes, and people, and animals, and buildings, and traffic lights, and elevators, and so on. Before object-oriented languages appeared, programming languages (such as Fortran, Pascal, Basic and C) were focussed on actions (verbs) rather than things or objects (nouns). Programmers living in a world of objects would get to the computer and have to program primarily with verbs. This paradigm shift made it a bit awkward to write programs. Now, with the availability of popular object-oriented languages such as Java and C++ and many others, programmers continue to live in an object-oriented world and when they get to the computer they can program in an object-oriented manner. This means they program in a manner similar to the way in which they perceive the world. This is a more natural process than procedural programming and has resulted in significant productivity enhancements.

One of the key problems with procedural programming is that the program units programmers created do not easily mirror real-world entities effectively. So they are not particularly reusable. It is not unusual for programmers to "start fresh" on each new project and wind up writing very similar software "from scratch." This wastes precious time and money resources as people repeatedly "reinvent the wheel." With object technology, the software entities created (called *objects*), if properly designed, tend to be much more reusable on future projects. Using libraries of reusable componentry such as *MFC (Microsoft Foundation Classes)* and those produced by Rogue Wave and many other software development organizations can greatly reduce the amount of effort it takes to implement certain kinds of systems (compared to the effort that would be required to reinvent these capabilities on new projects).

Some organizations report that software reuse is not, in fact, the key benefit they get from object-oriented programming. Rather, they indicate that object-oriented programming tends to produce software that is more understandable, better organized and easier to maintain. This can be significant because it has been estimated that as much as 80% of software costs are not associated with the original efforts to develop the software, but are in fact associated with the continued evolution and maintenance of that software throughout its lifetime.

Whatever the perceived benefits of object-orientation are, it is clear that object-oriented programming will be the key programming methodology for at least the next several decades.

Software Engineering Observation 1.1

Use a building block approach to creating programs. Avoid reinventing the wheel. Use existing pieces—this is called software reuse *and it is central to object-oriented programming.*

[*Note*: We will include many of these *Software Engineering Observations* throughout the text to explain concepts that affect and improve the overall architecture and quality of a software system, and particularly, of large software systems. We will also highlight *Good*

Programming Practices (practices that can help you write programs that are clearer, more understandable, more maintainable, and easier to test and debug), *Common Programming Errors* (problems to watch out for so you do not make these same errors in your programs), *Performance Tips* (techniques that will help you write programs that run faster and use less memory), *Portability Tips* (techniques that will help you write programs that can run, with little or no modification, on a variety of computers), *Testing and Debugging Tips* (techniques that will help you remove bugs from your programs, and more important, techniques that will help you write bug-free programs in the first place) and *Look and Feel Observations* (techniques that will help you design the "look" and "feel" of your graphical user interfaces for appearance and ease of use). Many of these techniques and practices are only guidelines; you will, no doubt, develop your own preferred programming style.]

The advantage of creating your own code is that you will know exactly how it works. You will be able to examine the code. The disadvantage is the time-consuming and complex effort that goes into designing and developing new code.

Performance Tip 1.1

Reusing proven code components instead of writing your own versions can improve program performance because these components are normally written to perform efficiently.

Software Engineering Observation 1.2

Extensive class libraries of reusable software components are available over the Internet and the World Wide Web. Many of these libraries are available at no charge.

1.11 JavaScript: Object-Based Scripting for the Web

JavaScript provides an attractive package for advancing the state of programming language education, especially at the introductory and intermediate levels. JavaScript makes World Wide Web pages "come alive."

JavaScript is an object-based language with strong support for proper software engineering techniques. You create and manipulate objects. For universities, these features are powerfully appealing. Students will learn *object-based* programming from the start. They will simply think in an object-based manner.

The fact that JavaScript is free for download in today's most popular Web browsers is appealing to colleges facing tight budgets and lengthy budget-planning cycles. Also, as bug fixes and new versions of JavaScript become available, these become available immediately over the Internet, so colleges can keep their JavaScript software current.

Does JavaScript provide the solid foundation of programming principles typically taught in first programming courses—the intended audience for this book? We think so.

The JavaScript chapters of this book are much more than just an introduction to JavaScript. They also present an introduction to the fundamentals of computer programming including control structures, functions, arrays, recursion, strings, objects, etc. Experienced programmers will be able to read Chapters 8 through 13 quickly and master JavaScript mostly by reading our live-code examples and examining the corresponding input/output screens. Nonprogrammers will learn computer programming in these carefully paced chapters with a large number of exercises. We cannot provide answers to all these exercises because this book is a textbook—college professors use the examples for homeworks, labs, short quizzes, major examinations and even term projects. We do, however, provide answers to many of the exercises in the companion product to this book called *The Internet and World Wide Web Programming Multimedia Cyber Classroom*. If you purchased our boxed product, *The Complete Internet and World Wide Web Programming Training Course*, you already have the *Cyber Classroom* CD. If you have the book and would like to order the CD separately please check our Web site for ordering instructions.

JavaScript is a powerful scripting language. Experienced programmers sometimes take pride in being able to create some weird, contorted, convoluted usage of the language. This is a poor programming practice. It makes programs difficult to read, more likely to behave strangely, more difficult to test and debug, and more difficult to adapt to changing requirements. This book is also geared for novice programmers, so we stress program *clarity*. The following is our first *Good Programming Practice*.

Good Programming Practice 1.1

Write your programs in a simple and straightforward manner. This is sometimes referred to as KIS ("keep it simple")*. Do not "stretch" the language by trying bizarre usages.*

You will hear that JavaScript is a portable scripting language, and that programs written in JavaScript can run on many different computers. Actually, *portability is an elusive goal.* Here is our first *Portability Tip* and our first *Test and Debugging Tip.*

Portability Tip 1.1

Although it is easier to write portable programs in JavaScript than in most other programming languages, there are differences among compilers, interpreters and computers that can make portability difficult to achieve. Simply writing programs in JavaScript does not guarantee portability. The programmer will occasionally need to deal directly with platform variations.

Testing and Debugging Tip 1.1

Always test your JavaScript programs on all systems on which you intend to run those programs.

We have done a careful walkthrough of the JavaScript documentation and audited our presentation against it for completeness and accuracy. However, JavaScript is a rich language, and there are some subtleties in the language and some topics we have not covered. The *Bibliography* section at the back of this book lists additional books and papers on JavaScript.

Good Programming Practice 1.2

Read the documentation for the version of JavaScript you are using to be sure you are aware of the rich collection of JavaScript features and that you are using these features correctly.

Testing and Debugging Tip 1.2

Your computer and compiler are good teachers. If after carefully reading your documentation you are not sure how a feature works, experiment and see what happens. Study each error or warning message you get when you browse pages containing JavaScript programs (referred to simply as scripts) and correct the programs to eliminate these messages.

In this book we explain how JavaScript works in its current implementations. JavaScript programs execute interpretively on the client's machine. Interpreters execute slowly compared to fully compiled machine code.

Performance Tip 1.2

Interpreters have an advantage over compilers for the JavaScript world, namely that an interpreted program can begin execution immediately as soon as it is downloaded to the client's machine, whereas a source program to be compiled must first suffer a potentially long delay as the program is compiled before it can be executed.

For organizations wanting to do heavy-duty information systems development, software packages called *Integrated Development Environments (IDEs)* are available from the major software suppliers. IDEs provide many tools for supporting the software-development process. Microsoft's Visual InterDev 6, which we discuss in Chapter 7, is an IDE for developing Internet-based and World-Wide-Web-based applications.

1.12 Browser Portability

One of the great challenges of developing Web-based applications is the great diversity of client-side browsers in use. Not only is the browser world divided into *Netscape Navigator*, *Microsoft Internet Explorer*, and many other Web browsers, but for any particular browser, many versions (1.0, 2.0, etc.) for many different platforms (Unix, Microsoft Windows, Apple Macintosh, IBM OS/2, Linux, etc.) are in use. There is great value to knowing the details of all these browsers when developing Web-based applications, but this is confusing to students learning this subject for the first time. We had to make a judgement call on this. We chose to include as many portable topics as possible (such as HTML, JavaScript, Cascading Style Sheets, e-commerce, database/SQL, Perl/CGI and XML, among others). But we also chose many Microsoft-Windows-specific topics such as the Internet Explorer 5 browser, the Jasc Paint Shop Pro 5 graphics package for Windows, Visual InterDev 6, Dynamic HTML, multimedia, VBScript, Personal Web Server (although we introduce Apache and Jigsaw and provide many URLs for more detailed information on these important Web servers), database access via ADO and Active Server Pages (ASP). For many of our readers, this amount of Microsoft-specific technology will not be appropriate.

Portability Tip 1.2

The Web world is highly fragmented and this makes it difficult for authors and Web developers to create universal solutions. The World Wide Web Consortium (W3C) is working towards the goal of creating a universal client-side platform.

Deitel & Associates, Inc. is a member of the World Wide Consortium.

1.13 Evolution of the *How to Program* Series: C and C++

For many years, the Pascal programming language was preferred for use in introductory and intermediate programming courses. The C language was evolved from a language called B by Dennis Ritchie at Bell Laboratories and was implemented in 1972—making C a contemporary of Pascal. C initially became widely known as the development language of the UNIX operating system. Today, virtually all new major operating systems are written in C and/or C++. Over the past two decades, C has become available for most computers. C is hardware independent. With careful design, it is possible to write C programs that are *portable* to most computers.

Many people said that C was too difficult a language for the courses in which Pascal was being used. In 1992, we published the first edition of *C How to Program* to encourage universities to try C instead of Pascal in these courses. In the book we urged instructors to please "trust us" that Pascal should be replaced in the introductory courses with C and that they would be using C for the next 10 years or so in these courses. We used the same pedagogic approach we had used in our college courses for a dozen years, but wrapped the concepts in C rather than Pascal. We found that students were able to handle C at about the same level as Pascal. But there was one noticeable difference. Students appreciated that they were learning a language (C) likely to be valuable to them in industry. Our industry clients appreciated the availability of C-literate graduates who could work immediately on substantial projects rather than first having to go through costly and time-consuming training programs.

C++, an extension of C, was developed by Bjarne Stroustrup in the early 1980s at Bell Laboratories. C++ provides a number of features that "spruce up" the C language, but more important, it provides capabilities for *object-oriented programming*.

C++ is a hybrid language—it is possible to program in either a C-like style (called procedural programming, in which the focus is on actions), an object-oriented style (in which the focus is on things) or both. [*Note:* Java, as we will see, is essentially a pure object-oriented language.]

One reason that C++ use has grown so quickly is that it extends C programming into the area of object orientation. For the huge community of C programmers this has been a powerful advantage. An enormous amount of C code has been written in industry over the last several decades. Because C++ is a superset of C, many organizations find it to be an ideal next step. Programmers can take their C code, compile it, often with nominal changes, in a C++ compiler and continue writing C-like code while mastering the object paradigm. Then the programmers can gradually migrate portions of the legacy C code into C++ as time permits. New systems can be entirely written in object-oriented C++. Such strategies have been appealing to many organizations. The downside is that even after adopting this strategy, companies tend to continue producing C-like code for many years. This, of course, means that they do not quickly realize the full benefits of object-oriented programming and they produce programs that are confusing and hard to maintain due to their hybrid design.

While we were writing *C How to Program*, we had already begun teaching C++ courses. Feeling that C++ would be of great interest to our C readers, we included a brief introduction to C++ at the back of the C book. We then went to work on *C++ How to Program*. Late in 1993 Prentice Hall urged us to write the second edition of *C How to Program*, explaining that the introductory market was still primarily using C with only incidental need for C++. We felt strongly about C++ based on the feedback we were getting in our industry courses, so we insisted on completing the C++ book first. We worked out a compromise solution. We would do the second edition of *C How to Program* first, as long as we could include a much enhanced, several-hundred-page section on C++. Prentice Hall agreed and *C How to Program: Second Edition* book was published in January, 1994. In May 1994 we published the first edition of *C++ How to Program,* a 950-page book devoted to the premise that C++ and OOP were now ready for prime time in introductory college courses for many schools that wanted to be at the leading edge of programming languages education.

Once again, we asked college instructors to please "trust us," that it was now time to shift from C and procedural programming in the introductory courses to C++ and object-oriented programming and that this would likely be stable for the next decade—and this only two years after we suggested to college instructors that they were likely to use C for a decade! Our credibility was in question.

1.14 Java and *Java How to Program*

Many people believe that the next major area in which microprocessors will have a profound impact is in intelligent consumer electronic devices. Recognizing this, Sun Microsystems funded an internal corporate research project code-named Green in 1991. The project resulted in the development of a C and C++ based language which its creator, James Gosling, called Oak after an oak tree outside his window at Sun. It was later discovered that there already was a computer language called Oak. When a group of Sun people visited a local coffee place, the name *Java* was suggested and it stuck.

But the Green project ran into some difficulties. The marketplace for intelligent consumer electronic devices was not developing as quickly as Sun had anticipated. Worse yet, a major contract for which Sun competed was awarded to another company. So the project was in danger of being canceled. By sheer good fortune, the World Wide Web exploded in popularity in 1993 and Sun people saw the immediate potential of using Java to create Web pages with so-called *dynamic content* (a subject we investigate in great detail in this book). This breathed new life into the project.

Sun formally announced Java at a trade show in May 1995. Ordinarily, an event like this would not have generated much attention. However, Java generated immediate interest in the business community because of the phenomenal interest in the World Wide Web. Java is now used to create Web pages with dynamic and interactive content, to develop large-scale enterprise applications, to enhance the functionality of Web servers (the computers that provide the content we see in our Web browsers), to provide applications for consumer devices (such as cell phones, pagers and personal digital assistants), and much more.

In 1995, we were carefully following the development of Java by Sun Microsystems. In November 1995 we attended an Internet conference in Boston. A representative from Sun Microsystems gave a rousing presentation on Java. As the talk proceeded, it became clear to us that Java would play a significant part in the development of interactive, multimedia Web pages. But we immediately saw a much greater potential for the language.

We saw Java as the proper language for teaching first-year programming language students the essentials of graphics, images, animation, audio, video, database, networking, multithreading and collaborative computing. We went to work on the first edition of *Java How to Program* which was published in time for fall 1996 classes. We once again asked instructors to please "trust us" that it was now time to shift from C++ in the introductory courses to Java and that instructors should now teach object-oriented programming as they were doing with C++, but with the addition of discussing Java's extensive class libraries of reusable software components that do graphics, graphical user interfaces, networking, multimedia, and the like. Once again, we suggested that Java would likely remain the key language in the introductory courses for a decade!

At this point it was not clear why anyone should believe us. It seemed like every two years we were urging instructors to shift their courses to a different programming language while asking that they please "trust us" and use the new language for a decade! Over the exciting decade of the 1990s, several things have become clear to us:

1. Programming language technology is moving so quickly that any attempt to forecast the direction of the technology for long periods is doomed to failure.
2. The developments in programming language technology are so exciting and so valuable that instructors responsible for introductory, college-level courses have

to be prepared to reevaluate the content of those courses much more frequently than in the past.

3. We as authors, and Prentice Hall as our publisher, need to produce new editions of our books and new books on emerging programming languages much more rapidly than in the past.

4. Capabilities such as graphics, graphical user interfaces, networking, client/server computing, Internet and World Wide Web technologies, multimedia, database and many more, that used to be accessible through technologies ancillary to programming languages, are now intimately associated with the programming languages themselves. It is now important to talk about these technologies extensively in the programming language textbooks we publish. The era of 500-page programming language textbooks is gone!

After establishing this pattern of recommending a new programming language every two years, we looked for the next major shift in 1998, but we did not see one clearly defined. So we took a diversion and worked on our *Visual Basic 6 How to Program* book, not to replace Java, but to be an appropriate introductory textbook more for the information technology curriculum than for the computer science curriculum. Sun kept us on our toes, though, by so enhancing Java in the Java 2 platform, that we were forced to write *Java How to Program: Third Edition* which was published in 1999.

In addition to its prominence in developing Internet- and intranet-based applications, Java is certain to become the language of choice for implementing software for devices that communicate over a network (such as cellular phones, pagers and personal digital assistants). Do not be surprised when your new stereo and other devices in your home will be networked together using Java technology! Although we do not teach Java in this book, we have included as a bonus for Java programmers Chapter 29 "Java Servlets."

1.15 Internet and World Wide Web How to Program

Throughout 1998 we saw an explosion of interest in the Internet and the World Wide Web. We immersed ourselves in these technologies and a clear picture started to emerge in our minds of the next direction to take in introductory programming courses. Our recent books on Java and Visual Basic included significant treatments of Internet and World Wide Web Programming. *Electronic commerce*, or *e-commerce*, as it is typically called, began to dominate the business, financial and computer industry news. We saw this as a total reconceptualization of the way organizations operate and transact their business. Should we be writing programming language principles textbooks, or was a new picture beginning to emerge where we should be writing textbooks focussed more on these enhanced capabilities that organizations want to incorporate into their information systems. We still had to provide a solid treatment of programming principles, but we felt compelled to do it in the context of the technologies that businesses and organizations need to create Internet-based and Web-based applications. With this realization, *Internet and World Wide Web How to Program* was born, and was published in December of 1999.

In this book you will learn computer programming and basic principles of computer science and information technology. Since the material we discuss must still be presented in typical college courses, we cannot use programming languages as rich as C++ or Java as these would take the entire course to present. Instead, we chose as our primary programming language JavaScript, a condensed programming language that is especially designed for developing Internet- and Web-based applications. Chapters 8 through 13 present a rich discussion of JavaScript and its capabilities, including dozens of working, live-code examples followed by screen images showing typical inputs and outputs of these programs.

After you have learned programming principles from the detailed JavaScript discussions, we present condensed treatments of the two other most popular Internet/Web scripting languages. In Chapter 22 and Chapter 26 we discuss Microsoft's VBScript, a language based on Microsoft's enormously popular Visual Basic. In Chapter 27 we discuss Perl (and CGI) programming; throughout the 1990s, Perl was the most widely used scripting language for building the server side of Internet-based and Web-based client/server applications. Perl/CGI programming is continuously being improved and is certain to remain popular for many years.

Internet and World Wide Web How to Program teaches programming languages and programming language principles. In addition, we focus on the broad range of important technologies that will help you build real-world Internet-based and Web-based applications.

1.16 Dynamic HTML

What is Dynamic HTML? This is an interesting question because if you walk into a computer store or scan some online software stores, you will not find a product by this name offered for sale. Rather Dynamic HTML, which has at least two versions—Microsoft's and Netscape's—consists of a number of technologies that are freely available for download and known by other names. Microsoft Dynamic HTML includes: HTML, JavaScript/JScript, Cascading Style Sheets, the Dynamic HTML Object Model and Event Model, ActiveX controls—each of which we discuss in this book—and other related technologies. It is geared to a world of developing high-performance, Web-based applications in which much of the application's work is performed directly on the client rather than placing burdens on servers and the Internet. Dynamic HTML is the key subject of most of Chapters 3 through 22 of this book that cover client-side programming.

In our Dynamic HTML presentation, we use *Microsoft's Dynamic HTML Object Model* rather than the more generic *Document Object Model*. Each of these models is accessible through Microsoft Internet Explorer 5, the browser included on the CD with this book.

Chapters 2 through 22 form the client-side programming portion of the book. They discuss Internet Explorer 5, HTML 4, JavaScript/JScript (ECMA common standard), Cascading Style Sheets (CSS), Microsoft's Dynamic HTML, and VBScript. The server-side programming portion of the book covers the three most popular paradigms for building the server side of Web-based applications development: Microsoft's Active Server Pages (ASP), Perl/CGI, and Java Servlets. The server side portion of the book also includes unique chapters on Electronic Commerce, Servers, Databases and XML.

This book is intended for several academic markets, namely the introductory course sequences in which C++, Java and Visual Basic are traditionally taught; upper-level elective courses for students who already know programming; and as a supplement in introductory courses where students are first becoming familiar with computers, the Internet and the Web. The book offers a solid one- or two-semester introductory programming experience or a solid one semester upper-level elective. The book is also intended for professional programmers in corporate training programs or doing self-study.

We will publish fresh editions of this book promptly in response to rapidly evolving Internet and Web technologies. [*Note:* Our publishing plans are updated regularly at our Web site **`http://www.deitel.com/`**. The contents and publication dates of our forthcoming publications are always subject to change. If you need more specific information, please email us at **`deitel@deitel.com`**.]

1.17 A Tour of the Book

In this section, we take a tour the subjects you will study in *Internet and World Wide Web How to Program*. Many of the chapters end with an Internet and World Wide Web Resources section that provides a listing of resources through which you can enhance your knowledge and use of the Internet and World Wide Web. In addition you may want to visit our Web site to stay informed of the latest correction.

Chapter 1—Introduction to Computers

In Chapter 1, we present some historical information about computers and computer programming, and introductory information about Dynamic HTML, the Internet and the World Wide Web. We also present an overview of the concepts you will learn in the remaining chapters in the book.

Chapter 2—Introduction to Internet Explorer 5 and the World Wide Web

Prior to the explosion of interest in the Internet and the World Wide Web, if you heard the term *browser,* you probably would have thought about browsing at a bookstore. Today "browser" has a whole new meaning. Now a browser is an important piece of software that enables you to browse the Internet ("surf" the Web). You have a world of information, services and products to browse. The two most popular browsers are *Microsoft's Internet Explorer* and *Netscape's Communicator*.

Using tools that are part of the Internet Explorer 5 software package (enclosed on the CD included with this book), we discuss how to use the Web to its fullest potential. These tools include, but are not limited to, the Internet browser, email, newsgroups and chat.

This chapter shows readers who are not familiar with the Internet and the World Wide Web how to begin browsing the Web with Internet Explorer. We demonstrate several commonly used features of Internet Explorer for searching the Web, keeping track of the sites you visit and transferring files between computers. We also discuss several programs that accompany Internet Explorer. We demonstrate sending email, receiving email and using Internet newsgroups with *Microsoft Outlook Express*. We demonstrate using Microsoft *NetMeeting* and *Microsoft Chat* to have live meetings and discussions with other people on the Internet. The chapter ends with a discussion of *plug-ins* that provide browser users access to the ever increasing number of programs and features that make your browsing experience more enjoyable and interactive.

Chapter 3—Introduction to Hypertext Markup Language 4 (HTML 4)

In this chapter, we begin unlocking the power of the Web with *HTML*—the *Hypertext Markup Language*. HTML is a *markup language* for identifying the elements of an HTML document (Web page) so that a browser, such as Microsoft's Internet Explorer or Netscape's Communicator, can render (i.e., display) that page on your computer screen.

We introduce the basics of creating Web pages in HTML using a technique we call the *live-code approach.* Every concept is presented in the context of a complete working

HTML document (or Web page) that is immediately followed by the screen output produced when that HTML document is rendered by Internet Explorer. We write many simple Web pages. Later chapters introduce more sophisticated HTML techniques, such as *tables*, which are particularly useful for presenting and manipulating information from *databases*.

We introduce basic HTML *tags* and *attributes*. A key issue when using HTML is the separation of the *presentation of a document* (i.e., how the document is rendered on the screen by a browser) from the *structure of that document*. This chapter begins our in-depth discussion of this issue. As the book proceeds, you will be able to create increasingly appealing and powerful Web pages.

Some key topics covered in this chapter include: incorporating text and images in an HTML document, linking to other HTML documents on the Web, formatting text (including fonts, font sizes, colors and alignment), incorporating special characters (such as copyright and trademark symbols) into an HTML document and separating parts of an HTML document with horizontal lines (called *horizontal rules*).

Chapter 4—Intermediate HTML 4

In this chapter, we discuss more substantial HTML elements and features. We demonstrate how to present information in *lists* and *tables*. We discuss how to collect information from people browsing a site. We explain how to use *internal linking* and *image maps* to make Web pages more navigable. We also discuss how to use *frames* to make attractive interactive Web sites. By the end of this chapter, you will be familiar with most commonly used HTML tags and features. You will then be able to create more complex and visually appealing Web sites.

Chapter 5—Paint Shop Pro

Knowledge of HTML alone is not quite enough to make attractive, successful Web pages. Great Web pages often come alive with rich graphics and multimedia that make Web pages "come alive." You can tap into an extensible pool of free graphics available at many popular Web sites. If you would like to create your own unique graphics, the enclosed CD includes a trial edition of Jasc Inc.'s *Paint Shop Pro 5*. This chapter explains how to use many of Paint Shop Pro's powerful graphics capabilities. This easy-to-use, inexpensive graphics package offers the functionality of more expensive packages. We use Paint Shop Pro to create a few images that can add pizzazz to your Web pages. [*Note: The version of paint Shop Pro included on the CD is a 30-day evaluation copy. Once you use it for the first time, your ability to access that software on the CD will expire after 30-days at which point, if you like the product you may wish to purchase it. If you prefer to use free graphics software packages, you may be able to find some by searching the Web.*]

Chapter 6—Microsoft FrontPage Express

In Chapters 3 and 4 we showed how to create Web pages working directly in HTML—the underlying "language of the Web." We will continue to work directly in HTML and Dynamic HTML throughout the book. Working at this level is appropriate for "heavy-duty" Web developers (i.e., the kind of people this book is intended to produce) who push the limits of the Web's capabilities. However, there is also a lightweight level at which to develop Web pages. There are many products generically referred to as *HTML editors*. These include products like *Microsoft's FrontPage* and *FrontPage Express* (the latter of which is included on the CD).

[Note: A FrontPage editor is included with Visual InterDev 6 Professional Edition which is on the CD with the student edition of this text. Microsoft allows us to distribute this version of the CD only in student editions of this book intended for academic use. Other readers wishing to learn Visual InterDev will need to purchase it separately.]

In this chapter, we walk through the process of creating Web pages quickly and conveniently with FrontPage Express. We repeat several of the examples from Chapters 3 and 4 to show how easy it is to work with FrontPage Express. This product is one of a class of products referred to as *WYSIWYG ("What You See Is What You Get") editors*. FrontPage Express presents an interface like that of Microsoft Word where you use point-and-click, drag-and-drop functionality to quickly layout and create professional-looking Web pages. You can find free demo versions of other HTML editors on the Web.

Chapter 7—Introduction to Microsoft Visual InterDev 6

[Note: Visual InterDev 6 Professional Edition is on the CD with the student edition of this text. Microsoft allows us to distribute this version of the CD only in student editions of this book intended for academic use. Other readers wishing to learn Visual InterDev will need to purchase it separately.]

A few years back, Microsoft recognized the commonality of the program development environments for its major programming languages and decided to offer a bundled package with Visual Basic, Visual C++, Visual J++ and Visual InterDev. This package, called *Visual Studio*, has become the standard development platform for the Microsoft Community.

Visual InterDev ("Internet Development") is an industrial-strength integrated development environment for developing Internet and World-Wide-Web based applications. In this chapter, we discuss the basics of the InterDev environment. In later chapters of the book, you can use InterDev with various server-side technologies such as Active Server Pages to quickly build powerful Web-based applications. *[Note: Chapter 7 is the only chapter of this book that uses Visual InterDev, but the reader may choose to use InterDev throughout the book. Readers not interested in using InterDev should simply skip Chapter 7.]*

Chapter 8—JavaScript/JScript: Introduction to Scripting

Chapter 8 presents our first JavaScript *programs* (also called *scripts*). Scripting helps Web-pages "come alive" by allowing a Web page developer to manipulate elements of a Web page dynamically as the client browses that page. Chapters 8 through 13 present the features of the JavaScript scripting language which are then used in Chapters 14 through 21 to demonstrate how to dynamically manipulate the contents of Web pages. JavaScript is interesting in that it enables us to present key fundamental computer-science concepts at the same depth as other programming languages (such as C, C++, Java and Visual Basic), but in the exciting context of the Internet and World Wide Web.

[*Note:* JavaScript was created by Netscape. Microsoft's version is called JScript. The languages are close. Netscape, Microsoft and other companies are cooperating with the European Computer Manufacturer's Association (ECMA) to produce a universal, client-side scripting language, the current version of which is referred to as ECMA-262. JavaScript and JScript each conform to this standard. We tested the JavaScript programs in Chapters 8 through 12. Each of these programs works in the latest Netscape and Microsoft browsers.]

Using our live-code approach, every concept is presented in the context of a complete working JavaScript program which is immediately followed by the screen output produced when the HTML document containing the program is loaded into a Web browser. The chapter introduces nonprogrammers to basic programming concepts and constructs. The scripts in this chapter illustrate how to write (*output*) text into a Web page for display to the user and how to obtain (*input*) data from the user at the keyboard. Some of the input and output is performed using the browser's ability to display predefined *graphical user interface (GUI)* windows (called *dialog boxes*) for input and output. This allows a nonprogrammer to concentrate on fundamental programming concepts and constructs rather than developing HTML forms containing GUI components and using the more complex GUI *event handling* in which a JavaScript program responds to the user interactions with an HTML form (we discuss these more powerful capabilities in Chapter 11). Chapter 8 also provides detailed treatments of *decision making* and *arithmetic operations*. After studying this chapter, the student will understand how to write simple, but complete, JavaScript programs.

Chapter 9—JavaScript/JScript: Control Structures I

Chapter 9 focusses on the program-development process. The chapter discusses how to take a *problem statement* (i.e., a *requirements document*) and from it develop a working JavaScript program, including performing intermediate steps in a program development tool called *pseudocode*. The chapter introduces some simple control structures used for decision making (**`if`** and **`if/else`**) and repetition (**`while`**). We examine counter-controlled repetition, sentinel-controlled repetition and introduce JavaScript's increment, decrement and assignment operators. The chapter uses simple flowcharts to show graphically the flow of control through each of the control structures. This chapter helps the student develop good programming habits in preparation for dealing with the more substantial programming tasks in the remainder of the text.

Chapter 10—JavaScript/JScript: Control Structures II

Chapter 10 discusses much of the material JavaScript has in common with the C programming language, especially the *sequence*, *selection* and *repetition* control structures. Here we introduce one additional control structure for decision making (**`switch`**) and two additional control structures for repetition (**`for`** and **`do/while`**). This chapter also introduces several more operators that allow programmers to define complex conditions in their decision making and repetition structures. The chapter uses flowcharts to show the flow of control through each of the control structures. The chapter concludes with a summary that enumerates each of the control structures. The techniques discussed in Chapters 9 and 10 constitute a large part of what has been traditionally taught in the universities under the topic of structured programming.

Chapter 11—JavaScript/JScript: Functions

Chapter 11 takes a deeper look inside scripts. Scripts contain data called *global* (or *script-level*) *variables* and executable units called *functions*. We explore functions in depth and include a discussion of functions that "call themselves," so-called *recursive* functions. We discuss predefined JavaScript functions, programmer-defined functions and recursion. The techniques presented in Chapter 11 are essential to the production of properly structured programs, especially the kinds of larger programs that Web programmers are likely to develop in real-world, Web-based applications. The *divide and conquer* strategy is presented as an effective means for solving complex problems by dividing them into simpler interacting components. The chapter offers a solid introduction to recursion and includes a table summarizing the many recursion examples and exercises in Chapters 11 through 13. In this chapter, we also introduce *events* and *event handling*—elements required for programming graphical user interfaces (GUIs) in HTML forms. Events are notifications of state change such as button clicks, mouse clicks, pressing a keyboard key, etc. JavaScript allows programmers to respond to various events by coding functions called *event handlers*. This begins our discussions of *event-driven programming*—the user drives the program by interacting with GUI components (causing *events* such as mouse clicks) and the scripts respond to the events by performing appropriate tasks (*event handling*). The event-driven programming techniques introduced here are used in scripts throughout the book. Dynamic HTML event handling is discussed in Chapter 16.

Chapter 12—JavaScript/JScript: Arrays

Chapter 12 explores the processing of data in lists and tables of values. We discuss the structuring of data into *arrays*, or groups, of related data item. The chapter presents numerous examples of both single-subscripted arrays and double-subscripted arrays. It is widely recognized that structuring data properly is just as important as using control structures effectively in the development of properly structured programs. Examples in the chapter investigate various common array manipulations, printing histograms (i.e., bar charts), sorting data, passing arrays to functions and an introduction to the field of survey data analysis (with simple statistics). This chapter also introduces JavaScript's **`for/in`** control structure that is specifically designed to work with collections of data stored in arrays.

A feature of this chapter is the discussion of elementary sorting and searching techniques and the presentation of binary searching (of a sorted array) as a dramatic improvement over linear searching. The end-of-chapter exercises include a variety of interesting and challenging problems such as improved sorting techniques, the design of an airline reservations system, and the *Knight's Tour* and *Eight Queens* problems that introduce the notions of heuristic programming so widely employed in the field of artificial intelligence. The chapter exercises also include a delightful simulation of the classic race between the tortoise and the hare, recursive quicksort and recursive maze traversals. A special section entitled "Building Your Own Computer" explains machine language programming and proceeds with the design and implementation of a computer simulator that allows the reader to write and run machine language programs. This unique feature of the text will be especially useful to the reader who wants to understand how computers really work.

Chapter 13—JavaScript/JScript: Objects

This chapter begins our discussion of *object-based programming* with JavaScript's built-in objects. The chapter discusses the terminology of *objects*. The chapter overviews the JavaScript **`Math`** object's methods and provides several examples of JavaScript's string, date and time processing capabilities with the **`String`** and **`Date`** objects. An interesting feature of the **`String`** object demonstrated here is a set of methods (functions associated with particular objects) that help a script programmer output HTML from a script by wrapping strings in HTML elements. The chapter also discusses JavaScript's **`Number`** and **`Boolean`** objects. Many of the features discussed in this chapter are used throughout the Dynamic HTML chapters (14 through 22) as we illustrate that every element of an HTML document is an object that can be manipulated by JavaScript statements.

Chapter 14—Dynamic HTML: Cascading Style Sheets (CSS)

In earlier versions of HTML, Web browsers controlled the appearance (i.e., the rendering) of every Web page. [If you placed an **`H1`** (i.e., a large heading) element in your document, the browser rendered it in any manner it so chose. With the advent of *Cascading Style Sheets*, you can now take control of the way the browser renders your page.] Applying Cascading Style Sheets to Web pages can give major portions of your Web site (or the whole Web site for that matter) their own distinctive look. Cascading Style Sheets technology allows you to specify the style of your page elements (spacing, margins, etc.) separately from the structure of your document (section headers, body text, links, etc.). This *separation of structure from content* allows greater manageability and makes changing the style of your document easier and faster.

Chapter 15—Dynamic HTML: DHTML Object Model and Collections

There is a massive switch occurring in the computer industry. The procedural programming style used since the inception of the industry is being replaced by the object-oriented style of programming. Object orientation has demonstrated its worth to the extent that the vast majority of major new software efforts use object technology in one form or another. Some languages make it easy for you to create your own objects by various means, either "from scratch" or by inheritance from object "blueprints" called classes. The scripting languages we discuss in this book are most commonly used to manipulate existing objects by sending them messages that either inquire about the objects' attributes or that ask the objects to perform certain supportable methods. In this Chapter we continue the discussion of object technology we began in Chapter 13, presenting Microsoft's Dynamic HTML object model. Working with this object model is a key to the power of Dynamic HTML in Chapters 14 through 21. As IE5 downloads your page from a server, it converts each of the elements on the page into an object. Objects store data (their *attributes*) and can perform functions (their methods). Through scripting languages (such as JavaScript), you can write commands that will *get* or *set* (i.e., read or write) an object's attributes. You can also write commands that call an object's methods to cause that object to perform its various functions.

Chapter 16—Dynamic HTML: Event Model

We have seen that HTML pages can be controlled via scripting. The HTML 4 specification includes HTML's *event model* that enables scripts to respond to user actions and change the Web page accordingly without having to download another Web page from the World Wide Web. This makes Web applications more responsive and user-friendly, and can reduce server load—a performance concern we discuss thoroughly in Chapters 24 through 29.

With the event model, scripts can respond to a user moving and/or clicking the mouse, scrolling up or down the screen or entering keystrokes. Content becomes more dynamic while interfaces become more intuitive. We discuss how to use the event model to respond to user actions. We give examples of event handling for many of the most common and useful events, which range from mouse capture, to error handling to form processing. For example, we use the **`onreset`** event to prompt a user to confirm that he or she really wants to reset a form. Included at the end of the chapter is a table of all DHTML events.

Chapter 17—Dynamic HTML: Filters and Transitions

Internet Explorer includes a set of filters that let the author perform complex image transformations completely in the Web browser without the need for further downloads from a Web server. Especially important is that the filters are scriptable, so the author can create stunning animations with a few lines of client-side JavaScript. We introduce the **`fliph`** and **`flipv`** filters, which can mirror text and images horizontally and vertically. The

chroma filter applies transparency to an image, and the **mask** filter applies an image mask. The **gray**, **xray**, and **invert** filters all apply simple transformations to images. The **shadow** and **dropShadow** filters both apply shadowing effects to text and images, and the **light** filter allows you to simulate light sources illuminating your document. The **alpha** filter allows you to create transparency gradients, and the **glow** filter allows you to create dynamic, glowing text. The **blur** filter applies a directional motion blur, and the **wave** filter applies a sine-wave distortion to your elements.

Internet Explorer also provides *transitions* that are similar to those in professional PowerPoint-like presentation packages, in which transitions between slides are marked with visual effects such as Box in, Circle out, Wipe left, Vertical blinds, Checkerboard across, Random dissolve, Split horizontal in, Strips right up and Random bars horizontal. Besides these transitions which are applied with the **revealTrans** filter, there is a **blendTrans** filter, which allows you to gradually fade in or fade out an HTML element over a set period of time.

Chapter 18—Dynamic HTML: Data Binding with Tabular Data Control

This is one of the most important chapters in the book for people who will build substantial, real-world, Web-based applications. Businesses thrive on data. Dynamic HTML helps Web application developers produce more responsive data-intensive applications.

With *data binding*, data need no longer reside exclusively on the server. The data can be maintained on the client and in a manner that distinguishes that data from the HTML code on the page. Typically, the data is sent from the server to the client and then all subsequent manipulations take place on that data directly on the client thus improving performance and responsiveness by eliminating server activity and network delays. Once the data is available on the client, the data can then be *sorted* (i.e., arranged into ascending or descending order) and *filtered* (i.e., only the portion of the data relevant to the user's needs is selected) in various ways. We present examples of each of these operations.

To bind external data to HTML elements, Internet Explorer employs software capable of connecting the browser to live data sources. These are known as *Data Source Objects (DSOs)*. There are several DSOs available in IE5—in this chapter we discuss the most popular DSO—the *Tabular Data Control (TDC)*. Returning data back to the server is covered in Chapter 25, in our discussion of the *Remote Data Services (RDS)* Data Source object.

Chapter 19—Dynamic HTML: Structured Graphics ActiveX Control

Although high-quality content is what visitors to your site are usually looking for, it may not be enough to hold their attention and keep them coming back. Eye-catching, animated graphics may help. This chapter explores the *Structured Graphics ActiveX Control* included with Internet Explorer 5. The Structured Graphics Control is a Web interface for the widely used *DirectAnimation* subset of Microsoft's *DirectX* software, used in many popular video games and graphical applications. This control allows you to create complex graphics containing lines, shapes, textures and fills. As with other elements of a Web page, the control is accessible through scripting which allows the graphics to be manipulated dynamically.

Chapter 20—Dynamic HTML: Path, Sequencer and Sprite ActiveX Controls

In this chapter we discuss three additional DirectAnimation ActiveX controls available for use with Internet Explorer 5: the *Path Control*, the *Sequencer Control* and the *Sprite Control*. Each of these controls allows Web-page designers to add animated multimedia effects to Web pages. The Path control allows you to control the positioning of elements on the screen. This is more elaborate than CSS absolute positioning, as you can define lines, ovals and other shapes as paths along which objects move. Every aspect of motion is controllable through scripting. The Sequencer Control allows you to perform tasks at specified time intervals. This is useful for presentation-like effects, especially when used with the transitions we covered in Chapter 17. The Sprite Control is a mechanism for creating animations for use on the Web. We also discuss, for comparison purposes, animated GIFs—another technique for producing web-based animations.

Chapter 21—Multimedia: Audio, Video, Speech Synthesis and Recognition

HTML is not just for text. Our focus in this chapter is on the explosion of audio, video and speech technology appearing on the Web. We discuss adding sound, video and animated characters to your Web pages (primarily using existing audio and video clips). Your first reaction may be a sense of caution, because these are complex technologies about which most readers have had little education. Yet, you will quickly see how easy it is to incorporate multimedia into your Web pages and control it with Dynamic HTML. This is one of the beauties of today's programming languages. They give the programmer easy access to complex technologies.

Multimedia files can be quite large. Some multimedia technologies require that the complete multimedia file be downloaded to the client before the audio or video begins playing. With *streaming audio* and *streaming video* technologies, the audios and videos can begin playing while the files are downloading, thus reducing delays. Streaming technologies are quite popular on the Web. This chapter demonstrates how to incorporate the *RealNetworks RealPlayer* into a Web page to receive streaming media.

The chapter also includes an extensive set of Internet and Web resources such as Web sites that show interesting ways in which designers use multimedia enhanced Web pages.

Chapter 22—Dynamic HTML: Client-Side Scripting with VBScript

In Chapter 22, we assume the reader is now familiar with the principles of programming, so we present Microsoft's *VBScript* condensed into a single chapter (exactly as we do with Perl scripting in Chapter 27). *JavaScript/JScript* has become the de facto standard for *client-side scripting*. All major browsers support this language which has been standardized through the *European Computer Manufacturers Association* as *ECMA-262*. VBScript is a subset of Visual Basic. It can certainly be used for client-side scripting, but it is a Microsoft-specific technology and is not supported by many leading browsers (although so-called *plug-ins* are available to help some of those browsers understand and process VBScript). So many people browsing Web pages containing VBScript will not experience the full functionality intended by the page designers. VBScript, however, has become the de facto standard for writing server side *Active Server Pages (ASP), a Microsoft-specific technology* which we discuss in detail in Chapter 26. Because we need to discuss VBScript before ASP, we have chosen to include this chapter as the last in our discussion of client-side scripting. This will prepare you to use VBScript on the client-side in Microsoft communities and in Microsoft-based *intranets* (i.e., internal networks that use the same communications protocols as the Internet). It will also prepare you to use VBScript with on the server side Active Server Pages.

Chapter 23—Electronic Commerce and Security
This is a unique chapter for an introductory programming textbook. The Web has caused a complete rethinking of the way systems should most effectively be designed and implemented. E-Commerce has been a major topic over the last few years in business publications, but it has been equally prominent in the computing literature. The Internet and especially the Web are causing a profound rethinking and restructuring of the way in which the world's business is conducted. Every major organization and most smaller groups are working hard to incorporate Internet and Web technology into existing systems and new information systems designs. This phenomenon is not a casual one; it is profound. In this chapter we discuss the fundamentals of conducting business on the Internet and the Web. Our goal is to give students an understanding of how important this topic is now and how it will continue to be important as they pursue their careers. We present a number of case studies, with the key goal of highlighting the common core of technologies needed to implement e-commerce systems. We emphasize the importance of Internet and Web technology, database technology, security technology and others. Then in the remainder of the server-side programming chapters, we put many of these technologies to work in constructing actual multitiered, client/server, database-intensive Web-based systems. The Internet and the Web "level the playing field" making it possible even for small companies to quickly establish a business presence in worldwide markets, something that was extraordinarily difficult to do just a few years ago. The chapter briefly introduces XML (the eXtensible Markup Language)—widely believed to be the hottest new e-commerce enabling technology. In Chapter 28, we present a detailed introduction to XML with live-code examples.

Chapter 24—Web Servers (PWS, IIS, Apache and Jigsaw)
We have worked hard to create a book that will help you construct complete Web-based multitiered, client/server, database-intensive systems. Through Chapter 22, we have focussed on the client side. Chapters 23 through 29 focus on the server side, discussing many technologies crucial to implementing successful Web-based systems. One of the crucial decisions you will make in building Web-based systems is what server(s) to use. The two most popular are *Apache* in the UNIX world and *Internet Information Server (IIS)* in the Microsoft world. Each of these is a "heavy-duty," "industrial strength" server designed to handle the high volumes of transactions that occur in active, real-world systems. These require considerable system resources and administrative support, as is typical of real systems. To help people enter the world of server programming, Microsoft provides *Personal Web Server (PWS)*—a lightweight version of IIS. PWS is easy to install and run on Windows-based systems, a large part of the intended audience for this book. We focus on PWS in our case studies so that students and professional readers with Windows 95 and Windows 98 systems will be able to run our server-side programs easily. We also provide (only) brief introductions to setting up and using three commercial-grade Web servers, namely IIS, Apache and Jigsaw. *Jigsaw* is a free Web server from the World Wide Web Consortium that is receiving considerable interest. *[Note: The world of server software is complex and evolving quickly. Our goal in this chapter is to give you a "handle" on setting up and using server-side software. Our organization does not currently provide software support on using these servers. We suggest you surf the Web sites we list at the back of Chapter 24 for organizations that may provide such help.]*

Chapter 25—Database: SQL, ADO and RDS

Chapter 25 discusses database concepts (the vast majority of organizations' data is stored in databases) and the Structured Query Language (SQL) for making database inquiries. The chapter also discusses Microsoft's database strategy called *universal database access (UDA)*. Two key elements of UDA are ActiveX Data Objects (ADO) and Remote Data Services (RDS). ADO, which we discuss in Chapter 25 and demonstrate in Chapter 26, is a high-level programming interface used by Microsoft languages such as Visual Basic, Visual C++, Visual J++, VBScript, etc. to access databases. RDS (which we discuss and demonstrate in this chapter) is a technology specifically designed for "connectionless access" from Web clients to databases. Because browsers do not maintain connections to HTTP servers, RDS provides a mechanism for getting database records to the client and returning those database records to the server for update. A number of other database packages are available (as "freeware" or "shareware") on the Internet.

Chapter 26—Active Server Pages (ASP)

In this chapter we discuss Microsoft's Active Server Pages (ASP), the first of the three server-side software development paradigms the book presents. Active Server Pages can be programmed in a variety of languages—by far the most popular of these is Microsoft's VBScript (which is discussed in Chapter 22). In a typical *multitiered Web-based application*, there is a *top-tier* containing the code that interacts directly with the user. This tier, called the *client*, is usually the browser (such as IE5) rendering a Web-page and executing scripting commands. These commands can be implemented in a variety of languages, but JavaScript has almost become the universal de facto standard *client-side scripting language*. Microsoft offers its version of JavaScript which it called *JScript*. We have tried to use the common portions only of these languages for most of the client-side scripting code in the book. The *bottom tier* is the database containing the organization's information. The *middle tier*, called the *server*, contains the *business logic*. It receives client requests from the top-tier, references the data stored in the database in the bottom tier, and responds to the client by creating a new HTML/Dynamic HTML page and sending the page to the client to be rendered by the browser. The HTML/Dynamic HTML sent to the client can be anything the programmer wishes—especially information retrieved from databases. Active Server Pages is Microsoft's technology for implementing middle-tier business logic. This a crucial chapter for those readers who will want to implement Web-based applications.

Chapter 27—CGI (Common Gateway Interface) and Perl 5

There are a variety of popular server-side technologies for developing Web-based applications. Historically, the most widely used (and the second such technology we cover in this book) has been Perl/CGI. Despite the onrush of the newer technologies from Microsoft and Sun—Active Server Pages (ASP) and Java Servlets (which we discuss in Chapter 29), respectively—the Perl/CGI community is well entrenched and will remain popular for the foreseeable future. Chapter 27 presents a nice introduction to CGI and Perl, including many real-world, live-code examples and discussions, including demonstrations of some of the most recent features of each of these technologies.

Chapter 28—XML (Extensible Markup Language)

Throughout the book we have been emphasizing HTML and Dynamic HTML. Each of these languages derives from SGML (Standardized General Markup Language) which became a world-class standard in 1986. SGML is widely employed in publishing applications worldwide, but it has not been incorporated into the mainstream computing and information technology curricula. Its sheer size and complexity has limited its use beyond heavy-duty, industrial-strength applications. XML (the eXtensible Markup Language) is an effort to make SGML-like technology available to a much broader community. XML is essentially a condensed subset of SGML with additional features for usability. XML is different in concept from HTML. HTML is a markup language. XML is a language for creating new markup languages. XML could be used, for example, to create HTML. The key to XML is that it is not limited to some fixed set of elements and tags as is HTML. Rather, XML allows you to define new elements and tags specific to your applications areas.

Two popular language created with XML are MathML (Mathematics Markup Language) and CML (Chemistry Markup Language) among others. We present examples of using MathML to transmit mathematical expressions over the Web, such that they can be rendered by a client browser. CML allows chemists to transmit information about the molecular structure of compounds.

The possible uses for XML are endless. Baseball fans might want to develop a language that lets them transmit structured information about games. Chess fans might want to transmit marked-up chess moves—an example we provide in this chapter. Businesses might want to transmit marked-up information about their financial transactions. Stock brokerage houses might want to transmit marked-up transaction information for buying and selling stocks and bonds. Clients might want to transmit marked-up purchase-order information to vendors. Actually all of this information can be transmitted in simple files without XML. But with XML, the information comes wrapped in elements that describe precisely what each type of information means, so the receiving programs, such as browsers, can work with the information more intelligently.

Chapter 29—Java™ Servlets (Bonus Chapter for Java Developers)

Java servlets represent a third popular way of building the server side of Web-based applications. We have discussed two of them, namely Microsoft's Active Server Pages and Perl/CGI. The underlying scripting languages—VBScript and Perl, respectively, are discussed in sufficient depth for the reader to understand the code examples in each of these chapters. In our recently published book *Java How to Program: Third Edition*, we provided a chapter-length treatment of Java servlets. Servlets are written in full-scale Java (not JavaScript/JScript), which requires a substantial book-length treatment to learn. We do not teach Java in *Internet and World Wide Web How to Program*, but we feel that servlets are important. So, we included (with slight revision) the chapter on servlets from our Java book. This chapter is provided as a "bonus section" for the portion of our audience that is familiar with Java. If you do not know Java, you may still enjoy reading the servlets chapter, although you may not be able to get as much out of it. When you finish studying the server-side chapters of *Internet and World Wide Web How to Program*, you will be familiar (at various levels of understanding) with the three most popular server-side implementation schemes—Microsoft's Active Server Pages, Perl/CGI and Sun Microsystems' Java servlets.

Well, there you have it! We have worked hard to create this book and its optional interactive multimedia *Cyber Classroom* version. The book is loaded with hundreds of working, live-code examples, programming tips, self-review exercises and answers, challenging exercises and projects and numerous study aids to help you master the material. The technologies we introduce will help you write Web-based applications quickly and effectively. As you read the book, if something is not clear, or if you find an error, please write to us at **deitel@deitel.com**. We will respond promptly, and we will post corrections and clarifications on our Web site

http://www.deitel.com/

Prentice Hall maintains **http://www.prenhall.com/deitel**—a Web site dedicated to our Prentice Hall textbooks, multimedia packages and Web-based training products. The site contains "Companion Web Sites" for each of our books that include frequently asked questions (FAQs), example downloads, errata, updates, additional self-test questions, and other resources.

You are about to start on a challenging and rewarding path. We hope you enjoy learning with *Internet and World Wide Web How to Program* as much as we enjoyed writing it!

1.18 Internet and World Wide Web Resources

http://www.deitel.com/
Please check this site for daily updates, corrections and additional resources for all Deitel & Associates, Inc. publications.

http://www.learnthenet.com/english/index.html
Learn the Net is a Web site containing a complete overview of the Internet, the World Wide Web and the underlying technologies. The site contains information that can help people Internet and Web get novices started.

http://www.w3.org/
The W3C homepage is a comprehensive description of the Web and where it is headed. The World Wide Web Consortium is an international joint effort with the goal of overseeing the development of the World Wide Web. The goals of the W3C are divided into categories: User Interface Domain, Technology and Society Domain, Architecture Domain and Web Accessibility Initiatives. For each Internet technology with which the W3C is involved, the site provides a description of the technology and its benefits to Web designers, the history of the technology and the future goals of the W3C in developing the technology. Topics discussed on the site include Hypertext Markup Language (HTML), Cascading Style Sheets (CSS), Document Object Model (DOM), multimedia, graphics, Hypertext Transfer Protocol (HTTP), Extensible Markup Language (XML) and Extensible Stylesheet Language (XSL). This site is of great benefit for understanding the standards of the World Wide Web. Each of these topics is discussed (at various levels of depth) in this book.

SUMMARY

[Note: Because this chapter is primarily a summary of the rest of the book we have not provided a summary section. In each of the remaining 28 chapters we provide a detailed summary of the points covered in that chapter.]

TERMINOLOGY

Active Server pages (ASP)
Ada
ALU (arithmetic and logic unit)
arithmetic and logic unit (ALU)
array
assembly language

bandwidth
Basic
bottom tier
browser
C
Cascading Style Sheets (CSS)
C++
central processing unit (CPU)
client
client/server computing
COBOL
compiler
computer
computer program
computer programmer
CPU (central processing unit)
database
data binding
disk
divide and conquer strategy
dynamic content
Dynamic HTML
e-commerce
ECMA-262
e-commerce
editor
electronic commerce
event-driven programming
execute phase
filtering data
filters
Fortran
FrontPage Express
function
hardware
high-level language
HTML (Hypertext Markup Language)
IDE (Integrated Development Environment)
input device
input/output (I/O)
input unit
Internet
Internet Explorer 5
interpreter
intranet
IP (Internet Protocol)
Java
JavaScript
JScript
KIS (keep it simple)
live-code approach
machine language
memory unit
method
Microsoft
Microsoft's Internet Explorer Web browser
middle tier
multimedia
multitasking
multithreading
Netscape's Communicator
objects
object-based programming (OBP)
object-oriented programming (OOP)
output device
output unit
Paint Shop Pro
Pascal
Path Control
Perl
personal computing
platforms
portability
presentation of a document
primary memory
problem statement
procedural programming
programming language
reusable componentry
secondary storage unit
Sequencer Control
server
servlets
software
software reuse
sorting data
speech
Sprite Control
streaming audio and video
Structured Graphics Control
structured programming
structure of a document
Sun Microsystems
syntax error
TCP (Transmission Control protocol)
TCP/IP
top tier
transitions
translator programs
VBScript

Visual InterDev
Web server
World Wide Web (WWW)
World Wide Web Consortium (W3C)
WYSIWYG

GOOD PROGRAMMING PRACTICES

1.1 Write your programs in a simple and straightforward manner. This is sometimes referred to as KIS ("keep it simple"). Do not "stretch" the language by trying bizarre usages.

1.2 Read the documentation for the version of JavaScript you are using. Refer to this documentation frequently to be sure you are aware of the rich collection of features and that you are using these features correctly.

PERFORMANCE TIPS

1.1 Reusing proven code components instead of writing your own versions can improve program performance because these components are normally written to perform efficiently.

1.2 Interpreters have an advantage over compilers for the Dynamic HTML world, namely that an interpreted program can begin execution immediately as soon as it is downloaded to the client's machine, whereas a source program to be compiled must first suffer a potentially long delay as the program is compiled before it can be executed.

PORTABILITY TIPS

1.1 Although it is easier to write portable programs in JavaScript than in most other programming languages, there are differences among compilers, interpreters and computers that can make portability difficult to achieve. Simply writing programs in JavaScript does not guarantee portability. The programmer will occasionally need to deal directly with compiler and computer variations.

1.2 The Web world is highly fragmented and this makes it difficult for authors and Web developers to create universal solutions. The World Wide Web Consortium (W3C) is working towards the goal of creating a universal client-side platform.

SOFTWARE ENGINEERING OBSERVATIONS

1.1 Use a building block approach to creating programs. Avoid reinventing the wheel. Use existing pieces—this is called software reuse and it is central to object-oriented programming.

1.2 Extensive class libraries of reusable software components are available over the Internet and the World Wide Web. Many of these libraries are available at no charge.

TESTING AND DEBUGGING TIPS

1.1 Always test your JavaScript programs on all systems on which you intend to run those programs.

1.2 Your computer and compiler are good teachers. If after carefully reading your documentation manual you are not sure how a feature works, experiment and see what happens. Study each error or warning message you get when you browse pages containing JavaScript programs and correct the programs to eliminate these messages.

SELF-REVIEW EXERCISES

1.1 Fill in the blanks in each of the following:

a) The company that popularized personal computing was __________.

b) The computer that made personal computing legitimate in business and industry was the __________.

c) Computers process data under the control of sets of instructions called __________.

d) The six key logical units of the computer are the __________, __________, __________, __________, __________ and __________.

e) The three classes of languages discussed in the chapter are __________, __________ and __________.

f) The programs that translate high-level language programs into machine language are called __________.

1.2 Fill in the blanks in each of the following sentences.

a) The __________ programming language was created by Professor Nicklaus Wirth and was intended for academic use.

b) One important capability of Ada is called __________ this allows programmers to specify that many activities are to occur in parallel.

c) The __________ is the grandparent of what is today called the Internet.

d) The information carrying capacity of a communications medium like the Internet is called __________.

e) The acronym TCP/IP stands for __________.

1.3 Fill in the blanks in each of the following statements.

a) The __________ allows computer users to locate and view multimedia-based documents on almost any subject over the Internet.

b) __________ of CERN developed the World Wide Web and several of the communications protocols that form the backbone of the Web.

c) __________ are essentially reusable software components that model items in the real world.

d) C initially became widely known as the development language of the __________ operating system.

e) In a client/server relationship, the __________ requests that some action be performed and the __________ performs the action and responds.

ANSWERS TO SELF-REVIEW EXERCISES

1.1 a) Apple. b) IBM Personal Computer. c) programs (or scripts). d) input unit, output unit, memory unit, arithmetic and logic unit, central processing unit, secondary storage unit. e) machine languages, assembly languages, high-level languages. f) compilers.

1.2 a) Pascal. b) multitasking. c) ARPAnet. d) bandwidth. e) Transmission Control Protocol/ Internet Protocol.

1.3 a) World Wide Web. b) Tim Berners-Lee. c) Objects. d) UNIX. e) client, server.

EXERCISES

1.4 Categorize each of the following items as either hardware or software:
a) CPU
b) Compiler
c) ALU
d) Interpreter
e) input unit
f) an editor program

1.5 Why might you want to write a program in a machine-independent language instead of a machine-dependent language? Why might a machine-dependent language be more appropriate for writing certain types of programs?

1.6 Fill in the blanks in each of the following statements:
a) Which logical unit of the computer receives information from outside the computer for use by the computer? __________.
b) The process of instructing the computer to solve specific problems is called __________.
c) What type of computer language uses English-like abbreviations for machine language instructions? __________.
d) Which logical unit of the computer sends information that has already been processed by the computer to various devices so that the information may be used outside the computer? __________.
e) Which logical unit of the computer retains information? __________.
f) Which logical unit of the computer performs calculations? __________.
g) Which logical unit of the computer makes logical decisions? __________.
h) The level of computer language most convenient to the programmer for writing programs quickly and easily is __________.
i) The only language that a computer can directly understand is called that computer's __________.
j) Which logical unit of the computer coordinates the activities of all the other logical units? __________.

1.7 Fill in the blanks in each of the following statements.
a) The two most popular World Wide Web browsers are Netscape Communicator and Microsoft __________.
b) A key issue when using HTML is the separation of the presentation of a document from the __________ of that document.
c) A function associated with a particular object is called a __________.
d) With the advent of __________ Style Sheets you can now take control of the way the browsers render your pages.
e) The data of an object is also referred to as that object's __________.
f) Visual effects such as Box in, Circle out, Wipe left, Vertical blinds, Checkerboard across, Random dissolve, Split horizontal in, Strips right up and Random bars horizontal are all examples of Internet Explorer 5 .
g) The process of arranging data into ascending or descending order is called __________.
h) The __________ Control allows you to perform tasks at specified time intervals.
i) With __________ audio and video technologies, audios and videos can begin playing while the files are downloading, thus reducing delays.
j) The __________ scripting language has become the de facto standard for writing server-side Active Server Pages.
k) The acronym XML stands for the __________ Markup Language.

l) The two most popular Web Servers are _________ in the UNIX world and _________ in the Microsoft world.
m) In a multitiered Web-based application, the middle tier is called the server and contains the __________.
n) MathML and ChemML are markup languages created from __________.

Introduction to Internet Explorer 5 and the World Wide Web

Objectives

- To become familiar with the Microsoft Internet Explorer 5 (IE5) Web browser's capabilities.
- To be able to use IE5 to search the "world of information" available on the World Wide Web.
- To be able to use Microsoft Outlook Express to send and receive email.
- To be able to use Microsoft NetMeeting to have online conferences with friends and colleagues.
- To feel comfortable using the Internet as an information tool.

Give us the tools, and we will finish the job.
Sir Winston Spencer Churchill

We must learn to explore all the options and possibilities that confront us in a complex and rapidly changing world.
James William Fulbright

Outline

2.1 Introduction

Prior to the explosion of interest in the Internet and the World Wide Web, if you heard the term *browser,* you probably would have thought about browsing at a bookstore. Today "browser" has a whole new meaning. Now a browser is an important piece of software that enables you to browse the Internet ("surf" the Web). You have a world of information, services and products to browse. The two most popular browsers are Microsoft's Internet Explorer and Netscape's Communicator—we will study Internet Explorer in depth.

You sit down at a computer and literally search the world in seconds with special Internet sites called *search engines*. Through your browser, you request your favorite search engine, then you type in your request, and the search engine responds in seconds, listing many Web sites that have information on the subject you requested. What a wonderful way to learn about the world in which we live—what a marvelous way to improve our productivity!

The Internet is also a wonderful medium for exchanging information. Using tools that are part of the Internet Explorer 5 software package (enclosed on the CD included with this book), we discuss how to use the Web to its fullest potential. These tools include the Internet browser, email, newsgroups, chat, and much more.

2.2 Connecting to the Internet

To connect to the Internet, you need a computer, a modem or network card, Internet software, and knowledge of how to install and run programs.

The first step to getting on the Internet, which we cannot cover here (because the method differs widely depending on your situation), is registering with an *Internet Service Provider* (ISP). An ISP connects your computer to the Internet through a modem or a network connection. If you are living on a college campus, you may have a free network connection available; contact your college computer support staff for more information on getting a network hookup. If you do not have a network connection available, then you will have to connect through a commercial ISP such as America Online, CompuServe, or many others.

Once you have signed up for your account (with your ISP), you should start the ***Internet Connection Wizard*** (ICW). This program should be located in your **Start** menu under **Programs-Accessories-Communications**. The screen that appears upon starting this program should look like Fig. 2.1.

Simply follow the instructions in **Internet Connection Wizard** to make the appropriate settings for your Internet connection with your computer. Making these settings will help things run more smoothly and will also help you reconnect to the Internet if you are ever disconnected accidentally.

If you are interested in learning more about the Internet and its features, click on the button labeled **Tutorial**, located in the first ICW screen.

Once your connection has been set up, you are ready to communicate over the Internet.

Performance Tip 2.1

You will get the best browsing performance when viewing the Web if you have as few programs as possible open on your system. This precaution will maximize the amount of memory available for your browser and its extensions to use.

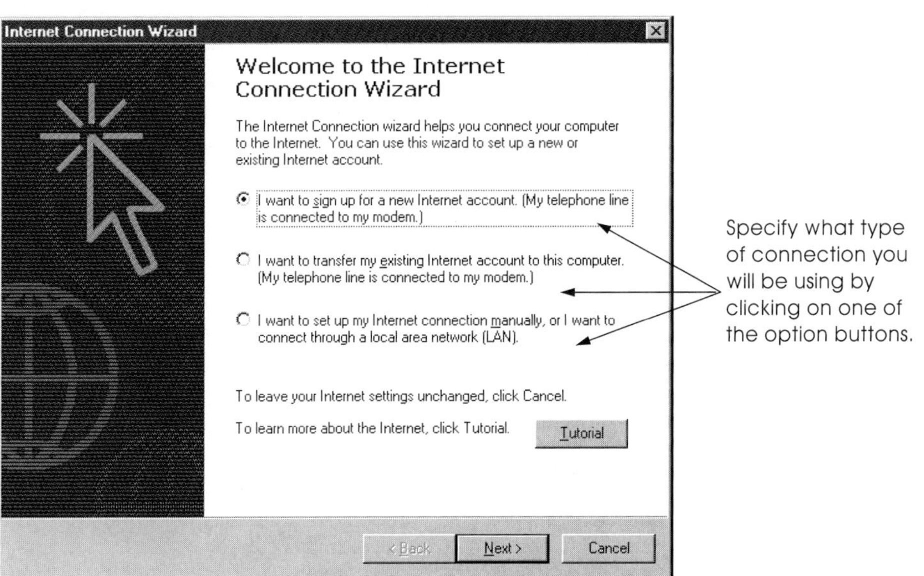

Fig. 2.1 Using **Internet Connection Wizard** to get on the Internet.

2.3 Features of Internet Explorer 5

The browser is a program that showcases certain files on the Internet in an accessible, visually pleasing way. Figure 2.2 shows the main browser window in Microsoft's Internet Explorer 5 (IE5).

A *URL (Uniform Resource Locator and Universal Resource Locator are both common usage)* is displayed in the **Address** bar, toward the top of the browser window. The URL describes the location of the file your browser is displaying or loading. If you are viewing a page on the Web, then the URL will usually begin with ***http://***. The acronym **http** stands for *HyperText Transfer Protocol*. This is the format of most URLs you will be viewing. We discuss additional types of URLs later in this chapter.

To go to a new URL, click anywhere inside the address bar. Once the current URL text is highlighted, type in the URL for the site you would like to visit (this overwrites the highlighted URL) and hit the *Enter* key.

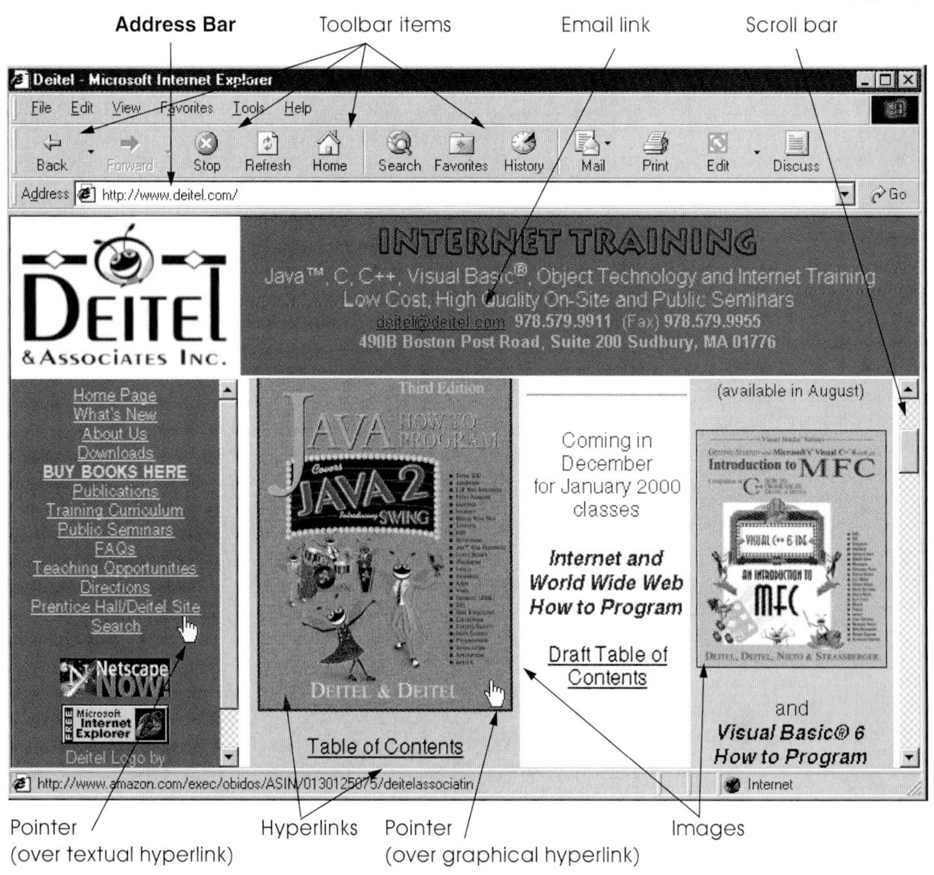

Fig. 2.2 Deitel & Associates, Inc. home page.

A *hyperlink* is a visual element on a Web page that, when clicked, loads a specified URL into the browser window. By clicking on this hyperlink (also known as an *anchor*), you will make your browser automatically load the new URL. Your mouse appears as a pointer by default. When it is passed over a hyperlink, it is transformed into a hand with the index finger pointing upward (to indicate that this is indeed a link). Originally used as a publishing tool for scientific texts, hyperlinking has been crucial to making the Internet a more interesting and dynamic environment for sharing information.

IE5 has built-in controls that record the URLs sites your browser has loaded. This record is called your *history* and is stored in chronological order by date. We discuss several ways to use this history. The simplest is to use the ***Forward*** and ***Back*** buttons located at the top of your browser window (Fig. 2.2). If you click on **Back**, then your browser will reload the last page you viewed in the browser. The **Forward** button loads the next page in your history (you can use the **Forward** button only after you have gone backward in your history). On pages that are frequently updated, you may want to click the ***Refresh*** button. This will cause your browser to reload an up-to-the-minute version of the current URL.

You can skip forward or backward several entries in your history at a time by clicking on the small arrow pointing down, located directly to the right of both the **Forward** and **Back** buttons. This will display a list of your last/next five sites in your history. You can go directly to one of these sites by highlighting and clicking its entry in this list.

As mentioned earlier, hyperlinks are used to direct your browser towards a specified URL. This URL could be another Web page, or it could lead to an email address or a file. If the hyperlink is targeted to an email address, clicking it will not load a new Web page. Instead, it will load your default email program and open a message addressed to the specified recipient email address. We will discuss emailing in greater detail later on in this chapter.

If a URL is targeted towards a file that the browser is incapable of displaying, then you will be given the option to *download* the file. When you download a file, you are making a copy of it on your computer. Examples of downloadable files are programs, documents and sound files.

The browser interface also enables you to download all elements of a Web page, including its code and any graphical elements that appear on the page. You save images on the page by right-clicking, choosing ***Save Picture As...*** from the options box that pops up, then specifying a location on your hard drive to save the image (Fig. 2.3). You can have the browser save the image as your background wallpaper by clicking ***Set as Wallpaper*** in the right-click menu (*wallpaper* is the background for your main operating system screen). To save the code of the page, click ***Save As..***. in the file menu and specify a location.

A new feature of IE5 that is related to the history function is the address bar *AutoComplete*. AutoComplete remembers all the URLs you have visited for a set time span (30 days by default). When you start typing a URL stored in the history, a scrollable drop-down menu like the one in Fig. 2.4 appears beneath your address bar, listing all URLs in the history that are potential matches for the URL you are entering. To go to one of these URLs, highlight your desired address in the AutoComplete bar (with your mouse or arrow keys), and either click on it or press *Enter*. Your browser will then load the file at the selected URL as if you had clicked a hyperlink targeting that URL.

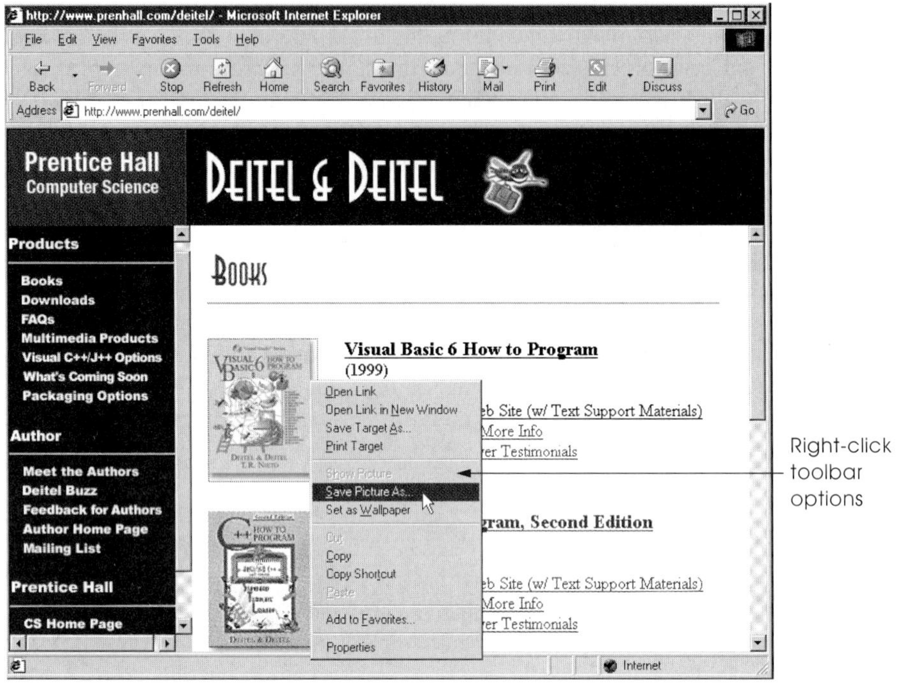

Fig. 2.3 Capturing a picture from a Web site.

Fig. 2.4 AutoComplete address options. (Courtesy of United States Senate.)

There is an extension of the AutoComplete feature for dealing with *forms* (areas on Web sites where you can enter information). While browsing the WWW, you will often encounter forms for entering and dispatching information. Examples of forms you might use are a username and password form to enter a site, or an address and credit card form for buying a book online. AutoComplete gives you the option (which you can decline if you like) to remember some of your common entries to forms. It will then provide an AutoComplete drop-down menu when you go to a place in a form where these commonly typed terms might be placed, thus saving you time.

The interactive history bar (Fig. 2.5) can be activated by clicking the button marked **History** in the row of buttons at the top of your browser window. The interactive history bar will show you your history over the past 30 days (or whatever length of time you specify). It has heading levels ordered chronologically by week, by day, alphabetically by site directory name and by individual URL. You can choose directories and URLs to visit with your mouse. This tool is useful for returning to a recently visited site for which you have forgotten the URL.

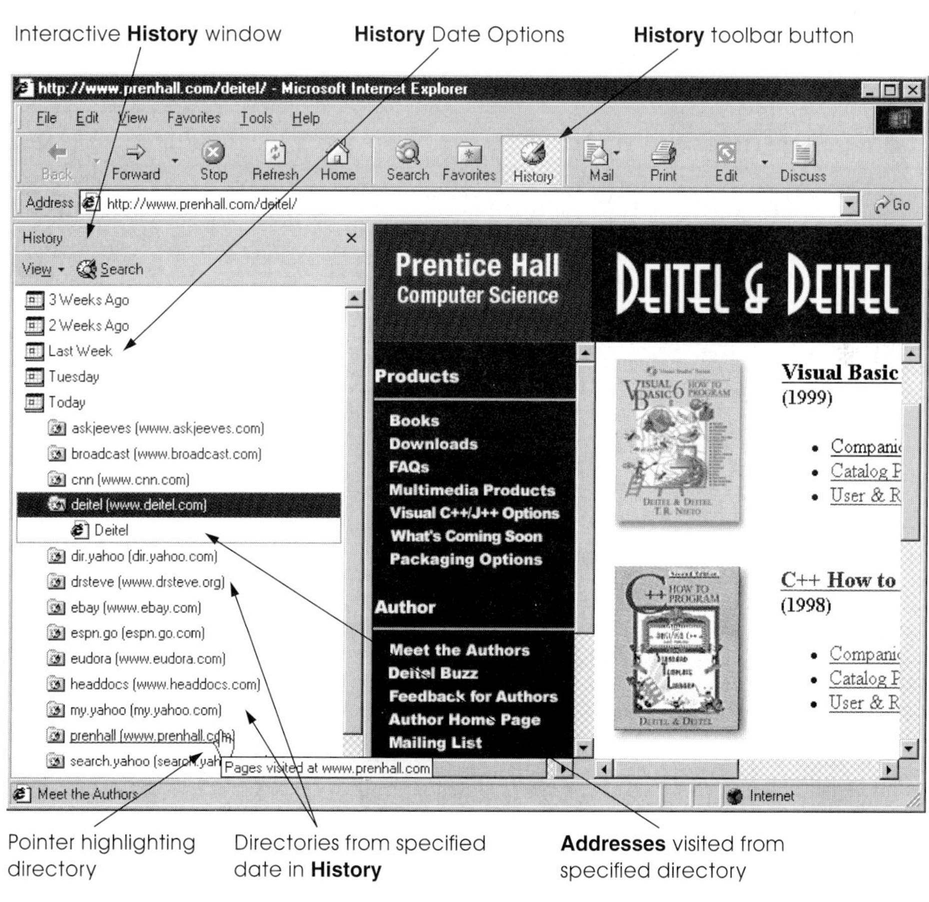

Fig. 2.5 **History** options.

2.4 Searching the Internet

The most commonly used method of finding a Web site related to a specific topic is to search the Internet by using sites called *search engines*. Search engines constantly explore Web pages throughout the Internet and keep searchable records of the sites they encounter. You can search through their catalogs by going to a search engine site such as *Yahoo* (**www.yahoo.com**), *AltaVista* (**www.altavista.com**), *Excite* (**www.excite.com**) and *InfoSeek* (**www.infoseek.com**), and then entering your desired topic. The search engine returns a list of hyperlinks to sites containing information on your topic.

IE5 has a nice feature that saves you time in querying the major search engines for a site that you want. This feature is accessible by clicking the **Search** button on the toolbar at the top of your browser window (Fig. 2.6). The window that appears after you click the **Search** button is easy to use. First, click the button next to the type of information for which you would like to search (you can select only one of these so-called *radio buttons*). Options include Web sites, addresses, businesses and online maps. After your specified search options load in the window, fill in the required fields in the search form and click the **Search** button. After a few seconds (the actual time depends significantly on the speed of your Internet connection and how busy the site is), the search results appear as hyperlinks in the search window. Click a link that interests you and let the surfing begin!

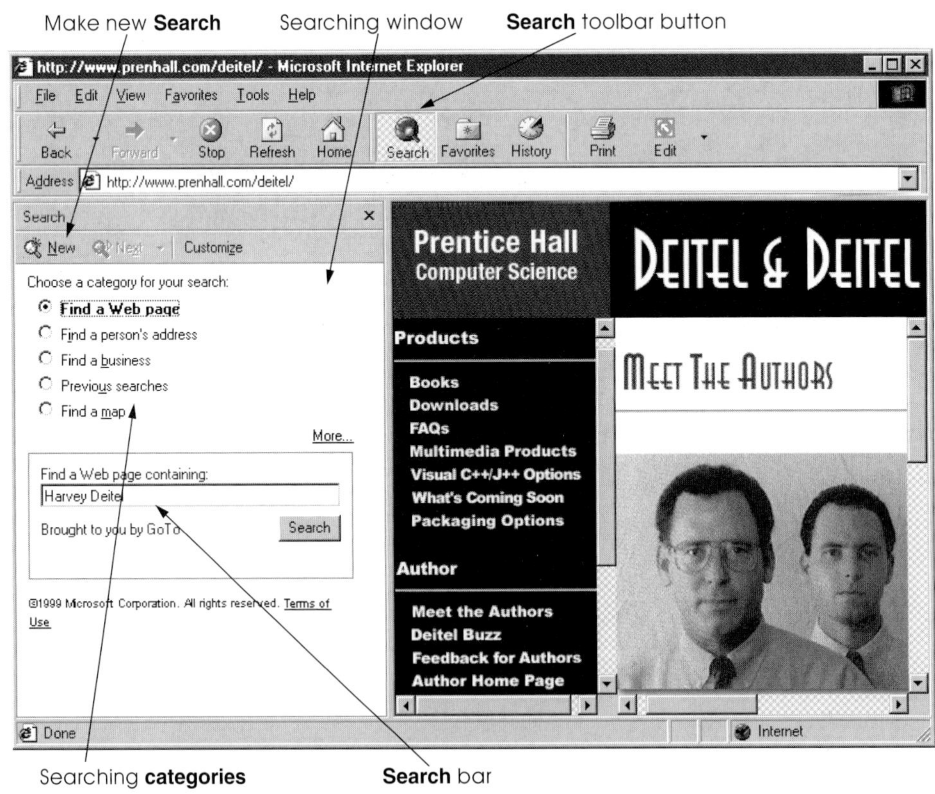

Fig. 2.6 Searching the Internet with IE5.

If you are not satisfied with the results of the search you can click on the button at the top of the search window labeled ***Next,*** and IE5 will automatically send your search string to another search engine.

2.5 Online Help and Tutorials

Solutions for most problems you may encounter while using Internet Explorer have been included with the software. IE5 includes an online ***Tour*** and a built-in ***Help*** feature. These can be accessed through the **Help** menu (Fig. 2.7).

When you click on **Tour**, your Web browser is directed to a site run by Microsoft, the developer of IE5. This site, which features an expanded version of the **Tour** available through the **Internet Connection Wizard**, presents a basic overview of the Internet, browsers and IE5, along with more specific information on IE5's features. This tour is navigated via hyperlinks.

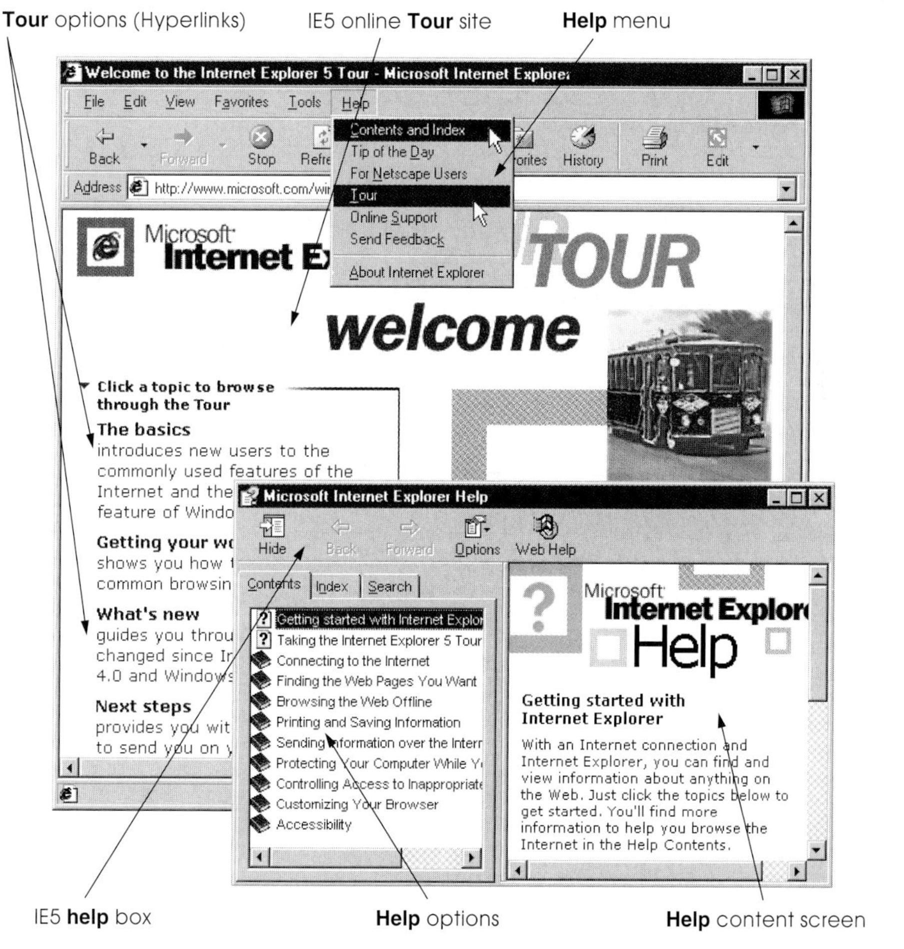

Fig. 2.7 Microsoft IE5 Online **Tour** and **Help** window.

If there is a menu item or a function that you do not understand in IE5, your best bet for finding assistance is the **Help** feature, accessible through the **Help** menu. There are three **Help** tabs here: ***Contents***, which provides a summary of the major **Help** topics available; ***Index***, which provides an alphabetical list of all **Help** topics available; and ***Search***, which provides you with a mechanism to search the **Help** index for a topic that gives answers to your question.

2.6 Keeping Track of Your Favorite Sites

As you browse the Web, you may identify sites that contain useful information, games and activities to which you would like to return. IE5 provides a mechanism called ***Favorites*** that allows you to save the URLs of sites you frequently visit, so you can easily return to those sites in the future (Fig. 2.8).

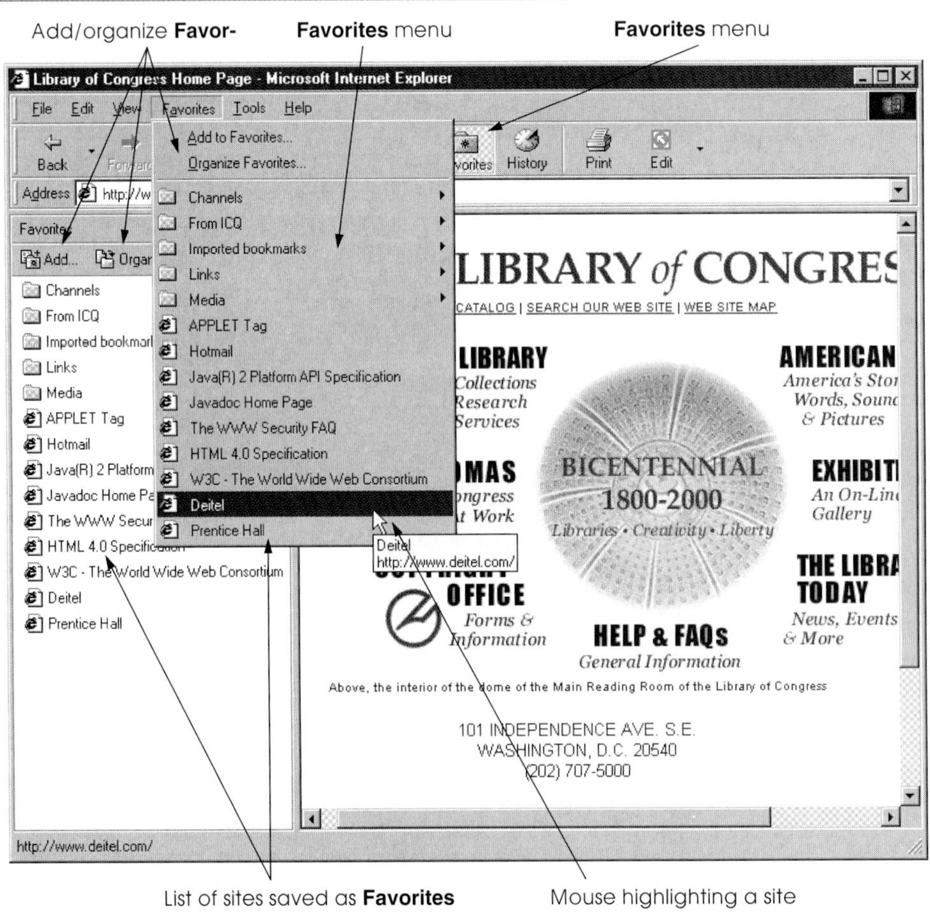

Fig. 2.8 The **Favorites** button and menu bar. (Courtesy of Library of Congress.)

When you visit a site that you would like to save as a favorite, select the ***Add to Favorites...*** option in the **Favorites** menu. The site will now be listed in the **Favorites** menu, identified by the page's title (the title is shown on the colored bar at the top of the browser window). You can later go to any site saved as a favorite by opening the **Favorites** menu and clicking the site.

Favorites functions are also accessible via clicking the **Favorites** button on the toolbar at the top of your browser window. IE5 also allows you to customize your favorites (Fig. 2.9).

Through the **Organize Favorites** dialog box, which is accessible by clicking **Organize Favorites...** in the **Favorites** menu, you can rename favorites, create folders to organize favorites, place favorites into and remove favorites from these folders, and delete favorites. All these options are available by clicking their buttons on the left of the **Organize Favorites** dialog box. The **Organize Favorites** box indicates how many times you have visited that site. You can have IE5 save the pages branching from a specific favorites site, so that you can view the info when not online. This option can be accessed by clicking the **Make available offline** checkbox.

2.7 FTP (File Transfer Protocol)

Earlier in this chapter, we touched upon downloading—the process of copying a file from the Internet to your hard drive. You will normally be downloading programs, or compressed versions of programs (i.e., programs that have been reformatted to take up less space), to install on your computer. Downloading is typically initiated on a Web page by clicking a hyperlink targeted at file on a Web site or *FTP* site. FTP stands for *File Transfer Protocol*, an old but still popular method for making data available over the internet. An FTP site URL begins with ***ftp://*** rather than **http://** (used with Web page addresses).

You typically access FTP sites via hyperlinks. You can also access FTP sites through the IE5 Web browser interface (see Fig. 2.10).

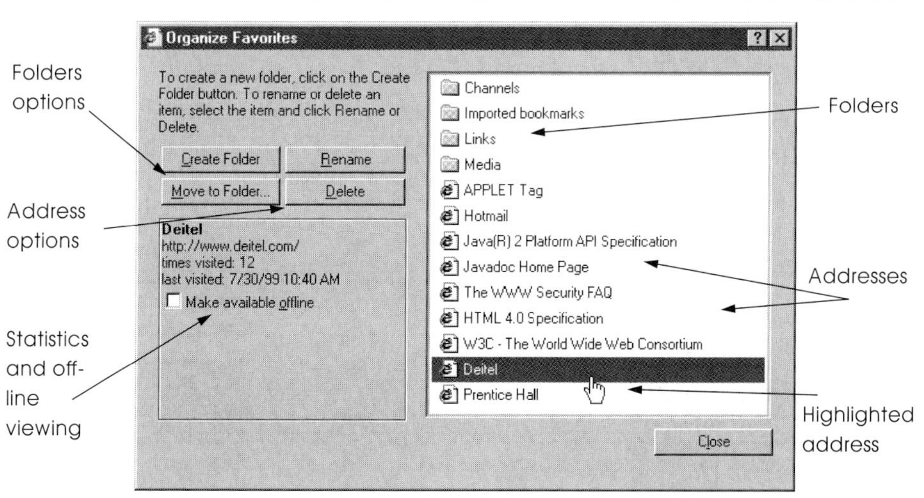

Fig. 2.9 **Organize Favorites** dialog.

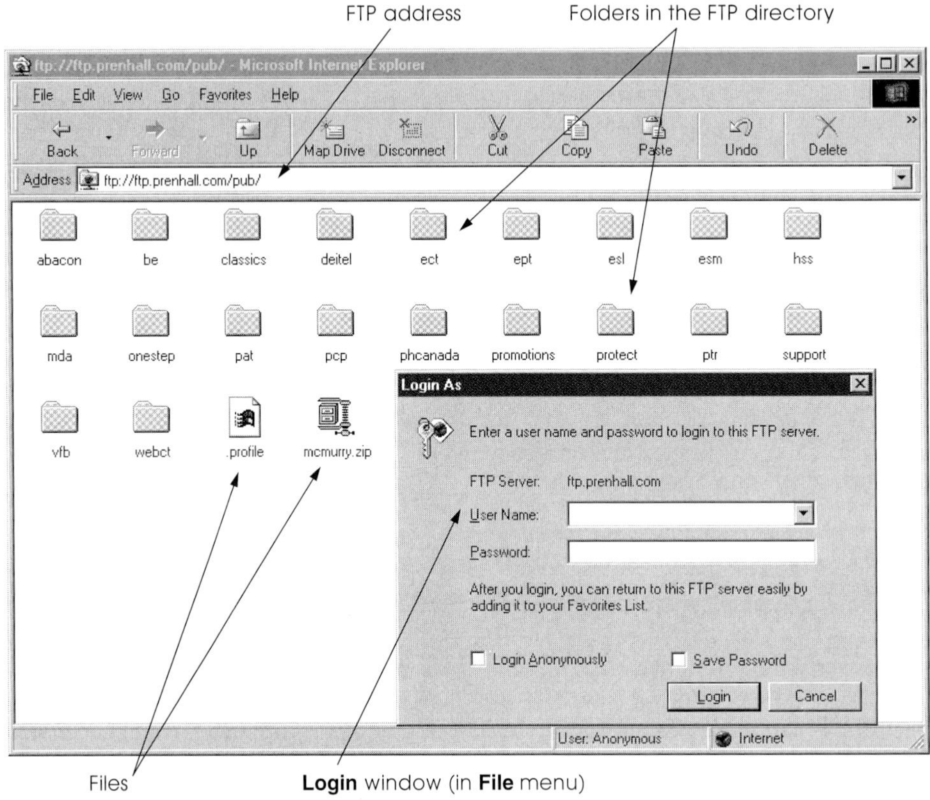

Fig. 2.10 Using IE5 to access FTP sites.

When you point your browser to the URL of an FTP site, you see the contents of the specified site directory. Two types of objects will appear in the directory: files available for download, and other directories to open. You can download a file by right-clicking on its icon, choosing **Save target as...** and specifying the location to which you would like to download the file. To enter another directory, double-click on its folder icon.

When you log on to an FTP site, IE5 automatically sends your email address and your name (which is set by default to **anonymous**). This occurs on FTP sites with *public access*. Many FTP sites on the Internet have *restricted access*—only people with specific usernames and passwords are allowed to access such sites. If you try to enter a restricted-access FTP site, a dialog box like the one in Fig. 2.10 appears for entering your information.

Sending a file to another location on the Internet is called *uploading* and can be done through the FTP protocol. To place a page on a Web site, you will usually have to upload it to a specific restricted-access FTP server (this is dependent on your ISP). This process involves uploading the file to a directory on the FTP site that is accessible through the Web.

2.8 Outlook Express and Electronic Mail

Electronic *mail*, or email for short, is a method of sending formatted messages and files over the Internet to other people. Depending on Internet traffic, an email message can go anywhere in the world in as little as a few seconds. Email is one of the most heavily used Internet services.

When you sign up with an Internet Service Provider, you are given an email address in the form of *username@domainname* (e.g., **deitel@deitel.com**). The domain name is normally a combination of your ISP's name (e.g., **aol**, **msn**, **prodigy**, etc.) and an extension specifying the type of email address. The most common domain types are **.com** and **.net** (commercial and network addresses, respectively), **.org** (non-profit organizations), **.edu** (educational institutions), **.mil** (military) and **.gov** (government). There are also a myriad of domain name suffixes reserved for addresses in countries around the world, such as **.uk** for Great Britain, and **.il** for Israel. Every email address must be unique.

There are many popular email programs such as Outlook, Netscape Messenger and Eudora. Many of these have special features and are available on the Internet for free download or for sale. The email program we discuss—Microsoft *Outlook Express*—is included and installed with IE5 (included on the CD). The opening screen of Outlook Express is shown in Fig. 2.11. The figure also shows the ***Internet Accounts*** dialog for adding email and news accounts to Outlook Express.

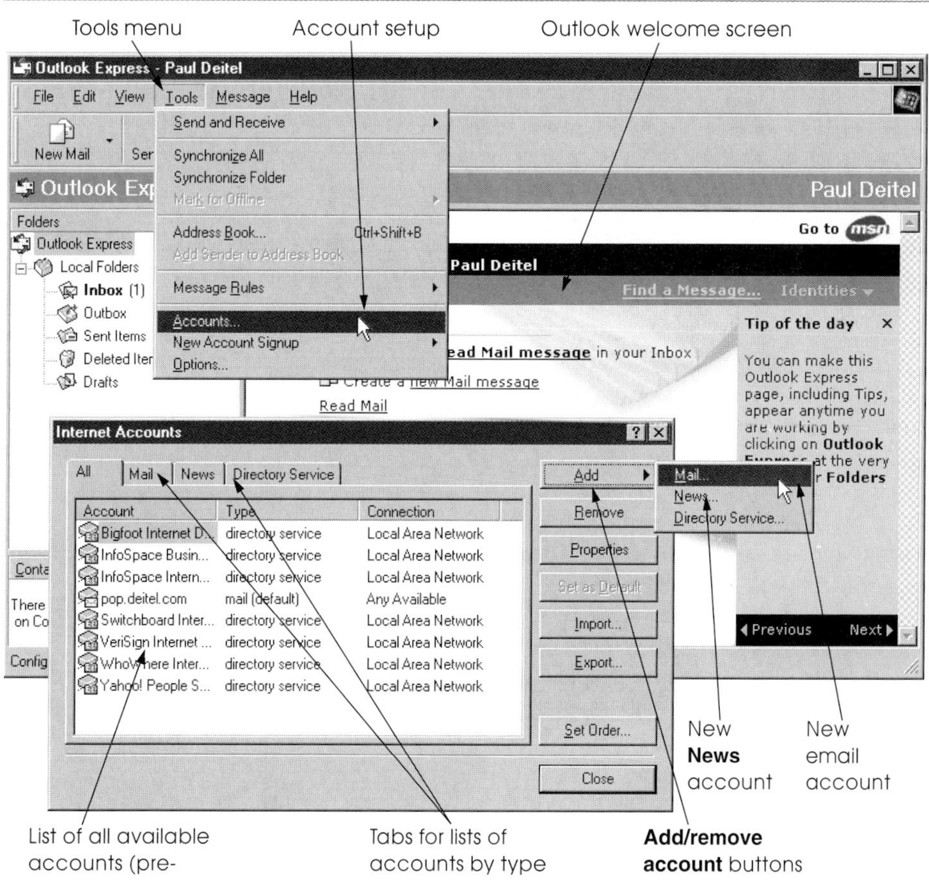

Fig. 2.11 Outlook Express opening screen and the **Internet Accounts** dialog.

When you start Outlook Express for the first time, you will have to enter information about your connection to the Internet and about your email account. You will do this in the dialog box that appears the first time the program is run. You will be asked for the names of your incoming and outgoing *email servers*. These are addresses of servers located at your ISP that administer your incoming and outgoing email. You should obtain the server addresses from your network administrator.

You can manage more than one email account with Outlook Express. You can add new accounts by clicking the **Accounts** option in the **Tools** menu; this will bring up a box listing all your accounts (there are a number of built-in accounts, as you will see). To add a new account, click the **Add** button in the upper-right corner of the box and select either a **Mail** or a **News** account. Figure 2.12 shows the account sign-up dialog box at various points in the sign-up process. We will discuss **News** accounts later in the chapter, but the sign-up process is nearly the same.

Outlook Express provides a straightforward interface for managing your accounts and messages. When you receive messages, you can save them on your hard drive for later access. Outlook Express allows you to create folders for saving messages.

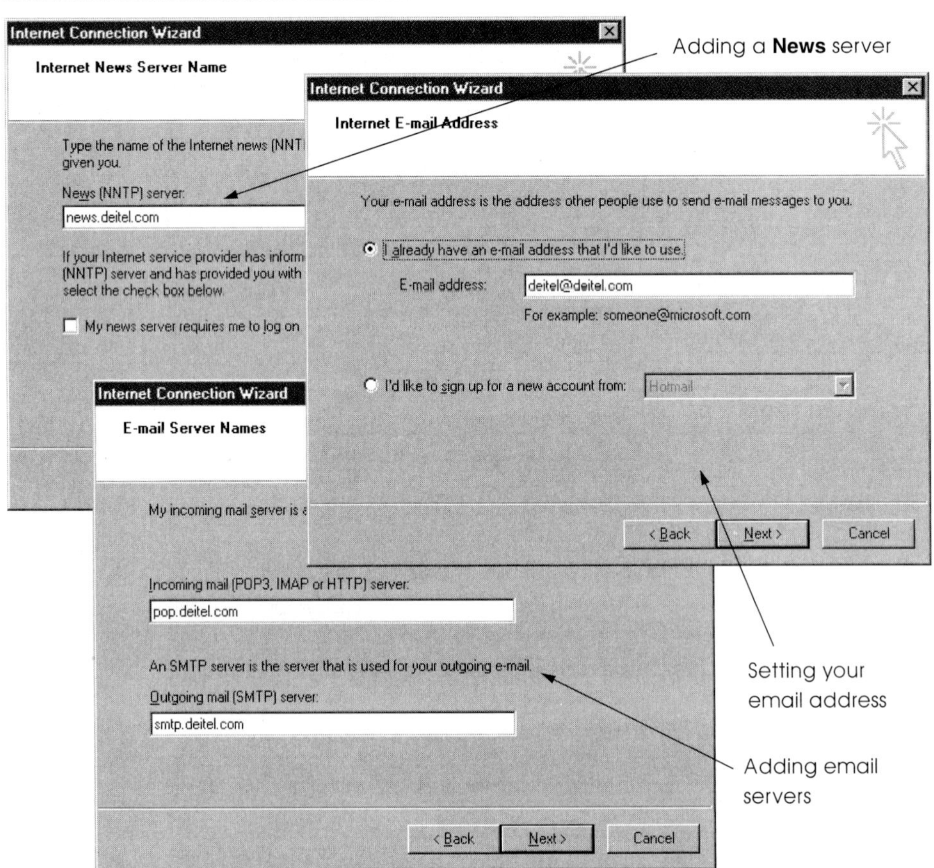

Fig. 2.12 Adding email and news accounts in Outlook Express.

Outlook Express automatically checks for new messages several times per hour (this frequency can be changed). When a new message arrives it is placed in your ***Inbox***. The **Inbox** setup is shown in Fig. 2.13.

The layout of the **Inbox** screen is fairly simple. Across the top of the window are buttons you can use to start **New Mail** messages and to **Reply** to, **Forward**, **Print**, **Delete** and **Send/Recv** messages. The right side of the window contains a list of messages in your inbox (listed by date and time received), the message subjects and the senders. Below this is a content preview of the selected message. To view the message in its entirety, double-click its entry in the **Inbox**. To do other things with the message (such as reply to its sender or print the message), highlight the message and click the appropriate button at the top of the screen. To move the message from the **Inbox** to another message box, highlight and drag the email entry to the left side of the screen and drop it into the selected message box.

The left side of the screen contains your folder structure and your *address book*. To add a new message box, right-click on **Local Folders** and select the **New Folder** option. In your address book, you can store the names and email addresses of people with whom you communicate frequently.

To set new entries for the address book, click on the **Addresses** button at the top of the window or click on the **Address Book...** entry in the **Tools** menu. The **Address Book** is shown in Fig. 2.14.

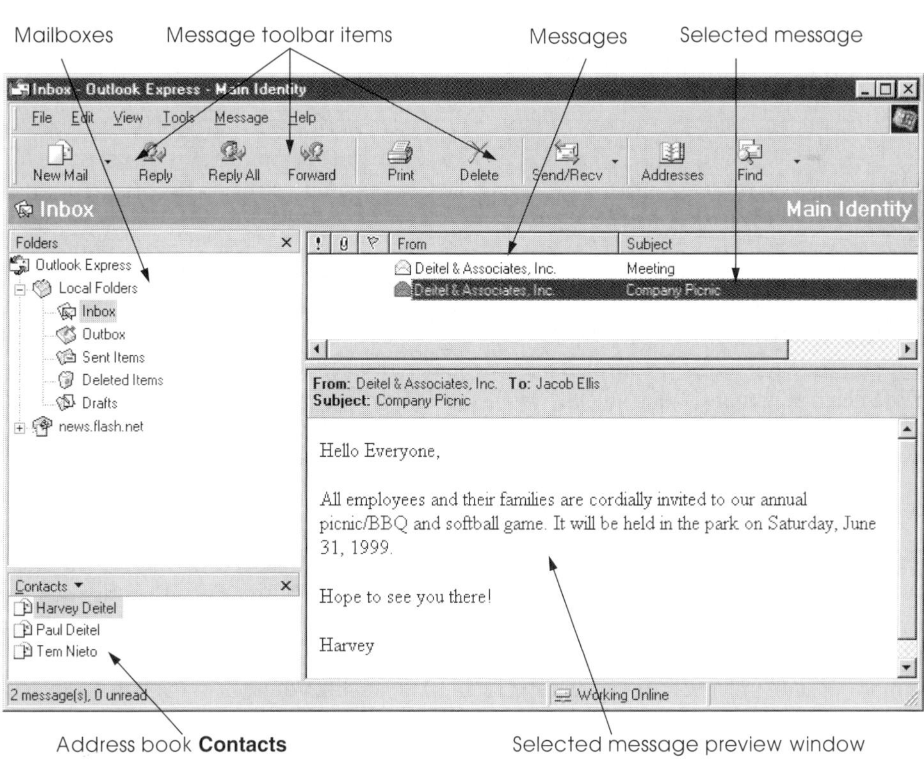

Fig. 2.13 The Outlook Express email main screen.

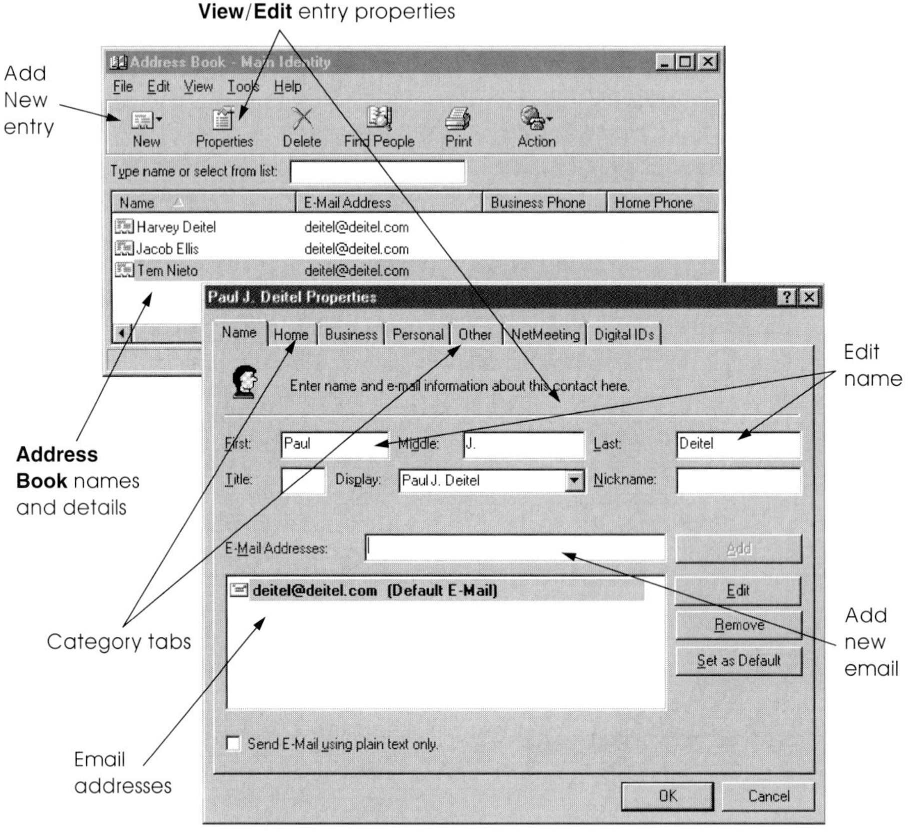

Fig. 2.14 Adding and modifying names in your **Address Book**.

All entries in the **Address Book** are listed in the main dialog box. You can send a message to anyone in your list by highlighting that person's entry, clicking the **Action** button, then clicking **Send Mail**. This sequence will open a blank message addressed to the selected recipient. To add an entry to the list, click the **New** button, then click **Contact**. This sequence will open a dialog box like the one in Fig. 2.14 and will give you a place to insert information on that person. You can also enter personal information, such as addresses and phone numbers, for reference outside Outlook Express.

When you initiate a new message through any source, a message box like the one in Fig. 2.15 opens.

There are several properties that can be associated with a message. The only mandatory property is the email address of the recipient, which should be put in the form described earlier in this chapter and placed in the field labeled **To:**. To send your message to more than one recipient, you can type in multiple email addresses in the **To:** field, separated by commas. You should always enter a subject in the **Subject** field. The **Subject** should give the recipient an idea of the message's contents before it is opened. The **CC:** (Carbon Copy) field is for sending messages to people who, although the message is not addressed to them directly, may be interested in the message. If you want to change the *priority* of the message, click the **Priority** button on the toolbar. High priority messages will be flagged to get the attention of the message recipient.

Finally, your message gets entered in the main window of the message box. You can format the text (font size, colors, styling) with the buttons above the message area. After you have entered your message, click **Send** and your message will be on its way to the designated recipient(s).

2.9 Outlook Express and Newsgroups

With a *newsgroup*, a person can post messages to a shared online viewing area. Other people can then view these messages, reply to them and post new messages. Imagine it as a way of sending email not to anyone in particular, but to a place where people interested in the email's subject can read it. Tens of thousands of newsgroups are available, on virtually any topic, and new groups are created daily.

Outlook Express has a built-in capability to view newsgroups. An Outlook Express newsgroup screen is shown in Fig. 2.16.

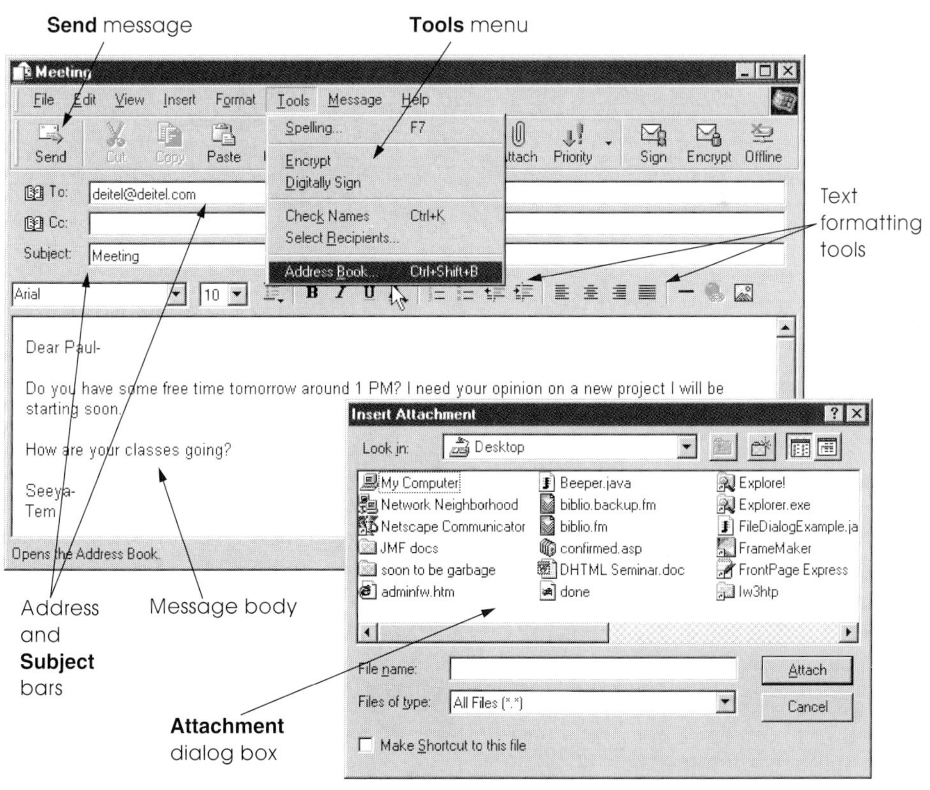

Fig. 2.15 An email message in Outlook Express.

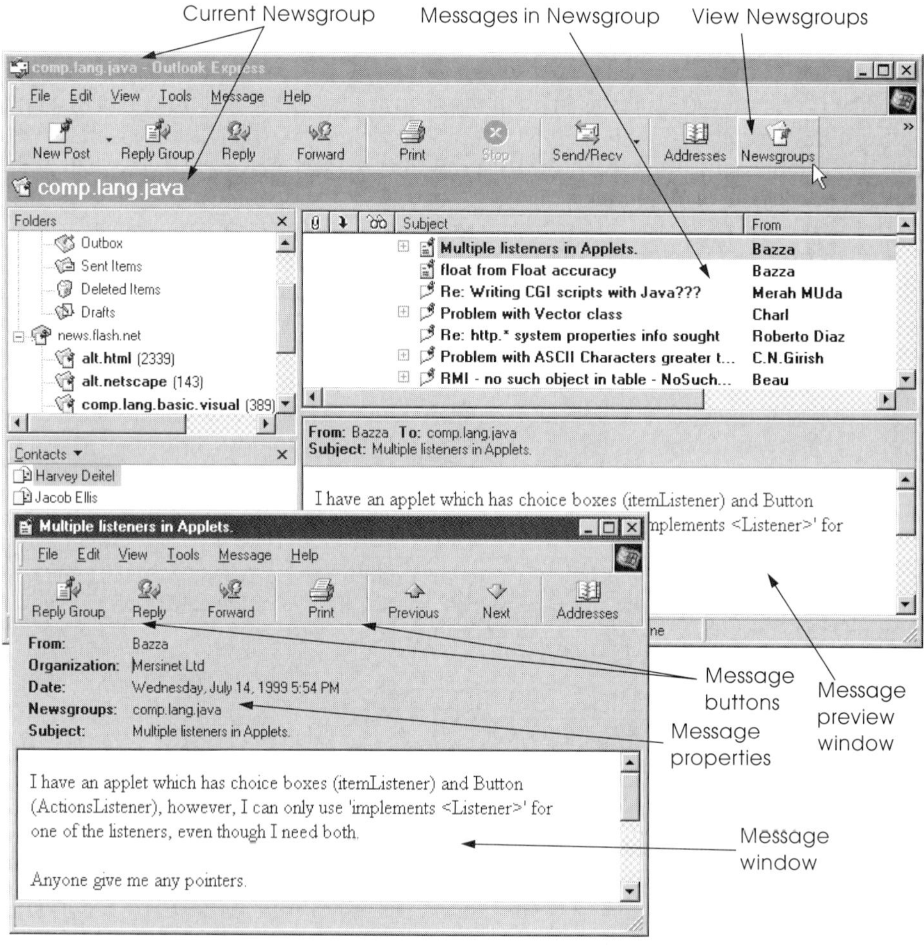

Fig. 2.16 Using **Outlook Express** to browse newsgroups.

To be able to view Newsgroups, you must first register your server settings with Outlook Express. Use the same process illustrated in Fig. 2.11, but select **News...** instead of **Mail...** on the popup menu.

After entering your server information, you can access newsgroups by clicking the **Newsgroups** button on the toolbar, or by clicking on the **Read News** hyperlink on the main Outlook screen. This action brings you to the main newsgroups screen, which ordinarily lists the groups to which you have subscribed. A subscribed newsgroup is comparable to a favorite site in IE5. The program will remember its location and give you easy access to its contents at the click of a button.

To search through and subscribe to newsgroups, click the **Newsgroups** button on the top of the main screen. Outlook Express will then download a list of all the available newsgroups (this search can take several minutes, as there are often tens of thousands of new-groups available on a server). Use the search bar to search the list by typing in keywords. When you find a group you like, double-click its entry and you will be "subscribed" to it. All groups you have subscribed to are listed underneath the mail folders on the left side of the screen and on the main newsgroups screen. To view the contents of a newsgroup, double-click its entry.

The look and functionality of the individual **Newsgroup** view is similar to that of the email message box. You will find message lists and previews in the same places. Posting a message to the group is done the same way you write a new email message. Likewise with replying to a message, printing and reading messages.

You can use a newsgroup to find information, to correspond with a group, to exchange news or to learn new subjects. Be cautious about entering too much personal information about yourself, because newsgroups are public forums.

2.10 Using FrontPage Express to Create Web Pages

Every Web site you view on the Web was created by someone. At one time, someone sat down and used a program or a coding language to define the text, formats and layouts of every page on the Internet. Many of these pages are designed with special programs that make the Web page authoring and editing process as simple as possible.

Included on your CD is a Web page authoring program called *FrontPage Express*. Chapter 6 explains FrontPage Express in detail. Here is a brief sampling of its uses and features, in case you want to get a head start on Web page production. Figure 2.17 shows a sample FrontPage Express window.

FrontPage Express has a straightforward interface. Most functions you can use to create and format textual and graphical elements are located on the buttons toolbar directly above the main editing area. These controls include buttons for changing text size, color, style, font and justification; for inserting images; and for creating hyperlinks. Experiment with these capabilities.

The pages you create using FrontPage Express are viewable with any Web browser (as long as you are careful to use browser-independent features). The files you create are then typically uploaded via FTP to a Web server.

2.11 NetMeeting and Chat

IE5 provides two programs for communicating with people over the Internet via live written text and other media such as audio and video. The first of these programs is *NetMeeting* (see Fig. 2.18). NetMeeting is designed for business and for work-related collaborations.

You can use NetMeeting to communicate with groups of people via textual and visual aids. These include sound (you can use a microphone to speak with people) and video (you can use video cameras to transmit live video). You can also use NetMeeting to share files (there are built-in mechanisms for the group editing of files and for the sharing of diagrams via the *whiteboard*, a drawing application that allows you to share visual effects with other people in the meeting).

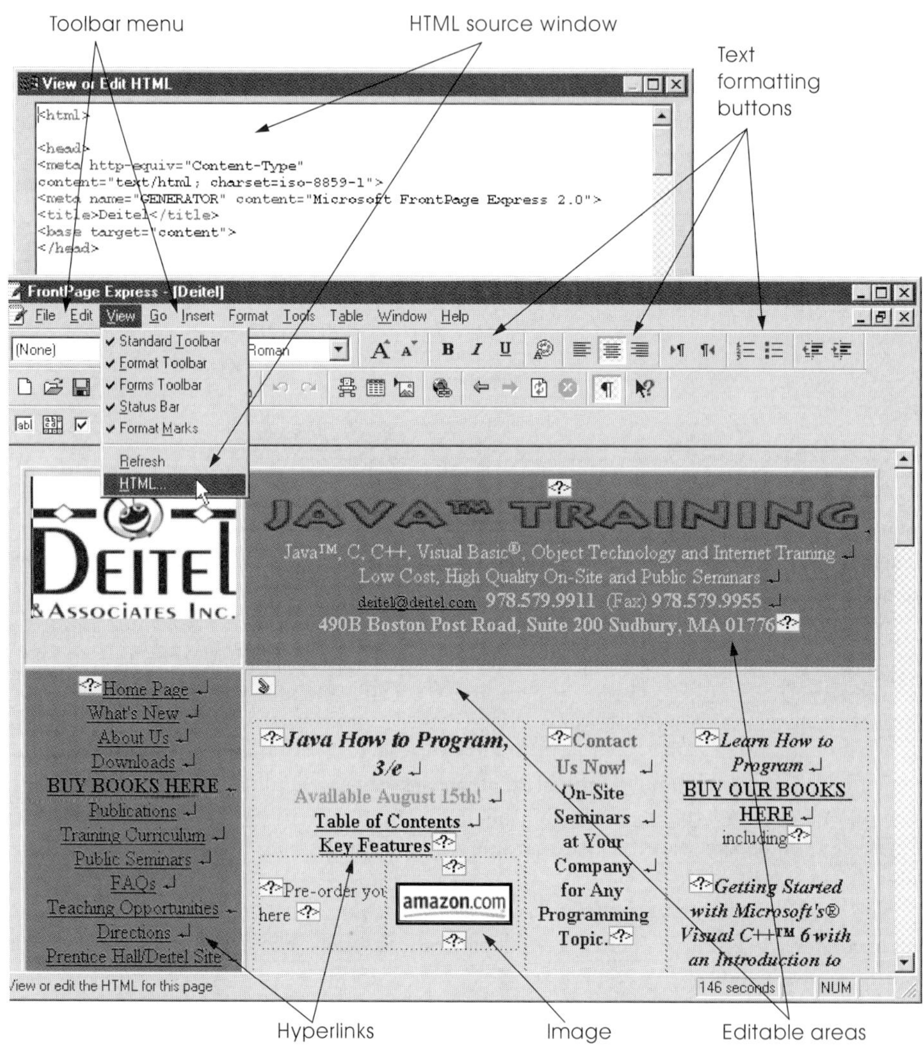

Fig. 2.17 Creating Web pages with FrontPage Express.

NetMeeting opens with a setup screen in which you set your initial options. Next, a screen appears that displays a list of the people who are available to chat using NetMeeting. You can also initiate a one-on-one meeting with an individual by using the **Call** button on the top toolbar. You can use the **Address Book** feature in NetMeeting to save commonly used addresses.

Once you begin a meeting, buttons appear on your screen and options become available on the toolbar for using the various communication media. You should experiment with these tools to determine how to use NetMeeting to its fullest potential.

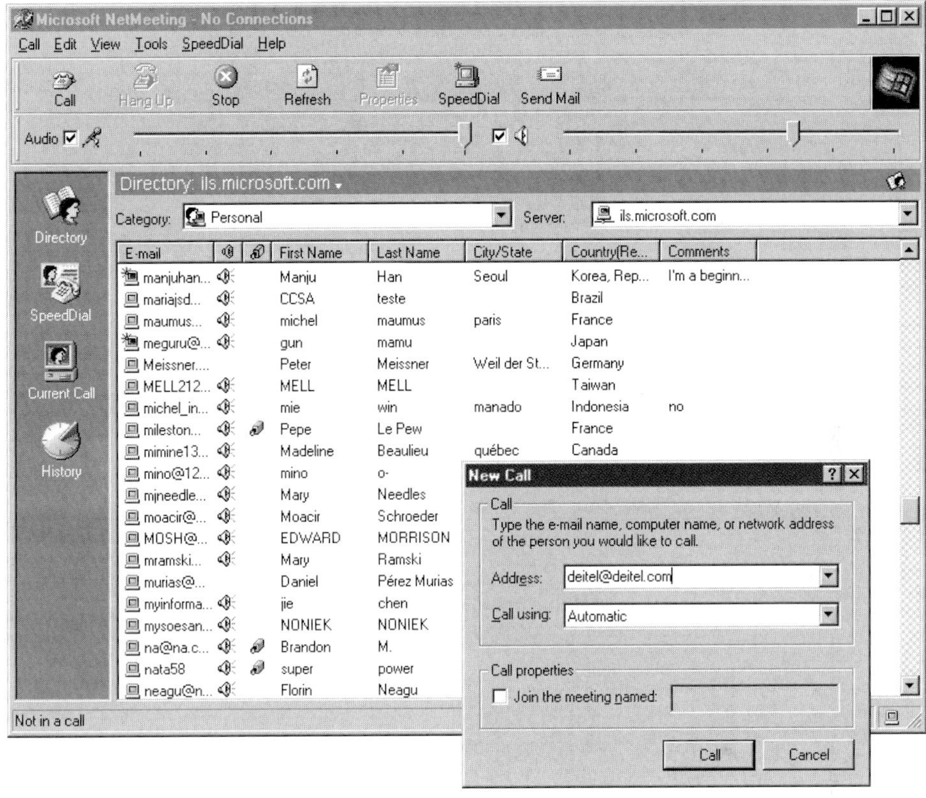

Fig. 2.18 Using NetMeeting to "speak" with people on the Internet.

Microsoft Chat is similar to NetMeeting, though its operation is simpler. Chat also offers a more casual atmosphere than NetMeeting. You start by choosing a "nickname" with which you would like to be referred to in the chat groups. Then connect with the server and you will be presented with a list of chat groups. Find one you like by scrolling down or searching, then join the chat by double-clicking on the group's entry.

Chat then displays a screen much like the one in Fig. 2.19. A list of people in the chat group appears on the right. You can start a private conversation with a person in this list by right-clicking on that person's name and selecting the appropriate option. You type text into the chat by typing it into the text bar at the bottom of the screen.

The group's conversation appears in the main screen. This is in plain text format (which can be styled using the toolbars above the conversation window) or in a delightful cartoon format. These two styles of chat can be toggled using the buttons in the middle of the toolbar above the conversation window. Have fun chatting with and meeting new people, but be cautious about revealing your true identity and contact information.

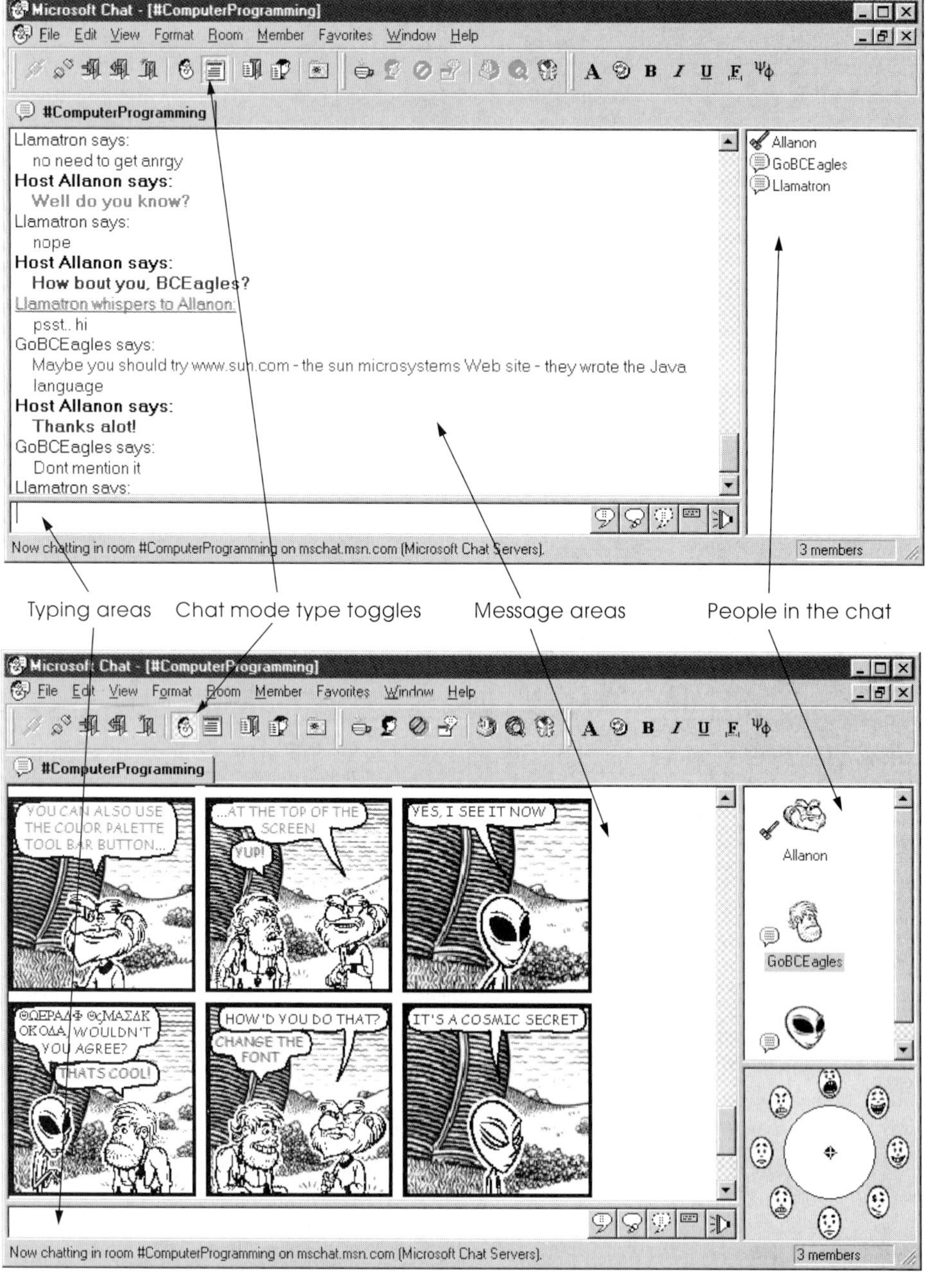

Fig. 2.19 Chatting with Microsoft Chat.

2.12 Controlling the Details

IE5 is installed with a myriad of default settings that affect the way sites are displayed, the security measures browsers take and the way browser outputs appear. Most of these settings are modifiable in the ***Internet Options*** dialog (Fig. 2.20).

Let us consider some of the more significant options that affect your browsing experience. If you have a slow connection and you do not mind less colorful pages being displayed in your browser, you might want to consider toggling off the ***Load Pictures*** setting, located under the **Advanced** tab. This stops the browser from loading images on a Web page. Images can require long load times, so this toggle can save precious minutes during every browsing session. Under the **Programs** tab, you can specify the default programs you want IE5 to use for such common Internet procedures as viewing newsgroups and sending email. Specifying these causes the designated programs to be accessed when there is a need for their respective technologies in your browsing. For example, if you designate **Outlook Express** as your default email program, then, when you click on an email hyperlink, **Outlook Express** will open a new email message for you to compose.

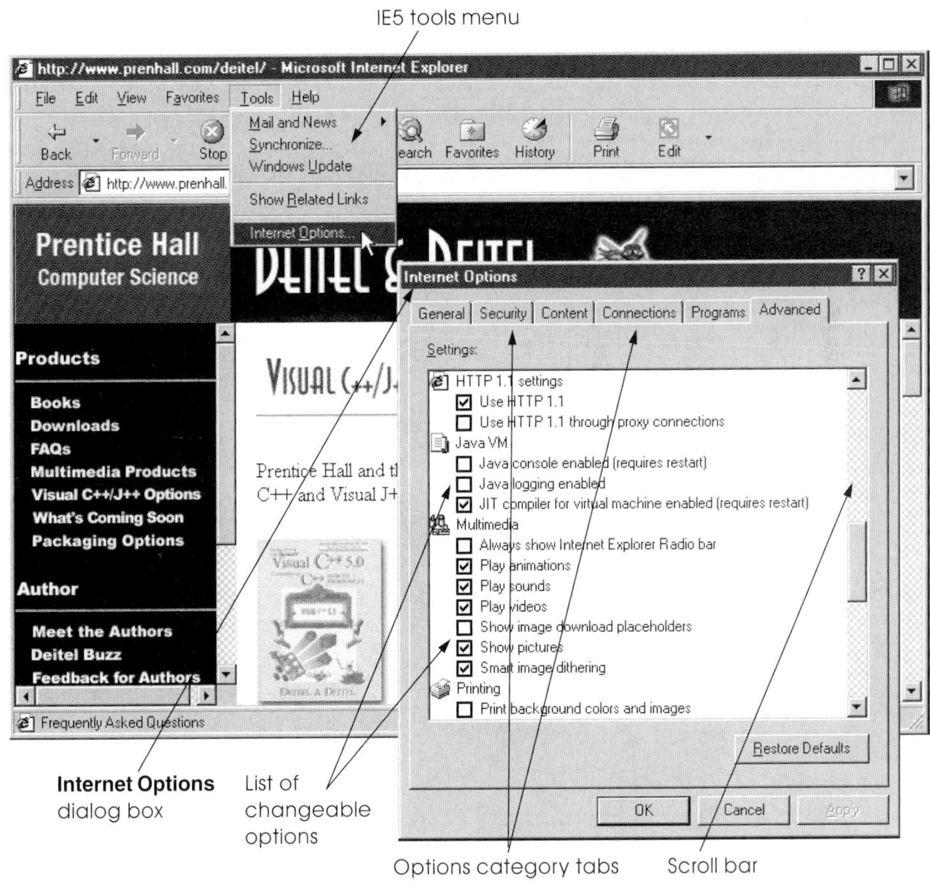

Fig. 2.20 Changing your **Internet Options** in IE5.

Under the **Security** tab, you can specify the level of caution IE5 should exercise when browsing sites in general and also for specific sites. There are four levels of security, the most lenient will not bother you much about downloading and *cookies* (files that are placed on your computer by Web sites to retain or gather information between sessions); the most secure will provide a constant flow of alerts and alarms about the security of your browsing. You should find a setting that balances your comfort level with the Internet against your tolerance for interruptions while browsing.

Finally, in the **General** options tab, you can specify a home page, which is the Web site that is loaded when the browser starts and also appears when you click the **Home** button on top of the browser window. You can designate here the length of time for which you would like to keep a history of URLs visited. By clicking on the **Settings...** button, you can set the amount of disk space you would like to reserve for your Web page *cache*. The cache is an area on your hard drive that a browser designates for automatically saving Web pages and their elements for rapid, future access. When you view a page that you have visited previously, IE5 checks the cache to see if it already has some elements on that page saved in the cache and so can save some download time. Having a large cache can considerably speed up Web browsing, whereas having a small cache can save disk space. However, caching can be a problem, as Internet Explorer does not always check to make sure that the cached page is the same as the latest version residing on the Web server. Clicking the **Refresh** button near the top of the browser window will remedy this by making Internet Explorer get the latest version of the desired Web page from the site.

Once your **Internet Options** are set, click the **Apply** button, then click **OK**. This sequence will apply your changes and will once again display the main browser window.

2.13 Plug-ins

With the advent of many new technologies in the past few years, an increasing number of programs and features are becoming available to make your browsing experience more enjoyable and interactive. Programs called *plug-ins* have been developed that work in conjunction with your browsers.

One of the most versatile plug-ins available on the Internet is *RealPlayer*, developed by Real Networks (Fig. 2.21). Download the most recent version of **RealPlayer** by clicking on the **Download Now** link on **`http://www.real.com`**. It is capable of playing live or prerecorded sound file, and even of playing video (with a fast enough connection). There are also a number of *channels* that you can access, including news, sports, comedy, talk shows and live events.

Another plug-in that provides Internet sound services but has a lesser following than RealAudio is the *Windows Media Player,* which is included with IE5. You can use this the same way you use RealPlayer. Each site with sound capabilities displays icons of the sound players the site supports.

Many Internet sites allow you to take advantage of **RealPlayer**. For example, the sites **`http://www.broadcast.com/`**, **`http://www.npr.org/`**, **`http://internetradio.about.com/`** and **`http://wmbr.mit.edu/stations/list.html`**. all feature either live Internet radio programs and sound or links to sites with live radio and sound events.

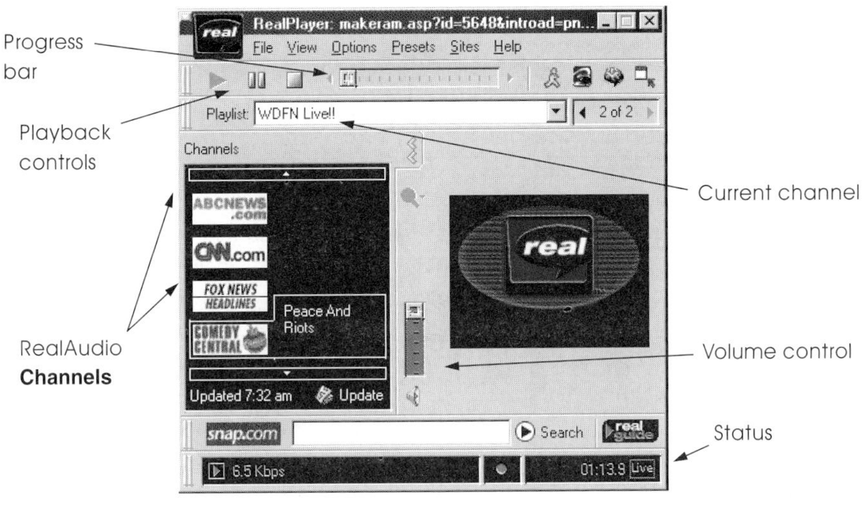

Fig. 2.21 **RealPlayer** dialog.

As useful as HTML is for transferring information, it is still a rather primitive markup language. The *Adobe Acrobat Reader* plug-in reads documents with advanced formatting. Figure 2.22 shows a file displayed with the *Adobe Acrobat Reader* plug-in.

The Acrobat reader is a multiplatform software plug-in (i.e., it works on many operating systems) that is capable of showing documents online without changing the original format of the document. Many manuals and forms are available for download in the Acrobat format (**`.pdf`**, or *Portable Data Format*). When you visit a site that requires the Acrobat reader, there will normally be a link to download the plug-in.

Macromedia *Shockwave* is a plug-in that, when installed and run with a site designed to take advantage of its capabilities, can produce breath-taking dynamic effects. You will be given an option to download this plug-in when you first encounter a Web site using its functions, or you can download the plug-in directly at **`http://www.shockwave.com`**. Figure 2.23 displays one of the thousands of Shockwave enabled sites on the Internet. Shockwave is used mostly for displaying motion on a Web page, so it is impossible to do it justice with a static screen capture.

In most cases, you are given an option or a link to download a plug-in whenever you visit a site that requires you to use the plug-in for the most effective browsing experience. If you cannot find a place to download a desired plug-in, you can probably find it at **`http://www.download.com`** or **`http://www.shareware.com`**. These sites have large searchable indexes and databases of almost every program available for download on the Internet.

2.14 Internet and World Wide Web Resources

There is a host of information on the Internet that no one could list in any book, let alone in one chapter; however, here are some useful Web sites that can get you started.

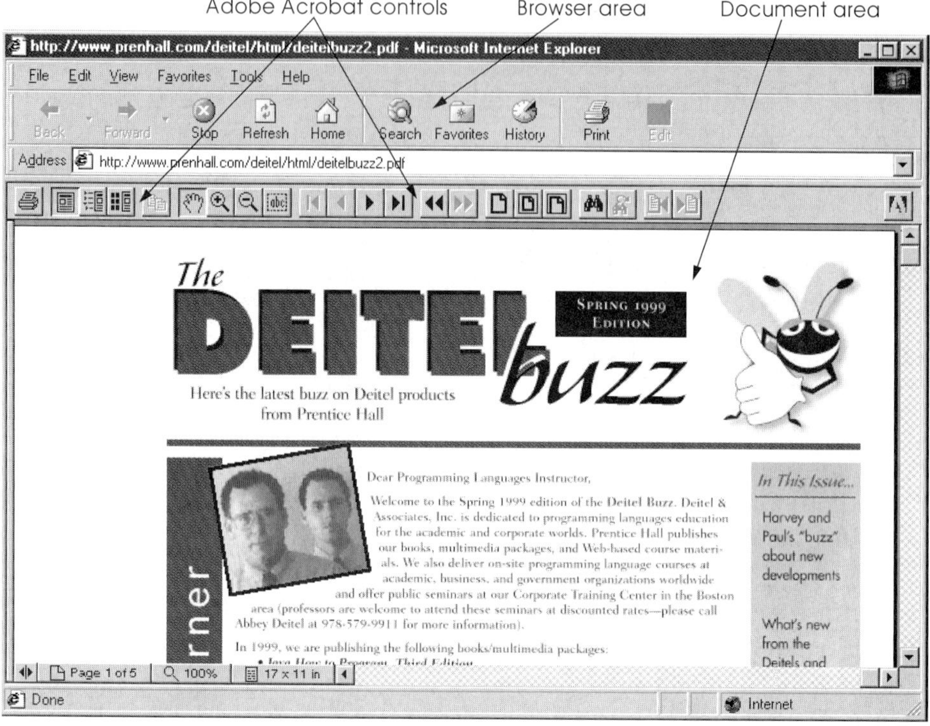

Fig. 2.22 "The Deitel Buzz" newsletter displayed from an Adobe Acrobat formatted file.c

http://www.altavista.com/
Altavista is one of the oldest search engines on the Internet. Developed by Digital several years ago, it is a very useful and comprehensive site.

http://www.yahoo.com/
Yahoo is one of the most popular sites on the Web. It serves both as a search engine and a site catalog.

http://www.excite.com/
Excite is a newer search engine which is often useful when neither Yahoo or Altavista provide useful search results.

http://www.askjeeves.com/)
AskJeeves is a search engine which allows users to type their requests in plain English and searches other search engines for the answer. It also catalogs commonly asked questions for faster response times.

http://www.broadcast.com/
broadcast.com is a comprehensive site for streaming audio and video. Hundreds of live events are available daily for listening with RealPlayer.

http://internetradio.about.com/
Internet Radio is another site that offers many live broadcasts from radio stations throughout the country, covering a broad range of topics.

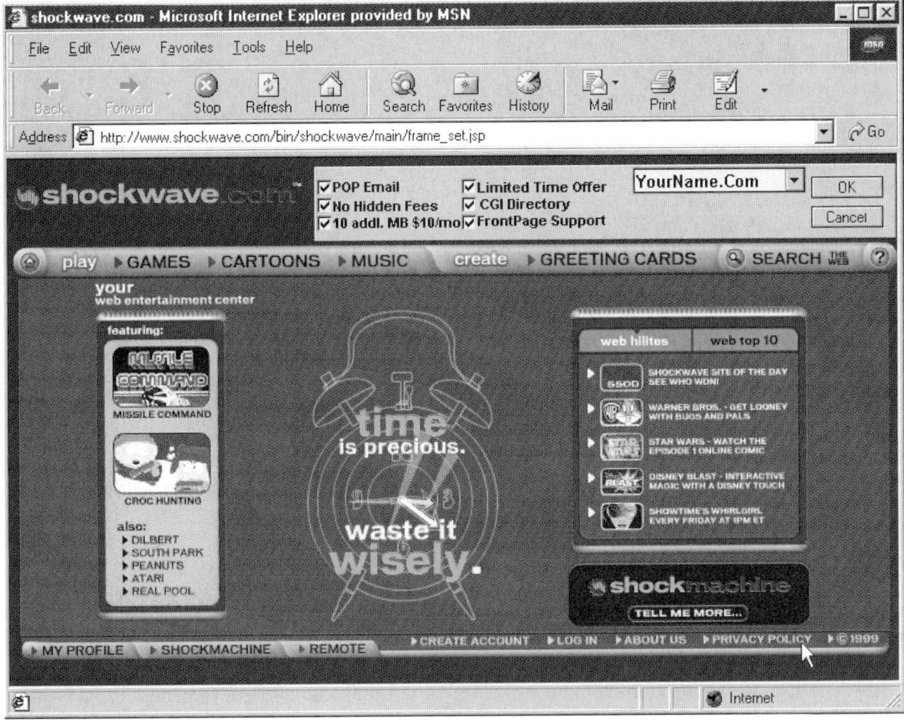

Fig. 2.23 An example of the Shockwave plug-in in use. (Courtesy of **shockwave.com**.)

SUMMARY

- A browser is an important piece of software that enables you to view pages on the Internet.
- The two most popular browsers are Microsoft's Internet Explorer and Netscape's Communicator.
- To connect to the Internet, you will need a computer, a modem and Internet software.
- The first step to getting onto the Internet is registering with an Internet Service Provider (ISP). Once you have signed up for your account (with your ISP), you should start the **Internet Connection Wizard**.
- If you are interested in learning more about the Internet and its features, click on the button labeled **Tutorial**, located in the first Internet Connection Wizard screen.
- The URL describes the location of the file your browser is displaying or loading.
- The URLs of files viewed on the Web normally begin with **http://**.
- A hyperlink is a visual element on a Web page that, when clicked, loads a specified URL into the browser window.
- IE5 has built-in controls that record the sites that your browser has loaded, called the history.
- If you click on **Back**, then your browser will automatically switch the URL to (and load) the previous page in your history. The **Forward** button loads the next page in your history.

- On pages that are frequently updated, you may want to click the **Refresh** button. This action will cause your browser to reload the current URL.
- If a URL addresses a file that the browser is incapable of loading, then you will be given the option to download the file.
- You save an image on the page by right-clicking it and choosing from the options box that pops up **Save Picture As...**.
- A nice new feature of IE5 is the address bar AutoComplete: when you start entering a URL stored in the history, a scrollable menu appears listing all URLs in the history that are potential matches for the URL you are entering.
- The interactive history bar can be activated by clicking the button marked **History** in the row of buttons at the top of your browser window. This shows you your history over the past month chronologically and alphabetically.
- Searching the Internet is usually done through sites called search engines. These search engines constantly explore Web pages all over the Internet through hyperlinks, recording characteristics of the sites they encounter.
- Solutions for many problems you might encounter while using Internet Explorer are accessible through an online **Tour** and a built-in **Help** feature, each accessible through the **Help** menu.
- IE5 provides a mechanism called **Favorites** that allows you to save the URLs of sites, to give you easy access to those sites in the future.
- When you visit a site that you would like to save as a favorite, select the **Add Favorites...** option in the **Favorites** menu. The site will be listed in the **Favorites** menu, identified its title.
- Through the **Organize Favorites** dialog box, you can rename favorites, create folders to organize favorites, place and remove favorites from these folders and delete favorites.
- Downloading is typically initiated on a Web page by clicking a hyperlink targeted at a file on a Web or FTP site.
- FTP stands for File Transfer Protocol, a popular method for sending files over the Internet. The address of an FTP site begins with `ftp://`.
- When you point your browser to the URL of an FTP site, you will be presented with the contents of the specified directory.
- Many FTP sites on the Web have restricted access. This means that only people with specific usernames and passwords will be allowed to access the FTP site.
- Sending a file to another location on the Internet is called uploading.
- Electronic mail, or email for short, is a method of sending formatted messages and files over the Internet to other people.
- When you sign up with an Internet Service Provider, you are given an email address in the form of *username*`@`*domainname*.
- Popular email programs include Microsoft Outlook, Netscape Messenger, and Eudora.
- Outlook Express allows you to manage more than one email account. You can add new accounts by clicking the **Accounts** option in the **Tools** menu.
- Outlook Express provides an easy interface for managing your accounts and messages. When you receive messages you have the option of saving them on your hard drive for later access. Outlook Express allows you to create folders for saving messages.
- Outlook Express checks for new messages several times per hour. When a new message arrives it is placed in your **Inbox**.

- To set new entries for the address book, click on the **Addresses** button at the top of the window, or click on the **Address Book...** entry in the **Tools** menu.
- All entries in the **Address Book** are listed in the main dialog box. You can send a message to anyone in your list by highlighting that person's entry, clicking the **Action** button, then clicking **Send Mail**.
- The only mandatory property is the email address of the recipient, which is put into the **To:** field.
- When you have entered your message, click **Send**, and your message will be on its way to the designated recipient.
- Using newsgroups, a person can post messages to online viewing areas. Other people can then view these messages, reply to them and post new messages.
- Outlook Express has a built-in capability to view Newsgroups. You must first register your newsgroup server settings with Outlook Express.
- A subscribed newsgroup is comparable to a favorite site in IE5. The program will remember its location and give you easy access to its contents at the click of a button.
- To search through and subscribe to newsgroups, click the **Newsgroups** button on the top of the main screen. Outlook Express will then download a list of all available newsgroups.
- To view the contents of a newsgroup, double-click on its entry.
- IE5 provides NetMeeting and Chat for communicating with people over the Internet via live written text and other media.
- You can use NetMeeting to communicate with groups of people via textual and visual aids.
- Microsoft Chat is similar to NetMeeting in its basic layout and procedures, though it is simpler and offers a more casual atmosphere than NetMeeting.
- Be cautious about revealing your true identity and contact information in NetMeeting and in Chat.
- IE5 is installed with a myriad of default settings, called **Internet Options**, that affect the way sites are displayed.
- Toggling off the **Load Pictures** setting will stop the browser from loading images from a Web page and so save time.
- Under the **Programs** tab, you can specify the default programs you want IE5 to use for such common Internet procedures as viewing newsgroups and sending email.
- Under the **Security** tab, you can specify the level of caution IE5 should exercise when browsing sites in general and also for specific sites.
- In the **General** options tab, you can specify a home page, which is the Web site that is loaded when IE5 starts.
- The most recent version of **RealPlayer** plays live or prerecorded sound files and videos.
- The Adobe Acrobat reader is a multiplatform software plug-in that is capable of showing documents online without changing the original format of the document.
- Macromedia Shockwave is a plug-in that when installed and run with a site designed to take advantage of its capabilities, can produce breath-taking dynamic effects.

TERMINOLOGY

Acrobat Portable Data Format (**.pdf**)
Active Desktop
Address bar
Address Book in Outlook Express
Adobe Acrobat reader
anchor
applets
AltaVista (`http://www.altavista.com`)

America OnLine
Ask Jeeves (**`http://www.askjeeves.com`**)
attachments to email
audio clip
audio conferencing
AutoComplete
Back button
background wallpaper
bookmark
browser
browsing the Web
cache
capturing an image
cartoon format in Microsoft Chat
channel
Chat (software from Microsoft)
chat group
chat room
collaboration
`.com`
CompuServe
Connecting to the Internet
Content Advisor and ratings
cookies
copying graphics from a Web site
copying text from a Web site
download file with FTP
`.edu`
electronic mail
email attachments
email server
Enter key
Excite (**`http://www.excite.com`**)
Favorites button and Menu Bar
Forward button
FrontPage Express
FTP (File Transfer Protocol)
FTP site
General tab of **Internet Options**
`.gov`
graphics
Help
history list
home page
`http://` (Hypertext Transfer Protocol)
`http://www.altavista.com`
`http://www.excite.com`
`http://www.infoseek.com`
`http://www.yahoo.com`
hyperlink
images
Inbox in Outlook Express
InfoSeek (**`http://www.infoseek.com/`**)
interactive history bar
Internet Explorer 5 (IE5)
Internet Connection Wizard
Internet options dialog box
Internet Service Provider (ISP)
ISP (Internet Service Provider)
links bar
Macromedia Shockwave
Menu
Microsoft
Microsoft Chat
`.mil`
multimedia
navigating the Web
`.net`
"netiquette"
NetMeeting conferences
Netscape
newsgroups
News Server
online help
online Web tutorial
`.org`
Organize Favorites dialog
Outlook Express (from Microsoft)
`.pdf` (Portable Data Format)
plug-ins
Programs tab of **Internet Options**
public-access FTP site
radio buttons
ratings and the **Content Advisor**
RealAudio **Channels**
Real Networks
RealPlayer plug-in
restricted-access FTP site
Save As...
Save as background...
Save Picture As...
search engine
searching the Internet
Security tab of **Internet Options**
Shockwave (from Macromedia)
shopping
subscribe to a newsgroup
surfing the Web
tables
toolbar

Tour
upload a file with FTP
URL (Uniform Resource Locator)
Usenet newsgroups
video clip
video conferencing
wallpaper
Web
Web browser
WebCrawler
Web page
Web server
Web site
whiteboard in NetMeeting
Windows Media Player
wizards
World Wide Web
Yahoo (**`http://www.yahoo.com`**)

PERFORMANCE TIP

2.1 You will get the best performance out of a browser when viewing the Web if you have as few programs as possible open in your system. This precaution will maximize the amount of memory available for your browser and its extensions to use.

SELF-REVIEW EXERCISES

2.1 Answer each of the following:
a) The two most popular browsers are _________ and _________.
b) A browser is used to view files on the _________.
c) The location of a file on the Internet is called its _________.
d) The element in a Web page that, when clicked, causes a new Web page to load is called a _________; when your mouse passes over this element, the mouse pointer changes into a _________ in IE5.
e) The record IE5 keeps of your Web travels is called the _________.
f) You can save an image from a Web page by right-clicking it and selecting _________.
g) The feature of IE5 that provides options for completing URLs is called _________.
h) The feature of IE5 that lets you save URLs of sites you visit often is called _________.

2.2 Expand the following acronyms:
a) HTTP
b) FTP
c) URL
d) WWW
e) email

2.3 State whether each of the following is *true* or *false*. If the statement is *false*, explain why.
a) There are about 1,000 newsgroups on the Internet.
b) You will have to download and install most plug-ins in order to use them.
c) NetMeeting and Chat are identical programs that do the same thing but look different.
d) FTP is a popular Internet mechanism by which files are uploaded and downloaded.
e) You can probably find a site on a topic you are looking for through a search engine.
f) You can access any FTP site by logging in as **`anonymous`**.

ANSWERS TO SELF-REVIEW EXERCISES

2.1 a) Internet Explorer, Netscape Navigator. b) Internet and the Web. c) URL. d) hyperlink, hand. e) history. f) **Save Picture as...**. g) AutoComplete. h) **Favorites**.

2.2 a) HyperText Transfer Protocol. b) File Transfer Protocol. c) Universal/Uniform Resource Locator. d) World Wide Web. e) Electronic mail.

2.3 a) False. There are tens of thousands of newsgroups, and more are added every day.
b) True.
c) False. NetMeeting is geared more for business use, and includes many features that can help the sharing of information. Chat is intended for more casual use on Chat servers.
d) True.
e) True.
f) False. Many FTP sites are private, and do not admit the general public.

EXERCISES

2.4 Search for the same terms on HotBot (**http://www.hotbot.com**), AltaVista (**http://www.altavista.com**) and Lycos (**http://www.lycos.com**). List the top three results from each search engine.

2.5 Use Internet Explorer's FTP capability to access both **ftp.cdrom.com** and **sunsite.unc.edu**. List the directory output for both sites.

2.6 Log on to a NetMeeting server and initiate a conversation with a friend.

2.7 Use Outlook Express to subscribe to the newsgroup **alt.html**

2.8 Find a local radio station on **http://www.broadcast.com** and listen to it using RealPlayer.

Introduction to HyperText Markup Language 4 (HTML 4)

Objectives

- To understand the key components of an HTML document.
- To be able to use basic HTML tags to write World Wide Web pages.
- To be able to use HTML to format text.
- To be able to add images to your Web pages.
- To understand how to create and use hyperlinks to transit between Web pages.

To read between the lines was easier than to follow the text.
Henry James

Mere colour, unspoiled by meaning, and annulled with definite form, can speak to the soul in a thousand different ways.
Oscar Wide

High thoughts must have high language.
Aristophanes

I've gradually risen from lower-class background to lower-class foreground.
Marvin Cohen

Outline

3.1 Introduction

Welcome to the wonderful world of opportunities being created by the World Wide Web. The Internet is now three decades old, but it was not until the World Wide Web became popular in the 1990s that this current explosion of opportunities began. It seems that exciting new developments occur almost daily—a pace of innovation unlike what we have seen with any other technology. In this chapter, you will begin developing your own Web pages. As the book proceeds, you will be able to create increasingly appealing and powerful Web pages. In the last portion of the book you will learn how to create complete Web-based applications.

We begin unlocking the power of the Web in this chapter with *HTML*—the *Hypertext Markup Language*. HTML is not a procedural programming language like C, Fortran, Cobol, or Pascal. Rather it is a *markup language* for identifying the elements of a page so that a browser, such as Microsoft's Internet Explorer or Netscape's Communicator, can render that page on your computer screen.

In this chapter we introduce the basics of creating Web pages in HTML. We write many simple Web pages. In later chapters we introduce more sophisticated HTML techniques, such as *tables*, which are particularly useful for presenting and manipulating information from databases.

In this chapter we introduce basic HTML *tags* and *attributes*. A key issue when using HTML is the separation of the *presentation of a document* (i.e., how the document is rendered on the screen by a browser) from the *structure of that document*. Over the next several chapters, we discuss this issue in depth.

3.2 Markup Languages

HTML is a *markup language*. It is used to format text and information. This "marking up" of information is different from the intent of traditional programming languages, which is to perform actions in a designated order. In the next several chapters, we discuss HTML markup in detail. (Note that we are specifically not doing action-oriented programming.) Then we introduce JavaScript and Dynamic HTML and show how you can introduce action-oriented programming into your HTML-based Web pages to make those pages "come alive" for the viewer.

In HTML, text is marked up with *elements*, delineated by *tags* that are keywords contained in pairs of angle brackets. For example, the HTML *element* itself, which indicates that we are writing a Web page to be rendered by a browser, begins with a start tag of **<HTML>** and terminates with an end tag of **</HTML>**, as shown in Fig 3.1.

Good Programming Practice 3.1

HTML tags are not case sensitive. However, keeping all the letters in one case improves program readability. We choose uppercase which we believe helps make the tags stand out from the surrounding code.

Common Programming Error 3.1

Forgetting to include closing tags for elements that require them is a syntax error, and can grossly affect the formatting and look of your page. However, unlike in conventional programming languages, a syntax error in HTML does not usually cause page display in browsers to fail completely.

These elements format your page in a specified way. Over the course of the next two chapters, we introduce many of the commonly used tags and how to use them.

3.3 Editing HTML

In this chapter we show how to write HTML in its *source-code form*. We create *HTML files*—also called *HTML documents*—using a text editor. In Chapter 6, we explain how to use a software package called *FrontPage Express* to create Web pages visually, without the need for the page developer to code with HTML directly.

A text editor called ***Notepad*** is built into Windows. It can be found inside the **Accessories** panel of your **Program** list, inside the **Start** menu.

You can also download a free HTML source-code editor called HTML-Kit at **http://www.chami.com/html-kit**. Programs like this can perform useful tasks, such as validating your code and speeding up some repetitive tasks. We will also introduce Microsoft's Visual InterDev in Chapter 7, a program that can be used for both simple HTML editing and more complex Web application development.

All HTML files typically have either the ***.htm*** or the ***.html*** file name extension (this is dependent on the server software). When HTML was first developed, most personal computers were running the Windows 3.1/DOS operating system, which allowed only three-character file name extensions. Current versions of Windows allow more characters in the extension, so the common usage has switched to **.html**. We recommend that you name all of your HTML files with the **.html** extension.

Good Programming Practice 3.2

Assign names to your files that describe their functionality. This practice can help you identify pages faster. It also helps people who want to link to your page, by giving them an easier-to-remember name for the file. For example, if you are writing an HTML document that will display your products, you might want to call it **`products.html`**.

As mentioned previously, making errors while coding in conventional programming languages like C, C++ and Java often produces a fatal error, preventing the program from running. Errors in HTML code are usually not fatal. The browser will make its best effort at rendering the page, but will probably not display the page as you intended. In our *Common Programming Errors* and *Testing and Debugging Tips,* we highlight common HTML errors and how to detect and correct them.

The file name of your *home page* (the first of your HTML pages that a user sees when browsing your Web site) should be ***`index.html`***, because when a browser does not request a specific file in a directory, the normal default Web server response is to return **`index.html`** (this may be different for your server) if it exists in that directory. For example, if you direct your browser to **`http://www.deitel.com`**, the server actually sends the file **`http://www.deitel.com/index.html`** to your browser.

3.4 Common Tags

Fig. 3.1 shows an HTML file that displays one line of text. Line 1

```
<HTML>
```

```
1  <HTML>
2
3  <!-- Fig. 3.1: main.html -->
4  <!-- Our first Web page -->
5
6  <HEAD>
7  <TITLE>Internet and WWW How to Program - Welcome</TITLE>
8  </HEAD>
9
10 <BODY>
11
12 <P>Welcome to Our Web Site!</P>
13
14 </BODY>
15 </HTML>
```

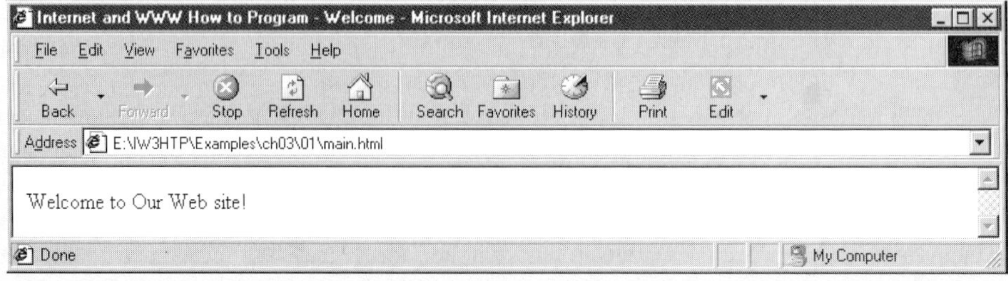

Fig. 3.1 Basic HTML file.

tells the browser that everything contained between the opening ***<HTML>*** tag and the closing ***</HTML>*** tag (line 15) is HTML. The **<HTML>** and **</HTML>** tags should always be the first and last lines of code in your HTML file, respectively.

Good Programming Practice 3.3

Always include the **<HTML>**...**</HTML>** *tags in the beginning and end of your HTML document. Place comments throughout your code. Comments in HTML are placed inside the* **<!--**...**-->** *tags. Comments help other programmers understand the code, assist in debugging, and list other useful information that you do not want the browser to render. Comments also help you understand your own code, especially if you have not looked at it for a while.*

We see our first comments on lines 3-4

```
<!-- Fig. 3.1: main.html -->
<!-- Our first Web page  -->
```

Comments in HTML always begin with **<!--** and end with **-->**. The browser ignores any text and/or tags placed inside a comment. We place comments at the top of each HTML document file giving the figure number, the file name, and a brief description of the file being coded. We also include abundant comments in the code, especially when we introduce new features.

Every HTML file is separated into a header element, which generally contains information about the document, and a body, which contains the page content. Information in the header element is not generally rendered in the display window, but may be made available to the user through other means.

Lines 6-8,

```
<HEAD>
<TITLE>Internet and WWW How to Program - Welcome</TITLE>
</HEAD>
```

show the header section of our Web page. Including a title is mandatory for every HTML document. To include a title in your Web page, enclose your chosen title between the pair of tags **<TITLE>**...**</TITLE>**, which are placed inside the header.

Good Programming Practice 3.4

Use a consistent title naming convention for all pages on your site. For example, if your site is called "Al's Web Site," then the title of your links page might best be "Al's Web Site - Links," etc. This practice presents a clearer picture to those browsing your site.

The **TITLE** element names your Web page. The title usually appears on the colored bar at the top of the browser window, and will also appear as the text identifying your page if a user adds your page to his or her list of **Favorites**. The title is also used by search engines for cataloging purposes, so picking a meaningful title can help the search engines direct a more focused group of people to your site.

Line 10

```
<BODY>
```

opens the ***BODY*** element. The body of an HTML document is the area where you place all content you would like browsers to display. This includes text, images, links, forms, etc. We discuss many elements that can be inserted in the **BODY** element later in this chapter.

These include backgrounds, link colors, and font faces. For now, we will use **<BODY>**...**</BODY>** in its simplest form. Remember to include the closing **</BODY>** tag at the end of the document right before the closing **</HTML>** tag.

Various elements enable you to place text in your HTML document. We see the *paragraph element* on line 12

```
<P>Welcome to Our Web Site!</P>
```

All text placed between the **<P>**...**</P>** tags forms one paragraph. This paragraph will be set apart from all other material on the page by a line of vertical space both before and after the paragraph. The HTML in line 12 causes the browser to render the enclosed text as shown in Fig. 3.1.

Our code example ends on lines 14–15 with

```
</BODY>
</HTML>
```

These two tags close the body and HTML sections of the document, respectively. As discussed earlier, the last tag in any HTML document should be **</HTML>**, which tells the browser that all HTML coding is complete. The closing **</BODY>** tag is placed before the **</HTML>** tag because the body section of the document is entirely enclosed by the HTML section. Therefore, the body section must be closed before the HTML section.

3.5 Headers

Headers are a simple form of text formatting that vary text size based on the header's "level." The six header elements (**H1** through **H6**) are often used to delineate new sections and subsections of a page. Figure 3.2 shows how they are used and their relative display sizes. Note that the actual size of the text of each header element is selected by the browser and can in fact vary significantly between browsers. Later in the book we discuss how you can "take control" of specifying these text sizes and other text attributes as well.

```
<HTML>

<!-- Fig. 3.2: header.html -->
<!-- HTML headers          -->

<HEAD>
<TITLE>Internet and WWW How to Program - Headers</TITLE>
</HEAD>

<BODY>

<!-- Centers everything in the CENTER element -->
<CENTER>
<H1>Level 1 Header</H1>     <!-- Level 1 header -->
<H2>Level 2 header</H2>     <!-- Level 2 header -->
<H3>Level 3 header</H3>     <!-- Level 3 header -->
<H4>Level 4 header</H4>     <!-- Level 4 header -->
```

Fig. 3.2 Header elements **H1** through **H6** (part 1 of 2).

```
18  <H5>Level 5 header</H5>    <!-- Level 5 header -->
19  <H6>Level 6 header</H6>    <!-- Level 6 header -->
20  </CENTER>
21
22  </BODY>
23  </HTML>
```

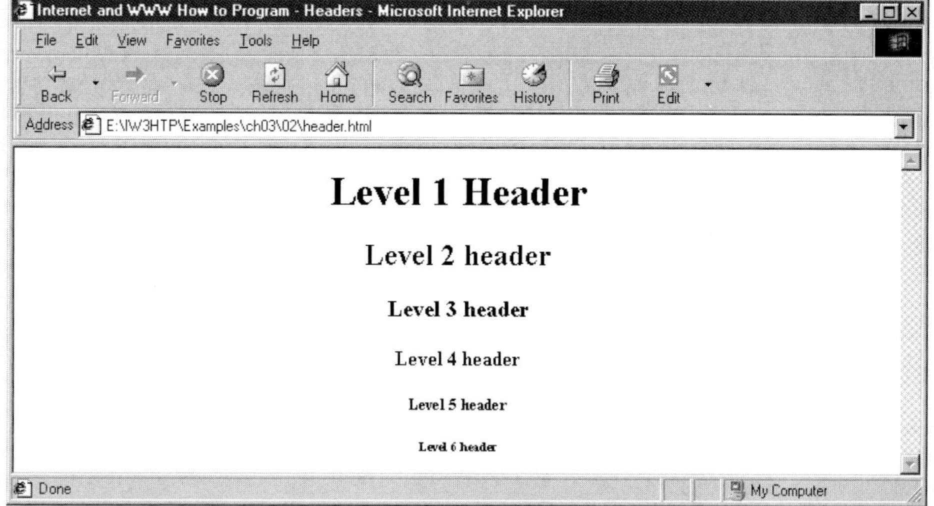

Fig. 3.2 Header elements **H1** through **H6** (part 2 of 2).

Good Programming Practice 3.5

Adding comments to the right of short HTML lines is a clean-looking way to comment your code.

Line 13

```
<CENTER>
```

introduces the ***CENTER*** element, which causes all the material between its **<CENTER>** and **</CENTER>** tags to be centered horizontally in the browser window. Most elements of an HTML page are left adjusted on the screen by default. Later, we discuss how to align individual elements.

Line 14

```
<H1>Level 1 Header</H1>
```

introduces the **H1** header element, with its opening tag ***<H1>*** and its closing tag ***</H1>***. Any text to be displayed is placed between the two tags. All six header elements, **H1** through **H6**, follow the same patterns but in successively smaller type font sizes.

Look-and-Feel Observation 3.1

Putting a header at the top of every Web page helps those viewing your pages understand what the purpose of each page is.

3.6 Text Styling

In HTML, text can be highlighted with bold, underlined, and/or italicized styles (Fig. 3.3).

Our first style, the *underline*, appears on line 11

```
<H1 ALIGN = "center"><U>Welcome to Our Web Site!</U></H1>
```

Notice the statement ***ALIGN* = "*center*"** inside the **<H1>** tag. This is the method by which any single element of the page can be aligned. This same attribute can be used in the **<P>** tag and in other elements such as images and tables. To right-align the element, include the statement **ALIGN = "right"** inside the opening tag of the element. The HTML 4.0 convention is to enclose the **ALIGN** value (**left**, **center**, or **right**) in quotation marks. This convention applies to most attribute values.

Good Programming Practice 3.6

When you have nested tags, always close them in the reverse order from that in which they were started. For example, if you have a word both italicized and underlined: **<EM><U>***Hello!***</U></EM>***, then close the* **U** *element before the* **EM** *element.*

As you can see, all text enclosed in the **<U>**...**</U>** tags is displayed underlined. A second style, the *emphasis* or *italic* style, is shown on line 14

```
about the wonders of <EM>HTML</EM>. We have been using
```

and is used in the same manner as the underline tag. The last style, the *strong* or *bold* style is shown on line 15

```
1   <HTML>
2
3   <!-- Fig. 3.3: main.html -->
4   <!-- Stylizing your text -->
5
6   <HEAD>
7   <TITLE>Internet and WWW How to Program - Welcome</TITLE>
8   </HEAD>
9
10  <BODY>
11  <H1 ALIGN = "center"><U>Welcome to Our Web Site!</U></H1>
12
13  <P>We have designed this site to teach
14  about the wonders of <EM>HTML</EM>. We have been using
15  <EM>HTML</EM> since <U>version<STRONG> 2.0</STRONG></U>,
16  and we enjoy the features that have been added recently. It
17  seems only a short time ago that we read our first <EM>HTML</EM>
18  book. Soon you will know about many of the great new features
19  of HTML 4.0.</P>
20
21  <H2 ALIGN = "center">Have Fun With the Site!</H2>
22
23  </BODY>
24  </HTML>
```

Fig. 3.3 Stylizing text on Web pages (part 1 of 2).

Fig. 3.3 Stylizing text on Web pages (part 2 of 2).

```
<EM>HTML</EM> ever since <U>version<STRONG> 2.0</STRONG></U>,
```

<STRONG> and **<EM>** are used instead of the tags **<B>** and **<I>** (the old standard usages for *bold* and *italic*). This is because the purpose of HTML is simply to mark up text, while the question of how it is presented is left to the browser itself. Therefore, the tags **<B>** and **<I>** are *deprecated* (i.e., their use in valid HTML is discouraged and their support in browsers will eventually disappear), because they overstep this boundary between content and presentation.

For example, people who have difficulty seeing can use special browsers that read aloud the text on the screen. These *text-based browsers* (which do not show images, colors or graphics) might read **STRONG** and **EM** with different inflections to convey the impact of the styled text to the user.

Look-and-Feel Observation 3.2

Be cautious when underlining text on your site, because hyperlinks are underlined by default in most browsers. Underlining plain text can be confusing to people browsing your site.

Look-and-Feel Observation 3.3

Use the **<STRONG>** *and* **<EM>** *tags instead of the* **<B>** *and* **<I>** *tags to ensure that your page is rendered properly by all browsers.*

You should also notice inside line 15

```
<U>version <STRONG>2.0</STRONG></U>
```

Here, the **U** and **STRONG** elements overlap each other. This causes the text included in both elements ("**2.0**") to have both styles applied.

You should also observe the order of the closing tags in the above example from line 15. Because the **STRONG** element started after the **U** element, the **STRONG** element's closing tag appears before that of **U**. Although the order of the closing tags does not always matter to the browser, it is good practice to close them in the reverse order from the order in which they were started.

3.7 Linking

The most important capability of HTML is its ability to create hyperlinks to documents elsewhere on the server and on different servers and thereby make possible a world-wide network of linked documents and information. In HTML, both text and images can act as *anchors* to *link* to other pages on the Web. We introduce anchors and links in Fig. 3.4.

The first link can be found on lines 18 and 19

```
<P>Yahoo: <A HREF = "http://www.yahoo.com">
http://www.yahoo.com</A></P>
```

Links are inserted using the **A** *(anchor) element*. The anchor element is unlike the elements we have seen thus far in that it requires certain attributes inside its opening tag in order to activate the hyperlink. The most important attribute is the location to which you would like the anchoring object to be linked. This location can be any accessible page, file or email URL. To specify the address you would like to link to, insert the ***HREF*** *attribute* into the anchor tag as follows: **<A HREF = "***address***">**. In this case, the address we are linking to is **http://www.yahoo.com**. The hyperlink created on line 18 activates the text on line 19, **http://www.yahoo.com** as an anchor to link to the indicated address.

```
1  <HTML>
2
3  <!-- Fig. 3.4: links.html         -->
4  <!-- Introduction to hyperlinks -->
5
6  <HEAD>
7  <TITLE>Internet and WWW How to Program - Links</TITLE>
8  </HEAD>
9
10 <BODY>
11
12 <CENTER>
13 <H2>Here are my favorite Internet Search Engines</H2>
14 <P><STRONG>Click on the Search Engine address to go to that
15 page.</STRONG></P>
16
17 <!-- Hyperlink form: <A HREF = "address"> -->
18 <P>Yahoo: <A HREF = "http://www.yahoo.com">
19 http://www.yahoo.com</A></P>
20
21 <P>AltaVista: <A HREF = "http://www.altavista.com">
22 http://www.altavista.com</A></P>
23
24 <P>Ask Jeeves: <A HREF = "http://www.askjeeves.com">
25 http://www.askjeeves.com</A></P>
26
```

Fig. 3.4 Linking to other Web pages (part 1 of 2).

```
27 <P>WebCrawler: <A HREF = "http://www.webcrawler.com">
28 http://www.webcrawler.com</A></P>
29 </CENTER>
30
31 </BODY>
32 </HTML>
```

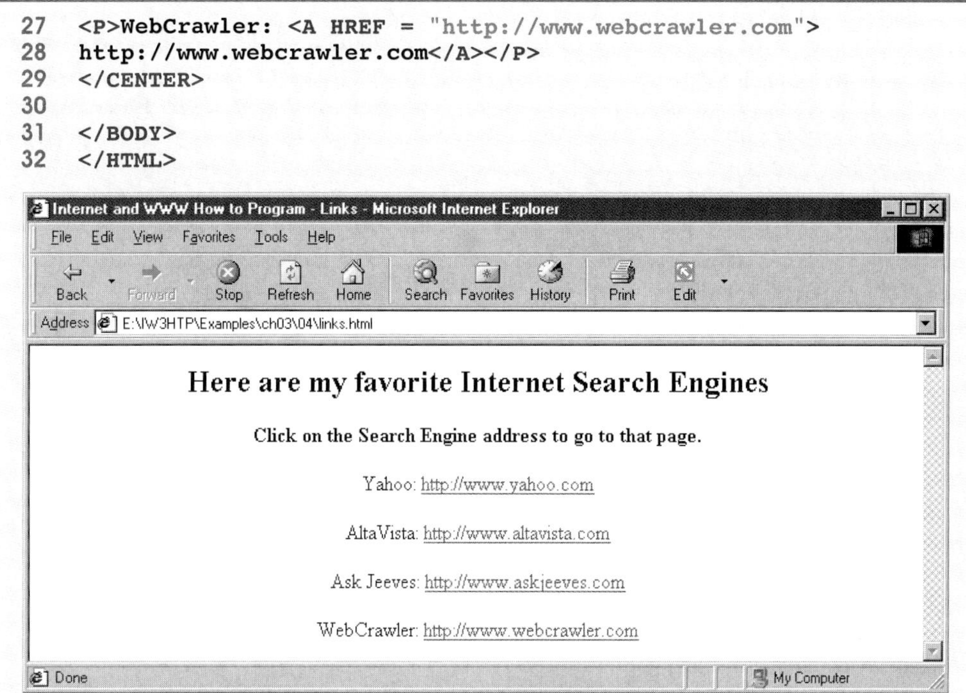

Fig. 3.4 Linking to other Web pages (part 2 of 2).

Anyone who loads your page and clicks on the hyperlinked word(s) will have their browser go to that page. Figure 3.4 contains several other examples of anchor tags.

Figure 3.4 also further demonstrates the function of the **P** element. Recall that the paragraph element adds vertical space around the paragraph area. On lines 18 through 28, there are four complete paragraph tags. Each one is a new paragraph and therefore has a line of vertical space around it.

Anchors can also link to email addresses. When someone clicks on this type of anchored link, their default email program initiates an email message to the linked address. This type of anchor is demonstrated in Fig. 3.5.

```
<HTML>

<!-- Fig. 3.5: contact.html  -->
<!-- Adding email hyperlinks -->

<HEAD>
<TITLE>Internet and WWW How to Program - Contact Page</TITLE>
</HEAD>

<BODY>

```

Fig. 3.5 Linking to an email address (part 1 of 2).

```
12 <!-- The correct form for hyperlinking to an email address -->
13 <!-- is <A HREF = "mailto:address"></A>                       -->
14 <P>My email address is <A HREF = "mailto:deitel@deitel.com">
15 deitel@deitel.com</A>. Click on the address and your browser
16 will open an email message and address it to me.
17 </P>
18
19 </BODY>
20 </HTML>
```

Fig. 3.5 Linking to an email address (part 2 of 2).

Email links use a syntax almost identical to that for links to other Web pages. We see an email link on lines 14 and 15:

```
<P>My email address is <A HREF = "mailto:deitel@deitel.com">
deitel@deitel.com</A>.
```

The form of an email anchor is **<A HREF = "mailto:***emailaddress***">**...**</A>**. It is important that this whole attribute, including the **mailto:**, be placed in quotation marks.

3.8 Images

We have been dealing exclusively with text. We now show how to incorporate images into Web pages (Fig 3.6).

```
<HTML>

<!-- Fig. 3.6: picture.html  -->
<!-- Adding images with HTML -->

<HEAD>
<TITLE>Internet and WWW How to Program - Welcome</TITLE>
</HEAD>

<BODY BACKGROUND = "background.gif">

<CENTER>
<!-- Format for entering images: <IMG SRC = "name"> -->
<IMG SRC = "deitel.gif" BORDER = "1" HEIGHT = "144"
     WIDTH = "200" ALT = "Harvey and Paul Deitel">
</CENTER>
```

Fig. 3.6 Placing images in HTML files (part 1 of 2).

```
17
18  </BODY>
19  </HTML>
```

Fig. 3.6 Placing images in HTML files (part 2 of 2).

For this page, an image background has been inserted in line 10

```
<BODY BACKGROUND = "background.gif">
```

As mentioned earlier, attributes can be added to the **BODY** tag to set certain characteristics of the page, one of which is ***BACKGROUND***. A background can consist of an image or a color. In this case, we are using an image. To use an image as a background, include the attribute **BACKGROUND =** "*filename*" inside the opening **<BODY>** tag. The filename of the image in this case is **background.gif**.

An image used as a background does not need to be large In fact, large background images greatly increase the time it takes for a page to load. The image used for the background in Fig. 3.6 is only 325 *pixels* wide and 85 *pixels* high—the browser *tiles* the image across and down the screen. The term pixel stands for "picture element". Each pixel represents one addressable dot of color on the screen.

Look-and-Feel Observation 3.4

Using an image for your background can be visually appealing. Make sure, however, that the image does not have any sharp color changes, as they can be disorienting to the user, making the text on top hard to read. Also try to use an image that tiles, that is, blends smoothly with the surrounding repetitions of itself.

The image in this code example is inserted in lines 14 and 15

```
<IMG SRC = "deitel.gif" BORDER = "1" HEIGHT = "144"
     WIDTH = "200" ALT = "Paul and Harvey Deitel">
```

You specify the location of the image file in the ***<IMG>*** *tag*. This is done by adding the **SRC =** "*location*" attribute. You can specify the ***HEIGHT*** and ***WIDTH*** of an image, measured in pixels. This image is 200 pixels wide and 144 pixels high.

Good Programming Practice 3.7

*Always include the **HEIGHT** and **WIDTH** of an image in the **IMG** tag. When the browser loads the HTML file, it will know immediately how much screen space to give the image and will therefore lay out the page properly, even before it downloads the image.*

Common Programming Error 3.2

Entering new dimensions for an image that change its inherent width-to-height ratio distorts the appearance of the image. For example, if your image is 200 pixels wide and 100 pixels high, you should always make sure that any new dimensions have a 2:1 width-to-height ratio.

You can add a border (black by default) to images with attribute ***BORDER* = *x***. If *x* is a number larger than 0, the width of the border will be that number of pixels. The image in this example has a border of 1 pixel, as indicated by the image attribute **BORDER = 1**.

An important image attribute is ***ALT***. In Fig. 3.6, the value of this attribute is

```
ALT = "Harvey and Paul Deitel"
```

ALT is provided for browsers that have images turned off, or that cannot view images (i.e., text-based browsers). The value of the **ALT** attribute will appear on-screen in place of the image, giving the user an idea of what was in the image.

Good Programming Practice 3.8

*Include a description of every image using the **ALT** attribute in the **IMG** tag.*

Now that we have discussed placing images on your Web page, we will show you how to transform images into anchors to link your site to other sites on the Internet (Fig. 3.7).

```
<HTML>

<!-- Fig. 3.7: navigationbar.html -->
<!-- Using images as link anchors -->

<HEAD>
<TITLE>Internet and WWW How to Program - Nav Bar</TITLE>
</HEAD>

<BODY BGCOLOR = "#CDCDCD">
<CENTER>

<A HREF = "main.html">
<IMG SRC = "buttons/about.jpg" WIDTH = "65" HEIGHT = "50"
   BORDER = "0" ALT = "Main Page"></A><BR>

<A HREF = "links.html">
<IMG SRC = "buttons/links.jpg" WIDTH = "65" HEIGHT = "50"
   BORDER = "0" ALT = "Links Page"></A><BR>

<A HREF = "list.html">
<IMG SRC = "buttons/list.jpg" WIDTH = "65" HEIGHT = "50"
   BORDER = "0" ALT = "List Example Page"></A><BR>
```

Fig. 3.7 Using images as link anchors (part 1 of 2).

```

<A HREF = "contact.html">
<IMG SRC = "buttons/contact.jpg" WIDTH = "65" HEIGHT = "50"
   BORDER = "0" ALT = "Contact Page"></A><BR>

<A HREF = "header.html">
<IMG SRC = "buttons/header.jpg" WIDTH = "65" HEIGHT = "50"
   BORDER = "0" ALT = "Header Page"></A><BR>

<A HREF = "table.html">
<IMG SRC = "buttons/table.jpg" WIDTH = "65" HEIGHT = "50"
   BORDER = "0" ALT = "Table Page"></A><BR>

<A HREF = "form.html">
<IMG SRC = "buttons/form.jpg" WIDTH = "65" HEIGHT = "50"
   BORDER = "0" ALT = "Feedback Form"></A><BR>
</CENTER>

</BODY>
</HTML>
```

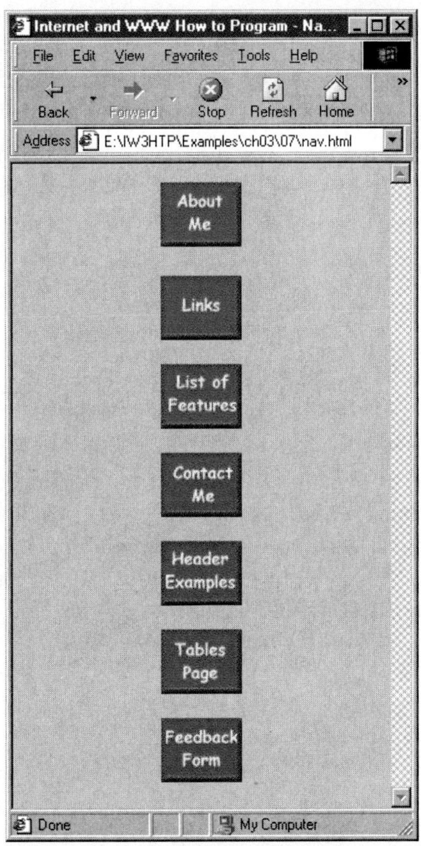

Fig. 3.7 Using images as link anchors (part 2 of 2).

We add a background on line 10 with

```
<BODY BGCOLOR = "#CDCDCD">
```

This is similar to the method we used in Fig. 3.6. The difference is that instead of using a background image, we use a solid background color. Because of this, the attribute name is ***BGCOLOR*** instead of **BACKGROUND**.

To indicate the color for your background, you can use either a preset color name, of which there are more than 100 (see the index of colors in Appendix E), or you can use a *hexadecimal* code to tell the browser what color you want to use (see the code **#CDCDCD** above). This method is also used to change your font color, as we show you in the next section. All colors are composed of varying shades of red, green and blue (so-called *RGB* colors). The first two characters in the "hex" color code represent the amount of red in the color, the second two represent the amount of green and the last two represent the blue. **00** is the weakest a color can get and **FF** is the strongest a color can get. Therefore, "**#FF0000**" is red, "**#00FF00**" is green, "**#0000FF**" is blue, "**#000000**" is black and "**#FFFFFF**" is white. For now, you can just use the preset colors in Appendix E. Later in the book, we explain how to find the hex code of any color you may want to use.

We see an image hyperlink in lines 13 through 15

```
<A HREF = "main.html">
<IMG SRC = "buttons/about.jpg" WIDTH = "65" HEIGHT = "50"
   BORDER = "0" ALT = "Main Page"></A>
```

Here we use the **A** element and the **IMG** element. The anchor works the same way as when it surrounds text; the image becomes an active hyperlink to a location somewhere on the Internet, indicated by the **HREF** attribute inside the **<A>** tag. Remember to close the anchor element when you want the hyperlink to end.

If you direct your attention to the **SRC** attribute of the **IMG** element,

```
SRC = "buttons/about.jpg"
```

you will see that it is not in the same form as that of the image in the previous example. This is because the image we are using here, **about.jpg**, resides in a subdirectory called **buttons**, which is in our main directory for the site. We have done this so that we can keep all our button graphics in the same place, making them easier to find and edit.

You can always refer to files in different directories simply by putting the directory name in the correct format in the **SRC** attribute. If, for example, there was a directory inside the **buttons** directory called **images**, and we wanted to put a graphic from that directory onto our page, we would just have to make the source attribute reflect the location of the image: **SRC = "buttons/images/filename"**.

You can even insert an image from a different Web site into your site (after obtaining permission from the site's owner, of course). Just make the **SRC** attribute reflect the location and name of the image file.

We introduce the *line break* element in line 15

```
BORDER = "0" ALT = "Main Page"></A><BR>
```

The ***BR*** element causes a line break to occur. If the **BR** element is placed inside a text area, the text begins a new line at the place of the **
** tag. We are using **
** here so that we can skip to the line below the image.

3.9 Formatting Text With <FONT>

We have seen how to make pages visually richer using backgrounds and images. Figure 3.8 shows how to add color and formatting to text.

We demonstrate the common methods of formatting in lines 15 through 17

```
<P><FONT COLOR = "red" SIZE = "+1" FACE = "Arial">We have
designed this site to teach about the wonders of
<EM>HTML</EM>.</FONT>
```

Here, several attributes of the ***FONT*** element are demonstrated. The first attribute is ***COLOR***, which indicates the color of the formatted text in the same manner in which you indicate a background color: You enter either a preset color name or a hex color code. Remember to include the quotation marks around the color name.

Note that you can set the font color for the whole document by putting a ***TEXT*** attribute into the **BODY** element and indicating the color in the same manner as above.

```
1  <HTML>
2
3  <!-- Fig. 3.8: main.html             -->
4  <!-- Formatting text size and color -->
5
6  <HEAD>
7  <TITLE>Internet and WWW How to Program - Welcome</TITLE>
8  </HEAD>
9
10 <BODY>
11
12 <H1 ALIGN = "center"><U>Welcome to Our Web Site!</U></H1>
13
14 <!-- Font tags change the formatting of text they enclose -->
15 <P><FONT COLOR = "red" SIZE = "+1" FACE = "Arial">We have
16 designed this site to teach about the wonders of
17 <EM>HTML</EM>.</FONT>
18
19 <FONT COLOR = "purple" SIZE = "+2" FACE = "Verdana">We have been
20 using <EM>HTML</EM> since <U>version<STRONG> 2.0</STRONG></U>,
21 and we enjoy the features that have been added recently.</FONT>
22
23 <FONT COLOR = "blue" SIZE = "+1" FACE = "Helvetica">It
24 seems only a short time ago that we read our first <EM>HTML</EM>
25 book.</FONT>
26
27 <FONT COLOR = "green" SIZE = "+2" FACE = "Times">Soon you will
28 know about many of the great new feature of HTML 4.0.</FONT></P>
29
30 <H2 ALIGN = "center">Have Fun With the Site!</H2></P>
31
32 </BODY>
33 </HTML>
```

Fig. 3.8 Using the **FONT** element to format text (part 1 of 2).

Fig. 3.8 Using the **FONT** element to format text (part 2 of 2).

The second attribute in the example is ***SIZE***, which is used to change the size of the text being formatted. To make the text larger, set **SIZE="+*x*"**. To make the text smaller, set **SIZE="-*x*"**. In each case, *x* is the number of font point sizes by which you want to enlarge or diminish the text.

The last font attribute shown in our example is ***FACE***. This attribute is used to change the font of the text you are formatting. Enter a font name in quotation marks, and the text will be changed to that font.

Common Programming Error 3.3

When using the font face attribute, be careful to only use common fonts like Times, Arial, Courier and Helvetica (just to name a few). Avoid more obscure fonts, because the browser default will be displayed instead (usually Times New Roman).

3.10 Special Characters, Horizontal Rules and More Line Breaks

In HTML, the old QWERTY typewriter setup no longer suffices for all our textual needs. HTML 4.0 has a provision for inserting special characters and symbols (Fig. 3.9).

```
<HTML>

<!-- Fig. 3.9: contact.html       -->
<!-- Inserting special characters -->

```

Fig. 3.9 Inserting special characters into HTML (part 1 of 2).

```
6  <HEAD>
7  <TITLE>Internet and WWW How to Program - Contact Page</TITLE>
8  </HEAD>
9
10 <BODY>
11
12 <!-- Special characters are entered using the form &code; -->
13 <P>My email address is <A HREF = "mailto:deitel@deitel.com">
14 deitel@deitel.com</A>. Click on the address and your browser
15 will automatically open an email message and address it to my
16 address.</P>
17
18 <P>All information on this site is <STRONG>&copy;</STRONG>
19 Deitel <STRONG>&amp;</STRONG> Associates, 1999.</P>
20
21 <!-- Text can be struck out with a set of <DEL>...</DEL>    -->
22 <!-- tags, it can be set in subscript with <SUB>...</SUB>, -->
23 <!-- and it can be set into superscript with <SUP...</SUP> -->
24 <DEL><P>You may copy up to 3.14 x 10<SUP>2</SUP> characters
25 worth of information from this site.</DEL><BR> Just make sure
26 you <SUB>do not copy more information</SUB> than is allowable.
27
28 <P>No permission is needed if you only need to use <STRONG>
29 &lt; &frac14;</STRONG> of the information presented here.</P>
30
31 </BODY>
32 </HTML>
```

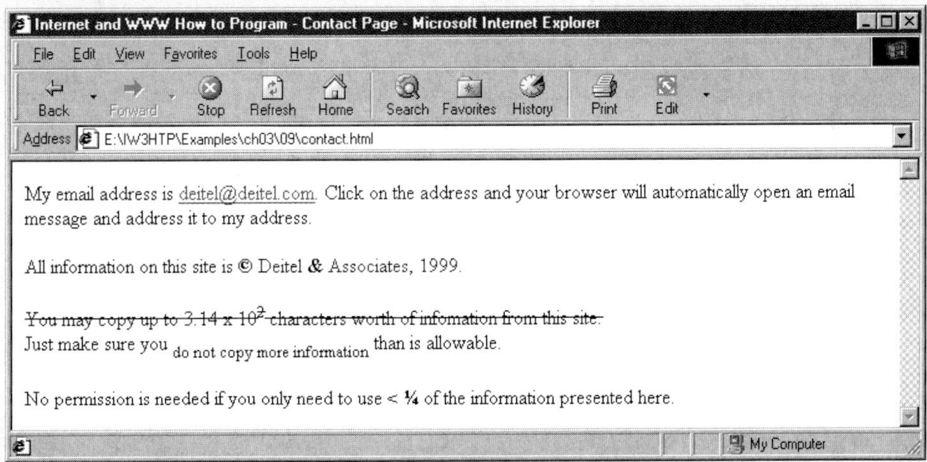

Fig. 3.9 Inserting special characters into HTML (part 2 of 2).

There are some *special characters* inserted into the text of lines 18 and 19

```
<P>All information on this site is <STRONG>&copy;</STRONG>
Deitel <STRONG>&amp;</STRONG> Associates, 1999.</P>
```

All special characters are inserted in their code form. The format of the code is always **&***code***;**. An example of this is **&**, which inserts an ampersand. Codes are often abbreviated forms of the character (like **amp** for ampersand and **copy** for copyright) and can also be in the form of *hex codes.* (For example, the hex code for an ampersand is 38, so another method of inserting an ampersand is to use **&**.) Please refer to the chart in Appendix C for a listing of special characters and their respective codes.

In lines 24 through 26, we introduce three new styles

```
<DEL><P>You may copy up to 3.14 x 10<SUP>2</SUP> characters
worth of information from this site.</DEL><BR> Just make sure
you <SUB>do not copy more information</SUB> than is allowable.
```

You can strike-through text with a horizontal line by including it in a ***DEL*** element. This could be used as an easy way to communicate revisions of an online document. To turn text into *superscript* (i.e., raised vertically to the top of the line and made smaller) or to turn text into *subscript* (the opposite of superscript, lowers text on a line and makes it smaller), use the ***SUP*** and ***SUB*** elements, respectively.

We touched on line breaks in Fig. 3.7. We now provide an example of a textual line break with a horizontal rule (Fig. 3.10).

```
<HTML>

<!-- Fig. 3.10: header.html            -->
<!-- Line breaks and horizontal rules -->

<HEAD>
<TITLE>Internet and WWW How to Program - Horizontal Rule</TITLE>
</HEAD>

<BODY>
<!-- Horizontal rules as inserted using the format: -->
<!-- <HR WIDTH = ".." SIZE = ".." ALIGN = "..">       -->
<HR WIDTH = "25%" SIZE = 1>
<HR WIDTH = "25%" SIZE = 2>
<HR WIDTH = "25%" SIZE = 3>

<P ALIGN = "left"><STRONG>Size:</STRONG>4
<STRONG>Width:</STRONG>75%
<HR WIDTH = "75%" SIZE = "4" ALIGN = "left">

<P ALIGN = "right"><STRONG>Size:</STRONG>12
<STRONG>Width:</STRONG>25%
<HR WIDTH = "25%" SIZE = "12" ALIGN = "right">

<P ALIGN = "center"><STRONG>Size:</STRONG>8
<STRONG>Width:</STRONG>50%
<STRONG><EM>No shade...</EM></STRONG>
<HR NOSHADE WIDTH = "50%" SIZE = "8" ALIGN = "center">

</BODY>
</HTML>
```

Fig. 3.10 Using horizontal rules (part 1 of 2).

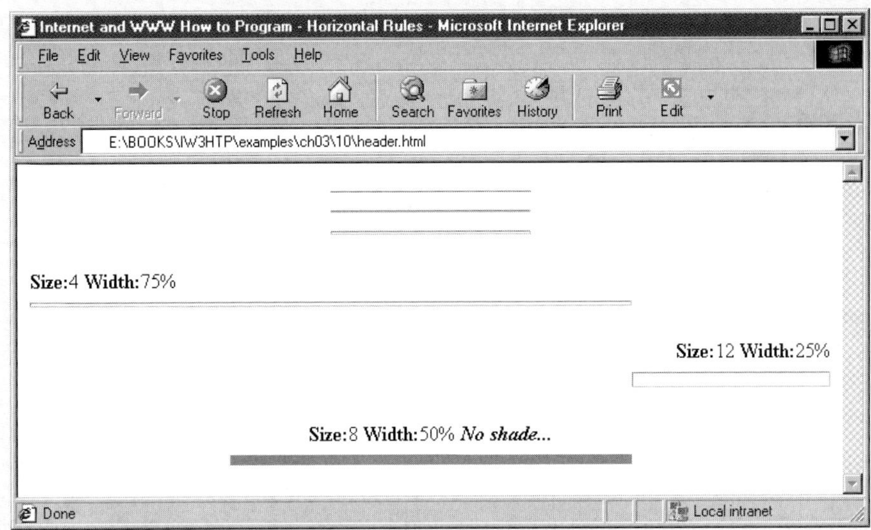

Fig. 3.10 Using horizontal rules (part 2 of 2).

Line 13

```
<HR WIDTH = "25%" SIZE = 1>
```

inserts a horizontal rule, indicated by the ***<HR>*** tag. A horizontal rule is a straight line going across the screen horizontally. The **HR** element also inserts a line break directly below it.

You can adjust the width of the horizontal rule by including the ***WIDTH*** attribute in the **HR** tag. You can set the width either by entering a number, which will indicate the width in pixels, or by entering a percentage, which indicates that the horizontal rule will occupy that percent of the screen width. For example, if you enter **WIDTH = "50%"**, and your screen resolution is 640 pixels, then the **HR** will measure 320 pixels across.

Look-and-Feel Observation 3.5

Inserting horizontal rules into your document can help break text up into meaningful units and so make the text easier to read.

This method of entering the width of an element is used with other elements in HTML 4, the most common being the ***TABLE*** element, which we discuss in the next chapter.

The **SIZE** attribute determines the height of the horizontal rule, in pixels. The **ALIGN** attribute, as we used with the **IMG** element, aligns the **HR** element horizontally on the page. The value of **ALIGN** can be either left, center or right. One final attribute of the **HR** element is ***NOSHADE***. This eliminates the default shading effect and instead displays the horizontal rule as a solid-color bar.

3.11 Internet and WWW Resources

There are many resources available on the World Wide Web that go into much more depth on the topics we cover. Visit the following sites for additional information on the topics in this chapter.

http://www.w3.org/
The *World Wide Web Consortium* (W3C), is the group that makes HTML recommendations. This Web site holds a variety of information about HTML—both its history and its present status.

http://www.w3.org/TR/REC-html40/
The *HTML 4.0 Specification* contains all the nuances and fine points in HTML 4.0.

http://www.freewebpromotion.com/harvillo/index.htm
Harvillo's Finest HTML Help. This site contains step-by-step instructions for beginners on building a Web page.

http://www2.utep.edu/~kross/tutorial
This University of Texas at El Paso site contains another guide for simple HTML programming. The site is helpful for beginners, because it focuses on teaching and gives specific examples.

SUMMARY

- HTML is not a procedural programming language like C, Fortran, Cobol or Pascal. It is a markup language that identifies the elements of a page so a browser can render that page on the screen.
- HTML is used to format text and information. This "marking up" of information is different from the intent of traditional programming languages, which is to perform actions in a designated order.
- In HTML, text is marked up with elements, delineated by tags that are keywords contained in pairs of angle brackets.
- Create HTML files—also called HTML documents—using a text editor. A text editor called **Notepad** is built into Windows. You can also download an HTML shareware source-code editor or use Microsoft's Visual InterDev.
- All HTML files require either the **.htm** or the **.html** file name extension.
- Making errors while coding in conventional programming languages like C, C++ and Java often produces a fatal error, preventing the program from running. Errors in HTML code are usually not fatal. The browser will make its best effort at rendering the page but will probably not display the page as you intended. In our Common Programming Errors and Testing and Debugging Tips we highlight common HTML errors and how to detect and correct them.
- The filename of your home page should be **index.html**. When a browser requests a directory, the default Web server response is to return **index.html**, if it exists in that directory.
- **<HTML>** tells the browser that everything contained between the opening **<HTML>** tag and the closing **</HTML>** tag is HTML.
- Comments in HTML always begin with **<!--** and end with **-->** and can span across several source lines. The browser ignores any text and/or tags placed inside a comment.
- Every HTML file is separated into a header section and a body.
- Including a title is mandatory for every HTML document. Use the **<TITLE>**...**</TITLE>** tags to do so. They are placed inside the header.
- **<BODY>** opens the **BODY** element. The body of an HTML document is the area where you place all content you would like browsers to display.
- All text between the **<P>**...**</P>** tags forms one paragraph. This paragraph will be set apart from all other material on the page by a line of vertical space both before and after the paragraph.
- Headers are a simple form of text formatting that typically increase text size based on the header's "level" (**H1** through **H6**). They are often used to delineate new sections and subsections of a page.
- The **CENTER** element causes all material between its **<CENTER>** and **</CENTER>** tags to be centered horizontally in the browser window.

- The attribute **ALIGN** is the method by which any single element of the page can be aligned. The HTML 4.0 convention is to enclose the **ALIGN** value (**left**, **center** or **right**) in quotation marks. This convention applies to most attribute values.
- The purpose of HTML is simply to mark up text, the question of how it is presented is left to the browser itself.
- People who have difficulty seeing can use special browsers that read the text on the screen aloud. These browsers (which are text based and do not show images, colors or graphics) might read **STRONG** and **EM** with different inflections to convey the impact of the styled text to the user.
- You should close tags in the reverse order from that in which they were started.
- The most important capability of HTML is creating hyperlinks to documents on any server to form a world-wide network of linked documents and information.
- Links are inserted using the **A** (anchor) element. To specify the address you would like to link to, insert the **HREF** attribute into the anchor tag, with the address as the value of **HREF**.
- Anchors can link to email addresses. When someone clicks on this type of anchored link, their default email program initiates an email message to the linked address.
- Attributes can be added to the **BODY** tag to set certain characteristics of the page. To use an image as a background, include the attribute **BACKGROUND** = "file.ext" inside the opening **<BODY>** tag.
- Large background images greatly increase the time it takes for a page to load. The browser tiles the image across and down the screen.
- The term pixel stands for "picture element". Each pixel represents one dot of color on the screen.
- You specify the location of the image file with the **SRC** = "location" attribute in the **<IMG>** tag. You can specify the **HEIGHT** and **WIDTH** of an image, measured in pixels. You can add a border by using the **BORDER** = "x" attribute.
- **ALT** is provided for browsers that cannot view pictures or that have images turned off (text-based browsers, for example). The value of the **ALT** attribute will appear on-screen in place of the image, giving the user an idea of what was in the image.
- **<BODY BGCOLOR = "#CDCDCD">** adds a solid background color. To indicate the color to use specify either a preset color name (Appendix E) or a hexadecimal code.
- All colors are composed of varying shades of red, green and blue (i.e., so-called RGB colors). The first two characters in the "hex" color code represent the amount of red in the color, the second two represent the amount of green and the last two represent the blue. **00** is the weakest a color can get and **FF** is the strongest a color can get.
- You can refer to files in different directories by including the directory name in the correct format in the **SRC** attribute. You can insert an image from a different Web site onto your site (after obtaining permission from the site's owner). Just make the **SRC** attribute reflects the location and name of the image file.
- The **BR** element forces a line break. If the **BR** element is placed inside a text area, the text begins a new line at the place of the **
** tag. Attribute **COLOR** indicates the color of the formatted text in the same manner in which you indicate a background color; you enter either a preset color name or a hex color code. Remember to include the quotation marks around the color name.
- Use **SIZE** to change the size of the text being formatted with **<FONT>**. To make the text larger, set the **SIZE** = "+x". To make the text smaller set **SIZE** = "-x". Use **FACE** to change the font of the text you are formatting.
- HTML 4.0 has a provision for inserting special characters and symbols. All special characters are inserted in the format of the code, always **&**code**;**. An example of this is **&**, which inserts an ampersand. Codes are often abbreviated forms of the character (like **amp** for ampersand and **copy**

for copyright) and can also be in the form of hex codes. (For example, the hex code for an ampersand is 38, so another method of inserting an ampersand is to use **&**.) Please refer to the chart in Appendix C for a listing of special characters and their respective codes.

- You can strike-through text with a horizontal line by including it in a **DEL** element. To turn text into superscript or subscript, use the **SUP** and **SUB** elements respectively.
- **<HR>** inserts a horizontal rule, a straight line going across the screen. You can adjust the width of it by including the **WIDTH** attribute, using a number of pixels or a percentage of screen width. **NOSHADE** will remove the 3D shading, rendering the **HR** as a solid-color bar. This method of entering the width of an element is used with other elements in HTML 4, for example the **TABLE** element.

TERMINOLOGY

<!--...--> (comment)
A element (anchor; **<A>**...**</A>**)
ALIGN = "center"
ALIGN = "left"
ALIGN = "right"
ALT
&
anchor
attributes of an HTML tag
BACKGROUND attribute of **BODY** element
BGCOLOR attribute of **BODY** element
<BODY>...**</BODY>**
bold
border of an image
CENTER element (**<CENTER>**...**</CENTER>**)
CLEAR = "all" in **
**
closing tag
color
COLOR in **<BODY>**
comments
content of an HTML element
DEL element
EM element (**<EM>**...**</EM>**)
emphasis
FACE = in **<FONT>**
FONT element (**<FONT>**...**</FONT>**)
FORM element (**<FORM>**...**</FORM>**)
FrontPage Express
HEAD element (**<HEAD>**...**</HEAD>**)
height
hexadecimal color codes
H5 element (**<H5>**...**</H5>**)
H4 element (**<H4>**...**</H4>**)
H1 element (**<H1>**...**</H1>**)
horizontal rule
<HR> element (horizontal rule)
HREF attribute of **<A>** element
H6 element (**<H6>**...**</H6>**)
H3 element (**<H3>**...**</H3>**)
.htm
.html
HTML (HyperText Markup Language)
HTML document
HTML element (**<HTML>**...**</HTML>**)
HTML file
HTML-Kit
HTML tags
H2 element (**<H2>**...**</H2>**)
hyperlink
hypertext
image
IMG element
index.html
italic
line break element (**
...</BR>**)
link
link attribute of **BODY** element...
mailto:
Markup Language
Name attribute of FRAME element
opening tag
paragraph element (**<P>**...**</P>**)
P element (paragraph; **<P>**...**</P>**)
presentation of a Web Page
RGB colors
SIZE = in **<FONT>**
source-code form
special characters
SRC attribute in **IMG** element
STRONG element (**<STRONG>**...**</STRONG>**)
structure of a Web page
SUB (subscript)
SUP (superscript)
tags in HTML

text-based browser
TEXT in **BODY**
tiling an image across the screen
TITLE element (**<TITLE>**...**</TITLE>**)
U element
unordered list (**<UL>**...**</UL>**)
Web site
WIDTH attribute
width by pixel
width by percentage
World Wide Web

COMMON PROGRAMMING ERRORS

3.1 Forgetting to include closing tags for elements that require them is a syntax error and can grossly affect the formatting and look of your page. However, unlike in conventional programming languages, a syntax error in HTML does not cause program failure.

3.2 Entering new dimensions for an image which change its inherent width-to-height ratio distorts the appearance of the image. For example, if your image is 200 pixels wide and 100 pixels high, you should always make sure that any new dimensions have a 2:1 width-to-height ratio.

3.3 When using the font face attribute, be careful to use only such common fonts like Times, Arial, Courier and Helvetica (just to name a few). Avoid more obscure fonts, because the browser default will be displayed instead (usually Times New Roman).

GOOD PROGRAMMING PRACTICES

3.1 HTML tags are not case sensitive. However, keeping all the letters in one case improves program readability. We choose uppercase which we believe helps make the tags stand out from the surrounding code

3.2 Assign names to your files that describe their functionality. This practice can help you identify pages faster. It also helps people who want to link to your page, by giving them an easier-to-remember name for the file. For example, if you are writing an HTML document that will display your products, you might want to call it **products.html**.

3.3 Always include the **<HTML>**...**</HTML>** tags in the beginning and end of your HTML document. Place comments throughout your code. Comments in HTML are placed inside **<!--** ...**-->** tags. Comments help other programmers understand the code, assist in debugging and list other useful information that you do not want the browser to render. Comments also help you understand your own code, especially if you have not looked at it for a while.

3.4 Use a consistent title naming convention for all pages on your site. For example, if your site is called "Al's Web Site," then the title of your links page might best be "Al's Web Site - Links." This practice presents a clearer picture to those browsing your site.

3.5 Adding comments to the right of short HTML lines is a clean-looking way to comment your code.

3.6 When you have nested tags, always close them in the reverse order from that in which they were started. For example, if you have a word both italicized and underlined: **<EM><U>**Hello! **</U></EM>**, then close the **U** element before the **EM** element

3.7 Always include the **HEIGHT** and **WIDTH** of an image in the **IMG** tag. When the browser loads the HTML file, it will know immediately how much screen space to give the image and will therefore lay out the page properly, even before it downloads the image.

3.8 Include a description of every image using the **ALT** attribute in every **IMG** tag.

LOOK-AND-FEEL OBSERVATIONS

3.1 Putting a header at the top of every Web page helps those viewing your pages understand what the purpose of each page is.

3.2 Be cautious when underlining text on your site, because hyperlinks are underlined by default in most browsers. Underlining plain text can be confusing to people browsing your site.

3.3 Use the **<STRONG>** and **<EM>** tags instead of the **<B>** and **<I>** tags to ensure that your page is rendered properly by all browsers.

3.4 Using an image for your background can be visually appealing. Make sure, however, that the image does not have any sharp color changes, as this can be disorienting to the user, making the text on top hard to read. Also try to use an image that tiles (blends smoothly with the surrounding repetitions of itself).

3.5 Inserting horizontal rules into your document can help break text up into meaningful units and so make the text easier to read.

SELF-REVIEW EXERCISES

3.1 State whether the following are *true* or *false*. If the answer is *false*, explain why.

a) You can specify the background of the page as an attribute in the **<HTML>** tag.
b) The use of the **EM** and **STRONG** elements is deprecated.
c) The name of your site home page should always be **homepage.html**.
d) It is a good programming practice to insert comments into your HTML document that explain what you are doing.
e) A hyperlink is inserted around text with the **LINK** element.

3.2 Fill in the blanks in each of the following:

a) The _______ element is used to insert a horizontal rule.
b) Superscript is formatted with the _______ element and subscript is formatted with the _______ element.
c) The _______ element is located within the **<HEAD>**...**</HEAD>** tags.
d) The smallest text header is the _______ element and the largest text header is _______.
e) The _______ element is used to format the size and color of text.
f) You can center a section of your page by enclosing it between _______ tags.

3.3 Identify each of the following as either an element or attribute.

a) **HTML**
b) **WIDTH**
c) **ALIGN**
d) **BR**
e) **SIZE**
f) **H3**
g) **A**
h) **SRC**

ANSWERS TO SELF-REVIEW EXERCISES

3.1 a) False. You specify the background with either the **BACKGROUND** or the **BGCOLOR** attribute in the **BODY** element. b) False. The use of the **U** and **B** elements is deprecated. **EM** and **STRONG** should be used instead. c) False. The name of your homepage should always be **index.html**. d) True. e) False. A hyperlink is inserted around text with the **A** (anchor) element.

3.2 a) **HR**. b) **SUP**, **SUB** c) **TITLE** d) **H6**, **H1** e) **FONT** f) **<CENTER>**...**</CENTER>**

3.3 a) Tag. b) Attribute. c) Attribute. d) Tag. e) Attribute. f) Tag. g) Tag. h) Attribute.

EXERCISES

3.4 Mark up the first paragraph of this chapter. Use **H1** for the section header, **P** for text, **STRONG** for the first word of every sentence, and **EM** for all capital letters.

3.5 Mark up the first paragraph again, this time using left-aligned horizontal rules to separate sentences. The size of each horizontal rule should be the same as the number of words in the preceding sentence. Every alternate horizontal rule should have the **NOSHADE** attribute applied.

3.6 Why is this code valid? (*Hint*: you can find the W3C specification for the **P** element at **http://www.w3.org/TR/REC-html40/struct/text.html**.)

```
<P>Here's some text...
<HR>
<P>And some more text...</P>
```

3.7 Why is this code invalid? (*Hint*: you can find the W3C specification for the **BR** element at the same URL given in Exercise 3.3.)

```
<P>Here's some text...<BR></BR>
And some more text...</P>
```

3.8 Given: We have an image named **deitel.gif** that is 200 pixels wide and 150 pixels high. Use the **WIDTH** and **HEIGHT** attributes of the **IMG** tag to a) increase image size by 100%; b) increase image size by 50%; c) change the width-to-height ratio to 2:1, keeping the width attained in a).

3.9 Create a link to each of the following: a) **index.html**, located in the **files** directory; b) index.html, located in the **text** subdirectory of the **files** directory; c) **index.html**, located in the **other** directory in your *parent directory* (*Hint*: **..** signifies parent directory.); d) A link to the President's email address (**president@whitehouse.gov**); e) An **FTP** link to the file named **README** in the **pub** directory of **ftp.cdrom.com** (*Hint*: remember to use **ftp://**).

Intermediate HTML 4

Objectives

- To be able to create lists of information.
- To be able to create tables with rows and columns of data.
- To be able to control the display and formatting of tables.
- To be able to create and use forms.
- To be able to create and use image maps to aid hyperlinking.
- To be able to make Web pages accessible to search engines.
- To be able to use the **<FRAMESET>** tag to create more interesting Web pages.

Yea, from the table of my memory
I'll wipe away all trivial fond records.
William Shakespeare

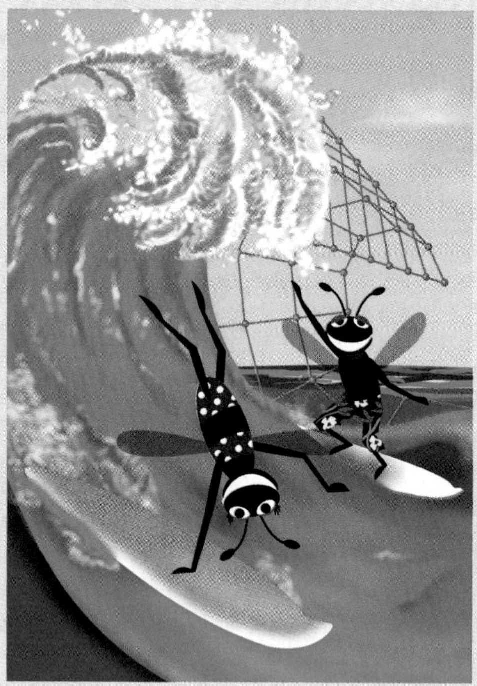

Outline

4.1 Introduction

In the previous chapter, we discussed some basic HTML features. We built several complete Web pages featuring text, hyperlinks, images, backgrounds, colors and such formatting tools as horizontal rules and line breaks.

In this chapter, we discuss more substantial HTML elements and features. We will see how to present information in *lists* and *tables*. We discuss how to use forms to collect information from people browsing a site. We explain how to use *internal linking* and *image maps* to make pages more navigable. We also discuss how to use *frames* to make attractive interactive Web sites.

By the end of this chapter, you will be familiar with most commonly used HTML tags and features. You will then be able to create more complex and visually appealing Web sites. Throughout the remainder of the book we introduce many more advanced HTML capabilities such as *scripting*, *Dynamic HTML*, *Perl/CGI*, *ASP* (*Active Server Pages*) and *XML* (*Extensible Markup Language*).

4.2 Unordered Lists

Figure 4.1 demonstrates displaying text in an *unordered list*. Here we reuse an HTML file from Chapter 3, adding an unordered list to enhance the look of the page. The *unordered list element* creates a list in which every line begins with a bullet mark. All entries in an unordered list must be enclosed within **<UL>**...**</UL>** tags, which open and close the unordered list element.

```
<HTML>

<!-- Fig. 4.1: links.html -->
<!-- Unordered Lists      -->

<HEAD>
<TITLE>Internet and WWW How to Program - Links</TITLE>
</HEAD>

<BODY>

<CENTER>
<H2>Here are my favorite Internet Search Engines</H2>
<P><STRONG>Click on the Search Engine address to go to that
page.</STRONG></P>

<!-- <UL> creates a new unordered (bullet) list -->
<!-- <LI> inserts a new entry into the list     -->
<UL>
<LI>Yahoo: <A HREF = "http://www.yahoo.com">
http://www.yahoo.com</A></LI>

<LI>Alta Vista: <A HREF = "http://www.altavista.com">
http://www.alta-vista.com</A></LI>

<LI>Ask Jeeves: <A HREF = "http://www.askjeeves.com">
http://www.askjeeves.com</A></LI>

<LI>WebCrawler: <A HREF = "http://www.webcrawler.com">
http://www.webcrawler.com</A></LI>
</UL>
</CENTER>

</BODY>
</HTML>
```

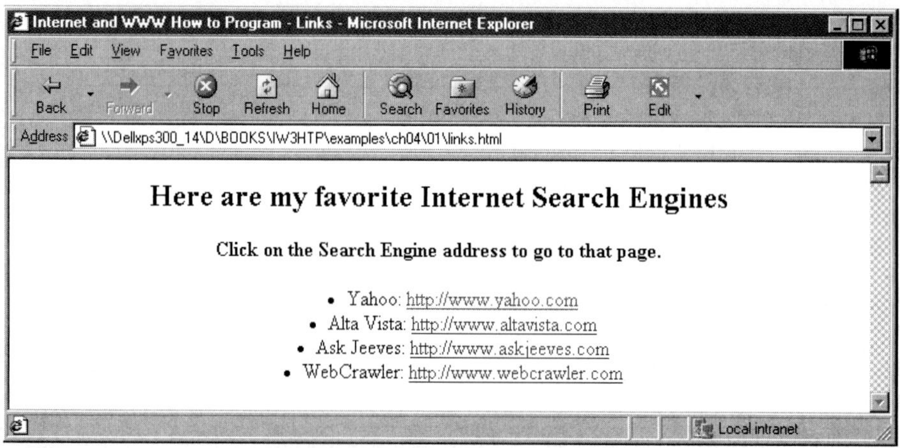

Fig. 4.1 Unordered lists with HTML.

The first list item appears on lines 20 and 21

```
<LI>Yahoo: <A HREF = "http://www.yahoo.com">
http://www.yahoo.com</A></LI>
```

Each entry in an unordered list is inserted with the **<*LI*>** (*list item*) tag, which creates a line break and inserts a bullet mark at the beginning of the line. You then insert and format any text. The closing tag of the list element (**</*LI*>**) is optional; we prefer to include it to maintain the clarity of the code. At the end of the list, close the **UL** element with the **</UL>** tag.

4.3 Nested and Ordered Lists

Figure 4.2 demonstrates *nested lists*. This feature is useful for displaying information in outline form.

```
<HTML>

<!-- Fig. 4.2: list.html                  -->
<!-- Advanced Lists: nested and ordered -->

<HEAD>
<TITLE>Internet and WWW How to Program - List</TITLE>
</HEAD>

<BODY>

<CENTER>
<H2><U>The Best Features of the Internet</U></H2>
</CENTER>

<UL>
<LI>You can meet new people from countries around
   the world.</LI>
<LI>You have access to new media as it becomes public:</LI>

   <!-- This starts a nested list, which uses a modified  -->
   <!-- bullet. The list ends when you close the <UL> tag -->
   <UL>
   <LI>New games</LI>
   <LI>New applications </LI>

      <!-- Another nested list, there is no nesting limit -->
      <UL>
      <LI>For business</LI>
      <LI>For pleasure</LI>
      </UL> <!-- This ends the double nested list -->
   <LI>Around the clock news</LI>
   <LI>Search engines</LI>
   <LI>Shopping</LI>
   <LI>Programming</LI>
      <UL>
      <LI>HTML</LI>
```

Fig. 4.2 Nested and ordered lists in HTML (part 1 of 2).

```
         <LI>Java</LI>
         <LI>Dynamic HTML</LI>
         <LI>Scripts</LI>
         <LI>New languages</LI>
         </UL>
      </UL>   <!-- This ends the first level nested list -->
   <LI>Links</LI>
   <LI>Keeping in touch with old friends</LI>
   <LI>It is the technology of the future!</LI>
   </UL>   <!-- This ends the primary unordered list -->

   <BR><CENTER><H2>My 3 Favorite <EM>CEO's</EM></H2></CENTER>

   <!-- Ordered lists are constructed in the same way as    -->
   <!-- unordered lists, except their starting tag is <OL> -->
   <OL>
   <LI>Bill Gates</LI>
   <LI>Steve Jobs</LI>
   <LI>Michael Dell</LI>
   </OL>

   </BODY>
   </HTML>
```

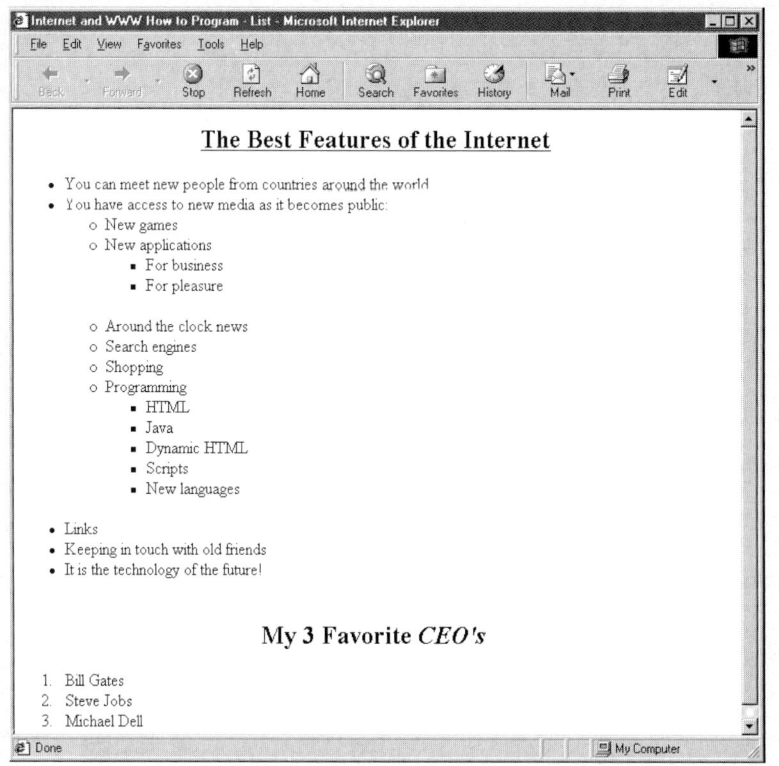

Fig. 4.2 Nested and ordered lists in HTML (part 2 of 2).

Our first nested list begins in lines 23 and 24

```
<UL>
<LI>New games</LI>
```

A nested list is written in the same way as the list we showed you in Fig. 3.2, except that the nested list is contained in another list element. Nesting the new list inside the original will indent the list one level and will change the bullet type to reflect the nesting.

Note the line of space that occurs when you close the unordered list element, for example between “For pleasure” and “Around the clock news” (Fig 4.2). Browsers insert a line of whitespace after every closed list.

Good Programming Practice 4.1

Indenting each level of a nested list in your code makes the code easier to edit and debug.

In Fig. 4.2, lines 16 through 47 show a list with three levels of nesting. When nesting lists, be sure to insert the closing **</UL>** tags in the appropriate places. Lines 53 through 57

```
<OL>
<LI>Bill Gates</LI>
<LI>Steve Jobs</LI>
<LI>Michael Dell</LI>
</OL>
```

define an *ordered list* element with the tags **<OL>**…**</OL>**. Every item in an ordered list begins with a sequence number. By default, ordered lists use decimal sequence numbers (1, 2, 3, …). Figure 4.3 demonstrates alternate labeling schemes for list items.

```
<HTML>

<!-- Fig. 4.3: list.html             -->
<!-- Different Types of Ordered Lists -->

<HEAD>
<TITLE>Internet and WWW How to Program - List</TITLE>
</HEAD>

<BODY>

<CENTER>
<H2>Web Site Outline</H2>
</CENTER>

<!-- Change the character style by specifying it in  -->
<!-- <OL TYPE = "style"> OR <LI TYPE = "style"> as    -->
<!-- decimal=1, uppercase Roman=I, lowercase Roman=i -->
<!-- uppercase Latin=A, lowercase Latin=a            -->
<OL>
<LI>Home page</LI>
<LI>Links page</LI>
   <OL TYPE = "I">
```

Fig. 4.3 Different types of ordered lists (part 1 of 2).

```
      <LI>Links to search engines</LI>
      <LI>Links to information sites</LI>
         <OL TYPE = "A">
         <LI>News sites</LI>
            <OL>
            <LI TYPE = "i">TV based</LI>
               <OL TYPE = "a">
               <LI>CNN</LI>
               <LI>Headline News</LI>
               </OL>
            <LI TYPE = "i">Text based</LI>
               <OL TYPE = "a">
               <LI>New York Times</LI>
               <LI>Washington Post</LI>
               </OL>
            </OL>
         <LI>Stock sites</LI>
         </OL>
      <LI>Links to "fun" sites</LI>
      </OL>
   <LI>Feedback page</LI>
   <LI>Contact page</LI>
   <LI>HTML Example Pages</LI>
   </OL>

   </BODY>
   </HTML>
```

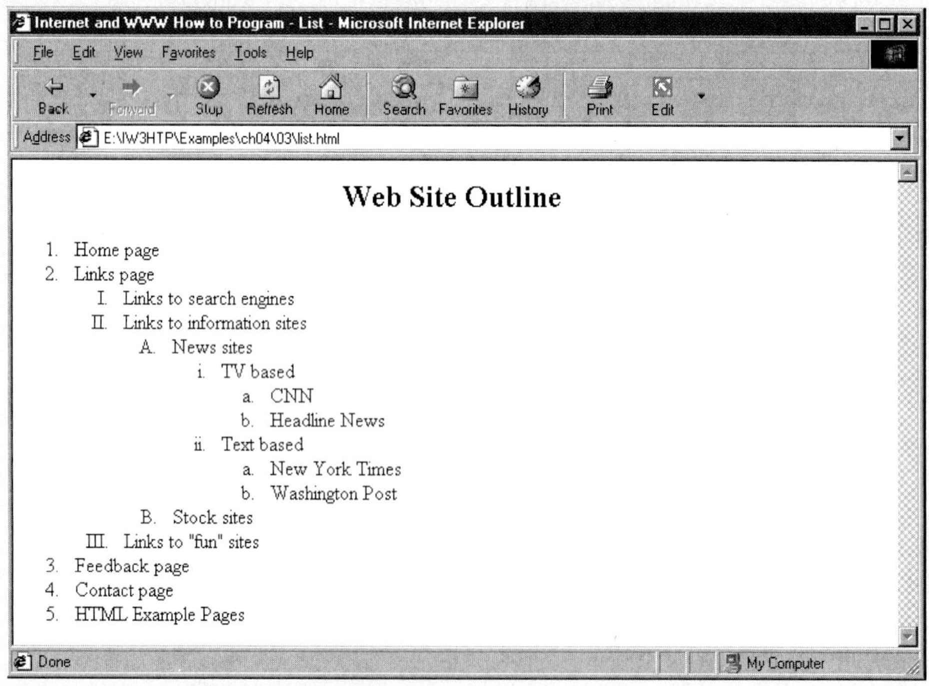

Fig. 4.3 Different types of ordered lists (part 2 of 2).

The four types of list item labeling appear in lines 23 and 24

```
<OL TYPE = "I">
<LI>Links to search engines</LI>
```

lines 26 and 27

```
<OL TYPE = "A">
<LI>News Sites</LI>
```

line 29

```
<LI TYPE = "i">TV based</LI>
```

and lines 30 and 31

```
<OL TYPE = "a">
<LI>CNN</LI>
```

To change the sequence type, use attribute ***TYPE*** in the **<OL>** opening tag. You can insert the **TYPE** attribute into an individual **<LI>** tag if you would like the change to affect just that list entry. The default type is ***TYPE* = "*1*"**, which uses the 1, 2, 3, … sequence. The second type, ***TYPE* = "*I*"**, makes an uppercase Roman numeral sequence (I, II, III, …). A variant of this second type is ***TYPE* = "*i*"**, which creates the lowercase Roman numeral sequence (i, ii, iii, …). The last two types are ***TYPE* = "*A*"** and ***TYPE* = "*a*"**, which produce uppercase and lowercase alphabetic sequences, respectively.

Look-and-Feel Observation 4.1

Using different types of ordered lists can add a well-organized look to your site and can help you categorize and outline information effectively.

4.4 Basic HTML Tables

Another way to format information using HTML 4.0 is to use *tables*. The table in Fig. 4.4 organizes data into rows and columns.

```
<HTML>

<!-- Fig. 4.4: table.html -->
<!-- Basic table design   -->

<HEAD>
<TITLE>Internet and WWW How to Program - Tables</TITLE>
</HEAD>

<BODY>

<H2>Table Example Page</H2>

<!-- The <TABLE> tag opens a new table and lets you put in -->
<!-- design options and instructions                        -->
<TABLE BORDER = "1" ALIGN = "center" WIDTH = "40%">
```

Fig. 4.4 HTML table (part 1 of 2).

```
17
18 <!-- Use the <CAPTION> tag to summarize the table's contents -->
19 <!-- (this helps the visually impaired)                       -->
20 <CAPTION>Here is a small sample table.</CAPTION>
21
22 <!-- The <THEAD> is the first (non-scrolling) horizontal   -->
23 <!-- section.Use it to format the table header area.       -->
24 <!-- <TH> inserts a header cell and displays bold text     -->
25 <THEAD>
26 <TR><TH>This is the head.</TH></TR>
27 </THEAD>
28
29 <!-- All of your important content goes in the <TBODY>. -->
30 <!-- Use this tag to format the entire section          -->
31 <!-- <TD> inserts a data cell, with regular text        -->
32 <TBODY>
33 <TR><TD ALIGN = "center">This is the body.</TD></TR>
34 </TBODY>
35
36 </TABLE>
37
38 </BODY>
39 </HTML>
```

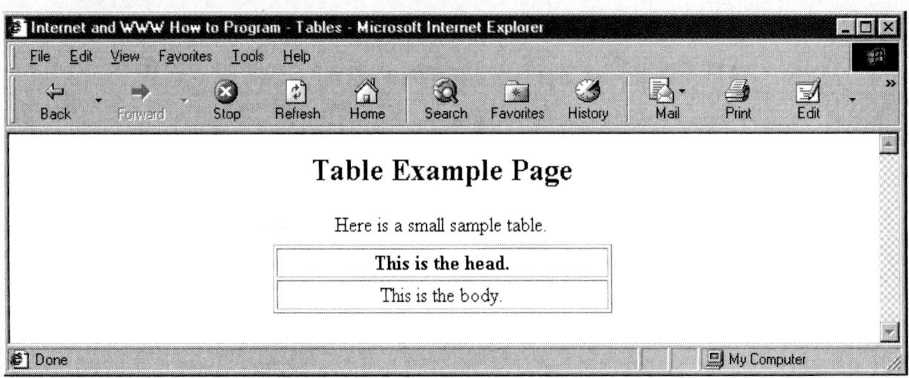

Fig. 4.4 HTML table (part 2 of 2).

All tags and text that apply to the table go inside the ***<TABLE>…</TABLE>*** tags, which begin on line 16

```
<TABLE BORDER = "1" ALIGN = "center" WIDTH = "40%">
```

There are a number of attributes that can be applied to the **TABLE** element. The ***BORDER*** *attribute* lets you set the width of the table's border in pixels. If you want all lines to be invisible, you can specify **BORDER = "0"**. You should experiment to find the best "look" for each table. In the table shown in Fig. 4.4, the value of the border attribute is set to **1**.

The horizontal alignment we saw before also applies to tables (**ALIGN = "left"**, **"center"** or **"right"**). The ***WIDTH*** attribute sets the width of the table, and is used exactly as in the **HR** element— you specify either a number of pixels or a percentage of the screen width.

Line 20

```
<CAPTION>Here is a small sample table.</CAPTION>
```

inserts a *caption* element into the table. The text inside the ***<CAPTION>**...**</CAPTION>*** tags is inserted directly above the table in the browser window. The caption text is also used to help *text-based browsers* interpret the table data.

Tables can be split into distinct horizontal and vertical sections. The first of these sections, the head area, appears in lines 25 through 27

```
<THEAD>
<TR><TH>This is the head.</TH></TR>
</THEAD>
```

Put all header information (for example, the titles of the table and column headers) inside the ***<THEAD>**...**</THEAD>*** tags.

The ***TR***, or *table row element*, is used for formatting the cells of individual rows. All of the cells in a row belong within the ***<TR>**...**</TR>*** tags of that row. In the next section we discuss how to use **TR** for row formatting.

The smallest area of the table we are able to format is the *data cell*. There are two types of data cells, located in the header (***<TH>**...**</TH>***) or in the table body (***<TD>**...**</TD>***). The code example above inserts a header cell. Header cells, which are usually placed in the **<THEAD>** area, are suitable for titles and column headings.

The second grouping section, the **TBODY** element, appears in lines 32 through 34

```
<TBODY>
<TR><TD ALIGN = "center">This is the body.</TD></TR>
</TBODY>
```

Like the **THEAD**, the ***TBODY*** is used for formatting and grouping purposes. Although there is only one row and one cell in the above example, most tables will use **TBODY** to house the majority of their content. In this code example, **TBODY** includes only one row and one data cell. The cell is marked by the ***<TD>**...**</TD>*** tags.

Regular data cells are left aligned by default. In the above example, notice that there is an **ALIGN** attribute included inside the opening **<TD>** tag. This attribute affects the horizontal alignment (we will see how to set vertical alignment in the next code example). The **ALIGN** attribute is used here in the same way as it is used to align other HTML tags.

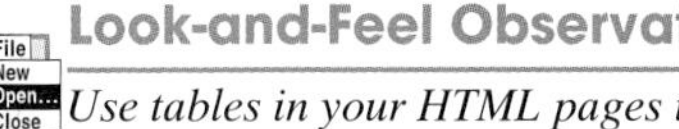

Look-and-Feel Observation 4.2

Use tables in your HTML pages to organize data attractively and effectively.

Common Programming Error 4.1

Forgetting to close any of the area formatting tags inside the table area can distort the table format. Be sure to check that every element is opened and closed in its proper place to make sure that the table appears as intended.

4.5 Intermediate HTML Tables and Formatting

In the previous section and code example, we explored the structure of a basic table. In Fig. 4.5, we extend our table example with more formatting attributes.

```
<HTML>

<!-- Fig. 4.5: table.html       -->
<!-- Intermediate table design -->

<HEAD>
<TITLE>Internet and WWW How to Program - Tables</TITLE>
</HEAD>
<BODY>

<H2 ALIGN = "center">Table Example Page</H2>

<TABLE BORDER = "1" ALIGN = "center" WIDTH = "40%">
   <CAPTION>Here is a small sample table.</CAPTION>

   <THEAD>
   <TR>
      <TH>This is the Head.</TH>
   </TR>
   </THEAD>

   <TBODY>
   <TR>
      <TD ALIGN = "center">This is the Body.</TD>
   </TR>
   </TBODY>

</TABLE>

<BR><BR>

<TABLE BORDER = "1" ALIGN = "center">

   <CAPTION>Here is a more complex sample table.</CAPTION>

   <!-- <COLGROUP> and <COL> are used to format entire    -->
   <!-- columns at once. SPAN determines how many columns -->
   <!-- the COL tag effects.                              -->
   <COLGROUP>
      <COL ALIGN = "right">
      <COL SPAN = "4" ALIGN = "center">
   </COLGROUP>

   <THEAD>

   <!-- ROWSPANs and COLSPANs combine the indicated number -->
   <!-- of cells vertically or horizontally                -->
   <TR BGCOLOR = "#8888FF">
      <TH ROWSPAN = "2">
         <IMG SRC = "deitel.gif" WIDTH = "200" HEIGHT = "144"
            ALT = "Harvey and Paul Deitel">
      </TH>
```

Fig. 4.5 A complex table with formatting and color (part 1 of 3).

```
53          <TH COLSPAN = "4" VALIGN = "top">
54             <H1>Camelid comparison</H1><BR>
55             <P>Approximate as of 8/99</P>
56           </TH>
57       </TR>
58
59       <TR BGCOLOR = "khaki" VALIGN = "bottom">
60          <TH># of Humps</TH>
61          <TH>Indigenous region</TH>
62          <TH>Spits?</TH>
63          <TH>Produces Wool?</TH>
64       </TR>
65
66       </THEAD>
67
68       <TBODY>
69
70       <TR>
71          <TH>Camels (bactrian)</TH>
72          <TD>2</TD>
73          <TD>Africa/Asia</TD>
74          <TD ROWSPAN = "2">Llama</TD>
75          <TD ROWSPAN = "2">Llama</TD>
76       </TR>
77
78       <TR>
79          <TH>Llamas</TH>
80          <TD>1</TD>
81          <TD>Andes Mountains</TD>
82       </TR>
83
84    </TBODY>
85    </TABLE>
86
87    </BODY>
88    </HMTL>
```

Fig. 4.5 A complex table with formatting and color (part 2 of 3).

The new table begins on line 32. The **COLGROUP** element, used for formatting groups of columns, is shown on lines 39 through 42

```
<COLGROUP>
   <COL ALIGN = "right">
   <COL SPAN = "4" ALIGN = "center">
</COLGROUP>
```

The ***COLGROUP*** element can be used to group and format columns. Each ***COL*** element in the **<COLGROUP>**...**</COLGROUP>** tags can format any number of columns (specified with the **SPAN** attribute). Any formatting to be applied to a column or group of columns can be specified in both the **COLGROUP** and **COL** tags. In this case, we align the text inside the leftmost column to the right, and center the text in the remaining four columns. Another useful attribute to use here is **WIDTH**, which specifies the width of the column.

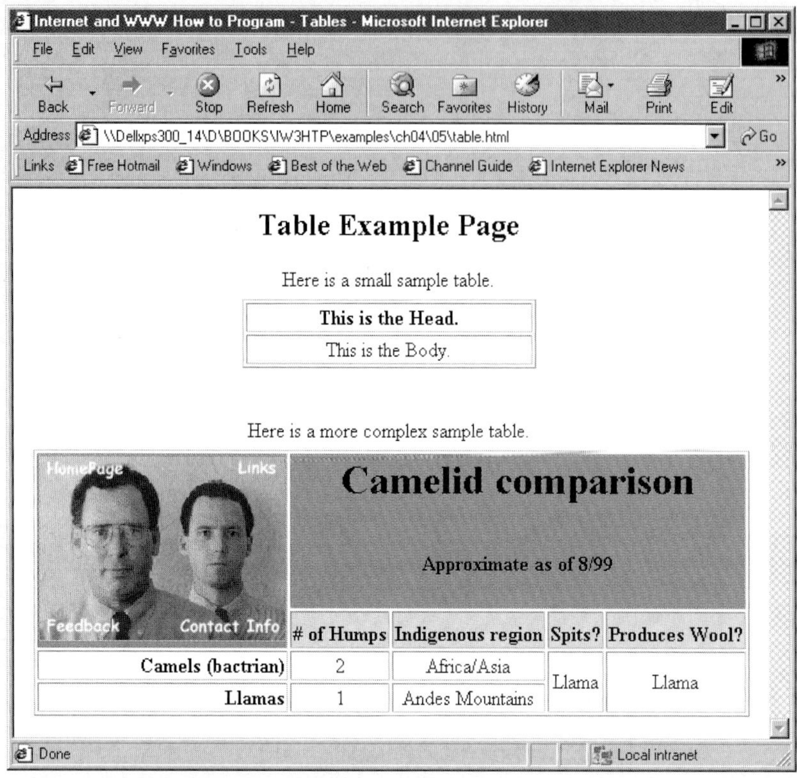

Fig. 4.5 A complex table with formatting and color (part 3 of 3).

Lines 48 and 49

```
<TR BGCOLOR = "#8888FF">
   <TH ROWSPAN = "2">
```

introduce several more table formatting capabilities. You can add a background color or image to any row or cell with the **BGCOLOR** and **BACKGROUND** attributes, which are used in the same way as in the **BODY** element.

It is possible to make some data cells larger than others. This effect is accomplished with the ***ROWSPAN*** and ***COLSPAN*** attributes, which can be placed inside any data cell opening tag. The attribute value extends the data cell to span the specified number of cells. Using our line of code, for example, **ROWSPAN = "2"** tells the browser that this data cell will span the area of two vertically adjacent cells. These cells will be joined vertically (and will thus span over two rows). An example of **COLSPAN** appears in line 53:

```
<TH COLSPAN = "4" VALIGN = "top">
```

where the header cell is widened to span four cells.

We also see here an example of vertical alignment formatting. The ***VALIGN*** attribute accepts the following values: **"top"**, **"middle"**, **"bottom"** and **"baseline"**. All cells in a row whose **VALIGN** attribute is set to **"baseline"** will have the first text line occur on a common baseline. The default vertical alignment in all data and header cells is **VALIGN = "middle"**.

The remaining code in Fig. 4.5 demonstrates other uses of the table attributes and elements outlined above.

Look-and-Feel Observation 4.3

*Using the **COLSPAN** and **ROWSPAN** attributes in your tables adds a nice look and can help you format the data cells to contain your information more effectively.*

Common Programming Error 4.2

*When using **COLSPAN** and **ROWSPAN** in table data cells, consider that the modified cells will cover the areas of other cells. Compensate for this in your code by reducing the number of cells in that row or column. If you do not, the formatting of your table will be distorted, and you may inadvertently create more columns and/or rows than you originally intended.*

4.6 Basic HTML Forms

HTML provides several mechanisms to collect information from people viewing your site; one is the *form* (Fig. 4.6).

```
<HTML>

<!-- Fig. 4.6: form.html      -->
<!-- Introducing Form Design -->

<HEAD>
<TITLE>Internet and WWW How to Program - Forms</TITLE>
</HEAD>

<BODY>
<H2>Feedback Form</H2>

<P>Please fill out this form to help us improve our site.</P>

<!-- This tag starts the form, gives the method of sending -->
<!-- information and the location of form scripts.         -->
<!-- Hidden inputs give the server non-visual information  -->
<FORM METHOD = "POST" ACTION = "/cgi-bin/formmail">

<INPUT TYPE = "hidden" NAME = "recipient"
   VALUE = "deitel@deitel.com">
<INPUT TYPE = "hidden" NAME = "subject"
   VALUE = "Feedback Form">
<INPUT TYPE = "hidden" NAME = "redirect"
   VALUE = "main.html">

<!-- <INPUT type = "text"> inserts a text box -->
<P><STRONG>Name:</STRONG>
<INPUT NAME = "name" TYPE = "text" SIZE = "25"></P>

```

Fig. 4.6 Simple form with basic fields and a text box (part 1 of 2).

```
31  <!-- Input types "submit" and "reset" insert buttons -->
32  <!-- for submitting or clearing the form's contents   -->
33  <INPUT TYPE = "submit" VALUE = "Submit Your Entries">
34  <INPUT TYPE = "reset" VALUE = "Clear Your Entries">
35  </FORM>
36
37  </BODY>
38  </HTML>
```

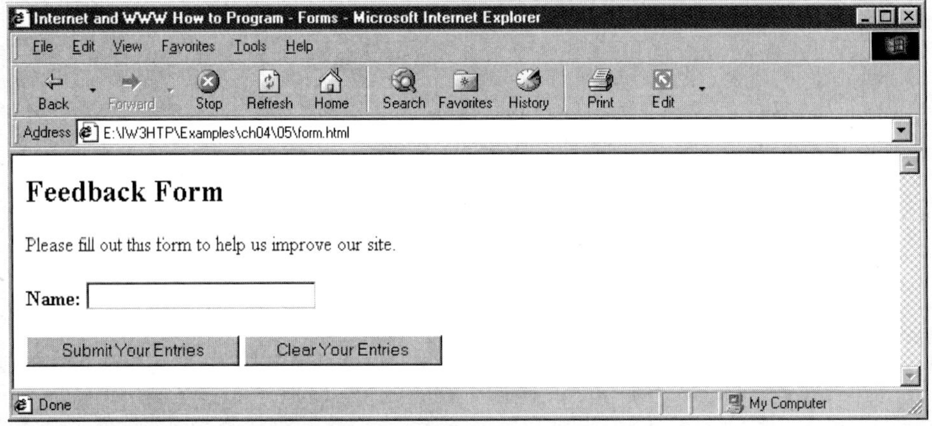

Fig. 4.6 Simple form with basic fields and a text box (part 2 of 2).

The form begins on line 18

```
<FORM METHOD = "POST" ACTION = "/cgi-bin/formmail">
```

with the ***FORM*** element. The ***METHOD*** attribute indicates the way the *Web server* will organize and send you the form output. Use ***METHOD* = "post"** in a form that causes changes to server data, for example when updating a database. The form data will be sent to the server as an *environment variable,* which scripts are able to access (you will learn how to do this in Chapter 27 when we cover Perl). The other possible value, ***METHOD* = "get"**, should be used when your form does not cause any changes in server-side data, for example when making a database request. The form data from **METHOD = "get"** is appended to the end of the URL (for example, **/cgi-bin/formmail?name=bob&order=5**). Because of this, the amount of data submitted using this **METHOD** is limited to 4K. Also be aware that **METHOD = "get"** is limited to standard characters, and can not submit any special characters, as discussed in Section 3.10.

A *Web server* is a machine that runs a software package such as Microsoft's PWS (Personal Web Server), Microsoft's IIS (Internet Information Server), Apache or Jigsaw. Each of these is described later in the book in Chapter 24 on "Servers." Web servers handle browser requests. When a browser requests a page or file somewhere on a server, the server processes the request and returns an answer to the browser. In this example, the data from the form goes to a CGI (Common Gateway Interface) script, which is a means of interfacing an HTML page with a script (i.e., a program) written in Perl, C, Tcl or other languages. The script then handles the data fed to it by the server and typically returns some information for the user. The **ACTION** attribute in the **FORM** tag is the path to this script; in this case, it is a common script which emails form data to an address. Most Internet Service Providers will have a script like this on their site, so you can ask your system administrator how to set up your HTML to use the script correctly.

There are several pieces of information (not seen by the user) that you need to insert in the form. Lines 20 through 25

```
<INPUT TYPE = "hidden" NAME = "recipient"
   VALUE = "deitel@deitel.com">
<INPUT TYPE = "hidden" NAME = "subject"
   VALUE = "Feedback Form">
<INPUT TYPE = "hidden" NAME = "redirect"
   VALUE = "main.html">
```

obtain this information by the use of *hidden input elements*. The **INPUT** element is common in forms and always requires the ***TYPE*** attribute. Two other attributes are ***NAME***, which provides a unique identification for the **INPUT** element, and ***VALUE***, which indicates the value that the ***INPUT*** element sends to the server upon submission.

As shown above, hidden inputs always have the attribute ***TYPE* = "*hidden*"**. The three hidden inputs shown are typical for this kind of CGI script: An email address to send the data to, the subject line of the email and a URL to which the user is redirected after submitting the form.

Good Programming Practice 4.2

*Place hidden **INPUT** elements in the beginning of a form, right after the opening **<FORM>** tag. This makes these elements easier to find and identify.*

The usage of an **<INPUT>** element is defined by the value of its **TYPE** attribute. We introduce another of these options in lines 28 and 29

```
<P><STRONG>Name: </STRONG>
<INPUT NAME = "name" TYPE = "text" SIZE = "25"></P>
```

The input ***TYPE* = "*text*"** inserts a one-line text box into the form. The value of this **INPUT** element and the information that the server sends to you from this **INPUT** is the text that the user types into the bar. A good use of the textual input element is for names or other one-line pieces of information.

We also use the ***SIZE*** attribute, whose value determines the width of the text input, measured in characters. You can also set a maximum number of characters that the text input will accept by inserting the **MAXLENGTH** = "*length*" attribute.

Good Programming Practice 4.3

*When using **INPUT** elements in forms, be sure to leave enough space for users to input the pertinent information.*

It is important to note here the placement of text relative to the **INPUT** element. You must make sure to include a textual identifier (in this case, **Name:**) adjacent to the **INPUT** element, to indicate the function of the element.

Common Programming Error 4.3

Forgetting to include textual labels for a form element is a design error. Without these labels, users will have no way of knowing what the function of individual form elements is.

There are two types of **INPUT** elements in lines 33 and 34

```
<INPUT TYPE = "submit" VALUE = "Submit Your Entries">
<INPUT TYPE = "reset" VALUE = "Clear Your Entries">
```

that should be inserted into every form. The ***TYPE* = "*submit*" INPUT** element places a button in the form that submits data to the server when clicked. The **VALUE** attribute changes the text displayed on the button (the default value is **"*submit*"**). The input element ***TYPE*** = **"*reset*"** inserts a button onto the form that, when clicked, clears all entries the user entered into the form. This can help the user correct mistakes or simply start over. As with the **submit** input, the **VALUE** attribute of the **RESET** input affects the text of the button on the screen, but does not affect functionality at all.

Good Programming Practice 4.4

*Be sure to close your form code with the **</FORM>** tag. Neglecting to include this can affect the actions of other forms on the same page.*

4.7 More Complex HTML Forms

We introduce additional form input options in Fig. 4.7.

```
<HTML>

<!-- Fig. 4.7: form.html     -->
<!-- Form Design Example 2 -->

<HEAD>
<TITLE>Internet and WWW How to Program - Forms</TITLE>
</HEAD>

<BODY>
<H2>Feedback Form</H2>

<P>Please fill out this form to help us improve our site.</P>

<FORM METHOD = "POST" ACTION = "/cgi-bin/formmail">

<INPUT TYPE = "hidden" NAME = "recipient"
   VALUE = "deitel@deitel.com">
<INPUT TYPE = "hidden" NAME = "subject"
   VALUE = "Feedback Form">
<INPUT TYPE = "hidden" NAME = "redirect"
   VALUE = "main.html">

<P><STRONG>Name: </STRONG>
<INPUT NAME = "name" TYPE = "text" SIZE = "25"></P>

<!-- <TEXTAREA> creates a textbox of the size given -->
<P><STRONG>Comments:</STRONG>
<TEXTAREA NAME = "comments" ROWS = "4" COLS = "36"></TEXTAREA>
</P>
```

Fig. 4.7 Form including textareas, password boxes and checkboxes (part 1 of 2).

```

<!-- <INPUT TYPE = "password"> inserts a textbox whose    -->
<!-- readout will be in *** instead of regular characters -->
<P><STRONG>Email Address:</STRONG>
<INPUT NAME = "email" TYPE = "password" SIZE = "25"></P>

<!-- <INPUT TYPE = "checkbox"> creates a checkbox -->
<P><STRONG>Things you liked:</STRONG><BR>

Site design
<INPUT NAME = "things" TYPE = "checkbox" VALUE = "Design">
Links
<INPUT NAME = "things" TYPE = "checkbox" VALUE = "Links">
Ease of use
<INPUT NAME = "things" TYPE = "checkbox" VALUE = "Ease">
Images
<INPUT NAME = "things" TYPE = "checkbox" VALUE = "Images">
Source code
<INPUT NAME = "things" TYPE = "checkbox" VALUE = "Code">
</P>

<INPUT TYPE = "submit" VALUE = "Submit Your Entries">
<INPUT TYPE = "reset" VALUE = "Clear Your Entries">
</FORM>

</BODY>
</HTML>
```

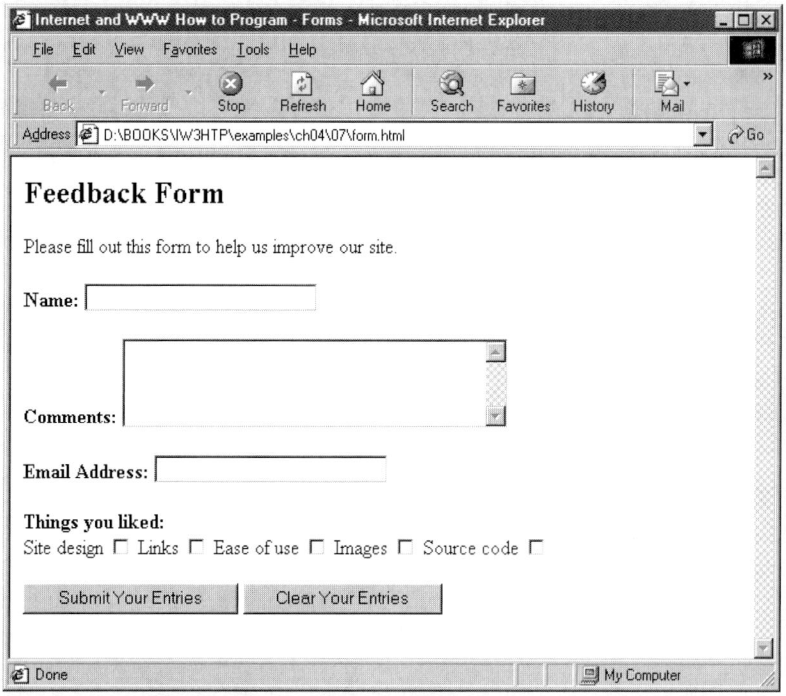

Fig. 4.7 Form including textareas, password boxes and checkboxes (part 2 of 2).

Line 29

```
<TEXTAREA NAME = "comments" ROWS = "4" COLS = "36"></TEXTAREA>
```

introduces the ***TEXTAREA*** element. This type of form component has its own element name. The **TEXTAREA** element inserts a box into the form. You specify the size of the box (which is scrollable) inside the opening **<TEXTAREA>** tag with the **ROWS** attribute, which sets the number of rows appearing in the **TEXTAREA**. With the **COLS** attribute, you specify how wide the **TEXTAREA** should be. This **TEXTAREA** is four rows of characters tall and 36 characters wide. Any default text that you want to place inside the **TEXTAREA** should be contained within the **<TEXTAREA>**...**</TEXTAREA>** tags.

The input ***TYPE* = "*password*"** in line 35

```
<INPUT NAME = "email" TYPE = "password" SIZE = "25"></P>
```

inserts a text box with the indicated size. The only difference between a password input and a text input is that, when data is entered into a password area, it appears on the screen as asterisks. The password is used for submitting sensitive information which the user would not want others to be able to read. It is just the browser that displays asterisks—the real form data is still submitted to the server.

Lines 40 through 49 introduce another form input **TYPE**.

```
Site design
<INPUT NAME = "things" TYPE = "checkbox" VALUE = "Design">
Links
<INPUT NAME = "things" TYPE = "checkbox" VALUE = "Links">
Ease of use
<INPUT NAME = "things" TYPE = "checkbox" VALUE = "Ease">
Images
<INPUT NAME = "things" TYPE = "checkbox" VALUE = "Images">
Source code
<INPUT NAME = "things" TYPE = "checkbox" VALUE = "Code">
```

Every **INPUT** element with **TYPE = "checkbox"** creates a new checkbox in the form. Checkboxes can be used individually or in groups. Each checkbox in a group should have the same **NAME** (in this case, **NAME = "things"**). This notifies the script handling the form that all of the checkboxes are related to one another, and are typically listed in the same output line in the email generated by the form.

Common Programming Error 4.4

When your form has several checkboxes with the same **NAME**, *you must make sure that they have different* **VALUE**s, *or else the script will have no way of distinguishing between them.*

Yet more form elements are introduced in Fig. 4.8.

```
<HTML>

<!-- Fig. 4.8: form.html    -->
<!-- Form Design Example 3 -->

```

Fig. 4.8 HTML form including radio buttons and pulldown lists (part 1 of 4).

```
<HEAD>
<TITLE>Internet and WWW How to Program - Forms</TITLE>
</HEAD>

<BODY>
<H2>Feedback Form</H2>

<P>Please fill out this form to help us improve our site.</P>

<FORM METHOD = "POST" ACTION = "/cgi-bin/formmail">

<INPUT TYPE = "hidden" NAME = "recipient"
   VALUE = "deitel@deitel.com">
<INPUT TYPE = "hidden" NAME = "subject"
   VALUE = "Feedback Form">
<INPUT TYPE = "hidden" NAME = "redirect"
   VALUE = "main.html">

<P><STRONG>Name: </STRONG>
<INPUT NAME = "name" TYPE = "text" SIZE = "25"></P>

<P><STRONG>Comments:</STRONG>
<TEXTAREA NAME = "comments" ROWS = "4" COLS = "36"></TEXTAREA>
</P>

<P><STRONG>Email Address:</STRONG>
<INPUT NAME = "email" TYPE = "password" SIZE = "25"></P>

<P><STRONG>Things you liked:</STRONG><BR>

Site design
<INPUT NAME = "things" TYPE = "checkbox" VALUE = "Design">
Links
<INPUT NAME = "things" TYPE = "checkbox" VALUE = "Links">
Ease of use
<INPUT NAME = "things" TYPE = "checkbox" VALUE = "Ease">
Images
<INPUT NAME = "things" TYPE = "checkbox" VALUE = "Images">
Source code
<INPUT NAME = "things" TYPE = "checkbox" VALUE = "Code">
</P>

<!-- <INPUT TYPE="radio"> creates a radio button. The      -->
<!-- difference between radio buttons and checkboxes is   -->
<!-- that only one radio button in a group can be selected -->
<P><STRONG>How did you get to our site?:</STRONG><BR>

Search engine
<INPUT NAME = "how get to site" TYPE = "radio"
   VALUE = "search engine" CHECKED>
Links from another site
<INPUT NAME = "how get to site" TYPE = "radio"
   VALUE = "link">
```

Fig. 4.8 HTML form including radio buttons and pulldown lists (part 2 of 4).

```
59  Deitel.com Web site
60  <INPUT NAME = "how get to site" TYPE = "radio"
61     VALUE = "deitel.com">
62  Reference in a book
63  <INPUT NAME = "how get to site" TYPE = "radio"
64     VALUE = "book">
65  Other
66  <INPUT NAME = "how get to site" TYPE = "radio"
67     VALUE = "other">
68  </P>
69
70  <!-- The <select> tag presents a drop down menu with -->
71  <!-- choices indicated by the <option> tags          -->
72  <P><STRONG>Rate our site (1-10):</STRONG>
73  <SELECT NAME = "rating">
74  <OPTION SELECTED>Amazing:-)
75  <OPTION>10
76  <OPTION>9
77  <OPTION>8
78  <OPTION>7
79  <OPTION>6
80  <OPTION>5
81  <OPTION>4
82  <OPTION>3
83  <OPTION>2
84  <OPTION>1
85  <OPTION>The Pits:-(
86  </SELECT></P>
87
88  <INPUT TYPE = "submit" VALUE = "Submit Your Entries">
89  <INPUT TYPE = "reset" VALUE = "Clear Your Entries">
90  </FORM>
91
```

Fig. 4.8 HTML form including radio buttons and pulldown lists (part 3 of 4).

In our final form code example, we introduce two new types of input options. The first of these is the *radio buttons*, introduced in lines 53 through 67

```
Search engine
<INPUT NAME = "how get to site" TYPE = "radio"
   VALUE ="search engine" CHECKED>
Links from another site
<INPUT NAME = "how get to site" TYPE = "radio"
   VALUE = "link">
Deitel.com Web site
<INPUT NAME = "how get to site" TYPE = "radio"
   VALUE = "deitel.com">
Reference in a book
<INPUT NAME = "how get to site" TYPE = "radio"
   VALUE = "book">
Other
<INPUT NAME = "how get to site" TYPE = "radio"
   VALUE = "other">
```

```
92  </BODY>
93  </HTML>
```

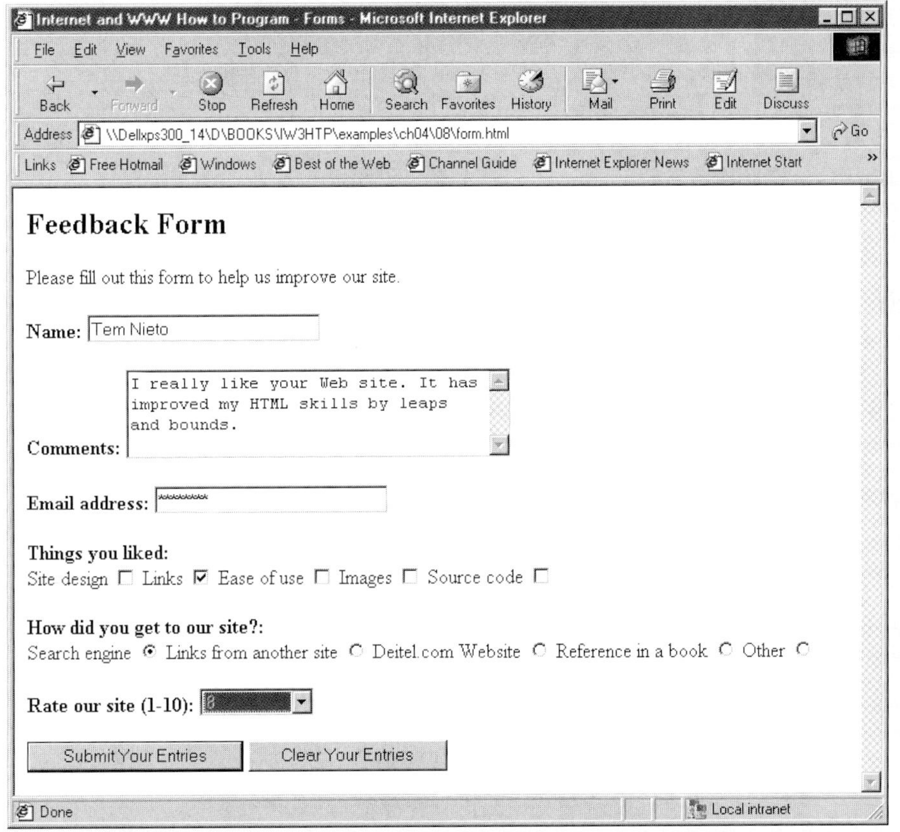

Fig. 4.8 HTML form including radio buttons and pulldown lists (part 4 of 4).

Inserted into forms with the **INPUT** attribute ***TYPE = "radio"***, radio buttons are similar in function and usage to checkboxes. Radio buttons are different in that only one in the group may be selected at any time. All of the **NAME** attributes of a group of radio inputs must be the same and all of the **VALUE** attributes different. Insert the attribute ***CHECKED*** to indicate which radio button you would like selected initially. The **CHECKED** attribute can also be applied to checkboxes.

Common Programming Error 4.5

When you are using a group of radio inputs in a form, forgetting to set the ***NAME*** *values to the same name will let the user select all the radio buttons at the same time: an undesired result.*

The last type of form input that we introduce here is the ***SELECT*** element, on lines 73 through 86 of our code. This will place a selectable list of items inside your form.

```
<SELECT NAME = "rating">
<OPTION SELECTED>Amazing:-)
<OPTION>10
<OPTION>9
<OPTION>8
<OPTION>7
<OPTION>6
<OPTION>5
<OPTION>4
<OPTION>3
<OPTION>2
<OPTION>1
<OPTION>The Pits:-(
</SELECT>
```

This type of type of form input is inserted using a **SELECT** element instead of an **INPUT** element. Inside the opening ***<SELECT>*** tag, be sure to include the **NAME** attribute.

To add an item to the list, insert an ***OPTION*** element in the ***<SELECT>***...***</SELECT>*** area, and type what you want the list item to display on the same line. If an option is selected, this text will be sent to you in the form output email. Although a closing tag for the **OPTION** element is optional, its use is deprecated and it is generally not included. When you have completed the list of **OPTION**s, close the **SELECT** area. The **SELECTED** attribute, like the **CHECKED** attribute for radio buttons and checkboxes, applies a default selection to your list.

The preceding code will generate a pull-down list of options, as shown in Fig. 4.8. There is another attribute that can be included in the opening **<SELECT>** tag which changes the appearance of the list: You can change the number of list options visible at one time by including the ***SIZE*** = "*x*" attribute inside the **<SELECT>** tag. Use this attribute if you prefer an expanded version of the list to the one-line expandable list.

4.8 Internal Linking

In Chapter 3, we discussed how to link one Web page to another by using textual and image anchors. Figure 4.9 introduces *internal linking*, which lets you assign a location name to any individual point in an HTML file. This location name can then be added to the page's URL, enabling you to link to that specific point on the page instead of being limited to linking to the top of the page.

```
<HTML>

<!-- Fig. 4.9: list.html  -->
<!-- Internal Linking     -->

<HEAD>
<TITLE>Internet and WWW How to Program - List</TITLE>
</HEAD>
```

Fig. 4.9 Using internal hyperlinks to make your pages more navigable (part 1 of 3).

```

<BODY>

<CENTER>
<!-- <A NAME = ".."></A> makes an internal hyperlink -->
<A NAME = "features"></A>
<H2><U>The Best Features of the Internet</U></H2>

<!-- An internal link's address is "xx.html#linkname" -->
<H3><A HREF = "#ceos">Go to <EM>Favorite CEO's</EM></A></H3>
</CENTER>

<UL>
<LI>You can meet new people from countries around the world.
<LI>You have access to new media as it becomes public:
   <UL>
   <LI>New games
   <LI>New applications
      <UL>
      <LI>For Business
      <LI>For Pleasure
      </UL>
   <LI>Around the Clock news
   <LI>Search Engines
   <LI>Shopping
   <LI>Programming
      <UL>
      <LI>HTML
      <LI>Java
      <LI>Dynamic HTML
      <LI>Scripts
      <LI>New languages
      </UL>
   </UL>
<LI>Links
<LI>Keeping In touch with old friends
<LI>It is the technology of the future!
</UL><BR><BR>

<A NAME = "ceos"></A>
<CENTER><H2>My 3 Favorite <EM>CEO's</EM></H2>
<H3><A HREF = "#features">Go to <EM>Favorite Features</EM></A>
</H3></CENTER>

<OL>
   <LI>Bill Gates
   <LI>Steve Jobs
   <LI>Michael Dell
</OL>

</BODY>

</HTML>
```

Fig. 4.9 Using internal hyperlinks to make your pages more navigable (part 2 of 3).

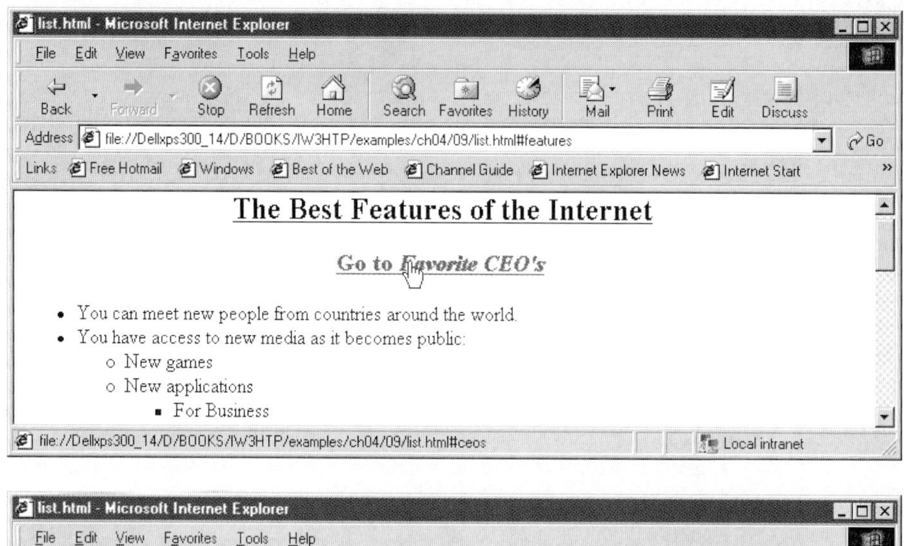

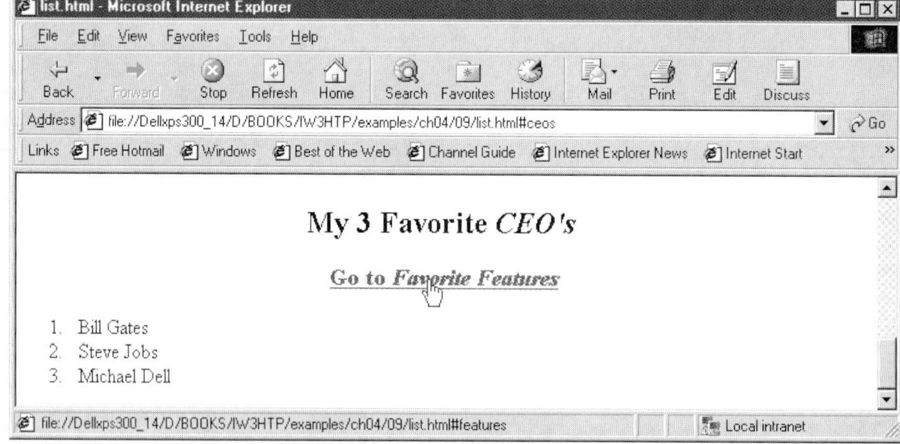

Fig. 4.9 Using internal hyperlinks to make your pages more navigable (part 3 of 3).

Line 14

```
<A NAME = "features"></A>
```

shows an internal hyperlink. A location on a page is marked by including a **NAME** attribute in an **A** element. Our line of code specifies its location on the page as having **NAME = "features"**. Since the name of the page is **list.html**, the URL of this point in the Web page is referred to as **list.html#features**.

Line 50

```
<H3><A HREF = "#features">Go to <EM>Favorite Features</EM></A>
```

shows the insertion of a regular hyperlink, the target destination being the internal hyperlink location **#features**. Clicking on this hyperlink in a browser would scroll the browser window to that point on the page. Examples of this occur in Fig 4.9, which shows two different screen captures from the same page, each at a different internal location. You can also link to an internal location on another page by using the URL of that location (using the format **HREF =** "*page.html#name*").

Look-and-Feel Observation 4.4

Internal hyperlinks are most useful in large HTML files with lots of information. You can link to various points on the page to save the user from having to scroll down and find a specific location.

4.9 Creating and Using Image Maps

We have seen that images can be used as anchors to link to other places on your site or elsewhere on the Internet. We now discuss how to create *image maps* (Fig. 4.10), which allow you to designate certain sections of the image as *hotspots* and then use these hotspots as anchors for linking.

```
<HTML>

<!-- Fig. 4.10: picture.html         -->
<!-- Creating and Using Imape Maps -->

<HEAD>
<TITLE>Internet and WWW How to Program - List</TITLE>
</HEAD>

<BODY BACKGROUND = "bckgrnd.gif">

<CENTER>
<!-- <MAP> opens and names an image map formatting area -->
<!-- and to be referenced later -->
<MAP NAME = "picture">

<!-- The "SHAPE = rect indicates a rectangular area, with  -->
<!-- coordinates of the upper-left and lower-right corners -->
<AREA HREF = "form.html" SHAPE = "rect"
   COORDS = "3, 122, 73, 143" ALT = "Go to the form">
<AREA HREF = "contact.html" SHAPE = "rect"
   COORDS = "109, 123, 199, 142" ALT = "Go to the contact page">
<AREA HREF = "main.html" SHAPE = "rect"
   COORDS = "1, 2, 72, 17" ALT = "Go to the homepage">
<AREA HREF = "links.html" SHAPE = "rect"
   COORDS = "155, 0, 199, 18" ALT = "Go to the links page">

<!-- The "SHAPE = polygon" indicates an area of cusotmizable -->
<!-- shape, with the coordinates of every vertex listed    -->
<AREA HREF = "mailto:deitel@deitel.com" SHAPE = "poly"
   COORDS = "28, 22, 24, 68, 46, 114, 84, 111, 99, 56, 86, 13"
   ALT = "Email the Deitels">

```

Fig. 4.10 A picture with links anchored to an image map (part 1 of 2).

```
34 <!-- The "SHAPE = circle" indicates a circular area with -->
35 <!-- center and radius listed                             -->
36 <AREA HREF = "mailto:deitel@deitel.com" SHAPE = "circle"
37    COORDS = "146, 66, 42" ALT = "Email the Deitels">
38 </MAP>
39
40 <!-- <IMG SRC=... USEMAP = "#name"> says that the indicated -->
41 <!-- image map will be used with this image                 -->
42 <IMG SRC = "deitel.gif" WIDTH = "200" HEIGHT = "144" BORDER = "1"
43    ALT = "Harvey and Paul Deitel" USEMAP = "#picture">
44 </CENTER>
45
46 </BODY>
47 </HTML>
```

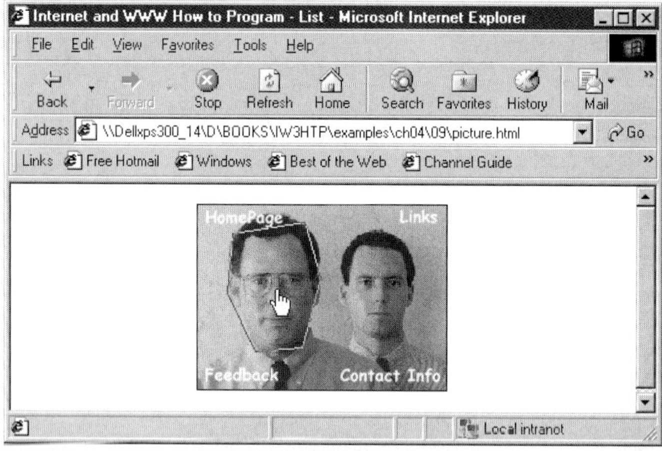

Fig. 4.10 A picture with links anchored to an image map (part 2 of 2).

All elements of an image map are contained inside the **<MAP>**...**</MAP>** tags. The required attribute for the ***MAP*** element is **NAME** (line 15)

```
<MAP NAME = "picture">
```

As we will see, this attribute is needed for referencing purposes. A hotspot on the image is designated with the ***AREA*** element. Every **<AREA>** tag has the following attributes: **HREF** sets the target for the link on that spot, ***SHAPE*** and ***COORDS*** set the characteristics of the area and **ALT** functions just as it does in **<IMG>** tags.

The first occurrence of the ***SHAPE* = "rect"** is on lines 19 and 20

```
<AREA HREF = "form.html" SHAPE = "rect"
   COORDS = "3, 122, 73, 143" ALT = "Go to the form">
```

This statement causes a *rectangular hotspot* to be drawn around the *coordinates* given in the **COORDS** element. A coordinate pair consists of two numbers, which are the locations of the point on the *x* and *y* axes. The *x* axis extends horizontally from the upper-left corner and the *y* axis vertically. Every point on an image has a unique *x–y* coordinate. In the case of a rectangular hotspot, the required coordinates are those of the upper-left and lower-right corners of the rectangle. In this case, the upper-left corner of the rectangle is located at 3 on the *x* axis and 122 on the *y* axis, annotated as (3, 122). The lower-right corner of the rectangle is at (73, 143).

Another map area is in lines 30 through 32

```
<AREA HREF = "mailto:deitel@deitel.com" SHAPE = "poly"
   COORDS = "28, 22, 24, 68, 46, 114, 84, 111, 99, 56, 86, 13"
   ALT = "Email the Deitels">
```

In this case, we use the ***SHAPE* = "poly"** **AREA** attribute. This creates a hotspot of no preset shape—you specify the shape of the hotspot in the **COORDS** attribute by listing the coordinates of every vertex, or corner of the hotspot. The browser will automatically connect these points with lines to form the area of the hotspot.

***SHAPE* = "circle"** is the last shape attribute that is commonly used in image maps. It creates a *circular hotspot*, and requires both the coordinates of the center of the circle and the radius of the circle, in pixels.

To use the image map with an **IMG** element, you must insert the **USEMAP = "#***name***"** attribute into the **IMG** element, where *name* is the value of the **NAME** attribute in the **MAP** element. Lines 42 and 43

```
<IMG SRC = "deitel.gif" WIDTH = "200" HEIGHT="144" BORDER="1"
   ALT = "Harvey and Paul Deitel" USEMAP = "#picture">
```

show how the image map **NAME = "picture"** is applied to the **IMG** element being inserted in the page.

Good Programming Practice 4.5

Keep the ***<MAP>...</MAP>*** *tags on the same page as the image that will use them. This will save time if you have to edit the image map.*

4.10 <META> Tags

People use search engines to find interesting Web sites. Search engines usually catalog sites by following links from page to page and saving identification and classification information for each page visited. The main HTML element that interacts with the search engines is the ***META*** tag (Fig. 4.11).

```
<!DOCTYPE HTML PUBLIC "-//W3C//DTD HTML 4.0 Transitional//EN">
<HTML>

<!-- Fig. 4.11: main.html         -->
<!-- <META> and <!DOCTYPE> tags -->

<HEAD>
<!-- <META> tags give search engines information they need -->
<!-- to catalog your site                                  -->
<META NAME = "keywords" CONTENT = "Webpage, design, HTML,
   tutorial, personal, help, index, form, contact, feedback,
   list, links, frame, deitel">
```

Fig. 4.11 Using **<META>** and **<DOCTYPE>** (part 1 of 2).

```
13
14  <META NAME = "description" CONTENT = "This Web site will help
15     you learn the basics of HTML and Webpage design through the
16     use of interactive examples and instruction.">
17
18  <TITLE>Internet and WWW How to Program - Welcome</TITLE>
19  </HEAD>
20
21  <BODY>
22
23  <H1 ALIGN = "center"><U>Welcome to Our Web Site!</U></H1>
24
25  <P><FONT COLOR = "red" SIZE = "+1" FACE = "Arial">We have
26  designed this site to teach about the wonders of
27  <EM>HTML</EM>.</FONT>
28
29  <FONT COLOR = "purple" SIZE = "+2" FACE = "Verdana">We have been
30  using <EM>HTML</EM> since <U>version<STRONG> 2.0</STRONG></U>,
31  and we enjoy the features that have been added recently.</FONT>
32
33  <FONT COLOR = "blue" SIZE = "+1" FACE = "Helvetica">It
34  seems only a short time ago that we read our first <EM>HTML</EM>
35  book.</FONT>
36
37  <FONT COLOR = "green" SIZE = "+2" FACE = "Times">Soon you will
38  know about many of the great new feature of HTML 4.0.</FONT></P>
39
40  <H2 ALIGN = "center">Have Fun With the Site!</H2></P>
41
42  </BODY>
43  </HTML>
```

Fig. 4.11 Using **<META>** and **<DOCTYPE>** (part 2 of 2).

Line 1

```
<!DOCTYPE HTML PUBLIC "-//W3C//DTD HTML 4.0 Transitional//EN">
```

tells the browser that the following HTML conforms to a **Transitional** subset of HTML version 4.0. Although browsers do not require this element in order to read your HTML file, it useful to include it at the beginning of every HTML document.

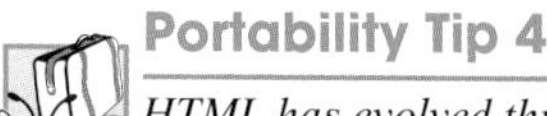

Portability Tip 4.1

HTML has evolved through many versions. Although the latest major version is 4, there are still many browsers and Web pages that are using version 3.2 or lower. Because each version of HTML introduces new features, it is important to tell the browser what version you are using, in order to get the best possible performance, compatibility and portability.

META tags contain two attributes that should always be used. The first of these, ***NAME***, is an identification of the type of **META** tag you are including. The ***CONTENT*** attribute provides information the search engine will be cataloging about your site.

Lines 10 through 12 demonstrate the **META** tag.

```
<META NAME = "keywords" CONTENT = "Webpage, design, HTML,
   tutorial, personal, help, index, form, contact, feedback,
   list, links, frame, deitel">
```

The **CONTENT** of a **META** tag with ***NAME* = "*keywords*"** provides search engines with a list of words that describe key aspects of your site. These words are used to match with searches—if someone searches for some of the terms in your **keywords META** tag, they have a better chance of being informed about your site in the search engine output. Thus, including **META** tags and their **CONTENT** information will draw more viewers—and better qualified viewers—to your site.

The ***description*** attribute value appears on lines 14 through 16

```
<META NAME = "description" CONTENT = "This Web site will help
you learn the basics of HTML and Webpage design through the
use of interactive examples and instruction.">
```

It is quite similar to the **keywords** value. Instead of giving a list of words describing your page, the **CONTENTS** of the keywords **META** element should be a readable 3 to 4 line description of your site, written in sentence form. This description is also used by search engines to catalog and display your site.

Software Engineering Observation 4.1

***META** elements are not visible to users of the sit, and must be placed inside the header section of your HTML document.*

4.11 <FRAMESET> Tag

All of the Web pages we have designed so far have the ability to link to other pages but can display only one page at a time. Figure 4.12 introduces *frames*, which can help you display more than one HTML file at a time. Frames, when used properly, can make your site more readable and usable for your users.

On line 1

```
<!DOCTYPE HTML PUBLIC "-//W3C//DTD HTML 4.0 Frameset//EN">
```

```
1   <!DOCTYPE HTML PUBLIC "-//W3C//DTD HTML 4.0 Frameset//EN">
2   <HTML>
3
4   <!-- Fig. 4.12: index.html -->
5   <!-- HTML Frames I         -->
6
7   <HEAD>
8   <META NAME = "keywords" CONTENT = "Webpage, design, HTML,
9      tutorial, personal, help, index, form, contact, feedback,
10     list, links, frame, deitel">
```

Fig. 4.12 Web site using two frames—navigational and content (part 1 of 2).

```

<META NAME = "description" CONTENT = "This Web site will help
   you learn the basics of HTML and Webpage design through the
   use of interactive examples and instruction.">

<TITLE>Internet and WWW How to Program - Main</TITLE>
</HEAD>

<!-- The <FRAMESET> tag gives the dimensions of your frame -->
<FRAMESET COLS = "110,*">

   <!-- The individual FRAME elements specify which pages -->
   <!-- appear in the given frames                       -->
   <FRAME NAME = "nav" SRC = "nav.html">
   <FRAME NAME = "main" SRC = "main.html">

   <NOFRAMES>
   <P>This page uses frames, but your browser does not support
   them.</P>
   <P>Get Internet Explorer 5 at the
      <A HREF = "http://www.microsoft.com/">
      Microsoft Web Site</A></P>
   </NOFRAMES>

</FRAMESET>
</HTML>
```

Fig. 4.12 Web site using two frames—navigational and content (part 2 of 2).

we encounter a slightly different **<!DOCTYPE>** tag. It now says **Frameset** instead of **Transitional**. This tag tells the browser that we will be using frames in the following code. You should include this modified version of the **<!DOCTYPE>** tag whenever you use frames in your HTML document.

The framed page begins with the opening ***FRAMESET*** tag, on line 20:

```
<FRAMESET COLS = "110,*">
```

This tag tells the browser that the page contains frames, the details of which will be set between the **<FRAMESET>**...**</FRAMESET>** tags. The **COLS** attribute of the opening **FRAMESET** tag gives the layout of the frameset. The value of ***COLS*** (or ***ROWS***, if you will be writing a frameset with a horizontal layout) gives the width of each frame, either in pixels or as a percentage of the screen. In this case, the attribute **COLS = "110,*"** tells the browser that there are two frames. The first one extends 110 pixels from the left edge of the screen, and the second frame fills the remainder of the screen (as indicated by the asterisk).

Now that we have defined the page layout, we have to specify what files will make up the frameset. We do this with the ***FRAME*** element in lines 24 and 25

```
<FRAME NAME = "nav" SRC = "nav.html">
<FRAME NAME = "main" SRC = "main.html">
```

In each **FRAME** element, the **SRC** attribute gives the URL of the page that will be displayed in the specified frame. In the preceding example, the first frame (which covers 110 pixels on the left side of the **FRAMESET**) will display the page **nav.html** and has the attribute **NAME = "nav"**. The second frame will display the page **main.html** and has the attribute **NAME = "main"**.

The purpose of a **NAME** attribute in the **FRAME** element is to identify that specific frame, enabling hyperlinks in a **FRAMESET** to load in their intended **FRAME**. For example,

```
<A HREF = "links.html" TARGET = "main">
```

would load **links.html** in the frame whose **NAME** attribute is **"main"**.

A target in an anchor element can also be set to a number of preset values: **TARGET="_blank"** loads the page in a new blank browser window, **TARGET="_self"** loads the page into the same window as the anchor element, **TARGET="_parent"** loads it in the parent **FRAMESET** (i.e., the **FRAMESET** which encapsulates the current frame) and **TARGET="_top"** loads the page into the full browser window (the page loads over the **FRAMESET**).

In lines 26 through 32 of the code example in Fig. 4.12, the **NOFRAMES** element displays HTML in those browsers that do not support frames.

Portability Tip 4.2

*Not everyone uses a browser that supports frames. Use the **NOFRAMES** element inside the **FRAMESET**, either to direct users to a non-framed version of your site or to provide links for downloading a frames-enabled browser.*

Look-and-Feel Observation 4.5

Frames are capable of enhancing your page, but are often misused. Never use frames to accomplish what you could with tables or other, simpler HTML formatting.

4.12 Nested <FRAMESET> Tags

You can use the **FRAMESET** element to create more complex layouts in a framed Web site by nesting **FRAMESET** areas as in Fig. 4.13.

The first level of **FRAMESET** tags is on lines 17 through 18

```
<FRAMESET COLS="110,*">
<FRAME NAME="nav" SCROLLING="no" NORESIZE SRC="nav.html">
```

The **FRAMESET** and **FRAME** elements here are constructed in the same manner as in Fig. 4.12. To this point, we have one frame that extends over the first 110 pixels of the screen starting at the left edge. The **SCROLLING** attribute, when set to **"no"**, prevents the browser from placing a scrolling bar on that frame. The **NORESIZE** attribute prevents the user from resizing the frame by using the mouse.

```
1  <!DOCTYPE html PUBLIC "-//W3C//DTD HTML 4.0 Frameset//EN">
2  <HTML>
3  
4  <!-- Fig. 4.13: index.html -->
5  <!-- HTML Frames II        -->
6  
7  <HEAD>
8  
9  <META NAME = "keywords" CONTENT = "Webpage, design, HTML,
10    tutorial, personal, help, index, form, contact, feedback,
11    list, links, frame, deitel">
12 
13 <META NAME = "description" CONTENT = "This Web site will help
14    you learn the basics of HTML and Webpage design through the
15    use of interactive examples and instruction.">
16 
17 <FRAMESET COLS = "110,*">
18    <FRAME NAME = "nav" SCROLLING = "no" SRC = "nav.html">
19 
20    <!-- Nested Framesets are used to change the formatting -->
21    <!-- and spacing of the frameset as a whole             -->
22    <FRAMESET ROWS = "175,*">
23       <FRAME NAME = "picture" SRC = "picture.html" NORESIZE>
24       <FRAME NAME = "main" SRC = "main.html">
25    </FRAMESET>
26 
27    <NOFRAMES>
28       <P>This page uses frames, but your browser doesn't
29          support them.</P>
30       <P>Get Internet Explorer 5 at the
31          <A HREF = "http://www.microsoft.com/">Microsoft
32          Web-Site</A></P>
33 
34    </NOFRAMES>
35 
36 </FRAMESET>
37 </HTML>
```

Fig. 4.13 Framed Web site with a nested frameset (part 1 of 2).

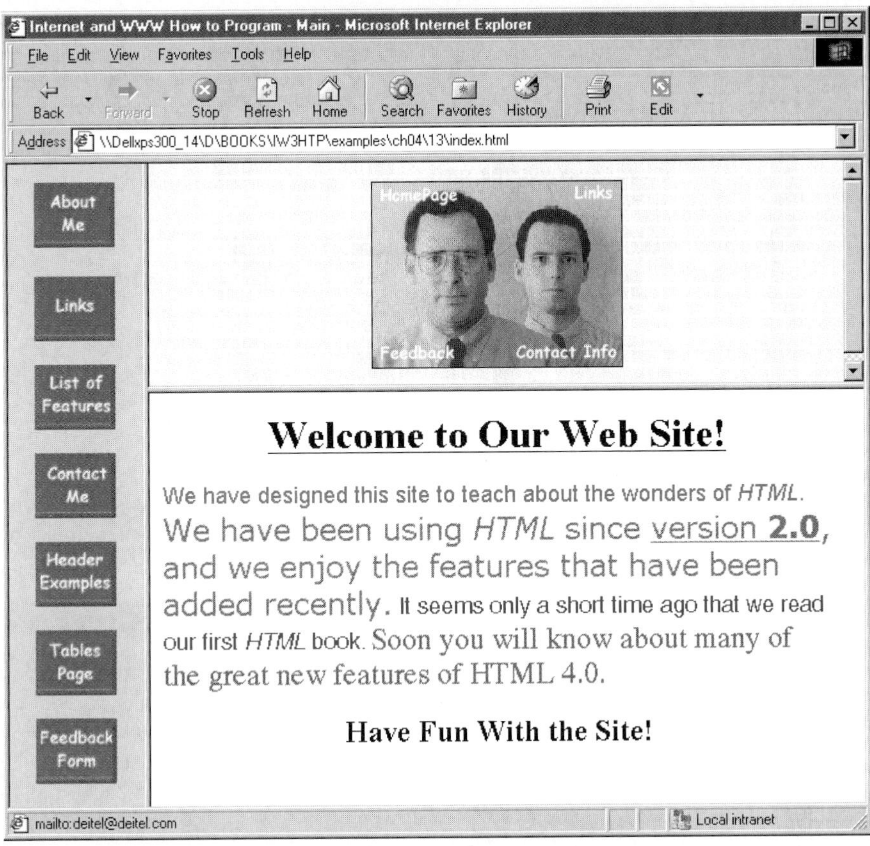

Fig. 4.13 Framed Web site with a nested frameset (part 2 of 2).

The second (nested) level of the **FRAMESET** element covers only the remaining **FRAME** area that was not included in the primary **FRAMESET**. Thus, any frames included in the second **FRAMESET** will not include the left-most 110 pixels of the screen. Lines 22 through 24 show the second level of **FRAMESET** tags.

```
<FRAMESET ROWS = "175,*">
   <FRAME NAME = "picture" SRC = "picture.html" NORESIZE>
   <FRAME NAME = "main" SRC = "main.html">
```

In this **FRAMESET** area, the first frame extends 175 pixels from the top of the screen, as indicated by the **ROWS = "175,*"**. Be sure to include the correct number of **FRAME** elements inside the second **FRAMESET** area. Also, be sure to include a **NOFRAME** element and to close both of the **FRAMESET** areas at the end of the Web page.

Testing and Debugging Tip 4.1

*When using nested **FRAMESET** elements, indent every level of **FRAME** tag. This makes the page clearer and easier to debug.*

Look-and-Feel Observation 4.6

*Nested **FRAMESET** elements can help you create visually pleasing, easy-to-navigate Web sites.*

4.13 Internet and WWW Resources

There are many Web sites that cover the more advanced and difficult features of HTML. Several of these sites are featured here.

`http://markradcliffe.co.uk/html/advancedhtml.htm`
This site gives pointers on techniques that can be used in addition to knowledge of basic HTML tags. The site mainly focuses on frames and tables.

`http://www.geocities.com/SiliconValley/Orchard/5212/`
Another page offering advanced tutorials is *Adam's Advanced HTML Page*. This page is geared to those looking to master the more advanced techniques of HTML. It includes instructions for creating tables, frames and marquees and other advanced topics.

`http://www.webdeveloper.com`
An excellent resource for creating and maintaining Web pages. This site contains extensive coverage of almost all topics related to creating Web pages and keeping them running. Its clean examples make learning even advanced topics very easy.

SUMMARY

- The unordered list element creates a list in which every line begins with a bullet mark. All entries in an unordered list must be enclosed within **<UL>**...**</UL>** tags, which open and close the unordered list element.
- Each entry in an unordered list is inserted with the **<LI>** tag, which creates a line break and inserts a bullet mark at the beginning of the line. You then insert and format any text. The closing list element tag (**</LI>**) is optional.
- Nested lists display information in outline form. A nested list is a list that appears in the bounds of another list element. Nesting the new list inside the original indents the list one level and changes the bullet type to reflect the nesting.
- Browsers insert a line of whitespace after every closed list.
- An ordered list (**<OL>**...**</OL>**) begins every new line with a sequence number instead of a bullet. By default, ordered lists use decimal sequence numbers (1,2,3, ...).
- To change the sequence type of a list, use the **TYPE** attribute in the **<OL>** opening tag or in an individual **<LI>** tag. The default type is **TYPE="1"**, which uses the 1, 2, 3, ... sequence. The second type, **TYPE="I"**, makes a capital Roman numeral sequence: I, II, III, and so on. **TYPE="i"** creates the lowercase Roman numeral sequence: i, ii, iii, etc. The last two types are **TYPE="A"** and **TYPE="a"**, which produce uppercase and lowercase alphabetic sequences, respectively.
- HTML tables organize data into rows and columns. All tags and text that apply to a table go inside the **<TABLE>**...**</TABLE>** tags. The **BORDER** attribute lets you set the width of the table's border in pixels. The **WIDTH** attribute sets the width of the table—you specify either a number of pixels or a percentage of the screen width.
- The text inside the **<CAPTION>**...**</CAPTION>** tags is inserted directly above the table in the browser window. The caption text is also used to help text-based browsers interpret the table data.
- Tables can be split into distinct horizontal and vertical sections. Put all header information (such as table titles and column headers) inside the **<THEAD>**...**</THEAD>** tags. The **TR** (table row)

element is used for formatting the cells of individual rows. All of the cells in a row belong within the **<TR>**...**</TR>** tags of that row.

- The smallest area of the table that we are able to format is the data cell. There are two types of data cells: ones located in the header (**<TH>**...**</TH>**) and ones located in the table body (**<TD>**...**</TD>**). Header cells, usually placed in the **<THEAD>** area, are suitable for titles and column headings.
- Like **THEAD**, the **TBODY** is used for formatting and grouping purposes. Most tables use **TBODY** to house the majority of their content.
- **TD** table data cells are left aligned by default. **TH** cells are centered by default.
- Just as you can use the **THEAD** and **TBODY** elements to format groups of table rows, you can use the **COLGROUP** element to group and format columns. **COLGROUP** is used by setting in its opening tag the number of columns it affects and the formatting it imposes on that group of columns.
- Each **COL** element contained inside the **<COLGROUP>**...**</COLGROUP>** tags can in turn format a specified number of columns.
- You can add a background color or image to any table row or cell with either the **BGCOLOR** or **BACKGROUND** attributes, which are used in the same way as in the **BODY** element.
- It is possible to make some table data cells larger than others by using the **ROWSPAN** and **COLSPAN** attributes. The attribute value extends the data cell to span the specified number of cells.
- The **VALIGN** (vertical alignment) attribute of a table data cell accepts the following values: **"top"**, **"middle"**, **"bottom"** and **"baseline"**.
- All cells in a table row whose **VALIGN** attribute is set to **"baseline"** will have the first text line on a common baseline.
- The default vertical alignment in all data and header cells is **VALIGN="middle"**.
- HTML provides several mechanisms—including the **FORM**—to collect information from people viewing your site.
- Use **METHOD = "post"** in a form that causes changes to server data, for example when updating a database. The form data will be sent to the server as an *environment variable,* which scripts are able to access (you will learn how to do this in Chapter 27 when we cover Perl). The other possible value, **METHOD = "get"**, should be used when your form does not cause any changes in server-side data, for example when making a database request. The form data from **METHOD = "get"** is appended to the end of the URL. Because of this, the amount of data submitted using this **METHOD** is limited to 4K. Also be aware that **METHOD = "get"** is limited to standard characters, and can not submit any special characters.
- A Web server is a machine that runs a software package such as Apache or IIS; servers are designed to handle browser requests. When a user uses a browser to request a page or file somewhere on the server, the server processes this request and returns an answer to the browser.
- The **ACTION** attribute in the **FORM** tag is the path to a script that processes the form data.
- The input element is common in forms, and always requires the **TYPE** attribute. Two other attributes are **NAME**, which provides a unique identification for the **INPUT**, and **VALUE**, which indicates the value that the **INPUT** element sends to the server upon submission.
- The input **TYPE="text"** inserts a one-line text bar into the form. The value of this **INPUT** element and the information that the server sends to you from this **INPUT** is the text that the user types into the bar. The **SIZE** attribute determines the width of the text input, measured in characters. You can also set a maximum number of characters that the text input will accept by inserting the **MAXLENGTH="***length***"** attribute.
- You must make sure to include a textual identifier (in this case, "**Name:**") adjacent to the **INPUT** element to indicate the function of the element.

- The **TYPE="submit" INPUT** element places a button in the form that submits data to the server when clicked. The **VALUE** attribute of the **submit** input changes the text displayed on the button.
- The **TYPE="reset"** input element places a button on the form that, when clicked, will clear all entries the user has entered into the form.
- The **TEXTAREA** element inserts a box into the form. You specify the size of the box (which is scrollable) inside the opening **<TEXTAREA>** tag with the **ROWS** attribute and the **COLS** attribute.
- Data entered in a **TYPE="password"** input appears on the screen as asterisks. The password is used for submitting sensitive information that the user would not want others to be able to read. It is just the browser that displays asterisks—the real form data is still submitted to the server.
- Every **INPUT** element with **TYPE="checkbox"** creates a new checkbox in the form. Checkboxes can be used individually or in groups. Each checkbox in a group should have the same **NAME** (in this case, **NAME="things"**).
- Inserted into forms by means of the **INPUT** attribute **TYPE="radio"**, radio buttons are different from checkboxes in that only one in the group may be selected at any time. All of the **NAME** attributes of a group of radio inputs must be the same and all of the **VALUE** attributes different.
- Insert the attribute **CHECKED** to indicate which radio button you would like selected initially.
- The **SELECT** element places a selectable list of items inside your form. To add an item to the list, insert an **OPTION** element in the **<SELECT>**...**</SELECT>** area, and type what you want the list item to display on the same line. You can change the number of list options visible at one time by including the **SIZE="*size*"** attribute inside the **<SELECT>** tag. Use this attribute if you prefer an expanded version of the list to the one-line expandable list.
- A location on a page is marked by including a **NAME** attribute in an **A** element. Clicking on this hyperlink in a browser would scroll the browser window to that point on the page.
- An image map allows you to designate certain sections of the image as hotspots and then use these hotspots as anchors for linking.
- All elements of an image map are contained inside the **<MAP>**...**</MAP>** tags. The required attribute for the **MAP** element is **NAME**.
- A hotspot on the image is designated with the **AREA** element. Every **<AREA>** tag has the following attributes: **HREF** sets the target for the link on that spot, **SHAPE** and **COORDS** set the characteristics of the area and **ALT** function just as it does in **<IMG>** tags.
- **SHAPE="rect"** creates a rectangular hotspot around the *coordinates* of a **COORDS** element.
- A coordinate pair consists of two numbers, which are the locations of the point on the x and y axes. The x axis extends horizontally from the upper-left corner and the y axis vertically. Every point on an image has a unique x–y coordinate, annotated as (x, y).
- In the case of a rectangular hotspot, the required coordinates are those of the upper-left and lower-right corners of the rectangle.
- The **SHAPE="poly"** creates a hotspot of no preset shape—you specify the shape of the hotspot in the **COORDS** attribute by listing the coordinates of every vertex, or corner of the hotspot.
- **SHAPE="circle"** creates a circular hotspot; it requires both the coordinates of the center of the circle and the length of the radius, in pixels.
- To use an image map with a graphic on your page, you must insert the **USEMAP="#*name*"** attribute into the **IMG** element, where "name" is the value of the **NAME** attribute in the **MAP** element.
- The main HTML element that interacts with search engines is the ***META*** element.
- **<!DOCTYPE HTML PUBLIC "-//W3C//DTD HTML 4.0 Transitional//EN">** tells the browser that the following HTML conforms to a transitional subset of HTML version 4.0.

- **META** tags contain two attributes that should always be used. The first of these, **NAME**, is an identification of the type of **META** tag you are including. The **CONTENT** attribute gives the information the search engine will be cataloging.
- The **CONTENT** of a **META** tag with **NAME="keywords"** provides the search engines with a list of words that describe the key aspects of your site. By including **META** tags and their content information, you can give precise information about your site to search engines. This will help you draw a more focused audience to your site.
- The **description** value of the **NAME** attribute in the **META** tag should be a 3 to 4 line description of your site, written in sentence form. This description is used by the search engine to catalog and display your site.
- **META** elements are not visible to users of the site and should be placed inside the header section of your HTML document.
- **<!DOCTYPE html PUBLIC "-//W3C//DTD HTML 4.0 Frameset//EN">** tells the browser that we are using frames in the following code. You should include this modified version of **<!DOCTYPE>** whenever you use frames in your HTML document.
- The **FRAMESET** tag tells the browser that the page contains frames.
- The value of **COLS** or **ROWS** gives the width of each frame, either in pixels or as a percentage of the screen.
- In each **FRAME** element, the **SRC** attribute gives the URL of the page that will be displayed in the specified frame.
- The purpose of a **NAME** attribute in the **FRAME** element is to give an identity to that specific frame, in order to enable hyperlinks in a **FRAMESET** to load their intended **FRAME**. The **TARGET** attribute in an anchor element is set to the **NAME** of the **FRAME** in which the new page should load.
- A target in an anchor element can be set to a number of preset values: **TARGET="_blank"** loads the page in a new blank browser window, **TARGET="self"** loads the page into the same window as the anchor element, **TARGET="_parent"** loads the page into the parent **FRAMESET** and **TARGET="_top"** loads the page into the full browser window.
- Not everyone who will be looking at your page will be using a browser that can handle frames. You therefore need to include a **NOFRAMES** element inside of the **FRAMESET**. You should include regular HTML tags and elements within the **<NOFRAMES>**...**</NOFRAMES>** tags. Use this area to direct the user to a non-framed version of the site or to provide links for downloading a frame-enabled browser.
- By nesting **FRAMESET** elements, you can create more complex layouts.

TERMINOLOGY

ACTION attribute in **FORM** element
AREA
BORDER property of **TABLE** element
CAPTION element
cell of a table
CELLSPACING property of **TABLE** element
CGI script
CHECKED
circular hotspot
COL element
COLGROUP element
COLS attribute of **TABLE** element
COLSPAN attribute of **TD** element
column of a table
COORDS attribute inside **AREA** element
data cell
DATAFIELD property of **TD** element
environment variable
<!DOCTYPE...>
form
FRAME element (**<FRAME>**...**</FRAME>**)
FRAMESET element

header cell
hotspot
image map
indenting lists
INPUT element (**<INPUT>**...**</INPUT>**)
INPUT Type="button"
INPUT Type="checkbox"
INPUT Type="password"
INPUT Type="radio"
INPUT Type="reset"
INPUT Type="submit"
INPUT Type="text"
INPUT Type="textarea"
internal linking
list
MAP element
MAXLENGTH="#"
<META> Tag
METHOD="get"
METHOD="post"
NAME attribute in **INPUT** element
NAME="recipient" in **INPUT** element
NAME="redirect" in **INPUT** element
NAME="subject" in **INPUT** element
nested lists
NOFRAMES
NORESIZE attribute in **FRAME**
OL (ordered list) element (**<OL>**...**</OL>**)
<OPTION>
rectangular hotspot
row of a table
ROWSPAN attribute of **TD** element
SCROLLING attribute in **FRAME**
SELECT element (**<SELECT>**...**</SELECT>**)
SHAPE attribute inside **AREA** element
SIZE attribute in **SELECT**
SRC attribute of **FRAME** element
table
TABLE element (**<TABLE>**...**</TABLE>**)
TARGET="_blank"
TARGET="_parent"
TARGET="_blank"
TARGET="_top"
TBODY
TD (table data) element (**<TD>**...**</TD>**)
text-based browser
TH (header cell) element (**<TH>**...**</TH>**)
THEAD element (**<THEAD>**...**</THEAD>**)
TR (table row) element (**<TR>**...**</TR>**)
TYPE=1 attribute of **<OL>**
TYPE=A attribute of **<OL>**
TYPE=a attribute of **<OL>**
TYPE=I attribute of **<OL>**
TYPE=i attribute of **<OL>**
UL (unordered list) element (**<UL>**...**</UL>**)
USEMAP="name" attribute in **IMG**
VALUE attribute of **INPUT** element
Web server
x–y scale

COMMON PROGRAMMING ERRORS

4.1 Forgetting to close any of the area formatting tags inside the table area can distort the table format. Be sure to check that every element is opened and closed in its proper place to make sure that the table appears as intended.

4.2 When using **COLSPAN** and **ROWSPAN** in table data cells, consider that the modified cells will cover the areas of other cells. Compensate for this in your code by reducing the number of cells in that row or column. If you do not, the formatting of your table will be distorted, and you may inadvertently create more columns and/or rows than you originally intended.

4.3 Forgetting to include textual labels for a form element is a design error. Without these labels, users will have no way of knowing what the function of individual form elements is.

4.4 When your form has several checkboxes with the same **NAME**, you must make sure that they have different **VALUE**s, or else the script will have no way of distinguishing between them.

4.5 When you are using a group of radio inputs in a form, forgetting to set the **NAME** values to be the same throughout the group will let the user select all the radio buttons at the same time: an undesired result.

GOOD PROGRAMMING PRACTICES

4.1 Indenting each level of a nested list in your code makes the code easier to edit and debug.

4.2 Place hidden **INPUT** elements in the beginning of a form, right after the opening **<FORM>** tag. This makes these elements easier to find and identify.

4.3 When using **INPUT** elements in forms, be sure to leave enough space for every user to input the pertinent information.

4.4 Be sure to close your form code with the **</FORM>** tag. Neglecting to include this can affect the actions of other forms on the same page.

4.5 Keep the **<MAP>**…**</MAP>** tags on the same page as the image that will use them. This will save time if you have to edit the image map.

LOOK-AND-FEEL OBSERVATIONS

4.1 Using different types of ordered lists can add a well-organized look to your site and can help you categorize and outline information effectively.

4.2 Use tables in your HTML pages to organize data attractively and effectively.

4.3 Using the **COLSPAN** and **ROWSPAN** attributes in your tables adds a nice look and can help you format the data cells to contain your information more effectively.

4.4 Internal hyperlinks are most useful in large HTML files with lots of information. You can link to various points on the page to save the user from having to scroll down and find a specific location.

4.5 Nested **FRAMESET** elements can help you create visually pleasing, easy-to-navigate Web sites.

PORTABILITY TIPS

4.1 HTML has evolved through many versions. Although the latest version is 4.0, there are still many browsers and Web pages that are using version 3.2 or lower. Because each version of HTML introduces new features, it is important to tell the browser what version you are using in order to get the best possible performance, compatibility and portability.

4.2 Not everyone uses a browser that supports frames. Use the **NOFRAMES** element inside the **FRAMESET**, either to direct users to a non-framed version of your site or to provide links for downloading a frames-enabled browser.

SOFTWARE ENGINEERING OBSERVATION

4.1 **META** elements are not visible to users of the site and must be placed inside the header section of your HTML document.

TESTING-AND-DEBUGGING TIP

4.1 When using nested **FRAMESET** elements, indent every level of **FRAME** tag. This makes the page clearer and easier to debug.

SELF-REVIEW EXERCISES

4.1 State whether the following are *true* or *false*. If the answer is *false*, explain why.

a) There is no limit to the number of levels to which you can nest an ordered or unordered list.

b) The width of all data cells in a table must be the same.
c) An ordered list can have only one type of numbering system. To initiate a new type of numbering, you must make a new ordered list.
d) The **THEAD** element is mandatory in a **TABLE**.
e) You are limited to a maximum of 100 internal links per page.
f) All browsers can render **FRAMESET**s.

4.2 Fill in the blanks in each of the following statements.
a) The ________ attribute in an **INPUT** element inserts a button that, when clicked, will clear the contents of the form.
b) The spacing of a **FRAMESET** is set by including the ________ attribute or the ________ attribute inside of the **<FRAMESET>** tag.
c) The ________ element inserts a new item in a list.
d) The ________ element tells the browser what version of HTML is included on the page. Two types of this element are ________ and ________.
e) The common shapes used in image maps are ________, ________ and ________.

4.3 Write HTML tags to accomplish the following.
a) Insert a framed Web page with the first frame extending 300 pixels across the page from the left side.
b) Insert an ordered list that will have numbering by lowercase Roman numerals.
c) Insert a scrollable list (in a form) that will always display four entries of the list.
d) Insert an image map onto a page using **deitel.gif** as an image and **MAP** with **NAME="hello"** as the image map, and have "hello" be the **ALT** text.

ANSWERS TO SELF-REVIEW EXERCISES

4.1 a) True.
b) False. You can specify the width of any column either in pixels or as a percentage of the total width of the table.
c) False. You can specify a numbering type for an individual list element by including the attribute **TYPE = "*name*"**.
d) False. The **THEAD** element is used only for formatting purposes and is optional (but it is recommended that you include it).
e) False. You can have an unlimited number of hyperlink locations on any page.
f) False. Text-based browsers are unable to render a **FRAMESET** and must therefore rely on the information that you include inside the **<NOFRAMES>…</NOFRAMES>** tag.

4.2 a) **TYPE = "reset"**. b) **COLS**, **ROWS**. c) **LI**. d) **<!DOCTYPE…>**, **TRANSITIONAL**, **FRAMESET**. e) **poly**, **circle**, **rect**.

4.3 a) **<FRAMESET COLS = "300,*">…</FRAMESET>**
b) **<OL TYPE = "i">…</OL>**
c) **<SELECT SIZE = "4">…</SELECT>**
d) **<IMG SRC = "deitel.gif" ALT = "hello" USEMAP = "#hello">**

EXERCISES

4.4 Categorize each of the following as an element or an attribute:
a) **SIZE**
b) **OL**
c) **LI**
d) **FRAME**
e) **CAPTION**

f) SELECT
g) TYPE

4.5 What will the **FRAMESET** produced by the following code look like? Assume that the pages being imported are blank with white backgrounds and that the dimensions of the screen are 800 by 600. Sketch the layout, approximating the dimensions.

```
<FRAMESET ROWS = "20%,*">
<FRAME SRC = "hello.html" NAME = "hello">
   <FRAMESET COLS = "150,*">
   <FRAME SRC = "nav.html" NAME = "nav">
   <FRAME SRC = "deitel.html" NAME = "deitel">
   <FRAMESET>
<FRAMESET>
```

4.6 Write the HTML code that produces the following Web page. The width of the table is 400 pixels and the border is one pixel wide. The header is enclosed in an **H2** element.

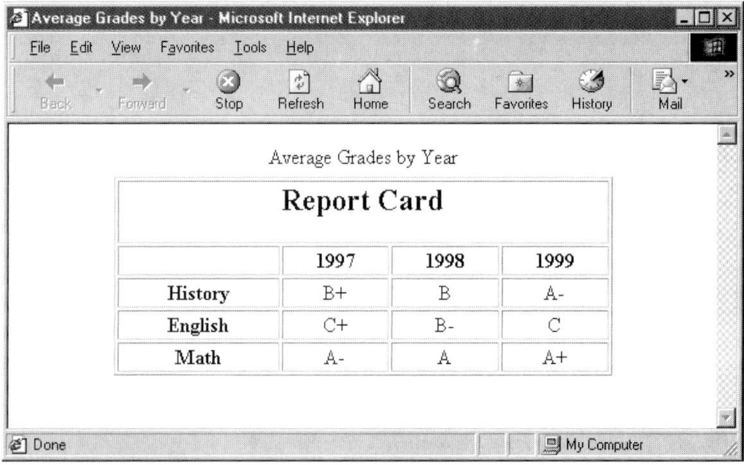

Report Card			
	1997	1998	1999
History	B+	B	A-
English	C+	B-	C
Math	A-	A	A+

4.7 Assume that you have a document with many subsections. Write the HTML code to create a frame with a table of contents on the left side of the window, and have each entry in the table of contents use internal linking to scroll down the document frame to the appropriate subsection.

Paint Shop Pro

Objectives

- To learn the basics of Paint Shop Pro 5.
- To learn how colors are represented in image files and what "color depth" and "transparency" are.
- To understand the difference between the GIF and JPEG formats, and to know when to use each.
- To be able to design images for your Web pages.
- To be able to take screen shots using Paint Shop Pro's built-in screen-capturing capability.
- To grasp the techniques of dithering, image layering, and other important image-preparation processes.

Now follow in this direction, now turn a different hue.
Theognis

There are occasions when it is undoubtedly better to incur loss than to make gain.
Titus Maccius Plautus

Beware lest you lose the substance by grasping at the shadow.
Aesop

Outline

5.1 Introduction

Knowledge of HTML is not quite enough to make successful Web pages. Plain text is fine, but images liven up your pages. Many images are available on the Internet for free downloading and use.

In this chapter we discuss how to create your own images quickly and conveniently using Jasc Inc.'s *Paint Shop Pro (*included on the CD with this book). This easy-to-use, inexpensive graphics package offers the functionality of more expensive packages. We use Paint Shop Pro to create a few images that can add pizzazz to your Web pages—a title picture, a navigation bar, and a few advanced photographic effects.

5.2 Image Basics

We begin by creating a basic title image for your Web page. Open Paint Shop Pro, and click **New...** in the **File** menu. The **New Image** dialog box that appears allows you to choose many initial settings for your image. You can select the **Height** and **Width** and the standard they are measured in: **Pixels**, **Inches**, or **Centimeters.**

You can also specify the initial **Background color** and the *color depth*, which is the maximum number of simultaneous colors in the image. This can be set to **2 Colors** (one bit per pixel), where each pixel would have a bit signifying whether it was "on" (black) or "off" (white). In **16 Colors** (four bits per pixel), each pixel has four bits signifying its color (2^4=16). In both 8-bit color depths (**Greyscale** and **256 Color**), there are 256 set colors that make up the *palette.* Each pixel takes 8 bits to refer to any one of the *palette entries.*

In the highest quality, 24 bits are used for every pixel—8 bits for each of the primary colors in light—red, green and blue. This allows for 16.7 million colors, a spectrum comparable to that of human vision and more than adequate for developing screen images.

Create a new image that is 300 pixels wide and 150 pixels high in 8-bit color depth with a white background. This should be a good size for a title image on your Web page. Familiarize yourself with the development environment (Fig 5.2). Notice that the status bar on the bottom gives information about any objects over which you move the mouse cursor.

In this case the cursor is over the image, so some vital image statistics are displayed with the cursor's location in the image's coordinate system. Image coordinates were explained in Chapter 3 in the discussion of image maps.

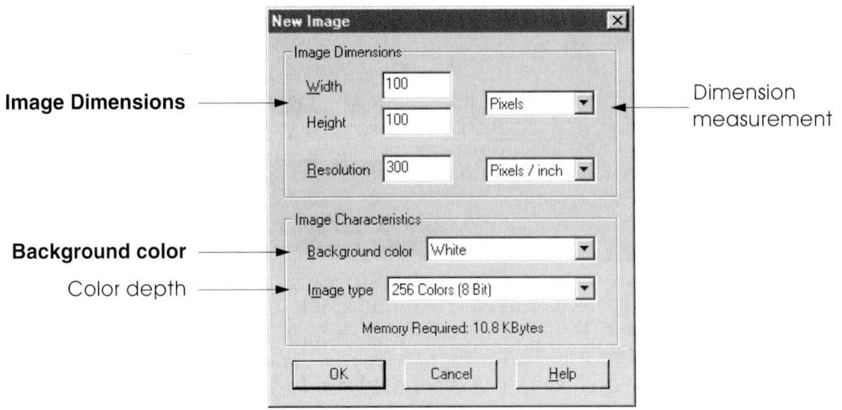

Fig. 5.1 Creating a **New Image** in Paint Shop Pro.

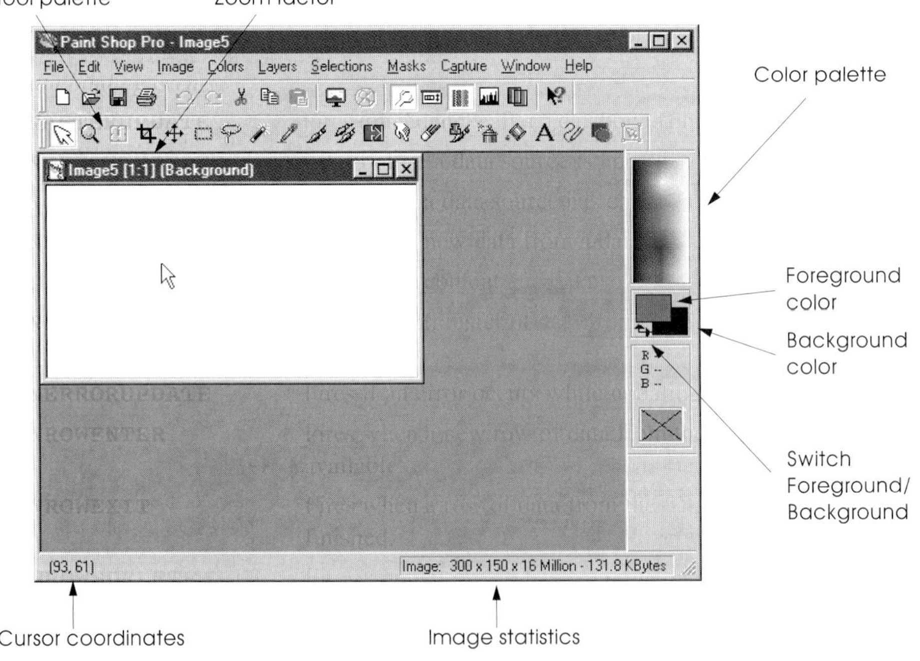

Fig. 5.2 Creating a new image in Paint Shop Pro.

The toolbar on the right side of the window is the *color palette*, where new colors can be selected. There are always two active colors—the *foreground color* and the *background color*. Click on the foreground color box. This will display the *color wheel* shown in Fig. 5.3. You can type in an RGB value or move the two selectors until you find the precise color you want. The outer selector determines the ***Hue*** (color), while the inner selector determines both ***Lightness*** (the amount of black vs. the amount of white) and ***Saturation*** (the amount of color vs. the amount of ***Lightness***). Note that the box labelled **HTML Code** displays the RGB value in hexadecimal notation, which can be used directly in HTML tags such as **<BODY>** or **<FONT>**.

Now we construct our title image. We use an RGB foreground color with a red value of 206, a green value of 140, and a blue value of 140.

Enter the color wheel again. Be sure to click on the foreground color box, as we are setting foreground color. Select this color by typing in the individual RGB values and then clicking **OK**. You should now see the color displayed in the foreground color box on the right side of the screen.

Now try to place some text. Select the text button on the tool palette and click inside the image window. The dialog box that appears (Fig. 5.4) allows you to fine-tune the properties of the text you are going to place in the image. Select a font and style you like and a large type size (25 "point" or so). As you enter text in the input area on the bottom of the dialog box, a sample will appear in the preview window directly above it.

Be sure to have the **Antialias** checkbox selected. *Antialiasing* is a process that smooths edges on scalable fonts by blending the color of the edge pixels with the color of the background on which the text is being placed. Without it, fonts can look jagged, an unattractive and distracting effect. Antialiasing can only be used in 24-bit and greyscale images.

If you have more than one line of text, you should make sure that the **Alignment** is set to **Center**. When your text looks good in the preview window, click OK. The color of your text will be the foreground color you selected previously. It will be surrounded by a dashed line, indicating that the text is *selected* and can be moved around. Move the cursor over the text, so that the cursor changes to a crosshair. This graphic indicates that the selection is ready to be moved. Drag the text to the center of the window.

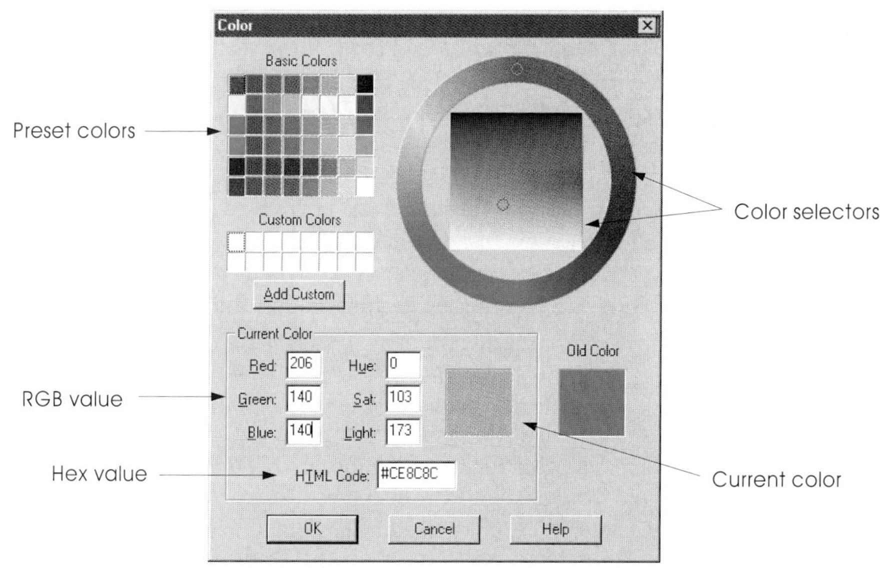

Fig. 5.3 Selecting a new **Color**.

Fig. 5.4 Adding **Text** to an image.

Now comes the fun part. In the **Image** menu, go to the **Effects** submenu and select the **Drop Shadow...** effect. The dialog box that appears (Fig. 5.5) allows you to modify the characteristics of the shadow that will be applied to your selected text. You can adjust both the **Horizontal** and **Vertical** offsets of the shadow by using the corresponding sliders in the **Offset** section. The **Color**, **Opacity**, and **Blur** of the shadow are also adjustable. You can see your adjustments being updated in "real time" in the small preview window. You can use the zoom buttons under the window and drag your mouse inside the window to preview a different area.

Use the settings shown in Fig. 5.5, and click **OK**. The drop shadow will be applied to the text. The dashed selection line expands to include both the text and the drop shadow. You can still move the shadowed text just as you did before. If you are satisfied with the position, right-click in the image area, and your selection will be placed on the image.

All that needs to be done now is to prepare the image for use on the Web. Keep in mind that most people will be viewing your images with their systems set to 8-bit color depth, able to see only 256 colors at a time. Using too many colors at once will create grainy images, as the viewer's browser *dithers* the image's colors to the 256 actually available on the system. Dithering is covered in depth in the next section.

For now, simply reduce the color depth of the image to 256 by using the **Decrease Color Depth** option in the **Colors** menu. The dialog box, shown in Fig. 5.6, presents you with several methods of reducing the color depth. The default, **Nearest color**, changes any colors missing from the palette to a nearest match. This is fine for now, so click the **OK** button.

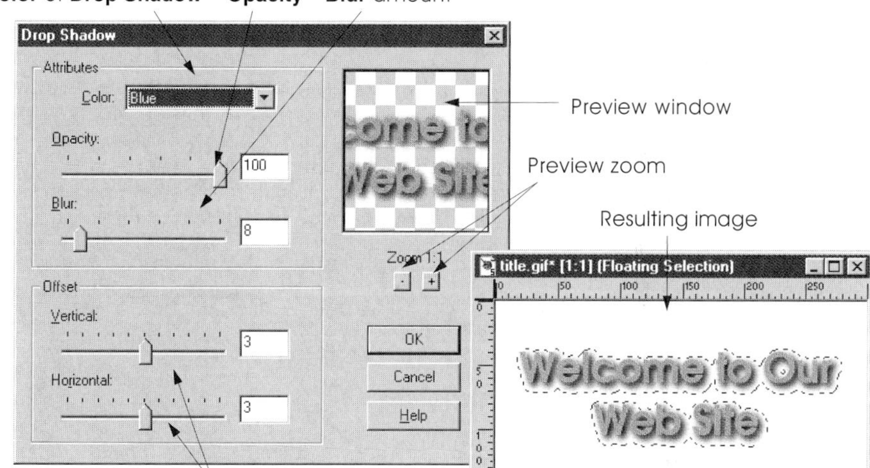

Fig. 5.5 Adding a **Drop Shadow** to text.

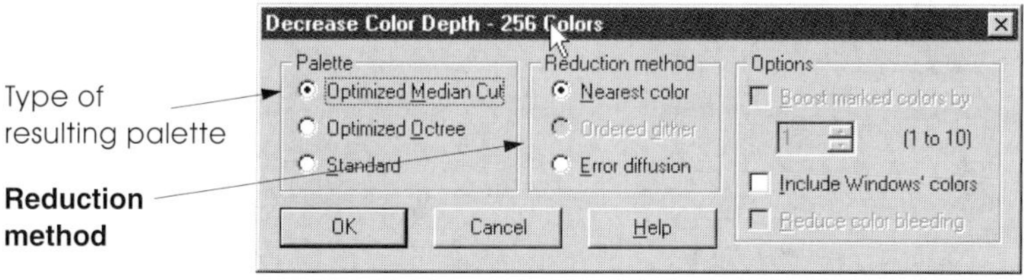

Fig. 5.6 Reducing **Color Depth** to **256 Colors**.

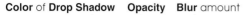

We also want our image background (the large white area) to be *transparent*. This is a process which designates one of the colors in the palette to instead show any background color or picture behind it. To do this, make sure your background color is set to white, and then select **Set Palette Transparency** in the **Colors** menu. In this menu, you can either choose a specific palette index (in 8 bits, clicking the foreground color box brings up the palette of 256 colors, where each color is listed in order) or simply set the current background color, which is what we want in this case. Select that, and click on the **Proof** button to see a preview in the actual image of which pixels will become transparent. The checkered background will not appear in the final image; it is simply Paint Shop Pro's way of showing you what is actually a transparent background and not simply white.

The title image for your Web page is now finished. In the **Save** menu, choose the **CompuServe Graphics Interchange (*.gif)** format for the picture. You can now insert the picture into your page using an **`<IMG>`** tag, as described in Chapter 3.

Look-and-Feel Observation 5.1

Because the drop shadow effect is so easy to do and looks so nice, it has become the most widely used image effect on the Web. If you are striving for originality in your pages, you might want to vary the settings or explore other effects Paint Shop Pro has to offer.

Images developed for use on a certain background color usually need to be redone if the background on your page changes. As you can see in Fig. 5.8, our image looks fine on the light background for which it was developed. Placing the image on a grey background, however, creates an unsightly effect. In this case, the effect occurs because the shadow was blurred over a white background and so the pixels of the blue shadow become gradually whiter towards the edges. They are not completely white, however, so the fact that white is the transparent color in this image does not matter. This effect is also noticeable with anti-aliased text, which uses the same process of blending with the background color.

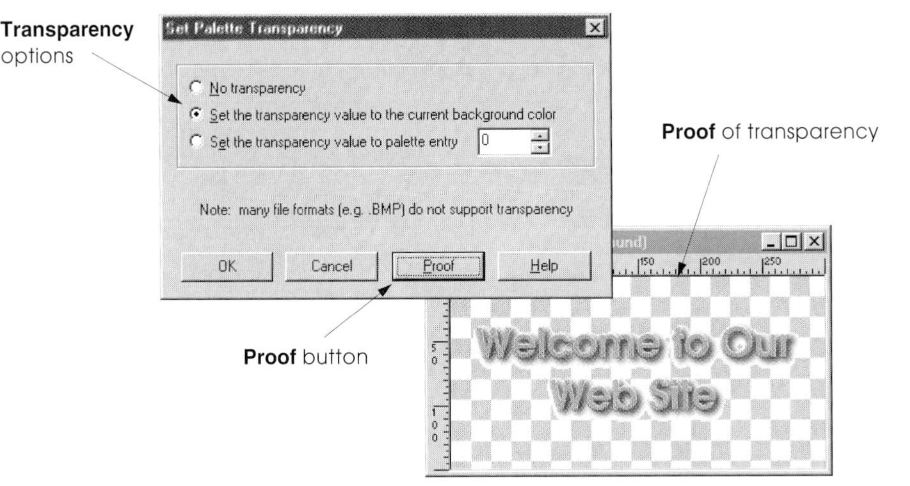

Fig. 5.7 Setting image **Transparency** and testing using the **Proof** button.

Fig. 5.8 A comparison of white transparency on white and grey backgrounds.

5.3 File Formats: GIF or JPEG?

The two major file formats used for images on the Web are *GIF* and *JPEG*. Whenever you compose images, you need to know the differences between these formats. What are they? Which format is better for which situation? How do you keep file size down while retaining picture quality?

The *Graphics Interchange Format (GIF)*, developed by CompuServe, is based on a palette of only 256 colors. It is best used in screenshots, line drawings, and other situations with sharp edges. It is well suited to the Web, because it has transparency, as demonstrated in the previous section. When reducing to 256 colors, Paint Shop Pro will perform *dithering* on the image, using colors already in the palette to simulate the desired color.

Performance Tip 5.1

A GIF file is typically larger than a JPEG file. If server space is a problem and your image has many more than 256 colors, it is a better idea to use the JPEG format.

Dithering can be effective, but it often destroys the quality of an image having hundreds or thousands of colors. Such richness is characteristic of real-world images such as photographs and scanned images, and it also occurs in computer art created with 3D rendering programs or advanced image packages. If you use the JPEG format, make sure to know its limitations. Its compression algorithms handle sharp edges and abrupt changes poorly. Also, JPEG is not a *lossless* format as GIF is, rather JPEG is a is a *lossy* format: Saving an image in JPEG format can reduce the quality of your image.

One feature that GIF and JPEG share is known as *interlacing (in GIF* terminology*)* or *progressive encoding (in JPEG terminology)*. This technique downloads a rough whole image and gradually increases the image's clarity, instead of downloading from the top of the image and moving downward as is done normally. This effect can often keep a user's attention focused while a large page loads.

Performance Tip 5.2

Do not place too many interlaced images on any one Web page; doing so can slow the rendering of the page.

Interlacing is easy to do in Paint Shop Pro. When you are saving an image, after you have selected an image type, click on the **Options...** button at the bottom right of the dialog box. This box shows you any special options for the image format you have selected. In Fig. 5.9 we see the **Save Options** for the JPEG and GIF formats and how to turn on **Interlacing/Progressive Encoding** in each of them.

Performance Tip 5.3

The JPEG format has scalable compression. *When saving a JPEG image, in the* **Save Options** *dialog, sliding the* **Compression** *slider to the left causes the image to retain high quality, but the file size also remains high. Sliding the* **Compression** *slider to the right causes the file size to decrease, but image quality suffers. This graduated scale helps you find a good balance between the file size and image quality.*

A newer image standard is making its mark on the Web. The *Portable Network Graphics (PNG*, pronounced *ping*) format was developed in response to a decision by the UniSys corporation to start charging royalties on the GIF format, on which UniSys holds a patent. PNG is actually a suitable replacement for both GIF and JPEG—it has the qualities of both formats. For example, PNG can encode in RGBA—The A stands for *alpha transparency*, which can make images transparent against any background and so solves problems like the one we saw in Fig. 5.8. Paint Shop Pro supports the PNG format, as do the latest versions of both Netscape Navigator and Internet Explorer. PNG is becoming increasingly used by Web developers and may soon dominate the Web. More information about the PNG format can be found at **`http://www.w3.org/Graphics/PNG/`**.

5.4 Tool Palette

The great power of Paint Shop Pro lies not in its filters (for instance, the drop shadow), but in its easy-to-use tools. The **Tool Palette** keeps the tools grouped on a single toolbar, which by default appears on the left side of the editing area. It can be dragged to other locations and docked on other sides (under the **Tool Bar**, for example).The most frequently used tools are highlighted in Fig. 5.10.

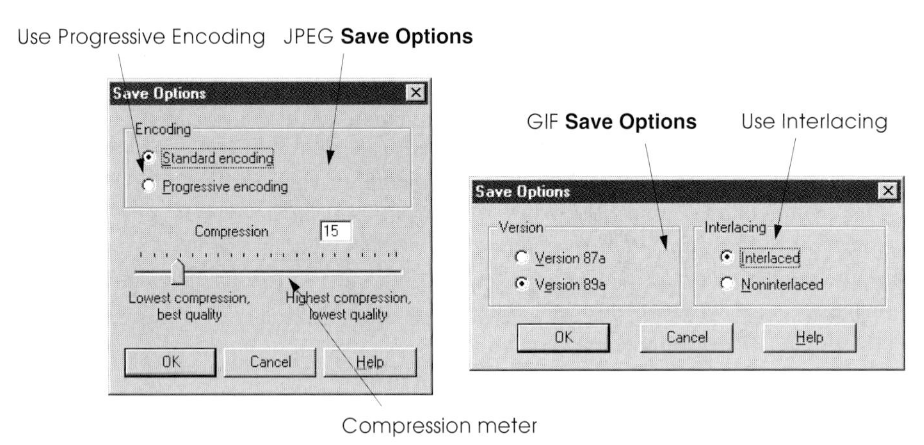

Fig. 5.9 **Save Options** for JPEG and GIF.

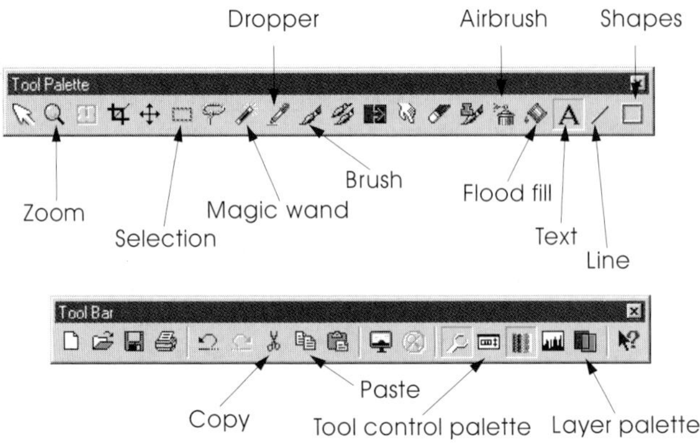

Fig. 5.10 Paint Shop Pro's **Tool Bar** and **Tool Palette**.

The *zoom tool* is fairly straightforward. Left-click the image to zoom in, right-click the image to zoom back out. The *zoom factor* is displayed on the title bar of the image, next to the image name. You can zoom in up to a 16:1 display-to-actual-size ratio, and out to 1:16.

The selection tool is something we are somewhat familiar with after creating the title image. Dragging inside the image selects a rectangular region whose borders are shown with a dashed line. Any filters, effects or tools you apply will take effect only in the selection area. The selection area can be moved by dragging it with the mouse; The area the selection occupied before it was moved is filled with the background color.

The *magic wand tool* is perhaps the most useful tool in Paint Shop Pro. Click in the image to select all adjacent pixels of the same colors. The **Tolerance** for this tool can be increased; this will let the tool select the color you clicked as well as similar colors. To do this click the *tool control palette* button on the **Tool Bar**. You can also change which method of approximation it uses (**Match Mode**) and how much larger the selection area will be than the actual matching pixels (**Feather**).

The tool control palette is important to learn, because it has many useful options that are not turned on by default. Check each tool and see what options it presents. For example, the *brush* and *airbrush* tools, which apply color to the image in simulated brush strokes, can have their **Brush Tip**s modified in many ways in the tool control palette.

The *flood fill tool* uses the same method as the magic wand, but it colors all the pixels in range instead of selecting them. In the control palette, it also offers an interesting feature called *gradient*, which fills an area with a gradual progression from the foreground color to the background color. We present an example using gradients later in the chapter.

With these tools, you can create a navigation bar for your site. Create a new image that is 625 pixels wide and 75 pixels high, with a white background and 24-bit color depth. This will span most of the browser window.

Testing and Debugging Tip 5.1

Keep in mind that most of your viewers will be using an 800 x 600 screen resolution. Two other common resolutions are 640 x 480 and 1024 x 768. Check your page in each of these resolutions to ensure that it displays as you intended.

Click the *shapes tool* on the **Tool Bar**, and check the tool control palette to make sure that it is set to a **Filled Rectangle**. Use the same foreground color as we did in the title image, and create a rectangle that fills a little less than 1/4 of the image width as shown in Fig. 5.12. Now use the magic wand tool to select the rectangle you created.

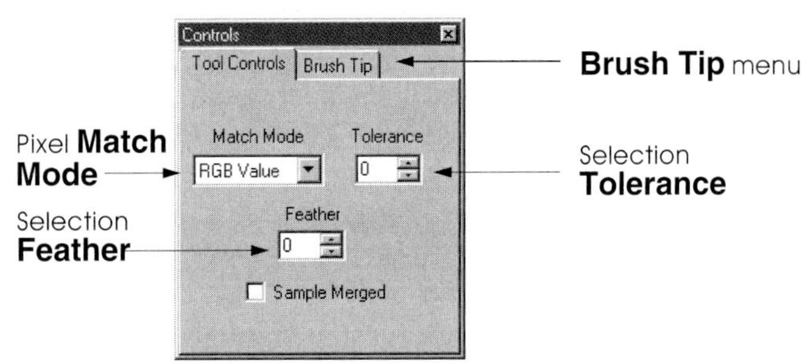

Fig. 5.11 **Controls** for the Magic wand tool.

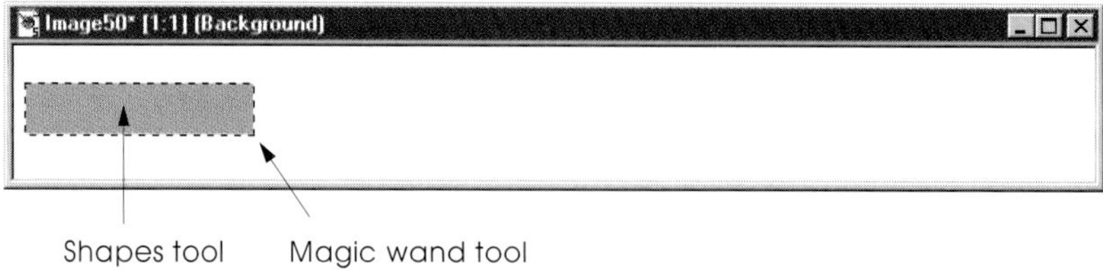

Fig. 5.12 Creating a rectangle and selecting it.

To duplicate this rectangle (once for each section that the navigation bar will link to), click the **Copy** button on the toolbar. This copies your selection to the clipboard. Now select **As New Selection** from the **Paste** submenu of the **Edit** menu, or press *CTRL+E* (*Ctrl* and *E* simultaneously). This will paste an active selection into the image. Move your cursor and click to place the image. Place it to the right of the first rectangle, as shown in Fig. 5.13. Repeat the **Paste** twice more, for a total of four rectangles spanning the length of the image.

If you think that you placed the rectangles unevenly, use the **Undo** command in the **Edit** menu. Paint Shop Pro keeps a history of your actions, so you can **Undo** your commands all the way back to the beginning of your session.

Once the placement is correct, draw a line connecting the rectangles. Click the line tool in the tool palette and change the line width to 5 in the control palette. Make sure that **Anti-alias** is turned off. Draw the line as shown by dragging the mouse across the image window. Releasing the mouse places the line, setting it to the active foreground color.

We want to apply some effects to the navigation bar, so select the whole bar by clicking with the magic wand tool anywhere in the foreground area. Any tools we now apply will affect only the selected area.

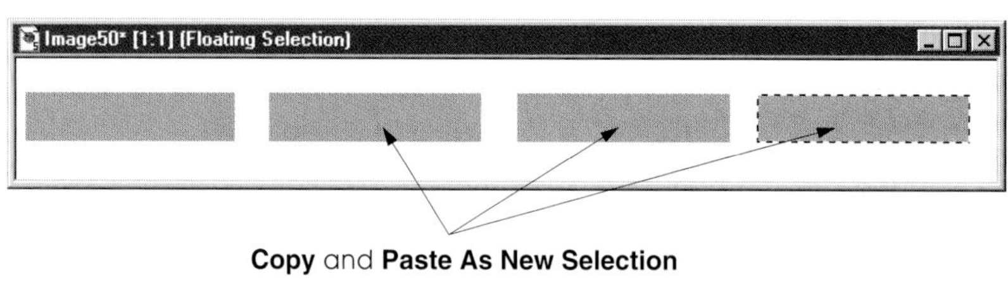

Fig. 5.13 Copying the rectangle 3 times.

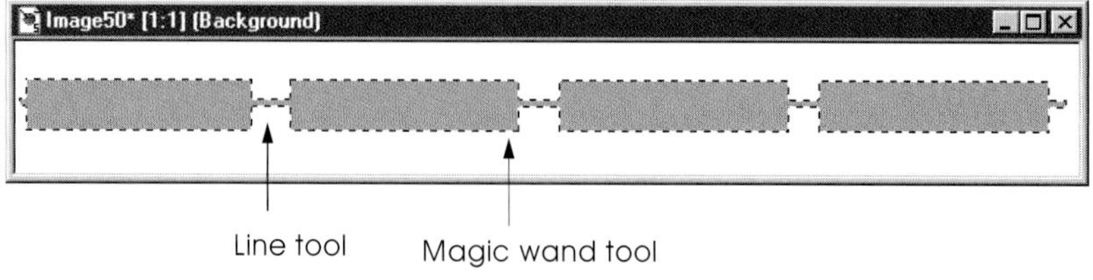

Fig. 5.14 Step 3: Connecting the rectangles with a line and selecting them.

Now select the *airbrush* tool. This tool simulates brush strokes on a canvas and can be customized in the control palette. You can change its brush **Size**, **Shape**, and **Hardness**. Another interesting option, located in the **Tool Controls** tab, is the ability to add a simulated **Texture** to your brush strokes. When this is applied, the brush stroke will be applied only in the pattern of the selected texture. Select the **Lava** texture, and set the brush size to around 20. Now select a light yellow color for the foreground. Move your cursor to the center of a rectangle, and click once. Holding down the mouse button too long will create too strong an effect. We want a subtle effect, as shown in Fig. 5.15. Repeat this procedure for the other three rectangles.

Now apply the same drop shadow that we used for the title image, to give your Web site a consistent look. Start the **Drop Shadow** filter as before. It should have the same settings as we applied to the title image drop shadow. Once you apply the drop shadow you can add the text. Use the color of the drop shadow for the text.

Look-and-Feel Observation 5.2

Too many colors will make your site look confusing and erratic. Pick three or four main colors, and use these as the prominent colors in your images and text. This will be easier for you to do with Cascading Style Sheets, discussed later in the book.

Do this by using the *dropper* tool. The dropper tool changes either the foreground color or the background color to any color present in the image. Simply move the dropper cursor over a color that you want, and click. Left-clicking will change the foreground to this color, right-clicking will change the background to this color.

Use the dropper to select the blue color of the drop shadow and enter text. If the text you added was too large, just press *Delete* and enter the text again with a smaller size. Do this until you find an appropriate size, and use that size text for all four text titles.

The rest is straightforward. Label each rectangle with the name of a section on your site. You could add some variations, such as altering the color of the text for each section label.

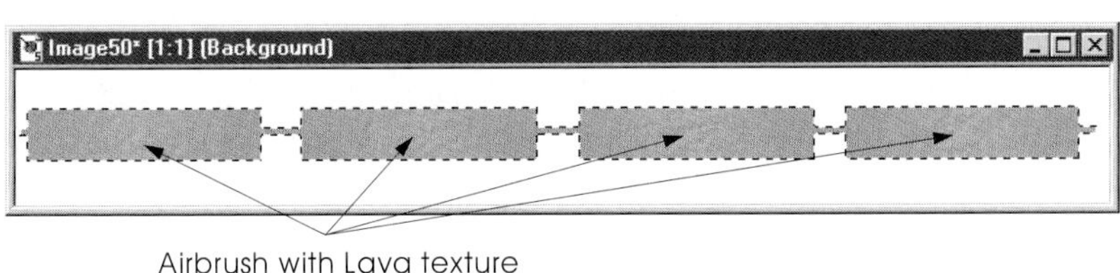

Fig. 5.15 Lightly airbrushing the rectangles with a texture.

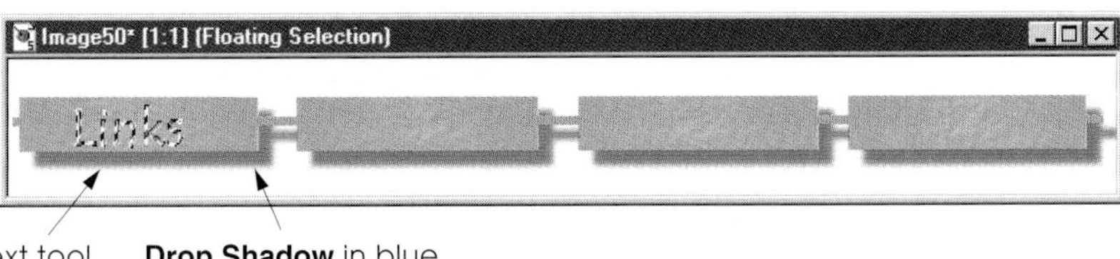

Fig. 5.16 Adding a **Drop Shadow** and text of the same color.

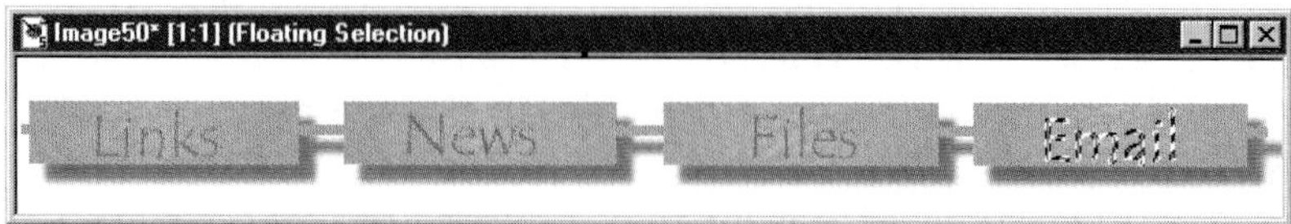

Fig. 5.17 A completed navigation bar.

Now that the image bar is completed, you need to make it an image map to function properly; we discussed how to do this in Chapter 3.

5.5 Screen Capturing

Paint Shop Pro does screen capturing as well as most programs written specifically for that purpose, and it adds the convenience of being able to edit the capture after it has been taken. To set up a capture select **Setup...** from the **Capture** menu (Fig. 5.18).

First, you will need to choose the type of area that you want to capture when you trigger the capture. **Area** gives you a cursor. Click once to start a rectangle, then move your mouse and click again to place the opposite corner of the rectangle. As you move the cursor, the borders of the resulting rectangle will move with it. The **Full screen** option will capture the whole screen. **Client area** will capture the input area of the active window (for example, the white area for text editing in Notepad). Making a screen capture with **Window** selected will capture the whole active window (for example, the whole Notepad window, including title bar and menus). The last option, **Object**, captures a specific object on the screen when you trigger the capture (we will show you how to do this shortly). Move the mouse cursor over objects like toolbars, pulldown menus, etc. A grey outline will surround the object; clicking with the mouse will capture this outlined area.

The next set of options lets you set the method you use to trigger the screen capture. The default method is to use a right-click, but the method can also be set to either a specific keystroke or a time-delay capture. You can specify whether or not you wish to include the cursor in your capture, and you can also specify that you would like to take multiple captures without switching back to Paint Shop Pro after each capture.

Once you have the settings you want, click **OK**. Select **Start...** in the **Capture** menu, or press *Shift* + *C*. This minimizes the Paint Shop Pro window. Switch to the program from which you want to take a screen capture and use whatever trigger you have set. Paint Shop Pro comes to the foreground with your screen capture in a new image ready to be edited or saved.

5.6 Layers

One of the most powerful features of Paint Shop Pro is the ability to edit images in *layers*. Any image can be composed of many layers, each having its own attributes and its own effects on other layers. Layers also make composing more complex images easier, because each element of an image can be moved easily if kept in its own layer. For example, if you were making a landscape, you might have one layer containing just the background scenery, one layer with trees, one layer with rocks, one layer with people in the foreground, and so on. The following example illustrates a simple use of layers in making a image for an Web page.

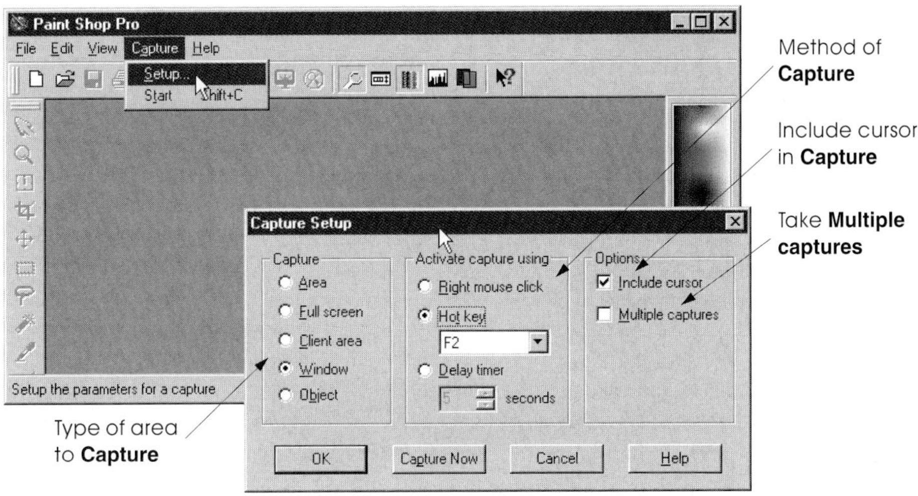

Fig. 5.18 Starting a screen capture.

Open the **`deitel.gif`** file from Figure 3.8. It is a 256-color **`.gif`** file, but layers are available only for 24-bit or greyscale images. Convert it to 24-bit format with the **Color** menu's **Increase Color Depth** option. Click the layer control palette button on the **Tool Bar**. This opens a window that allows you to control the separate layers in your image.

Each layer occupies one row in the window. A row displays that layer's name, its position relative to other layers and several properties that modify the function of the layer. At the bottom-left corner of the window is a button to add new layers.

Start by adding a new layer to the image. When layers are first added, they are transparent by default. You can tell which layer is selected by looking at the layer control palette. The name of the active layer is displayed in the title bar of the image to the right of the zoom factor. Fill your image with white using the flood fill tool. Now select the air brush and use black as your foreground color. Brush until your picture appears similar to the one in Fig. 5.20. The effect on the edges is achieved by lowering the brush **Density** in the tool control palette. Use white as your background color, so that if you make a mistake you can simply use the right mouse button to correct the error.

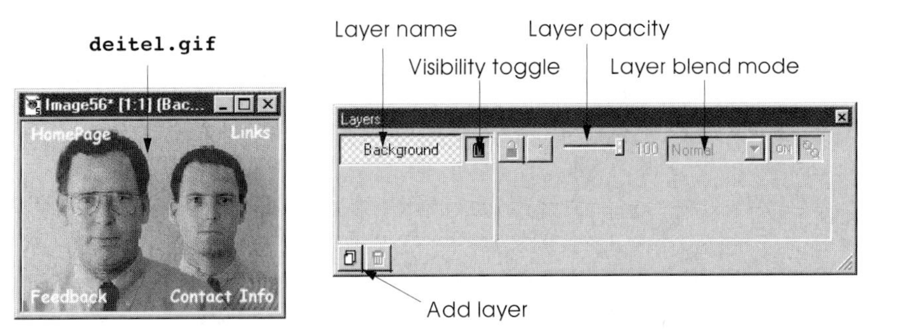

Fig. 5.19 Converting to 24-bit color depth and viewing the layer control palette.

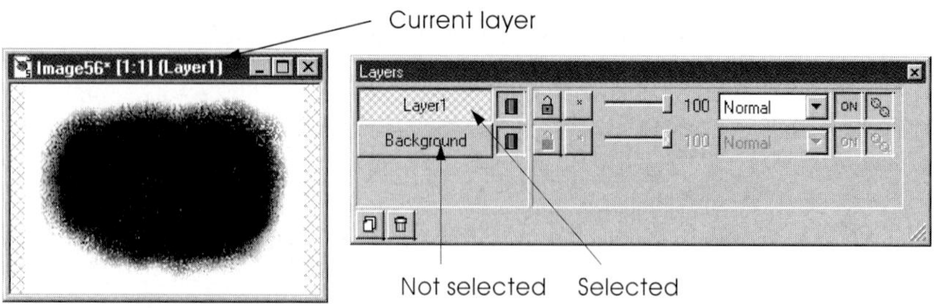

Fig. 5.20 Adding a new layer and airbrushing.

To check whether the correct area is covered, change the layer blend mode of **Layer1** from **Normal** to **Lighten**. The previously black area will become transparent, so that you can see the background, while the white remains as is. Try to cover only the area around the faces. When you are satisfied with the area of coverage, switch the layer blend mode back to **Normal**. Now click in the white area of the image with the magic wand tool. Our goal is to select all the non-white pixels in the image. Select **Invert** in the **Selections** menu. This action changes your current selection to everything that was not previously selected. We can now apply a filter—in this case, the **Cutout** filter. It is found in the **Effects** submenu of the **Image** menu.

The **Cutout** filter is similar to the **Drop shadow**. Instead of casting a shadow on the area surrounding the selection, the cutout filter casts a shadow on the selection, which appears to emanate from the surrounding area. Use the options shown in Fig. 5.21 to achieve the desired effect.

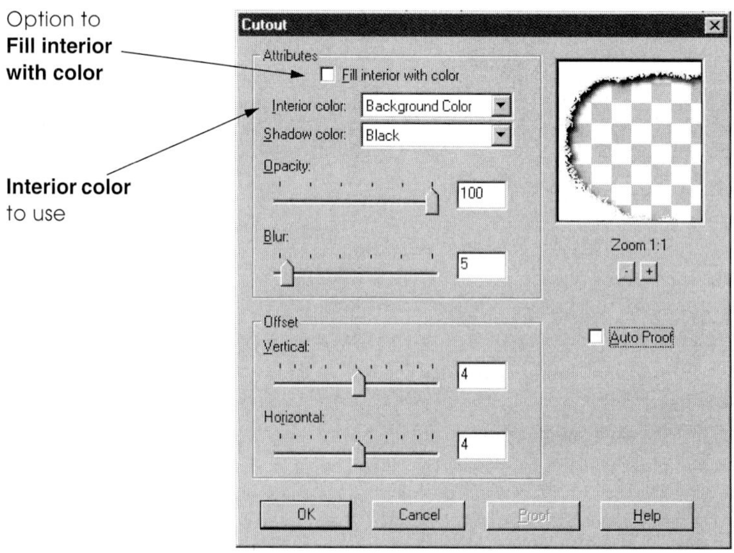

Fig. 5.21 Setting options for the **Cutout** effect.

The resulting image is shown in Fig 5.22. It can now be saved as a `.gif` file; such a file does not contain layer information, so the layers will be merged. It would also be a good idea to set white as a transparent color for this image.

Layering is a powerful technique. As another example, instead of using the **Cutout** filter on **Layer1** as we did in the last example, change the layer blend mode to **Lighten**. Now add another layer on top of the first two. Select a light red color for your foreground and a light green color for your background. Use the flood fill tool with **Radial Gradient** selected in the tool control palette. Change **Layer2**'s blend mode to **Difference** (near the bottom of the pull-down list). This makes the image look like a photographic negative, with an eerie tint contributed by the **Radial Gradient**.

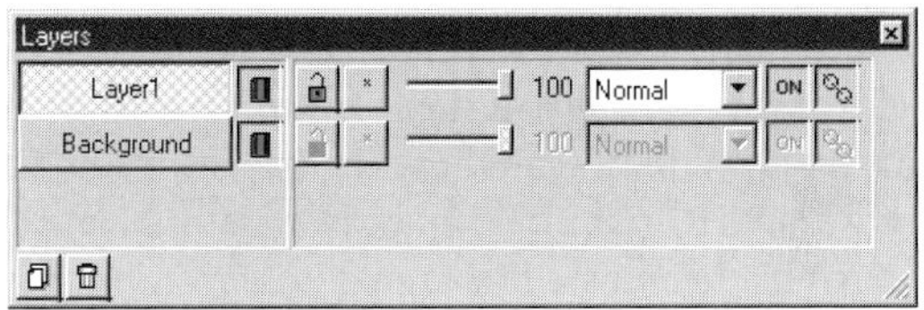

Fig. 5.22 Using layers to achieve a cutout effect.

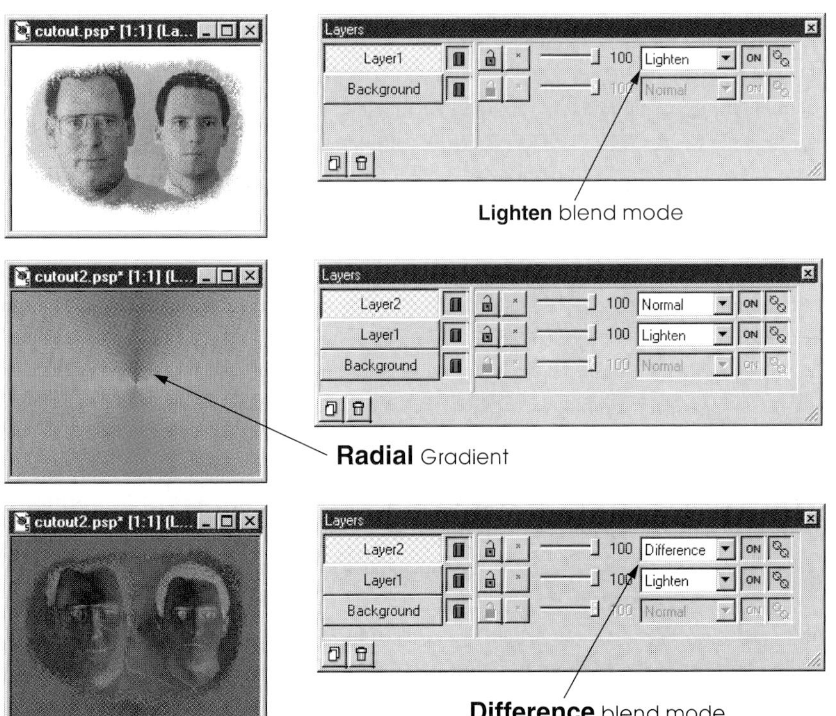

Fig. 5.23 Using layers for a negative image effect.

The effects shown in this chapter are just a small sample of Paint Shop Pro's capabilities. We saw only two image effects (filters) out of nearly forty that are included. The best way to learn is to practice using all the tools and effects included with Paint Shop Pro. If you are not sure how something works, press the *F1* key (i.e., the help key) for assistance.

5.7 Internet and World Wide Web Resources

Many resources are available on using Paint Shop Pro to create stunning new images for your Web page. To start, check out **http://www.jasc.com** (Jasc Inc.'s home page) to stay up to date on patches and general information about Paint Shop Pro. The majority of information on the Web, however, is available at user-run sites offering information and tutorials. For example, **http://psptips.com/5/** (Abstract Dimensions) has excellent in-depth tutorials, both for Paint Shop Pro beginners and for experts who want to learn new techniques. Another excellent site for tutorials, Paint Shop Pro Tips & Tricks, is located at **http://www.mardiweb.com/web/psp5/psp5.htm**. If you are looking for more diverse effects than those included in Paint Shop Pro, you can download new filters. PlugIn Com HQ (**http://pico.i-us.com**) is a storehouse of filters and effects, free for download and use. If you plan to develop images, make sure to look at the W3C site about the PNG image format, located at **http://www.w3.org/Graphics/PNG/**

SUMMARY

- Jasc Inc.'s Paint Shop Pro (included on the CD with this book) is an easy-to-use, inexpensive graphics package that offers the functionality of more expensive packages.
- Click **New...** in the **File** menu to create a new image. You can select the **Height** and **Width** and the standard they are measured in. You can specify the **Background color** and the color depth.
- Color depth is the maximum number of simultaneous colors in the image.
- In both 8-bit color depths (**Greyscale** and **256 Color**), there are 256 set colors that make up the palette. Each pixel takes 8 bits to refer to any one of the palette entries.
- In the highest quality, 24 bits are used for every pixel—8 bits for each of the primary colors in light—red, green and blue. This combination produces 16.7 million colors, a spectrum comparable to that of human vision.
- The status bar on the bottom of the Paint Shop Pro window gives information about any significant object over which you move your cursor.
- There are always two active colors: the foreground color and the background color.
- Clicking on the foreground color box displays the color wheel, where you can type in an RGB value, or move around the two selectors to find the precise color you want.
- The outer selector in the color wheel determines the **Hue** (color), while the inner selector determines both **Lightness** (the amount of black vs. the amount of white) and **Saturation** (the amount of color vs. the amount of **Lightness**).
- The dialog box that appears once you click with the text tool allows you to fine-tune the properties of the text you are going to place in the image.
- Antialiasing is a process that smooths edges on scalable fonts by blending the color of the edge pixels with the color of the background on which the text is being placed. Without it, fonts can look jagged, an unattractive and distracting effect.
- Antialiasing can be used only in 24-bit and greyscale images.
- A dashed line indicates a selection.

- You can adjust both the **Horizontal** and the **Vertical** offsets of the **Drop Shadow** effect by using the corresponding sliders in the **Offset** section. The **Color**, **Opacity** and **Blur** of the shadow are also adjustable.
- Most people will be viewing your Web page with their systems set to 8-bit color depth, able to see only 256 colors at a time. Using too many colors will create grainy images, as the viewer's browser dithers the image's colors to the 256 available to the system.
- The **Nearest Color** reduction method converts colors missing from the palette to a nearest match.
- Transparency is a process which designates one of the colors in the palette as instead showing any background color or picture behind it.
- A checkered background is Paint Shop Pro's way of showing you what is actually a transparent background and not simply white.
- When you develop images for a certain background color, you will usually need either to stick to that color or to develop new images if you want to switch.
- The two major file formats used for pictures on the Web are GIF and JPEG.
- The Graphics Interchange Format (GIF), developed by CompuServe, is based on a palette of only 256 colors. It is best used in screenshots, line drawings and other situations with sharp edges. It is well suited to the Web because it has transparency.
- A GIF file is typically larger than a JPEG file.
- When reducing to 256 colors, Paint Shop Pro will perform dithering on the image, using colors already in the palette to simulate the desired color.
- If you use the JPEG format, make sure to know its limitations. Its compression algorithms handle sharp edges and abrupt changes poorly. Also, JPEG is a lossy format.
- One feature that GIF and JPEG share is known as interlacing (in GIF) or progressive encoding (in JPEG). This is a technique that first downloads a rough whole image and then gradually increases its clarity, instead of downloading from the top and moving down as is done normally. This option can often keep a user's attention focused while a large page loads.
- The Portable Network Graphics (PNG, pronounced ping) format was developed in response to a decision by the UniSys corporation to start charging royalties on the GIF format, for which it holds a patent. PNG is a suitable replacement for both GIF and JPEG.
- Alpha transparency makes images transparent against any background.
- The **Tool Palette** keeps the tools grouped on a single toolbar that appears on the left side of the editing area. It can be dragged to other locations and docked on other sides.
- With the zoom tool selected, left-click inside the image to zoom in, and right-click inside the image to zoom back out. The zoom factor is displayed on the title bar of the image, next to the image name. You can zoom in, up to a 16:1 display-to-size ratio, and out, to 1:16.
- Dragging inside the image with the selection tool selects a rectangular region whose borders are shown with a dashed line. Any filters, effects or tools applied take effect only in the selection area.
- The selection area can be moved by dragging with the mouse; the area the selection occupied before it was moved is filled in with the background color.
- Click inside the image with the magic wand tool to select all adjacent pixels of the same colors. The **Tolerance** for this tool can be increased, to select colors similar to the one you clicked. To use this option, click the tool control palette button on the **Tool bar**. You can change the method of approximation that it uses (**Match Mode**) and how much larger the selection area will be than the actual matching pixels (**Feather**).
- The tool control palette is important, because it has many useful options that, by default, are not turned on. Check it with each tool and see what options it presents.

- The flood fill tool uses the same method as the magic wand, but it colors all the pixels in range instead of selecting them.
- **As New Selection** in the **Paste** submenu of the **Edit** menu pastes an active selection into the image. Move your cursor and click to place the image.
- Paint Shop Pro keeps a history of your actions, so that you can **Undo** your commands all the way back to the beginning of your session.
- Draw a line by clicking with the line tool selected and dragging across the image window.
- The airbrush tool simulates brush strokes on a canvas, and can be greatly customized in the control palette. You can change its brush **Size**, **Shape**, and **Hardness**. Another interesting option, located in the **Tool Controls** tab, is the ability to add a simulated **Texture** to your brush strokes.
- The dropper tool changes either the foreground color or the background color to any color present in the image. Move the dropper cursor over a color you want, and click. Left-clicking will change the foreground to this color and right-clicking will change the background to this color.
- To set up a screen capture, select **Setup...** from the **Capture** menu. You can choose the type of area that you want to capture when you trigger the capture. **Area** will give you a cursor. Click once to start a rectangle and then move your mouse and click again to place the opposite corner of the rectangle. As you move the cursor, the borders of the resulting rectangle will move with it. The **Full screen** option will capture the whole screen. **Client area** will capture the input area of the active window. **Window** will capture the whole active window. **Object** captures a specific object on the screen when you trigger the capture
- The next set of options lets you set the method you use to trigger the screen capture. The default is to use a right-click, but it can also be set to either a specific keystroke or a time-delay capture.
- You can specify whether you wish to include the cursor in a capture and that you would like to take multiple captures without switching back to Paint Shop Pro after each capture.
- Select **Start...** in the **Capture** menu to start your screen capture. This action will minimize the Paint Shop Pro window. Switch to the program in which you want to take a screen capture, and use whatever trigger you have set. Paint Shop Pro comes to the foreground with your capture in a new image ready to be edited or saved.
- Images can be comprised of many layers, each having its own attributes and effects on other layers.
- Layers make composing complex images easier, as each element of an image can be moved around easily if kept in its own layer.
- Each layer occupies one row in the layer control palette. A row displays that layer's name, its position relative to other layers and several properties that modify the function of the layer. At the bottom-left corner of the window is a button to add new layers.
- The name of the active layer is displayed in the title bar of the image right of the zoom factor.
- **Invert** in the **Selections** menu changes the current selection to everything not already selected.
- The **Cutout** filter is similar to the **Drop shadow**, but, instead of casting a shadow on the area surrounding the selection, the cutout filter casts a shadow on the selection, which appears to emanate from the surrounding area.
- The best way to learn is to practice using all the tools and effects included with Paint Shop Pro. If you are not sure about how something works, press *F1* for assistance.

TERMINOLOGY

Add Text dialog
airbrush tool
alpha transparency
Antialias checkbox
antialiasing
Background color in **New Image** dialog

Blur of shadow
brush tip
brush tool
Capture menu
Centimeters in **New Image** dialog
color depth
Color dialog
Color of shadow
color wheel
compression
Cutout filter
Decrease Color Depth in **Colors** menu
Difference layer blend mode
dithering
dropper tool
Drop Shadow... effect
Effects submenu of **Image** menu
8-bit color depth
Feather
filters
flood fill tool
foreground color
GIF (Graphics Interchange Format)
gradient
greyscale image
Hardness of a brush
hue
image layering
Image menu
Inches in **New Image** dialog
Increase Color Depth in **Colors** menu
interlacing
Invert in **Selections** menu
JPEG
Lava texture of a brush stroke
layer
layer control palette button on **Tool Bar**
Lighten layer blend mode
lightness
line tool
lossless format
magic wand tool
Match Mode
navigation bar
negative image effect
New Image dialog box
Normal layer blend mode
Opacity of shadow
Paint Shop Pro
palette
Pixels in **New Image** dialog
PNG (Portable Network Graphics) format
progressive encoding
Proof button
Radial Gradient
Reduction method
RGB value
saturation
scalable compression in JPEG
screen capturing
selection tool
Set Palette Transparency in **Colors** menu
Setup... in **Capture** menu
Shape of a brush
shapes tool
Size of a brush
text **Alignment**
text tool
Texture of a brush stroke
Tool Bar
Tool control palette button on **Tool Bar**
Tool Controls tab
Tool Palette
Tolerance
transparent
24-bit color depth
zoom factor
zoom tool

LOOK-AND-FEEL OBSERVATIONS

5.1 Because the drop shadow effect is so easy to achieve and looks so nice, it has become the most widely used image effect on the Web. If you are striving for originality in your pages, you might want to vary the settings or to explore other effects that Paint Shop Pro has to offer.

5.2 Too many colors will make your site look confusing and erratic. Pick three or four main colors, and use these as the prominent colors in your images and text. This will be easier for you to do with Cascading Style Sheets, discussed later in the book.

PERFORMANCE TIPS

5.1 A GIF file is typically larger than a JPEG file. If server space is a problem and your image has many more than 256 colors, it is a better idea to use the JPEG format

5.2 Do not place too many interlaced images on any one Web page—doing so can slow the rendering of the page.

5.3 The JPEG format has scalable compression. When saving a JPEG image, in the **Save Options** dialog, sliding the **Compression** slider to the left causes the image to retain high quality, but the file size also remains high. Sliding the **Compression** slider to the right causes the file size to decrease, but image quality suffers. This graduated scale helps you find a good balance between the file size and image quality.

TESTING AND DEBUGGING TIP

5.1 Keep in mind that most of your viewers will be using an 800 x 600 screen resolution. Two other common resolutions are 640 x 480 and 1024 x 768. Check your page in each of these resolutions to ensure that it displays as you intended.

SELF-REVIEW EXERCISES

5.1 Identify either GIF or JPEG as the optimal format for the following situations:
a) Line drawings
b) Photographs
c) Computer art
d) Transparent logos
e) Scanned images

5.2 State whether the following are true or false. If the answer is "false," explain why.
a) There are 16.7 million colors in a greyscale image.
b) Alpha transparency solves the current problems with antialiasing.
c) The GIF format supports layers.
d) Both GIF and JPEG support transparency.
e) 8-bit color depth yields 16 simultaneous colors.
f) There are two active colors at any time in Paint Shop Pro.
g) Decimal RGB values yield a greater range of colors than do hex RGB values.
h) Antialiasing prevents blurred edges on scalable text.
i) Saturation is a measure of hue vs. lightness.

ANSWERS TO SELF-REVIEW EXERCISES

5.1 a) GIF. b) JPEG. c) JPEG. d) GIF. e) JPEG.

5.2 a) False. There are 256 colors in a greyscale image.
b) True.
c) False. If you want to use layers on a GIF, you must first convert it to 24-bit color depth or greyscale.
d) False. Only GIF supports transparency.
e) False. 8-bit color depth yields 256 colors (2^8=256).
f) True.
g) False. Decimal and hex are different notations that specify the same range of colors.
h) False. Antialiasing prevents jagged edges, not blurred edges.
i) True.

EXERCISES

5.3 Create a new title image that reads "Welcome to my Web page". Apply the **Hot Wax Coating** effect (located in the **Other** submenu of the **Image** menu). Note: use white as a foreground color when you apply this effect.

5.4 Apply the airbrush tool with a texture to some selected text. Now invert the selection area and airbrush a different texture (in a different color) to the surrounding area. Apply a **Hot Wax Coating** again.

5.5 Place some large (72-point) black text on an image. Select **Expand...** in the **Modify** submenu of the **Selections** menu, and use 3 as your value. Now select **Blur More** in the **Blur** submenu of the **Image** menu. This blurs the text while keeping it selected. Now select a very light color, and airbrush the text using the **Marble** texture. Now emboss your text (**Emboss** in the **Other** submenu of the **Image** menu) and make it greyscale (**Grey Scale** in the **Colors** menu). This is an effective way of creating textured, 3D text. The depth of the texture on the lettering depends on the brightness of the color you choose.

5.6 Use the **Blur More** effect (in the **Blur** submenu of the **Image** menu) to add a drop shadow to text without using the built-in **Drop Shadow...** effect.

6

Microsoft FrontPage Express

Objectives

- To be able to use FrontPage Express effectively.
- To become familiar with developing Web pages in a visual environment.
- To understand how to insert images and links into Web pages.
- To use FrontPage to create advanced HTML elements such as tables and forms.
- To understand how to use the **MARQUEE** element to create dynamically scrolling text.
- To understand how to insert scripts into pages.

The test of greatness is the page of history.
William Hazlitt

The one in front has reached there, the one behind only hears about it.
West African saying

We must select the illusion which appeals to our temperament, and embrace it with passion, if we want to be happy.
Cyril Connolly

The symbolic view of things is a consequence of long absorption in images. Is sign language the real language of Paradise?
Hugo Ball

What you see is what you get (WYSIWYG).
Anonymous

All human knowledge takes the form of interpretation.
Walter Benjamin

Outline

6.1 Introduction

Now that you have a working knowledge of HTML, you are ready to start making your own Web pages. Successful Web pages are often huge undertakings. They need constant attention, maintenance and updating. They can also attract more attention if they are visually appealing. Many tools have appeared on the market to help the aspiring Web developer.

Many companies have written Web design software for nonprogrammers, making it easier for a wider range of people to establish a presence on the World Wide Web. This software is also useful for programmers. However, if you plan to build complex Web sites, then these graphics-based editing programs should only serve as aids. They often disrupt indentation and insert unnecessary tags, making it difficult to code manually when necessary. They are no substitute for in-depth knowledge of HTML, but are quite useful for speeding up tasks such as coding large tables.

In this chapter we discuss the features of Microsoft *FrontPage Express,* which is on the CD that accompanies this book. Perhaps the most popular of the graphics-based HTML editors, FrontPage Express is a versatile tool with a familiar interface similar to that of Microsoft Word. The short amount of time it takes to learn FrontPage Express is well worth the amount of effort it saves. FrontPage Express can more easily perform many of the tasks already discussed in previous chapters. It can insert text and font changes, and it can also create more complex HTML, such as for creating tables, forms, frames and much more.

6.2 Microsoft FrontPage Express

Upon starting FrontPage Express, you are welcomed with a blank page in the default viewing mode. This is a *WYSIWYG* (What You See Is What You Get) display. Unlike editors that simply display HTML code, FrontPage Express renders HTML elements exactly as a browser would. This is intended to give you more insight into how people will see your page on the Web, and saves you the often substantial amount of time that can be spent switching between browser and editor when writing HTML directly, tweaking code to make sure your page was displayed correctly.

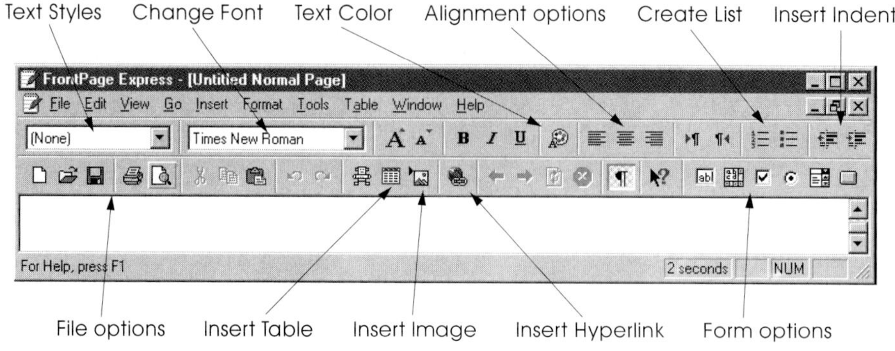

Fig. 6.1 A FrontPage Express window.

We can now easily recreate the example in Fig. 3.1 using FrontPage Express. Type in

```
Welcome to our Web Site!
```

in the text window. FrontPage express will automatically enclose this in a **P** element for proper formatting. Now to insert a title as we did in Fig. 3.1, right-click (click the second button on a two-button mouse) in the text area, and select ***Page Properties...*** from the pop-up menu. This causes the **Page Properties** dialog of Fig. 6.2 to appear.

Type in the title as shown and click **OK**. This inserts a **<TITLE>** tag inside the **<HEAD>**...**</HEAD>** element in your HTML code. Your page now appears exactly as it is in Fig. 3.1, shown here in FrontPage Express's WYSIWYG display instead of the browser window.

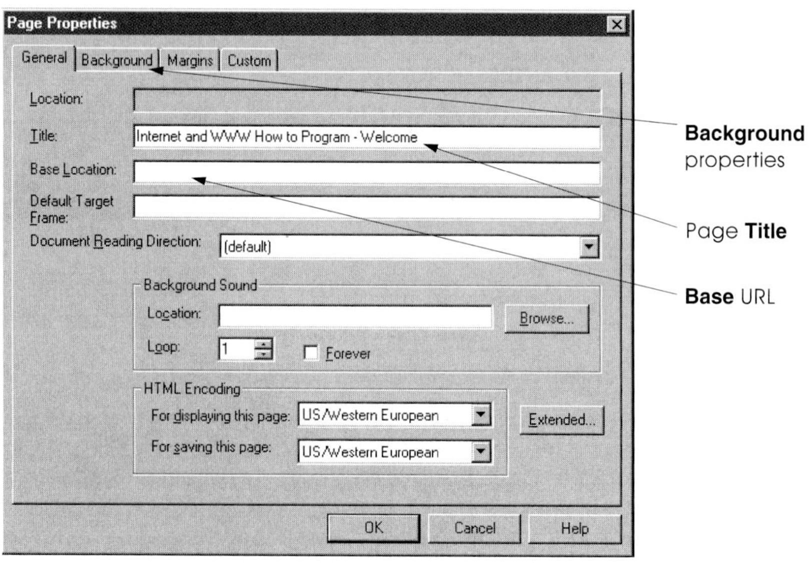

Fig. 6.2 Setting overall **Page Properties**.

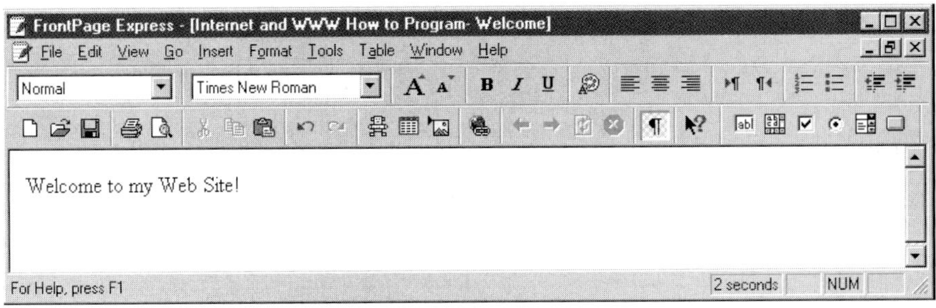

Fig. 6.3 Using FrontPage Express on example of Fig. 3.1.

Now that you have seen a basic example of WYSIWYG editing, remember that you are still programming in HTML. To view or edit your HTML directly select the ***HTML...*** option in the ***View*** menu. FrontPage automatically color codes your HTML to make viewing easier. The tag names, tag attributes, attribute values and page text are all displayed in different colors. This feature can be turned off by clicking off the checkbox titled ***Show Color Coding*** at the bottom of the dialog box.

There is also an option to switch between your **Current** code and your **Original** code. If you have modified your code since your last save, this is a useful option for reviewing any changes or updates you have made.

To save your file, click ***Save*** in the ***File*** menu. FrontPage Express will first give you a dialog box with the **`TITLE`** of your page and the address of a Web server on which to save the file. This will only work if your server has FrontPage Extensions installed. If it does not, simply click the ***As File...*** button in the dialog box and you can browse your hard drive for a location to save the file.

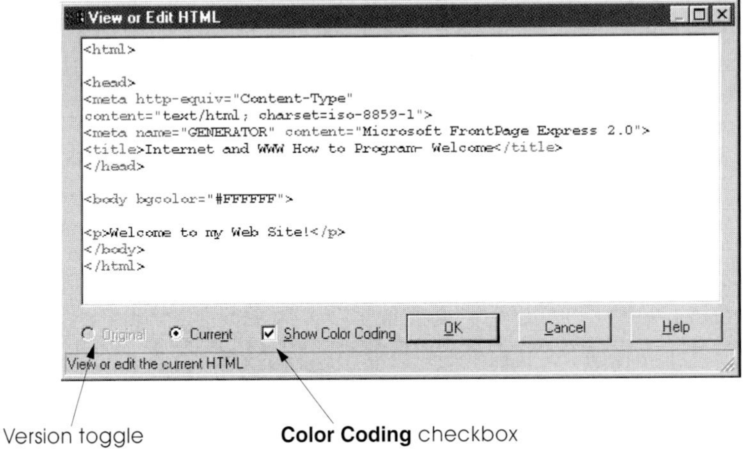

Fig. 6.4 Viewing the HTML source code.

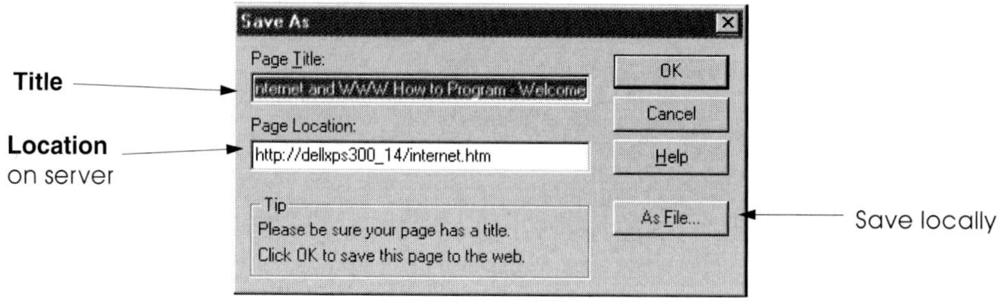

Fig. 6.5 Saving your HTML file.

6.3 Text Styles

FrontPage's screen appearance is like Microsoft Word's. There is a drop-down menu for changing text styles. Using this menu, you can quickly apply header tags (**<H1>**, **<H2>**, etc.), list tags (**<OL>**, **<UL>**), and several other tags used for stylizing text. Text can also be aligned left, right or centered using buttons on the top toolbar. Text can be increased or decreased in size indented and colored.

Type the screen text as shown in Fig. 6.6 into the window. Drag the mouse to highlight one line at a time and use the ***Change Style*** pull-down menu to apply the appropriate header tags. Now highlight all of the text, and click the align center button on the toolbar. Alignment options and text styles are also accessible through the **Paragraph...** option in the ***Format*** menu. The resulting HTML produced by FrontPage Express is shown in Fig. 6.6 (line 6 is split because it is too wide to fit on the page).

```
1   <html>
2   <head>
3
4   <meta http-equiv="Content-Type"
5   content="text/html; charset=iso-8859-1">
6   <meta name="GENERATOR" content="Microsoft FrontPage Express 2.0">
7   <title>Untitled Normal Page</title>
8   </head>
9
10  <body bgcolor="#FFFFFF">
11
12  <h1 align="center">Level 1 Header</h1>
13
14  <h2 align="center">Level 2 Header</h2>
15
16  <h3 align="center">Level 3 Header</h3>
17
18  <h4 align="center">Level 4 Header</h4>
19
20  <h5 align="center">Level 5 Header</h5>
21
22  <h6 align="center">Level 6 Header</h6>
23  </body>
24  </html>
```

Fig. 6.6 Applying header tags and centering using FrontPage Express (part 1 of 2).

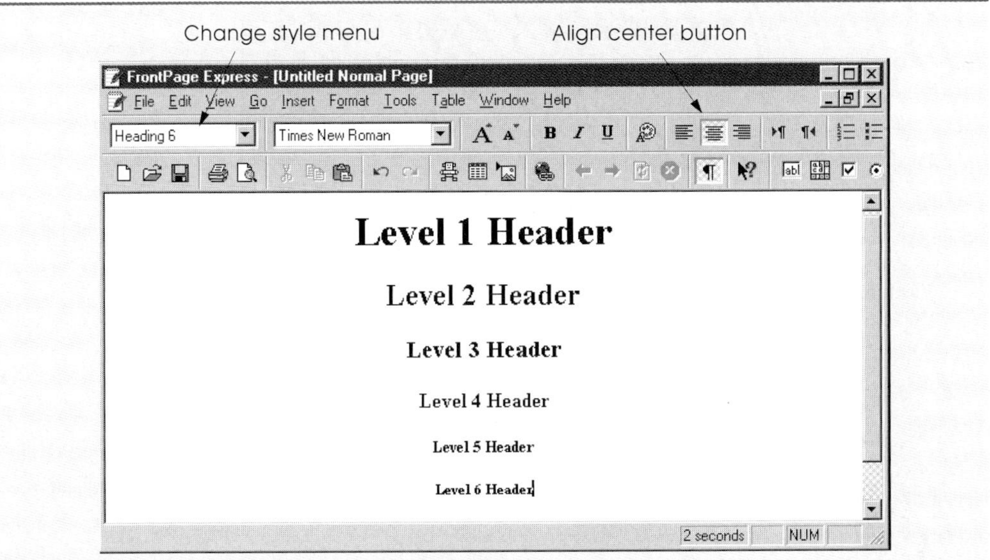

Fig. 6.6 Applying header tags and centering using FrontPage Express (part 2 of 2).

As you can see, FrontPage Express is prone to producing inefficient code. In this case, enclosing all the headers in a **CENTER** element would save both time and file space.

Software Engineering Observation 6.1

FrontPage Express uses a wide variety of techniques to manipulate the text, and often produces inefficient code. Make sure to check often to know exactly the kind of HTML code FrontPage Express is producing for you. Thorough knowledge of your page and what HTML elements are present will be necessary in later chapters.

FrontPage Express is capable of much more extensive text formatting. Perhaps you needed to place a mathematical formula on your Web page. For example, type

```
E=mc2
```

in the window, then highlight the text. You can now change the formatting of the equation by opening the ***Font...*** dialog box in the **Format** menu, and switching to the **Special Styles** tab. Click on the ***Code*** checkbox and return to the text by clicking **OK**. This applies a **CODE** element to the highlighted text, which designates formulas or computer code. Select the "2" in our formula and return to the **Special Styles** tab. Change the text to superscript as indicated in Fig. 6.7.

You can also access the **Font** dialog box by right-clicking highlighted text, and selecting ***Font Properties...*** from the pop-up menu that appears. The formula can be further emphasized by highlighting the text and using the ***Text Color*** button on the upper toolbar to make it stand out from surrounding text.

Good Programming Practice 6.1

When you press Enter *after typing text, FrontPage Express will enclose that text in a new set of* **<P>**...**</P>** *tags. If you want to insert only a* **
** *tag into your page hold down* Shift *while you press* Enter.

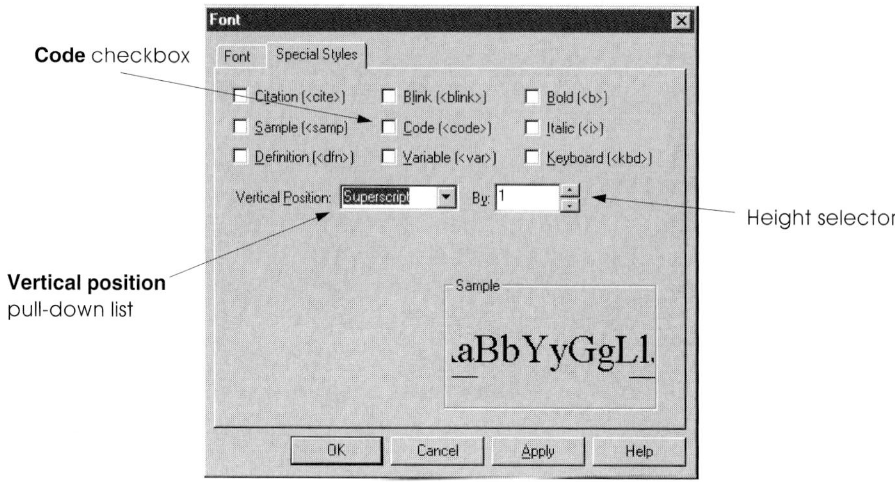

Fig. 6.7 Changing **Font** settings and adding special styles.

Good Programming Practice 6.2

You can manipulate the properties of almost any element displayed in the FrontPage Express window by right-clicking that element and selecting that element's properties from the window that pops up.

The **Change Style** pull-down menu (which we used previously in Fig. 6.6) is also useful for creating lists. Try entering the contents of a shopping list as shown Fig. 6.8, and applying the **Bulleted List** style.

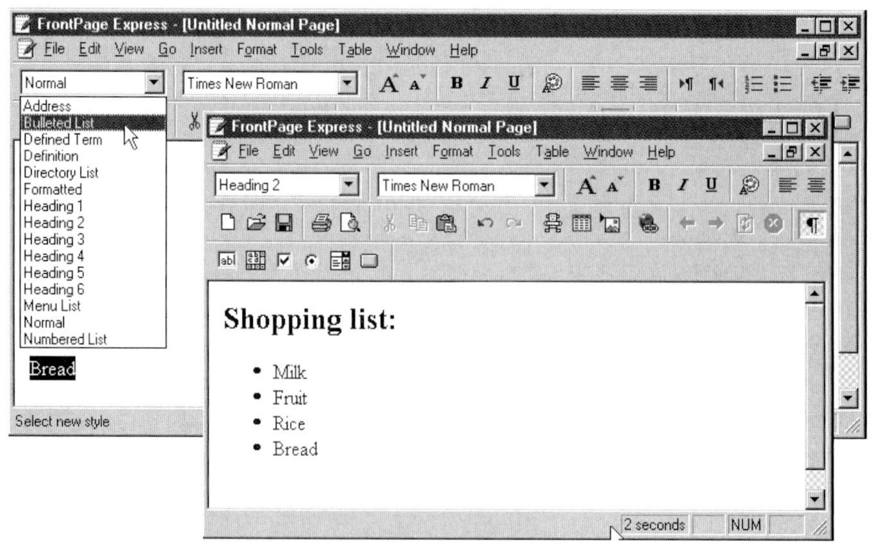

Fig. 6.8 Applying an unordered list and a header to text.

Apply an **H2** element to the title of the list. The **Change Style** pull-down menu has many more useful tags that were not covered in Chapters 3 and 4, such as the *definition list* (**<DL>**). There are two list elements in a definition list—the *defined term* (**<DT>**) and the *definition* (**<DD>**). Figure 6.9 shows the formatting produced by the definition list and the code FrontPage Express used to produce it.

To apply the definition list as shown, pull down the **Change Style** menu to **Defined Term**, and type in the term you want to define. When you press *Enter*, FrontPage Express then changes the style to **Definition**. The bold style was applied using the appropriate toolbar button (this applies to the **STRONG** element).

6.4 Images and Links

Inserting images using FrontPage Express is simply a matter of clicking a button and typing the image's path. The example of Fig. 6.10 is a repeat of the example in Fig. 3.8, using an image as a hyperlink.

Select ***Image...*** from the ***Insert*** menu, and browse your local hard drive directory for the image. You can also select ***From Location*** to use an image from the Web.

```
<dl>
    <dt><strong>FTP</strong></dt>
    <dd>File Transfer Protocol</dd>
    <dt><strong>GIF</strong></dt>
    <dd>Graphics Interchange Format</dd>
    <dt><strong>HTML</strong></dt>
    <dd>HyperText Markup Language</dd>
    <dt><strong>PNG</strong></dt>
    <dd>Portable Network Graphics</dd>
</dl>
```

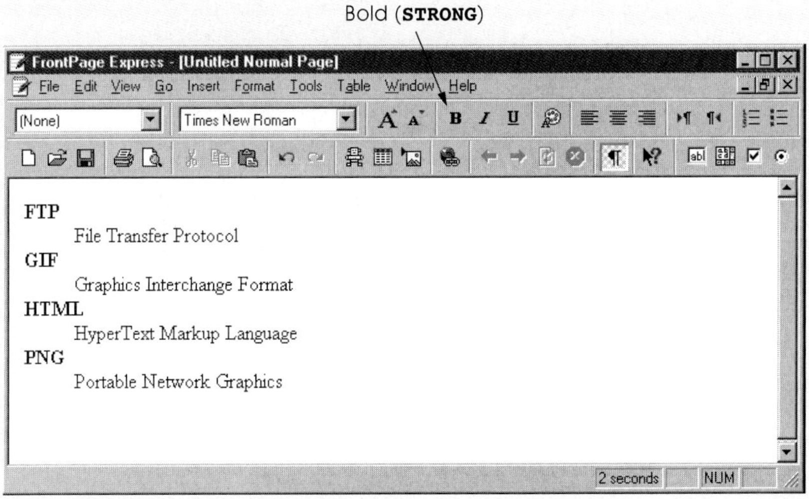

Bold (**STRONG**)

Fig. 6.9 Inserting a definition list using the **Change Style** menu.

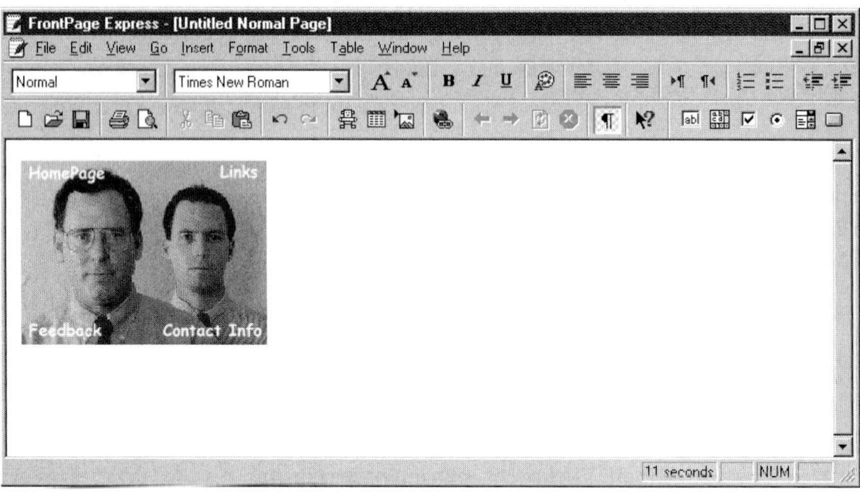

Fig. 6.10 Inserting an image into a Web page.

Common Programming Error 6.1

When you insert a local image into your code by using the **Browse...** *button, FrontPage Express sets an absolute path such as* **`C:/images/deitel.gif.`** *This will not work on the Web, so be sure to change this to a relative path such as* **`images/deitel.gif`**.

After inserting your image, highlight it and create a hyperlink using the ***Hyperlink...*** option in the ***Insert*** menu. First select the ***Hyperlink Type...*** that you want to use. There are some we have seen in previous chapters, such as **`http`** and **`mailto`**, and there are many new ones, such as **`https`**. **`https`** (Secure HyperText Transfer Protocol) is used to transfer sensitive information such as credit card numbers and personal data.

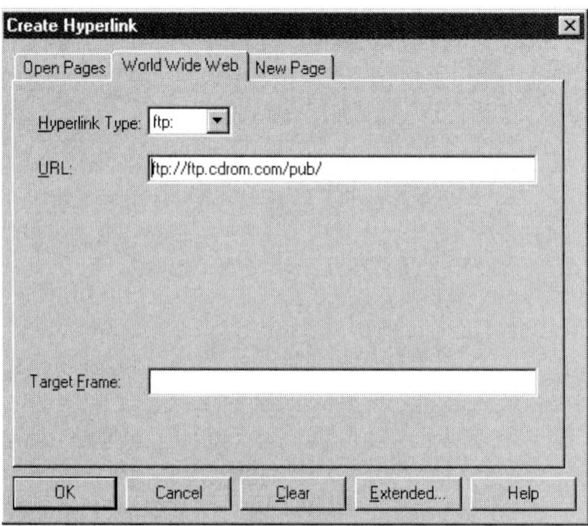

Fig. 6.11 Inserting a Hyperlink in a Web page.

Type in the URL to which the hyperlink will point. FrontPage Express adds a **BORDER=0** attribute to the **<IMG>** tag, removing the blue rectangle that would usually appear around the image.

You can add other attributes to the tag by using the ***Extended...*** button at the bottom of the dialog box. This button appears in many places throughout FrontPage Express and is often useful for adding unlisted attributes to fine-tune the appearance of the element.

6.5 Symbols and Lines

FrontPage Express also allows you to insert characters that are not located on the standard keyboard. This feature, accessed by the ***Symbol...*** option in the **Insert** menu, functions much like the Windows program **Character Map**. Select any listed character and click ***Insert*** to copy it into the text window.

In the coming example, we demonstrate how these symbols can be used in a Web page, along with another feature in FrontPage express, the ***Horizontal Line Properties*** menu. Begin by typing

This sentence is <π of the way down the page.

Use the ***Symbol*** menu to insert the two special characters into the sentence. Now click the ***Horizontal Line*** option in the **Insert** menu. This will insert the line (an **HR** element) directly into the page, so right-click the line and select **Horizontal Line Properties...** from the popup menu. Make this line 1 pixel high, spanning 40% of the width of the page.

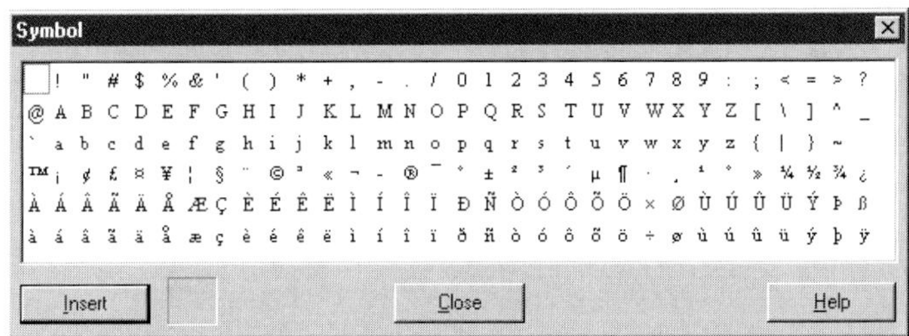

Fig. 6.12 Adding symbols and nonstandard letters.

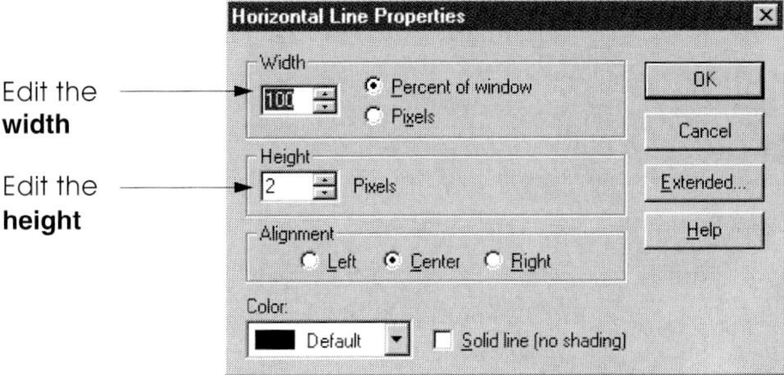

Fig. 6.13 Setting the properties of a **Horizontal Line** element.

Next type the following text

`This sentence is <∫ of the way down the page.`

Again, insert a horizontal rule. This time set it 3 pixels high and spanning 60% of the page width. Type in the last two sentences as they appear in Fig. 5.11. The third horizontal line is 80% of the page width and 10 pixels high.

6.6 Tables

As useful as tables are, they are hard and confusing to code accurately in HTML. FrontPage Express offers a simple method of dealing with this problem. To create a table click ***Insert Table...*** in the ***Table*** menu. You can select the number of rows and columns, the overall width of the table and several other related settings. Figure 6.15 is a simple table created this way with the default size of 2 rows by 2 columns.

Once the table is placed, you can manipulate the table size. You can click in a cell and press the *Delete* key to remove the cell. You can highlight two adjacent cells and use the ***Merge Cells...*** option in the **Table** menu to merge the cells into one. FrontPage Express uses the **COLSPAN** and **ROWSPAN** attributes of the **<TD>** tag to accomplish this. Using the ***Split Cells...*** option allows you to split a cell into any number of rows or columns. Figure 6.16 shows a table two cells high and two cells wide that has had its top two cells merged, and its lower left cell split into five columns. A caption has also been added using the ***Insert Caption*** command, also located in the **Table** menu.

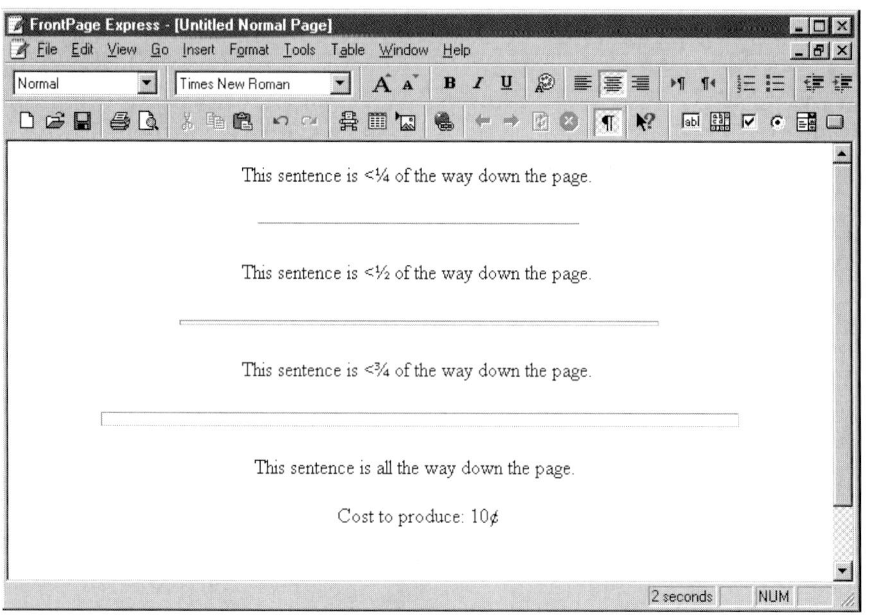

Fig. 6.14 Demonstrating symbols and horizontal lines on one page.

More complex tables are created with the ***Table Properties...*** command (Fig. 6.17). You can add colors or background images and change the width and alignment. Individual cells are customized by clicking a cell and clicking ***Cell Properties...*** in the **Table** menu.

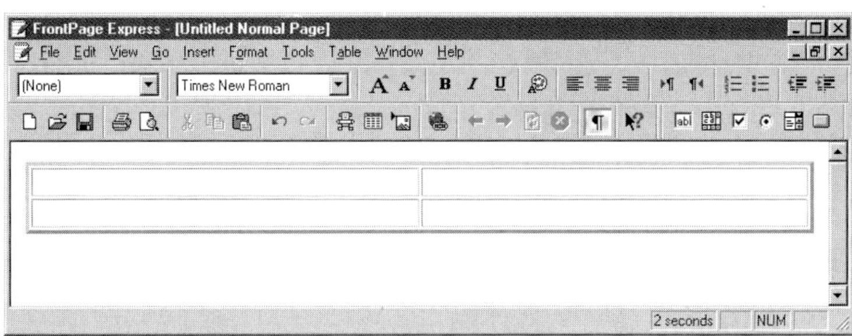

Fig. 6.15 A default table.

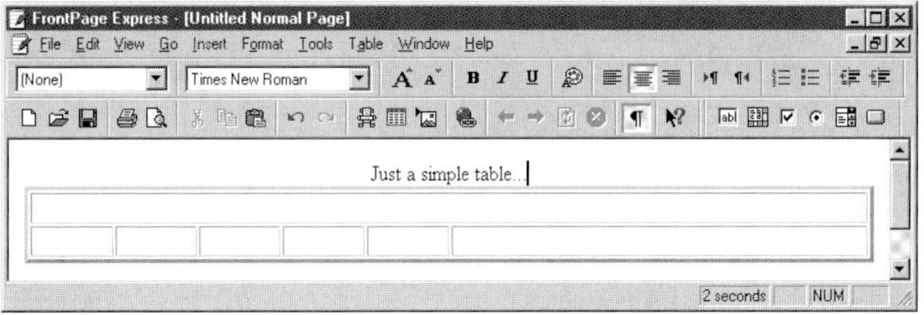

Fig. 6.16 A basic table.

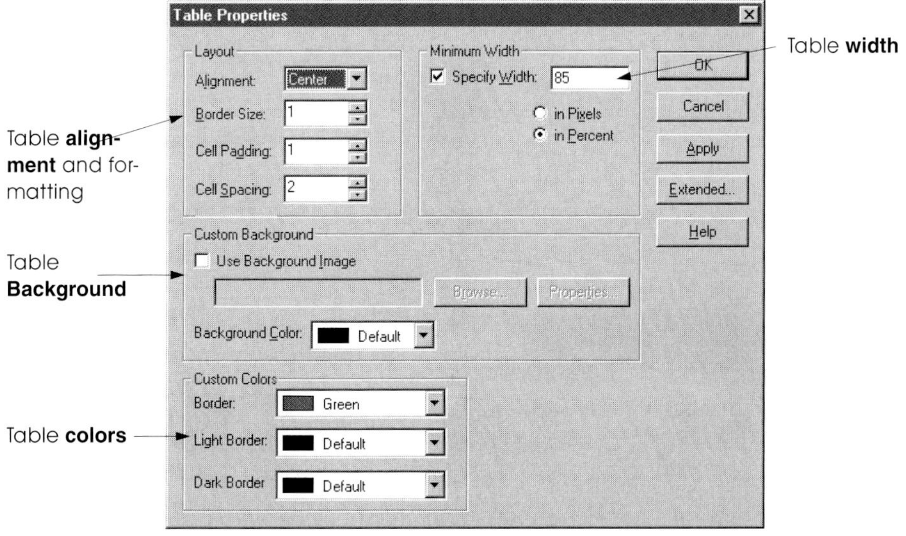

Fig. 6.17 Adjusting table colors and alignment in **Table Properties**.

In Fig. 6.18, we recreate the table of Fig. 4.5. Begin by making a table 4 rows tall and 5 columns wide. Click the top left cell, and click ***Select Column*** in the **Table** menu. This will highlight the left-most column in the table. Now control-click (hold control down as you click) the lower two selected cells, this will deselect them and; turn them white again. Now that only the top two are selected, merge them using the **Merge Cells** command.

Now to make space for the title, click in the same cell as before, but this time use the ***Select Row*** command. Unselect the top left cell, and click on **Merge Cells.** Repeat this process for the rest of the oversized cells, and then start typing in the text and insert the image (Fig 6.19).

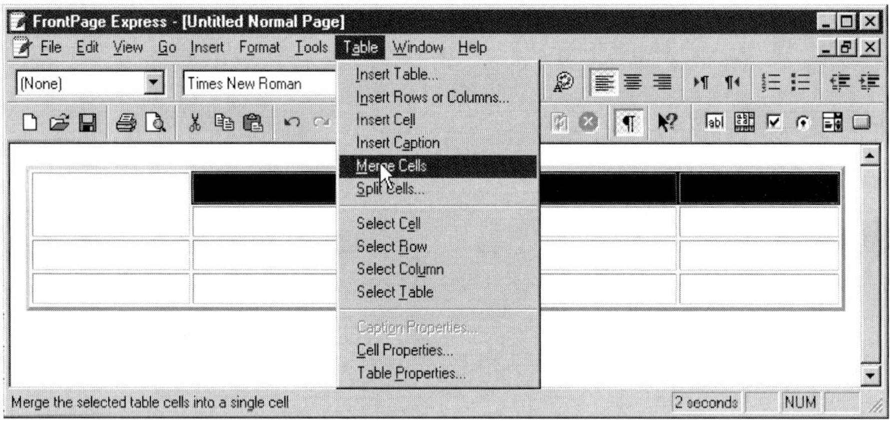

Fig. 6.18 A 4x5 table with the top left cell expanded.

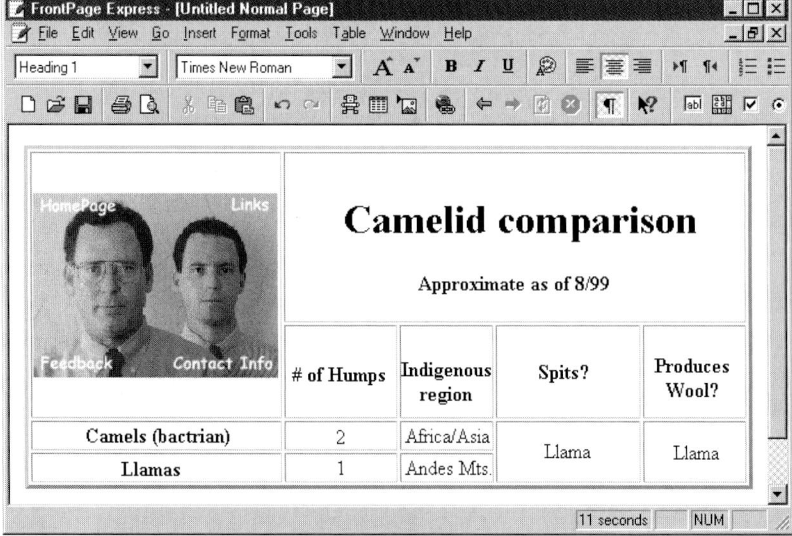

Fig. 6.19 An almost completed table.

Remember to shade the upper rows just as they were in Fig. 4.5. Do this by right-clicking the cells and selecting **Cell Properties...** from the pop-up menu that appears. Select the proper color from the ***Background Color*** pull-down menu.

6.7 Forms

All the necessary HTML coding needed for installing a feedback form or other form on your page can be done with FrontPage Express. After you insert any form field, a dotted line will be drawn around the field. Any other form fields placed inside this line will lie inside the same set of **<FORM>**...**</FORM>** tags as the original form.

A text box is easily inserted by clicking the ***One-Line Text Box*** button on the toolbar or by clicking **One-Line Text Box** in the ***Form-Field*** submenu of the **Insert** menu. Once placed, the placed text box can be stretched wider or narrower with the mouse, or its width can be changed in the ***Form Field Properties...*** menu, accessed by right-clicking on the field or by double-clicking the text box.

In the **Text Box Properties** dialog that appears, the **NAME** and **VALUE** attributes of the form field can be set along with the width (this corresponds to the **SIZE** attribute) and whether this box is a **TYPE = "password"**.

Multiline text boxes can also be placed from the ***Form-Field*** submenu, and their properties are almost identical to normal text boxes, except that they have an additional attribute of height (measured in lines).

The drop-down **SELECT** menu is also added through the **Form Field** submenu. In the **Form Field Properties...** menu, new entries can be added, removed, modified or moved up and down in the order you want them to appear on the page. A single entry can also be made the default selection by toggling **Selected** or **Not Selected** when you add or modify a menu item (Fig 6.20).

Now that we have completed the basics of forms in FrontPage Express, we are ready to make a real form that could be used on any Web page—a typical "rate-my-Web site" form. To start, place all the form fields as they appear in Fig. 6.21.

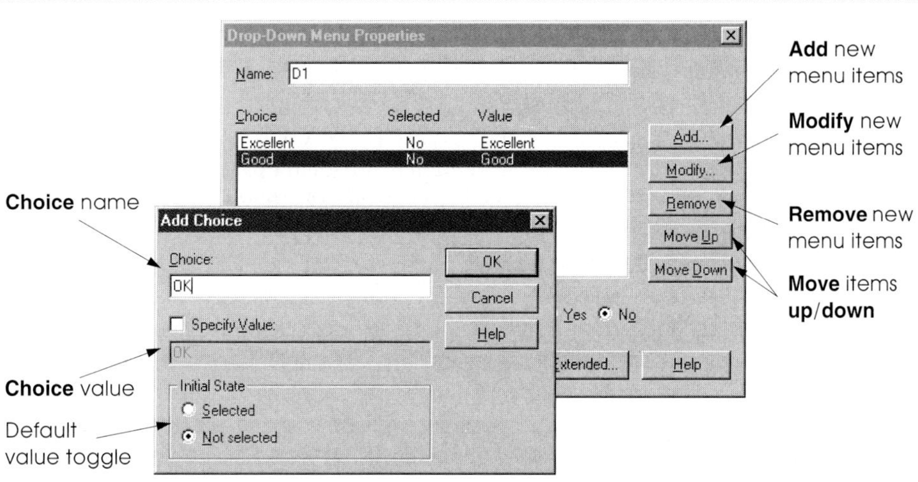

Fig. 6.20 Adding a new item to a drop-down form menu.

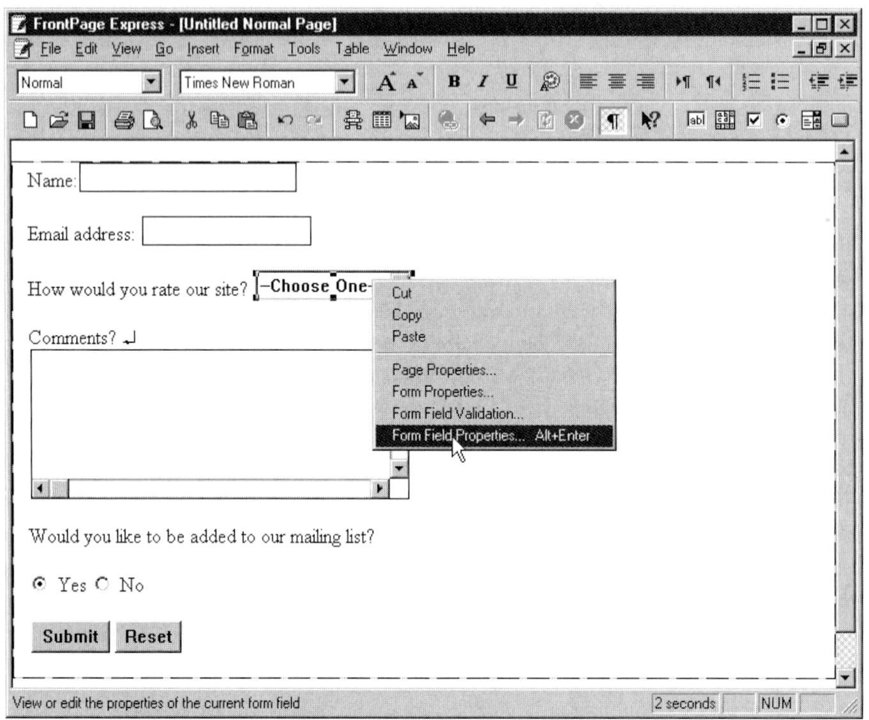

Fig. 6.21 A brief form for user input.

Stretch the text boxes to the proper width using your mouse. Now right-click on the drop-down menu and click on the **Form Field Properties...** menu. You can also access the properties dialog box by double-clicking that form field. Begin adding choices by clicking ***Add...*** and then typing in the choice name. If you want the **`VALUE`** of the choice to be different than the name, click on ***Specify Value*** and type in the value. You can also move any choices up or down in the order they appear on screen with the ***Move Up*** and ***Move Down*** buttons.

This example only has one set of radio buttons. If you want to put more than one set in, you can change the group name of a radio button in its **Form Field Properties...**. Only one radio button in each set may be selected and only one may be set as default.

To set the ***Reset*** and ***Submit*** buttons, click ***Push Button*** in the Form section on the toolbar. The placed button defaults to **Submit**, but by accessing their **Form Field Properties**, you can change them to ***Normal*** or **Reset** buttons.

Now that all the fields have been placed, modify the form itself by right-clicking anywhere inside the dotted line that delineates the form, and select **Form Properties...**. In the resulting dialog box, you can add any hidden fields that a CGI script might require. By clicking the **Settings...** button, you can also set the **`ACTION`** and **`METHOD`** attributes of your form, which should be provided to you by your ISP (Fig. 6.22).

Here we add the properties for the CGI example from Figure 4.6 using FrontPage Express' **Form Properties** dialog box.

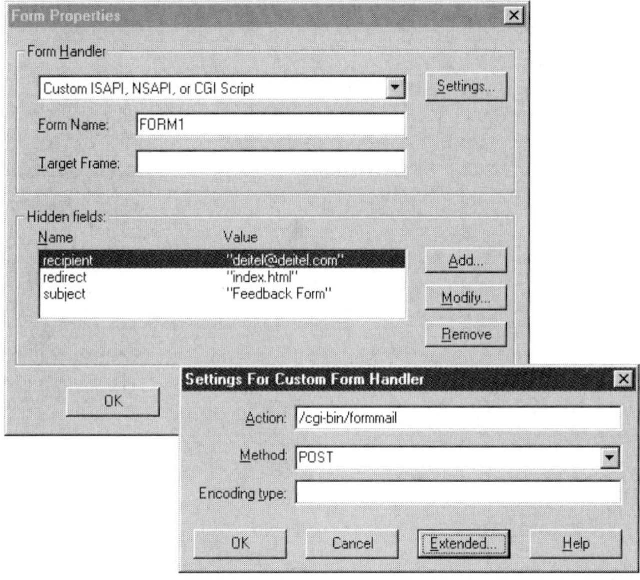

Fig. 6.22 Using the **Form Properties** dialog box.

6.8 Marquees and Scripts

The **<MARQUEE>** tag is a nonstandard tag, supported only by Microsoft Internet Explorer. It is meant as a mimic of the Marquee screen saver, included with Windows. Any text inside a **<MARQUEE>**...**</MARQUEE>** element will scroll slowly across the screen and repeat, depending on the settings you choose. Figure 6.22 illustrates the ***Marquee...*** properties box, located in the **Insert** menu.

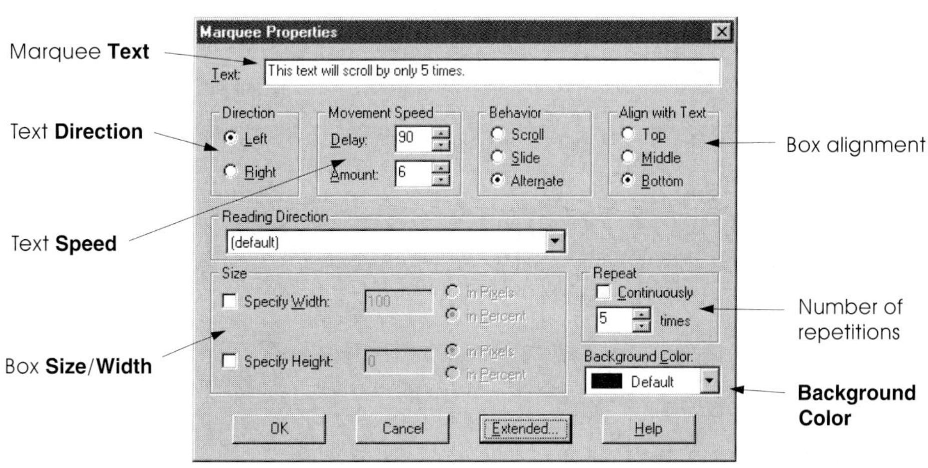

Fig. 6.23 Inserting a **<MARQUEE>** element for scrolling Web page text.

You can choose the **Text** that scrolls by, the **Direction** it scrolls, and the **Speed** at which it scrolls by. You can also specify the width and height of the box in which the text will scroll, and its background color. You can also choose whether or not it will scroll by continuously and, if not, how many times it will iterate. Figure 6.24 shows two screen captures of the **MARQUEE** element in action.

Good Programming Practice 6.3

Netscape will not display any **<MARQUEE>** *elements that you put on your page, so use them sparingly, and do not put any critical information inside them.*

While not providing much support for scripts, FrontPage Express does give you the ability to insert them into your Web page. By clicking **Script...** in the **Insert** menu, you are given a dialog box (Fig. 6.25) in which you can type your complete script in JavaScript or VBScript. We discuss how to program JavaScripts for use in your Web pages in Chapters 8 through 13.

SUMMARY

- Upon starting FrontPage Express, you are welcomed with a blank page in the default viewing mode. This is a WYSIWYG (What You See Is What You Get) display. FrontPage Express renders HTML elements as a browser would.
- FrontPage express automatically encloses text that you type in a **P** element for proper formatting.
- To insert a title right-click in the text area, and select **Page Properties...** from the pop-up menu. Type in the title as shown, and click **OK**. This inserts a **<TITLE>** tag inside the **<HEAD>**...**</HEAD>** element in your HTML code.

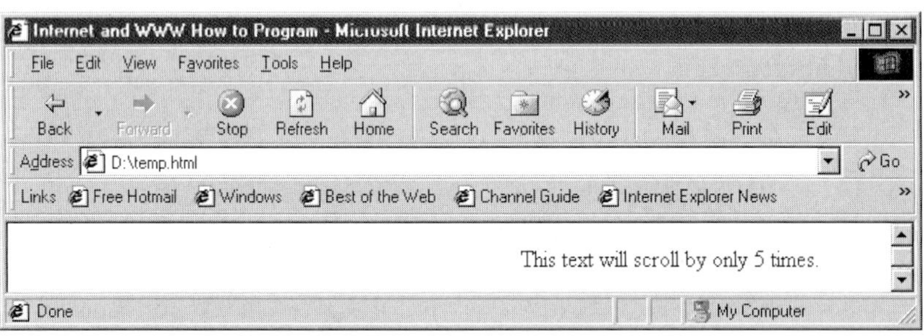

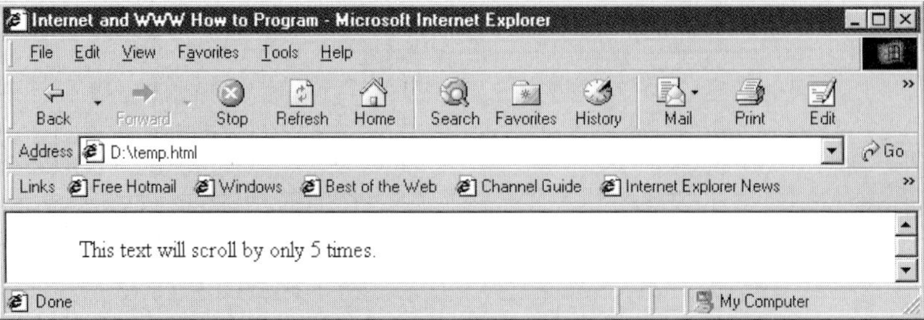

Fig. 6.24 The **MARQUEE** element in action.

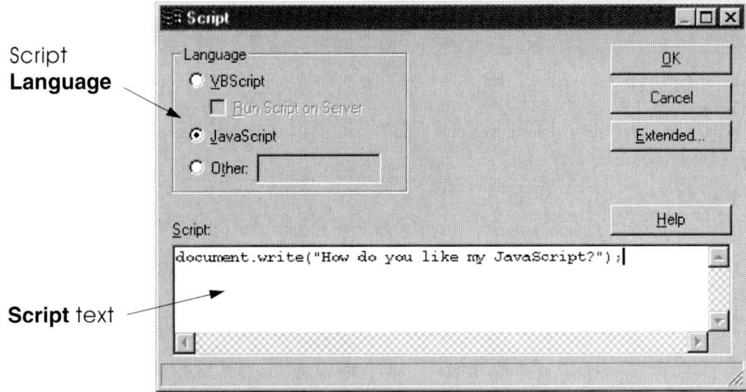

Fig. 6.25 Adding a script to the HTML file.

- To view or edit HTML directly, select the **HTML...** option in the **View** menu. FrontPage automatically color codes HTML to make viewing easier. The tag names, tag attributes, attribute values and page text are all displayed in different colors. This feature can be turned off by clicking off the checkbox titled **Show Color Coding** at the bottom of the dialog box. There is an option to switch between your **Current** code and your **Original** code if you modified your code since the last save.
- To save your file, click **Save** in the **File** menu. FrontPage Express will first give you a dialog box with the **TITLE** of your page, and the address of a Web server on which to save the file. This will only work if your server has FrontPage Extensions installed. If it does not, click the **As File...** button in the dialog box and you can browse your hard drive for a location to save the file.
- Using the **Change Style** menu, you can quickly apply header tags (**<H1>**, **<H2>**, etc.), list tags (**<OL>**, **<UL>**) and several other tags used for stylizing text.
- Text can be aligned left, center or right using buttons on the top toolbar. Text can be increased or decreased in size, indented and colored.
- FrontPage Express is prone to producing inefficient code.
- The **Font...** dialog box in the **Format** menu allows you to apply special styles to selected text. You can also access the **Font** dialog box by right-clicking highlighted text, and selecting **Font Properties...** from the pop-up menu that appears.
- The **Change Style** pull-down menu is useful for creating lists.
- The items in a definition list (**<DL>**) are the defined term (**<DT>**) and the definition (**<DD>**). To apply the definition list, pull down the **Change Style** menu to **Defined Term** and type the term you want to define. When you press Enter, FrontPage Express changes the style to **Definition**.
- Inserting images using FrontPage Express is simply a matter of selecting **Image...** from the **Insert** menu and typing the image's path. You can either **Browse** your local hard drive for the image or select **From Location** to use an image on the Web.
- Create a hyperlink using the **Hyperlink...** option in the **Insert** menu. First select the **Hyperlink Type...** that you want to use, then type in the address of the link.
- **https** (Secure HyperText Transfer Protocol) is used in transfer of sensitive information such as credit card numbers and personal data.
- You can add other attributes to many tags by using the **Extended...** button at the bottom of a dialog box. This button appears in many places throughout FrontPage Express and is often useful for adding unlisted attributes to fine-tune the appearance of the element.

- FrontPage Express allows you to insert characters that are not on a standard keyboard. This feature, accessed by the **Symbol...** option in the **Insert** menu, functions like the Windows **Character Map**. Select any listed character and click **Insert** to copy it into the text window.
- Click on the **Horizontal Line** option in the **Insert** menu to insert a line (an **HR** element) directly into the page. Right-click the line and select **Horizontal Line Properties...** from the popup menu to change the properties of this line.
- To create a table, click **Insert Table...** in the **Table** menu. You can select the number of rows and columns, the overall width of the table and several other related settings. Once the table is placed, options exist for manipulating the table size. You can click in a cell and press the Delete key to remove the cell. You can highlight two adjacent cells and use the **Merge Cells...** option in the **Table** menu to merge the cells into one. FrontPage Express uses the **COLSPAN** and **ROWSPAN** attributes of the **<TD>** tag to accomplish this. Using the **Split Cells...** option allows you to split a cell into any number of rows or columns. A caption may be added using the **Insert Caption** command located in the **Table** menu.
- More advanced tables can be created by using the **Table Properties...** command. You can add colors or background images to the whole table and change width and alignment. This can also be done to individual cells by clicking on a cell and clicking **Cell Properties...** in the **Table** menu.
- All the necessary HTML coding needed for installing a feedback or other form on your page can be done with FrontPage Express. After you insert any form field, a dotted line will be automatically drawn around the field. Any other form fields placed inside this line will lie inside the same set of **<FORM>**...**</FORM>** tags as the original form.
- A text box is inserted by clicking the **One-Line Text Box** button on the toolbar, or by clicking **One-Line Text Box** in the **Form-Field** submenu of the **Insert** menu. The placed text box can be stretched wider or narrower with the mouse, or its width can be changed in the **Form Field Properties...** menu, accessed by right-clicking on the field. In this menu both the **NAME** and **VALUE** attributes of the form field can also be set. Multiline text boxes can be placed from the same submenu, and their properties are almost identical to normal text boxes, except that they have an additional attribute of width.
- A drop-down menu is added through the **Form-Field** submenu. In the **Form Field Properties...** menu, new entries can be added, removed, modified or moved up and down in the order you want them to appear on the page. A single entry is made the default selection by toggling **Selected** or **Not Selected** when you add or modify a menu item. When adding entries, if you want the **VALUE** of the choice to be different than the name, click on **Specify Value** and type the value.
- If you want to insert more than one set of radio buttons in your form, you can change the group name of a radio button in its **Form Field Properties...**. Only one radio button in each set may be selected, and only one may be set as default.
- To insert the **Reset** and **Submit** buttons, click **Push Button** in the Form section on the toolbar. The placed buttons default to **Submit**, but by accessing their **Form Field Properties...**, you can change them to **Normal** or **Reset** buttons.
- You can modify a form by right-clicking anywhere inside the dotted line that delineates the form, and select **Form Properties...**. In the resulting dialog box, you can add any hidden fields that your CGI script might require. By clicking the **Settings...** button, you can also set the **ACTION** and **METHOD** attributes of your form, which should be provided to you by your ISP.
- The **<MARQUEE>** tag is a nonstandard tag, supported only by Microsoft Internet Explorer. It is meant as a mimic of the Marquee screen saver, included with Windows. Any text inside a **<MARQUEE>**...**</MARQUEE>** element will scroll slowly across the screen and repeat, depending on the settings you choose. You can choose the **Text** that scrolls by, the **Direction** it scrolls and the **Speed** at which it scrolls by. You can also specify the width and height of the box in which

the text will scroll, and its background color. You can also choose whether or not it will scroll by continuously, and if not, how many times it will iterate.

- While not providing much support for scripts, FrontPage Express does give you the ability to insert them into your Web page. By clicking **Script...** in the **Insert** menu, you are given a dialog box in which you can type your complete script.

TERMINOLOGY

absolute path
Add... in **Form Field Properties...**
Align Center button
As File... in the **Save** menu
Background Color in **Cell Properties**
Cell Properties... in **Table** menu
Change Style pull-down menu
Code checkbox
COLSPAN
Current toggle and **Original** toggle.
DD element (definition; **<DD>**...)
Direction of a **MARQUEE** tag
DL element (definition list; **<DL>**...**</DL>**)
DT element (defined term; **<DT>**...**</DT>**)
Font...in the **Format** menu
Font Properties... pop-up menu
<FORM>
Form Field Properties... menu
Form Properties...
From Location in **Image**
ftp
Horizontal Line in **Insert** menu
Horizontal Line Properties menu
HTML... in **View** menu
https
Hyperlink... in the **Insert** menu
Hyperlink Type...
Image... in **Insert** menu
Insert Caption in **Table** menu
Insert in ***Symbol*** menu
Insert Table... in **Table** menu
mailto
<MARQUEE>
Marquee... in **Insert** menu
Merge Cells... in **Table** menu
Move Down in **Add** menu
Move Up in **Add** menu
NAME
Normal option in **Push Button** menu
One-Line Text Box button
Page Properties... *pop-up* menu.
Paragraph...in the **Format** menu
Push Button button
relative path
Reset option in **Push Button** menu
right-clicking
ROWSPAN
Save in the ***File*** menu
Script... in **Insert** menu
Select Column in the **Table** menu
Selected and **Not Selected** toggles
Select Row in **Table** menu
Show Color Coding
Special Styles tab
Specify value in ***Add*** menu
Speed of a **MARQUEE** tag
Split Cells... in **Table** menu
Symbol... option in the **Insert** menu
Table Properties...
<TD>
Text Color button
Text of a **MARQUEE** tag
VALUE
WYSIWYG

COMMON PROGRAMMING ERROR

6.1 When you insert a local image into your code by using the **Browse...** button, FrontPage Express sets an absolute path such as **C:\images\deitel.gif**. This will not work on the Web, so be sure to change this to a relative path such as **images/deitel.gif**.

GOOD PROGRAMMING PRACTICES

6.1 When you press Enter after typing text, FrontPage Express will put that text in a new set of **<P>**...**</P>** tags. If you only want to insert a **
** tag into your page, then hold down *Shift* while you press *Enter*.

6.2 You can manipulate the properties of almost any element displayed in the FrontPage Express window by right-clicking that element and selecting that element's properties from the window that pops up.

6.3 Netscape will not display any **<MARQUEE>** elements that you put on your page, so use them sparingly, and do not put any critical information inside them.

SOFTWARE ENGINEERING OBSERVATION

6.1 FrontPage Express uses a wide variety of techniques to manipulate the text and often produces inefficient code. Make sure to check often to know exactly the kind of HTML code FrontPage Express is producing for you. Thorough knowledge of your page and what HTML elements are present will be necessary in later chapters.

SELF-REVIEW EXERCISES

6.1 What color does FrontPage Express use for the following types of code in the *HTML...* option in the View menu?

a) Plain text
b) Tags
c) Attributes
d) Attribute Values

6.2 What button that appears in many dialog boxes allows you to insert unlisted attributes directly into your HTML code?

6.3 What action gives you access to the properties of an item?

6.4 State whether the following are true or false:

a) FrontPage Express renders most HTML elements correctly in its WYSIWYG display.
b) FrontPage Express sometimes inserts superfluous HTML tags.
c) The **MARQUEE** element can be rendered properly by all browsers.
d) **https** is the same as **http**.
e) FrontPage Express delineates a **FORM** element with a dotted line.
f) FrontPage Express inserts local images using a relative path.

ANSWERS TO SELF-REVIEW EXERCISES

6.1 a) Black. b) Purple. c) Red. d) Blue.

6.2 **Extended...**

6.3 Right-clicking.

6.4
a) True.
b) True.
c) False. The **MARQUEE** element is supported only by Internet Explorer.
d) False. **https** is a secure version of **http**, permitting the transmission of sensitive information such as credit card numbers.
e) True.
f) False. FrontPage Express inserts images with an absolute path. You must change this to a relative path so the images may be displayed properly on the Web.

EXERCISES

6.5 Create the following table using FrontPage Express:

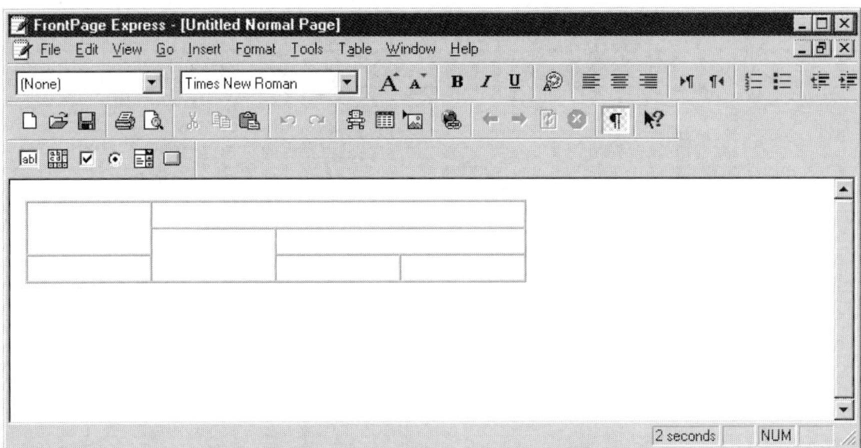

6.6 Create the following form using FrontPage Express.

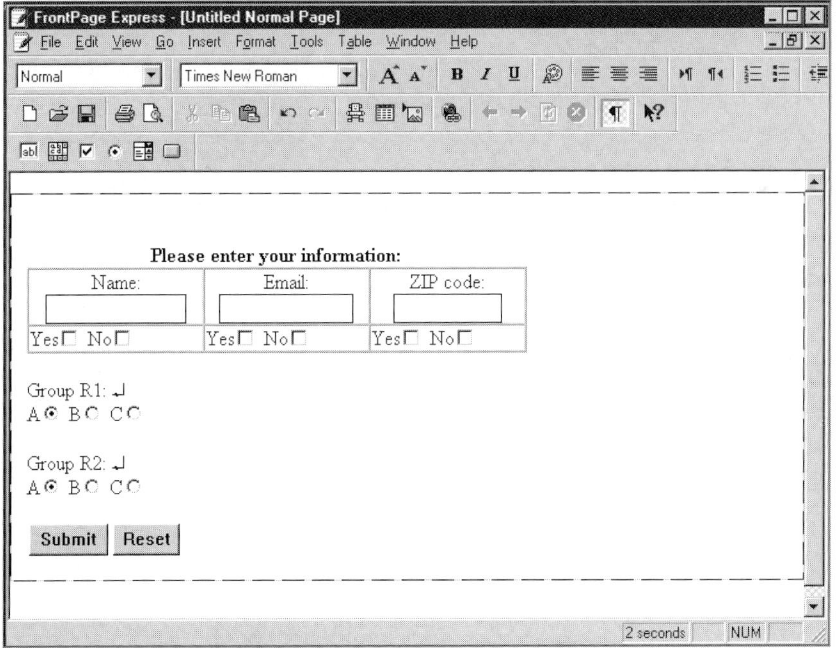

6.7 Create a personal Web page using FrontPage Express.

7

Introduction to Microsoft Visual InterDev 6

Objectives

- To understand the possible uses of Visual InterDev in designing a dynamic Web site.
- To understand the layout of the main Visual InterDev screen.
- To understand the functions of the various windows and toolbars.
- To be able to start a new project in Visual InterDev.
- To be able to open a file and edit it using both **Design** and **Source** views.
- To be able to set up a site hierarchy using the site designer.

The Park [Central Park, New York City] throughout is a single work of art, and as such subject to the primary law of every work of art, namely, that it shall be framed upon a single, noble motive, to which the design of all its parts, in some more or less subtle way, shall be confluent and helpful.
Frederick Law Olmsted and Calvert Vaux

A new beauty has been added to the splendor of the world—the beauty of speed.
Fillipo Tommaso Marinetti

The most advanced nations are always those who navigate the most.
Ralph Waldo Emerson

Beware the ides of March.
William Shakespeare, *Julius Caesar*

Outline

7.1 Introduction

In previous chapters we discussed a variety of programs that simplify the process of creating Web pages. In this chapter we present *Microsoft Visual InterDev 6*, a software package that combines a powerful HTML WYSIWYG editor with a thorough source-editing interface that will simplify all the coding you will be doing throughout the book. Visual InterDev is an *Integrated Development Environment* (IDE) that will help you produce powerful Web-based, multitier, client/server database-intensive applications. Note that "InterDev" is a combination of the words in "Internet Development."

[*Note:* Microsoft allowed us to include the *Professional Edition* of *Visual InterDev 6* only with the version of this book sold to students through academic channels. The version of this book sold to the general public does not include *Visual InterDev 6*. At the time of this writing, Microsoft did not offer a version of *Visual InterDev 6* free for download. We introduce Visual InterDev in this chapter, but it is not used anywhere else in this book.]

7.2 Web Servers

A *Web server* is a computer that is designed to act as a hub for a number of computers that form a *network*. If you think of individual networks as localized systems of roads, then their servers are the traffic lights at the main intersections. They handle all of the incoming and outgoing data of the network, and make sure that everything that arrives at the server is sent on the right road to reach its destination. The *Internet* is, in essence, a network connecting many smaller networks (the "information superhighway"). All information accessible on the Internet exists on some server, and when you view that information, you are accessing the files on that server somewhere in the world. When information is uploaded to the Internet, it is placed on a server.

Visual InterDev 6 helps you create complex Web sites and powerful Web-based applications. It interacts with the server on which the Web site will be placed. Many of the tasks that Visual InterDev is capable of are only possible through this close interaction with a server. In order to create even a Web site with Visual InterDev, you must specify a server with which the program should connect and share information.

If your computer is not on a LAN (*Local Area Network*, many of which connect to create the Internet), then you will need to create a server on your own computer to use when developing your Web site with Visual InterDev. You can do this quickly and easily with Microsoft's *Personal Web Server*. When you install Visual InterDev, if the program does not detect a connection to a server, then it will automatically install Personal Web Server. Follow the prompts through the installation, leaving the default location settings intact. You will be asked to name your server—the name does not matter as long as it is one word containing alphanumeric characters. Be sure to write down the exact name of the server for later reference. Once your server connection is established, you will be ready to create your first project with Visual InterDev 6.

7.3 Creating a New Visual InterDev Project

To start creating your first Web site using Visual InterDev, you must create a shell of a site on your server from which you will be working. You can do this through the ***New Project*** dialog box that appears whenever you start Visual InterDev (see Fig. 7.1).

There are three tabs in the **New Project** box—***New***, ***Existing*** and ***Recent***. The **New** tab is used to create new projects. This is the tab we will be selecting now (it is also displayed by default). The **Existing** and **Recent** tabs are for opening projects that you have previously saved. The next time you start Visual InterDev, if you would like to continue working on an existing project, it will appear in the **Existing** tab, and also in the **Recent** tab (if it has been accessed recently in relation to other saved projects).

In the left side of the dialog box, you designate what type of project you are going to create—**Visual InterDev** or **Visual Studio**. These basically use the same environment, but for different purposes. Initially, we will ignore the last option—for now, be sure that **Visual InterDev** is always highlighted when you are creating a new project. If you highlight the wrong project type, then Visual InterDev will create the wrong default files when beginning your project.

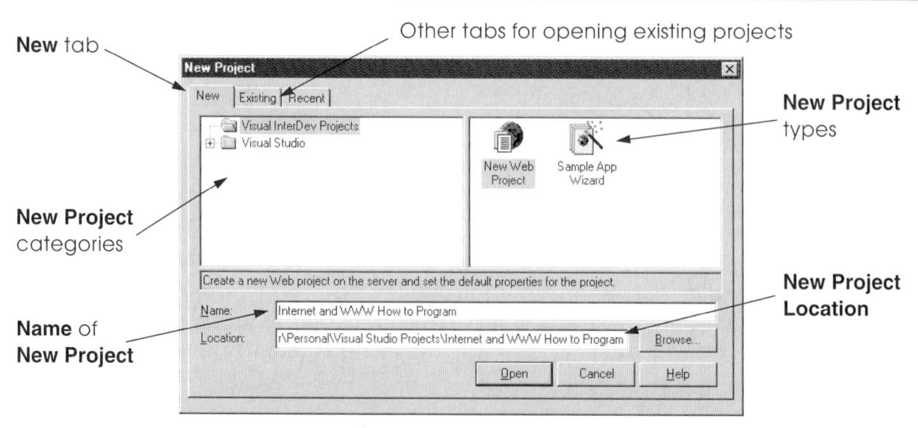

Fig. 7.1 Add **New Project** dialog box.

Common Programming Error 7.1

*Having the wrong type of project highlighted—***Visual Studio***—when beginning a new project will cause Visual InterDev to create a new project in a different format from what you are expecting.*

On the right side of the **New Project** dialog box, you can choose the type of project you would like to create. Whenever beginning a new Web page project, make sure that the ***New Web Project*** icon is highlighted. The **Sample App Wizard** (Fig. 7.1) will be covered in a later chapter.

In the field labeled ***Name***, enter the name of your new project. You should leave the default location as is (unless there is a different location on your hard drive in which you would like to create the project). Click the **Open** button to create your new project in the designated location.

There are four more dialogs that must be completed to finish the creation of your project (see Fig. 7.2).

The project setup window that appears on your screen after you open your new project for the first time will ask you for the server Visual InterDev that you will be communicating with when you are designing your topic. If you will be using the Personal Web Server as your server for Visual InterDev, enter its designated name (which was set in Section 7.2) in the server name text box. Below the text box you are asked whether you want to work in ***Master Mode*** or in ***Local Mode***. When working in **Master Mode**, any changes you make to the project will be immediately added to the version of your project on the server. When working in **Local Mode**, all changes to the project will be kept on your computer until you choose to update the server. **Local Mode** is used most often in situations where you are working on a site accessible to the public, and would like to test all changes to the site before making them official. Click **Next** to go to the second step in the setup process.

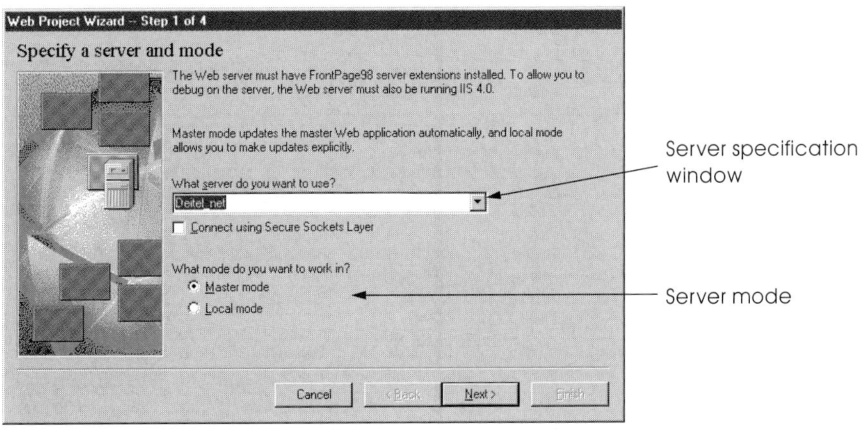

Fig. 7.2 Step 1: Specifying a server.

The second setup window (Fig. 7.3) prompts you to enter the name for your new application. By default it selects the same name you gave to the project. For now, use the name of your project as the name of your application and click **Next**.

The third and fourth setup windows (Fig. 7.4 and Fig. 7.5) ask you to choose a *layout* (where navigation bars are placed) and a *theme* (the predominant colors and styles) for your site. Visual InterDev has a built-in process that can add preset layouts and themes. When you highlight a layout or theme, a preview will appear in the window on the left of the setup box. While you are unfamiliar with the interface of Visual InterDev, we recommend that you choose the **<none>** option in both the layout and theme setup windows. After your layout option is highlighted in the third setup window, click **Next**. Highlight your theme option in the fourth window and click **Finish** to complete the project creation process.

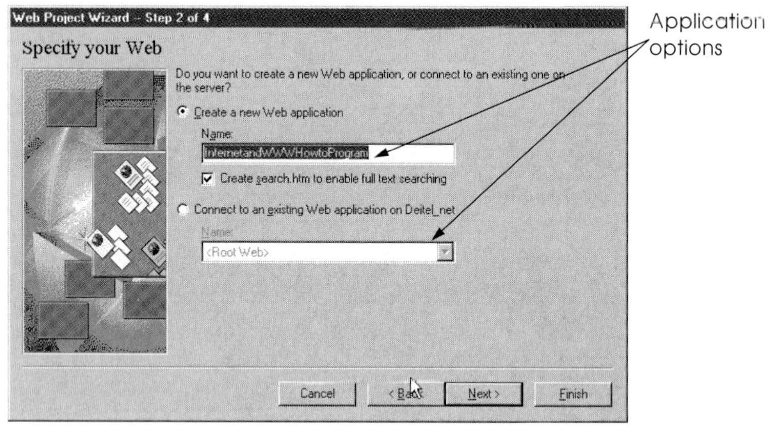

Fig. 7.3 Step 2: Naming your new project.

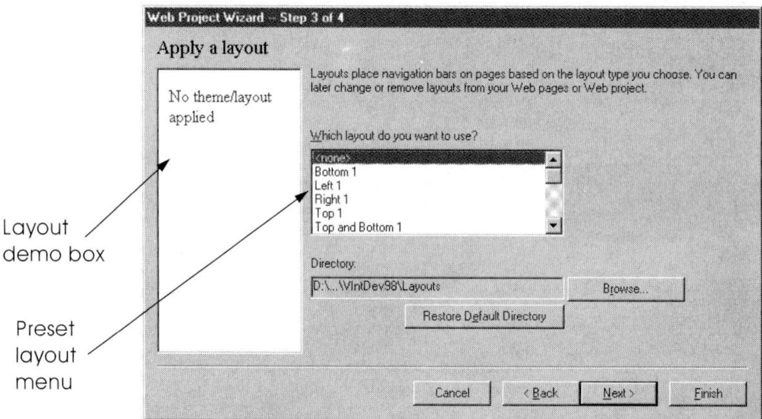

Fig. 7.4 Step 3: Selecting a layout for your site.

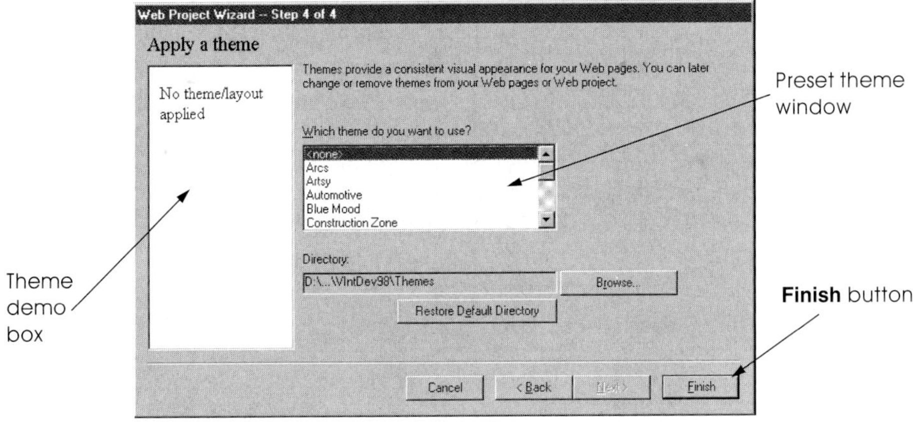

Fig. 7.5 **Web Project Wizard** dialog boxes.

Upon completing the setup for your new project, Visual InterDev will create a new directory on your chosen server. Inside this main directory a number of folders will be created containing basic information for your site, along with all files needed for your chosen layout and theme. In the main directory for your project Visual InterDev will create two files—**`global.asa`**, and **`search.htm`**. These files have to do with a database integration capability that Visual InterDev builds into sites and should be ignored for now. We discuss working with databases in Chapter 25.

7.4 Adding New Items

The interface of Visual InterDev 6 is designed to simplify building, editing, testing and publishing your Web sites and Web-based applications. Figure 7.6 illustrates the process of adding an item to your site.

To add an item to an open project, select the ***Add Item...*** option located in the ***Project*** *menu*. On the right side of the **Add Item** dialog box are the four types of files you can create—***HTML Page***, ***ASP Page***, ***Style Sheet*** and ***Site Diagram***. The **ASP Page** and **Style Sheet** file types are not explained in this book (see the Visual InterDev documentation for more information on this file types). **Site Diagram** will be covered later in this chapter. For now you should make sure that the **HTML Page** icon is highlighted. Enter a name for your HTML file. We call our new file **main** (the **`.htm`** suffix is appended automatically). Click the **Open** button after entering the file name. Visual InterDev now creates a new blank HTML file called **`main.htm`**, located in the main directory of your project.

7.5 Project Explorer

Visual InterDev has a number of windows that simplify editing your pages. These windows can be positioned on your screen for easy access. When you start Visual InterDev for the first time, only the **Project Explorer** window is on the screen. It is located by default along the right side of the main screen. This window is *anchored* to the side of the main Visual InterDev screen (as are all other windows by default). If you prefer that the **Project**

Explorer (or any other window on the screen) be *floating* instead of anchored (when a window is floating, it is separate from the main Visual InterDev screen and you can move it around as you desire) double-click on the blue title bar at the top of the window. To reattach any floating window double-click on its title bar. Windows can be resized by placing your mouse on an edge of the window and dragging the window to your desired size. An unanchored view of the *Project Explorer* can be seen in Fig. 7.7.

The **Project Explorer** is used to display the directories and files of your project. When an item is added to your project, it will appear in the **Project Window** in its designated location. You can view the contents of a directory inside your project by clicking the directory name. To edit any item in your project, simply double-click its entry in the **Project Explorer** and an editing window will open in the main area of the Visual InterDev screen.

You can access many of the options for modifying your project and its files by right-clicking on the main project directory. The resulting menu (Fig. 7.7) shows options such as **Add** (which is the equivalent of the **Add Item...** in the **View** menu), ***View in Browser***, which lets you preview the site or a selected file in a browser environment. The ***Get Latest Version***, ***Get Working Copy***, ***Release Working Copy*** and ***Discard Changes*** options are used when you are working in **Local Mode** to update the version of the project on your computer with the version on the server, or vice versa. A theme or layout can be applied to the selected project or file (if you did not exercise these options when creating the project) using the ***Apply Theme and Layout...*** option. The options in this menu will be discussed later in this chapter.

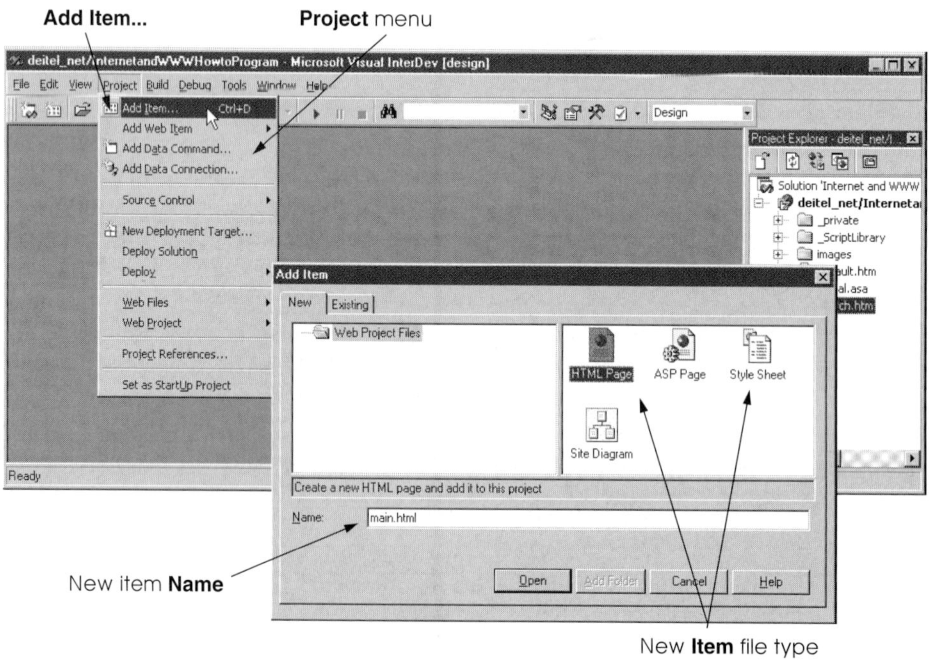

Fig. 7.6 **Add Item** dialog box.

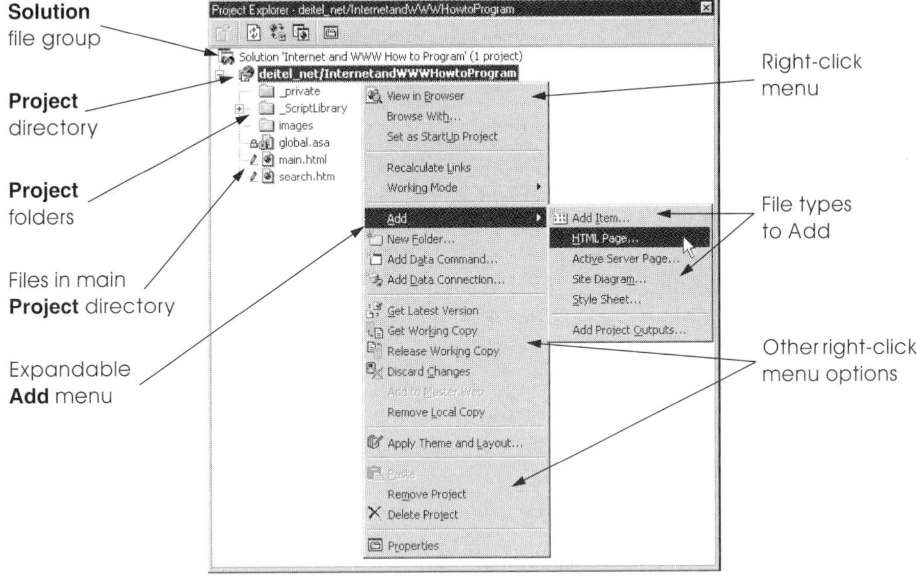

Fig. 7.7 **Project Explorer** window.

7.6 Toolbox Window

Another window that you should always have on the screen when editing pages is the ***Toolbox*** window. You can insert the ***Toolbox*** window (which is anchored by default against the left side of the Visual InterDev screen) by selecting the **Toolbox** option in the **View** menu (Fig. 7.8).

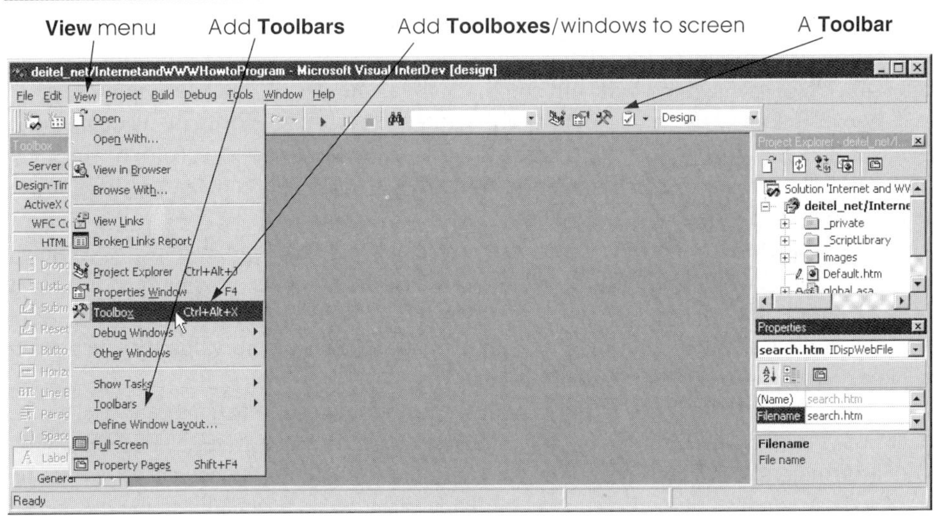

Fig. 7.8 Inserting windows into your view.

As you learned in Chapters 3 and 4, HTML includes many elements that place visual items on your Web page. Examples include form **INPUT** elements, horizontal rules, line breaks, etc. The **Toolbox** provides a shortcut to placing these elements directly into the page-editing screens (we discuss these later in the chapter). To position one of these elements, click in the place on your page where you would like to insert the element, then locate and double-click the button representing the desired element in the **Toolbox** window. You are also able to add elements by dragging them from the toolbar to a location on the page.

Visual InterDev is intended for total Web-site and Web-based application design. The HTML editing capabilities of Visual InterDev represent only a small portion of InterDev's impressive capabilities. Visual InterDev condenses five toolboxes into one interface (Fig. 7.9).

The four main versions of the **Toolbox** window are (from left to right)—***Server Objects***, ***Design Time Controls***, ***ActiveX Controls*** and ***HTML***. For now, we will be using only the **HTML** toolbox.

When you open a file, the **Toolbox** will change to the version most suited to your type of file. So when you open an HTML file and you have the **Toolbox** on your screen, the **HTML Toolbox** will automatically appear. To switch between toolboxes click on the name of the **Toolbox** you would like to see.

7.7 Toolbars and the Properties Window

There are a number of toolbars that can be inserted at the top of the Visual InterDev screen. Toolbars contain shortcut buttons grouped by task. They help reduce your design time by eliminating the necessity of having to type in a code word or pull down a menu whenever you want to do something. Toolbars are inserted by highlighting the **Toolbars** option in the **View** menu, then choosing the desired **Toolbar** to be inserted. When editing HTML it is always helpful to use the HTML toolbar. When you open many of the functions in Visual InterDev any associated toolbars will automatically be inserted at the top of the screen.

When editing a page, you should also insert the ***Properties Window***, which appears by default on the right side of the screen, directly below the **Project Explorer**. It can be inserted on the screen by selecting the **Properties Window** option in the **View** menu. An unanchored **Properties** window is shown in Fig. 7.10.

The **Properties** window is used mostly to create *styles* for your Web pages. Setting a style is a method of indicating the way you want certain elements on your page to appear. In the **Properties** window, the property is listed on the left, with its value on the right. When you click a value cell, a button appears on the right of the value cell that, when clicked, expands into a list of possible values.

Styles help you make your site visually pleasing and can help you give the various pages of your site a uniform look and feel. There are many ways styles can be configured with your individual Web pages and with your site as a whole. Styles and the use of the **Properties** window are explored in detail later in the book, especially in the chapter on "Cascading Style Sheets."

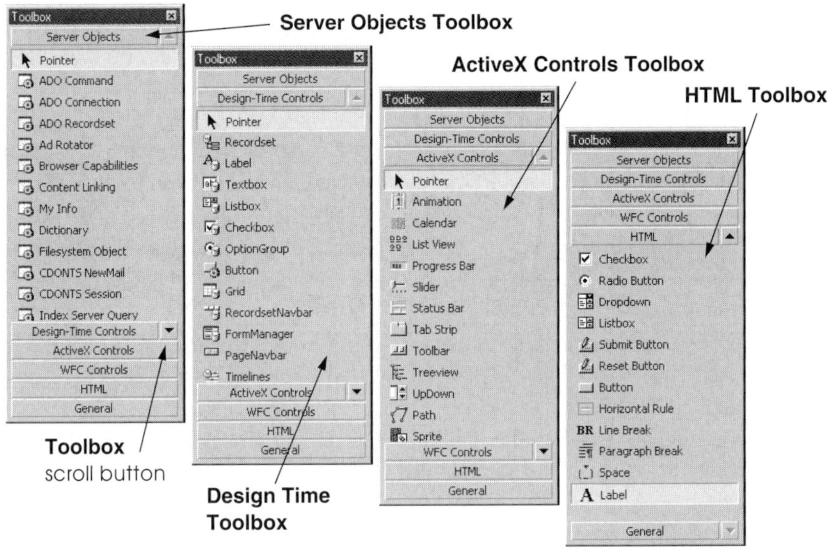

Fig. 7.9 Five different Visual InterDev **Toolboxes**.

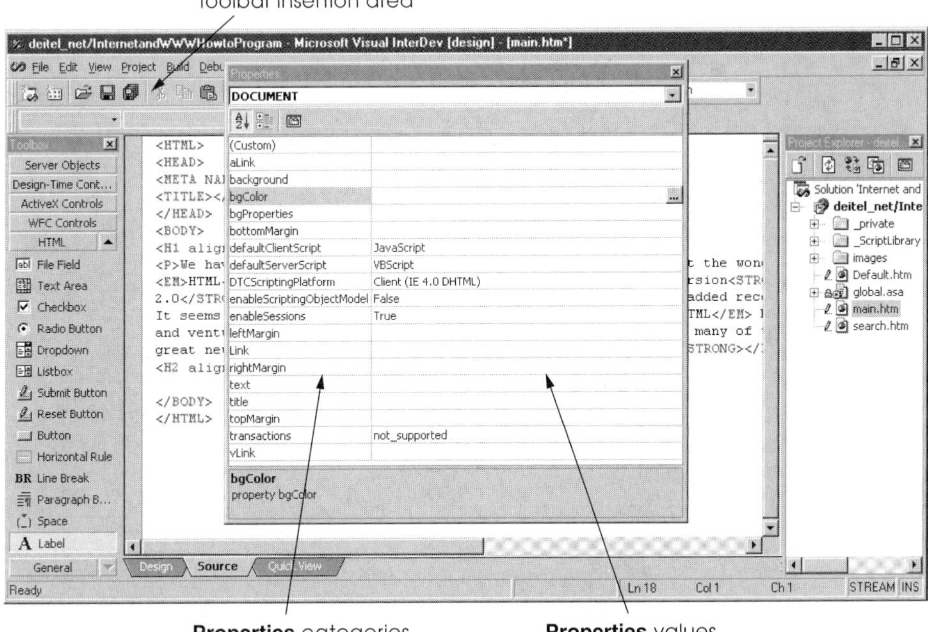

Fig. 7.10 Page **Properties** window (unanchored).

7.8 Project Edit Window

Visual InterDev 6 includes an advanced editor to help design visually impressive and technically complex sites and pages. To enter the *editor mode* for a file, double-click on the file's entry in the **Project Explorer**.

The Visual InterDev page editor includes three views—***Design*** view, which allows you to edit your page in a WYSIWYG interface; ***Source*** view, which allows you to edit the source of your page directly and ***Quick View***, which allows you to view your page as it would appear in a browser. You can switch between views at any time when editing a file by clicking on the appropriate tab on the bottom of the editor window. Figure 7.11 shows a sample editor screen in **Design** view. In this example, we modify the file **main.htm**, which we created in Section 7.4.

In Chapter 6 we discussed the basics of WYSIWYG page editing using FrontPage Express. The **Design** view in Visual InterDev improves on the concepts and interface of the FrontPage Express editor.

When you load an HTML page, the HTML toolbar will automatically be inserted into the toolbar area at the top of the screen. The toolbar contains buttons for text formatting, styling, coloring, alignment, lists, indentation and hyperlinks. If you have the **Toolbox** open (we opened the toolbox in Section 7.6), then it will automatically be switched to the **HTML Toolbox** when you open an HTML program. The **HTML Toolbox** contains shortcut buttons for elements like form inputs and other visual elements like horizontal rules and line breaks. Other design elements and tools can be found in the HTML menu. For table creation and design, look in the **Table** menu.

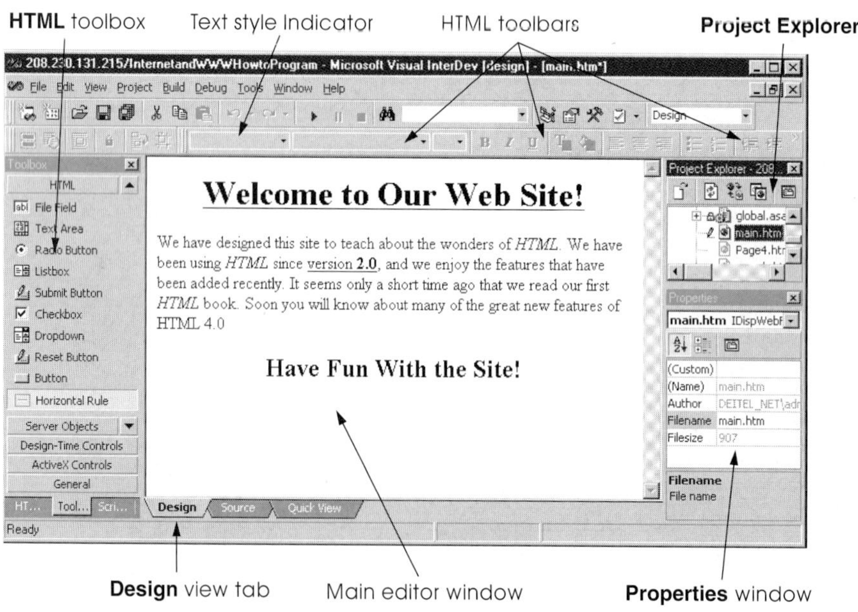

Fig. 7.11 Page editor **Design** view.

The design view that we use most often throughout this book is the **Source** view. In Chapters 3 and 4 we used a bland type of source view that used same-color text and no automatic formatting and spacing conventions. In Chapter 6, we saw FrontPage Express's source mode, which inserted many superfluous tags into the HTML source. The Visual InterDev **Source** view (Fig. 7.12), is a vast improvement over what we have previously used to edit and view the HTML source.

Visual InterDev automatically color codes source code (Fig. 7.12) to enhance visibility and to make editing easier. A feature of the **Source** view is its integration with scripting and Web-based application development.

Most WYSIWYG page editors cannot render pages to show you how they will look on the Internet. With these editors, to view a page as it will actually be rendered in a browser environment, you have to save the file you are working on and open it in a browser. Visual InterDev eliminates this step with **Quick View** (Fig. 7.13).

The **Quick View** editing mode uses the currently installed version of Internet Explorer to render your page. You can therefore use **Quick View** to see how your page will look to many people viewing it on the Internet.

If you would like to view your page in an actual Web browser, select the ***View in Browser*** option in the **View** menu. If you would like to change the browser that renders your page, select the ***Browse With...*** option in the **View** menu.

While editing any page, it is important to save your work every few minutes to prevent loss of information in case your system fails. You can save your changes by clicking the *Save* button on the file toolbar, or by selecting **Save** in the **File** menu.

Software Engineering Observation 7.1

Save your work every few minutes to prevent loss of information.

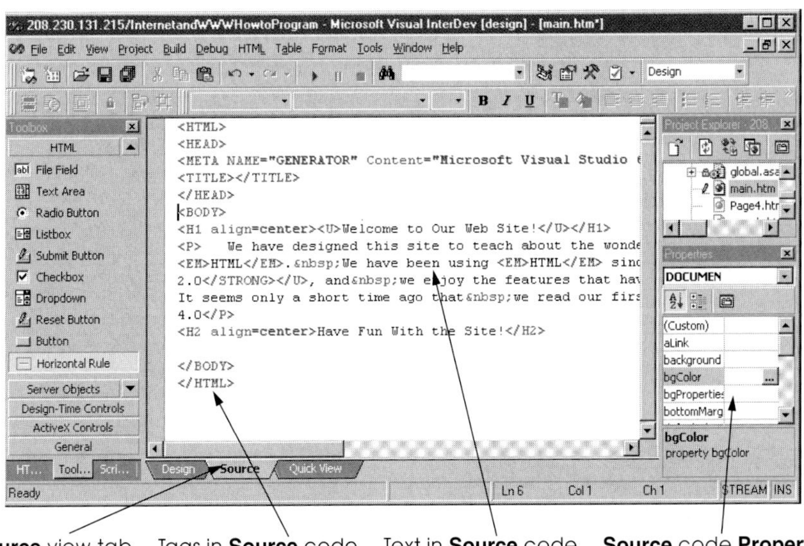

Fig. 7.12 Page editor **Source** view.

Fig. 7.13 Page editor **Quick View** mode.

7.9 Site Design View

Visual InterDev 6 provides the *Site Designer* tool for organizing the layout of your site and for updating connections between your pages. To access the Site Designer for your project, you must first add a ***Site Diagram*** file to your projects directory. This can be done through the **Add Item...** option in the **Project** menu (which we also used in Fig. 7.6) or through the **Add** list in the **Project Explorer** right-click menu (see Fig. 7.7). Give your **Site Diagram** a name you can remember and find easily (you can add more than one **Site Diagram**—if you plan to, then you may want to name each one according to its function). A **Site Diagram** for our project is in Fig. 7.14.

The Site Designer helps make and track connections between pages in your project. To bring an icon for a page into the **Site Diagram**, right-click in the main area and choose the ***Add Existing File...*** option. You can add new pages to your project using the Site Designer by selecting the ***New HTML Page*** option in the right-click menu. This menu can also be used to change the settings of the pages on the **Site Diagram**.

When a page is added to the **Site Diagram**, it appears in the form of a box with its name displayed at the top of the box. You can change the file name by clicking on it and typing in the new name.

You can take advantage of the Site Designer only when there is more than one file designated in the **Site Diagram**, as in Fig. 7.15.

When you have more than one file in the **Site Diagram**, you can create a link between the pages by dragging them close to one another until a dashed line appears. This dashed line indicates that a link has been inserted into each page, connecting one page to the other.

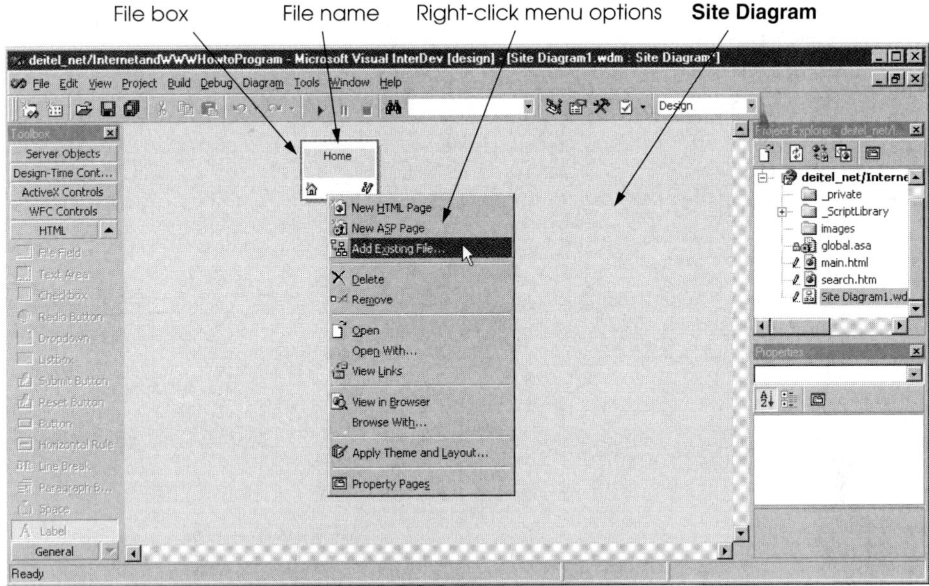

Fig. 7.14 Site design view: **Add Existing File...**.

You can also create a hierarchy of pages using the Site Designer. The level of importance in this hierarchy extends from top to bottom, with the top-most files being on the first tier, and the bottom-most files being in the lowest tier. If you applied a **Layout** to your site in Section 7.3, this hierarchy can be used by Visual InterDev to automatically create *navigation bars* throughout your site. You can define the content of these navigation bars by position in the hierarchy—for example, you can have a third-tier page link to all other third-tier pages in the project and to its parent page on the second tier—so the hierarchy of your site can turn out to be important to the way people navigate through your site.

Figure 7.15 also shows two steps in the procedure of changing a file's place in the hierarchy. In the first screen we see a three-level hierarchy in the process of being changed. As shown, you can use the mouse to drag the bottom-most file onto the second tier of the site. The new possible links of this page are displayed with dotted lines. In the second screen, we see the new hierarchy of the site.

The Site Designer also has the capability to keep track of the pages in your ***Site Diagram*** and correct any *broken links* (links that refer to a page that has moved or has been deleted) that may occur. For example, if you change the name of a page in your **Site Diagram**, then all links to it from other pages in the **Site Diagram** will be automatically corrected to the new page name. This tool can save you time when making changes to your site.

As your project gets larger, the Site Designer should be regularly updated to reflect changes in hierarchy and additions of files. This will help you keep your site working to its fullest potential throughout the life of your project.

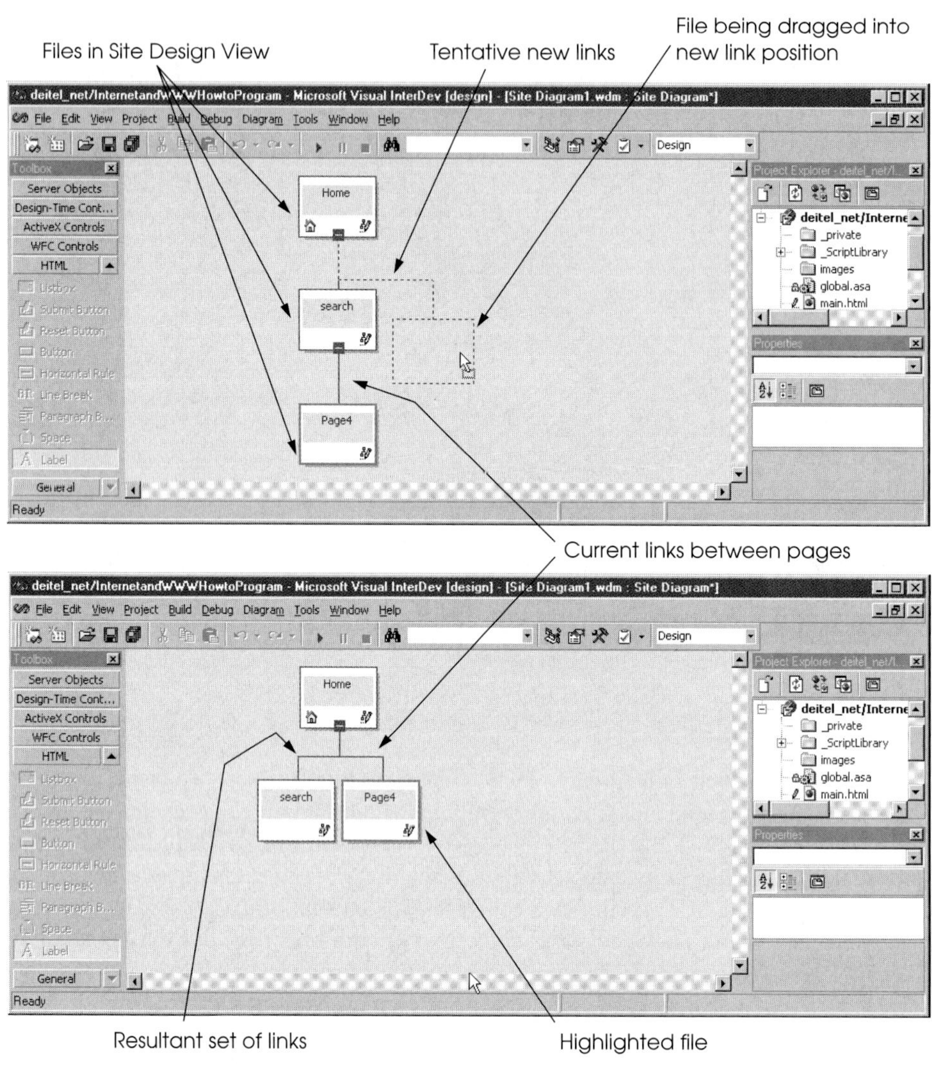

Fig. 7.15 Changing the site structure in site design view.

7.10 Internet and World Wide Web Resources

If you have trouble using Visual InterDev, the best place to look for support is Microsoft's site. Located at **`http://msdn.microsoft.com/vinterdev/`**, the Microsoft Visual InterDev Home Page has tutorials, samples and articles written by professionals who use InterDev. Another resource, located at **`http://bdcnet.net/programming/visual_interdev.htm`**, lists a number of major Web sites related to programming with Visual InterDev.

SUMMARY

- Microsoft Visual InterDev 6 combines a powerful HTML WYSIWYG editor with a thorough source editing interface that simplifies all the coding you do throughout the book and will help you to produce powerful Web-based, multitier, client/server database-intensive applications.
- A Web server is a computer that responds to file requests by browsers.
- In order to create even a bare-bones Web site with Visual InterDev, you must specify a server with which the program should connect and share information.
- If you are working on an LAN, you are connected to a server. You can use this server when designing a Web site with Visual InterDev.
- If you are not connected to a server, you must create a server on your own computer with Microsoft's Personal Web Server, which is included on the CD.
- To start creating your first Web site using Visual InterDev, you must create a shell of a site on your server through the **New Project** dialog box that appears whenever you start Visual InterDev.
- On the right side of the **New Project** dialog, you can choose what type of project you would like to create. Whenever beginning a new project, make sure that the **New Web Project** icon is highlighted.
- The project setup window that appears on your screen after you open your new project for the first time will ask you for the server Visual InterDev that you will be communicating with when you are designing your topic.
- When working in **Master Mode**, any changes you make to the project will be immediately added to the version of your project on the server.
- When working in **Local Mode**, all changes to the project are kept on your computer until you choose to update the server.
- The second setup window prompts you to enter the name for your new application.
- The third and fourth setup windows ask you to choose a layout and a theme for your site.
- Upon completing the setup for your new project, Visual InterDev creates a new directory on your chosen server. Inside this main directory a number of folders are created containing basic information for your site, along with all files necessary for your chosen layout and theme.
- The interface of Visual InterDev 6 simplifies building, editing, testing and publishing your Web site and Web-based applications.
- To add an item to an open project, select the **Add Item...** option located in the **Project** menu. Enter a name for your HTML file. Click the **Open** button when done entering the file name and Visual InterDev will create your new blank HTML file in the main directory of your project.
- Visual InterDev has a number of tools that simplify editing your pages immensely. These tools can all be positioned on your screen for easy access.
- When you start Visual InterDev for the first time, only the **Project Explorer** window is on the screen, located along the right side of the main screen by default.
- If you prefer that any window on the screen be floating instead of anchored double-click on the blue title bar at the top of the window. To reattach any floating window double-click on its title bar.
- The **Project Explorer** displays the directories and files of your project. When an item is added to your project, it appears in the **Project Window** in its designated location.
- You can access many of the options for modifying your project and its files by right-clicking on the main project directory.
- A window that you should always have on the screen when editing pages is the **Toolbox** window. You can insert the **Toolbox** window by selecting the **Toolbox** option in the **View** menu.

- The **Toolbox** provides a shortcut to placing elements into page-editing screens. To position one of these elements, designate the place on your page where you would like to insert the element, then locate and double-click the button representing the desired element in the **Toolbox** window.
- Visual InterDev condenses four toolboxes into one interface—**Server Objects**, **Design Time Controls**, **ActiveX controls** and **HTML**.
- There are a number of **Toolbars** that can be inserted onto the top of the Visual InterDev screen. Toolbars contain shortcut buttons grouped by task and are inserted by highlighting the **Toolbars** option in the **View** menu, then choosing the desired **Toolbar** to be inserted.
- When editing a page you should also insert the **Properties Window**, which is used mostly for creating styles for your Web pages.
- Visual InterDev 6 includes an advanced editor to help design visually impressive and technically complex sites and pages. To enter the editor mode for a file, double-click on the file's entry in the **Project Explorer**.
- The Visual InterDev page editor includes three different views.
- **Design** view allows you to edit your page in a WYSIWYG interface.
- **Source** view allows you to edit the source of your page directly.
- **Quick View** allows you to view your page as it would appear in a browser.
- You can switch between views at any time when editing a file by clicking on the appropriate tab on the bottom of the editor window.
- When you load an HTML page, the HTML toolbar will automatically be inserted into the toolbar area at the top of the screen.
- The design view that we use most throughout this book is **Source** view. Visual InterDev **Source** view, is a vast improvement over we what have previously used to edit and view source. A feature of the **Source** view that will be used later in the book is its integration with scripting and Web-based application development.
- The **Quick View** editing mode renders your page as it would be rendered in Internet Explorer 4.
- If you would like to view your page in an actual Web browser, select the **View in Browser** option in the **View** menu.
- Visual InterDev 6 provides the Site Designer tool for organizing the layout of your site and for automatically updating connections between your pages.
- To access the Site Designer for your project, you must first add a **Site Diagram** file to your projects directory. This can be done through the **Add Item...** option in the **Project** menu.
- To bring an icon for a page into the **Site Diagram** right-click in the main area and choose the **Add Existing File...** option.
- You can add new pages to your project using the Site Designer by selecting the **New HTML Page** option in the right-click menu.
- When you have more than one file in the **Site Diagram,** you can create a link between the pages by dragging them close to one another until a dashed line appears. This dashed line indicates that a link has been inserted into each page, connecting one page to the other.
- You can also create a hierarchy of pages using the Site Designer. This hierarchy can be used by Visual InterDev to automatically create navigation bars throughout your site.
- The Site Designer also has the capability to keep track of the pages in your **Site Diagram** and correct any errors with their links that may occur.
- As your project gets larger, the Site Designer should be regularly updated to reflect changes in link hierarchy and additions of files.

TERMINOLOGY

ActiveX Controls toolbox
Add Item... in Project menu
anchored window
Apply Theme and Layout...
ASP Page
Browse With...
client-side programming
Design Time Controls toolbox
Design view
Discard Changes
Existing tab of **New Project** dialog box
floating window
Get Latest Version
Get Working Copy
global.asa
HTML Page
HTML toolbox
Integrated Design Environment (IDE)
Internet
LAN (local area network)
Local Mode
Master Mode
Name
navigation bar
network
New Project dialog box
New tab of **New Project** dialog box
New Web Project icon
<none> option in the project setup
Personal Web Server (PWS)
preset theme
Project Explorer
Project menu
Properties Window
PWS
Quick View
Recent tab on New Project dialog box
Release Working Copy
Sample App Wizard
search.htm
Server Objects toolbox
server-side programming
site designer
Site Diagram
Source view
styles
Style Sheet
theme
Toolbars
Toolbox
View in Browser
View menu
Visual InterDev 6
Web Project Wizard
Web server
WYSIWYG HTML editor

COMMON PROGRAMMING ERROR

7.1 Having the wrong type of project highlighted—**Visual Studio**—when beginning a new project will cause Visual InterDev to create a new project in a different format from what you are expecting.

SOFTWARE ENGINEERING OBSERVATION

7.1 Save your work every few minutes to prevent loss of information.

SELF-REVIEW EXERCISES

7.1 Fill in the blanks in each of the following:

a) The __________ window is used to modify styles in your Web page.

b) The three modes in the Visual InterDev WYSIWYG editor are ________, ________ and __________.

c) To create a new HTML file, you must select the ________ item option in the ________ menu.

d) In __________ mode, all changes made to pages in your project are automatically made on the copy of your project in the server.

e) If you are not connected to a Web server, Visual InterDev will automatically install __________ onto your system.
f) In order to access the site designer, you must first create a __________ file.

7.2 State whether each of the following are true or false. If the answer is false, explain why.
a) The **Toolbox** automatically changes to fit the type of file you are working on.
b) Visual InterDev is a strictly client-side programming device and does not have anything to do with servers.
c) You can edit your page's content while in-site designer mode.
d) You have to manually add any toolbars that you need to use.
e) You can view and edit the directory structure and files of your project in the **Project Explorer**.

ANSWERS TO SELF-REVIEW EXERCISES

7.1 a) **Properties** b) **Design**, **Source**, **Quick View** c) **Add Item...**, **View** d) **Master** e) Personal Web Server f) **Site Diagram**.

7.2 a) True.
b) False. Visual InterDev is intended to design dynamic client-side and server-side Web sites.
c) False. Site Designer is used to create and modify the hierarchy and links between the pages in your site. You can edit page's content in the page edit window, accessible by double-clicking the desired file in the **Project Explorer** window.
d) False. Toolbars will automatically be inserted onto the top of your screen to help with the current task.
e) True.

EXERCISES

7.3 Create a **New Project** called **InternetProgramming** with no preset theme or layout. After the project is created, add a new HTML file called `index.html`. Save your changes and close Visual InterDev.

7.4 Start Visual InterDev, locate and open the project you created in Exercise 7.3.

7.5 Add a **Site Diagram** to your project. Add the file you created in Exercise 7.3 `index.html` to the **Site Diagram**. While in the site designer, add two HTML pages called `contact.html` and `links.html`. Link the three pages in the **Site Diagram**, making the two new files second tier, and `index.html` first tier. Save your changes and close the site designer.

7.6 Open your `index.html` file. Type in a paragraph describing yourself. Use the WYSIWYG tools to create a header element, and style the text using colors, bold, italics and underline. Save and close your page.

7.7 Open the `contact.html` page and use the hyperlinks placed by the site designer to go to `index.html`. Save and close your project.

JavaScript/JScript: Introduction to Scripting

Objectives

- To be able to write simple JavaScript programs.
- To be able to use input and output statements.
- To understand basic memory concepts.
- To be able to use arithmetic operators.
- To understand the precedence of arithmetic operators.
- To be able to write decision-making statements.
- To be able to use relational and equality operators.

Comment is free, but facts are sacred.
C. P. Scott

The creditor hath a better memory than the debtor.
James Howell

When faced with a decision, I always ask, "What would be the most fun?"
Peggy Walker

Equality, in a social sense, may be divided into that of condition and that of rights.
James Fenimore Cooper

Outline

8.1 Introduction

In the first seven chapters, we introduced the Internet and World Wide Web, creating HTML documents and several tools that help Web page designers create HTML documents. In this chapter, we begin our introduction to the *JavaScript scripting language,* which facilitates a disciplined approach to designing computer programs that enhance the functionality and appearance of Web pages.

We now introduce JavaScript programming and present examples that illustrate several important features of JavaScript. Each example is analyzed one line at a time. In Chapters 9 and 10, we present a detailed treatment of *program development* and *program control* in JavaScript. *Note:* Microsoft's version of JavaScript is called *JScript.* JavaScript was originally created by Netscape. Both Netscape and Microsoft have been instrumental in the standardization of JavaScript/JScript by the *ECMA (European Computer Manufacturer's Association)* as *ECMAScript.* For information on the current ECMAScript standard, visit:

`http://www.ecma.ch/stand/ecma-262.htm`

Throughout this book we refer to JavaScript and JScript generically as JavaScript—the most commonly used name in industry.

8.2 A Simple Program: Printing a Line of Text in a Web Page

JavaScript uses notations that may appear strange to nonprogrammers. We begin by considering a simple *script* (or *program*) that displays the line of text "**`Welcome to JavaScript Programming!`**" in the body of an HTML document. The Internet Explorer Web browser contains the *JavaScript interpreter,* which processes the commands in a script written in JavaScript. The script and its output are shown in Fig. 8.1.

This program illustrates several important features of implementing a JavaScript in an HTML document. We consider each line of the HTML document and script in detail. We have given each HTML document line numbers for the reader's convenience; those line numbers are not part of the HTML document or of the JavaScript programs. Lines 9 and 10 do the "real work" of the script, namely displaying the phrase **`Welcome to JavaScript Programming!`** in the Web page. But let us consider each line in order.

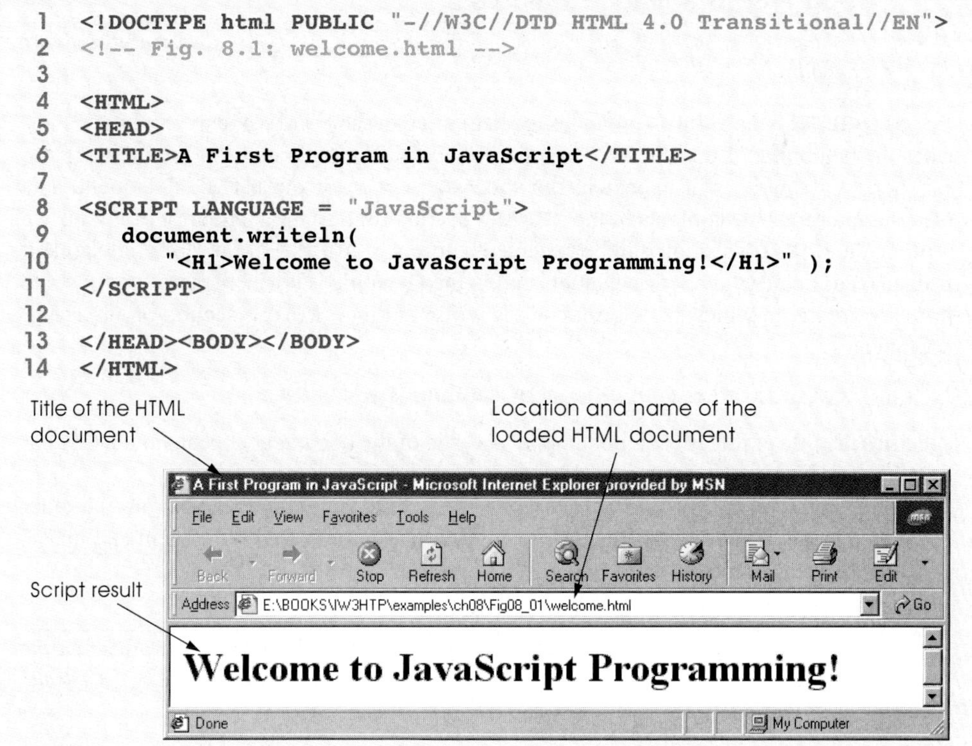

```
1  <!DOCTYPE html PUBLIC "-//W3C//DTD HTML 4.0 Transitional//EN">
2  <!-- Fig. 8.1: welcome.html -->
3
4  <HTML>
5  <HEAD>
6  <TITLE>A First Program in JavaScript</TITLE>
7
8  <SCRIPT LANGUAGE = "JavaScript">
9     document.writeln(
10       "<H1>Welcome to JavaScript Programming!</H1>" );
11 </SCRIPT>
12
13 </HEAD><BODY></BODY>
14 </HTML>
```


Fig. 8.1 A first program in JavaScript.

The **DOCTYPE** element in line 1 indicates that the document type is an HTML 4.0 document. Line 2

```
<!-- Fig. 8.1: welcome.html -->
```

is an HTML comment indicating the figure number and file name for this HTML document. Programmers insert HTML comments to *document* or *describe* the purpose of parts of an HTML document and to improve readability. Comments also help other people read and understand your HTML documents. We begin every HTML document with a comment indicating figure number and file name.

Good Programming Practice 8.1

HTML documents should begin with a comment describing the purpose of the document.

Line 3 is simply a blank line. Blank lines and space characters are often used throughout HTML documents and scripts to make them easier to read. Together, blank lines, space characters and tab characters are known as *whitespace* (space characters and tabs are known specifically as *whitespace characters*). Such characters are generally ignored by the browser. In many cases, such characters are used for readability and clarity. The spacing displayed by a browser in a Web page is determined by the HTML elements used to format the page. Several conventions for using whitespace characters are discussed in this chapter and the next several chapters, as these spacing conventions become needed.

Good Programming Practice 8.2

Use blank lines, space characters and tab characters in an HTML document to enhance readability.

The **<HTML>** tag at line 4 indicates the beginning of the HTML document. Line 5 indicates the beginning of the **<HEAD>** section of the HTML document. For the moment, the JavaScripts we write will appear in the **<HEAD>** section of the HTML document. The browser interprets the contents of the **<HEAD>** section first, so the JavaScript programs we write in the **<HEAD>** section will be executed before the **<BODY>** of the HTML document is displayed. In later JavaScript chapters and in the Dynamic HTML chapters, we illustrate *inline scripting,* in which JavaScript code is written in the **<BODY>** section of an HTML document. Line 6

```
<TITLE>A First Program in JavaScript</TITLE>
```

specifies the title of this HTML document. The title of the document appears in the title bar of the browser when the document is loaded.

Line 7 is simply a blank line to separate the **<SCRIPT>** tag at line 8 from the other HTML elements. This effect helps the script stand out in the HTML document and makes the document easier to read.

Good Programming Practice 8.3

Place a blank line before the ***<SCRIPT>*** *tag and after the* ***</SCRIPT>*** *tag to separate the script from the surrounding HTML elements and to make the script stand out in the document.*

Line 8

```
<SCRIPT LANGUAGE = "JavaScript">
```

uses the ***<SCRIPT>*** tag to indicate to the browser that the text that follows is part of a script. The ***LANGUAGE*** attribute specifies the *scripting language* used in the script—in this case, **JavaScript**. [*Note:* Even though Microsoft calls the language JScript, the **LANGUAGE** attribute specifies **JavaScript**, to adhere to the ECMAScript standard.] Both Microsoft Internet Explorer and Netscape Navigator use JavaScript as the default scripting language. Therefore, the preceding line can be written simply as

```
<SCRIPT>
```

with no **LANGUAGE** attribute specified.

Portability Tip 8.1

Specify the scripting language with the **LANGUAGE** *attribute of the* **<SCRIPT>** *tag, to ensure that all browsers in which the HTML document is loaded know the language of the script. Although it is unlikely at this time, future Web browsers may not use* **JavaScript** *as the default scripting language.*

Lines 9 and 10

```
document.writeln(
   "<H1>Welcome to JavaScript Programming!</H1>" );
```

instruct the browser's JavaScript interpreter to perform an *action*, namely to display in the Web page the *string* of characters contained between the *double quotation (") marks*. A string is sometimes called a *character string*, a *message* or a *string literal*. We refer to characters between double quotation marks generically as strings. Whitespace characters in strings are not ignored by the browser.

Software Engineering Observation 8.1

*Strings in JavaScript can also be enclosed in single quotation (**'**) marks.*

Lines 9 and 10 use the browser's ***document** object,* which represents the HTML document currently being displayed in the browser. The **document** object allows a script programmer to specify HTML text to be displayed in the HTML document. The browser contains a complete set of objects that allow script programmers to access and manipulate every element of an HTML document. In the next several chapters, we overview some of these objects. Chapters 14 through 22 provide in-depth coverage of many more objects that a script programmer can manipulate.

An object resides in the computer's memory and contains information used by the script. The term *object* normally implies that *attributes* (*data*) and *behaviors* (*methods*) are associated with the object. The object's methods use the attributes to provide useful services to the *client of the object*—the script that calls the methods. In the preceding statement, we call the **document** object's ***writeln** method* to write a line of HTML text in the HTML document being displayed. The parentheses following the method name **writeln** contain the *arguments* that the method requires to perform its task (or its action). Method **writeln** instructs the browser to display the argument string. If the string contains HTML elements, the browser interprets these elements and renders them on the screen. In this example, the browser displays the phrase **Welcome to JavaScript Programming!** as an **H1**-level HTML head, because the phrase is enclosed in an **H1** element. [*Note:* Using **writeln** to write a line of HTML text into the **document** does not necessarily write a line of text in the HTML document. The text displayed in the browser is entirely dependent on the contents of the string written, which is subsequently rendered by the browser. The browser will interpret the HTML elements as it normally does to render the final text in the document.]

The code elements in lines 9 and 10, including **document.writeln**, its *argument* in the parentheses (the string) and the *semicolon* (**;**), together are called a *statement*. Every statement should end with a semicolon (also known as the *statement terminator*), although this practice is not required by JavaScript.

Good Programming Practice 8.4

Always include the semicolon at the end of a statement to explicitly terminate the statement. This clarifies where one statement ends and the next statement begins.

Line 11

```
</SCRIPT>
```

indicates the end of the script.

Common Programming Error 8.1

*Forgetting the ending **</SCRIPT>** tag for a script may prevent the browser from interpreting the script properly and may prevent the HTML document from loading properly.*

The **</HEAD>** tag at line 13 indicates the end of the **<HEAD>** section. Also on line 13, the tags **<BODY>** and **</BODY>** specify that this HTML document has an empty body—no HTML appears in the **BODY** element. Line 14 indicates the end of this HTML document.

We are now ready to view our HTML document in Internet Explorer. Open this HTML document in the browser. If the script contains no syntax errors, the preceding script should produce the output shown in Fig. 8.1.

Common Programming Error 8.2

JavaScript is case sensitive. Not using the proper uppercase and lowercase letters is a syntax error. *A syntax error occurs when the script interpreter cannot recognize a statement. The interpreter normally issues an error message to help the programmer locate and fix the incorrect statement. Syntax errors are violations of the language rules. You will be notified of a syntax error when the interpreter attempts to execute the statement containing the error. The JavaScript interpreter in Internet Explorer reports all syntax errors by indicating in a separate popup window that a "*runtime error*" occurred (a problem occurred while the interpreter was running the script).*

Testing and Debugging Tip 8.1

When the interpreter reports a syntax error, the error may not be on the line indicated by the error messages. First, check the line where the error was reported. If that line does not contain errors, check the preceding several lines in the script.

Some older Web browsers do not support scripting. In such browsers, the actual text of a script will often display in the Web page. To prevent this from happening, many script programmers enclose the script code in an HTML comment so the browser ignores the script if it does not support scripts. The syntax used is as follows:

```
<SCRIPT LANGUAGE = "JavaScript">
<!--
    script code here
// -->
</SCRIPT>
```

When a browser that does not support scripts encounters the preceding code, it ignores the **<SCRIPT>** and **</SCRIPT>** tags and the script code in the HTML comment. Browsers that do support scripting will interpret the JavaScript code as expected. [*Note:* The *JavaScript single-line comment* **//** (see section 8.3 for an explanation) before the ending HTML comment delimiter (**-->**) is required in some browsers for the script to interpret properly.]

Portability Tip 8.2

Some browsers do not support the **<SCRIPT></SCRIPT>** *tags. If your document is to be rendered with such browsers, the script code between these tags should be enclosed in an HTML comment so the script text does not display as part of the Web page.*

Welcome to JavaScript Programming! can be displayed in several ways. Figure 8.2 uses two JavaScript statements to produce one line of text in the HTML document. In this example, we also changed the color of the text displayed.

The majority of this HTML document is identical to Fig. 8.1, so we concentrate only on lines 9 and 10 of Fig. 8.2

```
document.write( "<FONT COLOR='magenta'><H1>Welcome to " );
document.writeln( "JavaScript Programming!</H1></FONT>" );
```

```
1  <!DOCTYPE html PUBLIC "-//W3C//DTD HTML 4.0 Transitional//EN">
2  <HTML>
3  <!-- Fig. 8.2: welcome.html -->
4
5  <HEAD>
6  <TITLE>Printing a Line with Multiple Statements</TITLE>
7
8  <SCRIPT LANGUAGE = "JavaScript">
9     document.write( "<FONT COLOR='magenta'><H1>Welcome to " );
10    document.writeln( "JavaScript Programming!</H1></FONT>" );
11 </SCRIPT>
12
13 </HEAD><BODY></BODY>
14 </HTML>
```

Fig. 8.2 Printing on one line with separate statements.

which display one line of text in the HTML document. The first statement uses **`document`** method ***`write`*** to display a string. Unlike **`writeln`**, **`write`** does not position the output cursor in the HTML document at the beginning of the next line after writing its argument. [*Note:* The output cursor keeps track of where the next character will be placed in the HTML document.] The next character written in the HTML document appears immediately after the last character written with **`write`**. Thus, when line 10 executes, the first character written, "**`J`**," appears immediately after the last character displayed with **`write`** (the space character inside the right double quote on line 9). Each **`write`** or **`writeln`** statement resumes writing characters where the last **`write`** or **`writeln`** stopped writing characters. So after a **`writeln`**, the next output appears on the next line. In effect, the preceding two statements result in one line of HTML text.

It is important to note that the preceding discussion has nothing to do with the actual rendering of the HTML text. Remember that the browser does not create a new line of text unless the browser window is too narrow for the text being rendered or an HTML element is encountered that causes the browser to start a new line—e.g., **
** to start a new line, **<P>** to start a new paragraph, etc.

Common Programming Error 8.3

Many people confuse the writing of HTML text with the rendering of HTML text. Writing HTML text creates the HTML that will be rendered by the browser for presentation to the user.

In the next example, we demonstrate that a single statement can cause the browser to display multiple lines by using line break HTML tags (**
**) throughout the string of

HTML text in a **`write`** or **`writeln`** method call. Figure 8.3 demonstrates using line break HTML tags.

Lines 8 and 9

```
document.writeln(
   "<H1>Welcome to<BR>JavaScript<BR>Programming!</H1>" );
```

produce three separate lines of text in the HTML document. Remember that statements in JavaScript are separated with semicolons (**`;`**). Therefore, lines 8 and 9 represent one statement. JavaScript allows large statements to be split over many lines. However, you cannot split a statement in the middle of a string.

Common Programming Error 8.4

Splitting a statement in the middle of a string is a syntax error.

The first several programs display text in the HTML document. Sometimes it is useful to display information in windows called *dialog boxes* that "pop up" on the screen to grab the user's attention. Dialog boxes are typically used to display important messages to the user who is browsing the Web page. JavaScript allows you to easily display a dialog box containing a message. The program of Fig. 8.4 displays **`Welcome to JavaScript Programming`**! as three lines in a predefined dialog box called an ***`alert`*** *dialog*.

```
1  <!DOCTYPE html PUBLIC "-//W3C//DTD HTML 4.0 Transitional//EN">
2  <HTML>
3  <!-- Fig. 8.3: welcome.html -->
4
5  <HEAD><TITLE>Printing Multiple Lines</TITLE>
6
7  <SCRIPT LANGUAGE = "JavaScript">
8     document.writeln(
9        "<H1>Welcome to<BR>JavaScript<BR>Programming!</H1>" );
10 </SCRIPT>
11
12 </HEAD><BODY></BODY>
13 </HTML>
```

Fig. 8.3 Printing on multiple lines with a single statement.

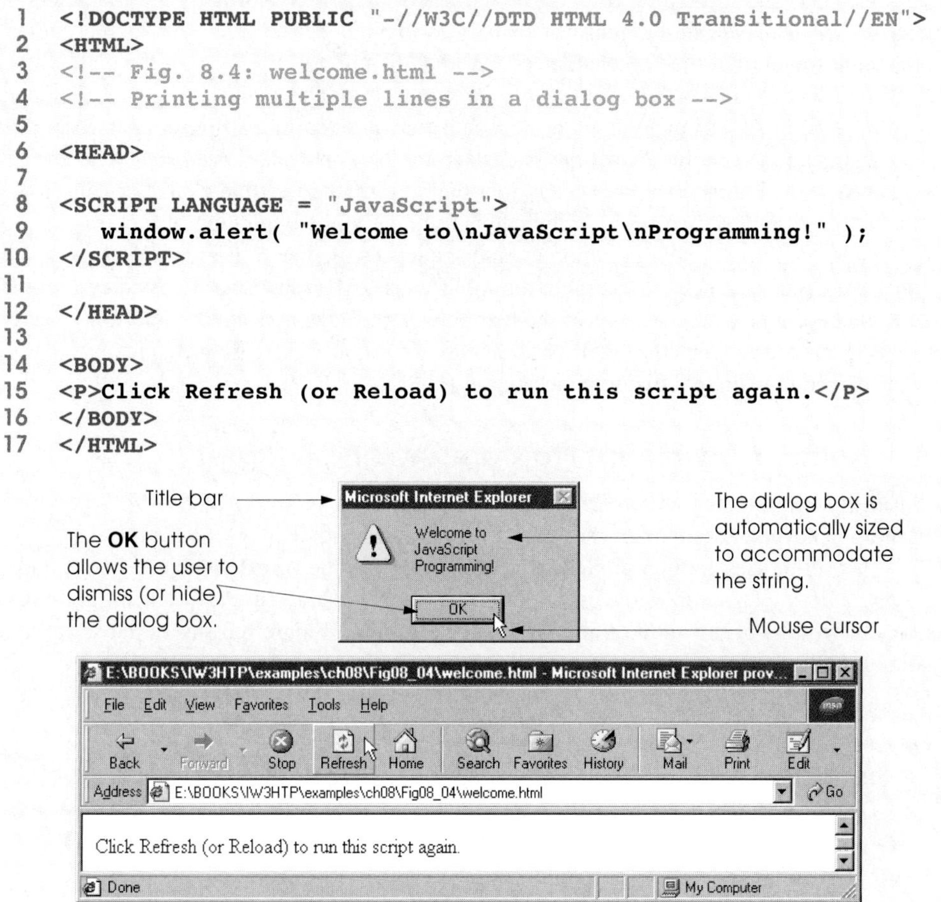

```
1  <!DOCTYPE HTML PUBLIC "-//W3C//DTD HTML 4.0 Transitional//EN">
2  <HTML>
3  <!-- Fig. 8.4: welcome.html -->
4  <!-- Printing multiple lines in a dialog box -->
5
6  <HEAD>
7
8  <SCRIPT LANGUAGE = "JavaScript">
9     window.alert( "Welcome to\nJavaScript\nProgramming!" );
10 </SCRIPT>
11
12 </HEAD>
13
14 <BODY>
15 <P>Click Refresh (or Reload) to run this script again.</P>
16 </BODY>
17 </HTML>
```


Fig. 8.4 Displaying multiple lines in a dialog box.

Line 9 in the script

```
window.alert( "Welcome to\nJavaScript\nProgramming!" );
```

uses the browser's ***window*** object to display an alert dialog box. Method ***alert*** of the **window** object requires as its argument the string to display. Executing the preceding statement displays the dialog box shown in the first window of Fig. 8.4. The *title bar* of the dialog contains the string **Microsoft Internet Explorer,** to indicate that the browser is presenting a message to the user. The dialog box automatically includes an **OK** button that allows the user to *dismiss (hide) the dialog* by pressing the button. This is accomplished by positioning the *mouse cursor* (also called the *mouse pointer*) over the **OK** button and clicking the mouse.

Common Programming Error 8.5

Dialog boxes display plain text—they do not render HTML. Therefore, specifying HTML elements as part of a string to display in a dialog box results in the actual characters of the tags being displayed.

Note that the alert dialog contains three lines of plain text. Normally the characters in a string are displayed in a dialog box exactly as they appear between the double quotes. Notice, however, that the two characters "\" and "**n**" are not displayed in the dialog box. The *backslash* (\) in a string is an *escape character*. It indicates that a "special" character is to be used in the string. When a backslash is encountered in a string of characters, the next character is combined with the backslash to form an *escape sequence*. The escape sequence **\n** is the *newline character*. In a dialog box, the newline character causes the *cursor* (the current screen position indicator) to move to the beginning of the next line in the dialog box. Some other common escape sequences are listed in Fig. 8.5. The **\n**, **\t** and **\r** escape sequences in the table do not affect HTML rendering unless they are in a **PRE** element (this element displays the text between its tags in a fixed-width font exactly as it is formatted between the tags). The other escape sequences result in characters that will be displayed in plain text dialog boxes and in HTML.

8.3 Another JavaScript Program: Adding Integers

Our next script inputs two *integers* (whole numbers such as 7, –11, 0, 31914) typed by a user at the keyboard, computes the sum of these values and displays the result.

This script uses another predefined dialog box from the **window** object, one called a ***prompt*** *dialog,* that allows the user to input a value for use in the script. The program displays the results of the addition in the HTML document. Figure 8.6 shows the script and some sample screen captures. [Note: In later JavaScript chapters, we will obtain input via GUI components in HTML forms, as introduced in Chapter 4].

Escape sequence	Description
`\n`	Newline. Position the screen cursor to the beginning of the next line.
`\t`	Horizontal tab. Move the screen cursor to the next tab stop.
`\r`	Carriage return. Position the screen cursor to the beginning of the current line; do not advance to the next line. Any characters output after the carriage return overwrite the previous characters output on that line.
`\\`	Backslash. Used to represent a backslash character in a string.
`\"`	Double quote. Used to represent a double quote character in a string contained in double quotes. For example, `window.alert( "\"in quotes\"" );` displays **"in quotes"** in an **alert** dialog.
`\'`	Single quote. Used to represent a single quote character in a string. For example, `window.alert( '\'in quotes\'' );` displays **'in quotes'** in an **alert** dialog.

Fig. 8.5 Some common escape sequences.

```
<!DOCTYPE html PUBLIC "-//W3C//DTD HTML 4.0 Transitional//EN">
<HTML>
<!-- Fig. 8.6: Addition.html -->

<HEAD>
<TITLE>An Addition Program</TITLE>

<SCRIPT LANGUAGE = "JavaScript">
   var firstNumber,   // first string entered by user
       secondNumber,  // second string entered by user
       number1,       // first number to add
       number2,       // second number to add
       sum;           // sum of number1 and number2

   // read in first number from user as a string
   firstNumber = window.prompt( "Enter first integer", "0" );

   // read in second number from user as a string
   secondNumber = window.prompt( "Enter second integer", "0" );

   // convert numbers from strings to integers
   number1 = parseInt( firstNumber );
   number2 = parseInt( secondNumber );

   // add the numbers
   sum = number1 + number2;

   // display the results
   document.writeln( "<H1>The sum is " + sum + "</H1>" );
</SCRIPT>

</HEAD>
<BODY>
<P>Click Refresh (or Reload) to run the script again</P>
</BODY>
</HTML>
```

Fig. 8.6 An addition script "in action" (part 1 of 2).

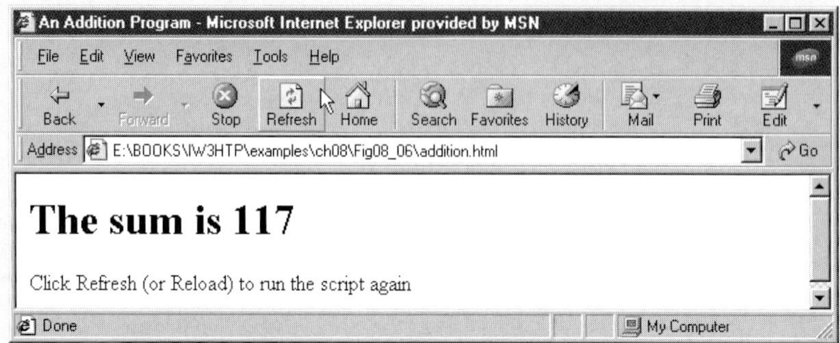

Fig. 8.6 An addition script "in action" (part 2 of 2).

Lines 9 through 13

```
var firstNumber,    // first string entered by user
    secondNumber,   // second string entered by user
    number1,        // first number to add
    number2,        // second number to add
    sum;            // sum of number1 and number2
```

are a *declaration.* The keyword **`var`** at the beginning of the statement indicates that the words **`firstNumber`**, **`secondNumber`**, **`number1`**, **`number2`** and **`sum`** are the names of *variables.* A variable is a location in the computer's memory where a value can be stored for use by a program. All variables should be declared with a name in a **`var`** statement before they are used in a program. Although using **`var`** to declare variables is not required, we will see in Chapter 11, "JavaScript/JScript: Functions," that **`var`** sometimes ensures proper behavior of a script.

A variable name can be any valid *identifier*. An identifier is a series of characters consisting of letters, digits, underscores (**`_`**) and dollar signs (**`$`**) that does not begin with a digit and does not contain any spaces. Some valid identifiers are **`Welcome`**, **`$value`**, **`_value`**, **`m_inputField1`** and **`button7`**. The name **`7button`** is not a valid identifier because it begins with a digit, and the name **`input field`** is not a valid identifier because it contains a space. Remember that JavaScript is *case sensitive*—uppercase and lowercase letters are different, so **`firstNumber`**, **`FiRsTnUmBeR`** and **`FIRSTNUMBER`** are different identifiers.

Good Programming Practice 8.5

Choosing meaningful variable names helps a script to be "self-documenting" (one that is easy to understand by simply reading it, rather than having to read manuals or excessive comments).

Good Programming Practice 8.6

By convention, variable name identifiers begin with a lowercase first letter. Every word in the name after the first word should begin with a capital first letter. For example, identifier ***`firstNumber`*** *has a capital* ***`N`*** *in its second word* ***`Number`****.*

Common Programming Error 8.6

Splitting a statement in the middle of an identifier is normally a syntax error.

Declarations (like statements) end with a semicolon (**;**) and can be split over several lines (as shown here) with each variable in the declaration separated by a comma—known as a *comma-separated list* of variable names. Several variables may be declared either in one declaration or in multiple declarations. We could have written five declarations, one for each variable, but the preceding single declaration is more concise.

Programmers often indicate the purpose of each variable in the program by placing a JavaScript comment at the end of each line in the declaration. In lines 9 through 13, *single-line comments* that begin with the characters **//** are used to state the purpose of each variable in the script. This form of comment is called a single-line comment because the comment terminates at the end of the line. A **//** comment can begin at any position in a line of JavaScript code and continues until the end of that line. Comments do not cause the browser to perform any action when the script is interpreted; rather, comments are ignored by the JavaScript interpreter.

Good Programming Practice 8.7

Some programmers prefer to declare each variable on a separate line. This format allows for easy insertion of a descriptive comment next to each declaration.

Another comment notation facilitates writing *multiple-line comments.* For example,

```
/* This is a multiple-line
   comment. It can be
   split over many lines. */
```

is a comment that can spread over several lines. Such comments begin with delimiter **/*** and end with delimiter ***/**. All text between the delimiters of the comment is ignored by the compiler.

Common Programming Error 8.7

Forgetting one of the delimiters of a multiple-line comment is a syntax error.

Common Programming Error 8.8

Nesting multiple-line comments (placing a multiple-line comment between the delimiters of another multiple-line comment) is a syntax error.

Note: JavaScript adopted comments delimited with **/*** and ***/** from the C programming language and single-line comments delimited with **//** from the C++ programming language. JavaScript programmers generally use C++-style single-line comments in preference to C-style comments. Throughout this book, we use C++-style single-line comments.

Line 15

```
// read in first number from user as a string
```

is a single-line comment indicating the purpose of the statement at line 16.

Line 16

```
firstNumber = window.prompt( "Enter first integer", "0" );
```

allows the user to enter a string representing the first of the two integers that will be added. The **window** object's ***prompt*** method displays the following **prompt** dialog:

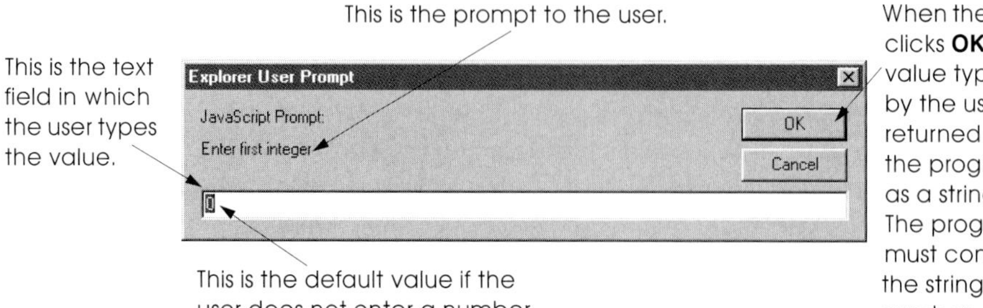
This is the prompt to the user.
When the user clicks OK, the value typed by the user is returned to the program as a string. The program must convert the string to a number.
This is the text field in which the user types the value.
Explorer User Prompt
JavaScript Prompt:
Enter first integer
OK
Cancel
0
This is the default value if the user does not enter a number.

The first argument to **prompt** indicates to the user what to do in the text field. This message is called a *prompt* because it directs the user to take a specific action. The optional second argument is the default string to display in the text field—if the second argument is not supplied, the text field does not contain a default value. The user types characters in the text field, then clicks the **OK** button to return the string to the program. [If you type and nothing appears in the text field, position the mouse pointer in the text field and click the mouse to activate the text field.] Unfortunately, JavaScript does not provide a simple form of input that is analogous to writing a line of text with **document.write** and **document.writeln**. For this reason, we normally receive input from a user through a GUI component such as the **prompt** dialog in this program or through an HTML form GUI component, as we will see in later chapters.

Technically, the user can type anything in the text field of the **prompt** dialog. For this program, if the user either types a non-integer value or clicks the **Cancel** button, a run-time logic error will occur and the sum of the two values will appear in the HTML document as *NaN* (*not a number*). In Chapter 13, "JavaScript: Objects," we discuss the **Number** object and its methods that can be used to determine whether a value is not a number.

The result of the call to **window.prompt** (a string containing the characters typed by the user) is given to variable **firstNumber** with the *assignment operator* **=**. The statement is read as, "**firstNumber**, *gets* the value of **window.prompt("Enter first integer", "0")**." The **=** operator is called a *binary operator* because it has two *operands*—**firstNumber** and the result of the expression **window.prompt("Enter first integer", "0")**. This whole statement is called an *assignment statement,* because it assigns a value to a variable. The expression to the right of the assignment operator **=** is always evaluated first.

Lines 18 and 19

```
// read in second number from user as a string
secondNumber = window.prompt( "Enter second integer", "0" );
```

consist of a single-line comment (line 18) that indicates the purpose of the statement at line 19. The statement displays a **prompt** dialog in which the user types a string representing the second of the two integers that will be added.

Lines 22 and 23

```
number1 = parseInt( firstNumber );
number2 = parseInt( secondNumber );
```

convert the two strings input by the user to **int** values that can be used in a calculation. Function ***parseInt*** converts its string argument to an integer. The integer returned by

parseInt in line 22 is assigned to variable **number1**. Any subsequent references to **number1** in the program use this same integer value. The integer returned by **parseInt** in line 23 is assigned to variable **number2**. Any subsequent references to **number2** in the program use this same integer value. [Note: We refer to **parseInt** as a *function* rather than a *method* because we do not precede the function call with an object name (such as **document** or **window**) and a dot operator (**.**). The term method implies that the function belongs to a particular object. For example, method **writeln** belongs to the **document** object and method **prompt** belongs to the **window** object.]

The assignment statement at line 26

```
sum = number1 + number2;
```

calculates the sum of the variables **number1** and **number2** and assigns the result to variable **sum** by using the assignment operator =. The statement is read as, "**sum** *gets* the value of **number1 + number2**." Most calculations are performed in assignment statements.

Good Programming Practice 8.8

Place spaces on either side of a binary operator. This makes the operator stand out and makes the program more readable.

After performing the calculation on line 26, on line 29 of the script,

```
document.writeln( "<H1>The sum is " + sum + "</H1>" );
```

displays the result of the addition using **document.writeln**. The expression

```
"<H1>The sum is " + sum + "</H1>"
```

from the preceding statement uses the operator **+** to "add" a string (the literal "**<H1>The sum is** ") and **sum** (the variable containing the integer result of the addition on line 26). JavaScript has a version of the **+** operator for *string concatenation* that enables a string and a value of another data type (including another string) to be concatenated—the result of this operation is a new (and normally longer) string. If we assume that **sum** contains the value **117**, the expression evaluates as follows: JavaScript determines that the two operands of the **+** operator (the string "**<H1>The sum is** " and the integer **sum**) are different types and one of them is a string. Next, the value of variable **sum** is automatically converted to a string and concatenated with "**<H1>The sum is** ", which results in the string "**<H1>The sum is 117**". Next, the string "**</H1>**" is concatenated to produce the string "**<H1>The sum is 117</H1>**". This string is rendered by the browser as part of the HTML document. Note that the automatic conversion of integer **sum** occurs because it is concatenated with the string literal "**<H1>The sum is** ". Also note that the space between **is** and **117** is part of the string "**<H1>The sum is** ".

Common Programming Error 8.9

Confusing the **+** *operator used for string concatenation with the* **+** *operator used for addition can lead to strange results. For example, assuming integer variable* **y** *has the value* **5**, *the expression* **"y + 2 = " + y + 2** *results in the string* **"y + 2 = 52"**, *not* **"y + 2 = 7"**, *because first the value of* **y** *is concatenated with the string* **"y + 2 = "**, *then the value* **2** *is concatenated with the new larger string* **"y + 2 = 5"**. *The expression* **"y + 2 = " + (y + 2)** *produces the desired result.*

After the browser interprets the **<HEAD>** section of the HTML document (which contains the JavaScript), it then interprets the **<BODY>** of the HTML document (lines 33 through 35) and renders the HTML. If you click your browser's **Refresh** (or **Reload**) button, the browser will reload the HTML document so that you can execute the script again and add two new integers. [*Note:* In some cases, it may be necessary to hold the Shift key while clicking your browser's **Refresh** (or **Reload**) button to ensure that the HTML document reloads properly.]

8.4 Memory Concepts

Variable names such as **number1**, **number2** and **sum** actually correspond to *locations* in the computer's memory. Every variable has a *name,* a *type* and a *value.*

In the addition program of Fig. 8.6, when the statement

```
number1 = parseInt( firstNumber );
```

executes, the string **firstNumber** (previously entered by the user in a **prompt** dialog) is converted to an integer and placed into a memory location to which the name **number1** has been assigned by the compiler. Suppose the user entered the string **45** as the value for **firstNumber**. The program converts **firstNumber** to an integer, and the computer places that integer value **45** into location **number1** as shown in Fig. 8.7.

Whenever a value is placed in a memory location, this new value replaces the previous value in that location. The previous value is lost.

When the statement

```
number2 = Integer.parseInt( secondNumber );
```

executes, suppose the user entered the string **72** as the value for **secondNumber**. The program converts **secondNumber** to an integer and the computer places that integer value **72** into location **number2** and memory appears as shown in Fig. 8.8.

Once the program has obtained values for **number1** and **number2**, it adds these values and places the sum into variable **sum**. The statement

```
sum = number1 + number2;
```

number1	45

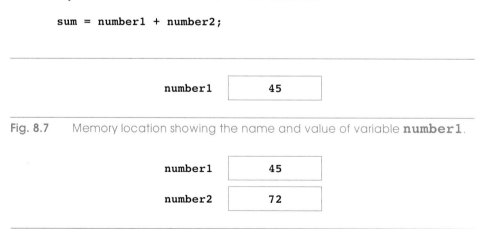

Fig. 8.7 Memory location showing the name and value of variable **number1**.

number1	45
number2	72

Fig. 8.8 Memory locations after values for variables **number1** and **number2** have been input.

performs the addition also replaces **sum**'s previous value. After **sum** is calculated, memory appears as shown in Fig. 8.9. Note that the values of **number1** and **number2** appear exactly as they did before they were used in the calculation of **sum**. These values were used, but not destroyed, as the computer performed the calculation. When a value is read from a memory location, the process is nondestructive.

8.5 Arithmetic

Many scripts perform arithmetic calculations. The *arithmetic operators* are summarized in Fig. 8.10. Note the use of various special symbols not used in algebra. The *asterisk* (*) indicates multiplication; the *percent sign* (%) is the *modulus operator*, which is discussed shortly. The arithmetic operators in Fig. 8.10 are called binary operators, because each operates on two operands. For example, the expression **sum + value** contains the binary operator **+** and the two operands **sum** and **value**.

JavaScript provides the modulus operator, %, which yields the remainder after division. The expression **x % y** yields the remainder after **x** is divided by **y**. Thus, **7.4 % 3.1** yields **1.2** and **17 % 5** yields **2**. In later chapters, we consider many interesting applications of the modulus operator such as determining whether one number is a multiple of another. There is no arithmetic operator for exponentiation in JavaScript. (Chapter 10 shows how to perform exponentiation in JavaScript.)

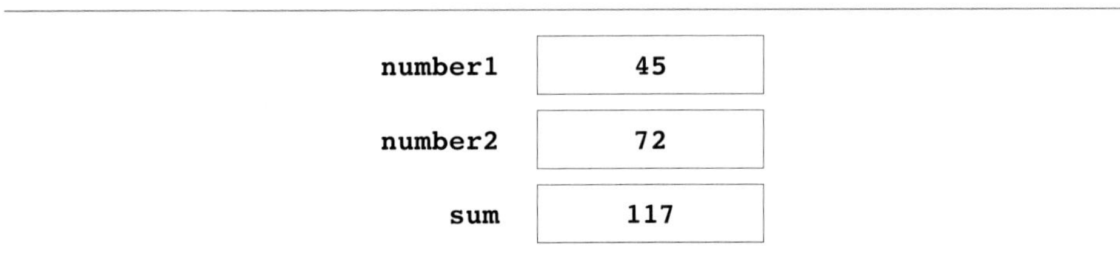

Fig. 8.9 Memory locations after a calculation.

JavaScript operation	Arithmetic operator	Algebraic expression	JavaScript expression
Addition	+	$f + 7$	`f + 7`
Subtraction	-	$p - c$	`p - c`
Multiplication	*	bm	`b * m`
Division	/	x / y or $\frac{x}{y}$ or $x \div y$	`x / y`
Modulus	%	$r \bmod s$	`r % s`

Fig. 8.10 Arithmetic operators.

Arithmetic expressions in JavaScript must be written in *straight-line form* to facilitate entering programs into the computer. Thus, expressions such as "**a** divided by **b**" must be written as **a / b** so that all constants, variables and operators appear in a straight line. The following algebraic notation is generally not acceptable to computers:

$$\frac{a}{b}$$

Parentheses are used in JavaScript expressions in the same manner as in algebraic expressions. For example, to multiply **a** times the quantity **b + c** we write:

```
a * ( b + c )
```

JavaScript applies the operators in arithmetic expressions in a precise sequence determined by the following *rules of operator precedence,* which are generally the same as those followed in algebra:

1. Operators in expressions contained between a left parenthesis and its corresponding right parenthesis are evaluated first. Thus, *parentheses may be used to force the order of evaluation to occur in any sequence desired by the programmer.* Parentheses are said to be at the "highest level of precedence." In cases of *nested* or *embedded* parentheses, the operators in the innermost pair of parentheses are applied first.

2. Multiplication, division and modulus operations are applied next. If an expression contains several multiplication, division and modulus operations, operators are applied from left to right. Multiplication, division and modulus are said to have the same level of precedence.

3. Addition and subtraction operations are applied last. If an expression contains several addition and subtraction operations, operators are applied from left to right. Addition and subtraction have the same level of precedence.

The rules of operator precedence enable JavaScript to apply operators in the correct order. When we say that operators are applied from left to right, we are referring to the *associativity* of the operators—the order in which operators of equal priority are evaluated. We will see that some operators associate from right to left. Figure 8.11 summarizes these rules of operator precedence. This table will be expanded as additional JavaScript operators are introduced. A complete precedence chart is included in Appendix B.

Now let us consider several expressions in light of the rules of operator precedence. Each example lists an algebraic expression and its JavaScript equivalent.

The following is an example of an arithmetic mean (average) of five terms:

Algebra: $m = \dfrac{a + b + c + d + e}{5}$

JavaScript: **m = (a + b + c + d + e) / 5;**

The parentheses are required because division has higher precedence than addition. The entire quantity **(a + b + c + d + e)** is to be divided by **5**. If the parentheses are erroneously omitted, we obtain **a + b + c + d + e / 5**, which evaluates as

$$a + b + c + d + \frac{e}{5}$$

Operator(s)	Operation(s)	Order of evaluation (precedence)
( )	Parentheses	Evaluated first. If the parentheses are nested, the expression in the innermost pair is evaluated first. If there are several pairs of parentheses "on the same level" (not nested), they are evaluated left to right.
*, / or %	Multiplication Division Modulus	Evaluated second. If there are several, they are evaluated left to right.
+ or -	Addition Subtraction	Evaluated last. If there are several, they are evaluated left to right.

Fig. 8.11 Precedence of arithmetic operators.

The following is an example of the equation of a straight line:

Algebra: $y = mx + b$

JavaScript: `y = m * x + b;`

No parentheses are required. The multiplication is applied first, because multiplication has a higher precedence than addition. The assignment occurs last because it has a lower precedence than multiplication and addition.

The following example contains modulus (`%`), multiplication, division, addition and subtraction operations:

Algebra: $z = pr\%q + w/x - y$

JavaScript:

```
z  =  p  *  r  %  q  +  w  /  x  -  y;
   6     1     2     4     3     5
```

The circled numbers under the statement indicate the order in which JavaScript applies the operators. The multiplication, modulus and division are evaluated first in left-to-right order (they associate from left to right), because they have higher precedence than addition and subtraction. The addition and subtraction are applied next. These are also applied left to right.

Not all expressions with several pairs of parentheses contain nested parentheses. For example, the expression

```
a * (b + c) + c * (d + e)
```

does not contain nested parentheses. Rather, the parentheses are said to be "on the same level."

To develop a better understanding of the rules of operator precedence, consider how a second-degree polynomial ($y = ax^2 + bx + c$) is evaluated.

```
y  =  a  *  x  *  x  +  b  *  x  +  c;
   6     1     2     4     3     5
```

The circled numbers under the statement indicate the order in which JavaScript applies the operators. There is no arithmetic operator for exponentiation in JavaScript, so x^2 is represented as **x * x**.

Suppose **a**, **b**, **c** and **x** are initialized as follows: **a = 2**, **b = 3**, **c = 7** and **x = 5**. Figure 8.12 illustrates the order in which the operators are applied in the preceding second-degree polynomial.

As in algebra, it is acceptable to place unnecessary parentheses in an expression to make the expression clearer. These unnecessary parentheses are also called *redundant parentheses*. For example, the preceding assignment statement might be parenthesized as

```
y = (a * x * x) + (b * x) + c;
```

Good Programming Practice 8.9

Using parentheses for more complex arithmetic expressions even when the parentheses are not necessary can make the arithmetic expressions easier to read.

Step 1. **y = 2 * 5 * 5 + 3 * 5 + 7;**

2 * 5 is 10 *(Leftmost multiplication)*

Step 2. **y = 10 * 5 + 3 * 5 + 7;**

10 * 5 is 50 *(Leftmost multiplication)*

Step 3. **y = 50 + 3 * 5 + 7;**

3 * 5 is 15 *(Multiplication before addition)*

Step 4. **y = 50 + 15 + 7;**

50 + 15 is 65 *(Leftmost addition)*

Step 5. **y = 65 + 7;**

65 + 7 is 72 *(Last addition)*

Step 6. **y = 72;** *(Last operation—assignment)*

Fig. 8.12 Order in which a second-degree polynomial is evaluated.

8.6 Decision Making: Equality and Relational Operators

This section introduces a version of JavaScript's **`if`** *structure* that allows a program to make a decision based on the truth or falsity of a *condition.* If the condition is met (the condition is *true*), the statement in the body of the **`if`** structure is executed. If the condition is not met (the condition is *false),* the body statement is not executed. We will see an example shortly.

Conditions in **`if`** structures can be formed by using the *equality operators* and *relational operators* summarized in Fig. 8.13. The relational operators all have the same level of precedence and associate left to right. The equality operators both have the same level of precedence, which is lower than the precedence of the relational operators. The equality operators also associate left to right.

Common Programming Error 8.10

It is a syntax error if the operators **==**, **!=**, **>=** *and* **<=** *contain spaces between their symbols, as in* **= =**, **! =**, **> =** *and* **< =**, *respectively.*

Common Programming Error 8.11

Reversing the operators **!=**, **>=** *and* **<=**, *as in* **=!**, **=>** *and* **=<**, *are all syntax errors.*

Common Programming Error 8.12

Confusing the equality operator **==** *with the assignment operator* **=** *is a logic error. The equality operator should be read "is equal to" and the assignment operator should be read "gets" or "gets the value of." Some people prefer to read the equality operator as "double equals" or "equals equals."*

The following script uses six **`if`** statements to compare two values input into **`prompt`** dialogs by the user. If the condition in any of these **`if`** statements is satisfied, the assignment statement associated with that **`if`** is executed. The user inputs two values through input dialogs. The values are stored in the variables **`first`** and **`second`**. Then, the comparisons are performed and the results of the comparison are displayed in an information dialog. The script and sample outputs are shown in Fig. 8.14.

Standard algebraic equality operator or relational operator	JavaScript equality or relational operator	Sample JavaScript condition	Meaning of JavaScript condition
Equality operators			
=	`==`	`x == y`	**x** is equal to **y**
≠	`!=`	`x != y`	**x** is not equal to **y**
Relational operators			
>	`>`	`x > y`	**x** is greater than **y**
<	`<`	`x < y`	**x** is less than **y**
≥	`>=`	`x >= y`	**x** is greater than or equal to **y**
≤	`<=`	`x <= y`	**x** is less than or equal to **y**

Fig. 8.13 Equality and relational operators.

```
<!DOCTYPE html PUBLIC "-//W3C//DTD HTML 4.0 Transitional//EN">
<HTML>
<!-- Fig. 8.14: comparison.html -->
<!-- Using if statements, relational operators, -->
<!-- and equality operators -->

<HEAD>
<TITLE>Performing Comparisons</TITLE>

<SCRIPT LANGUAGE = "JavaScript">
   var first,   // first string entered by user
       second;  // second string entered by user

   // read first number from user as a string
   first = window.prompt( "Enter first integer:", "0" );

   // read second number from user as a string
   second = window.prompt( "Enter second integer:", "0" );

   document.writeln( "<H1>Comparison Results</H1>" );
   document.writeln( "<TABLE BORDER = '1' WIDTH = '100%'>" );

   if ( first == second )
      document.writeln( "<TR><TD>" + first + " == " + second +
                        "</TD></TR>" );

   if ( first != second )
      document.writeln( "<TR><TD>" + first + " != " + second +
                        "</TD></TR>" );

   if ( first < second )
      document.writeln( "<TR><TD>" + first + " < " + second +
                        "</TD></TR>" );

   if ( first > second )
      document.writeln( "<TR><TD>" + first + " > " + second +
                        "</TD></TR>" );

   if ( first <= second )
      document.writeln( "<TR><TD>" + first + " <= " + second +
                        "</TD></TR>" );

   if ( first >= second )
      document.writeln( "<TR><TD>" + first + " >= " + second +
                        "</TD></TR>" );

   // Display results
   document.writeln( "</TABLE>" );
</SCRIPT>

</HEAD>
```

Fig. 8.14 Using equality and relational operators (part 1 of 4).

```
52  <BODY>
53  <P>Click Refresh (or Reload) to run the script again</P>
54  </BODY>
55  </HTML>
```

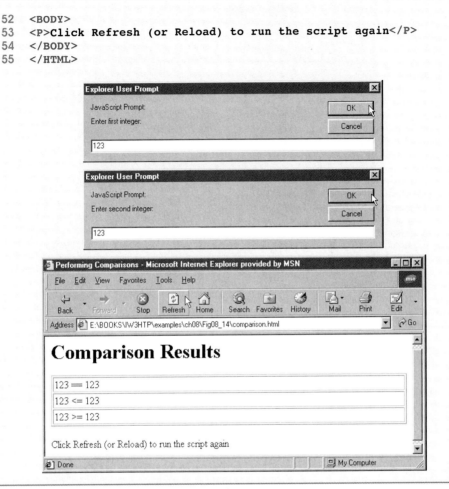

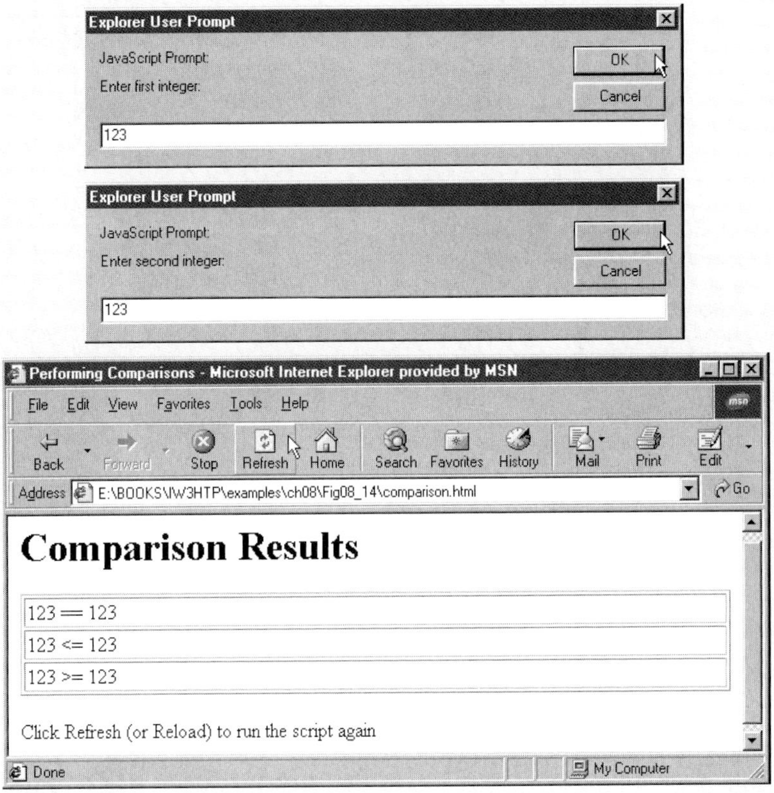

Fig. 8.14 Using equality and relational operators (part 2 of 4).

Lines 11 and 12

```
var first,    // first string entered by user
    second;   // second string entered by user
```

declare the variables used in the script. Remember that variables may be declared in one declaration or in multiple declarations. If more than one name is declared in a declaration (as in this example), the names are separated by commas (**,**). This is referred to as a comma-separated list. Once again, notice the comment at the end of each line indicating the purpose of each variable in the program.

Line 15

```
first = window.prompt( "Enter first integer:", "0" );
```

uses **window.prompt** to allow the user to input the first value and store it in **first**.

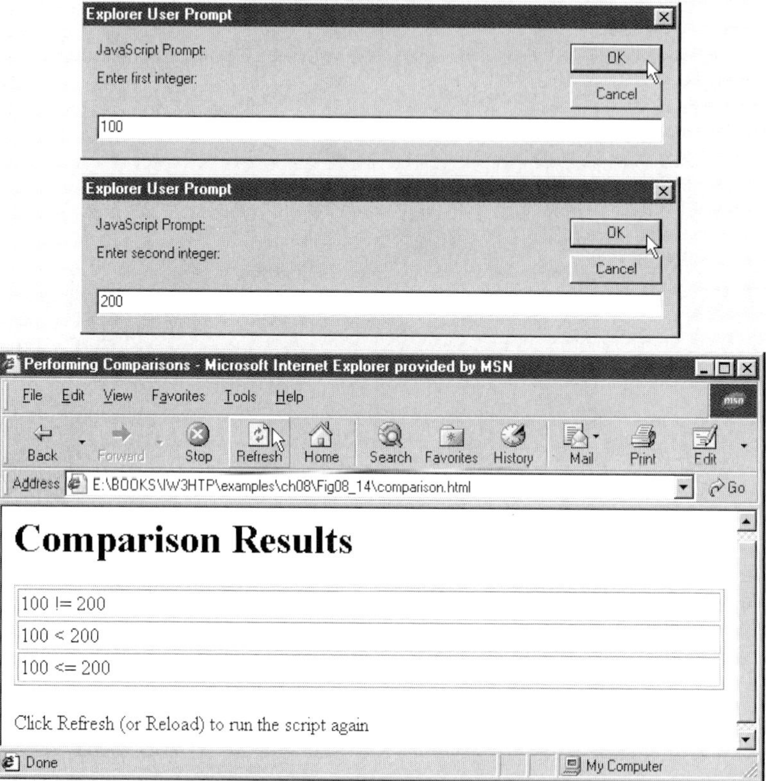

Fig. 8.14 Using equality and relational operators (part 3 of 4).

Line 18

```
second = window.prompt( "Enter second integer:", "0" );
```

uses **window.prompt** to allow the user to input the second value and store it in **second**.

Line 20 outputs a line of HTML text containing the **<H1>** head **Comparison Results**. Line 21 outputs a line of HTML text that indicates the start of a **<TABLE>** that has a 1-pixel border and is 100% of the browser window's width.

The **if** structure from lines 23 though 25

```
if ( first == second )
   document.writeln( "<TR><TD>" + first + " == " + second +
                     "</TD></TR>" );
```

compares the values of variables **number1** and **number2** to test for equality. If the values are equal, the statement at lines 24 and 25 outputs a line of HTML text representing one row of an HTML table (as indicated with the **<TR>** and **</TR>** tags). The text in the row contains the result of **first + " == " + second**. As in Fig. 8.6, the **+** operator is used in this expression to perform string concatenation. If the conditions are true in one or more of the **if** structures starting at lines 27, 31, 35, 39 and 43, the corresponding **document.writeln** statement(s) output a line of HTML text representing a row in the HTML table.

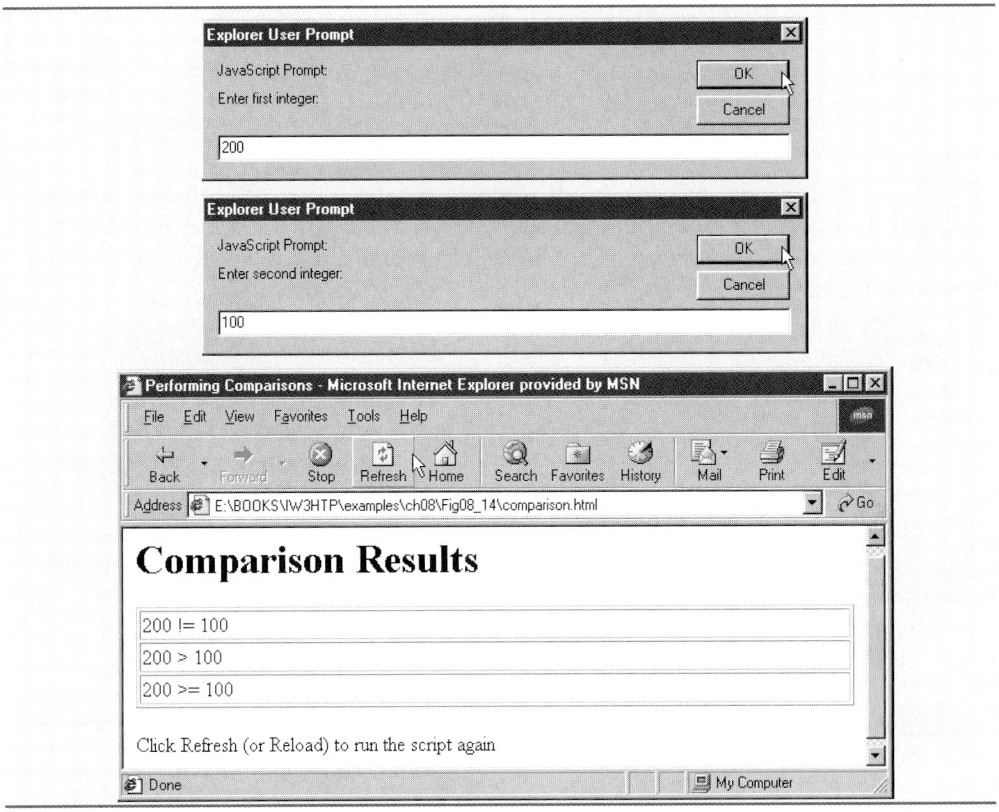

Explorer User Prompt
JavaScript Prompt:
Enter first integer:
200
OK
Cancel

Explorer User Prompt
JavaScript Prompt:
Enter second integer:
100
OK
Cancel

Performing Comparisons - Microsoft Internet Explorer provided by MSN
Address E:\BOOKS\IW3HTP\examples\ch08\Fig08_14\comparison.html

Comparison Results

200 != 100
200 > 100
200 >= 100

Click Refresh (or Reload) to run the script again

Fig. 8.14 Using equality and relational operators (part 4 of 4).

Notice the indentation in the **if** statements throughout the program. Such indentation enhances program readability.

Good Programming Practice 8.10

Indent the statement in the body of an **if** *structure to make the body of the structure stand out and to enhance program readability.*

Good Programming Practice 8.11

Place only one statement per line in a program. This enhances program readability.

Common Programming Error 8.13

Forgetting the left and right parentheses for the condition in an **if** *structure is a syntax error. The parentheses are required.*

Notice that there is no semicolon (**;**) at the end of the first line of each **if** structure. Such a semicolon would result in a logic error at execution time. For example,

```
if ( first == second ) ;
   document.writeln( "<TR><TD>" + first + " == " + second +
                     "</TD></TR>" );
```

would actually be interpreted by JavaScript as

```
if ( first == second )
   ;
document.writeln( "<TR><TD>" + first + " == " + second +
                  "</TD></TR>" );
```

where the semicolon on the line by itself—called the *empty statement*—is the statement to execute if the condition in the **if** structure is true. When the empty statement executes, no task is performed in the program. The program then continues with the assignment statement, which executes regardless of whether the condition is true or false.

Common Programming Error 8.14

Placing a semicolon immediately after the right parenthesis of the condition in an **if** *structure is normally a logic error. The semicolon would cause the body of the* **if** *structure to be empty, so the* **if** *structure itself would perform no action, regardless of whether its condition is true. Worse yet, the intended body statement of the* **if** *structure would now become a statement in sequence with the* **if** *structure and would always be executed.*

Notice the use of spacing in Fig. 8.14. Remember that whitespace characters such as tabs, newlines and spaces are normally ignored by the compiler. So, statements may be split over several lines and may be spaced according to the programmer's preferences without affecting the meaning of a program. It is incorrect to split identifiers and string literals. Ideally, statements should be kept small, but it is not always possible to do so.

Good Programming Practice 8.12

A lengthy statement may be spread over several lines. If a single statement must be split across lines, choose breaking points that make sense, such as after a comma in a comma-separated list, or after an operator in a lengthy expression. If a statement is split across two or more lines, indent all subsequent lines.

The chart in Fig. 8.15 shows the precedence of the operators introduced in this chapter. The operators are shown top to bottom in decreasing order of precedence. Notice that all these operators, with the exception of the assignment operator **=**, associate from left to right. Addition is left associative, so an expression like **x + y + z** is evaluated as if it had been written **(x + y) + z**. The assignment operator **=** associates from right to left, so an expression like **x = y = 0** is evaluated as if it had been written **x = (y = 0)**, which, as we will soon see, first assigns the value **0** to variable **y** and then assigns the result of that assignment, **0**, to **x**.

Good Programming Practice 8.13

Refer to the operator precedence chart when writing expressions containing many operators. Confirm that the operators in the expression are performed in the order you expect. If you are uncertain about the order of evaluation in a complex expression, use parentheses to force the order, exactly as you would do in algebraic expressions. Be sure to observe that some operators, such as assignment (=), associate right to left rather than left to right.

We have introduced many important features of JavaScript, including displaying data, inputting data from the keyboard, performing calculations and making decisions. In Chapter 9, we build on the techniques of Chapter 8 as we introduce *structured programming*. You will become more familiar with indentation techniques. We will study how to specify and vary the order in which statements are executed—this order is called *flow of control*.

Operators	Associativity	Type
`()`	left to right	parentheses
`* / %`	left to right	multiplicative
`+ -`	left to right	additive
`< <= > >=`	left to right	relational
`== !=`	left to right	equality
`=`	right to left	assignment

Fig. 8.15 Precedence and associativity of the operators discussed so far.

8.7 JavaScript Internet and World Wide Web Resources

There are a tremendous number of resources for JavaScript programmers on the Internet and World Wide Web. This section lists a variety of JScript, JavaScript and ECMAScript resources available on the Internet and provides a brief description of each. Additional resources for these topics are presented in the subsequent JavaScript chapters and in other chapters as necessary.

http://www.ecma.ch/stand/ecma-262.htm
JScript is Microsoft's version of *JavaScript*—a scripting language that is standardized by the *ECMA (European Computer Manufacturer's Association)* as *ECMAScript*. This site is the home of the standard document for ECMAScript.

http://msdn.microsoft.com/scripting/default.htm
The *Microsoft Windows Script Technologies* page includes an overview of JScript complete with tutorials, FAQ, demos, tools for download and newsgroups.

http://www.webteacher.com/javatour/framehol.htm
Webteacher.com is an excellent source for tutorials that focus on teaching with detailed explanations and examples. This site is particularly useful for nonprogrammers.

http://wsabstract.com/
Website Abstraction is devoted to JavaScript with specialized tutorials and many free scripts. This is a good site for beginners, as well as those with experience who are looking for help in a specific area of JavaScript.

http://builder.cnet.com/Programming/JsTips/
This site provides 30 tips for using JavaScript to improve your HTML programming. Tips are divided into the following categories: controlling windows, tips to add fun and functionality, tips to simplify your scripts and tips to master syntax.

SUMMARY

- The JavaScript language facilitates a disciplined approach to designing computer programs that enhance Web pages.
- JScript is Microsoft's version of JavaScript—a scripting language that is standardized by the ECMA (European Computer Manufacturer's Association) as ECMAScript.
- Together, blank lines, space characters and tab characters are known as whitespace (space characters and tabs are known specifically as whitespace characters).

- The spacing displayed by a browser in a Web page is determined by the HTML elements used to format the page.
- The **<HTML>** tag indicates the beginning of the HTML document.
- Often JavaScripts appear in the **<HEAD>** section of the HTML document.
- The browser interprets the contents of the **<HEAD>** section first.
- The **<SCRIPT>** tag indicates to the browser that the text that follows is part of a script. Attribute **LANGUAGE** specifies the scripting language used in the script—such as **JavaScript**. [Note: Even though Microsoft calls the language JScript, the **LANGUAGE** attribute specifies **JavaScript** to adhere to the ECMAScript standard.]
- Both Microsoft Internet Explorer and Netscape Navigator use JavaScript as the default scripting language. Therefore, the **LANGUAGE** attribute can be omitted.
- A string of characters can be contained between the double quotation (**"**) marks or single quotation (**'**) marks.
- A string is sometimes called a character string, a message or a string literal.
- The browser's **document** object represents the HTML document currently being displayed in the browser. The **document** object allows a script programmer to specify HTML text to be displayed in the HTML document.
- The browser contains a complete set of objects that allow script programmers to access and manipulate every element of an HTML document.
- An object resides in the computer's memory and contains information used by the script. The term object normally implies that attributes (data) and behaviors (methods) are associated with the object. The object's methods use the attributes to provide useful services to the client of the object—the script that calls the methods.
- The **document** object's **writeln** method writes a line of HTML text in the HTML document being displayed. Method **writeln** instructs the browser to display the string of HTML text based on the contents of the string.
- The parentheses following a method name contain the arguments that the method requires to perform its task (or its action).
- Using **writeln** to write a line of HTML text into the **document** does not guarantee that a corresponding line of text will appear in the HTML document. The text displayed is dependent on the contents of the string written which is subsequently rendered by the browser. The browser will interpret the HTML elements as it normally does to render the final text in the document.
- Every statement should end with a semicolon (also known as the statement terminator), although none is required by JavaScript.
- JavaScript is case sensitive. Not using the proper uppercase and lowercase letters is a syntax error.
- Unlike **writeln**, **document** method **write** does not position the output cursor in the HTML document at the beginning of the next line of HTML text after writing its argument.
- Each **write** or **writeln** statement resumes writing characters where the last **write** or **writeln** stopped writing characters.
- Sometimes it is useful to display information in windows called dialog boxes that "pop up" on the screen to grab the user's attention. Dialog boxes are typically used to display important messages to the user who is browsing the Web page. The browser's **window** object displays an alert dialog box with method **alert**. Method **alert** requires as its argument the string to display.
- Normally the characters in a string are displayed exactly as they appear between the double quotes. When a backslash is encountered in a string of characters, the next character is combined with the

backslash to form an escape sequence. The escape sequence **\n** is the newline character. It causes the cursor in the HTML document to move to the beginning of the next line in the dialog box.

- The keyword **var** is used to declare the names of variables. A variable is a location in the computer's memory where a value can be stored for use by a program. Though not required, all variables should be declared with a name in a **var** statement before they are used in a program.
- A variable name can be any valid identifier. An identifier is a series of characters consisting of letters, digits, underscores (**_**) and dollar signs (**$**) that does not begin with a digit and does not contain any spaces.
- Declarations end with a semicolon (**;**) and can be split over several lines (as shown here) with each variable in the declaration separated by a comma (a comma-separated list of variable names). Several variables may be declared in one declaration or in multiple declarations.
- Programmers often indicate the purpose of each variable in the program by placing a JavaScript comment at the end of each line in the declaration. A single-line comment begins with the characters **//** and terminate at the end of the line. Comments do not cause the browser to perform any action when the script is interpreted; rather, comments are ignored by the JavaScript interpreter.
- Multiple-line comments begin with delimiter **/*** and end with delimiter ***/**. All text between the delimiters of the comment is ignored by the compiler.
- The **window** object's **prompt** method displays a dialog into which the user can type a value. The first argument is a message (called a prompt) that directs the user to take a specific action. The optional second argument is the default string to display in the text field.
- A variable is assigned a value with an assignment statement using the assignment operator **=**. The = operator is called a binary operator because it has two operands.
- Function **parseInt** converts its string argument to an integer.
- JavaScript has a version of the **+** operator for string concatenation that enables a string and a value of another data type (including another string) to be concatenated.
- Variable names correspond to locations in the computer's memory. Every variable has a name, a type, a size and a value.
- When a value is placed in a memory location, this value replaces the previous value in that location. When a value is read out of a memory location, the process is nondestructive.
- The arithmetic operators are binary operators because they each operate on two operands.
- Operators in arithmetic expressions are applied in a precise sequence determined by the rules of operator precedence.
- Parentheses may be used to force the order of evaluation of operators to occur in any sequence desired by the programmer.
- When we say operators are applied from left to right, we are referring to the associativity of the operators. Some operators associate from right to left.
- Java's **if** structure allows a program to make a decision based on the truth or falsity of a condition. If the condition is met (the condition is true), the statement in the body of the **if** structure is executed. If the condition is not met (the condition is false), the body statement is not executed.
- Conditions in **if** structures can be formed by using the equality operators and relational operators.

TERMINOLOGY

\n newline escape sequence.
addition operator (**+**)
alert dialog
alert method of the **window** object
argument to a method
arithmetic expressions in straight-line form

arithmetic operator
assignment operator (**=**)
assignment statement
attribute
automatic conversion
backslash (****) escape character
behavior
binary operator
blank line
case sensitive
character string
client of an object
comma-separated list
comment
condition
data
decision making
declaration
dialog box
division operator (**/**)
document object
double quotation (**"**) marks
ECMA
ECMAScript
empty statement
equality operators
error message
escape sequence
European Computer Manufacturer's Association
false
<HEAD> section of the HTML document
identifier
if structure
inline scripting
integer
interpreter
JavaScript
JScript
JavaScript interpreter
LANGUAGE attribute of the **<SCRIPT>** tag
location in the computer's memory
logic error
meaningful variable names
method
modulus operator (**%**)
multiple-line comment (**/*** and ***/**)
multiplication operator (*****)
name of a variable
object
operand
operator associativity
operator precedence
parentheses
parseInt function
perform an action
program
prompt
prompt dialog
prompt method of the **window** object
redundant parentheses
relational operators
remainder after division
rules of operator precedence
runtime error
script
scripting language
<SCRIPT></SCRIPT>
self-documenting
semicolon (**;**) statement terminator
single-line comment (**//**)
single quotation (**'**) marks
statement
string concatenation
string concatenation operator (**+**)
string literal
string of characters
subtraction operator (**-**)
syntax error
text field
true
type of a variable
value of a variable
var keyword
variable
violation of the language rules
whitespace characters
whole number
window object
writeln method of the **document** object
write method of the **document** object

COMMON PROGRAMMING ERRORS

8.1 Forgetting the ending **</SCRIPT>** tag for a script may prevent the browser from interpreting the script properly and may prevent the HTML document from loading properly.

8.2 JavaScript is case sensitive. Not using the proper uppercase and lowercase letters is a syntax error. A syntax error occurs when the script interpreter cannot recognize a statement. The interpreter normally issues an error message to help the programmer locate and fix the incorrect statement. Syntax errors are violations of the language rules. You will be notified of a syntax error when the interpreter attempts to execute the statement containing the error. The JavaScript interpreter in Internet Explorer reports all syntax errors by indicating in a separate popup window that a "runtime error" occurred (a problem occurred while the interpreter was running the script).

8.3 Splitting a statement in the middle of a string is a syntax error.

8.4 Many people confuse the writing of HTML text with the rendering of HTML text. Writing HTML text creates the HTML that will be rendered by the browser for presentation to the user.

8.5 Dialog boxes display plain text—they do not render HTML. Therefore, specifying HTML elements as part of a string to display in a dialog box results in the actual characters of the tags being displayed.

8.6 Splitting a statement in the middle of an identifier is normally a syntax error.

8.7 Forgetting one of the delimiters of a multiple-line comment is a syntax error.

8.8 Nesting multiple-line comments (placing a multiple-line comment between the delimiters of another multiple-line comment) is a syntax error.

8.9 Confusing the **+** operator used for string concatenation with the **+** operator used for addition can lead to strange results. For example, assuming integer variable **y** has the value **5**, the expression **"y + 2 = " + y + 2** results in the string **"y + 2 = 52"**, not **"y + 2 = 7"**, because first the value of **y** is concatenated with the string **"y + 2 = "**, then the value **2** is concatenated with the new larger string **"y + 2 = 5"**. The expression **"y + 2 = " + (y + 2)** produces the desired result.

8.10 It is a syntax error if the operators **==**, **!=**, **>=** and **<=** contain spaces between their symbols, as in **= =**, **! =**, **> =** and **< =**, respectively.

8.11 Reversing the operators **!=**, **>=** and **<=**, as in **=!**, **=>** and **=<**, all each syntax errors.

8.12 Confusing the equality operator **==** with the assignment operator **=** is a logic error. The equality operator should be read "is equal to" and the assignment operator should be read "gets" or "gets the value of." Some people prefer to read the equality operator as "double equals" or "equals equals."

8.13 Forgetting the left and right parentheses for the condition in an **if** structure is a syntax error. The parentheses are required.

8.14 Placing a semicolon immediately after the right parenthesis of the condition in an **if** structure is normally a logic error. The semicolon would cause the body of the **if** structure to be empty, so the **if** structure itself would perform no action, regardless of whether its condition is true. Worse yet, the intended body statement of the **if** structure would now become a statement in sequence with the **if** structure and would always be executed.

GOOD PROGRAMMING PRACTICES

8.1 HTML documents should begin with a comment describing the purpose of the document.

8.2 Use blank lines, space characters and tab characters in an HTML document to enhance readability.

8.3 Place a blank line before the **<SCRIPT>** tag and after the **</SCRIPT>** tag to separate the script from the surrounding HTML elements and to make the script stand out in the document.

8.4 Always include the semicolon at the end of a statement to explicitly terminate the statement. This clarifies where one statement ends and the next statement begins.

8.5 Choosing meaningful variable names helps a script to be "self-documenting" (one that is easy to understand by simply reading it, rather than having to read manuals or excessive comments).

8.6 By convention, variable name identifiers begin with a lowercase first letter. Every word in the name after the first word should begin with a capital first letter. For example, identifier **`firstNumber`** has a capital **`N`** in its second word **`Number`**.

8.7 Some programmers prefer to declare each variable on a separate line. This format allows for easy insertion of a descriptive comment next to each declaration.

8.8 Place spaces on either side of a binary operator. This makes the operator stand out and makes the program more readable.

8.9 Using parentheses for more complex arithmetic expressions even when the parentheses are not necessary can make the arithmetic expressions easier to read.

8.10 Indent the statement in the body of an **`if`** structure to make the body of the structure stand out and to enhance program readability.

8.11 Place only one statement per line in a program. This enhances program readability.

8.12 A lengthy statement may be spread over several lines. If a single statement must be split across lines, choose breaking points that make sense, such as after a comma in a comma-separated list, or after an operator in a lengthy expression. If a statement is split across two or more lines, indent all subsequent lines.

8.13 Refer to the operator precedence chart when writing expressions containing many operators. Confirm that the operators in the expression are performed in the order you expect. If you are uncertain about the order of evaluation in a complex expression, use parentheses to force the order, exactly as you would do in algebraic expressions. Be sure to observe that some operators, such as assignment (**`=`**), associate right to left rather than left to right.

PORTABILITY TIPS

8.1 Specify the scripting language with the **`LANGUAGE`** attribute of the **`<SCRIPT>`** tag, to ensure that all browsers in which the HTML document is loaded know the language of the script. Although it is unlikely at this time, future Web browsers may not use **`JavaScript`** as the default scripting language.

8.2 Some browsers do not support the **`<SCRIPT></SCRIPT>`** tags. If your document is to be rendered with such browsers, the script code between these tags should be enclosed in an HTML comment so the script text does not display as part of the Web page.

SOFTWARE ENGINEERING OBSERVATION

8.1 Strings in JavaScript can also be enclosed in single quotation (**`'`**) marks.

TESTING AND DEBUGGING TIP

8.1 When the interpreter reports a syntax error, the error may not be on the line indicated by the error messages. First, check the line where the error was reported. If that line does not contain errors, check the preceding several lines in the script.

SELF-REVIEW EXERCISES

8.1 Fill in the blanks in each of the following.

a) ________ begins a single-line comment.
b) Every statement should end with a ________.
c) The ________ structure is used to make decisions.
d) ________, ________, ________ and ________ are known as whitespace.
e) The ________ object displays alert dialogs and prompt dialogs.
f) ________ are reserved for use by JavaScript.
g) Methods ________ and ________ of the ________ object write HTML text into an HTML document.

8.2 State whether each of the following is *true* or *false*. If *false*, explain why.

a) Comments cause the computer to print the text after the **//** on the screen when the program is executed.
b) JavaScript considers the variables **number** and **NuMbEr** to be identical.
c) The modulus operator (**%**) can be used only with any numeric operands.
d) The arithmetic operators *****, **/**, **%**, **+** and **-** all have the same level of precedence.
e) Method **parseInt** converts an integer to a string.

8.3 Write JavaScript statements to accomplish each of the following:

a) Declare variables **c**, **thisIsAVariable**, **q76354** and **number**.
b) Display a dialog asking the user to enter an integer. Show a default value of **0** in the text field.
c) Convert a string to an integer and store the converted value in variable **age**. Assume that the string is stored in **stringValue**.
d) If the variable **number** is not equal to **7**, display **"The variable number is not equal to 7"** in a message dialog.
e) Output a line of HTML text that will display the message **"This is a JavaScript program"** on one line in the HTML document.
f) Output a line of HTML text that will display the message **"This is a JavaScript program"** on two lines in the HTML document. Use only one statement.

8.4 Identify and correct the errors in each of the following statements:

a)
```
if ( c < 7 );
   window.alert( "c is less than 7" );
```
b)
```
if ( c => 7 )
   window.alert( "c is equal to or greater than 7" );
```

8.5 Write a statement (or comment) to accomplish each of the following:

a) State that a program will calculate the product of three integers.
b) Declare the variables **x**, **y**, **z** and **result**.
c) Declare the variables **xVal**, **yVal** and **zVal**.
d) Prompt the user to enter the first value, read the value from the user and store it in the variable **xVal**.
e) Prompt the user to enter the second value, read the value from the user and store it in the variable **yVal**.
f) Prompt the user to enter the third value, read the value from the user and store it in the variable **zVal**.
g) Convert **xVal** to an integer and store the result in the variable **x**.
h) Convert **yVal** to an integer and store the result in the variable **y**.
i) Convert **zVal** to an integer and store the result in the variable **z**.

j) Compute the product of the three integers contained in variables **x**, **y** and **z**, and assign the result to the variable **result**.
k) Write a line of HTML text containing the string **"The product is "** followed by the value of the variable **result**.

8.6 Using the statements you wrote in Exercise 8.5, write a complete program that calculates and prints the product of three integers.

ANSWERS TO SELF-REVIEW EXERCISES

8.1 a) **//**. b) Semicolon (**;**). c) **if**. d) Blank lines, space characters, newline characters and tab characters. e) **window**. f) Keywords. g) **write**, **writeln**, **document**.

8.2 a) False. Comments do not cause any action to be performed when the program is executed. They are used to document programs and improve their readability.
b) False. JavaScript is case sensitive, so these variables are distinct.
c) True.
d) False. The operators *, / and % are on the same level of precedence and the operators + and - are on a lower level of precedence.
e) False. Function **parseInt** converts a string to an integer value.

8.3 a) `var c, thisIsAVariable, q76354, number;`
b) `value = window.prompt( "Enter an integer", "0" );`
c) `var age = parseInt( stringValue );`
d)
```
if ( number != 7 )
   window.alert( "The variable number is not equal to 7" );
```
e) `document.writeln( "This is a JavaScript program" );`
f) `document.writeln( "This is a<BR>JavaScript program" );`

8.4 a) Error: Semicolon after the right parenthesis of the condition in the **if** statement. Correction: Remove the semicolon after the right parenthesis. [*Note:* The result of this error is that the output statement will be executed whether or not the condition in the **if** statement is true. The semicolon after the right parenthesis is considered an empty statement—a statement that does nothing. We will learn more about the empty statement in the next chapter.]
b) Error: The relational operator => is incorrect. Correction: Change => to >=.

8.5
```
a) // Calculate the product of three integers
b) var x, y, z, result;
c) var xVal, yVal, zVal;
d) xVal = window.prompt( "Enter first integer:", "0" );
e) yVal = window.prompt( "Enter second integer:", "0" );
f) zVal = window.prompt( "Enter third integer:", "0" );
g) x = parseInt( xVal );
h) y = parseInt( yVal );
i) z = parseInt( zVal );
j) result = x * y * z;
k) document.writeln(
       <H1>"The product is " + result + "</H1>" );
```

8.6 The program is:

```
<!DOCTYPE html PUBLIC "-//W3C//DTD HTML 4.0 Transitional//EN">
<!-- Exercise 8.6: product.html -->

<HTML>
<HEAD>
<TITLE>Product of Three Integers</TITLE>

<SCRIPT LANGUAGE = "JavaScript">
   // Calculate the product of three integers
   var x, y, z, result;
   var xVal, yVal, zVal;

   xVal = window.prompt( "Enter first integer:", "0" );
   yVal = window.prompt( "Enter second integer:", "0" );
   zVal = window.prompt( "Enter third integer:", "0" );

   x = parseInt( xVal );
   y = parseInt( yVal );
   z = parseInt( zVal );

   result = x * y * z;
   document.writeln( "<H1>The product is " + result + "<H1>" );
</SCRIPT>

</HEAD><BODY></BODY>
</HTML>
```

EXERCISES

8.7 Fill in the blanks in each of the following:

a) __________ are used to document a program and improve its readability.
b) A dialog capable of receiving input from the user is displayed with method ________ of class __________.
c) A JavaScript statement that makes a decision is __________.
d) Calculations are normally performed by __________ statements.
e) A dialog capable of showing a message to the user is displayed with method ________ of class __________.

8.8 Write JavaScript statements that accomplish each of the following:

a) Display the message **"Enter two numbers"** using the **window** object.
b) Assign the product of variables **b** and **c** to variable **a**.
c) State that a program performs a sample payroll calculation (*Hint:* use text that helps to document a program).

8.9 State whether each of the following is *true* or *false*. If *false*, explain why.

a) JavaScript operators are evaluated from left to right.
b) The following are all valid variable names: **_under_bar_**, **m928134**, **t5**, **j7**, **her_sales$**, **his_$account_total**, **a**, **b$**, **c**, **z**, **z2**.
c) A valid JavaScript arithmetic expression with no parentheses is evaluated from left to right.
d) The following are all invalid variable names: **3g, 87, 67h2, h22, 2h.**

8.10 Fill in the blanks in each of the following:

a) What arithmetic operations have the same precedence as multiplication? __________.
b) When parentheses are nested, which set of parentheses is evaluated first in an arithmetic expression? __________.
c) A location in the computer's memory that may contain different values at various times throughout the execution of a program is called a __________.

8.11 What displays in the message dialog when each of the following JavaScript statements is performed? Assume **`x = 2`** and **`y = 3`**.

a) **`window.alert( "x = " + x );`**
b) **`window.alert( "The value of x + x is " + ( x + x ) );`**
c) **`window.alert( "x =" );`**
d) **`window.alert( ( x + y ) + " = " + ( y + x ) );`**

8.12 Which of the following JavaScript statements contain variables whose values are destroyed (changed or replaced)?

a) **`p = i + j + k + 7;`**
b) **`window.alert( "variables whose values are destroyed" );`**
c) **`window.alert( "a = 5" );`**
d) **`stringVal = window.prompt( "Enter string:" );`**

8.13 Given $y = ax^3 + 7$, which of the following are correct statements for this equation?

a) **`y = a * x * x * x + 7;`**
b) **`y = a * x * x * (x + 7);`**
c) **`y = (a * x) * x * (x + 7);`**
d) **`y = (a * x) * x * x + 7;`**
e) **`y = a * (x * x * x) + 7;`**
f) **`y = a * x * (x * x + 7);`**

8.14 State the order of evaluation of the operators in each of the following JavaScript statements and show the value of **`x`** after each statement is performed.

a) **`x = 7 + 3 * 6 / 2 - 1;`**
b) **`x = 2 % 2 + 2 * 2 - 2 / 2;`**
c) **`x = ( 3 * 9 * ( 3 + ( 9 * 3 / ( 3 ) ) ) );`**

8.15 Write a script that displays the numbers 1 to 4 on the same line with each pair of adjacent numbers separated by one space. Write the program using the following methods.

a) Using one **`document.writeln`** statement.
b) Using four **`document.write`** statements.

8.16 Write a script that asks the user to enter two numbers, obtains the two numbers from the user and outputs HTML text that displays the sum, product, difference and quotient of the two numbers. Use the techniques shown in Fig. 8.6.

8.17 Write a script that asks the user to enter two integers, obtains the numbers from the user and outputs HTML text that displays the larger number followed by the words "**`is larger`**" in an information message dialog. If the numbers are equal, output HTML text that displays the message "**`These numbers are equal`**." Use the techniques shown in Fig. 8.14.

8.18 Write a script that inputs three integers from the user and displays the sum, average, product, smallest and largest of these numbers in an **`alert`** dialog.

8.19 Write a script that inputs from the user the radius of a circle and outputs HTML text that displays the circle's diameter, circumference and area. Use the constant value 3.14159 for π. Use the GUI techniques shown in Fig. 8.6. [*Note:* You may also use the predefined constant **`Math.PI`** for the value of π. This constant is more precise than the value 3.14159. The **`Math`** object is defined by

JavaScript and provides many common mathematical capabilities.] Use the following formulas (*r* is the radius): *diameter* = $2r$, *circumference* = $2\pi r$, *area* = πr^2.

8.20 Write a script that outputs HTML text that displays in the HTML document an oval, an arrow and a diamond using asterisks (*) as follows (Note: Use the **<PRE>** and **</PRE>** tags to specify that the asterisks should be displayed using a fixed-width font):

8.21 Modify the program you created in Exercise 8.20 to display the shapes without using the **<PRE>** and **</PRE>** tags. Does the program display the shapes exactly as in Exercise 8.20?

8.22 What does the following code print?

```
document.writeln( "*\n**\n***\n****\n*****" );
```

8.23 What does the following code print?

```
document.writeln( "*" );
document.writeln( "***" );
document.writeln( "*****" );
document.writeln( "****" );
document.writeln( "**" );
```

8.24 What does the following code print?

```
document.write( "*<BR>" );
document.write( "***<BR>" );
document.write( "*****<BR>" );
document.write( "****<BR>" );
document.writeln( "**" );
```

8.25 What does the following code print?

```
document.write( "*<BR>" );
document.writeln( "***" );
document.writeln( "*****" );
document.write( "****<BR>" );
document.writeln( "**" );
```

8.26 Write a script that reads five integers and determines and outputs HTML text that displays the largest and the smallest integers in the group. Use only the programming techniques you learned in this chapter.

8.27 Write a script that reads an integer and determines and outputs HTML text that displays whether it is odd or even. (*Hint:* Use the modulus operator. An even number is a multiple of 2. Any multiple of 2 leaves a remainder of zero when divided by 2.)

8.28 Write a script that reads in two integers and determines and outputs HTML text that displays whether the first is a multiple of the second. (*Hint:* Use the modulus operator.)

8.29 Write a script that outputs HTML text that displays in the HTML document a checkerboard pattern as follows:

8.30 Write a script that inputs five numbers and determines and outputs HTML text that displays the number of negative numbers input, the number of positive numbers input and the number of zeros input.

8.31 Write a script that reads a first name and a last name from the user as two separate inputs and concatenates the first name and last name separated by a space. Output HTML text that displays the concatenated name in the HTML document.

8.32 Write a script that inputs one number consisting of five digits from the user, separates the number into its individual digits and outputs HTML text that displays the digits separated from one another by three spaces each. For example, if the user types in the number **42339**, the script should display

```
4   2   3   3   9
```

(*Hint*: This exercise is possible with the techniques you learned in this chapter. You will need to use both division and modulus operations to "pick off" each digit.)

For the purpose of this exercise assume that the user enters the correct number of digits. What happens when you execute the program and type a number with more than five digits? What happens when you execute the program and type a number with fewer than five digits?

8.33 Using only the programming techniques you learned in this chapter, write a script that calculates the squares and cubes of the numbers from 0 to 10 and outputs HTML text that displays the resulting values in an HTML table format as follows:

number	square	cube
0	0	0
1	1	1
2	4	8
3	9	27
4	16	64
5	25	125
6	36	216
7	49	343
8	64	512
9	81	729
10	100	1000

[*Note:* This program does not require any input from the user.]

JavaScript/JScript: Control Structures I

Objectives

- To understand basic problem-solving techniques.
- To be able to develop algorithms through the process of top-down, stepwise refinement.
- To be able to use the **`if`** and **`if/else`** selection structures to choose among alternative actions.
- To be able to use the **`while`** repetition structure to execute statements in a script repeatedly.
- To understand counter-controlled repetition and sentinel-controlled repetition.
- To be able to use the increment, decrement and assignment operators.

Let's all move one place on.
Lewis Carroll

The wheel is come full circle.
William Shakespeare, *King Lear*

How many apples fell on Newton's head before he took the hint!
Robert Frost, Comment

Outline

9.1 Introduction

Before writing a script to solve a problem, it is essential to have a thorough understanding of the problem and a carefully planned approach to solving the problem. When writing a script, it is equally essential to understand the types of building blocks that are available and to employ proven program construction principles. In this chapter and in Chapter 10, we discuss these issues in our presentation of the theory and principles of structured programming. The techniques you learn here are applicable to most high-level languages, including JavaScript.

9.2 Algorithms

Any computing problem can be solved by executing a series of actions in a specific order. A *procedure* for solving a problem in terms of

1. the *actions* to be executed, and
2. the *order* in which these actions are to be executed

is called an *algorithm*. The following example demonstrates that correctly specifying the order in which the actions are to be executed is important.

Consider the "rise-and-shine algorithm" followed by one junior executive for getting out of bed and going to work: (1) get out of bed, (2) take off pajamas, (3) take a shower, (4) get dressed, (5) eat breakfast, (6) carpool to work.

This routine gets the executive to work well-prepared to make critical decisions. Suppose, however, that the same steps are performed in a slightly different order: (1) get out of bed, (2) take off pajamas, (3) get dressed, (4) take a shower, (5) eat breakfast, (6) carpool to work.

In this case, our junior executive shows up for work soaking wet. Specifying the order in which statements are to be executed in a computer program is called *program control*. In this chapter and Chapter 10, we investigate the program control capabilities of JavaScript.

9.3 Pseudocode

Pseudocode is an artificial and informal language that helps programmers develop algorithms. The pseudocode we present here is particularly useful for developing algorithms that will be converted to structured portions of JavaScript programs. Pseudocode is similar to everyday English; it is convenient and user-friendly, although it is not an actual computer programming language.

Pseudocode is not actually executed on computers. Rather, it helps the programmer "think out" a program before attempting to write it in a programming language, such as JavaScript. In this chapter, we give several examples of pseudocode.

Software Engineering Observation 9.1

Pseudocode is often used to "think out" a program during the program design process. Then the pseudocode program is converted to a programming language such as JavaScript.

The style of pseudocode we present consists purely of characters, so programmers may conveniently type pseudocode using an editor program. The computer can produce a fresh printed copy of a pseudocode program on demand. Carefully prepared pseudocode may be converted easily to a corresponding JavaScript program. This is done in many cases simply by replacing pseudocode statements with their JavaScript equivalents.

Pseudocode normally describes only executable statements—the actions that are performed when the program is converted from pseudocode to JavaScript and is run. Declarations are not executable statements. For example, the declaration

```
var value1;
```

instructs the JavaScript interpreter to reserve space in memory for the variable **value1**. This declaration does not cause any action—such as input, output or a calculation—to occur when the script executes. Some programmers choose to list variables and mention the purpose of each at the beginning of a pseudocode program.

9.4 Control Structures

Normally, statements in a program are executed one after the other in the order in which they are written. This is called *sequential execution*. Various JavaScript statements we will soon discuss enable the programmer to specify that the next statement to be executed may be one other than the next one in sequence. This is called *transfer of control*.

During the 1960s, it became clear that the indiscriminate use of transfers of control was the root of much difficulty experienced by software development groups. The finger of blame was pointed at the **goto** *statement,* which allows the programmer to specify a transfer of control to one of a very wide range of possible destinations in a program. The notion of so-called *structured programming* became almost synonymous with "**goto** *elimination.*" JavaScript does not have a **goto** statement.

The research of Bohm and Jacopini[1] had demonstrated that programs could be written without any **goto** statements. The challenge of the era for programmers was to shift their styles to "**goto**-less programming." It was not until the 1970s that programmers started taking structured programming seriously. The results have been impressive, as software development groups have reported reduced development times, more frequent on-time delivery of systems and more frequent within-budget completion of software projects. The key to these successes is that structured programs are clearer, easier to debug and modify, and more likely to be bug-free in the first place.

Bohm and Jacopini's work demonstrated that all programs could be written in terms of only three *control structures*, namely the *sequence structure*, the *selection structure* and the *repetition structure*. The sequence structure is built into JavaScript. Unless directed otherwise, the computer executes JavaScript statements one after the other in the order in which they are written. The *flowchart* segment of Fig. 9.1 illustrates a typical sequence structure in which two calculations are performed in order.

A flowchart is a graphical representation of an algorithm or of a portion of an algorithm. Flowcharts are drawn using certain special-purpose symbols such as rectangles, diamonds, ovals and small circles; these symbols are connected by arrows called *flowlines,* which indicate the order in which the actions of the algorithm execute.

Like pseudocode, flowcharts are often useful for developing and representing algorithms, although pseudocode is strongly preferred by many programmers. Flowcharts show clearly how control structures operate; that is all we use them for in this text. The reader should carefully compare the pseudocode and flowchart representations of each control structure.

Consider the flowchart segment for the sequence structure on the left side of Fig. 9.1. We use the *rectangle symbol* (or *action symbol*) to indicate any type of action, including a calculation or an input/output operation. The flowlines in the figure indicate the order in which the actions are performed—first, **grade** is added to **total**, then **1** is added to **counter**. JavaScript allows us to have as many actions as we want in a sequence structure. As we will soon see, anywhere a single action may be placed, we may place several actions in sequence.

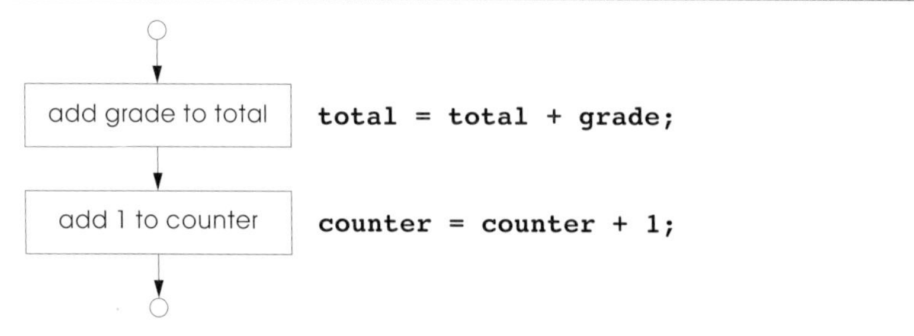

Fig. 9.1 Flowcharting JavaScript's sequence structure.

1. Bohm, C., and G. Jacopini, "Flow Diagrams, Turing Machines, and Languages with Only Two Formation Rules," *Communications of the ACM,* Vol. 9, No. 5, May 1966, pp. 336–371.

In a flowchart that represents a *complete* algorithm, an *oval symbol* containing the word "Begin" is the first symbol used in the flowchart; an oval symbol containing the word "End" indicates where the algorithm ends. In a flowchart that shows only a portion of an algorithm, as in Fig. 9.1, the oval symbols are omitted in favor of using *small circle symbols,* also called *connector symbols.*

Perhaps the most important flowcharting symbol is the *diamond symbol,* also called the *decision symbol,* which indicates that a decision is to be made. We will discuss the diamond symbol in the next section.

JavaScript provides three types of selection structures; we discuss each of these in this chapter and in Chapter 10. The **if** selection structure performs (selects) an action if a condition is true or skips the action if the condition is false. The **if/else** selection structure performs an action if a condition is true and performs a different action if the condition is false. The **switch** selection structure (Chapter 10) performs one of many different actions, depending on the value of an expression.

The **if** structure is called a *single-selection structure* because it selects or ignores a single action (or, as we will soon see, a single group of actions). The **if/else** structure is called a *double-selection structure* because it selects between two different actions (or groups of actions). The **switch** structure is called a *multiple-selection structure* because it selects among many different actions (or groups of actions).

JavaScript provides four types of repetition structures, namely **while**, **do/while**, **for** and **for/in** (**do/while** and **for** are covered in Chapter 10; **for/in** is covered in Chapter 12). Each of the words **if**, **else**, **switch**, **while**, **do**, **for** and **in** is a JavaScript *keyword.* These words are reserved by the language to implement various features, such as JavaScript's control structures. Keywords cannot be used as identifiers (such as for variable names). A complete list of JavaScript keywords is shown in Fig. 9.2.

Common Programming Error 9.1

Using a keyword as an identifier is a syntax error.

JavaScript Keywords				
break	**case**	**continue**	**delete**	**do**
else	**false**	**for**	**function**	**if**
in	**new**	**null**	**return**	**switch**
this	**true**	**typeof**	**var**	**void**
while	**with**			
Keywords that are reserved but not used by JavaScript				
catch	**class**	**const**	**debugger**	**default**
enum	**export**	**extends**	**finally**	**import**
super	**try**			

Fig. 9.2 JavaScript keywords.

As we have shown, JavaScript has only eight control structures: sequence, three types of selection and four types of repetition. Each program is formed by combining as many of each type of control structure as is appropriate for the algorithm the program implements. As with the sequence structure of Fig. 9.1, we will see that each control structure is flowcharted with two small circle symbols, one at the entry point to the control structure and one at the exit point.

Single-entry/single-exit control structures make it easy to build programs—the control structures are attached to one another by connecting the exit point of one control structure to the entry point of the next. This process is similar to the way a child stacks building blocks, so we call this *control-structure stacking*. We will learn that there is only one other way control structures may be connected—*control-structure nesting*. Thus, algorithms in JavaScript programs are constructed from only eight different types of control structures combined in only two ways.

9.5 The `if` Selection Structure

A selection structure is used to choose among alternative courses of action in a program. For example, suppose that the passing grade on an examination is 60 (out of 100). Then the pseudocode statement

If student's grade is greater than or equal to 60
Print "Passed"

determines if the condition "student's grade is greater than or equal to 60" is true or false. If the condition is true, then "Passed" is printed, and the next pseudocode statement in order is "performed" (remember that pseudocode is not a real programming language). If the condition is false, the print statement is ignored, and the next pseudocode statement in order is performed. Note that the second line of this selection structure is indented. Such indentation is optional, but it is highly recommended because it emphasizes the inherent structure of structured programs. The JavaScript interpreter ignores whitespace characters: blanks, tabs and newlines used for indentation and vertical spacing. Programmers insert these whitespace characters to enhance program clarity.

Good Programming Practice 9.1

Consistently applying reasonable indentation conventions throughout your programs improves program readability. We suggest a fixed-size tab of about 1/4 inch or three spaces per indent.

The preceding pseudocode *If* statement may be written in JavaScript as

```
if ( studentGrade >= 60 )
   document.writeln( "Passed" );
```

Notice that the JavaScript code corresponds closely to the pseudocode. This similarity is why pseudocode is a useful program development tool. The statement in the body of the **`if`** structure outputs the character string **`"Passed"`** in the HTML document.

The flowchart of Fig. 9.3 illustrates the single-selection **`if`** structure. This flowchart contains what is perhaps the most important flowcharting symbol—the *diamond symbol* (or *decision symbol*) which indicates that a decision is to be made. The decision symbol contains an expression, such as a condition, that can be either **`true`** or **`false`**. The decision symbol has two flowlines emerging from it. One indicates the path to follow in the program when the expression in the symbol is true; the other indicates the path to follow in the program when the expression is false. A decision can be made on any expression that evaluates to a value of JavaScript's boolean type (any expression that evaluates to **`true`** or **`false`**).

Software Engineering Observation 9.2

In JavaScript, any non-zero numeric value in a condition evaluates to **`true`**, *and 0 evaluates to* **`false`**. *For strings, any string containing 1 or more characters evaluates to* **`true`** *and the empty string (the string containing no characters) evaluates to* **`false`**. *Also, a variable that has been declared with* **`var`** *but has not been assigned a value evaluates to* **`false`**.

Note that the **`if`** structure is a single-entry/single-exit structure. We will soon learn that the flowcharts for the remaining control structures also contain (besides small circle symbols and flowlines) only rectangle symbols to indicate the actions to be performed and diamond symbols to indicate decisions to be made. This is the *action/decision model of programming*.

We can envision eight bins, each containing only control structures of one of the eight types. These control structures are empty. Nothing is written in the rectangles or in the diamonds. The programmer's task, then, is to assemble a program from as many of each type of control structure as the algorithm demands, combining those control structures in only two possible ways (stacking or nesting), and then filling in the actions and decisions in a manner appropriate for the algorithm. We will discuss the variety of ways in which actions and decisions may be written.

9.6 The `if/else` Selection Structure

The **`if`** selection structure performs an indicated action only when the condition evaluates to **`true`**; otherwise, the action is skipped. The **`if/else`** selection structure allows the programmer to specify that a different action is to be performed when the condition is true than when the condition is false. For example, the pseudocode statement

If student's grade is greater than or equal to 60
    Print "Passed"
else
    Print "Failed"

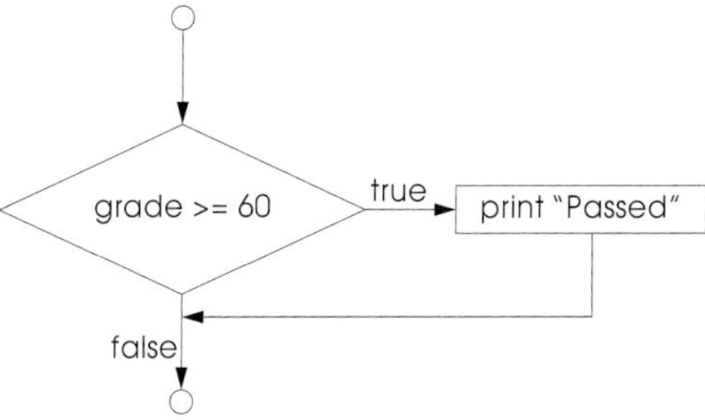

Fig. 9.3 Flowcharting the single-selection **`if`** structure.

prints *Passed* if the student's grade is greater than or equal to 60 and prints *Failed* if the student's grade is less than 60. In either case, after printing occurs, the next pseudocode statement in sequence (the next statement after the whole **if/else** structure) is "performed." Note that the body of the *else* is also indented.

Good Programming Practice 9.2

Indent both body statements of an **if/else** *structure.*

The indentation convention you choose should be carefully applied throughout your programs (both in pseudocode and in JavaScript). It is difficult to read programs that do not use uniform spacing conventions.

The preceding pseudocode *if/else* structure may be written in JavaScript as

```
if ( studentGrade >= 60 )
   document.writeln( "Passed" );
else
   document.writeln( "Failed" );
```

The flowchart of Fig. 9.4 nicely illustrates the flow of control in the **if/else** structure. Once again, note that the only symbols in the flowchart (besides small circles and arrows) are rectangles (for actions) and a diamond (for a decision). We continue to emphasize this action/decision model of computing. Imagine again a deep bin containing as many empty double-selection structures as might be needed to build a JavaScript algorithm. The programmer's job is to assemble the selection structures (by stacking and nesting) with other control structures required by the algorithm and to fill in the empty rectangles and empty diamonds with actions and decisions appropriate to the algorithm being implemented.

JavaScript provides an operator called the *conditional operator* (**?:**) that is closely related to the **if/else** structure. The operator **?:** is JavaScript's only *ternary operator*—it takes three operands. The operands together with the **?:** form a *conditional expression.* The first operand is a boolean expression, the second is the value for the conditional expression if the condition evaluates to true and the third is the value for the conditional expression if the condition evaluates to false. For example, the statement

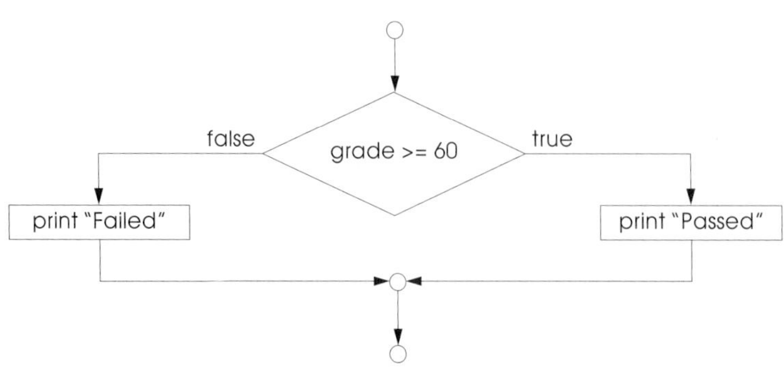

Fig. 9.4 Flowcharting the double-selection **if/else** structure.

```
document.writeln(
   studentGrade >= 60 ? "Passed" : "Failed" );
```

contains a conditional expression that evaluates to the string **"Passed"** if the condition **studentGrade >= 60** is true and evaluates to the string **"Failed"** if the condition is false. Thus, this statement with the conditional operator performs essentially the same operation as the preceding **if/else** statement. The precedence of the conditional operator is low, so the entire conditional expression is normally placed in parentheses.

*Nested **if/else** structures* test for multiple cases by placing **if/else** structures inside **if/else** structures. For example, the following pseudocode statement will print **A** for exam grades greater than or equal to 90, **B** for grades in the range 80 to 89, **C** for grades in the range 70 to 79, **D** for grades in the range 60 to 69 and **F** for all other grades:

```
If student's grade is greater than or equal to 90
   Print "A"
else
   If student's grade is greater than or equal to 80
      Print "B"
   else
      If student's grade is greater than or equal to 70
         Print "C"
      else
         If student's grade is greater than or equal to 60
            Print "D"
         else
            Print "F"
```

This pseudocode may be written in JavaScript as

```
if ( studentGrade >= 90 )
   document.writeln( "A" );
else
   if ( studentGrade >= 80 )
      document.writeln( "B" );
   else
      if ( studentGrade >= 70 )
         document.writeln( "C" );
      else
         if ( studentGrade >= 60 )
            document.writeln( "D" );
         else
            document.writeln( "F" );
```

If **studentGrade** is greater than or equal to 90, the first four conditions will be true, but only the **document.writeln** statement after the first test will be executed. After that particular **document.writeln** is executed, the **else** part of the "outer" **if/else** statement is skipped.

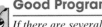

If there are several levels of indentation, each level should be indented the same additional amount of space.

Most JavaScript programmers prefer to write the preceding **if** structure as

```
if ( grade >= 90 )
   document.writeln( "A" );
else if ( grade >= 80 )
   document.writeln( "B" );
else if ( grade >= 70 )
   document.writeln( "C" );
else if ( grade >= 60 )
   document.writeln( "D" );
else
   document.writeln( "F" );
```

The two forms are equivalent. The latter form is popular because it avoids the deep indentation of the code to the right. Such deep indentation often leaves little room on a line, forcing lines to be split and decreasing program readability.

It is important to note that the JavaScript interpreter always associates an **else** with the previous **if**, unless told to do otherwise by the placement of braces (**{}**). This is referred to as the *dangling-else problem*. For example,

```
if ( x > 5 )
   if ( y > 5 )
      document.writeln( "x and y are > 5" );
else
   document.writeln( "x is <= 5" );
```

appears to indicate with its indentation that if **x** is greater than **5**, the **if** structure in its body determines whether **y** is also greater than **5**. If so, the string **"x and y are > 5"** is output. Otherwise, it *appears* that if **x** is not greater than **5**, the **else** part of the **if/else** structure outputs the string **"x is <= 5"**.

Beware! The preceding nested **if** structure does not execute as it appears. The interpreter actually interprets the preceding structure as

```
if ( x > 5 )
   if ( y > 5 )
      document.writeln( "x and y are > 5" );
   else
      document.writeln( "x is <= 5" );
```

in which the body of the first **if** structure is an **if/else** structure. This structure tests whether **x** is greater than **5**. If so, execution continues by testing whether **y** is also greater than **5**. If the second condition is true, the proper string—**"x and y are > 5"**—is displayed. However, if the second condition is false, the string **"x is <= 5"** is displayed, even though we know **x** is greater than **5**.

To force the preceding nested **if** structure to execute as it was originally intended, the structure must be written as follows:

```
if ( x > 5 ) {
   if ( y > 5 )
      document.writeln( "x and y are > 5" );
}
else
   document.writeln( "x is <= 5" );
```

The braces (**{}**) indicate to the interpreter that the second **if** structure is in the body of the first **if** structure and that the **else** is matched with the first **if** structure. In Exercises 9.21 and 9.22 you will investigate the dangling-else problem further.

The **if** selection structure normally expects only one statement in its body. To include several statements in the body of an **if**, enclose the statements in braces (**{** and **}**). A set of statements contained within a pair of braces is called a *compound statement.*

Software Engineering Observation 9.3

A compound statement can be placed anywhere in a program that a single statement can be placed.

Software Engineering Observation 9.4

Unlike individual statements, a compound statement does not end with a semicolon. However, each statement within the braces of a compound statement should end with a semicolon.

The following example includes a compound statement in the **else** part of an **if/else** structure.

```
if ( grade >= 60 )
   document.writeln( "Passed" );
else {
   document.writeln( "Failed<BR>" );
   document.writeln( "You must take this course again." );
}
```

In this case, if **grade** is less than 60, the program executes both statements in the body of the **else** and prints

```
Failed.
You must take this course again.
```

Notice the braces surrounding the two statements in the **else** clause. These braces are important. Without the braces, the statement

```
document.writeln( "You must take this course again." );
```

would be outside the body of the **else** part of the **if** and would execute regardless of whether the grade is less than 60.

Common Programming Error 9.2

Forgetting one or both of the braces that delimit a compound statement can lead to syntax errors or logic errors.

Syntax errors (such as when one brace in a compound statement is left out of the program) are caught by the interpreter when it attempts to interpret the code containing the syntax error. A *logic error* (such as the one caused when both braces in a compound statement are left out of the program) also has its effect at execution time. A *fatal logic error* causes a program to fail and terminate prematurely. A *nonfatal logic error* allows a program to continue executing, but the program produces incorrect results.

Software Engineering Observation 9.5

*Just as a compound statement can be placed anywhere a single statement can be placed, it is also possible to have no statement at all (the empty statement). The empty statement is represented by placing a semicolon (**;**) where a statement would normally be.*

Common Programming Error 9.3

Placing a semicolon after the condition in an **`if`** *structure leads to a logic error in single-selection* **`if`** *structures and a syntax error in double-selection* **`if`** *structures (if the* **`if`** *part contains a nonempty body statement).*

Good Programming Practice 9.4

Some programmers prefer to type the beginning and ending braces of compound statements before typing the individual statements within the braces. This helps avoid omitting one or both of the braces.

9.7 The `while` Repetition Structure

A *repetition structure* allows the programmer to specify that an action is to be repeated while some condition remains true. The pseudocode statement

While there are more items on my shopping list
    Purchase next item and cross it off my list

describes the repetition that occurs during a shopping trip. The condition "there are more items on my shopping list" may be true or false. If it is true, then the action "Purchase next item and cross it off my list" is performed. This action will be performed repeatedly while the condition remains true. The statement(s) contained in the *while* repetition structure constitute the body of the *while*. The *while* structure body may be a single statement or a compound statement. Eventually, the condition will become false (when the last item on the shopping list has been purchased and crossed off the list). At this point, the repetition terminates, and the first pseudocode statement after the repetition structure is executed.

Common Programming Error 9.4

Not providing in the body of a **`while`** *structure an action that eventually causes the condition in the* **`while`** *to become false is a logic error. Normally, such a repetition structure will never terminate—an error called an "infinite loop." Browsers handle infinite loops differently. For example, Internet Explorer allows the user to terminate the script containing the infinite loop.*

Common Programming Error 9.5

Spelling the keyword **`while`** *with an uppercase* **`W`** *as in* **`While`** *(remember that JavaScript is a case-sensitive language) is a syntax error. All of JavaScript's reserved keywords, such as* **`while`**, **`if`** *and* **`else`**, *contain only lowercase letters.*

As an example of a **`while`** structure, consider a program segment designed to find the first power of 2 larger than 1000. Suppose variable **`product`** has been initialized to 2. When the following **`while`** structure finishes executing, **`product`** contains the result:

```
var product = 2;

while ( product <= 1000 )
   product = 2 * product;
```

The flowchart of Fig. 9.5 illustrates the flow of control of the preceding **`while`** repetition structure. Once again, note that (besides small circles and arrows) the flowchart contains only a rectangle symbol and a diamond symbol.

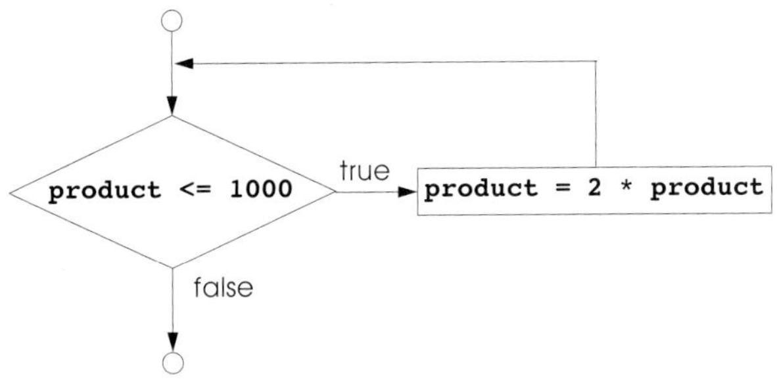

Fig. 9.5 Flowcharting the **while** repetition structure.

When the **while** structure is entered, **product** is 2. Variable **product** is repeatedly multiplied by 2, taking on the values 4, 8, 16, 32, 64, 128, 256, 512 and 1024 successively. When **product** becomes 1024, the condition **product <= 1000** in the **while** structure becomes **false**. This terminates the repetition with 1024 as **product**'s final value. Execution continues with the next statement after the **while**. [*Note:* If a **while** structure's condition is initially **false** the body statement(s) will never be performed.]

Imagine, again, a deep bin of empty **while** structures that may be stacked and nested with other control structures to form a structured implementation of an algorithm's flow of control. The empty rectangles and diamonds are then filled in with appropriate actions and decisions. The flowchart clearly shows the repetition. The flowline emerging from the rectangle wraps back to the decision, which is tested each time through the loop until the decision eventually becomes false. At this point, the **while** structure is exited, and control passes to the next statement in the program.

9.8 Formulating Algorithms: Case Study 1 (Counter-Controlled Repetition)

To illustrate how algorithms are developed, we solve several variations of a class-averaging problem. Consider the following problem statement:

> *A class of ten students took a quiz. The grades (integers in the range 0 to 100) for this quiz are available to you. Determine the class average on the quiz.*

The class average is equal to the sum of the grades divided by the number of students (10 in this case). The algorithm for solving this problem on a computer must input each of the grades, perform the averaging calculation and display the result.

Let us use pseudocode to list the actions to be executed and specify the order in which these actions should be executed. We use *counter-controlled repetition* to input the grades one at a time. This technique uses a variable called a *counter* to control the number of times a set of statements will execute. In this example, repetition terminates when the counter exceeds 10. In this section, we present a pseudocode algorithm (Fig. 9.6) and the corresponding program (Fig. 9.7). In the next section, we show how pseudocode algorithms are developed. Counter-controlled repetition is often called *definite repetition* because the number of repetitions is known before the loop begins executing.

```
Set total to zero
Set grade counter to one

While grade counter is less than or equal to ten
    Input the next grade
    Add the grade into the total
    Add one to the grade counter

Set the class average to the total divided by ten
Print the class average
```

Fig. 9.6 Pseudocode algorithm that uses counter-controlled repetition to solve the class-average problem.

Note the references in the algorithm to a total and a counter. A *total* is a variable used to accumulate the sum of a series of values. A counter is a variable used to count—in this case, to count the number of grades entered. Variables used to store totals should normally be initialized to zero before being used in a program.

Good Programming Practice 9.5

Variables to be used in calculations should be initialized before their use.

```
<!DOCTYPE html PUBLIC "-//W3C//DTD HTML 4.0 Transitional//EN">
<HTML>
<!-- Fig. 9.7: average.html -->

<HEAD>
<TITLE>Class Average Program</TITLE>

<SCRIPT LANGUAGE = "JavaScript">
   var total,          // sum of grades
       gradeCounter,   // number of grades entered
       gradeValue,     // grade value
       average,        // average of all grades
       grade;          // grade typed by user

   // Initialization Phase
   total = 0;          // clear total
   gradeCounter = 1;   // prepare to loop

   // Processing Phase
   while ( gradeCounter <= 10 ) {  // loop 10 times

      // prompt for input and read grade from user
      grade = window.prompt( "Enter integer grade:", "0" );

      // convert grade from a String to an integer
      gradeValue = parseInt( grade );
```

Fig. 9.7 Class-average program with counter-controlled repetition (part 1 of 3).

```

         // add gradeValue to total
         total = total + gradeValue;

         // add 1 to gradeCounter
         gradeCounter = gradeCounter + 1;
      }

      // Termination Phase
      average = total / 10;  // calculate the average

      // display average of exam grades
      document.writeln(
         "<H1>Class average is " + average + "</H1>" );
   </SCRIPT>

   </HEAD>
   <BODY>
   Click Refresh (or Reload) to run the script again
   </BODY>
   </HTML>
```

Fig. 9.7 Class-average program with counter-controlled repetition (part 2 of 3).

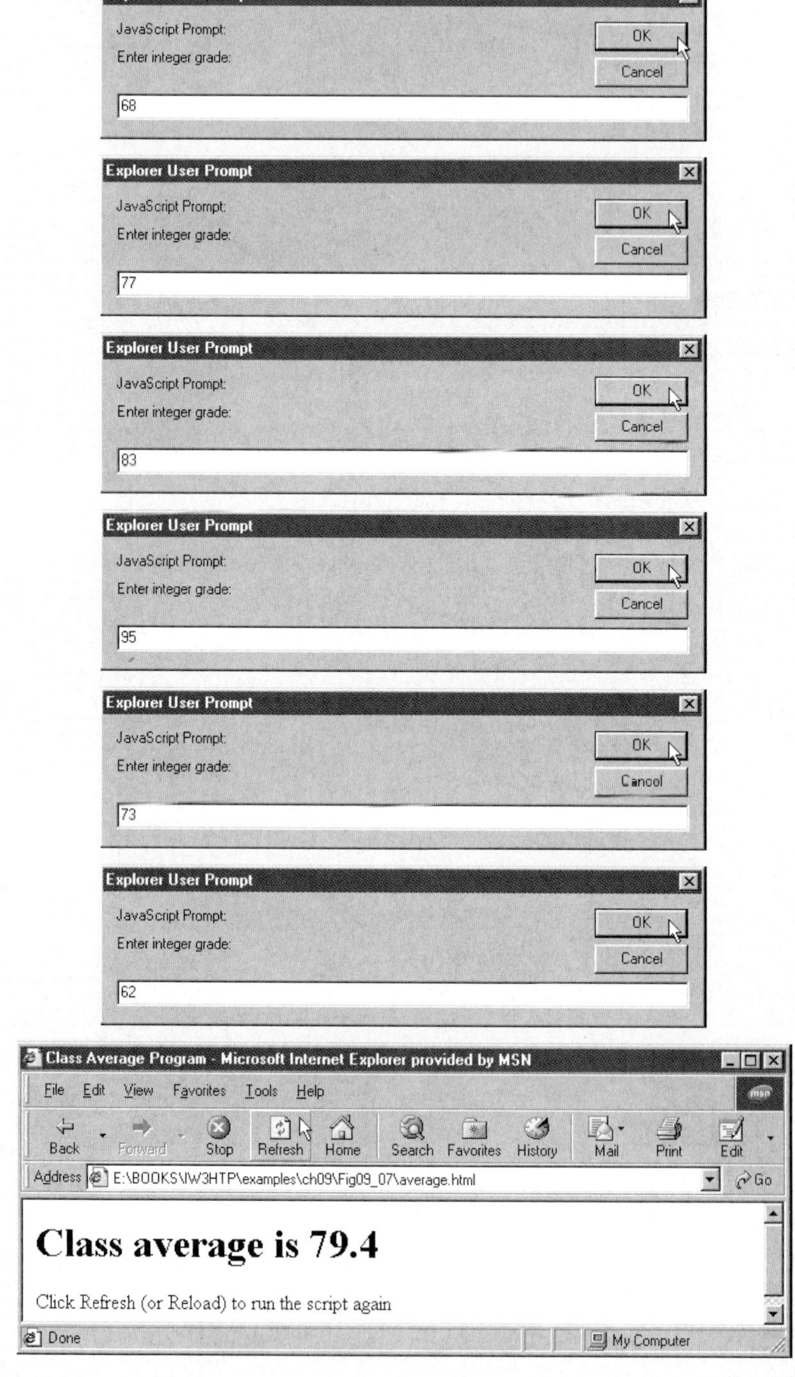

Fig. 9.7 Class-average program with counter-controlled repetition (part 3 of 3).

Lines 9 through 13,

```
var total,          // sum of grades
    gradeCounter,   // number of grades entered
    gradeValue,     // grade value
    average,        // average of all grades
    grade;          // grade typed by user
```

declare variables **total**, **gradeCounter**, **gradeValue**, **average** and **grade**. The variable **grade** will store the string the user types into the **prompt** dialog. The variable **gradeValue** will store the value of **grade** when its string representation that was returned from the **prompt** dialog is converted to an integer.

Lines 16 and 17,

```
total = 0;          // clear total
gradeCounter = 1;   // prepare to loop
```

are assignment statements that initialize **total** to **0** and **gradeCounter** to **1**.

Note that variables **total** and **gradeCounter** are initialized before they are used in a calculation. Uninitialized variables used in calculations result in logic errors and produce the value ***NaN*** *(not a number)*.

Common Programming Error 9.6

Not initializing a variable that will be used in a calculation results in a logic error. You must initialize the variable before it is used in a calculation.

Testing and Debugging Tip 9.1

Initialize variables that will be used in calculations.

Line 20,

```
while ( gradeCounter <= 10 ) {  // loop 10 times
```

indicates that the **while** structure should continue as long as the value of the variable **gradeCounter** is less than or equal to 10.

Line 23,

```
grade = window.prompt( "Enter integer grade:", "0" );
```

corresponds to the pseudocode statement *"Input the next grade."* The statement displays a **prompt** dialog with the prompt "**Enter integer grade:**" on the screen. The default value displayed in the dialog box's text field is **0**.

After the user enters the **grade**, it is converted from a string to an integer with line 26:

```
gradeValue = parseInt( grade );
```

Note that we must convert the string to an integer in this example. Otherwise, the addition statement at line 29 will be a string concatenation statement rather than a numeric sum.

Next, the program updates the **total** with the new **gradeValue** entered by the user. Line 29,

```
total = total + gradeValue;
```

adds **gradeValue** to the previous value of **total** and assigns the result to **total**. This statement seems a bit strange, because it does not follow the rules of algebra. Keep in mind that operator precedence causes JavaScript to evaluate the addition (**+**) operation before the assignment (**=**) operation. The value of the expression on the right side of the assignment always replaces the value of the variable on the left side of the assignment.

The program is now ready to increment the variable **gradeCounter** to indicate that a grade has been processed and read the next grade from the user. Line 32,

```
gradeCounter = gradeCounter + 1;
```

adds **1** to **gradeCounter**, so the condition in the **while** structure will eventually become **false** and terminate the loop. After this statement executes, the program continues by testing the condition in the **while** at line 20. If the condition is still true, the statements from lines 23 through 32 are repeated. Otherwise the program continues execution with the first statement in sequence after the body of the loop.

Line 36,

```
average = total / 10;  // calculate the average
```

assigns the results of the average calculation to variable **average**. Lines 39 and 40,

```
document.writeln(
   "<H1>Class average is " + average + "</H1>" );
```

write a line of HTML text in the document that displays the string **"Class average is "** followed by the value of variable **average** as an **<H1>** head in the browser.

After saving the HTML document, load it into Internet Explorer to execute the script. Note that this script reads only integer values from the user. In the sample program execution of Fig. 9.7, the sum of the values entered (100, 88, 93, 55, 68, 77, 83, 95, 73 and 62) is 794. Although the script reads only integers, the averaging calculation in the program does not produce an integer. Rather, the calculation produces a *floating-point number* (a number containing a decimal point). The average for the 10 integers input by the user in this example is 79.4.

Software Engineering Observation 9.6

If the string passed to **parseInt** *contains a floating-point numeric value,* **parseInt** *simply truncates the floating-point part. For example, the string "27.95" results in the integer 27 and the string -123.45 results in the integer -123. If the string passed to* **parseInt** *is not a numeric value,* **parseInt** *returns* **NaN** *(not a number).*

JavaScript actually represents all numbers as floating-point numbers in memory. Floating-point numbers often develop through division, as shown in this example. When we divide 10 by 3, the result is 3.3333333…, with the sequence of 3s repeating infinitely. The computer allocates only a fixed amount of space to hold such a value, so the stored floating-point value can only be an approximation. Despite the fact that floating-point numbers are not always "100% precise," they have numerous applications. For example, when we speak of a "normal" body temperature of 98.6 we do not need to be precise to a large number of digits. When we view the temperature on a thermometer and read it as 98.6, it may actually be 98.5999473210643. The point here is that few applications require high-precision floating-point values, so calling this number simply 98.6 is fine for most applications.

Common Programming Error 9.7

Using floating-point numbers in a manner that assumes they are precisely represented real numbers can lead to incorrect results. Real numbers are represented only approximately by computers. For example, no fixed-size floating-point representation of PI can ever be precise because PI is a transcendental number whose value cannot be expressed in a finite amount of space.

9.9 Formulating Algorithms with Top-Down, Stepwise Refinement: Case Study 2 (Sentinel-Controlled Repetition)

Let us generalize the class-average problem. Consider the following problem:

> *Develop a class-averaging program that will process an arbitrary number of grades each time the program is run.*

In the first class-average example, the number of grades (10) was known in advance of our inputting the data. In this example, no indication is given of how many grades are to be entered. The program must process an arbitrary number of grades. How can the program determine when to stop the input of grades? How will it know when to calculate and display the class average?

One way to solve this problem is to use a special value called a *sentinel value* (also called a *signal value,* a *dummy value* or a *flag value*) to indicate "end of data entry." The user types grades in until all legitimate grades have been entered. The user then types the sentinel value to indicate that the last grade has been entered. Sentinel-controlled repetition is often called *indefinite repetition,* because the number of repetitions is not known before the loop begins executing.

Clearly, the sentinel value must be chosen so that it cannot be confused with an acceptable input value. Because grades on a quiz are normally nonnegative integers from 0 to 100, –1 is an acceptable sentinel value for this problem. Thus, a run of the class-average program might process a stream of inputs such as 95, 96, 75, 74, 89 and –1. The program would then compute and print the class average for the grades 95, 96, 75, 74 and 89 (–1 is the sentinel value, so it should not enter into the average calculation).

Common Programming Error 9.8

Choosing a sentinel value that is also a legitimate data value results in a logic error and may prevent a sentinel-controlled loop from terminating properly.

We approach the class-average program with a technique called *top-down, stepwise refinement,* a technique that is essential to the development of well-structured algorithms. We begin with a pseudocode representation of the *top:*

> *Determine the class average for the quiz*

The top is a single statement that conveys the overall purpose of the program. As such, the top is, in effect, a complete representation of a program. Unfortunately, the top rarely conveys a sufficient amount of detail from which to write the JavaScript algorithm. So, we now begin the refinement process. We divide the top into a series of smaller tasks and list these in the order in which they need to be performed, creating the following *first refinement*:

> *Initialize variables*
> *Input, sum up and count the quiz grades*
> *Calculate and print the class average*

Here, only the sequence structure has been used—the steps listed are to be executed in order, one after the other.

Software Engineering Observation 9.7

Each refinement, as well as the top itself, is a complete specification of the algorithm; only the level of detail varies.

To proceed to the next level of refinement (the *second refinement*), we commit to specific variables. We need a running total of the numbers, a count of how many numbers have been processed, a variable to receive the string representation of each grade as it is input, a variable to store the value of the grade after it is converted to an integer and a variable to hold the calculated average. The pseudocode statement

Initialize variables

may be refined as follows:

Initialize total to zero
Initialize gradeCounter to zero

Notice that only the variables *total* and *gradeCounter* are initialized before they are used; the variables *average*, *grade* and *gradeValue* (for the calculated average, the user input and the integer representation of the *grade*, respectively) need not be initialized, because their values are determined as they are calculated or input.

The pseudocode statement

Input, sum up and count the quiz grades

requires a repetition structure (a loop) that successively inputs each grade. Because we do not know how many grades are to be processed, we will use sentinel-controlled repetition. The user at the keyboard will type legitimate grades in one at a time. After the last legitimate grade is typed, the user will type the sentinel value. The program will test for the sentinel value after each grade is input and will terminate the loop when the sentinel value is entered by the user. The second refinement of the preceding pseudocode statement is then

Input the first grade (possibly the sentinel)
While the user has not as yet entered the sentinel
    Add this grade into the running total
    Add one to the grade counter
    Input the next grade (possibly the sentinel)

Notice that in pseudocode, we do not use braces around the pseudocode that forms the body of the *while* structure. We simply indent the pseudocode under the *while* to show that it belongs to the body of the *while*. Remember, pseudocode is only an informal program development aid.

The pseudocode statement

Calculate and print the class average

may be refined as follows:

If the counter is not equal to zero
    Set the average to the total divided by the counter
    Print the average
else
    Print "No grades were entered"

Notice that we are testing for the possibility of division by zero—a *logic error* that, if undetected, would cause the program to produce invalid output. The complete second refinement of the pseudocode algorithm for the class-average problem is shown in Fig. 9.8.

Testing and Debugging Tip 9.2

When performing division by an expression whose value could be zero, explicitly test for this case and handle it appropriately in your program (such as printing an error message) rather than allowing the division by zero to occur.

Good Programming Practice 9.6

Include completely blank lines in pseudocode programs to make the pseudocode more readable. The blank lines separate pseudocode control structures and separate the phases of the programs.

Software Engineering Observation 9.8

Many algorithms can be divided logically into three phases: an initialization phase that initializes the program variables; a processing phase that inputs data values and adjusts program variables accordingly; and a termination phase that calculates and prints the results.

The pseudocode algorithm in Fig. 9.8 solves the more general class-averaging problem. This algorithm was developed after only two levels of refinement. Sometimes more levels are necessary.

Software Engineering Observation 9.9

The programmer terminates the top-down, stepwise refinement process when the pseudocode algorithm is specified in sufficient detail for the programmer to be able to convert the pseudocode to a JavaScript program. Implementing the JavaScript program is then normally straightforward.

```
Initialize total to zero
Initialize gradeCounter to zero

Input the first grade (possibly the sentinel)
While the user has not as yet entered the sentinel
    Add this grade into the running total
    Add one to the grade counter
    Input the next grade (possibly the sentinel)

If the counter is not equal to zero
    Set the average to the total divided by the counter
    Print the average
else
    Print "No grades were entered"
```

Fig. 9.8 Pseudocode algorithm that uses sentinel-controlled repetition to solve the class-average problem.

Good Programming Practice 9.7

When converting a pseudocode program to JavaScript, keep the pseudocode in the JavaScript program as comments.

Software Engineering Observation 9.10

Experience has shown that the most difficult part of solving a problem on a computer is developing the algorithm for the solution. After a correct algorithm has been specified, the process of producing a working JavaScript program from the algorithm is normally straightforward.

Software Engineering Observation 9.11

Many experienced programmers write programs without ever using program development tools like pseudocode. These programmers feel that their ultimate goal is to solve the problem on a computer, and that writing pseudocode merely delays the production of final outputs. Although this may work for simple and familiar problems, it can lead to serious errors on large, complex projects.

The JavaScript program and a sample execution are shown in Fig. 9.9. Although each grade is an integer, the averaging calculation is likely to produce a number with a decimal point (a real number).

```
<!DOCTYPE html PUBLIC "-//W3C//DTD HTML 4.0 Transitional//EN">
<HTML>
<!-- Fig. 9.9: Average2.html -->

<HEAD>
<TITLE>Class Average Program:
       Sentinel-controlled Repetition</TITLE>

<SCRIPT LANGUAGE = "JavaScript">
   var gradeCounter,  // number of grades entered
       gradeValue,    // grade value
       total,         // sum of grades
       average,       // average of all grades
       grade;         // grade typed by user

   // Initialization phase
   total = 0;           // clear total
   gradeCounter = 0;   // prepare to loop

   // Processing phase
   // prompt for input and read grade from user
   grade = window.prompt(
              "Enter Integer Grade, -1 to Quit:", "0" );

   // convert grade from a String to an integer
   gradeValue = parseInt( grade );

```

Fig. 9.9 Class-average program with sentinel-controlled repetition (part 1 of 3).

```
    while ( gradeValue != -1 ) {
       // add gradeValue to total
       total = total + gradeValue;

       // add 1 to gradeCounter
       gradeCounter = gradeCounter + 1;

       // prompt for input and read grade from user
       grade = window.prompt(
                  "Enter Integer Grade, -1 to Quit:", "0" );

       // convert grade from a String to an integer
       gradeValue = parseInt( grade );
    }

    // Termination phase
    if ( gradeCounter != 0 ) {
       average = total / gradeCounter;

       // display average of exam grades
       document.writeln(
          "<H1>Class average is " + average + "</H1>" );
    }
    else
       document.writeln( "<P>No grades were entered</P>" );
</SCRIPT>
</HEAD>

<BODY>
<P>Click Refresh (or Reload) to run the script again</P>
</BODY>
</HTML>
```

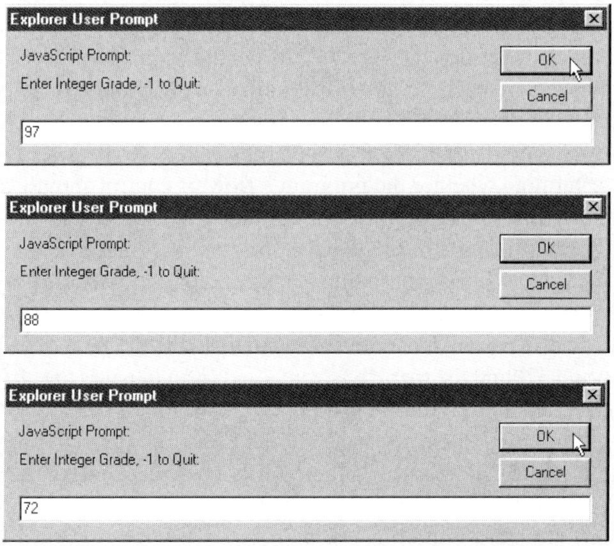

Fig. 9.9 Class-average program with sentinel-controlled repetition (part 2 of 3).

Fig. 9.9 Class-average program with sentinel-controlled repetition (part 3 of 3).

In this example, we see that control structures may be stacked on top of one another (in sequence) just as a child stacks building blocks. The **`while`** structure (lines 28 through 41) is immediately followed by an **`if`**/**`else`** structure (lines 44 through 52) in sequence. Much of the code in this program is identical to the code in Fig. 9.7, so we concentrate in this example on the new features and issues.

Line 18 initializes **`gradeCounter`** to **`0`**, because no grades have been entered yet. Remember that this program uses sentinel-controlled repetition. To keep an accurate record of the number of grades entered, variable **`gradeCounter`** is incremented only when a valid grade value is entered.

Notice the difference in program logic for sentinel-controlled repetition compared with the counter-controlled repetition in Fig. 9.7. In counter-controlled repetition, we read a value from the user during each iteration of the **`while`** structure's body for the specified number of iterations. In sentinel-controlled repetition, we read one value (lines 22 and 23) and convert it to an integer (line 26) before the program reaches the **`while`** structure. This value is used to determine whether the program's flow of control should enter the body of the **`while`** structure. If the **`while`** structure condition is **`false`** (the user typed the sentinel as the first grade), the body of the **`while`** structure does not execute (no grades were entered). If, on the other hand, the condition is **`true`**, the body begins execution and the value entered by the user is processed (added to the **`total`** at line 30). After the value is processed, **`gradeCounter`** is incremented by 1 (line 33), the next **`grade`** is input from the user (lines 36 and 37) and the **`grade`** is converted to an integer (line 40), before the end of the **`while`** structure's body. As the closing right brace (**`}`**) of the body is reached, at line 41, execution continues with the next test of the **`while`** structure condition (line 28) using the new value just entered by the user to determine whether the **`while`** structure's body should execute again. Notice that the next value is always input from the user immediately before the **`while`** structure condition is evaluated. This order allows us to determine whether the value just entered by the user is the sentinel value *before* that value is processed (added to the **total**). If the value entered is the sentinel value, the **while** structure terminates and the value is not added to the **total**.

Good Programming Practice 9.8

In a sentinel-controlled loop, the prompts requesting data entry should explicitly remind the user what the sentinel value is.

Notice the compound statement in the **while** loop in Fig 9.9. Without the braces, the last four statements in the body of the loop would fall outside the loop, causing the computer to interpret this code incorrectly as follows:

```
while ( gradeValue != -1 )
   // add gradeValue to total
   total = total + gradeValue;

// add 1 to gradeCounter
gradeCounter = gradeCounter + 1;

// prompt for input and read grade from user
grade = window.prompt(
           "Enter Integer Grade, -1 to Quit:", "0" );

// convert grade from a String to an integer
gradeValue = parseInt( grade );
```

This interpretation would cause an infinite loop in the program if the user does not input the sentinel **-1** as the input value at lines 22 and 23 (before the **while** structure) in the program.

Common Programming Error 9.9

Omitting the curly braces that are needed to delineate a compound statement can lead to logic errors such as infinite loops.

9.10 Formulating Algorithms with Top-Down, Stepwise Refinement: Case Study 3 (Nested Control Structures)

Let us work through another complete problem. We will once again formulate the algorithm using pseudocode and top-down, stepwise refinement, and we will write a corresponding JavaScript program.

Consider the following problem statement:

A college offers a course that prepares students for the state licensing exam for real estate brokers. Last year, several of the students who completed this course took the licensing examination. Naturally, the college wants to know how well its students did on the exam. You have been asked to write a program to summarize the results. You have been given a list of these 10 students. Next to each name is written a 1 if the student passed the exam and a 2 if the student failed.

Your program should analyze the results of the exam as follows:

1. *Input each test result (a 1 or a 2). Display the message "Enter result" on the screen each time the program requests another test result.*
2. *Count the number of test results of each type.*

3. *Display a summary of the test results indicating the number of students who passed and the number of students who failed.*
4. *If more than 8 students passed the exam, print the message "Raise tuition."*

After reading the problem statement carefully, we make the following observations about the problem:

1. The program must process test results for 10 students. A counter-controlled loop will be used.
2. Each test result is a number—either a 1 or a 2. Each time the program reads a test result, the program must determine whether the number is a 1 or a 2. We test for a 1 in our algorithm. If the number is not a 1, we assume that it is a 2. (An exercise at the end of the chapter considers the consequences of this assumption.)
3. Two counters are used to keep track of the exam results—one to count the number of students who passed the exam, and one to count the number of students who failed the exam.
4. After the program has processed all the results, it must decide whether more than eight students passed the exam.

Let us proceed with top-down, stepwise refinement. We begin with a pseudocode representation of the top:

Analyze exam results and decide if tuition should be raised

Once again, it is important to emphasize that the top is a complete representation of the program but that several refinements are likely to be needed before the pseudocode can be naturally evolved into a JavaScript program. Our first refinement is

Initialize variables
Input the ten exam grades and count passes and failures
Print a summary of the exam results and decide whether tuition should be raised

Here, too, even though we have a complete representation of the entire program, further refinement is necessary. We now commit to specific variables. Counters are needed to record the passes and failures, a counter will be used to control the looping process and a variable is needed to store the user input. The pseudocode statement

Initialize variables

may be refined as follows:

Initialize passes to zero
Initialize failures to zero
Initialize student to one

Notice that only the counters for the number of passes, number of failures and number of students are initialized. The pseudocode statement

Input the ten quiz grades and count passes and failures

requires a loop that successively inputs the result of each exam. Here it is known in advance that there are precisely 10 exam results, so counter-controlled looping is appropriate. Inside the loop (*nested* within the loop), a double-selection structure will determine whether each exam result is a pass or a failure and will increment the appropriate counter accordingly. The refinement of the preceding pseudocode statement is then

While student counter is less than or equal to ten
  Input the next exam result

  If the student passed
    Add one to passes
  else
    Add one to failures

  Add one to student counter

Notice the use of blank lines to set off the *if/else* control structure to improve program readability. The pseudocode statement

Print a summary of the exam results and decide whether tuition should be raised

may be refined as follows:

Print the number of passes
Print the number of failures
If more than eight students passed
  Print "Raise tuition"

The complete second refinement appears in Fig. 9.10. Notice that blank lines are also used to set off the *while* structure for program readability.

This pseudocode is now sufficiently refined for conversion to JavaScript. The JavaScript program and two sample executions are shown in Fig. 9.11.

Initialize passes to zero
Initialize failures to zero
Initialize student to one

While student counter is less than or equal to ten
  Input the next exam result

  If the student passed
    Add one to passes
  else
    Add one to failures

  Add one to student counter

Print the number of passes
Print the number of failures
If more than eight students passed
  Print "Raise tuition"

Fig. 9.10 Pseudocode for examination-results problem.

```
<!DOCTYPE html PUBLIC "-//W3C//DTD HTML 4.0 Transitional//EN">
<HTML>
<!-- Fig. 9.11: analysis.html -->

<HEAD>
<TITLE>Analysis of Examination Results</TITLE>

<SCRIPT LANGUAGE = "JavaScript">
   // initializing variables in declarations
   var passes = 0,       // number of passes
       failures = 0,     // number of failures
       student = 1,      // student counter
       result;           // one exam result

   // process 10 students; counter-controlled loop
   while ( student <= 10 ) {
      result = window.prompt(
                  "Enter result (1=pass,2=fail)", "0" );

      if ( result == "1" )
         passes = passes + 1;
      else
         failures = failures + 1;

      student = student + 1;
   }

   // termination phase
   document.writeln( "<H1>Examination Results</H1>" );
   document.writeln(
      "Passed: " + passes + "<BR>Failed: " + failures );

   if ( passes > 8 )
      document.writeln( "<BR>Raise Tuition" );
</SCRIPT>

</HEAD>
<BODY>
<P>Click Refresh (or Reload) to run the script again</P>
</BODY>
</HTML>
```

Fig. 9.11 JavaScript program for examination-results problem (part 1 of 5).

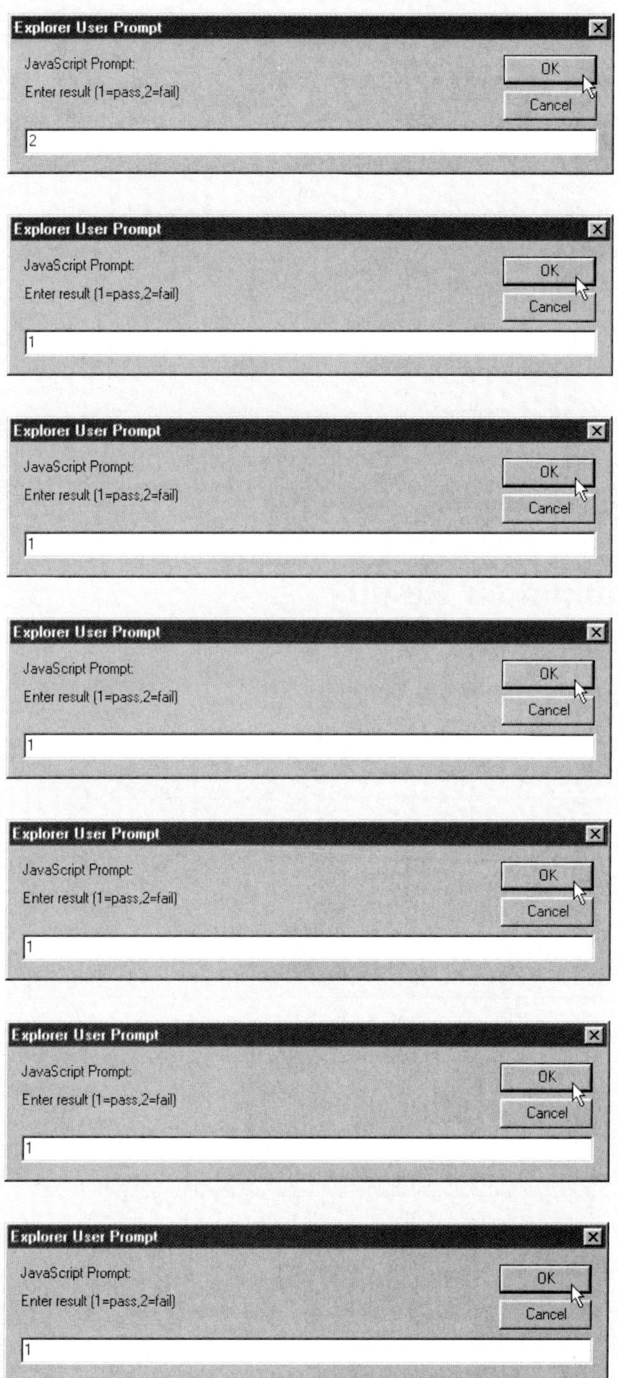

Fig. 9.11 JavaScript program for examination-results problem (part 2 of 5).

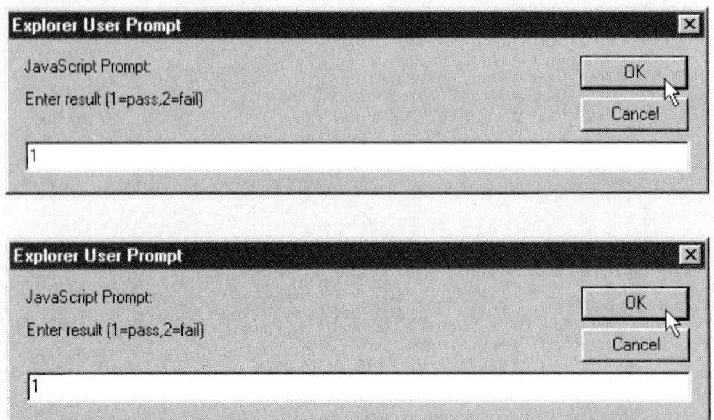

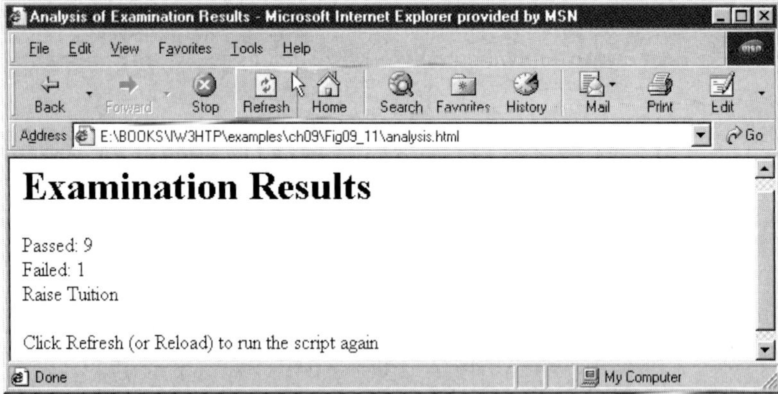

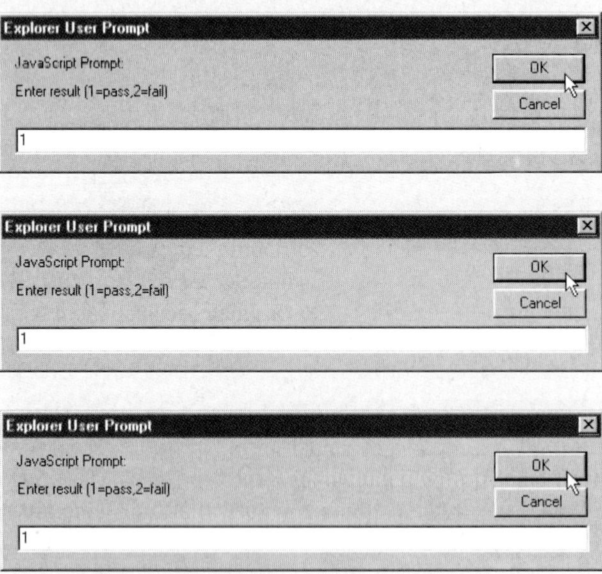

Fig. 9.11 JavaScript program for examination-results problem (part 3 of 5).

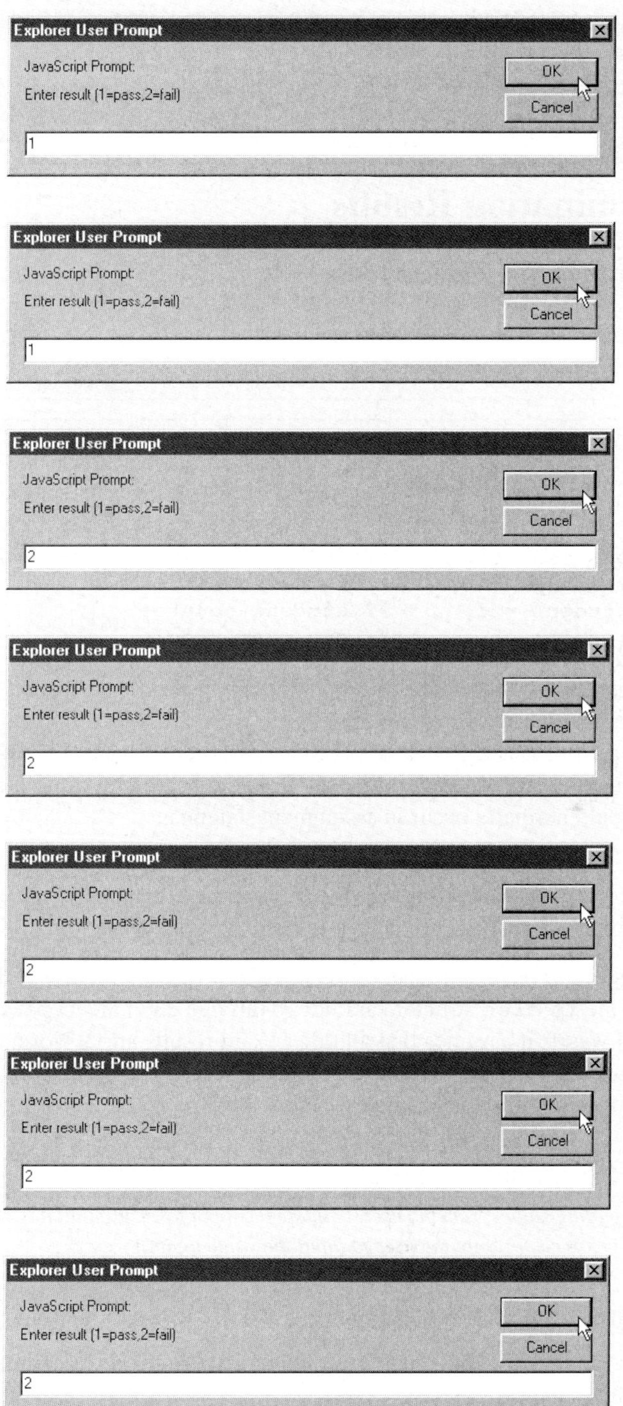

Fig. 9.11 JavaScript program for examination-results problem (part 4 of 5).

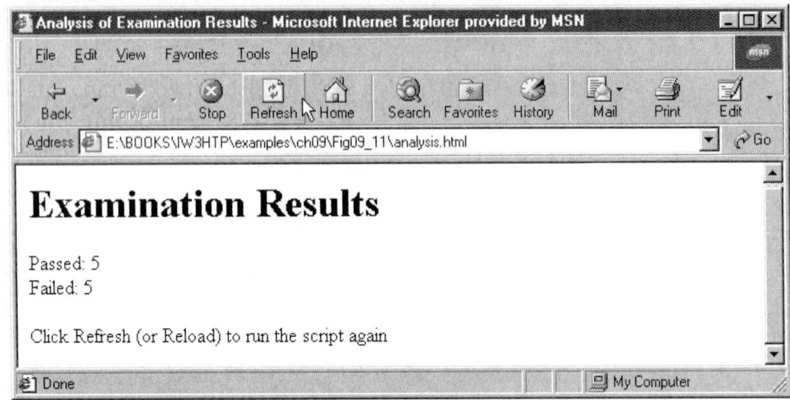

Fig. 9.11 JavaScript program for examination-results problem (part 5 of 5).

Lines 10 through 13,

```
var passes = 0,        // number of passes
    failures = 0,      // number of failures
    student = 1,       // student counter
    result;            // one exam result
```

declare the variables used to process the examination results. Note that we have taken advantage of a feature of JavaScript that allows variable initialization to be incorporated into declarations (**passes** is assigned **0**, **failures** is assigned **0** and **student** is assigned **1**). Looping programs may require initialization at the beginning of each repetition; such initialization would normally occur in assignment statements.

Testing and Debugging Tip 9.3

Initializing variables when they are declared in methods helps the programmer avoid incorrect results and interpreter messages warning of uninitialized data.

The processing of the exam results occurs in the **while** structure at lines 16 through 26. Notice that the **if/else** structure at lines 20 through 23 in the loop tests only whether the exam result was 1; it assumes that all other exam results are 2. Normally, you should validate the values input by the user (determine whether the values are correct). In the exercises, we ask you to modify this example to validate the input values to ensure that they are either 1 or 2.

Good Programming Practice 9.9

When inputting values from the user, validate the input to ensure that it is correct. If an input value is incorrect, prompt the user to input the value again.

9.11 Assignment Operators

JavaScript provides several assignment operators for abbreviating assignment expressions. For example, the statement

```
c = c + 3;
```

can be abbreviated with the *addition assignment operator* **+=** as

```
c += 3;
```

The **+=** operator adds the value of the expression on the right of the operator to the value of the variable on the left of the operator and stores the result in the variable on the left of the operator. Any statement of the form

variable = *variable operator expression*;

where *operator* is one of the binary operators **+**, **-**, *****, **/** or **%** (or others we will discuss later in the text), can be written in the form

variable operator= *expression*;

Thus the assignment **c += 3** adds **3** to **c**. Figure 9.12 shows the arithmetic assignment operators, sample expressions using these operators and explanations.

Performance Tip 9.1

Programmers can write programs that execute a bit faster when the "abbreviated" assignment operators are used, because the variable on the left side of the assignment does not have to be evaluated twice.

Performance Tip 9.2

Many of the performance tips we mention in this text result in nominal improvements, so the reader may be tempted to ignore them. Significant performance improvement is often realized when a supposedly nominal improvement is placed in a loop that may repeat a large number of times.

9.12 Increment and Decrement Operators

JavaScript provides the unary *increment operator* (**++**) and *decrement operator* (**--**) which are summarized in Fig. 9.13. If a variable **c** is incremented by 1, the increment operator **++** can be used rather than the expressions **c = c + 1** or **c += 1**. If an increment or decrement operator is placed before a variable, it is referred to as the *preincrement* or *predecrement operator*, respectively. If an increment or decrement operator is placed after a variable, it is referred to as the *postincrement* or *postdecrement operator*, respectively.

Assignment operator	Initial variable value	Sample expression	Explanation	Assigns
`+=`	`c = 3`	`c += 7`	`c = c + 7`	**10** to **c**
`-=`	`d = 5`	`d -= 4`	`d = d - 4`	**1** to **d**
`*=`	`e = 4`	`e *= 5`	`e = e * 5`	**20** to **e**
`/=`	`f = 6`	`f /= 3`	`f = f / 3`	**2** to **f**
`%=`	`g = 12`	`g %= 9`	`g = g % 9`	**3** to **g**

Fig. 9.12 Arithmetic assignment operators.

Operator	Called	Sample expression	Explanation
++	preincrement	**++a**	Increment **a** by 1, then use the new value of **a** in the expression in which **a** resides.
++	postincrement	**a++**	Use the current value of **a** in the expression in which **a** resides, then increment **a** by 1.
--	predecrement	**--b**	Decrement **b** by 1, then use the new value of **b** in the expression in which **b** resides.
--	postdecrement	**b--**	Use the current value of **b** in the expression in which **b** resides, then decrement **b** by 1.

Fig. 9.13 The increment and decrement operators.

Preincrementing (predecrementing) a variable causes the variable to be incremented (decremented) by 1, then the new value of the variable is used in the expression in which it appears. Postincrementing (postdecrementing) the variable causes the current value of the variable to be used in the expression in which it appears, then the variable value is incremented (decremented) by 1.

The script of Fig. 9.14 demonstrates the difference between the preincrementing version and the postincrementing version of the ++ increment operator. Postincrementing the variable **c** causes it to be incremented after it is used in the **document.writeln** method call (line 14). Preincrementing the variable **c** causes it to be incremented before it is used in the **document.writeln** method call (line 20). The program displays the value of **c** before and after the ++ operator is used. The decrement operator (**--**) works similarly.

Good Programming Practice 9.10

For readability, unary operators should be placed next to their operands with no intervening spaces.

```
1  <!DOCTYPE html PUBLIC "-//W3C//DTD HTML 4.0 Transitional//EN">
2  <HTML>
3  <!-- Fig. 9.14: increment.html -->
4
5  <HEAD>
6  <TITLE>Preincrementing and Postincrementing</TITLE>
7
8  <SCRIPT LANGUAGE = "JavaScript">
9     var c;
10
11    c = 5;
12    document.writeln( "<H3>Postincrementing</H3>" );
13    document.writeln( c );            // print 5
14    document.writeln( "<BR>" + c++ ); // print 5 then increment
15    document.writeln( "<BR>" + c );   // print 6
16
```

Fig. 9.14 Differences between preincrementing and postincrementing (part 1 of 2).

```
    c = 5;
    document.writeln( "<H3>Preincrementing</H3>" );
    document.writeln( c );                  // print 5
    document.writeln( "<BR>" + ++c );  // increment then print 6
    document.writeln( "<BR>" + c );    // print 6
</SCRIPT>

</HEAD><BODY></BODY>
</HTML>
```

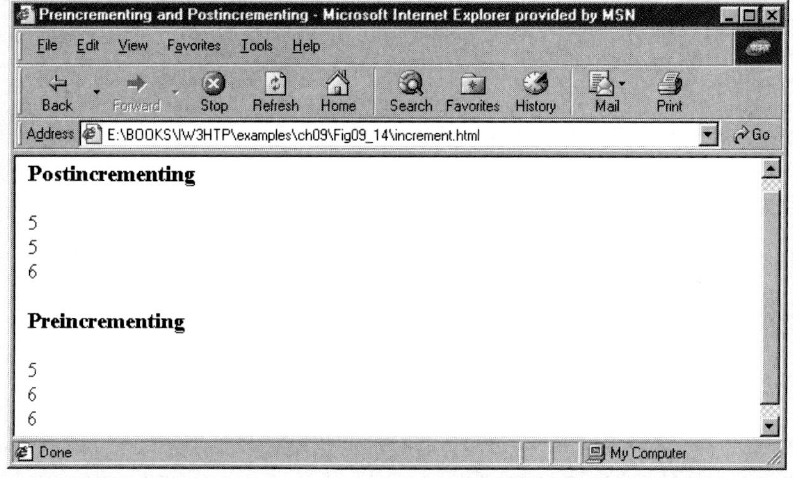

Fig. 9.14 Differences between preincrementing and postincrementing (part 2 of 2).

The three assignment statements in Fig 9.11 (lines 21, 23 and 25, respectively),

```
passes = passes + 1;
failures = failures + 1;
student = student + 1;
```

can be written more concisely with assignment operators as

```
passes += 1;
failures += 1;
student += 1;
```

with preincrement operators as

```
++passes;
++failures;
++student;
```

or with postincrement operators as

```
passes++;
failures++;
student++;
```

It is important to note here that when incrementing or decrementing a variable in a statement by itself, the preincrement and postincrement forms have the same effect, and the predecrement and postdecrement forms have the same effect. It is only when a variable appears in the context of a larger expression that preincrementing the variable and post-incrementing the variable have different effects. Predecrementing and postdecrementing behave similarly.

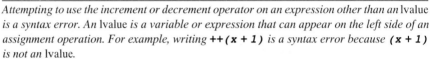

Common Programming Error 9.10

Attempting to use the increment or decrement operator on an expression other than an lvalue *is a syntax error. An* lvalue *is a variable or expression that can appear on the left side of an assignment operation. For example, writing* `++(x + 1)` *is a syntax error because* `(x + 1)` *is not an* lvalue.

The chart in Fig. 9.15 shows the precedence and associativity of the operators introduced up to this point. The operators are shown from top to bottom in decreasing order of precedence. The second column describes the associativity of the operators at each level of precedence. Notice that the conditional operator (`?:`), the unary operators increment (`++`) and decrement (`--`) and the assignment operators `=`, `+=`, `-=`, `*=`, `/=` and `%=` associate from right to left. All other operators in the operator precedence chart of Fig. 9.15 associate from left to right. The third column names the groups of operators.

9.13 A Note on Data Types

Unlike its predecessor languages C, C++ and Java, JavaScript does not require variables to have a type before they can be used in a program. A variable in JavaScript can contain a value of any data type, and in many situations JavaScript automatically converts between values of different types for you. For this reason, JavaScript is referred to as a *loosely typed language*.

When a variable is declared in JavaScript but is not given a value, that variable has an *undefined* value. Attempting to use the value of such a variable is normally a logic error.

When variables are declared, they are not assigned default values unless specified otherwise by the programmer. To indicate that a variable does not contain a value, you can assign the value **`null`** to the variable.

Operators	Associativity	Type
`()`	left to right	parentheses
`++ --`	right to left	unary
`* / %`	left to right	multiplicative
`+ -`	left to right	additive
`< <= > >=`	left to right	relational
`== !=`	left to right	equality
`?:`	right to left	conditional
`= += -= *= /= %=`	right to left	assignment

Fig. 9.15 Precedence and associativity of the operators discussed so far.

9.14 JavaScript Internet and World Wide Web Resources

There are a tremendous number of resources for JavaScript programmers on the Internet and World Wide Web. This section lists a variety of JavaScript, JavaScript and ECMAScript resources available on the Internet and provides a brief description of each. Additional resources for these topics are presented at the ends of chapters 10 through 13 (on JavaScript) and in other chapters as necessary.

http://www.javascriptmall.com/
The *JavaScript Mall* provides free scripts, FAQs, tools for web pages and a class in JavaScript. The mall is a helpful resource for web page design.

http://builder.cnet.com/Programming/kahn
This site offers recent and backdated columns containing tips on JavaScript. It also includes nifty tools to aid in JavaScript programming.

http://developer.netscape.com/docs/manuals/communicator/jsref/contents.htm
This *JavaScript Reference* explores JavaScript syntax piece by piece.

http://www.javascripts.com/toc.cfm
Javascripts.com contains an archive of over 2700 scripts to cut and paste and a tutorial section comprised of 30 demo scripts with explanations.

http://www.hidaho.com/colorcenter/
JavaScript for testing backgrounds by combining colors and textures.

http://javascript.internet.com
"Cut & Paste" JavaScript Library has more than 300 free scripts! Simply click on the source code to obtain JavaScript buttons, clocks, games, cookies and more.

http://www.infohiway.com/javascript/indexf.htm
Here you will find close to 200 free JavaScripts

SUMMARY

- Any computing problem can be solved by executing a series of actions in a specific order.
- A procedure for solving a problem in terms of the actions to be executed and the order in which these actions are to be executed is called an algorithm.
- Specifying the order in which statements are to be executed in a computer program is called program control.
- Pseudocode is an artificial and informal language that helps programmers develop algorithms.
- Pseudocode is not actually executed on computers. Rather, it helps the programmer "think out" a program before attempting to write it in a programming language such as JavaScript.
- Carefully prepared pseudocode may be converted easily to a corresponding JavaScript program.
- Pseudocode normally describes only executable statements—the actions that are performed when the program is converted from pseudocode to JavaScript and is run.
- Normally, statements in a program are executed one after the other, in the order in which they are written. This is called sequential execution.
- Various JavaScript statements enable the programmer to specify that the next statement to be executed may be other than the next one in sequence. This is called transfer of control.
- All programs can be written in terms of only three control structures, namely the sequence structure, the selection structure and the repetition structure.

- A flowchart is a graphical representation of an algorithm or of a portion of an algorithm. Flowcharts are drawn using certain special-purpose symbols, such as rectangles, diamonds, ovals and small circles; these symbols are connected by arrows called flowlines, which indicate the order in which the actions of the algorithm execute.
- Flowcharts are often useful for developing and representing algorithms, although pseudocode is strongly preferred by many programmers.
- JavaScript provides three types of selection structures. The **`if`** selection structure either performs (selects) an action if a condition is true or skips the action if the condition is false. The **`if/else`** selection structure performs an action if a condition is true and performs a different action if the condition is false. The **`switch`** selection structure performs one of many different actions, depending on the value of an expression.
- The **`if`** structure is called a single-selection structure, because it selects or ignores a single action (or as we will soon see, a single group of actions).
- The **`if/else`** structure is called a double-selection structure, because it selects between two different actions (or groups of actions).
- The **`switch`** structure is called a multiple-selection structure, because it selects among many different actions (or groups of actions).
- JavaScript provides four types of repetition structures, namely **`while`**, **`do/while`**, **`for`** and **`for/in`**.
- Keywords cannot be used as identifiers (such as for variable names).
- Single-entry/single-exit control structures make it easy to build programs. Control structures are attached to one another by connecting the exit point of one control structure to the entry point of the next—this is called control-structure stacking. There is only one other way control structures may be connected—control-structure nesting.
- A selection structure is used to choose among alternative courses of action in a program.
- The JavaScript interpreter ignores whitespace characters: blanks, tabs and newlines used for indentation and vertical spacing. Programmers insert these whitespace characters to enhance program clarity.
- A decision can be made on any expression that evaluates to a value of JavaScript's boolean type (any expression that evaluates to **`true`** or **`false`**).
- The **`if/else`** selection structure allows the programmer to specify that different actions are to be performed when the condition is true and when the condition is false.
- The indentation convention you choose should be carefully applied throughout your programs. It is difficult to read programs that do not use uniform spacing conventions.
- JavaScript provides an operator called the conditional operator (**`?:`**) that is closely related to the **`if/else`** structure. Operator **`?:`** is JavaScript's only ternary operator—it takes three operands. The operands together with the **`?:`** form a conditional expression. The first operand is a boolean expression, the second is the value for the conditional expression if the condition evaluates to true and the third is the value for the conditional expression if the condition evaluates to false.
- Nested **`if/else`** structures test for multiple cases by placing **`if/else`** structures inside **`if/else`** structures.
- The JavaScript interpreter always associates an **`else`** with the previous **`if`** unless told to do otherwise by the placement of braces (**`{}`**).
- The **`if`** selection structure normally expects only one statement in its body. To include several statements in the body of an **`if`**, enclose the statements in braces (**`{`** and **`}`**). A set of statements contained within a pair of braces is called a compound statement.

- A logic error has its effect at execution time. A fatal logic error causes a program to fail and terminate prematurely. A nonfatal logic error allows a program to continue executing, but the program produces incorrect results.
- A repetition structure allows the programmer to specify that an action is to be repeated while some condition remains true.
- Counter-controlled repetition is often called definite repetition, because the number of repetitions is known before the loop begins executing.
- Uninitialized variables used in mathematical calculations result in logic errors and produce the value **NaN** *(not a number).*
- JavaScript represents all numbers as floating-point numbers in memory. Floating-point numbers often develop through division. The computer allocates only a fixed amount of space to hold such a value, so the stored floating-point value can only be an approximation.
- In sentinel-controlled repetition, a special value called a sentinel value (also called a signal value, a dummy value or a flag value) indicates "end of data entry." Sentinel-controlled repetition is often called indefinite repetition, because the number of repetitions is not known in advance.
- The sentinel value must be chosen so that it is not confused with an acceptable input value.
- Top-down, stepwise refinement is a technique that is essential to the development of well-structured algorithms. The top is a single statement that conveys the overall purpose of the program. As such, the top is, in effect, a complete representation of a program. The stepwise refinement process divides the top into a series of smaller tasks. The programmer terminates the top-down, stepwise refinement process when the pseudocode algorithm is specified in sufficient detail for the programmer to be able to convert the pseudocode to a JavaScript program. Implementing the JavaScript program is then normally straightforward.
- JavaScript provides the arithmetic assignment operators **+=**, **-=**, ***=**, **/=** and **%=** that help abbreviate certain common types of expressions.
- The increment operator, **++**, and the decrement operator, **--**, increment or decrement a variable by 1. If the operator is prefixed to the variable, the variable is incremented or decremented by 1 first, then used in its expression. If the operator is postfixed to the variable, the variable is used in its expression, then incremented or decremented by 1.
- JavaScript does not require variables to have a type before they can be used in a program. A variable in JavaScript can contain a value of any data type, and in many situations JavaScript automatically converts between values of different types for you. For this reason, JavaScript is referred to as a *loosely typed language.*
- When a variable is declared in JavaScript but is not given a value, that variable has an *undefined* value. Attempting to use the value of such a variable is normally a logic error.
- When variables are declared, they are not assigned default values unless specified otherwise by the programmer. To indicate that a variable does not contain a value, you can assign the value **null** to the variable.

TERMINOLOGY

-- operator
++ operator
?: operator
action
action/decision model
algorithm
arithmetic assignment operators:
    +=, **-=**, ***=**, **/=** and **%=**
block
body of a loop
compound statement
conditional operator (**?:**)

control structure
counter-controlled repetition
decision
decrement operator (`--`)
definite repetition
double-selection structure
empty statement (`;`)
`if` selection structure
`if`/**`else`** selection structure
increment operator (`++`)
indefinite repetition
infinite loop
initialization
logic error
loop-continuation condition
loop counter
nested control structures
postdecrement operator
postincrement operator
predecrement operator
preincrement operator
pseudocode
repetition
repetition structures
selection
sentinel value
sequential execution
single-entry/single-exit control structures
single-selection structure
stacked control structures
structured programming
syntax error
top-down, stepwise refinement
unary operator
`while` repetition structure
whitespace characters

COMMON PROGRAMMING ERRORS

9.1 Using a keyword as an identifier is a syntax error.

9.2 Forgetting one or both of the braces that delimit a compound statement can lead to syntax errors or logic errors.

9.3 Placing a semicolon after the condition in an **`if`** structure leads to a logic error in single-selection **`if`** structures and a syntax error in double-selection **`if`** structures (if the **`if`** part contains a nonempty body statement).

9.4 Not providing in the body of a **`while`** structure an action that eventually causes the condition in the **`while`** to become false is a logic error. Normally, such a repetition structure will never terminate—an error called an "infinite loop." Browsers handle infinite loops differently. For example, Internet Explorer allows the user to terminate the script containing the infinite loop.

9.5 Spelling the keyword **`while`** with an uppercase **`W`** as in **`While`** (remember that JavaScript is a case-sensitive language) is a syntax error. All of JavaScript's reserved keywords, such as **`while`**, **`if`** and **`else`**, contain only lowercase letters.

9.6 Not initializing a variable that will be used in a calculation results in a logic error. You must initialize the variable before it is used in a calculation.

9.7 Using floating-point numbers in a manner that assumes they are precisely represented real numbers can lead to incorrect results. Real numbers are represented only approximately by computers. For example, no fixed-size floating-point representation of PI can ever be precise because PI is a transcendental number whose value cannot be expressed in a finite amount of space.

9.8 Choosing a sentinel value that is also a legitimate data value results in a logic error and may prevent a sentinel-controlled loop from terminating properly.

9.9 Omitting the curly braces that are needed to delineate a compound statement can lead to logic errors such as infinite loops.

9.10 Attempting to use the increment or decrement operator on an expression other than an lvalue is a syntax error. An lvalue is a variable or expression that can appear on the left side of an assignment operation. For example, writing **`++(x + 1)`** is a syntax error because **`(x + 1)`** is not an lvalue.

GOOD PROGRAMMING PRACTICES

9.1 Consistently applying reasonable indentation conventions throughout your programs improves program readability. We suggest a fixed-size tab of about 1/4 inch or three spaces per indent.

9.2 Indent both body statements of an **`if/else`** structure.

9.3 If there are several levels of indentation, each level should be indented the same additional amount of space.

9.4 Some programmers prefer to type the beginning and ending braces of compound statements before typing the individual statements within the braces. This helps avoid omitting one or both of the braces.

9.5 Variables to be used in calculations should be initialized before their use.

9.6 Include completely blank lines in pseudocode programs to make the pseudocode more readable. The blank lines separate pseudocode control structures and separate the phases of the programs.

9.7 When converting a pseudocode program to JavaScript, keep the pseudocode in the JavaScript program as comments.

9.8 In a sentinel-controlled loop, the prompts requesting data entry should explicitly remind the user what the sentinel value is.

9.9 When inputting values from the user, validate the input to ensure that it is correct. If an input value is incorrect, prompt the user to input the value again.

9.10 For readability, unary operators should be placed next to their operands with no intervening spaces.

PERFORMANCE TIPS

9.1 Programmers can write programs that execute a bit faster when the "abbreviated" assignment operators are used, because the variable on the left side of the assignment does not have to be evaluated twice.

9.2 Many of the performance tips we mention in this text result in nominal improvements, so the reader may be tempted to ignore them. Significant performance improvement is often realized when a supposedly nominal improvement is placed in a loop that may repeat a large number of times.

SOFTWARE ENGINEERING OBSERVATIONS

9.1 Pseudocode is often used to "think out" a program during the program design process. Then the pseudocode program is converted to a programming language such as JavaScript.

9.2 In JavaScript, any non-zero numeric value in a condition evaluates to **`true`**, and 0 evaluates to **`false`**. For strings, any string containing 1 or more characters evaluates to **`true`** and the empty string (the string containing no characters) evaluates to **`false`**. Also, a variable that has been declared with **`var`** but has not been assigned a value evaluates to **`false`**.

9.3 A compound statement can be placed anywhere in a program that a single statement can be placed.

9.4 Unlike individual statements, a compound statement does not end with a semicolon. However, each statement within the braces of a compound statement should end with a semicolon.

9.5 Just as a compound statement can be placed anywhere a single statement can be placed, it is also possible to have no statement at all (the empty statement). The empty statement is represented by placing a semicolon (**`;`**) where a statement would normally be.

9.6 If the string passed to **parseInt** contains a floating-point numeric value, **parseInt** simply truncates the floating-point part. For example, the string "27.95" results in the integer 27 and the string -123.45 results in the integer -123. If the string passed to **parseInt** is not a numeric value, **parseInt** returns **NaN** (not a number).

9.7 Each refinement, as well as the top itself, is a complete specification of the algorithm; only the level of detail varies.

9.8 Many algorithms can be divided logically into three phases: an initialization phase that initializes the program variables; a processing phase that inputs data values and adjusts program variables accordingly; and a termination phase that calculates and prints the results.

9.9 The programmer terminates the top-down, stepwise refinement process when the pseudocode algorithm is specified in sufficient detail for the programmer to be able to convert the pseudocode to a JavaScript program. Implementing the JavaScript program is then normally straightforward.

9.10 Experience has shown that the most difficult part of solving a problem on a computer is developing the algorithm for the solution. After a correct algorithm has been specified, the process of producing a working JavaScript program from the algorithm is normally straightforward.

9.11 Many experienced programmers write programs without ever using program development tools like pseudocode. These programmers feel that their ultimate goal is to solve the problem on a computer, and that writing pseudocode merely delays the production of final outputs. Although this may work for simple and familiar problems, it can lead to serious errors on large, complex projects.

TESTING AND DEBUGGING TIPS

9.1 Initialize variables that will be used in calculations.

9.2 When performing division by an expression whose value could be zero, explicitly test for this case and handle it appropriately in your program (such as printing an error message) rather than allowing the division by zero to occur.

9.3 Initializing variables when they are declared in methods helps the programmer avoid incorrect results and interpreter messages warning of uninitialized data.

SELF-REVIEW EXERCISES

9.1 Answer each of the following questions.

a) All programs can be written in terms of three types of control structures: _________, _________ and _________.
b) The _________ selection structure is used to execute one action when a condition is true and another action when that condition is false.
c) Repetition of a set of instructions a specific number of times is called _______ repetition.
d) When it is not known in advance how many times a set of statements will be repeated, a _________ value can be used to terminate the repetition.

9.2 Write four different JavaScript statements that each add 1 to variable **x** which contains a number.

9.3 Write JavaScript statements to accomplish each of the following:

a) Assign the sum of **x** and **y** to **z** and increment the value of **x** by 1 after the calculation. Use only one statement.
b) Test whether the value of the variable **count** is greater than 10. If it is, print **"Count is greater than 10"**.

c) Decrement the variable **x** by 1, then subtract it from the variable **total**. Use only one statement.
d) Calculate the remainder after **q** is divided by **divisor** and assign the result to **q**. Write this statement two different ways.

9.4 Write a JavaScript statement to accomplish each of the following tasks.
a) Declare variables **sum** and **x**.
b) Assign **1** to variable **x**.
c) Assign **0** to variable **sum**.
d) Add variable **x** to variable **sum** and assign the result to variable **sum**.
e) Print **"The sum is: "** followed by the value of variable **sum**.

9.5 Combine the statements that you wrote in Exercise 9.4 into a JavaScript program that calculates and prints the sum of the integers from 1 to 10. Use the **while** structure to loop through the calculation and increment statements. The loop should terminate when the value of **x** becomes 11.

9.6 Determine the values of each variable after the calculation is performed. Assume that, when each statement begins executing, all variables have the integer value 5.
a) `product *= x++;`
b) `quotient /= ++x;`

9.7 Identify and correct the errors in each of the following:
a)
```
while ( c <= 5 ) {
   product *= c;
   ++c;
```
b)
```
if ( gender == 1 )
   document.writeln( "Woman" );
else;
   document.writeln( "Man" );
```

9.8 What is wrong with the following **while** repetition structure?
```
while ( z >= 0 )
   sum += z;
```

ANSWERS TO SELF-REVIEW EXERCISES

9.1 a) Sequence, selection and repetition. b) **if/else**. c) Counter-controlled (or definite). d) Sentinel, signal, flag or dummy.

9.2
```
x = x + 1;
x += 1;
++x;
x++;
```

9.3 a) `z = x++ + y;`
b)
```
if ( count > 10 )
   document.writeln( "Count is greater than 10" );
```
c) `total -= --x;`
d)
```
q %= divisor;
q = q % divisor;
```

9.4 a) `var sum, x;`
b) `x = 1;`
c) `sum = 0;`
d) `sum += x;` or `sum = sum + x;`
e) `document.writeln( "The sum is: " + sum );`

9.5 The solution is:

```
<!DOCTYPE html PUBLIC "-//W3C//DTD HTML 4.0 Transitional//EN">
<!-- Exercise 9.5: sum.html -->

<HTML>
<HEAD><TITLE>Sum the Integers from 1 to 10</TITLE>

<SCRIPT LANGUAGE = "JavaScript">
   var sum, x;

   x = 1;
   sum = 0;

   while ( x <= 10 ) {
      sum += x;
      ++x;
   }

   document.writeln( "The sum is: " + sum );
</SCRIPT>

</HEAD><BODY></BODY>
</HTML>
```

9.6 a) **product = 25, x = 6;**
b) **quotient = 0.833333..., x = 6;**

9.7 a) Error: Missing the closing right brace of the **while** body.
Correction: Add closing right brace after the statement **++c;**.
b) Error: Semicolon after **else** results in a logic error. The second output statement will always be executed.
Correction: Remove the semicolon after **else**.

9.8 The value of the variable **z** is never changed in the **while** structure body. Therefore, if the loop-continuation condition **(z >= 0)** is true, an infinite loop is created. To prevent the infinite loop, **z** must be decremented so that it eventually becomes less than 0.

EXERCISES

9.9 Identify and correct the errors in each of the following. [*Note:* There may be more than one error in each piece of code.]

a)
```
if ( age >= 65 );
   document.writeln( "Age greater than or equal to 65" );
else
   document.writeln( "Age is less than 65 )";
```

b)
```
var x = 1, total;
while ( x <= 10 ) {
   total += x;
   ++x;
}
```

```
c) While ( x <= 100 )
       total += x;
       ++x;
d) while ( y > 0 ) {
       document.writeln( y );
       ++y;
```

9.10 What does the following program print?

```
<!DOCTYPE html PUBLIC "-//W3C//DTD HTML 4.0 Transitional//EN">
<HTML>
<HEAD><TITLE>Mystery Script</TITLE>

<SCRIPT LANGUAGE = "JavaScript">
   var y, x = 1, total = 0;

   while ( x <= 10 ) {
      y = x * x;
      document.writeln( y + "<BR>" );
      total += y;
      ++x;
   }

   document.writeln( "<BR>Total is " + total );
</SCRIPT>

</HEAD><BODY></BODY>
</HTML>
```

For Exercises 9.11 through 9.14, perform each of these steps:

a) Read the problem statement.
b) Formulate the algorithm using pseudocode and top-down, stepwise refinement.
c) Write a JavaScript program.
d) Test, debug and execute the JavaScript program.
e) Process three complete sets of data.

9.11 Drivers are concerned with the mileage obtained by their automobiles. One driver has kept track of several tankfuls of gasoline by recording miles driven and gallons used for each tankful. Develop a JavaScript program that will input the miles driven and gallons used (both as integers) for each tankful. The program should calculate and output HTML text that displays the miles per gallon obtained for each tankful and print the combined miles per gallon obtained for all tankfuls up to this point. Use **prompt** dialogs to obtain the data from the user.

9.12 Develop a JavaScript program that will determine whether a department store customer has exceeded the credit limit on a charge account. For each customer, the following facts are available:

a) Account number
b) Balance at the beginning of the month
c) Total of all items charged by this customer this month
d) Total of all credits applied to this customer's account this month
e) Allowed credit limit

The program should input each of these facts from **prompt** dialogs as integers, calculate the new balance (= *beginning balance* + *charges* – *credits*), display the new balance and determine whether the new balance exceeds the customer's credit limit. For those customers whose credit limit is exceeded, the program should output HTML text that displays the message, "Credit limit exceeded."

9.13 A large company pays its salespeople on a commission basis. The salespeople receive $200 per week plus 9% of their gross sales for that week. For example, a salesperson who sells $5000 worth of merchandise in a week receives $200 plus 9% of $5000, or a total of $650. You have been supplied with a list of items sold by each salesperson. The values of these items are as follows:

Item	Value
1	239.99
2	129.75
3	99.95
4	350.89

Develop a JavaScript program that inputs one salesperson's items sold for last week, calculates that salesperson's earnings and outputs HTML text that displays that salesperson's earnings. There is no limit to the number of items sold by a salesperson.

9.14 Develop a JavaScript program that will determine the gross pay for each of three employees. The company pays "straight-time" for the first 40 hours worked by each employee and pays "time-and-a-half" for all hours worked in excess of 40 hours. You are given a list of the employees of the company, the number of hours each employee worked last week and the hourly rate of each employee. Your program should input this information for each employee, determine the employee's gross pay and output HTML text that displays the employee's gross pay. Use **`prompt`** dialogs to input the data.

9.15 The process of finding the largest value (the maximum of a group of values) is used frequently in computer applications. For example, a program that determines the winner of a sales contest would input the number of units sold by each salesperson. The salesperson who sells the most units wins the contest. Write a pseudocode program and then a JavaScript program that inputs a series of 10 single-digit numbers as characters, determines the largest of the numbers and outputs HTML text that displays the largest number. Your program should use three variables as follows:

`counter:` A counter to count to 10 (to keep track of how many numbers have been input, and to determine when all 10 numbers have been processed)

`number:` The current digit input to the program

`largest:` The largest number found so far.

9.16 Write a JavaScript program that utilizes looping to print the following table of values. Output the results in an HTML table.

N	10*N	100*N	1000*N
1	10	100	1000
2	20	200	2000
3	30	300	3000
4	40	400	4000
5	50	500	5000

9.17 Using an approach similar to Exercise 9.15, find the *two* largest values among the 10 digits entered. (*Note:* You may input each number only once.)

9.18 Modify the program in Fig. 9.11 to validate its inputs. On any input, if the value entered is other than 1 or 2, keep looping until the user enters a correct value.

9.19 What does the following program print?

```
<!DOCTYPE html PUBLIC "-//W3C//DTD HTML 4.0 Transitional//EN">
<HTML>
<HEAD><TITLE>Mystery Script</TITLE>

<SCRIPT LANGUAGE = "JavaScript">
   var count = 1;

   while ( count <= 10 ) {
      document.writeln(
         count % 2 == 1 ? "****<BR>" : "++++++++<BR>" );
      ++count;
   }
</SCRIPT>

</HEAD><BODY></BODY>
</HTML>
```

9.20 What does the following program print?

```
<!DOCTYPE html PUBLIC "-//W3C//DTD HTML 4.0 Transitional//EN">
<HTML>
<HEAD><TITLE>Mystery Script</TITLE>

<SCRIPT LANGUAGE = "JavaScript">
   var row = 10, column;

   while ( row >= 1 ) {
      column = 1;

      while ( column <= 10 ) {
         document.write( row % 2 == 1 ? "<" : ">" );
         ++column;
      }

      --row;
      document.writeln( "<BR>" );
   }
</SCRIPT>

</HEAD><BODY></BODY>
</HTML>
```

9.21 *(Dangling-Else Problem)* Determine the output for each of the following when **x** is **9** and **y** is **11** and when **x** is **11** and **y** is **9**. Note that the interpreter ignores the indentation in a JavaScript program. Also, the JavaScript interpreter always associates an **else** with the previous **if** unless told to do otherwise by the placement of braces (**{}**). Because, on first glance, the programmer may not be sure which **if** an **else** matches, this is referred to as the "dangling-else" problem. We have eliminated the indentation from the following code to make the problem more challenging. (*Hint:* Apply indentation conventions you have learned.)

a)
```
if ( x < 10 )
if ( y > 10 )
document.writeln( "*****<BR>" );
else
document.writeln( "#####<BR>" );
document.writeln( "$$$$$<BR>" );
```

b)
```
if ( x < 10 ) {
if ( y > 10 )
document.writeln( "*****<BR>" );
}
else {
document.writeln( "#####<BR>" );
document.writeln( "$$$$$<BR>" );
}
```

9.22 *(Another Dangling-Else Problem)* Modify the following code to produce the output shown. Use proper indentation techniques. You may not make any changes other than inserting braces and changing the indentation of the code. The interpreter ignores indentation in a JavaScript program. We have eliminated the indentation from the following code to make the problem more challenging. [*Note:* It is possible that no modification is necessary.]

```
if ( y == 8 )
if ( x == 5 )
document.writeln( "@@@@@<BR>" );
else
document.writeln( "#####<BR>" );
document.writeln( "$$$$$<BR>" );
document.writeln( "&&&&&<BR>" );
```

a) Assuming **x = 5** and **y = 8**, the following output is produced.

```
@@@@@
$$$$$
&&&&&
```

b) Assuming **x = 5** and **y = 8**, the following output is produced.

```
@@@@@
```

c) Assuming **x = 5** and **y = 8**, the following output is produced.

```
@@@@@
&&&&&
```

d) Assuming **x = 5** and **y = 7**, the following output is produced. [*Note:* The last three output statements after the **else** are all part of a compound statement.]

```
#####
$$$$$
&&&&&
```

9.23 Write a script that reads in the size of the side of a square and outputs HTML text that displays a hollow square of that size out of asterisks. Use a **prompt** dialog to read the size from the user. Your program should work for squares of all side sizes between 1 and 20.

9.24 A palindrome is a number or a text phrase that reads the same backward as forward. For example, each of the following five-digit integers is a palindrome: 12321, 55555, 45554 and 11611. Write a script that reads in a five-digit integer and determines whether it is a palindrome. If the number is not five digits, output HTML text that displays an **alert** dialog indicating the problem to the user. When the user dismisses the **alert** dialog, allow the user to enter a new value.

9.25 Write a script that inputs an integer containing only 0s and 1s (a "binary" integer) and outputs HTML text that displays the decimal equivalent. (*Hint:* Use the modulus and division operators to pick off the "binary" number's digits one at a time from right to left. Just as in the decimal number system the rightmost digit has a positional value of 1 and the next digit left has a positional value of 10, then 100, then 1000, etc., in the binary number system the rightmost digit has a positional value of 1, the next digit left has a positional value of 2, then 4, then 8, etc. Thus the decimal number 234 can be interpreted as 4 * 1 + 3 * 10 + 2 * 100. The decimal equivalent of binary 1101 is 1 * 1 + 0 * 2 + 1 * 4 + 1 * 8 or 1 + 0 + 4 + 8 or 13.)

9.26 Write a script that outputs HTML text that displays the following checkerboard pattern:

```
* * * * * * * *
 * * * * * * * *
* * * * * * * *
 * * * * * * * *
* * * * * * * *
 * * * * * * * *
* * * * * * * *
 * * * * * * * *
```

Your program may use only three output statements, one of the form

```
document.write( "* " );
```

one of the form

```
document.write( " " );
```

and one of the form

```
document.writeln( "<BR>" );
```

[*Hint:* Repetition structures are required in this exercise.]

9.27 Write a script that outputs HTML text that keeps displaying in the browser window the multiples of the integer 2, namely 2, 4, 8, 16, 32, 64, etc. Your loop should not terminate (you should create an infinite loop). What happens when you run this program?

9.28 What's wrong with the following statement? Provide the correct statement to add one to the sum of **x** and **y**.

```
document.writeln( ++(x + y) );
```

9.29 Write a script that reads three nonzero values entered by the user in **prompt** dialogs and determines whether they could represent the sides of a triangle.

9.30 Write a script that reads three nonzero integers and determines whether they could be the sides of a right triangle.

9.31 A company wants to transmit data over the telephone, but they are concerned that their phones may be tapped. All of their data is transmitted as four-digit integers. They have asked you to write a program that will encrypt their data so that it may be transmitted more securely. Your script should read a four-digit integer entered by the user in a **`prompt`** dialog and encrypt it as follows: Replace each digit by *(the sum of that digit plus 7) modulus 10*. Then swap the first digit with the third, and swap the second digit with the fourth. Then output HTML text that displays the encrypted integer. Write a separate program that inputs an encrypted four-digit integer and decrypts it to form the original number.

9.32 The factorial of a nonnegative integer n is written $n!$ (pronounced "n factorial") and is defined as follows:

$$n! = n \cdot (n - 1) \cdot (n - 2) \cdot \ldots \cdot 1 \quad \text{(for values of } n \text{ greater than or equal to 1)}$$

and

$$n! = 1 \quad (\text{for } n = 0).$$

For example, $5! = 5 \cdot 4 \cdot 3 \cdot 2 \cdot 1$, which is 120.

a) Write a script that reads a nonnegative integer from a **`prompt`** dialog and computes its factorial.

b) Write a script that estimates the value of the mathematical constant e by using the formula

$$e = 1 + \frac{1}{1!} + \frac{1}{2!} + \frac{1}{3!} + \ldots$$

c) Write a script that computes the value of e^x by using the formula:

$$e^x = 1 + \frac{x}{1!} + \frac{x^2}{2!} + \frac{x^3}{3!} + \ldots$$

10

JavaScript/JScript: Control Structures II

Objectives

- To be able to use the **`for`** and **`do/while`** repetition structures to execute statements in a program repeatedly.
- To understand multiple selection using the **`switch`** selection structure.
- To be able to use the **`break`** and **`continue`** program control statements.
- To be able to use the logical operators.

Who can control his fate?
William Shakespeare, *Othello*

The used key is always bright.
Benjamin Franklin

Outline

10.1 Introduction

Before you write a program to solve a particular problem, it is essential to have a thorough understanding of the problem and a carefully planned approach to solving the problem. When you are writing a program, it is equally essential to understand the types of building blocks that are available and to employ proven program construction principles. In this chapter, we discuss all of these issues in our presentation of the theory and principles of structured programming. The techniques that you will learn here are applicable to most high-level languages, including JavaScript.

10.2 Essentials of Counter-Controlled Repetition

Counter-controlled repetition requires:

1. The *name* of a control variable (or loop counter).
2. The *initial value* of the control variable.
3. The *increment* (or *decrement*) by which the control variable is modified each time through the loop (also known as *each iteration of the loop*).
4. The condition that tests for the *final value* of the control variable to determine whether looping should continue.

To see the four elements of counter-controlled repetition, consider the simple script shown in Fig. 10.1, which displays lines of HTML text that illustrate the seven different font sizes supported by HTML. The declaration at line 9

```
var counter = 1;                // initialization
```

names the control variable (**counter**), reserves space for it in memory and sets it to an *initial value* of **1**. Declarations that include initialization are, in effect, executable statements.

```
<!DOCTYPE html PUBLIC "-//W3C//DTD HTML 4.0 Transitional//EN">
<HTML>
<!-- Fig. 10.1: WhileCounter.html -->

<HEAD>
<TITLE>Counter-Controlled Repetition</TITLE>

<SCRIPT LANGUAGE = "JavaScript">
   var counter = 1;              // initialization

   while ( counter <= 7 ) {      // repetition condition
      document.writeln( "<P><FONT SIZE = '" + counter +
         "'>HTML font size " + counter + "</FONT></P>" );
      ++counter;                 // increment
   }
</SCRIPT>

</HEAD><BODY></BODY>
</HTML>
```

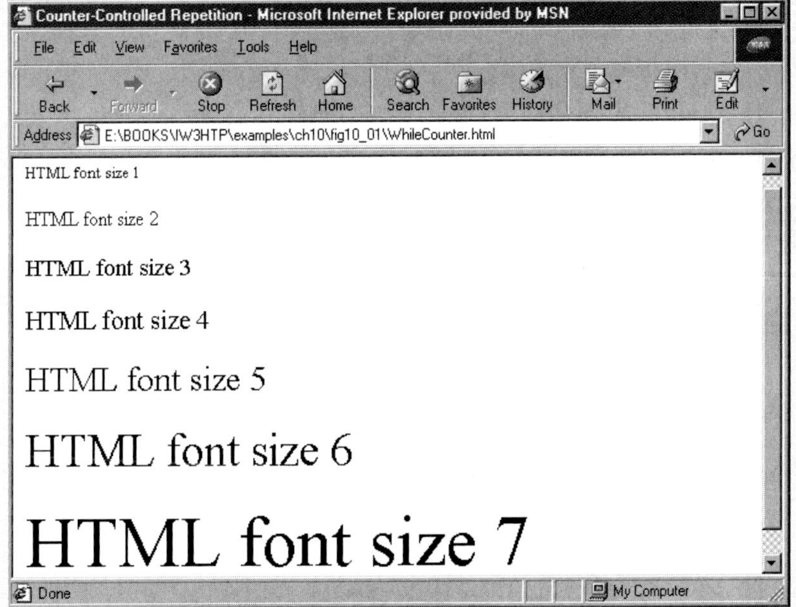

Fig. 10.1 Counter-controlled repetition.

The declaration and initialization of **counter** could also have been accomplished with the following declaration and statement:

```
var counter;                   // declare counter
counter = 1;                   // initialize counter to 1
```

The declaration is not executable, but the assignment statement is. We use both methods of initializing variables throughout the book.

Lines 12 and 13 in the **while** structure

```
document.writeln( "<P><FONT SIZE = '" + counter +
   "'>HTML font size " + counter + "</FONT></P>" );
```

write a paragraph consisting of the string "**HTML font size**" concatenated with the control variable **counter**'s value that represents the font size. This text is enclosed in a **<FONT>** tag that specifies the font size of the text. Notice the use of the single quotes that are placed around the value of **counter** in the concatenated string. For example, if **counter** is 5, the preceding statement produces the HTML

```
<P><FONT SIZE='5'>HTML font size 5</FONT></P>
```

Because the double quote character is used to specify the beginning and end of a string literal in JavaScript, it cannot be used in the contents of the string unless it is preceded by a \ to create the escape sequence \". HTML allows either single quotes (') or double quotes (") to be placed around the value specified for an attribute (such as the **SIZE** attribute of the **<FONT>** tag). JavaScript allows single quotes to be placed in a string literal and HTML allows single quotes to delimit an attribute value, so we use single quotes to delimit the attribute value for **SIZE** in the script. [*Note:* Although it is considered a good programming practice, HTML does not require attribute values to be enclosed in quotes. Therefore, the preceding HTML can be written as

```
<P><FONT SIZE=5>HTML font size 5</FONT></P>
```

without quotes around **SIZE** value **5**, and the browser will produce the same output.]

Common Programming Error 10.1

Placing a double-quote (") character inside a string literal causes a runtime error when the script is interpreted. To display a double-quote (") character as part of a string literal, the double quote (") character must be preceded by a \ to form the escape sequence \".

Testing and Debugging Tip 10.1

When writing HTML text from a script, use single-quote (') characters to delimit attribute values in string literals.

Line 14 in the **while** structure

```
++counter;                  // increment
```

increments the control variable by 1 for each iteration of the loop (i.e., each time the body of the loop is performed). The loop-continuation condition (line 11) in the **while** structure tests whether the value of the control variable is less than or equal to **7** (the *final value* for which the condition is **true**). Note that the body of this **while** is performed even when the control variable is **7**. The loop terminates when the control variable exceeds **7** (**counter** becomes **8**).

Good Programming Practice 10.1

Control counting loops with integer values.

Good Programming Practice 10.2

Indent the statements in the body of each control structure.

Good Programming Practice 10.3

Put a blank line before and after each major control structure, to make it stand out in the program.

Good Programming Practice 10.4

Too many levels of nesting can make a program difficult to understand. As a general rule, try to avoid using more than three levels of nesting.

Good Programming Practice 10.5

Vertical spacing above and below control structures, and indentation of the bodies of control structures within the control structure headers, gives programs a two-dimensional appearance that enhances readability.

10.3 The `for` Repetition Structure

The **`for`** *repetition structure* handles all the details of counter-controlled repetition. Figure 10.2 illustrates the power of the **`for`** structure by reimplementing the script of Fig. 10.1.

The script operates as follows. When the **`for`** structure (line 11) begins executing, the control variable **`counter`** is declared and is initialized to **`1`** (the first two elements of counter-controlled repetition—declaring the control variable's *name* and providing the control variable's *initial value*). Next, the loop-continuation condition **`counter <= 7`** is checked. The condition contains the *final value* (**`7`**) of the control variable. Because the initial value of **`counter`** is **`1`**, the condition is satisfied (i.e., **`true`**), so the body statement (lines 12 and 13) writes a line of HTML text in the document. Variable **`counter`** is then incremented in the expression **`++counter`** and the loop continues execution with the loop-continuation test. Because the control variable is now equal to 2, the final value is not exceeded, so the program performs the body statement again (i.e., performs the next iteration of the loop). This process continues until the control variable **`counter`** is incremented to 8—this causes the loop-continuation test to fail and repetition terminates.

```
1  <!DOCTYPE html PUBLIC "-//W3C//DTD HTML 4.0 Transitional//EN">
2  <HTML>
3  <!-- Fig. 10.2: ForCounter.html -->
4
5  <HEAD>
6  <TITLE>Counter-Controlled Repetition</TITLE>
7
8  <SCRIPT LANGUAGE = "JavaScript">
9     // Initialization, repetition condition and incrementing
10    // are all included in the for structure header.
11    for ( var counter = 1; counter <= 7; ++counter )
12       document.writeln( "<P><FONT SIZE = '" + counter +
13          "'>HTML font size " + counter + "</FONT></P>" );
14 </SCRIPT>
15
16 </HEAD><BODY></BODY>
17 </HTML>
```

Fig. 10.2 Counter-controlled repetition with the **`for`** structure (part 1 of 2).

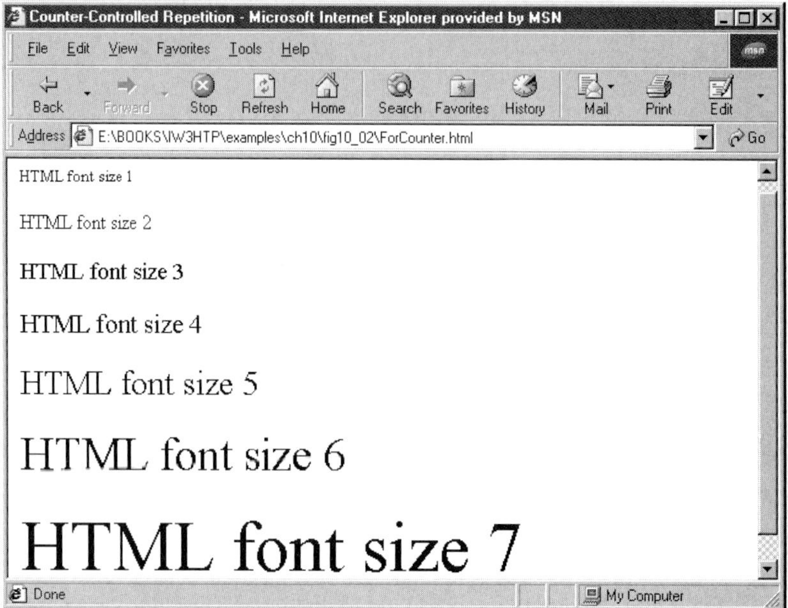

Fig. 10.2 Counter-controlled repetition with the **for** structure (part 2 of 2).

The program continues by performing the first statement after the **for** structure (in this case, the script terminates, because the interpreter reaches the end of the script).

Note that **counter** is declared inside the **for** in this example, but this practice is not required. Variable **counter** could have been declared before the **for** structure or not declared at all. Remember that JavaScript does not explicitly require variables to be declared before they are used. If a variable is used without being declared, the JavaScript interpreter creates the variable at the point of its first use in the script.

Figure 10.3 takes a closer look at the **for** structure of Fig. 10.2. The **for** structure's first line (including the keyword **for** and everything in parentheses after **for**) is often called the ***for** structure header*. Notice that the **for** structure "does it all"—it specifies each of the items needed for counter-controlled repetition with a control variable. If there is more than one statement in the body of the **for**, braces (**{** and **}**) are required to define the body of the loop.

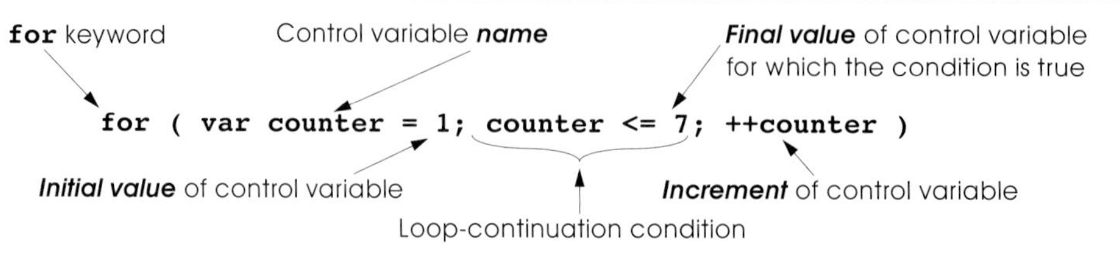

Fig. 10.3 Components of a typical **for** header.

Notice that Fig. 10.3 uses the loop-continuation condition **counter <= 7**. If the programmer incorrectly wrote **counter < 7**, the loop would be executed only 6 times. This is an example of a common logic error called an *off-by-one error.*

Common Programming Error 10.2

Using an incorrect relational operator or using an incorrect final value of a loop counter in the condition of a **while**, **for** *or* **do/while** *structure can cause an off-by-one error or an infinite loop.*

Good Programming Practice 10.6

Using the final value in the condition of a **while** *or* **for** *structure and using the* **<=** *relational operator will help avoid off-by-one errors. For a loop used to print the values 1 to 10, for example, the loop-continuation condition should be* **counter <= 10** *rather than* **counter < 10** *(which is an off-by-one error) or* **counter < 11** *(which is correct). Many programmers prefer so-called zero-based counting, in which, to count 10 times through the loop,* **counter** *would be initialized to zero and the loop-continuation test would be* **counter < 10**.

The general format of the **for** structure is

```
for ( initialization; loopContinuationTest; increment )
   statement
```

where the *initialization* expression names the loop's control variable and provides its initial value, *loopContinuationTest* is the expression that tests the loop-continuation condition (containing the final value of the control variable for which the condition is true) and *increment* is an expression that increments the control variable. The **for** structure can be represented by an equivalent **while** structure, with *initialization*, *loopContinuationTest* and *increment* placed as follows:

```
initialization;

while ( loopContinuationTest ) {
   statement
   increment;
}
```

There is an exception to this rule that we will discuss in Section 10.7.

If the *initialization* expression in the **for** structure header is the first definition of the control variable, the control variable can still be used after the **for** structure in the script. The part of a script in which a variable name can be used is known as the variable's *scope*. Scope is discussed in detail in Chapter 11, "Functions."

Good Programming Practice 10.7

Place only expressions involving the control variables in the initialization and increment sections of a **for** *structure. Manipulations of other variables should appear either before the loop (if they execute only once, like initialization statements) or in the loop body (if they execute once per iteration of the loop, like incrementing or decrementing statements).*

The three expressions in the **for** structure are optional. If *loopContinuationTest* is omitted, JavaScript assumes that the loop-continuation condition is **true**, thus creating an infinite loop. One might omit the *initialization* expression if the control variable is initialized elsewhere in the program before the loop. One might omit the *increment* expression if the increment is calculated by statements in the body of the **for** or if no increment is needed. The increment expression in the **for** structure acts like a stand-alone statement at the end of the body of the **for**. Therefore, the expressions

```
counter = counter + 1
counter += 1
++counter
counter++
```

are all equivalent in the incrementing portion of the **for** structure. Many programmers prefer the form **counter++** because the incrementing of the control variable occurs after the loop body is executed. The postincrementing form therefore seems more natural. Because the variable being incremented here does not appear in an expression, preincrementing and postincrementing both have the same effect. The two semicolons in the **for** structure are required.

Common Programming Error 10.3

Using commas instead of the two required semicolons in a **for** *header is a syntax error.*

Common Programming Error 10.4

Placing a semicolon immediately to the right of the right parenthesis of a **for** *header makes the body of that* **for** *structure an empty statement. This is normally a logic error.*

Software Engineering Observation 10.1

Placing a semicolon immediately after a **for** *header is sometimes used to create a so-called* delay loop. *Such a* **for** *loop with an empty body still loops the indicated number of times, doing nothing other than the counting. You might use a delay loop, for example, to slow down a program that is producing outputs on the screen too quickly for you to read them. [Chapter 15 introduces better techniques to create delays in programs, so you should never use delay loops.]*

The initialization, loop-continuation condition and increment portions of a **for** structure can contain arithmetic expressions. For example, assume that **x = 2** and **y = 10**. If **x** and **y** are not modified in the loop body, the statement

```
for ( var j = x; j <= 4 * x * y; j += y / x )
```

is equivalent to the statement

```
for ( var j = 2; j <= 80; j += 5 )
```

The "increment" of a **for** structure may be negative, in which case it is really a decrement and the loop actually counts downward.

If the loop-continuation condition is initially **false**, the body of the **for** structure is not performed. Instead, execution proceeds with the statement following the **for** structure.

The control variable is frequently printed or used in calculations in the body of a **for** structure, but it does not have to be. It is common to use the control variable for controlling repetition while never mentioning it in the body of the **for** structure.

Testing and Debugging Tip 10.2

Although the value of the control variable can be changed in the body of a **for** *loop, avoid changing it, because doing so can lead to subtle errors.*

The **for** structure is flowcharted much like the **while** structure. For example, the flowchart of the **for** statement

```
for ( var counter = 1; counter <= 7; ++counter )
   document.writeln( "<P><FONT SIZE = '" + counter +
      "'>HTML font size " + counter + "</FONT></P>" );
```

is shown in Fig. 10.4. This flowchart makes it clear that the initialization occurs only once and that incrementing occurs each time *after* the body statement is performed. Note that (besides small circles and arrows) the flowchart contains only rectangle symbols and a diamond symbol. Imagine, again, that the programmer has access to a deep bin of empty **for** structures—as many as the programmer might need to stack and nest with other control structures to form a structured implementation of an algorithm's flow of control. The rectangles and diamonds are then filled with actions and decisions appropriate to the algorithm.

10.4 Examples Using the for Structure

The following examples show methods of varying the control variable in a **for** structure. In each case, we write the appropriate **for** header. Note the change in the relational operator for loops that decrement the control variable.

a) Vary the control variable from **1** to **100** in increments of **1**.

```
for ( var i = 1; i <= 100; ++i )
```

b) Vary the control variable from **100** to **1** in increments of **-1** (decrements of **1**).

```
for ( var i = 100; i >= 1; --i )
```

Common Programming Error 10.5

Not using the proper relational operator in the loop-continuation condition of a loop that counts downward (such as using **i <= 1** *in a loop counting down to 1) is usually a logic error that will yield incorrect results when the program runs.*

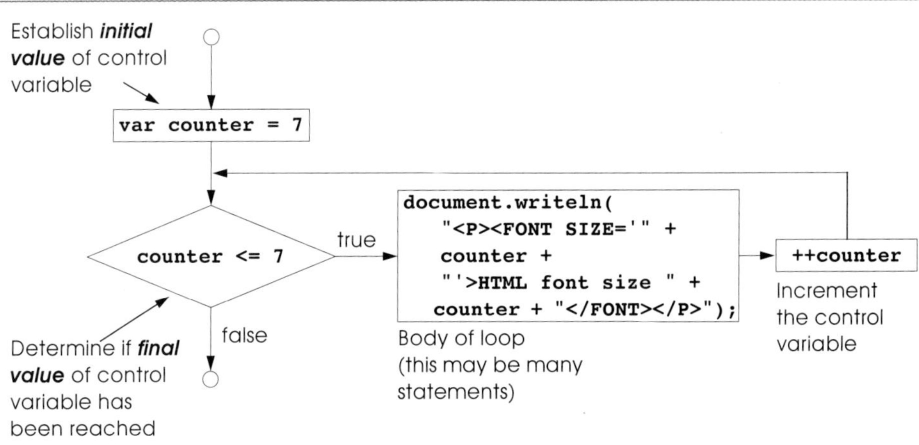

Fig. 10.4 Flowcharting a typical **for** repetition structure.

c) Vary the control variable from **7** to **77** in steps of **7**.

```
for ( var i = 7; i <= 77; i += 7 )
```

d) Vary the control variable from **20** to **2** in steps of **-2**.

```
for ( var i = 20; i >= 2; i -= 2 )
```

e) Vary the control variable over the following sequence of values: **2**, **5**, **8**, **11**, **14**, **17**, **20**.

```
for ( var j = 2; j <= 20; j += 3 )
```

f) Vary the control variable over the following sequence of values: **99**, **88**, **77**, **66**, **55**, **44**, **33**, **22**, **11**, **0**.

```
for ( var j = 99; j >= 0; j -= 11 )
```

The next two scripts demonstrate the **for** repetition structure. Figure 10.5 uses the **for** structure to sum all the even integers from **2** to **100**. Notice the increment expression adds **2** to the control variable **number** after the body is executed during each iteration of the loop. The loop terminates when **number** has the value 102 (which is not added to the sum).

```
<!DOCTYPE html PUBLIC "-//W3C//DTD HTML 4.0 Transitional//EN">
<HTML>
<!-- Fig. 10.5: Sum.html -->

<HEAD>
<TITLE>Sum the Even Integers from 2 to 100</TITLE>

<SCRIPT LANGUAGE = "JavaScript">
   var sum = 0;

   for ( var number = 2; number <= 100; number += 2 )
      sum += number;

   document.writeln( "<BIG>The sum of the even integers " +
      "from 2 to 100 is " + sum + "</BIG>" );
</SCRIPT>

</HEAD><BODY></BODY>
</HTML>
```

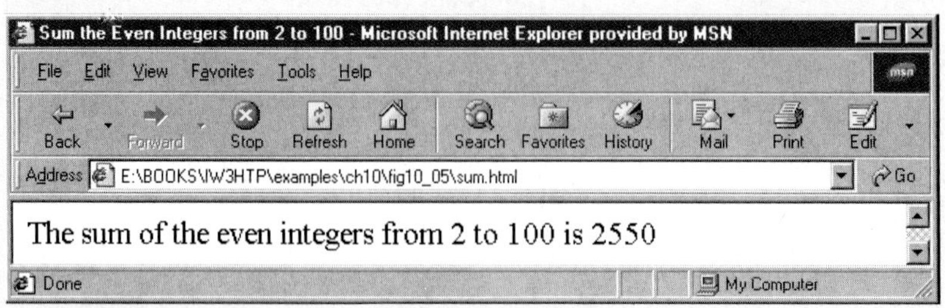

Fig. 10.5 Summation with **for**.

Note that the body of the **for** structure in Fig. 10.5 could actually be merged into the rightmost portion of the **for** header, by using a *comma* as follows:

```
for ( var number = 2; number <= 100;
      sum += number, number += 2)
   ;
```

Similarly, the initialization **sum = 0** could be merged into the initialization section of the **for** structure.

Good Programming Practice 10.8

*Although statements preceding a **for** and in the body of a **for** can often be merged into the **for** header, avoid doing so because it makes the program more difficult to read.*

Good Programming Practice 10.9

For clarity, limit the size of control structure headers to a single line if possible.

The next example computes compound interest (compounded yearly) using the **for** structure. Consider the following problem statement:

> *A person invests $1000.00 in a savings account yielding 5% interest. Assuming that all interest is left on deposit, calculate and print the amount of money in the account at the end of each year for 10 years. Use the following formula for determining these amounts:*
>
> $a = p(1 + r)^n$
>
> *where*
>
> p is the principal (original) amount invested,
> r is the annual interest rate,
> n is the number of years and
> a is the amount on deposit at the end of the nth year.

This problem involves a loop that performs the indicated calculation for each of the 10 years the money remains on deposit. The solution is the script shown in Fig. 10.6.

```
<!DOCTYPE html PUBLIC "-//W3C//DTD HTML 4.0 Transitional//EN">
<HTML>
<!-- Fig. 10.6: interest.html -->

<HEAD>
<TITLE>Calculating Compound Interest</TITLE>

<SCRIPT LANGUAGE = "JavaScript">
   var amount, principal = 1000.0, rate = .05;

   document.writeln( "<TABLE BORDER = '1' WIDTH = '100%'>" );
   document.writeln( "<TR><TD WIDTH = '100'><B>Year</B></TD>" );
   document.writeln(
      "<TD><B>Amount on deposit</B></TD></TR>" );

```

Fig. 10.6 Calculating compound interest with **for** (part 1 of 2).

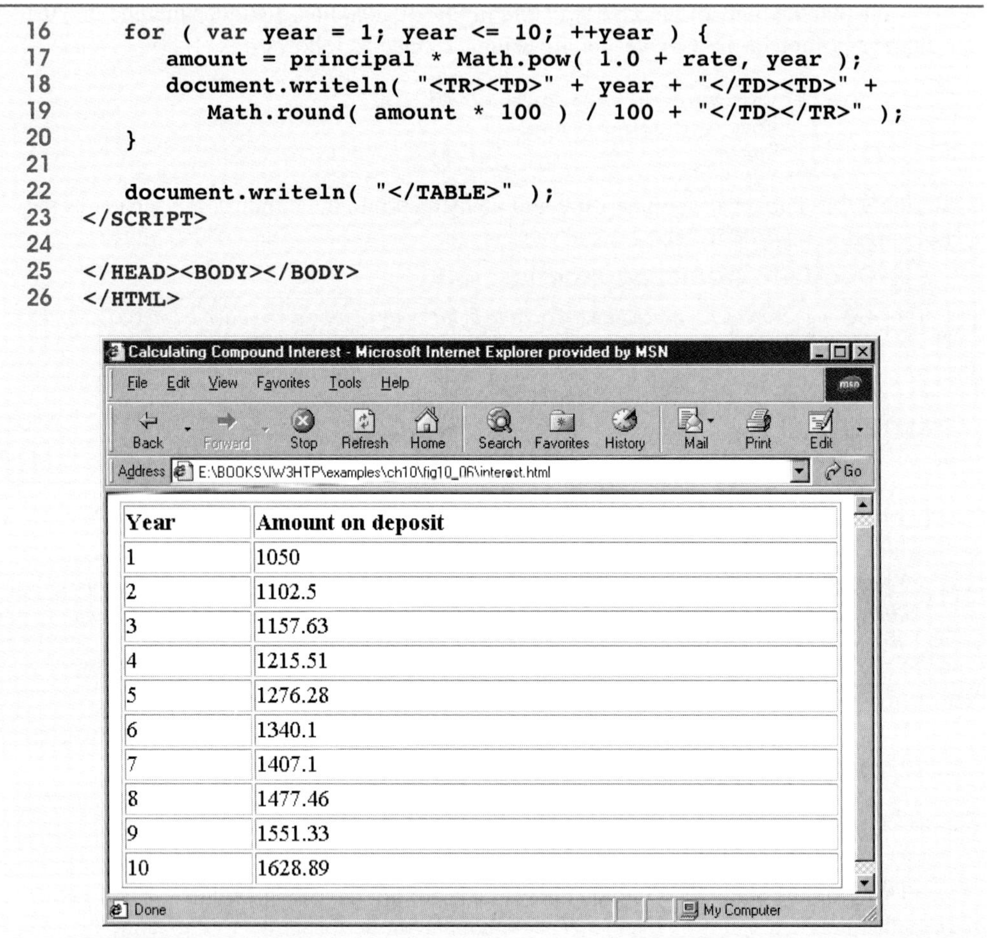

```
16      for ( var year = 1; year <= 10; ++year ) {
17         amount = principal * Math.pow( 1.0 + rate, year );
18         document.writeln( "<TR><TD>" + year + "</TD><TD>" +
19            Math.round( amount * 100 ) / 100 + "</TD></TR>" );
20      }
21
22      document.writeln( "</TABLE>" );
23   </SCRIPT>
24
25   </HEAD><BODY></BODY>
26   </HTML>
```


Year	Amount on deposit
1	1050
2	1102.5
3	1157.63
4	1215.51
5	1276.28
6	1340.1
7	1407.1
8	1477.46
9	1551.33
10	1628.89

Fig. 10.6 Calculating compound interest with **for** (part 2 of 2).

Line 9

```
var amount, principal = 1000.0, rate = .05;
```

declares three variables and initializes **principal** to **1000.0** and **rate** to **.05**.

Lines 11 through 14

```
document.writeln( "<TABLE BORDER = '1' WIDTH = '100%'>" );
document.writeln( "<TR><TD WIDTH='100'><B>Year</B></TD>" );
document.writeln(
   "<TD><B>Amount on deposit</B></TD></TR>" );
```

write HTML text that begins the definition of an HTML **<TABLE>** element that has a **BORDER** of **1** and a **WIDTH** of **100%** (the table is the entire width of the browser window). After the first statement writes the initial attributes of the table, the second and third statements create a row in the table (**<TR>**) in which the first column (indicated with the first **<TD>** tag) has a **WIDTH** of **100** pixels and contains the bold text **Year** and the second column contains the bold text **Amount on deposit**.

The **for** structure (line 16) executes its body 10 times, varying control variable **year** from 1 to 10 in increments of 1 (note that **year** represents *n* in the problem statement). JavaScript does not include an exponentiation operator. Instead, we use the **Math** object's **pow** method for this purpose. **Math.pow(x, y)** calculates the value of **x** raised to the **y**th power. Method **Math.pow** takes two numbers as arguments and returns the result.

Line 17

```
amount = principal * Math.pow( 1.0 + rate, year );
```

performs this calculation from the problem statement

$$a = p\,(1 + r)^{\,n}$$

where *a* is **amount**, *p* is **principal**, *r* is **rate** and *n* is **year** in line 17.

Lines 18 and 19

```
document.writeln( "<TR><TD>" + year + "</TD><TD>" +
   Math.round( amount * 100 ) / 100 + "</TD></TR>" );
```

write a line of HTML text that creates another row in the table. The first column is the current **year** value, and the second column is the result of the expression

```
Math.round( amount * 100 ) / 100
```

which multiplies the current value of **amount** by 100 to convert the value from dollars to cents, then uses the **Math** object's ***round*** method to round the value to the closest integer. The result is then divided by 100, to produce a dollar value that has a maximum of 2 digits to the right of the decimal point. Unlike many other programming languages, JavaScript does not provide numeric formatting capabilities that allow you to precisely control the display format of a number.

When the loop terminates, line 22

```
document.writeln( "</TABLE>" );
```

writes the **</TABLE>** tag to terminate the HTML table definition.

Variables **amount**, **principal** and **rate** are used to represent numbers in this script. Remember that JavaScript represents all numbers as floating-point numbers. This is convenient in this example, because we are dealing with fractional parts of dollars and we need a type that allows decimal points in its values. Unfortunately, this can cause trouble. Here is a simple explanation of what can go wrong when using floating-point numbers to represent dollar amounts (assuming that dollar amounts are displayed with two digits to the right of the decimal point): Two dollar amounts stored in the machine could be 14.234 (which would normally be rounded to 14.23 for display purposes) and 18.673 (which would normally be rounded to 18.67 for display purposes). When these amounts are added, they produce the internal sum 32.907, which would normally be rounded to 32.91 for display purposes. Thus your printout could appear as

```
   14.23
 + 18.67
 -------
   32.91
```

but a person adding the individual numbers as printed would expect the sum 32.90! You have been warned!

10.5 The `switch` Multiple-Selection Structure

Previously, we discussed the **`if`** single-selection structure and the **`if`**/**`else`** double-selection structure. Occasionally, an algorithm will contain a series of decisions in which a variable or expression is tested separately for each of the values it may assume and different actions are taken for each. JavaScript provides the **`switch`** multiple-selection structure to handle such decision making. The script of Fig. 10.7 demonstrates one of three different HTML list formats determined by the value input by the user.

```
<!DOCTYPE html PUBLIC "-//W3C//DTD HTML 4.0 Transitional//EN">
<HTML>
<!-- Fig. 10.7: SwitchTest.html -->

<HEAD>
<TITLE>Switching between HTML List Formats</TITLE>

<SCRIPT LANGUAGE = "JavaScript">
   var choice,              // user's choice
       startTag,            // starting list item tag
       endTag,              // ending list item tag
       validInput = true,   // indicates if input is valid
       listType;            // list type as a string

   choice = window.prompt( "Select a list style:\n" +
               "1 (bullet), 2 (numbered), 3 (lettered)", "1" );

   switch ( choice ) {
      case "1":
         startTag = "<UL>";
         endTag = "</UL>";
         listType = "<H1>Bullet List</H1>"
         break;
      case "2":
         startTag = "<OL>";
         endTag = "</OL>";
         listType = "<H1>Ordered List: Numbered</H1>"
         break;
      case "3":
         startTag = "<OL TYPE = 'A'>";
         endTag = "</OL>";
         listType = "<H1>Ordered List: Lettered</H1>"
         break;
```

Fig. 10.7 An example using **`switch`** (part 1 of 3).

```
      default:
         validInput = false;
   }

   if ( validInput == true ) {
      document.writeln( listType + startTag );

      for ( var i = 1; i <= 3; ++i )
         document.writeln( "<LI>List item " + i + "</LI>" );

      document.writeln( endTag );
   }
   else
      document.writeln( "Invalid choice: " + choice );
</SCRIPT>

</HEAD>
<BODY>
<P>Click Refresh (or Reload) to run the script again</P>
</BODY>
</HTML>
```

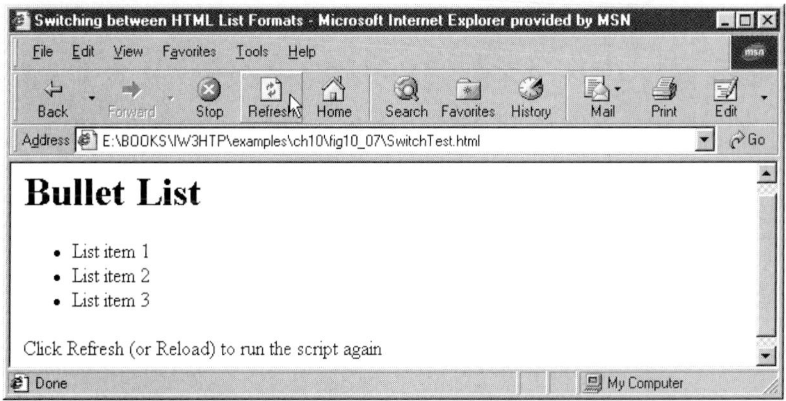

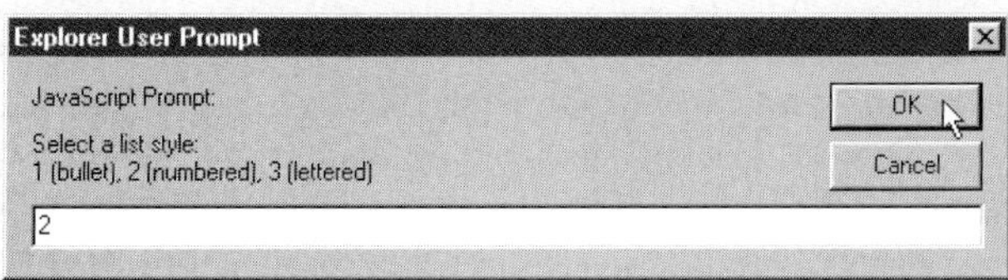

Fig. 10.7 An example using **`switch`** (part 2 of 3).

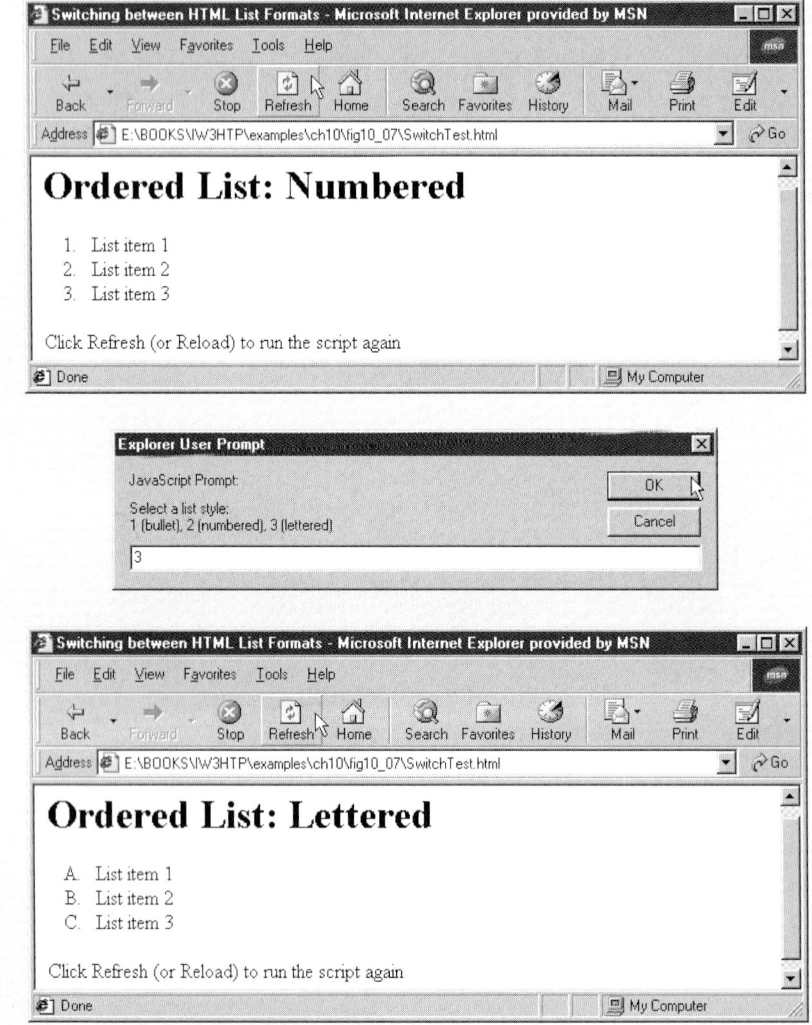

Fig. 10.7 An example using **`switch`** (part 3 of 3).

Line 9 in the script declares the instance variable **`choice`**. This variable will store the user's choice that determines which type of HTML list to display. Lines 10 and 11 declare variables **`startTag`** and **`endTag`** that store the HTML tags that indicate the HTML list type the user chooses. Line 12 declares variable **`validInput`** and initializes it to **`true`**. This boolean variable is used in the script to determine whether the user made a valid choice (**`true`**). If a choice is invalid, the script will set this variable's value to **`false`**. Line 13 declares variable **`listType`** that will store a string indicating the HTML list type. This string will appear before the list in the HTML document.

Lines 15 and 16,

```
choice = window.prompt( "Select a list style:\n" +
            "1 (bullet), 2 (numbered), 3 (lettered)", "1" );
```

prompt the user to enter a 1 to display a bullet (unordered) list, a 2 to display a numbered (ordered) list and a 3 to display a lettered (ordered) list.

Lines 18 through 36 define a **switch** structure that assigns to the variables **startTag**, **endTag** and **listType** values based on the value input by the user in the **prompt** dialog. The **switch** structure consists of a series of ***case*** *labels* and an optional ***default*** *case*.

When the flow of control reaches the **switch** structure, the *controlling expression* (**choice** in this example) in the parentheses following keyword **switch** is evaluated. The value of this expression is compared with the value in each of the ***case*** *labels* starting with the first **case** label. Assume the user entered **2**. Remember that the value typed by the user in a **prompt** dialog is returned as a string. So, the string **2** is compared to the string in each **case** in the **switch**. If a match occurs (**case "2":**), the statements for that **case** are executed. For the string **2**, lines 25 through 27,

```
startTag = "<OL>";
endTag = "</OL>";
listType = "<H1>Ordered List: Numbered</H1>"
```

set **startTag** to **"<OL>"** to indicate an ordered list (such lists are numbered by default), set **endTag** to **"</OL>"** to indicate the end of an ordered list and set **listType** to **"<H1>Ordered List: Numbered</H1>"**. Line 28,

```
break;
```

exits the **switch** structure immediately with the **break** statement. The **break** statement causes program control to proceed with the first statement after the **switch** structure. The **break** statement is used because the **case**s in a **switch** statement would otherwise run together. If **break** is not used anywhere in a **switch** structure, then each time a match occurs in the structure, the statements for all the remaining **case**s will be executed. If no match occurs between the controlling expression's value and a **case** label, the **default** case executes and sets boolean variable **validInput** to **false**.

Next, the flow of control continues with the **if** structure at line 38, which tests variable **validInput** to determine whether its value is **true**. If so, lines 39 through 44 write the **listType**, the **startTag**, three list items (**<LI>**) and the **endTag**. Otherwise, the script writes text in the HTML document indicating that an invalid choice was made.

Each **case** can have multiple actions (statements). The **switch** structure is different from other structures in that braces are not required around multiple actions in a **case** of a **switch**. The general **switch** structure (using a **break** in each **case**) is flowcharted in Fig. 10.8. [*Note:* As an exercise, flowchart the general **switch** structure without **break** statements.]

The flowchart makes it clear that each **break** statement at the end of a **case** causes control to exit from the **switch** structure immediately. The **break** statement is not required for the last **case** in the **switch** structure (or the **default** case, when it appears last), because program control automatically continues with the next statement after the **switch** structure.

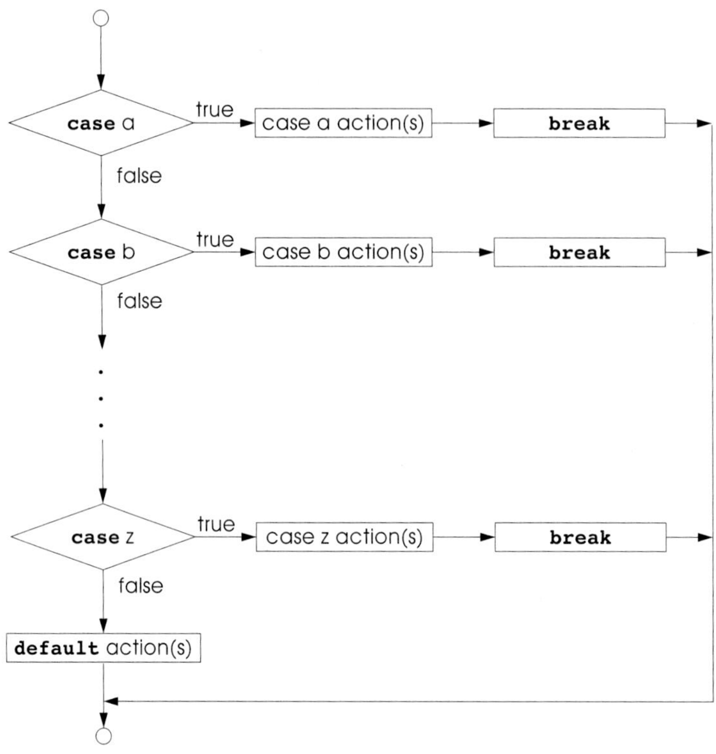

Fig. 10.8 The **switch** multiple-selection structure.

Common Programming Error 10.6

*Forgetting a **break** statement when one is needed in a **switch** structure is a logic error.*

Good Programming Practice 10.10

*Provide a **default** case in **switch** statements. Cases not explicitly tested in a **switch** statement without a **default** case are ignored. Including a **default** case focuses the programmer on processing exceptional conditions. However, there are situations in which no **default** processing is needed.*

Good Programming Practice 10.11

*Although the **case** clauses and the **default** case clause in a **switch** structure can occur in any order, it is considered a good programming practice to place the **default** clause last.*

Good Programming Practice 10.12

*In a **switch** structure, when the **default** clause is listed last, the **break** for that **case** statement is not required. Some programmers include this **break** for clarity and for symmetry with other cases.*

Note that having several **case** labels listed together (such as **case 1: case 2:** with no statements between the cases) simply means that the same set of actions is to occur for each of the cases.

Again, note that (besides small circles and arrows) the flowchart contains only rectangle symbols and diamond symbols. Imagine, again, that the programmer has access to a deep bin of empty **switch** structures—as many as the programmer might need to stack and nest with other control structures to form a structured implementation of an algorithm's flow of control. Again, the rectangles and diamonds are filled with actions and decisions appropriate to the algorithm. Although nested control structures are common, it is rare to find nested **switch** structures in a program.

10.6 The do/while Repetition Structure

The **do/while** repetition structure is similar to the **while** structure. In the **while** structure, the loop-continuation condition is tested at the beginning of the loop before the body of the loop is performed. The **do/while** structure tests the loop-continuation condition *after* the loop body is performed; therefore, *the loop body is always executed at least once.* When a **do/while** terminates, execution continues with the statement after the **while** clause. Note that it is not necessary to use braces in the **do/while** structure if there is only one statement in the body. However, the braces are usually included to avoid confusion between the **while** and **do/while** structures. For example,

```
while ( condition )
```

is normally regarded as the header to a **while** structure. A **do/while** with no braces around the single statement body appears as

```
do
   statement
while ( condition );
```

which can be confusing. The last line—**while(** *condition* **);**—may be misinterpreted by the reader as a **while** structure containing an empty statement (the semicolon by itself). Thus, the **do/while** with one statement is often written as follows, to avoid confusion:

```
do {
   statement
} while ( condition );
```

Good Programming Practice 10.13

Some programmers always include braces in a **do/while** *structure even if the braces are not necessary. This helps eliminate ambiguity between the* **while** *structure and the* **do/while** *structure containing one statement.*

Common Programming Error 10.7

Infinite loops are caused when the loop-continuation condition never becomes **false** *in a* **while**, **for** *or* **do/while** *structure. To prevent this, make sure there is not a semicolon immediately after the header of a* **while** *or* **for** *structure. In a counter-controlled loop, make sure the control variable is incremented (or decremented) in the body of the loop. In a sentinel-controlled loop, make sure the sentinel value is eventually input.*

The script in Fig. 10.9 uses a **do/while** structure to display each of the six different HTML header types (**H1** through **H6**). Control variable **counter** is declared is and initialized to **1** at line 9. Upon entering the **do/while** structure, lines 12 and 13 write a line of HTML text in the document. The value of control variable **counter** is used both to create the starting and ending header tags (e.g., **<H1>** and **</H1>**) and to create the line of text to display (e.g., **This is an H1 level head**). Line 15 increments the **counter** before the loop-continuation test is performed at the bottom of the loop.

```
1  <!DOCTYPE html PUBLIC "-//W3C//DTD HTML 4.0 Transitional//EN">
2  <HTML>
3  <!-- Fig. 10.9: DoWhileTest.html -->
4
5  <HEAD>
6  <TITLE>Using the do/while Repetition Structure</TITLE>
7
8  <SCRIPT LANGUAGE = "JavaScript">
9     var counter = 1;
10
11    do {
12       document.writeln( "<H" + counter + ">This is an H" +
13          counter + " level head" + "</H" + counter + ">" );
14
15       ++counter;
16    } while ( counter <= 6 );
17 </SCRIPT>
18
19 </HEAD><BODY></BODY>
20 </HTML>
```

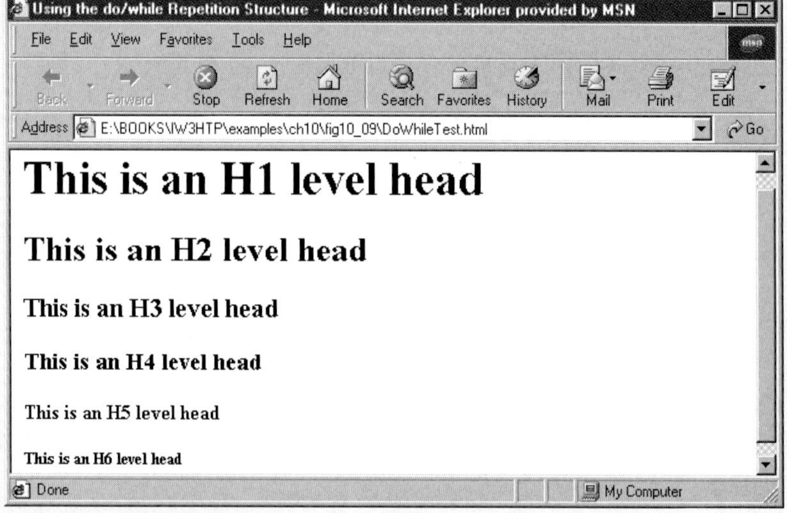

Fig. 10.9 Using the **do/while** repetition structure.

The **do/while** flowchart (Fig. 10.10) makes it clear that the loop-continuation condition is not executed until the action is performed at least once. The flowchart contains only a rectangle and a diamond. Imagine, also, that the programmer has access to a bin of empty **do/while** structures—as many as the programmer might need to stack and nest with other control structures to form a structured implementation of an algorithm. The rectangles and diamonds are filled with actions and decisions appropriate to the algorithm.

10.7 The break and continue Statements

The ***break*** and ***continue*** statements alter the flow of control. The **break** statement, when executed in a **while**, **for**, **do/while** or **switch** structure, causes immediate exit from that structure. Execution continues with the first statement after the structure. Common uses of the **break** statement are to escape early from a loop or to skip the remainder of a **switch** structure (as in Fig. 10.7). Figure 10.11 demonstrates the **break** statement in a **for** repetition structure.

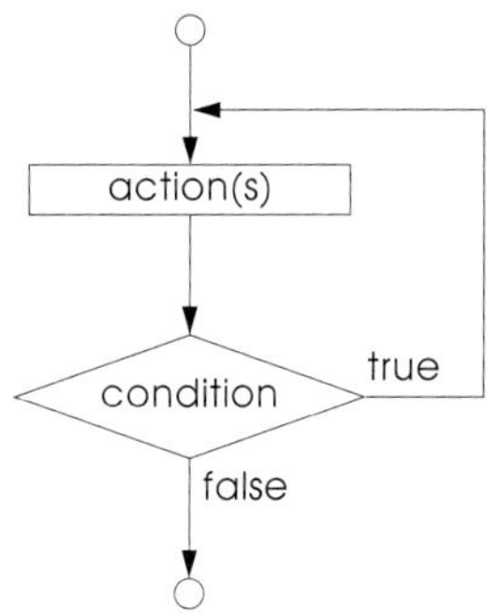

Fig. 10.10 Flowcharting the **do/while** repetition structure.

```
<!DOCTYPE html PUBLIC "-//W3C//DTD HTML 4.0 Transitional//EN">
<HTML>
<!-- Fig. 10.11: BreakTest.html -->

<HEAD>
<TITLE>Using the break Statement in a for Structure</TITLE>

<SCRIPT LANGUAGE = "JavaScript">
   for ( var count = 1; count <= 10; ++count ) {
      if ( count == 5 )
         break;   // break loop only if count == 5

      document.writeln( "Count is: " + count + "<BR>" );
   }

   document.writeln( "Broke out of loop at count = " + count );
</SCRIPT>
```

Fig. 10.11 Using the **break** statement in a **for** structure (part 1 of 2).

```
18
19  </HEAD><BODY></BODY>
20  </HTML>
```

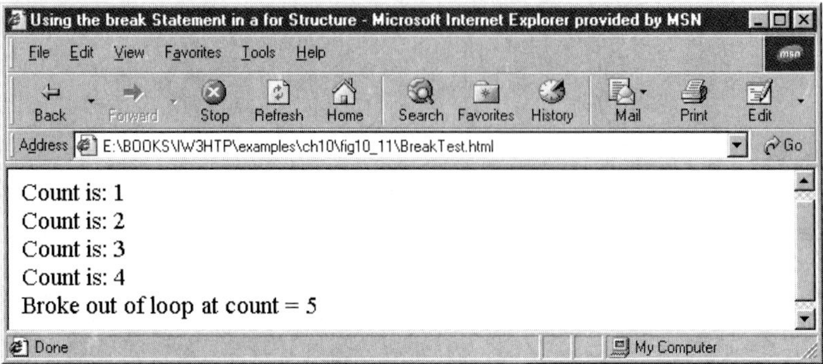

Fig. 10.11 Using the **break** statement in a **for** structure (part 2 of 2).

During each iteration of the **for** structure at line 9, the value of **count** is written in the HTML document. When the **if** structure at line 10 in the **for** structure detects that **count** is **5**, **break** (line 11) is executed. This statement terminates the **for** structure, and the program proceeds to line 16 (the next statement in sequence immediately after the **for**), where the script writes the value of **count** when the loop terminated (i.e., 5). The loop fully executes its body only four times.

The **continue** statement, when executed in a **while**, **for** or **do/while** structure, skips the remaining statements in the body of that structure and proceeds with the next iteration of the loop. In **while** and **do/while** structures, the loop-continuation test is evaluated immediately after the **continue** statement is executed. In the **for** structure, the increment expression is executed, then the loop-continuation test is evaluated.

Figure 10.12 uses **continue** in a **for** structure to the **document.writeln** statement at line 14 when the **if** structure at line 10 determines that the value of **count** is **5**. When the **continue** statement executes, the remainder of the **for** structure's body is skipped. Program control continues with the increment of the **for** structure control variable followed by the loop-continuation test to determine whether the loop should continue executing.

```
1   <!DOCTYPE html PUBLIC "-//W3C//DTD HTML 4.0 Transitional//EN">
2   <HTML>
3   <!-- Fig. 10.12: ContinueTest.html -->
4
5   <HEAD>
6   <TITLE>Using the break Statement in a for Structure</TITLE>
7
8   <SCRIPT LANGUAGE = "JavaScript">
9      for ( var count = 1; count <= 10; ++count ) {
10        if ( count == 5 )
11           continue;  // skip remaining code in loop
12                      // only if count == 5
```

Fig. 10.12 Using the **continue** statement in a **for** structure (part 1 of 2).

```
        document.writeln( "Count is: " + count + "<BR>" );
    }

    document.writeln( "Used continue to skip printing 5" );
</SCRIPT>

</HEAD><BODY></BODY>
</HTML>
```

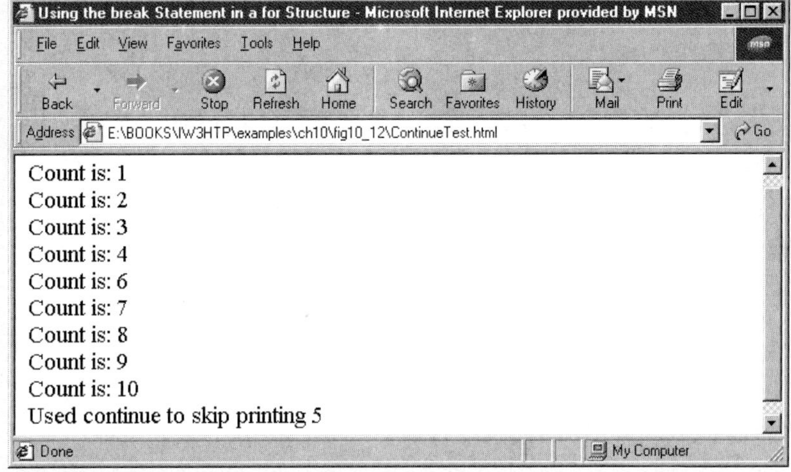

Fig. 10.12 Using the **continue** statement in a **for** structure (part 2 of 2).

Good Programming Practice 10.14

Some programmers feel that **break** *and* **continue** *violate structured programming. Because the effects of these statements can be achieved by structured programming techniques, these programmers do not use* **break** *and* **continue**.

Performance Tip 10.1

The **break** *and* **continue** *statements, when used properly, perform faster than the corresponding structured techniques.*

Software Engineering Observation 10.2

There is a tension between achieving quality software engineering and achieving the best-performing software. Often, one of these goals is achieved at the expense of the other. For all but the most performance-intensive situations, the following "rule of thumb" should be followed: First make your code simple and correct; then make it fast and small, but only if necessary.

10.8 The Labeled break and continue Statements

The **break** statement can break out of an immediately enclosing **while**, **for**, **do/while** or **switch** structure. To break out of a nested set of structures, you can use the *labeled* **break** *statement*. This statement, when executed in a **while**, **for**, **do/while** or

switch, causes immediate exit from that structure and any number of enclosing repetition structures; program execution resumes with the first statement after the enclosing *labeled statement* (a statement preceded by a label). The labeled statement can be a compound statement (a set of statements enclosed in curly braces, **{}**). Labeled **break** statements are commonly used to terminate nested looping structures containing **while**, **for**, **do/while** or **switch** structures. Figure 10.13 demonstrates the labeled **break** statement in a nested **for** structure.

```
<!DOCTYPE html PUBLIC "-//W3C//DTD HTML 4.0 Transitional//EN">
<HTML>
<!-- Fig. 10.13: BreakLabelTest.html -->

<HEAD>
<TITLE>Using the break Statement with a Label</TITLE>

<SCRIPT LANGUAGE = "JavaScript">
   stop: {   // labeled compound statement
      for ( var row = 1; row <= 10; ++row ) {
         for ( var column = 1; column <= 5 ; ++column ) {

            if ( row == 5 )
               break stop; // jump to end of stop block

            document.write( "* " );
         }

         document.writeln( "<BR>" );
      }

      // the following line is skipped
      document.writeln( "This line should not print" );
   }

   document.writeln( "End of script" );
</SCRIPT>

</HEAD><BODY></BODY>
</HTML>
```

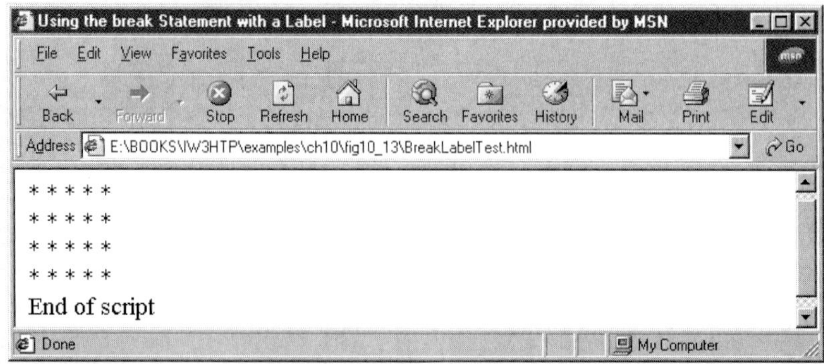

Fig. 10.13 Using a labeled **break** statement in a nested **for** structure.

The labeled compound statement (lines 9 through 24) begins with a *label* (an identifier followed by a colon). Here we use the label "**stop:**." The compound statement is enclosed between the braces at the end of line 9 and line 24, and includes both the nested **for** structure starting at line 10 and the **document.writeln** statement at line 23. When the **if** structure at line 13 detects that **row** is equal to **5**, the statement at line 14

```
break stop;
```

executes. This statement terminates both the **for** structure at line 11 and its enclosing **for** structure at line 10, and the program proceeds to the statement at line 26 (the first statement in sequence after the labeled compound statement). The inner **for** structure fully executes its body only four times. Notice that the **document.writeln** statement at line 23 never executes, because it is included in the labeled compound statement and the outer **for** structure never completes.

The **continue** statement proceeds with the next iteration (repetition) of the immediately enclosing **while**, **for** or **do/while** structure. The *labeled* ***continue*** *statement*, when executed in a repetition structure (**while**, **for** or **do/while**), skips the remaining statements in that structure's body and any number of enclosing repetition structures, then proceeds with the next iteration of the enclosing *labeled repetition structure* (a repetition structure preceded by a label). In labeled **while** and **do/while** structures, the loop-continuation test is evaluated immediately after the **continue** statement is executed. In a labeled **for** structure, the increment expression is executed, then the loop-continuation test is evaluated. Figure 10.14 uses the labeled **continue** statement in a nested **for** structure to cause execution to continue with the next iteration of the outer **for** structure.

```
<!DOCTYPE html PUBLIC "-//W3C//DTD HTML 4.0 Transitional//EN">
<HTML>
<!-- Fig. 10.14: ContinueLabelTest.html -->

<HEAD>
<TITLE>Using the continue Statement with a Label</TITLE>

<SCRIPT LANGUAGE = "JavaScript">
   nextRow:   // target label of continue statement
      for ( var row = 1; row <= 5; ++row ) {
         document.writeln( "<BR>" );

         for ( var column = 1; column <= 10; ++column ) {

            if ( column > row )
               continue nextRow; // next iteration of
                                 // labeled loop

            document.write( "* " );
         }
      }
</SCRIPT>

```

Fig. 10.14 Using a labeled **continue** statement in a nested **for** structure (part 1 of 2).

```
24 </HEAD><BODY></BODY>
25 </HTML>
```

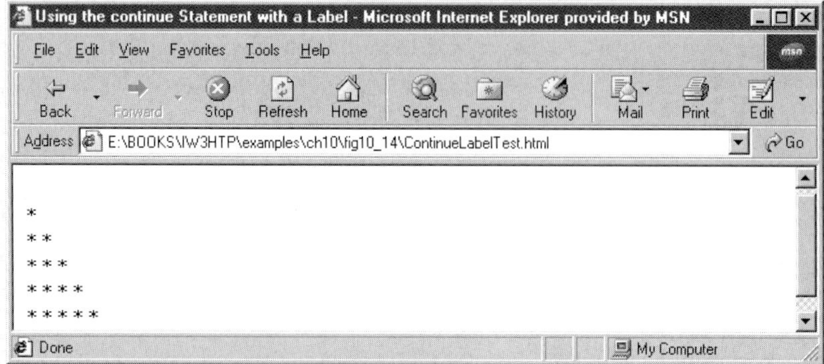

Fig. 10.14 Using a labeled **continue** statement in a nested **for** structure (part 2 of 2).

The labeled **for** structure (lines 9 through 21) starts with the **nextRow** label at line 9. When the **if** structure at line 15 in the inner **for** structure detects that **column** is greater than **row**, the statement

```
continue nextRow;
```

executes and program control continues with the increment of the control variable of the outer **for** loop. Even though the inner **for** structure counts from 1 to 10, the number of ***** characters output on a row never exceeds the value of **row**.

10.9 Logical Operators

So far we have studied only such *simple conditions* as **count <= 10**, **total > 1000** and **number != sentinelValue**. These conditions were expressed in terms of the relational operators **>**, **<**, **>=** and **<=** and in terms of the equality operators **==** and **!=**. Each decision tested one condition. To test multiple conditions in the process of making a decision, we performed these tests in separate statements or in nested **if** or **if/else** structures.

JavaScript provides *logical operators* that may be used to form more complex conditions by combining simple conditions. The logical operators are **&&** *(logical AND),* **||** *(logical OR)* and **!** *(logical NOT,* also called *logical negation).* We will consider examples of each of these.

Suppose that at some point in a program we wish to ensure that two conditions are *both* **true** before we choose a certain path of execution. In this case, we can use the logical **&&** operator as follows:

```
if ( gender == 1 && age >= 65 )
   ++seniorFemales;
```

This **if** statement contains two simple conditions. The condition **gender == 1** might be evaluated to determine, for example, whether a person is a female. The condition **age >=**

65 is evaluated to determine whether a person is a senior citizen. The two simple conditions are evaluated first, because the precedences of **==** and **>=** are both higher than the precedence of **&&**. The **if** statement then considers the combined condition

```
gender == 1 && age >= 65
```

This condition is **true** *if and only if* both of the simple conditions are **true**. Finally, if this combined condition is indeed **true**, the count of **seniorFemales** is incremented by **1**. If either or both of the simple conditions are **false**, the program skips the incrementing and proceeds to the statement following the **if** structure. The preceding combined condition can be made more readable by adding redundant parentheses:

```
( gender == 1 ) && ( age >= 65 )
```

The table of Fig. 10.15 summarizes the **&&** operator. The table shows all four possible combinations of **false** and **true** values for *expression1* and *expression2*. Such tables are often called *truth tables*. JavaScript evaluates to **false** or **true** all expressions that include relational operators, equality operators and/or logical operators.

Now let us consider the **||** (logical OR) operator. Suppose we wish to ensure that either *or* both of two conditions are **true** before we choose a certain path of execution. In this case, we use the **||** operator as in the following program segment:

```
if ( semesterAverage >= 90 || finalExam >= 90 )
   document.writeln( "Student grade is A" );
```

This statement also contains two simple conditions. The condition **semesterAverage >= 90** is evaluated to determine whether the student deserves an "A" in the course because of a solid performance throughout the semester. The condition **finalExam >= 90** is evaluated to determine whether the student deserves an "A" in the course because of an outstanding performance on the final exam. The **if** statement then considers the combined condition

```
semesterAverage >= 90 || finalExam >= 90
```

and awards the student an "A" if either or both of the simple conditions are **true**. Note that the message "**Student grade is A**" is *not* printed only when both of the simple conditions are **false**. Figure 10.16 is a truth table for the logical OR operator (**||**).

expression1	expression2	expression1 && expression2
false	false	false
false	true	false
true	false	false
true	true	true

Fig. 10.15 Truth table for the **&&** (logical AND) operator.

expression1	expression2	expression1 || expression2
`false`	`false`	`false`
`false`	`true`	`true`
`true`	`false`	`true`
`true`	`true`	`true`

Fig. 10.16 Truth table for the `||` (logical OR) operator.

The **`&&`** operator has a higher precedence than the `||` operator. Both operators associate from left to right. An expression containing **`&&`** or `||` operators is evaluated only until truth or falsity is known. Thus, evaluation of the expression

```
gender == 1 && age >= 65
```

will stop immediately if **`gender`** is not equal to **`1`** (the entire expression is **`false`**), and continue if **`gender`** is equal to **`1`** (the entire expression could still be **`true`** if the condition **`age >= 65`** is **`true`**). This performance feature for evaluation of logical AND and logical OR expressions is called *short-circuit evaluation.*

JavaScript provides the **`!`** (logical negation) operator to enable a programmer to "reverse" the meaning of a condition (a **`true`** value becomes **`false`** and a **`false`** value becomes **`true`**). Unlike the logical operators **`&&`** and `||` which combine two conditions (binary operators), the logical negation operator has only a single condition as an operand (unary operator). The logical negation operator is placed before a condition to choose a path of execution if the original condition (without the logical negation operator) is **`false`**, such as in the following program segment:

```
if ( ! ( grade == sentinelValue ) )
   document.writeln( "The next grade is " + grade );
```

The parentheses around the condition **`grade == sentinelValue`** are needed because the logical negation operator has a higher precedence than the equality operator. Figure 10.17 is a truth table for the logical negation operator.

In most cases, the programmer can avoid using logical negation by expressing the condition differently with an appropriate relational or equality operator. For example, the preceding statement may also be written as follows:

```
if ( grade != sentinelValue )
   document.writeln( "The next grade is " + grade );
```

expression	!expression
`false`	`true`
`true`	`false`

Fig. 10.17 Truth table for operator **`!`** (logical negation).

This flexibility can help a programmer express a condition in a more convenient manner.

The script of Fig. 10.18 demonstrates all the logical operators by producing their truth tables. The script produces an HTML table containing the results.

In the output of Fig. 10.18, the strings "false" and "true" indicate **false** and **true** for the operands in each condition. The result of the condition is shown as **true** or **false**. Note that when you add a boolean value to a string, JavaScript automatically adds the string "false" or "true" based on the boolean value. Lines 9 through 30 build an HTML table containing the results.

An interesting feature of JavaScript is that most non-boolean values can be converted by JavaScript into a boolean **true** or **false** value. Non-zero numeric values are considered to be **true**. The numeric value zero is considered to be **false**. Any string that contains characters is considered to be **true**. The empty string (i.e., the string containing no characters) is considered to be **false**. The value **null** and a variable that has been declared but not initialized are considered to be **false**. All objects (such as the browser's **document** and **window** objects and JavaScript's **Math** object) are considered **true**.

```
1  <!DOCTYPE html PUBLIC "-//W3C//DTD HTML 4.0 Transitional//EN">
2  <HTML>
3  <!-- Fig. 10.18: LogicalOperators.html -->
4
5  <HEAD>
6  <TITLE>Demonstrating the Logical Operators</TITLE>
7
8  <SCRIPT LANGUAGE = "JavaScript">
9     document.writeln( "<TABLE BORDER = '1' WIDTH = '100%'>" );
10
11    document.writeln(
12       "<TR><TD WIDTH = '25%'>Logical AND (&&)</TD>" +
13       "<TD>false && false: " + ( false && false ) +
14       "<BR>false && true: " + ( false && true ) +
15       "<BR>true && false: " + ( true && false ) +
16       "<BR>true && true: " + ( true && true ) + "</TD>" );
17
18    document.writeln(
19       "<TR><TD WIDTH = '25%'>Logical OR (||)</TD>" +
20       "<TD>false || false: " + ( false || false ) +
21       "<BR>false || true: " + ( false || true ) +
22       "<BR>true || false: " + ( true || false ) +
23       "<BR>true || true: " + ( true || true ) + "</TD>" );
24
25    document.writeln(
26       "<TR><TD WIDTH = '25%'>Logical NOT (!)</TD>" +
27       "<TD>!false: " + ( !false ) +
28       "<BR>!true: " + ( !true ) + "</TD>" );
29
30    document.writeln( "</TABLE>" );
31 </SCRIPT>
32
33 </HEAD><BODY></BODY>
34 </HTML>
```

Fig. 10.18 Demonstrating the logical operators (part 1 of 2).

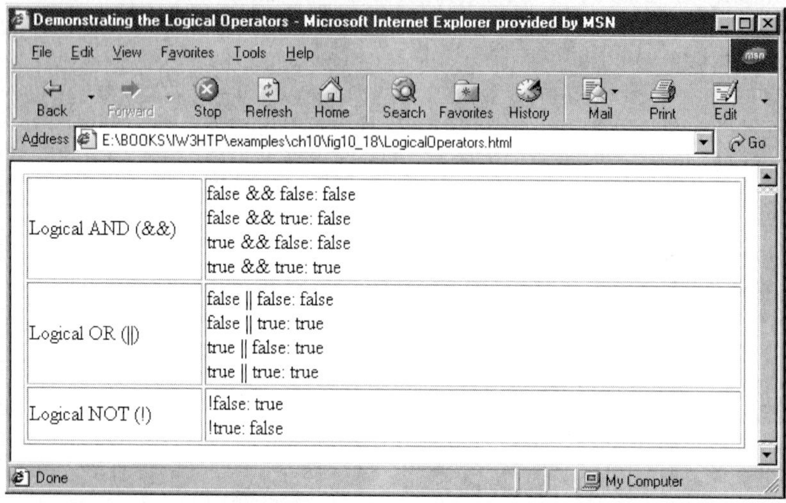

Fig. 10.18 Demonstrating the logical operators (part 2 of 2).

The chart in Fig. 10.19 shows the precedence and associativity of the JavaScript operators introduced up to this point. The operators are shown from top to bottom in decreasing order of precedence.

10.10 Structured Programming Summary

Just as architects design buildings by employing the collective wisdom of their profession, so should programmers design programs. Our field is younger than architecture is, and our collective wisdom is considerably sparser. We have learned that structured programming produces programs that are easier than unstructured programs to understand and hence are easier to test, debug, modify and even prove correct in a mathematical sense.

<table>
<tr><th>Operators</th><th>Associativity</th><th>Type</th></tr>
<tr><td><code>()</code></td><td>left to right</td><td>parentheses</td></tr>
<tr><td><code>++ -- !</code></td><td>right to left</td><td>unary</td></tr>
<tr><td><code>* / %</code></td><td>left to right</td><td>multiplicative</td></tr>
<tr><td><code>+ -</code></td><td>left to right</td><td>additive</td></tr>
<tr><td><code>< <= > >=</code></td><td>left to right</td><td>relational</td></tr>
<tr><td><code>== !=</code></td><td>left to right</td><td>equality</td></tr>
<tr><td><code>&&</code></td><td>left to right</td><td>logical AND</td></tr>
<tr><td><code>||</code></td><td>left to right</td><td>logical OR</td></tr>
<tr><td><code>?:</code></td><td>right to left</td><td>conditional</td></tr>
<tr><td><code>= += -= *= /= %=</code></td><td>right to left</td><td>assignment</td></tr>
</table>

Fig. 10.19 Precedence and associativity of the operators discussed so far.

Figure 10.20 summarizes JavaScript's control structures. Small circles are used in the figure to indicate the single entry point and the single exit point of each structure. Connecting individual flowchart symbols arbitrarily can lead to unstructured programs. Therefore, the programming profession has chosen to combine flowchart symbols to form a limited set of control structures and to build structured programs by properly combining control structures in two simple ways.

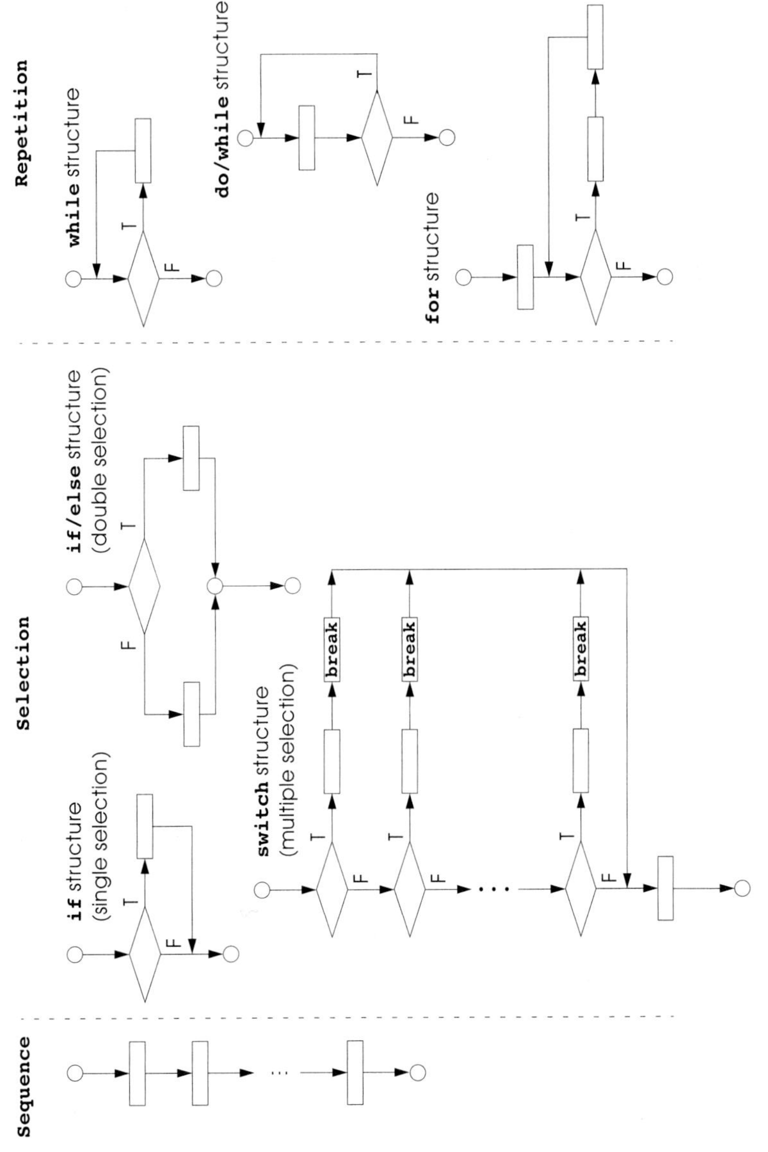

Fig. 10.20 JavaScript's single-entry/single-exit sequence, selection and repetition structures.

For simplicity, only single-entry/single-exit control structures are used—there is only one way to enter and only one way to exit each control structure. Connecting control structures in sequence to form structured programs is simple—the exit point of one control structure is connected to the entry point of the next control structure (the control structures are simply placed one after another in a program)—we have called this "control structure stacking." The rules for forming structured programs also allow for control structures to be nested.

Figure 10.21 shows the rules for forming properly structured programs. The rules assume that the rectangle flowchart symbol may be used to indicate any action, including input/output.

Applying the rules of Fig. 10.21 always results in a structured flowchart with a neat, building-block appearance. For example, repeatedly applying rule 2 to the simplest flowchart (Fig. 10.22) results in a structured flowchart containing many rectangles in sequence (Fig. 10.23). Notice that rule 2 generates a stack of control structures; so, let us call rule 2 the *stacking rule.*

Rule 3 is called the *nesting rule*. Repeatedly applying rule 3 to the simplest flowchart results in a flowchart with neatly nested control structures. For example, in Fig. 10.24, the rectangle in the simplest flowchart is first replaced with a double-selection (**if**/**else**) structure. Then rule 3 is applied again to both of the rectangles in the double-selection structure, by replacing each of these rectangles with double-selection structures. The dashed box around each of the double-selection structures represent the rectangle in the original simplest flowchart that was replaced.

Rules for Forming Structured Programs
1) Begin with the "simplest flowchart" (Fig. 10.22).
2) Any rectangle (action) can be replaced by two rectangles (actions) in sequence.
3) Any rectangle (action) can be replaced by any control structure (sequence, **if**, **if**/**else**, **switch**, **while**, do/**while** or **for**).
4) Rules 2 and 3 may be applied as often as you like and in any order.

Fig. 10.21 Rules for forming structured programs.

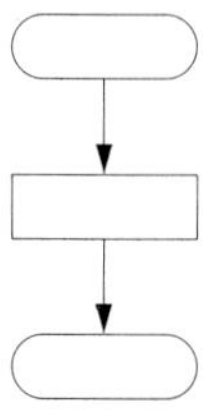

Fig. 10.22 The simplest flowchart.

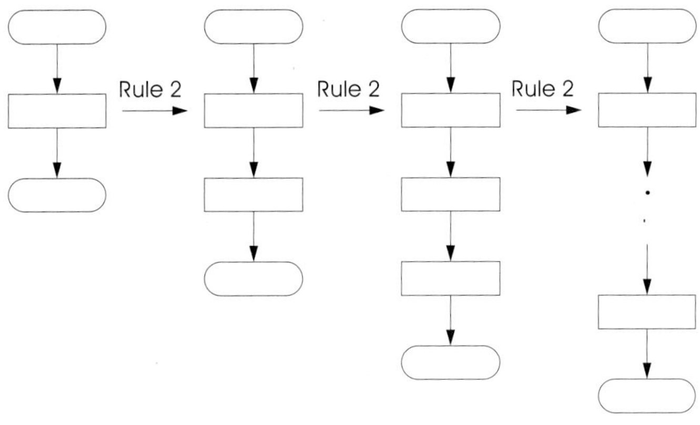

Fig. 10.23 Repeatedly applying rule 2 of Fig. 10.21 to the simplest flowchart.

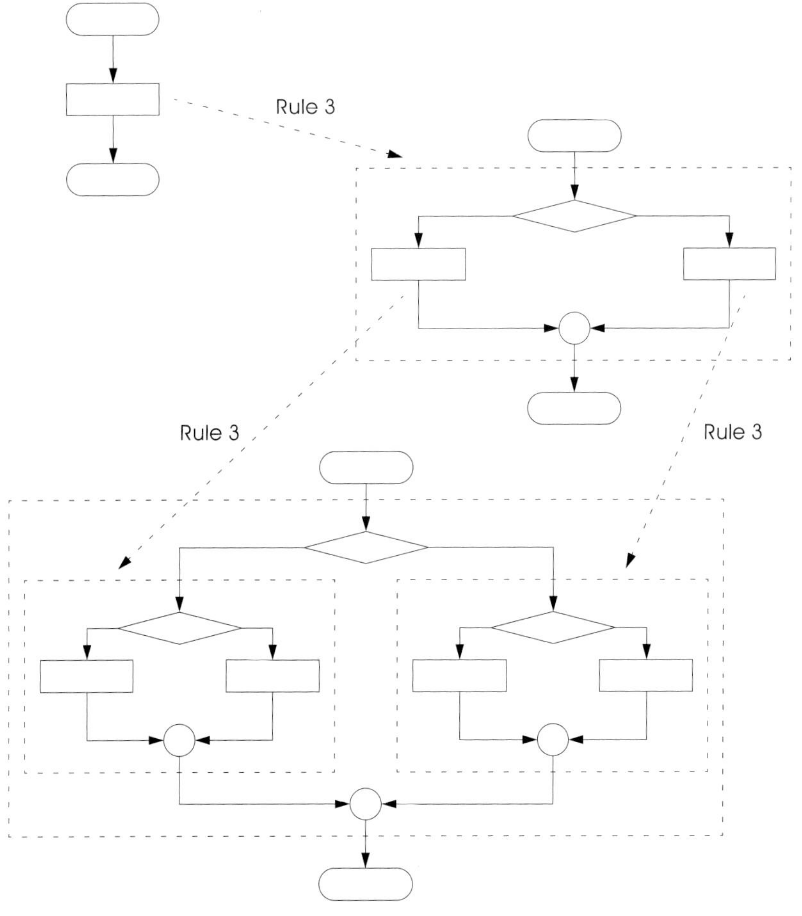

Fig. 10.24 Applying rule 3 of Fig. 10.21 to the simplest flowchart.

Rule 4 generates larger, more involved and more deeply nested structures. The flowcharts that emerge from applying the rules in Fig. 10.21 constitute the set of all possible structured flowcharts and hence the set of all possible structured programs.

The beauty of the structured approach is that we use only seven simple single-entry/single-exit pieces and that we assemble them in only two simple ways. Figure 10.25 shows the kinds of stacked building blocks that emerge from applying rule 2 and the kinds of nested building blocks that emerge from applying rule 3. The figure also shows the kind of overlapped building blocks that cannot appear in structured flowcharts (because of the elimination of the **goto** statement).

If the rules in Fig. 10.21 are followed, an unstructured flowchart (such as that in Fig. 10.26) cannot be created. If you are uncertain about whether a particular flowchart is structured, apply the rules of Fig. 10.21 in reverse to try to reduce the flowchart to the simplest flowchart. If the flowchart is reducible to the simplest flowchart, the original flowchart is structured; otherwise, it is not.

Structured programming promotes simplicity. Bohm and Jacopini have given us the result that only three forms of control are needed:

- sequence
- selection
- repetition

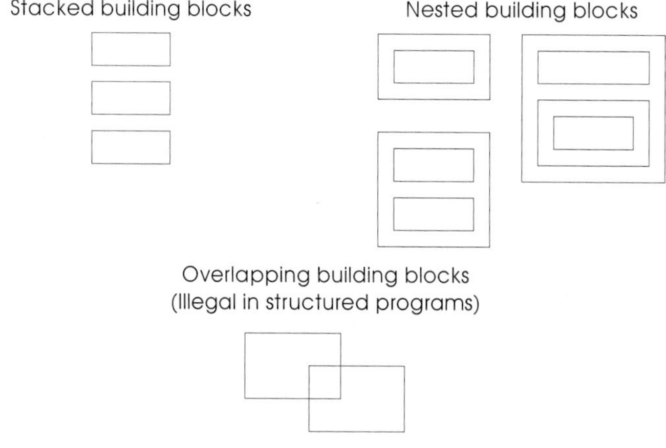

Fig. 10.25 Stacked, nested and overlapped building blocks.

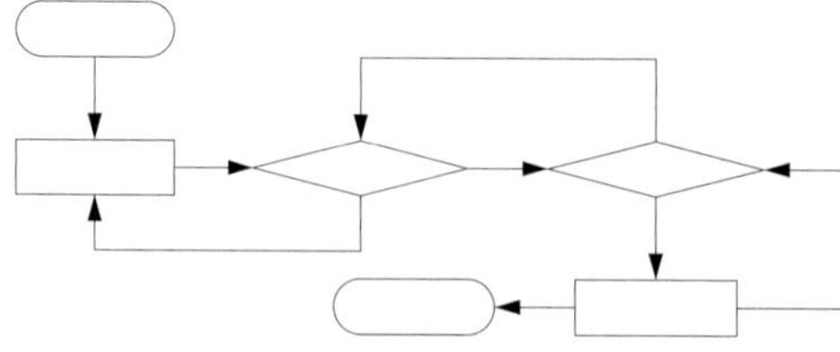

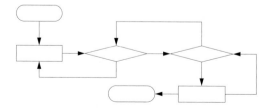

Fig. 10.26 An unstructured flowchart.

Sequence is trivial. Selection is implemented in one of three ways:

- **if** structure (single selection)
- **if/else** structure (double selection)
- **switch** structure (multiple selection)

In fact, it is straightforward to prove that the simple **if** structure is sufficient to provide any form of selection—everything that can be done with the **if/else** structure and the **switch** structure can be implemented by combining **if** structures (although perhaps not as smoothly).

Repetition is implemented in one of four ways:

- **while** structure
- **do/while** structure
- **for** structure
- **for/in** structure (discussed in Chapter 12)

It is straightforward to prove that the **while** structure is sufficient to provide any form of repetition. Everything that can be done with the **do/while** structure and the **for** structure can be done with the **while** structure (although perhaps not as elegantly).

Combining these results illustrates that any form of control ever needed in a JavaScript program can be expressed in terms of:

- sequence
- **if** structure (selection)
- **while** structure (repetition)

These control structures can be combined in only two ways—stacking and nesting. Indeed, structured programming promotes simplicity.

In this chapter, we discussed how to compose programs from control structures containing actions and decisions. In Chapter 11, we introduce another program structuring unit called the *function*. We will learn to compose large programs by combining functions that, in turn, are composed of control structures. We will also discuss how functions promote software reusability.

SUMMARY

- Counter-controlled repetition requires the name of a control variable (or loop counter), the initial value of the control variable, the increment (or decrement) by which the control variable is modified each time through the loop (also known as *each iteration of the loop*) and the condition that tests for the final value of the control variable to determine whether looping should continue.
- Because the double quote character is used to specify the beginning and end of a string literal in JavaScript, it cannot be used in the contents of the string unless it is preceded by a \ to create the escape sequence `\"`.
- HTML allows either single quotes (`'`) or double quotes (`"`) to be placed around the value specified for an attribute.
- JavaScript allows single quotes to be placed in a string literal.
- Although it is considered a good programming practice, HTML does not require attribute values to be enclosed in quotes.

- The **for** repetition structure handles all the details of counter-controlled repetition.
- JavaScript does not require variables to be declared before they are used. If a variable is used without being declared, the JavaScript interpreter creates the variable at the point of its first use in the script.
- The **for** structure's first line (including the keyword **for** and everything in parentheses after **for**) is often called the **for** *structure header*.
- If there is more than one statement in the body of the **for**, braces (**{** and **}**) are required to define the body of the loop.
- The general format of the **for** structure is

  for (*initialization***;** *loopContinuationTest***;** *increment* **)**
  statement

  where the *initialization* expression names the loop's control variable and provides its initial value, the *loopContinuationTest* expression is the loop-continuation condition (containing the final value of the control variable for which the condition is **true**) and *increment* is an expression that increments the control variable.
- In most cases the **for** structure can be represented by an equivalent **while** structure with initialization, loopContinuationTest and increment placed as follows:

  *initialization***;**

  while (*loopContinuationTest* **) {**
  statement
  *increment***;**
  }
- The three expressions in the **for** structure are optional. If *loopContinuationTest* is omitted, JavaScript assumes that the loop-continuation condition is **true**, thus creating an infinite loop. One might omit the *initialization* expression if the control variable is initialized elsewhere in the program before the loop. One might omit the *increment* expression if the increment is calculated by statements in the body of the **for** or if no increment is needed.
- The increment expression in the **for** structure acts like a stand-alone statement at the end of the body of the **for**.
- The initialization, loop-continuation condition and increment portions of a **for** structure can contain arithmetic expressions.
- The "increment" of a **for** structure may be negative, in which case it is really a decrement and the loop actually counts downward.
- If the loop-continuation condition is initially **false**, the body of the **for** structure is not performed.
- JavaScript does not include an exponentiation operator. The **Math** object's **pow** method calculates the value of **x** raised to the **y**th power and returns the result.
- The **Math** object's **round** method rounds its argument to the closest integer.
- JavaScript provides the **switch** multiple-selection structure to handle a series of decisions in which a variable or expression is tested separately for each of the values it may assume and different actions are taken.
- The **switch** structure consists of a series of **case** *labels* and an optional **default** *case*. When the flow of control reaches the **switch** structure, the controlling expression in the parentheses following keyword **switch** is evaluated. The value of this expression is compared with the value in each of the **case** labels, starting with the first **case** label. If a match occurs, the statements for

that **case** are executed. If no match occurs between the controlling expression's value and the value in a **case** label, the statements in the **default** case execute.

- Each **case** can have multiple actions (statements). The **switch** structure is different from other structures, in that braces are not required around multiple actions in a **case** of a **switch**.
- The **break** statement at the end of a **case** causes control to immediately exit the **switch**. The **break** statement is not required for the last **case** in the **switch** structure (or the **default** case when it appears last) because program control automatically continues with the next statement after the **switch** structure.
- Having several **case** labels listed together simply means that the same set of actions is to occur for each of the cases.
- The **do/while** structure tests the loop-continuation condition after the loop body is performed; therefore, the loop body is always executed at least once.
- Braces are not necessary in the **do/while** structure if there is only one statement in the body. The braces are usually included to avoid confusion between the **while** and **do/while** structures.
- The **break** statement, when executed in a **while**, **for**, **do/while** or **switch** structure, causes immediate exit from that structure.
- The **continue** statement, when executed in a **while**, **for** or **do/while** structure, skips the remaining statements in the body of that structure and proceeds with the next iteration of the loop.
- The labeled **break** statement, when executed in a **while**, **for**, **do/while** or **switch**, causes immediate exit from that structure and any number of enclosing repetition structures; program execution resumes with the first statement after the enclosing labeled statement (i.e., a statement preceded by a label). The labeled statement can be a compound statement.
- The labeled **continue** statement, when executed in a repetition structure (**while**, **for** or **do/while**), skips the remaining statements in that structure's body and in any number of enclosing repetition structures, and proceeds with the next iteration of the enclosing labeled loop.
- JavaScript provides logical operators that may be used to form more complex conditions by combining simple conditions. The logical operators are **&&** (logical AND), **||** (logical OR) and **!** (logical NOT, also called logical negation).
- A logical AND (**&&**) condition is **true** if and only if both of its operands are **true**.
- A logical OR (**||**) condition is **true** if either or both of its operands are **true**.
- An expression containing **&&** or **||** operators is evaluated only until truth or falsity is known. This performance feature for evaluation of logical AND and logical OR expressions is called short-circuit evaluation.
- The unary logical negation (**!**) operator reverses the meaning of a condition.
- JavaScript uses only single-entry/single-exit control structures—there is only one way to enter and only one way to exit each control structure.
- Structured programming promotes simplicity. Only three forms of control are needed: sequence, selection and repetition.
- Selection is implemented in one of three ways: the **if** structure (single selection), the **if/else** structure (double selection) and the **switch** structure (multiple selection).
- Repetition is implemented in one of four ways: the **while** structure, the **do/while** structure, the **for** structure and the **for/in** structure.
- Any form of control ever needed in a JavaScript program can be expressed in terms of: the sequence structure, the **if** structure (selection) and the **while** structure (repetition). These control structures can be combined in only two ways—stacking and nesting.

TERMINOLOGY

&& operator
|| operator
! operator
break
case label
continue
counter-controlled repetition
default case in **switch**
definite repetition
do/**while** repetition structure
for repetition structure
infinite loop
labeled **break** statement
labeled compound statement
labeled **continue** statement
labeled repetition structure
logical AND (**&&**)
logical negation (**!**)
logical operators
logical OR (**||**)
loop-continuation condition
multiple selection
nested control structures
off-by-one error
repetition structures
scrollbar
scroll box
short-circuit evaluation
single-entry/single-exit control structures
stacked control structures
switch selection structure
while repetition structure

COMMON PROGRAMMING ERRORS

10.1 Placing a double-quote (**"**) character inside a string literal causes a runtime error when the script is interpreted. To display a double-quote (**"**) character as part of a string literal, the double quote (**"**) character must be preceded by a **** to form the escape sequence **\"**.

10.2 Using an incorrect relational operator or using an incorrect final value of a loop counter in the condition of a **while**, **for** or do/**while** structure can cause an off-by-one error or an infinite loop.

10.3 Using commas instead of the two required semicolons in a **for** header is a syntax error.

10.4 Placing a semicolon immediately to the right of the right parenthesis of a **for** header makes the body of that **for** structure an empty statement. This is normally a logic error.

10.5 Not using the proper relational operator in the loop-continuation condition of a loop that counts downward (such as using **i <= 1** in a loop counting down to 1) is usually a logic error that will yield incorrect results when the program runs.

10.6 Forgetting a **break** statement when one is needed in a **switch** structure is a logic error.

10.7 Infinite loops are caused when the loop-continuation condition never becomes **false** in a **while**, **for** or do/**while** structure. To prevent this, make sure there is not a semicolon immediately after the header of a **while** or **for** structure. In a counter-controlled loop, make sure the control variable is incremented (or decremented) in the body of the loop. In a sentinel-controlled loop, make sure the sentinel value is eventually input.

GOOD PROGRAMMING PRACTICES

10.1 Control counting loops with integer values.

10.2 Indent the statements in the body of each control structure.

10.3 Put a blank line before and after each major control structure, to make it stand out in the program.

10.4 Too many levels of nesting can make a program difficult to understand. As a general rule, try to avoid using more than three levels of nesting.

10.5 Vertical spacing above and below control structures, and indentation of the bodies of control structures within the control structure headers, gives programs a two-dimensional appearance that enhances readability.

10.6 Using the final value in the condition of a **`while`** or **`for`** structure and using the <= relational operator will help avoid off-by-one errors. For a loop used to print the values 1 to 10, for example, the loop-continuation condition should be **`counter <= 10`** rather than **`counter < 10`** (which is an off-by-one error) or **`counter < 11`** (which is correct). Many programmers prefer so-called zero-based counting, in which, to count 10 times through the loop, **`counter`** would be initialized to zero and the loop-continuation test would be **`counter < 10`**.

10.7 Place only expressions involving the control variables in the initialization and increment sections of a **`for`** structure. Manipulations of other variables should appear either before the loop (if they execute only once, like initialization statements) or in the loop body (if they execute once per iteration of the loop, like incrementing or decrementing statements).

10.8 Although statements preceding a **`for`** and in the body of a **`for`** can often be merged into the **`for`** header, avoid doing so because it makes the program more difficult to read.

10.9 For clarity, limit the size of control structure headers to a single line if possible.

10.10 Provide a **`default`** case in **`switch`** statements. Cases not explicitly tested in a **`switch`** statement without a **`default`** case are ignored. Including a **`default`** case focuses the programmer on processing exceptional conditions. However, there are situations in which no **`default`** processing is needed.

10.11 Although the **`case`** clauses and the **`default`** case clause in a **`switch`** structure can occur in any order, it is considered good programming practice to place the **`default`** clause last.

10.12 In a **`switch`** structure, when the **`default`** clause is listed last, the **`break`** for that **`case`** statement is not required. Some programmers include this **`break`** for clarity and for symmetry with other cases.

10.13 Some programmers always include braces in a **`do/while`** structure even if the braces are not necessary. This helps eliminate ambiguity between the **`while`** structure and the **`do/while`** structure containing one statement.

10.14 Some programmers feel that **`break`** and **`continue`** violate structured programming. Because the effects of these statements can be achieved by structured programming techniques, these programmers do not use **`break`** and **`continue`**.

PERFORMANCE TIP

10.1 The **`break`** and **`continue`** statements, when used properly, perform faster than the corresponding structured techniques.

SOFTWARE ENGINEERING OBSERVATIONS

10.1 Placing a semicolon immediately after a **`for`** header is sometimes used to create a so-called delay loop. Such a **`for`** loop with an empty body still loops the indicated number of times, doing nothing other than the counting. You might use a delay loop, for example, to slow down a program that is producing outputs on the screen too quickly for you to read them.

10.2 There is a tension between achieving quality software engineering and achieving the best-performing software. Often, one of these goals is achieved at the expense of the other. For all but the most performance-intensive situations, the following "rule of thumb" should be followed: First make your code simple and correct; then make it fast and small, but only if necessary. [Chapter 15 introduces better techniques to create delays in programs, so you should never use delay loops.]

TESTING AND DEBUGGING TIPS

10.1 When writing HTML text from a script, use single-quote (') characters to delimit attribute values in string literals.

10.2 Although the value of the control variable can be changed in the body of a **for** loop, avoid changing it, because doing so can lead to subtle errors.

SELF-REVIEW EXERCISES

10.1 State whether each of the following is *true* or *false*. If *false*, explain why.
   a) The **default** case is required in the **switch** selection structure.
   b) The **break** statement is required in the default case of a **switch** selection structure.
   c) The expression **(x > y && a < b)** is true if either **x > y** is true or **a < b** is true.
   d) An expression containing the **||** operator is true if either or both of its operands is true.

10.2 Write a JavaScript statement or a set of statements to accomplish each of the following:
   a) Sum the odd integers between 1 and 99. Use a **for** structure. Assume that the integer variables **sum** and **count** have been declared.
   b) Calculate the value of **2.5** raised to the power of **3**. Use the **pow** method.
   c) Print the integers from 1 to 20 by using a **while** loop and the counter variable **x**. Assume that the variable **x** has been declared but not initialized. Print only five integers per line. [*Hint:* Use the calculation **x % 5**. When the value of this is 0, print a newline character; otherwise, print a tab character. Use the **document.write("<BR>")** to output a line break in the HTML document.]
   d) Repeat Exercise 10.2 c), but using a **for** structure.

10.3 Find the error in each of the following code segments and explain how to correct it.

a)
```
x = 1;

while ( x <= 10 );
   x++;
}
```

b)
```
for ( y = .1; y != 1.0; y += .1 )
   document.write( y + " " );
```

c)
```
switch ( n ) {
   case 1:
      document.writeln( "The number is 1" );
   case 2:
      document.writeln( "The number is 2" );
      break;
   default:
      document.writeln( "The number is not 1 or 2" );
      break;
}
```

d) The following code should print the values 1 to 10.
```
n = 1;
while ( n < 10 )
   document.writeln( n++ );
```

ANSWERS TO SELF-REVIEW EXERCISES

10.1 a) False. The **default** case is optional. If no default action is needed, then there is no need for a **default** case. b) False. The **break** statement is used to exit the **switch** structure. The

break statement is not required for the last case in a **switch** structure. c) False. Both of the relational expressions must be true in order for the entire expression to be true when using the **&&** operator. d) True.

10.2 a)
```
sum = 0;
for ( count = 1; count <= 99; count += 2 )
   sum += count;
```
b) `Math.pow( 2.5, 3 )`

c)
```
x = 1;

while ( x <= 20 ) {
   document.write( x + "  " );

   if ( x % 5 == 0 )
      document.write( "<BR>" );

   ++x;
}
```
d)
```
for ( x = 1; x <= 20; x++ ) {
   document.write( x + "  " );

   if ( x % 5 == 0 )
      document.write( "<BR>" );
}
```

or

```
for ( x = 1; x <= 20; x++ )

   if ( x % 5 == 0 )
      document.write( x + "<BR>" );
   else
      document.write( x + "  " );
```

10.3 a) Error: The semicolon after the **while** header causes an infinite loop and there is a missing left brace.
Correction: Replace the semicolon by a **{** or remove both the **;** and the **}**.

b) Error: Using a floating-point number to control a **for** repetition structure may not work, because floating-point numbers are represented approximately by most computers.
Correction: Use an integer, and perform the proper calculation in order to get the values you desire.
```
for ( y = 1; y != 10; y++ )
   document.writeln( y / 10 );
```
c) Error: Missing **break** statement in the statements for the first **case**.
Correction: Add a **break** statement at the end of the statements for the first **case**. Note that this is not necessarily an error if the programmer wants the statement of **case 2:** to execute every time the **case 1:** statement executes.

d) Error: Improper relational operator used in the **while** repetition-continuation condition.
Correction: Use **<=** rather than **<** or change **10** to **11**.

EXERCISES

10.4 Find the error in each of the following. [*Note:* There may be more than one error.]

a)
```
For ( x = 100, x >= 1, x++ )
    document.writeln( x );
```

b) The following code should print whether integer **value** is odd or even:
```
switch ( value % 2 ) {
   case 0:
      document.writeln( "Even integer" );
   case 1:
      document.writeln( "Odd integer" );
}
```

c) The following code should output the odd integers from 19 to 1:
```
for ( x = 19; x >= 1; x += 2 )
   document.writeln( x );
```

d) The following code should output the even integers from 2 to 100:
```
counter = 2;
do {
   document.writeln( counter );
   counter += 2;
} While ( counter < 100 );
```

10.5 What does the following script do?

```
<!DOCTYPE html PUBLIC "-//W3C//DTD HTML 4.0 Transitional//EN">
<HTML>
<HEAD><TITLE>Mystery</TITLE>

<SCRIPT LANGUAGE = "JavaScript">
   for ( var i = 1; i <= 10; i++ ) {

      for ( var j = 1; j <= 5; j++ )
         document.writeln( "@" );

      document.writeln( "<BR>" );
   }
</SCRIPT>

</HEAD><BODY></BODY>
</HTML>
```

10.6 Write a script that finds the smallest of several integers. Assume that the first value read specifies the number of values to be input from the user.

10.7 Write a script that calculates the product of the odd integers from 1 to 15 and then outputs HTML text that displays the results.

10.8 The *factorial* method is used frequently in probability problems. The factorial of a positive integer *n* (written *n!* and pronounced "n factorial") is equal to the product of the positive integers from 1 to *n*. Write a script that evaluates the factorials of the integers from 1 to 5. Display the results in an HTML table format.

10.9 Modify the compound interest program of Fig. 10.6 to repeat its steps for interest rates of 5, 6, 7, 8, 9 and 10%. Use a **for** loop to vary the interest rate.

10.10 Write a script that outputs HTML to display the following patterns separately one below the other. Use **for** loops to generate the patterns. All asterisks (*) should be printed by a single statement of the form **document.write("*");** (this causes the asterisks to print side by side). A statement of the form **document.writeln("<BR>");** can be used to position to the next line. A statement of the form **document.write(" ");** can be used display a space for the last two patterns. There should be no other output statements in the program. (*Hint:* The last two patterns require that each line begin with an appropriate number of blanks. You may need to use the HTML **<PRE></PRE>** tags.)

```
(A)          (B)          (C)          (D)
*            **********   **********            *
**           *********     *********           **
***          ********       ********          ***
****         *******         *******         ****
*****        ******           ******        *****
******       *****             *****       ******
*******      ****               ****      *******
********     ***                 ***     ********
*********    **                   **    *********
**********   *                     *   **********
```

10.11 One interesting application of computers is the drawing of graphs and bar charts (sometimes called "histograms"). Write a script that reads five numbers (each between 1 and 30). For each number read, your program should output HTML text that displays a line containing that number of adjacent asterisks. For example, if your program reads the number seven, it should output HTML text that displays *******.

10.12 *("The Twelve Days of Christmas" Song)* Write a script that uses repetition and **switch** structures to print the song "The Twelve Days of Christmas." One **switch** structure should be used to print the day (i.e., "First," "Second," etc.). A separate **switch** structure should be used to print the remainder of each verse. You can find the words at the site

http://www.santas.net/twelvedaysofchristmas.htm

10.13 A mail order house sells five different products whose retail prices are: product 1— $2.98, product 2—$4.50, product 3—$9.98, product 4—$4.49, and product 5—$6.87. Write a script that reads a series of pairs of numbers as follows:

a) Product number
b) Quantity sold for one day

Your program should use a **switch** structure to help determine the retail price for each product. Your program should calculate and ouput HTML that displays the total retail value of all products sold last week. Use a **prompt** dialog to obtain the product number from the user. Use a sentinel-controlled loop to determine when the program should stop looping and display the final results.

10.14 Modify the program in Fig. 10.6 to use only integers to calculate the compound interest. (*Hint:* Treat all monetary amounts as integral numbers of pennies. Then "break" the result into its dollar portion and cents portion by using the division and modulus operations, respectively. Insert a period.)

10.15 Assume **i = 1**, **j = 2**, **k = 3** and **m = 2**. What does each of the following statements print? Are the parentheses necessary in each case?

a) **document.writeln(i == 1);**
b) **document.writeln(j == 3);**
c) **document.writeln(i >= 1 && j < 4);**
d) **document.writeln(m <= 99 & k < m);**

e) `document.writeln( j >= i || k == m );`
f) `document.writeln( k + m < j | 3 - j >= k );`
g) `document.writeln( !( k > m ) );`

10.16 Write a script that outputs HTML text to display an HTML table of the binary, octal, and hexadecimal equivalents of the decimal numbers in the range 1 through 256. If you are not familiar with these number systems, first read Appendix D.

10.17 Calculate the value of π from the infinite series

$$\pi = 4 - \frac{4}{3} + \frac{4}{5} - \frac{4}{7} + \frac{4}{9} - \frac{4}{11} + \cdots$$

Print a table that shows the value of π as approximated by one term of this series, by two terms, by three terms, etc. How many terms of this series do you have to use before you first get 3.14? 3.141? 3.1415? 3.14159?

10.18 *(Pythagorean Triples)* A right triangle can have sides that are all integers. The set of three integer values for the sides of a right triangle is called a Pythagorean triple. These three sides must satisfy the relationship that the sum of the squares of two of the sides is equal to the square of the hypotenuse. Write a script to find all the Pythagorean triples for **side1**, **side2** and the **hypotenuse** that have no member larger than 500. Use a triple-nested **for** loop that tries all possibilities. This approach is an example of "brute force" computing. You will learn in more advanced computer science courses that there are large numbers of interesting problems for which there is no known algorithmic approach other than using sheer brute force.

10.19 Modify Exercise 10.10 to combine your code from the four separate triangles of asterisks into a single script that prints all four patterns side by side making clever use of nested **for** loops.

```
*            **********   **********            *
**           *********     *********           **
***          ********       ********          ***
****         *******         *******         ****
*****        ******           ******        *****
******       *****             *****       ******
*******      ****               ****      *******
********     ***                 ***     ********
*********    **                   **    *********
**********   *                     *   **********
```

10.20 *(De Morgan's Laws)* In this chapter, we discussed the logical operators **&&**, **||** and **!**. De Morgan's Laws can sometimes make it more convenient for us to express a logical expression. These laws state that the expression **!(***condition1* **&&** *condition2***)** is logically equivalent to the expression **(!***condition1* **||** **!***condition2***)**. Also, the expression **!(***condition1* **||** *condition2***)** is logically equivalent to the expression **(!***condition1* **&&** **!***condition2***)**. Use De Morgan's Laws to write equivalent expressions for each of the following, and then write a program to show that the original expression and the new expression are equivalent in each case.

a) `!( x < 5 ) && !( y >= 7 )`
b) `!( a == b ) || !( g != 5 )`
c) `!( ( x <= 8 ) && ( y > 4 ) )`
d) `!( ( i > 4 ) || ( j <= 6 ) )`

10.21 Write a script that prints the following diamond shape. You may use output statements that print a single asterisk (*****), a single space or a single newline character. Maximize your use of repetition (with nested **for** structures) and minimize the number of output statements.

10.22 Modify the program you wrote in Exercise 10.21 to read an odd number in the range 1 to 19 to specify the number of rows in the diamond. Your program should then display a diamond of the appropriate size.

10.23 A criticism of the **break** statement and the **continue** statement is that each is unstructured. Actually, **break** statements and **continue** statements can always be replaced by structured statements, although coding the replacement can be awkward. Describe in general how you would remove any **break** statement from a loop in a program and replace that statement with some structured equivalent. (*Hint:* The **break** statement "jumps out of" a loop from the body of that loop. The other way to leave is by failing the loop-continuation test. Consider using in the loop-continuation test a second test that indicates "early exit because of a 'break' condition.") Use the technique you developed here to remove the break statement from the program of Fig. 10.11.

10.24 What does the following script do?

```
<!DOCTYPE html PUBLIC "-//W3C//DTD HTML 4.0 Transitional//EN">
<HTML>
<HEAD><TITLE>Mystery</TITLE>

<SCRIPT LANGUAGE = "JavaScript">
   for ( i = 1; i <= 5; i++ ) {
      for ( j = 1; j <= 3; j++ ) {
         for ( k = 1; k <= 4; k++ )
            document.write( "*" );
         document.writeln( "<BR>" );
      }
      document.writeln( "<BR>" );
   }
</SCRIPT>

</HEAD><BODY></BODY>
</HTML>
```

10.25 Describe in general how you would remove any **continue** statement from a loop in a program and replace that statement with some structured equivalent. Use the technique you developed here to remove the **continue** statement from the program of Fig. 10.12.

11

JavaScript/JScript: Functions

Objectives

- To understand how to construct programs modularly from small pieces called functions.
- To be able to create new functions.
- To understand the mechanisms used to pass information between functions.
- To introduce simulation techniques using random number generation.
- To understand how the visibility of identifiers is limited to specific regions of programs.
- To understand how to write and use functions that call themselves.

Form ever follows function.
Louis Henri Sullivan

E pluribus unum.
(One composed of many.)
Virgil

O! call back yesterday, bid time return.
William Shakespeare, *Richard II*

Call me Ishmael.
Herman Melville, *Moby Dick*

When you call me that, smile.
Owen Wister

Outline

11.1 Introduction

Most computer programs that solve real-world problems are much larger than the programs presented in the first few chapters. Experience has shown that the best way to develop and maintain a large program is to construct it from small, simple pieces or *modules*. This technique is called *divide and conquer*. This chapter describes many key features of JavaScript that facilitate the design, implementation, operation and maintenance of large scripts.

11.2 Program Modules in JavaScript

Modules in JavaScript are called *functions*. JavaScript programs are written by combining new functions that the programmer writes with "prepackaged" functions and objects available in JavaScript. The "prepackaged" functions that belong to JavaScript objects (such as **`Math.pow`** and **`Math.round`**, introduced previously) are often called *methods*. The term method implies that the function belongs to a particular object; however, the terms function and method can be used interchangeably. We will refer to functions that belong to a particular JavaScript object as methods; all others are referred to as functions.

JavaScript provides several objects that have a rich collection of methods for performing common mathematical calculations, string manipulations, date and time manipulations, and manipulations of collections of data called ***`Array`**s*. These make the programmer's job easier, because they provide many of the capabilities programmers need. Some common predefined objects of JavaScript and their methods are discussed in Chapter 12, "JavaScript: Arrays" and Chapter 13, "JavaScript: Objects."

Good Programming Practice 11.1

Familiarize yourself with the rich collection of objects and methods provided by JavaScript.

Software Engineering Observation 11.1

Avoid reinventing the wheel. When possible, use JavaScript objects and methods instead of writing new functions. This reduces program development time and avoids introducing new errors.

Portability Tip 11.1

Using the methods built into JavaScript objects helps make programs more portable.

Performance Tip 11.1

Do not try to rewrite existing methods of JavaScript objects to make them more efficient. You usually will not be able to increase the performance of these methods.

The programmer can write functions to define specific tasks that may be used at many points in a script. These are sometimes referred to as *programmer-defined functions.* The actual statements defining the function are written only once, and these statements are hidden from other functions.

A function is *invoked* (i.e., made to perform its designated task) by a *function call.* The function call specifies the function name and provides information (as *arguments*) that the called function needs to do its task. A common analogy for this structure is the hierarchical form of management. A boss (the *calling function* or *caller*) asks a worker (the *called function*) to perform a task and *return* (i.e., report back) the results when the task is done. The boss function does not know *how* the worker function performs its designated tasks. The worker may call other worker functions, and the boss will be unaware of this. We will soon see how this "hiding" of implementation details promotes good software engineering. Figure 11.1 shows the **boss** function communicating with several worker functions in a hierarchical manner. Note that **worker1** acts as a "boss" function to **worker4** and **worker5**. Relationships among functions may be other than the hierarchical structure shown in this figure.

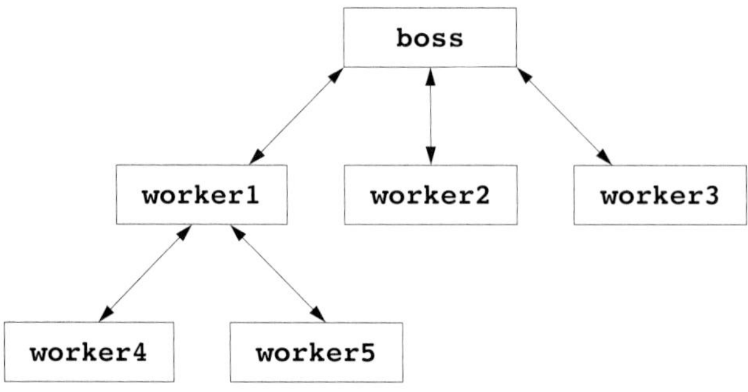

Fig. 11.1 Hierarchical boss function/worker function relationship.

Functions (and methods) are called (invoked) by writing the name of the function (or method), followed by a left parenthesis, followed by the argument (or a comma-separated list of arguments) of the function, followed by a right parenthesis. For example, a programmer desiring to convert a string stored in variable **inputValue** to a floating-point number, to add it to variable **total**, might write

```
total += parseFloat( inputValue );
```

When this statement is executed, JavaScript function ***parseFloat*** converts the string contained in the parentheses (stored in variable **inputValue** in this case) to a floating-point value, then that value is added to **total**. The variable **inputValue** is the argument of the **parseFloat** function. Function **parseFloat** method takes a string representation of a floating-point number as an argument and returns the corresponding floating-point numeric value.

Function (and method) arguments may be constants, variables or expressions. If **s1 = "22.3"** and **s2 = "45"**, then the statement

```
total += parseFloat( s1 + s2 );
```

evaluates the expression **s1 + s2**, concatenates the strings **s1** and **s2** (resulting in the string **"22.345"**), converts the result into a floating-point number and adds the floating-point number to variable **total**.

11.3 Programmer-Defined Functions

Functions allow the programmer to modularize a program. All variables declared in function definitions are *local variables*—they are known only in the function in which they are defined. Most functions have a list of *parameters* that provide the means for communicating information between functions via function calls. A function's parameters are also considered to be local variables. When a function is called, the arguments in the function call are assigned to the corresponding parameters in the function definition.

There are several motivations for modularizing a program with functions. The divide-and-conquer approach makes program development more manageable. Another motivation is *software reusability*—using existing functions as building blocks to create new programs. With good function naming and definition, programs can be created from standardized functions rather than being built by using customized code. For example, we did not have to define how to convert strings to integers and floating-point numbers—JavaScript already provides function **parseInt** to convert a string to an integer and function **parseFloat** to convert a string to a floating-point number. A third motivation is to avoid repeating code in a program. Packaging code as a function allows that code to be executed from several locations in a program by calling the function.

Software Engineering Observation 11.2

Each function should be limited to performing a single, well-defined task, and the function name should effectively express that task. This promotes software reusability.

Software Engineering Observation 11.3

If you cannot choose a concise name that expresses what the function does, it is possible that your function is attempting to perform too many diverse tasks. It is usually best to break such a function into several smaller functions.

11.4 Function Definitions

Each script we have presented has consisted of a series of statements and control structures in sequence. These scripts have been executed as the browser loads the Web page and evaluates the **<HEAD>** section of the page. We now consider how programmers write their own customized functions and call them in a script.

Consider a script (Fig. 11.2) that uses a function **square** to calculate the squares of the integers from 1 to 10. [*Note:* We continue to show many examples in which the **BODY** element of the HTML document is empty and the document is created directly by a JavaScript. In later chapters we show many examples in which JavaScripts interact with the elements in the **BODY** of a document.]

The **for** structure at lines 13 through 15

```
for ( var x = 1; x <= 10; ++x )
   document.writeln( "The square of " + x + " is " +
                     square( x ) + "<BR>" );
```

outputs HTML that displays the results of squaring the integers from 1 to 10. Each iteration of the loop calculates the **square** of the current value of control variable **x** and outputs the result by writing a line in the HTML document. Function **square** is *invoked* or *called* on line 15 in the **for** structure with the expression

```
1  <!DOCTYPE html PUBLIC "-//W3C//DTD HTML 4.0 Transitional//EN">
2  <HTML>
3  <!-- Fig. 11.2: SquareInt.html -->
4
5  <HEAD>
6  <TITLE>A Programmer-Defined square Function</TITLE>
7
8  <SCRIPT LANGUAGE = "JavaScript">
9     document.writeln(
10       "<H1>Square the numbers from 1 to 10</H1>" );
11
12    // square the numbers from 1 to 10
13    for ( var x = 1; x <= 10; ++x )
14       document.writeln( "The square of " + x + " is " +
15                         square( x ) + "<BR>" );
16
17    // The following square function's body is executed only
18    // when the function is explicitly called.
19
20    // square function definition
21    function square( y )
22    {
23       return y * y;
24    }
25 </SCRIPT>
26
27 </HEAD><BODY></BODY>
28 </HTML>
```

Fig. 11.2 Using programmer-defined function **square** (part 1 of 2).

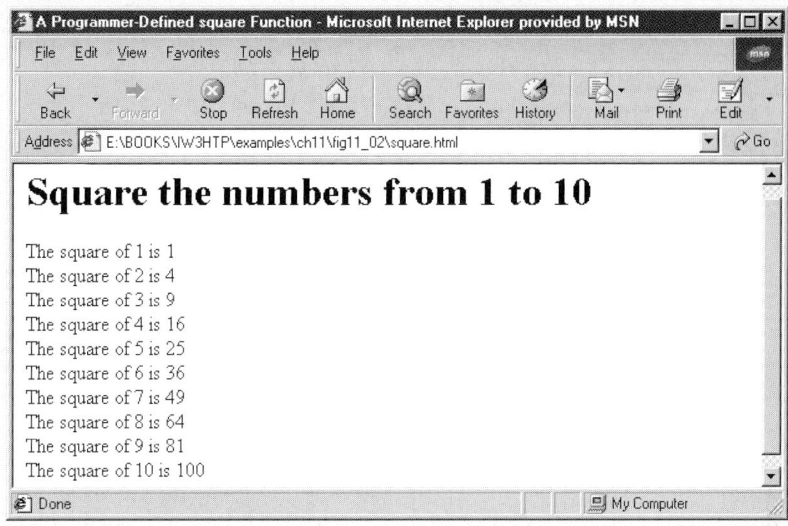

Fig. 11.2 Using programmer-defined function **square** (part 2 of 2).

```
square( x )
```

When program control reaches this expression, function **square** (defined at line 21) is called. In fact, the **()** represent the *function call operator* which has high precedence. At this point, a copy of the value of **x** (the argument to the function call) is made automatically by the program and program control transfers to the first line of function **square**. Function **square** receives the copy of the value of **x** in the parameter **y**. Then **square** calculates **y * y**. The result is passed back to the point in line 15 where **square** was invoked. Lines 14 and 15 concatenate **"The square of "**, the value of **x**, **" is "**, the value returned by function **square**, and a **
** tag, then write that line of text in the HTML document. This process is repeated ten times.

The definition of function **square** (line 21) shows that **square** expects a single parameter **y**—this will be the name used in the body of function **square** to manipulate the value passed to **square** from line 15. Note that the JavaScript keyword **var** is not used to declare variables in the parameter list of a function. The ***return*** *statement* in **square** passes the result of the calculation **y * y** back to the calling function.

Common Programming Error 11.1

*Using the JavaScript **var** keyword to declare a variable in a function parameter list results in a JavaScript runtime error.*

Note that function **square** follows the rest of the script. When the **for** structure terminates, JavaScript will not continue to flow sequentially into function **square**. A function must explicitly be called for the code in its body to execute. Thus, when the **for** structure terminates in this example, the script terminates.

Good Programming Practice 11.2

Place a blank line between function definitions to separate the functions and enhance program readability.

Software Engineering Observation 11.4

Statements that are enclosed in the body of a function definition will not be executed by the JavaScript interpreter unless the function is explicitly invoked (called).

The format of a function definition is

```
function function-name ( parameter-list )
{
    declarations and statements
}
```

The *function-name* is any valid identifier. The *parameter-list* is a comma-separated list containing the names of the parameters received by the function when it is called (remember that the arguments in the function call are assigned to the corresponding parameter in the function definition). There should be one argument in the function call for each parameter in the function definition. If a function does not receive any values, the *parameter-list* is empty (the function name is followed by an empty set of parentheses).

The *declarations* and *statements* within braces form the *function body*. The function body is also referred to as a *block*. A block is a compound statement that includes declarations.

Common Programming Error 11.2

Forgetting to return a value from a function that is supposed to return a value is a logic error.

Common Programming Error 11.3

Placing a semicolon after the right parenthesis enclosing the parameter list of a function definition results in a JavaScript runtime error.

Common Programming Error 11.4

Redefining a function parameter as a local variable in the function is a logic error.

Common Programming Error 11.5

Passing to a function an argument that is not compatible with the corresponding parameter's expected type is a logic error and may result in a JavaScript runtime error.

Good Programming Practice 11.3

Although it is not incorrect to do so, do not use the same names for the arguments passed to a function and the corresponding parameters in the function definition. This helps avoid ambiguity.

Good Programming Practice 11.4

Choosing meaningful function names and meaningful parameter names makes programs more readable and helps avoid excessive use of comments.

Software Engineering Observation 11.5

A function should usually be no longer than one printed page. Better yet, a function should usually be no longer than half a printed page. Regardless of how long a function is, it should perform one task well. Small functions promote software reusability.

Software Engineering Observation 11.6

Scripts should be written as collections of small functions. This makes programs easier to write, debug, maintain and modify.

Software Engineering Observation 11.7

A function requiring a large number of parameters may be performing too many tasks. Consider dividing the function into smaller functions that perform the separate tasks. The function header should fit on one line if possible.

Testing and Debugging Tip 11.1

Small functions are easier to test, debug and understand than large ones.

There are three ways to return control to the point at which a function was invoked. If the function does not return a result, control is returned when the function-ending right brace is reached or by executing the statement

```
return;
```

If the function does return a result, the statement

return *expression*;

returns the value of *expression* to the caller. When a **return** statement is executed, control returns immediately to the point at which a function was invoked.

The script in our next example (Fig. 11.3) uses a programmer-defined function called **maximum** to determine and return the largest of three floating-point values.

```
<!DOCTYPE html PUBLIC "-//W3C//DTD HTML 4.0 Transitional//EN">
<HTML>
<!-- Fig. 11.3: maximum.html -->

<HEAD>
<TITLE>Finding the Maximum of Three Values</TITLE>

<SCRIPT LANGUAGE = "JavaScript">
   var input1 = window.prompt( "Enter first number", "0" );
   var input2 = window.prompt( "Enter second number", "0" );
   var input3 = window.prompt( "Enter third number", "0" );

   var value1 = parseFloat( input1 );
   var value2 = parseFloat( input2 );
   var value3 = parseFloat( input3 );

   var maxValue = maximum( value1, value2, value3 );

   document.writeln( "First number: " + value1 +
                     "<BR>Second number: " + value2 +
                     "<BR>Third number: " + value3 +
                     "<BR>Maximum is: " + maxValue );
```

Fig. 11.3 Programmer-defined **maximum** function (part 1 of 2).

```
23
24       // maximum method definition (called from line 17)
25       function maximum( x, y, z )
26       {
27          return Math.max( x, Math.max( y, z ) );
28       }
29    </SCRIPT>
30
31    </HEAD>
32    <BODY>
33    <P>Click Refresh (or Reload) to run the script again</P>
34    </BODY>
35    </HTML>
```

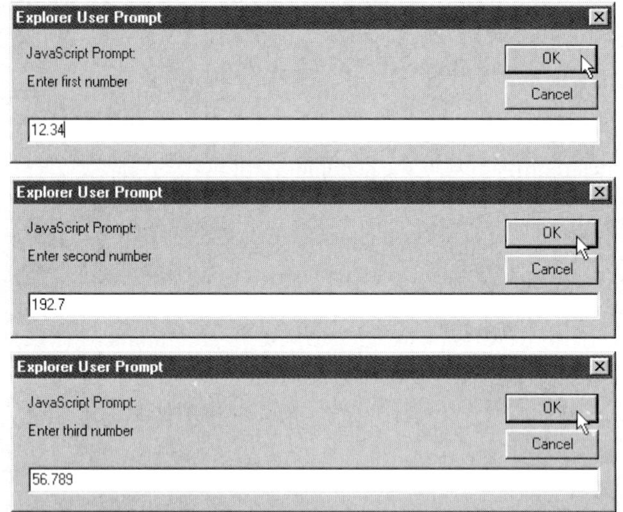

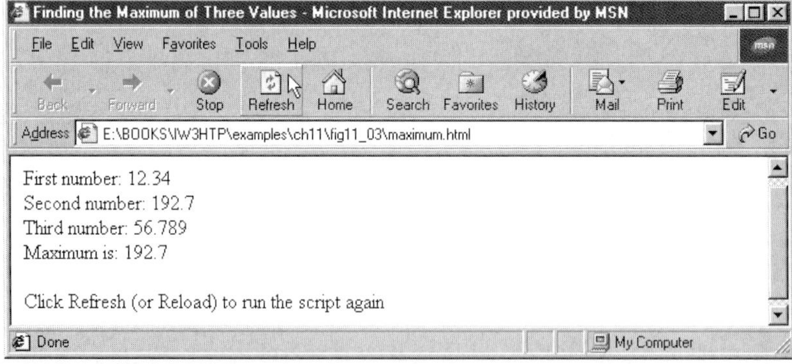

Fig. 11.3 Programmer-defined **maximum** function (part 2 of 2).

The three floating-point values are input by the user via **prompt** dialogs (lines 9 through 11). Lines 13 through 15 use function **parseFloat** to convert the strings input by the user to floating-point values. The statement at line 17

```
var maxValue = maximum( value1, value2, value3 );
```

passes the three floating-point values to function **maximum** (defined at line 25), which determines the largest floating-point value. This value is returned to line 17 by the **return** statement in function **maximum**. The value returned is assigned to variable **maxValue**. The three floating-point values input by the user and the **maxValue** value are concatenated and displayed by the **document.writeln** statement at lines 19 through 22.

Notice the implementation of the function **maximum** (line 25). The first line indicates that the function's name is **maximum** and that the function takes three parameters (**x**, **y** and **z**) to accomplish its task. Also, the body of the function contains the statement

```
return Math.max( x, Math.max( y, z ) );
```

which returns the largest of the three floating-point values using two calls to the **Math** object's **max** method. First, method **Math.max** is invoked with the values of variables **y** and **z** to determine the larger of these two values. Next, the value of variable **x** and the result of the first call to **Math.max** are passed to method **Math.max**. Finally, the result of the second call to **Math.max** is returned to the point at which **maximum** was invoked (i.e., line 17). Note once again that the script terminates before sequentially reaching the definition of function **maximum**. The statement in the body of function **maximum** is executed only when the function is invoked from line 17.

11.5 Random Number Generation

We now take a brief and, it is hoped, entertaining diversion into a popular programming application, namely simulation and game playing. In this section and the next section, we will develop a nicely structured game-playing program that includes multiple functions. The program uses most of the control structures we have studied.

There is something in the air of a gambling casino that invigorates people, from the high-rollers at the plush mahogany-and-felt craps tables to the quarter-poppers at the one-armed bandits. It is the *element of chance,* the possibility that luck will convert a pocketful of money into a mountain of wealth. The element of chance can be introduced through the **Math** object's ***random*** method. (Remember, we are calling **random** a method because it belongs to the **Math** object.)

Consider the following statement:

```
var randomValue = Math.random();
```

Method **random** generates a floating-point value from 0.0 up to (but not including) 1.0. If **random** truly produces values at random, every value from 0.0 up to (but not including) 1.0 has an equal *chance* (or *probability*) of being chosen each time **random** is called.

The range of values produced directly by **random** is often different from what is needed in a specific application. For example, a program that simulates coin tossing might require only 0 for "heads" and 1 for "tails." A program that simulates rolling a six-sided die would require random integers in the range 1 to 6. A program that randomly predicts the next type of spaceship (out of four possibilities) that will fly across the horizon in a video game might require random integers in the range 0 through 3 or 1 through 4.

To demonstrate method **random**, let us develop a program that simulates 20 rolls of a six-sided die and displays the value of each roll. We use the multiplication operator (*) in conjunction with **random** as follows:

```
Math.floor( 1 + Math.random() * 6 )
```

First, the preceding expression multiplies the result of a call to **Math.random()** by **6** to produce a number in the range 0.0 up to (but not including) 6.0. This is called *scaling* the range of the random numbers. The number 6 is called the *scaling factor*. Next, we add 1 to this result to *shift* the range of numbers to produce a number in the range 1.0 up to (but not including 7.0. Finally, we use method ***Math.floor*** to *round* the result down to the closest integer value in the range 1 to 6. **Math** method **floor** rounds its floating-point number argument to the closest integer not greater than its argument's value—e.g., 1.75 is rounded to 1 and -1.25 is rounded to -2. Figure 11.4 confirms that the results are in the range 1 to 6.

To show that these numbers occur with approximately equal likelihood, let us simulate 6000 rolls of a die with the program of Fig. 11.5. Each integer from 1 to 6 should appear approximately 1000 times. Use your browser's **Refresh** (or **Reload**) button to execute the script again.

```
<!DOCTYPE html PUBLIC "-//W3C//DTD HTML 4.0 Transitional//EN">
<HTML>
<!-- Fig. 11.4: RandomInt.java -->

<HEAD>
<TITLE>Shifted and Scaled Random Integers</TITLE>

<SCRIPT LANGUAGE = "JavaScript">
   var value;

   document.writeln( "<H1>Random Numbers</H1>" +
                     "<TABLE BORDER = '1' WIDTH = '50%'><TR>" );

   for ( var i = 1; i <= 20; i++ ) {
      value = Math.floor( 1 + Math.random() * 6 );
      document.writeln( "<TD>" + value + "</TD>" );

      if ( i % 5 == 0 && i != 20 )
         document.writeln( "</TR><TR>" );
   }

   document.writeln( "</TR></TABLE>" );
</SCRIPT>

</HEAD>
<BODY>
<P>Click Refresh (or Reload) to run the script again</P>
</BODY>
</HTML>
```

Fig. 11.4 Shifted and scaled random integers (part 1 of 2).

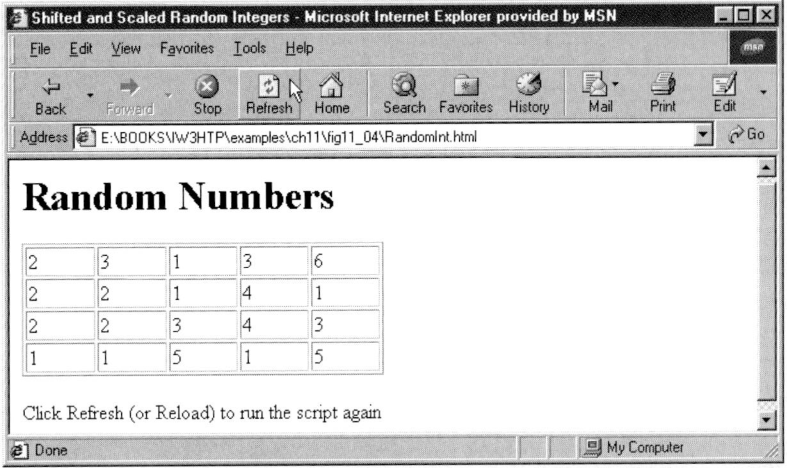

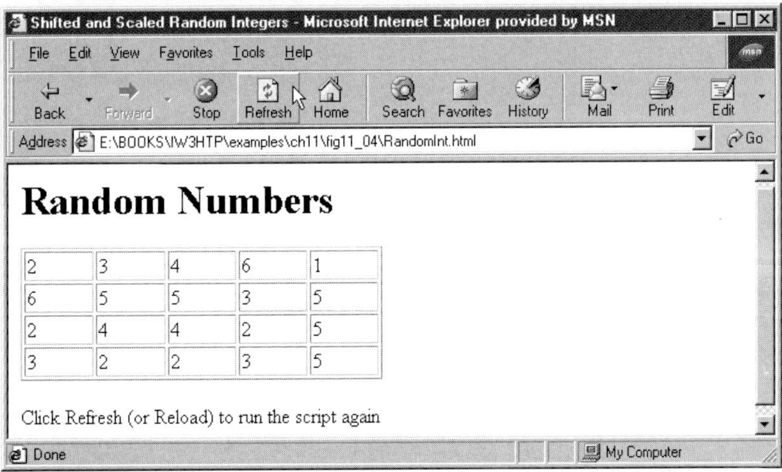

Fig. 11.4 Shifted and scaled random integers (part 2 of 2).

```
<!DOCTYPE html PUBLIC "-//W3C//DTD HTML 4.0 Transitional//EN">
<HTML>
<!-- Fig. 11.5: RollDie.html -->

<HEAD>
<TITLE>Roll a Six-Sided Die 6000 Times</TITLE>

```

Fig. 11.5 Rolling a six-sided die 6000 times (part 1 of 3).

```
<SCRIPT LANGUAGE = "JavaScript">
   var frequency1 = 0, frequency2 = 0,
       frequency3 = 0, frequency4 = 0,
       frequency5 = 0, frequency6 = 0, face;

   // summarize results
   for ( var roll = 1; roll <= 6000; ++roll ) {
      face = Math.floor( 1 + Math.random() * 6 );

      switch ( face ) {
         case 1:
            ++frequency1;
            break;
         case 2:
            ++frequency2;
            break;
         case 3:
            ++frequency3;
            break;
         case 4:
            ++frequency4;
            break;
         case 5:
            ++frequency5;
            break;
         case 6:
            ++frequency6;
            break;
      }
   }

   document.writeln( "<TABLE BORDER = '1' WIDTH = '50%'>" );
   document.writeln( "<TR><TD><B>Face</B></TD>" +
                     "<TD><B>Frequency</B></TD></TR>" );
   document.writeln( "<TR><TD>1</TD><TD>" + frequency1 +
                     "</TD></TR>" );
   document.writeln( "<TR><TD>2</TD><TD>" + frequency2 +
                     "</TD></TR>" );
   document.writeln( "<TR><TD>3</TD><TD>" + frequency3 +
                     "</TD></TR>" );
   document.writeln( "<TR><TD>4</TD><TD>" + frequency4 +
                     "</TD></TR>" );
   document.writeln( "<TR><TD>5</TD><TD>" + frequency5 +
                     "</TD></TR>" );
   document.writeln( "<TR><TD>6</TD><TD>" + frequency6 +
                     "</TD></TR></TABLE>" );
</SCRIPT>

</HEAD>
<BODY>
<P>Click Refresh (or Reload) to run the script again</P>
</BODY>
</HTML>
```

Fig. 11.5 Rolling a six-sided die 6000 times (part 2 of 3).

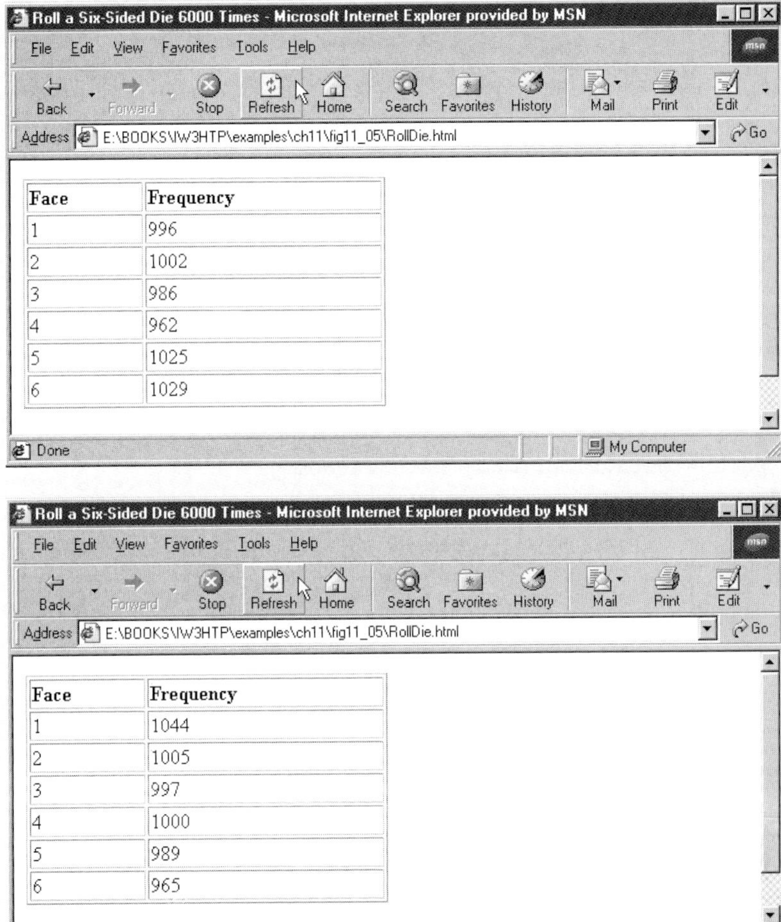

Fig. 11.5 Rolling a six-sided die 6000 times (part 3 of 3).

As the program output shows, by scaling and shifting we used **`Math`** method **`random`** to realistically simulate the rolling of a six-sided die. Note that we used nested control structures to determine the number of times each side of the six-sided die occurred. The **`for`** loop at lines 14 through 37 iterates 6000 times. During each iteration of the loop, line 15 produces a value from 1 to 6. The nested **`switch`** structure at lines 17 through 36 uses the **`face`** value that was randomly chosen as its controlling expression. Based on the value of **`face`**, one of the six counter variables is incremented during each iteration of the loop. Note that *no* **`default`** case is provided in this **`switch`** structure because the statement at line 15 only produces the values 1, 2, 3, 4, 5 and 6. In this example, the **`default`** case would never be executed. After we study **`Array`**s in Chapter 12, we will show how to replace the entire **`switch`** structure in this program with a single-line statement. Run the program several times and observe the results. Notice that a *different* sequence of random numbers is obtained each time the script executes, so the results should vary.

The values produced directly by **random** are always in the range

```
0.0 ≤ Math.random() < 1.0
```

Previously we demonstrated how to write a single statement to simulate the rolling of a six-sided die with the statement

```
face = Math.floor( 1 + Math.random() * 6 );
```

which always assigns an integer (at random) to variable **face** in the range $1 \le$ **face** ≤ 6. Note that the width of this range (i.e., the number of consecutive integers in the range) is 6 and the starting number in the range is 1. Referring to the preceding statement, we see that the width of the range is determined by the number used to scale **random** with the multiplication operator (6 in the preceding statement) and the starting number of the range is equal to the number (1 in the preceding statement) added to **Math.random() * 6**. We can generalize this result as follows:

```
face = Math.floor( a + Math.random() * b );
```

where **a** is the *shifting value* (which is equal to the first number in the desired range of consecutive integers) and **b** is the *scaling factor* (which is equal to the width of the desired range of consecutive integers). In the exercises, we will see that it is possible to choose integers at random from sets of values other than ranges of consecutive integers.

11.6 Example: A Game of Chance

One of the most popular games of chance is a dice game known as "craps," which is played in casinos and back alleys throughout the world. The rules of the game are straightforward:

> *A player rolls two dice. Each die has six faces. These faces contain 1, 2, 3, 4, 5 and 6 spots, respectively. After the dice have come to rest, the sum of the spots on the two upward faces is calculated. If the sum is 7 or 11 on the first throw, the player wins. If the sum is 2, 3 or 12 on the first throw (called "craps"), the player loses (i.e., the "house" wins). If the sum is 4, 5, 6, 8, 9 or 10 on the first throw, that sum becomes the player's "point." To win, you must continue rolling the dice until you "make your point" (i.e., roll your point value). The player loses by rolling a 7 before making the point.*

The script in Fig. 11.6 simulates the game of craps.

```
<!DOCTYPE html PUBLIC "-//W3C//DTD HTML 4.0 Transitional//EN">
<HTML>
<!-- Fig. 11.6: Craps.html -->

<HEAD>
<TITLE>Program that Simulates the Game of Craps</TITLE>

<SCRIPT LANGUAGE = "JavaScript">
   // variables used to test the state of the game
   var WON = 0, LOST = 1, CONTINUE_ROLLING = 2;

```

Fig. 11.6 Program to simulate the game of craps (part 1 of 5).

```
   // other variables used in program
   var firstRoll = true,                    // true if first roll
       sumOfDice = 0,                       // sum of the dice
       myPoint = 0,    // point if no win/loss on first roll
       gameStatus = CONTINUE_ROLLING;       // game not over yet

   // process one roll of the dice
   function play()
   {
      if ( firstRoll ) {                   // first roll of the dice
         sumOfDice = rollDice();

         switch ( sumOfDice ) {
            case 7: case 11:                // win on first roll
               gameStatus = WON;
               craps.point.value = ""; // clear point field
               break;
            case 2: case 3: case 12:        // lose on first roll
               gameStatus = LOST;
               craps.point.value = ""; // clear point field
               break;
            default:                        // remember point
               gameStatus = CONTINUE_ROLLING;
               myPoint = sumOfDice;
               craps.point.value = myPoint;
               firstRoll = false;
         }
      }
      else {
         sumOfDice = rollDice();

         if ( sumOfDice == myPoint )      // win by making point
            gameStatus = WON;
         else
            if ( sumOfDice == 7 )          // lose by rolling 7
               gameStatus = LOST;
      }

      if ( gameStatus == CONTINUE_ROLLING )
         window.status = "Roll again";
      else {
         if ( gameStatus == WON )
            window.status = "Player wins. " +
               "Click Roll Dice to play again.";
         else
            window.status = "Player loses. " +
               "Click Roll Dice to play again.";

         firstRoll = true;
      }
   }

```

Fig. 11.6 Program to simulate the game of craps (part 2 of 5).

```
   // roll the dice
   function rollDice()
   {
      var die1, die2, workSum;

      die1 = Math.floor( 1 + Math.random() * 6 );
      die2 = Math.floor( 1 + Math.random() * 6 );
      workSum = die1 + die2;

      craps.firstDie.value = die1;
      craps.secondDie.value = die2;
      craps.sum.value = workSum;

      return workSum;
   }
</SCRIPT>

</HEAD>
<BODY>
<FORM NAME = "craps">
   <TABLE BORDER = "1">
   <TR><TD>Die 1</TD>
      <TD><INPUT NAME = "firstDie" TYPE = "text"></TD></TR>
   <TR><TD>Die 2</TD>
      <TD><INPUT NAME = "secondDie" TYPE = "text"></TD></TR>
   <TR><TD>Sum</TD>
      <TD><INPUT NAME = "sum" TYPE = "text"></TD></TR>
   <TR><TD>Point</TD>
      <TD><INPUT NAME = "point" TYPE = "text"></TD></TR>
   <TR><TD><INPUT TYPE = "button" VALUE = "Roll Dice"
                  ONCLICK = "play()"></TD></TR>
   </TABLE>
</FORM>
</BODY>
</HTML>
```

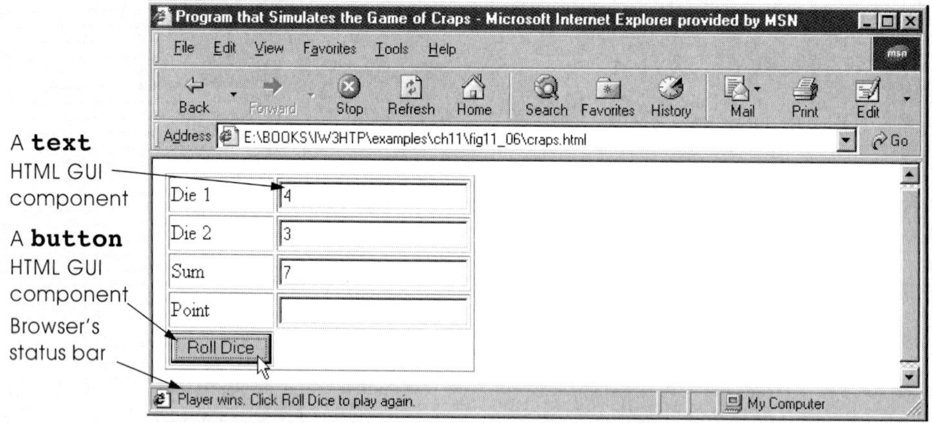

Fig. 11.6 Program to simulate the game of craps (part 3 of 5).

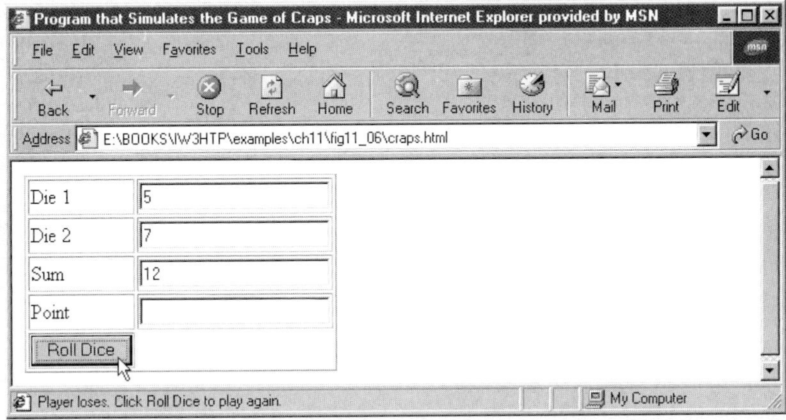

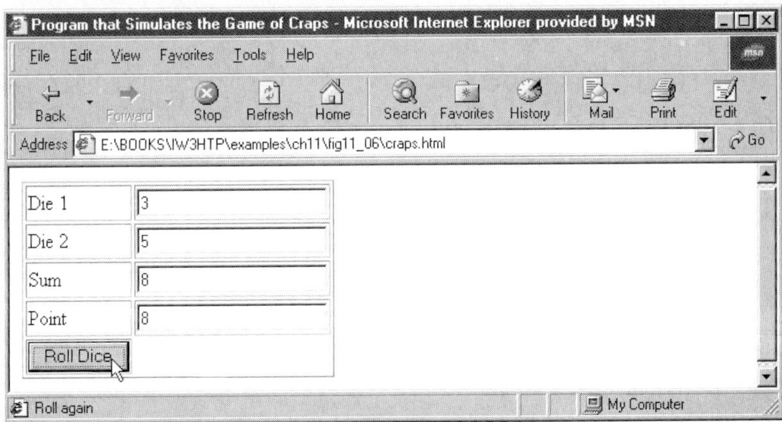

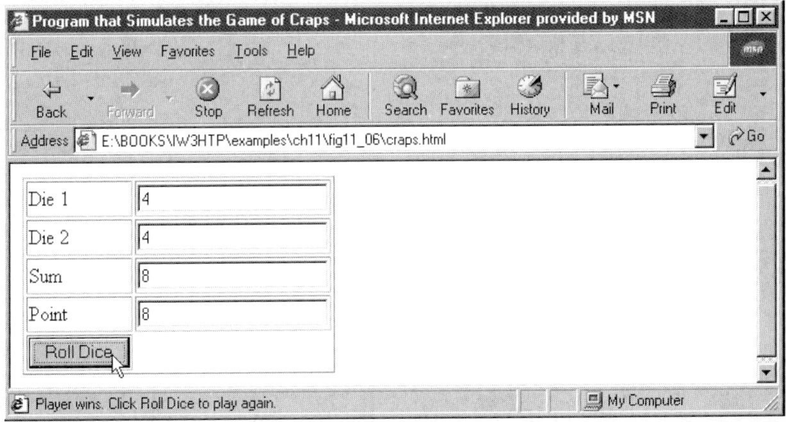

Fig. 11.6 Program to simulate the game of craps (part 4 of 5).

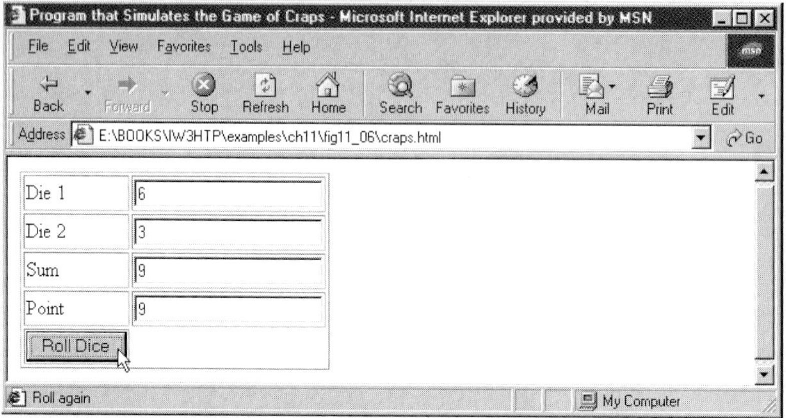

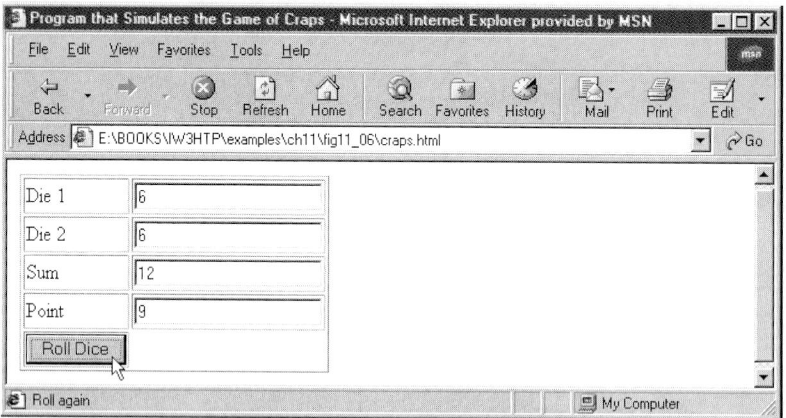

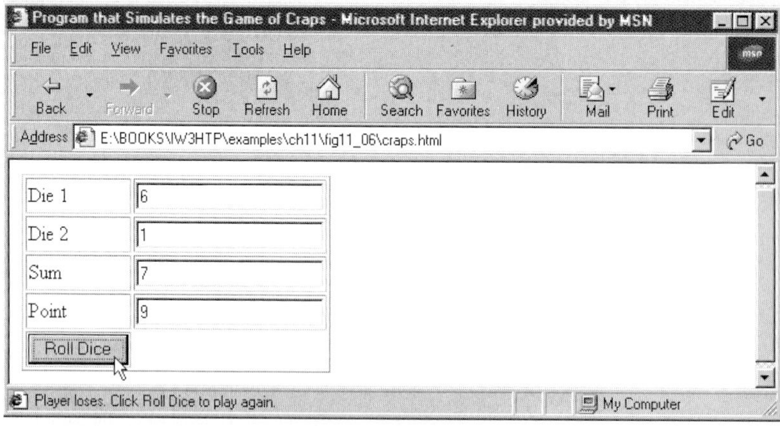

Fig. 11.6 Program to simulate the game of craps (part 5 of 5).

Notice that the player must roll two dice on the first and all subsequent rolls. When you execute the script, click the **Roll Dice** button to play the game. The *status bar* in the lower-left corner of the browser window displays the results of each roll. The screen captures show four separate executions of the script (a win and a loss on the first roll, and a win and a loss after the first roll).

Until now, all user interactions with scripts have been through either a **prompt** dialog (into which the user could type an input value for the program) or an **alert** dialog (in which a message was displayed to the user and the user could click **OK** to dismiss the dialog). Although these are valid ways to receive input from a user and to display messages in a JavaScript program, they are fairly limited in their capabilities—a **prompt** dialog can obtain only one value at a time from the user, and a message dialog can display only one message. It is much more common to receive multiple inputs from the user at once via an HTML *form* (such as the user entering name and address information) or to display many pieces of data at once (such as the values of the dice, the sum of the dice and the point, in this example). To begin our introduction to more elaborate user interfaces, this program uses an HTML form (discussed in Chapter 4) and introduces a new graphical user interface concept—graphical user interface *event handling*. This is our first example in which the JavaScript executes in response to the user's interaction with a GUI component in an HTML form. This interaction causes an *event*. Scripts are often used to respond to events.

Before we discuss the script code, we first discuss the **<BODY>** section (lines 82 through 97) of the HTML document. The GUI components in this section are used extensively in the script.

Line 83,

```
<FORM NAME = "craps">
```

begins the definition of an HTML **<FORM>** with its ***NAME*** attribute set to **craps**. The **NAME** attribute **craps** enables script code to refer to the elements of the form. This attribute helps a script distinguish between multiple forms in the same HTML document. Similarly, the **NAME** attribute is specified for each GUI component in the form, so that the script code can individually refer to each GUI component.

In this example, we decided to place the form's GUI components in an HTML **<TABLE>**, so line 84

```
<TABLE BORDER = "1">
```

begins the definition of the HTML table and indicates that it has a 1-pixel border.

Lines 85 and 86

```
<TR><TD>Die 1</TD>
    <TD><INPUT NAME = "firstDie" TYPE = "text"></TD></TR>
```

define the first row of the table. The left column contains the text **Die 1** and the right column contains the text field named **firstDie**.

Lines 87 and 88

```
<TR><TD>Die 2</TD>
    <TD><INPUT NAME = "secondDie" TYPE = "text"></TD></TR>
```

define the second row of the table. The left column contains the text **Die 2** and the right column contains the text field named **secondDie**.

Lines 89 and 90

```
<TR><TD>Sum</TD>
    <TD><INPUT NAME = "sum" TYPE = "text"></TD></TR>
```

define the third row of the table. The left column contains the text **Sum** and the right column contains the text field named **sum**.

Lines 91 and 92

```
<TR><TD>Point</TD>
    <TD><INPUT NAME = "point" TYPE = "text"></TD></TR>
```

define the fourth row of the table. The left column contains the text **Point** and the right column contains the text field named **point**.

Lines 93 and 94,

```
<TR><TD><INPUT TYPE = "button" VALUE = "Roll Dice"
                ONCLICK = "play()"></TD></TR>
```

define the last row of the table. The left column contains the button **Roll Dice**. The button's attribute ***ONCLICK*** is used to indicate the action to take when the user of this HTML document clicks the **Roll Dice** button. In this example, the script function **play** will be called in response to a button click.

This style of programming is known as *event-driven programming*—the user interacts with a GUI component, the script is notified of the event and the script processes the event. The user's interaction with the GUI "drives" the program. The clicking of the button is known as the *event*. The function that is called when an event occurs is known as an *event handling function* or *event handler*. When a GUI event occurs in a form, the browser *automatically calls* the specified event handling function. Before any event can be processed, each GUI component must know which event handling function will be called when a particular event occurs. Most HTML GUI components have several different event types. The event model is discussed in detail in Chapter 14, "Dynamic HTML: Event Model." By specifying **ONCLICK = "play()"** for the **Roll Dice** button, we enable the browser to *listen for events* (button click events in particular). This is called *registering the event handler* with the GUI component (we also like to call it the *start listening* line, because the browser is now listening for button click events from the button). If not event handler is specified for the **Roll Dice** button, the script will not respond when the user presses the button.

Lines 95 and 96 end the **<TABLE>** and **<FORM>** definitions, respectively.

The game is reasonably involved. The player may win or lose on the first roll, or may win or lose on any roll. Line 10 of the program

```
var WON = 0, LOST = 1, CONTINUE_ROLLING = 2;
```

creates variables that define the three states of a game of craps—game won, game lost or continue rolling the dice. Unlike many other programming languages, JavaScript does not provide a mechanism to define a *constant variable* (the value of such a variable cannot be modified). For this reason, we purposely used all capital letters for these variable names to indicate that we do not intend to modify these variables and to make them stand out in the program.

Good Programming Practice 11.5

Use only uppercase letters (with underscores between words) in the names of variables that should be used as constants. This makes these constants stand out in a program.

Good Programming Practice 11.6

Using meaningfully named variables rather than constants (such as 2) makes programs more readable.

Lines 13 through 16

```
var firstRoll = true,                    // true if first roll
    sumOfDice = 0,                       // sum of the dice
    myPoint = 0,    // point if no win/loss on first roll
    gameStatus = CONTINUE_ROLLING;   // game not over yet
```

declare several variables that are used throughout the script. Variable **firstRoll** indicates whether the next roll of the dice is the first roll in the current game. Variable **sumOfDice** maintains the sum of the dice for the last roll. Variable **myPoint** stores the "point" if the player does not win or lose on the first roll. Variable **gameStatus** keeps track of the current state of the game (**WON**, **LOST** or **CONTINUE_ROLLING**).

We define a function **rollDice** (line 65) to roll the dice and to compute and display their sum. Function **rollDice** is defined once, but it is called from two places in the program (lines 22 and 41). Function **rollDice** takes no arguments, so it has an empty parameter list. Function **rollDice** returns the sum of the two dice.

The user clicks the "**Roll Dice**" button to roll the dice. This invokes function **play** (line 19) of the script. Function **play** checks the boolean variable **firstRoll** (line 21) to determine whether it is **true** or **false**. If it is **true**, this is the first roll of the game. Line 22 calls **rollDice** (defined at line 65), which picks two random values from 1 to 6, displays the value of the first die, the second die and the sum of the dice in the first three text fields and returns the sum of the dice (we discuss function **rollDice** in detail shortly). After the first roll, the nested **switch** structure at line 24 determines whether the game is won or lost, or whether the game should continue with another roll. After the first roll, if the game is not over, **sumOfDice** is saved in **myPoint** and displayed in the text field **point** in the HTML form. Notice how the text field's value is changed at lines 27, 31 and 36. The expression

```
craps.point.value
```

specifies that the script would like to change the ***value*** property of the text field **point**. The **value** property specifies the text to display in the text field. To access this property, we specify the name of the form (**craps**) that contains the text field followed by a *dot operator* (**.**) followed by the name of the text field we would like to manipulate. The dot operator is also known as the *field access operator* or the *member access operator*. In the preceding expression, the dot operator is used to access the **point** member of the **craps** form. Similarly, the second member access operator is used to access the **value** member (or property) of the **point** text field. Actually, we will see in the Dynamic HTML chapters that every element of an HTML document can be accessed in a manner similar to that shown here.

The program proceeds to the nested **if/else** structure at line 50, which sets the **window** object's **status** property (**window.status** at lines 51, 54 and 57) to

```
Roll again.
```

if **gameStatus** is equal to **CONTINUE**, to

```
Player wins. Click Roll Dice to play again.
```

if **gameStatus** is equal to **WON** and to

```
Player loses. Click Roll Dice to play again.
```

if **gameStatus** is equal to **LOST**. The **window** object's **status** property displays the string assigned to it in the status bar of the browser. If the game was won or lost, line 60 sets **firstRoll** to **true** to indicate that the next roll of the dice is the first roll of the next game.

The program then waits for the user to click the button "**Roll Dice**" again. Each time the user presses **Roll Dice**, function **play** is called, which, in turn, calls the **rollDice** function to produce a new value for **sumOfDice**. If **sumOfDice** matches **myPoint**, **gameStatus** is set to **WON**, the **if/else** structure at line 50 executes and the game is complete. If **sum** is equal to **7**, **gameStatus** is set to **LOST**, the **if/else** structure at line 50 executes and the game is complete. Clicking the "**Roll Dice**" button starts a new game. Throughout the program, the four text fields in the HTML form are updated with the new values of the dice and the sum on each roll, and the text field **point** is also updated each time a new game begins.

Function **rollDice** (line 65) defines its own local variables **die1**, **die2** and **workSum** at line 67. Because these variables are defined inside the body of **rollDice**, they are known only in that function. If these three variable names are used elsewhere in the program, they will be entirely separate variables in memory. Lines 69 and 70 pick two random values in the range 1 to 6 and assign them to variables **die1** and **die2** respectively. Lines 73 through 75

```
craps.firstDie.value = die1;
craps.secondDie.value = die2;
craps.sum.value = workSum;
```

assign the values of **die1**, **die2** and **workSum** to the corresponding text fields in the HTML form **craps**. Note that the integer values are automatically converted to strings when they are assigned to each text field's **value** property. Line 77 returns the value of workSum for use in function **play**.

Software Engineering Observation 11.8

Variables that are defined inside the body of a function are known only in that function. If the same variable names are used elsewhere in the program, they will be entirely separate variables in memory.

Note the interesting use of the various program control mechanisms we have discussed. The craps program uses two functions—**play** and **rollDice**—and the **switch**, **if/else** and nested **if** structures. Note also the use of multiple **case** labels in the **switch** structure to execute the same statements (lines 25 and 29). In the exercises, we investigate various interesting characteristics of the game of craps.

11.7 Duration of Identifiers

Chapters 8 through 10 used identifiers for variable names. The attributes of variables include name, value and data type (such as string, number or boolean). We also use identifiers as names for user-defined functions. Actually, each identifier in a program has other attributes, including *duration* and *scope* (discussed in section 11.8).

An identifier's *duration* (also called its *lifetime*) is the period during which that identifier exists in memory. Some identifiers exist briefly, some are repeatedly created and destroyed and others exist for the entire execution of a script.

Identifiers that represent local variables in a function (i.e., parameters and variables declared in the function body) have *automatic duration*. Automatic duration variables are *automatic*ally created when program control enters the function in which they are declared, they exist while the function in which they are declared is active; and they are *automatic*ally destroyed when the function in which they are declared is exited. For the remainder of the text, we will refer to variables of automatic duration as local variables.

Software Engineering Observation 11.9

Automatic duration is a means of conserving memory, because automatic duration variables are created when program control enters the function in which they are declared and are destroyed when the function in which they are declared is exited.

Software Engineering Observation 11.10

Automatic duration is an example of the principle of least privilege. *This principle states that each component of a system should have sufficient rights and privileges to accomplish its designated task, but no additional rights or privileges. This helps prevent accidental and/or malicious errors from occurring in systems. Why have variables stored in memory and accessible when they are not needed?*

JavaScript also has identifiers of *static duration*. Identifiers of static duration are typically defined in the **<HEAD>** section of the HTML document and exist from the point at which the **<HEAD>** section of the HTML document is interpreted until the browsing session terminates (the browser is closed by the user). Even though static duration variables exist after the **<HEAD>** section of the document is interpreted, this does not mean that these identifiers can be used throughout the script. Duration and *scope* (where a name can be used) are separate issues, as shown in Section 11.8. Static duration variables are globally accessible to the script—i.e., every function in the script can potentially use these variables. For the remainder of the text, we refer to variables of static duration as *global variables* or *script-level variables*.

11.8 Scope Rules

The *scope* of an identifier for a variable or function is the portion of the program in which the identifier can be referenced. A local variable declared in a function can be used only in that function. The scopes for an identifier are *global scope* and *function* (or *local*) *scope*.

Identifiers declared inside a function have *function* (or *local*) *scope*. Function scope begins with the opening left brace (**{**) of the function in which the identifier is declared and ends at the terminating right brace (**}**) of the function. Local variables of a function have function scope; so do function parameters, which are also local variables of the function. If a local variable in a function has the same name as a global variable, the global variable is "hidden" from the body of the function.

Good Programming Practice 11.7

Avoid local variable names that hide global variable names. This can be accomplished by avoiding the use of duplicate identifiers in a script.

The script of Fig. 11.7 demonstrates scoping issues with global variables and local variables. This example also demonstrates the event ***ONLOAD***, which calls an event handler when the **<BODY>** of the HTML document is loaded into the browser.

```
<!DOCTYPE html PUBLIC "-//W3C//DTD HTML 4.0 Transitional//EN">
<HTML>
<!-- Fig. 11.7: scoping.html -->

<HEAD>
<TITLE>A Scoping Example</TITLE>

<SCRIPT LANGUAGE = "JavaScript">
   var x = 1;        // global variable

   function start()
   {
      var x = 5;    // variable local to function start

      document.writeln( "local x in start is " + x );

      functionA();    // functionA has local x
      functionB();    // functionB uses global variable x
      functionA();    // functionA reinitializes local x
      functionB();    // global variable x retains its value

      document.writeln(
         "<P>local x in start is " + x + "</P>" );
   }

   function functionA()
   {
      var x = 25;   // initialized each time functionA is called

      document.writeln( "<P>local x in functionA is " + x +
                        " after entering functionA" );
      ++x;
      document.writeln( "<BR>local x in functionA is " + x +
                        " before exiting functionA</P>" );
   }

   function functionB()
   {
      document.writeln( "<P>global variable x is " + x +
                        " on entering functionB" );
      x *= 10;
```

Fig. 11.7 A scoping example. (part 1 of 2)

```
42         document.writeln( "<BR>global variable x is " + x +
43                           " on exiting functionB</P>" );
44     }
45  </SCRIPT>
46
47  </HEAD>
48  <BODY ONLOAD = "start()"></BODY>
49  </HTML>
```

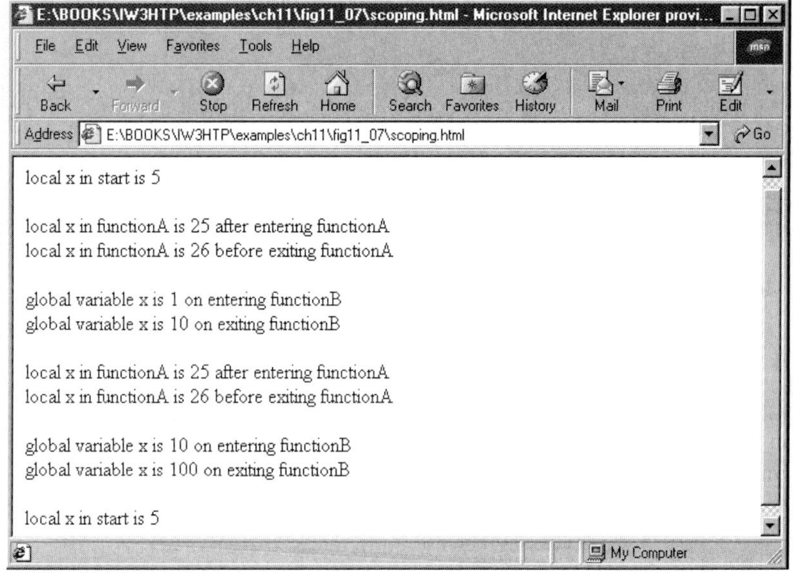

Fig. 11.7 A scoping example. (part 2 of 2)

Global variable **x** (line 9) is declared and initialized to 1. This global variable is hidden in any block (or function) that declares a variable named **x**. Function **start** (line 11) declares a local variable **x** (line 13) and initializes it to **5**. This variable is output in a line of HTML text to show that the global variable **x** is hidden in **start**. The script defines two other functions—**functionA** and **functionB**—that each take no arguments and return nothing. Each function is called twice from function **start**.

Function **functionA** defines local variable **x** (line 28) and initializes it to **25**. When **functionA** is called, the variable is output in a line of HTML text to show that the global variable **x** is hidden in **functionA**, then the variable is incremented and output in a line of HTML text again before exiting the function. Each time this function is called, local variable **x** is recreated and initialized to **25**.

Function **functionB** does not declare any variables. Therefore, when it refers to variable **x**, the global variable **x** is used. When **functionB** is called, the global variable is output in a line of HTML text, multiplied by **10** and output in a line of HTML text again before exiting the function. The next time function **functionB** is called, the global variable has its modified value, **10**. Finally, the program outputs local variable **x** in **start** in a line of HTML text again to show that none of the function calls modified the value of **x** in **start** because the functions all referred to variables in other scopes.

11.9 Recursion

The programs we have discussed are generally structured as functions that call one another in a disciplined, hierarchical manner. For some problems, it is useful to have functions call themselves. A *recursive function* is a function that calls itself either directly or indirectly through another function. Recursion is an important topic discussed at length in upper-level computer science courses. In this section and the next, simple examples of recursion are presented. This book contains an extensive treatment of recursion. Figure 11.12 (at the end of Section 11.11) summarizes the recursion examples and exercises in the book.

We consider recursion conceptually first, then examine several programs containing recursive functions. Recursive problem-solving approaches have a number of elements in common. A recursive function is called to solve a problem. The function actually knows how to solve only the simplest case(s) or so-called *base case(s)*. If the function is called with a base case, the function returns a result. If the function is called with a more complex problem, the function divides the problem into two conceptual pieces: a piece that the function knows how to do (base case) and a piece that the function does not know how to do. To make recursion feasible, the latter piece must resemble the original problem, but be a slightly simpler or slightly smaller version of the original problem. Because this new problem looks like the original problem, the function invokes (calls) a fresh copy of itself to go to work on the smaller problem—this is referred to as a *recursive call* and is also called the *recursion step*. The recursion step also normally includes the keyword **`return`** because its result will be combined with the portion of the problem the function knew how to solve to form a result that will be passed back to the original caller.

The recursion step executes while the original call to the function is still open (i.e., it has not finished executing). The recursion step can result in many more recursive calls, as the function divides each new subproblem into two conceptual pieces. For the recursion to eventually terminate, each time the function calls itself with a slightly simpler version of the original problem, the sequence of smaller and smaller problems must converge on the base case. At that point, the function recognizes the base case, returns a result to the previous copy of the function and a sequence of returns ensues up the line until the original function call eventually returns the final result to the caller. This sounds exotic compared to the conventional problem solving we performed to this point. As an example of these concepts at work, let us write a recursive program to perform a popular mathematical calculation.

The factorial of a nonnegative integer n, written $n!$ (and pronounced "n factorial"), is the product

$$n \cdot (n - 1) \cdot (n - 2) \cdot \ldots \cdot 1$$

with 1! equal to 1 and 0! defined to be 1. For example, 5! is the product $5 \cdot 4 \cdot 3 \cdot 2 \cdot 1$, which is equal to 120.

The factorial of an integer (**`number`** in the following example) greater than or equal to 0, can be calculated *iteratively* (nonrecursively) using **`for`** as follows:

```
var factorial = 1;

for ( var counter = number; counter >= 1; --counter )
   factorial *= counter;
```

A recursive definition of the factorial function is arrived at by observing the following relationship:

$$n! = n \cdot (n-1)!$$

For example, 5! is clearly equal to 5 * 4!, as is shown by the following:

$$5! = 5 \cdot 4 \cdot 3 \cdot 2 \cdot 1$$
$$5! = 5 \cdot (4 \cdot 3 \cdot 2 \cdot 1)$$
$$5! = 5 \cdot (4!)$$

The evaluation of 5! would proceed as shown in Fig. 11.8. Figure 11.8a shows how the succession of recursive calls proceeds until 1! is evaluated to be 1, which terminates the recursion. Figure 11.8b shows the values returned from each recursive call to its caller until the final value is calculated and returned.

The program of Fig. 11.9 uses recursion to calculate and print the factorials of the integers 0 to 10. The recursive function **`factorial`** first tests (line 21) to see if a terminating condition is **`true`** (i.e., is **`number`** less than or equal to 1). If **`number`** is indeed less than or equal to 1, **`factorial`** returns 1, no further recursion is necessary and the function returns. If **`number`** is greater than 1, line 24

```
return number * factorial( number - 1 );
```

expresses the problem as the product of **`number`** and a recursive call to **`factorial`** evaluating the factorial of **`number - 1`**. Note that **`factorial( number - 1 )`** is a slightly simpler problem than the original calculation **`factorial( number )`**.

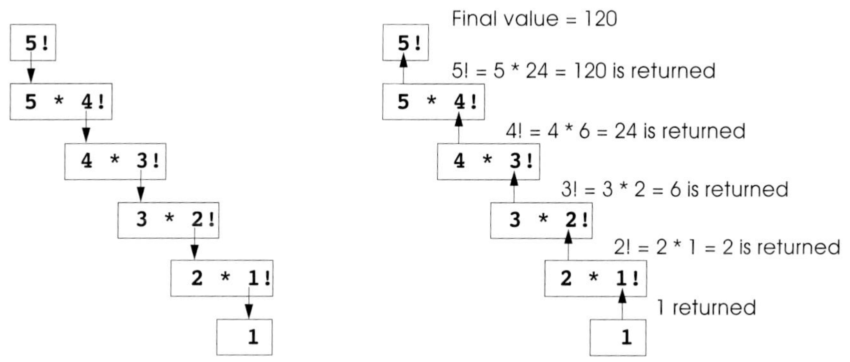

a) Procession of recursive calls. b) Values returned from each recursive call.

Fig. 11.8 Recursive evaluation of *5!*.

```
1  <!DOCTYPE html PUBLIC "-//W3C//DTD HTML 4.0 Transitional//EN">
2  <HTML>
3  <!-- Fig. 11.9: FactorialTest.html -->
4
```

Fig. 11.9 Calculating factorials with a recursive function (part 1 of 2).

```
<HEAD>
<TITLE>Recursive Factorial Function</TITLE>

<SCRIPT LANGUAGE = "JavaScript">
   document.writeln( "<H1>Factorials of 1 to 10</H1>" );
   document.writeln( "<TABLE BORDER = '1' WIDTH = '100%'>" );

   for ( var i = 0; i <= 10; i++ )
      document.writeln( "<TR><TD>" + i + "!</TD><TD>" +
                        factorial( i ) + "</TD></TR>" );

   document.writeln( "</TABLE>" );

   // Recursive definition of function factorial
   function factorial( number )
   {
      if ( number <= 1 )  // base case
         return 1;
      else
         return number * factorial( number - 1 );
   }
</SCRIPT>

</HEAD><BODY></BODY>
</HTML>
```

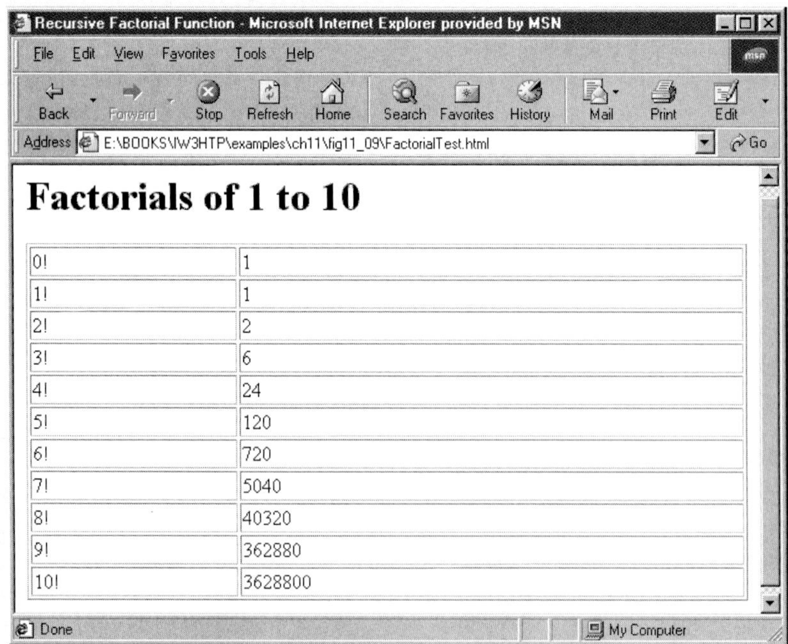

Fig. 11.9 Calculating factorials with a recursive function (part 2 of 2).

Function **`factorial`** (line 19) receives as its argument the value for which to calculate the factorial. As can be seen in the screen capture of Fig. 11.9, factorial values become large quickly. Because JavaScript uses floating-point numeric representations, we are able to calculate factorials of larger numbers.

Common Programming Error 11.6

Forgetting to return a value from a recursive function when one is needed results in a logic error.

Common Programming Error 11.7

Either omitting the base case or writing the recursion step incorrectly so that it does not converge on the base case will cause infinite recursion, eventually exhausting memory. This is analogous to the problem of an infinite loop in an iterative (nonrecursive) solution.

Testing and Debugging Tip 11.2

Internet Explorer displays a message when a script takes an unusually long time to execute. This allows the user of the Web page to recover from a script that contains an infinite loop or infinite recursion.

11.10 Example Using Recursion: The Fibonacci Series

The Fibonacci series

0, 1, 1, 2, 3, 5, 8, 13, 21, …

begins with 0 and 1 and has the property that each subsequent Fibonacci number is the sum of the previous two Fibonacci numbers.

The series occurs in nature and, in particular, describes a form of spiral. The ratio of successive Fibonacci numbers converges on a constant value of 1.618…. This number, too, repeatedly occurs in nature and has been called the *golden ratio* or the *golden mean.* Humans tend to find the golden mean aesthetically pleasing. Architects often design windows, rooms and buildings whose length and width are in the ratio of the golden mean. Postcards are often designed with a golden mean length/width ratio.

The Fibonacci series may be defined recursively as follows:

$$fibonacci(\ 0\ ) = 0$$
$$fibonacci(\ 1\ ) = 1$$
$$fibonacci(\ n\ ) = fibonacci(\ n - 1\ ) + fibonacci(\ n - 2\ )$$

Note that there are two base cases for the Fibonacci calculation—*fibonacci(0)* is defined to be 0 and *fibonacci(1)* is defined to be 1. The script of Fig. 11.10 calculates the ith Fibonacci number recursively using function **`fibonacci`**. Lines 32 through 41 define an HTML form (**`myForm`**) consisting of two text fields and a button. The user enters an integer in the first text field (**`number`**), indicating the ith Fibonacci number to calculate, and presses the **Calculate** button. When the event occurs, function **`getFibonacciValue`** (defined at line 10) executes in response to the user interface event and calls recursive function **`fibonacci`** (defined at line 20) to calculate the specified Fibonacci number. Notice that Fibonacci numbers tend to become large quickly. In Fig. 11.10, the screen captures show the results of calculating several Fibonacci numbers.

```
<!DOCTYPE html PUBLIC "-//W3C//DTD HTML 4.0 Transitional//EN">
<HTML>
<!-- Fig. 11.10: FibonacciTest.html -->

<HEAD>
<TITLE>Recursive Fibonacci Function</TITLE>

<SCRIPT LANGUAGE = "JavaScript">
   // Event handler for button HTML component in myForm
   function getFibonacciValue()
   {
      var value = parseInt( document.myForm.number.value );
      window.status =
         "Calculating Fibonacci number for " + value;
      document.myForm.result.value = fibonacci( value );
      window.status = "Done calculating Fibonacci number";
   }

   // Recursive definition of function fibonacci
   function fibonacci( n )
   {
      if ( n == 0 || n == 1 )  // base case
         return n;
      else
         return fibonacci( n - 1 ) + fibonacci( n - 2 );
   }
</SCRIPT>

</HEAD>

<BODY>
<FORM NAME = "myForm">
   <TABLE BORDER = "1">
   <TR><TD>Enter an integer</TD>
      <TD><INPUT NAME = "number" TYPE = "text"></TD>
      <TD><INPUT TYPE = "button" VALUE = "Calculate"
                 ONCLICK = "getFibonacciValue()"</TR>
   <TR><TD>Fibonacci value</TD>
      <TD><INPUT NAME = "result" TYPE = "text"></TD></TR>
   </TABLE>
</FORM></BODY>
</HTML>
```

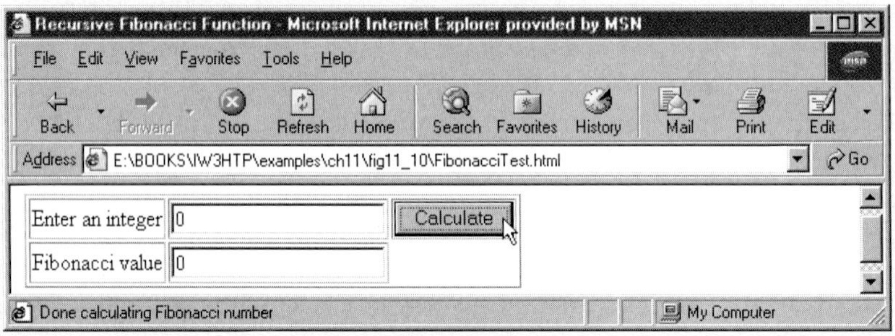

Fig. 11.10 Recursively generating Fibonacci numbers (part 1 of 3).

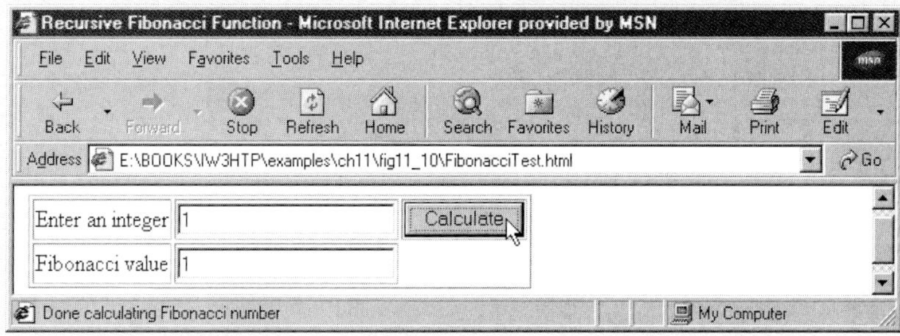

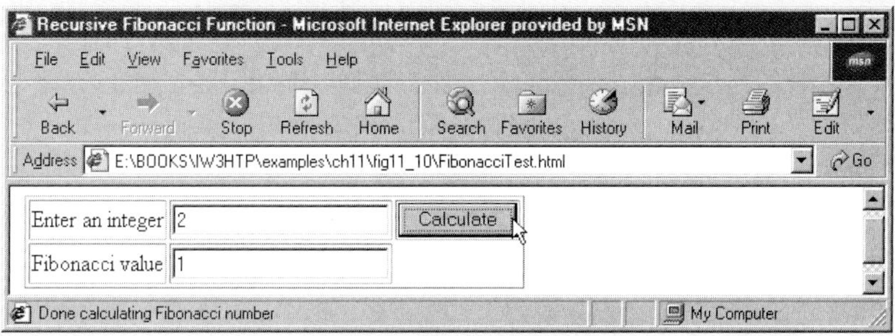

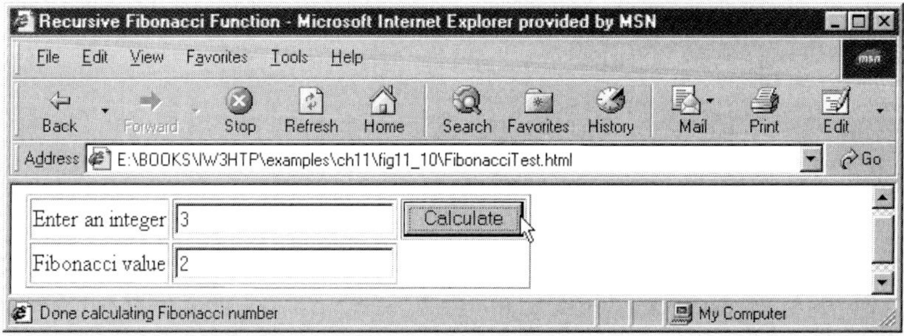

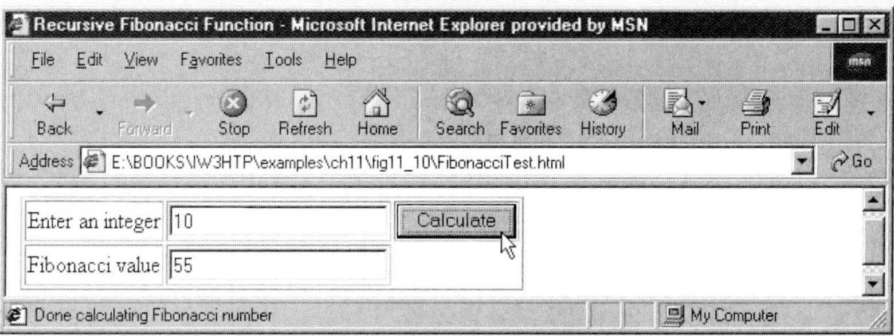

Fig. 11.10 Recursively generating Fibonacci numbers (part 2 of 3).

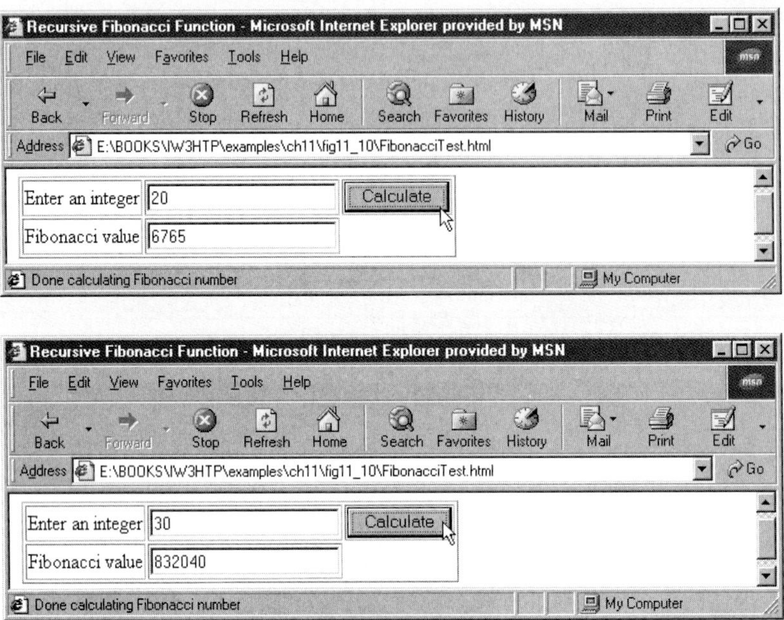

Fig. 11.10 Recursively generating Fibonacci numbers (part 3 of 3).

The event handling in this example is similar to the event handling of the **Craps** script in Fig. 11.6. Lines 36 and 37

```
<TD><INPUT TYPE = "button" VALUE = "Calculate"
          ONCLICK = "getFibonacciValue()"</TR>
```

define the form's button and specify function **getFibonacciValue** as the event handler for the button's **ONCLICK** event. When function **getFibonacciValue** is called, it converts from a string to an integer the value the user typed into the number text field (line 12). Then, the value is displayed in the browser's status bar (lines 13 and 14). Next, the value is passed to function **fibonacci** (line 15), and the result is displayed in the text field **result** (line 15). Finally, a message is displayed in the browser's status bar, indicating that the call to function **fibonacci** is complete.

The call to **fibonacci** (line 15) from **getFibonacciValue** is not a recursive call, but all subsequent calls to **fibonacci** are recursive. Each time **fibonacci** is invoked, it immediately tests for the base case—**n** equal to 0 or 1. If this is true, **n** is returned (*fibonacci(0)* is 0 and *fibonacci(1)* is 1). Interestingly, if **n** is greater than 1, the recursion step generates *two* recursive calls, each of which is for a slightly simpler problem than the original call to **fibonacci**. Figure 11.11 shows how function **fibonacci** would evaluate **fibonacci(3)**—we abbreviate **fibonacci** as **f** to make the figure more readable.

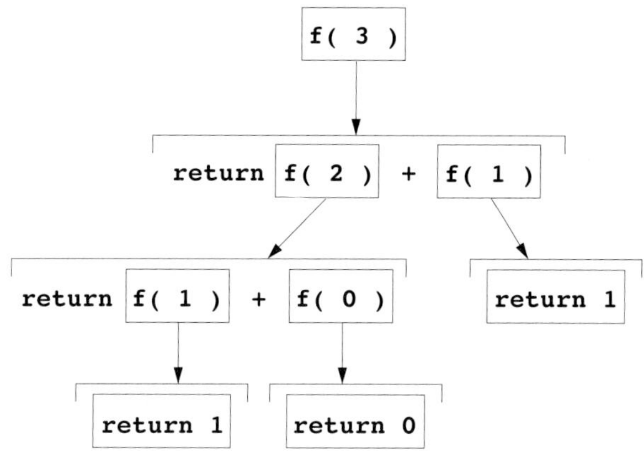

Fig. 11.11 Set of recursive calls to function **fibonacci**.

This figure raises some interesting issues about the order in which JavaScript interpreters will evaluate the operands of operators. This is a different issue from the order in which operators are applied to their operands, namely the order dictated by the rules of operator precedence. From Fig. 11.11 it appears that while evaluating **f(3)**, two recursive calls will be made, namely **f(2)** and **f(1)**. But in what order will these calls be made? Most programmers assume the operands will be evaluated left to right. In JavaScript this is true.

The C and C++ languages (on which many of JavaScript's features are based) do not specify the order in which the operands of most operators (including +) are evaluated. Therefore, the programmer can make no assumption in those languages about the order in which these calls execute. The calls could in fact execute **f(2)** first, then **f(1)**, or the calls could execute in the reverse order: **f(1)**, then **f(2)**. In this program and in most other programs, it turns out the final result would be the same. But in some programs the evaluation of an operand may have *side effects* that could affect the final result of the expression.

The JavaScript language specifies that the order of evaluation of the operands is left to right. Thus, the function calls are in fact **f(2)** first, then **f(1)**.

Good Programming Practice 11.8

Do not write expressions that depend on the order of evaluation of the operands of an operator. This often results in programs that are difficult to read, debug, modify and maintain.

A word of caution is in order about recursive programs like the one we use here to generate Fibonacci numbers. Each invocation of the **fibonacci** function that does not match one of the base cases (i.e., 0 or 1) results in two more recursive calls to the **fibonacci** function. This rapidly gets out of hand. Calculating the Fibonacci value of 20 using the program in Fig. 11.10 requires 21,891 calls to the **fibonacci** function; calculating the Fibonacci value of 30 requires 2,692,537 calls to the **fibonacci** function.

As you try larger values, you will notice that each consecutive Fibonacci number you ask the script to calculate results in a substantial increase in calculation time and number of calls to the **fibonacci** function. For example, the Fibonacci value of 31 requires 4,356,617 calls and the Fibonacci value of 32 requires 7,049,155 calls. As you can see, the number of calls to Fibonacci is increasing quickly—1,664,080 additional calls between Fibonacci of 30 and 31 and 2,692,538 additional calls between Fibonacci of 31 and 32. This difference in number of calls made between Fibonacci of 31 and 32 is more than 1.5 times the difference between Fibonacci of 30 and 31. Problems of this nature humble even the world's most powerful computers! Computer scientists study, in the field of complexity theory, how hard algorithms have to work to do their jobs. Complexity issues are discussed in detail in the upper-level computer science curriculum course generally called "Algorithms."

Performance Tip 11.2

Avoid Fibonacci-style recursive programs, which result in an exponential "explosion" of calls.

11.11 Recursion vs. Iteration

In the previous sections, we studied two functions that can easily be implemented either recursively or iteratively. In this section we compare the two approaches and discuss why the programmer might choose one approach over the other in a particular situation.

Both iteration and recursion are based on a control structure: Iteration uses a repetition structure (such as **`for`**, **`while`** or **`do/while`**); recursion uses a selection structure (such as **`if`**, **`if/else`** or **`switch`**). Both iteration and recursion involve repetition: Iteration explicitly uses a repetition structure; recursion achieves repetition through repeated function calls. Iteration and recursion each involve a termination test: Iteration terminates when the loop-continuation condition fails; recursion terminates when a base case is recognized. Iteration with counter-controlled repetition and recursion each gradually approach termination: Iteration keeps modifying a counter until the counter assumes a value that makes the loop-continuation condition fail; recursion keeps producing simpler versions of the original problem until the base case is reached. Both iteration and recursion can occur infinitely: An infinite loop occurs with iteration if the loop-continuation test never becomes false; infinite recursion occurs if the recursion step does not reduce the problem each time via a sequence that converges on the base case or if the base case is incorrect.

Recursion has many negatives. It repeatedly invokes the mechanism, and consequently the overhead, of function calls. This effect can be expensive in both processor time and memory space. Each recursive call causes another copy of the function (actually, only the function's variables) to be created; this effect can consume considerable memory. Iteration normally occurs within a function, so the overhead of repeated function calls and extra memory assignment is omitted. So why choose recursion?

Software Engineering Observation 11.11

Any problem that can be solved recursively can also be solved iteratively (nonrecursively). A recursive approach is normally chosen in preference to an iterative approach when the recursive approach more naturally mirrors the problem and results in a program that is easier to understand and debug. Another reason to choose a recursive solution is that an iterative solution may not be apparent.

Performance Tip 11.3

Avoid using recursion in performance-oriented situations. Recursive calls take time and consume additional memory.

Common Programming Error 11.8

Accidentally having a nonrecursive function call itself, either directly, or indirectly through another function, can cause infinite recursion.

Most programming textbooks introduce recursion much later than we have done here. We feel that recursion is a sufficiently rich and complex topic that it is better to introduce it earlier and spread the examples over the remainder of the JavaScript chapters. Figure 11.12 summarizes the recursion examples and exercises in the text.

Let us reconsider some observations we make repeatedly throughout the book. Good software engineering is important. High performance is often important. Unfortunately, these goals are often at odds with one another. Good software engineering is key to making more manageable the task of developing larger and more complex software systems. High performance in these systems is key to realizing the systems of the future, which will place ever greater computing demands on hardware. Where do functions fit in here?

Software Engineering Observation 11.12

Modularizing programs in a neat, hierarchical manner promotes good software engineering, sometimes at the expense of performance.

Performance Tip 11.4

A heavily modularized program—as compared to a monolithic (i.e., one-piece) program without functions—makes potentially large numbers of function calls, and these consume execution time and space on a computer's processor(s). But monolithic programs are difficult to program, test, debug, maintain and evolve. So modularize your programs judiciously, always keeping in mind the delicate balance between performance and good software engineering.

Chapter	Recursion examples and exercises
11	Factorial function
	Fibonacci function
	Greatest common divisor
	Sum of two integers
	Multiply two integers
	Raising an integer to an integer power
	Towers of Hanoi
	Visualizing recursion
12	Sum the elements of an array
	Print an array
	Print an array backward
	Check if a string is a palindrome
	Minimum value in an array
	Selection sort
	Eight Queens
	Linear search
	Binary search
	Quicksort
	Maze traversal
13	Printing a string input at the keyboard backward

Fig. 11.12 Summary of recursion examples and exercises in the text.

11.12 JavaScript Global Functions

JavaScript provides seven functions that are available globally in a JavaScript. We have already used two of these functions—**`parseInt`** and **`parseFloat`**. The global functions are summarized in Fig. 11.13.

Global function	Description
`escape`	This function takes a string argument and returns a string in which all spaces, punctuation, accent characters and any other character that is not in the ASCII character set (see Appendix C, "Character Set") are encoded in a hexadecimal format (see Appendix F, "Number Systems") that can be represented on all platforms.
`eval`	This function takes a string argument representing JavaScript code to execute. The JavaScript interpreter evaluates the code and executes it when the **`eval`** function is called. This function allows JavaScript code to be stored as strings and executed dynamically.
`isFinite`	This function takes a numeric argument and returns **`true`** if the value of the argument is not **`NaN`**, **`Number.POSITIVE_INFINITY`** or **`Number.NEGATIVE_INFINITY`**; otherwise the function returns **`false`**.
`isNaN`	This function takes a numeric argument and returns **`true`** if the value of the argument is not a number; otherwise the function returns **`false`**. The function is commonly used with the return value of **`parseInt`** or **`parseFloat`** to determine whether the result is a proper numeric value.
`parseFloat`	This function takes a string argument and attempts to convert the beginning of the string into a floating-point value. If the conversion is not successful, the function returns **`NaN`**; otherwise, it returns the converted value (e.g., **`parseFloat( "abc123.45" )`** returns **`NaN`** and **`parseFloat( "123.45abc" )`** returns the floating-point value **`123.45`**.
`parseInt`	This function takes a string argument and attempts to convert the beginning of the string into an integer value. If the conversion is not successful, the function returns **`NaN`**; otherwise, it returns the converted value (e.g., **`parseInt( "abc123" )`** returns **`NaN`** and **`parseInt( "123abc" )`** returns the integer value **`123`**. This function takes an optional second argument between 2 and 36 specifying the *radix* (or *base*) of the number. For example, 2 indicates that the first argument string is in *binary* format, 8 indicates that the first argument string is in *octal* format and 16 indicates that the first argument string is in *hexadecimal* format. See Appendix F, "Number Systems" for more information on binary, octal and hexadecimal numbers.
`unescape`	This function takes a string as its argument and returns a string in which all characters that we previously encoded with **`escape`** are decoded.

Fig. 11.13 **`JavaScript`** global functions.

Actually, the global functions in Fig. 11.13 are all part of JavaScript's ***Global** object*. The **Global** object contains all the global variables in the script, all the user-defined functions in the script and the functions of Fig. 11.13. Because global functions and user-defined functions are part of the **Global** object, some JavaScript programmers refer to these functions as methods. We will use the term "method" only when referring to a function that is called for a particular object (such as **Math.random()**). As a JavaScript programmer, you do not need to use the **Global** object directly; JavaScript does this for you.

SUMMARY

- Experience has shown that the best way to develop and maintain a large program is to construct it from small, simple pieces or modules. This technique is called divide and conquer.
- Modules in JavaScript are called functions. JavaScript programs are written by combining new functions that the programmer writes with "prepackaged" functions and objects available in JavaScript.
- The "prepackaged" functions that belong to JavaScript objects are often called *methods*. The term *method* implies that the function belongs to a particular object.
- The programmer can write programmer-defined functions to define specific tasks that may be used at many points in a script. The actual statements defining the function are written only once, and these statements are hidden from other functions.
- A function is invoked by a function call. The function call specifies the function name and provides information (as arguments) that the called function needs to do its task.
- Functions allow the programmer to modularize a program.
- All variables declared in function definitions are local variables—they are known only in the function in which they are defined.
- Most functions have parameters that provide the means for communicating information between functions via function calls. A function's parameters are also considered to be local variables.
- The divide-and-conquer approach to program development makes program development more manageable.
- Using existing functions as building blocks to create new programs promotes software reusability. With good function naming and definition, programs can be created from standardized functions rather than be built by using customized code.
- The **()** represent the *function call operator.*
- The **return** *statement* passes the result of a function call back to the calling function.
- The format of a function definition is

```
function function-name( parameter-list )
{
    declarations and statements
}
```

  The *function-name* is any valid identifier. The *parameter-list* is a comma-separated list containing the names of the parameters received by the function when it is called. There should be one argument in the function call for each parameter in the function definition. If a function does not receive any values, the *parameter-list* is empty (i.e., the function name is followed by an empty set of parentheses).
- The declarations and statements within braces form the function body. The function body is also referred to as a block. A block is a compound statement that includes declarations. Variables can be declared in any block and blocks can be nested.

- There are three ways to return control to the point at which a function was invoked. If the function does not return a result, control is returned when the function-ending right brace is reached or by executing the statement

```
return;
```

- If the function does return a result, the statement

```
return expression;
```

- returns the value of *expression* to the caller. When a **return** statement is executed, control returns immediately to the point at which a function was invoked.
- The **Math** object's **max** method determines the larger of its two argument values.
- The **Math** object's ***random*** method generates a floating-point value from 0.0 up to (but not including) 1.0.
- **Math** method **floor** rounds its floating-point number argument to the closest integer not greater than its argument's value.
- The values produced directly by **random** are always in the range

```
0.0 ≤ Math.random() < 1.0
```

- We can generalize picking a random number from a range of values by writing:

```
value = Math.floor( a + Math.random() * b );
```

- where **a** is the *shifting value* (the first number in the desired range of consecutive integers) and **b** is the *scaling factor* (the width of the desired range of consecutive integers).
- Graphical user interface *event handling* enables JavaScript code to execute in response to the user's interaction with a GUI component in an HTML form. This interaction causes an *event*. Scripts are often used to respond to events.
- Specifying the **NAME** attribute of an HTML **<FORM>** enables script code to refer to the elements of the form. This attribute helps a script distinguish between multiple forms in the same HTML document. Similarly, the **NAME** attribute is specified for each GUI component in the form, so the script code can individually refer to each GUI component.
- An HTML button's attribute **ONCLICK** indicates the action to take when the user clicks the button.
- When the user interacts with a GUI component, the script is notified of the event, and the script processes the event. The user's interaction with the GUI "drives" the program. This style of programming is known as *event-driven programming*.
- The clicking of the button (or any other GUI interaction) is known as the *event*. The function that is called when an event occurs is known as an *event handling function* or *event handler*. When a GUI event occurs in a form, the browser *automatically calls* the specified event handling function.
- The **value** property specifies the text to display in an HTML text field GUI component.
- The *dot operator* (**.**) is known as the *field access operator* or the *member access operator*.
- Each identifier in a program has many attributes, including *duration* and *scope*.
- An identifier's duration or lifetime is the period during which that identifier exists in memory.
- Identifiers that represent local variables in a function have automatic duration. Automatic duration variables are *automatic*ally created when program control enters the function in which they are declared, they exist while the function in which they are declared is active; and they are *automatic*ally destroyed when the function in which they are declared is exited.
- Identifiers of static duration are typically defined in the **<HEAD>** section of the HTML document and exist from the point at which the **<HEAD>** section of the HTML document is interpreted until the browsing session terminates.

- Variables of static duration are normally called *global variables* or *script-level variables.*
- The scope of an identifier for a variable or function is the portion of the program in which the identifier can be referenced. The scopes for an identifier are *global scope* and function (or local) scope.
- Event **ONLOAD** calls an event handler when the **<BODY>** of the HTML document is loaded into the browser.
- Identifiers declared inside a function have function (or local) scope. Function scope begins with the opening left brace (**{**) of the function in which the identifier is declared and ends at the terminating right brace (**}**) of the function. Local variables of a function have function scope, as do function parameters, which are also local variables of the function.
- If a local variable in a function has the same name as a global variable, the global variable is "hidden" from the body of the function.
- A recursive function is a function that calls itself either directly or indirectly.
- If a recursive function is called with a base case, the function returns a result. If the function is called with a more complex problem, the function divides the problem into two or more conceptual pieces: a piece that the function knows how to do, and a slightly smaller version of the original problem. Because this new problem looks like the original problem, the function launches a recursive call to work on the smaller problem.
- For recursion to terminate, each time the recursive function calls itself with a slightly simpler version of the original problem, the sequence of smaller and smaller problems must converge on the base case. When the function recognizes the base case, the result is returned to the previous function call and a sequence of returns ensues all the way up the line until the original call of the function eventually returns the final result.
- Both iteration and recursion are based on a control structure: Iteration uses a repetition structure; recursion uses a selection structure.
- Both iteration and recursion involve repetition: Iteration explicitly uses a repetition structure; recursion achieves repetition through repeated function calls.
- Iteration and recursion each involve a termination test: Iteration terminates when the loop-continuation condition fails; recursion terminates when a base case is recognized.
- Iteration and recursion can occur infinitely: An infinite loop occurs with iteration if the loop-continuation test never becomes false; infinite recursion occurs if the recursion step does not reduce the problem in a manner that converges on the base case.
- Recursion repeatedly invokes the mechanism, and consequently the overhead, of function calls. This effect can be expensive in both processor time and memory space.
- Function **escape** takes a string argument and returns a string in which all spaces, punctuation, accent characters and any other character that is not in the ASCII character set (see Appendix C, "Character Set") are encoded in a hexadecimal format that can be represented on all platforms.
- Function **eval** takes a string argument representing JavaScript code to execute. The JavaScript interpreter evaluates the code and executes it when the **eval** function is called.
- Function **isFinite** takes a numeric argument and returns **true** if the value of the argument is not **NaN**, **Number.POSITIVE_INFINITY** or **Number.NEGATIVE_INFINITY**; otherwise the function returns **false**.
- Function **isNaN** takes a numeric argument and returns **true** if the value of the argument is not a number; otherwise the function returns **false**.
- Function **parseFloat** takes a string argument and attempts to convert the beginning of the string into a floating-point value. If the conversion is not successful, the function returns **NaN**; otherwise, it returns the converted value.

- Function **parseInt** takes a string argument and attempts to convert the beginning of the string into an integer value. If the conversion is not successful, the function returns **NaN**; otherwise, it returns the converted value. This function takes an optional second argument between 2 and 36 specifying the *radix* (or *base*) of the number.
- Function **unescape** takes a string as its argument and returns a string in which all characters that we previously encoded with **escape** are decoded.
- JavaScript's global functions are all part of the **Global** *object,* which also contains all the global variables in the script and all the user-defined functions in the script.

TERMINOLOGY

argument in a function call
automatic duration
automatic variable
base case in recursion
block
call a function
called function
caller
calling function
compound statement
converge on the base case
copy of a value
divide and conquer
dot operator (**.**)
duration
escape function
eval function
event
event-driven programming
event handler
event handling function
field access operator (**.**)
floor method of the **Math** object
function
function argument
function body
function call
function call operator, **()**
function definition
function keyword
function name
function parameter
function scope
Global object
global scope
global variable
invoke a function
isFinite function
isNaN function
iteration
lifetime
local scope
local variable
max method of the **Math** object
member access operator (**.**)
method
modularize a program
module
NAME attribute of an HTML **<FORM>**
ONCLICK
ONLOAD
parameter in a function definition
parseFloat function
parseInt function
programmer-defined function
random method of the **Math** object
random number generation
recursion
recursion step
recursive call
recursive function
respond to an event
return statement
scaling
scaling factor
scope
script-level variable
shifting
shifting value
side effect
signature
simulation
software engineering
software reusability
static duration
unescape function
value property of an HTML text field

COMMON PROGRAMMING ERRORS

11.1 Using the JavaScript **var** keyword to declare a variable in a function parameter list results in a JavaScript runtime error.

11.2 Forgetting to return a value from a function that is supposed to return a value is a logic error.

11.3 Placing a semicolon after the right parenthesis enclosing the parameter list of a function definition results in a JavaScript runtime error.

11.4 Redefining a function parameter as a local variable in the function is a logic error.

11.5 Passing to a function an argument that is not compatible with the corresponding parameter's expected type is a logic error and may result in a JavaScript runtime error.

11.6 Forgetting to return a value from a recursive function when one is needed results in a logic error.

11.7 Either omitting the base case or writing the recursion step incorrectly so that it does not converge on the base case will cause infinite recursion, eventually exhausting memory. This is analogous to the problem of an infinite loop in an iterative (nonrecursive) solution.

11.8 Accidentally having a nonrecursive function call itself, either directly, or indirectly through another function, can cause infinite recursion.

GOOD PROGRAMMING PRACTICES

11.1 Familiarize yourself with the rich collection of objects and methods provided by JavaScript.

11.2 Place a blank line between function definitions to separate the functions and enhance program readability.

11.3 Although it is not incorrect to do so, do not use the same names for the arguments passed to a function and the corresponding parameters in the function definition. This helps avoid ambiguity.

11.4 Choosing meaningful function names and meaningful parameter names makes programs more readable and helps avoid excessive use of comments.

11.5 Use only uppercase letters (with underscores between words) in the names of variables that should be used as constants. This makes these constants stand out in a program.

11.6 Using meaningfully named variables rather than constants (such as 2) makes programs more readable.

11.7 Avoid local variable names that hide global variable names. This effect can be accomplished by avoiding the use of duplicate identifiers in a script.

11.8 Do not write expressions that depend on the order of evaluation of the operands of an operator. This often results in programs that are difficult to read, debug, modify and maintain.

PERFORMANCE TIPS

11.1 Do not try to rewrite existing methods of JavaScript objects to make them more efficient. You usually will not be able to increase the performance of these methods.

11.2 Avoid Fibonacci-style recursive programs, which result in an exponential "explosion" of calls.

11.3 Avoid using recursion in performance-oriented situations. Recursive calls take time and consume additional memory.

11.4 A heavily modularized program—as compared to a monolithic (i.e., one-piece) program without functions—makes potentially large numbers of function calls, and these consume execution time and space on a computer's processor(s). But monolithic programs are difficult to program, test, debug, maintain and evolve. So modularize your programs judiciously, always keeping in mind the delicate balance between performance and good software engineering.

PORTABILITY TIP

11.1 Using the methods built into JavaScript objects helps make programs more portable.

SOFTWARE ENGINEERING OBSERVATIONS

11.1 Avoid reinventing the wheel. When possible, use JavaScript objects and methods instead of writing new functions. This reduces program development time and avoids introducing new errors.

11.2 Each function should be limited to performing a single, well-defined task, and the function name should effectively express that task. This promotes software reusability.

11.3 If you cannot choose a concise name that expresses what the function does, it is possible that your function is attempting to perform too many diverse tasks. It is usually best to break such a function into several smaller functions.

11.4 Statements that are enclosed in the body of a function definition will not be executed by the JavaScript interpreter unless the function is explicitly invoked (called).

11.5 A function should usually be no longer than one printed page. Better yet, a function should usually be no longer than half a printed page. Regardless of how long a function is, it should perform one task well. Small functions promote software reusability.

11.6 Scripts should be written as collections of small functions. This makes programs easier to write, debug, maintain and modify.

11.7 A function requiring a large number of parameters may be performing too many tasks. Consider dividing the function into smaller functions that perform the separate tasks. The function header should fit on one line if possible.

11.8 Variables that are defined inside the body of a function are known only in that function. If the same variable names are used elsewhere in the program, they will be entirely separate variables in memory.

11.9 Automatic duration is a means of conserving memory, because automatic duration variables are created when program control enters the function in which they are declared and are destroyed when the function in which they are declared is exited.

11.10 Automatic duration is an example of the principle of least privilege. This principle states that each component of a system should have sufficient rights and privileges to accomplish its designated task, but no additional rights or privileges. This helps prevent accidental and/or malicious errors from occurring in systems. Why have variables stored in memory and accessible when they are not needed?

11.11 Any problem that can be solved recursively can also be solved iteratively (nonrecursively). A recursive approach is normally chosen in preference to an iterative approach when the recursive approach more naturally mirrors the problem and results in a program that is easier to understand and debug. Another reason to choose a recursive solution is that an iterative solution may not be apparent.

11.12 Modularizing programs in a neat, hierarchical manner promotes good software engineering, sometimes at the expense of performance.

TESTING AND DEBUGGING TIPS

11.1 Small functions are easier to test, debug and understand than large ones.

11.2 Internet Explorer displays a message when a script takes an unusually long time to execute. This allows the user of the Web page to recover from a script that contains an infinite loop or infinite recursion.

SELF-REVIEW EXERCISES

11.1 Answer each of the following:

a) Program modules in JavaScript are called __________.
b) A function is invoked with a __________.
c) A variable known only within the function in which it is defined is called a __________.
d) The ________ statement in a called function can be used to pass the value of an expression back to the calling function.
e) The keyword __________ indicates the beginning of a function definition.

11.2 For the following program, state the scope (either global scope or function scope) of each of the following elements.

a) The variable **x**.
b) The variable **y**.
c) The function **cube**.
d) The function **output**.

```
<!DOCTYPE html PUBLIC "-//W3C//DTD HTML 4.0 Transitional//EN">
<!-- Exercise 11.2: scoping.html -->

<HEAD>
<TITLE>Scoping</TITLE>

<SCRIPT LANGUAGE = "JavaScript">
   var x;

   function output()
   {
      for ( var x = 1; x <= 10; x++ )
         document.writeln( cube( x ) + "<BR>" );
   }

   function cube( y )
   {
      return y * y * y;
   }
</SCRIPT>

</HEAD><BODY ONLOAD = "output()"></BODY>
</HTML>
```

11.3 Answer each of the following:

a) Programmer-defined functions, global variables and JavaScript's global functions are all part of the __________ object.
b) Function __________ determines if its argument is or is not a number.

c) Function __________ takes a string argument and returns a string in which all spaces, punctuation, accent characters and any other character that is not in the ASCII character set are encoded in a hexadecimal format.
d) Function __________ takes a string argument representing JavaScript code to execute.
e) Function __________ takes a string as its argument and returns a string in which all characters that we previously encoded with **escape** are decoded.

11.4 Answer each of the following:
a) The __________ of an identifier is the portion of the program in which the identifier can be used.
b) The three ways to return control from a called function to a caller are __________, __________ and __________.
c) A recursive function typically has two components: one that provides a means for the recursion to terminate by testing for a __________ case and one that expresses the problem as a recursive call for a slightly simpler problem than the original call.
d) The __________ function is used to produce random numbers.
e) A function that calls itself either directly or indirectly is a __________ function.
f) Variables declared in a block or in a function's parameter list are of __________ duration.

11.5 Find the error in each of the following program segments and explain how the error can be corrected:

```
a) method g() {
      document.writeln( "Inside method g" );
   }
b) // This function should return the sum of its arguments
   function sum( x, y ) {
      var result;
      result = x + y;
   }
c) var sum( n ) {
      if ( n == 0 )
         return 0;
      else
         n + sum( n - 1 );
   }
d) function f( a ); {
      document.writeln( a );
   }
```

11.6 Write a complete JavaScript script to prompt the user for the radius of a sphere and call function **sphereVolume** to calculate and display the volume of that sphere. Use the statement

```
volume = ( 4.0 / 3.0 ) * Math.PI * Math.pow( radius, 3 )
```

to calculate the volume. The user should input the radius through an HTML text field in a **<FORM>** and press an HTML button to initiate the calculation.

ANSWERS TO SELF-REVIEW EXERCISES

11.1 a) functions. b) function call. c) Local variable. d) **return**. e) **function**.

11.2 a) Global scope. b) Function scope. c) Global scope. d) Global scope.

11.3 a) **Global**. b) **isNaN**. c) **escape**. d) **eval**. e) **unescape**.

11.4 a) Scope. b) **return;** or **return** *expression***;** or encountering the closing right brace of a function. c) Base. d) **Math.random**. e) Recursive. f) Automatic.

11.5
a) Error: **method** is not a keyword used to begin a function definition.
Correction: Change **method** to **function**.
b) Error: The function is supposed to return a value, but does not. Correction: Delete variable **result** and place the following statement in the function:
```
return x + y;
```
or add the following statement at the end of the function body:
```
return result;
```
c) Error: The result of **n + sum(n - 1)** is not returned by this recursive function, resulting in a syntax error.
Correction: Rewrite the statement in the **else** clause as
```
return n + sum(n - 1);
```
d) Error: The semicolon after the right parenthesis that encloses the parameter list.
Correction: Delete the semicolon after the right parenthesis of the parameter list.

11.6 The following solution calculates the volume of a sphere using the radius entered by the user.

```
<!DOCTYPE html PUBLIC "-//W3C//DTD HTML 4.0 Transitional//EN">
<HTML>
<!-- Exercise 11.6: volume.html -->

<HEAD>
<TITLE>Calculating Sphere Volumes</TITLE>

<SCRIPT LANGUAGE = "JavaScript">
   function displayVolume()
   {
      var radius = parseFloat( myForm.radiusField.value );
      window.status = "Volume is " + sphereVolume( radius );
   }

   function sphereVolume( r )
   {
      return ( 4.0 / 3.0 ) * Math.PI * Math.pow( r, 3 );
   }
</SCRIPT>

</HEAD>

<BODY>
<FORM NAME = "myForm">
   Enter radius of sphere<BR>
   <INPUT NAME = "radiusField" TYPE = "text">
   <INPUT NAME = "calculate" TYPE = "button" VALUE = "Calculate"
         ONCLICK = "displayVolume()">
</FORM>
</BODY>
</HTML>
```

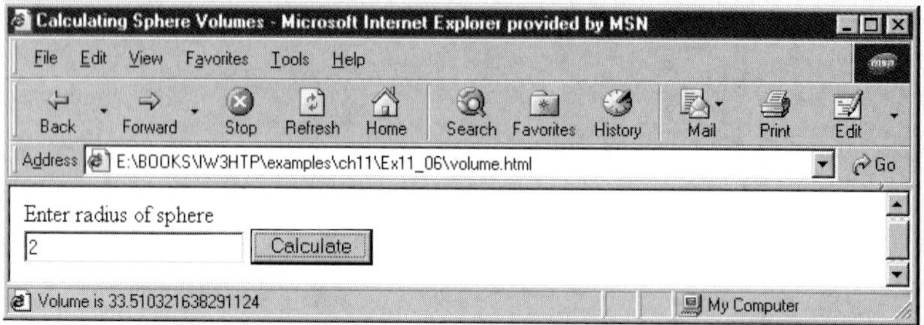

EXERCISES

11.7 Write a script that uses a function **circleArea** to prompt the user for the radius of a circle and to calculate and print the area of that circle.

11.8 A parking garage charges a $2.00 minimum fee to park for up to three hours. The garage charges an additional $0.50 per hour for each hour *or part thereof* in excess of three hours. The maximum charge for any given 24-hour period is $10.00. Assume that no car parks for longer than 24 hours at a time. Write a script that calculates and displays the parking charges for each customer who parked a car in this garage yesterday. You should input from the user the hours parked for each customer. The program should display the charge for the current customer and should calculate and display the running total of yesterday's receipts. The program should use the function **calculateCharges** to determine the charge for each customer. Use the techniques described in Self-Review Exercise 11.6 to obtain the input from the user.

11.9 Write function **distance**, which calculates the distance between two points (x1, y1) and (x2, y2). All numbers and return values should be floating-point values. Incorporate this function into a script that enables the user to enter the coordinates of the points through an HTML form.

11.10 Answer each of the following questions.

a) What does it mean to choose numbers "at random?"
b) Why is the **Math.random** function useful for simulating games of chance?
c) Why is it often necessary to scale and/or shift the values produced by **Math.random**?
d) Why is computerized simulation of real-world situations a useful technique?

11.11 Write statements that assign random integers to the variable *n* in the following ranges:

a) $1 \le n \le 2$
b) $1 \le n \le 100$
c) $0 \le n \le 9$
d) $1000 \le n \le 1112$
e) $-1 \le n \le 1$
f) $-3 \le n \le 11$

11.12 For each of the following sets of integers, write a single statement that will print a number at random from the set.

a) 2, 4, 6, 8, 10.
b) 3, 5, 7, 9, 11.
c) 6, 10, 14, 18, 22.

11.13 Write a function **integerPower(base, exponent)** that returns the value of

$$base^{exponent}$$

For example, **integerPower(3, 4) = 3 * 3 * 3 * 3**. Assume that **exponent** is a positive, nonzero integer and **base** is an integer. Function **integerPower** should use **for** or **while** to control the calculation. Do not use any math library functions. Incorporate this function into a script that reads integer values from an HTML form for **base** and **exponent** and performs the calculation with the **integerPower** function. The HTML form should consist of two text fields and a button to initiate the calculation. The user should interact with the program by typing numbers in both text fields then clicking the button.

11.14 Define a function **hypotenuse** that calculates the length of the hypotenuse of a right triangle when the other two sides are given. The function should take two floating-point arguments and return the hypotenuse as a floating-point number. Incorporate this function into a script that reads integer values for **side1** and **side2** and performs the calculation with the **hypotenuse** function. The HTML form should consist of two text fields and a button to initiate the calculation. The user should interact with the program by typing numbers in both text fields then clicking the button. Determine the length of the hypotenuse for each of the following triangles.

Triangle	Side 1	Side 2
1	3.0	4.0
2	5.0	12.0
3	8.0	15.0

11.15 Write a function **multiple** that determines for a pair of integers whether the second integer is a multiple of the first. The function should take two integer arguments and return **true** if the second is a multiple of the first and **false** otherwise. Incorporate this function into a script that inputs a series of pairs of integers (one pair at a time using **JTextFields**). The HTML form should consist of two text fields and a button to initiate the calculation. The user should interact with the program by typing numbers in both text fields then clicking the button.

11.16 Write a script that inputs integers (one at a time) and passes them one at a time to function **isEven**, which uses the modulus operator to determine if an integer is even. The function should take an integer argument and return **true** if the integer is even and **false** otherwise. Use sentinel-controlled looping and a **prompt** dialog.

11.17 Write a function **squareOfAsterisks** that displays a solid square of asterisks whose side is specified in integer parameter **side**. For example, if **side** is **4**, the function displays

```
****
****
****
****
```

Incorporate this function into a script that reads an integer value for **side** from the user at the keyboard and performs the drawing with the **squareOfAsterisks** function.

11.18 Modify the function created in Exercise 11.17 to form the square out of whatever character is contained in parameter **fillCharacter**. Thus if **side** is **5** and **fillCharacter** is "**#**", this function should print

```
#####
#####
#####
#####
#####
```

11.19 Use techniques similar to those developed in Exercises 11.17 and 11.18 to produce a program that graphs a wide range of shapes.

11.20 Write program segments that accomplish each of the following:

a) Calculate the integer part of the quotient when integer **a** is divided by integer **b**.

b) Calculate the integer remainder when integer **a** is divided by integer **b**.

c) Use the program pieces developed in a) and b) to write a function **displayDigits** that receives an integer between **1** and **99999** and prints it as a series of digits, each pair of which is separated by two spaces. For example, the integer **4562** should be printed as

```
4  5  6  2.
```

d) Incorporate the function developed in c) into a script that inputs an integer from a **prompt** dialog and invokes **displayDigits** by passing the function the integer entered.

11.21 Implement the following functions:

a) Function **celsius** returns the Celsius equivalent of a Fahrenheit temperature using the calculation

```
C = 5.0 / 9.0 * ( F - 32 );
```

b) Function **fahrenheit** returns the Fahrenheit equivalent of a Celsius temperature using the calculation

```
F = 9.0 / 5.0 * C + 32;
```

c) Use these functions to write a script that enables the user to enter either a Fahrenheit temperature and display the Celsius equivalent or enter a Celsius temperature and display the Fahrenheit equivalent.

Your HTML document should contain two buttons—one to initiate the conversion from Fahrenheit to Celcius and one to initiate the conversion from Celcius to Fahrenheit.

11.22 Write a function **minimum3** that returns the smallest of three floating-point numbers. Use the **Math.min** function to implement **minimum3**. Incorporate the function into a script that reads three values from the user and determines the smallest value. Display the result in the status bar.

11.23 An integer number is said to be a *perfect number* if its factors, including 1 (but not the number itself), sum to the number. For example, 6 is a perfect number because 6 = 1 + 2 + 3. Write a function **perfect** that determines whether parameter **number** is a perfect number. Use this function in a script that determines and displays all the perfect numbers between 1 and 1000. Print the factors of each perfect number to confirm that the number is indeed perfect. Challenge the computing power of your computer by testing numbers much larger than 1000. Display the results in a **<TEXTAREA>**.

11.24 An integer is said to be *prime* if it is divisible by only 1 and itself. For example, 2, 3, 5 and 7 are prime, but 4, 6, 8 and 9 are not.

a) Write a function that determines whether a number is prime.

b) Use this function in a script that determines and prints all the prime numbers between 1 and 10,000. How many of these 10,000 numbers do you really have to test before being sure that you have found all the primes? Display the results in a **<TEXTAREA>**.

c) Initially you might think that $n/2$ is the upper limit for which you must test to see whether a number is prime, but you only need go as high as the square root of n. Why? Rewrite the program and run it both ways. Estimate the performance improvement.

11.25 Write a function that takes an integer value and returns the number with its digits reversed. For example, given the number 7631, the function should return 1367. Incorporate the function into a script that reads a value from the user. Display the result of the function in the status bar.

11.26 The *greatest common divisor (GCD)* of two integers is the largest integer that evenly divides each of the two numbers. Write a function **gcd** that returns the greatest common divisor of two integers. Incorporate the function into a script that reads two values from the user. Display the result of the function in the browser's status bar.

11.27 Write a function **qualityPoints** that inputs a student's average and returns 4 if a student's average is 90–100, 3 if the average is 80–89, 2 if the average is 70–79, 1 if the average is 60–69 and 0 if the average is lower than 60. Incorporate the function into a script that reads a value from the user. Display the result of the function in the browser's status bar.

11.28 Write a script that simulates coin tossing. Let the program toss the coin each time the user presses the "**Toss**" button. Count the number of times each side of the coin appears. Display the results. The program should call a separate function **flip** that takes no arguments and returns **false** for tails and **true** for heads. [*Note:* If the program realistically simulates the coin tossing, each side of the coin should appear approximately half the time.]

11.29 Computers are playing an increasing role in education. Write a program that will help an elementary school student learn multiplication. Use **Math.random** to produce two positive one-digit integers. It should then display a question such as

```
How much is 6 times 7?
```

The student then types the answer into a text field. Your program checks the student's answer. If it is correct, display the string **"Very good!"** in the browser's status bar and generate a new question. If the answer is wrong, display the string **"No. Please try again."** in the browser's status bar, and let the student try the same question again repeatedly until the student finally gets it right. A separate function should be used to generate each new question. This function should be called once when the script begins execution and each time the user answers the question correctly.

11.30 The use of computers in education is referred to as *computer-assisted instruction* (CAI). One problem that develops in CAI environments is student fatigue. This can be eliminated by varying the computer's dialogue to hold the student's attention. Modify the program of Exercise 11.29 so the various comments are printed for each correct answer and each incorrect answer as follows:

Responses to a correct answer

```
Very good!
Excellent!
Nice work!
Keep up the good work!
```

Responses to an incorrect answer

```
No. Please try again.
Wrong. Try once more.
Don't give up!
No. Keep trying.
```

Use random number generation to choose a number from 1 to 4 that will be used to select an appropriate response to each answer. Use a **switch** structure to issue the responses.

11.31 More sophisticated computer-aided instruction systems monitor the student's performance over a period of time. The decision to begin a new topic is often based on the student's success with previous topics. Modify the program of Exercise 11.30 to count the number of correct and incorrect responses typed by the student. After the student types 10 answers, your program should calculate the percentage of correct responses. If the percentage is lower than 75%, print **Please ask your instructor for extra help** and reset the program so another student can try the program.

11.32 Write a script that plays the "guess the number" game as follows: Your program chooses the number to be guessed by selecting a random integer in the range 1 to 1000. The script displays the prompt **Guess a number between 1 and 1000** next to a text field. The player types a first guess into the text field and presses a button to submit the guess to the script. If the player's guess is incorrect, your program should display **Too high. Try again.** or **Too low. Try again.** in the browser's status bar to help the player "zero in" on the correct answer and should clear the text field so the user can enter the next guess. When the user enters the correct answer, display **Congratulations. You guessed the number!** in the status bar and clear the text field so the user can play again. [*Note:* The guessing technique employed in this problem is similar to a *binary search.*]

11.33 Modify the program of Exercise 11.32 to count the number of guesses the player makes. If the number is 10 or fewer, display **Either you know the secret or you got lucky!** If the player guesses the number in 10 tries, display **Ahah! You know the secret!** If the player makes more than 10 guesses, display **You should be able to do better!** Why should it take no more than 10 guesses? Well with each "good guess" the player should be able to eliminate half of the numbers. Now show why any number 1 to 1000 can be guessed in 10 or fewer tries.

11.34 Write a recursive function **power (base, exponent)** that when invoked returns

$$base^{exponent}$$

for example, **power(3, 4) = 3 * 3 * 3 * 3**. Assume that **exponent** is an integer greater than or equal to 1. (*Hint:* The recursion step would use the relationship

$$base^{exponent} = base \cdot base^{exponent - 1}$$

and the terminating condition occurs when **exponent** is equal to **1** because

$$base^{1} = base$$

Incorporate this function into a script that enables the user to enter the **base** and **exponent.**)

11.35 *(Towers of Hanoi)* Every budding computer scientist must grapple with certain classic problems and the Towers of Hanoi (see Fig. 11.14) is one of the most famous of these. Legend has it that in a temple in the Far East, priests are attempting to move a stack of disks from one peg to another. The initial stack had 64 disks threaded onto one peg and arranged from bottom to top by decreasing size. The priests are attempting to move the stack from this peg to a second peg under the constraints that exactly one disk is moved at a time and at no time may a larger disk be placed above a smaller disk. A third peg is available for temporarily holding disks. Supposedly, the world will end when the priests complete their task, so there is little incentive for us to facilitate their efforts.

Let us assume that the priests are attempting to move the disks from peg 1 to peg 3. We wish to develop an algorithm that will print the precise sequence of peg-to-peg disk transfers.

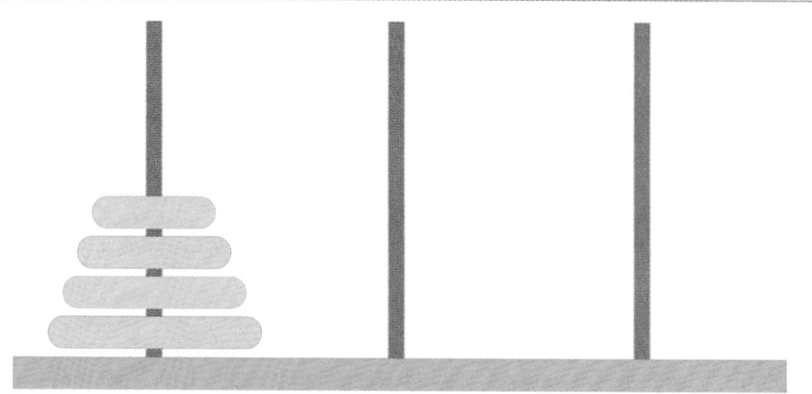

Fig. 11.14 The Towers of Hanoi for the case with four disks.

If we were to approach this problem with conventional functions, we would rapidly find ourselves hopelessly knotted up in managing the disks. Instead, if we attack the problem with recursion in mind, it immediately becomes tractable. Moving n disks can be viewed in terms of moving only $n - 1$ disks (and hence the recursion) as follows:

a) Move $n - 1$ disks from peg 1 to peg 2, using peg 3 as a temporary holding area.
b) Move the last disk (the largest) from peg 1 to peg 3.
c) Move the $n - 1$ disks from peg 2 to peg 3, using peg 1 as a temporary holding area.

The process ends when the last task involves moving $n = 1$ disk (i.e., the base case). This is accomplished by trivially moving the disk without the need for a temporary holding area.

Write a script to solve the Towers of Hanoi problem. Allow the user to enter the number of disks in a text field. Use a recursive **`tower`** function with four parameters:

a) The number of disks to be moved
b) The peg on which these disks are initially threaded
c) The peg to which this stack of disks is to be moved
d) The peg to be used as a temporary holding area

Your program should display in a **`<TEXTAREA>`** the precise instructions it will take to move the disks from the starting peg to the destination peg. For example, to move a stack of three disks from peg 1 to peg 3, your program should display the following series of moves:

1 → 3 (This means move one disk from peg 1 to peg 3.)
1 → 2
3 → 2
1 → 3
2 → 1
2 → 3
1 → 3

11.36 Any program that can be implemented recursively can be implemented iteratively, although sometimes with more difficulty and less clarity. Try writing an iterative version of the Towers of Hanoi. If you succeed, compare your iterative version with the recursive version developed in Exercise 11.35. Investigate issues of performance, clarity and your ability to demonstrate the correctness of the programs.

11.37 *(Visualizing Recursion)* It is interesting to watch recursion "in action." Modify the factorial function of Fig. 11.9 to display its local variable and recursive call parameter. For each recursive call, display the outputs on a separate line and add a level of indentation. Do your utmost to make the outputs clear, interesting and meaningful. Your goal here is to design and implement an output format that helps a person understand recursion better. You may want to add such display capabilities to the many other recursion examples and exercises throughout the text.

11.38 The greatest common divisor of integers **`x`** and **`y`** is the largest integer that evenly divides both **`x`** and **`y`**. Write a recursive function **`gcd`** that returns the greatest common divisor of **`x`** and **`y`**. The **`gcd`** of **`x`** and **`y`** is defined recursively as follows: If **`y`** is equal to **`0`**, then **`gcd( x, y )`** is **`x`**; otherwise, **`gcd( x, y )`** is **`gcd( y, x % y )`**, where **`%`** is the modulus operator. Use this function to replace the one you wrote in the script of Exercise 11.26.

11.39 Exercises 11.29 through 11.31 developed a computer-assisted instruction program to teach an elementary school student multiplication. This exercise suggests enhancements to that program.

a) Modify the program to allow the user to enter a grade-level capability. A grade level of 1 means to use only single-digit numbers in the problems, a grade level of 2 means to use numbers as large as two digits, etc.
b) Modify the program to allow the user to pick the type of arithmetic problems he or she wishes to study. An option of 1 means addition problems only, 2 means subtraction problems only, 3 means multiplication problems only, 4 means division problems only and 5 means to randomly intermix problems of all these types.

11.40 What does the following function do?

```
// Parameter b must be a positive
// integer to prevent infinite recursion
function mystery( a, b )
{
   if ( b == 1 )
      return a;
   else
      return a + mystery( a, b - 1 );
}
```

11.41 After you determine what the program of Exercise 11.40 does, modify the function to operate properly after removing the restriction of the second argument being nonnegative. Also, incorporate the function into a script that enables the user to enter two integers and test the function.

11.42 Find the error in the following recursive function and explain how to correct it:

```
function sum( n )
{
   if ( n == 0 )
      return 0;
   else
      return n + sum(n);
}
```

11.43 Modify the craps program of Fig. 11.6 to allow wagering. Initialize variable **bankBalance** to 1000 dollars. Prompt the player to enter a **wager**. Check that **wager** is less than or equal to **bankBalance**, and if not, have the user reenter **wager** until a valid **wager** is entered. After a correct **wager** is entered, run one game of craps. If the player wins, increase **bankBalance** by **wager** and print the new **bankBalance**. If the player loses, decrease **bankBalance** by **wager**, print the new **bankBalance**, check if **bankBalance** has become zero, and if so, print the message "**Sorry. You busted!**" As the game progresses, print various messages to create some "chatter," such as "**Oh, you're going for broke, huh?**" or "**Aw c'mon, take a chance!**" or "**You're up big. Now's the time to cash in your chips!**". Implement the "chatter" as a separate function that randomly chooses the string to display.

12

JavaScript/JScript: Arrays

Objectives

- To introduce the array data structure.
- To understand the use of arrays to store, sort and search lists and tables of values.
- To understand how to declare an array, initialize an array and refer to individual elements of an array.
- To be able to pass arrays to functions.
- To understand basic sorting techniques.
- To be able to declare and manipulate multiple-subscript arrays.

With sobs and tears he sorted out
Those of the largest size ...
Lewis Carroll

Attempt the end, and never stand to doubt;
Nothing's so hard, but search will find it out.
Robert Herrick

Now go, write it before them in a table,
and note it in a book.
Isaiah 30:8

'Tis in my memory lock'd,
And you yourself shall keep the key of it.
William Shakespeare

Outline

12.1 Introduction

This chapter serves as an introduction to the important topic of data structures. *Arrays* are data structures consisting of related data items (sometimes called *collections* of data items). JavaScript arrays are "dynamic" entities, in that they can change size after they are created. Many of the techniques demonstrated in this chapter are used frequently in the Dynamic HTML chapters, as we introduce the collections that allow a script programmer to manipulate every element of an HTML document dynamically.

12.2 Arrays

An array is a group of memory locations that all have the same name and are normally of the same type (although this is not required). To refer to a particular location or element in the array, we specify the name of the array and the *position number* of the particular element in the array.

Figure 12.1 shows an array of integer values called **c**. This array contains 12 *elements.* Any one of these elements may be referred to by giving the name of the array followed by the position number of the particular element in square brackets (**[]**). The first element in every array is the *zeroth element.* Thus, the first element of array **c** is referred to as **c[0]**, the second element of array **c** is referred to as **c[1]**, the seventh element of array **c** is referred to as **c[6]** and, in general, the *i*th element of array **c** is referred to as **c[i-1]**. Array names follow the same conventions as other identifiers.

The position number in square brackets is more formally called a *subscript* (or an index). A subscript must be an integer or an integer expression. If a program uses an expression as a subscript, the expression is evaluated first, to determine the subscript. For example, if we assume that variable **a** is equal to **5** and that variable **b** is equal to **6**, then the statement

```
c[ a + b ] += 2;
```

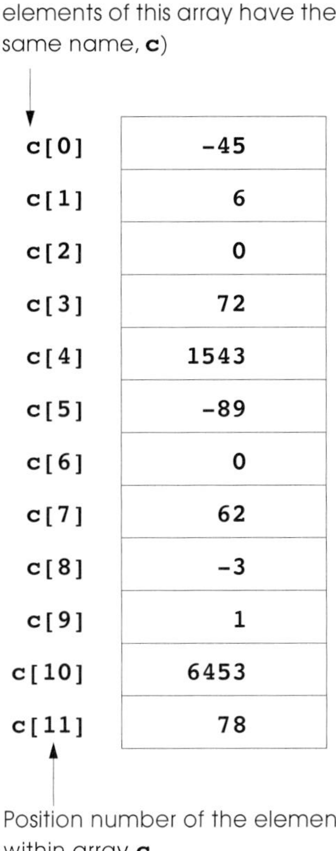

Fig. 12.1 A 12-element array.

adds 2 to array element **c[11]**. Note that a subscripted array name is an *lvalue*—it can be used on the left side of an assignment to place a new value into an array element.

Let us examine array **c** in Fig. 12.1 more closely. The *name* of the array is **c**. The *length* of the array is determined by the following expression:

```
c.length
```

Every array in JavaScript *knows* its own length. The array's 12 elements are referred to as **c[0]**, **c[1]**, **c[2]**, ..., **c[11]**. The *value* of **c[0]** is **-45**, the value of **c[1]** is **6**, the value of **c[2]** is **0**, the value of **c[7]** is **62** and the value of **c[11]** is **78**. To calculate the sum of the values contained in the first three elements of array **c** and store the result in variable **sum**, we would write

```
sum = c[ 0 ] + c[ 1 ] + c[ 2 ];
```

To divide the value of the seventh element of array **c** by **2** and assign the result to the variable **x**, we would write

```
x = c[ 6 ] / 2;
```

Common Programming Error 12.1

It is important to note the difference between the "seventh element of the array" and "array element seven." Because array subscripts begin at 0, the "seventh element of the array" has a subscript of 6, while "array element seven" has a subscript of 7 and is actually the eighth element of the array. This confusion is a source of "off-by-one" errors.

The brackets used to enclose the subscript of an array are an operator in JavaScript. Brackets have the same level of precedence as parentheses. The chart in Fig. 12.2 shows the precedence and associativity of the operators introduced to this point in the text. They are shown top to bottom in decreasing order of precedence with their associativity and type.

12.3 Declaring and Allocating Arrays

Arrays occupy space in memory. Actually, an array in JavaScript is an ***Array** object*. The programmer uses *operator* **new** to dynamically allocate the number of elements required by each array. Operator **new** creates an object as the program executes by obtaining enough memory to store an object of the type specified to the right of **new**. The process of creating new objects is also known as *creating an instance* or *instantiating an object,* and operator **new** is known as the *dynamic memory allocation operator*. **Array** objects are allocated with **new** because arrays are considered to be objects and all objects must be created with **new**. To allocate 12 elements for integer array **c**, use the statement

```
var c = new Array( 12 );
```

The preceding statement can also be performed in two steps as follows:

```
var c;                 // declares the array
c = new Array( 12 );   // allocates the array
```

When arrays are allocated, the elements are not initialized.

Operators	Associativity	Type
`() [] .`	left to right	highest
`++ -- !`	right to left	unary
`* / %`	left to right	multiplicative
`+ -`	left to right	additive
`< <= > >=`	left to right	relational
`== !=`	left to right	equality
`&&`	left to right	logical AND
`||`	left to right	logical OR
`?:`	right to left	conditional
`= += -= *= /= %=`	right to left	assignment

Fig. 12.2 Precedence and associativity of the operators discussed so far.

Common Programming Error 12.2

Assuming that the elements of an array are initialized when the array is allocated may result in logic errors.

Memory may be reserved for several arrays with a single declaration. The following declaration reserves 100 elements for array **b** and 27 elements for array **x**:

```
var b = new Array( 100 ), x = new Array( 27 );
```

12.4 Examples Using Arrays

The script of Fig. 12.3 uses the **new** operator to dynamically allocate an **Array** of five elements and an empty array. The script demonstrates initializing an **Array** of existing elements and also shows that an **Array** can grow dynamically to accommodate new elements. The two **Array** objects are displayed as HTML tables. [*Note:* Many of the scripts in this chapter are executed in response to the **<BODY>**'s **ONLOAD** event.]

```
<!DOCTYPE HTML PUBLIC "-//W3C//DTD HTML 4.0 Transitional//EN">
<HTML>
<!-- Fig. 12.3: InitArray.html -->

<HEAD>
<TITLE>Initializing an Array</TITLE>

<SCRIPT LANGUAGE = "JavaScript">
   // this function is called when the <BODY> element's
   // ONLOAD event occurs
   function initializeArrays()
   {
      var n1 = new Array( 5 );    // allocate 5-element Array
      var n2 = new Array();       // allocate empty Array

      // assign values to each element of Array n1
      for ( var i = 0; i < n1.length; ++i )
         n1[ i ] = i;

      // create and initialize five-elements in Array n2
      for ( i = 0; i < 5; ++i )
         n2[ i ] = i;

      outputArray( "Array n1 contains", n1 );
      outputArray( "Array n2 contains", n2 );
   }

   // output "header" followed by a two-column table
   // containing subscripts and elements of "theArray"
   function outputArray( header, theArray )
   {
      document.writeln( "<H2>" + header + "</H2>" );
      document.writeln( "<TABLE BORDER = '1' WIDTH = '100%'>" );
```

Fig. 12.3 Initializing the elements of an array to zeros (part 1 of 2).

```
34         document.writeln( "<TR><TD WIDTH = '100'><B>Subscript</B>"
35                           + "<TD><B>Value</B></TR>" );
36
37         for ( var i = 0; i < theArray.length; i++ )
38            document.writeln( "<TR><TD>" + i + "<TD>" +
39                              theArray[ i ] + "</TR>" );
40
41         document.writeln( "</TABLE>" );
42      }
43   </SCRIPT>
44
45   </HEAD><BODY ONLOAD = "initializeArrays()"></BODY>
46   </HTML>
```

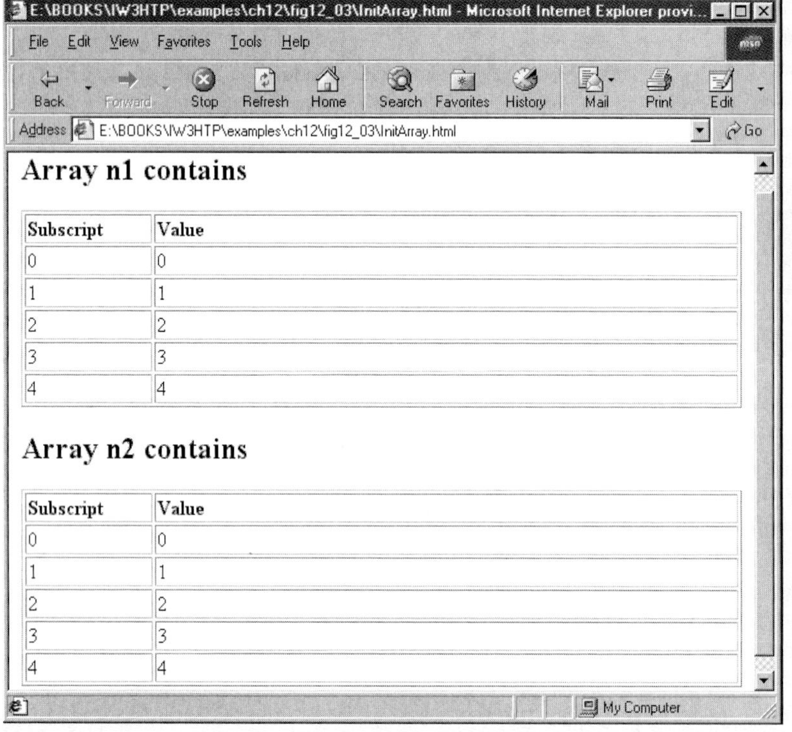

Fig. 12.3 Initializing the elements of an array to zeros (part 2 of 2).

Function **initializeArrays** (defined at line 11) is called by the browser as the event handler for the **<BODY>**'s **ONLOAD** event. Line 13 creates **Array n1** as an array of 5 elements. Line 14 creates **Array n2** as an empty array.

Lines 17 and 18

```
for ( var i = 0; i < n1.length; ++i )
   n1[ i ] = i;
```

use a **for** structure to initialize the elements of **n1** to their subscript numbers (0 to 4). Note the use of zero-based counting (remember, subscripts start at 0), so the loop can access every element of the array. Also, note the expression **n1.length** in the **for** structure condition to determine the length of the array. In this example, the length of the array is 5, so the loop continues executing as long as the value of control variable **i** is less than 5. For a five-element array, the subscript values are 0 through 4, so using the less than operator, **<**, guarantees that the loop does not attempt to access an element beyond the end of the array.

Lines 21 and 22

```
for ( i = 0; i < 5; ++i )
   n2[ i ] = i;
```

use a **for** structure to add five elements to the **Array n2** and initialize each element to its subscript numbers (0 to 4). Note that **Array n2** grows dynamically to accommodate the values assigned to each element of the array.

Lines 24 and 25 invoke function **outputArray** (defined at line 30) to display the contents of each array as HTML tables. Function **outputArray** receives two arguments—a string to be output before the HTML table that displays the contents of the array and the array to output. Lines 32 through 35 output the header string and begin the definition of the HTML table with two columns—**Subscript** and **Value**.

Lines 37 through 39

```
for ( var i = 0; i < theArray.length; i++ )
   document.writeln( "<TR><TD>" + i + "<TD>" +
                     theArray[ i ] + "</TR>" );
```

use a **for** structure to output HTML text that defines each row of the table. Once again, note the use of zero-based counting so that the loop can access every element of the array. Line 41 terminates the definition of the HTML table.

If an **Array**'s element values are known in advance, the elements of the **Array** can be allocated and initialized in the array declaration. There are two ways in which the initial values can be specified. The statement

```
var n = [ 10, 20, 30, 40, 50 ];
```

uses a comma-separated *initializer list* enclosed in square brackets (**[** and **]**) to create a five-element **Array** with subscripts of **0**, **1**, **2**, **3** and **4**. In this case, the array size is determined by the number of values in the initializer list. Note that the preceding declaration does not require the **new** operator to create the **Array** object—this is provided automatically by the interpreter when it encounters an array declaration that includes an initializer list. The statement

```
var n = new Array( 10, 20, 30, 40, 50 );
```

also creates a five-element array with subscripts of **0**, **1**, **2**, **3** and **4**. In this case, the initial values of the array elements are specified as arguments in the parentheses following **new Array**. The array size is determined by the number of values in parentheses. It is also possible to reserve a space in an **Array** for a value to be specified later by using a comma as a *place holder* in the initializer list. For example, the statement

```
var n = [ 10, 20, , 40, 50 ];
```

creates a five-element array with no value specified for the third element (**n[2]**).

The script of Fig. 12.4 creates three **Array** objects to demonstrate initializing arrays with initializer lists and displays each array in an HTML table using the same function **outputArray** discussed in Fig. 12.3. Notice that when **Array integers2** is displayed in the Web page, the elements with subscripts 1 and 2 (the second and third elements of the array) appear in the Web page as "**undefined**." These are the two elements of the array for which we did not supply values in the declaration at line 16 in the script.

```
1  <!DOCTYPE HTML PUBLIC "-//W3C//DTD HTML 4.0 Transitional//EN">
2  <HTML>
3  <!-- Fig. 12.4: InitArray.html -->
4
5  <HEAD>
6  <TITLE>Initializing an Array with a Declaration</TITLE>
7
8  <SCRIPT LANGUAGE = "JavaScript">
9     function start()
10    {
11       // Initializer list specifies number of elements and
12       // value for each element.
13       var colors = new Array( "cyan", "magenta",
14                               "yellow", "black" );
15       var integers1 = [ 2, 4, 6, 8 ];
16       var integers2 = [ 2, , , 8 ];
17
18       outputArray( "Array colors contains", colors );
19       outputArray( "Array integers1 contains", integers1 );
20       outputArray( "Array integers2 contains", integers2 );
21    }
22
23    // output "header" followed by a two-column table
24    // containing subscripts and elements of "theArray"
25    function outputArray( header, theArray )
26    {
27       document.writeln( "<H2>" + header + "</H2>" );
28       document.writeln( "<TABLE BORDER = '1' WIDTH = '100%'>" );
29       document.writeln( "<TR><TD WIDTH = '100'><B>Subscript</B>"
30                         + "<TD><B>Value</B></TR>" );
31
32       for ( var i = 0; i < theArray.length; i++ )
33          document.writeln( "<TR><TD>" + i + "<TD>" +
34                            theArray[ i ] + "</TR>" );
35
36       document.writeln( "</TABLE>" );
37    }
38 </SCRIPT>
39
40 </HEAD><BODY ONLOAD = "start()"></BODY>
41 </HTML>
```

Fig. 12.4 Initializing the elements of an array with a declaration. (part 1 of 2)

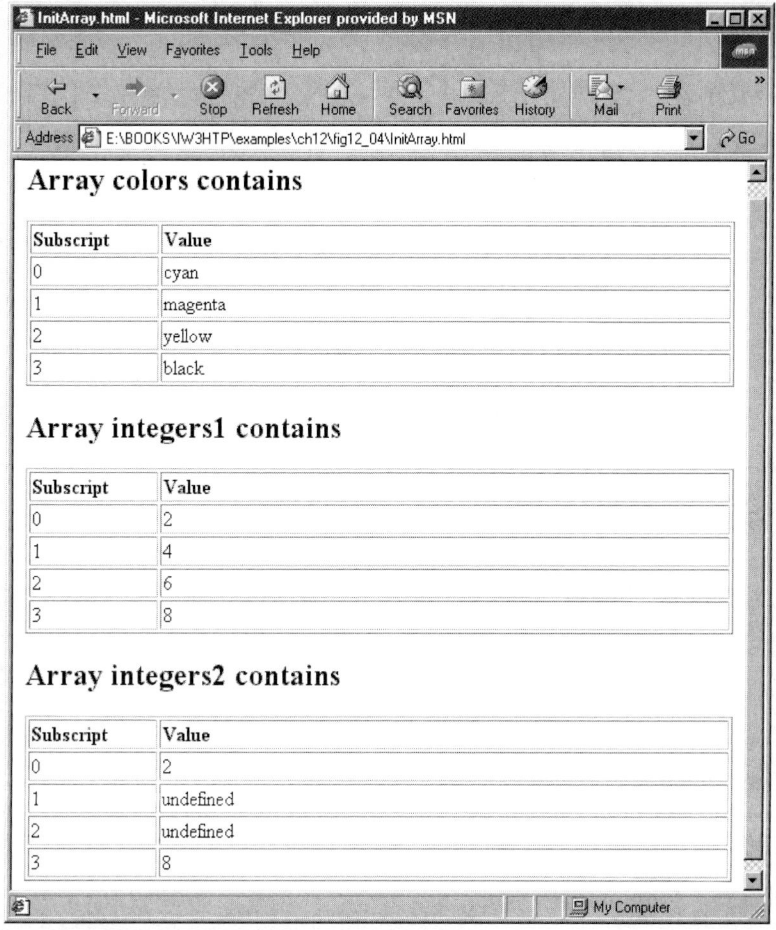

Fig. 12.4 Initializing the elements of an array with a declaration. (part 2 of 2)

The script of Fig. 12.5 sums the values contained in the 10-element integer array called **theArray**—declared, allocated and initialized at line 11 in function **start** (which is called in response to the **<BODY>**'s **ONLOAD** event). The statement at line 15 in the body of the first **for** loop does the totaling. It is important to remember that the values being supplied as initializers for array **theArray** normally would be read into the program. For example, in a script the user could enter the values through an HTML form.

```
1  <!DOCTYPE HTML PUBLIC "-//W3C//DTD HTML 4.0 Transitional//EN">
2  <HTML>
3  <!-- Fig. 12.5: SumArray.html -->
4
5  <HEAD>
6  <TITLE>Sum the Elements of an Array</TITLE>
```

Fig. 12.5 Computing the sum of the elements of an array (part 1 of 2).

```
7
8   <SCRIPT LANGUAGE = "JavaScript">
9      function start()
10     {
11        var theArray = [ 1, 2, 3, 4, 5, 6, 7, 8, 9, 10 ];
12        var total1 = 0, total2 = 0;
13
14        for ( var i = 0; i < theArray.length; i++ )
15           total1 += theArray[ i ];
16
17        document.writeln( "Total using subscripts: " + total1 );
18
19        for ( var element in theArray )
20           total2 += theArray[ element ];
21
22        document.writeln( "<BR>Total using for/in: " + total2 );
23     }
24  </SCRIPT>
25
26  </HEAD><BODY ONLOAD = "start()"></BODY>
27  </HTML>
```

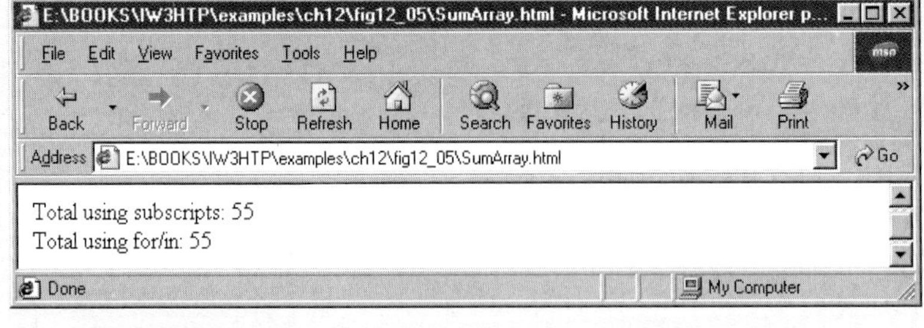

Fig. 12.5 Computing the sum of the elements of an array (part 2 of 2).

In this example, we introduce for the first time JavaScript's ***for/in*** control structure, which enables a script to perform a task ***for*** *each element* ***in*** *an array* (or, as we will see in the Dynamic HTML chapters, for each element in a collection). This is also known as *iterating over the array elements*. Lines 19 and 20

```
for ( var element in theArray )
   total2 += theArray[ element ];
```

show the syntax of a **for/in** structure. Inside the parentheses, we declare the **element** variable that will be used to select each element in the object to the right of keyword **in** (**theArray**, in this case). In the preceding **for/in** structure, JavaScript automatically determines the number of elements in the array. As the JavaScript interpreter iterates over **theArray**'s elements, variable **element** is assigned a value that can be used as a subscript for **theArray**. In the case of an **Array**, the value assigned is a subscript in the range from 0 up to (but not including) **theArray.length**. Each value is added to **total2** to produce the sum of the elements in the array.

Our next example uses arrays to summarize the results of data collected in a survey. Consider the problem statement:

Forty students were asked to rate the quality of the food in the student cafeteria on a scale of 1 to 10 (1 means awful and 10 means excellent). Place the 40 responses in an integer array and summarize the results of the poll.

This is a typical array processing script (see Fig. 12.6). We wish to summarize the number of responses of each type (i.e., 1 through 10). The array **`responses`** is a 40-element integer array of the students' responses to the survey. We use an 11-element array **`frequency`** to count the number of occurrences of each response. We ignore the first element, **`frequency[ 0 ]`**, because it is more logical to have the response 1 increment **`frequency[ 1 ]`** than **`frequency[ 0 ]`**. This allows us to use each response directly as a subscript on the **`frequency`** array. Each element of the array is used as a counter for one of the survey responses.

Good Programming Practice 12.1

Strive for program clarity. It is sometimes worthwhile to trade off the most efficient use of memory or processor time in favor of writing clearer programs.

```
<!DOCTYPE HTML PUBLIC "-//W3C//DTD HTML 4.0 Transitional//EN">
<HTML>
<!-- Fig. 12.6: StudentPoll.html -->

<HEAD>
<TITLE>Student Poll Program</TITLE>

<SCRIPT LANGUAGE = "JavaScript">
   function start()
   {
      var responses = [ 1, 2, 6, 4, 8, 5, 9, 7, 8, 10,
                        1, 6, 3, 8, 6, 10, 3, 8, 2, 7,
                        6, 5, 7, 6, 8, 6, 7, 5, 6, 6,
                        5, 6, 7, 5, 6, 4, 8, 6, 8, 10 ];
      var frequency = [ , 0, 0, 0, 0, 0, 0, 0, 0, 0, 0 ];

      for ( var answer in responses )
         ++frequency[ responses[ answer ] ];

      document.writeln( "<TABLE BORDER = '1' WIDTH = '100%'>" );
      document.writeln( "<TR><TD WIDTH = '100'><B>Rating</B>" +
                        "<TD><B>Frequency</B></TR>" );

      for ( var rating = 1;
            rating < frequency.length; ++rating )
         document.writeln( "<TR><TD>" + rating + "<TD>" +
                           frequency[ rating ] + "</TR>" );

      document.writeln( "</TABLE>" );
   }
</SCRIPT>
</HEAD><BODY ONLOAD = "start()"></BODY>
</HTML>
```

Fig. 12.6 A simple student-poll analysis program (part 1 of 2).

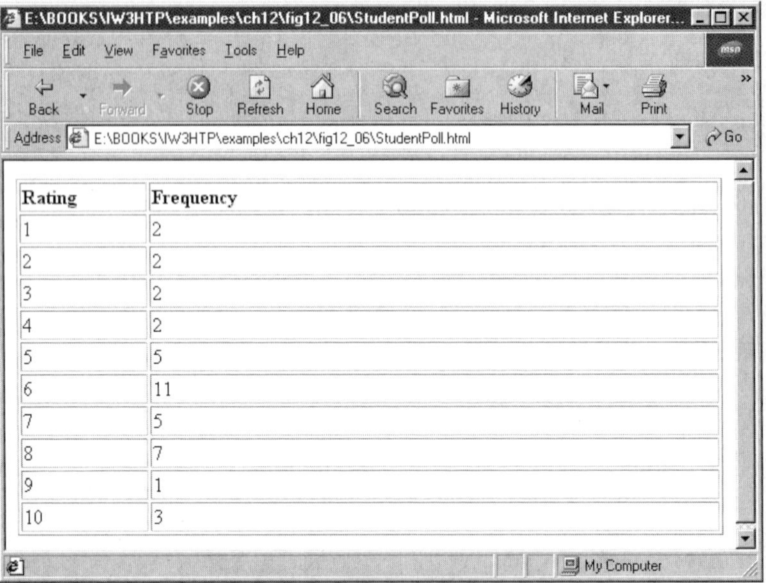

Rating	Frequency
1	2
2	2
3	2
4	2
5	5
6	11
7	5
8	7
9	1
10	3

Fig. 12.6 A simple student-poll analysis program (part 2 of 2).

Function **start** (defined at line 9) is called in response to the **<BODY>**'s **ONLOAD** event. The **for/in** loop at lines 17 and 18

```
for ( var answer in responses )
   ++frequency[ responses[ answer ] ];
```

takes the responses one at a time from the array **response** and increments one of the 10 counters in the **frequency** array (**frequency[1]** to **frequency[10]**). The key statement in the loop is

```
++frequency[ responses[ answer ] ];
```

This statement increments the appropriate **frequency** counter, depending on the value of **responses[answer]**.

Let us consider several iterations of the **for** loop. As the JavaScript interpreter iterates over the array **responses**, variable **answer** will be assigned the subscript values from 0 to 39 (the 40 subscripts of array responses). When the value of variable **answer** is **0**, the expression **responses[answer]** is the value of the first element of **responses** (**1**), so **++frequency[responses[answer]];** is actually interpreted as

```
++frequency[ 1 ];
```

which increments array element one (the second element of the array). In evaluating the expression, start with the value in the innermost set of square brackets (**answer**). Once you know the value of **answer**, plug that value into the expression and evaluate the next outer set of square brackets (**responses[answer]**). Then, use that value as the subscript for the **frequency** array to determine which counter to increment.

When **answer** is **1**, **responses[answer]** is the value of the second element of array **responses** (**2**), so **++frequency[responses[answer]];** is actually interpreted as

```
++frequency[ 2 ];
```

which increments array element two (the third element of the array).

When **answer** is **2**, **responses[answer]** is the value of the third element of array **responses** (**6**), so **++frequency[responses[answer]];** is actually interpreted as

```
++frequency[ 6 ];
```

which increments array element six (the seventh element of the array) and so on. Note that, regardless of the number of responses processed in the survey, only an 11-element array is required (ignoring element zero) to summarize the results, because all the response values are between 1 and 10, and the subscript values for an 11-element array are 0 through 10. Also note that the results are correct, because the elements of the **frequency** array were initialized to zero with the initializer list in the declaration at line 15.

If the data contained on invalid value, such as 13, the program would attempt to add **1** to **frequency[13]**. This is outside the bounds of the array. When a value is assigned to an element of an **Array** that is outside the current bounds, JavaScript automatically allocates more memory, so the **Array** will contain the appropriate number of elements. Thus, if the script encounters the expression **++frequency[13]**, the JavaScript interpreter allocates memory for elements 11, 12 and 13 of the **frequency** array and adds 1 to **frequency[13]**. Unfortunately, the new elements of the array are not initialized, so the preceding expression does not result in a valid value.

Common Programming Error 12.3

Referring to an element outside the **Array** *bounds is normally a logic error.*

Testing and Debugging Tip 12.1

When a program is looping through an **Array** *using subscripts, the* **Array** *subscript should never go below 0 and should always be less than the total number of elements in the* **Array** *(one less than the size of the* **Array***). Make sure the loop-terminating condition prevents accessing elements outside this range.*

Testing and Debugging Tip 12.2

Programs should validate the correctness of all input values, to prevent erroneous information from affecting a program's calculations.

Testing and Debugging Tip 12.3

When iterating over all the elements of an **Array***, use a* **for***/***in** *control structure to ensure that you manipulate only the existing elements of the* **Array***.*

Software Engineering Observation 12.1

JavaScript automatically reallocates an **Array** *when a value is assigned to an element that is outside the bounds of the original* **Array***. Elements between the last element of the original* **Array** *and the new element have undefined values.*

The script in Fig. 12.7 reads numbers from an array and graphs the information in the form of a *bar chart* (or *histogram*)—each number is printed, then a bar consisting of that many asterisks is displayed beside the number in an HTML table. The nested **for** loop (lines 18 through 27) formats each row of the HTML table. Note the loop continuation condition of the inner **for** structure at line 23 (**j <= theArray[i]**). Each time the inner **for** structure is reached, it counts from **1** to **theArray[i]**, thus using a value in array **theArray** to determine the final value of the control variable **j** and the number of asterisks to display. [*Note:* Function **start** (line 9) handles the **<BODY>**'s **ONLOAD** event.]

Chapter 11 indicated that there is a more elegant way to implement the dice-rolling program of Fig. 11.5. The program rolled a single six-sided die 6000 times. An array version of this script is shown in Fig. 12.8. Lines 17 through 36 of Fig. 11.5 are replaced by line 16 of this program, which uses the random **face** value as the subscript for array **frequency** to determine which element should be incremented during each iteration of the loop. Because the random number calculation on line 15 produces numbers from 1 to 6 (the values for a six-sided die), the **frequency** array must be large enough to allow subscript values of 1 to 6. The smallest number of elements required for an array to have these subscript values is seven elements (subscript values from 0 to 6). In this program, we ignore element 0 of array **frequency**. Also, lines 23 through 25 of this program replace lines 42 through 53 from Fig. 11.5. Because we can loop through array **frequency**, we do not have to enumerate each HTML table row as we did in Fig. 11.5.

```
1  <!DOCTYPE HTML PUBLIC "-//W3C//DTD HTML 4.0 Transitional//EN">
2  <HTML>
3  <!-- Fig. 12.7: Histogram.html -->
4
5  <HEAD>
6  <TITLE>Histogram Printing Program</TITLE>
7
8  <SCRIPT LANGUAGE = "JavaScript">
9     function start()
10    {
11       var theArray = [ 19, 3, 15, 7, 11, 9, 13, 5, 17, 1 ];
12
13       document.writeln( "<TABLE BORDER = '1' WIDTH = '100%'>" );
14       document.writeln( "<TR><TD WIDTH = '100'><B>Element</B>" +
15                         "<TD WIDTH = '100'><B>Value</B>" +
16                         "<TD><B>Histogram</B></TR>" );
17
18       for ( var i in theArray ) {
19          document.writeln( "<TR><TD>" + i +
20                            "<TD>" + theArray[ i ] + "<TD>" );
21
22          // print a bar
23          for ( var j = 1; j <= theArray[ i ]; ++j )
24             document.writeln( "*" );
25
26          document.writeln( "</TR>" );
27       }
28
```

Fig. 12.7 A program that prints histograms (part 1 of 2).

```
      document.writeln( "</TABLE>" );
   }
</SCRIPT>

</HEAD><BODY ONLOAD = "start()"></BODY>
</HTML>
```

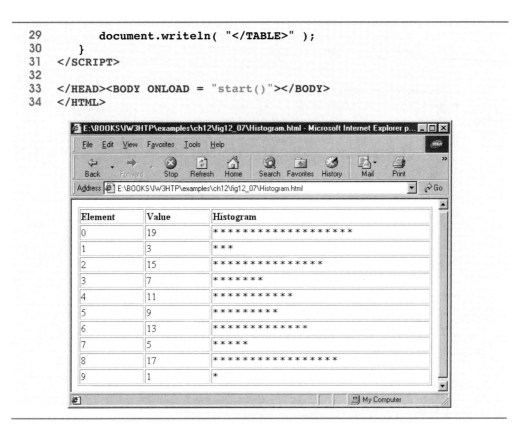

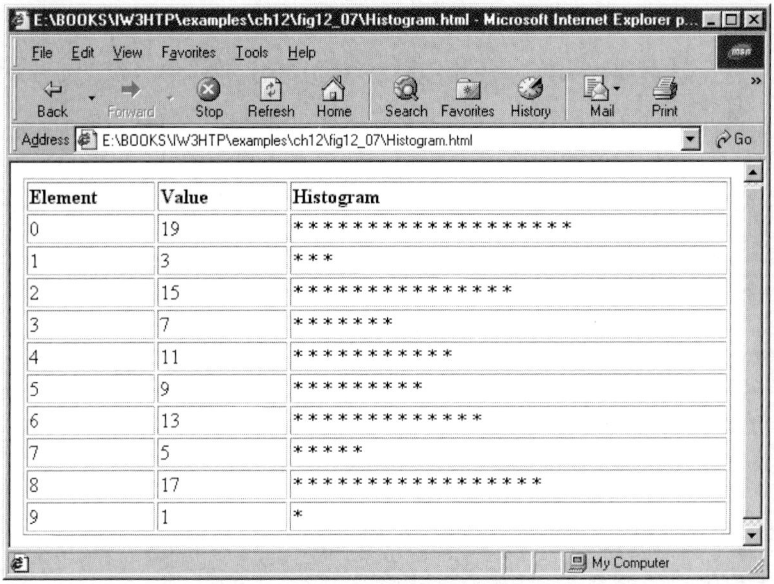

Element	Value	Histogram
0	19	*******************
1	3	***
2	15	***************
3	7	*******
4	11	***********
5	9	*********
6	13	*************
7	5	*****
8	17	*****************
9	1	*

Fig. 12.7 A program that prints histograms (part 2 of 2).

```
<!DOCTYPE HTML PUBLIC "-//W3C//DTD HTML 4.0 Transitional//EN">
<HTML>
<!-- Fig. 12.8: RollDie.html -->

<HEAD>
<TITLE>Roll a Six-Sided Die 6000 Times</TITLE>

<SCRIPT LANGUAGE = "JavaScript">
   var face, frequency = [ , 0, 0, 0, 0, 0, 0 ];

   // summarize results
   for ( var roll = 1; roll <= 6000; ++roll ) {
      face = Math.floor( 1 + Math.random() * 6 );
      ++frequency[ face ];
   }

   document.writeln( "<TABLE BORDER = '1' WIDTH = '100%'>" );
   document.writeln( "<TR><TD WIDTH = '100'><B>Face</B>" +
      "<TD><B>Frequency</B></TR>" );

```

Fig. 12.8 Dice-rolling program using arrays instead of **switch** (part 1 of 2).

```
      for ( face = 1; face < frequency.length; ++face )
         document.writeln( "<TR><TD>" + face + "<TD>" +
                           frequency[ face ] + "</TR>" );

      document.writeln( "</TABLE>" );
   </SCRIPT>

   </HEAD>
   <BODY>
   <P>Click Refresh (or Reload) to run the script again</P>
   </BODY>
   </HTML>
```

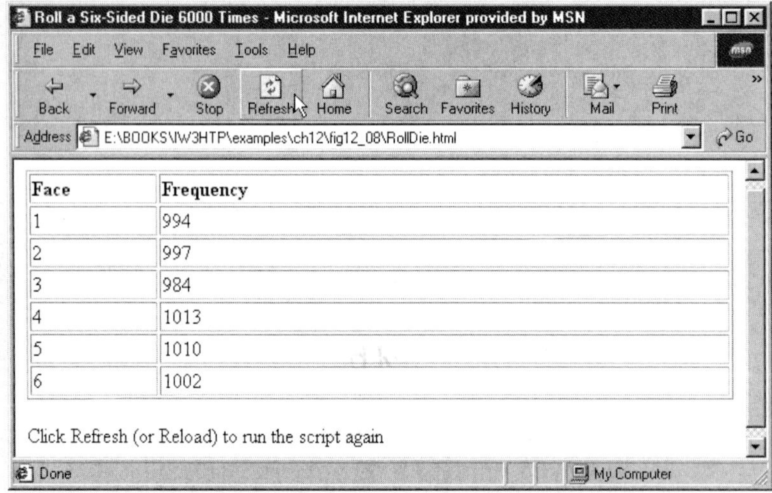

Fig. 12.8 Dice-rolling program using arrays instead of **`switch`** (part 2 of 2).

12.5 References and Reference Parameters

Two ways to pass arguments to functions (or methods) in many programming languages are *call-by-value* and *call-by-reference* (also called *pass-by-value* and *pass-by-reference*). When an argument is passed to a function by using call-by-value, a *copy* of the argument's value is made and is passed to the called function. In JavaScript, numbers and boolean values are passed to functions by value.

Testing and Debugging Tip 12.4

With call-by-value, changes to the called function's copy do not affect the original variable's value in the calling function. This prevents the accidental side effects that so greatly hinder the development of correct and reliable software systems.

With call-by-reference, the caller gives the called function the ability to directly access the caller's data and to modify that data if the called function so chooses. This is accomplished by passing to the called function the actual *location in memory* (also called the *address*) where the data resides. Call-by-reference can improve performance because it can eliminate the overhead of copying large amounts of data, but call-by-reference can weaken security because the called function can access the caller's data. In JavaScript, all objects and **Array**s are passed to functions by reference.

Software Engineering Observation 12.2

Unlike other languages, JavaScript does not allow the programmer to choose whether to pass each argument using call-by-value or call-by-reference. Numbers and boolean values are always passed using call-by-value. Objects are not passed to functions; rather, references to objects are passed to functions. When a function receives a reference to an object, the function can manipulate the object directly.

Software Engineering Observation 12.3

When returning information from a function via a **return** *statement, numbers and boolean values are always returned by value (i.e., a copy is returned) and objects are always returned by reference (i.e., a reference to the object is returned).*

To pass a reference to an object into a function, simply specify in the function call the reference name. Normally, the reference name is the identifier that is used to manipulate the object in the program. Mentioning the reference by its parameter name in the body of the called function actually refers to the original object in memory, and the original object can be accessed directly by the called function.

Because **Array**s are objects in JavaScript, **Array**s are passed to functions call-by-reference—a called function can access the elements of the caller's original **Array**s. The name of an array is actually a reference to an object that contains the array elements and the **length** variable, which indicates the number of elements in the array. In the next section, we demonstrate call-by-value and call-by-reference, using arrays.

Performance Tip 12.1

Passing arrays by reference makes sense for performance reasons. If arrays were passed by value, a copy of each element would be passed. For large, frequently passed arrays, this would waste time and would consume considerable storage for the copies of the arrays.

12.6 Passing Arrays to Functions

To pass an array argument to a function, specify the name of the array (a reference to the array) without any brackets. For example, if array **hourlyTemperatures** has been declared as

```
var hourlyTemperatures = new Array( 24 );
```

the function call

```
modifyArray( hourlyTemperatures );
```

passes array **hourlyTemperatures** to function **modifyArray**. In JavaScript, every array object "knows" its own size (via the **length** instance variable). Thus, when we pass an array object into a function, we do not separately pass the size of the array as an argument. In fact, Fig. 12.3 illustrated this concept when we passed **Array**s **n1** and **n2** to function **outputArray** to display each **Array**'s contents.

Although entire arrays are passed by using call-by-reference, *individual numeric and boolean array elements are passed by call-by-value exactly as simple numeric and boolean variables are passed* (the objects referred to by individual elements of an Array of objects are still passed by call-by-reference). Such simple single pieces of data are called *scalars* or *scalar quantities*. To pass an array element to a function, use the subscripted name of the array element as an argument in the function call.

For a function to receive an **Array** through a function call, the function's parameter list must specify a parameter that will be used to refer to the **Array** in the body of the function. Unlike other programming languages, JavaScript does not provide a special syntax for this purpose. JavaScript simply requires specifying the identifier for the **Array** in the parameter list. For example, the function header for function **modifyArray** might be written as

```
function modifyArray( b )
```

indicating that **modifyArray** expects to receive a parameter named **b** (the argument supplied in the calling function must be an **Array**). Because arrays are passed by reference, when the called function uses the array name **b**, it refers to the actual array in the caller (array **hourlyTemperatures** in the preceding call).

Software Engineering Observation 12.4

JavaScript does not check the number of arguments or types of arguments that are passed to a function. It is possible to pass any number of values to a function. JavaScript will attempt to perform conversions when the values are used

The script of Fig. 12.9 demonstrates the difference between passing an entire array and passing an array element. [*Note:* Function **start** (defined at line 10) is called in response to the **<BODY>**'s **ONLOAD** event.]

```
1  <!DOCTYPE HTML PUBLIC "-//W3C//DTD HTML 4.0 Transitional//EN">
2  <HTML>
3  <!-- Fig. 12.9: PassArray.html -->
4
5  <HEAD>
6  <TITLE>Passing Arrays and Individual Array
7        Elements to Functions</TITLE>
8
9  <SCRIPT LANGUAGE = "JavaScript">
10    function start()
11    {
12       var a = [ 1, 2, 3, 4, 5 ];
13
14       document.writeln( "<H2>Effects of passing entire " +
15                         "array call-by-reference</H2>" );
16       outputArray(
17          "The values of the original array are: ", a );
18
19       modifyArray( a );  // array a passed call-by-reference
20
21       outputArray(
22          "The values of the modified array are: ", a );
23
```

Fig. 12.9 Passing arrays and individual array elements to functions (part 1 of 2).

```
      document.writeln( "<H2>Effects of passing array " +
         "element call-by-value</H2>" +
         "a[3] before modifyElement: " + a[ 3 ] );

      modifyElement( a[ 3 ] );

      document.writeln(
         "<BR>a[3] after modifyElement: " + a[ 3 ] );
   }

   // outputs "header" followed by the contents of "theArray"
   function outputArray( header, theArray )
   {
      document.writeln(
         header + theArray.join( " " ) + "<BR>" );
   }

   // function that modifies the elements of an array
   function modifyArray( theArray )
   {
      for ( var j in theArray )
         theArray[ j ] *= 2;
   }

   // function that attempts to modify the value passed
   function modifyElement( e )
   {
      e *= 2;
      document.writeln( "<BR>value in modifyElement: " + e );
   }
</SCRIPT>

</HEAD><BODY ONLOAD = "start()"></BODY>
</HTML>
```

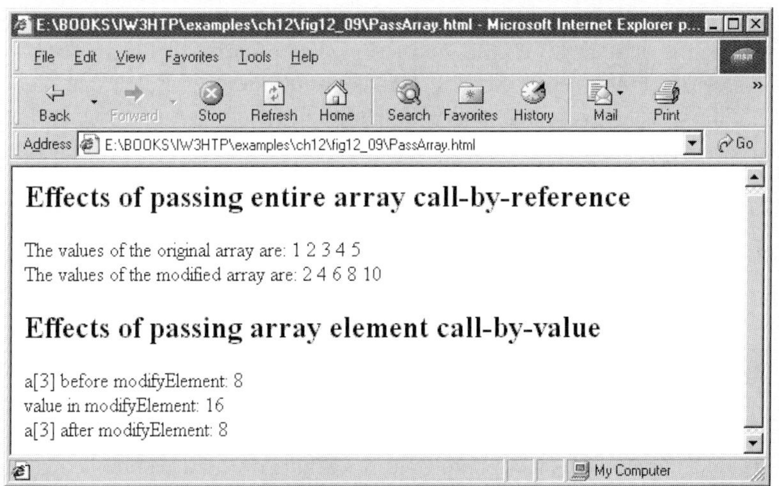

Fig. 12.9 Passing arrays and individual array elements to functions (part 2 of 2).

The statement at lines 16 and 17 invokes function **outputArray** to display the contents of array **a** before it is modified. Function outputArray (defined at line 35) receives a string to output and the array to output. The statement at lines 37 and 38

```
document.writeln(
   header + theArray.join( " " ) + "<BR>" );
```

uses **Array** method **join** to create a string containing all the elements in **theArray**. Method **join** takes as its argument a string containing the *separator* that should be used to separate the elements of the array in the string that is returned. If the argument is not specified, the empty string is used as the separator.

Line 19 invokes function **modifyArray** and passes it array **a**. The **modifyArray** function multiplies each element by 2. To illustrate that array **a**'s elements were modified, the statement at lines 21 and 22 invokes function **outputArray** again to display the contents of array **a** after it is modified. As the screen capture shows, the elements of **a** are indeed modified by **modifyArray**.

To show the value of **a[3]** before the call to **modifyElement**, lines 24 through 26 output the value of **a[3]** (and other information). Line 28 invokes **modifyElement** and passes **a[3]**. Remember that **a[3]** is actually one integer value in the array **a**. Also, remember that numeric values and boolean values are always passed to functions call-by-value. Therefore, a copy of **a[3]** is passed. Function **modifyElement** multiplies its argument by 2 and stores the result in its parameter **e**. The parameter of function **modifyElement** is a local variable in that function, so when the function terminates, the local variable is destroyed. Thus, when control is returned to **start**, the unmodified value of **a[3]** is displayed by the statement at lines 30 and 31.

12.7 Sorting Arrays

Sorting data (placing the data into some particular order, such as ascending or descending) is one of the most important computing scripts. A bank sorts all checks by account number, so that it can prepare individual bank statements at the end of each month. Telephone companies sort their lists of accounts by last name and, within that, by first name, to make it easy to find phone numbers. Virtually every organization must sort some data—in many cases, massive amounts of data. Sorting data is an intriguing problem that has attracted some of the most intense research efforts in the field of computer science. In this chapter we discuss one of the simplest sorting schemes. In the exercises, we investigate more complex schemes that yield superior performance.

Performance Tip 12.2

Sometimes, the simplest algorithms perform poorly. Their virtue is that they are easy to write, test and debug. More complex algorithms are sometimes needed to realize maximum performance.

Figure 12.10 sorts the values of the 10-element array **a** into ascending order. The technique we use is called the *bubble sort* or the *sinking sort* because the smaller values gradually "bubble" their way to the top of the array (toward the first element) like air bubbles rising in water, while the larger values sink to the bottom of the array. The technique makes several passes through the array. On each pass, successive pairs of elements are compared. If a pair is in increasing order (or the values are equal), we leave the values as they are. If a pair is in decreasing order, their values are swapped in the array. The script contains functions **start**, **outputArray**, **bubbleSort** and **swap**. Function **start** (line 9) initializes the array and invokes functions **outputArray** and **bubbleSort** to display the array and sort the array, respectively. Function **bubbleSort** (line 27) is called from **start** to sort array **a**. Function **swap** (line 41) is called from **bubbleSort** to exchange two elements of the array. [*Note:* Function **start** (line 9) handles the **<BODY>**'s **ONLOAD** event.]

```
1  <!DOCTYPE html PUBLIC "-//W3C//DTD HTML 4.0 Transitional//EN">
2  <HTML>
3  <!-- Fig. 12.10: BubbleSort.html -->
4  
5  <HEAD>
6  <TITLE>Sorting an Array with Bubble Sort</TITLE>
7  
8  <SCRIPT LANGUAGE = "JavaScript">
9     function start()
10    {
11       var a = [ 10, 1, 9, 2, 8, 3, 7, 4, 6, 5 ];
12 
13       document.writeln( "<H1>Sorting an Array</H1>" );
14       outputArray( "Data items in original order: ", a );
15       bubbleSort( a );  // sort the array
16       outputArray( "Data items in ascending order: ", a );
17    }
18 
19    // outputs "header" followed by the contents of "theArray"
20    function outputArray( header, theArray )
21    {
22       document.writeln(
23          "<P>" + header + theArray.join( " " ) + "</P>" );
24    }
25 
26    // sort the elements of an array with bubble sort
27    function bubbleSort( theArray )
28    {
29       // control number of passes of theArray
30       for ( var pass = 1; pass < theArray.length; ++pass )
31 
32          // one pass - control's number of comparison per pass
33          for ( var i = 0; i < theArray.length - 1; ++i )
34 
35             // perform one comparison
36             if ( theArray[ i ] > theArray[ i + 1 ] )
37                swap( theArray, i, i + 1 );  // swap elements
38    }
39 
40    // swap two elements of an array
41    function swap( theArray, first, second )
42    {
43       var hold;  // temporary holding area for swap
44 
```

Fig. 12.10 Sorting an array with bubble sort (part 1 of 2).

```
45          hold = theArray[ first ];
46          theArray[ first ] = theArray[ second ];
47          theArray[ second ] = hold;
48      }
49   </SCRIPT>
50
51   </HEAD><BODY ONLOAD = "start()"></BODY>
52   </HTML>
```

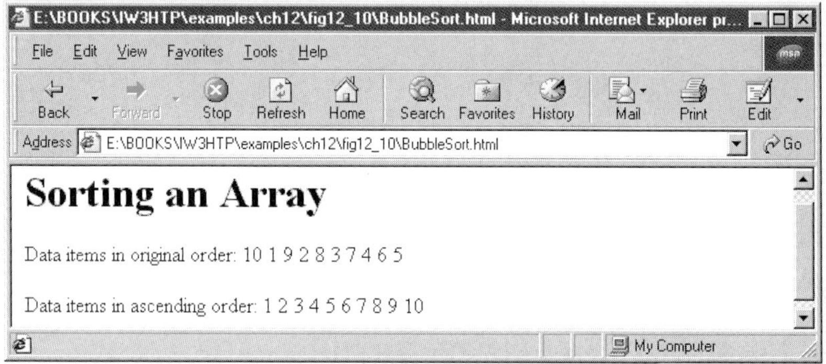

Fig. 12.10 Sorting an array with bubble sort (part 2 of 2).

The call to **outputArray** at line 14 displays the original values of array **a**. Line 15 invokes function **bubbleSort** and passes array **a** as the array to sort.

Function **bubbleSort** receives the array as parameter **theArray**. The nested **for** loop at lines 29 through 37

```
// control number of passes of theArray
for ( var pass = 1; pass < theArray.length; ++pass )

   // one pass - control's number of comparison per pass
   for ( var i = 0; i < theArray.length - 1; ++i )

      // perform one comparison
      if ( theArray[ i ] > theArray[ i + 1 ] )
         swap( theArray, i, i + 1 );   // swap elements
```

performs the sort. The outer loop controls the number of passes of the array. The inner loop controls the comparisons and swapping (if necessary) of the elements during each pass.

Function **bubbleSort** first compares **theArray[0]** to **theArray[1]**, then **theArray[1]** to **theArray[2]**, then **theArray[2]** to **theArray[3]** and so on until it completes the pass by comparing **theArray[8]** to **theArray[9]**. Although there are 10 elements, only nine comparisons are performed. Because of the way successive comparisons are performed, a large value may move down the array (sink) many positions on a single pass, but a small value may move up (bubble) only one position. On the first pass, the largest value is guaranteed to sink to the bottom element of the array, element **theArray[9]**. On the second pass, the second largest value is guaranteed to sink to element **theArray[8]**. On the ninth pass, the ninth largest value sinks to **theArray[1]**. This leaves the smallest value in **theArray[0]**, so only nine passes are needed to sort a 10-element array.

If a comparison reveals that the two elements are in descending order, function **swap** is invoked to exchange the two elements so they will be in ascending order in the array. Function **swap** receives a reference to the array (which it calls **theArray**) and two integers representing the subscripts of the two elements of the array to exchange. The exchange is performed by the three assignments

```
hold = theArray[ first ];
theArray[ first ] = theArray[ second ];
theArray[ second ] = hold;
```

where the extra variable **hold** temporarily stores one of the two values being swapped. The swap cannot be performed with only the two assignments

```
theArray[ first ] = theArray[ second ];
theArray[ second ] = theArray[ first ];
```

If **theArray[first]** is **7** and **theArray[second]** is **5**, after the first assignment both elements contain **5** and the value **7** is lost. Hence the need for the extra variable **hold**.

The chief virtue of the bubble sort is that it is easy to program. However, the bubble sort runs slowly. This becomes apparent when sorting large arrays. In the exercises, we will develop more efficient versions of the bubble sort and investigate some far more efficient sorts than the bubble sort. More advanced courses (often titled "Data Structures" or "Algorithms" or "Computational Complexity") investigate sorting and searching in greater depth.

The **Array** object in JavaScript has a built-in method ***sort*** for sorting arrays. Figure 12.11 demonstrates the **Array** object's **sort** method.

```
<!DOCTYPE html PUBLIC "-//W3C//DTD HTML 4.0 Transitional//EN">
<HTML>
<!-- Fig. 12.11: sort.html -->

<HEAD>
<TITLE>Sorting an Array with Array Method sort</TITLE>

<SCRIPT LANGUAGE = "JavaScript">
   function start()
   {
      var a = [ 10, 1, 9, 2, 8, 3, 7, 4, 6, 5 ];

      document.writeln( "<H1>Sorting an Array</H1>" );
      outputArray( "Data items in original order: ", a );
      a.sort( compareIntegers );  // sort the array
      outputArray( "Data items in ascending order: ", a );
   }

   // outputs "header" followed by the contents of "theArray"
   function outputArray( header, theArray )
   {
      document.writeln( "<P>" + header +
         theArray.join( " " ) + "</P>" );
   }

```

Fig. 12.11 Sorting an array with **sort** (part 1 of 2).

```
26     // comparison function for use with sort
27     function compareIntegers( value1, value2 )
28     {
29        return parseInt( value1 ) - parseInt( value2 );
30     }
31  </SCRIPT>
32
33  </HEAD><BODY ONLOAD = "start()"></BODY>
34  </HTML>
```

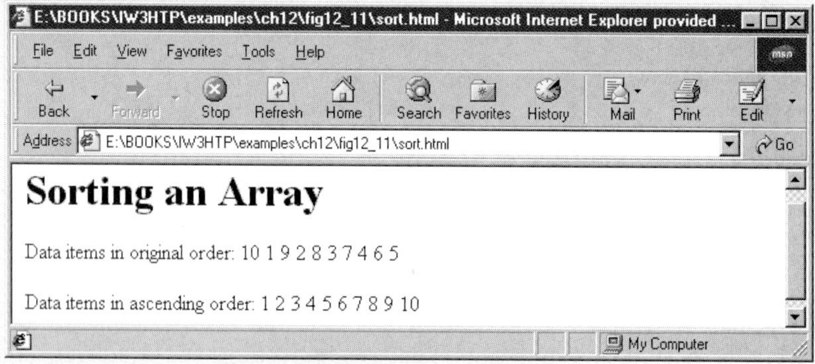

Fig. 12.11 Sorting an array with **sort** (part 2 of 2).

By default, **Array** method **sort** uses string comparisons to determine the sorting order of the **Array** elements. The strings are compared by the ASCII values of their characters. [*Note:* String comparison is discussed in more detail in Chapter 13, "JavaScript: Objects."] In this example, we would like once again to sort an array of integers.

Method **sort** takes as its optional argument the name of a function (called the *comparator function*) that compares its two arguments and returns one of the following:

- a negative value if the first argument is less than the second,
- zero if the arguments are equal, or
- a positive value if the first argument is greater than the second.

Function **compareIntegers** (defined at line 27) is used in this example as the comparator function for method **sort**. It calculates the difference between the integer values of its two arguments (function **parseInt** is used to ensure that the arguments are properly handled as integers). If the first argument is less than the second, the difference will be a negative value. If the arguments are equal, the difference will be zero. If the first argument is greater than the second, the difference will be a positive value.

Line 15

```
a.sort( compareIntegers );  // sort the array
```

invokes **Array** object **a**'s **sort** method and passes function **compareIntegers** as an argument. In JavaScript, functions are actually considered to be data and can be assigned to variables and passed to functions like any other data. Here, method **sort** receives function **compareIntegers** as an argument, then uses the function to compare elements of the **Array a** to determine their sorting order.

Software Engineering Observation 12.5

Functions in JavaScript are considered to be data. Therefore, functions can be assigned to variables, stored in **`Array`***s and passed to functions like other data types.*

12.8 Searching Arrays: Linear Search and Binary Search

Often, a programmer will be working with large amounts of data stored in arrays. It may be necessary to determine whether an array contains a value that matches a certain *key value.* The process of locating a particular element value in an array is called *searching.* In this section we discuss two searching techniques—the simple *linear search* technique and the more efficient *binary search* technique. Exercises 12.31 and 12.32 at the end of this chapter ask you to implement recursive versions of the linear search and the binary search.

In the script of Fig. 12.12, function **`linearSearch`** (defined at line 33) uses a **`for`** structure containing an **`if`** structure to compare each element of an array with a *search key* (lines 35 through 37). If the search key is found, the function returns the subscript (line 37) value for the element to indicate the exact position of the search key in the array. [*Note:* The loop in the **`linearSearch`** function terminates and the function returns control to the caller as soon as the **`return`** statement in its body executes.] If the search key is not found, the function returns **`-1`** to indicate that the search key was not found. (We return **`-1`** because it is not a valid subscript number.)

If the array being searched is not in any particular order, it is just as likely that the value will be found in the first element as the last. On average, therefore, the program will have to compare the search key with half the elements of the array.

The program contains a 100-element array (defined at line 9) filled with the even integers from 0 to 198. The user types the search key in a text field (defined in the HTML form at lines 46 through 54) and presses the **Search** button to start the search. [*Note:* The array is passed to **`linearSearch`** even though the array is a global variable. This is done because an array is normally passed to a function for searching.]

```
1  <!DOCTYPE HTML PUBLIC "-//W3C//DTD HTML 4.0 Transitional//EN">
2  <HTML>
3  <!-- Fig. 12.12: LinearSearch.html -->
4
5  <HEAD>
6  <TITLE>Linear Search of an Array</TITLE>
7
8  <SCRIPT LANGUAGE = "JavaScript">
9     var a = new Array( 100 );  // create an Array
10
11    // fill Array with even integer values from 0 to 198
12    for ( var i = 0; i < a.length; ++i )
13       a[ i ] = 2 * i;
14
15    // function called when "Search" button is pressed
16    function buttonPressed()
17    {
18       var searchKey = searchForm.inputVal.value;
19
```

Fig. 12.12 Linear search of an array (part 1 of 3).

```
        // Array a is passed to linearSearch even though it
        // is a global variable. Normally an array will
        // be passed to a method for searching.
        var element = linearSearch( a, parseInt( searchKey ) );

        if ( element != -1 )
           searchForm.result.value =
              "Found value in element " + element;
        else
           searchForm.result.value = "Value not found";
     }

     // Search "theArray" for the specified "key" value
     function linearSearch( theArray, key )
     {
        for ( var n = 0; n < theArray.length; ++n )
           if ( theArray[ n ] == key )
              return n;

        return -1;
     }
  </SCRIPT>

  </HEAD>

  <BODY>
  <FORM NAME = "searchForm">
     <P>Enter integer search key<BR>
     <INPUT NAME = "inputVal" TYPE = "text">
     <INPUT NAME = "search" TYPE = "button" VALUE = "Search"
            ONCLICK = "buttonPressed()"><BR></P>

     <P>Result<BR>
     <INPUT NAME = "result" TYPE = "text" SIZE = "30"></P>
  </FORM>
  </BODY>
  </HTML>
```

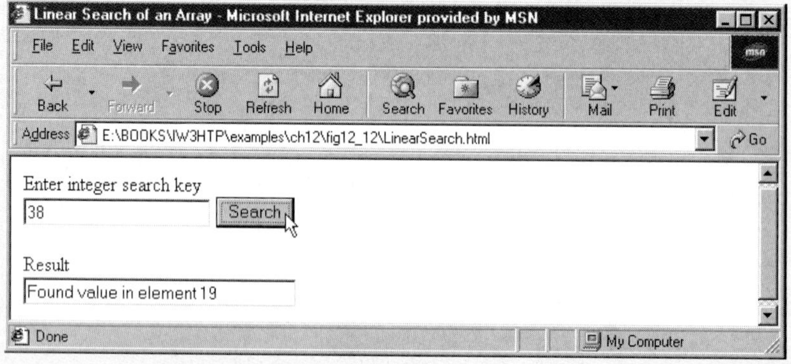

Fig. 12.12 Linear search of an array (part 2 of 3).

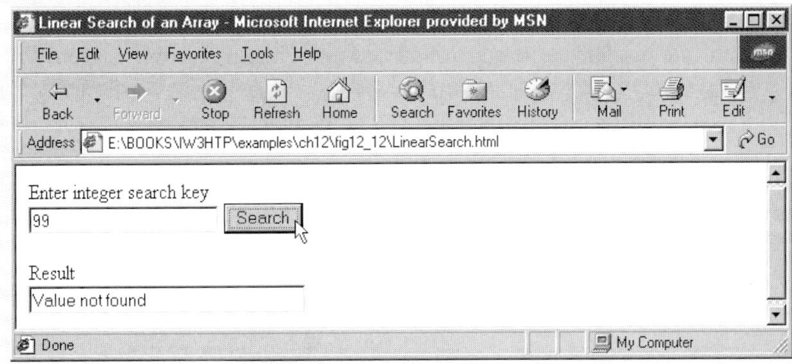

Fig. 12.12 Linear search of an array (part 3 of 3).

The linear search function works well for small arrays or for unsorted arrays. However, for large arrays, linear searching is inefficient. If the array is sorted, the high-speed binary search technique can be used.

After each comparison, the binary search algorithm eliminates half of the elements in the array being searched. The algorithm locates the middle array element and compares it to the search key. If they are equal, the search key has been found and the subscript of that element is returned. Otherwise, the problem is reduced to searching half of the array. If the search key is less than the middle array element, the first half of the array is searched; otherwise, the second half of the array is searched. If the search key is not the middle element in the specified subarray (piece of the original array), the algorithm is repeated on one quarter of the original array. The search continues until the search key is equal to the middle element of a subarray or until the subarray consists of one element that is not equal to the search key (i.e., the search key is not found).

In a worst-case scenario, searching an array of 1024 elements will take only 10 comparisons using a binary search. Repeatedly dividing 1024 by 2 (because after each comparison we are able to eliminate half of the array) yields the values 512, 256, 128, 64, 32, 16, 8, 4, 2 and 1. The number 1024 (2^{10}) is divided by 2 only ten times to get the value 1. Dividing by 2 is equivalent to one comparison in the binary search algorithm. An array of 1,048,576 (2^{20}) elements takes a maximum of 20 comparisons to find the key. An array of one billion elements takes a maximum of 30 comparisons to find the key. When searching a sorted array, this is a tremendous increase in performance over the linear search that required comparing the search key to an average of half the elements in the array. For a one-billion-element array, this is a difference between an average of 500 million comparisons and a maximum of 30 comparisons! The maximum number of comparisons needed for the binary search of any sorted array is the exponent of the first power of 2 greater than the number of elements in the array.

Figure 12.13 presents the iterative version of function **`binarySearch`** (line 35). Function **`binarySearch`** is called from function **`buttonPressed`**—the event handler for the **`search`** button in the HTML form. Function **`binarySearch`** receives two arguments—an array called **`theArray`** (the array to search) and **`key`** (the search key). The array is passed to **`binarySearch`**, even though the array is global variable. Once again, this is done because an array is normally passed to a function for searching. If **key** matches the **middle** element of a subarray, **middle** (the subscript of the current element) is returned, to indicate that the value was found and the search is complete. If **key** does not match the **middle** element of a subarray, the **low** subscript or the **high** subscript (both declared in the function) is adjusted, so that a smaller subarray can be searched. If **key** is less than the middle element, the **high** subscript is set to **middle - 1** and the search is continued on the elements from **low** to **middle - 1**. If **key** is greater than the middle element, the **low** subscript is set to **middle + 1** and the search is continued on the elements from **middle + 1** to **high**. These comparisons are performed by the nested **if/else** structure at lines 49 through 54.

```
1  <!DOCTYPE HTML PUBLIC "-//W3C//DTD HTML 4.0 Transitional//EN">
2  <HTML>
3  <!-- Fig. 12.13: BinarySearch.html -->
4  
5  <HEAD>
6  <TITLE>Binary Search of an Array</TITLE>
7  
8  <SCRIPT LANGUAGE = "JavaScript">
9     var a = new Array( 15 );
10 
11    for ( var i = 0; i < a.length; ++i )
12       a[ i ] = 2 * i;
13 
14    // function called when "Search" button is pressed
15    function buttonPressed()
16    {
17       var searchKey = searchForm.inputVal.value;
18 
19       searchForm.result.value =
20          "Portions of array searched\n";
21 
22       // Array a is passed to binarySearch even though it
23       // is a global variable. This is done because normally
24       // an array is passed to a method for searching.
25       var element = binarySearch( a, parseInt( searchKey ) );
26 
27       if ( element != -1 )
28          searchForm.result.value +=
29             "\nFound value in element " + element;
30       else
31          searchForm.result.value += "\nValue not found";
32    }
33 
34    // Binary search
35    function binarySearch( theArray, key )
36    {
37       var low = 0;                       // low subscript
38       var high = theArray.length - 1;    // high subscript
39       var middle;                        // middle subscript
```

Fig. 12.13 Binary search of a sorted array (part 1 of 3).

```

      while ( low <= high ) {
         middle = ( low + high ) / 2;

         // The following line is used to display the part
         // of theArray currently being manipulated during
         // each iteration of the binary search loop.
         buildOutput( theArray, low, middle, high );

         if ( key == theArray[ middle ] )  // match
            return middle;
         else if ( key < theArray[ middle ] )
            high = middle - 1;  // search low end of array
         else
            low = middle + 1;   // search high end of array
      }

      return -1;   // searchKey not found
   }

   // Build one row of output showing the current
   // part of the array being processed.
   function buildOutput( theArray, low, mid, high )
   {
      for ( var i = 0; i < theArray.length; i++ ) {
         if ( i < low || i > high )
            searchForm.result.value += "    ";
         else if ( i == mid ) // mark middle element in output
            searchForm.result.value += a[ i ] +
               ( theArray[ i ] < 10 ? "*  " : "* " );
         else
            searchForm.result.value += a[ i ] +
               ( theArray[ i ] < 10 ? "   " : "  " );
      }

      searchForm.result.value += "\n";
   }
</SCRIPT>

</HEAD>

<BODY>
<FORM NAME = "searchForm">
   <P>Enter integer search key<BR>
   <INPUT NAME = "inputVal" TYPE = "text">
   <INPUT NAME = "search" TYPE = "button" VALUE = "Search"
         ONCLICK = "buttonPressed()"><BR></P>
   <P>Result<BR><TEXTAREA NAME = "result" ROWS = "7" COLS = "60">
               </TEXTAREA></P>
</FORM>
</BODY>
</HTML>
```

Fig. 12.13 Binary search of a sorted array (part 2 of 3).

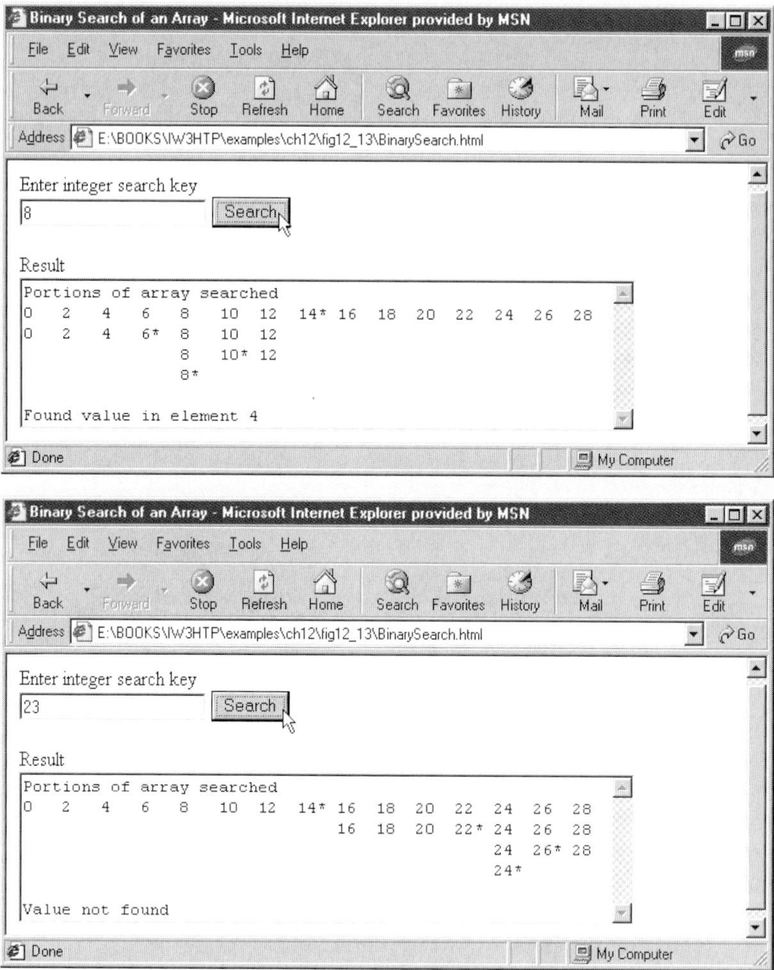

Fig. 12.13 Binary search of a sorted array (part 3 of 3).

The program uses a 15-element array. The first power of 2 greater than the number of array elements is 16 (2^4)—at most four comparisons are required to find the **key**. To illustrate this, function **binarySearch** calls function **buildOutput** from line 47 to output each subarray during the binary search process. The middle element in each subarray is marked with an asterisk (*) to indicate the element to which the **key** is compared. Each search in this example results in a maximum of four lines of output—one per comparison.

12.9 Multiple-Subscripted Arrays

Multiple-subscripted arrays with two subscripts are often used to represent *tables* of values consisting of information arranged in *rows* and *columns*. To identify a particular table element, we must specify the two subscripts—by convention, the first identifies the element's row and the second identifies the element's column. Arrays that require two subscripts to identify a particular element are called *double-subscripted arrays* (also called *two-dimensional arrays*). Note that multiple-subscripted arrays can have more than two subscripts. JavaScript does not support multiple-subscripted arrays directly, but does allow the programmer to specify single-subscripted arrays whose elements are also single-subscripted arrays, thus achieving the same effect. Figure 12.14 illustrates a double-subscripted array, **a**, containing three rows and four columns (i.e., a 3-by-4 array). In general, an array with *m* rows and *n* columns is called an *m-by-n array*.

Every element in array **a** is identified in Fig. 12.14 by an element name of the form **a[i][j]**; **a** is the name of the array and **i** and **j** are the subscripts that uniquely identify the row and column of each element in **a**. Notice that the names of the elements in the first row all have a first subscript of **0**; the names of the elements in the fourth column all have a second subscript of **3**.

Multiple-subscripted arrays can be initialized in declarations like a single-subscripted array. A double-subscripted array **b** with two rows and two columns could be declared and initialized with

```
var b = [ [ 1, 2 ], [ 3, 4 ] ];
```

The values are grouped by row in square brackets. So, **1** and **2** initialize **b[0][0]** and **b[0][1]**, and **3** and **4** initialize **b[1][0]** and **b[1][1]**. The compiler determines the number of rows by counting the number of sub-initializer lists (represented by sets of square brackets) in the main initializer list. The compiler determines the number of columns in each row by counting the number of initializer values in the sub-initializer list for that row.

Multiple-subscripted arrays are maintained as arrays of arrays. The declaration

```
var b = [ [ 1, 2 ], [ 3, 4, 5 ] ];
```

creates array **b** with row **0** containing two elements (**1** and **2**) and row **1** containing three elements (**3**, **4** and **5**).

A multiple-subscripted array in which each row has a different number of columns can be allocated dynamically as follows:

```
var b;
b = new Array( 2 );    // allocate rows
b[ 0 ] = new Array( 5 ); // allocate columns for row 0
b[ 1 ] = new Array( 3 ); // allocate columns for row 1
```

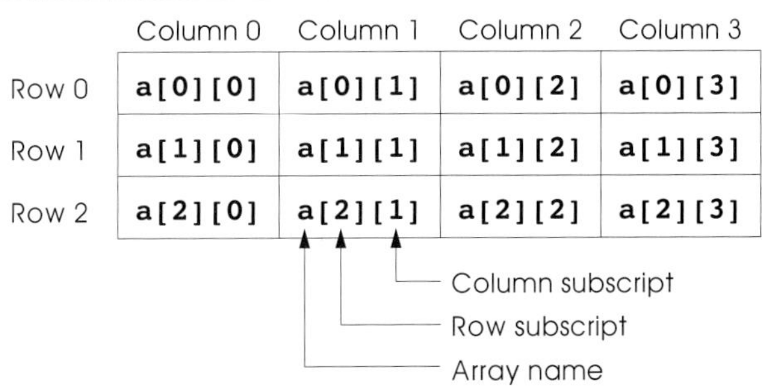

Column 0
Column 1
Column 2
Column 3
Row 0
a[0][0]
a[0][1]
a[0][2]
a[0][3]
Row 1
a[1][0]
a[1][1]
a[1][2]
a[1][3]
Row 2
a[2][0]
a[2][1]
a[2][2]
a[2][3]
Column subscript
Row subscript
Array name

Fig. 12.14 A double-subscripted array with three rows and four columns.

The preceding code creates a two-dimensional array with two rows. Row **0** has five columns and row **1** has three columns.

Figure 12.15 initializes double-subscripted arrays in declarations and uses nested **for/in** loops to *traverse the arrays* (i.e., manipulate every element of the array).

The program declares two arrays in function **start** (which is called in response to the **<BODY>**'s **ONLOAD** event). The declaration of **array1** (line 11) provides six initializers in two sublists. The first sublist initializes the first row of the array to the values 1, 2 and 3; and the second sublist initializes the second row of the array to the values 4, 5 and 6. The declaration of **array2** (line 13) provides six initializers in three sublists. The sublist for the first row explicitly initializes the first row to have two elements, with values 1 and 2, respectively. The sublist for the second row initializes the second row to have one element with value 3. The sublist for the third row initializes the third row to the values 4, 5 and 6.

```
1  <!DOCTYPE html PUBLIC "-//W3C//DTD HTML 4.0 Transitional//EN">
2  <HTML>
3  <!-- Fig. 12.15: InitArray.html -->
4
5  <HEAD>
6  <TITLE>Initializing Multidimensional Arrays</TITLE>
7
8  <SCRIPT LANGUAGE = "JavaScript">
9     function start()
10    {
11       var array1 = [ [ 1, 2, 3 ],          // first row
12                      [ 4, 5, 6 ] ];        // second row
13       var array2 = [ [ 1, 2 ],             // first row
14                      [ 3 ],                // second row
15                      [ 4, 5, 6 ] ];        // third row
16
17       outputArray( "Values in array1 by row", array1 );
18       outputArray( "Values in array2 by row", array2 );
19    }
20
21    function outputArray( header, theArray )
22    {
23       document.writeln( "<H2>" + header + "</H2><TT>" );
24
25       for ( var i in theArray ) {
26
27          for ( var j in theArray[ i ] )
28             document.write( theArray[ i ][ j ] + " " );
29
30          document.writeln( "<BR>" );
31       }
32
33       document.writeln( "</TT>" );
34    }
35 </SCRIPT>
36
37 </HEAD><BODY ONLOAD = "start()"></BODY>
38 </HTML>
```

Fig. 12.15 Initializing multidimensional arrays (part 1 of 2).

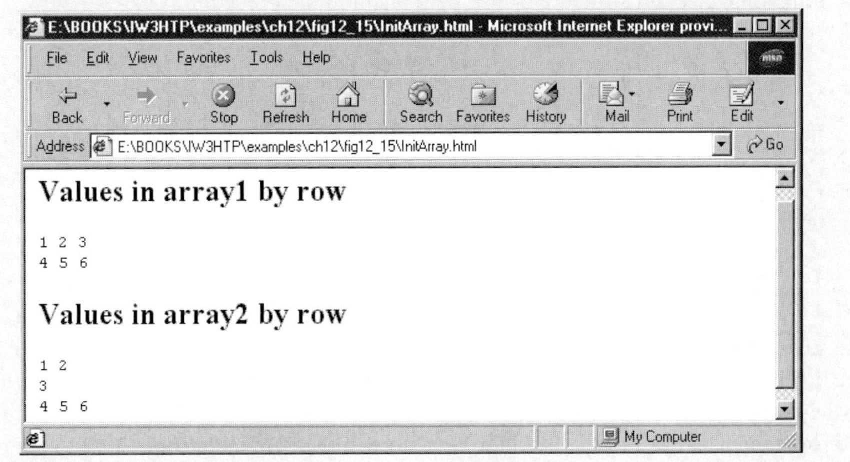

Fig. 12.15 Initializing multidimensional arrays (part 2 of 2).

Function **start** calls function **outputArray** from lines 17 and 18 to display each array's elements in the Web page. Function **outputArray** receives two arguments—a string **header** to output before the array and the array to output (called **theArray**). Note the use of a nested **for/in** structure to output the rows of each double-subscripted array. The outer **for/in** structure iterates over the rows of the array. The inner **for/in** structure iterates over the columns of the current row being processed. The nested **for/in** structure in this example could have been written with **for** structures as follows:

```
for ( var i = 0; i < theArray.length; ++i ) {
   for ( var j = 0; j < theArray[ i ].length; ++j )
      document.write( theArray[ i ][ j ] + " " );
   document.writeln( "<BR>" );
}
```

In the outer **for** structure, the expression **theArray.length** determines the number of rows in the array. In the inner **for** structure, the expression **theArray[i].length** determines the number of columns in each row of the array. This condition enables the loop to determine, for each row, the exact number of columns.

Many common array manipulations use **for** or **for/in** repetition structures. For example, the following **for** structure sets all the elements in the third row of array **a** in Fig. 12.14 to zero:

```
for ( int col = 0; col < a[ 2 ].length; ++col )
   a[ 2 ][ col ] = 0;
```

We specified the *third* row, therefore we know that the first subscript is always **2** (**0** is the first row and **1** is the second row). The **for** loop varies only the second subscript (i.e., the column subscript). The preceding **for** structure is equivalent to the assignment statements

```
a[ 2 ][ 0 ] = 0;
a[ 2 ][ 1 ] = 0;
a[ 2 ][ 2 ] = 0;
a[ 2 ][ 3 ] = 0;
```

The following **for/in** structure is also equivalent to the preceding **for** structure

```
for ( var col in a[ 2 ] )
   a[ 2 ][ col ] = 0;
```

The following nested **for** structure determines the total of all the elements in array **a**.

```
var total = 0;

for ( var row = 0; row < a.length; ++row )
   for ( var col = 0; col < a[ row ].length; ++col )
      total += a[ row ][ col ];
```

The **for** structure totals the elements of the array, one row at a time. The outer **for** structure begins by setting the **row** subscript to **0**, so the elements of the first row may be totaled by the inner **for** structure. The outer **for** structure then increments **row** to **1**, so the second row can be totaled. Then, the outer **for** structure increments **row** to **2**, so the third row can be totaled. The result can be displayed when the nested **for** structure terminates. The preceding **for** structure is equivalent to the following **for/in** structure

```
var total = 0;

for ( var row in a )
   for ( var col in a[ row ] )
      total += a[ row ][ col ];
```

The script of Fig. 12.16 performs several other common array manipulations on 3-by-4 array **grades**. Each row of the array represents a student, and each column represents a grade on one of the four exams the students took during the semester. The array manipulations are performed by four functions. Function **minimum** (line 31) determines the lowest grade of any student for the semester. Function **maximum** (line 44) determines the highest grade of any student for the semester. Function **average** (line 58) determines a particular student's semester average. Function **outputArray** (line 69) displays the double-subscripted array in a tabular format.

```
1  <!DOCTYPE html PUBLIC "-//W3C//DTD HTML 4.0 Transitional//EN">
2  <HTML>
3  <!-- Fig. 12.16: DoubleArray.html -->
4
5  <HEAD>
6  <TITLE>Double-subscripted Array Example</TITLE>
7
8  <SCRIPT LANGUAGE = "JavaScript">
9     function start()
10    {
11       var grades = [ [ 77, 68, 86, 73 ],
12                      [ 96, 87, 89, 81 ],
13                      [ 70, 90, 86, 81 ] ];
14
```

Fig. 12.16 Example of using double-subscripted arrays (part 1 of 3).

```
      document.writeln( "<PRE>" );
      outputArray( grades );

      document.writeln(
         "\n\nLowest grade: " + minimum( grades ) +
         "\nHighest grade: " + maximum( grades ) );

      // calculate average for each student (i.e., each row)
      for ( var i in grades )
         document.write( "\nAverage for student " + i +
            " is " + average( grades[ i ] ) );

      document.writeln( "</PRE>" );
   }

   // find the minimum grade
   function minimum( grades )
   {
      var lowGrade = 100;

      for ( var i in grades )
         for ( var j in grades[ i ] )
            if ( grades[ i ][ j ] < lowGrade )
               lowGrade = grades[ i ][ j ];

      return lowGrade;
   }

   // find the maximum grade
   function maximum( grades )
   {
      var highGrade = 0;

      for ( var i in grades )
         for ( var j in grades[ i ] )
            if ( grades[ i ][ j ] > highGrade )
               highGrade = grades[ i ][ j ];

      return highGrade;
   }

   // determine the average grade for a particular
   // student (or set of grades)
   function average( setOfGrades )
   {
      var total = 0;

      for ( var i in setOfGrades )
         total += setOfGrades[ i ];

      return total / setOfGrades.length;
   }

```

Fig. 12.16 Example of using double-subscripted arrays (part 2 of 3).

```
      // output grades
      function outputArray( grades )
      {
         document.write( "               " );  // align heads

         for ( var i in grades[ 0 ] )
            document.write( "[" + i + "]   " );

         for ( var i in grades ) {
            document.write( "<BR>grades[" + i + "]    " );

            for ( var j in grades[ i ] )
               document.write( grades[ i ][ j ] + "    " );
         }
      }
   </SCRIPT>

   </HEAD><BODY ONLOAD = "start()"></BODY>
   </HTML>
```

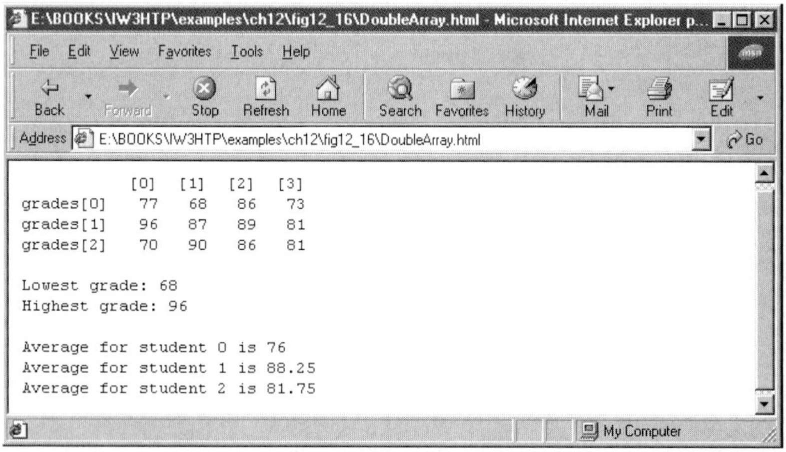

```
              [0]  [1]  [2]  [3]
grades[0]     77   68   86   73
grades[1]     96   87   89   81
grades[2]     70   90   86   81

Lowest grade: 68
Highest grade: 96

Average for student 0 is 76
Average for student 1 is 88.25
Average for student 2 is 81.75
```

Fig. 12.16 Example of using double-subscripted arrays (part 3 of 3).

Functions **minimum**, **maximum** and **ouputArray** each process array **grades**. Each function loops through array **grades**, using nested **for/in** structures. The following nested **for/in** structure is from the function **minimum** definition:

```
var lowGrade = 100;

for ( var i in grades )
   for ( var j in grades[ i ] )
      if ( grades[ i ][ j ] < lowGrade )
         lowGrade = grades[ i ][ j ];
```

The outer **for/in** structure iterates over the rows of the array starting with the first row. The inner **for/in** structure iterates over the four grades of the current row and compares each grade to **lowGrade**. If a grade is less than **lowGrade**, **lowGrade** is set to that grade. The outer **for/in** structure then begins processing the next row. The elements of the second row are compared to variable **lowGrade**. The outer **for** structure then begins processing the next row. The elements of the third row are compared to the **lowGrade** variable. When execution of the nested structure is complete, **lowGrade** contains the smallest grade in the double-subscripted array. Function **maximum** works similarly to function **minimum**.

Function **average** takes one argument—a single-subscripted array of test results for a particular student. When **average** is called, the argument is **grades[i]**, which specifies that a particular row of the double-subscripted array **grades** is to be passed to **average**. For example, the argument **grades[1]** represents the four values (a single-subscripted array of grades) stored in the second row of the double-subscripted array **grades**. Remember that, in JavaScript, a double-subscripted array is an array with elements that are single-subscripted arrays. Function **average** calculates the sum of the array elements, divides the total by the number of test results and returns the floating-point result.

SUMMARY

- Arrays are data structures consisting of related data items (sometimes called collections).
- Arrays are "dynamic" entities, in that they can change size after they are created.
- An array is a group of memory locations that all have the same name and are normally of the same type (although this is not required).
- To refer to a particular location or element in the array, specify the name of the array and the position number of the particular element in the array.
- The first element in every array is the zeroth element.
- The position number in square brackets is called a subscript (or an index). A subscript must be an integer or an integer expression.
- The length of an array is determined by arrayName**.length**.
- An array in JavaScript is an **Array** object. Operator **new** is used to dynamically allocate the number of elements required by an array. Operator **new** creates an object as the program executes, by obtaining enough memory to store an object of the type specified to the right of **new**.
- The process of creating new objects is also known as creating an instance or instantiating an object, and operator **new** is known as the dynamic memory allocation operator.
- An array can be initialized with a comma-separated initializer list enclosed in square brackets (**[** and **]**). The array size is determined by the number of values in the initializer list. When using an initializer list in an array declaration, the **new** operator is not required to create the **Array** object—this operator is provided automatically by the interpreter.
- It is possible to reserve a space in an **Array** for a value to be specified later, by using a comma as a place holder in the initializer list.
- JavaScript's **for/in** control structure enables a script to perform a task **for** each element **in** an array. This is also known as iterating over the array elements.
- The basic syntax of a **for/in** structure is

```
for ( var element in arrayName )
   statement
```

- where element is the name of the variable to which the **for/in** structure assigns a subscript number and arrayName is the array over which to iterate.

- When a value is assigned to an element of an **Array** that is outside the current bounds, JavaScript automatically allocates more memory so the **Array** contains the appropriate number of elements. The new elements of the array are not initialized.
- Two ways to pass arguments to functions (or methods) in many programming languages are call-by-value and call-by-reference (also called pass-by-value and pass-by-reference).
- When an argument is passed to a function by using call-by-value, a copy of the argument's value is made and passed to the called function. Numbers and boolean values are passed by value.
- With call-by-reference, the caller gives the called function the ability to directly access the caller's data and to modify that data. This effect is accomplished by passing to the called function the location or address in memory where the data resides. All objects and **Array**s are passed by reference.
- To pass a reference to an object into a function, specify in the function call the reference name. The reference name is the identifier that is used to manipulate the object in the program.
- Because **Array**s are objects in JavaScript, **Array**s are passed to functions by call-by-reference—a called function can access the elements of the caller's original **Array**s.
- The name of an array is actually a reference to an object that contains the array elements and the **length** variable, which indicates the number of elements in the array.
- Placing data into some particular order, such as ascending or descending, is called sorting the data.
- In the sorting technique called bubble sort (or sinking sort), the smaller values gradually "bubble" their way to the top of the array (i.e., toward the first element), like air bubbles rising in water, while the larger values sink to the bottom of the array.
- The bubble sort makes several passes through the array. On each pass, successive pairs of elements are compared. If a pair is in increasing order (or the values are equal), the values are left in their current order. If a pair is in decreasing order, their values are swapped in the array. Because of the way the successive comparisons are made, a large value may move down the array (sink) many positions on a single pass, but a small value can move up (bubble) only one position.
- The chief virtue of the bubble sort is that it is easy to program. However, the bubble sort runs slowly. This defect becomes apparent when sorting large arrays.
- The **Array** object in JavaScript has a built-in method, **sort**, for sorting arrays. By default, **Array** method **sort** uses string comparisons to determine the sorting order of the **Array** elements.
- Method **sort** takes as its optional argument the comparator function that compares its two arguments and returns a negative value if the first argument is less than the second, zero if the arguments are equal or a positive value if the first argument is greater than the second.
- The process of locating a particular element value (the key value) in an array is called searching.
- Linear search compares each element of an array with a search key. If the search key is found, the linear search normally returns the subscript for the element to indicate the exact position of the search key in the array. If the search key is not found, the linear search normally returns **-1** to indicate that the search key was not found.
- If the array being searched with a linear search is not in any particular order, it is just as likely that the value will be found in the first element as the last. On average, the program will have to compare the search key with half the elements of the array.
- Linear search works well for small arrays or for unsorted arrays. However, for large arrays linear searching is inefficient.
- If an array is sorted, the binary search technique can be used to locate a search key. The binary search algorithm eliminates half of the elements in the array being searched after each comparison. The algorithm locates the middle array element and compares it to the search key. If they are equal,

the search key has been found and the subscript of that element is returned. Otherwise, the problem is reduced to searching half of the array. If the search key is less than the middle array element, the first half of the array is searched; otherwise, the second half of the array is searched.

- The maximum number of comparisons needed for the binary search of any sorted array is the exponent of the first power of 2 greater than the number of elements in the array.
- Multiple-subscripted arrays with two subscripts are often used to represent tables of values consisting of information arranged in rows and columns. Two subscripts identify a particular table element—the first identifies the element's row and the second identifies the element's column.
- Arrays requiring two subscripts to identify a particular element are called double-subscripted arrays (or two-dimensional arrays). Multiple-subscripted arrays can have more than two subscripts.
- JavaScript does not support multiple-subscripted arrays directly, but does allow single-subscripted arrays whose elements are also single-subscripted arrays, thus achieving the same effect.
- In general, an array with m rows and n columns is called an m-by-n array.
- Multiple-subscripted arrays can be initialized with initializer lists. The compiler determines the number of rows by counting the number of sub-initializer lists (represented by sets of square brackets) in the main initializer list. The compiler determines the number of columns in each row by counting the number of initializer values in the sub-initializer list for that row.

TERMINOLOGY

a[i]
a[i][j]
array
array initializer list
Array object
binary search of an array
bounds of an array
bubble sort
call-by-reference
call-by-value
collection
column subscript
comma-separated initializer list
comparator function
creating an instance
data structure
declare an array
double-subscripted array
dynamic memory allocation operator (**new**)
element of an array
for/**in** repetition structure
index of an element
initialize an array
initializer
initializer list
instantiating an object
iterating over an array's elements
length of an **Array**
linear search of an array
location in an array
lvalue
m-by-*n* array
multiple-subscripted array
name of an array
new operator
off-by-one error
pass-by-reference
pass-by-value
passing arrays to functions
pass of a bubble sort
place holder in an initializer list (**,**)
position number of an element
related data items
reserve a space in an **Array**
row subscript
searching an array
search key
single-subscripted array
sinking sort
sorting an array
sort method of the **Array** object
square brackets **[ ]**
subscript
table of values
tabular format
temporary area for exchange of values
value of an element
zeroth element

COMMON PROGRAMMING ERRORS

12.1 It is important to note the difference between the "seventh element of the array" and "array element seven." Because array subscripts begin at 0, the "seventh element of the array" has a subscript of 6, while "array element seven" has a subscript of 7 and is actually the eighth element of the array. This confusion is a source of "off-by-one" errors.

12.2 Assuming that the elements of an array are initialized when the array is allocated may result in logic errors.

12.3 Referring to an element outside the **Array** bounds is normally a logic error.

GOOD PROGRAMMING PRACTICE

12.1 Strive for program clarity. It is sometimes worthwhile to trade off the most efficient use of memory or processor time in favor of writing clearer programs.

PERFORMANCE TIPS

12.1 Passing arrays by reference makes sense for performance reasons. If arrays were passed by value, a copy of each element would be passed. For large, frequently passed arrays, this would waste time and would consume considerable storage for the copies of the arrays.

12.2 Sometimes, the simplest algorithms perform poorly. Their virtue is that they are easy to write, test and debug. More complex algorithms are sometimes needed to realize maximum performance.

SOFTWARE ENGINEERING OBSERVATIONS

12.1 JavaScript automatically reallocates an **Array** when a value is assigned to an element that is outside the bounds of the original **Array**. Elements between the last element of the original **Array** and the new element have undefined values.

12.2 Unlike other languages, JavaScript does not allow the programmer to choose whether to pass each argument using call-by-value or call-by-reference. Numbers and boolean values are always passed using call-by-value. Objects are not passed to functions; rather, references to objects are passed to functions. When a function receives a reference to an object, the function can manipulate the object directly.

12.3 When returning information from a function via a **return** statement, numbers and boolean values are always returned by value (i.e., a copy is returned) and objects are always returned by reference (i.e., a reference to the object is returned).

12.4 JavaScript does not check the number of arguments or types of arguments that are passed to a function. It is possible to pass any number of values to a function. JavaScript will attempt to perform conversions when the values are used

12.5 Functions in JavaScript are considered to be data. Therefore, functions can be assigned to variables, stored in **Array**s and passed to functions like other data types.

TESTING AND DEBUGGING TIPS

12.1 When looping through an **Array** using subscripts, the **Array** subscript should never go below 0 and should always be less than the total number of elements in the **Array** (one less than the size of the **Array**). Make sure the loop-terminating condition prevents accessing elements outside this range.

12.2 Programs should validate the correctness of all input values, to prevent erroneous information from affecting a program's calculations.

12.3 When iterating over all the elements of an **`Array`**, use a **`for/in`** control structure to ensure that you manipulate only the existing elements of the **`Array`**.

12.4 With call-by-value, changes to the called function's copy do not affect the original variable's value in the calling function. This prevents the accidental side effects that so greatly hinder the development of correct and reliable software systems.

SELF-REVIEW EXERCISES

12.1 Answer each of the following:

a) Lists and tables of values can be stored in __________.
b) The elements of an array are related by the fact that they have the same __________ and normally the same __________.
c) The number used to refer to a particular element of an array is called its __________.
d) The process of placing the elements of an array in order is called __________ the array.
e) Determining whether an array contains a certain key value is called __________ the array.
f) An array that uses two subscripts is referred to as a __________ array.

12.2 State whether each of the following is *true* or *false*. If *false*, explain why.

a) An array can store many different types of values.
b) An array subscript should normally be a floating-point value.
c) An individual array element that is passed to a function and modified in that function will contain the modified value when the called function completes execution.

12.3 Answer the following questions regarding an array called **`fractions`**.

a) Declare an array with 10 elements and initialize the elements of the array to **`0`**.
b) Name the fourth element of the array.
c) Refer to array element 4.
d) Assign the value **`1.667`** to array element 9.
e) Assign the value **`3.333`** to the seventh element of the array.
f) Sum all the elements of the array using a **`for/in`** repetition structure. Define variable **`x`** as a control variable for the loop.

12.4 Answer the following questions regarding an array called **`table`**.

a) Declare and create the array with 3 rows and 3 columns.
b) How many elements does the array contain?
c) Use a **`for/in`** repetition structure to initialize each element of the array to the sum of its subscripts. Assume the variables **`x`** and **`y`** are declared as control variables.

12.5 Find the error in each of the following program segments and correct the error.

a) Assume **`var b = new Array( 10 );`**

```
for ( var i = 0; i <= b.length; ++i )
   b[ i ] = 1;
```

b) Assume **`var a = [ [ 1, 2 ], [ 3, 4 ] ];`**

```
   a[ 1, 1 ] = 5;
```

ANSWERS TO SELF-REVIEW EXERCISES

12.1 a) Arrays. b) Name, type. c) Subscript. d) Sorting. e) Searching. f) Double-subscripted.

12.2 a) True. b). False. An array subscript must be an integer or an integer expression. c) False for individual primitive-data-type elements of an array because they are passed with call-by-value. If a reference to an array is passed, then modifications to the array elements are reflected in the original. Also, an individual element of an object type passed to a function is passed with call-by-reference, and changes to the object will be reflected in the original array element.

12.3 a) **var fractions = [0, 0, 0, 0, 0, 0, 0, 0, 0, 0];**
b) **fractions[3]**
c) **fractions[4]**
d) **fractions[9] = 1.667;**
e) **fractions[6] = 3.333;**
f)
```
var total = 0;
for ( var x in fractions )
   total += fractions[ x ];
```

12.4 a)
```
var table = new Array( new Array( 3 ),
                       new Array( 3 ),
                       new Array( 3 ) );
```
b) Nine.
c)
```
for ( var x in table )
   for ( var y in table[ x ] )
      table[ x ][ y ] = x + y;
```

12.5 a) Error: Referencing an array element outside the bounds of the array (**b[10]**). [*Note:* This is actually a logic error not a syntax error.]
Correction: Change the **<=** operator to **<**.
b) Error: Array subscripting done incorrectly.
Correction: Change the statement to **a[1][1] = 5;**.

EXERCISES

12.6 Fill in the blanks in each of the following:
a) JavaScript stores lists of values in __________.
b) When referring to an array element, the position number contained within brackets is called a __________.
c) The names of the four elements of array **p** are ________, ________, ________ and ________.
d) The process of placing the elements of an array into either ascending or descending order is called __________.
e) In a double-subscripted array, the first subscript identifies the __________ of an element and the second subscript identifies the __________ of an element.
f) An *m*-by-*n* array contains __________ rows, __________ columns and ________ elements.
g) The name of the element in row 3 and column 5 of array **d** is __________.
h) The name of the element in the third row and fifth column of array **d** is __________.

12.7 State whether each of the following is *true* or *false*. If *false*, explain why.
a) To refer to a particular location or element within an array, we specify the name of the array and the value of the particular element.
b) An array declaration reserves space for the array.
c) To indicate that 100 locations should be reserved for integer array **p**, the programmer writes the declaration
```
p[ 100 ];
```
d) A JavaScript program that initializes the elements of a 15-element array to zero must contain at least one **for** statement.
e) A JavaScript program that totals the elements of a double-subscripted array must contain nested **for** statements.

12.8 Write JavaScript statements to accomplish each of the following:

a) Display the value of the seventh element of array **f**.
b) Initialize each of the five elements of single-subscripted array **g** to **8**.
c) Total the elements of array **c** of 100 numeric elements.
d) Copy 11- element array **a** into the first portion of array **b**, containing 34 elements.
e) Determine and print the smallest and largest values contained in 99-element floating-point array **w**.

12.9 Consider a 2-by-3 array **t** that will store integers.

a) Write a statement that declares and creates array **t**.
b) How many rows does **t** have?
c) How many columns does **t** have?
d) How many elements does **t** have?
e) Write the names of all the elements in the second row of **t**.
f) Write the names of all the elements in the third column of **t**.
g) Write a single statement that sets the element of **t** in row 1 and column 2 to zero.
h) Write a series of statements that initializes each element of **t** to zero. Do not use a repetition structure.
i) Write a nested **for** structure that initializes each element of **t** to zero.
j) Write a series of statements that determines and prints the smallest value in array **t**.
k) Write a statement that displays the elements of the first row of **t**.
l) Write a statement that totals the elements of the fourth column of **t**.
m) Write a series of statements that prints the array **t** in neat, tabular format. List the column subscripts as headings across the top and list the row subscripts at the left of each row.

12.10 Use a single-subscripted array to solve the following problem: A company pays its salespeople on a commission basis. The salespeople receive $200 per week plus 9% of their gross sales for that week. For example, a salesperson who grosses $5000 in sales in a week receives $200 plus 9% of $5000, or a total of $650. Write a script (using an array of counters) that obtains the gross sales for each employee through an HTML form and determines how many of the salespeople earned salaries in each of the following ranges (assume each salesperson's salary is truncated to an integer amount):

a) $200-$299
b) $300-$399
c) $400-$499
d) $500-$599
e) $600-$699
f) $700-$799
g) $800-$899
h) $900-$999
i) $1000 and over

12.11 The bubble sort presented in Fig. 12.10 is inefficient for large arrays. Make the following simple modifications to improve the performance of the bubble sort.

a) After the first pass, the largest number is guaranteed to be in the highest-numbered element of the array; after the second pass, the two highest numbers are "in place"; and so on. Instead of making nine comparisons on every pass, modify the bubble sort to make eight comparisons on the second pass, seven on the third pass and so on.
b) The data in the array may already be in the proper order or near-proper order, so why make nine passes if fewer will suffice? Modify the sort to check at the end of each pass whether any swaps have been made. If none has been made, the data must already be in the proper order, so the program should terminate. If swaps have been made, at least one more pass is needed.

12.12 Write statements that perform the following single-subscripted array operations:
a) Set the 10 elements of array **counts** to zeros.
b) Add 1 to each of the 15 elements of array **bonus**.
c) Display the five values of array **bestScores** separated by spaces.

12.13 Use a single-subscripted array to solve the following problem. Read in 20 numbers, each of which is between 10 and 100, inclusive. As each number is read, print it only if it is not a duplicate of a number already read. Provide for the "worst case" in which all 20 numbers are different. Use the smallest possible array to solve this problem.

12.14 Label the elements of 3-by-5 double-subscripted array **sales** to indicate the order in which they are set to zero by the following program segment:

```
for ( var row in sales )
   for ( var col in sales[ row ] )
      sales[ row ][ col ] = 0;
```

12.15 Write a script to simulate the rolling of two dice. The script should use **Math.random** to roll the first die and should use **Math.random** again to roll the second die. The sum of the two values should then be calculated. [*Note:* Since each die can show an integer value from 1 to 6, the sum of the values will vary from 2 to 12, with 7 being the most frequent sum and 2 and 12 being the least frequent sums. Figure 12.17 shows the 36 possible combinations of the two dice. Your program should roll the dice 36,000 times. Use a single-subscripted array to tally the numbers of times each possible sum appears. Display the results in an HTML table. Also, determine whether the totals are reasonable (e.g., there are six ways to roll a 7, so approximately one sixth of all the rolls should be 7).]

12.16 Write a script that runs 1000 games of craps and answers the following questions:
a) How many games are won on the first roll, second roll, ..., twentieth roll and after the twentieth roll?
b) How many games are lost on the first roll, second roll, ..., twentieth roll and after the twentieth roll?
c) What are the chances of winning at craps? [*Note:* You should discover that craps is one of the fairest casino games. What do you suppose this means?]
d) What is the average length of a game of craps?
e) Do the chances of winning improve with the length of the game?

	1	2	3	4	5	6
1	2	3	4	5	6	7
2	3	4	5	6	7	8
3	4	5	6	7	8	9
4	5	6	7	8	9	10
5	6	7	8	9	10	11
6	7	8	9	10	11	12

Fig. 12.17 The 36 possible outcomes of rolling two dice.

12.17 What does the following program do?

```
<!DOCTYPE html PUBLIC "-//W3C//DTD HTML 4.0 Transitional//EN">
<HTML>
<!-- Exercise 12.16: WhatDoesThisDo.html -->

<HEAD><TITLE>What Does This Do?</TITLE>

<SCRIPT LANGUAGE = "JavaScript">
   var a = [ 1, 2, 3, 4, 5, 6, 7, 8, 9, 10 ];
   var result = whatIsThis( a, a.length );

   document.writeln( "<H1>Result is: " + result + "<H1>" );

   function whatIsThis( b, size )
   {
      if ( size == 1 )
         return b[ 0 ];
      else
         return b[ size - 1 ] + whatIsThis( b, size - 1 );
   }
</SCRIPT>

</HEAD>
<BODY></BODY></HTML>
```

12.18 (*Airline Reservations System*) A small airline has just purchased a computer for its new automated reservations system. You have been asked to program the new system. You are to write a program to assign seats on each flight of the airline's only plane (capacity: 10 seats).

Your program should display the following menu of alternatives:

```
Please type 1 for "smoking"
Please type 2 for "nonsmoking"
```

If the person types 1, your program should assign a seat in the smoking section (seats 1-5). If the person types 2, your program should assign a seat in the nonsmoking section (seats 6-10). Your program should then print a boarding pass indicating the person's seat number and whether it is in the smoking or nonsmoking section of the plane.

Use a single-subscripted array to represent the seating chart of the plane. Initialize all the elements of the array to 0 to indicate that all seats are empty. As each seat is assigned, set the corresponding elements of the array to 1 to indicate that the seat is no longer available.

Your program should, of course, never assign a seat that has already been assigned. When the smoking section is full, your program should ask the person if it is acceptable to be placed in the nonsmoking section (and vice versa). If yes, make the appropriate seat assignment. If no, print the message `"Next flight leaves in 3 hours."`

12.19 What does the following program do?

```
<!DOCTYPE html PUBLIC "-//W3C//DTD HTML 4.0 Transitional//EN">
<HTML>
<!-- Exercise 12.19: WhatDoesThisDo2.html -->

```

```
<HEAD><TITLE>What Does This Do?</TITLE>

<SCRIPT LANGUAGE = "JavaScript">
   var a = [ 1, 2, 3, 4, 5, 6, 7, 8, 9, 10 ];

   someFunction( a, 0 );

   function someFunction( b, x )
   {
      if ( x < b.length ) {
         someFunction( b, x + 1 );
         document.writeln( b[ x ] + " " );
      }
   }
</SCRIPT>

</HEAD>
<BODY></BODY></HTML>
```

12.20 Use a double-subscripted array to solve the following problem. A company has four salespeople (1 to 4) who sell five different products (1 to 5). Once a day, each salesperson passes in a slip for each different type of product actually sold. Each slip contains

1. the salesperson number,
2. the product number, and
3. the total dollar value of that product sold that day.

Thus, each salesperson passes in between 0 and 5 sales slips per day. Assume that the information from all of the slips for last month is available. Write a script that will read all this information for last month's sales and summarize the total sales by salesperson by product. All totals should be stored in the double-subscripted array **sales**. After processing all the information for last month, display the results in an HTML table format with each of the columns representing a particular salesperson and each of the rows representing a particular product. Cross total each row to get the total sales of each product for last month; cross total each column to get the total sales by salesperson for last month. Your tabular printout should include these cross totals to the right of the totaled rows and to the bottom of the totaled columns.

12.21 (*Turtle Graphics*) The Logo language, which is popular among young computer users, made the concept of *turtle graphics* famous. Imagine a mechanical turtle that walks around the room under the control of a JavaScript program. The turtle holds a pen in one of two positions, up or down. While the pen is down, the turtle traces out shapes as it moves; while the pen is up, the turtle moves about freely without writing anything. In this problem you will simulate the operation of the turtle and create a computerized sketchpad as well.

Use a 20-by-20 array **floor** that is initialized to zeros. Read commands from an array that contains them. Keep track of the current position of the turtle at all times and of whether the pen is currently up or down. Assume that the turtle always starts at position (0,0) of the floor, with its pen up. The set of turtle commands your script must process are as follows:

Command	Meaning
1	Pen up
2	Pen down
3	Turn right
4	Turn left
5,10	Move forward 10 spaces (or a number other than 10)
6	Print the 20-by-20 array
9	End of data (sentinel)

Suppose that the turtle is somewhere near the center of the floor. The following "program" would draw and print a 12-by-12 square, then leave the pen in the up position:

```
2
5,12
3
5,12
3
5,12
3
5,12
1
6
9
```

As the turtle moves with the pen down, set the appropriate elements of array **floor** to **1**s. When the **6** command (print) is given, wherever there is a **1** in the array, display an asterisk or some other character you choose. Wherever there is a zero, display a blank. Write a script to implement the turtle graphics capabilities discussed here. Write several turtle graphics programs to draw interesting shapes. Add other commands to increase the power of your turtle graphics language.

12.22 (*Knight's Tour*) One of the more interesting puzzlers for chess buffs is the Knight's Tour problem, originally proposed by the mathematician Euler. The question is this: Can the chess piece called the knight move around an empty chessboard and touch each of the 64 squares once and only once? We study this intriguing problem in depth here.

The knight makes L-shaped moves (over two in one direction and then over one in a perpendicular direction). Thus, from a square in the middle of an empty chessboard, the knight can make eight different moves (numbered 0 through 7) as shown in Fig. 12.18.

a) Draw an 8-by-8 chessboard on a sheet of paper and attempt a Knight's Tour by hand. Put a **1** in the first square you move to, a **2** in the second square, a **3** in the third, etc. Before starting the tour, estimate how far you think you will get, remembering that a full tour consists of 64 moves. How far did you get? Was this close to your estimate?
b) Now let us develop a script that will move the knight around a chessboard. The board is represented by an 8-by-8 double-subscripted array **board**. Each of the squares is initialized to zero. We describe each of the eight possible moves in terms of both their horizontal and vertical components. For example, a move of type 0 as shown in Fig. 12.18 consists of moving two squares horizontally to the right and one square vertically upward. Move 2 consists of moving one square horizontally to the left and two squares vertically upward. Horizontal moves to the left and vertical moves upward are indicated with negative numbers. The eight moves may be described by two single-subscripted arrays, **horizontal** and **vertical**, as follows:

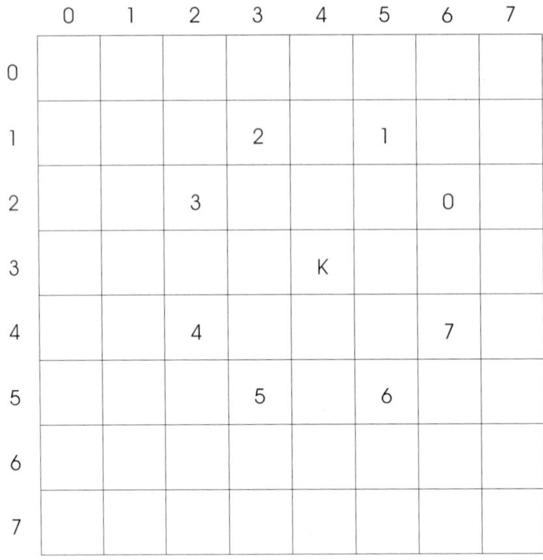

Fig. 12.18 The eight possible moves of the knight.

```
horizontal[ 0 ] = 2
horizontal[ 1 ] = 1
horizontal[ 2 ] = -1
horizontal[ 3 ] = -2
horizontal[ 4 ] = -2
horizontal[ 5 ] = -1
horizontal[ 6 ] = 1
horizontal[ 7 ] = 2

vertical[ 0 ] = -1
vertical[ 1 ] = -2
vertical[ 2 ] = -2
vertical[ 3 ] = -1
vertical[ 4 ] = 1
vertical[ 5 ] = 2
vertical[ 6 ] = 2
vertical[ 7 ] = 1
```

Let the variables **currentRow** and **currentColumn** indicate the row and column of the knight's current position. To make a move of type **moveNumber**, where **moveNumber** is between 0 and 7, your script uses the statements

```
currentRow += vertical[ moveNumber ];
currentColumn += horizontal[ moveNumber ];
```

Keep a counter that varies from **1** to **64**. Record the latest count in each square the knight moves to. Test each potential move to see whether the knight has already visited that square. Test every potential move to ensure that the knight does not land off the chessboard. Write a script to move the knight around the chessboard. Run the script. How many moves did the knight make?

c) After attempting to write and run a Knight's Tour script, you have probably developed some valuable insights. We will use these to develop a *heuristic* (or strategy) for moving the knight. Heuristics do not guarantee success, but a carefully developed heuristic greatly improves the chance of success. You may have observed that the outer squares are more troublesome than the squares nearer the center of the board. In fact, the most troublesome or inaccessible squares are the four corners.

Intuition may suggest that you should attempt to move the knight to the most troublesome squares first and leave open those that are easiest to get to, so that, when the board gets congested near the end of the tour, there will be a greater chance of success.

We may develop an "accessibility heuristic" by classifying each of the squares according to how accessible it is, then always moving the knight (using the knight's L-shaped moves) to the most inaccessible square. We label a double-subscripted array **accessibility** with numbers indicating from how many squares each particular square is accessible. On a blank chessboard, each center square is rated as **8**, each corner square is rated as **2** and the other squares have accessibility numbers of **3**, **4** or **6**, as follows:

```
2  3  4  4  4  4  3  2
3  4  6  6  6  6  4  3
4  6  8  8  8  8  6  4
4  6  8  8  8  8  6  4
4  6  8  8  8  8  6  4
4  6  8  8  8  8  6  4
3  4  6  6  6  6  4  3
2  3  4  4  4  4  3  2
```

Write a version of the Knight's Tour using the accessibility heuristic. The knight should always move to the square with the lowest accessibility number. In case of a tie, the knight may move to any of the tied squares. Therefore, the tour may begin in any of the four corners. [*Note:* As the knight moves around the chessboard, your script should reduce the accessibility numbers as more squares become occupied. In this way, at any given time during the tour, each available square's accessibility number will remain equal to precisely the number of squares from which that square may be reached.] Run this version of your script. Did you get a full tour? Modify the script to run 64 tours, one starting from each square of the chessboard. How many full tours did you get?

d) Write a version of the Knight's Tour script which, when encountering a tie between two or more squares, decides what square to choose by looking ahead to those squares reachable from the "tied" squares. Your script should move to the square for which the next move would arrive at a square with the lowest accessibility number.

12.23 (*Knight's Tour: Brute Force Approaches*) In Exercise 12.22 we developed a solution to the Knight's Tour problem. The approach used, called the "accessibility heuristic," generates many solutions and executes efficiently.

As computers continue increasing in power, we will be able to solve more problems with sheer computer power and relatively unsophisticated algorithms. Let us call this approach "brute force" problem solving.

a) Use random number generation to enable the knight to walk around the chessboard (in its legitimate L-shaped moves, of course) at random. Your script should run one tour and print the final chessboard. How far did the knight get?

b) Most likely, the preceding script produced a relatively short tour. Now modify your script to attempt 1000 tours. Use a single-subscripted array to keep track of the number of tours of each length. When your script finishes attempting the 1000 tours, it should print this information in neat tabular format. What was the best result?

c) Most likely, the preceding script gave you some "respectable" tours but no full tours. Now "pull all the stops out," and simply let your script run until it produces a full tour. (*Caution:* This version of the script could run for hours on a powerful computer.) Once again, keep a table of the number of tours of each length, and print this table when the first full tour is found. How many tours did your script attempt before producing a full tour? How much time did it take?

d) Compare the brute force version of the Knight's Tour with the accessibility-heuristic version. Which required a more careful study of the problem? Which algorithm was more difficult to develop? Which required more computer power? Could we be certain (in advance) of obtaining a full tour with the accessibility-heuristic approach? Could we be certain (in advance) of obtaining a full tour with the brute force approach? Argue the pros and cons of brute force problem solving in general.

12.24 (*Eight Queens*) Another puzzler for chess buffs is the Eight Queens problem. Simply stated: Is it possible to place eight queens on an empty chessboard so that no queen is "attacking" any other—that is, no two queens are in the same row, the same column or along the same diagonal? Use the thinking developed in Exercise 12.22 to formulate a heuristic for solving the Eight Queens problem. Run your script. [*Hint:* It is possible to assign a value to each square of the chessboard indicating how many squares of an empty chessboard are "eliminated" if a queen is placed in that square. Each of the corners would be assigned the value 22, as in Fig. 12.19.] Once these "elimination numbers" are placed in all 64 squares, an appropriate heuristic might be to place the next queen in the square with the smallest elimination number. Why is this strategy intuitively appealing?

12.25 (*Eight Queens: Brute Force Approaches*) In this exercise you will develop several brute force approaches to solving the Eight Queens problem introduced in Exercise 12.24.

a) Solve the Eight Queens exercise, using the random brute force technique developed in Exercise 12.23.
b) Use an exhaustive technique (i.e., try all possible combinations of eight queens on the chessboard).
c) Why do you suppose the exhaustive brute force approach may not be appropriate for solving the Knight's Tour problem?
d) Compare and contrast the random brute force and exhaustive brute force approaches.

12.26 (*Knight's Tour: Closed Tour Test*) In the Knight's Tour, a full tour occurs when the knight makes 64 moves touching each square of the chessboard once and only once. A closed tour occurs when the 64th move is one move away from the square in which the knight started the tour. Modify the script you wrote in Exercise 12.22 to test for a closed tour, if a full tour has occurred.

12.27 (*The Sieve of Eratosthenes*) A prime integer is an integer that is evenly divisible by only itself and 1. The Sieve of Eratosthenes is an algorithm for finding prime numbers. It operates as follows:

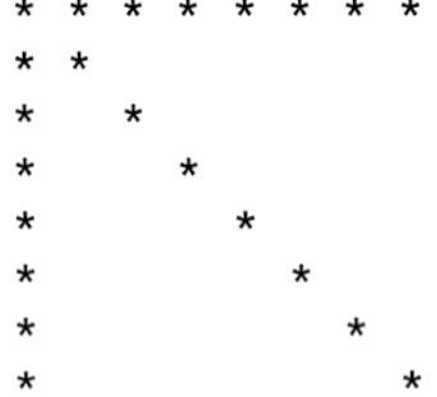

```
* * * * * * * *
* *
*   *
*     *
*       *
*         *
*           *
*             *
```

Fig. 12.19 The 22 squares eliminated by placing a queen in the upper left corner.

a) Create an array with all elements initialized to 1 (true). Array elements with prime subscripts will remain 1. All other array elements will eventually be set to zero.
b) Starting with array subscript 2 (subscript 1 must be prime), every time an array element is found whose value is 1, loop through the remainder of the array and set to zero every element whose subscript is a multiple of the subscript for the element with value 1. For array subscript 2, all elements beyond 2 in the array that are multiples of 2 will be set to zero (subscripts 4, 6, 8, 10, etc.); for array subscript 3, all elements beyond 3 in the array that are multiples of 3 will be set to zero (subscripts 6, 9, 12, 15, etc.); and so on.

When this process is complete, the array elements that are still set to one indicate that the subscript is a prime number. These subscripts can then be printed. Write a script that uses an array of 1000 elements to determine and print the prime numbers between 1 and 999. Ignore element 0 of the array.

12.28 (*Bucket Sort*) A bucket sort begins with a single-subscripted array of positive integers to be sorted and a double-subscripted array of integers with rows subscripted from 0 to 9 and columns subscripted from 0 to *n* - 1, where *n* is the number of values in the array to be sorted. Each row of the double-subscripted array is referred to as a bucket. Write a function **`bucketSort`** that takes an integer array as an argument and performs as follows:

a) Place each value of the single-subscripted array into a row of the bucket array based on the value's ones digit. For example, 97 is placed in row 7, 3 is placed in row 3 and 100 is placed in row 0. This is called a "distribution pass."
b) Loop through the bucket array row by row and copy the values back to the original array. This is called a "gathering pass." The new order of the preceding values in the single-subscripted array is 100, 3 and 97.
c) Repeat this process for each subsequent digit position (tens, hundreds, thousands, etc.).

On the second pass, 100 is placed in row 0, 3 is placed in row 0 (because 3 has no tens digit) and 97 is placed in row 9. After the gathering pass, the order of the values in the single-subscripted array is 100, 3 and 97. On the third pass, 100 is placed in row 1, 3 is placed in row 0 and 97 is placed in row 0 (after the 3). After the last gathering pass, the original array is now in sorted order.

Note that the double-subscripted array of buckets is ten times the size of the integer array being sorted. This sorting technique provides better performance than a bubble sort, but requires much more memory. The bubble sort requires space for only one additional element of data. This comparison is an example of the space-time trade-off: The bucket sort uses more memory than the bubble sort, but performs better. This version of the bucket sort requires copying all the data back to the original array on each pass. Another possibility is to create a second double-subscripted bucket array and repeatedly swap the data between the two bucket arrays.

RECURSION EXERCISES

12.29 (*Selection Sort*) A selection sort searches an array looking for the smallest element in the array, then swaps that element with the first element of the array. The process is repeated for the subarray beginning with the second element. Each pass of the array places one element in its proper location. For an array of *n* elements, *n* - 1 passes must be made, and for each subarray, *n* - 1 comparisons must be made to find the smallest value. When the subarray being processed contains one element, the array is sorted. Write recursive function **`selectionSort`** to perform this algorithm.

12.30 (*Palindromes*) A palindrome is a string that is spelled the same way forward and backward. Some examples of palindromes are: "radar," "able was i ere i saw elba" and (if blanks are ignored) "a man a plan a canal panama." Write a recursive function **`testPalindrome`** that returns 1 if the string stored in the array is a palindrome and 0 otherwise. The function should ignore spaces and punctuation in the string.

12.31 (*Linear Search*) Modify Fig. 12.12 to use recursive function **linearSearch** to perform a linear search of the array. The function should receive an integer array and the size of the array as arguments. If the search key is found, return the array subscript; otherwise, return –1.

12.32 (*Binary Search*) Modify the script of Fig. 12.13 to use a recursive function **binarySearch** to perform the binary search of the array. The function should receive an integer array and the starting subscript and ending subscript as arguments. If the search key is found, return the array subscript; otherwise, return –1.

12.33 (*Eight Queens*) Modify the Eight Queens script you created in Exercise 12.24 to solve the problem recursively.

12.34 (*Print an array*) Write a recursive function **printArray** that takes an array and the size of the array as arguments and returns nothing. The function should stop processing and return when it receives an array of size zero.

12.35 (*Print a string backward*) Write a recursive function **stringReverse** that takes a string as an argument, prints the string backward and returns nothing. All **String** objects in JavaScript have method **charAt** to select characters in the string. For example, **s.charAt(0)** returns the first character in **s**.

12.36 (*Find the minimum value in an array*) Write a recursive function **recursiveMinimum** that takes an array and the array size as arguments and returns the smallest element of the array. The function should stop processing and return when it receives an array of one element.

12.37 (*Quicksort*) In the examples and exercises of this chapter, we discussed three sorting techniques: bubble sort, bucket sort and selection sort. We now present the recursive sorting technique called Quicksort. The basic algorithm for a single-subscripted array of values is as follows:

a) *Partitioning Step:* Take the first element of the unsorted array and determine its final location in the sorted array (i.e., all values to the left of the element in the array are less than the element and all values to the right of the element in the array are greater than the element). We now have one element in its proper location and two unsorted subarrays.
b) *Recursive Step:* Perform step 1 on each unsorted subarray.

Each time step 1 is performed on a subarray, another element is placed in its final location of the sorted array and two unsorted subarrays are created. When a subarray consists of one element, it must be sorted, therefore that element is in its final location.

The basic algorithm seems simple enough, but how do we determine the final position of the first element of each subarray? As an example, consider the following set of values (the element in bold is the partitioning element—it will be placed in its final location in the sorted array):

37 2 6 4 89 8 10 12 68 45

a) Starting from the rightmost element of the array, compare each element to **37** until an element less than **37** is found, then swap **37** and that element. The first element less than **37** is 12, so **37** and 12 are swapped. The new array is

   12 2 6 4 89 8 10 **37** 68 45

   Element 12 is in italic to indicate that it was just swapped with **37**.
b) Starting from the left of the array, but beginning with the element after 12, compare each element to **37** until an element greater than **37** is found, then swap **37** and that element. The first element greater than **37** is 89, so **37** and 89 are swapped. The new array is

   12 2 6 4 **37** 8 10 *89* 68 45

c) Starting from the right, but beginning with the element before 89, compare each element to **37** until an element less than **37** is found, then swap **37** and that element. The first element less than **37** is 10, so **37** and 10 are swapped. The new array is

   12 2 6 4 *10* 8 **37** 89 68 45

d) Starting from the left, but beginning with the element after 10, compare each element to **37** until an element greater than **37** is found, then swap **37** and that element. There are no more elements greater than **37**, so when we compare **37** to itself we know that **37** has been placed in its final location of the sorted array.

Once the partition has been applied on the above array, there are two unsorted subarrays. The subarray with values less than 37 contains 12, 2, 6, 4, 10 and 8. The subarray with values greater than 37 contains 89, 68 and 45. The sort continues with both subarrays being partitioned in the same manner as the original array.

Based on the preceding discussion, write recursive function **`quickSort`** to sort a single-subscripted array. The function should receive as arguments an array, a starting subscript and an ending subscript. Function **`quicksort`** should call **`partition`** to perform the partitioning step.

12.38 (*Maze Traversal*) The following grid of #s and dots (**.**) is a double-subscripted array representation of a maze.

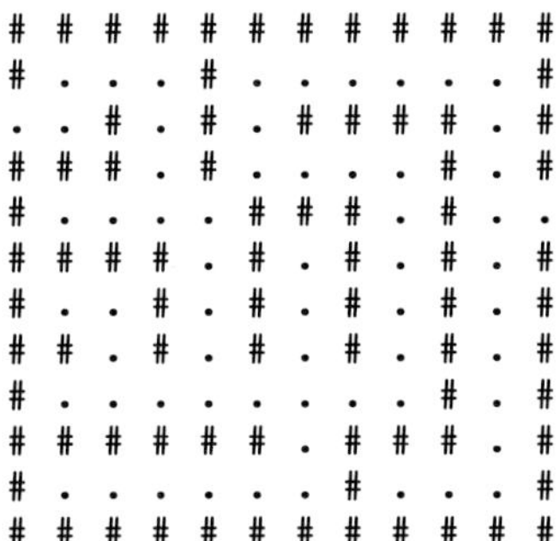

```
# # # # # # # # # # # #
# . . . # . . . . . . #
. . # . # . # # # # . #
# # # . # . . . . # . #
# . . . . # # # . # . .
# # # # . # . # . # . #
# . . # . # . # . # . #
# # . # . # . # . # . #
# . . . . . . . . # . #
# # # # # # . # # # . #
# . . . . . . # . . . #
# # # # # # # # # # # #
```

In the preceding double-subscripted array, the #s represent the walls of the maze and the dots represent squares in the possible paths through the maze. Moves can be made only to a location in the array that contains a dot.

There is a simple algorithm for walking through a maze that guarantees finding the exit (assuming there is an exit). If there is not an exit, you will arrive at the starting location again. Place your right hand on the wall to your right, and begin walking forward. Never remove your hand from the wall. If the maze turns to the right, you follow the wall to the right. As long as you do not remove your hand from the wall, eventually you will arrive at the exit of the maze. There may be a shorter path than the one you have taken, but you are guaranteed to get out of the maze if you follow the algorithm.

Write recursive function **`mazeTraverse`** to walk through the maze. The function should receive as arguments a 12-by-12 array of strings representing the maze and the starting location of the maze. As **`mazeTraverse`** attempts to locate the exit from the maze, it should place the string "**`X`**" in each square in the path. The function should display the maze after each move so the user can watch as the maze is solved.

12.39 (*Generating Mazes Randomly*) Write a function **`mazeGenerator`** that takes as an argument a double-subscripted 12-by-12 array and randomly produces a maze. The function should also provide the starting and ending locations of the maze. Try your function **`mazeTraverse`** from Exercise 12.38, using several randomly generated mazes.

12.40 (*Mazes of Any Size*) Generalize functions **`mazeTraverse`** and **`mazeGenerator`** of Exercises 12.38 and 12.39 to process mazes of any width and height.

12.41 (*Simulation: The Tortoise and the Hare*) In this problem you will recreate one of the truly great moments in history, namely, the classic race of the tortoise and the hare. You will use random number generation to develop a simulation of this memorable event.

Our contenders begin the race at "square 1" of 70 squares. Each square represents a possible position along the race course. The finish line is at square 70. The first contender to reach or pass square 70 is rewarded with a pail of fresh carrots and lettuce. The course weaves its way up the side of a slippery mountain, so occasionally the contenders lose ground.

There is a clock that ticks once per second. With each tick of the clock, your script should adjust the position of the animals according to the following rules:

Animal	Move type	Percentage of the time	Actual move
Tortoise	Fast plod	50%	3 squares to the right
	Slip	20%	6 squares to the left
	Slow plod	30%	1 square to the right
Hare	Sleep	20%	No move at all
	Big hop	20%	9 squares to the right
	Big slip	10%	12 squares to the left
	Small hop	30%	1 square to the right
	Small slip	20%	2 squares to the left

Use variables to keep track of the positions of the animals (i.e., position numbers are 1–70). Start each animal at position 1 (i.e., the "starting gate"). If an animal slips left before square 1, move the animal back to square 1.

Generate the percentages in the preceding table by producing a random integer, i, in the range $1 \le i \le 10$. For the tortoise, perform a "fast plod" when $1 \le i \le 5$, a "slip" when $6 \le i \le 7$ or a "slow plod" when $8 \le i \le 10$. Use a similar technique to move the hare.

Begin the race by printing

```
BANG !!!!!
AND THEY'RE OFF !!!!!
```

Then, for each tick of the clock (i.e., each repetition of a loop), print a 70-position line showing the letter **T** in the position of the tortoise and the letter **H** in the position of the hare. Occasionally, the contenders will land on the same square. In this case, the tortoise bites the hare and your script should print **OUCH!!!** beginning at that position. All print positions other than the **T**, the **H** or the **OUCH!!!** (in case of a tie) should be blank.

After each line is printed, test whether either animal has reached or passed square 70. If so, print the winner and terminate the simulation. If the tortoise wins, print **TORTOISE WINS!!! YAY!!!** If the hare wins, print **Hare wins. Yuch.** If both animals win on the same tick of the clock, you may want to favor the turtle (the "underdog") or you may want to print **It's a tie.** If neither animal wins, perform the loop again to simulate the next tick of the clock. When you are ready to run your script, assemble a group of fans to watch the race. You'll be amazed at how involved your audience gets!

Later in the book we introduce a number of Dynamic HTML capabilities, such as graphics, images, animation and sound. As you study those features, you might enjoy enhancing your tortoise-and-hare contest simulation.

SPECIAL SECTION: BUILDING YOUR OWN COMPUTER

In the next several problems, we take a temporary diversion away from the world of high-level language programming. We "peel open" a computer and look at its internal structure. We introduce machine-language programming and write several machine-language programs. To make this diversion an especially valuable experience, we then build a computer (through the technique of software-based *simulation)* on which you can execute your machine-language programs!

12.42 (*Machine-Language Programming*) Let us create a computer we will call the Simpletron. As its name implies, it is a simple machine, but as we will soon see, a powerful one as well. The Simpletron runs programs written in the only language it directly understands, that is, Simpletron Machine Language or SML for short.

The Simpletron contains an *accumulator*—a "special register" in which information is put before the Simpletron uses that information in calculations or examines it in various ways. All information in the Simpletron is handled in terms of *words.* A word is a signed four-digit decimal number such as **+3364**, **-1293**, **+0007**, **-0001**, etc. The Simpletron is equipped with a 100-word memory and these words are referenced by their location numbers **00**, **01**, ..., **99**.

Before running an SML program, we must *load* or place the program into memory. The first instruction (or statement) of every SML program is always placed in location **00**. The simulator will start executing at this location.

Each instruction written in SML occupies one word of the Simpletron's memory (thus, instructions are signed four-digit decimal numbers). We shall assume that the sign of an SML instruction is always plus, but the sign of a data word may be either plus or minus. Each location in the Simpletron's memory may contain either an instruction, a data value used by a program or an unused (and hence undefined) area of memory. The first two digits of each SML instruction are the *operation code* specifying the operation to be performed. SML operation codes are summarized in Fig. 12.20.

Operation code	Meaning
Input/output operations:	
var READ = 10;	Read a word from the keyboard into a specific location in memory.
var WRITE = 11;	Write a word from a specific location in memory to the screen.
Load/store operations:	
var LOAD = 20;	Load a word from a specific location in memory into the accumulator.
var STORE = 21;	Store a word from the accumulator into a specific location in memory.
Arithmetic operations:	
var ADD = 30;	Add a word from a specific location in memory to the word in the accumulator (leave result in the accumulator).
var SUBTRACT = 31;	Subtract a word from a specific location in memory from the word in the accumulator (leave result in the accumulator).

Fig. 12.20 Simpletron Machine Language (SML) operation codes (part 1 of 2).

Operation code	Meaning
`var DIVIDE = 32;`	Divide a word from a specific location in memory into the word in the accumulator (leave result in the accumulator).
`var MULTIPLY = 33;`	Multiply a word from a specific location in memory by the word in the accumulator (leave result in the accumulator).
Transfer of control operations:	
`var BRANCH = 40;`	Branch to a specific location in memory.
`var BRANCHNEG = 41;`	Branch to a specific location in memory if the accumulator is negative.
`var BRANCHZERO = 42;`	Branch to a specific location in memory if the accumulator is zero.
`var HALT = 43;`	Halt—the program has completed its task.

Fig. 12.20 Simpletron Machine Language (SML) operation codes (part 2 of 2).

The last two digits of an SML instruction are the *operand*—the address of the memory location containing the word to which the operation applies. Let's consider several simple SML programs.

The first SML program (Example 1) reads two numbers from the keyboard and computes and prints their sum. The instruction **+1007** reads the first number from the keyboard and places it into location **07** (which has been initialized to zero). Then instruction **+1008** reads the next number into location **08**. The *load* instruction, **+2007**, puts the first number into the accumulator and the *add* instruction, **+3008**, adds the second number to the number in the accumulator. *All SML arithmetic instructions leave their results in the accumulator.* The *store* instruction, **+2109**, places the result into memory location **09**, from which the *write* instruction, **+1109**, takes the number and prints it (as a signed four-digit decimal number). The *halt* instruction, **+4300**, terminates execution.

Example 1 Location	Number	Instruction
00	+1007	(Read A)
01	+1008	(Read B)
02	+2007	(Load A)
03	+3008	(Add B)
04	+2109	(Store C)
05	+1109	(Write C)
06	+4300	(Halt)
07	+0000	(Variable A)
08	+0000	(Variable B)
09	+0000	(Result C)

The second SML program (Example 2) reads two numbers from the keyboard and determines and prints the larger value. Note the use of the instruction **+4107** as a conditional transfer of control, much the same as JavaScript's **if** statement.

Example 2 **Location**	**Number**	**Instruction**
00	+1009	(Read A)
01	+1010	(Read B)
02	+2009	(Load A)
03	+3110	(Subtract B)
04	+4107	(Branch negative to 07)
05	+1109	(Write A)
06	+4300	(Halt)
07	+1110	(Write B)
08	+4300	(Halt)
09	+0000	(Variable A)
10	+0000	(Variable B)

Now write SML programs to accomplish each of the following tasks.

a) Use a sentinel-controlled loop to read ten positive numbers. Compute and print their sum.

b) Use a counter-controlled loop to read seven numbers, some positive and some negative, and compute and print their average.

c) Read a series of numbers and determine and print the largest number. The first number read indicates how many numbers should be processed.

12.43 (*A Computer Simulator*) It may at first seem outrageous, but in this problem you are going to build your own computer. No, you will not be soldering components together. Rather, you will use the powerful technique of *software-based simulation* to create a *software model* of the Simpletron. You will not be disappointed. Your Simpletron simulator will turn the computer you are using into a Simpletron, and you will actually be able to run, test and debug the SML programs you wrote in Exercise 12.42. Your Simpletron will be an event-driven program—you will click a button to execute each SML instruction and you will be able to see the instruction "in action."

When you run your Simpletron simulator, it should begin by displaying:

```
*** Welcome to Simpletron! ***
*** Please enter your program one instruction  ***
*** (or data word) at a time into the input    ***
*** text field. I will display the location    ***
*** number and a question mark (?). You then   ***
*** type the word for that location. Press the ***
*** Done button to stop entering your program. ***
```

The HTML document should display a form containing at least an **input** text field into which the user will type each instruction, one at a time, and a **done** button for the user to click when the complete SML program has been entered. Simulate the memory of the Simpletron with a single-subscripted array called **memory** that has 100 elements. Now assume that the simulator is running and let us examine the dialog as we enter the program of Example 2 of Exercise 12.42:

```
00 ? +1009
01 ? +1010
02 ? +2009
03 ? +3110
04 ? +4107
05 ? +1109
06 ? +4300
07 ? +1110
08 ? +4300
09 ? +0000
10 ? +0000
```

Your program should prompt the user with the memory location followed by a question mark. Each of the values to the right of a question mark is typed by the user into the **input** text field. When the **done** button is clicked, the program should display

```
*** Program loading completed ***
*** Program execution begins   ***
```

The SML program has now been placed (or loaded) in array **memory**. The Simpletron should provide an "**Execute next instruction**" button the user can click to execute each instruction in your SML program. Execution begins with the instruction in location **00** and, as in JavaScript, continues sequentially, unless directed to some other part of the program by a transfer of control.

Use the variable **accumulator** to represent the accumulator register. Use the variable **instructionCounter** to keep track of the location in memory that contains the instruction being performed. Use the variable **operationCode** to indicate the operation currently being performed (i.e., the left two digits of the instruction word). Use the variable **operand** to indicate the memory location on which the current instruction operates. Thus, **operand** is the rightmost two digits of the instruction currently being performed. Do not execute instructions directly from memory. Rather, transfer the next instruction to be performed from memory into variable **instructionRegister**. Then, "pick off" the left two digits and place them in **operationCode**, and "pick off" the right two digits and place them in **operand**. Each of the preceding registers should have a corresponding text field in which its current value can be displayed at all times. When Simpletron begins execution, the special registers are all initialized to 0.

Now let us "walk through" execution of the first SML instruction, **+1009** in memory location **00**. This is called an *instruction execution cycle.*

The **instructionCounter** tells us the location of the next instruction to be performed. We *fetch* the contents of that location from **memory** by using the JavaScript statement

```
instructionRegister = memory[ instructionCounter ];
```

The operation code and the operand are extracted from the instruction register by the statements

```
operationCode = instructionRegister / 100;
operand = instructionRegister % 100;
```

Now the Simpletron must determine that the operation code is actually a *read* (versus a *write*, a *load*, etc.). A **switch** differentiates among the twelve operations of SML.

In the **switch** structure, the behavior of various SML instructions is simulated as follows (we leave the others to the reader):

read:	Display an input dialog with the prompt "**Enter an integer**." Read the value entered, convert it to an integer and store it in location **memory[operand]**.
load:	**accumulator = memory[operand];**
add:	**accumulator += memory[operand];**
branch:	We will discuss the branch instructions shortly.
halt:	This instruction prints the message ***** Simpletron execution terminated *****

When the SML program completes execution, the name and contents of each register as well as the complete contents of memory should be displayed. Such a printout is often called a *computer dump* (and, no, a computer dump is not a place where old computers go). To help you program your dump function, a sample dump format is shown in Fig. 12.21. Note that a dump after executing a Simpletron program would show the actual values of instructions and data values at the moment execution terminated. The sample dump assumes the output will be sent to the display screen with a series of **document.print** and **document.println** function calls. However, we encourage you to experiment with a version that can be displayed on the script using a **<TEXTAREA>** or text fields.

Let us proceed with the execution of our program's first instruction, namely the **+1009** in location **00**. As we have indicated, the **switch** statement simulates execution of this instruction by prompting the user to enter a value into the input dialog, reading the value, converting the value to an integer and storing it in memory location **memory[operand]**. Because your Simpletron is event driven, it waits for the user to type a value into the **input** text field and press the *Enter key*. The value is then read into location **09**.

At this point, simulation of the first instruction is completed. All that remains is to prepare the Simpletron to execute the next instruction. Because the instruction just performed was not a transfer of control, we need merely increment the instruction counter register as follows:

```
++instructionCounter;
```

This action completes the simulated execution of the first instruction. When the user clicks the **Execute next instruction** button, the entire process (i.e., the instruction execution cycle) begins again with the fetch of the next instruction to be executed.

```
REGISTERS:
accumulator          +0000
instructionCounter      00
instructionRegister  +0000
operationCode           00
operand                 00

MEMORY:
       0     1     2     3     4     5     6     7     8     9
 0 +0000 +0000 +0000 +0000 +0000 +0000 +0000 +0000 +0000 +0000
10 +0000 +0000 +0000 +0000 +0000 +0000 +0000 +0000 +0000 +0000
20 +0000 +0000 +0000 +0000 +0000 +0000 +0000 +0000 +0000 +0000
30 +0000 +0000 +0000 +0000 +0000 +0000 +0000 +0000 +0000 +0000
40 +0000 +0000 +0000 +0000 +0000 +0000 +0000 +0000 +0000 +0000
50 +0000 +0000 +0000 +0000 +0000 +0000 +0000 +0000 +0000 +0000
60 +0000 +0000 +0000 +0000 +0000 +0000 +0000 +0000 +0000 +0000
70 +0000 +0000 +0000 +0000 +0000 +0000 +0000 +0000 +0000 +0000
80 +0000 +0000 +0000 +0000 +0000 +0000 +0000 +0000 +0000 +0000
90 +0000 +0000 +0000 +0000 +0000 +0000 +0000 +0000 +0000 +0000
```

Fig. 12.21 A sample dump.

Now let us consider how the branching instructions—the transfers of control—are simulated. All we need to do is adjust the value in the instruction counter appropriately. Therefore, the unconditional branch instruction (**40**) is simulated within the **switch** as

```
instructionCounter = operand;
```

The conditional "branch if accumulator is zero" instruction is simulated as

```
if ( accumulator == 0 )
   instructionCounter = operand;
```

At this point you should implement your Simpletron simulator and run each of the SML programs you wrote in Exercise 12.42. You may embellish SML with additional features and provide for these in your simulator.

Your simulator should check for various types of errors. During the program loading phase, for example, each number the user types into the Simpletron's **memory** must be in the range **-9999** to **+9999**. Your simulator should test that each number entered is in this range, and, if not, keep prompting the user to reenter the number until the user enters a correct number.

During the execution phase, your simulator should check for various serious errors, such as attempts to divide by zero, attempts to execute invalid operation codes, accumulator overflows (i.e., arithmetic operations resulting in values larger than **+9999** or smaller than **-9999**) and the like. Such serious errors are called *fatal errors.* When a fatal error is detected, your simulator should print an error message such as

```
*** Attempt to divide by zero ***
*** Simpletron execution abnormally terminated ***
```

and should print a full computer dump in the format we have discussed previously. This dump will help the user locate the error in the program.

12.44 (*Modifications to the Simpletron Simulator*) In Exercise 12.43, you wrote a software simulation of a computer that executes programs written in Simpletron Machine Language (SML). In this exercise, we propose several modifications and enhancements to the Simpletron Simulator.

a) Extend the Simpletron Simulator's memory to contain 1000 memory locations, to enable the Simpletron to handle larger programs.
b) Allow the simulator to perform modulus calculations. This requires an additional Simpletron Machine Language instruction.
c) Allow the simulator to perform exponentiation calculations. This requires an additional Simpletron Machine Language instruction.
d) Modify the simulator to use hexadecimal values rather than integer values to represent Simpletron Machine Language instructions.
e) Modify the simulator to allow output of a newline. This requires an additional Simpletron Machine Language instruction.
f) Modify the simulator to process floating-point values in addition to integer values.
g) Modify the simulator to handle string input. [*Hint:* Each Simpletron word can be divided into two groups, each holding a two-digit integer. Each two-digit integer represents the ASCII decimal equivalent of a character. Add a machine-language instruction that will input a string and store the string beginning at a specific Simpletron memory location. The first half of the word at that location will be a count of the number of characters in the string (i.e., the length of the string). Each succeeding half-word contains one ASCII character expressed as two decimal digits. The machine-language instruction converts each character into its ASCII equivalent and assigns it to a "half-word."]

h) Modify the simulator to handle output of strings stored in the format of part g). [*Hint:* Add a machine-language instruction that will print the string beginning at a certain Simpletron memory location. The first half of the word at that location is a count of the number of characters in the string (i.e., the length of the string). Each succeeding half-word contains one ASCII character expressed as two decimal digits. The machine-language instruction checks the length and prints the string by translating each two-digit number into its equivalent character.]

12.45 The Fibonacci series

0, 1, 1, 2, 3, 5, 8, 13, 21, …

begins with the terms 0 and 1 and has the property that each succeeding term is the sum of the two preceding terms.

a) Write a *nonrecursive* function **fibonacci(n)** that calculates the *n*th Fibonacci number. Incorporate this function into a script that enables the user to enter the value of **n**.
b) Determine the largest Fibonacci number that can be printed on your system.

13

JavaScript/JScript: Objects

Objectives

- To understand object-based programming terminology and concepts.
- To understand encapsulation and data hiding.
- To appreciate the value of object orientation.
- To be able to use the **`Math`** object.
- To be able to use the **`String`** object.
- To be able to use the **`Date`** object.
- To be able to use the **`Boolean`** and **`Number`** objects.

My object all sublime
I shall achieve in time.
W. S. Gilbert

Is it a world to hide virtues in?
William Shakespeare, *Twelfth Night*

Good as it is to inherit a library, it is better to collect one.
Augustine Birrell

A philosopher of imposing stature doesn't think in a vacuum. Even his most abstract ideas are, to some extent, conditioned by what is or is not known in the time when he lives.
Alfred North Whitehead

Outline

13.1 Introduction

Most JavaScript programs demonstrated to this point illustrate basic computer programming concepts. These programs provide you with the foundation you need to build powerful and complex scripts as part of your Web pages. As you proceed beyond this chapter, you will use JavaScript to manipulate every element of an HTML document from a script.

This chapter presents a more formal treatment of *objects*. The chapter overviews—and serves as a reference for—several of JavaScript's built-in objects and demonstrates many of their capabilities. In the chapters on Dynamic HTML that follow this chapter, you will be introduced to a wide variety of objects provided by the browser that enable scripts to interact with the different elements of an HTML document.

13.2 Thinking About Objects

Now we begin our introduction to objects. We will see that objects are a natural way of thinking about the world and of writing scripts that manipulate HTML documents.

In Chapters 8 through 12, we used built-in JavaScript objects—**`Math`** and **`Array`**—and we used objects provided by the Web browser—**`document`** and **`window`**—to perform tasks in our scripts. Because JavaScript uses objects to perform many tasks, JavaScript is commonly referred to as an *object-based programming language*. As we have seen, JavaScript also contains many constructs from the "conventional" methodology of structured programming supported by many other programming languages. In the first six JavaScript chapters, we concentrated on these "conventional" parts of JavaScript, as they are important components of all JavaScript programs.

Our strategy in this section is to introduce the basic concepts (i.e., "object think") and terminology (i.e., "object speak") of object-based programming, so we can properly refer to the object-based concepts as we encounter them in the remainder of the text.

Let us start by introducing some of the key terminology of object orientation. Look around you in the real world. Everywhere you look you see them—objects! People, animals, plants, cars, planes, buildings, computers and the like. Humans think in terms of objects. We have the marvelous ability of *abstraction,* which enables us to view screen images as objects such as people, planes, trees and mountains rather than as individual dots of color (called *pixels,* for "picture elements"). We can, if we wish, think in terms of beaches rather than grains of sand, forests rather than trees and houses rather than bricks.

We might be inclined to divide objects into two categories—animate objects and inanimate objects. Animate objects are "alive" in some sense. They move around and do things. Inanimate objects, like towels, seem not to do much at all. They just kind of "sit around." All these objects, however, do have some things in common. They all have *attributes,* such as size, shape, color, weight and the like; and they all exhibit *behaviors*—for example, a ball rolls, bounces, inflates and deflates; a baby cries, sleeps, crawls, walks and blinks; a car accelerates, decelerates, brakes and turns; a towel absorbs water.

Humans learn about objects by studying their attributes and observing their behaviors. Different objects can have similar attributes and can exhibit similar behaviors. Comparisons can be made, for example, between babies and adults and between humans and chimpanzees. Cars, trucks, little red wagons and skateboards have much in common.

Objects *encapsulate* data (attributes) and methods (behavior); the data and methods of an object are intimately tied together. Objects have the property of *information hiding.* Programs communicate with objects through well-defined *interfaces.* Normally, implementation details of objects are hidden within the objects themselves.

Most people reading this book probably drive (or have driven) an automobile—a perfect example of an object. Surely it is possible to drive an automobile effectively without knowing the details of how engines, transmissions and exhaust systems work internally. Millions of human years of research and development have been performed for automobiles and have resulted in extremely complex objects containing thousands of parts (attributes). All of this complexity is hidden (encapsulated) from the driver. The driver only sees the friendly user interface of behaviors that enable the driver to make the car go faster by pressing the gas pedal, go slower by pressing the brake pedal, turn left or right by turning the steering wheel, go forward or backward by selecting the gear, and turn on and off by turning the key in the ignition.

Like the designers of an automobile, the designers of World Wide Web browsers have defined a set of objects that encapsulate the elements of an HTML document and expose to a JavaScript programmer attributes and behaviors that enable a JavaScript program to interact with (or script) the elements (objects) in an HTML document. The browser's **window** object provides attributes and behaviors that enable a script to manipulate a browser window. When a string is assigned to the **window** object's **status** property (attribute), that string is displayed in the status bar of the browser window. The **window** object's **alert** method (behavior) allows the programmer to display a message in a separate window. We will soon see that the browser's **document** object contains attributes and behaviors that provide access to every element of an HTML document. Similarly, JavaScript provides objects that encapsulate various capabilities in a script. For example, the

JavaScript **Array** object provides attributes and behaviors that enable a script to manipulate a collection of data. The **Array** object's **length** property (attribute) contains the number of elements in the **Array**. The **Array** object's **sort** method (behavior) orders the elements of the **Array**.

Indeed, with object technology, we will build most future software by combining "standardized, interchangeable parts" called objects. These parts allow programmers to create new programs without having to "reinvent the wheel." Objects will allow programmers to speed and enhance the quality of future software development efforts.

13.3 Math Object

The **Math** object's methods allow the programmer to perform many common mathematical calculations. As shown previously, an object's methods are called by writing the name of the object followed by a dot operator (**.**) and the name of the method. In parentheses following the method name is the argument (or a comma-separated list of arguments) to the method. For example, a programmer desiring to calculate and display the square root of **900.0** might write

```
document.writeln( Math.sqrt( 900.0 ) );
```

When this statement is executed, the method **Math.sqrt** is called to calculate the square root of the number contained in the parentheses (**900.0**). The number **900.0** is the argument of the **Math.sqrt** method. The preceding statement would display **30.0**. Invoking the **sqrt** method of the **Math** object is also referred to as *sending the* ***sqrt*** *message to* ***Math*** *object*. Similarly, invoking the **writeln** method of the **document** object is also referred to as *sending the* ***writeln*** *message to the* ***document*** *object.*

Common Programming Error 13.1

Forgetting to invoke a ***Math*** *method by preceding the method name with the object name* ***Math*** *and a dot operator (*__.__*) is an error.*

Software Engineering Observation 13.1

The primary difference between invoking a function and invoking a method is that a function does not require an object name and a dot operator to call the function.

Some **Math** object methods are summarized in Fig. 13.1.

Method	Description	Example
abs(x)	absolute value of *x*	if **x > 0** then **abs(x)** is **x** if **x = 0** then **abs(x)** is **0** if **x < 0** then **abs(x)** is **-x**
ceil(x)	rounds *x* to the smallest integer not less than *x*	**ceil(9.2)** is **10.0** **ceil(-9.8)** is **-9.0**

Fig. 13.1 Commonly used **Math** object methods (part 1 of 2).

Method	Description	Example
`cos( x )`	trigonometric cosine of *x* (*x* in radians)	`cos( 0.0 )` is `1.0`
`exp( x )`	exponential method e^x	`exp( 1.0 )` is `2.71828` `exp( 2.0 )` is `7.38906`
`floor( x )`	rounds *x* to the largest integer not greater than *x*	`floor( 9.2 )` is `9.0` `floor( -9.8 )` is `-10.0`
`log( x )`	natural logarithm of *x* (base *e*)	`log( 2.718282 )` is `1.0` `log( 7.389056 )` is `2.0`
`max( x, y )`	larger value of *x* and *y*	`max( 2.3, 12.7 )` is `12.7` `max( -2.3, -12.7 )` is `-2.3`
`min( x, y )`	smaller value of *x* and *y*	`min( 2.3, 12.7 )` is `2.3` `min( -2.3, -12.7 )` is `-12.7`
`pow( x, y )`	*x* raised to power *y* (x^y)	`pow( 2.0, 7.0 )` is `128.0` `pow( 9.0, .5 )` is `3.0`
`round( x )`	rounds *x* to the closest integer	`round( 9.75 )` is `10` `round( 9.25 )` is `9`
`sin( x )`	trigonometric sine of *x* (*x* in radians)	`sin( 0.0 )` is `0.0`
`sqrt( x )`	square root of *x*	`sqrt( 900.0 )` is `30.0` `sqrt( 9.0 )` is `3.0`
`tan( x )`	trigonometric tangent of *x* (*x* in radians)	`tan( 0.0 )` is `0.0`

Fig. 13.1 Commonly used **Math** object methods (part 2 of 2).

The **Math** object also defines several commonly used mathematical constants, summarized in Fig. 13.2. [Note: By convention, the names of these constants are written in all uppercase letters.]

Good Programming Practice 13.1

Use the mathematical constants of the **Math** *object rather than explicitly typing the numeric value of the constant.*

Constant	Description	Value
Math.E	Euler's constant.	Approximately 2.718.
Math.LN2	Natural logarithm of 2.	Approximately 0.693.
Math.LN10	Natural logarithm of 10.	Approximately 2.302.
Math.LOG2E	Base 2 logarithm of Euler's constant.	Approximately 1.442.

Fig. 13.2 Properties of the **Math** object. (part 1 of 2)

Constant	Description	Value
Math.LOG10E	Base 10 logarithm of Euler's constant.	Approximately 0.434.
Math.PI	PI—the ratio of a circle's circumference to its diameter.	Approximately 3.141592653589793.
Math.SQRT1_2	Square root of 0.5.	Approximately 0.707.
Math.SQRT2	Square root of 2.0.	Approximately 1.414.

Fig. 13.2 Properties of the **Math** object. (part 2 of 2)

13.4 String Object

In this section, we introduce Java's string and character processing capabilities. The techniques discussed here are appropriate for developing text editors, word processors, page layout software, computerized typesetting systems and other kinds of text-processing software.

13.4.1 Fundamentals of Characters and Strings

Characters are the fundamental building blocks of JavaScript programs. Every program is composed of a sequence of characters that—when grouped together meaningfully—is interpreted by the computer as a series of instructions used to accomplish a task.

A string is a series of characters treated as a single unit. A string may include letters, digits and various *special characters,* such as **+**, **-**, *****, **/**, **$** and others. A string is an object of type **String**. *String literals* or *string constants* (often called *anonymous* ***String*** *objects*) are written as a sequence of characters in double quotation marks or single quotation marks as follows:

```
"John Q. Doe"                  (a name)
'9999 Main Street'             (a street address)
"Waltham, Massachusetts"       (a city and state)
'(201) 555-1212'               (a telephone number)
```

A **String** may be assigned to a variable in a declaration. The declaration

```
var color = "blue";
```

initializes variable **color** as a **String** object containing the string **"blue"**.

Strings can be compared with the relational operators (**<**, **<=**, **>** and **>=**) and the equality operators (**==** and **!=**).

13.4.2 Methods of the String Object

The **String** object encapsulates the attributes and behaviors of a string of characters. The **String** object provides many methods (behaviors) for selecting characters from a string, combining strings (called *concatenation*), obtaining substrings of a string, searching for substrings within a string, tokenizing a string and converting strings to all uppercase or lowercase letters. The **String** object also provides several methods that generate HTML tags. Figure 13.3 summarizes many **String** methods. Figures 13.4 through 13.7 demonstrate some of these methods.

Method	Description
charAt(*index* **)**	Returns the character at the specified *index*. If there is no character at that *index*, **charAt** returns an empty string. The first character is located at *index* 0.
charCodeAt(*index* **)**	Returns the Unicode value of the character at the specified *index*. If there is no character at that *index*, **charCodeAt** returns **NaN**.
concat(*string* **)**	Concatenates its argument to the end of the string that invokes the method. This method is the same as adding two strings with the string concatenation operator **+** (e.g., **s1.concat(s2)** is the same as **s1 + s2**). The original strings are not modified.
fromCharCode(*value1*, *value2*, ...**)**	Converts a list of Unicode values into a string containing the corresponding characters.
indexOf(*substring*, *index* **)**	Searches for the first occurrence of *substring* starting from position *index* in the string that invokes the method. The method returns the starting index of *substring* in the source string (-1 if *substring* is not found). If the *index* argument is not provided, the method begins searching from index 0 in the source string.
lastIndexOf(*substring*, *index* **)**	Searches for the last occurrence of *substring* starting from position *index* and searching toward the beginning of the string that invokes the method. The method returns the starting index of *substring* in the source string (-1 if *substring* is not found). If the *index* argument is not provided, the method begins searching from end of the source string.
slice(*start*, *end* **)**	Returns a string containing the portion of the string from index *start* through index *end*. If the *end* index is not specified, the method returns a string from the *start* index to the end of the source string. A negative *end* index specifies an offset from the end of the string starting from a position one past the end of the last character (so, -1 indicates the last character position in the string).
split(*string* **)**	Splits the source string into an array of strings (tokens) where its *string* argument specifies the delimiter (i.e., the characters that indicate the end of each token in the source string).
substr(*start*, *length* **)**	Returns a string containing *length* characters starting from index *start* in the source string. If *length* is not specified, a string containing characters from *start* to the end of the source string is returned.
substring(*start*, *end* **)**	Returns a string containing the characters from index *start* up to but not including index *end* in the source string.
toLowerCase()	Returns a string in which all uppercase letters are converted to lowercase letters. Non-letter characters are not changed.
toUpperCase()	Returns a string in which all lowercase letters are converted to uppercase letters. Non-letter characters are not changed.
toString()	Returns the same string as the source string.

Fig. 13.3 Methods of the **String** object (part 1 of 2).

Method	Description
valueOf()	Returns the same string as the source string.
Methods that generate HTML tags	
anchor(*name* **)**	Wraps the source string in an anchor element (**<A></A>**) with *name* as the anchor name.
big()	Wraps the source string in a **<BIG></BIG>** element.
blink()	Wraps the source string in a **<BLINK></BLINK>** element.
bold()	Wraps the source string in a **<B></B>** element.
fixed()	Wraps the source string in a**<TT></TT>** element.
fontcolor(*color* **)**	Wraps the source string in a **<FONT></FONT>** element with *color* as the font color.
fontsize(*size* **)**	Wraps the source string in a **<FONT></FONT>** element with *size* as the HTML font size.
italics()	Wraps the source string in an **<I></I>** element.
link(*url* **)**	Wraps the source string in an anchor element (**<A></A>**) with *url* as the hyperlink location.
small()	Wraps the source string in a **<SMALL></SMALL>** element.
strike()	Wraps the source string in a **<STRIKE></STRIKE>** element.
sub()	Wraps the source string in a **** element.
sup()	Wraps the source string in a **** element.

Fig. 13.3 Methods of the **String** object (part 2 of 2).

13.4.3 Character Processing Methods

The script of Fig. 13.4 demonstrates some of the **String** object's character processing methods: ***charAt*** (returns the character at a specific position); ***charCodeAt*** (returns the Unicode value of the character at a specific position); ***fromCharCode*** (creates a string from a list of Unicode values); ***toLowerCase*** (returns the lowercase version of a string); and ***toUpperCase*** (returns the uppercase version of a string).

```
<!DOCTYPE HTML PUBLIC "-//W3C//DTD HTML 4.0 Transitional//EN">
<HTML>
<!-- Fig. 13.4: CharacterProcessing.html -->

<HEAD>
<TITLE>Character Processing Methods</TITLE>

<SCRIPT LANGUAGE = "JavaScript">
   var s = "ZEBRA";
   var s2 = "AbCdEfG";
```

Fig. 13.4 String methods **charAt**, **charCodeAt**, **fromCharCode**, **toLowercase** and **toUpperCase** (part 1 of 2).

```
11
12     document.writeln( "<P>Character at index 0 in '" +
13        s + "' is " + s.charAt( 0 ) );
14     document.writeln( "<BR>Character code at index 0 in '" +
15        s + "' is " + s.charCodeAt( 0 ) + "</P>" );
16
17     document.writeln( "<P>'" +
18        String.fromCharCode( 87, 79, 82, 68 ) +
19        "' contains character codes 87, 79, 82 and 68</P>" )
20
21     document.writeln( "<P>'" + s2 + "' in lowercase is '" +
22        s2.toLowerCase() + "'" );
23     document.writeln( "<BR>'" + s2 + "' in uppercase is '" +
24        s2.toUpperCase() + "'</P>" );
25  </SCRIPT>
26
27  </HEAD><BODY></BODY>
28  </HTML>
```

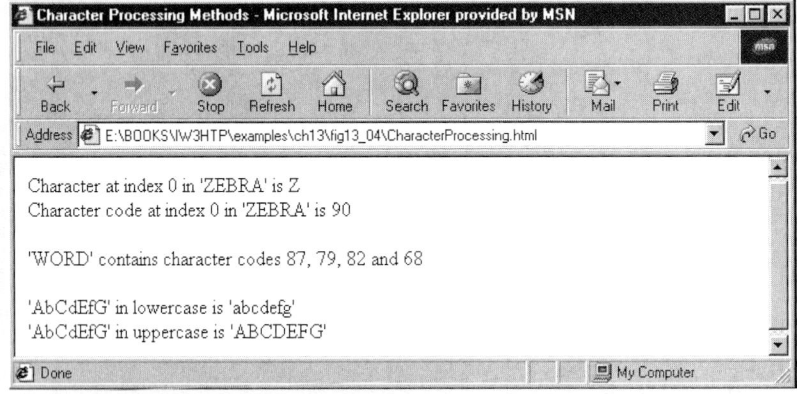

Fig. 13.4 String methods **charAt**, **charCodeAt**, **fromCharCode**, **toLowercase** and **toUpperCase** (part 2 of 2).

Lines 12 and 13

```
document.writeln( "<P>Character at index 0 in '" +
   s + "' is " + s.charAt( 0 ) );
```

display the first character in **String s** (**"ZEBRA"**) using **String** method **charAt**. Method ***charAt*** returns a string containing the character at the specified index (**0** in this example). Indices for the characters in a string start at 0 (the first character) and go up to (but not including) the string's **length** (i.e., if the string contains five characters, the indices are 0 through 4). If the index is outside the bounds of the string, the method returns an empty string.

Lines 14 and 15

```
document.writeln( "<BR>Character code at index 0 in '" +
   s + "' is " + s.charCodeAt( 0 ) + "</P>" );
```

display the character code for the first character in **String s** (**"ZEBRA"**) by using **String** method ***charCodeAt***. Method **charCodeAt** returns the Unicode value of the character at the specified index (**0** in this example). If the index is outside the bounds of the string, the method returns **NaN**.

String method ***fromCharCode*** receives as its argument a comma-separated list of Unicode values and builds a string containing the character representation of those Unicode values. Lines 17 through 19

```
document.writeln( "<P>'" +
   String.fromCharCode( 87, 79, 82, 68 ) +
   "' contains character codes 87, 79, 82 and 68</P>" )
```

display the string "**WORD**", which consists of the character codes 87, 79, 82 and 68. Notice that the **String** object is used to call method **fromCharCode**. Appendix C, "Character Set," contains the character codes ASCII character set—a subset of the Unicode character set that contains only English characters.

The statements at lines 21 and 23 use **String** methods ***toLowerCase*** and ***toUpperCase*** to display versions of **String s2** (**"AbCdEfG"**) in all lowercase letters and all uppercase letters, respectively.

13.4.4 Searching Methods

Often it is useful to search for a character or a sequence of characters in a string. For example, if you are creating your own word processor, you may want to provide a capability for searching through the document. The script of Fig. 13.5 demonstrates the **String** object methods ***indexOf*** and ***lastIndexOf*** that search for a specified substring in a string. All the searches in this example are performed on the global string **letters** (initialized at line 9 with **"abcdefghijklmnopqrstuvwxyzabcdefghijklm"** in the script).

The user types a substring in the HTML form **searchForm**'s **inputVal** text field and presses button **search** (with the label **Search** on the screen) to search for the substring in **letters**. Function **buttonPressed** (defined at line 11) is called to respond to the **ONCLICK** event of button **search** and perform the searches. The results of each search are displayed in the appropriate text field of **searchForm**.

```
1  <!DOCTYPE HTML PUBLIC "-//W3C//DTD HTML 4.0 Transitional//EN">
2  <HTML>
3  <!-- Fig. 13.5: SearchingStrings.html -->
4
5  <HEAD>
6  <TITLE>Searching Strings with indexOf and lastIndexOf</TITLE>
7
8  <SCRIPT LANGUAGE = "JavaScript">
9     var letters = "abcdefghijklmnopqrstuvwxyzabcdefghijklm";
10
11    function buttonPressed()
12    {
13       searchForm.first.value =
14          letters.indexOf( searchForm.inputVal.value );
```

Fig. 13.5 Searching **Strings** with **indexOf** and **lastIndexOf** (part 1 of 3).

```
         searchForm.last.value =
            letters.lastIndexOf( searchForm.inputVal.value );
         searchForm.first12.value =
            letters.indexOf( searchForm.inputVal.value, 12 );
         searchForm.last12.value =
            letters.lastIndexOf( searchForm.inputVal.value, 12 );
      }
   </SCRIPT>

   </HEAD>
   <BODY>
   <FORM NAME = "searchForm">
      <H1>The string to search is:<BR>
         abcdefghijklmnopqrstuvwxyzabcdefghijklm</H1>
      <P>Enter substring to search for
      <INPUT NAME = "inputVal" TYPE = "text">
      <INPUT NAME = "search" TYPE = "button" VALUE = "Search"
         ONCLICK = "buttonPressed()"><BR></P>

      <P>First occurrence located at index
      <INPUT NAME = "first" TYPE = "text" SIZE = "5">
      <BR>Last occurrence located at index
      <INPUT NAME = "last" TYPE = "text" SIZE = "5">
      <BR>First occurrence from index 12 located at index
      <INPUT NAME = "first12" TYPE = "text" SIZE = "5">
      <BR>Last occurrence from index 12 located at index
      <INPUT NAME = "last12" TYPE = "text" SIZE = "5"></P>
   </FORM>
   </BODY>
   </HTML>
```

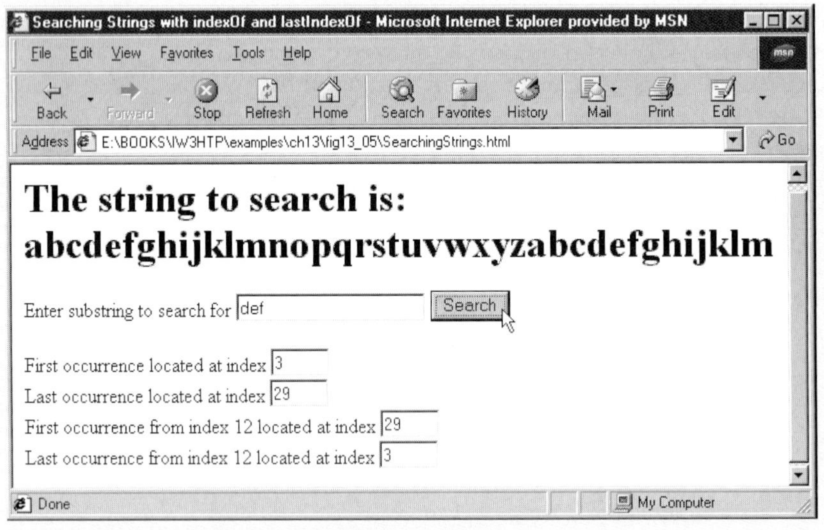

Fig. 13.5 Searching **Strings** with **indexOf** and **lastIndexOf** (part 2 of 3).

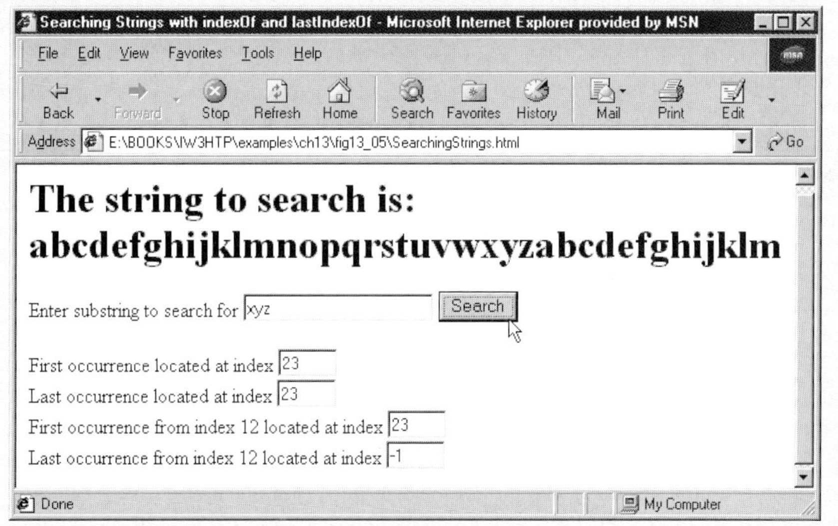

Fig. 13.5 Searching **String**s with **indexOf** and **lastIndexOf** (part 3 of 3).

Lines 13 and 14

```
searchForm.first.value =
   letters.indexOf( searchForm.inputVal.value );
```

use **String** method **indexOf** to determine the location of the first occurrence in string **letters** of the string **searchForm.inputVal.value** (i.e., the string the user typed in the **inputVal** text field). If the substring is found, the index at which the first occurrence of the substring begins is returned; otherwise, -1 is returned.

Lines 15 and 16

```
searchForm.last.value =
   letters.lastIndexOf( searchForm.inputVal.value );
```

use **String** method **lastIndexOf** to determine the location of the last occurrence in **letters** of the string in the **inputVal** text field. If the substring is found, the index at which the last occurrence of the substring begins is returned; otherwise, -1 is returned.

Lines 17 and 18

```
searchForm.first12.value =
   letters.indexOf( searchForm.inputVal.value, 12 );
```

use **String** method **indexOf** to determine the location of the first occurrence in string **letters** of the string in the **inputVal** text field, starting from index **12** in **letters**. If the substring is found, the index at which the first occurrence of the substring (starting from index **12**) begins is returned; otherwise, -1 is returned.

Lines 19 and 20

```
searchForm.last12.value =
   letters.lastIndexOf( searchForm.inputVal.value, 12 );
```

use **String** method **lastIndexOf** to determine the location of the last occurrence in **letters** of the string in the **inputVal** text field starting from index **12** in **letters**. If the substring is found, the index at which the first occurrence of the substring (starting from index **12**) begins is returned; otherwise, -1 is returned.

Software Engineering Observation 13.2

***String** methods **indexOf** or **lastIndexOf**, with their optional second argument (the starting index from which to search), are particularly useful for continuing a search through a large amount of text.*

13.4.5 Splitting Strings and Obtaining Substrings

When you read a sentence, your mind breaks the sentence into individual words, or *tokens,* each of which conveys meaning to you. The process of breaking a string into tokens is called *tokenization*. Interpreters also perform tokenization. They break up statements into such individual pieces as keywords, identifiers, operators and other elements of a programming language. In this section, we demonstrate **String** method ***split*** that breaks a string into its component tokens. Tokens are separated from one another by *delimiters*, typically white-space characters such as blank, tab, newline and carriage return. Other characters may also be used as delimiters to separate tokens. The program of Fig. 13.6 demonstrates **String** method **split**. The HTML document displays a form containing a text field where the user types a sentence to tokenize. The results of the tokenization process are displayed in an HTML **TEXTAREA** GUI component. The script of Fig. 13.6 also demonstrates **String** method ***substring*** which returns a portion of a string.

```
<!DOCTYPE HTML PUBLIC "-//W3C//DTD HTML 4.0 Transitional//EN">
<HTML>
<!-- Fig. 13.6: SplitAndSubString.html -->

<HEAD>
<TITLE>String Method split and substring</TITLE>

<SCRIPT LANGUAGE = "JavaScript">
   function splitButtonPressed()
   {
      var strings = myForm.inputVal.value.split( " " );
      myForm.output.value = strings.join( "\n" );

      myForm.outputSubstring.value =
         myForm.inputVal.value.substring( 0, 10 );
   }
</SCRIPT>
</HEAD>

<BODY>
<FORM NAME = "myForm">
   <P>Enter a sentence to split into words<BR>
   <INPUT NAME = "inputVal" TYPE = "text" SIZE = "40">
   <INPUT NAME = "splitButton" TYPE = "button" VALUE = "Split"
         ONCLICK = "splitButtonPressed()"></P>
```

Fig. 13.6 Using **String** method split and **Array** method **join** (part 1 of 2).

```
26
27      <P>The sentence split into words is<BR>
28      <TEXTAREA NAME = "output" ROWS = "8" COLS = "34">
29      </TEXTAREA></P>
30
31      <P>The first 10 characters of the input string are
32      <INPUT NAME = "outputSubstring" TYPE = "text" SIZE = "15">
33      </P>
34   </FORM>
35   </BODY>
36   </HTML>
```

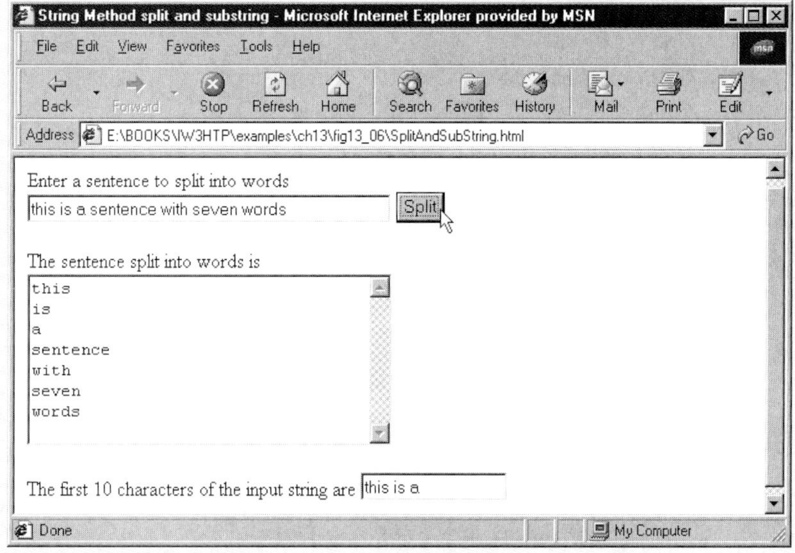

Fig. 13.6 Using **String** method split and **Array** method **join** (part 2 of 2).

The user types a sentence into form **myForm**'s **inputVal** text field and presses button **splitButton** (labeled **Split** on the screen) to tokenize the string. Function **splitButtonPressed** (line 9) handles **splitButton**'s **ONCLICK** event.

Line 11

```
var strings = myForm.inputVal.value.split( " " );
```

uses **String** method **split** to tokenize the string **myForm.inputVal.value**. The argument to method **split** is the *delimiter string*—the string that determines the end of each token in the original string. In this example, the space character is used as the delimiter for tokens. The delimiter string can contain multiple characters that should be used as delimiters. Method **split** returns an array of strings containing the tokens. Line 12

```
myForm.output.value = strings.join( "\n" );
```

uses **Array** method **join** to combine the strings in array **strings** and separate each string with a newline character (**\n**). The resulting string is assigned to the **value** property of the HTML form's **output** GUI component (an HTML **TEXTAREA**).

Lines 14 and 15

```
myForm.outputSubstring.value =
   myForm.inputVal.value.substring( 0, 10 );
```

use **String** method **substring** to obtain a string containing the first 10 characters of the string the user entered in text field **inputVal**. The method returns the substring from the *starting index* (**0** in this example) up to but not including the *ending index* (**10** in this example). If the ending index is greater than the length of the string, the substring returned includes the characters from the starting index to the end of the original string.

13.4.6 HTML Markup Methods

The script of Fig. 13.7 demonstrates the **String** object's methods that generate HTML markup tags. When a markup method is applied to a string, the string is automatically wrapped in the appropriate HTML tag. These methods are particularly useful for generating HTML dynamically during script processing. [*Note:* Internet Explorer ignores the **BLINK** element.]

```
<!DOCTYPE HTML PUBLIC "-//W3C//DTD HTML 4.0 Transitional//EN">
<HTML>
<!-- Fig. 13.7: MarkupMethods.html -->

<HEAD>
<TITLE>HTML Markup Methods of the String Object</TITLE>

<SCRIPT LANGUAGE = "JavaScript">
   var anchorText = "This is an anchor",
       bigText = "This is big text",
       blinkText = "This is blinking text",
       boldText = "This is bold text",
       fixedText = "This is monospaced text",
       fontColorText = "This is red text",
       fontSizeText = "This is size 7 text",
       italicText = "This is italic text",
       linkText = "Click here to go to anchorText",
       smallText = "This is small text",
       strikeText = "This is strike out text",
       subText = "subscript",
       supText = "superscript";

   document.writeln( anchorText.anchor( "top" ) );
   document.writeln( "<BR>" + bigText.big() );
   document.writeln( "<BR>" + blinkText.blink() );
   document.writeln( "<BR>" + boldText.bold() );
   document.writeln( "<BR>" + fixedText.fixed() );
   document.writeln(
      "<BR>" + fontColorText.fontcolor( "red" ) );
   document.writeln( "<BR>" + fontSizeText.fontsize( 7 ) );
   document.writeln( "<BR>" + italicText.italics() );
   document.writeln( "<BR>" + smallText.small() );
```

Fig. 13.7 HTML markup methods of the **String** object (part 1 of 2).

```
33       document.writeln( "<BR>" + strikeText.strike() );
34       document.writeln(
35          "<BR>This is text with a " + subText.sub() );
36       document.writeln(
37          "<BR>This is text with a " + supText.sup() );
38       document.writeln( "<BR>" + linkText.link( "#top" ) );
39    </SCRIPT>
40
41    </HEAD><BODY></BODY>
42    </HTML>
```

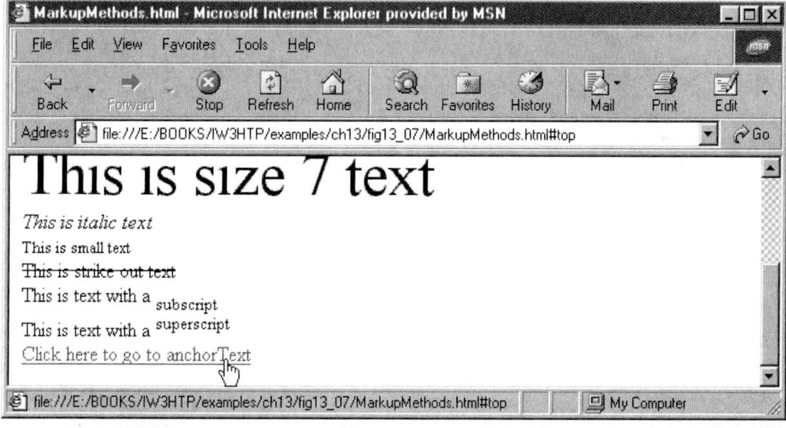

Fig. 13.7 HTML markup methods of the **String** object (part 2 of 2).

Lines 9 through 21 define the strings that are used to call each of the HTML markup methods of the **String** object. Line 23

```
document.writeln( anchorText.anchor( "top" ) );
```

uses **String** method ***anchor*** to format the string in variable **anchorText** (**"This is an anchor"**) as

```
<A NAME = "top">This is an anchor</A>
```

The **NAME** of the anchor is supplied as the argument to the method. This anchor will be used later in the example as the target of a hyperlink.

Line 24

```
document.writeln( "<BR>" + bigText.big() );
```

uses **String** method ***big*** to make the size of the displayed text bigger than normal text by formatting the string in variable **bigText** (**"This is big text"**) as

```
<BIG>This is big text</BIG>
```

Line 25

```
document.writeln( "<BR>" + blinkText.blink() );
```

uses **String** method ***blink*** to make the string blink in the Web page by formatting the string in variable **blinkText** (**"This is blinking text"**) as

```
<BLINK>This is blinking text</BLINK>
```

Line 26

```
document.writeln( "<BR>" + boldText.bold() );
```

uses **String** method ***bold*** to display bold text by formatting the string in the variable **boldText** (**"This is bold text"**) as

```
<B>This is bold text</B>
```

Line 27

```
document.writeln( "<BR>" + fixedText.fixed() );
```

uses **String** method ***fixed*** to display text in a fixed-width font by formatting the string in variable **fixedText** (**"This is monospaced text"**) as

```
<TT>This is monospaced text</TT>
```

Lines 28 and 29

```
document.writeln(
   "<BR>" + fontColorText.fontcolor( "red" ) );
```

uses **String** method ***fontcolor*** to change the color of the displayed text by formatting the string in variable **fontColorText** (**"This is red text"**) as

```
<FONT COLOR = "red">This is red text</FONT>
```

The argument to the method is the HTML color for the text. This color can be specified either as the HTML color name or as a hexadecimal value. For example, red in hexadecimal format would be **"FF0000"**.

Line 30

```
document.writeln( "<BR>" + fontSizeText.fontsize( 7 ) );
```

uses **String** method ***fontsize*** to change the HTML size of the displayed text by formatting the string in variable **fontSizeText** (**"This is size 7 text"**) as

```
<FONT SIZE = "7">This is size 7 text</FONT>
```

The argument to the method is the HTML font size (1 to 7) for the text.

Line 31

```
document.writeln( "<BR>" + italicText.italics() );
```

uses **String** method ***italics*** to display italic text by formatting the string in variable **italicText** (**"This is italic text"**) as

```
<I>This is italic text</I>
```

Line 32

```
document.writeln( "<BR>" + smallText.small() );
```

uses **String** method ***small*** to make the size of the displayed text smaller than normal text by formatting the string in variable **smallText** (**"This is small text"**) as

```
<SMALL>This is small text</SMALL>
```

Line 33

```
document.writeln( "<BR>" + strikeText.strike() );
```

uses **String** method ***strike*** to display struck-out text (i.e., text with a line through it) by formatting the string in variable **strikeText** (**"This is strike out text"**) as

```
<STRIKE>This is strike out text</STRIKE>
```

Lines 34 and 35

```
document.writeln(
   "<BR>This is text with a " + subText.sub() );
```

use **String** method ***sub*** to display subscript text by formatting the string in variable **subText** (**"subscript"**) as

```
<SUB>subscript</SUB>
```

Notice that the resulting line in the HTML document displays the word **subscript** smaller than the rest of the line and slightly below the line. Lines 36 and 37

```
document.writeln(
   "<BR>This is text with a " + supText.sup() );
```

use **String** method ***sup*** to display superscript text by formatting the string in variable **supText** (**"superscript"**) as

```
<SUP>superscript</SUP>
```

Notice that the resulting line in the HTML document displays the word **superscript** smaller than the rest of the line and slightly above the line.

Line 38

```
document.writeln( "<BR>" + linkText.link( "#top" ) );
```

uses **String** method ***link*** to create a hyperlink by formatting the string in variable **linkText** (**"Click here to go to anchorText"**) as

```
<A HREF = "#top">Click here to go to anchorText</A>
```

The target of the hyperlink (**#top** in this example) is the argument to the method and can be any URL. In this example, the hyperlink target is the anchor created at line 23. If you make your browser window short and scroll to the bottom of the Web page, then click this link, the browser will reposition to the top of the Web page.

13.5 Date Object

JavaScript's ***Date*** object provides methods for date and time manipulations. Date and time processing can be performed based on the computer's *local time zone* or based on World Time Standard's *Universal Coordinated Time (UTC)*—formerly called *Greenwich Mean Time (GMT)*. Most methods of the **Date** object have a local time zone and a UTC version. The methods of the **Date** object are summarized in Fig. 13.8.

Method	Description
getDate() **getUTCDate()**	Returns a number from 1 to 31 representing the day of the month in local time or UTC, respectively.
getDay() **getUTCDay()**	Returns a number from 0 (Sunday) to 6 (Saturday) representing the day of the week in local time or UTC, respectively.
getFullYear() **getUTCFullYear()**	Returns the year as four-digit number in local time or UTC, respectively.
getHours() **getUTCHours()**	Returns a number from 0 to 23 representing hours since midnight in local time or UTC, respectively.
getMilliseconds() **getUTCMilliSeconds()**	Returns a number from 0 to 999 representing the number of milliseconds in local time or UTC, respectively. The time is stored in hours, minutes, seconds and milliseconds.
getMinutes() **getUTCMinutes()**	Returns a number from 0 to 59 representing the minutes for the time in local time or UTC, respectively.
getMonth() **getUTCMonth()**	Returns a number from 0 (January) to 11 (December) representing the month in local time or UTC, respectively.
getSeconds() **getUTCSeconds()**	Returns a number from 0 to 59 representing the seconds for the time in local time or UTC, respectively.
getTime()	Returns the number of milliseconds between January 1, 1970 and the time in the **Date** object.
getTimezoneOffset()	Returns the difference in minutes between the current time on the local computer and UTC—previously known as Greenwich Mean Time (GMT).
setDate(*val* **)** **setUTCDate(** *val* **)**	Sets the day of the month (1 to 31) in local time or UTC, respectively.
setFullYear(*y*, *m*, *d* **)** **setUTCFullYear(** *y*, *m*, *d* **)**	Sets the year in local time or UTC, respectively. The second and third arguments representing the month and the date are optional. If an optional argument is not specified, the current value in the **Date** object is used.

Fig. 13.8 Methods of the **Date** object (part 1 of 2).

Method	Description
setHours(*h*, *m*, *s*, *ms* **)** **setUTCHours(** *h*, *m*, *s*, *ms* **)**	Sets the hour in local time or UTC, respectively. The second, third and fourth arguments representing the minutes, seconds and milliseconds are optional. If an optional argument is not specified, the current value in the **Date** object is used.
setMilliSeconds(*ms* **)** **setUTCMilliseconds(** *ms* **)**	Sets the number of milliseconds in local time or UTC, respectively.
setMinutes(*m*, *s*, *ms* **)** **setUTCMinutes(** *m*, *s*, *ms* **)**	Sets the minute in local time or UTC, respectively. The second and third arguments representing the seconds and milliseconds are optional. If an optional argument is not specified, the current value in the **Date** object is used.
setMonth(*m*, *d* **)** **setUTCMonth(** *m*, *d* **)**	Sets the month in local time or UTC, respectively. The second argument representing the date is optional. If the optional argument is not specified, the current date value in the **Date** object is used.
setSeconds(*s*, *ms* **)** **setUTCSeconds(** *s*, *ms* **)**	Sets the second in local time or UTC, respectively. The second argument representing the milliseconds is optional. If this argument is not specified, the current millisecond value in the **Date** object is used.
setTime(*ms* **)**	Sets the time based on its argument—the number of elapsed milliseconds since January 1, 1970.
toLocaleString()	Returns a string representation of the date and time in a form specific to the locale of the computer. For example, September 13, 1999 at 3:42:22 PM is represented as *09/13/99 15:47:22* in the United States and *13/09/99 15:47:22* in Europe.
toUTCString()	Returns a string representation of the date and time in the form: *13 Sep 1999 15:47:22 UTC*
toString()	Returns a string representation of the date and time in a form specific to the locale of the computer (*Mon Sep 13 15:47:22 EDT 1999* in the United States).
valueOf()	The time in number of milliseconds since midnight, January 1, 1970.

Fig. 13.8 Methods of the **Date** object (part 2 of 2).

The script of Fig. 13.9 demonstrates many of the local time zone methods in Fig. 13.8. Line 9 creates a new **Date** object with the statement

```
var current = new Date();
```

The **new** operator allocates the memory for the **Date** object, then the **Date** object's *constructor* is called with no arguments. A constructor is an initializer method for an object. Constructors are called automatically when an object is allocated with **new**. The **Date** constructor with no arguments initializes the **Date** object with the current date and time.

```
<!DOCTYPE HTML PUBLIC "-//W3C//DTD HTML 4.0 Transitional//EN">
<HTML>
<!-- Fig. 13.9: DateTime.html -->

<HEAD>
<TITLE>Date and Time Methods</TITLE>

<SCRIPT LANGUAGE = "JavaScript">
   var current = new Date();

   document.writeln(
      "<H1>String representations and valueOf</H1>" );
   document.writeln( "toString: " + current.toString() +
      "<BR>toLocaleString: " + current.toLocaleString() +
      "<BR>toUTCString: " + current.toUTCString() +
      "<BR>valueOf: " + current.valueOf() );

   document.writeln(
      "<H1>Get methods for local time zone</H1>" );
   document.writeln( "getDate: " + current.getDate() +
      "<BR>getDay: " + current.getDay() +
      "<BR>getMonth: " + current.getMonth() +
      "<BR>getFullYear: " + current.getFullYear() +
      "<BR>getTime: " + current.getTime() +
      "<BR>getHours: " + current.getHours() +
      "<BR>getMinutes: " + current.getMinutes() +
      "<BR>getSeconds: " + current.getSeconds() +
      "<BR>getMilliseconds: " + current.getMilliseconds() +
      "<BR>getTimezoneOffset: " +
      current.getTimezoneOffset() );

   document.writeln(
      "<H1>Specifying arguments for a new Date</H1>" );
   var anotherDate = new Date( 1999, 2, 18, 1, 5, 0, 0 );
   document.writeln( "Date: " + anotherDate );

   document.writeln(
      "<H1>Set methods for local time zone</H1>" );
   anotherDate.setDate( 31 );
   anotherDate.setMonth( 11 );
   anotherDate.setFullYear( 1999 );
   anotherDate.setHours( 23 );
   anotherDate.setMinutes( 59 );
   anotherDate.setSeconds( 59 );
   document.writeln( "Modified date: " + anotherDate );
</SCRIPT>

</HEAD><BODY></BODY>
</HTML>
```

Fig. 13.9 Demonstrating date and time methods of the **Date** object (part 1 of 2).

Date and Time Methods - Microsoft Internet Explorer provided by MSN

File Edit View Favorites Tools Help

Back Forward Stop Refresh Home Search Favorites History Mail Print Edit

Address E:\BOOKS\IW3HTP\examples\ch13\fig13_09\DateTime.html Go

String representations and valueOf

toString: Mon Sep 13 21:09:09 EDT 1999
toLocaleString: 09/13/1999 21:09:09
toUTCString: Tue, 14 Sep 1999 01:09:09 UTC
valueOf: 937271349800

Get methods for local time zone

getDate: 13
getDay: 1
getMonth: 8
getFullYear: 1999
getTime: 937271349800
getHours: 21
getMinutes: 9
getSeconds: 9
getMilliseconds: 800
getTimezoneOffset: 240

Done My Computer

Date and Time Methods - Microsoft Internet Explorer provided by MSN

File Edit View Favorites Tools Help

Back Forward Stop Refresh Home Search Favorites History Mail Print Edit

Address E:\BOOKS\IW3HTP\examples\ch13\fig13_09\DateTime.html Go

Specifying arguments for a new Date

Date: Thu Mar 18 01:05:00 EST 1999

Set methods for local time zone

Modified date: Fri Dec 31 23:59:59 EST 1999

Done My Computer

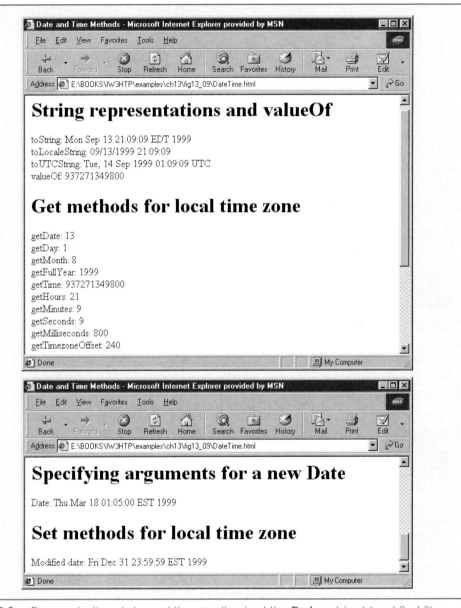

Fig. 13.9 Demonstrating date and time methods of the **`Date`** object (part 2 of 2).

Software Engineering Observation 13.3

When an object is allocated with **`new`***, the object's constructor is called automatically to initialize the object before it is used in the program.*

Lines 13 through 16 demonstrate the methods **`toString`**, **`toLocaleString`**, **`toUTCString`** and **`valueOf`**. Notice that method **`valueOf`** returns a large integer value representing the total number of milliseconds between midnight, January 1, 1970 and the date and time stored in **`Date`** object **`current`**.

Lines 20 through 30 demonstrate the **Date** object's *get* methods for the local time zone. Notice that method **getFullYear** returns the year as a four-digit number. Also, notice that method **getTimeZoneOffset** returns the difference in minutes between the local time zone and UTC time (a difference of four hours at the time of the sample execution).

Line 34

```
var anotherDate = new Date( 1999, 2, 18, 1, 5, 0, 0 );
```

demonstrates creating a new **Date** object and supplying arguments to the **Date** constructor for *year*, *month*, *date*, *hours*, *minutes*, *seconds* and *milliseconds*. Note that the *hours*, *minutes*, *seconds* and *milliseconds* arguments are all optional. If any one of these arguments is not specified, a zero is supplied in its place. For the *hours*, *minutes* and *seconds* arguments, if the argument to the right of any of these arguments is specified, that argument must also be specified (e.g., if the *minutes* argument is specified, the *hours* argument must be specified; if the *milliseconds* argument is specified, all the arguments must be specified).

Lines 39 through 44 demonstrate the **Date** object *set* methods for the local time zone.

Software Engineering Observation 13.4

Methods **getFullYear** *and* **setFullYear** *use four-digit years to avoid problems with dates at the beginning of the 21st century. In particular, two-digit year format would cause a problem for year 2000—00 could be treated by many computers as 1900 rather than 2000. This is commonly known as the Y2K (year 2000) bug.*

Date objects represent the month internally as a integer from 0 to 11. These values are off-by-one from what you might expect (i.e., 1 for January, 2 for February, ..., and 12 for December). When creating a **Date** object, you must specify 0 to indicate January, 1 to indicate February, ..., and 11 to indicate December.

Common Programming Error 13.2

Assuming months are represented as numbers from 1 to 12 leads to off-by-one errors when you are processing **Dates**.

The **Date** object provides two other methods that can be called without creating a new **Date** object—***Date.parse*** and ***Date.UTC***. Method **Date.parse** receives as its argument a string representing a date and time, and returns the number of milliseconds between midnight, January 1, 1970 and the specified date and time. This value can be converted to a **Date** object with the statement

```
var theDate = new Date( numberOfMilliseconds );
```

which passes to the **Date** constructor the number of milliseconds since midnight, January 1, 1970 for the **Date** object.

Method **parse** converts the string using the following rules:

- Short dates can be specified in the form **MM-DD-YY**, **MM-DD-YYYY**, **MM/DD/YY** or **MM/DD/YYYY**. The month and day are not required to be two-digits. The year should be specified as a four-digit number to avoid the Y2K problem mentioned previously.
- Long dates that specify the complete month name (e.g., "January"), date and year can specify the month, date and year in any order. The year should be specified as a four-digit number to avoid the Y2K problem mentioned previously.

- Text in parentheses within the string is treated as a comment and ignored. Commas and whitespace characters are treated as delimiters.
- All month and day names must have at least two characters. The names are not required to be unique. If the names are identical, the name is resolved as the last match (e.g., "Ju" represents "July" rather than "June").
- If the name of the day of the week is supplied, it is ignored.
- All standard time zones (e.g., EST for Eastern Standard Time), Universal Coordinated Time (UTC) and Greenwich Mean Time (GMT) are recognized.
- When specifying hours, minutes, and seconds, separate each by colons.
- When using 24-hour clock format, "PM" should not be used for times after 12 noon.

`Date` method **`UTC`** returns the number of milliseconds between midnight, January 1, 1970 and the date and time specified as its arguments. The arguments to the **`UTC`** method include the required *year*, *month* and *date*, and the optional *hours*, *minutes*, *seconds* and *milliseconds*. If any of the *hours*, *minutes*, *seconds* or *milliseconds* arguments is not specified, a zero is supplied in its place. For the *hours*, *minutes* and *seconds* arguments, if the argument to the right of any of these arguments is specified, that argument must also be specified (e.g., if the *minutes* argument is specified, the *hours* argument must be specified; if the *milliseconds* argument is specified, all the arguments must be specified). As with the result of **`Date.parse`**, the result of **`Date.UTC`** can be converted to a **`Date`** object by creating a new **`Date`** object with the result of **`Date.UTC`** as its argument.

13.6 Boolean and Number Objects

JavaScript provides the ***`Boolean`*** and ***`Number`*** objects as object *wrappers* for boolean **`true`**/**`false`** values and numbers, respectively. These wrappers define methods and properties useful in manipulating boolean values and numbers.

When a boolean value is required in a JavaScript program, JavaScript automatically creates a **`Boolean`** object to store the value. JavaScript programmers can create **`Boolean`** objects explicitly with the statement

```
var b = new Boolean( booleanValue );
```

The constructor argument *booleanValue* specifies whether the value of the **`Boolean`** object should be **`true`** or **`false`**. If *booleanValue* is **`false`**, **`0`**, **`null`**, **`Number.NaN`** or the empty string (`""`), or if no argument is supplied, the new **`Boolean`** object contains **`false`**. Otherwise, the new **`Boolean`** object contains **`true`**. Figure 13.10 summarizes the methods of the **`Boolean`** object.

Method	Description
`toString()`	Returns the string "**`true`**" if the value of the **`Boolean`** object is true; otherwise, returns the string "**`false`**."
`valueOf()`	Returns the value **`true`** if the **`Boolean`** object is **`true`**; otherwise, returns **`false`**.

Fig. 13.10 Methods of the **`Boolean`** object.

JavaScript automatically creates **Number** objects to store numeric values in a JavaScript program. JavaScript programmers can create a **Number** object with the statement

```
var n = new Number( numericValue );
```

The constructor argument *numericValue* is the number to store in the object. Although you can explicitly create **Number** objects, normally they are created when needed by the JavaScript interpreter. Figure 13.11 summarizes the methods and properties of the **Number** object.

SUMMARY

- Objects are a natural way of thinking about the world.
- Because JavaScript uses objects to perform many tasks, JavaScript is commonly referred to as an object-based programming language.
- Humans think in terms of objects. We have the marvelous ability of abstraction, which enables us to view screen images as objects such as people, planes, trees and mountains rather than as individual dots of color (called pixels for "picture elements").

Method or property	Description
toString(*radix* **)**	Returns the string representation of the number. The optional *radix* argument (a number from 2 to 36) specifies the base of the number. For example, a radix of 2 results in the binary representation of the number, a radix of 8 results in the octal representation of the number, a radix of 10 results in the decimal representation of the number and a radix of 16 results in the hexadecimal representation of the number. See appendix D, "Number Systems," for a review of the binary, octal, decimal and hexadecimal number systems.
valueOf()	Returns the numeric value.
Number.MAX_VALUE	This property represents the largest value that can be stored in a JavaScript program—approximately 1.79E+308
Number.MIN_VALUE	This property represents the smallest value that can be stored in a JavaScript program—approximately 2.22E–308
Number.NaN	This property represents *not a number*—a value returned from arithmetic expressions that do not result in a number (e.g., the expression **parseInt("hello")** cannot convert the string **"hello"** into a number, so **parseInt** would return **Number.NaN**). To determine whether a value is **NaN**, test the result with function **isNaN** which returns **true** if the value is **NaN**; otherwise, it returns **false**.
Number.NEGATIVE_INFINITY	This property represents a value less than **-Number.MAX_VALUE**.
Number.POSITIVE_INFINITY	This property represents a value greater than **Number.MAX_VALUE**.

Fig. 13.11 Methods and properties of the **Number** object.

- All objects have attributes and exhibit behaviors. Humans learn about objects by studying their attributes and observing their behaviors.
- Objects encapsulate data (attributes) and methods (behavior).
- Objects have the property of information hiding.
- Programs communicate with objects by using well-defined interfaces.
- World Wide Web browsers have a set of objects that encapsulate the elements of an HTML document and expose to a JavaScript programmer attributes and behaviors that enable a JavaScript program to interact with (or script) the elements (i.e., objects) in an HTML document.
- **`Math`** object methods allow programmers to perform many common mathematical calculations.
- An object's methods are called by writing the name of the object followed by a dot operator (**`.`**) and the name of the method. In parentheses following the method name is the argument (or a comma-separated list of arguments) to the method.
- Invoking (or calling) a method of an object is called "sending a message to the object."
- Characters are the fundamental building blocks of JavaScript programs. Every program is composed of a sequence of characters that—when grouped together meaningfully—is interpreted by the computer as a series of instructions used to accomplish a task.
- A string is a series of characters treated as a single unit.
- A string may include letters, digits and various special characters, such as **`+`**, **`-`**, **`*`**, **`/`**, **`$`** and others.
- String literals or string constants (often called anonymous **`String`** objects) are written as a sequence of characters in double quotation marks or single quotation marks.
- String method **`charAt`** returns the character at a specific index in a string. Indices for the characters in a string start at 0 (the first character) and go up to (but not including) the string's **`length`** (i.e., if the string contains five characters, the indices are 0 through 4). If the index is outside the bounds of the string, the method returns an empty string.
- **`String`** method **`charCodeAt`** returns the Unicode value of the character at a specific index in a string. If the index is outside the bounds of the string, the method returns **`NaN`**.
- **`String`** method **`fromCharCode`** creates a string from a list of Unicode values.
- **`String`** method **`toLowerCase`** returns the lowercase version of a string.
- **`String`** method **`toUpperCase`** returns the uppercase version of a string.
- **`String`** method **`indexOf`** determines the location of the first occurrence of its argument in the string used to call the method. If the substring is found, the index at which the first occurrence of the substring begins is returned; otherwise, -1 is returned. This method receives an optional second argument specifying the index from which to begin the search.
- **`String`** method **`lastIndexOf`** determines the location of the last occurrence of its argument in the string used to call the method. If the substring is found, the index at which the first occurrence of the substring begins is returned; otherwise, -1 is returned. This method receives an optional second argument specifying the index from which to begin the search.
- The process of breaking a string into tokens is called tokenization. Tokens are separated from one another by delimiters, typically white-space characters such as blank, tab, newline and carriage return. Other characters may also be used as delimiters to separate tokens.
- **`String`** method **`split`** breaks a string into its component tokens. The argument to method **`split`** is the delimiter string—the string that determines the end of each token in the original string. Method **`split`** returns an array of strings containing the tokens.
- **`String`** method **`substring`** returns the substring from the starting index (its first argument) up to but not including the ending index (its second argument). If the ending index is greater than the

length of the string, the substring returned includes the characters from the starting index to the end of the original string.

- **String** method **anchor** wraps the string that calls the method in HTML element **<A></A>** with the **NAME** of the anchor supplied as the argument to the method.
- **String** method **big** makes the size of the displayed text bigger than normal text by wrapping the string that calls the method in a **<BIG></BIG>** HTML element.
- **String** method **blink** make a string blink in a Web page by wrapping the string that calls the method in a **<BLINK></BLINK>** HTML element.
- **String** method **bold** displays bold text by wrapping the string that calls the method in HTML element **<B></B>**.
- **String** method **fixed** displays text in a fixed-width font by wrapping the string that calls the method in a **<TT></TT>** HTML element.
- **String** method **fontcolor** changes the color of the displayed text by wrapping the string that calls the method in a **<FONT></FONT>** element. The argument to the method is the HTML color for the text, which can be specified as either the HTML color name or as a hexadecimal value.
- **String** method **fontsize** changes the HTML size of the displayed text by wrapping the string that calls the method in a **<FONT></FONT>** element. The argument to the method is the HTML font size (1 to 7) for the text.
- **String** method **italics** displays italic text by wrapping the string that calls the method in an **<I></I>** HTML element.
- **String** method **small** makes the size of the displayed text smaller than normal text by wrapping the string that calls the method in a **<SMALL></SMALL>** HTML element.
- **String** method **strike** displays struck-out text (i.e., text with a line through it) by wrapping the string that calls the method in a **<STRIKE></STRIKE>** HTML element.
- **String** method **sub** displays subscript text by wrapping the string that calls the method in a **** HTML element.
- **String** method **sup** displays superscript text by wrapping the string that calls the method in a **** HTML element.
- **String** method **link** creates a hyperlink by wrapping the string that calls the method in HTML element **<A></A>**. The target of the hyperlink (i.e, value of the **HREF** property) is the argument to the method and can be any URL.
- JavaScript's **Date** object provides methods for date and time manipulations.
- Date and time processing can be performed based on the computer's local time zone or based on World Time Standard's Universal Coordinated Time (UTC)—formerly called Greenwich Mean Time (GMT).
- Most methods of the **Date** object have a local time zone and a UTC version.
- **Date** method **parse** receives as its argument a string representing a date and time and returns the number of milliseconds between midnight, January 1, 1970 and the specified date and time.
- **Date** method **UTC** returns the number of milliseconds between midnight, January 1, 1970 and the date and time specified as its arguments. The arguments to the **UTC** method include the required year, month and date, and the optional hours, minutes, seconds and milliseconds. If any of the hours, minutes, seconds or milliseconds arguments is not specified, a zero is supplied in its place. For the hours, minutes and seconds arguments, if the argument to the right of any of these arguments is specified, that argument must also be specified (e.g., if the minutes argument is specified, the hours argument must be specified; if the milliseconds argument is specified, all the arguments must be specified).

- JavaScript provides the **Boolean** and **Number** objects as object wrappers for boolean **true**/**false** values and numbers, respectively.
- When a boolean value is required in a JavaScript program, JavaScript automatically creates a **Boolean** object to store the value.
- JavaScript programmers can create **Boolean** objects explicitly with the statement

```
var b = new Boolean( booleanValue );
```

The argument *booleanValue* specifies whether the value of the **Boolean** object should be **true** or **false**. If *booleanValue* is **false**, **0**, **null**, **Number.NaN** or the empty string (" "), or if no argument is supplied, the new **Boolean** object contains **false**. Otherwise, the new **Boolean** object contains **true**.

- JavaScript automatically creates **Number** objects to store numeric values in a JavaScript program.
- JavaScript programmers can create a **Number** object with the statement

```
var n = new Number( numericValue );
```

The argument *numericValue* is the number to store in the object. Although you can explicitly create **Number** objects, normally they are created when needed by the JavaScript interpreter.

TERMINOLOGY

abs method of **Math**
abstraction
anchor method of **String**
anonymous **String** object
attribute
behavior
big method of **String**
blink method of **String**
bold method of **String**
Boolean object
bounds of the string
ceil method of **Math**
character
charAt method of **String**
charCodeAt method of **String**
concat method of **String**
cos method of **Math**
date
Date object
delimiters
double quotation marks
E property of Math
empty string
encapsulation
ending index
exp method of **Math**
fixed method of **String**
floor method of **Math**
fontcolor method of **String**
fontsize method of **String**
fromCharCode method of **String**
getDate method of **Date**
getDay method of **Date**
getFullYear method of **Date**
getHours method of **Date**
getMilliseconds method of **Date**
getMinutes method of **Date**
getMonth method of **Date**
getSeconds method of **Date**
getTime method of **Date**
getTimezoneOffset method of **Date**
getUTCDate method of **Date**
getUTCDay method of **Date**
getUTCFullYear method of **Date**
getUTCHours method of **Date**
getUTCMilliSeconds method of **Date**
getUTCMinutes method of **Date**
getUTCMonth method of **Date**
getUTCSeconds method of **Date**
Greenwich Mean Time (GMT)
hiding
index in a string
indexOf method of **String**
information hiding
italics method of **String**
lastIndexOf method of **String**
link method of **String**
local time zone
LN10 property of Math
LN2 property of Math

log method of **Math**
LOG10E property of Math
LOG2E property of Math
Math object
max method of **Math**
MAX_SIZE property of **Number**
min method of **Math**
MIN_SIZE property of **Number**
NaN property of **Number**
NEGATIVE_INFINITY property of **Number**
Number object
object
object-based programming language
object wrapper
parse method of **Date**
PI property of Math
POSITIVE_INFINITY property of **Number**
pow method of **Math**
round method of **Math**
search a string
sending a message to an object
setDate method of **Date**
setFullYear method of **Date**
setHours method of **Date**
setMilliSeconds method of **Date**
setMinutes method of **Date**
setMonth method of **Date**
setSeconds method of **Date**
setTime method of **Date**
setUTCDate method of **Date**
setUTCFullYear method of **Date**
setUTCHours method of **Date**
setUTCMilliseconds method of **Date**
setUTCMinutes method of **Date**
setUTCMonth method of **Date**
setUTCSeconds method of **Date**
single quotation marks
sin method of **Math**
slice method of **String**
small method of **String**
special characters
split method of **String**
sqrt method of **Math**
SQRT1_2 property of Math
SQRT2 property of Math
starting index
strike method of **String**
string
string constant
string literal
sub method of **String**
substring
substring method of **String**
substr method of **String**
sup method of **String**
sup method of **String**
tan method of **Math**
time
token
tokenization
toLocaleString method of **Date**
toLowerCase method of **String**
toString method of **Date**
toString method of **String**
toUpperCase method of **String**
toUTCString method of **Date**
Unicode
Universal Coordinated Time (UTC)
UTC method of **Date**
valueOf method of **Boolean**
valueOf method of **Date**
valueOf method of **Number**
valueOf method of **String**
well-defined interfaces
wrap in HTML tags

COMMON PROGRAMMING ERRORS

13.1 Forgetting to invoke a **Math** method by preceding the method name with the object name **Math** and a dot operator (**.**) is an error.

13.2 Assuming months are represented as numbers from 1 to 12 leads to off-by-one errors when you are processing **Date**s.

GOOD PROGRAMMING PRACTICE

13.1 Use the mathematical constants of the **Math** object rather than explicitly typing the numeric value of the constant.

SOFTWARE ENGINEERING OBSERVATIONS

13.1 The primary difference between invoking a function and invoking a method is that a function does not require an object name and a dot operator to call the function.

13.2 **String** methods **indexOf** or **lastIndexOf**, with their optional second argument (the starting index from which to search), are particularly useful for continuing a search through a large amount of text.

13.3 When an object is allocated with **new**, the object's constructor is called automatically to initialize the object before it is used in the program.

13.4 Methods **getFullYear** and **setFullYear** use four-digit years to avoid problems with dates at the beginning of the 21st century. In particular, two-digit year format would cause a problem for year 2000–00 could be treated by many computers as 1900 rather than 2000. This is commonly known as the Y2K (year 2000) bug.

SELF-REVIEW EXERCISES

13.1 Fill in the blank(s) in each of the following:

a) Because JavaScript uses objects to perform many tasks, JavaScript is commonly referred to as an ________.
b) All objects have ________ and exhibit ________.
c) The methods of the ________ object allow programmers to perform many common mathematical calculations.
d) Invoking (or calling) a method of an object is referred to as ________.
e) String literals or string constants are written as a sequence of characters in ________ or ________.
f) Indices for the characters in a string start at ________.
g) **String** methods ________ and ________ search for the first and last occurrence of a substring in a **String**, respectively.
h) The process of breaking a string into tokens is called ________.
i) **String** method ________ formats a **String** as a hyperlink.
j) Date and time processing can be performed based on the ________ or based on World Time Standard's ________.
k) **Date** method ________ receives as its argument a string representing a date and time, and returns the number of milliseconds between midnight, January 1, 1970 and the specified date and time.

ANSWERS TO SELF-REVIEW EXERCISES

13.1 a) object-based programming language. b) attributes, behaviors. c) **Math**. d) sending a message to the object. e) double quotation marks, single quotation marks. f) 0. g) **indexOf**, **lastIndexOf**. h) tokenization. i) **link**. j) computer's local time zone, Universal Coordinated Time (UTC). k) **parse**.

EXERCISES

13.2 Write a script that tests whether the examples of the **Math** method calls shown in Fig. 13.1 actually produce the indicated results.

13.3 Write a script that tests as many of the math library functions in Fig. 6.2 as you can. Exercise each of these functions by having your program display tables of return values for a diversity of argument values in an HTML **TEXTAREA**.

13.4 **`Math`** method **`floor`** may be used to round a number to a specific decimal place. For example, the statement

```
y = Math.floor( x * 10 + .5 ) / 10;
```

rounds **`x`** to the tenths position (the first position to the right of the decimal point). The statement

```
y = Math.floor( x * 100 + .5 ) / 100;
```

rounds **`x`** to the hundredths position (i.e., the second position to the right of the decimal point). Write a script that defines four functions to round a number **`x`** in various ways:

a) **`roundToInteger( number )`**
b) **`roundToTenths( number )`**
c) **`roundToHundredths( number )`**
d) **`roundToThousandths( number )`**

For each value read, your program should display the original value, the number rounded to the nearest integer, the number rounded to the nearest tenth, the number rounded to the nearest hundredth and the number rounded to the nearest thousandth.

13.5 Modify the solution to Exercise 13.4 to use **`Math`** method **`round`** instead of method **`floor`**.

13.6 Write a script that uses relational and equality operators to compare two **`String`**s input by the user through an HTML form. Output in an HTML **`TEXTAREA`** whether the first string is less than, equal to or greater than the second.

13.7 Write a script that uses random number generation to create sentences. Use four arrays of strings called **`article`**, **`noun`**, **`verb`** and **`preposition`**. Create a sentence by selecting a word at random from each array in the following order: **`article`**, **`noun`**, **`verb`**, **`preposition`**, **`article`** and **`noun`**. As each word is picked, concatenate it to the previous words in the sentence. The words should be separated by spaces. When the final sentence is output, it should start with a capital letter and end with a period. The program should generate 20 sentences and output them to an HTML **`TEXTAREA`**.

The arrays should be filled as follows: the **`article`** array should contain the articles **`"the"`**, **`"a"`**, **`"one"`**, **`"some"`** and **`"any"`**; the **`noun`** array should contain the nouns **`"boy"`**, **`"girl"`**, **`"dog"`**, **`"town"`** and **`"car"`**; the **`verb`** array should contain the verbs **`"drove"`**, **`"jumped"`**, **`"ran"`**, **`"walked"`** and **`"skipped"`**; the **`preposition`** array should contain the prepositions **`"to"`**, **`"from"`**, **`"over"`**, **`"under"`** and **`"on"`**.

After the preceding script is written, modify the script to produce a short story consisting of several of these sentences. (How about the possibility of a random term paper writer!)

13.8 *(Limericks)* A limerick is a humorous five-line verse in which the first and second lines rhyme with the fifth, and the third line rhymes with the fourth. Using techniques similar to those developed in Exercise 13.7, write a script that produces random limericks. Polishing this program to produce good limericks is a challenging problem, but the result will be worth the effort!

13.9 *(Pig Latin)* Write a script that encodes English language phrases into pig Latin. Pig Latin is a form of coded language often used for amusement. Many variations exist in the methods used to form pig Latin phrases. For simplicity, use the following algorithm:

To form a pig Latin phrase from an English language phrase, tokenize the phrase into an array of words using **`String`** method **`split`**. To translate each English word into a pig Latin word, place the first letter of the English word at the end of the word and add the letters "**`ay`**." Thus the word "**`jump`**" becomes "**`umpjay`**," the word "**`the`**" becomes "**`hetay`**," and the word "**`computer`**" becomes "**`omputercay`**." Blanks between words remain as blanks. Assume the following: The English phrase consists of words separated by blanks, there are no punctuation marks and all words have two or more letters. Function **`printLatinWord`** should display each word. Each token (i.e., word in the sentence) is passed to method **`printLatinWord`** to print the pig Latin word. Enable the user to input the sentence through an HTML form. Keep a running display of all the converted sentences in an HTML **TEXTAREA**.

13.10 Write a script that inputs a telephone number as a string in the form **(555) 555-5555**. The script should use **String** method **split** to extract the area code as a token, the first three digits of the phone number as a token and the last four digits of the phone number as a token. Display the area code in one text field and the seven-digit phone number in another text field.

13.11 Write a script that inputs a line of text, tokenizes the line with **String** method **split** and outputs the tokens in reverse order.

13.12 Write a script that inputs text from an HTML form and outputs the text in uppercase and lowercase letters.

13.13 Write a script that inputs several lines of text and a search character and uses **String** method **indexOf** to determine the number of occurrences of the character in the text.

13.14 Write a script based on the program of Exercise 13.13 that inputs several lines of text and uses **String** method **indexOf** to determine the total number of occurrences of each letter of the alphabet in the text. Uppercase and lowercase letters should be counted together. Store the totals for each letter in an array, and print the values in tabular format in an HTML **TEXTAREA** after the totals have been determined.

13.15 Write a script that reads a series of strings and outputs in an HTML **TEXTAREA** only those strings beginning with the letter "**b**."

13.16 Write a script that reads a series of strings and outputs in an HTML **TEXTAREA** only those strings ending with the letters "**ED**."

13.17 Write a script that inputs an integer code for a character and displays the corresponding character.

13.18 Modify your solution to exercise 13.17 so that it generates all possible three-digit codes in the range 000 to 255 and attempts to display the corresponding characters. Display the results in an HTML **TEXTAREA**.

13.19 Write your own version of the **String** method **indexOf** and use it in a script.

13.20 Write your own version of the **String** method **lastIndexOf** and use it in a script.

13.21 Write a program that reads a five-letter word from the user and produces all possible three-letter words that can be derived from the letters of the five-letter word. For example, the three-letter words produced from the word "bathe" include the commonly used words "ate", "bat", "bet", "tab", "hat", "the" and "tea." Output the results in an HTML **TEXTAREA**.

13.22 *(Printing Dates in Various Formats)* Dates are printed in several common formats. Write a script that reads a date from an HTML form and creates a **Date** object in which to store that date. Then, use the various methods of the **Date** object that convert **Date**s into strings to display the date in several formats.

SPECIAL SECTION: ADVANCED STRING MANIPULATION EXERCISES

The preceding exercises are keyed to the text and designed to test the reader's understanding of fundamental string manipulation concepts. This section includes a collection of intermediate and advanced string manipulation exercises. The reader should find these problems challenging, yet entertaining. The problems vary considerably in difficulty. Some require an hour or two of program writing and implementation. Others are useful for lab assignments that might require two or three weeks of study and implementation. Some are challenging term projects.

13.23 *(Text Analysis)* The availability of computers with string manipulation capabilities has resulted in some rather interesting approaches to analyzing the writings of great authors. Much attention has been focused on whether William Shakespeare ever lived. Some scholars believe there is substantial evidence indicating that Christopher Marlowe or other authors actually penned the masterpieces attributed to Shakespeare. Researchers have used computers to find similarities in the writings of these two authors. This exercise examines three methods for analyzing texts with a computer.

a) Write a script that reads several lines of text from the keyboard and prints a table indicating the number of occurrences of each letter of the alphabet in the text. For example, the phrase

```
To be, or not to be: that is the question:
```

contains one "a," two "b's," no "c's," etc.

b) Write a script that reads several lines of text and prints a table indicating the number of one-letter words, two-letter words, three-letter words, etc. appearing in the text. For example, the phrase

```
Whether 'tis nobler in the mind to suffer
```

contains

Word length	Occurrences
1	0
2	2
3	1
4	2 (including 'tis)
5	0
6	2
7	1

c) Write a script that reads several lines of text and prints a table indicating the number of occurrences of each different word in the text. The first version of your program should include the words in the table in the same order in which they appear in the text. For example, the lines

```
To be, or not to be: that is the question:
Whether 'tis nobler in the mind to suffer
```

contain the words "to" three times, the word "be" two times, the word "or" once, etc. A more interesting (and useful) printout should then be attempted in which the words are sorted alphabetically.

13.24 *(Check Protection)* Computers are frequently employed in check-writing systems such as payroll and accounts payable applications. Many strange stories circulate regarding weekly paychecks being printed (by mistake) for amounts in excess of $1 million. Incorrect amounts are printed by computerized check-writing systems because of human error and/or machine failure. Systems designers build controls into their systems to prevent such erroneous checks from being issued.

Another serious problem is the intentional alteration of a check amount by someone who intends to cash a check fraudulently. To prevent a dollar amount from being altered, most computerized check-writing systems employ a technique called *check protection.*

Checks designed for imprinting by computer contain a fixed number of spaces in which the computer may print an amount. Suppose a paycheck contains eight blank spaces in which the computer is supposed to print the amount of a weekly paycheck. If the amount is large, then all eight of those spaces will be filled, for example:

```
1,230.60 (check amount)
--------
12345678 (position numbers)
```

On the other hand, if the amount is less than $1000, then several of the spaces would ordinarily be left blank. For example,

```
   99.87
--------
12345678
```

contains three blank spaces. If a check is printed with blank spaces, it is easier for someone to alter the amount of the check. To prevent a check from being altered, many check-writing systems insert *leading asterisks* to protect the amount as follows:

```
***99.87
--------
12345678
```

Write a script that inputs a dollar amount to be printed on a check, and then prints the amount in check-protected format with leading asterisks if necessary. Assume that nine spaces are available for printing the amount.

13.25 *(Writing the Word Equivalent of a Check Amount)* Continuing the discussion of the previous exercise, we reiterate the importance of designing check-writing systems to prevent alteration of check amounts. One common security method requires that the check amount be written both in numbers and "spelled out" in words as well. Even if someone is able to alter the numerical amount of the check, it is extremely difficult to change the amount in words.

Many computerized check-writing systems do not print the amount of the check in words. Perhaps the main reason for this omission is the fact that most high-level languages used in commercial applications do not contain adequate string manipulation features. Another reason is that the logic for writing word equivalents of check amounts is somewhat involved.

Write a script that inputs a numeric check amount and writes the word equivalent of the amount. For example, the amount 112.43 should be written as

```
ONE HUNDRED TWELVE and 43/100
```

13.26 *(Morse Code)* Perhaps the most famous of all coding schemes is the Morse code, developed by Samuel Morse in 1832 for use with the telegraph system. The Morse code assigns a series of dots and dashes to each letter of the alphabet, each digit and a few special characters (such as period, comma, colon, and semicolon). In sound-oriented systems, the dot represents a short sound and the dash represents a long sound. Other representations of dots and dashes are used with light-oriented systems and signal-flag systems.

Separation between words is indicated by a space, or, quite simply, by the absence of a dot or dash. In a sound-oriented system, a space is indicated by a short period of time during which no sound is transmitted. The international version of the Morse code appears in Fig. 13.12.

Write a script that reads an English language phrase and encodes the phrase into Morse code. Also write a program that reads a phrase in Morse code and converts the phrase into the English language equivalent. Use one blank between each Morse-coded letter and three blanks between each Morse-coded word.

Character	Code	Character	Code
A	.-	T	-
B	-...	U	..-
C	-.-.	V	...-
D	-..	W	.--
E	.	X	-..-
F	..-.	Y	-.--
G	--.	Z	--..
H	....		
I	..	Digits	
J	.---	1	.----
K	-.-	2	..---
L	.-..	3	...--
M	--	4	....-
N	-.	5	.....
O	---	6	-....
P	.--.	7	--...
Q	--.-	8	---..
R	.-.	9	----.
S	...	0	-----

Fig. 13.12 The letters of the alphabet as expressed in international Morse code.

13.27 *(A Metric Conversion Program)* Write a script that will assist the user with metric conversions. Your program should allow the user to specify the names of the units as strings (i.e., centimeters, liters, grams etc. for the metric system and inches, quarts, pounds etc. for the English system) and should respond to simple questions such as

```
"How many inches are in 2 meters?"
"How many liters are in 10 quarts?"
```

Your program should recognize invalid conversions. For example, the question

```
"How many feet in 5 kilograms?"
```

is not a meaningful question because **"feet"** is a unit of length while **"kilograms"** is a unit of mass.

SPECIAL SECTION: CHALLENGING STRING MANIPULATION PROJECTS

13.28 *(Project: A Spelling Checker)* Many popular word processing software packages have built-in spell checkers.

In this project, you are asked to develop your own spell-checker utility. We make suggestions to help get you started. You should then consider adding more capabilities. Use a computerized dictionary (if you have access to one) as a source of words.

Why do we type so many words with incorrect spellings? In some cases, it is because we simply do not know the correct spelling, so we make a "best guess." In some cases, it is because we transpose two letters (e.g., "defualt" instead of "default"). Sometimes we double-type a letter accidentally (e.g., "hanndy" instead of "handy"). Sometimes we type a nearby key instead of the one we intended (e.g., "biryhday" instead of "birthday"). And so on.

Design and implement a spell-checker application in Java. Your program should maintain an array **`wordList`** of strings. Enable the user to enter these strings.

Your program should ask a user to enter a word. The program should then look up that word in the **`wordList`** array. If the word is present in the array, your program should print "**`Word is spelled correctly`**."

If the word is not present in the array, your program should print "**`word is not spelled correctly`**." Then your program should try to locate other words in **`wordList`** that might be the word the user intended to type. For example, you can try all possible single transpositions of adjacent letters to discover that the word "default" is a direct match to a word in **`wordList`**. Of course, this implies that your program will check all other single transpositions, such as "edfault," "dfeault," "deafult," "defalut," and "defautl." When you find a new word that matches one in **`wordList`**, print that word in a message, such as "**`Did you mean "default?"`**."

Implement other tests, such as replacing each double letter with a single letter and any other tests you can develop to improve the value of your spell checker.

13.29 *(Project: A Crossword Puzzle Generator)* Most people have worked a crossword puzzle, but few have ever attempted to generate one. Generating a crossword puzzle is suggested here as a string manipulation project requiring substantial sophistication and effort.

There are many issues the programmer must resolve to get even the simplest crossword puzzle generator program working. For example, how does one represent the grid of a crossword puzzle inside the computer? Should one use a series of strings, or should double-subscripted arrays be used?

The programmer needs a source of words (i.e., a computerized dictionary) that can be directly referenced by the program. In what form should these words be stored to facilitate the complex manipulations required by the program?

The really ambitious reader will want to generate the "clues" portion of the puzzle, in which the brief hints for each "across" word and each "down" word are printed for the puzzle worker. Merely printing a version of the blank puzzle itself is not a simple problem.

14

Dynamic HTML: Cascading Style Sheets™ (CSS)

Objectives

- To take control of the appearance of a Web site by creating your own style sheets.
- To use a style sheet to give all the pages of a Web site the same look and feel.
- To use the **CLASS** attribute to apply styles.
- To specify the precise font, size, color and other properties of displayed text.
- To specify element backgrounds and colors.
- To understand the box model and be able to control the margins, borders, padding.
- To truly separate content and presentation.

Fashions fade, style is eternal.
Yves Saint Laurent

A style does not go out of style as long as it adapts itself to its period. When there is an incompatibility between the style and a certain state of mind, it is never the style that triumphs.
Coco Chanel

How liberating to work in the margins, outside a central perception.
Don DeLillo

Our words have wings, but fly not where we would.
George Eliot

There are aphorisms that, like airplanes, stay up only while they are in motion.
Vladimir Nabokov

Outline

14.1 Introduction

Cascading Style Sheets (*CSS*) allow you to specify the style of your page elements (spacing, margins, etc.) separately from the structure of your document (section headers, body text, links, etc.). This *separation of structure from content* allows greater manageability and makes changing the style of your document easier.

14.2 Inline Styles

There are many ways to declare styles for a document. Figure 14.1 presents *inline styles* in which an individual element's style is declared using the ***STYLE*** *attribute*.

```
<!DOCTYPE html PUBLIC "-//W3C//DTD HTML 4.0 Transitional//EN">
<HTML>

<!-- Fig. 14.1: inline.html -->
<!-- Using inline styles    -->

<HEAD><TITLE>Inline Styles</TITLE></HEAD>

<BODY>

<P>Here is some text</P>

<!-- The STYLE attribute allows you to declare inline   -->
<!-- styles. Separate multiple styles with a semicolon. -->
<P STYLE = "font-size: 20pt">Here is some more text</P>
<P STYLE = "font-size: 20pt; color: #0000FF">Even more text</P>
```

Fig. 14.1 Inline styles (part 1 of 2).

```
17
18  </BODY>
19  </HTML>
```

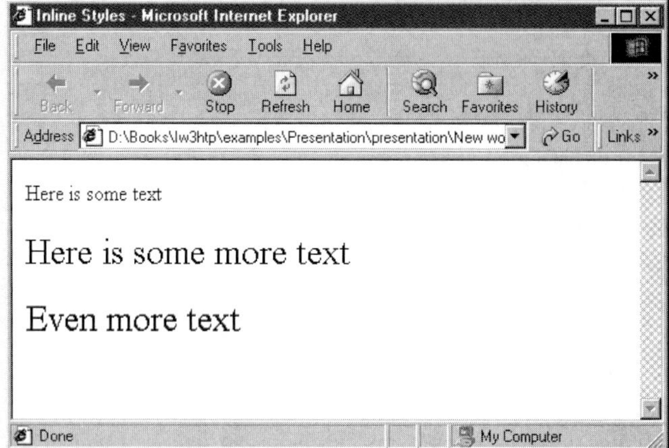

Fig. 14.1 Inline styles (part 2 of 2).

Our first inline style declaration appears on line 15:

```
<P STYLE = "font-size: 20pt">Here is some more text</P>
```

The ***STYLE*** *attribute* allows you to specify a style for an element. Each *CSS property* (in this case, **font-size**) is followed by a colon then the value of that attribute. In the preceding HTML line we declare the **P** element (of only that line) to have 20-point text size.

Line 16

```
<P STYLE = "font-size: 20pt; color: #0000FF">Even more text</P>
```

specifies two properties separated by a semicolon. In this line we also set the **color** of the text to blue using the hex code **#0000FF**. Color names (see Appendix E) may be used in place of hex codes as we will see in the next example. Note that inline styles override any other styles applied by the methods we cover later in this chapter.

14.3 Creating Style Sheets with the STYLE Element

In Fig. 14.2 we declare, in the header section of the document, styles that may be applied to the entire document.

```
<!DOCTYPE html PUBLIC "-//W3C//DTD HTML 4.0 Transitional//EN">
<HTML>

<!-- Fig. 14.2: declared.html                          -->
<!-- Declaring a style sheet in the header section. -->

```

Fig. 14.2 Declaring styles in the header section of a document (part 1 of 2).

```
<HEAD>
<TITLE>Style Sheets</TITLE>

<!-- This begins the style sheet section. -->
<STYLE TYPE = "text/css">

   EM    { background-color: #8000FF;
           color: white }

   H1    { font-family: Arial, sans-serif }

   P     { font-size: 18pt }

   .blue { color: blue }

</STYLE>
</HEAD>

<BODY>

<!-- This CLASS attribute applies the .blue style -->
<H1 CLASS = "blue">A Heading</H1>
<P>Here is some text. Here is some text. Here is some text.
Here is some text. Here is some text.</P>

<H1>Another Heading</H1>
<P CLASS = "blue">Here is some more text. Here is some more text.
Here is some <EM>more</EM> text. Here is some more text.</P>

</BODY>
</HTML>
```

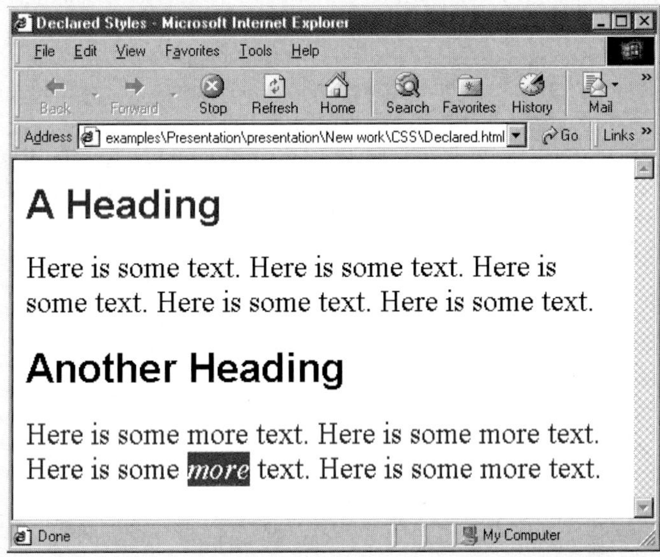

Fig. 14.2 Declaring styles in the header section of a document (part 2 of 2).

The element in the header section on line 11

```
<STYLE TYPE = "text/css">
```

begins the *style sheet*. Styles that are placed here apply to the whole document, not just a single element. The ***TYPE*** *attribute* specifies the *MIME type* of the following style sheet. MIME is a standard for specifying the format of content—some other MIME types are **text/html**, **image/gif**, and **text/javascript**. Regular text style sheets always use the MIME type **text/css**.

Look-and-Feel Observation 14.1

Without style sheets, the browser completely controls the look and feel of Web pages. With style sheets, the designer can specify the look and feel of all elements on a Web page.

The body of the **STYLE** sheet on lines 13 through 20

```
EM    { background-color: #8000FF;
        color: white }

H1    { font-family: Arial, sans-serif }

P     { font-size: 18pt }

.blue { color: blue }
```

declares the *CSS rules* for this style sheet. We declare rules for the **EM**, **H1** and **P** elements. All **EM**, **H1** and **P** elements in this document will be modified in the specified manner. CSS is a powerful tool for applying universal formatting. Notice that each rule body begins and ends with a curly brace (**{** and **}**). We also declare a *style class* named **blue** on line 20. All class declarations are preceded with a period and are applied to elements only of that specific class (as we will see below).

The CSS rules in a style sheet use the same format as inline styles—the property is followed by a colon (**:**) and the value of that property. Multiple properties are separated with a semicolon (**;**) as in the preceding **EM** style rule.

The ***color*** property specifies the color of text in an element. The ***background-color*** property specifies the background color of the element (like the **BGCOLOR** attribute in HTML does).

The ***font-family*** property (line 16) specifies the name of the font that should be displayed. In this case, we use the **Arial** font. The second value, ***sans-serif***, is a *generic font family*. Generic font families allow you to specify a type of font instead of a specific font. This allows much greater flexibility in your site display. In this example, if the **Arial** font is not found on the system, the browser will instead display another **sans-serif** font (such as **Helvetica** or **Verdana**). Other generic font families are ***serif*** (e.g., **Times New Roman** or **Georgia**), ***cursive*** (e.g., **Script**), ***fantasy*** (e.g., **Critter**) and ***monospace*** (e.g., **Courier** or **Fixedsys**).

The ***font-size*** property specifies the size to use to render the font—in this case we use 18 points. Other possible measurements besides **pt** are covered later in the chapter. You can also use the relative values ***xx-small***, ***x-small***, ***small***, ***smaller***, ***medium***, ***large***, ***larger***, ***x-large*** and ***xx-large***.

On line 28

```
<H1 CLASS = "blue">A Heading</H1>
```

the ***CLASS*** *attribute* applies a style class, in this case **blue** (this was declared as **.blue** in the **STYLE** sheet). Note that the text appears on screen with *both* the properties of an **H1** element and the properties of the **.blue** style class applied.

On lines 33 and 34

```
<P CLASS = "blue">Here is some more text. Here is some more text.
Here is some <EM>more</EM> text. Here is some more text.</P>
```

The **P** element and the **.blue** class style are both applied to the whole text. All styles applied to an element (the *parent element*) also apply to elements inside that element (*child elements*). The word inside the **EM** element *inherits* the **P** style (namely, the 18-point font size of line 18), but it conflicts with the **color** attribute of the **blue** class. Since styles declared in child element are more specific (have greater *specificity*) than parent element styles, the **EM** style overrides the styles set in the **blue** class.

14.4 Conflicting Styles

Figure 14.3 has more examples of *inheritance* and *specificity*.

```
<!DOCTYPE html PUBLIC "-//W3C//DTD HTML 4.0 Transitional//EN">
<HTML>

<!-- Fig 14.3: advanced.html     -->
<!-- More advanced style sheets -->

<HEAD>
<TITLE>More Styles</TITLE>
<STYLE TYPE = "text/css">

   A.nodec  { text-decoration: none }

   A: hover { text-decoration: underline;
              color: red;
              background-color: #CCFFCC }

   LI EM    { color: red;
              font-weight: bold }

   UL       { margin-left: 75px }

   UL UL    { text-decoration: underline;
              margin-left: 15px }

```

Fig. 14.3 Inheritance in style sheets (part 1 of 2).

```
</STYLE>
</HEAD>

<BODY>

<H1>Shopping list for <EM>Monday</EM>:</H1>
<UL>
<LI>Milk</LI>
<LI>Bread
   <UL>
   <LI>White bread</LI>
   <LI>Rye bread</LI>
   <LI>Whole wheat bread</LI>
   </UL></LI>
<LI>Rice</LI>
<LI>Potatoes</LI>
<LI>Pizza <EM>with mushrooms</EM></LI>
</UL>

<P><A CLASS = "nodec" HREF = "http://food.com">Go to the Grocery
   store</A></P>

</BODY>
</HTML>
```

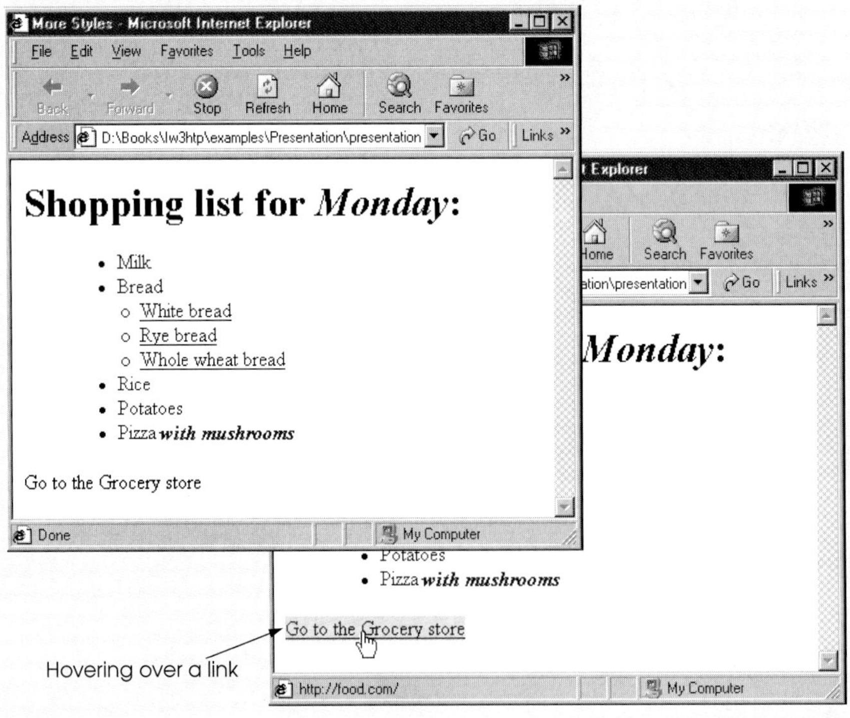

Fig. 14.3 Inheritance in style sheets (part 2 of 2).

Line 11

```
A.nodec  { text-decoration: none }
```

applies the ***text-decoration*** *property* to all **A** elements whose **CLASS** attribute is set to **nodec**. The default browser rendering of an **A** element is to underline, but here we set it to **none**. The **text-decoration** property applies *decorations* to text within an element. Other possible values are ***overline***, ***line-through*** and ***blink***.

The **.nodec** appended to **A** is an extension of class styles—this style will apply only to **A** elements that specify **nodec** as their class.

Lines 13 through 15

```
A: hover { text-decoration: underline;
           color: red;
           background-color: #CCFFCC }
```

specify a style for **hover**, which is a *pseudo-class*. Pseudo-classes give the author access to content not specifically declared in the document. The **hover** pseudo-class is dynamically activated when the user moves the mouse cursor over an **A** element.

Portability Tip 14.1

Browsers are not required to support the **blink** *value of the* **text-decoration** *property, so do not use it as a mechanism for important highlighting.*

Portability Tip 14.2

Always test DHTML programs on all intended client platforms to ensure that the display is reasonable, especially for those client platforms with older browsers.

Lines 16 and 17

```
LI EM   { color: red;
          font-weight: bold }
```

declare a style for all **EM** elements that are children of **LI** elements. In the screen output of Fig. 14.3 notice that **Monday** is not made red and bold, because it is not encapsulated by an **LI** element as **with mushrooms** is.

The declaration syntax for applying rules to multiple elements is similar. If you instead wanted to apply the rule on lines 17 and 18 to both **LI** and **EM** elements, you would separate the elements with commas, as follows:

```
LI, EM  { color: red;
          font-weight: bold }
```

Lines 22 and 23

```
UL UL   { text-decoration: underline;
          margin-left: 15px }
```

specify that all nested lists (**UL** elements that are children of **UL** elements) will be underlined and have a left-hand margin of 15 pixels (margins and the box model will be covered in Section 14.9).

A pixel is a *relative-length* measurement—it varies in size based on screen resolution. Other relative lengths are **em** (the size of the font), **ex** (the so-called "x-height" of the font, which is usually set to the height of a lowercase x) and percentages (e.g., **margin-left: 10%**). To set an element to display text at 150% of its normal size, you could use the syntax

```
font-size: 1.5em
```

The other units of measurement available in CSS are *absolute-length* measurements, i.e., units that do not vary in size based on the system. These are **in** (inches), **cm** (centimeters), **mm** (millimeters), **pt** (points—1 **pt**=1/72 **in**) and **pc** (picas—1 **pc** = 12 **pt**).

Good Programming Practice 14.1

Whenever possible, use relative length measurements. If you use absolute length measurements, you might override styles preset by the user.

Software Engineering Observation 14.1

There are three possible sources for styles sheets—browser defaults, preset user styles, and author styles (e.g., in the ***STYLE*** *section of a document). Author styles have a greater precedence than preset user styles, so any conflicts will be resolved in favor of the author styles.*

In Fig. 14.3, the whole list is indented because of the 75-pixel left-hand margin for top-level **UL** elements, but the nested list is indented only 15 pixels (not another 75 pixels) because the child **UL** element's **margin-left** property overrides the parent **UL** element's **margin-left** property.

14.5 Linking External Style Sheets

As we have seen, style sheets are an efficient way to give a document a uniform theme. With *external linking*, you can give your whole Web site the same uniform look—separate pages on your site could all utilize the same style sheet, and you would have to modify only a single file to make changes to styles across your whole Web site. Figure 14.4 shows the external style sheet, and Fig. 14.5 shows the syntax for including the external style sheet.

```
A       { text-decoration: none }

A:hover { text-decoration: underline;
          color: red;
          background-color: #CCFFCC }

LI EM   { color: red;
          font-weight: bold}

UL      { margin-left: 2cm }

UL UL   { text-decoration: underline;
          margin-left: .5cm }
```

Fig. 14.4 An external style sheet (**styles.css**).

```
<!DOCTYPE html PUBLIC "-//W3C//DTD HTML 4.0 Transitional//EN">
<HTML>

<!-- Fig. 14.5: imported.html              -->
<!-- Linking external style sheets  -->

<HEAD>
<TITLE>Importing style sheets</TITLE>
<LINK REL = "stylesheet" TYPE = "text/css" HREF = "styles.css">
</HEAD>

<BODY>

<H1>Shopping list for <EM>Monday</EM>:</H1>
<UL>
<LI>Milk</LI>
<LI>Bread
   <UL>
   <LI>White bread</LI>
   <LI>Rye bread</LI>
   <LI>Whole wheat bread</LI>
   </UL></LI>
<LI>Rice</LI>
<LI>Potatoes</LI>
<LI>Pizza <EM>with mushrooms</EM></LI>
</UL>

<A HREF = "http://food.com">Go to the Grocery store</A>

</BODY>
</HTML>
```

Fig. 14.5 Linking an external style sheet.

Line 9

```
<LINK REL = "stylesheet" TYPE = "text/css" HREF = "styles.css">
```

shows a ***LINK*** *element*, which specifies a *relationship* between the current document and another document using the ***REL*** *attribute*. In this case, we declare the linked document to be a **stylesheet** for this document. We use the **TYPE** attribute to specify the MIME type as **text/css** and provide the URL for the stylesheet with the **HREF** attribute.

Software Engineering Observation 14.2

Style sheets are reusable. Creating style sheets once and reusing them reduces programming effort.

Software Engineering Observation 14.3

The **LINK** *element can be placed only in the header section. Other relationships you can specify between documents are* **next** *and* **previous***, which would allow you to link a whole series of documents. This could let browsers print a large collection of related documents at once (in Internet Explorer, select* **Print all linked documents** *in the* **Print...** *submenu of the* **File** *menu).*

14.6 Positioning Elements

In the past, controlling the positioning of elements in an HTML document was difficult; positioning was basically up to the browser. CSS introduces the **position** property and a capability called *absolute positioning*, which gives us greater control over how our documents are displayed (Fig. 14.6).

```
<!DOCTYPE html PUBLIC "-//W3C//DTD HTML 4.0 Transitional//EN">
<HTML>

<!-- Fig 14.6: positioning.html        -->
<!-- Absolute positioning of elements -->

<HEAD>
<TITLE>Absolute Positioning</TITLE>
</HEAD>

<BODY>

<IMG SRC = "i.gif" STYLE = "position: absolute; top: 0px;
   left: 0px; z-index: 1">
<H1 STYLE = "position: absolute; top: 50px; left: 50px;
   z-index: 3">Positioned Text</H1>
<IMG SRC = "circle.gif" STYLE = "position: absolute; top: 25px;
   left: 100px; z-index: 2">

</BODY>
</HTML>
```

Fig. 14.6 Positioning elements with CSS (part 1 of 2).

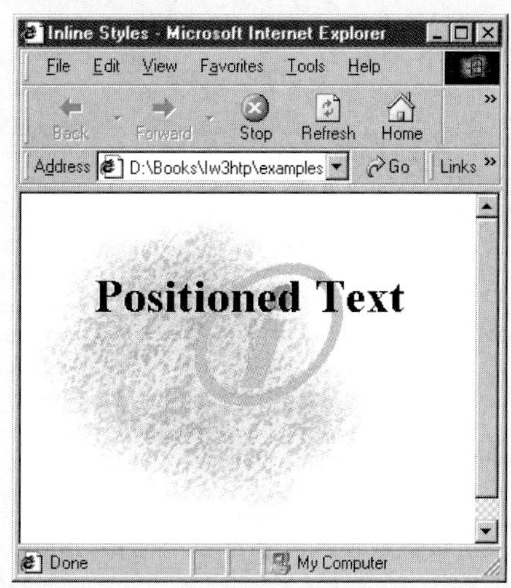

Fig. 14.6 Positioning elements with CSS (part 2 of 2).

Lines 13 and 14

```
<IMG SRC = "i.gif" STYLE = "position: absolute; top: 0px;
   left: 0px; z-index: 1">
```

position the first **IMG** element (**i.gif**) on the page. Specifying an element's **position** as ***absolute*** removes it from the normal flow of elements on the page and instead, positions the element according to distance from the ***top***, ***left***, ***right*** or ***bottom*** margins of its parent element. Here we position the element to be **0** pixels away from both the **top** and **left** margins of the **BODY** element (the parent element).

The ***z-index*** *attribute* allows you to properly layer overlapping elements. Elements that have higher **z-index** values are displayed in front of elements with lower **z-index** values. In this example, **i.gif**, with a **z-index** of 1, is displayed at the back; **circle.gif**, with a **z-index** of 2, is displayed in front of that; the **H1** element ("Positioned Text"), with a **z-index** of 3, is displayed in front of both of the others. If you do not specify **z-index**, the elements that occur later in the document are displayed in front of those that occur earlier.

Absolute positioning is not the only way to specify page layout—*relative positioning* is shown in Fig. 14.7.

```
<!DOCTYPE html PUBLIC "-//W3C//DTD HTML 4.0 Transitional//EN">
<HTML>

<!-- Fig 14.7: positioning2.html        -->
<!-- Relative positioning of elements -->

<HEAD>
<TITLE>Relative Positioning</TITLE>
```

Fig. 14.7 Relative positioning of elements (part 1 of 2).

```

<STYLE TYPE = "text/css">

   P       { font-size: 2em;
             font-family: Verdana, Arial, sans-serif }

   SPAN    { color: red;
             font-size: .6em;
             height: 1em }

   .super  { position: relative;
             top: -1ex }

   .sub    { position: relative;
             bottom: -1ex }

   .shiftl { position: relative;
             left: -1ex }

   .shiftr { position: relative;
             right: -1ex }
</STYLE>
</HEAD>

<BODY>

<P>
Text text text text <SPAN CLASS = "super">superscript</SPAN>
text text text text <SPAN CLASS = "sub">subscript</SPAN>
text Text text <SPAN CLASS = "shiftl">left-shifted</SPAN>
text text text <SPAN CLASS = "shiftr">right-shifted</SPAN>
Text text text text text
</P>

</BODY>
</HTML>
```

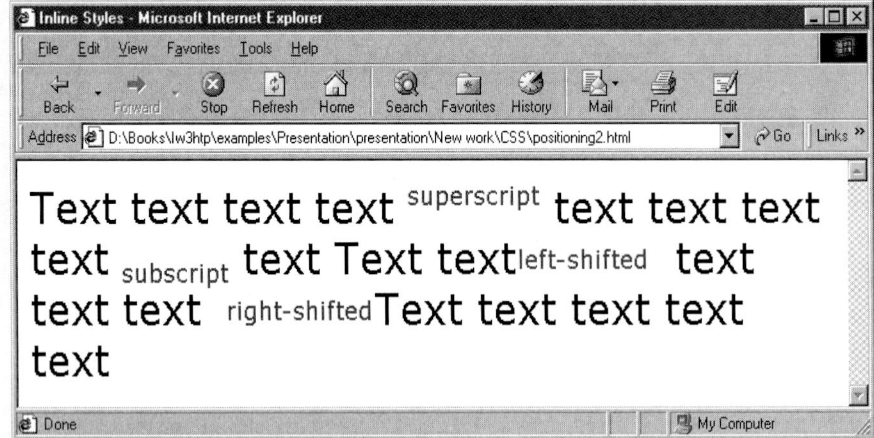

Fig. 14.7 Relative positioning of elements (part 2 of 2).

Setting the **`position`** property to ***`relative`***, as in lines 19 and 20,

```
.super  { position: relative;
          top: -1ex }
```

will first lay out the element on the page, then offset the element by the specified **`top`**, **`bottom`**, **`left`** or **`right`** values. Unlike absolute positioning, relative positioning keeps elements in the general flow of elements on the page.

Common Programming Error 14.1

Since relative positioning keeps elements in the flow of text in your documents, be careful to avoid overlapping text unintentionally.

14.7 Backgrounds

CSS also gives you more control over backgrounds than simple HTML attributes. We have used the **`background-color`** property in previous examples. You can also add background images to your documents using CSS. In Fig. 14.8, we add a corporate watermark to the bottom-right corner of the document—this watermark stays fixed in the corner, even when the user scrolls up or down the screen.

```
<!DOCTYPE html PUBLIC "-//W3C//DTD HTML 4.0 Transitional//EN">
<HTML>

<!-- Fig. 14.8: background.html                  -->
<!-- Adding background images and indentation -->

<HEAD>
<TITLE>Background Images</TITLE>

<STYLE TYPE = "text/css">

   BODY  { background-image: url(watermark.gif);
           background-position: bottom right;
           background-repeat: no-repeat;
           background-attachment: fixed }

   P     { font-size: 2em;
           color: #AA5588;
           text-indent: 1em;
           font-family: Arial, sans-serif }

   .dark { font-weight: bold }

</STYLE>
</HEAD>

<BODY>

<P>
This is some sample text to fill in the page.
```

Fig. 14.8 Adding a background image with CSS (part 1 of 2).

```
31  <SPAN CLASS = "dark">This is some sample
32  text to fill in the page.</SPAN>
33  This is some sample text to fill in the page.
34  This is some sample text to fill in the page.
35  This is some sample text to fill in the page.
36  This is some sample text to fill in the page.
37  </P>
38
39  </BODY>
40  </HTML>
```

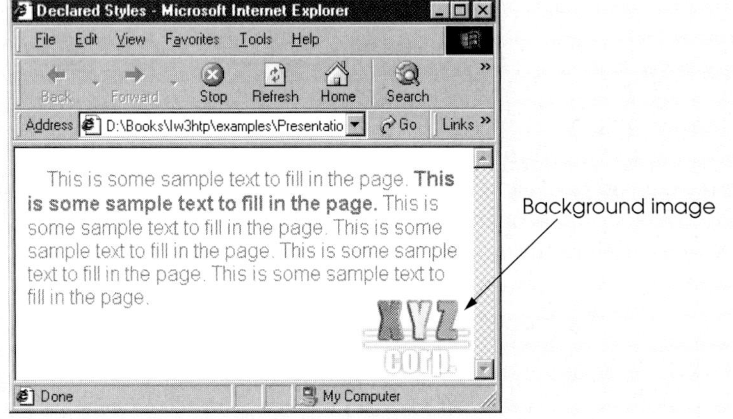

Fig. 14.8 Adding a background image with CSS (part 2 of 2).

The code that adds the background image in the bottom-right corner of the window is on lines 12 through 15:

```
BODY  { background-image: url(watermark.gif);
        background-position: bottom right;
        background-repeat: no-repeat;
        background-attachment: fixed }
```

The ***background-image** property* specifies the URL of the image to use, in the format **url(fileLocation)**. You can also specify ***background-color*** to use in case the image is not found.

The ***background-position** property* positions the image on the page. You can use the keywords **top**, **bottom**, **center**, **left** and **right** individually or in combination for vertical and horizontal positioning. You can also position using lengths, specifying the horizontal length followed by the vertical length. For example, to position the image centered vertically (positioned at 50% of the distance across the screen) and 30 pixels from the top, you would use

```
background-position: 50% 30px;
```

The **background-repeat** property controls the *tiling* of the background image (tiling was discussed in Section 3.8). Here we set the tiling to **no-repeat** so that only one copy of the background image is placed on screen. The **background-repeat** property can be set to ***repeat*** (the default) to tile the image vertically and horizontally, to ***x-repeat*** to tile the image only horizontally or ***y-repeat*** to tile the image only vertically.

The final property setting, ***background-attachment: fixed***, fixes the image in the position specified by **background-position**. Scrolling the browser window will not move the image from its set position. The default value, **scroll**, moves the image as the user scrolls the browser window down.

On line 19, we introduce a new text-formatting property:

```
text-indent: 1em;
```

This indents the first line of text in the element by the specified amount. You might use this to make your Web page read more like a novel, in which the first line of every paragraph is indented.

Another new property is introduced on line 22:

```
.dark { font-weight: bold }
```

The ***font-weight*** *property* specifies the "boldness" of affected text. Values besides ***bold*** and ***normal*** (the default) are ***bolder*** (bolder than **bold** text) and ***lighter*** (lighter than **normal** text). You can also specify the value using multiples of 100 from 100 to 900 (i.e., **100**, **200**, ..., **900**). Text specified as **normal** is equivalent to **400** and **bold** text is equivalent to **700**. Most systems do not have fonts that can be scaled this finely so using the **100**...**900** values might not display the desired effect.

Another CSS property you can use to format text is the ***font-style*** *property*, which allows you to set text to ***none***, ***italic*** or ***oblique*** (**oblique** will default to **italic** if the system does not have a separate font file for oblique text, which is normally the case).

We introduce the ***SPAN*** *element* in lines 31 and 32:

```
<SPAN CLASS = "dark">This is some sample
text to fill in the page.</SPAN>
```

SPAN is a generic grouping element—it does not apply any inherent formatting to its contents. Its main use is to apply styles or ***ID*** *attributes* to a block of text. It is displayed inline (a so-called *inline-level element*) with other text, with no line breaks. A similar element is the ***DIV*** *element*, which also applies no inherent styles, but is displayed on its own line, with margins above and below (a so-called *block-level element*).

14.8 Element Dimensions

The dimensions of each element on the page can be set using CSS (Fig. 14.9).

```
<!DOCTYPE html PUBLIC "-//W3C//DTD HTML 4.0 Transitional//EN">
<HTML>

<!-- Fig. 14.9: width.html                    -->
<!-- Setting box dimensions and aligning text -->

```

Fig. 14.9 Setting box dimensions and aligning text (part 1 of 2).

```
<HEAD>
<TITLE>Box Dimensions</TITLE>
<STYLE TYPE = "text/css">

   DIV { background-color: #FFCCFF;
         margin-bottom: .5em }

</STYLE>
</HEAD>

<BODY>

<DIV STYLE = "width: 20%">Here is some
text that goes in a box which is
set to stretch across twenty precent
of the width of the screen.</DIV>

<DIV STYLE = "width: 80%; text-align: center">
Here is some CENTERED text that goes in a box
which is set to stretch across eighty precent of
the width of the screen.</DIV>

<DIV STYLE = "width: 20%; height: 30%; overflow: scroll">
This box is only twenty percent of
the width and thirty percent of the height.
What do we do if it overflows? Set the
overflow property to scroll!</DIV>

</BODY>
</HTML>
```

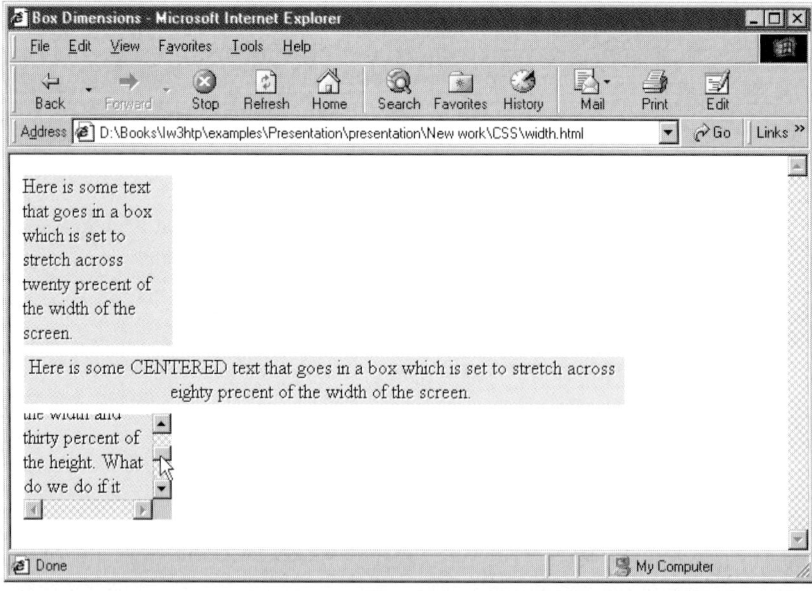

Fig. 14.9 Setting box dimensions and aligning text (part 2 of 2).

The inline style of line 19,

```
<DIV STYLE = "width: 20%">Here is some
```

shows how to set the ***width*** of an element on screen; here we indicate that this **DIV** element should occupy 20% of the screen width (which 20% of the screen depends on how the element is aligned, most elements are left-aligned by default). The height of an element can be set similarly, using the **height** property. Relative lengths and absolute lengths may also be used to specify **height** and **width**. For example, you could set the width of an element using

```
width: 10em
```

to have the element's width be equal to 10 times the size of the font.

Line 24,

```
<DIV STYLE = "width: 80%; text-align: center">
```

shows that text within an element can be ***center***ed—other values for the ***text-align*** property are ***left*** and ***right***.

One problem with setting both element dimensions is that content inside might sometimes exceed the set boundaries, in which case the element is simply made large enough for all the content to fit. However, as we see on line 29

```
<DIV STYLE = "width: 20%; height: 30%; overflow: scroll">
```

we can set the ***overflow*** *property* to ***scroll***; this adds scrollbars if the text overflows the boundaries.

14.9 Text Flow and the Box Model

A browser normally places text and elements on screen in the order they are in the HTML file. However, as we saw with absolute positioning, it is possible to remove elements from the normal flow of text. *Floating* allows you to move an element to one side of the screen—other content in the document will then flow around the floated element. In addition, each block-level element has a box drawn around it, known as the *box model*—the properties of this box are easily adjusted (Fig. 14.10).

Line 21

```
<DIV STYLE = "text-align: center">Centered Text</DIV>
```

shows that text inside an element can be aligned by setting the **text-align** property, whose possible values are **left**, **center**, **right** and **justify**.

In addition to text, whole elements can be *floated* to the left or right of a document. This means that any nearby text will wrap around the floated element. For example, in lines 24 and 25

```
<DIV STYLE = "float: right; margin: .5em">This is some floated
text, floated text, floated text, floated text.</DIV>
```

we float a **DIV** element to the **right** side of the screen. As you can see, the text from lines 27 through 34 flows cleanly to the left and underneath this **DIV** element.

The second property we set in line 24, ***margin***, determines the distance between the edge of the element and any text outside the element. When elements are rendered on the screen using the box model, the content of each element is surrounded by *padding*, a *border* and *margins* (Fig. 14.11).

```
1  <!DOCTYPE html PUBLIC "-//W3C//DTD HTML 4.0 Transitional//EN">
2  <HTML>
3
4  <!-- Fig. 14.10: floating.html           -->
5  <!-- Floating elements and element boxes -->
6
7  <HEAD>
8  <TITLE>Flowing Text Around Floating Elements</TITLE>
9  <STYLE TYPE = "text/css">
10
11    DIV { background-color: #FFCCFF;
12          margin-bottom: .5em;
13          font-size: 1.5em;
14          width: 50% }
15
16 </STYLE>
17 </HEAD>
18
19 <BODY>
20
21 <DIV STYLE = "text-align: center">Centered text</DIV>
22 <DIV STYLE = "text-align: right">Right-aligned text</DIV>
23
24 <DIV STYLE = "float: right; margin: .5em">This is some floated
25 text, floated text, floated text, floated text.</DIV>
26 <P>
27 Here is some flowing text, flowing text, flowing text.
28 Here is some flowing text, flowing text, flowing text.
29 Here is some flowing text, flowing text, flowing text.
30 Here is some flowing text, flowing text, flowing text.
31 Here is some flowing text, flowing text, flowing text.
32 Here is some flowing text, flowing text, flowing text.
33 Here is some flowing text, flowing text, flowing text.
34 Here is some flowing text, flowing text, flowing text.
35 </P>
36
37 <P><DIV STYLE ="float: right; padding: .5em">This is some floated
38 text, floated text, floated text, floated text.</DIV>
39 Here is some flowing text, flowing text, flowing text.
40 Here is some flowing text, flowing text, flowing text.
41 Here is some flowing text, flowing text, flowing text.
42 <SPAN STYLE = "clear: right">Here is some unflowing text.
43 Here is some unflowing text.</SPAN>
44 </P>
45
46 </BODY>
47 </HTML>
```

Fig. 14.10 Floating elements, aligning text and setting box dimensions (part 1 of 2).

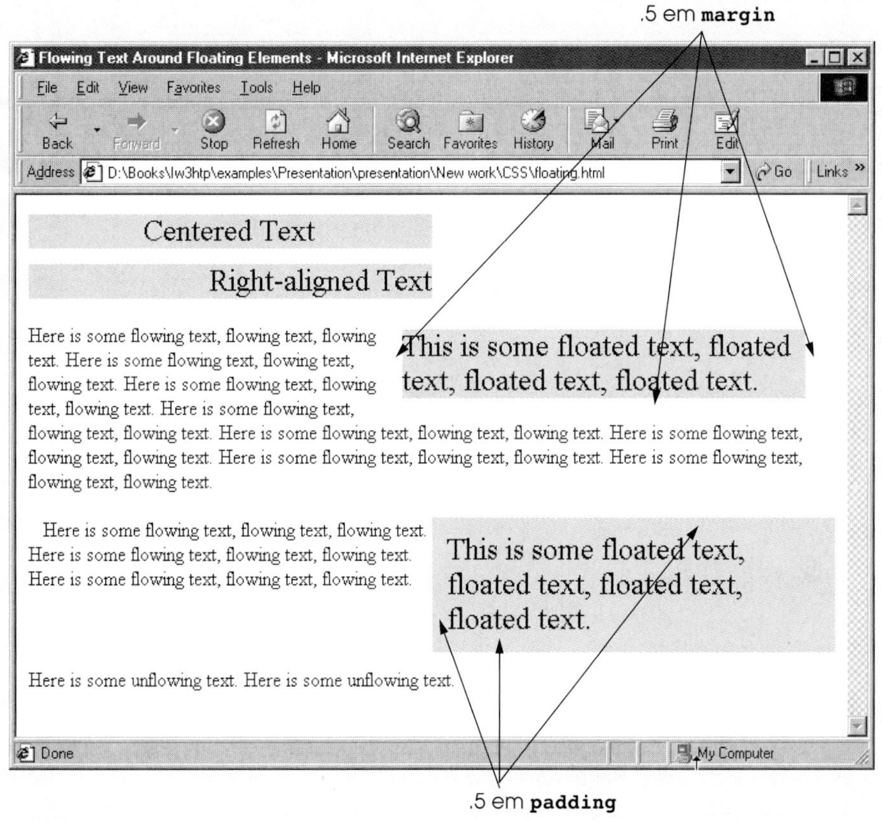

Fig. 14.10 Floating elements, aligning text and setting box dimensions (part 2 of 2).

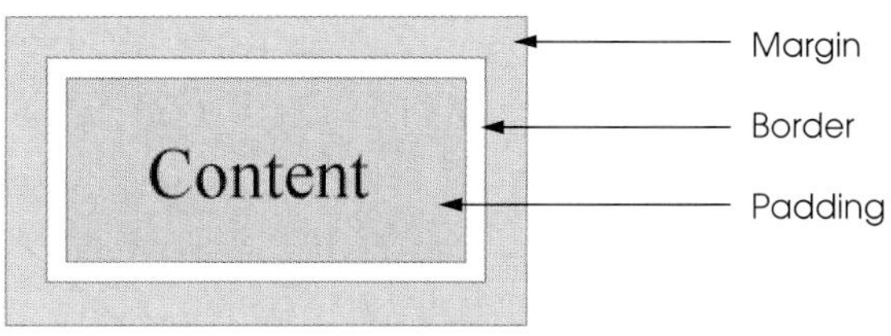

Fig. 14.11 Box model for block-level elements.

Margins for individual sides of an element can be specified by using ***margin-top***, ***margin-right***, ***margin-left***, and ***margin-bottom***.

A related property, ***padding***, is set for the **DIV** element in line 37:

```
<DIV STYLE = "float: right; padding: .5em">This is some floated
```

The *padding* is the distance between the content inside an element and the edge of the element. Like the margin, the padding can be set for each side of the box with **padding-top**, **padding-right**, **padding-left**, and **padding-bottom**.

Line 42

```
<SPAN STYLE = "clear: right">Here is some unflowing text.
```

shows that you can interrupt the flow of text around a **`float`**ed element by setting the ***`clear`*** *property* to the same direction the element is **`float`**ed—**`right`** or **`left`**. Setting the **`clear`** property to ***`all`*** interrupts the flow on both sides of the document. Note that the box model only applies to block-level elements such as **`DIV`**, **`P`** and **`H1`**—the box model does not apply to inline-level elements such as **`EM`**, **`STRONG`** and **`SPAN`**.

Another property included around every block-level element on screen is the border. The border lies between the padding space and the margin space, and has numerous properties to adjust its appearance (Fig. 14.12).

```
<!DOCTYPE html PUBLIC "-//W3C//DTD HTML 4.0 Transitional//EN">
<HTML>

<!-- Fig. 14.12: borders.html         -->
<!-- Setting borders of an element -->

<HEAD>
<TITLE>Borders</TITLE>
<STYLE TYPE = "text/css">

   BODY    { background-color: #CCFFCC }

   DIV     { text-align: center;
             margin-bottom: 1em;
             padding: .5em }

   .thick  { border-width: thick }

   .medium { border-width: medium }

   .thin   { border-width: thin }

   .groove { border-style: groove }

   .inset  { border-style: inset }

   .outset { border-style: outset }

   .red    { border-color: red }

   .blue   { border-color: blue }

</STYLE>
</HEAD>

<BODY>

<DIV CLASS = "thick groove">This text has a border</DIV>
```

Fig. 14.12 Applying borders to elements (part 1 of 2).

```
39   <DIV CLASS = "medium groove">This text has a border</DIV>
40   <DIV CLASS = "thin groove">This text has a border</DIV>
41
42   <P CLASS = "thin red inset">A thin red line...</P>
43   <P CLASS = "medium blue outset">And a thicker blue line</P>
44
45   </BODY>
46   </HTML>
```

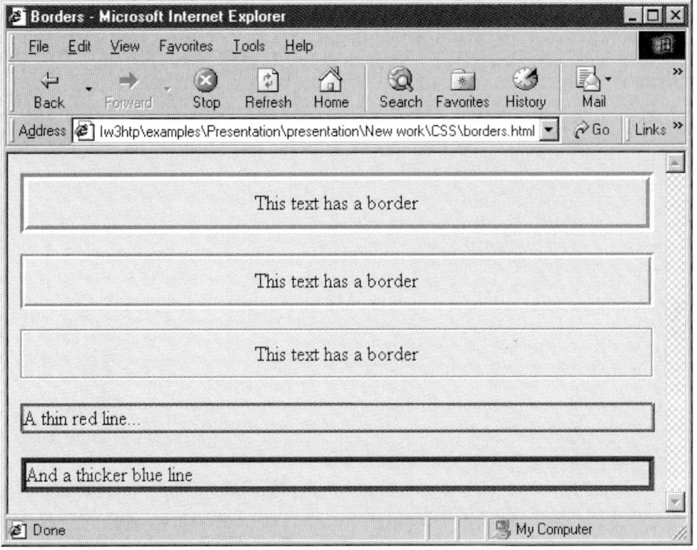

Fig. 14.12 Applying borders to elements (part 2 of 2).

In this example, we set three properties: the ***border-width***, ***border-style*** and ***border-color***. The **border-width** property may be set to any of the CSS lengths, or the predefined values of ***thin***, ***medium*** or ***thick***. The **border-color** sets the color used for the border (this has different meanings for different borders).

As with padding and margins, each of the border properties may be set for individual sides of the box (e.g., ***border-top-style*** or ***border-left-color***).

Also, as shown on line 38,

```
<DIV CLASS = "thick groove">This text has a border</DIV>
```

it is possible to assign more than one class to an HTML element using the **CLASS** attribute.

The **border-style**s are ***none***, ***hidden***, ***dotted***, ***dashed***, ***solid***, ***double***, ***groove***, ***ridge***, ***inset*** and ***outset***. Figure 14.13 illustates these border styles.

Portability Tip 14.3

Keep in mind that the **dotted** *and* **dashed** *styles are available only for Macintosh systems.*

As you can see, the **groove** and **ridge** **border-style**s have opposite effects, as do **inset** and **outset**.

```
<!DOCTYPE html PUBLIC "-//W3C//DTD HTML 4.0 Transitional//EN">
<HTML>

<!-- Fig. 14.13: borders2.html   -->
<!-- Various border-styles       -->

<HEAD>
<TITLE>Borders</TITLE>

<STYLE TYPE = "text/css">

   BODY    { background-color: #CCFFCC }

   DIV     { text-align: center;
             margin-bottom: .3em;
             width: 50%;
             position: relative;
             left: 25%;
             padding: .3em }
</STYLE>
</HEAD>

<BODY>

<DIV STYLE = "border-style: solid">Solid border</DIV>
<DIV STYLE = "border-style: double">Double border</DIV>
<DIV STYLE = "border-style: groove">Groove border</DIV>
<DIV STYLE = "border-style: ridge">Ridge border</DIV>
<DIV STYLE = "border-style: inset">Inset border</DIV>
<DIV STYLE = "border-style: outset">Outset border</DIV>
</BODY>
</HTML>
```

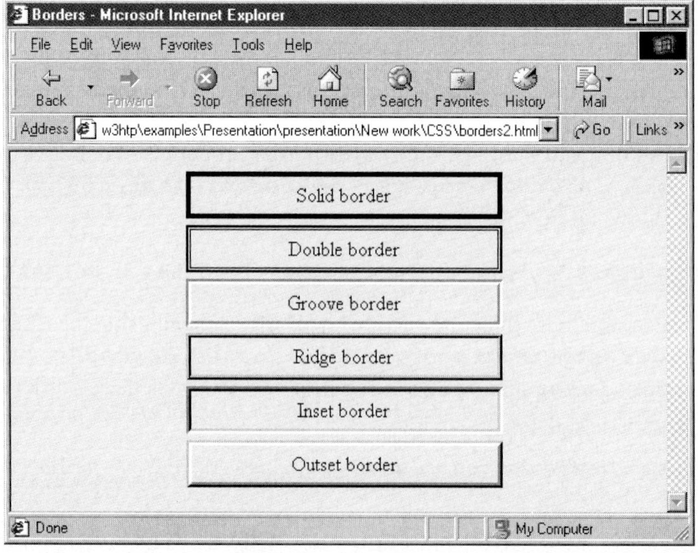

Fig. 14.13 Various `border-style`s.

14.10 User Style Sheets

An important issue to keep in mind when adding style sheets to your site is what kind of users will be viewing your site. Users have the option to define their own *user style sheets* to format pages based on their own preferences—for example, visually impaired people might want to increase the text size on all pages they view. As a Web-page author, if you are not careful, you might inadvertantly override user preferences with the styles defined on your Web pages. This section explores possible conflicts between *user styles* and *author styles*. Figure 14.4 is a simple example of a Web page using the **em** measurement for the **font-size** property to increase text size on the page.

```
<!DOCTYPE html PUBLIC "-//W3C//DTD HTML 4.0 Transitional//EN">
<HTML>

<!-- Fig. 14.14: user.html  -->
<!-- User styles            -->

<HEAD>
<TITLE>User Styles</TITLE>

<STYLE TYPE = "text/css">

   .note { font-size: 1.5em }

</STYLE>
</HEAD>

<BODY>

<P>Thanks for visiting my Web site. I hope you enjoy it.</P>
<P CLASS = "note">Please Note: This site will be moving soon.
Please check periodically for updates.</P>

</BODY>
</HTML>
```

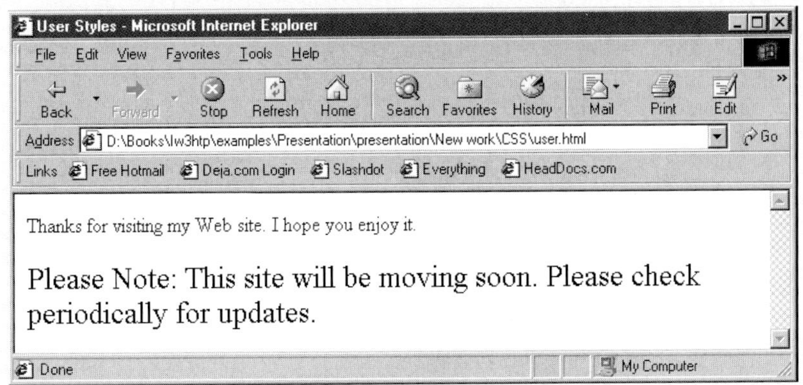

Fig. 14.14 Modifying text size with the **em** measurement.

In line 12

```
.note { font-size: 1.5em }
```

we multiply by 1.5 the font size of all elements with **`CLASS = "note"`** (see lines 20 and 21). Assuming the default browser font size of 12 points, this same text size increase could also have been accomplished by specifying

```
.note { font-size:  18pt }
```

However, what if the user had defined their own **`font-size`** in a user style sheet? Because the CSS specification gives precedence to author styles over user styles, this conflict would be resolved with the author style overriding the user style. This can be avoided by using relative measurements (such as **`em`** or **`ex`**) instead of absolute measurements (such as **`pt`**).

Adding a user style sheet (Fig. 14.15) in Internet Explorer 5 is done by selecting **Internet Options...** located in the **Tools** menu. In the dialog box that appeares, click on **Accessibility...**, check the **Format documents using my style sheet** check box and type in the location of your user style sheet. Note that you also have the option of overriding colors, font styles, and font sizes specified on Web pages with your own user styles.

User style sheets are created in the same format as the linked external style sheet shown in Fig. 14.4. A sample user style sheet is shown in Fig. 14.16.

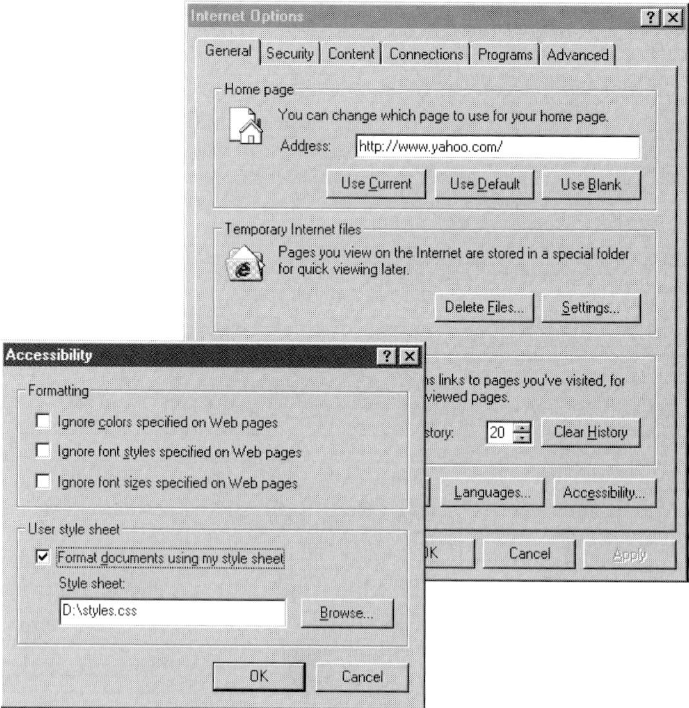

Fig. 14.15 Adding a user style sheet in Internet Explorer 5.

The Web page shown in Fig. 14.14 is re-rendered in Figure 14.17, this time with the user style sheet from 14.16 applied.

Because the code for this page uses a relative **`font-size`** measurement of **`1.5em`**, it multiplies the original size of the affected text (**`20pt`**) by **`1.5`** times, giving it an effective size of **`30pt`**.

14.11 Internet and World Wide Web Resources

`http://www.w3.org/TR/REC-CSS2/`

The W3C *Cascading Style Sheets, Level 2* specification contains a list of all the CSS properties. The specification is also filled with helpful examples detailing the use of many of the properties.

`http://style.webreview.com`

This site has several charts of CSS properties, including a listing of which browsers support which attributtes, and to what extent.

`http://www.w3.org/TR/REC-CSS1-961217.html`

This site contains the W3C *Cascading Style Sheets, Level 1* specification.

SUMMARY

- The inline style allows you to declare a style for an individual element using the **`STYLE`** attribute in that element's opening HTML tag.
- Each CSS property is followed by a colon then the value of that attribute.
- The **`color`** property sets the color of text. Color names and hex codes may be used as the value.
- Styles that are placed in the **`<STYLE>`** section apply to the whole document.

```
BODY      { font-size: 20pt;
            background-color: #CCFFCC }
A         { color: red }
```

Fig. 14.16 A sample user style sheet.

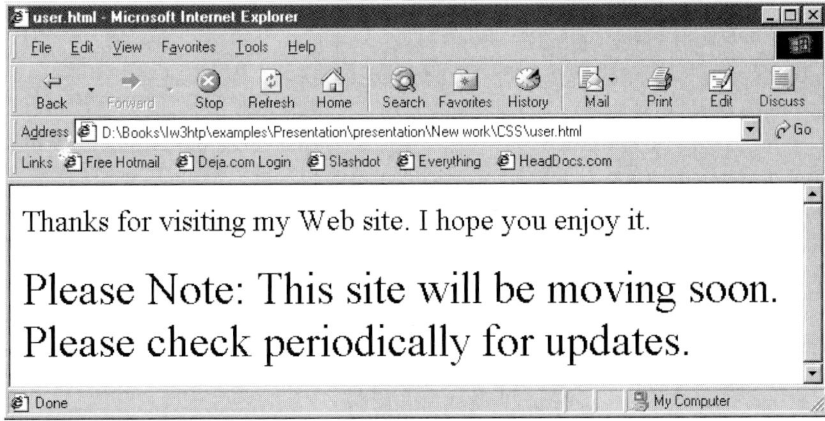

Fig. 14.17 A Web page with user styles enabled.

- The **TYPE** attribute of the **STYLE** element specifies the MIME type (the specific format of binary encoding) of the following style sheet. Regular text style sheets always use **text/css**.
- Each rule body begins and ends with a curly brace (**{** and **}**).
- All style class declarations are preceded with a period and are applied to elements only of that specific class.
- The CSS rules in a style sheet to follow the same format as used with inline styles—the property is followed by a colon (**:**) and the value of that property. Multiple properties are separated with a semicolon (**;**).
- The **background-color** attribute specifies the background color of the element.
- The **font-family** attribute specifies the name of the font that should be displayed.
- Generic font families allow you to specify a type of font instead of a specific font. This allows much greater flexibility in your site display.
- The **font-size** property specifies the size to use to render the font.
- The **CLASS** attribute applies a style class to an element.
- All styles applied to an element (the parent element) also apply to elements inside that element (child elements).
- Pseudo-classes give the author access to content not specifically declared in the document.
- The **hover** pseudo-class is dynamically activated when the user moves the mouse cursor over an **A** element.
- The **text-decoration** property applies decorations to text within an element, such as **underline**, **overline**, **line-through** and **blink**
- To apply rules to multiple elements separate the elements with commas.
- A pixel is a relative-length measurement—it varies in size based on screen resolution. Other relative lengths are **em** (the size of the font), **ex** (the so-called "x-height" of the font, which is usually set to the height of a lowercase x) and percentages.
- The other units of measurement available in CSS are absolute-length measurements, i.e., units that do not vary in size based on the system. These are **in** (inches), **cm** (centimeters), **mm** (millimeters), **pt** (points—1 **pt**=1/72 **in**) and **pc** (picas—1 **pc** = 12 **pt**).
- With external linking, you can give your whole Web site the same uniform look—separate pages on your site could all utilize the same style sheet, and you would have to modify only a single file to make changes to styles across your whole Web site.
- The **LINK** element specifies a relationship between the current document and another document using the **REL** attribute.
- CSS introduces the **position** property and a capability called absolute positioning, which gives us greater control over how our documents are displayed.
- Specifying an element's **position** as **absolute** removes it from the normal flow of elements on the page, and positions it according to distance from the **top**, **left**, **right** or **bottom** margins of its parent element.
- The **z-index** property allows you to properly layer overlapping elements. Elements that have higher **z-index** values are displayed in front of elements with lower **z-index** values.
- Unlike absolute positioning, relative positioning keeps elements in the general flow of elements on the page, and offsets them by the specified **top**, **left**, **right** or **bottom** values.
- The **background-image** property specifies the URL of the image to use, in the format **url(fileLocation)**. Specify the **background-color** to use if the image is not found.

- The **background-position** property positions the image on the page. You can use the properties **top**, **bottom**, **center**, **left** and **right** individually or in combination for vertical and horizontal positioning. You can also position using lengths, specifying the horizontal length followed by the vertical length.
- The **background-repeat** property controls the tiling of the background image. Setting the tiling to **no-repeat** will display only one copy of the background image on screen. The **background-repeat** property can be set to **repeat** (the default) to tile the image vertically and horizontally, to **x-repeat** to tile the image only horizontally or **y-repeat** to tile the image only vertically.
- The property setting **background-attachment: fixed** fixes the image in the position specified by **background-position**. Scrolling the browser window will not move the image from its set position. The default value, **scroll**, moves the image as the user scrolls the browser window down.
- The **text-indent** property indents the first line of text in the element by the specified amount.
- The **font-weight** property specifies the "boldness" of affected text. Values besides **bold** and **normal** (the default) are **bolder** (bolder than **bold** text) and **lighter** (lighter than **normal** text). You can also specify the value using multiples of 100 from 100 to 900 (i.e., **100**, **200**, ..., **900**). Text specified as **normal** is equivalent to **400** and **bold** text is equivalent to **700**. Most systems do not have fonts that can be scaled this finely so using the **100**...**900** values might not display the desired effect.
- The **font-style** property allows you to set text to **none**, **italic** or **oblique** (**oblique** will default to **italic** if the system does not have a separate font file for oblique text, which is normally the case).
- **SPAN** is a generic grouping element—it does not apply any inherent formatting to its contents. Its main use is to apply styles or **ID** attributes to a block of text. It is displayed inline (a so-called inline element) with other text, with no line breaks. A similar element is the **DIV** element, which also applies no inherent styles, but is displayed on a separate line, with margins above and below (a so-called block-level element).
- The dimensions of each element on the page can be set using CSS using the **height** and **width** properties.
- Text within an element can be **center**ed using **text-align**—other values for the **text-align** property are **left** and **right**.
- One problem with setting both element dimensions is that content inside might sometimes exceed the set boundaries, in which case the element is simply made large enough for all the content to fit. However, you can set the **overflow** property to **scroll**; this adds scroll bars if the text overflows the boundaries we have set for it.
- A browser normally places text and elements on screen in the order they appear in the HTML file. However, it is possible to remove elements from the normal flow of text. Floating allows you to move an element to one side of the screen—other content in the document will then flow around the floated element.
- Each block-level element has a box drawn around it, known as the box model—the properties of this box are easily adjusted (Fig. 14.9).
- The **margin** property determines the distance between the element's edge and any outside text.
- CSS uses a box model to render elements on screen—the content of each element is surrounded by padding, a border and margins
- Margins for individual sides of an element can be specified by using **margin-top**, **margin-right**, **margin-left** and **margin-bottom**.

- The padding, as opposed to the margin, is the distance between the content inside an element and the edge of the element. Padding can be set for each side of the box with **padding-top**, **padding-right**, **padding-left** and **padding-bottom**.
- You can interrupt the flow of text around a **float**ed element by setting the **clear** property to the same direction the element is **float**ed—**right** or **left**. Setting the **clear** property to **all** interrupts the flow on both sides of the document.
- Another property included around every block-level element on screen is the border. The border lies between the padding space and the margin space and has numerous properties to adjust its appearance
- The **border-width** property may be set to any of the CSS lengths, or the predefined values of **thin**, **medium** or **thick**.
- The **border-style**s available are **none**, **hidden**, **dotted**, **dashed**, **solid**, **double**, **groove**, **ridge**, **inset** and **outset**. Keep in mind that the **dotted** and **dashed** styles are available only for Macintosh systems.
- The **border-color** property sets the color used for the border.
- It is possible to assign more than one class to an HTML element using the **CLASS** attribute.

TERMINOLOGY

absolute-length measurement
absolute positioning
Arial font
background
background-attachment
background-color
background-image
background-position
background-repeat
blink
block-level element
border
border-color
border-style
border-width
bottom
box model
Cascading Style Sheet (CSS) specification
child element
CLASS attribute of an element
clear: all
clear: left
clear: right
cm (centimeters)
colon (**:**) in a CSS rule
color
CSS rule
cursive generic font family
dashed border style
dotted border style
double border style
em (size of font)
embedded style sheet
ex (x-height of font)
fantasy generic font family
float property
font-style property
generic font family
groove border style
height property
hidden border style
hover pseudo-class
HREF attribute of **<LINK>** element
importing a style sheet
in (inches)
inline-level element
inline styles
inset border style
large font size
larger font size
left
line-through text decoration
<LINK> element
linking to an external style sheet
margin
margin-bottom property
margin-left property
margin-right property
margin-top property
medium border width

medium font size
mm (millimeters)
monospace generic font family
none border style
outset border style
overflow property
overline text decoration
padding
parent element
pc (picas)
position: absolute
position: relative
pseudo-class
pt (points)
REL attribute of **<LINK>** element
relative-length measurement
relative positioning
ridge border style
right
rule in CSS
sans-serif generic font family
scroll
separation of structure from content
serif generic font family
small font size
smaller font size
solid border style
style
STYLE attribute
style class
style in header of document
style sheet (CSS rules separate text file)
text-align
text/css MIME type
text-decoration
text flow
text-indent
thick border width
thin border width
top
user style sheet
width
x-large font size
x-repeat
x-small font size
xx-large font size
xx-small font size
y-repeat
z-index

COMMON PROGRAMMING ERROR

14.1 Since relative positioning keeps elements in the flow of text in your documents, be careful to avoid overlapping text unintentionally.

GOOD PROGRAMMING PRACTICE

14.1 Whenever possible, use relative length measurements. If you use absolute length measurements, you might override styles preset by the user.

LOOK-AND-FEEL OBSERVATION

14.1 Without style sheets, the browser completely controls the look and feel of Web pages. With style sheets, the designer can specify the look and feel of all elements on a Web page.

PORTABILITY TIPS

14.1 Browsers are not required to support the blink value of the text-decoration property, so do not use it as a mechanism for important highlighting.

14.1 Always test DHTML programs on all intended client platforms to ensure that the display is reasonable, especially for those client platforms with older browsers.

14.1 Keep in mind that the **dotted** and **dashed** border styles are available only for Macintosh systems.

SOFTWARE ENGINEERING OBSERVATIONS

14.1 There are three possible sources for styles sheets—browser defaults, preset user styles, and author styles (e.g., in the **STYLE** section of a document). Author styles have a greater precedence than preset user styles, so any conflicts will be resolved in favor of the author styles.

14.2 Style sheets are reusable. Creating style sheets once and reusing them reduces programming effort.

14.3 The **LINK** element can be placed only in the header section. Other relationships you can specify between documents are **next** and **previous**, which would allow you to link a whole series of documents. This could let browsers print a large collection of related documents at once (in Internet Explorer, select **Print all linked documents** in the **Print...** submenu of the **File** menu).

SELF-REVIEW EXERCISES

14.1 Assume that the size of the base font on a system is 12 points.

a) How big is 36 point font in ems?
b) How big is 8 point font in ems?
c) How big is 24 point font in picas?
d) How big is 12 point font in inches?
e) How big is 1 inch font in picas?

14.2 Fill in the blanks in the following questions:

a) Using the ________ element allows you to use external style sheets in your pages.
b) To apply a CSS rule to more than one element at a time, separate the element names with a ________.
c) Pixels are a ________ length measurement unit.
d) The **hover** ________-________ is activated when the user moves the mouse cursor over the specified element.
e) Setting the **overflow** property to ________ provides a mechanism for containing inner content without compromising specified box dimensions.
f) While ________ is a generic inline element that applies no inherent formatting, the ________ is a generic block-level element that applies no inherent formatting.
g) Setting the **background-repeat** property to ________ will tile the specified **background-image** only vertically.
h) If you **float** an element, you can stop the flowing text by using the ________ property.
i) The ________ property allows you to indent the first line of text in an element.
j) Three components of the box model are the ________, ________ and ________.

ANSWERS TO SELF-REVIEW EXERCISES

14.1 a) 3 ems. b) .75 ems. c) 2 picas. d) 1/6 inch. e) 6 picas.

14.2 a) **LINK**. b) comma. c) relative. d) pseudo-element. e) **scroll**. f) **SPAN**, **DIV**. g) **y-repeat**. h) **clear**. i) **text-indent**. j) content, padding, border or margin.

EXERCISES

14.3 Write a CSS rule that makes all text 1.5 times larger than the base font of the system and colors it red.

14.4 Write a CSS rule that removes the underline from all links inside list items (**`LI`**) and shifts them left by 3 **`em`**s.

14.5 Write a CSS rule that places a background image halfway down the page, tiling horizontally. The image should remain in place when the user scrolls up or down.

14.6 The **`EM`** element typically applies an italic effect to text. Create a rule so that it underlines text instead.

14.7 Write a CSS rule that gives all **`H1`** and **`H2`** elements a padding of .5 **`em`**s, a **`groove`**d border style and a margin of .5 **`em`**s.

14.8 Write a CSS rule that changes the color of all elements with attribute **`CLASS="greenMove"`** to green and shifts them down 25 pixels and right 15 pixels.

14.9 Write a CSS rule that sets an element to occupy 60% of the screen width and that is centered horizontally.

15

Dynamic HTML: Object Model and Collections

Objectives

- To use the Dynamic HTML Object Model and scripting to create dynamic Web pages.
- To understand the Dynamic HTML object hierarchy.
- To use the **`all`** and **`children`** collections to enumerate all of the HTML elements of a Web page.
- To use dynamic styles and dynamic positioning.
- To use the **`frames`** collection to access objects in a separate frame on your Web page.
- To use the **`navigator`** object to determine which browser is being used to access your page.

Absolute freedom of navigation upon the seas...

Woodrow Wilson

Our children may learn about heroes of the past. Our task is to make ourselves architects of the future.

Jomo Mzee Kenyatta

The complex is made over into the simple, the hypothetical into the dogmatic, and the relative into an absolute.

Walter Lippmann

The thing that impresses me most about America is the way parents obey their children.

Duke of Windsor

The test of greatness is the page of history.

William Hazlitt

Outline

15.1 Introduction

In this chapter we introduce the Dynamic HTML object model. The object model gives Web authors great control over the presentation of their pages by giving them access to all elements on their Web page. The whole Web page—elements, forms, frames, tables, etc. is represented in an object hierarchy. Using scripting, an author is able to retrieve and modify any properties or attributes of the Web page dynamically.

This chapter begins by examining several of the objects available in the object hierarchy. Toward the end of the chapter there is a diagram of the extensive object hierarchy, with explanations of the various objects and properties and links to Web sites with further information on the topic.

Software Engineering Observation 15.1

With Dynamic HTML, HTML elements can be treated as objects, and attributes of these elements can be treated as properties of those objects. Then, objects identified with an **`ID`** *attribute can be scripted with languages like JavaScript, JScript and VBScript to achieve dynamic effects.*

15.2 Object Referencing

The simplest way to reference an element is by its **`ID`** attribute. The element is represented as an object, and its various HTML attributes become properties that can be manipulated by scripting. Figure 15.1 uses this method to read the ***`innerHTML`*** *property* of a **`P`** element.

```
<!DOCTYPE html PUBLIC "-//W3C//DTD HTML 4.0 Transitional//EN">
<HTML>

<!-- Fig. 15.1: example1.html  -->
<!-- Object Model Introduction -->

<HEAD>
```

Fig. 15.1 Object referencing with the Dynamic HTML Object Model (part 1 of 2).

```
8  <TITLE>Object Model</TITLE>
9
10 <SCRIPT LANGUAGE = "JavaScript">
11    function start()
12    {
13       alert( pText.innerText );
14       pText.innerText = "Thanks for coming.";
15    }
16 </SCRIPT>
17
18 </HEAD>
19
20 <BODY ONLOAD = "start()">
21
22 <P ID = "pText">Welcome to our Web page!</P>
23
24 </BODY>
25 </HTML>
```

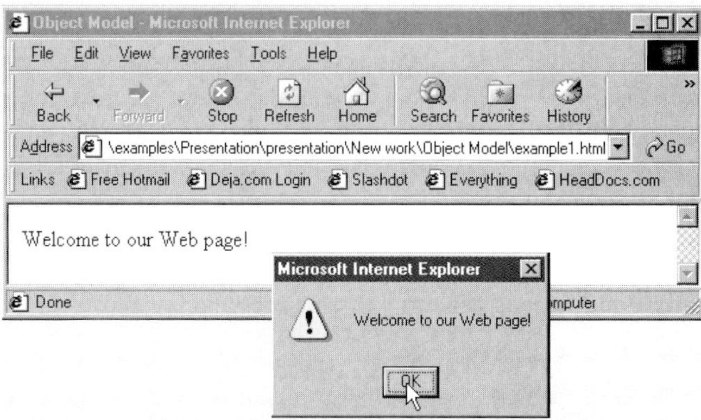

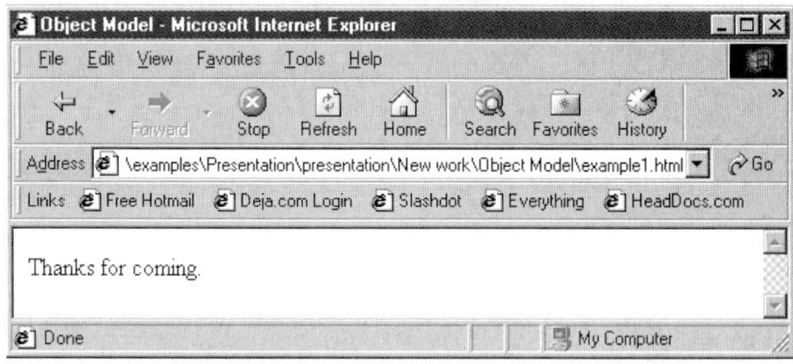

Fig. 15.1 Object referencing with the Dynamic HTML Object Model (part 2 of 2).

Line 20

```
<BODY ONLOAD = "start()">
```

uses the ***ONLOAD** event* to call the JavaScript **start** function when the document is finished loading. Events are covered in depth in the next chapter. Once function **start** has been called, it pops up an **`alert`** box with the value **`pText.innerText`**. The object **`pText`** refers to the **`P`** element whose **`ID`** is set to **`pText`** (line 22). The **`innerText`** property of the object refers to the text contained in that element (**`Welcome to our Web page!`**). The next line of the **`start`** function, line 14, sets the **`innerText`** property of **`pText`** to a different value—changing the text displayed on screen, as we do here, is an example of a Dynamic HTML ability called *dynamic content*.

15.3 Collections `all` and `children`

Included in the Dynamic HTML Object Model is the notion of *collections*. Collections are basically arrays of related objects on a page. There are several special collections in the object model (some collections are listed at the end of this chapter, in Figs. 15.10 and 15.11). The Dynamic HTML Object Model includes a special collection, **`all`**. The ***`all`** collection* is a collection of all the HTML elements in a document, in the order in which they appear. This provides an easy way of referring to any specific element, especially if it does not have an **`ID`**. The script in Fig. 15.2 loops through the **`all`** collection, and displays the list of HTML elements on the page by writing to the ***`innerHTML`** property* of a **`P`** element.

Lines 15 and 16 in function **`start`**

```
for ( var loop = 0; loop < document.all.length; ++loop )
   elements += "<BR>" + document.all[ loop ].tagName;
```

```
1  <!DOCTYPE html PUBLIC "-//W3C//DTD HTML 4.0 Transitional//EN">
2  <HTML>
3
4  <!-- Fig 15.2: all.html         -->
5  <!-- Using the all collection -->
6
7  <HEAD>
8  <TITLE>Object Model</TITLE>
9
10 <SCRIPT LANGUAGE = "JavaScript">
11    var elements = "";
12
13    function start()
14    {
15       for ( var loop = 0; loop < document.all.length; ++loop )
16          elements += "<BR>" + document.all[ loop ].tagName;
17
18       pText.innerHTML += elements;
19    }
20 </SCRIPT>
21 </HEAD>
22
23 <BODY ONLOAD = "start()">
24
25 <P ID = "pText">Elements on this Web page:</P>
26
27 </BODY>
28 </HTML>
```

Fig. 15.2 Looping through the **`all`** collection (part 1 of 2).

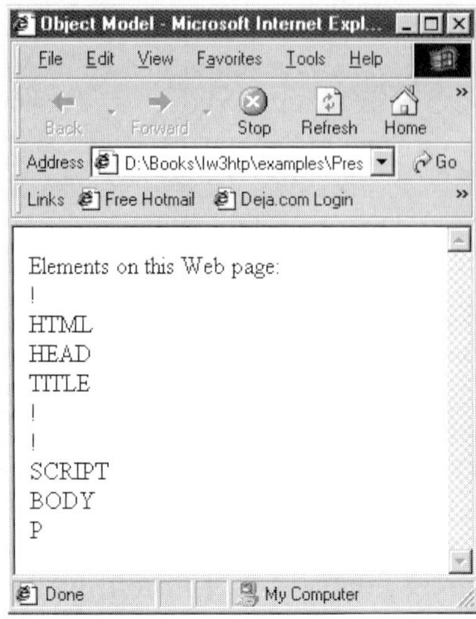

Fig. 15.2 Looping through the **all** collection (part 2 of 2).

loop through the elements of the **all** collection and displays each element's name. The **all** collection is a property of the **document** object (discussed in more detail later in this chapter). The ***length*** *property* of the **all** collection (and other collections) specifies the number of elements in the collection. For each element in the collection, we append to **elements** the name of the HTML element (determined with the ***tagName*** *property*). When the loop terminates, we write the names of the elements to **pText.innerHTML**—the ***innerHTML*** *property* is similar to the **innerText** property, but it can include HTML formatting. Note that both the **!DOCTYPE** element and the **<!--** (comment) elements are represented with a **tagName** property of **!** in the document.

When we use the **document.all** collection, we refer to all the HTML elements in the document. However, every element has its own **all** collection, consisting of all the elements contained within that element. For example, the **all** collection of the **BODY** element contains the **P** element in line 25.

A collection similar to the **all** collection is the **children** collection—the **children** collection of any element contains only those elements that are direct child elements of that element. For example, an **HTML** element has only two children: the **HEAD** element and the **BODY** element. In Fig. 15.3 we use the **children** collection and recursion to walk through all the elements in the document.

Function **child** uses recursion to view all the elements on the page—it starts at the level of the **HTML** element (**document.all[1]** on line 33) and begins walking through all the children of that element. If it encounters an element that has its own children (line 21), it recursively calls the **child** function, passing the object of the new element through which the function should loop. As that loop finishes, the loop which called it proceeds to the next element in its own array of **children**. We use the **tagName** property to gather the names of the tags we encounter while looping through the document, and place them in the string **elements**. The script adds **UL** and **LI** tags to display the element in a hierarchical manner on the page. When the original call to function child completes, line 34

```
myDisplay.outerHTML += elements;">
```

changes the ***outerHTML*** *property* of the **P** element **myDisplay** to string **elements**. Property **outerHTML** is similar to property **innerHTML** we introduced in the previous example, but it includes the enclosing HTML tags (tags **<P ID = "myDisplay">** and **</P>** in this case) as well as the content inside them.

```
<!DOCTYPE html PUBLIC "-//W3C//DTD HTML 4.0 Transitional//EN">
<HTML>

<!-- Fig 15.3: children.html -->
<!-- The children collection -->

<HEAD>
<TITLE>Object Model</TITLE>

<SCRIPT LANGUAGE = "JavaScript">
   var elements = "<UL>";

   function child( object )
   {
      var loop = 0;

      elements += "<LI>" + object.tagName + "<UL>";

      for ( loop = 0; loop < object.children.length; loop++ ) {

         if ( object.children[loop].children.length )
            child( object.children[ loop ] );
         else
            elements += "<LI>" + object.children[ loop ].tagName
                        + "</LI>";
      }

      elements += " </UL> ";
   }
</SCRIPT>
</HEAD>

<BODY ONLOAD = "child( document.all[ 1 ] );
                myDisplay.outerHTML += elements;">

<P>Welcome to our <STRONG>Web</STRONG> page!</P>

<P ID = "myDisplay">
Elements on this Web page:
</P>

</BODY>
</HTML>
```

Fig. 15.3 Navigating the object hierarchy using collection **children** (part 1 of 2).

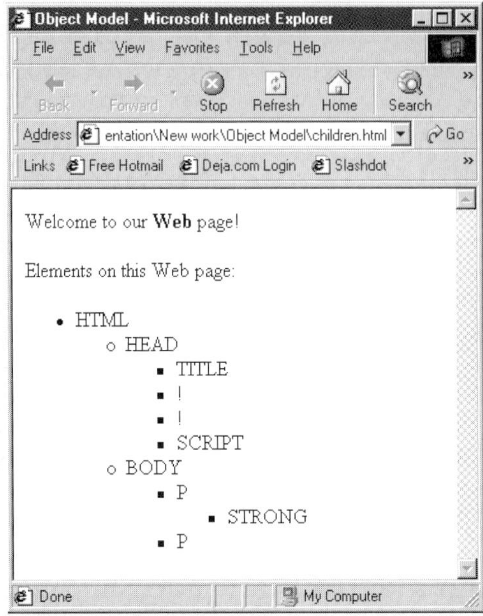

Fig. 15.3 Navigating the object hierarchy using collection **`children`** (part 2 of 2).

15.4 Dynamic Styles

An element's style can be changed dynamically. Often such a change is made in response to user events, which are discussed in the next chapter. Figure 15.4 is a simple example of changing styles in response to user input.

```
<!DOCTYPE html PUBLIC "-//W3C//DTD HTML 4.0 Transitional//EN">
<HTML>

<!-- Fig. 15.4: dynamicstyle.html -->
<!-- Dynamic Styles               -->

<HEAD>
<TITLE>Object Model</TITLE>

<SCRIPT LANGUAGE = "JavaScript">
   function start()
   {
      var inputColor = prompt( "Enter a color name for the " +
                               "background of this page", "" );
      document.body.style.backgroundColor = inputColor;
   }
</SCRIPT>
</HEAD>

```

Fig. 15.4 Dynamic styles (part 1 of 2).

```
20  <BODY ONLOAD = "start()">
21
22  <P>Welcome to our Web site!</P>
23
24  </BODY>
25  </HTML>
```

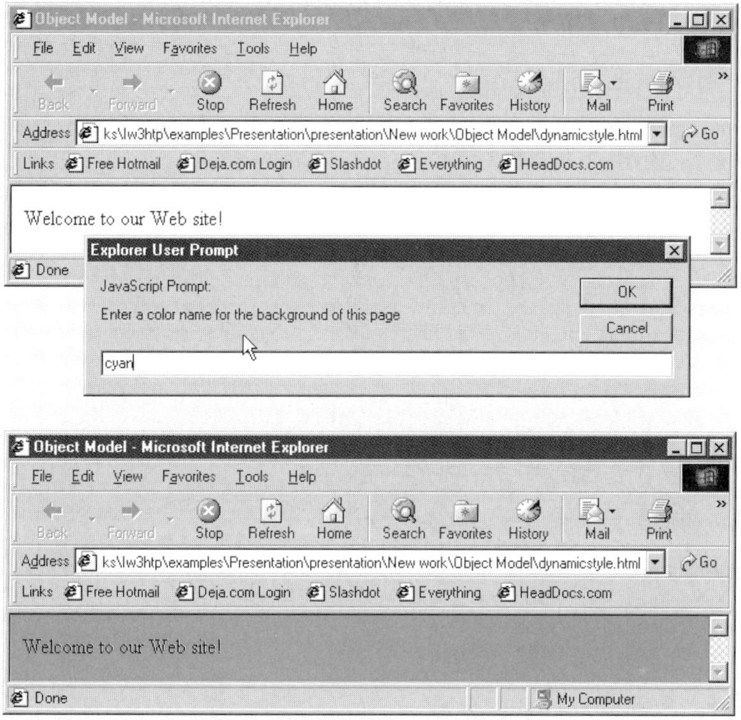

Fig. 15.4 Dynamic styles (part 2 of 2).

Function **start**, in lines 11 through 16

```
function start()
{
   var inputColor = prompt( "Enter a color name for the " +
                            "background of this page", "" );
   document.body.style.backgroundColor = inputColor;
}
```

prompt's the user to enter a color name, then sets the background color to that value. We refer to the background color as **document.body.style.backgroundColor**—the **body** property of the **document** object refers to the **BODY** element. We then use the **style** object (a property of most HTML elements) to set the **background-color** CSS property. (This is referred to as **backgroundColor** in JavaScript, to avoid confusion with the subtraction (**-**) operator. This naming convention is consistent for most of the CSS properties. For example, **borderWidth** correlates to the **border-width** CSS property, and **fontFamily** correlates to the **font-family** CSS property).

The Dynamic HTML object model also allows you to change the **CLASS** attribute of an element—instead of changing many individual styles at a time, you can have preset style classes for easily altering element styles. Fig 15.5 prompts the user to enter the name of a style class, and then changes the screen text to that style.

As in the previous example, we prompt the user for information—in this case, we ask for the name of a style class to apply, either **bigText** or **smallText**. Once we have this information, we then use the **className** property to change the style class of **pText**.

15.5 Dynamic Positioning

Another important feature of Dynamic HTML is *dynamic positioning*, by means of which HTML elements can be positioned with scripting. This is done by declaring an element's CSS **position** property to be either **absolute** or **relative**, and then moving the element by manipulating any of the **top**, **left**, **right** or **bottom** CSS properties.

```
<!DOCTYPE html PUBLIC "-//W3C//DTD HTML 4.0 Transitional//EN">
<HTML>

<!-- Fig. 15.5: dynamicstyle2.html -->
<!-- More Dynamic Styles           -->

<HEAD>
<TITLE>Object Model</TITLE>

<STYLE>

   .bigText   { font-size: 3em;
                font-weight: bold }

   .smallText { font-size: .75em }

</STYLE>

<SCRIPT LANGUAGE = "JavaScript">
   function start()
   {
      var inputClass = prompt( "Enter a className for the text "
                               + "(bigText or smallText)", "" );
      pText.className = inputClass;
   }
</SCRIPT>
</HEAD>

<BODY ONLOAD = "start()">

<P ID = "pText">Welcome to our Web site!</P>

</BODY>
</HTML>
```

Fig. 15.5 Dynamic styles in action (part 1 of 2).

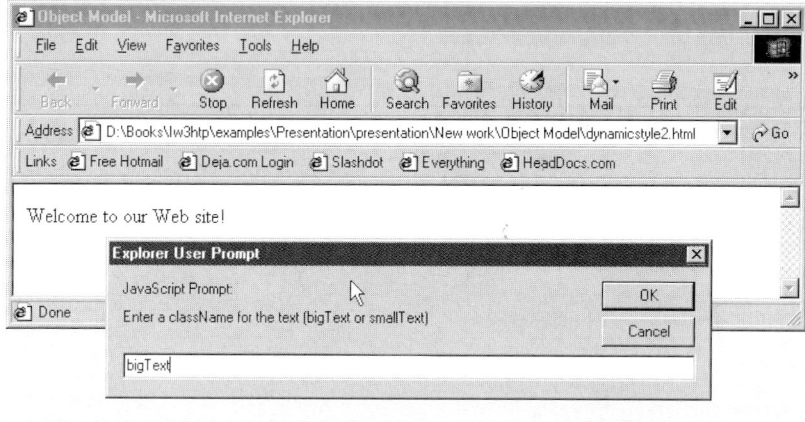

Fig. 15.5 Dynamic styles in action (part 2 of 2).

This example is a combination of dynamic positioning, dynamic styles, and dynamic content—we vary the position of the element on the page by accessing its CSS **`left`** attribute, we use scripting to vary the **`color`**, **`fontFamily`** and **`fontSize`** attributes, and we use the element's **`innerHTML`** property to alter the content of the element.

In order to constantly update the content of the **`P`** element, in line 20

```
window.setInterval( "run()", 100 );
```

we use a new function, **`setInterval`**. This function takes two parameters—a function name, and how often to run that function (in this case, every **`100`** milliseconds). A similar JavaScript function is **`setTimeout`**, which takes the same parameters but instead waits the specified amount of time before calling the named function only once. There are also JavaScript functions for stopping either of these two timers—the **`clearTimeout`** and **`clearInterval`** functions. To stop a specific timer, the parameter you pass to either of these functions should be the value that the corresponding set time function returned. For example, if you started a **`setTimeout`** timer with

```
timer1 = window.setTimeout( "timedFunction()", 2000 );
```

you could then stop the timer by calling

```
window.clearTimeout( timer1 );
```

which would stop the timer before it fired.

```
<!DOCTYPE html PUBLIC "-//W3C//DTD HTML 4.0 Transitional//EN">
<HTML>

<!-- Fig. 15.6: dynamicposition.html -->
<!-- Dynamic Positioning            -->

<HEAD>
<TITLE>Dynamic Positioning</TITLE>

<SCRIPT LANGUAGE = "JavaScript">
   var speed = 5;
   var count = 10;
   var direction = 1;
   var firstLine = "Text growing";
   var fontStyle = [ "serif", "sans-serif", "monospace" ];
   var fontStylecount = 0;

   function start()
   {
      window.setInterval( "run()", 100 );
   }

   function run()
   {
      count += speed;

      if ( ( count % 200 ) == 0 ) {
         speed *= -1;
         direction = !direction;

         pText.style.color =
            ( speed < 1 ) ? "red" : "blue" ;
         firstLine =
            ( speed < 1 ) ? "Text shrinking" : "Text growing";
         pText.style.fontFamily =
            fontStyle[ ++fontStylecount % 3 ];
      }

      pText.style.fontSize = count / 3;
      pText.style.left = count;
      pText.innerHTML = firstLine + "<BR> Font size: " +
                        count + "px";
   }
</SCRIPT>
</HEAD>

<BODY ONLOAD = "start()">

```

Fig. 15.6 Dynamic positioning (part 1 of 2).

```
<P ID = "pText" STYLE = "position: absolute; left: 0;
                           font-family: serif; color: blue">
Welcome!</P>

</BODY>
</HTML>
```

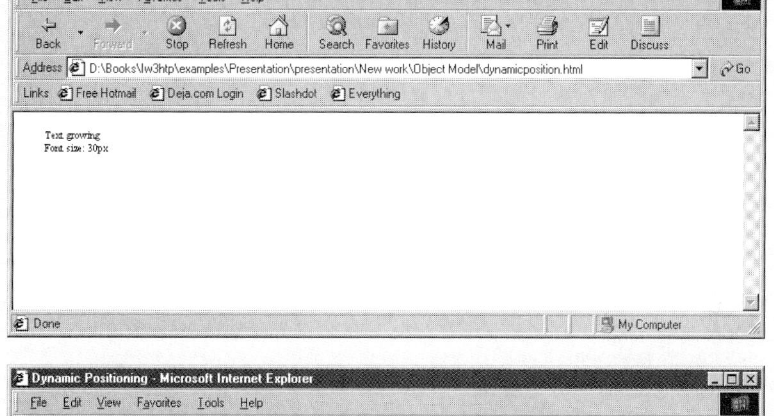

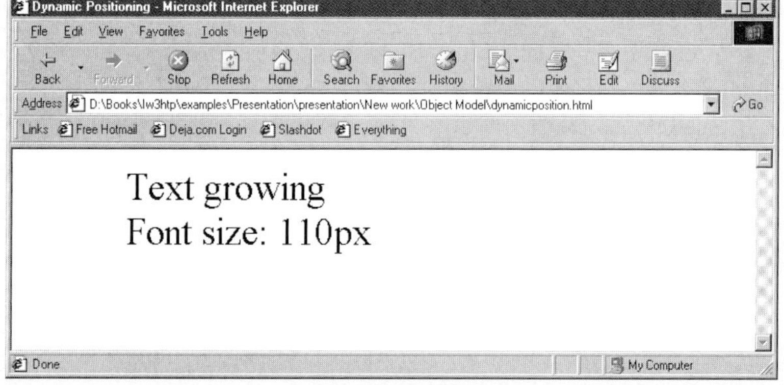

Fig. 15.6 Dynamic positioning (part 2 of 2).

15.6 Using the `frames` Collection

One problem that you might run into while developing applications is communication between frames in the browsers. The referencing we have used certainly allows for access to objects and HTML elements on the same page, but what if those elements and objects are on separate pages? Figures 15.7 and 15.8 solve this problem by using the **frames** collection. [*Note:* Because Fig. 15.7 and Fig. 15.8 compose one example, we use consecutive lines numbers across the two figures.]

```
<!DOCTYPE html PUBLIC "-//W3C//DTD HTML 4.0 Frameset//EN">
<HTML>

<!-- Fig 15.7: index.html          -->
<!-- Using the frames collection -->

<HEAD>
   <TITLE>Frames collection</TITLE>
</HEAD>

<FRAMESET ROWS = "100, *">
   <FRAME SRC = "top.html">
   <FRAME SRC = "">
</FRAMESET>

</HTML>
```

Fig. 15.7 **FRAMESET** file for cross-frame scripting.

```
<!DOCTYPE html PUBLIC "-//W3C//DTD HTML 4.0 Transitional//EN">
<HTML>

<!-- Fig 15.8: top.html     -->
<!-- Cross-frame scripting -->

<HEAD>
<TITLE>The frames collection</TITLE>

<SCRIPT LANGUAGE = "JavaScript">
   function start()
   {
      var text = prompt( "What is your name?", "" );
      parent.frames( "lower" ).document.write( "<H1>Hello, " +
                                                text + "</H1>" );
   }
</SCRIPT>
</HEAD>

<BODY ONLOAD = "start()">

<H1>Cross-frame scripting!</H1>

```

Fig. 15.8 Accessing other frames.

```
40
41  </BODY>
42  </HTML>
```

Fig. 15.8 Accessing other frames.

Lines 30 and 31 of Fig. 15.8

```
parent.frames( "lower" ).document.write( "<H1>Hello, " +
                                          text + "</H1>" );
```

apply changes to the lower frame. To reference the lower frame, we first reference the **`parent`** frame of the current frame, then use the **`frames`** collection. We use a new notation here—**`frames( "lower" )`**—to refer to the element in the frames collection with an **`ID`** or **`NAME`** of lower. The **`<FRAME>`** tag for the lower frame appears second in the HTML file, so the frame is second in the **`frames`** collection. We then use the familiar **`document.write`** method in that frame to update it with the user input from our **`prompt`** on line 29.

15.7 `navigator` Object

One of the most appealing aspects of the Internet is its diversity. Unfortunately, because of this diversity, standards are often compromised. The most popular browsers currently on the market, Netscape's Navigator and Microsoft's Internet Explorer, each has many features that give the Web author great control over the browser, but most of their features are incompatible. Each, however, supports the **`navigator`** object, which contains information about the Web browser that is viewing the page. This allows Web authors to determine which browser the user has—this is especially important when the page uses browser-specific features, because it allows the author to redirect users to a page that can be viewed properly in their own browsers. (This is done in Fig. 15.9.)

When the page loads, function **`start`** is called. It checks the value of the property **`navigator.appName`**—this property of the **`navigator`** object contains the name of the application (for IE, this property is "**`Microsoft Internet Explorer`**"; for

Netscape, it is "**Netscape**"). If the browser viewing this page is not Internet Explorer, in line 21 we redirect the browser to the file "**NSversion.html**" by using the property **document.location**. (This is the URL of the document being viewed.)

In line 15, we also check the version of the browser by using the property **navigator.appVersion**. The value of **appVersion** is not a simple integer, however—it is a string containing other information, such as the current Operating System. We therefore use the **substring** method to retrieve the first character of the string, which is the actual version number. If the version number is **4** or greater, we redirect to **newIEversion.html**. Otherwise, we redirect the browser to **oldIEversion.html**

As we see here, the **navigator** object is crucial in providing browser-specific pages so that as many users as possible can view your site properly.

Portability Tip 15.1

Always make provisions for other browsers if you are using a browser-specific technology or feature on your Web page.

```
1  <!DOCTYPE html PUBLIC "-//W3C//DTD HTML 4.0 Transitional//EN">
2  <HTML>
3
4  <!-- Fig 15.9: navigator.html    -->
5  <!-- Using the navigator object -->
6
7  <HEAD>
8  <TITLE>The navigator Object</TITLE>
9
10 <SCRIPT LANGUAGE = "JavaScript">
11    function start()
12    {
13       if ( navigator.appName == "Microsoft Internet Explorer" ) {
14
15          if ( navigator.appVersion.substring( 1, 0 ) >= "4" )
16             document.location = "newIEversion.html";
17          else
18             document.location = "oldIEversion.html";
19       }
20       else
21          document.location = "NSversion.html";
22    }
23 </SCRIPT>
24 </HEAD>
25
26 <BODY ONLOAD = "start()">
27
28 <P>Redirecting your browser to the appropriate page,
29 please wait...</P>
30
31 </BODY>
32 </HTML>
```

Fig. 15.9 Using the **navigator** object to redirect users.

15.8 Summary of the DHTML Object Model

As you have seen in the preceding sections, the objects and collections supported by Internet Explorer allow the script programmer tremendous flexibility in manipulating the elements of a Web page. We have shown how to access the objects in a page, how to navigate the objects in a collection, how to change element styles dynamically and how to change the position of elements dynamically.

The Dynamic HTML object model provided by Internet Explorer allows a script programmer to access every element in an HTML document. Literally every element in a document is represented by a separate object. The diagram in Fig. 15.10 shows many of the important objects and collections supported in Internet Explorer. The table of Fig. 15.11 provides a brief description of each object and collection in the diagram of Fig. 15.10. For a comprehensive listing of all objects and collections supported by Internet Explorer, browse the Microsoft *DHTML, HTML and CSS* Web site,

```
http://msdn.microsoft.com/workshop/c-frame.htm#
/workshop/author/default.asp
```

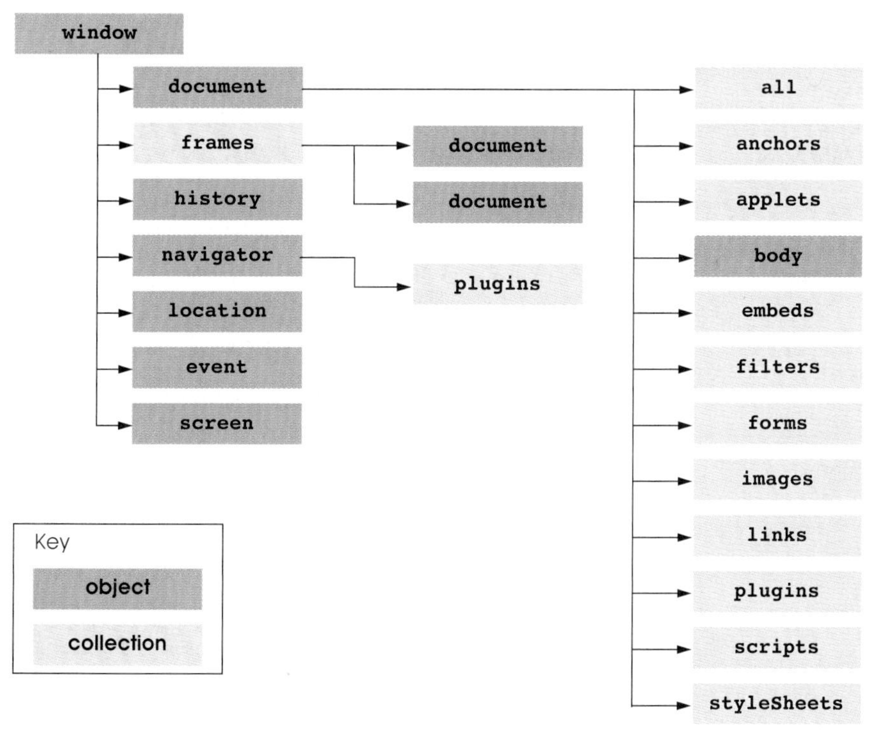

Fig. 15.10 The DHTMLObject Model.

This site provides detailed information on HTML, Dynamic HTML and Cascading Style Sheets technologies. The *DHTML References* section of this site provides detailed descriptions of every object, event and collection used in DHTML. For each object, all the properties, methods and collections supported by that object are discussed. For each collection, all the properties and methods supported by that collection are discussed.

Object or collection	Description
Objects	
`window`	This object represents the browser window and provides access to the **`document`** object contained in the **`window`**. If the **`window`** contains frames, a separate **`window`** object is created automatically for each frame, to provide access to the **`document`** rendered in that frame. Frames are considered to be subwindows in the browser.
`document`	This object represents the HTML document rendered in a **`window`**. The document object provides access to every element in the HTML document and allows dynamic modification of the HTML document.
`body`	This object provides access to the **`BODY`** element of an HTML document.
`history`	This object keeps track of the sites visited by the browser user. The object provides a script programmer with the ability to move forward and backward through the visited sites, but for security reasons does not allow the actual site URLs to be manipulated.
`navigator`	This object contains information about the Web browser, such as the name of the browser, the version of the browser, the operating system on which the browser is running and other information that can help a script writer customize the user's browsing experience.
`location`	This object contains the URL of the rendered document. When this object is set to a new URL, the browser immediately switches (navigates) to the new location.
`event`	This object can be used in an event handler to obtain information about the event that occurred (e.g., the mouse coordinates during a mouse event).
`screen`	The object contains information about the computer screen for the computer on which the browser is running. Information such as the width and height of the screen in pixels can be used to determine the size at which elements should be rendered in a Web page.
Collections	
`all`	Many objects have an **`all`** collection that provides access to every element contained in the object. For example, the **`body`** object's **`all`** collection provides access to every element in the **`BODY`** element of an HTML document.

Fig. 15.11 Objects in the Internet Explorer 5 object model (part 1 of 2).

Object or collection	Description
anchors	This collection contains all anchor elements (**A**) that have a **NAME** or **ID** attribute. The elements appear in the collection in the order they were defined in the HTML document.
applets	This collection contains all the **APPLET** elements in the HTML document. Currently, the most common **APPLET** elements are Java™ applets.
embeds	This collection contains all the **EMBED** elements in the HTML document.
forms	This collection contains all the **FORM** elements in the HTML document. The elements appear in the collection in the order they were defined in the HTML document.
frames	This collection contains **window** objects that represent each frame in the browser window. Each frame is treated as its own subwindow.
images	This collection contains all the **IMG** elements in the HTML document. The elements appear in the collection in the order they were defined in the HTML document.
links	This collection contains all the anchor elements (**A**) with an **HREF** property. This collection also contains all the **AREA** elements that represent links in an image map.
plugins	Like the **embeds** collection, this collection contains all the **EMBED** elements in the HTML document.
scripts	This collection contains all the **SCRIPT** elements in the HTML document.
styleSheets	This collection contains **styleSheet** objects that represent each **STYLE** element in the HTML document and each style sheet included in the HTML document via **LINK**.

Fig. 15.11 Objects in the Internet Explorer 5 object model (part 2 of 2).

SUMMARY

- The Dynamic HTML object model gives Web authors great control over the presentation of their pages by giving them access to all elements on their Web page. The whole Web page—elements, forms, frames, tables, etc. is represented in an object hierarchy. Using scripting, an author is able to retrieve and modify any properties or attributes of the Web page dynamically.
- The simplest way to reference an element by its **ID** attribute. The element is represented as an object and its various HTML attributes become properties that can be manipulated by scripting.
- The **innerText** property of the object refers to the text contained in that element
- Changing the text displayed on screen is a Dynamic HTML ability called dynamic content.
- Collections are basically arrays of related objects on a page. There are several special collections in the object model.
- The **all** collection is a collection of all the HTML elements in a document in the order in which they appear.
- The **length** property of the a collection specifies the size of the collection.
- Property **innerHTML** is similar to property **innerText**, but it can include HTML formatting.

- Every element has its own **all** collection consisting of all the elements contained in that element.
- The **children** collection of any element contains only elements which are direct children elements of that element. For example, an **HTML** element has only two children: the **HEAD** element and the **BODY** element.
- The **tagName** property contains the name of the tags we encounter while looping through the document, and place them in the string **elements**.
- The **outerHTML** property is similar to the **innerHTML** property, but it includes the enclosing HTML tags as well as the content inside them.
- The **className** property of an element is used to change that element's style class.
- An important feature of Dynamic HTML is dynamic positioning, in which HTML elements can be positioned with scripting. This is done by declaring an element's CSS **position** property to be either **absolute** or **relative**, and then moving the element by manipulating any of the **top**, **left**, **right**, or **bottom** CSS properties.
- Function **setInterval** takes two parameters—a function name and how often to call it.
- Function **setTimeout** takes the same parameters as **setInterval**, but instead waits the specified amount of time before calling the named function only once.
- There are also JavaScript functions for stopping the **setTimeout** and **setInterval** timers—the **clearTimeout** and **clearInterval** functions. To stop a specific timer, the parameter you pass to either of these functions should be the value that the corresponding set time function returned.
- The **frames** collections contains all the frames in a document.
- The **navigator** object contains information about the Web browser that is viewing the page. This allows Web authors to determine which browser the user has.
- The **navigator.appName** property contains the name of the application—for IE, this property is "**Microsoft Internet Explorer**", and for Netscape it is "**Netscape**".
- The version of the browser is accessible through the **navigator.appVersion** property. The value of **appVersion** is not a simple integer, however—it is a string containing other information such as the current Operating System.
- The **navigator** object is crucial in providing browser-specific pages so that as many users as possible can view your site properly.

TERMINOLOGY

all collection
all collection of an element
background-color CSS property
body property of **document** object
bottom CSS property
children collection
className property
clearTimeout JavaScript function
clearInterval JavaScript function
collection
document object
document.all.length
dynamic content
Dynamic HTML Object Model
dynamic style
dynamic positioning
fontSize property
ID attribute
innerText property
innerHTML property
outerHTML property
length property of a collection
left CSS property
loop through a collection
object referencing
onload event
position: absolute
position: relative

prompt dialog box
JavaScript
recursion
reference an object
right CSS property
setInterval JavaScript function
setTimeout JavaScript function
style object
tagName property
top CSS property
window.setInterval
window.setTimeout

PORTABILITY TIP

15.1 Always make provisions for other browsers if you are using a browser-specific technology or feature on your Web page.

SOFTWARE ENGINEERING OBSERVATION

15.1 With Dynamic HTML, HTML elements can be treated as objects and attributes of these elements can be treated as properties of those objects. Then, objects identified with an ID attribute can be scripted with languages like JavaScript, JScript and VBScript to achieve dynamic effects.

SELF-REVIEW EXERCISES

15.1 Answer the following questions true or false; If false, state why.
a) An HTML element may be referred to in JavaScript by its **ID** attribute.
b) Only the **document** object has an **all** collection.
c) An element's tag is accessed with the **tagName** property.
d) You can change an element's style class dynamically with the **style** property.
e) The **frames** collection contains all the frames on a page.
f) The **setTimeout** method calls a function repeatedly at a set time interval.
g) The **browser** object is often used to determine which Web browser is viewing the page.
h) The browser may be sent to a new URL by setting the **document.url** property.
i) Collection **links** contains all links in a document with specified **NAME** or **ID** attributes.

15.2 Fill in the blanks for each of the following.
a) The ________ property refers to the text inside an element
b) The ________ property refers to the text inside an element, including HTML tags.
c) The ________ property refers to the text and HTML inside an element *and* the enclosing HTML tags.
d) The ________ property contains the length of a collection.
e) An element's CSS **position** property must be set to ________ or ________ in order to reposition it dynamically.
f) The ________ property contains the name of the browser viewing the Web page.
g) The ________ property contains the version of the browser viewing the Web page.
h) The ________ collection contains all **IMG** elements on a page.
i) The ________ object contains information about the sites that a user previously visited.
j) CSS properties may be accessed using the ________ object.

ANSWERS TO SELF-REVIEW EXERCISES

15.1 a) True. b) False. All elements have an **all** collection. c) True. d) False; this is done with the **className** property. e) True. f) False; the **setInterval** method does this. g) False; the navigator object does this. h) False; use the **document.location** object to send the browser to a different URL. i) False; the **anchors** collection contains all links in a document.

15.2 a) **innerText**. b) **innerHTML**. c) **outerHTML**. d) **length**. e) **absolute**, **relative**. f) **navigator.appName**. g) **navigator.appVersion**. h) **images**. i) **history**. j) **style**.

EXERCISES

15.3 Modify Fig.15.9 to display a greeting to the user which contains the name and version of their browser.

15.4 Use the **screen** object to get the size of the user's screen, then use this information to place an image (using dynamic positioning) in the middle of the page.

15.5 Write a script that loops through the elements in a page and places enclosing **<STRONG>**...**</STRONG>** tags around all text inside all **P** elements.

15.6 Write a script that prints out the length of all collections on a page.

15.7 Create a Web page in which users are allowed to select their favorite layout and formatting through the use of the **className** property.

15.8 *(15 Puzzle)* Write a Web page that enables the user to play the game of 15. There is a 4-by-4 board (implemented as an HTML table) for a total of 16 slots. One of the slots is empty. The other slots are occupied by 15 tiles, randomly numbered from 1 through 15. Any tile next to the currently empty slot can be moved into the currently empty slot by clicking on the tile. Your program should create the board with the tiles out of order. The user's goal is to arrange the tiles into sequential order row by row. Using the DHTML object model and the **ONCLICK** event presented in Chapter 11, write a script that allows the user swap the positions of a tile and the open position. [*Hint:* The **ONCLICK** event should be specified for each table cell.]

15.9 Modify your solution to Exercise 15.8 to determine when the game is over, then prompt the user to determine if they would like to play again. If so, scramble the numbers.

15.10 Modify your solution to Exercise 15.9 to use an image that is split into 16 equally sized pieces. Discard one of the pieces ad randomly place the other 15 pieces in the HTML table.

16

Dynamic HTML: Event Model

Objectives

- To understand the notion of events, event handlers and event bubbling.
- To be able to create event handlers that respond to mouse and keyboard events.
- To be able to use the event object to be made aware of, and ultimately, respond to user actions.
- To understand how to recognize and respond to the most popular events.

The wisest prophets make sure of the event first.
Horace Walpole

Do you think I can listen all day to such stuff?
Lewis Carroll

The user should feel in control of the computer; not the other way around. This is achieved in applications that embody three qualities: responsiveness, permissiveness, and consistency.
Inside Macintosh, Volume 1
Apple Computer, Inc., 1985

We are responsible for actions performed in response to circumstances for which we are not responsible.
Allan Massie

Outline

16.1 Introduction

We have seen that HTML pages can be controlled via scripting. Dynamic HTML with the *event model* exists so that scripts can respond to user actions and change the page accordingly. This makes Web applications more responsive and user-friendly, and can reduce server load—a concern we will learn more about in Chapters 24 through 29.

With the event model, scripts can respond to a user moving the mouse, scrolling up or down the screen or entering keystrokes. Content becomes more dynamic while interfaces become more intuitive.

In this chapter we discuss how to use the event model to respond to user actions. We give examples of event handling for 10 of the most common and useful events, which range from mouse capture to error handling to form processing. For example, we use the **ONRESET** event to prompt a user to confirm that they want to reset a form. Included at the end of the chapter is a table of all DHTML events.

16.2 Event ONCLICK

One of the most common events is **ONCLICK**. When the user clicks the mouse, the **ONCLICK** event *fires*. With JavaScript we are able to respond to **ONCLICK** and other events. Figure 16.1 is an example of simple event handling for the **ONCLICK** event.

The script beginning on line 12

```
<SCRIPT LANGUAGE = "JavaScript" FOR = "para" EVENT = "ONCLICK">
```

introduces a new notation. The **FOR** attribute of the **SCRIPT** element specifies another element (in this case, the **<P>** element in line 22) that is identified by its **ID** attribute (in this case, **para**). When the event specified in the **EVENT** attribute occurs for the element with **ID** specified in the **FOR** attribute, the enclosed script (line 14) runs.

```
1  <!DOCTYPE html PUBLIC "-//W3C//DTD HTML 4.0 Transitional//EN">
2  <HTML>
3
4  <!-- Fig 16.1: onclick.html                -->
5  <!-- Demonstrating the ONCLICK event -->
6
7  <HEAD>
8  <TITLE>DHTML Event Model - ONCLICK</TITLE>
9
10 <!-- The FOR attribute declares the script for a certain -->
11 <!-- element, and the EVENT for a certain event.           -->
12 <SCRIPT LANGUAGE = "JavaScript" FOR = "para" EVENT = "ONCLICK">
13
14    alert( "Hi there" );
15
16 </SCRIPT>
17 </HEAD>
18
19 <BODY>
20
21 <!-- The ID attribute gives a unique identifier -->
22 <P ID = "para">Click on this text!</P>
23
24 <!-- You can specify event handlers inline -->
25 <INPUT TYPE = "button" VALUE = "Click Me!"
26    ONCLICK = "alert( 'Hi again' )">
27
28 </BODY>
29 </HTML>
```

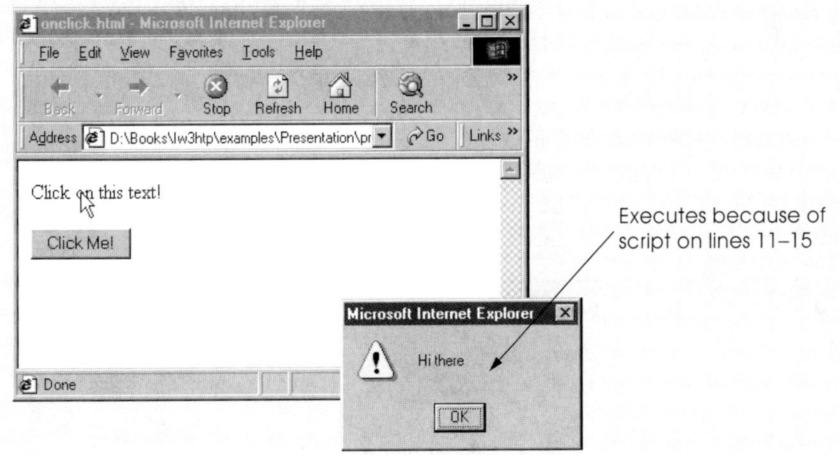

Fig. 16.1 Triggering an **ONCLICK** event (part 1 of 2).

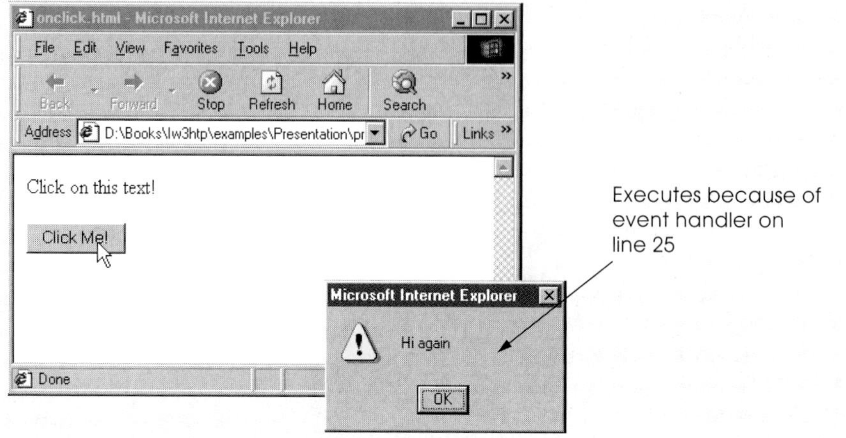

Fig. 16.1 Triggering an **ONCLICK** event (part 2 of 2).

Line 22

```
<P ID = "para">Click on this text!</P>
```

sets the **ID** for this **P** element to match that mentioned **SCRIPT** tag. The ***ID** attribute* specifies a unique identifier for an HTML element. When the **ONCLICK** event for this element is *fired* the script in line 14 executes.

Another way to handle events is with inline scripting. As we see in lines 25 and 26,

```
<INPUT TYPE = "button" VALUE = "Click Me!"
   ONCLICK = "alert( 'Hi again' )";>
```

specifying the event as an HTML attribute allows you to insert script directly. Inline scripting like this is often used to pass a value to an event handler, based on the clicked element.

16.3 Event ONLOAD

The **ONLOAD** event fires whenever an element finishes loading successfully, and is often used in the **BODY** tag to initiate scripts as soon as the page has been loaded into the client. In Fig. 16.2 we use the **ONLOAD** event for this purpose, updating a timer that indicates how many seconds have elapsed since the document has been loaded.

```
<HTML>

<!-- Fig. 16.2: onload.html         -->
<!-- Demonstrating the ONLOAD event -->

<HEAD>
<TITLE>DHTML Event Model - ONLOAD</TITLE>
<SCRIPT LANGUAGE = "JavaScript">

```

Fig. 16.2 Demonstrating the **ONLOAD** event (part 1 of 2).

```
10  var seconds = 0;
11
12  function startTimer(){
13     // 1000 milliseconds = 1 second
14     window.setInterval( "updateTime()", 1000 );
15  }
16
17  function updateTime(){
18     seconds++;
19     soFar.innerText = seconds;
20  }
21
22  </SCRIPT>
23  </HEAD>
24
25  <BODY ONLOAD = "startTimer()">
26
27  <P>Seconds you have spent viewing this page so far:
28  <A ID = "soFar" STYLE = "font-weight: bold">0</A></P>
29
30  </BODY>
31  </HTML>
```

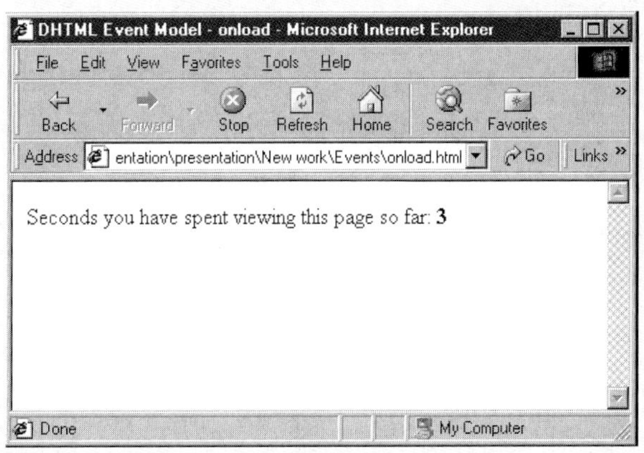

Fig. 16.2 Demonstrating the **ONLOAD** event (part 2 of 2).

Our reference to the **ONLOAD** event occurs in line 26:

```
<BODY ONLOAD = "startTimer()">
```

After the **BODY** section is loaded, the **ONLOAD** event is triggered. This calls function **startTimer**, which in turn uses the **window.setInterval** method to call function **updateTime** every **1000** milliseconds. Other uses of the **ONLOAD** event are to open a popup window once your page has loaded, or to trigger a script when an image or applet loads.

16.4 Error Handling with ONERROR

With the Web being as dynamic a medium as it is, there are occasions when, for example, the object your script refers to might change location, rendering your scripts invalid. The error dialog box presented by browsers is usually confusing to the user. To restrain this dialog box from appearing in order and to handle errors more elegantly, you can use the **ONERROR** event to launch error-handling code. In Fig. 16.3, we use the **ONERROR** event to launch a script that writes error messages to the status bar of the browser.

```
<!DOCTYPE html PUBLIC "-//W3C//DTD HTML 4.0 Transitional//EN">
<HTML>

<!-- Fig 16.3: onerror.html                    -->
<!-- Demonstrating the ONERROR event   -->

<HEAD>
<TITLE>DHTML Event Model - ONERROR</TITLE>
<SCRIPT LANGUAGE = "JavaScript">

// Specify that if an ONERROR event is triggered in the window
// function handleError should execute
window.onerror = handleError;

function doThis() {
     alrrt( "hi" ); // alert misspelled, creates an error
}

// The ONERROR event passes three values to the function: the
// name of the error, the url of the file, and the line number.
function handleError( errType, errURL, errLineNum )
{
   // Writes to the status bar at the bottom of the window.
   window.status = "Error: " + errType + " on line " +
      errLineNum;

   // Returning a value of true cancels the browser's reaction.
   return true;
}

</SCRIPT>
</HEAD>

<BODY>

<INPUT ID = "mybutton" TYPE = "button" VALUE = "Click Me!"
   ONCLICK = "doThis()">

</BODY>
</HTML>
```

Fig. 16.3 Handling script errors by handling an **ONERROR** event (part 1 of 2).

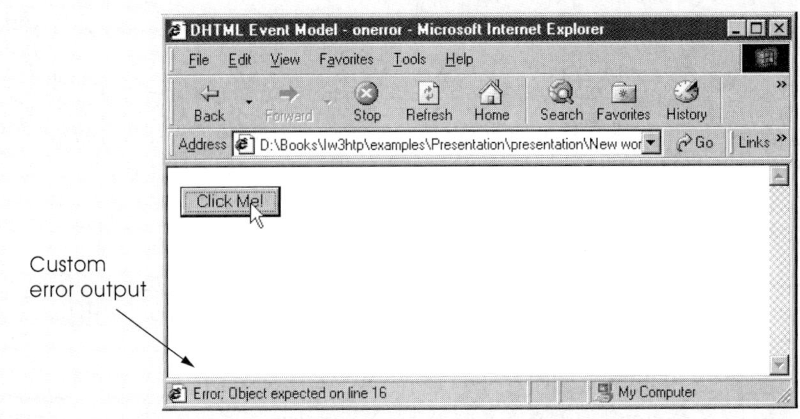

Fig. 16.3 Handling script errors by handling an **ONERROR** event (part 2 of 2).

Line 13

```
window.onerror = handleError;
```

indicates that function **handleError** is to execute when an **ONERROR** event is triggered in the **window** object.

The misspelled function name (**alrrt**) in line 16

```
alrrt( "hi" );
```

intentionally creates an error; the code in line 13 then calls the **handleError** function.

The function definition beginning in line 21

```
function handleError( errType, errURL, errLineNum ) {
```

accepts three parameters from the **ONERROR** event, which is one of the few events that passes parameters to an event handler. The parameters are the type of error that occurred, the URL of the file that had the error, and the line number on which the error occurred.

In lines 24 and 25

```
window.status = "Error: " + errType + " on line " +
   errLineNum;
```

we use the parameters passed to the function by **ONERROR** to write information about the scripting error to the status bar at the bottom of the browser window (Fig. 16.3). This mechanism provides a neat way of handling errors without confusing users browsing your site.

Line 28

```
return true;
```

returns **true** to the event handler, stopping the browser's default response (the intrusive dialog box we choose to avoid). Error handling is useful because of the diversity of browser software available on the Web—chances are that if you are using an advanced feature of

JavaScript, there will be some browsers that cannot view your site properly. If a browser triggers an **ONERROR** event, you could then give the user a custom message such as "Your browser does not support some features on this site. It may not render properly."

Software Engineering Observation 16.1

Use error handling on your Web site to prevent incompatible browsers from complaining about scripts they cannot process.

16.5 Tracking the Mouse with Event ONMOUSEMOVE

Event **ONMOUSEMOVE** fires constantly whenever the mouse is in motion. In Fig. 16.4 we use this event to update a coordinate display that gives the position of the mouse in the coordinate system of the object containing the mouse cursor.

Our event handling in this example occurs in lines 12 and 13

```
coordinates.innerText = event.srcElement.tagName +
   " (" + event.offsetX + ", " + event.offsetY + ")";
```

The **event** object (line 12) contains much information about the triggered event. Property **srcElement** is a pointer to the element object that triggered the event. We use this pointer to access the name (**tagName**) of the element and display it in the **innerText** (line 12) of **coordinates** (line 21).

```
1  <!DOCTYPE html PUBLIC "-//W3C//DTD HTML 4.0 Transitional//EN">
2  <HTML>
3
4  <!-- Fig 16.4: onmousemove.html          -->
5  <!-- Demonstrating the ONMOUSEMOVE event -->
6
7  <HEAD>
8  <TITLE>DHTML Event Model - ONMOUSEMOVE event</TITLE>
9  <SCRIPT LANGUAGE = "JavaScript">
10    function updateMouseCoordinates()
11    {
12          coordinates.innerText = event.srcElement.tagName +
13             " (" + event.offsetX + ", " + event.offsetY + ")";
14    }
15
16 </SCRIPT>
17 </HEAD>
18
19 <BODY ONMOUSEMOVE = "updateMouseCoordinates()">
20
21 <SPAN ID = "coordinates">(0, 0)</SPAN><BR>
22 <IMG SRC = "deitel.gif" STYLE = "position: absolute; top: 100;
23    left: 100">
24
25 </BODY>
26 </HTML>
```

Fig. 16.4 Demonstrating the **ONMOUSEMOVE** event (part 1 of 2).

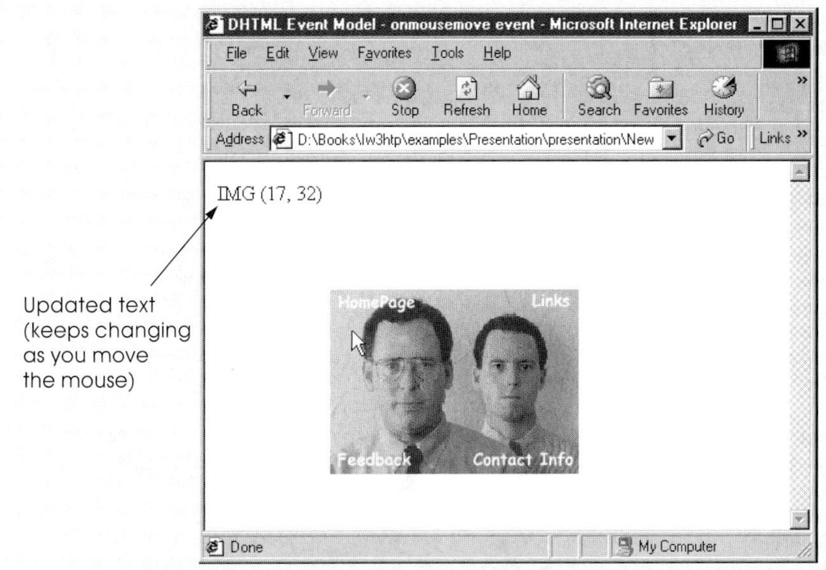

Fig. 16.4 Demonstrating the **ONMOUSEMOVE** event (part 2 of 2).

The **offsetX** and **offsetY** properties of the **event** object give the location of the mouse cursor relative to the top-left corner of the object on which the event was triggered. Notice that when you move the cursor over the image, the coordinate display changes to the image's coordinate system. This is because it is now the image over which the **ONMOUSEMOVE** event is being triggered. Figure 16.5 is a table of 14 of the 28 properties of the **event** object.

Property of event	Description
altkey	This value is **true** if *ALT* key was pressed when event fired.
button	Returns which mouse button was pressed by user (1: left- mouse button, 2: right-mouse button, 3: left and right buttons, 4: middle button, 5: left and middle buttons, 6: right and middle, 7: all three buttons).
cancelBubble	Set to **false** to prevent this event from bubbling.
clientX / **clientY**	The coordinates of the mouse cursor inside the client area (i.e., the active area where the Web page is displayed, excluding scrollbars, navigation buttons, etc.).
ctrlKey	This value is **true** if *CTRL* key was pressed when event fired.
offsetX / **offsetY**	The coordinates of the mouse cursor relative to the object that fired the event.
propertyName	The name of the property that changed in this event.
recordset	A reference to a datafield's recordset (see Chapter 18, "Data Binding").

Fig. 16.5 Properties of the **event** object (part 1 of 2).

Property of event	Description
returnValue	Set to **false** to cancel the default browser action.
screenX / **screenY**	The coordinates of the mouse cursor on the screen coordinate system.
shiftKey	This value is **true** if *Shift* key was pressed when event fired.
srcElement	A reference to the object that fired the event.
type	The name of the event that fired.
x / **y**	The coordinates of the mouse cursor relative to this element's parent element.

Fig. 16.5 Properties of the **event** object (part 2 of 2).

The properties of the **event** object contain much information any events that occur on your page, and are easily used to create Web pages that are truly dynamic and responsive to the user.

16.6 Rollovers with ONMOUSEOVER and ONMOUSEOUT

Two more events fired by mouse movement are ***ONMOUSEOVER*** and ***ONMOUSEOUT***. When the mouse cursor moves over an element, **ONMOUSEOVER** is fired for that element. When the mouse cursor leaves the element, the **ONMOUSEOUT** event is fired. Figure 16.6 uses these events to achieve a *rollover effect* that updates text when the mouse cursor moves over that text. We also introduce a technique for creating rollover images.

```
<!DOCTYPE html PUBLIC "-//W3C//DTD HTML 4.0 Transitional//EN">
<HTML>

<!-- Fig 16.6: onmouseoverout.html      -->
<!-- Events ONMOUSEOVER and ONMOUSEOUT -->

<HEAD>
<TITLE>DHTML Event Model - ONMOUSEOVER and ONMOUSEOUT</TITLE>
<SCRIPT LANGUAGE = "JavaScript">

   captionImage1 = new Image();
   captionImage1.src = "caption1.gif";
   captionImage2 = new Image();
   captionImage2.src = "caption2.gif";

   function mOver()
   {
      if ( event.srcElement.id == "tableCaption" ) {
         event.srcElement.src = captionImage2.src;
         return;
      }

```

Fig. 16.6 Events **ONMOUSEOVER** and **ONMOUSEOUT**.

```
         // If the element which triggered ONMOUSEOVER has an ID,
         // Change its color to its ID.
         if ( event.srcElement.id )
            event.srcElement.style.color = event.srcElement.id;
      }

      function mOut()
      {
         if ( event.srcElement.id == "tableCaption" ) {
            event.srcElement.src = captionImage1.src;
            return;
         }

         // If it has an ID, change the text inside to the text of
         // the ID.
         if ( event.srcElement.id )
            event.srcElement.innerText = event.srcElement.id;
      }

      document.onmouseover = mOver;
      document.onmouseout = mOut;

   </SCRIPT>
   </HEAD>

   <BODY STYLE = "background-color: wheat">

   <H1>Guess the Hex Code's Actual Color</H1>

   <P>Can you tell a color from its hexadecimal RGB code value?
   Look at the hex code, guess the color. To see what color it
   corresponds to, move the mouse over the hex code. Moving the
   mouse out will display the color name.</P>

   <TABLE STYLE = "width: 50%; border-style: groove;
      text-align: center; font-family: monospace;
      font-weight: bold">

      <CAPTION>
         <IMG SRC = "caption1.gif" ID = "tableCaption">
      </CAPTION>

      <TR>
         <TD><A ID = "Black">#000000</A>
         <TD><A ID = "Blue">#0000FF</A>
         <TD><A ID = "Magenta">#FF00FF</A>
         <TD><A ID = "Gray">#808080</A>
      </TR>
      <TR>
         <TD><A ID = "Green">#008000</A>
         <TD><A ID = "Lime">#00FF00</A>
         <TD><A ID = "Maroon">#800000</A>
```

Fig. 16.6 Events **ONMOUSEOVER** and **ONMOUSEOUT**.

```
75         <TD><A ID = "Navy">#000080</A>
76      </TR>
77      <TR>
78         <TD><A ID = "Olive">#808000</A>
79         <TD><A ID = "Purple">#800080</A>
80         <TD><A ID = "Red">#FF0000</A>
81         <TD><A ID = "Silver">#C0C0C0</A>
82      </TR>
83      <TR>
84         <TD><A ID = "Cyan">#00FFFF</A>
85         <TD><A ID = "Teal">#008080</A>
86         <TD><A ID = "Yellow">#FFFF00</A>
87         <TD><A ID = "White">#FFFFFF</A>
88      <TR>
89   </TABLE>
90
91   </BODY>
92   </HTML>
```

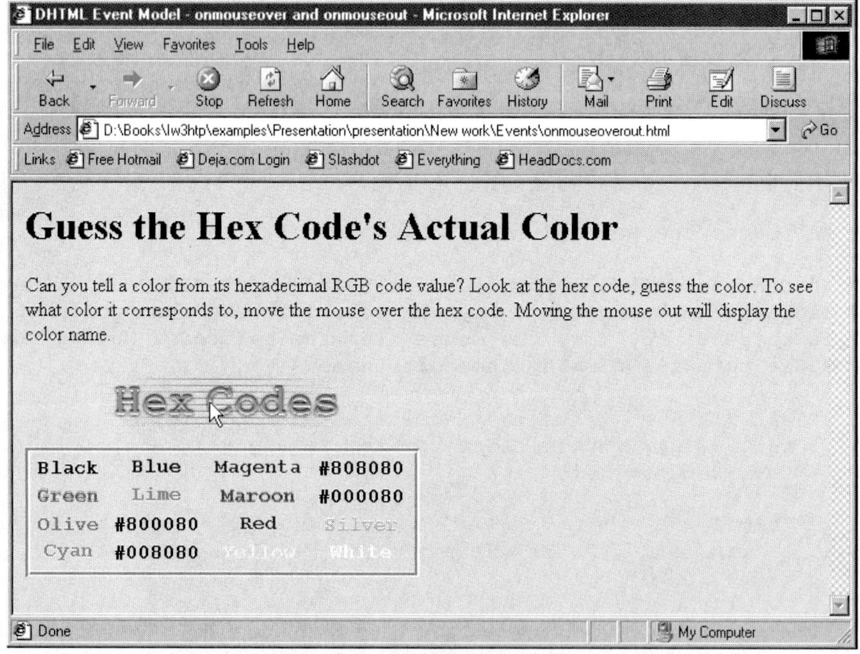

Fig. 16.6 Events **ONMOUSEOVER** and **ONMOUSEOUT**.

To create a rollover effect for the image in the table caption, lines 11 through 14

```
captionImage1 = new Image();
captionImage1.src = "caption1.gif";
captionImage2 = new Image();
captionImage2.src = "caption2.gif";
```

create two new JavaScript **Image** objects—**captionImage1** and **captionImage2**. The image **captionImage2** will be displayed when the mouse is hovering over the image. The image **captionImage1** is displayed when the mouse is not over the image. We set the **src** properties of the **Image** objects to the two images we are using (lines 12 and 14). Creating **Image** objects allows us to pre-load the desired images—if we had not done this, then the browser would only begin to download the rollover image once we moved the mouse over the image. If the image is large or the connection is slow, this causes a noticeable delay in the image update.

Lines 18 through 21 in the **mOver** function

```
if ( event.srcElement.id == "tableCaption" ) {
   event.srcElement.src = captionImage2.src;
   return;
}
```

handle the **ONMOUSEOVER** event for the image by setting its **SRC** attribute (**event.srcElement.src**) to the **src** property of the appropriate **Image** object (**captionImage2.src**). The same task is performed with the **captionImage1** object in the **mOut** function (lines 31 through 34).

We handle the **ONMOUSEOVER** event for the table cells in lines 25 and 26

```
if ( event.srcElement.id )
   event.srcElement.style.color = event.srcElement.id;
```

As mentioned earlier, the **event** object contains much information about the triggered event. In particular, the **id** property of the **srcElement** object is the **ID** attribute of that element. This code checks whether an **ID** is specified, and if it is, the code changes the color of the element to match the color name in the **ID**. As you can see in the code for the table (lines 57 through 89), each **ID** is one of the 16 basic HTML colors.

Lines 38 and 39

```
if ( event.srcElement.id )
   event.srcElement.innerText = event.srcElement.id;
```

handle the **ONMOUSEOUT** event by changing the text in the table cell the cursor just left to match the color that it represents.

16.7 Form Processing with ONFOCUS and ONBLUR

The **ONFOCUS** and **ONBLUR** events are particularly useful when dealing with forms (Fig. 16.7).

```
<!DOCTYPE html PUBLIC "-//W3C//DTD HTML 4.0 Transitional//EN">
<HTML>

<!-- Fig 16.7: onfocusblur.html                    -->
<!-- Demonstrating the ONFOCUS and ONBLUR events   -->

```

Fig. 16.7 Events **ONFOCUS** and **ONBLUR** (part 1 of 3)

```
<HEAD>
<TITLE>DHTML Event Model - ONFOCUS and ONBLUR</TITLE>
<SCRIPT LANGUAGE = "JavaScript">

   var helpArray = [ "Enter your name in this input box.",
                    "Enter your email address in this input box, \
                     in the format user@domain.",
                    "Check this box if you liked our site.",
                    "In this box, enter any comments you would \
                     like us to read.",
                    "This button submits the form to the \
                     server-side script",
                    "This button clears the form",
                    "This TEXTAREA provides context-sensitive \
                     help. Click on any input field or use the \
                     TAB key to get more information about the \
                     input field." ];

   function helpText( messageNum )
   {
      myForm.helpBox.value = helpArray[ messageNum ];
   }
</SCRIPT>
</HEAD>

<BODY>

<FORM ID = "myForm">
Name: <INPUT TYPE = "text" NAME = "name"
   ONFOCUS = "helpText(0)" ONBLUR = "helpText(6)"><BR>
Email: <INPUT TYPE = "text" NAME = "email"
   ONFOCUS = "helpText(1)" ONBLUR = "helpText(6)"><BR>
Click here if you like this site
<INPUT TYPE = "checkbox" NAME = "like" ONFOCUS = "helpText(2)"
   ONBLUR = "helpText(6)"><BR><HR>

Any comments?<BR>
<TEXTAREA NAME = "comments" ROWS = 5 COLS = 45 ONFOCUS =
   "helpText(3)" ONBLUR = "helpText(6)"></TEXTAREA><BR>
<INPUT TYPE = "submit" VALUE = "Submit" ONFOCUS = "helpText(4)"
   ONBLUR = "helpText(6)">
<INPUT TYPE = "reset" VALUE = "Reset" ONFOCUS = "helpText(5)"
   ONBLUR = "helpText(6)">

<TEXTAREA NAME = "helpBox" STYLE = "position: absolute;
   right: 0; top: 0" ROWS = 4 COLS = 45>
This TEXTAREA provides context-sensitive help. Click on any
input field or use the TAB key to get more information about the
input field.</TEXTAREA>
</FORM>

</BODY>
</HTML>
```

Fig. 16.7 Events **ONFOCUS** and **ONBLUR** (part 2 of 3)

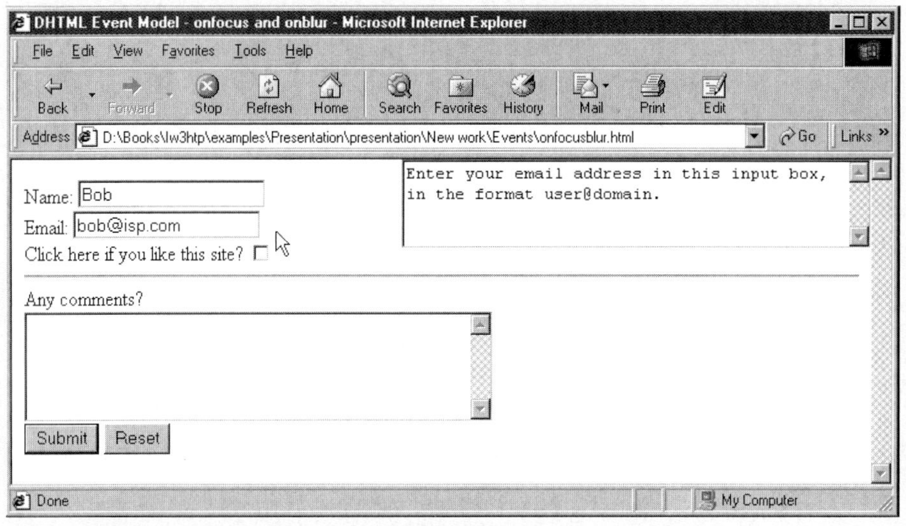

Fig. 16.7 Events **ONFOCUS** and **ONBLUR** (part 3 of 3)

The **ONFOCUS** event fires when an element gains focus (i.e., when the user clicks on a form field or when the user uses the *Tab* key to highlight the element) and **ONBLUR** fires when an element loses focus. In line 27 of function **helpText**

```
myForm.helpBox.value = helpArray[ messageNum ];
```

we see that the function simply changes the text inside the text box in the upper-right corner based on the **messageNum** passed to it. The elements of the form, for example on lines 35 and 36

```
Name: <INPUT TYPE = "text" NAME = "name"
   ONFOCUS = "helpText(0)" ONBLUR = "helpText(6)"><BR>
```

each pass a different value to the **helpText** function when they gain focus and the **ONFOCUS** event is fired. When elements lose focus, they all pass the value 6 to **helpText** so that the default message ("**This TEXTAREA provides context-sensitive help. Click on any**...") is displayed in **helpBox**. In this way, there is constantly a message in the help box—if the user clicks elsewhere on the page without specifically focusing on another form field, the default message is displayed again.

16.8 More Form Processing with ONSUBMIT and ONRESET

Two more functions that are useful for dealing with forms are **ONSUBMIT** and **ONRESET**. These events fire when a form is submitted or reset, respectively (Fig. 16.8).

Line 31

```
window.event.returnValue = false;
```

Setting the **returnValue** property to **false** cancels the default action of the event on the element, which in this case is for the browser to submit the form.

```
<!DOCTYPE html PUBLIC "-//W3C//DTD HTML 4.0 Transitional//EN">
<HTML>

<!-- Fig 16.8: onsubmitreset.html                          -->
<!-- Demonstrating the ONSUBMIT and ONRESET events -->

<HEAD>
<TITLE>DHTML Event Model - ONSUBMIT and ONRESET events</TITLE>
<SCRIPT LANGUAGE = "JavaScript">

   var helpArray = [ "Enter your name in this input box.",
                     "Enter your email address in this input box, \
                      in the format user@domain.",
                     "Check this box if you liked our site.",
                     "In this box, enter any comments you would \
                      like us to read.",
                     "This button submits the form to the \
                      server-side script",
                     "This button clears the form",
                     "This TEXTAREA provides context-sensitive \
                      help. Click on any input field or use the \
                      TAB key to get more information about the \
                      input field." ];

   function helpText( messageNum )
   {
      myForm.helpBox.value = helpArray[ messageNum ];
   }

   function formSubmit() {
      window.event.returnValue = false;

      if ( confirm ( "Are you sure you want to submit?" ) )
         window.event.returnValue = true;
   }

   function formReset() {
      window.event.returnValue = false;

      if ( confirm ( "Are you sure you want to reset?" ) )
         window.event.returnValue = true;
   }

</SCRIPT>
</HEAD>

<BODY>

<FORM ID = "myForm" ONSUBMIT = "formSubmit()"
   ONRESET = "formReset()">
Name: <INPUT TYPE = "text" NAME = "name" ONFOCUS =  "helpText(0)"
   ONBLUR = "helpText(6)"><BR>
```

Fig. 16.8 Events **ONSUBMIT** and **ONRESET** (part 1 of 2)

```
53 Email: <INPUT TYPE = "text" NAME = "email"
54    ONFOCUS = "helpText(1)" ONBLUR = "helpText(6)"><BR>
55 Click here if you like this site
56 <INPUT TYPE = "checkbox" NAME = "like" ONFOCUS = "helpText(2)"
57    ONBLUR = "helpText(6)"><HR>
58
59 Any comments?<BR>
60 <TEXTAREA NAME = "comments" ROWS = 5 COLS = 45
61    ONFOCUS = "helpText(3)" ONBLUR = "helpText(6)"></TEXTAREA><BR>
62 <INPUT TYPE = "submit" VALUE = "Submit" ONFOCUS = "helpText(4)"
63    ONBLUR = "helpText(6)">
64 <INPUT TYPE = "reset" VALUE = "Reset" ONFOCUS = "helpText(5)"
65    ONBLUR = "helpText(6)">
66
67 <TEXTAREA NAME = "helpBox" STYLE = "position: absolute; right:0;
68    top: 0" ROWS = 4 COLS = 45>
69 This TEXTAREA provides context-sensitive help. Click on any
70 input field or use the TAB key to get more information about the
71 input field.</TEXTAREA>
72 </FORM>
73
74 </BODY>
75 </HTML>
```

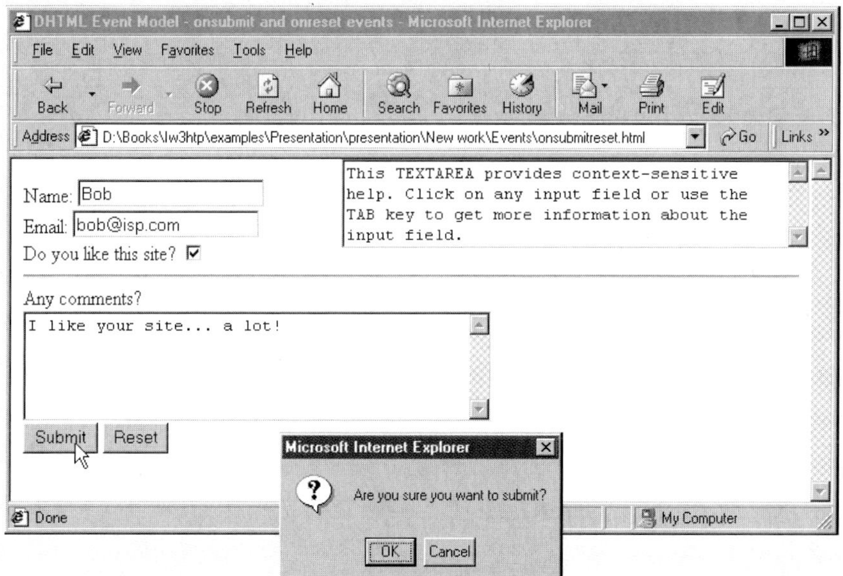

Fig. 16.8 Events **ONSUBMIT** and **ONRESET** (part 2 of 2)

Line 33

```
if ( confirm ( "Are you sure you want to submit?" ) )
```

pops up a dialog box asking the user a question. If the user clicks **OK**, function **confirm** returns **true**. If the user clicks **Cancel**, **confirm** returns **false**.

Based on this information, line 34

```
window.event.returnValue = true;
```

sets the **returnValue** back to **true**, since the user has confirmed that the form should indeed be submitted (based on the **if** statement on line 33, which executes line 34 if the user clicks **OK**).

16.9 Event Bubbling

Event bubbling, a crucial part of the event model, is the process whereby events fired in child elements also "bubble" up to their parent elements for handling. If you intend to handle an event in a child element, you might need to cancel the bubbling of that event in that child element's event-handling code using the **cancelBubble** property of the **event** object, as shown in Fig. 16.9.

```
<!DOCTYPE html PUBLIC "-//W3C//DTD HTML 4.0 Transitional//EN">
<HTML>

<!-- Fig 16.9: bubbling.html  -->
<!-- Disabling event bubbling -->

<HEAD>
<TITLE>DHTML Event Model - Event Bubbling</TITLE>

<SCRIPT LANGUAGE = "JavaScript">
   function documentClick()
   {
      alert( "You clicked in the document" );
   }

   function paragraphClick( value )
   {
      alert( "You clicked the text" );
      if ( value )
         event.cancelBubble = true;
   }

   document.onclick = documentClick;
</SCRIPT>
</HEAD>

<BODY>

<P ONCLICK = "paragraphClick( false )">Click here!</P>
<P ONCLICK = "paragraphClick( true )">Click here, too!</P>
</BODY>
</HTML>
```

Fig. 16.9 Event bubbling (part 1 of 2).

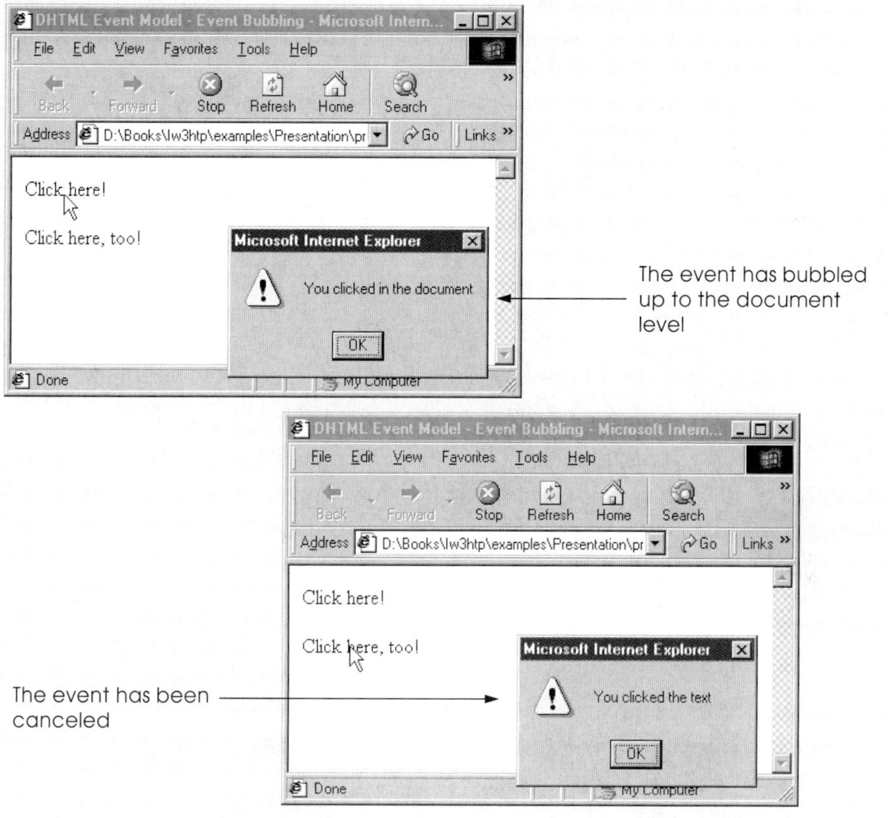

Fig. 16.9 Event bubbling (part 2 of 2).

Common Programming Error 16.1

Forgetting to cancel event bubbling when necessary may cause unexpected results in your scripts.

As we see, clicking on the first **P** element (line 29) first triggers the statement

```
ONCLICK = paragraphClick( false )
```

then also triggers the

```
document.onclick = documentClick
```

statement in line 23, since the **ONCLICK** event has bubbled up to the document level. This is probably not the desired result. However, clicking on the second **P** element (line 30) passes a value of **true** to function **paragraphClick**, so that the **if** statement on line 19 executes line 20

```
event.cancelBubble = true;
```

which disables the event bubbling for this event by setting the **cancelBubble** property of the **event** object to **true**.

16.10 More DHTML Events

The events we covered in this chapter are among the most common in use. The remaining DHTML events and their descriptions are listed in Fig. 16.10.

Event	Description
Clipboard events	
ONBEFORECUT	Fires before a selection is cut to the clipboard.
ONBEFORECOPY	Fires before a selection is copied to the clipboard.
ONBEFOREPASTE	Fires before a selection is pasted from the clipboard.
ONCOPY	Fires when a selection is copied to the clipboard.
ONCUT	Fires when a selection is cut to the clipboard.
ONABORT	Fires if image transfer has been interrupted by user.
ONPASTE	Fires when a selection is pasted from the clipboard.
Data binding events	
ONAFTERUPDATE	Fires immediately after a databound object has been updated.
ONBEFOREUPDATE	Fires before a data source is updated.
ONCELLCHANGE	Fires when a data source has changed.
ONDATAAVAILABLE	Fires when new data from a data source become available.
ONDATASETCHANGED	Fires when content at a data source has changed.
ONDATASETCOMPLETE	Fires when transfer of data from the data source has completed.
ONERRORUPDATE	Fires if an error occurs while updating a data field.
ONROWENTER	Fires when a new row of data from the data source is available.
ONROWEXIT	Fires when a row of data from the data source has just finished.
ONROWSDELETE	Fires when a row of data from the data source is deleted.
ONROWSINSERTED	Fires when a row of data from the data source is inserted.
Keyboard Events	
ONHELP	Fires when the user initiates help (i.e., by pressing the *F1* key).
ONKEYDOWN	Fires when the user pushes down a key.
ONKEYPRESS	Fires when the user presses a key.
ONKEYUP	Fires when the user ends a keypress.

Fig. 16.10 Dynamic HTML events (part 1 of 3).

Event	Description
MARQUEE *Events*	
ONBOUNCE	Fires when a scrolling **MARQUEE** bounces back in the other direction.
ONFINISH	Fires when a **MARQUEE** finishes its scrolling.
ONSTART	Fires when a **MARQUEE** begins a new loop.
Mouse events	
ONCONTEXTMENU	Fires when the context menu is shown (right-click).
ONDBLCLICK	Fires when the mouse is double-clicked.
ONDRAG	Fires during a mouse drag.
ONDRAGEND	Fires when a mouse drag ends.
ONDRAGENTER	Fires when something is dragged onto an area.
ONDRAGLEAVE	Fires when something is dragged out of an area.
ONDRAGOVER	Fires when a drag is held over an area.
ONDRAGSTART	Fires when a mouse drag begins.
ONDROP	Fires when a mouse button is released over a valid target during a drag.
ONMOUSEDOWN	Fires when a mouse button is pressed down.
ONMOUSEUP	Fires when a mouse button is released.
Miscellaneous Events	
ONAFTERPRINT	Fires immediately after the document prints.
ONBEFOREEDITFOCUS	Fires before an element gains focus for editing.
ONBEFOREPRINT	Fires before a document is printed.
ONBEFOREUNLOAD	Fires before a document is unloaded (i.e., the window was closed or a link was clicked).
ONCHANGE	Fires when a new choice is made in a **SELECT** element, or when a text input is changed and the element loses focus.
ONFILTERCHANGE	Fires when a filter changes properties or finishes a transition (see Chapter 17, Filters and Transitions).
ONLOSECAPTURE	Fires when the **releaseCapture** method is invoked.
ONPROPERTYCHANGE	Fires when the property of an object is changed.
ONREADYSTATECHANGE	Fires when the **readyState** property of an element changes.
ONRESET	Fires when a form resets (i.e., the user clicks an **<INPUT TYPE = "reset">**).

Fig. 16.10 Dynamic HTML events (part 2 of 3).

Event	Description
ONRESIZE	Fires when the size of an object changes (i.e., the user resizes a window or frame).
ONSCROLL	Fires when a window or frame is scrolled.
ONSELECT	Fires when a text selection begins (applies to **INPUT** or **TEXTAREA**).
ONSELECTSTART	Fires when the object is selected.
ONSTOP	Fires when the user stops loading the object.
ONUNLOAD	Fires when a page is about to unload.

Fig. 16.10 Dynamic HTML events (part 3 of 3).

SUMMARY

- The event model exists so that scripts can respond to user actions and change the page accordingly. This makes Web applications more responsive and user-friendly, and can lessen server load greatly if applied correctly.
- With the event model, scripts can respond to a user moving the mouse, scrolling up or down the screen or entering keystrokes. Content becomes more dynamic and interfaces become more intuitive.
- One of the most common events is **ONCLICK**. When the user clicks the mouse, **ONCLICK** fires.
- The **FOR** attribute of the **SCRIPT** element specifies an element by its **ID** attribute. When the event specified in the **EVENT** attribute occurs for the element with **ID** specified in the **FOR** attribute, the designated script runs.
- Specifying an event as an HTML attribute allows you to insert script directly into your HTML code. Inline scripting is usually used to pass a certain value to a event handler based on the element that was clicked.
- The **ONLOAD** event fires whenever an element finishes loading successfully, and is often used in the **BODY** tag to initiate scripts as soon as the page has been loaded into the client.
- You can use the **ONERROR** event to write error-handling code.
- The syntax **window.onerror** = *functionName* says that *functionName* will run if the **ONERROR** event is triggered in the **window** object.
- Event handlers can accept three parameters from the **ONERROR** event (one of the few events that passes parameters to an event handler). The **ONERROR** event passes the type of error that occurred, the URL of the file that had the error and the line number on which the error occurred.
- Returning a value of **true** in an error handler stops the browser's default response (the intrusive dialog box).
- Writing a function to ignore other script errors is not a good idea—try writing scripts that will adjust or stop their actions if an error in loading the page has been detected.
- Event **ONMOUSEMOVE** fires constantly whenever the mouse is in motion.
- The **event** object contains much information about the triggered event.
- Property **srcElement** of the event **object** is a pointer to the element that triggered the event.
- The **offsetX** and **offsetY** properties of the **event** object give the location of the cursor relative to the top-left corner of the object on which the event was triggered.

- Notice that when you move the mouse cursor over an element like an image, the **offsetX** and **offsetY** properties change to that element's coordinate system. This is because it is now the element over which the **ONMOUSEMOVE** is being triggered.
- Whenever the mouse cursor moves over an element, it fires event **ONMOUSEOVER** for that element. Once the mouse cursor leaves the element, an **ONMOUSEOUT** event is fired.
- The **id** property of the **srcElement** object is the **ID** attribute of that element.
- Events **ONFOCUS** and **ONBLUR** fire when an element gains or loses focus, respectively.
- The events **ONSUBMIT** and **ONRESET** fire when a form is submitted or reset, respectively.
- The code **window.event.returnValue = false** cancels the default browser action.
- Event bubbling, a crucial part of the event model, is the process whereby events fired in child elements also "bubble" up to their parent elements for handling. If you intend to handle an event in a child element, you might need to cancel the bubbling of that event in that child element's event-handling code using the **cancelBubble** property of the **event** object.

TERMINOLOGY

alert dialog box
altKey property of **event** object
button property of **event** object
cancelBubble property of **event** object
clientX property of **event** object
clientY property of **event** object
confirm method of **window** object
ctrlKey property of **event** object
cursor (of the mouse)
Dynamic HTML event model
EVENT attribute of **SCRIPT** element
event bubbling
event handler
event model
event object (property of the **window** object)
events in DHTML
fire an event
FOR attribute of **SCRIPT** element
innerText property of an HTML element
keyboard events
mouse cursor
mouse events
offsetX property of **event** object
offsetY property of **event** object
ONAFTERPRINT event
ONAFTERUPDATE event
ONBEFORECOPY event
ONBEFORECUT event
ONBEFOREEDITFOCUS event
ONBEFOREPASTE event
ONBEFOREPRINT event
ONBEFOREUNLOAD event
ONBEFOREUPDATE event
ONBLUR event
ONBOUNCE event
ONCELLCHANGE event
ONCHANGE event
ONCLICK event
ONCONTEXTMENU event
ONCOPY event
ONCUT event
ONDATAAVAILABLE event
ONDATASETCHANGED event
ONDATASETCOMPLETE event
ONDBLCLICK event
ONDRAG event
ONDRAGEND event
ONDRAGENTER event
ONDRAGLEAVE event
ONDRAGOVER event
ONDRAGSTART event
ONDROP event
ONERRORUPDATE event
ONFINISH event
ONFOCUS event
ONHELP event
ONKEYDOWN event
ONKEYPRESS event
ONKEYUP event
ONLOAD event
ONLOSECAPTURE event
ONMOUSEDOWN event
ONMOUSEMOVE event
ONMOUSEOUT event
ONMOUSEOVER event
ONMOUSEUP event

ONPASTE event
ONPROPERTYCHANGE event
ONREADYSTATECHANGE event
ONRESET event
ONRESIZE event
ONROWEXIT event
ONROWSDELETE event
ONROWSINSERTED event
ONSCROLL event
ONSELECT event
ONSELECTSTART event
ONSTART event
ONSTOP event
ONSUBMIT event
ONUNLOAD event
position of the mouse cursor
propertyName property of **event** object
recordset property of **event** object
returnValue property of **event**
screenX property of event
screenY property of event
setInterval method of **window** object
shiftkey property of **event**
srcElement property of **event**
status bar at bottom of a window
status property of **window** object
Tab key to switch between fields on a form
tagName property of **event** object
trigger an event
type property of event
x property of **event** object
y property of **event** object

COMMON PROGRAMMING ERROR

16.1 Forgetting to cancel event bubbling when necessary may cause unexpected results in your scripts.

SOFTWARE ENGINEERING OBSERVATION

16.1 Use error handling on your Web site to prevent incompatible browsers from complaining about scripts they cannot process.

SELF-REVIEW EXERCISES

16.1 Fill in the blanks in each of the following:

a) The state of three special keys can be retrieved using the **event** object. These keys are ________, ________ and ________.

b) If a child element does not handle an event, ________ ________ lets the event rise through the object hierarchy handling.

c) Using the ________ property of the **SCRIPT** element allows you to specify to which element the script applies.

d) The ________ property of the **event** object specifies whether to continue bubbling the current event.

e) Setting **window.returnValue** to ________ cancels the default browser action for the event.

f) The reference for the **ID** of an element that fired an event (using the **event** object) is ________.

g) The ________ event will fire when an image finished loading.

h) Three events that fire when the user clicks the mouse are ________, ________ and ________.

ANSWERS TO SELF-REVIEW EXERCISES

16.1 *Ctrl*, *Alt* and *Shift*. b) event bubbling. c) **FOR**. d) **returnValue**. e) false. f) **event.srcElement.id**. g) **ONCLICK**, **ONMOUSEDOWN**, h) **ONMOUSEUP**.

EXERCISES

16.2 Write an error handler that changes the **ALT** text of an image to "Error Loading" if the image loading is not completed.

16.3 You have a server-side script that cannot handle any ampersands (**&**) in the form data. Write a function that converts all ampersands in a form field to "and" when the field loses focus (**ONBLUR**).

16.4 Write a function that responds to a click anywhere on the page by displaying with **alert()** the event name if the user held *Shift* during the mouse click, or the name of the element that triggered the event if the user held *Ctrl* during the mouse click.

16.5 Use CSS absolute positioning, **ONMOUSEMOVE** and **event.x**/**event.y** to have a sentence of text follow the mouse as the user moves the mouse over the Web page. Disable this feature if the user double-clicks (**ONDBLCLICK**).

16.6 Modify Exercise 16.5 to have an image follow the mouse as the user moves the mouse over the Web page.

17

Dynamic HTML: Filters and Transitions

Objectives

- To use filters to achieve special effects.
- To combine filters to achieve an even greater variety of special effects.
- To be able to create animated visual transitions between Web pages.
- To be able to modify filters dynamically using DHTML.

Between the motion and the act falls the shadow.
Thomas Stearns Eliot, *The Hollow Men*

...as through a filter, before the clear product emerges.
F. Scott Fitzgerald

There is strong shadow where there is much light.
Johann Wolfgang von Goethe

When all things are equal, translucence in writing is more effective than transparency, just as glow is more revealing than glare.
James Thurber

...one should disdain the superficial and let the true beauty of one's soul shine through.
Fran Lebowitz

Modernity exists in the form of a desire to wipe out whatever came earlier, in the hope of reaching at least a point that could be called a true present, a point of origin that marks a new departure.
Paul de Man

Outline

17.1 Introduction

Just a few years back it was not realistic to offer the kinds of dramatic visual effects you will see in this chapter because desktop processing power was insufficient. Today with powerful processors, these visual effects are realizable without delays. Just as you expect to see dramatic visual effects on TV weather reports, Web users appreciate visual effects when browsing Web pages.

In the past, achieving these kinds of effects, if you could get them at all, demanded frequent trips back and forth to the server. With the consequent delays, the beauty of the effects was lost.

Performance Tip 17.1

With Dynamic HTML, many visual effects are implemented directly in the client-side browser (Internet Explorer 5 for this book), so no server-side processing delays are incurred. The DHTML code that initiates these effects is generally quite small and is coded directly into the HTML Web page.

You will be able to achieve a great variety of effects. You may transition between pages with *random dissolves* and *horizontal and vertical blinds* effects, among others. You can convert colored images to gray in response to user actions; this could be used, for example, to indicate that some option is not currently selectable. You can make letters *glow* for emphasis. You can create *drop shadows* to give text a three-dimensional appearance.

In this chapter we discuss both *filters* and *transitions*. Applying filters to text and images causes changes that are persistent. Transitions are temporary phenomena: applying a transition allows you to transfer from one page to another with a pleasant visual effect such as a random dissolve. Filters and transitions do not add content to your pages—rather, they present existing content in an engaging manner to help hold the user's attention.

Each of the visual effects achievable with filters and transitions is programmable, so these effects may be adjusted dynamically by programs that respond to user-initiated events like mouse clicks and keystrokes. Filters and transitions are so easy to use that virtually any Web page designer or programmer can incorporate these effects with minimal effort.

Look-and-Feel Observation 17.1

Experiment by applying combinations of filters to the same element. You may discover some eye-pleasing effects that are particularly appropriate for your applications.

Part of the beauty of DHTML filters and transitions is that they are built right into Internet Explorer. You do not need to spend time working with sophisticated graphics packages preparing images that will be downloaded (slowly) from servers. When Internet Explorer renders your page, it applies all the special effects and does this while running on the client computer without lengthy waits for files to download from the server.

Look-and-Feel Observation 17.2

DHTML's effects are programmable. They can be applied dynamically to elements of your pages in response to user events such as mouse clicks and keystrokes.

Filters and transitions are included with the *CSS* ***filter*** *property*. They give you the same kind of graphics capabilities you get through presentation software like Microsoft's PowerPoint. You can have new pages or portions of pages fade in and fade out. You can have a page randomly dissolve into the next page. You can make portions of the page transparent or semitransparent so that you can see what is behind them. You can make elements glow for emphasis. You can blur text or an image to give it the illusion of motion. You can create drop shadows on elements to give them a three-dimensional effect. And you can combine effects to generate an even greater variety of effects.

Software Engineering Observation 17.1

Filters and transitions can be applied to block-level elements such as ***DIV*** *or* ***P****, and can only be applied to inline-level elements such as* ***STRONG*** *or* ***EM*** *if the element has its* ***height*** *or* ***width*** *CSS properties set.*

Portability Tip 17.1

Filters and transitions are a Microsoft technology available only in Windows-based versions of Internet Explorer 5. Do not use these capabilities if you are writing for other browsers. If you are writing for an audience with a diversity of browsers and you use DHTML filters and transitions, you should also make alternate provisions.

17.2 Flip filters: `flipv` and `fliph`

The ***flipv*** and ***fliph*** *filters* mirror text or images vertically and horizontally, respectively. In Fig. 17.1 we demonstrate these effects using both filters to flip text.

In line 30

```
<TD STYLE = "filter: fliph">Text</TD>
```

filters are applied in the **STYLE** attribute. The value of the **filter** property is the name of the filter. In this case, the filter is **fliph**, which flips the affected object horizontally.

In line 36

```
<TD STYLE = "filter: flipv fliph">Text</TD>
```

we see that more than one filter can be applied at once. Enter multiple filters as values of the **filter** attribute, separated by spaces. In this case the **flipv** filter is also applied, which flips the affected object vertically.

```
1  <!DOCTYPE html PUBLIC "-//W3C//DTD HTML 4.0 Transitional//EN">
2  <HTML>
3
4  <!-- Fig. 17.1: flip.html   -->
5  <!-- Using the flip filters -->
6
7  <HEAD>
8  <TITLE>The flip filter</TITLE>
9
10 <STYLE TYPE = "text/css">
11    BODY  { background-color: #CCFFCC }
12
13    TABLE { font-size: 3em;
14            font-family: Arial, sans-serif;
15            background-color: #FFCCCC;
16            border-style: ridge ;
17            border-collapse: collapse }
18
19    TD    { border-style: groove;
20            padding: 1ex }
21 </STYLE>
22 </HEAD>
23
24 <BODY>
25
26 <TABLE>
27
28    <TR>
29       <!-- Filters are applied in style declarations -->
30       <TD STYLE = "filter: fliph">Text</TD>
31       <TD>Text</TD>
32    </TR>
33
34    <TR>
35       <!-- More than one filter can be applied at once -->
36       <TD STYLE = "filter: flipv fliph">Text</TD>
37       <TD STYLE = "filter: flipv">Text</TD>
38    </TR>
39
40 </TABLE>
41
42 </BODY>
43 </HTML>
```

Fig. 17.1 Using the **flip** filter (part 1 of 2).

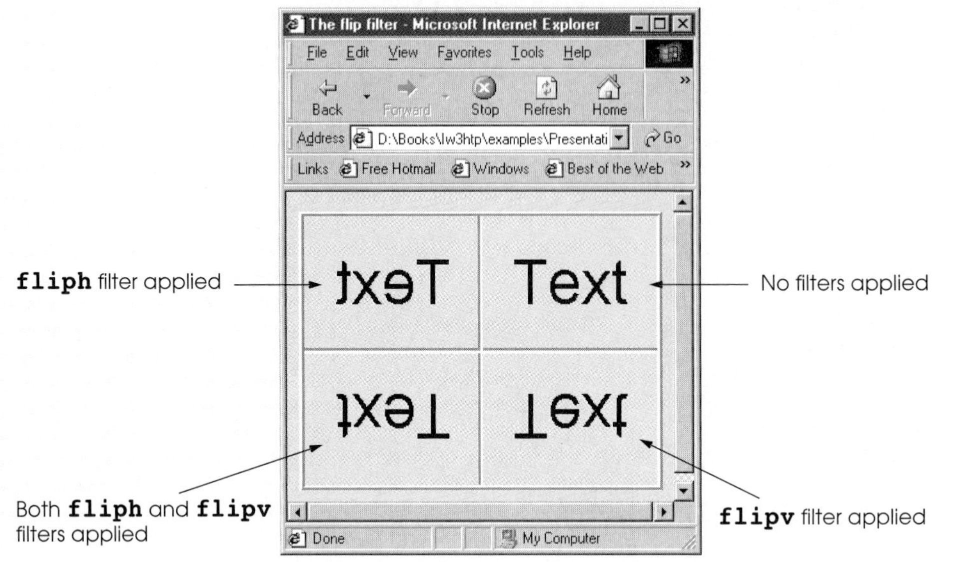

Fig. 17.1 Using the **flip** filter (part 2 of 2).

17.3 Transparency with the chroma Filter

The ***chroma*** *filter* allows you to apply *transparency effects* dynamically, without using a graphics editor to hard-code transparency into the image. However, as we noted in Chapter 5, using transparency on images that have antialiasing often produces unsightly effects. In Fig. 17.2 we alter the transparency of an image using object model scripting, based on a user selection from a **SELECT** element.

```
<!DOCTYPE html PUBLIC "-//W3C//DTD HTML 4.0 Transitional//EN">
<HTML>

<!-- Fig 17.2: chroma.html                                  -->
<!-- Applying transparency using the chroma filter  -->

<HEAD>
<TITLE>Chroma Filter</TITLE>

<SCRIPT LANGUAGE = "JavaScript">

   function changecolor()
   {
      if ( colorSelect.value ) { // if the user selected a color,

         // parse the value to hex and set the filter color.
         chromaImg.filters( "chroma" ).color =
            parseInt( colorSelect.value, 16 );
```

Fig. 17.2 Changing values of the **chroma** filter (part 1 of 2).

```
            chromaImg.filters( "chroma" ).enabled = true;
         }
         else // if the user selected "None",

            // disable the filter.
            chromaImg.filters( "chroma" ).enabled = false;
      }

   </SCRIPT>
   </HEAD>

   <BODY>

   <H1>Chroma Filter:</H1>

   <IMG ID = "chromaImg" SRC = "trans.gif" STYLE =
      "position: absolute; filter: chroma">

   <!-- The ONCHANGE event fires when a selection is changed -->
   <SELECT ID = "colorSelect" ONCHANGE = "changecolor()">
      <OPTION VALUE = "">None
      <OPTION VALUE = "00FFFF">Cyan
      <OPTION VALUE = "FFFF00">Yellow
      <OPTION VALUE = "FF00FF">Magenta
      <OPTION VALUE = "000000" SELECTED>Black
   </SELECT>

   </BODY>
   </HTML>
```

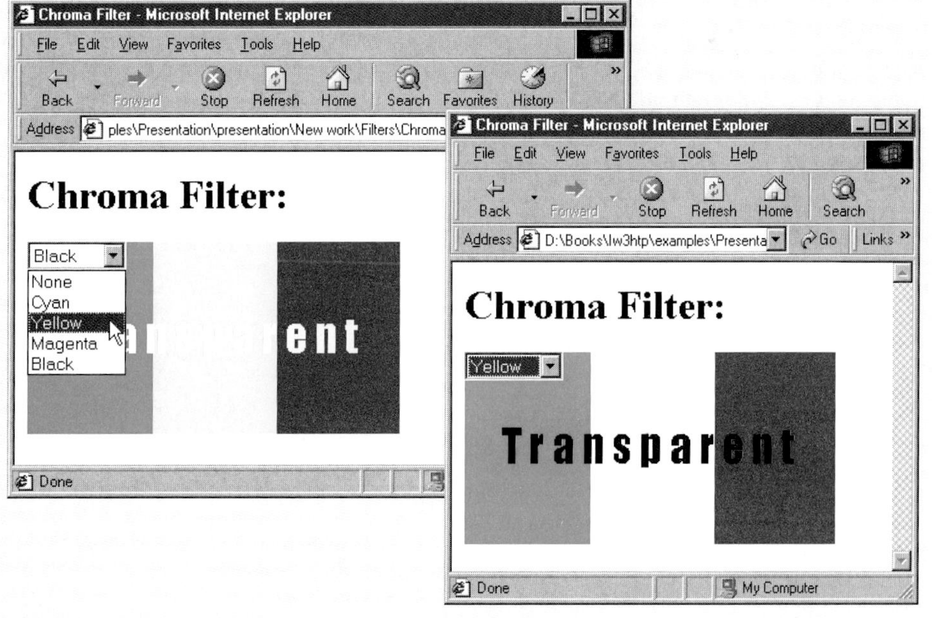

Fig. 17.2 Changing values of the `chroma` filter (part 2 of 2).

In lines 17 and 18

```
chromaImg.filters( "chroma" ).color =
   parseInt( colorSelect.value, 16 );
```

we set the filter properties dynamically using JavaScript. In this case **colorSelect.value**, the value of the **colorSelect** drop-down list (line 38), is a string. We use the **parseInt** function to convert the value to a hexadecimal integer for setting the **color** property of the **chroma** filter. The second parameter of **parseInt**, **16** in this case, specifies the base of the integer (base 16 is hexadecimal).

In line 19

```
chromaImg.filters( "chroma" ).enabled = true;
```

we turn on the filter. Each filter has a property named ***enabled***. If this property is set to **true**, the filter is applied. If it is set to **false**, the filter is not applied. So, in line 24

```
chromaImg.filters( "chroma" ).enabled = false;
```

we say that if the user selected **None** (line 39) from the drop-down list, the filter is disabled.

In line 38

```
<SELECT ID = "trSelect" ONCHANGE = "changecolor()">
```

we use a new event, ***ONCHANGE***. This event fires whenever the **VALUE** of a form field changes, which in this case happens whenever the user makes a different selection in the **colorSelect** drop-down list.

17.4 Creating Image masks

Applying the ***mask*** *filter* to an image allows you to create an *image mask*, in which the background of an element is a solid color and the foreground of an element is transparent to the image or color behind it. In Fig. 17.3 we add the **mask** filter to an **H1** element which overlaps an image. The foreground of that **H1** element (the text inside it) is transparent to the image behind it.

```
<!DOCTYPE html PUBLIC "-//W3C//DTD HTML 4.0 Transitional//EN">
<HTML>

<!-- Fig 17.3: mask.html            -->
<!-- Placing a mask over an image -->

<HEAD>
<TITLE>Mask Filter</TITLE>
</HEAD>

<BODY>

<H1>Mask Filter</H1>

```

Fig. 17.3 Using the **mask** filter (part 1 of 2).

```
15 <!-- Filter parameters are specified in parentheses, in   -->
16 <!-- the form param1 = value1, param2 = value2, etc.       -->
17 <DIV STYLE = "position: absolute; top: 125; left: 20;
18    filter: mask( color = #CCFFFF )">
19 <H1 STYLE = "font-family: Courier, monospace">
20 AaBbCcDdEeFfGgHhIiJj<BR>
21 KkLlMmNnOoPpQqRrSsTt
22 </H1>
23 </DIV>
24
25 <IMG SRC = "gradient.gif" WIDTH = "400" HEIGHT = "200">
26 </BODY>
27 </HTML>
```

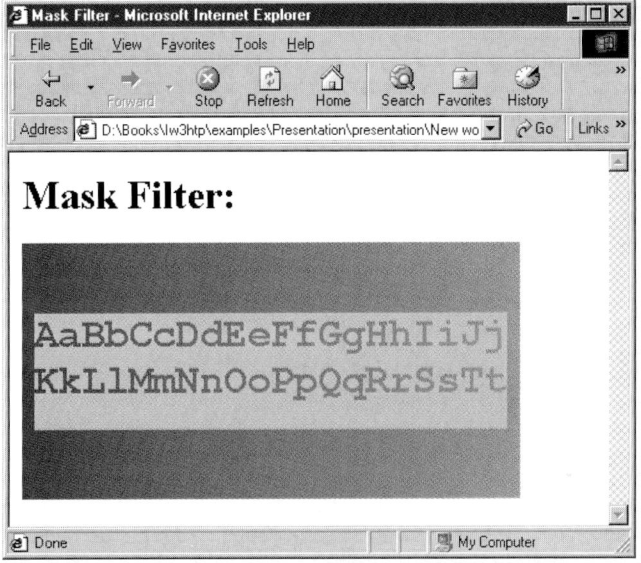

Fig. 17.3 Using the **mask** filter (part 2 of 2).

In line 18

```
filter: mask( color = #CCFFFF )
```

is a color parameter for the **mask** filter that specifies what color the mask will be. Parameters are always specified in the format *param* = *value*.

17.5 Miscellaneous Image filters: invert, gray and xray

The following three image filters apply simple image effects to images or text. The ***invert*** *filter* applies a *negative image effect*—dark areas become light, and light areas become dark. The ***gray*** *filter* applies a *grayscale image effect*, in which all color is stripped from the image and all that remains is brightness data. The ***xray*** *filter* applies an xray effect, which is basically just an inversion of the grayscale effect. Figure 17.4 demonstrates applying these filters, alone and in combination, to a simple image.

```
<!DOCTYPE html PUBLIC "-//W3C//DTD HTML 4.0 Transitional//EN">
<HTML>

<!-- Fig 17.4: misc.html                                   -->
<!-- Image filters to invert, grayscale, or xray an image -->

<HEAD>
<TITLE>Misc. Image filters</TITLE>

<STYLE TYPE = "text/css">
   .cap { font-weight: bold;
          background-color: #DDDDAA;
          text-align: center }
</STYLE>
</HEAD>

<BODY>
<TABLE>
   <TR CLASS = "cap">
      <TD>Normal</TD>
      <TD>Grayscale</TD>
      <TD>Xray</TD>
      <TD>Invert</TD>
   </TR>

   <TR>
      <TD><IMG SRC = "harvey.jpg"></TD>
      <TD><IMG SRC = "harvey.jpg" STYLE = "filter: gray"></TD>
      <TD><IMG SRC = "harvey.jpg" STYLE = "filter: xray"></TD>
      <TD><IMG SRC = "harvey.jpg" STYLE = "filter: invert"></TD>
   </TR>
</TABLE>

</BODY>
</HTML>
```

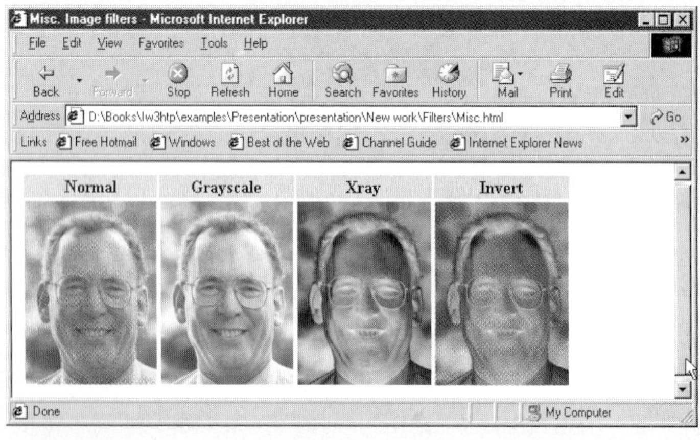

Fig. 17.4 Filters `invert`, `gray` and `xray`.

Each of our filters in lines 28 through 30 applies a separate image effect to **harvey.jpg**.

Look-and-Feel Observation 17.3

*A good use of the **invert** filter is to signify that something has just been clicked or selected.*

17.6 Adding shadows to Text

A simple filter that adds depth to your text is the ***shadow*** *filter*. This filter creates a shadowing effect that gives your text a three-dimensional look (Fig. 17.5).

In lines 31 through 33

```
<H1 ID = "shadowText" STYLE = "position: absolute; top: 50;
         left: 50; padding: 10; filter: shadow(direction = 0,
         color = red )">Shadow Direction: 0</H1>
```

```
1  <!DOCTYPE html PUBLIC "-//W3C//DTD HTML 4.0 Transitional//EN">
2  <HTML>
3  
4  <!-- Fig 17.5: shadow.html       -->
5  <!-- Applying the shadow filter -->
6  
7  <HEAD>
8  <TITLE>Shadow Filter</TITLE>
9  
10 <SCRIPT LANGUAGE = "JavaScript">
11    var shadowDirection = 0;
12 
13    function start()
14    {
15       window.setInterval( "runDemo()", 500 );
16    }
17 
18    function runDemo()
19    {
20       shadowText.innerText =
21          "Shadow Direction: " + shadowDirection % 360;
22       shadowText.filters( "shadow" ).direction =
23          ( shadowDirection % 360 );
24       shadowDirection += 45;
25    }
26 </SCRIPT>
27 </HEAD>
28 
29 <BODY ONLOAD = "start()">
30 
31 <H1 ID = "shadowText" STYLE = "position: absolute; top: 50;
32          left: 50; padding: 10; filter: shadow( direction = 0,
33          color = red )">Shadow Direction: 0</H1>
34 </BODY>
35 </HTML>
```

Fig. 17.5 Applying a **shadow** filter to text (part 1 of 2).

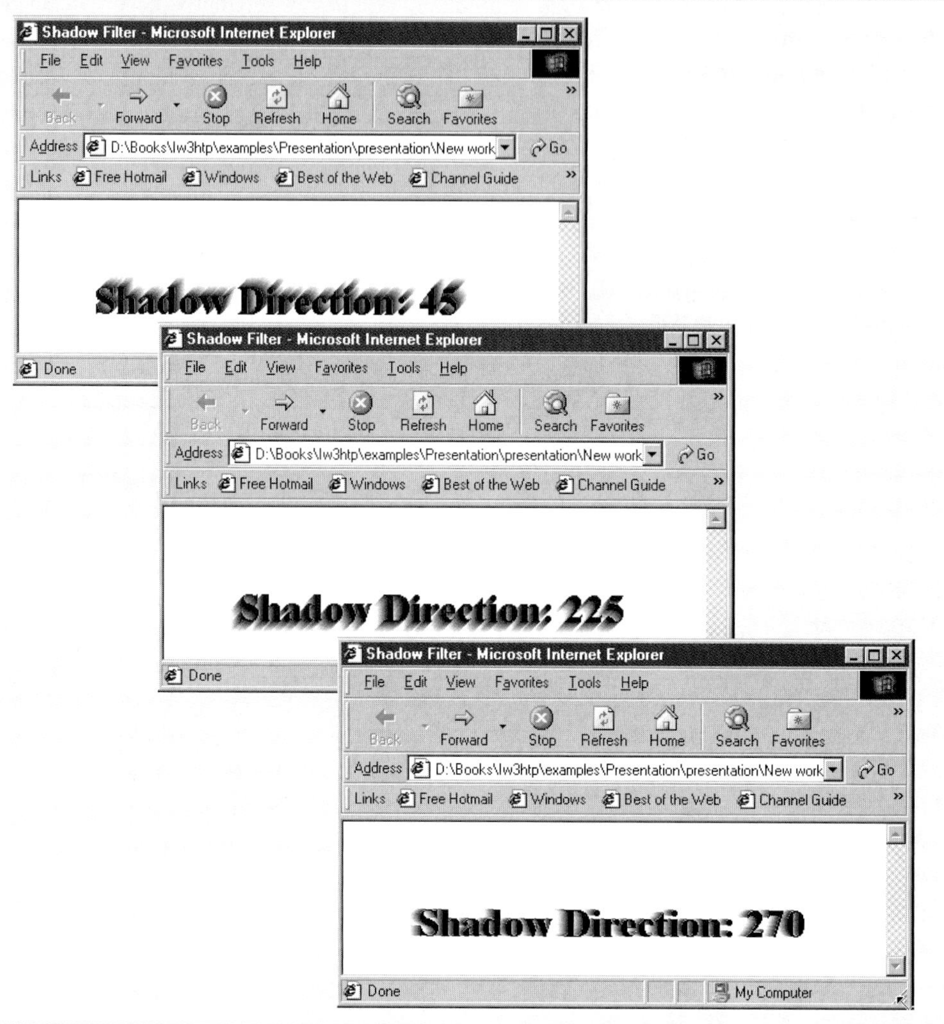

Fig. 17.5 Applying a **shadow** filter to text (part 2 of 2).

we apply the **shadow** filter to text. Property **direction** of the **shadow** filter determines in which direction the shadow effect is applied—this can be set to any of eight directions expressed in angular notation: **0** (up), **45** (above-right), **90** (right), **135** (below-right), **180** (below), **225** (below-left), **270** (left) and **315** (above-left). Property **color** specifies the color of the shadow that is applied to the text. Lines 20 through 24 in function **runDemo**

```
shadowText.innerText =
   "Shadow Direction: " + shadowDirection % 360;
shadowText.filters( "shadow" ).direction =
   ( shadowDirection % 360 );
shadowDirection += 45;
```

cycle through all values of the **direction** property, from **0** to **315**, and update property **innerText** of the **H1** element (**shadowText**) to match the current shadow direction.

Note that we apply a **padding** CSS style to the **H1** element. Otherwise, the shadow effect is partially cut off by the border of the element. Increasing the **padding** gives greater distance between the text and the border of the element, allowing the full effect to be displayed.

Software Engineering Observation 17.2

Some filters may be cut off by element borders—make sure to increase the padding in that element if this happens.

17.7 Creating Gradients with alpha

In Chapter 5 we saw a brief example of the gradient effect, which is a gradual progression from a starting color to a target color. Internet Explorer 5 allows you to create the same type of effect dynamically using the ***alpha** filter* (Fig 17.6). It is also often used for transparency effects not achievable with the **chroma** filter.

```
<!DOCTYPE html PUBLIC "-//W3C//DTD HTML 4.0 Transitional//EN">
<HTML>

<!-- Fig 17.6: alpha.html                      -->
<!-- Applying the alpha filter to an image -->

<HEAD>
<TITLE>Alpha Filter</TITLE>
<SCRIPT LANGUAGE = "JavaScript">
   function run()
   {
      pic.filters( "alpha" ).opacity = opacityButton.value;
      pic.filters( "alpha" ).finishopacity = opacityButton2.value;
      pic.filters( "alpha" ).style = styleSelect.value;
   }
</SCRIPT>
</HEAD>

<BODY>

<DIV ALIGN = "center" ID = "pic"
     STYLE = "position: absolute; left:0; top: 0;
              filter: alpha( style = 2, opacity = 100,
              finishopacity = 0 )">
   <IMG SRC = "flag.gif">
</DIV>

<TABLE STYLE = "position: absolute; top: 250; left: 0;
   background-color: #CCFFCC" BORDER = "1">

   <TR>
      <TD>Opacity (0-100):</TD>
      <TD><INPUT TYPE = "text" ID = "opacityButton" SIZE = "3"
         MAXLENGTH = "3" VALUE = "100"></TD>
   </TR>
```

Fig. 17.6 Applying the **alpha** filter (part 1 of 2).

```

      <TR>
         <TD>FinishOpacity (0-100):</TD>
         <TD><INPUT TYPE = "text" ID = "opacityButton2" SIZE = "3"
            MAXLENGTH = "3" VALUE = "0"></TD>
      </TR>

      <TR>
         <TD>Style:</TD>
         <TD><SELECT ID = "styleSelect">
            <OPTION VALUE = "1">Linear
            <OPTION VALUE = "2" SELECTED>Circular
            <OPTION VALUE = "3">Rectangular
            </SELECT></TD>
      </TR>

      <TR>
         <TD ALIGN = "center" COLSPAN = "2"><INPUT TYPE = "button"
            VALUE = "Apply" ONCLICK = "run()"></TD>
      </TR>
   </TABLE>

   </BODY>
   </HTML>
```

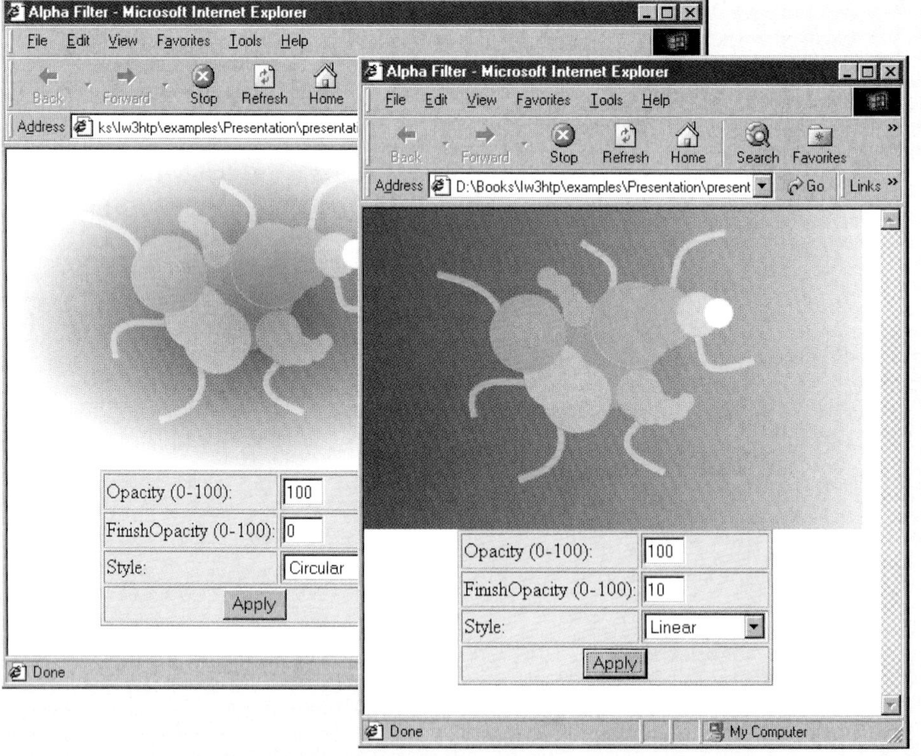

Fig. 17.6 Applying the **`alpha`** filter (part 2 of 2).

In lines 21 through 24

```
<DIV ALIGN = "center" ID = "pic"
     STYLE = "position: absolute; left:0; top: 0; filter:
              alpha( style = 2, opacity = 100,
              finishopacity = 0 )">
```

we apply the **alpha** filter to a **DIV** element containing an image. The **style** property of the filter determines in what style the opacity is applied; a value of 0 applies *uniform opacity*, a value of 1 applies a *linear gradient*, a value of 2 applies a *circular gradient*, and a value of 3 applies a *rectangular gradient*.

The **opacity** and **finishopacity** properties are both percentages determining at what percent opacity the specified gradient will start and finish, respectively. Additional attributes are **startX**, **startY**, **finishX**, and **finishY**. These allow you to specify at what *x-y* coordinates the gradient starts and finishes in that element.

17.8 Making Text glow

The **glow** filter allows you to add an aura of color around your text. The color and strength can both be specified (Fig. 17.7).

```
<!DOCTYPE html PUBLIC "-//W3C//DTD HTML 4.0 Transitional//EN">
<HTML>

<!-- Fig 17.7: glow.html       -->
<!-- Applying the glow filter -->

<HEAD>
<TITLE>Glow Filter</TITLE>
<SCRIPT LANGUAGE = "JavaScript">
   var strengthIndex = 1;
   var counter = 1;
   var upDown = true;
   var colorArray = [ "FF0000", "FFFF00", "00FF00",
                      "00FFFF", "0000FF", "FF00FF" ];
   function apply()
   {
      glowSpan.filters( "glow" ).color =
         parseInt( glowColor.value, 16);
      glowSpan.filters( "glow" ).strength =
         glowStrength.value;
   }

   function startdemo()
   {
      window.setInterval( "rundemo()", 150 );
   }

```

Fig. 17.7 Applying changes to the **glow** filter (part 1 of 3).

```
   function rundemo()
   {
      if ( upDown )
         glowSpan.filters( "glow" ).strength = strengthIndex++;
      else
         glowSpan.filters( "glow" ).strength = strengthIndex--;

      if ( strengthIndex == 1 ) {
         upDown = !upDown;
         counter++;
         glowSpan.filters( "glow" ).color =
            parseInt( colorArray[ counter % 6 ], 16 );
      }

      if ( strengthIndex == 10 ) {
         upDown = !upDown;
      }
   }
</SCRIPT>
</HEAD>

<BODY STYLE = "background-color: #00AAAA">
<H1>Glow Filter:</H1>

<SPAN ID = "glowSpan" STYLE = "position: absolute; left: 200;
   top: 100; padding: 5; filter: glow( color = red,
   strength = 5 )">
   <H2>Glowing Text</H2>
</SPAN>

<TABLE BORDER = 1 STYLE = "background-color: #CCFFCC">
   <TR>
      <TD>Color (Hex)</TD>
      <TD><INPUT ID = "glowColor" TYPE = "text" SIZE = 3
         MAXLENGTH = 3 VALUE = FF0000></TD>
   </TR>
   <TR>
      <TD>Strength (1-255)</TD>
      <TD><INPUT ID = "glowStrength" TYPE = "text" SIZE = 3
         MAXLENGTH = 3 VALUE = 5></TD>
   </TR>
   <TR>
      <TD COLSPAN = 2>
         <INPUT TYPE = "BUTTON" VALUE = "Apply"
            ONCLICK = "apply()">
         <INPUT TYPE = "BUTTON" VALUE = "Run Demo"
            ONCLICK = "startdemo()"></TD>
   </TR>
</TABLE>

</BODY>
</HTML>
```

Fig. 17.7 Applying changes to the **glow** filter (part 2 of 3).

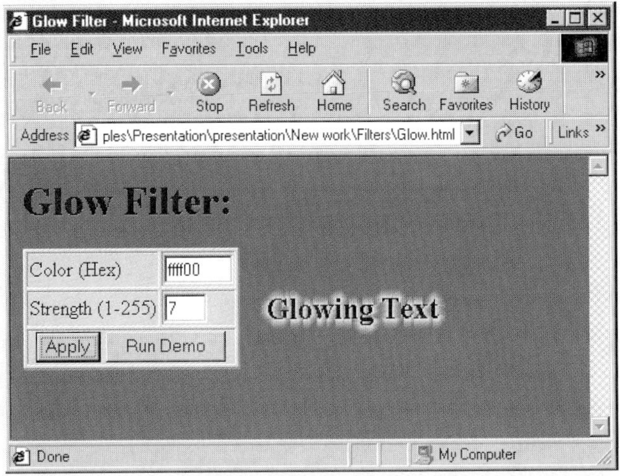

Fig. 17.7 Applying changes to the **glow** filter (part 3 of 3).

Lines 13 and 14

```
var colorArray = [ "FF0000", "FFFF00", "00FF00",
                   "00FFFF", "0000FF", "FF00FF" ];
```

establish an array of color values to cycle through in the demo.

Lines 38 and 39

```
glowSpan.filters( "glow" ).color =
   parseInt( colorArray[ counter % 6 ], 16 );
```

change the **color** attribute of the **glow** filter based on **counter**, which is incremented (line 37) every time the value of **strengthIndex** becomes 1. As in the example with the **chroma** filter, we use the **parseInt** function to assign a proper hex value (taken from the **colorArray** we declared in lines 13 and 14) to the **color** property.

Lines 30 through 33

```
if ( upDown )
   glowSpan.filters( "glow" ).strength = strengthIndex++;
else
   glowSpan.filters( "glow" ).strength = strengthIndex--;
```

are an **if**/**else** structure that increments or decrements the **strength** property of the **glow** filter based on the value of **upDown**, which is toggled in the **if** structures at lines 35 and 42 when **strengthIndex** reaches either 1 or 10.

Clicking the **Run Demo** button starts a cycle that oscillates the filter **strength**, cycling through the colors in **colorArray** after every loop.

Common Programming Error 17.1

When the **glow** *filter is set to a large* **strength**, *the effect is often cut off by the borders of the element. Add CSS* **padding** *to prevent this.*

17.9 Creating Motion with `blur`

The **`blur`** filter creates an illusion of motion by blurring text or images in a certain direction. As we see in Fig 17.8, the **`blur`** filter can be applied in any of eight directions and its strength may vary.

```
<!DOCTYPE html PUBLIC "-//W3C//DTD HTML 4.0 Transitional//EN">
<HTML>

<!-- Fig 17.8: blur.html -->
<!-- The blur filter    -->

<HEAD>
<TITLE>Blur Filter</TITLE>
<SCRIPT LANGUAGE = "JavaScript">
   var strengthIndex = 1;
   var blurDirection = 0;
   var upDown = 0;
   var timer;

   function reBlur()
   {
      blurImage.filters( "blur" ).direction =
         document.forms( "myForm" ).Direction.value;
      blurImage.filters( "blur" ).strength =
         document.forms( "myForm" ).Strength.value;
      blurImage.filters( "blur" ).add =
         document.forms( "myForm" ).Add.checked;
   }

   function startDemo()
   {
      timer = window.setInterval( "runDemo()", 5 );
   }

   function runDemo( )
   {
      document.forms( "myForm" ).Strength.value = strengthIndex;
      document.forms( "myForm" ).Direction.value =
         ( blurDirection % 360 );

      if( strengthIndex == 35 || strengthIndex == 0 )
         upDown = !upDown;

      blurImage.filters( "blur" ).strength =
         ( upDown ? strengthIndex++ : strengthIndex-- );

      if ( strengthIndex == 0 )
         blurImage.filters( "blur" ).direction =
            ( ( blurDirection += 45 ) % 360 );
   }

</SCRIPT>
```

Fig. 17.8 Using the **`blur`** filter with the **`add`** property **`false`** then **`true`** (part 1 of 3).

```
</HEAD>

<BODY>
<FORM NAME = "myForm">

<TABLE BORDER = "1" STYLE = "background-color: #CCFFCC">
<CAPTION>Blur filter controls</CAPTION>

   <TR>
      <TD>Direction:</TD>
      <TD><SELECT NAME = "Direction">
         <OPTION VALUE = "0">above
         <OPTION VALUE = "45">above-right
         <OPTION VALUE = "90">right
         <OPTION VALUE = "135">below-right
         <OPTION VALUE = "180">below
         <OPTION VALUE = "225">below-left
         <OPTION VALUE = "270">left
         <OPTION VALUE = "315">above-left
      </SELECT></TD>
   </TR>

   <TR>
      <TD>Strength:</TD>
      <TD><INPUT NAME = "Strength" SIZE = "3" MAXLENGTH = "3"
         VALUE = "0"></TD>
   </TR>

   <TR>
      <TD>Add original?</TD>
      <TD><INPUT TYPE = "checkbox" NAME = "Add"></TD>
   </TR>

   <TR>
      <TD ALIGN = "center" COLSPAN = "2"><INPUT TYPE = "button"
         VALUE = "Apply" ONCLICK = "reBlur();"></TD>
   </TR>

   <TR>
      <TD COLSPAN = "2">
      <INPUT TYPE = "button" VALUE = "Start demo"
        ONCLICK = "startDemo();">
      <INPUT TYPE = "button" VALUE = "Stop demo"
        ONCLICK = "window.clearInterval( timer );"></TD>
   </TR>

</TABLE>
</FORM>

<DIV ID = "blurImage" STYLE = "position: absolute; top: 0;
   left: 300; padding: 0; filter:
   blur( add = 0, direction = 0, strength = 0 )
   background-color: white;">
```

Fig. 17.8 Using the `blur` filter with the `add` property `false` then `true` (part 2 of 3).

```
    <IMG ALIGN = "center" SRC = "shapes.gif">
</DIV>

</BODY>
</HTML>
```

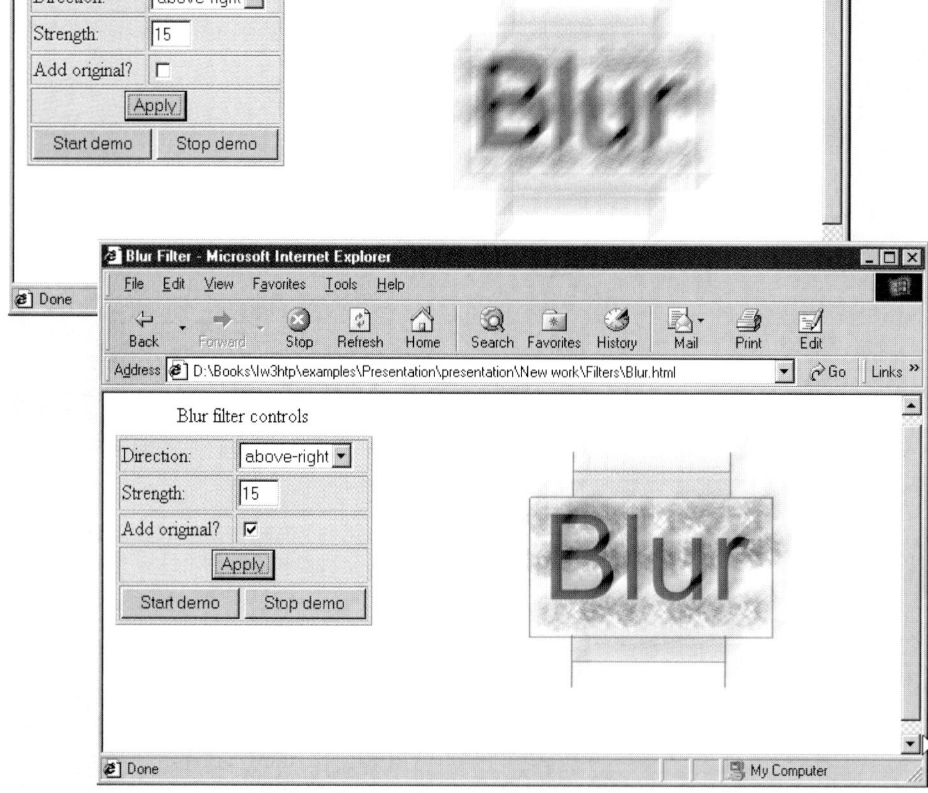

Fig. 17.8 Using the **blur** filter with the **add** property **false** then **true** (part 3 of 3).

The three properties of the **blur** filter are **add**, **direction**, and **strength**. The **add** property, when set to **true**, adds a copy of the original image over the blurred image, creating a more subtle blurring effect; Fig. 17.8 demonstrates the contrast between setting this to **true** or **false**.

The **direction** property determines in which direction the **blur** filter will be applied. This is expressed in angular form (as we saw in Fig. 17.5 with the **shadow** filter). The **strength** property determines how strong the blurring effect will be.

Lines 21 and 22

```
blurImage.filters( "blur" ).add =
     document.forms( "myForm" ).Add.checked;
```

assign to the **add** property of the **blur** filter the boolean **checked** property of the **Add** checkbox—if the box was checked, the value is **true**.

Lines 43 and 44

```
blurImage.filters( "blur" ).direction =
   ( ( blurDirection += 45 ) % 360 )
```

increment the **direction** property whenever the **strength** of the **blur** filter is 0 (i.e., whenever an iteration has completed). The value assigned to the **direction** property cycles through all the multiples of 45 between 0 and 360.

17.10 Using the wave Filter

The ***wave*** *filter* allows you to apply *sine-wave distortions* to text and images on your Web pages (Fig. 17.9).

```
<!DOCTYPE html PUBLIC "-//W3C//DTD HTML 4.0 Transitional//EN">
<HTML>

<!-- Fig 17.9: wave.html        -->
<!-- Applying the wave filter -->

<HEAD>
<TITLE>Wave Filter</TITLE>

<SCRIPT LANGUAGE = "JavaScript">
   var wavePhase = 0;

   function start()
   {
      window.setInterval( "wave()", 5 );
   }

   function wave()
   {
      wavePhase++;
      flag.filters( "wave" ).phase = wavePhase;
   }
</SCRIPT>
</HEAD>

<BODY ONLOAD = "start();">

<SPAN ID = "flag"
   STYLE = "align: center; position: absolute;
   left: 30; padding: 15;
   filter: wave(add = 0, freq = 1, phase = 0, strength = 10)">
```

Fig. 17.9 Adding a **wave** filter to text (part 1 of 2).

```
32  <H1>Here's some waaaavy text</H1>
33  </SPAN>
34
35  </BODY>
36  </HTML>
```

Fig. 17.9 Adding a **wave** filter to text (part 2 of 2).

The **wave** filter, as seen in line 31,

```
filter: wave(add = 0, freq = 1, phase = 0, strength = 10)">
```

has many properties. The **add** property, as in the case of the **blur** filter, adds a copy of the text or image underneath the filtered effect. The **add** property is usually useful only when applying the **wave** filter to images.

Performance Tip 17.2

Applying the **wave** *filter to images is processor intensive—if your viewers have inadequate processor power, your pages may act sluggishly on their systems.*

The **freq** property determines the *frequency of the wave* applied—i.e., how many complete sine waves will be applied in the affected area. Increasing this property creates a more pronounced wave effect, but makes the text harder to read.

The **phase** property indicates the *phase shift of the wave*. Increasing this property does not modify any physical attributes of the wave, but merely shifts it in space. This property is useful for creating a gentle waving effect, as we do in this example. The last property, **strength**, is the amplitude of the sine wave that is applied.

In the script, lines 20 and 21

```
wavePhase++;
flag.filters( "wave" ).phase = wavePhase;
```

increment the phase shift of the wave in every call to the **wave** function.

17.11 Advanced Filters: dropShadow and light

Two filters that apply advanced image processing effects are the **dropShadow** and **light** filters. The ***dropShadow** filter*, as you can probably tell, applies an effect similar to the drop shadow we applied to our images with Paint Shop Pro in Chapter 5—it creates a blacked-out version of the image, and places it behind the image, offset by a specified number of pixels.

The ***light** filter* is the most powerful and advanced filter available in Internet Explorer 5. It allows you to simulate the effect of a light source shining on your page. With scripting, this filter can be used with dazzling results. Figure 17.10. combines these two filters to create an interesting effect.

```
<!DOCTYPE html PUBLIC "-//W3C//DTD HTML 4.0 Transitional//EN">
<HTML>

<!-- Fig 17.10: dropshadow.html                          -->
<!-- Using the light filter with the dropshadow filter -->

<HEAD>
<TITLE>DHTML dropShadow and light Filters</TITLE>

<SCRIPT LANGUAGE = "JavaScript">
   function setlight( )
   {
      dsImg.filters( "light" ).addPoint( 150, 150,
         125, 255, 255, 255, 100);
   }

   function run()
   {
      eX = event.offsetX;
      eY = event.offsetY;

      xCoordinate = Math.round( eX-event.srcElement.width/2, 0 );
      yCoordinate = Math.round( eY-event.srcElement.height/2, 0 );

```

Fig. 17.10 Applying **light** filter with a **dropshadow** (part 1 of 2).

```
25         dsImg.filters( "dropShadow" ).offx = xCoordinate / -3;
26         dsImg.filters( "dropShadow" ).offy = yCoordinate / -3;
27
28         dsImg.filters( "light" ).moveLight(0, eX, eY, 125, 1);
29      }
30   </SCRIPT>
31   </HEAD>
32
33   <BODY ONLOAD = "setlight()" STYLE = "background-color: green">
34
35   <IMG ID = "dsImg" SRC = "circle.gif"
36      STYLE = "top: 100; left: 100; filter: dropShadow( offx = 0,
37      offy = 0, color = black ) light()" ONMOUSEMOVE = "run()">
38
39   </BODY>
40   </HTML>
```

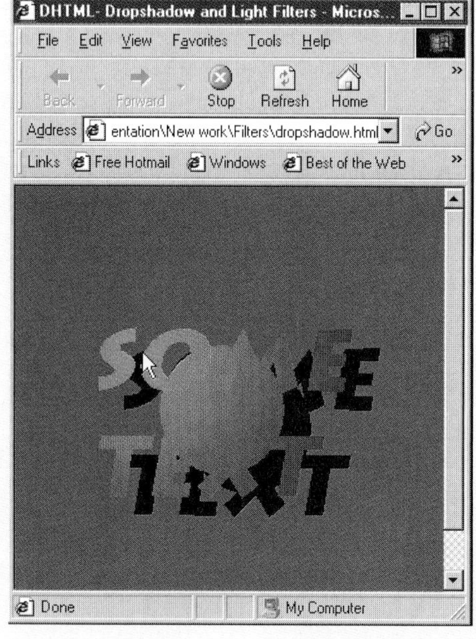

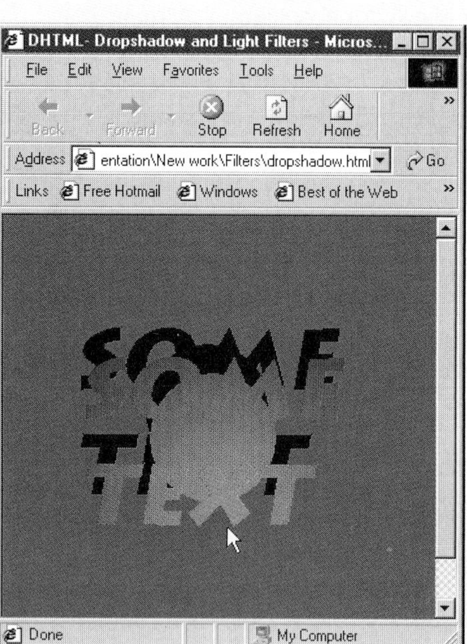

Fig. 17.10 Applying **`light`** filter with a **`dropshadow`** (part 2 of 2).

Let us begin by examining the **`dropshadow`** filter. In lines 35 through 37

```
<IMG ID = "dsImg" SRC = "circle.gif"
   STYLE = "top: 100; left: 100; filter: dropShadow( offx = 0,
   offy = 0, color = black ) light()" ONMOUSEMOVE = "run()">
```

we apply the **`dropShadow`** filter to our image. The **`offx`** and **`offy`** properties determine by how many pixels the drop shadow will be offset (see Chapter 5). The **`color`** property specifies the color of the drop shadow. Note that we also declare the **light** filter in line 37, although we do not give it any initial parameters—all the parameters and methods of the light **filter** are set by scripting. Lines 13 and 14

```
dsImg.filters( "light" ).addPoint(150, 150,
   125, 255, 255, 255, 100);
```

call the ***addPoint*** method of the **light** filter. This adds a *point light source*—a source of light which emanates from a single point and radiates in all directions. The first two parameters (**150, 150**) set the *x-y* coordinates at which to add the point source. In this case we place the source at the center of the image, which is 300-by-300 pixels.

The next parameter (**125**) sets the *height* of the point source. This simulates how far above the surface the light is situated. Small values create a small but high-intensity circle of light on the image, while large values cast a circle of light which is darker, but spreads over a greater distance.

The next three parameters (**255**, **255**, **255**) specify the RGB value of the light, in decimal. In this case we set the light to a color of white (**#FFFFFF**).

The last value (**100**), is a strength percentage—we set our light in this case to radiate with 100% strength.

This point light source will create a pleasant lighting effect, but it is static. We can use scripting to animate the light source in response to user actions. We use the **ONMOUSEMOVE** event (line 37) to have the light source follow the mouse cursor as the user moves it over the image. Lines 19 through 28

```
eX = event.offsetX;
eY = event.offsetY;

xCoordinate = Math.round( eX-event.srcElement.width/2, 0 );
yCoordinate = Math.round( eY-event.srcElement.height/2, 0 );

dsImg.filters( "dropShadow" ).offx = xCoordinate / -3;
dsImg.filters( "dropShadow" ).offy = yCoordinate / -3;

dsImg.filters( "light" ).moveLight(0, eX, eY, 125, 1);
```

of the **run** function animate both the **dropshadow** and **light** filters in response to user actions. First we set the variables **xCoord** and **yCoord** to the distance between the current cursor position (**eX** and **eY**, which were set to **event.offsetX** and **event.offsetY** on lines 19 and 20) to the middle of the image (**event.srcElement.width / 2** or **event.srcElement.height / 2**). In the next two lines of code we set the **offx** and **offy** properties of the **dropShadow** filter relative to the current *x-y* coordinates of the image. We divide by a certain amount to create an effect of height (shadows cast by objects far from light sources only move a small amount when the light source moves by a larger amount).

We then call the **moveLight** method to update the position of the light source as well. The first parameter (**0**) is the index of the light source on the page. Multiple light sources have index numbers assigned to them in the order in which they are added. The next two parameters (**event.offsetX**, **event.offsetY**) specify the *x-y* coordinates to which we should move the light source. We use the **offsetX** and **offsetY** properties of the

`event` object to move the light source to the current mouse cursor position over the image. The next parameter (**`125`**) specifies the height to which we move the light source. In this case, we keep the light source as the same level it was when we declared it. The last parameter (**`1`**) indicates that the values we are using are absolute. To move your light source by relative amounts instead, use a value of **`0`** for the last parameter of the **`moveLight`** function.

As you can see, combining the **`dropShadow`** and **`light`** filters creates a stunning effect that responds to user actions. The point source is not the only type of light source available for the light filter. Figure 17.11 demonstrates the use of a *cone light source* for illuminating an image.

```
<!DOCTYPE html PUBLIC "-//W3C//DTD HTML 4.0 Transitional//EN">
<HTML>

<!-- Fig 17.11: conelight.html         -->
<!-- Automating the cone light source -->

<HEAD><TITLE>Cone lighting</TITLE>

<SCRIPT LANGUAGE = "JavaScript">
   var upDown = true;
   var counter = 0;
   var moveRate = -2;

   function setLight()
   {
      marquee.filters( "light" ).addCone( 0, marquee.height, 8,
         marquee.width/2, 30, 255, 150, 255, 50, 15 );
      marquee.filters( "light" ).addCone( marquee.width,
         marquee.height, 8, 200, 30, 150, 255, 255, 50, 15 );
      marquee.filters( "light" ).addCone( marquee.width/2,
         marquee.height, 4, 200, 100, 255, 255, 150, 50, 50 );

      window.setInterval( "moveLight()", 100 );
   }

   function moveLight()
   {
      counter++;

      if ( ( counter % 30 ) == 0 )
         upDown = !upDown;

      if( ( counter % 10 ) == 0 )
         moveRate *= -1;

      if ( upDown ) {
         marquee.filters( "light" ).moveLight( 0,-1,-1,3,0 );
         marquee.filters( "light" ).moveLight( 1,1,-1,3,0 );
        marquee.filters( "light" ).moveLight( 2,moveRate,0,3,0 );
      }
```

Fig. 17.11 Dynamic cone source lighting (part 1 of 2).

```
         else {
            marquee.filters( "light" ).moveLight( 0,1,1,3,0 );
            marquee.filters( "light" ).moveLight( 1,-1,1,3,0 );
           marquee.filters( "light" ).moveLight( 2,moveRate,0,3,0 );
         }
      }
   </SCRIPT>

   <BODY STYLE = "background-color: #000000" ONLOAD = "setLight()">

   <IMG ID = "marquee" SRC = "marquee.gif"
      STYLE = "filter: light; position: absolute; left: 100;
      top: 100">

   </BODY>
   </HTML>
```

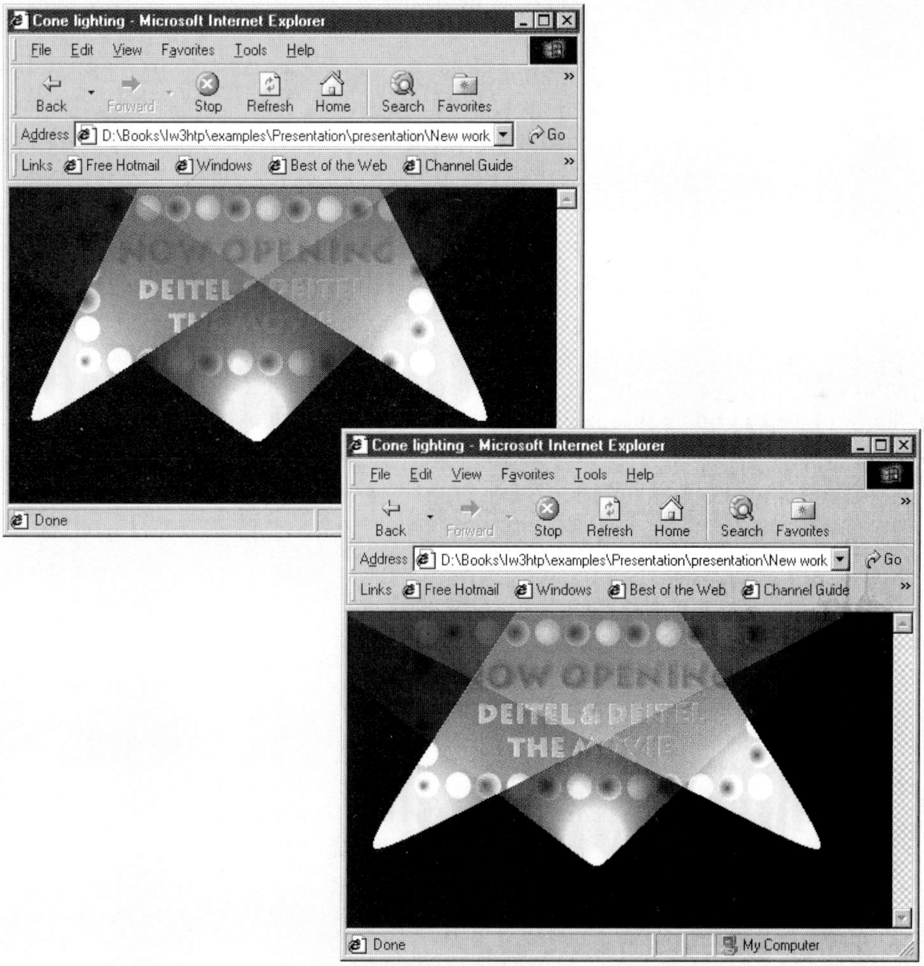

Fig. 17.11 Dynamic cone source lighting (part 2 of 2).

In lines 16 and 17

```
marquee.filters( "light" ).addCone( 0, marquee.height, 8,
   marquee.width/2, 30, 255, 150, 255, 50, 15 );
```

we add our first cone light source using the **addCone** method. The parameters of this method are similar to the **addPoint** method. The first two parameters specify the *x-y* coordinates of the light source, and the third parameter specifies the simulated height above the page at which the light should be placed. The next two parameters (**marquee.width/2**, **30**) are new—they specify the *x-y* coordinates at which the cone source is targeted. The next three parameters (**255**, **150**, **255**) specify the RGB value of the light which is cast, just as we did in the **addPoint** method. The next parameter (**50**) specifies the strength of the cone source, in a percentage (also equivalent to the strength parameter in the **addPoint** method). The last value (**15**) specifies the *spread* of the light source, in degrees (this can be set in the range **0**–**90**). In this case we set the spread of the cone to **15** degrees, illuminating relatively narrow area.

In line 37

```
marquee.filters( "light" ).moveLight( 0,-1,-1,3,0 );
```

we use the **moveLight** method once again. When used on cone sources, the **moveLight** method moves the target of the light. In this case we set the last parameter to **0** to move the light by a relative amount, not an absolute amount, as we did in Fig 17.10.

17.12 Transitions I: Filter blendTrans

The transitions included with Internet Explorer 5 give the author control of many scriptable PowerPoint type effects. Transitions are set as values of the **filter** CSS property, just as regular filters are. We then use scripting to begin the transition. Figure 17.12 is a simple example of the **blendTrans** transition, which creates a smooth fade-in/fade-out effect.

```
<!DOCTYPE html PUBLIC "-//W3C//DTD HTML 4.0 Transitional//EN">
<HTML>

<!-- Fig 17.12: blendtrans.html -->
<!-- Blend transition           -->

<HEAD>
<TITLE>Using blendTrans</TITLE>

<SCRIPT LANGUAGE = "JavaScript">
   function blendOut()
   {
      textInput.filters( "blendTrans" ).apply();
      textInput.style.visibility = "hidden";
      textInput.filters( "blendTrans" ).play();
   }
</SCRIPT>
</HEAD>
```

Fig. 17.12 Using the **blendTrans** transition (part 1 of 2).

```
19
20  <BODY>
21
22  <DIV ID = "textInput" ONCLICK = "blendOut()"
23     STYLE = "width: 300; filter: blendTrans( duration = 3 )">
24     <H1>Some fading text</H1>
25  </DIV>
26
27  </BODY>
28  </HTML>
```

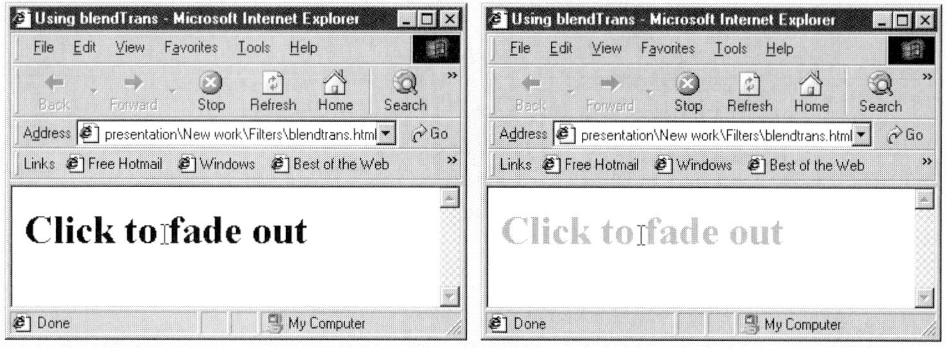

Fig. 17.12 Using the **blendTrans** transition (part 2 of 2).

First, line 23

```
STYLE = "width: 300; filter:blendTrans( duration = 3 )">
```

sets the filter to **blendTrans** and the **duration** parameter to 3. This determines how long the transition will take. All the rest of our work is done by scripting. In lines 13 through 15

```
textInput.filters( "blendTrans" ).apply();
textInput.style.visibility = "hidden";
textInput.filters( "blendTrans" ).play();
```

we invoke two methods of **blendTrans**. The **apply** method (line 13) initializes the transition for the affected element. Once this is done, we set the **visibility** of the element to **hidden**—this takes effect when we invoke the **play** method on line 15.

Figure 17.13 is a more complex example of the **blendTrans** transition. We use this to transition between two separate images.

```
<!DOCTYPE html PUBLIC "-//W3C//DTD HTML 4.0 Transitional//EN">
<HTML>

<!-- Fig 17.13: blendtrans2.html -->
<!-- Blend Transition            -->

<HEAD>
<TITLE>Blend Transition II</TITLE>
```

Fig. 17.13 Blending between images with **blendTrans** (part 1 of 3).

```
<SCRIPT LANGUAGE = "JavaScript">
   var whichImage = true;

   function blend()
   {
      if ( whichImage ) {
         image1.filters( "blendTrans" ).apply();
         image1.style.visibility = "hidden";
         image1.filters( "blendTrans" ).play();
      }
      else {
         image2.filters( "blendTrans" ).apply();
         image2.style.visibility = "hidden";
         image2.filters( "blendTrans" ).play();
      }
   }

   function reBlend ( fromImage )
   {
      if ( fromImage ) {
         image1.style.zIndex -= 2;
         image1.style.visibility = "visible";
      }
      else {
         image1.style.zIndex += 2;
         image2.style.visibility = "visible";
      }

      whichImage = !whichImage;
      blend();
   }
</SCRIPT>
</HEAD>

<BODY STYLE = "color: darkblue; background-color: lightblue"
      ONLOAD = "blend()">

<H1>Blend Transition Demo</H1>

<IMG ID = "image2" SRC = "cool12.jpg"
   ONFILTERCHANGE = "reBlend( false )"
   STYLE = "position: absolute; left: 50; top: 50; width: 300;
   filter: blendTrans( duration = 4 ); z-index: 1">

<IMG ID = "image1" SRC = "cool8.jpg"
   ONFILTERCHANGE = "reBlend( true )"
   STYLE = "position: absolute; left: 50; top: 50; width: 300;
   filter: blendTrans( duration = 4 ); z-index: 2">

</BODY>
</HTML>
```

Fig. 17.13 Blending between images with **blendTrans** (part 2 of 3).

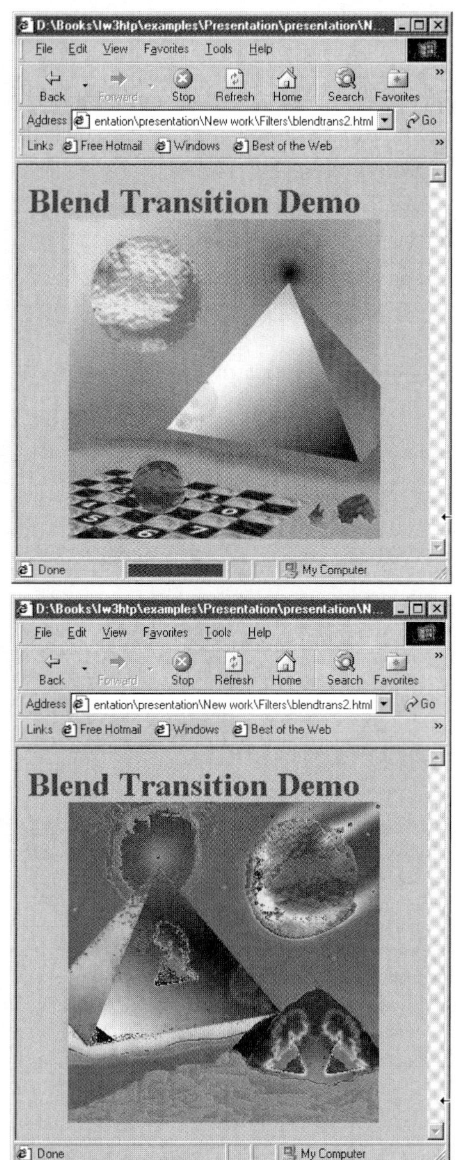

Fig. 17.13 Blending between images with **`blendTrans`** (part 3 of 3).

We begin by placing two overlapping images on the page, with IDs **`image1`** and **`image2`** (lines 49 though 57). The **`BODY`** tag's **`ONLOAD`** event (line 45) calls function **`blend`** as the body loads. The **`blend`** function checks the value of the **`whichImage`** variable, and because it is set to **`true`**, begins a fade transition on **`image1`**. Because there are two images in the same place, when **`image1`** fades out it appears that **`image2`** fades in to replace it. When the transition is complete, **`image1`**'s **`ONFILTERCHANGE`** event (line 55) fires. This calls function **`reBlend`**, which in lines 30 and 31

```
image1.style.zIndex -= 2;
image1.style.visibility = "visible";
```

changes the **zIndex** (the JavaScript version of the **z-index** CSS property) of **image1** so that it is now below **image2**. Once this is done, the image is made visible again. The function then toggles the **whichImage** property, and calls function **blend** so that the whole process starts again, now transitioning from **image2** back to **image1**.

17.13 Transitions II: Filter revealTrans

The **revealTrans** filter allows you to transition using professional-style transitions, from *box out* to *random dissolve*. Figure 17.14 cycles through all 24 of these, transitioning from one image to another.

The script in this example is almost the same as the script in the **blendTrans** example. In line 48

```
image2.filters("revealTrans").transition = counter % 24;
```

we set the **transition** property of the image, which determines what visual transition will be used here. There are 25 different visual transitions (their names are listed in the **transitionName** array for updating the **DIV** element **transitionDisplay**.

```
1  <!DOCTYPE html PUBLIC "-//W3C//DTD HTML 4.0 Transitional//EN">
2  <HTML>
3
4  <!-- Fig 17.14: revealtrans.html -->
5  <!-- Cycling through 24 transitions -->
6  <HEAD>
7  <TITLE>24 DHTML Transitions</TITLE>
8
9  <SCRIPT>
10    var transitionName =
11      ["Box In", "Box Out",
12       "Circle In", "Circle Out",
13       "Wipe Up", "Wipe Down", "Wipe Right", "Wipe Left",
14       "Vertical Blinds", "Horizontal Blinds",
15       "Checkerboard Across", "Checkerboard Down",
16       "Random Dissolve",
17       "Split Vertical In", "Split Vertical Out",
18       "Split Horizontal In", "Split Horizontal Out",
19       "Strips Left Down", "Strips Left Up",
20       "Strips Right Down", "Strips Right Up",
21       "Random Bars Horizontal", "Random Bars Vertical",
22       "Random"];
23
24    var counter = 0;
25    var whichImage = true;
26
27    function blend()
28    {
29       if ( whichImage ) {
30          image1.filters( "revealTrans" ).apply();
```

Fig. 17.14 Transitions using **revealTrans** (part 1 of 5).

```
            image1.style.visibility = "hidden";
            image1.filters( "revealTrans" ).play();
         }
         else {
            image2.filters( "revealTrans" ).apply();
            image2.style.visibility = "hidden";
            image2.filters( "revealTrans" ).play();
         }
      }

      function reBlend( fromImage )
      {
         counter++;

         if ( fromImage ) {
            image1.style.zIndex -= 2;
            image1.style.visibility = "visible";
            image2.filters("revealTrans").transition = counter % 24;
         }
         else {
            image1.style.zIndex += 2;
            image2.style.visibility = "visible";
            image1.filters("revealTrans").transition = counter % 24;
         }

         whichImage = !whichImage;
         blend();
        transitionDisplay.innerHTML = "Transition " + counter % 24 +
            ":<BR> " + transitionName[ counter % 24 ];
      }
   </SCRIPT>
   </HEAD>

   <BODY STYLE = "color: white; background-color: lightcoral"
         ONLOAD = "blend()">

      <IMG ID = "image2" SRC = "icontext.gif"
           STYLE = "position: absolute; left: 10; top: 10;
           width: 300; z-index:1; visibility: visible;
           filter: revealTrans( duration = 2, transition = 0 )"
           ONFILTERCHANGE = "reBlend( false )">

      <IMG ID = "image1" SRC = "icons2.gif"
           STYLE = "position: absolute; left: 10; top: 10;
           width: 300; z-index:1; visibility: visible;
           filter: revealTrans( duration = 2, transition = 0 )"
           ONFILTERCHANGE = "reBlend( true )">

   <DIV ID = "transitionDisplay" STYLE = "position: absolute;
      top: 10; left: 325">Transition 0:<BR> Box In</DIV>

   </BODY>
   </HTML>
```

Fig. 17.14 Transitions using **revealTrans** (part 2 of 5).

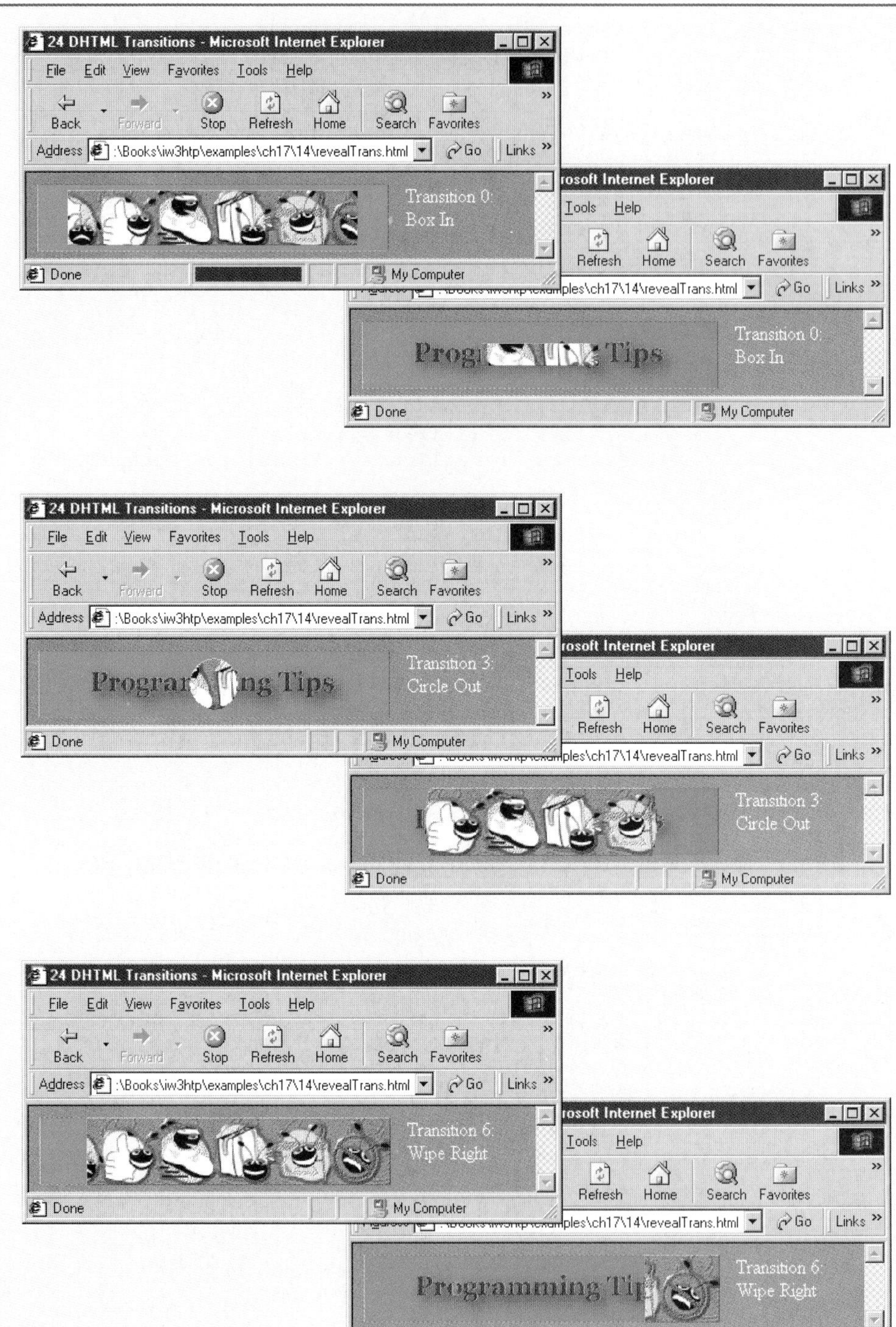

Fig. 17.14 Transitions using **revealTrans** (part 3 of 5).

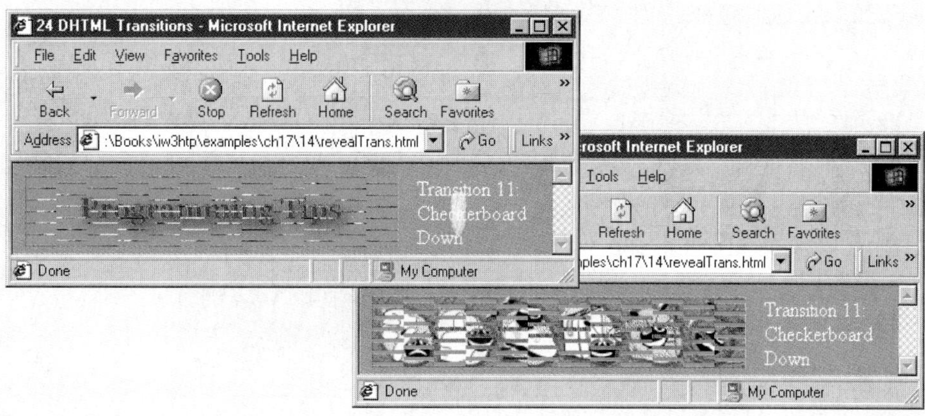

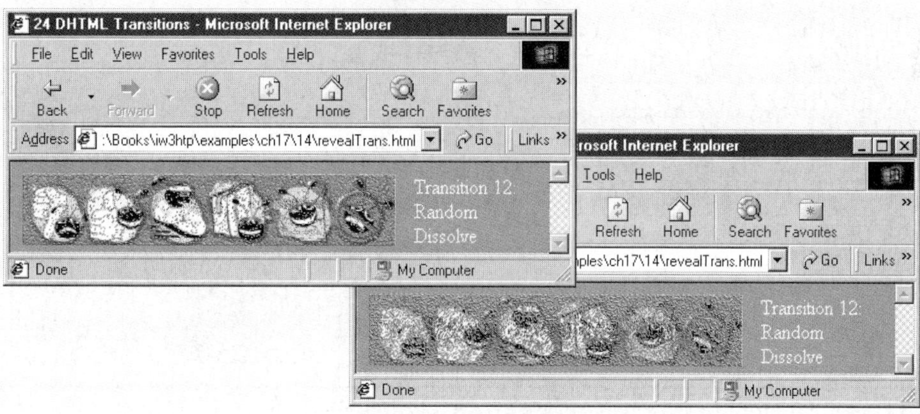

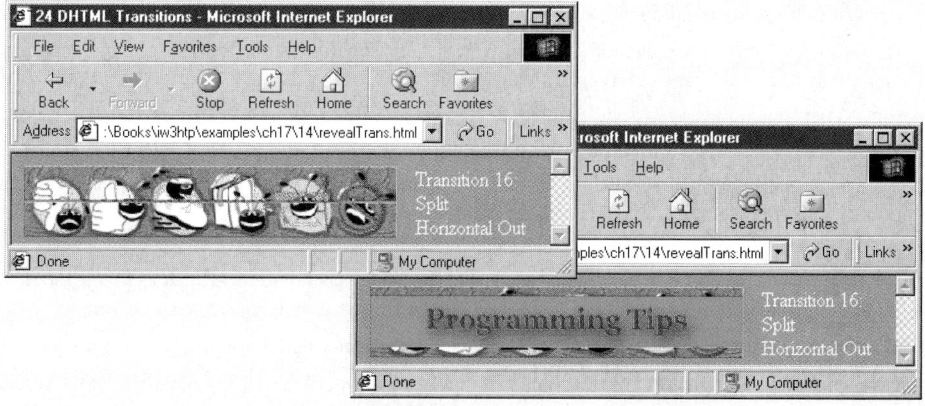

Fig. 17.14 Transitions using `revealTrans` (part 4 of 5).

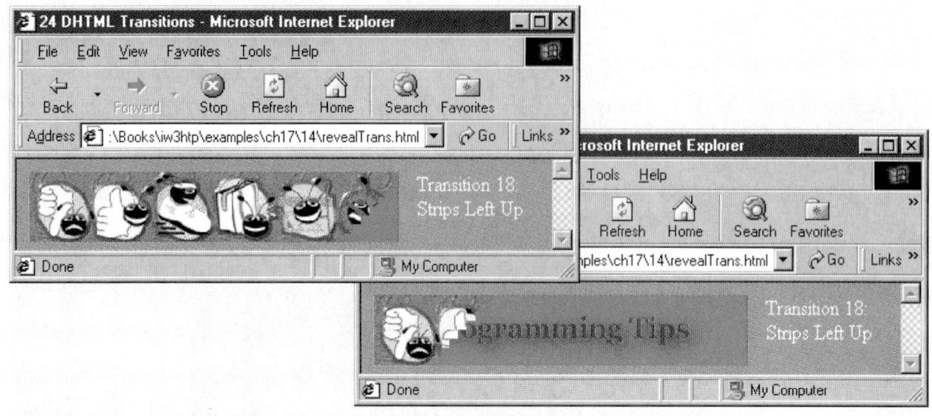

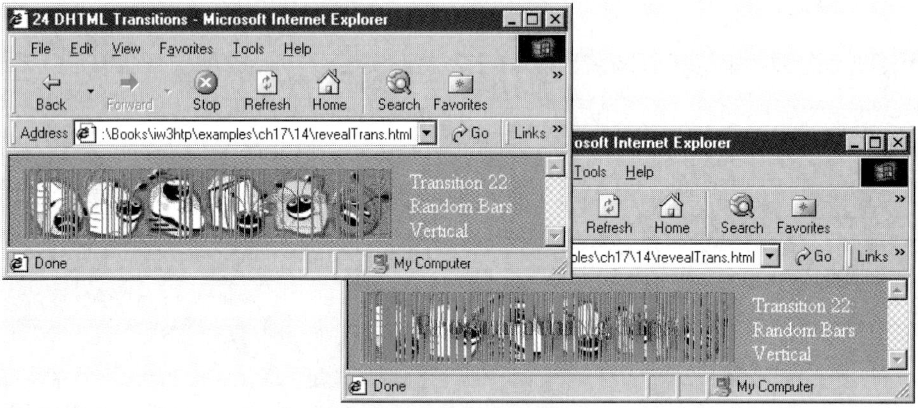

Fig. 17.14 Transitions using **`revealTrans`** (part 5 of 5).

SUMMARY

- Applying filters to text and images causes changes that are persistent.
- Transitions are temporary phenomena: applying a transition allows you to transfer from one page to another with a pleasant visual effect such as a random dissolve.
- Filters and transitions do not add content to your pages—rather, they present existing content in an engaging manner to help hold the user's attention.
- Each of the visual effects achievable with filters and transitions is programmable, so these effects may be adjusted dynamically by programs that respond to user-initiated events like mouse clicks and keystrokes.
- When Internet Explorer renders your page, it applies all the special effects and does this while running on the client computer without lengthy waits for files to download from the server.
- The **`flipv`** and **`fliph`** filters mirror text or images vertically and horizontally, respectively.
- Filters are applied in the **`STYLE`** attribute. The **`filter`** property's value is the name of the filter.
- One filter can be applied at once. Enter multiple filters as values of the **`filter`** attribute, separated by spaces.

- The **chroma** filter allows you to apply transparency effects dynamically, without using a graphics editor to hard-code transparency into the image. However, as we noted in Chapter 5, using transparency on images that have anti-aliasing often produces unsightly effects.
- Use the **parseInt** function to convert a string to a hexadecimal integer for setting the **color** property of the **chroma** filter. The second parameter of **parseInt** specifies the base of the integer.
- Each filter has a property named **enabled**. If this property is set to **true**, the filter is applied. If it is set to **false**, the filter is not applied.
- The **ONCHANGE** event fires whenever the **VALUE** of a form field changes.
- Applying the **mask** filter to an image allows you to create an image mask, in which the background of an element is a solid color and the foreground of an element is transparent to the image or color behind it.
- Parameters for filters are always specified in the format *param = value*.
- The **invert** filter applies a negative image effect—dark areas become light, and light areas become dark.
- The **gray** filter applies a grayscale image effect, in which all color is stripped from the image and all that remains is brightness data.
- The **xray** filter applies an xray effect which is basically just an inversion of the grayscale effect.
- A simple filter that adds depth to your text is the **shadow** filter. This filter creates a shadowing effect that gives your text a three-dimensional look. The **direction** property of the **shadow** filter determines in which direction the shadow effect will be applied—this can be set to any of eight directions, expressed in angular notation: **0** (up), **45** (above-right), **90** (right), **135** (below-right), **180** (below), **225** (below-left), **270** (left), and **315** (above-left). The **color** property of the **shadow** filter specifies the color of the shadow which will be applied to the text.
- Internet Explorer 5 allows you to create gradient effects dynamically using the **alpha** filter. The **style** property of the filter determines in what style the opacity is applied; a value of 0 applies uniform opacity, a value of 1 applies a linear gradient, a value of 2 applies a circular gradient, and a value of 3 applies a rectangular gradient. The **opacity** and **finishopacity** properties are both percentages determining at what percent opacity the specified gradient will start and finish, respectively. Additional attributes are **startX**, **startY**, **finishX**, and **finishY**. These allow you to specify at what x-y coordinates the gradient starts and finishes in that element.
- The **glow** filter allows you to add an aura of color around your text. The **color** and **strength** can both be specified.
- The **blur** filter creates an illusion of motion by blurring text or images in a certain direction. The **blur** filter can be applied in any of eight directions, and its strength may vary. The **add** property, when set to **true**, adds a copy of the original image over the blurred image, creating a more subtle blurring effect. The **direction** property determines in which direction the **blur** filter will be applied. This is expressed in angular form (as with the **shadow** filter). The **strength** property determines how strong the blurring effect will be.
- The **wave** filter allows you to apply sine-wave distortions to text and images on your Web pages.
- The **add** property, as in the case of the **blur** filter, adds a copy of the text or image underneath the filtered effect. The **add** property is usually only useful when applying the **wave** filter to images. The **freq** property determines the frequency of the wave applied—i.e., how many complete sine waves will be applied in the affected area. Increasing this property would create a more pronounced wave effect, but makes the text harder to read. The **phase** property indicates the phase shift of the wave. Increasing this property does not modify any physical attributes of the wave, but merely shifts it in space. This property is useful for creating a gentle waving effect, as we do in this example. The last property, **strength**, is the amplitude of the sine wave that is applied.

- Two filters that apply advanced image processing effects are the **dropShadow** and **light** filters. The **dropShadow** filter applies an effect similar to the drop shadow we applied to our images in Chapter 5—it creates a blacked-out version of the image, and places it behind the image, offset by a specified number of pixels.
- The **light** filter is the most powerful and advanced filter available in Internet Explorer 5. It allows you to simulate the effect of a light source shining on your page.
- The **offx** and **offy** properties of the **dropShadow** filter determine by how many pixels the drop shadow will be offset. The **color** property specifies the color of the drop shadow.
- All the parameters and methods of the light **filter** are done by scripting. The **addPoint** method adds a point light source—a source of light which emanates from a single point and radiates in all directions. The first two parameters set the x-y coordinates at which to add the point source. The next parameter sets the height of the point source.This simulates how far above the surface the light is situated. Small values create a small but high-intensity circle of light on the image, while large values cast a circle of light which is darker, but spreads over a greater distance. The next three parameters specify the RGB value of the light, in decimal. In this case we set the light to a color of white. The last parameter is a strength percentage.
- The **moveLight** method updates the position of the light source. The first parameter is the index of the light source on the page. Multiple light sources have index numbers assigned to them in the order they are added. The next two parameters specify the x-y coordinates to which we should move the light source. The next parameter specifies the height to which we move the light source. Setting the last parameter to **1** indicates that the values we are using are absolute. To move your light source by relative amounts instead, use a value of **0** for the last parameter of the **moveLight** function.
- The parameters of the **addCone** method are similar to the **addPoint** method. The first two parameters specify the x-y coordinates of the light source, and the third parameter specifies the simulated height above the page at which the light should be placed. The next two parameters specify the x-y coordinates at which the cone source is targeted. The next three parameters specify the RGB value of the light which is cast, just as we did in the **addPoint** method. The next parameter specifies the strength of the cone source, in a percentage The last value specifies the spread of the light source, in degrees (this can be set in the range **0**–**90**).
- The transitions included with Internet Explorer 5 give the author control of scriptable PowerPoint type effects. Transitions are set as values of the **filter** CSS property, just as regular filters are. We then use scripting to begin the transition.
- The **duration** parameter of **blendTrans** determines how long the transition will take.
- The **apply** method initializes the transition for the affected element. The **play** method then begins the transition.
- The **revealTrans** filter allows you to transition using professional-style transitions, from Box Out to Random Dissolve. The **transition** property determines what visual transition will be used. There are 24 different visual transitions.

TERMINOLOGY

add property of **blur** filter
add property of **wave** filter
addCone method of **light** filter
addPoint method of **light** filter
alpha filter
blendTrans filter
blur filter
chroma filter
CSS **filter** property
direction property of **blur** filter
direction property of **shadow** filter
dropShadow filter

duration of **blendTrans** filter
enabled property of each filter
fade-in/fade-out effect
filter
circular gradient
color property of **chroma** filter
color property of **dropshadow** filter
color property of **glow** filter
color property of **shadow** filter
combining filters
cone light source
filter:gray
filter:invert
filter:light
filter:mask
filter property with **STYLE** attribute
filter:shadow
filter **strength**
filter:wave
filter:xray
finishopacity property of **alpha** filter
finishx property of **alpha** filter
finishy property of **alpha** filter
flipH filter
flipV filter
freq property of **wave** filter
glow filter
gradient
gray filter
grayscale image effect
height of light source
horizontal blinds transition
illusion of motion by blurring
image mask
invert filter
light filter
linear opacity
mask filter
moveLight property of **light** filter
negative image effect with **invert** filter
filter:alpha
filter:blur
filter:chroma
filter:dropshadow
filter:flipH
filter:flipV
filter:glow
offx property of **dropshadow** filter
offy property of **dropshadow** filter
opacity property of **alpha** filter
padding (CSS)
phase property of **wave** filter
phase shift of a wave
point light source
radial opacity
random dissolve transition
rectangular opacity
revealTrans filter
shadow filter
sine-wave distortions
spread of cone light source
startx property of **alpha** filter
starty property of **alpha** filter
strength property of **blur** filter
strength property of **glow** filter
strength property of **wave** filter
style property of **alpha** filter
three-dimensional effect with **shadow** filter
transition effects
transparency effects
uniform opacity
vertical blinds transition
visibility
visual filters
wave filter
xray filter

COMMON PROGRAMMING ERROR

17.1 When the **glow** filter is set to a large **strength**, the effect is often cut off by the borders of the element. Add CSS **padding** to prevent this.

LOOK-AND-FEEL OBSERVATIONS

17.1 Experiment by applying combinations of filters to the same element. You may discover some eye-pleasing effects that are particularly appropriate for your applications.

17.2 DHTML's effects are programmable. They can be applied dynamically to elements of your pages in response to user events such as mouse clicks and keystrokes.

17.3 A good use of the **invert** filter is to signify that something has just been clicked or selected.

PERFORMANCE TIPS

17.1 With Dynamic HTML many visual effects are implemented directly in the client-side browser (Internet Explorer 5 for this book), so no server-side processing delays are incurred. The DHTML code that initiates these effects is generally quite small and is coded directly into the HTML Web page.

17.2 Applying the **wave** filter to images is processor intensive—if your viewers have inadequate processor power, your pages may act sluggishly on their systems.

PORTABILITY TIP

17.1 Filters and transitions are a Microsoft technology available only in Windows-based versions of Internet Explorer 5. Do not use these capabilities if you are writing for other browsers. If you are writing for an audience with a diversity of browsers and you use DHTML filters and transitions, you should also make alternate provisions.

SOFTWARE ENGINEERING OBSERVATION

17.1 Filters and transitions can be applied to block-level elements such as **DIV** or **P**, and can only be applied to inline-level elements such as **STRONG** or **EM** if the element has its **height** or **width** CSS properties set.

SELF-REVIEW EXERCISES

17.1 State whether each of the following is *true* or *false*; if *false* state why:

a) You can determine the strength of the **shadow** filter.
b) The **flip** filter flips text horizontally.
c) The **mask** filter makes the foreground of an element transparent.
d) The **freq** property of the wave filter determines how many sine waves are applied to that element.
e) Increasing the margin of an element prevents the **glow** filter from being clipped by the element's border.
f) The **apply** method begins a transition.
g) The **invert** filter creates a negative image effect.
h) The **add** property adds a duplicate image below the affected image.

17.2 Fill in the blanks in the following questions:

a) You must use the __________ function to pass a value to the **color** property.
b) The last parameter of the **moveLight** method determines whether the move is ________ or __________.
c) The amplitude of the **wave** filter is controlled by the __________ property.
d) There are __________ **direction**s in which the **blur** filter can be applied.
e) There are two coordinate pairs in the parameters of the **addCone** method: the ________ and the __________.
f) There are __________ different transition styles for the **revealTrans** transition.
g) The two properties of the **dropShadow** filter that specify the offset of the shadow are __________ and __________.
h) The four styles of opacity are __________, __________, __________ and __________.
i) The __________ filter creates a grayscale version of the effected image.

ANSWERS TO SELF-REVIEW EXERCISES

17.1 a) False; there is no **strength** property for the **shadow** filter. b) False; the **fliph** filter flips text horizontally. c) True. d) True. e) False; increasing the padding of an element prevents clipping. f) False; the **play** method begins a transition. g) True. h) True.

17.2 a) **parseInt**. b) relative, absolute. c) **strength**. d) eight. e) source, target. f) 24 g) **offx**, **offy**. h) uniform, linear, circular, rectangular. i) **gray**.

EXERCISES

17.3 Create a Web page which applies the **invert** filter to an image if the user moves the mouse over the image.

17.4 Create a Web page which applies the **glow** filter to a hyperlink if the user moves the mouse over the over the link.

17.5 Write a script that **blur**s images and slowly unblurs them when they are finished loading into the browser (use event **ONLOAD** for the image).

17.6 Write a script that creates a cone **light** filter which tracks mouse movements across the page.

17.7 Write a script which uses the **blendTrans** filter to transition into an image after the image fully loads (use event **ONLOAD** for the image).

17.8 Write a script that changes the attributes of an **alpha** filter every 20 seconds (see **setInterval** in Chapter 15). Change both the color and the style of the **alpha** filter every time.

17.9 *(Slide Show)* Use the **revealTrans** filter to present your own slide show in a Web page. On each transition display a new image.

17.10 *(Image Selector)* Design a Web page that allows the user to choose from a series of images and allows the user to view the image in color and in grayscale.

18

Dynamic HTML: Data Binding with Tabular Data Control

Objectives

- To understand Dynamic HTML's notion of data binding and how to bind data to HTML elements.
- To be able to sort and filter data directly on the client without involving the server.
- To be able to bind a **`TABLE`** and other HTML elements to data source objects (DSOs).
- To be able to filter data to select only records appropriate for a particular application.
- To be able to navigate backwards and forwards through a database with the **`Move`** methods.

Let's look at the record.
Alfred Emanuel Smith

It is a capital mistake to theorize before one has data.
Sir Arthur Conan Doyle

The more the data banks record about each one of us, the less we exist.
Marshall McLuhan

Poor fellow, he suffers from files.
Aneurin Bevan

Outline

18.1 Introduction

This is one of the most important chapters for people who will build substantial, real-world, Web-based applications. Businesses and organizations thrive on data. Dynamic HTML helps Web application developers produce more responsive data-intensive applications.

Performance Tip 18.1

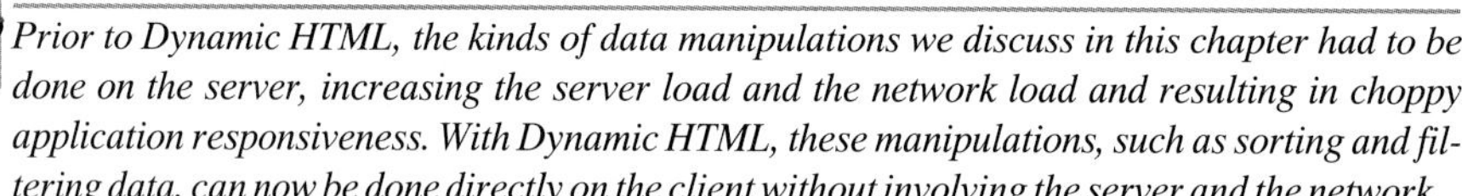

Prior to Dynamic HTML, the kinds of data manipulations we discuss in this chapter had to be done on the server, increasing the server load and the network load and resulting in choppy application responsiveness. With Dynamic HTML, these manipulations, such as sorting and filtering data, can now be done directly on the client without involving the server and the network.

With *data binding*, data need no longer reside exclusively on the server. The data can be maintained on the client and in a manner that distinguishes that data from the HTML code on the page. Typically, the data is sent to the client and then all subsequent manipulations take place on that data directly on the client thus eliminating server activity and network delays.

Performance Tip 18.2

With Dynamic HTML (rather than server-based database processing) it is more likely that a larger amount of data will be sent to the client on the first request. This initial downloading of the data by Internet Explorer is performed in a manner that enables processing to begin immediately on the portion of the data that has arrived.

Also, with the kind of data binding technology we discuss in this chapter, changes to data made on the client do not propagate back to the server. This is not a problem for a great many popular applications. If you do need to access the database directly and have the changes that you make on the client actually update the original database, you can use Microsoft's *Remote Data Services* (RDS), which we discuss in Chapter 25.

Once the data is available on the client, the data can then be sorted and filtered in various ways. We present examples of each of these operations.

In order to bind external data to HTML elements, Internet Explorer employs software capable of connecting the browser to live data sources. These are known as *Data Source Objects* (DSOs). There are several DSOs available in IE5—in this chapter we discuss the most popular DSO, namely the *Tabular Data Control (TDC)*. As we said, in Chapter 25 we discuss Remote Data Services, which is another DSO.

Software Engineering Observation 18.1

Data-bound properties can be modified with Dynamic HTML even after the browser renders the page.

18.2 Simple Data Binding

The Tabular Data Control (TDC) is an *ActiveX control* (a proprietary Microsoft software technology), and is added to the page with an **OBJECT** element. Figure 18.2 demonstrates a simple use of data binding with the TDC to update the contents of a **SPAN** element (the data file used in this example is listed in Fig. 18.1).

```
@ColorName@|@ColorHexRGBValue@
@aqua@|@#00FFFF@
@black@|@#000000@
@blue@|@#0000FF@
@fuchsia@|@#FF00FF@
@gray@|@#808080@
@green@|@#008000@
@lime@|@#00FF00@
@maroon@|@#800000@
@navy@|@#000080@
@olive@|@#808000@
@purple@|@#800080@
@red@|@#FF0000@
@silver@|@#C0C0C0@
@teal@|@#008080@
@yellow@|@#FFFF00@
@white@|@#FFFFFF@
```

Fig. 18.1 HTML color table data (**HTMLStandardColors.txt**).

```
<!DOCTYPE html PUBLIC "-//W3C//DTD HTML 4.0 Transitional//EN">
<HTML>

<!-- Fig 18.2: introdatabind.html                          -->
<!-- Simple data binding and recordset manipulation        -->

<HEAD>
<TITLE>Intro to Data Binding</TITLE>

```

Fig. 18.2 Simple data binding. (part 1 of 3)

```
<!-- This OBJECT element inserts an ActiveX control for -->
<!-- handling and parsing our data. The PARAM tags      -->
<!-- give the control starting parameters such as URL.  -->
<OBJECT ID = "Colors"
   CLASSID = "CLSID:333C7BC4-460F-11D0-BC04-0080C7055A83">
   <PARAM NAME = "DataURL" VALUE = "HTMLStandardColors.txt">
   <PARAM NAME = "UseHeader" VALUE = "TRUE">
   <PARAM NAME = "TextQualifier" VALUE = "@">
   <PARAM NAME = "FieldDelim" VALUE = "|">
</OBJECT>

<SCRIPT LANGUAGE = "JavaScript">
   recordSet = Colors.recordset;

   function reNumber()
   {
      if ( !recordSet.EOF )
         recordNumber.innerText = recordSet.absolutePosition;
      else
         recordNumber.innerText = " ";
   }

   function forward()
   {
      if( !recordSet.EOF )
         recordSet.MoveNext();
      else
         recordSet.MoveFirst();

      colorSample.style.backgroundColor = colorRGB.innerText;
      reNumber();
   }

</SCRIPT>
</HEAD>

<BODY ONLOAD = "reNumber()" ONCLICK = "forward()">

<H1>HTML Color Table</H1>
<H3>Click to move forward in the recordset.</H3>

<P><STRONG>Color Name: </STRONG>
<SPAN ID = "colorName" STYLE = "font-family: monospace"
   DATASRC = "#Colors" DATAFLD = "ColorName"></SPAN><BR>

<STRONG>Color RGB Value: </STRONG>
<SPAN ID = "colorRGB" STYLE = "font-family: monospace"
   DATASRC = "#Colors" DATAFLD = "ColorHexRGBValue"></SPAN>
<BR>

Currently viewing record number
<SPAN ID = "recordNumber" STYLE = "font-weight: 900"></SPAN>
<BR>
```

Fig. 18.2 Simple data binding. (part 2 of 3)

```
63
64  <SPAN ID = "colorSample" STYLE = "background-color: aqua;
65     color: 888888; font-size: 30pt">Color Sample</SPAN>
66  </P>
67
68  </BODY>
69  </HTML>
```

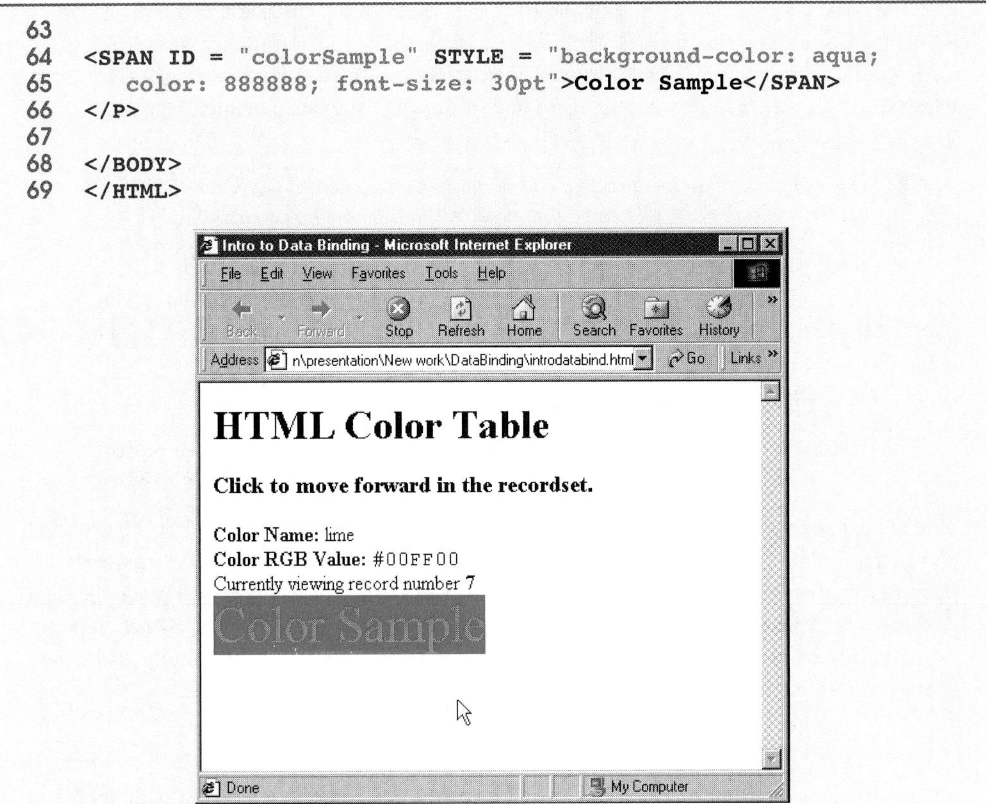

Fig. 18.2 Simple data binding. (part 3 of 3)

Line 1 of Fig. 18.1

```
@ColorName@|@ColorHexRGBValue@
```

begins our data file with a *header row*. This row specifies the names of the columns below (**ColorName** and **ColorHexRGBValue**). In this case, the data in each field is encapsulated in *text qualifiers* (**@**), and the fields are separated with a *field delimiter* (**|**).

Moving on to Fig. 18.2, the first thing you probably notice is the new **OBJECT** element, on lines 13 through 19

```
<OBJECT ID = "Colors"
   CLASSID = "CLSID:333C7BC4-460F-11D0-BC04-0080C7055A83">
   <PARAM NAME = "DataURL" VALUE = "HTMLStandardColors.txt">
   <PARAM NAME = "UseHeader" VALUE = "TRUE">
   <PARAM NAME = "TextQualifier" VALUE = "@">
   <PARAM NAME = "FieldDelim" VALUE = "|">
</OBJECT>
```

The **OBJECT** element here inserts the Tabular Data Control—one of the Microsoft ActiveX controls built into Internet Explorer 5. Attribute **CLASSID** specifies the ActiveX control to add to the Web page—here we use the **CLASSID** of the Tabular Data Control.

The **PARAM** tag specifies parameters for the object in the **OBJECT** element. Attribute **NAME** is the parameter name and attribute **VALUE** is the value. Parameter **DataURL** is the URL of the data source (**HTMLStandrardColors.txt**). Parameter **UseHeader**, when set to **true**, specifies that the first line of our data file has a header row.

Common Programming Error 18.1

*Forgetting to set the **UseHeader** parameter to **true** when you have a header row in your data source is an error that can cause problems in referencing columns.*

The third parameter, **TextQualifier**, sets the *text qualifier* of our data (in this case to **@**). A text qualifier is the character placed on both ends of the field data. The fourth parameter, **FieldDelim**, sets the *field delimiter* of our data (in this case to **|**). The field is the character delimiting separate data fields.

Lines 52 and 53

```
<SPAN ID = "colorName" STYLE = "font-family: monospace"
   DATASRC = "#Colors" DATAFLD = "ColorName"></SPAN><BR>
```

bind the data to a **SPAN** element. The **DATASRC** attribute refers to the **ID** of the TDC object (**Colors**, in this case) preceded with a hash mark (**#**), and the **DATAFLD** attribute specifies the name of the field to bind it to (**ColorName**, in this case). This will place the data contained in the first *record* (i.e., row) of the **ColorName** column into the **SPAN** element.

So far, we only have a static display of data. We can update it dynamically with some simple scripting. Line 22

```
recordSet = Colors.recordset;
```

assigns the ***recordset*** *property* of the **Colors** object (our TDC **OBJECT** element) to the variable **recordSet**. A *recordset* is simply a set of data—in our case, it is the current row of data from the data source. To move the recordset to a different row in the data source, line 35

```
recordSet.MoveNext();
```

calls the ***MoveNext*** *method* of the **recordSet** object. This will move the current recordset forward by one row, automatically updating the **SPAN** to which we bound our data. Note that line 34

```
if( !recordSet.EOF )
```

checks to make sure that the boolean ***EOF*** property of the **recordSet** is not **true**. If it were, that would indicate that we had reached the end of the data source.

Common Programming Error 18.2

*Trying to use the **MoveNext** or **MovePrevious** methods past the boundaries of the data source creates a JavaScript error.*

If **EOF** is **true**, line 37

```
recordSet.MoveFirst();
```

uses the ***MoveFirst*** *method* to move back to the first recordset in the file.

18.3 Moving a Recordset

Most applications will probably need more functionality than simply moving forward. Figure 18.3 demonstrates creating a user interface for moving throughout a data source.

```
<!DOCTYPE html PUBLIC "-//W3C//DTD HTML 4.0 Transitional//EN">
<HTML>

<!-- Fig 18.3: moving.html        -->
<!-- Moving through a recordset -->

<HEAD>
<TITLE>Dynamic Recordset Viewing</TITLE>
<OBJECT ID = "Colors"
   CLASSID = "CLSID:333C7BC4-460F-11D0-BC04-0080C7055A83">
   <PARAM NAME = "DataURL" VALUE = "HTMLStandardColors.txt">
   <PARAM NAME = "UseHeader" VALUE = "TRUE">
   <PARAM NAME = "TextQualifier" VALUE = "@">
   <PARAM NAME = "FieldDelim" VALUE = "|">
</OBJECT>

<SCRIPT LANGUAGE = "JavaScript">
   recordSet = Colors.recordset;

   function update()
   {
      h1Title.style.color = colorRGB.innerText;
   }

   function move( whereTo )
   {
      switch( whereTo ) {

         case "first":
            recordSet.MoveFirst();
            update();
            break;

         // If recordset is at beginning, move to end.
         case "previous":

            if( recordSet.BOF )
               recordSet.MoveLast();
            else
               recordSet.MovePrevious();

            update();
            break;

```

Fig. 18.3 Moving through a recordset using JavaScript (part 1 of 3).

```
            // If recordset is at end, move to beginning.
            case "next":

               if( recordSet.EOF )
                  recordSet.MoveFirst();
               else
                  recordSet.MoveNext();

               update();
               break;

            case "last":
               recordSet.MoveLast();
               update();
               break;
         }
      }

   </SCRIPT>

   <STYLE TYPE = "text/css">
     INPUT { background-color: khaki;
             color: green;
             font-weight: bold }
   </STYLE>
   </HEAD>

   <BODY STYLE = "background-color: darkkhaki">

   <H1 STYLE = "color: black" ID = "h1Title">HTML Color Table</H1>

   <SPAN STYLE = "position: absolute; left: 200; width: 270;
      border-style: groove; text-align: center;
      background-color: cornsilk; padding: 10">
   <STRONG>Color Name: </STRONG>
   <SPAN ID = "colorName" STYLE = "font-family: monospace"
      DATASRC = "#Colors" DATAFLD = "ColorName">ABC</SPAN><BR>

   <STRONG>Color RGB Value: </STRONG>
   <SPAN ID = "colorRGB" STYLE = "font-family: monospace"
      DATASRC = "#Colors" DATAFLD = "ColorHexRGBValue">ABC
   </SPAN><BR>

   <INPUT TYPE = "button" VALUE = "First"
      ONCLICK = "move( 'first' );">

   <INPUT TYPE = "button" VALUE = "Previous"
      ONCLICK = "move( 'previous' );">

   <INPUT TYPE = "button" VALUE = "Next"
      ONCLICK = "move( 'next' );">

```

Fig. 18.3 Moving through a recordset using JavaScript (part 2 of 3).

```
97  <INPUT TYPE = "button" VALUE = "Last"
98     ONCLICK = "move( 'last' );">
99  </SPAN>
100
101 </BODY>
102 </HTML>
```

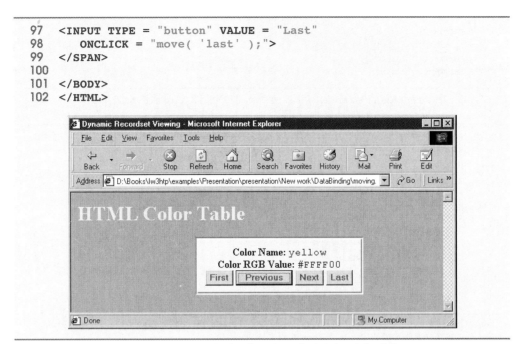

Fig. 18.3 Moving through a recordset using JavaScript (part 3 of 3).

The **`switch`** on lines 27 through 60 handles the commands issued by clicking the buttons. The two new functions we use are ***`MoveLast`*** and ***`MovePrevious`***, which are self-explanatory.

Line 37

```
if( recordSet.BOF )
```

determines if the recordset is pointing to the beginning of the file (***`BOF`***), so that we can redirect it. This is for the same reason that we checked for **`EOF`** in Fig. 18.2—using the ***`MovePrevious`*** when the recordset points to the first record in a data file that causes an error.

18.4 Binding to an `IMG`

Many different types of HTML elements can be bound to data sources. In Fig. 18.5 we bind an **`IMG`** element to the data source shown in Fig. 18.4.

```
image
numbers/0.gif
numbers/1.gif
numbers/2.gif
numbers/3.gif
numbers/4.gif
numbers/5.gif
```

Fig. 18.4 The **`images.txt`** data source file for Fig. 18.5 (part 1 of 2).

```
numbers/6.gif
numbers/7.gif
numbers/8.gif
numbers/9.gif
```

Fig. 18.4 The **images.txt** data source file for Fig. 18.5 (part 2 of 2).

```
<!DOCTYPE html PUBLIC "-//W3C//DTD HTML 4.0 Transitional//EN">
<HTML>

<!-- Fig. 18.5: bindimg.html  -->
<!-- Binding data to an image -->

<HEAD>
<TITLE>Binding to a IMG</TITLE>

<OBJECT ID = "Images"
   CLASSID = "CLSID:333C7BC4-460F-11D0-BC04-0080C7055A83">
   <PARAM NAME = "DataURL" VALUE = "images.txt">
   <PARAM NAME = "UseHeader" VALUE = "True">
</OBJECT>

<SCRIPT LANGUAGE = "JavaScript">

   recordSet = Images.recordset;

   function move( whereTo )
   {
      switch( whereTo ) {

         case "first":
            recordSet.MoveFirst();
            break;

         case "previous":

            if ( recordSet.BOF )
               recordSet.MoveLast();
            else
                recordSet.MovePrevious();

            break;

         case "next":

            if ( recordSet.EOF )
               recordSet.MoveFirst();
            else
               recordSet.MoveNext();

            break;

```

Fig. 18.5 Binding data to an **IMG** element (part 1 of 2).

```
46            case "last":
47               recordSet.MoveLast();
48               break;
49         }
50      }
51
52   </SCRIPT>
53   </HEAD>
54
55   <BODY>
56
57   <IMG DATASRC = "#Images" DATAFLD = "image"
58        STYLE = "position: relative; left: 45px"><BR>
59
60   <INPUT TYPE = "button" VALUE = "First"
61      ONCLICK = "move( 'first' );">
62
63   <INPUT TYPE = "button" VALUE = "Previous"
64      ONCLICK = "move( 'previous' );">
65
66   <INPUT TYPE = "button" VALUE = "Next"
67      ONCLICK = "move( 'next' );">
68
69   <INPUT TYPE = "button" VALUE = "Last"
70      ONCLICK = "move( 'last' );">
71
72   </BODY>
73   </HTML>
```

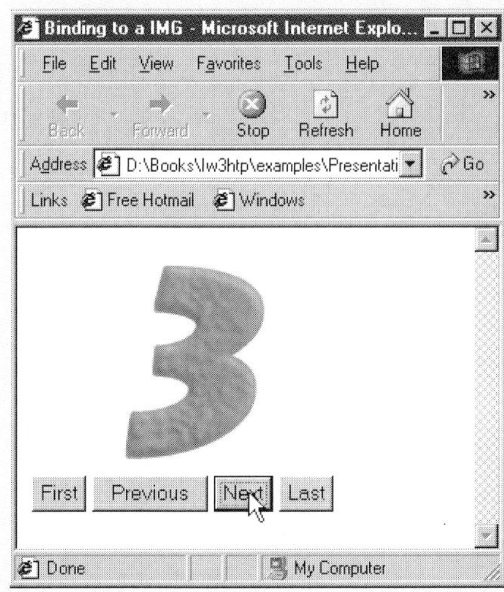

Fig. 18.5 Binding data to an **IMG** element (part 2 of 2).

Lines 57 and 58

```
<IMG DATASRC = "#Images" DATAFLD = "image"
   STYLE = "position: relative; left: 45px"><BR>
```

bind our data source to an **IMG** element. When binding to an **IMG** element, changing the recordset updates the **SRC** attribute of the image. Thus, clicking any of the navigation buttons under the image changes the image displayed on screen.

18.5 Binding to a TABLE

Binding data to a **TABLE** element (Fig. 18.6) is perhaps the most useful feature of data binding. This is done somewhat differently from the data binding we have seen thus far.

```
<!DOCTYPE html PUBLIC "-//W3C//DTD HTML 4.0 Transitional//EN">
<HTML>

<!-- Fig 18.6: tablebind.html      -->
<!-- Using Data Binding with tables -->

<HEAD>
<TITLE>Data Binding and Tables</TITLE>
<OBJECT ID = "Colors"
   CLASSID = "CLSID:333C7BC4-460F-11D0-BC04-0080C7055A83">
   <PARAM NAME = "DataURL" VALUE = "HTMLStandardColors.txt">
   <PARAM NAME = "UseHeader" VALUE = "TRUE">
   <PARAM NAME = "TextQualifier" VALUE = "@">
   <PARAM NAME = "FieldDelim" VALUE = "|">
</OBJECT>
</HEAD>

<BODY STYLE = "background-color: darkseagreen">

<H1>Binding Data to a <CODE>TABLE</CODE></H1>

<TABLE DATASRC = "#Colors" STYLE = "border-style: ridge;
   border-color: darkseagreen; background-color: lightcyan">

   <THEAD>
   <TR STYLE = "background-color: mediumslateblue">
      <TH>Color Name</TH>
      <TH>Color RGB Value</TH>
   </TR>
   </THEAD>

   <TBODY>
      <TR STYLE = "background-color: lightsteelblue">
         <TD><SPAN DATAFLD = "ColorName"></SPAN></TD>
         <TD><SPAN DATAFLD = "ColorHexRGBValue"
            STYLE = "font-family: monospace"></SPAN></TD>
      </TR>
   </TBODY>

</TABLE>

</BODY>
</HTML>
```

Fig. 18.6 Binding data to a **TABLE** element (part 1 of 2).

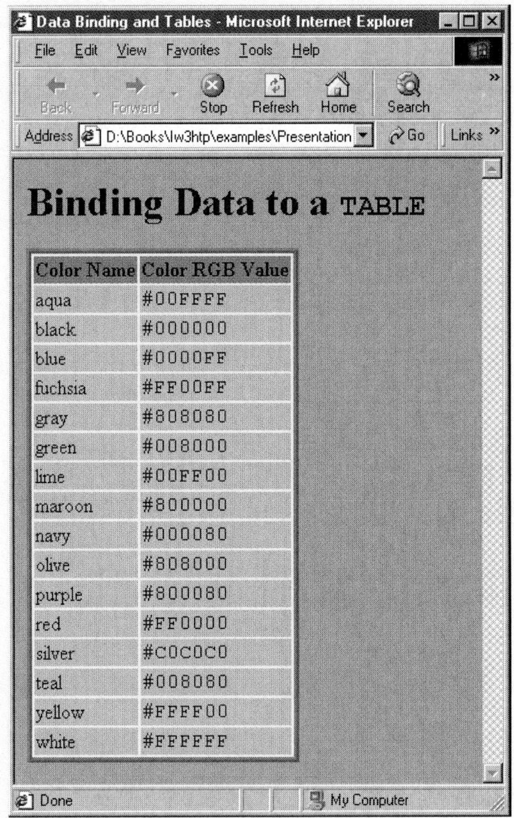

Fig. 18.6 Binding data to a **TABLE** element (part 2 of 2).

Lines 22 and 23

```
<TABLE DATASRC = "#Colors" STYLE = "border-style: ridge;
   border-color: darkseagreen; background-color: lightcyan">
```

begin binding the table by adding the **DATASRC** attribute to the opening **TABLE** tag. We complete the data binding in lines 34 through 36

```
<TD><SPAN DATAFLD = "ColorName"></SPAN></TD>
<TD><SPAN DATAFLD = "ColorHexRGBValue"
   STYLE = "font-family: monospace"></SPAN></TD>
```

by adding the **DATAFLD** attribute to **SPAN** tags that reside in the table cells. Note that in the file we only have one row of table cells—Internet Explorer iterates through the data file, and creates a table row for each recordset it finds.

18.6 Sorting TABLE Data

If you are working with a large data source, your client will probably need some way to sort the data. This is accomplished with the ***Sort*** *property* of the TDC (Fig 18.7).

```
<!DOCTYPE html PUBLIC "-//W3C//DTD HTML 4.0 Transitional//EN">
<HTML>

<!-- Fig 18.7: sorting.html -->
<!-- Sorting TABLE data      -->

<HEAD>
<TITLE>Data Binding and Tables</TITLE>
<OBJECT ID = "Colors"
   CLASSID = "CLSID:333C7BC4-460F-11D0-BC04-0080C7055A83">
   <PARAM NAME = "DataURL" VALUE = "HTMLStandardColors.txt">
   <PARAM NAME = "UseHeader" VALUE = "TRUE">
   <PARAM NAME = "TextQualifier" VALUE = "@">
   <PARAM NAME = "FieldDelim" VALUE = "|">
</OBJECT>
</HEAD>

<BODY STYLE = "background-color: darkseagreen">

<H1>Sorting Data</H1>

<TABLE DATASRC = "#Colors" STYLE = "border-style: ridge;
   border-color: darkseagreen; background-color: lightcyan">
   <CAPTION>
   Sort by:

   <SELECT ONCHANGE = "Colors.Sort = this.value;
      Colors.Reset();">
      <OPTION VALUE = "ColorName">Color Name (Ascending)
      <OPTION VALUE = "-ColorName">Color Name (Descending)
      <OPTION VALUE = "ColorHexRGBValue">Color RGB Value
         (Ascending)
      <OPTION VALUE = "-ColorHexRGBValue">Color RGB Value
         (Descending)
   </SELECT>
   </CAPTION>

   <THEAD>
   <TR STYLE = "background-color: mediumslateblue">
      <TH>Color Name</TH>
      <TH>Color RGB Value</TH>
   </TR>
   </THEAD>

   <TBODY>
   <TR STYLE = "background-color: lightsteelblue">
      <TD><SPAN DATAFLD = "ColorName"></SPAN></TD>
      <TD><SPAN DATAFLD = "ColorHexRGBValue"
         STYLE = "font-family: monospace"></SPAN></TD>
   </TR>
   </TBODY>

</TABLE>
```

Fig. 18.7 Sorting data in a **TABLE** (part 1 of 2).

```
54
55  </BODY>
56  </HTML>
```

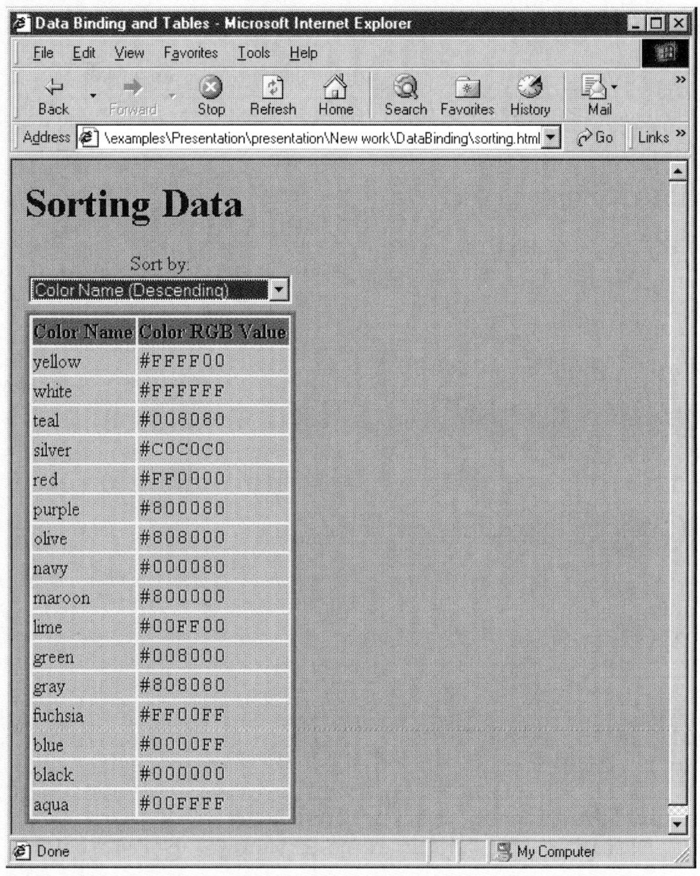

Fig. 18.7 Sorting data in a **TABLE** (part 2 of 2).

Lines 27 and 28

```
<SELECT ONCHANGE = "Colors.Sort = this.value;
   Colors.Reset();">
```

sort our data by specifying the column by which to sort in the **Sort** property of the TDC. This example sets property **Sort** to the value of the selected **OPTION** tag (**this.value**) when the **ONCHANGE** event is fired. JavaScript keyword **this** refers to the element in which the statement resides (i.e., the **SELECT** element). Therefore, the **value** property refers to the currently selected **OPTION** tag. After setting the **Sort** property, we invoke the ***Reset*** *method* of the TDC to display our data in its new sort order.

Lines 29 and 30

```
<OPTION VALUE = "ColorName">Color Name (Ascending)
<OPTION VALUE = "-ColorName">Color Name (Descending)
```

set the **VALUE** attributes of the **OPTION** tags to the column names in our data file. By default, a column will be sorted in ascending order. To sort in descending order, the column name is preceded with a minus sign (**-**).

18.7 Advanced Sorting and Filtering

The TDC allows for sorting by multiple columns. Combined with *filtering*, this provides a powerful means of data rendering (Fig. 18.9).

Note that line 16

```
<PARAM NAME = "Sort" VALUE = "+Title">
```

sets the **Sort** property of the TDC using a **PARAM** tag instead of scripting. This is useful for providing an initial sorting order (in this case alphabetically by **Title**).

Line 28

```
SPAN    { cursor: hand; }
```

introduces the ***cursor*** CSS attribute, which specifies what the mouse cursor will look like when hovering over an object. In this case we set the property to ***hand*** (the same hand that appears when you move your cursor over a link). This lets the user know that a **SPAN** is clickable when the cursor is moved over it.

```
@Title:String@|@Authors:String@|@Copyright:String@|@Edition:String@|@Type:String@
@C How to Program@|@Deitel,Deitel@|@1992@|@1@|@BK@
@C How to Program@|@Deitel,Deitel@|@1994@|@2@|@BK@
@C++ How to Program@|@Deitel,Deitel@|@1994@|@1@|@BK@
@C++ How to Program@|@Deitel,Deitel@|@1998@|@2@|@BK@
@Java How to Program@|@Deitel,Deitel@|@1997@|@1@|@BK@
@Java How to Program@|@Deitel,Deitel@|@1998@|@2@|@BK@
@Java How to Program@|@Deitel,Deitel@|@2000@|@3@|@BK@
@Visual Basic 6 How to Program@|@Deitel,Deitel,Nieto@|@1999@|@1@|@BK@
@Internet and World Wide Web How to Program@|@Deitel,Deitel@|@2000@|@1@|@BK@
@The Complete C++ Training Course@|@Deitel,Deitel@|@1996@|@1@|@BKMMCD@
@The Complete C++ Training Course@|@Deitel,Deitel@|@1998@|@2@|@BKMMCD@
@The Complete Java Training Course@|@Deitel,Deitel@|@1997@|@1@|@BKMMCD@
@The Complete Java Training Course@|@Deitel,Deitel@|@1998@|@2@|@BKMMCD@
@The Complete Java Training Course@|@Deitel,Deitel@|@2000@|@3@|@BKMMCD@
@The Complete Visual Basic 6 Training Course@|@Deitel,Deitel,Nieto@|@1999@|@1@|@BKMMCD@
@The Complete Internet and World Wide Web Programming Training Course@|@Deitel,Deitel@|@2000@|@1@|@BKMMCD@
```

Fig. 18.8 **DBPublications.txt** data file for Fig. 18.9.

```
<!DOCTYPE html PUBLIC "-//W3C//DTD HTML 4.0 Transitional//EN">
<HTML>

<!-- Fig 18.9: advancedsort.html -->
<!-- Sorting and filtering data  -->

<HEAD>
<TITLE>Data Binding - Sorting and Filtering</TITLE>

<OBJECT ID = "Publications"
   CLASSID = "CLSID:333C7BC4-460F-11D0-BC04-0080C7055A83">
   <PARAM NAME = "DataURL" VALUE = "DBPublications.txt">
   <PARAM NAME = "UseHeader" VALUE = "TRUE">
   <PARAM NAME = "TextQualifier" VALUE = "@">
   <PARAM NAME = "FieldDelim" VALUE = "|">
   <PARAM NAME = "Sort" VALUE = "+Title">
</OBJECT>

<STYLE>

 A       { font-size: 9pt;
           text-decoration: underline;
           cursor: hand;
           color: blue }

 CAPTION { cursor: hand; }

 SPAN    { cursor: hand; }

</STYLE>

<SCRIPT LANGUAGE = "JavaScript">
   var sortOrder;

   function reSort( column, order )
   {
      if ( order )
         sortOrder = "";
      else
         sortOrder = "-";

      if ( event.ctrlKey ) {
         Publications.Sort += "; " + sortOrder + column;
         Publications.Reset();
      }
      else {
         Publications.Sort = sortOrder + column;
         Publications.Reset();
      }

      spanSort.innerText = "Current sort: " + Publications.Sort;
   }

```

Fig. 18.9 Advanced sorting and filtering (part 1 of 4).

```
    function filter( filterText, filterColumn )
    {
       Publications.Filter = filterColumn + "=" + filterText;
       Publications.Reset();
       spanFilter.innerText =
          "Current filter: " + Publications.Filter;
    }

    function clearAll()
    {
        Publications.Sort = " ";
        spanSort.innerText = "Current sort: None";
        Publications.Filter = " ";
        spanFilter.innerText = "Current filter: None";
        Publications.Reset();
     }
</SCRIPT>
</HEAD>

<BODY>
<H1>Advanced Sorting</H1>
Click on the link next to a column head to sort by that column.
To sort by more than one column at a time, hold down CTRL while
you click another sorting link. Click on any cell to filter by
the data of that cell. To clear filters and sorts, click on the
green caption bar.

<TABLE DATASRC = "#Publications" BORDER = 1 CELLSPACING = 0
   CELLPADDING = 2 STYLE = "background-color: papayawhip;">

   <CAPTION STYLE = "background-color: lightgreen; padding: 5"
      ONCLICK = "clearAll()">
      <SPAN ID = "spanFilter" STYLE = "font-weight: bold;
         background-color: lavender">Current filter: None
         </SPAN>
      <SPAN ID = "spanSort" STYLE = "font-weight: bold;
         background-color: khaki">Current sort: None</SPAN>
   </CAPTION>

   <THEAD>
   <TR>
      <TH>Title <BR>
         (<A ONCLICK = "reSort( 'Title', true )">
            Ascending</A>
         <A ONCLICK = "reSort( 'Title', false )">
            Descending</A>)
      </TH>

      <TH>Authors <BR>
         (<A ONCLICK = "reSort( 'Authors', true )">
            Ascending</A>
         <A ONCLICK = "reSort( 'Authors', false )">
            Descending</A>)
```

Fig. 18.9 Advanced sorting and filtering (part 2 of 4).

```
         </TH>

         <TH>Copyright <BR>
            (<A ONCLICK = "reSort( 'Copyright', true )">
               Ascending</A>
            <A ONCLICK = "reSort( 'Copyright', false )">
               Descending</A>)
         </TH>

         <TH>Edition <BR>
            (<A ONCLICK = "reSort( 'Edition', true )">
               Ascending</A>
            <A ONCLICK = "reSort( 'Edition', false )">
               Descending</A>)
         </TH>

         <TH>Type <BR>
            (<A ONCLICK = "reSort( 'Type', true )">
               Ascending</A>
            <A ONCLICK = "reSort( 'Type', false )">
               Descending</A>)
         </TH>
      </TR>
      </THEAD>

      <TR>
         <TD><SPAN DATAFLD = "Title" ONCLICK =
            "filter( this.innerText, 'Title' )"></SPAN></A>
         </TD>

         <TD><SPAN DATAFLD = "Authors" ONCLICK =
            "filter( this.innerText, 'Authors')"></SPAN>
         </TD>

         <TD><SPAN DATAFLD = "Copyright" ONCLICK =
            "filter( this.innerText, 'Copyright' )"></SPAN>
         </TD>

         <TD><SPAN DATAFLD = "Edition" ONCLICK =
            "filter( this.innerText, 'Edition' )"></SPAN>
         </TD>

         <TD><SPAN DATAFLD = "Type" ONCLICK =
            "filter( this.innerText, 'Type' )"></SPAN>
         </TD>

      </TR>

   </TABLE>

   </BODY>
   </HTML>
```

Fig. 18.9 Advanced sorting and filtering (part 3 of 4).

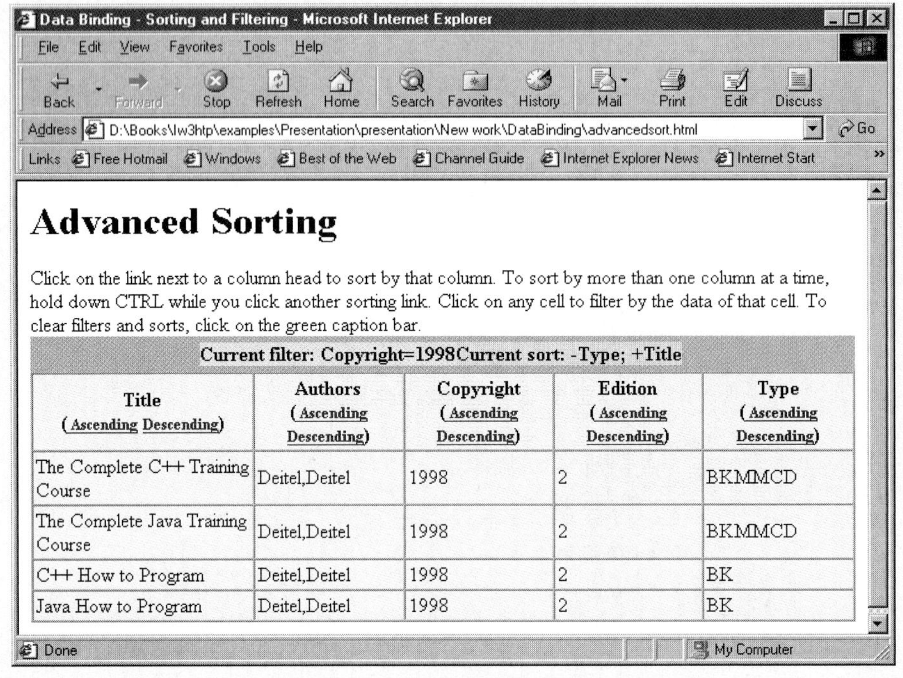

Fig. 18.9 Advanced sorting and filtering (part 4 of 4).

When a user clicks the **Ascending** or **Descending** links in any of the column heads, the table resorts by that column. To do this, each column head has an associated **ONCLICK** event that calls the **reSort** function, passing the name of the column to sort and a boolean value that specifies the sort order (**true** for ascending, **false** for descending).

The user can sort by multiple columns by holding *CTRL* while clicking a link. Line 42

```
if ( event.ctrlKey )
```

checks the boolean value ***event.ctrlKey***, which returns **true** if *CTRL* was pressed when the event was triggered. If the user did press *CTRL*, line 43

```
Publications.Sort += "; " + sortOrder + column;
```

adds another sort criterion to property **Sort**, separated from the first with a semicolon (**"; "**).

The **Filter** property allows you to filter out all records that do not have a cell matching the text you specify. It should be in the format *ColumnName = FilterText*. In this example, the user can click on any cell to filter by the text inside that cell. Any cell, when clicked, calls the **filter** function, passing as parameters the text of the cell (**this.innerText**) and the column by which to filter. In the **filter** function, line 56

```
Publications.Filter = filterColumn + "=" + filterText;
```

sets the **Filter** property of the TDC to the column and text by which that column should be filtered. In this case the filter tests for equality using the equality operator **=** (which is different from the JavaScript equality operator **==**). Any of the normal equality operators (**=**, **<>**) and relational operators (**>**, **<**, **>=**, **<=**) may be used for filtering.

18.8 Data Binding Elements

Exactly how a data source is displayed by the browser depends on the HTML element the data is bound to—different elements may use the data for different purposes. Figure 18.10 lists some elements that can be bound to data with the TDC, and the attributes of those elements that reflect data changes.

18.9 Internet and the World Wide Web Resources

http://www.microsoft.com/data
The Microsoft *Universal Data Access Technologies* Web site provides information about Microsoft database access strategies and data source objects.

http://www.msdn.microsoft.com/resources/schurmandhtml.asp
This Web site for the Microsoft Press book for *Dynamic HTML in Action, Second Edition* (by Eric M. Schurman and William J. Pardi) provides information about Dynamic HTML and Microsoft database access.

Element	Bindable property/attribute
A	**HREF**
DIV	Contained text
FRAME	**HREF**
IFRAME	**HREF**
IMG	**SRC**
INPUT TYPE = "button"	**VALUE** (button text)
INPUT TYPE = "checkbox"	**CHECKED** (use a boolean value in the data)
INPUT TYPE = "hidden"	**VALUE**
INPUT TYPE = "password"	**VALUE**
INPUT TYPE = "radio"	**CHECKED** (use a boolean value in the data)
INPUT TYPE = "text"	**VALUE**
MARQUEE	Contained text
PARAM	**VALUE**
SELECT	Selected **OPTION**
SPAN	Contained text
TABLE	Cell elements (see Section 18.6)
TEXTAREA	Contained text (**VALUE**)

Fig. 18.10 HTML elements that allow data binding.

SUMMARY

- With data binding, data need no longer resides exclusively on the server. The data can be maintained on the client and in a manner that distinguishes that data from the HTML code on the page.
- If you need to access the database directly and have changes you make on the client to update the original database, you can use Microsoft's Remote Data Services.
- Once the data is available on the client, the Web application designer can provide various functionality, especially the ability to sort and filter the data in various ways.
- When a Web page is loaded with data-bound elements, the client retrieves the data from the data source specified by the TDC. The data is then formatted for display on the Web page and remains accessible on the client.
- The Tabular Data Control (TDC) is an ActiveX control that can be added to the page with an **OBJECT** tag.
- A header row in a data source specifies the names of the columns. The data in each field can be encapsulated in text qualifiers and the fields are separated with a field delimiter.
- An **OBJECT** tag is used to insert the ActiveX Tabular Data Control. The **CLASSID** attribute specifies the ActiveX control identifier.
- The **PARAM** tag specifies parameters for the object in the **OBJECT** tag. The **NAME** attribute is the parameter name, and the **VALUE** attribute is the value. The **DataURL** parameter is the URL of the data source. The **UseHeader** parameter specifies that the first line of the data file has a header row when set to **TRUE**. The **TextQualifier** parameter sets the text qualifier of our data. The **FieldDelim** parameter sets the field delimiter of our data.
- The **DATASRC** attribute refers to the **ID** of the TDC object, and the **DATAFLD** attribute specifies the name of the field to bind it to (**ColorName**, in this case).
- A recordset is simply a set of data—in our case, it is the current row of data from the data source.
- The **MoveNext** method moves the current recordset forward by one row, automatically updating the **bound** element.
- The **EOF** property indicates whether the recordset has reached the end of the data source.
- The **MoveFirst** method moves the recordset to the first row in the file.
- The **BOF** property indicates whether the recordset points to the first row of the data source.
- When binding to an **IMG** element, changing the recordset updates the **SRC** attribute of the image.
- To bind to a table, add the **DATASRC** attribute to the opening **TABLE** tag. Then add the **DATAFLD** attribute to **SPAN** tags that reside in the table cells. Internet Explorer iterates through the data file, and creates a table row for each row it finds.
- The **Sort** property of the ActiveX control determines by what column the data is sorted. Once the **Sort** property is set, call the **Reset** method to display the data in its new sort order. By default, a column will be sorted in ascending order—to sort in descending order, the column name is preceded with a minus sign (**-**).
- Setting the **Sort** property of the TDC using a **PARAM** tag instead of scripting is useful for providing an initial sorting order.
- The **cursor** CSS attribute specifies what the mouse cursor will look like when hovering over an object. The value **hand** makes the mouse appear as the same hand that appears when you move your cursor over a link.
- The boolean value **event.ctrlKey** returns **true** if *CTRL* was held down when the event was triggered.

- An additional sort criterion can be added to the **Sort** property, separated from the first with a semicolon.
- The **Filter** property allows you to filter out all records that do not have a cell that matches the text you specify. It should be in the format *ColumnName = FilterText.*
- Any of the normal equality operators (=, <>) and relational operators (>, <, >=, <=) can be used for filtering.

TERMINOLOGY

ActiveX control
ascending sort order
ASP (Active Server Pages)
binding
BOF (beginning-of-file) property of **recordset**
bound elements
CLASSID property
column in a database
current record of a **recordset**
database
data binding
data-bound elements
DATAFLD attribute
data source
data source object (DSO)
DATASRC attribute
DataURL property of Tabular Data Control
descending sort order
DSO (data source object)
EOF (end-of-file) property of **recordset**
field of a record
field delimiter
FieldDelim property of Tabular Data Control
filter data
Filter property of Tabular Data Control
header row
minus sign (**-**) for descending sort order
MoveFirst method of **recordset**
MoveLast method of **recordset**
Move methods
MoveNext method of **recordset**
MovePrevious method of **recordset**
multicolumn sort
record
recordset
Remote Data Services (RDS)
sort in ascending order
sort in descending order
Sort property of Tabular Data Control
Tabular Data Control (**CLSID:333C7BC4-460F-11D0-BC04-0080C7055A83**)
Tabular Data Control (TDC) DSO of IE5
text qualifier
TextQualifer property of TDC
UseHeader property of Tabular Data Control

COMMON PROGRAMMING ERRORS

18.1 Forgetting to set the **UseHeader** parameter to true when you have a header row in your data source is an error that can cause problems in referencing columns.

18.2 Trying to use the **MoveNext** or **MovePrevious** methods past the boundaries of the data source creates a JavaScript error.

PERFORMANCE TIPS

18.1 Prior to Dynamic HTML, the kinds of data manipulations we discuss in this chapter had to be done on the server, increasing the server load and the network load and resulting in choppy application responsiveness. With Dynamic HTML, these manipulations, such as sorting and filtering data, can now be done directly on the client without involving the server and the network.

18.2 With Dynamic HTML (rather than server-based database processing) it is more likely that a larger amount of data will be sent to the client on the first request. This initial downloading of the data by Internet Explorer is performed in a manner that enables processing to begin immediately on the portion of the data that has arrived.

SOFTWARE ENGINEERING OBSERVATION

18.1 Data bound properties may be modified with Dynamic HTML even after the browser renders the page.

SELF-REVIEW EXERCISES

18.1 Answer the following questions true or false; if false, state why:

a) A TDC recordset is one row of data.
b) You can bind any HTML element to data sources.
c) The **CLASSID** attribute for the TDC never changes.
d) **SPAN** elements display bound data as inner text.
e) **IMG** elements display bound data as **ALT** text.
f) You separate multiple sort criteria of the **Sort** property with a comma (**,**).
g) The equality operator (**=**) is the only operator that can be used in filtering data.
h) Calling **MoveNext** when **EOF** is true will move the recordset to the first row of data.
i) Calling **MoveLast** when **EOF** is true causes an error.

18.2 Fill in the blank for each of the following:

a) When binding data to a table, the ________ attribute is placed in the opening **TABLE** tag and the ________ attribute is placed inside the table cells.
b) The TDC is an ________ control.
c) To sort in descending order, precede the sort criterion with a ________.
d) To display data with recently applied sorting, call the ________ method.
e) The ________ parameter specifies that the data source has a header row.
f) A ________ encapsulates text in a data source and a ________ separates fields in a data source.
g) The ________ CSS property changes the appearance of the mouse cursor.

ANSWERS TO SELF-REVIEW EXERCISES

18.1 a) True. b) False; only some HTML elements may be bound to data (Fig. 18.1). c) True. d) True. e) False; data bound to **IMG** elements affects the **SRC** attribute of that **IMG**. f) False; you separate them with a semicolon (**;**). g) False; any of the equality operators or relational operators can be used. h) False; this causes an error. i) False; the recordset will move to the last row of data.

18.2 a) **DATASRC**, **DATAFLD**. b) ActiveX. c) minus sign. (**-**). d) **Reset**. e) **UseHeader**. f) text qualifier, field delimiter. g) **cursor**.

EXERCISES

18.3 Create a data source file with two columns: one for URLs, and one for URL descriptions. Bind the first column to an **A** element on a page and the second to a **SPAN** element contained within the **A** element.

18.4 Bind the data source file you created in Exercise 18.3 to a **TABLE** to create a table of clickable links.

18.5 Add a dropdown **SELECT** list to Fig. 18.9 that allows you to choose the binary operator used for filter matching, from any of **=**, **>**, **<**, **>=** or **<=**.

18.6 Create a data source with a set of name/password pairs. Bind these fields to an **INPUT TYPE = "text"** and **INPUT TYPE = "password"** and provide navigation buttons to allow the user to move throughout the data source.

18.7 Apply the transitions you learned in Chapter 17 to Fig. 18.5 to create a virtual slideshow.

19

Dynamic HTML: Structured Graphics ActiveX Control

Objectives

- To be able to use the Structured Graphics Control to create various shapes.
- To understand the Structured Graphics Control methods for modifying lines and borders
- To understand the Structured Graphics Control methods for modifying colors and fill styles
- To be able to enable event capturing for the Structured Graphics Control
- To be able to import external lists of methods into the Structured Graphics Control
- To be able to scale, rotate, and translate shapes in the Structured Graphics Control

One picture is worth ten thousand words.
Chinese proverb

Treat nature in terms of the cylinder, the sphere, the cone, all in perspective.
Paul Cezanne

Nothing ever becomes real till it is experienced—even a proverb is no proverb to you till your life has illustrated it.
John Keats

Capture its reality in paint!
Paul Cezanne

Outline

19.1 Introduction

Although high-quality content is what visitors to your site are usually looking for, it may not be enough to hold their attention and keep them coming back. Eye-catching graphics may help. This chapter explores the *Structured Graphics* ActiveX Control included with Internet Explorer 5.

The Structured Graphics Control, like the Tabular Data Control we discussed in the previous chapter, is an ActiveX control that you can add to your page with an **OBJECT** tag. Like the TDC, the Structured Graphics Control is easily accessible through scripting. Unlike the TDC, the Structured Graphics Control is meant primarily for visual presentations, and not for displaying data and content.

The Structured Graphics control is a Web interface for the widely used *DirectAnimation* subset of Microsoft's *DirectX* software, used in many high-end video games and graphical applications. To explore the Structured Graphics Control and DirectAnimation further, visit Microsoft's DirectAnimation reference site at

http://www.microsoft.com/directx/dxm/help/da/default.htm

19.2 Shape Primitives

The Structured Graphics Control allows you to create simple shapes by using methods that can be called via scripting or through **PARAM** tags inside **OBJECT** elements. Fig 19.1 demonstrates most of the shapes included in the Structured Graphics Control.

We begin in lines 13 through 15

```
<OBJECT ID = "shapes" STYLE = "background-color: #CCCCFF;
   width: 500; height: 400"
   CLASSID = "CLSID:369303C2-D7AC-11d0-89D5-00A0C90833E6">
```

by inserting the Structured Graphics ActiveX Control. We give it an **ID** of **shapes** for reference purposes. Note that this is a different **CLASSID** from that for the Tabular Data Control in Chapter 17.

```
<!DOCTYPE html PUBLIC "-//W3C//DTD HTML 4.0 Transitional//EN">
<HTML>

<!-- Fig 19.1: shapes.html  -->
<!-- Creating simple shapes -->

<HEAD>
   <TITLE>Structured Graphics - Shapes</TITLE>
</HEAD>

<BODY>

   <OBJECT ID = "shapes" STYLE = "background-color: #CCCCFF;
      width: 500; height: 400"
      CLASSID = "CLSID:369303C2-D7AC-11d0-89D5-00A0C90833E6">

      <PARAM NAME = "Line0001"
         VALUE = "SetLineColor( 0, 0, 0 )">
      <PARAM NAME = "Line0002"
         VALUE = "SetLineStyle( 1, 1 )">
      <PARAM NAME = "Line0003"
         VALUE = "SetFillColor( 0, 255, 255 )">
      <PARAM NAME = "Line0004"
         VALUE = "SetFillStyle( 1 )">

      <PARAM NAME = "Line0005"
         VALUE = "Oval( 0, -175, 25, 50, 45 )">
      <PARAM NAME = "Line0006"
         VALUE = "Arc( -200, -125, 100, 100, 45, 135, 0 )">
      <PARAM NAME = "Line0007"
         VALUE = "Pie( 100, -100, 150, 150, 90, 120, 0 )">
      <PARAM NAME = "Line0008"
         VALUE = "Polygon(5, 0, 0, 10, 20, 0, -30,
                          -10, -10, -10, 25)">
      <PARAM NAME = "Line0009"
         VALUE = "Rect( -185, 0, 60, 30, 25 )">
      <PARAM NAME = "Line0010"
         VALUE = "RoundRect( 200, 100, 35, 60, 10, 10, 25 )">

      <PARAM NAME = "Line0011"
         VALUE = "SetFont( 'Arial', 65, 400, 0, 0, 0 )">
      <PARAM NAME = "Line0012"
         VALUE = "Text( 'Shapes', -200, 200 , -35 )">

      <PARAM NAME = "Line0013"
           VALUE = "SetLineStyle( 2,1 )">
      <PARAM NAME = "Line0014"
         VALUE = "PolyLine( 5, 100, 0, 120, 175, -150, -50,
                           -75, -75, 75, -75)">
   </OBJECT>

</BODY>
</HTML>
```

Fig. 19.1 Creating shapes with the Structured Graphics ActiveX Control (part 1 of 2).

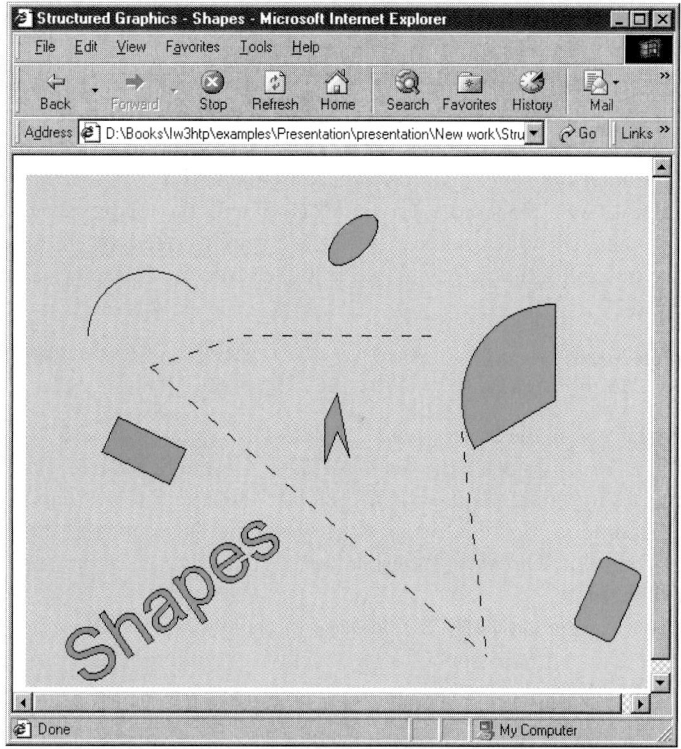

Fig. 19.1 Creating shapes with the Structured Graphics ActiveX Control (part 2 of 2).

The first **PARAM** tag in lines 17 and 18

```
<PARAM NAME = "Line0001"
   VALUE = "SetLineColor( 0, 0, 0 )">
```

calls the ***SetLineColor*** *method* of the Structured Graphics Control. The **NAME** attribute determines the order in which the function is called.

Common Programming Error 19.1

Forgetting to assign successive line numbers (i.e., ***NAME = "Line0001"****,* ***NAME = "Line0002"****) to method calls prevents the intended methods from being called.*

The order of calls must be **Line0001**, **Line0002**, **Line0003**, and so on. The method **SetLineColor** sets the color of lines and borders of shapes that are drawn. It takes an RGB triplet in decimal notation as its three parameters—in this case, we set the line color to black (**0, 0, 0**).

Lines 19 and 20

```
<PARAM NAME = "Line0002"
   VALUE = "SetLineStyle( 1, 1 )">
```

call the ***SetLineStyle*** *method.* Its two parameters set the *line style* and *line width*, respectively. A value of **1** for line style creates a solid line (the default), a value of **0** does not draw any lines or borders, and a value of **2** creates a dashed line. The line width is specified in pixels. In order to create a dashed line with the **SetLineStyle** method, you must set the line width to **1**.

Method ***SetFillColor*** (lines 21 and 22) sets the foreground color with which to fill shapes. Like method **SetLineColor**, it takes a decimal RGB triplet as its parameters. We set the foreground color to cyan (**0**, **255**, **255**). The ***SetFillStyle*** *method* (lines 23 and 24) determines the style in which a shape is filled with color—a value of **1**, as we set here, fills shapes with the solid color we declared with the method **SetFillColor**. There are 14 possible fill styles, some of which we demonstrate later in this chapter. Fig. 19.2 lists all the possible fill styles available with the Structured Graphics Control.

Lines 26 and 27

```
<PARAM NAME = "Line0005"
   VALUE = "Oval( 0, -175, 25, 50, 45 )">
```

create our first shape with the ***Oval*** *method*. The first two parameters, (**0, -175**), specify *x–y* coordinates at which to place the oval. All shapes in the Structured Graphics Control effectively have a surrounding box—when you place the image at a certain *x–y* position, it is the upper-left corner of that box which is placed at that position. It is important to note that, inside the control, the point (0,0) (also known as the *origin*) is at the *center* of the control, not at the upper left.

The next two parameters (**25, 50**) specify the height and width of the oval, respectively. The last parameter (**45**) specifies the clockwise rotation of the oval relative to the *x*-axis, expressed in degrees.

Number	Fill Style
0	None
1	Solid fill
2	None
3	Horizontal lines
4	Vertical lines
5	Diagonal lines
6	Diagonal lines
7	Cross-hatch
8	Diagonal cross-hatch
9	Horizontal Gradient
10	Vertical Gradient
11	Circular Gradient
12	Line Gradient
13	Rectangular Gradient
14	Shaped Gradient

Fig. 19.2 Fill styles available for the **SetFillStyle** method.

Lines 28 and 29

```
<PARAM NAME = "Line0006"
   VALUE = "Arc( -200, -125, 100, 100, 45, 135, 0 )">
```

create another shape, an *arc*. The **Arc** *method* takes 7 parameters: the *x-y* coordinates of the arc, the height and width of the box that the arc encloses, the starting angle of the arc in degrees, the size of the arc relative to the starting angle, also in degrees, and the rotation of the arc. The ***Pie*** *method* (lines 30 and 31) takes the same parameters as the **Arc** method, but it fills the arc with the foreground color, thus creating a *pie* shape.

Lines 32 through 34, create a *polygon* using the ***Polygon*** *method*. The first parameter specifies the number of vertices in the polygon; each successive pair of parameters thereafter specifies the *x–y* coordinates of the next vertex of the polygon. The last point of the polygon is automatically connected to the first, to close the polygon.

Lines 35 and 36

```
<PARAM NAME = "Line0009"
   VALUE = "Rect( -185, 0, 60, 30, 25 )">
```

create a *rectangle* using the ***Rect*** *method*. Here the first two parameters specify the coordinates, the next two specify height and width respectively, and the last parameter specifies rotation in degrees.

Lines 37 and 38

```
<PARAM NAME = "Line0010"
   VALUE = "RoundRect( 200, 100, 35, 60, 10, 10, 25 )">
```

add a *rounded rectangle*. The ***RoundRect*** *method* is almost identical to the **Rect** method, but it adds two new parameters, which specify the width and height of the rounded arc at the corners of the rectangle—in this case, 10 pixels wide and 10 pixels high (**10, 10**).

Lines 40 through 43

```
<PARAM NAME = "Line0011"
   VALUE = "SetFont( 'Arial', 65, 400, 0, 0, 0 )">
<PARAM NAME = "Line0012"
   VALUE = "Text( 'Shapes', -200, 200 , -35 )">
```

add text to our Structured Graphics Control with two methods, ***SetFont*** and ***Text***. The **SetFont** method sets the font style to use when we place text with the **Text** method. Here we tell **SetFont** to use a font face of **Arial** that is **65** points high, has a boldness of **400** (this is similar to the CSS **font-weight** property, with values ranging from 100 to 700) and is neither italic (**0**), underline (**0**) nor strikethrough (**0**). Then, we use the **Text** method to place the text (**Shapes**) on the screen, positioned at (**-200**, **200**), with a rotation of **-35** degrees.

In lines 45 through 48 we use the ***PolyLine*** *method* to draw a line with multiple line segments. Before we draw the line, we call the **SetLineStyle** method again to override the settings we gave it before—in this case, we set the line style to dashed, with a width of **1** pixel (**2**, **1**). The **PolyLine** method itself operates much like the **Polygon** method—the first parameter declares the number of points in the line, and each successive pair declares the *x–y* coordinates of the next vertex.

19.3 Moving Shapes with `Translate`

The Structured Graphics Control provides several scriptable methods that allow you to move and transform shapes on the screen. Fig 19.3 provides an example of using the ***`Translate`*** *function* to move an oval.

```
<!DOCTYPE html PUBLIC "-//W3C//DTD HTML 4.0 Transitional//EN">
<HTML>

<!-- Fig 19.3: bounce.html                    -->
<!-- Textures and the Translate method -->

<HEAD>
   <TITLE>Structured Graphics - Translate</TITLE>

<SCRIPT LANGUAGE = "JavaScript">
   var x = 15;
   var y = 15;
   var upDown = -1;
   var leftRight = 1;

   function start()
   {
      window.setInterval( "run()", 50 );
   }

   function run()
   {
      // if the ball hits the top or bottom side...
      if ( y == -100 || y == 50 )
         upDown *= -1;

      // if the ball hits the left or right side...
      if ( x == -150 || x == 100 )
         leftRight *= -1;

      // Move the ball and increment our counters
      ball.Translate( leftRight * 5, upDown * 5, 0 );
      y += upDown * 5;
      x += leftRight * 5;
   }

</SCRIPT>
</HEAD>

<BODY ONLOAD = "start()">

   <OBJECT ID = "ball" STYLE = "background-color: ffffff;
      width: 300; height: 200; border-style: groove;
      position: absolute; top: 50; left: 50;"
      CLASSID = "CLSID:369303C2-D7AC-11d0-89D5-00A0C90833E6">

      <PARAM NAME = "Line0001" VALUE = "SetLineStyle( 0 )">
```

Fig. 19.3 Methods `SetTextureFill` and `Translate` (part 1 of 2).

```
48         <PARAM NAME = "Line0002"
49            VALUE = "SetTextureFill( 0, 0, 'ball.gif', 0 )">
50         <PARAM NAME = "Line0003"
51            VALUE = "Oval( 15, 15, 50, 50 )">
52      </OBJECT>
53
54   </BODY>
55   </HTML>
```

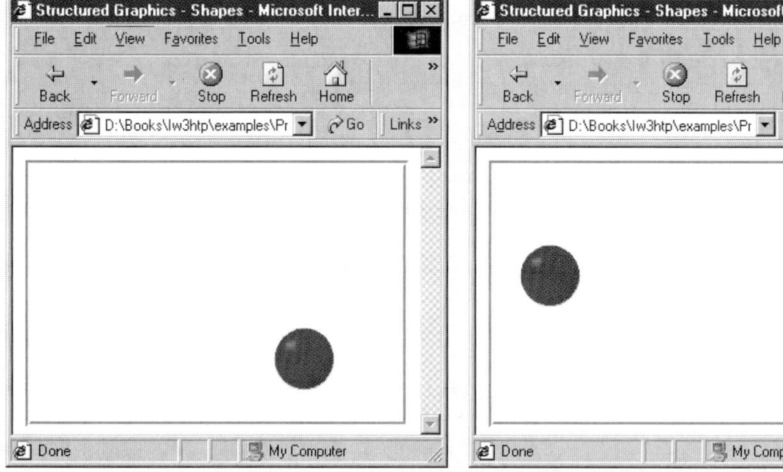

Fig. 19.3 Methods **SetTextureFill** and **Translate** (part 2 of 2).

In this example, we create a ball that bounces around inside the Structured Graphics Control box. Instead of the **SetFillColor** method, we use the ***SetTextureFill*** *method* (line 49) to fill the oval we create with a *texture*. A texture is a picture that is placed on the surface of a polygon. The first two parameters, (**0, 0**), specify the *x–y* coordinates inside the shape at which the texture will begin. The next parameter (**'ball.gif'**) specifies the location of the texture to use, and the last parameter (**0**) specifies that the texture should be stretched to fit inside the shape. A last parameter of **1** would instead tile the texture as many times as necessary inside the shape.

Now that the shape is in place, we use the ***Translate*** *method* to *translate* the shape—that is, to move the shape in coordinate space without deforming it. In every call to function **run**, we determine whether the ball has reached the edge of the box (lines 24 and 28)—if this is the case, we reverse the ball's direction to simulate a bounce. Then, in line 32

```
ball.Translate( leftRight * 5, upDown * 5, 0 );
```

we call the **Translate** function, passing it three parameters, which determine the relative distance to move the **ball** along the *x*, *y* and *z* axes, respectively.

19.4 Rotation

Another useful method for moving shapes is ***Rotate***, which can rotate shapes in 3D space. Fig. 19.4 demonstrates using the **Rotate** method, along with some new fill style effects.

```
<!DOCTYPE html PUBLIC "-//W3C//DTD HTML 4.0 Transitional//EN">
<HTML>

<!-- Fig 19.4: gradient.html -->
<!-- Gradients and rotation  -->

<HEAD>
<TITLE>Structured Graphics - Gradients</TITLE>

<SCRIPT LANGUAGE = "JavaScript">
   var speed = 5;
   var counter = 180;

   function start()
   {
      window.setInterval( "run()", 100 );
   }

   function run()
   {
      counter += speed;

      // accelerate half the time...
      if ( ( counter % 360 ) > 180 )
         speed *= ( 5 / 4 );

      // deccelerate the other half.
      if ( ( counter % 360 ) < 180 )
         speed /= ( 5 / 4 );

      pies.Rotate( 0, 0, speed );
   }
</SCRIPT>

</HEAD>

<BODY ONLOAD = "window.setInterval( 'run()', 100 )">

   <OBJECT ID = "pies" STYLE = "background-color:blue;
      width: 300; height: 200;"
      CLASSID = "CLSID:369303C2-D7AC-11d0-89D5-00A0C90833E6">

      <PARAM NAME = "Line0001"
         VALUE = "SetFillColor( 255, 0, 0, 0, 0, 0 )">
      <PARAM NAME = "Line0002"
         VALUE = "SetFillStyle( 13 )">
      <PARAM NAME = "Line0003"
         VALUE = "Pie( -75, -75, 150, 150, 90, 120, 300 )">

      <PARAM NAME = "Line0004"
         VALUE = "SetFillStyle( 9 )">
      <PARAM NAME = "Line0005"
         VALUE = "Pie( -75, -75, 150, 150, 90, 120, 180 )">
```

Fig. 19.4 Using gradients and **Rotate** (part 1 of 2).

```
54
55          <PARAM NAME = "Line0006"
56             VALUE = "SetFillStyle( 11 )">
57          <PARAM NAME = "Line0007"
58             VALUE = "Pie( -75, -75, 150, 150, 90, 120, 60 )">
59      </OBJECT>
60
61   </BODY>
62   </HTML>
```

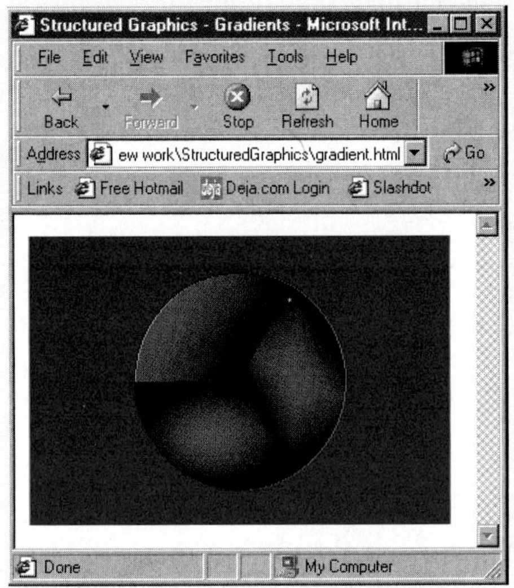

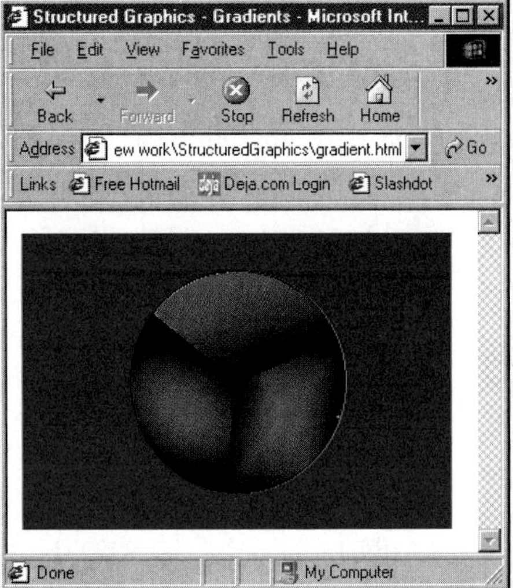

Fig. 19.4 Using gradients and **`Rotate`** (part 2 of 2).

In this example we create 3 pie shapes that we place together to form a circle. Line 30

```
pies.Rotate( 0, 0, speed );
```

calls function **`Rotate`** to rotate the circle around the *z*-axis (like the **`Translate`** method, the three parameters of the **`Rotate`** function specify rotation in the *x*, *y* and *z* coordinate planes, respectively). Lines 23 through 29 in the JavaScript code provide a mechanism for varying the speed of rotation about the *z* axis.

The gradient fills are set with the **`SetFillStyle`** method (lines 46, 51, and 56). A parameter of **`9`** for **`SetFillStyle`** fills the shape with a linear gradient from the foreground color to the background color. The background color is specified with the method **`SetFillColor`** in lines 43 and 44

```
<PARAM NAME = "Line0001"
   VALUE = "SetFillColor( 255, 255, 255, 0, 0, 0 )">
```

by adding a second RGB triplet—here we set the foreground color to white (**`255, 255, 255`**) and the background color to black (**`0,0,0`**). The two other parameters we use for **`SetFillStyle`**, **`11`** and **`13`**, fill the pies with circular and rectangular gradients, respectively.

19.5 Mouse Events and External Source Files

To provide interaction with the user, the Structured Graphics Control can process the Dynamic HTML events **ONMOUSEUP**, **ONMOUSEDOWN**, **ONMOUSEMOVE**, **ONMOUSEOVER**, **ONMOUSEOUT**, **ONCLICK** and **ONDBLCLICK** (see Chapter 16). By default, the Structured Graphics Control does not capture these mouse events, because doing so takes a small amount of processing power. The ***MouseEventsEnabled*** *property* allows you to turn on capturing for these events. In Fig. 19.6, we use mouse events to trigger another feature of the Structured Graphics Control, one which allows you to keep a set of method calls in a separate source file (Fig. 19.5) and invoke them by calling the ***SourceURL*** *method*.

```
SetLineStyle( 1, 3 )
SetFillStyle( 1 )
Oval( 20, 20, 50, 50, 0 )

SetLineStyle( 1, 1 )
PolyLine( 2, 45, 20, 45, 70, 0 )
PolyLine( 2, 45, 20, 45, 70, 90 )
PolyLine( 2, 45, 20, 45, 70, 45 )
PolyLine( 2, 45, 20, 45, 70, 135 )

SetFillColor( 0, 255, 0 )
Oval( 30, 30, 30, 30, 0 )
SetFillColor( 255,0,0 )
Oval( 35, 35, 20, 20, 0 )
```

Fig. 19.5 External source file **newoval.txt** for Fig. 19.6.

```
<!DOCTYPE html PUBLIC "-//W3C//DTD HTML 4.0 Transitional//EN">
<HTML>

<!-- Fig 19.6: bounce2.html            -->
<!-- SourceURL and MouseEventsEnabled -->

<HEAD>
<TITLE>Structured Graphics - Shapes</TITLE>

<SCRIPT FOR = "ball" EVENT = "ONCLICK" LANGUAGE = "JavaScript">
   ball.SourceURL = "newoval.txt";
</SCRIPT>

<SCRIPT LANGUAGE = "JavaScript">
   var x = 20;
   var y = 20;
   var upDown = -1;
   var leftRight = 1;

   function start()
   {
      window.setInterval( "run()", 50 );
   }
```

Fig. 19.6 Using **SourceURL** and **MouseEventsEnabled** (part 1 of 2).

```

   function run()
   {
      if ( y == -100 || y == 50 )
         upDown *= -1;

      if ( x == -150 || x == 100 )
         leftRight *= -1;

      ball.Translate( leftRight * 5, upDown * 5, 0 );
      y += upDown * 5;
      x += leftRight *5;
   }

</SCRIPT>
</HEAD>

<BODY ONLOAD = "start()">

   <OBJECT ID = "ball"
      STYLE = "width: 300; height: 200; border-style: groove;
      position: absolute; top: 10; left: 10;"
      CLASSID = "clsid:369303C2-D7AC-11d0-89D5-00A0C90833E6">

      <PARAM NAME = "Line0001" VALUE = "SetLineStyle(0)">
      <PARAM NAME = "Line0002"
         VALUE = "SetTextureFill( 0, 0, 'ball.gif', 0 )">
      <PARAM NAME = "Line0003"
         VALUE = "Oval( 20, 20, 50, 50 )">
      <PARAM NAME = "MouseEventsEnabled" VALUE = "1">
   </OBJECT>

</BODY>
</HTML>
```

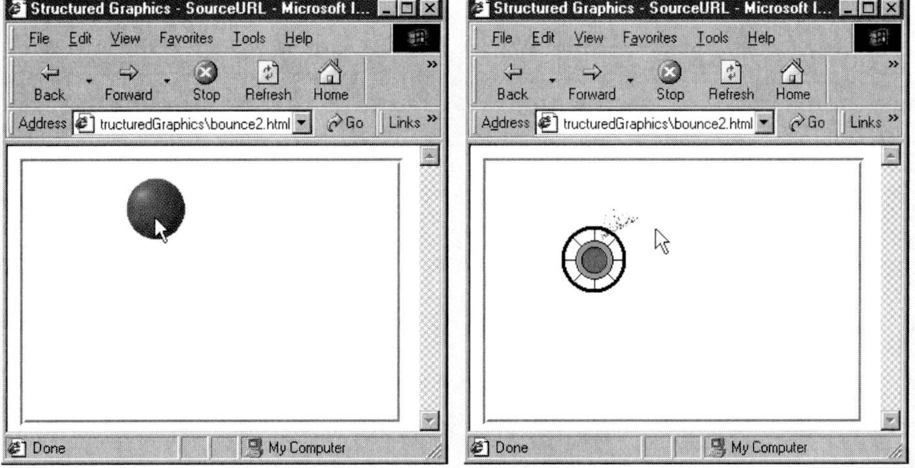

Fig. 19.6 Using **SourceURL** and **MouseEventsEnabled** (part 2 of 2).

We toggle the mouse-event capturing in line 53

```
<PARAM NAME = "MouseEventsEnabled" VALUE = "1">
```

by setting the **MouseEventsEnabled** property to a value of **1** (true) to turn event capturing on. Now lines 10 through 12

```
<SCRIPT FOR = "oval1" EVENT = "ONCLICK" LANGUAGE = "JavaScript">
   ball.SourceURL = "newoval.txt";
</SCRIPT>
```

designate a script for the **ONCLICK** event of our Structured Graphics object. This event calls method **SourceURL** to load the set of instructions in **newoval.txt** (Fig 19.5). Each command is on a separate line, consisting of only the method call and its parameters.

19.6 Scaling

The third type of shape transformation that the Structured Graphics Control provides is *scaling*, which modifies the size of an object while retaining its position and shape. Figure 19.7 provides an example of scaling, using the ***Scale** method.*

```
<!DOCTYPE html PUBLIC "-//W3C//DTD HTML 4.0 Transitional//EN">
<HTML>

<!-- Fig 19.7: scaling.html -->
<!-- Scaling a shape        -->

<HEAD>
<TITLE>Structured Graphics - Scaling</TITLE>

<SCRIPT LANGUAGE = "JavaScript">
   var speedX = 0;
   var speedY = 0;
   var speedZ = 0;
   var scale = 1;

   function start()
   {
      window.setInterval( "run()", 100 );
   }

   function run()
   {
      drawing.Rotate( speedX, speedY, speedZ );
      drawing.Scale( scale, scale, scale );
   }

   function rotate( axis )
   {
      axis = ( axis ? 0 : 5 );
   }
</SCRIPT>

```

Fig. 19.7 Rotating a shape in three dimensions and scaling up and down (part 1 of 4).

```
</HEAD>

<BODY ONLOAD = "window.setInterval( 'run()', 100 )">

<DIV STYLE = "position: absolute; top: 25; left: 220">
<INPUT TYPE = "BUTTON" VALUE = "Rotate-X"
   ONCLICK = "speedX = ( speedX ? 0 : 5 )"><BR>
<INPUT TYPE = "BUTTON" VALUE = "Rotate-Y"
   ONCLICK = "speedY = ( speedY ? 0 : 5 )"><BR>
<INPUT TYPE = "BUTTON" VALUE = "Rotate-Z"
   ONCLICK = "speedZ = ( speedZ ? 0 : 5 )"><BR>
<BR>
<INPUT TYPE = "BUTTON" VALUE = "Scale Up"
   ONCLICK = "scale = ( scale * 10 / 9 )"><BR>
<INPUT TYPE = "BUTTON" VALUE = "Scale Down"
   ONCLICK = "scale = ( scale * 9 / 10 )">
</DIV>

<OBJECT ID = "drawing" STYLE = " position: absolute;
   z-index: 2; width: 200; height: 300;"
   CLASSID = "CLSID:369303C2-D7AC-11d0-89D5-00A0C90833E6">

   <PARAM NAME = "Line0001" VALUE = "SetFillColor( 0,0,0 )">
   <PARAM NAME = "Line0002" VALUE = "SetFillStyle( 0 )">
   <PARAM NAME = "Line0003" VALUE = "SetLineStyle( 1, 3 )">

   <PARAM NAME = "Line0004"
          VALUE = "Oval( -25, -100, 50, 50, 0 )">

   <PARAM NAME = "Line0005"
      VALUE = "PolyLine(2, 0, -50, 0, 50 )">

   <PARAM NAME = "Line0006"
      VALUE = "PolyLine( 3, -30, -25, 0, -15, 30, -25 )">

   <PARAM NAME = "Line0007"
      VALUE = "PolyLine( 3, -15, 90, 0, 50, 15, 90 )">

   <PARAM NAME = "Line0008"
      VALUE = "SetFillColor ( 255, 0, 0 )">
   <PARAM NAME = "Line0009"
      VALUE = "Oval( -15, -85, 7, 7, 0 )">
   <PARAM NAME = "Line0010"
      VALUE = "Oval( 5, -85, 7, 7, 0 )">

   <PARAM NAME = "Line0011"
      VALUE = "SetLineStyle( 1, 2 )">
   <PARAM NAME = "Line0012"
      VALUE = "SetLineColor( 255, 0, 0 )">
   <PARAM NAME = "Line0013"
      VALUE = "SetFont( 'Courier', 25, 200, 0, 0, 0 )">
   <PARAM NAME = "Line0014"
      VALUE = "Text( 'Hello', -35, -115 , 0 )">
```

Fig. 19.7 Rotating a shape in three dimensions and scaling up and down (part 2 of 4).

```
</OBJECT>

<OBJECT ID = "background" STYLE = " position:absolute;
   z-index: 1; width: 200; height: 300; background-color: none"
   CLASSID = "CLSID:369303C2-D7AC-11d0-89D5-00A0C90833E6">

   <PARAM NAME = "Line0001"
      VALUE = "SetFillColor( 38, 250, 38 )">
   <PARAM NAME = "Line0002"
      VALUE = "Oval( -75, -125, 150, 250, 0 )">
</OBJECT>
</BODY>
</HTML>
```

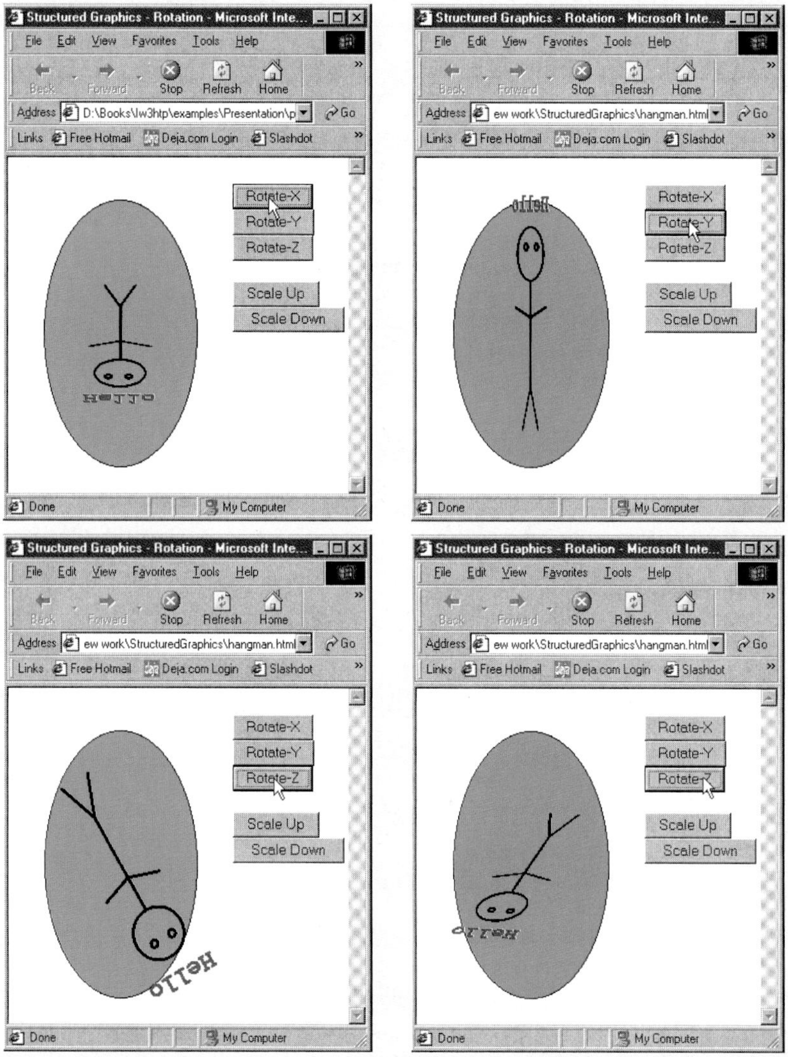

Fig. 19.7 Rotating a shape in three dimensions and scaling up and down (part 3 of 4).

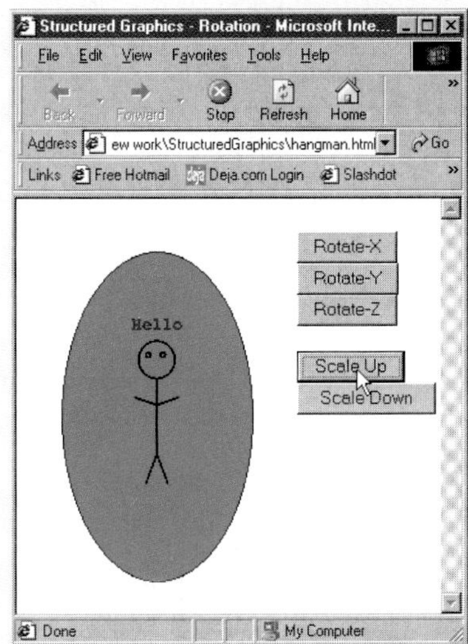

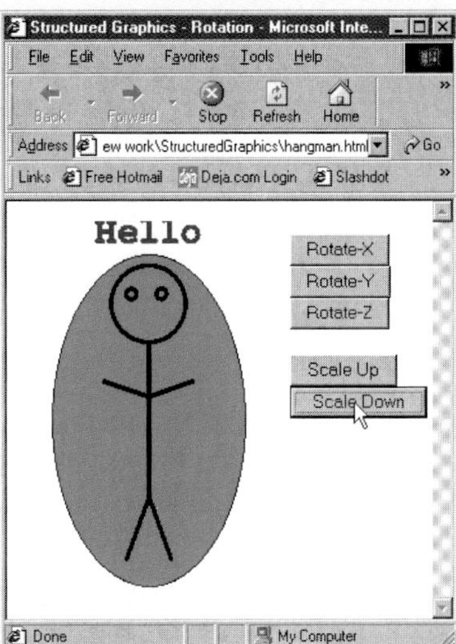

Fig. 19.7 Rotating a shape in three dimensions and scaling up and down (part 4 of 4).

In this example we use two separate controls—the first (lines 51 through 86) for our rotating foreground, and the second (lines 88 through 96) for the oval in the background. We position these over each other using the **`position`** and **`z-index`** CSS attributes. We then use the five buttons to the side of the Structured Graphics Controls to control rotation and scaling of the upper layer. In line 24

```
drawing.Scale( scale, scale, scale );
```

the **`Scale`** method scales object **`drawing`** uniformly in the three dimensions based on the variable **`scale`**.

SUMMARY

- The Structured Graphics Control is an ActiveX control that you can add with an **`OBJECT`** tag. The Structured Graphics Control is easily accessible through script for creating dynamic Web pages.
- The Structured Graphics Control is a Web interface for the widely used DirectAnimation subset of Microsoft's DirectX software, used in many high-end games and graphical applications.
- The Structured Graphics control allows you to create simple shapes by using functions that can be called via scripting or through **`PARAM`** tags inside **`OBJECT`** elements.
- The **`NAME`** attribute of the **`PARAM`** tag method determines the order in which the function specified in the **`VALUE`** attribute is called. The order of calls must be **`Line0001`**, **`Line0002`**, **`Line0003`**, and so on.
- The **`SetLineColor`** function sets the color of lines and borders of shapes that are drawn. It takes an RGB triplet in decimal notation as its three parameters.
- The two parameters of the **`SetLineStyle`** function set the line style and line width, respectively. A value of **`1`** for line style creates a solid line (the default). A value of **`0`** does not draw any lines or borders, and a value of **`2`** creates a dashed line. The line width is specified in pixels.
- The **`SetFillColor`** method sets the foreground color with which to fill shapes.

- The **SetFillStyle** method determines the style in which a shape is filled with color—a value of **1** fills shapes with the solid color declared with the **SetFillColor** method. There are 14 possible fill styles.
- The first two parameters of the **Oval** method specify *x–y* coordinates at which to place the oval. The next two parameters specify the height and width of the oval respectively. The last parameter specifies the clockwise rotation of the oval relative to the *x*-axis, expressed in degrees.
- All shapes in the Structured Graphics control effectively have a surrounding box—when you place the image at a certain *x-y* coordinate, it is the upper left corner of that box that is placed at that coordinate. Inside the control, the point *(0, 0)* (also known as the origin) is at the center of the control, not at the upper left.
- The **Arc** method takes 7 parameters: the *x–y* coordinates of the arc, the height and width of the box in which the arc is enclosed, the starting angle of the arc in degrees, the size of the arc relative to the starting angle (also in degrees) and the rotation of the arc.
- The **Pie** method takes the same parameters as the **Arc** method, but it fills in the arc with the foreground color, thus creating a pie shape.
- The first parameter of method **Polygon** specifies the number of vertices in the polygon, and then each successive pair of numbers specifies the *x–y* coordinates of the next vertex in the polygon.
- The **Rect** method creates a rectangle. The first two parameters specify the coordinates, the next two specify height and width respectively, and the last parameter specifies rotation in degrees.
- The **RoundRect** method is almost identical to the **Rect** method, but it adds two new parameters, which specify the height and width of the rounded arcs at the corners of the rectangle.
- The **SetFont** method sets the font style to use when placing text with the **Text** method.
- The **PolyLine** method draws a line with multiple segments. The **PolyLine** method functions much like the **Polygon** method—the first parameter declares the number of points in the line, and then each successive pair declares the *x–y* coordinates of another vertex.
- The **SetTextureFill** method fills a shape with a texture. A texture is a picture that is placed on the surface of a polygon. The first two parameters specify at what *x–y* coordinates inside the shape the texture will begin. The next parameter specifies the location of the texture to use. A last parameter of **0** specifies that the texture should be stretched to fit inside the shape. A last parameter of **1** would instead tile the texture as many times as necessary inside the shape.
- The **Translate** method moves a shape in coordinate space without deforming it. Its three parameters determine the relative distance to move along the *x*, *y* and *z* axes, respectively (the *z*-axis is the third-dimensional coordinate axis).
- The **Rotate** method rotates shapes in 3D space. The three parameters of the **Rotate** function specify rotation in the x, y and z coordinate planes, respectively.
- A parameter of **9** for **SetFillStyle** fills the shape with a linear gradient from the foreground color to the background color.
- A background color can be specified with the **SetFillColor** method by adding a second RGB triplet to the parameters.
- Two other parameters for **SetFillStyle**, **11** and **13**, fill shapes with circular and rectangular gradients, respectively.
- To provide interaction with the user, the Structured Graphics control can process the Dynamic HTML mouse events **ONMOUSEUP**, **ONMOUSEDOWN**, **ONMOUSEMOVE**, **ONMOUSEOVER**, **ONMOUSEOUT**, **ONCLICK** and **ONDBLCLICK**.
- By default, the Structured Graphics Control does not capture mouse events, because doing so takes a small amount of processing power.

- The Structure Graphics Control allows you to keep a set of method calls in a separate source file and to invoke those methods by calling the **SourceURL** function.
- Turn event capturing on by calling the **MouseEventsEnabled** method with a **VALUE** of **1** (true).
- Each command in a file targeted by **SourceURL** is on a separate line and consists of only the method call and its parameters.

TERMINOLOGY

arc
Arc method
CLSID:369303C2-D7AC-11d0-89D5-00A0C90833E6 (Structured Graphics Control)
DirectAnimation
DirectX
Line0001 (Line0002, etc.)
line style
line width
mouse events
OBJECT tag
origin
ONCLICK event
ONDBLCLICK event
ONMOUSEDOWN event
ONMOUSEMOVE event
ONMOUSEOUT event
ONMOUSEOVER event
ONMOUSEUP event
oval
Oval method
PARAM tag
pie
Pie method
polygon
Polygon method
PolyLine method
Rect method
rectangle
Rotate method
rounded rectangle
RoundRect method
Scale method
SetFillColor method
SetFillStyle method
SetFont method
SetLineColor method
SetLineStyle method
SetTextureFill method
SourceURL method
Structured Graphics
Text method
texture
translate
Translate method

COMMON PROGRAMMING ERROR

19.1 Forgetting to assign successive line numbers (i.e., **NAME = "Line0001"**, **NAME = "Line0002"**) to method calls prevents the intended methods from being called.

SELF-REVIEW EXERCISES

19.1 Fill in the blanks for the following questions:

a) The Structured Graphics control is a subset of Microsoft's _________ software package.
b) The Structured Graphics control captures only _________-related events.
c) The _________ method allows you to draw a multi-segmented line.
d) There are _________ different styles for the **SetFillStyle** method.
e) The _________ method allows you to import external lists of commands.
f) A _________ is an image that is placed on the surface of a polygon.
g) The _________ method moves shapes in the Structured Graphics Control without distorting or rotating them.
h) To place text with the **Text** method, the _________ method must first be called to set the properties of the text to be placed.

19.2 Answer the following questions true or false; if false, state why.

a) By default, event capturing is turned on for the Structured Graphics control.
b) The **SetLineColor** and **SetLineStyle** methods also apply to shape borders.
c) The **Pie** method has the same parameters as the **Arc** method.
d) Calling **SetFillStyle** with an argument of **1** fills shapes with a solid color.
e) The dotted line style may be used at any line width.
f) The **SetFillTexture** method specifies whether the texture is tiled or stretched.

ANSWERS TO SELF-REVIEW EXERCISES

19.1 a) DirectX. b) mouse. c) **PolyLine**. d) 15. e) **SourceURL**. f) texture. g) **Translate**. h) **SetFont**.

19.2 a) False. It is off by default. b) True. c) True. d) True. e) False. It may be used only with lines that are 1 pixel wide. f) True.

EXERCISES

19.3 Modify example 19.2 to do the following:

a) speed up when the ball is clicked;
b) change the ball's shape when it hits a wall;
c) have the ball stop if the user moves the mouse cursor over the ball and resume moving if the user moves the mouse cursor off the ball.

19.4 Use scripting to create a page that displays 50 ovals in randomly selected sizes, shapes, locations, colors and fill styles.

19.5 Use the primitive shapes to create simple pictures of a person, a car, a house, a bicycle, and a dog.

19.6 Look up the **Spline** method mentioned in the documentation at the URL provided in Section 19.1, and use it to create a figure-eight shape.

19.7 Write a script that draws a series of eight concentric circles, each separation being 10 pixels.

19.8 Write a script that draws four triangles of different sizes. Each triangle should be filled with a different color (or fill style).

19.9 Create a web page that uses JavaScript and the Structured Graphics Control to create an interactive hangman game.

19.10 Write a script that uses the Structured Graphics Control to draw a cube.

19.11 Modify Exercise 19.10 to continuously rotate the cube.

19.12 Modify Exercise 19.10 to rotate the cube in response to the user moving the mouse. The cube should rotate in the direction the user drags the mouse. [Hint: Use the **ONMOUSEDOWN** event to determine when the user begins a drag and use the **ONMOUSEUP** event to determine when the drag operation terminates.]

19.13 Modify Exercise 19.12 to determine the speed at which the cube rotates by calculating the distance between two consecutive **ONMOUSEMOVE** events.

20

Dynamic HTML: Path, Sequencer and Sprite ActiveX Controls

Objectives

- To be able to use the DirectAnimation multimedia ActiveX controls, including the Path, Sequencer and Sprite controls.
- To add animation to Web pages with the DirectAnimation ActiveX controls.
- To use the Path Control to specify the path along which an animated Web page element moves.
- To use the Sequencer Control to control the timing and synchronization of actions on a Web page.
- To use the Sprite Control to create animated images for a Web page.

There is a natural hootchy-kootchy motion to a goldfish.
Walt Disney

Isn't life a series of images that change as they repeat themselves?
Andy Warhol

Between the motion and the act falls the shadow.
Thomas Stearns Eliot, The Hollow Men

The wheel is come full circle.
William Shakespeare

Grass grows, birds fly, waves pound the sand.
Muhammad Ali

Outline

20.1 Introduction

In this chapter we discuss the remaining three DirectAnimation ActiveX controls available for use with Internet Explorer 5: the *Path Control*, the *Sequencer Control*, and the *Sprite Control*. Each one of these controls allows a Web page designer to add certain multimedia effects to Web pages. When used with one another, with the Structured Graphics Control we discussed in the last chapter, and with other Dynamic HTML effects, they help create stunning visual presentations for your content.

Performance Tip 20.1

Multimedia is performance intensive. Internet bandwidth and processor speed are still precious resources. Multimedia-based Web applications must be carefully designed to use resources wisely, or they may perform poorly.

20.2 DirectAnimation Path Control

The *DirectAnimation Path Control* allows you to control the position of elements on your page. This is more advanced than dynamic CSS positioning, because it allows you to define paths that the targeted elements follow. This gives you the ability to create professional presentations, especially when integrated with other Dynamic HTML features such as filters and transitions. Figure 20.1 uses the Path Control to create a short linear path for an **H1** element.

```
<!DOCTYPE html PUBLIC "-//W3C//DTD HTML 4.0 Transitional//EN">
<HTML>

<!-- Fig. 20.1: path1.html        -->
<!-- Introducing the path control -->

<HEAD>
   <TITLE>Path control</TITLE>
</HEAD>

<BODY STYLE = "background-color: #9C00FF">
```

Fig. 20.1 Demonstrating the DirectAnimation Path Control (part 1 of 2).

```
12
13  <H1 ID = "headertext" STYLE = "position: absolute">
14  Path animation:</H1>
15
16  <OBJECT ID = "oval"
17     CLASSID = "CLSID:D7A7D7C3-D47F-11D0-89D3-00A0C90833E6">
18     <PARAM NAME = "AutoStart" VALUE = "1">
19     <PARAM NAME = "Repeat" VALUE = "-1">
20     <PARAM NAME = "Duration" VALUE = "2">
21     <PARAM NAME = "Bounce" VALUE = "1">
22     <PARAM NAME = "Shape"
23       VALUE = "PolyLine( 2, 0, 0, 200, 50 )">
24     <PARAM NAME = "Target" VALUE = "headerText">
25  </OBJECT>
26
27  </BODY>
28  </HTML>
```

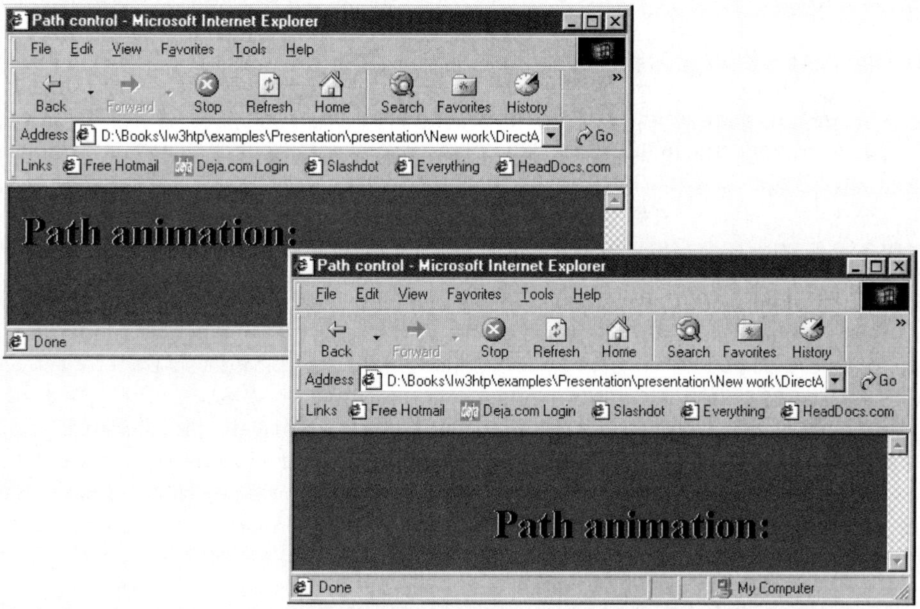

Fig. 20.1 Demonstrating the DirectAnimation Path Control (part 2 of 2).

Lines 16 through 25

```
<OBJECT ID = "oval"
   CLASSID = "CLSID:D7A7D7C3-D47F-11D0-89D3-00A0C90833E6">
   <PARAM NAME = "AutoStart" VALUE = "1">
   <PARAM NAME = "Repeat" VALUE = "-1">
   <PARAM NAME = "Duration" VALUE = "2">
   <PARAM NAME = "Bounce" VALUE = "1">
   <PARAM NAME = "Shape"
      VALUE = "PolyLine( 2, 0, 0, 200, 50 )">
   <PARAM NAME = "Target" VALUE = "headerText">
</OBJECT>
```

use the **OBJECT** element to place the Path Control on the page. The **CLASSID** attribute used here identifies the DirectAnimation Path Control. The **PARAM** tags in the **OBJECT** element specify certain properties of the control. Setting ***AutoStart*** to a nonzero value (**1** in this case) starts the element along the path as soon as the page loads (setting a zero value would prevent it from starting automatically, in which case a script would have to call the **Play** method to start the path). The ***Repeat*** method determines how many times the path will be traversed—setting the value to **-1**, as we do here, specifies that the path should loop continuously. The ***Duration*** *method* specifies the amount of time that it will take to traverse the path, in seconds.

The ***Bounce*** *method*, when set to **1**, reverses the element's direction on the path when it reaches the end. Setting the value to **0** would instead return the element to the beginning of the path when the path has been traversed. The ***Shape*** *method* is what actually determines the path of the element—as we saw with the Structured Graphics Control, the ***PolyLine*** *method* creates a path with multiple line segments. In this case we declare a path with **2** points, located at (**0, 0**) and (**200, 50**). Finally, the ***Target*** *method* specifies the **ID** of the element that is targeted by the path control. Note that line 13

```
<H1 ID = "headertext" STYLE = "position: absolute">
```

sets the CSS attribute **position** to **absolute**—this allows the Path Control to actually move the element around the screen. Otherwise, the element would be static, locked in the position determined by the browser when the page loads.

20.3 Multiple Path Controls

The Path Control also allows you to set paths for multiple objects present on your page. To do this, you must add a separate **OBJECT** tag for each object you wish to control. Figure 20.2 creates **PolyLine** paths for seven separate objects for a pleasant splash screen effect.

Each **OBJECT** element in our program controls a separate **SPAN** element. As the page loads, these elements move separately into place, creating a visually pleasing effect. Note that because we did not specify the **z-index** properties, the **z-index** of elements that overlap each other is determined by their order of declaration in the HTML source. Elements declared later in the HTML file are displayed above elements declared earlier.

```
<!DOCTYPE html PUBLIC "-//W3C//DTD HTML 4.0 Transitional//EN">
<HTML>

<!-- Fig 20.2: path2.html         -->
<!-- Controlling multiple paths -->
<HEAD>
   <TITLE>Path Control - Multiple paths</TITLE>

<STYLE TYPE = "text/css">

  SPAN { position: absolute;
         font-family: sans-serif;
         font-size: 2em;
```

Fig. 20.2 Controlling multiple elements with the Path Control (part 1 of 4).

```
            font-weight: bold;
            filter: shadow( direction = 225 );
            padding: 9px;
         }

</STYLE>
</HEAD>

<BODY STYLE = "background-color: lavender">

<IMG SRC = "icons2.gif"
     STYLE = "position: absolute; left: 30; top: 110">

<SPAN ID = "titleTxt"
      STYLE = "left: 500; top: 500; color: white">
Multimedia Cyber Classroom<BR>
Programming Tip Icons</SPAN>

<SPAN ID = "CPEspan"
      STYLE = "left: 75; top: 500; color: red">
Common Programming Errors</SPAN>

<SPAN ID = "GPPspan"
      STYLE = "left: 275; top: 500; color: orange">
Good Programming Practices</SPAN>

<SPAN ID = "PERFspan"
      STYLE = "left: 475; top: 500; color: yellow">
Performance Tips</SPAN>

<SPAN ID = "PORTspan"
      STYLE = "left: 100; top: -50; color: green">
Portability Tips</SPAN>

<SPAN ID = "SEOspan"
      STYLE = "left: 300; top: -50; color: blue">
Software Engineering Observations</SPAN>

<SPAN ID = "TDTspan"
      STYLE = "left: 500; top: -50; color: violet">
Testing and Debugging Tips</SPAN>

<OBJECT ID = "CyberPath"
   CLASSID = "CLSID:D7A7D7C3-D47F-11D0-89D3-00A0C90833E6">
   <PARAM NAME = "Target" VALUE = "titleTxt">
   <PARAM NAME = "Duration" VALUE = "10">
   <PARAM NAME = "Shape"
      VALUE = "PolyLine( 2, 500, 500, 100, 10 )">
   <PARAM NAME = "AutoStart" VALUE = 1>
</OBJECT>

<OBJECT ID = "CPEPath"
   CLASSID = "CLSID:D7A7D7C3-D47F-11D0-89D3-00A0C90833E6">
```

Fig. 20.2 Controlling multiple elements with the Path Control (part 2 of 4).

```
      <PARAM NAME = "Target" VALUE = "CPEspan">
      <PARAM NAME = "Duration" VALUE = "4">
      <PARAM NAME = "Shape"
         VALUE = "PolyLine( 3, 75, 500, 300, 170, 35, 175 )">
      <PARAM NAME = "AutoStart" VALUE = 1>
   </OBJECT>

   <OBJECT ID = "GPPPath"
      CLASSID = "CLSID:D7A7D7C3-D47F-11D0-89D3-00A0C90833E6">
      <PARAM NAME = "Target" VALUE = "GPPspan">
      <PARAM NAME = "Duration" VALUE = "5">
      <PARAM NAME = "Shape"
         VALUE = "PolyLine( 3, 275, 500, 300, 340, 85, 205 )">
      <PARAM NAME = "AutoStart" VALUE = 1>
   </OBJECT>

   <OBJECT ID = "PERFPath"
      CLASSID = "CLSID:D7A7D7C3-D47F-11D0-89D3-00A0C90833E6">
      <PARAM NAME = "Target" VALUE = "PERFspan">
      <PARAM NAME = "Duration" VALUE = "6">
      <PARAM NAME = "Shape"
         VALUE = "PolyLine( 3, 475, 500, 300, 340, 140, 235 )">
      <PARAM NAME = "AutoStart" VALUE = 1>
   </OBJECT>

   <OBJECT ID = "PORTPath"
      CLASSID = "CLSID:D7A7D7C3-D47F-11D0-89D3-00A0C90833E6">
      <PARAM NAME = "Target" VALUE = "PORTspan">
      <PARAM NAME = "Duration" VALUE = "7">
      <PARAM NAME = "Shape"
         VALUE = "PolyLine( 3, 600, -50, 300, 340, 200, 265 )">
      <PARAM NAME = "AutoStart" VALUE = 1>
   </OBJECT>

   <OBJECT ID = "SEOPath"
      CLASSID = "CLSID:D7A7D7C3-D47F-11D0-89D3-00A0C90833E6">
      <PARAM NAME = "Target" VALUE = "SEOspan">
      <PARAM NAME = "Duration" VALUE = "8">
      <PARAM NAME = "Shape"
         VALUE = "PolyLine( 3, 300, -50, 300, 340, 260, 295 )">
      <PARAM NAME = "AutoStart" VALUE = 1>
   </OBJECT>

   <OBJECT ID = "TDTPath"
      CLASSID = "CLSID:D7A7D7C3-D47F-11D0-89D3-00A0C90833E6">
      <PARAM NAME = "Target" VALUE = "TDTspan">
      <PARAM NAME = "Duration" VALUE = "9">
      <PARAM NAME = "Shape"
         VALUE = "PolyLine( 3, 500, -50, 300, 340, 310, 325 )">
      <PARAM NAME = "AutoStart" VALUE = 1>
   </OBJECT>
   </BODY>
   </HTML>
```

Fig. 20.2 Controlling multiple elements with the Path Control (part 3 of 4).

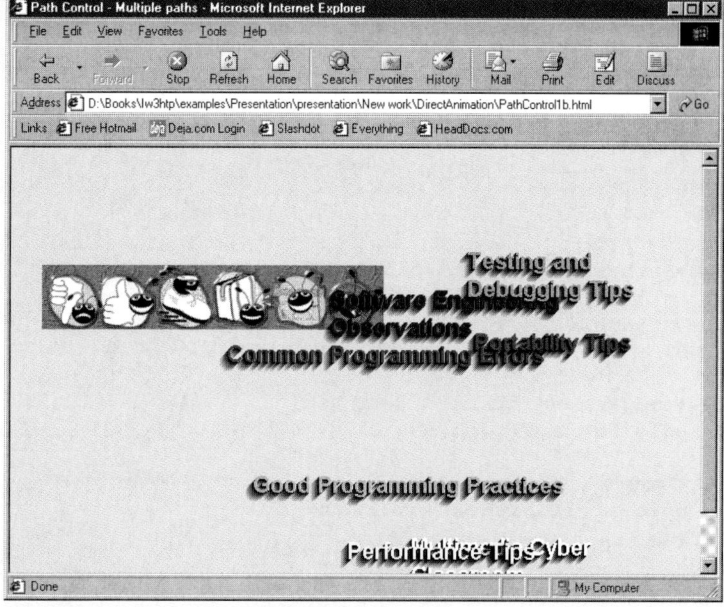

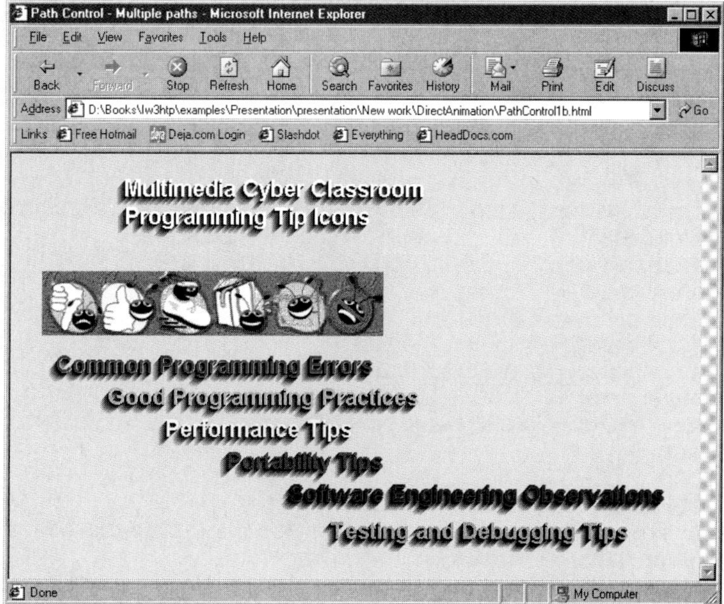

Fig. 20.2 Controlling multiple elements with the Path Control (part 4 of 4).

20.4 Time Markers for Path Control

A useful feature of the Path Control is the ability to execute certain actions at any point along an object's path. This is done with the **`AddTimeMarker`** *method*, which creates a *time marker* that can be handled with simple JavaScript event handling. Figure 20.3 has two separate time markers for an image that follows an *oval* path.

```
<!DOCTYPE html PUBLIC "-//W3C//DTD HTML 4.0 Transitional//EN">
<HTML>

<!-- Fig 20.3: path3.html         -->
<!-- Oval paths and time markers -->

<HEAD>
<TITLE>Path control - Advanced Paths</TITLE>

<SCRIPT LANGUAGE = "JavaScript" FOR = "oval"
   EVENT = "ONMARKER ( marker )">

   if ( marker == "mark1" )
      pole.style.zIndex +=  2;

   if ( marker == "mark2" )
      pole.style.zIndex -=  2;
</SCRIPT>
</HEAD>

<BODY STYLE = "background-color: #9C00FF">

<IMG ID = "pole" SRC = "pole.gif" STYLE = "position: absolute;
   left: 350; top: 80; z-index: 3; height: 300">

<IMG ID = "largebug" SRC = "animatedbug_large.gif"
     STYLE = "position: absolute; z-index: 4">

<OBJECT ID = "oval"
   CLASSID = "CLSID:D7A7D7C3-D47F-11D0-89D3-00A0C90833E6">
   <PARAM NAME = "AutoStart" VALUE = "-1">
   <PARAM NAME = "Repeat" VALUE = "-1">
   <PARAM NAME = "Relative" VALUE = "1">
   <PARAM NAME = "Duration" VALUE = "8">
   <PARAM NAME = "Shape" VALUE = "Oval( 100, 80, 300, 60 )">
   <PARAM NAME = "Target" VALUE = "largebug">
   <PARAM NAME = "AddTimeMarker1" VALUE = "2, mark1, 0">
   <PARAM NAME = "AddTimeMarker2" VALUE = "6, mark2, 0">
</OBJECT>

<OBJECT ID = "swarmPath"
   CLASSID = "CLSID:D7A7D7C3-D47F-11D0-89D3-00A0C90833E6">
   <PARAM NAME = "AutoStart" VALUE = "-1">
   <PARAM NAME = "Repeat" VALUE = "-1">
   <PARAM NAME = "Relative" VALUE = "1">
   <PARAM NAME = "Duration" VALUE = "15">
   <PARAM NAME = "Shape"
      VALUE = "Polygon(6, 0, 0, 400, 300, 450, 50, 320, 300,
                       150, 180, 50, 250 )">
   <PARAM NAME = "Target" VALUE = "swarm">
```

Fig. 20.3 Adding time markers for script interaction (part 1 of 2).

```
</OBJECT>

<SPAN ID = "swarm"
   STYLE = "position:absolute; top: 0; left: 0; z-index: 1">

<IMG SRC = "animatedbug_small.gif"
   STYLE = "position:absolute; top: 25; left: -30">
<IMG SRC = "animatedbug_small.gif"
   STYLE = "position:absolute; top: 0; left: 0">
<IMG SRC = "animatedbug_small.gif"
   STYLE = "position:absolute; top: 15; left: 70">
<IMG SRC = "animatedbug_small.gif"
   STYLE = "position:absolute; top: 30; left: 5">
<IMG SRC = "animatedbug_small.gif"
   STYLE = "position: absolute; top: 10; left: 30">
<IMG SRC = "animatedbug_small.gif"
   STYLE = "position: absolute; top: 40; left: 40">
<IMG SRC = "animatedbug_small.gif"
   STYLE = "position: absolute; top: 65; left: 15">

</SPAN>
</BODY>
</HTML>
```

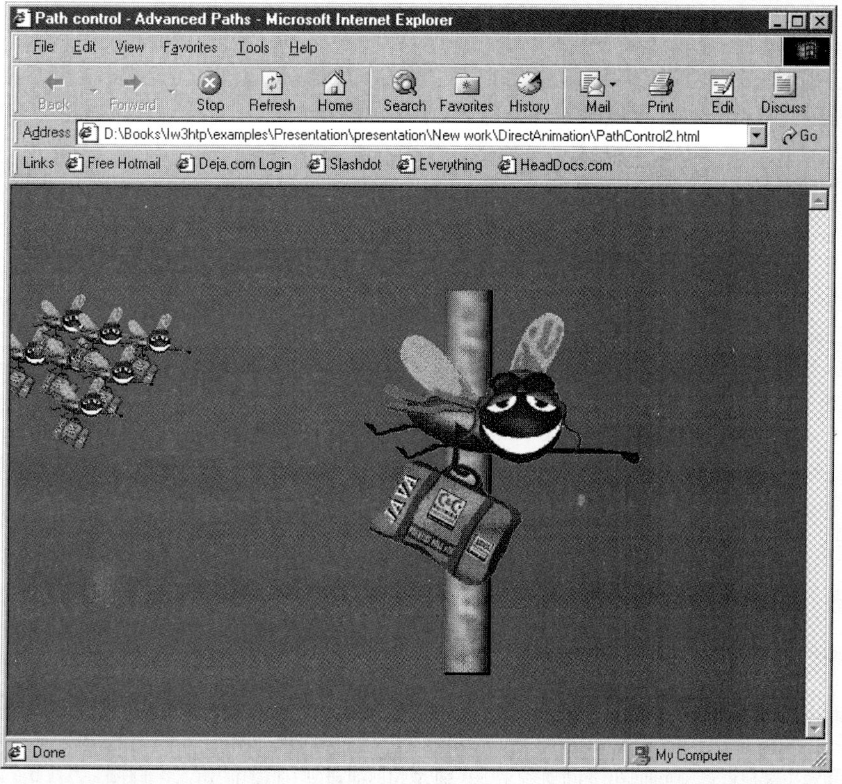

Fig. 20.3 Adding time markers for script interaction (part 2 of 2).

Line 35

```
<PARAM NAME = "Shape" VALUE = "Oval( 100, 80, 300, 60 )">
```

places the image with the **ID** of **largebug** on an oval path using the ***Oval*** *method*. This is very similar to the **Oval** method from the Structured Graphics Control in that the first two parameters specify the *x–y* coordinates of the oval and the next two parameters specify the width and height of the oval, respectively.

Line 37

```
<PARAM NAME = "AddTimeMarker1" VALUE = "2, mark1, 0">
```

introduces the ***AddTimeMarker*** *method*. The **1** appended to the **AddTimeMarker** function is a sequential identifier—much like **Line0001** is used in the Structured Graphics Control. The first parameter in the **VALUE** attribute determines at which point our time marker is placed along the path, specified in seconds—when this point is reached, event **ONMARKER** is fired. The second parameter gives an identifying name to the event, which is later passed on to the event handler for the **ONMARKER** function. The last parameter specifies whether to fire the **ONMARKER** event every time the object's path loops past the time marker (as we do here by setting the parameter to **0**) or to fire the event just the first time that the time marker is passed (by setting the parameter to **1**).

Lines 10 through 18

```
<SCRIPT LANGUAGE = "JavaScript" FOR = "oval"
   EVENT = "ONMARKER ( marker )">

   if ( marker == "mark1" )
      pole.style.zIndex += 2;

   if ( marker == "mark2" )
      pole.style.zIndex -= 2;
</SCRIPT>
```

create an event handler for the **ONMARKER** event. The parameter that the **ONMARKER** event receives (here defined as **marker** in line 11) identifies which marker fired the event. The **if** control structures following then change the **zIndex** attribute of element **pole** to correspond to the time marker in our Path Control that actually fired the event. These events fire when the large image is at the leftmost and rightmost extremes of its oval path, so this creates the appearance that the bee image is flying alternately behind and in front of the pole image.

20.5 DirectAnimation Sequencer Control

Thus far, we have been using the JavaScript function **window.setInterval** to control timed events on our Web pages. The Sequencer Control provides a simpler interface for calling functions or performing actions, at time intervals that you can set easily. Figure 20.4 uses the Sequencer Control to display 4 lines of text sequentially—when the fourth line of text has displayed, the Sequencer Control then starts that fourth line on a **PolyLine** path, using the ***Play*** *method* of the Path Control.

Lines 57 through 59

```
<OBJECT ID = "sequencer"
   CLASSID = "CLSID:B0A6BAE2-AAF0-11d0-A152-00A0C908DB96">
</OBJECT>
```

add the Sequencer Control to our Web page. Notice that we do not include any **PARAM** tags inside the **OBJECT** element—here, we set all the parameters for the Sequencer Control via scripting.

```
1  <!DOCTYPE html PUBLIC "-//W3C//DTD HTML 4.0 Transitional//EN">
2  <HTML>
3
4  <!-- Fig 20.4: sequencer.html -->
5  <!-- Sequencer Control         -->
6
7  <HEAD>
8
9  <STYLE TYPE = "text/css">
10
11    DIV { font-size: 2em;
12          color: white;
13          font-weight: bold }
14
15 </STYLE>
16
17 <SCRIPT FOR = "sequencer" EVENT = "ONINIT">
18    sequencer.Item( "showThem" ).at( 2.0, "show( line1 )" );
19    sequencer.Item( "showThem" ).at( 4.0, "show( line2 )" );
20    sequencer.Item( "showThem" ).at( 6.0, "show( line3 )" );
21    sequencer.Item( "showThem" ).at( 7.0, "show( line4 )" );
22    sequencer.Item( "showThem" ).at( 8.0, "runPath()" );
23 </SCRIPT>
24
25 <SCRIPT>
26    function show( object )
27    {
28       object.style.visibility = "visible";
29    }
30
31    function start()
32    {
33       sequencer.Item( "showThem" ).Play();
34    }
35
36    function runPath()
37    {
38       pathControl.Play();
39    }
40 </SCRIPT>
41 </HEAD>
```

Fig. 20.4 Using the DirectAnimation Sequencer Control (part 1 of 3).

```

<BODY STYLE = "background-color: limegreen" ONLOAD = "start()">

<DIV ID = "line1" STYLE = "position: absolute; left: 50;
   top: 10; visibility: hidden">Sequencer DirectAnimation</DIV>

<DIV ID = "line2" STYLE = "position: absolute; left: 70;
   top: 60; visibility: hidden">ActiveX Control</DIV>

<DIV ID = "line3" STYLE = "position: absolute; left: 90;
   top: 110; visibility: hidden">Controls time intervals</DIV>

<DIV ID = "line4" STYLE = "position: absolute; left: 110;
   top:160; visibility: hidden">For dynamic effects</DIV>

<OBJECT ID = "sequencer"
   CLASSID = "CLSID:B0A6BAE2-AAF0-11d0-A152-00A0C908DB96">
</OBJECT>

<OBJECT ID = "pathControl"
   CLASSID = "CLSID:D7A7D7C3-D47F-11D0-89D3-00A0C90833E6">
   <PARAM NAME = "AutoStart" VALUE = "0">
   <PARAM NAME = "Repeat" VALUE = "1">
   <PARAM NAME = "Relative" VALUE = "1">
   <PARAM NAME = "Duration" VALUE = "2">
   <PARAM NAME = "Shape" VALUE = "PolyLine( 2, 0, 0, 250, 0 )">
   <PARAM NAME = "Target" VALUE = "line4">
</OBJECT>

</BODY>
</HTML>
```

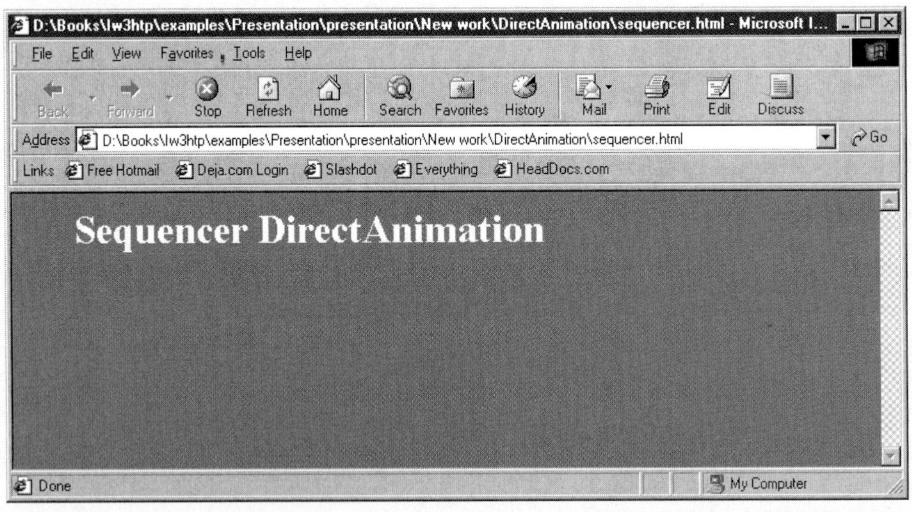

Fig. 20.4 Using the DirectAnimation Sequencer Control (part 2 of 3).

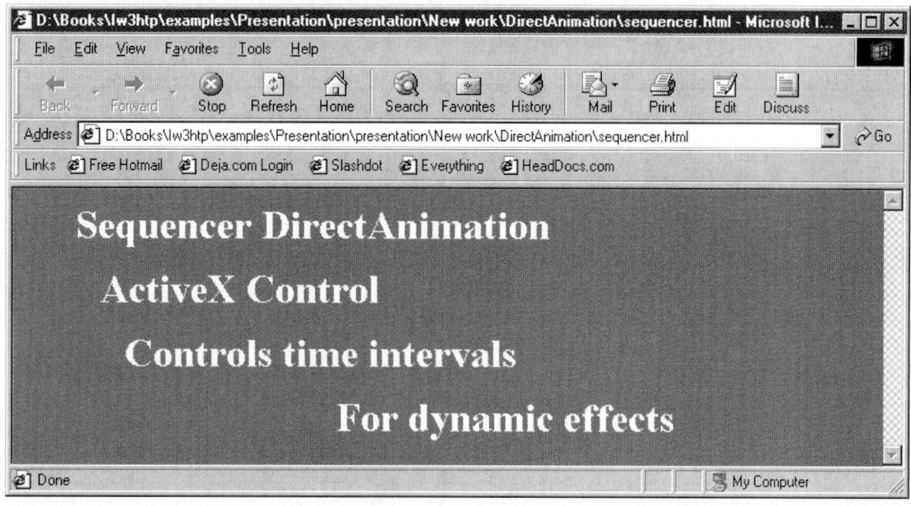

Fig. 20.4 Using the DirectAnimation Sequencer Control (part 3 of 3).

Lines 17 through 23

```
<SCRIPT FOR = "sequencer" EVENT = "ONINIT">
   sequencer.Item( "showThem" ).at( 2.0, "show( line1 )" );
   sequencer.Item( "showThem" ).at( 4.0, "show( line2 )" );
   sequencer.Item( "showThem" ).at( 6.0, "show( line3 )" );
   sequencer.Item( "showThem" ).at( 7.0, "show( line4 )" );
   sequencer.Item( "showThem" ).at( 8.0, "runPath()" );
</SCRIPT>
```

use a JavaScript event handler for the ***ONINIT*** *event* that fires when the sequencer loads. The **Item** object creates a grouping of events using a common name (in this case, **showThem**). The **at** method of the **Item** object takes two parameters: how many seconds to wait, and what action to perform when that time has expired. In this case, we call the **show** function for specific lines in the text at 2, 4, 6 and 7 seconds after the **ONINIT** event fires, and we call the **runPath** function after 8 seconds elapse.

We then use the **runPath** function to initiate a Path Control by scripting. Line 38

```
pathControl.Play();
```

calls the Path Control's **Play** method to start the targeted element (**line4**) along the path.

20.6 DirectAnimation Sprite Control

The images we have been using thus far have all been static. Some standards exist for standardized animation (the most common of which is an *animated GIF*), but none provides the dynamic control over animation that the Sprite Control provides. It allows you to control the rate of playback for images or even for individual *frames.* (An animation is composed of many individual frames which create the illusion of motion). Figure 20.6 uses the Sprite Control to add a simple animation to a Web page. The source image containing all the frames is displayed in Fig. 20.5.

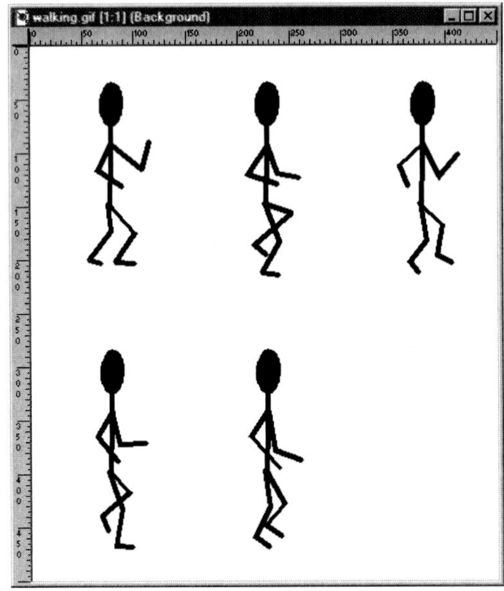

Fig. 20.5 Source image for Sprite Control (**`walking.gif`**).

```
<!DOCTYPE html PUBLIC "-//W3C//DTD HTML 4.0 Transitional//EN">
<HTML>

<!-- Fig 20.6: sprite.html -->
<!-- Sprite Control        -->

<HEAD>
   <TITLE>Sprite Control</TITLE>
</HEAD>

<BODY>

<OBJECT ID = "walking" STYLE = "width: 150; height: 250"
   CLASSID  = "CLSID:FD179533-D86E-11d0-89D6-00A0C90833E6">
   <PARAM NAME = "Repeat" value = -1>
   <PARAM NAME = "NumFrames" VALUE = 5>
   <PARAM NAME = "NumFramesAcross" VALUE = 3>
   <PARAM NAME = "NumFramesDown" VALUE = 2>
   <PARAM NAME = "SourceURL" VALUE = "walking.gif">
   <PARAM NAME = "AutoStart" VALUE = -1>
</OBJECT>

</BODY>
</HTML>
```

Fig. 20.6 Simple animation with the Sprite Control (part 1 of 2).

Fig. 20.6 Simple animation with the Sprite Control (part 2 of 2).

The **OBJECT** tag (lines 13 through 21) inserts the Sprite Control. The **height** and **width** CSS properties are needed to display the image correctly—they should be equal to the size of one frame in your file.

Setting the **REPEAT** attribute to a nonzero **VALUE** (**-1**) loops the animation indefinitely. The next attribute, **NumFrames**, specifies how many frames are present in the animation source image (Fig 20.5). The next two attributes—**NumFramesAcross** and **NumFramesDown**—specify how many rows and columns of frames there are in the animation file. The **SourceURL** property gives a path to the file containing all the frames of the animation, and setting the **AutoStart** property to a nonzero **VALUE** starts the animation automatically when the page loads.

What distinguishes Sprite Control from other animation formats is that it can do much more than simply loop through frames repeatedly—it can, through Dynamic HTML, respond to user actions, as we demonstrate in Fig. 20.7.

This example introduces several new aspects of the Sprite Control. The ***PlayRate*** *method* controls the rate at which frames are displayed—**1** is the default value. Method ***MouseEventsEnabled***, as with the Structured Graphics Control, allows the object to capture certain mouse events.

In lines 10 through 16 and 18 through 24, we provide event handlers for the events **ONMOUSEOVER** and **ONMOUSEOUT**. When the user moves the mouse over the Sprite Control, the event handler calls the ***Stop*** *method*, which stops the animation in place, and sets the **PlayRate** method to **-3** . (The **PlayRate** method is writable only at runtime or when the animation is stopped.) This plays the animation in reverse at three times the normal speed. The script then calls the **Play** function to restart the animation. The **ONMOUSEOUT** event handler sets the **PlayRate** back to the default of **1** when the user moves the mouse cursor off the animation.

```
<!DOCTYPE html PUBLIC "-//W3C//DTD HTML 4.0 Transitional//EN">
<HTML>

<!-- Fig 20.7: sprite2.html      -->
<!-- Events with Sprite Control -->

<HEAD>
<TITLE>Sprite Control</TITLE>

<SCRIPT LANGUAGE = "JavaScript" FOR = "bounce"
   EVENT = "ONMOUSEOVER">

   bounce.Stop();
   bounce.PlayRate = -3;
   bounce.Play();
</SCRIPT>

<SCRIPT LANGUAGE = "JavaScript" FOR = "bounce"
   EVENT = "ONMOUSEOUT">

   bounce.Stop();
   bounce.PlayRate = 1;
   bounce.Play();
</SCRIPT>
</HEAD>

<BODY>

<H1>Sprite Control</H1>

<OBJECT ID = "bounce" STYLE = "width:75; height:75"
   CLASSID  = "CLSID:FD179533-D86E-11d0-89D6-00A0C90833E6">
   <PARAM NAME = "Repeat" value = -1>
   <PARAM NAME = "PlayRate" VALUE = 1>
   <PARAM NAME = "NumFrames" VALUE = 22>
   <PARAM NAME = "NumFramesAcross" VALUE = 4>
   <PARAM NAME = "NumFramesDown" VALUE = 6>
   <PARAM NAME = "SourceURL" VALUE = "bounce.jpg">
   <PARAM NAME = "MouseEventsEnabled" VALUE = "True">
   <PARAM NAME = "AutoStart" VALUE = -1>
</OBJECT>

</BODY>
</HTML>
```

Fig. 20.7 Responding to mouse events with the Sprite Control (part 1 of 2).

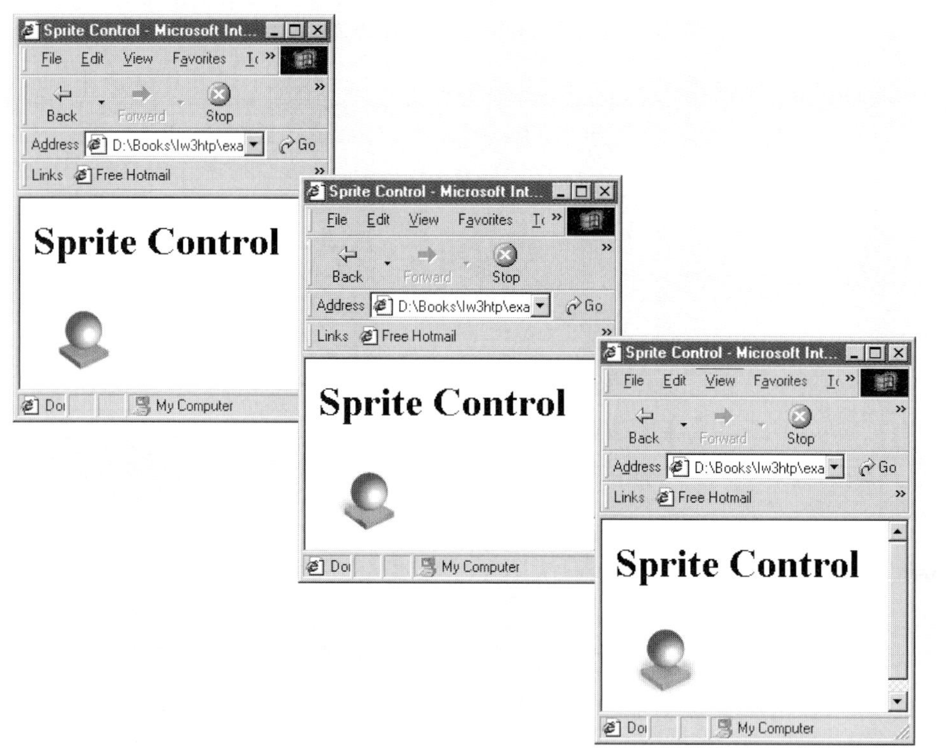

Fig. 20.7 Responding to mouse events with the Sprite Control (part 2 of 2).

20.7 Animated GIFs

Although the Sprite Control is useful for adding animation to Web pages, it is a new, proprietary format specific to Internet Explorer. The most popular method of creating animated graphics is a format known as *Animated GIF*. As with the Sprite Control, Animated GIFs are composed of a number of frames, which in this case are all in the GIF image format. However, unlike the images used with Sprite Control, GIF images must be assembled into animated GIF images by special graphics applications. One such program is Animation Shop, which is bundled with the Paint Shop Pro package on the CD included with this book. Figure 20.8 is a screen capture of the Animation Shop application. The screen capture the file **`animatedbug_large.gif`** loaded into Animation Shop. This image was used to demonstrate the Path Control in Figure 20.3.

As you can see here, the file is comprised of two separate frames. The Animated GIF format includes many features such as specifying the amount of time each separate frame is displayed. Animation Shop itself has many useful features that you are able to apply, such as image transparency and transitions between frames (these are very similar to the transitions we covered in Chapter 17).

Performance Tip 20.2

Animated GIFs with a large number of frames can become extremely large. Make sure to use small images when possible and to minimize the amount of frames used.

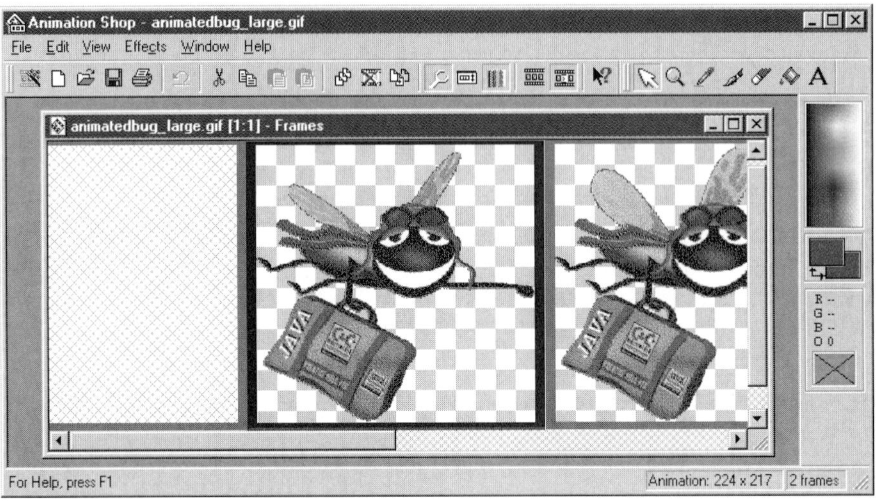

Fig. 20.8 Viewing an Animated Gif in Animation Shop

Summary

- The DirectAnimation Path Control allows you to control the positions of elements on your page.
- Setting **AutoStart** to a nonzero value starts the element along a path as soon as the page loads. Setting a zero value would prevent it from starting automatically, in which case a script would have to call the **Play** method to start the path. The **Repeat** method determines how many times the path will be traversed—setting the value to **-1** specifies that the path should loop continuously. The **Duration** method specifies the amount of time that it will take to traverse the path, in seconds. The **Bounce** method, when set to **1**, reverses the element's direction on the path when it reaches the end. Setting the value to **0** would instead return the element to the beginning of the path when the path has been traversed.
- The **PolyLine** method creates a path with multiple line segments.
- The **Target** method specifies the **ID** of the element that is targeted by the Path Control.
- Setting the CSS attribute **position** to **absolute** allows the Path Control to move an element around the screen. Otherwise, the element would be static, locked in the position determined by the browser when the page loads.
- The Path Control also allows you to set paths for multiple objects present on your page. To do this, you must add a separate **OBJECT** tag for each object you wish to control.
- The **z-index** of elements that overlap is determined by their order of declaration in the HTML source (elements declared later in the HTML file are displayed above elements declared earlier).
- A useful feature of the Path Control is the ability to execute certain actions at any point along an object's path. This is done with the **AddTimeMarker** method, which creates a time marker that can be handled with simple JavaScript event handling.
- The number appended to the **AddTimeMarker** function is a sequential identifier, much like **Line0001** is used in Structured Graphics Control. The first parameter in the **VALUE** attribute determines at which point our time marker is placed along the path, specified in seconds—when this point is reached, the **ONMARKER** event is fired. The second parameter gives an identifying name to the event, which is later passed on to the event handler for the **ONMARKER** event. The last pa-

rameter specifies whether to fire the **ONMARKER** event every time the object's path loops past the time marker (as we do here by setting the parameter to **0**) or to fire the event just the first time that the time marker is passed (by setting the parameter to **1**).

- The parameter received by the **ONMARKER** event identifies which marker fired the event.
- The Sequencer Control provides a simpler interface for calling functions or performing actions at time intervals that you can set easily.
- The **ONINIT** event fires when the Sequencer Control has loaded.
- The **Item** object of the Sequencer Control creates a grouping of events using a common name.
- The **at** method of the **Item** object takes two parameters: how many seconds to wait, and what action to perform when that time has expired.
- The **Play** method of the Path Control starts the targeted element along the path.
- The Sprite Control allows you to display animated images composed of individual frames.
- The **OBJECT** tag inserts the Sprite Control. The **height** and **width** CSS properties are needed to display the image correctly—they should be equal to the size of one frame in your file. Setting attribute **REPEAT** to a nonzero **VALUE** loops the animation indefinitely. **NumFrames** specifies how many frames are present in the animation source image. Attributes **NumFramesAcross** and **NumFramesDown** specify how many rows and columns of frames there are in the animation file. Property **SourceURL** gives a path to the file containing the frames of the animation. Setting property **AutoStart** to a nonzero **VALUE** starts the animation automatically when the page loads.
- Sprite Control method **PlayRate** controls the rate at which frames are displayed (**1** is the default value). The **MouseEventsEnabled** method, as with the Structured Graphics Control, allows the object to capture certain mouse events. The **Stop** method stops the animation in place. Method **PlayRate** is writable only at runtime or when the animation is stopped.

TERMINOLOGY

animated GIF
AddTimeMarker method
at method of **Item** object
AutoStart
Bounce method
CLASSID
Duration method
Item object of Sequencer Control
MouseEventsEnabled
NumFrames
NumFramesAcross
NumFramesDown
ONINIT event
ONMARKER event
Oval method
Path Control
Play method
PlayRate method of the Sprite Control
PolyLine method
position: absolute
Relative method
REPEAT attribute
Repeat method
Sequencer Control
Shape method
SourceURL
splash screen effect
Sprite Control
Stop method
Target method
time marker
visibility: hidden
window.setInterval
z-index

PERFORMANCE TIPS

20.1 Multimedia is performance intensive. Internet bandwidth and processor speed are still precious resources. Multimedia-based Web applications must be carefully designed to use resources wisely, or they may perform poorly.

20.2 Animated GIFs with a large number of frames can become extremely large. Make sure to use small images when possible and to minimize the amount of frames used.

SELF-REVIEW EXERCISES

20.1 Answer the following questions true or false; if false, explain why:

a) The **z-index** of elements in which the **z-index** property is not declared specifically is determined by the order of their appearance in the HTML document.
b) The parameters for the Path Control **PolyLine** method are the same as those for the Structured Graphics Control **PolyLine**.
c) A time marker will fire the **ONMARKER** event only once.
d) You can control multiple paths with a single Path Control **OBJECT**.
e) The **ONINIT** event fires when the Sequencer Control has finished loading.
f) The **PlayRate** method of the Sprite Control is always writable.
g) All ActiveX controls use the same **CLASSID** attribute.

20.2 Fill in the blanks in the following questions:

a) The _______ Control allows you to perform scripted actions on your Web page at timed intervals.
b) The _______ Control allows you to place animated images on your web page.
c) The _______ Control can move elements around your page dynamically.
d) The _______ method is used to create a time marker for the Path Control.
e) An element's CSS **position** property must be set to _______ for the Path Control to successfully target that object.
f) The _______ method determines over how many iterations the Path Control will continue on a certain path.

ANSWERS TO SELF-REVIEW EXERCISES

20.1 a) True. b) True. c) False; this depends on the last parameter of the **AddTimeMarker** method and may be set to fire every time the time marker is reached. d) False; multiple controls are needed if you want to control multiple paths. e) True. f) False; it is writable only at run-time or when the animation is stopped. g) False; each uses a unique **CLASSID**.

20.2 a) Sequencer. b) Sprite. c) Path. d) **AddTimeMarker**. e) **absolute**. f) **Repeat**.

EXERCISES

20.3 Use the Path Control to have the logo on your Web page follow an **Oval** path around the page.

20.4 Use the Path Control to simulate the motion of text inside a **MARQUEE** tag.

20.5 Modify Exercise 20.4 by adding time markers that change the color of the text every loop.

20.6 Use the Sequencer Control to create a slideshow of images.

20.7 Use Paint Shop Pro to create a sprite that simulates a rotating planet. Modify Fig. 20.3 so that the sprite, animated with the Sprite control, rotates around a larger planet in the center of the page.

20.8 Create your own animated GIF with Animation Shop Pro.

21

Multimedia: Audio, Video, Speech Synthesis and Recognition

Objectives

- To enhance Web pages with sound and video.
- To use **<BGSOUND>** to add background sounds.
- To use the **<IMG>** element's **DYNSRC** property to incorporate video into Web pages.
- To use **<EMBED>** to add sound or video to Web pages.
- To use the Windows Media Player ActiveX control to play a variety of media formats in Web pages.
- To use the Microsoft Agent ActiveX control to create animated characters that speak to users and respond to spoken commands from users.
- To embed a RealPlayer™ ActiveX control to allow streaming audio and video to appear in a Web page.

The wheel that squeaks the loudest … gets the grease.
John Billings (Henry Wheeler Shaw)

We'll use a signal I have tried and found far-reaching and easy to yell. Waa-hoo!
Zane Grey

TV gives everyone an image, but radio gives birth to a million images in a million brains.
Peggy Noonan

Noise proves nothing. Often a hen who has merely laid an egg cackles as if she had laid an asteroid.
Mark Twain, *Following the Equator*

Outline

21.1 Introduction

Just a few years back, the typical desktop computer's power, although considered substantial at the time, made it impossible to think of integrating high-quality audio and video into applications. Today's computers typically include CD-ROMs, sound cards, and other hardware and special software to make computer multimedia a reality. Economical desktop machines are so powerful that they can store and play DVD-quality sound and video. Given this, we expect to see a huge advance in the kinds of programmable multimedia capabilities available through programming languages.

The multimedia revolution occurred first on the desktop, with the widespread availability of CD-ROMs. This platform is rapidly evolving towards DVD technology, but our focus in this chapter is on the explosion of sound and video technology appearing on the World Wide Web. In general, we expect the desktop to lead with the technology, because the Web is so dependent on bandwidth, and, for the foreseeable future, Internet bandwidths for the masses are likely to lag considerably those available on the desktop. One thing that we have learned—having been in this industry for nearly four decades now—is to plan for the impossible. In the computer and communications fields, the impossible has repeatedly become reality, and this has happened so many times as to be almost routine.

In this chapter, we discuss adding sound, video and animated characters to your Web-based applications. Your first reaction may be a sense of caution, because you realize that these are complex technologies and most readers have had little if any education in these areas. This is one of the beauties of today's programming languages. They give the programmer easy access to complex technologies and hide most of the complexity.

Performance Tip 21.1

Multimedia is performance intensive. Internet bandwidth and processor speed are still precious resources. Multimedia-based Web applications must be carefully designed to use resources wisely, or they may perform poorly.

Multimedia files can be quite large. Some multimedia technologies require that the complete multimedia file be downloaded to the client before the audio or video begins playing. With streaming audio and streaming video technologies, the audios and videos can begin playing while the files are downloading, thus reducing delays. Streaming technologies are becoming very popular on the Web.

Creating audio and video to incorporate into Web pages often requires complex and powerful software. Rather than discuss how to create media clips, this chapter focuses on using existing audio and video clips to enhance Web pages. The chapter also includes an extensive set of Internet and World Wide Web resources. Some of these resources are Web sites that show you interesting ways in which Web site designers use multimedia to enhance Web pages. Many of the resource sites contain useful information for Web developers who plan to add multimedia to the sites they implement.

21.2 Adding Background Sounds with the BGSOUND Element

Some Web sites provide background audio to give the site some "atmosphere." There are several ways in which to add sound to a Web page. The simplest is the ***BGSOUND*** element.

Portability Tip 21.1

*The **BGSOUND** element is specific to Internet Explorer.*

The **BGSOUND** element has four key properties—***SRC***, ***LOOP***, ***BALANCE*** and ***VOLUME***. If you would like to change the property values via a script, you can assign a scripting name to the **BGSOUND** element's ***ID*** property.

Software Engineering Observation 21.1

*The **BGSOUND** element should be placed in the **HEAD** section of the HTML document.*

The **SRC** property specifies the URL of the audio clip to play. Internet Explorer supports a wide variety of audio formats.

Software Engineering Observation 21.2

*The audio clip specified with **BGSOUND**'s **SRC** property can be any type supported by Internet Explorer.*

The **LOOP** property specifies the number of times the audio clip should play. The value **-1** (the default) specifies that the audio clip should loop until the user browses a different Web page or until the user clicks the browser's **Stop** button. A positive integer can be specified for this property, to indicate the exact number of times the audio clip should loop. Negative values (except **-1**) and zero values for this property result in the audio clip's playing once.

The **BALANCE** property specifies the balance between the left and right speakers. The value for this property is between **-10000** (sound only from the left speaker) and **10000** (sound only from the right speaker). The default value **0** indicates that the sound should be balanced between the two speakers.

Software Engineering Observation 21.3

***BGSOUND** property **BALANCE** cannot be set via scripting.*

The **VOLUME** property determines the volume of the audio clip. The value for this property is between **-10000** (minimum volume) and **0** (maximum volume). The default value **0** indicates that the sound should play at its maximum volume.

Software Engineering Observation 21.4

*The volume specified with **BGSOUND** property **VOLUME** is relative to the current volume setting on the client computer. If the client computer has sound turned off, the **VOLUME** property has no effect.*

Portability Tip 21.2

*On most computers, the minimum audible volume for **BGSOUND** property **VOLUME** is a value much greater than **-10000**. This value will be machine dependent.*

The HTML document of Fig 21.1 demonstrates the **BGSOUND** element and scripting the element's properties. The audio clip used in this example came from the Microsoft Developer Network's downloads site,

http://msdn.microsoft.com/downloads/default.asp

This site contains many free images and sounds.

```
<!DOCTYPE HTML PUBLIC "-//W3C//DTD HTML 4.0 Transitional//EN">
<HTML>
<!-- Fig. 21.1: BackroundAudio.html -->

<HEAD><TITLE>The BGSOUND Element</TITLE>
<BGSOUND ID = "audio" SRC = "jazzgos.mid" LOOP = "1"></BGSOUND>

<SCRIPT LANGUAGE = "JavaScript">
   function changeProperties()
   {
      var loop = parseInt( audioForm.loopit.value );
      audio.loop = ( isNaN( loop ) ? 1 : loop );

      var vol = parseInt( audioForm.vol.value );
      audio.volume = ( isNaN( vol ) ? 0 : vol );
   }
</SCRIPT>
</HEAD>

<BODY>
   <H1>Background Music via the BGSOUND Element</H1>
   <H2>Jazz Gospel</H2>

   This sound is from the free sound downloads at the
   <A HREF = "http://msdn.microsoft.com/downloads/default.asp">
      Microsoft Developer Network</a> downloads site.
   <HR>
   Use the fields below to change the number of iterations
   and the volume for the audio clip<BR>
   Press <B>Stop</B> to stop playing the sound.<BR>
   Press <B>Refresh</B> to begin playing the sound again.
```

Fig. 21.1 Demonstrating background audio with **BGSOUND** (part 1 of 2).

```
32
33      <FORM NAME = "audioForm"><P>
34         Loop [-1 = loop forever]
35         <INPUT NAME = "loopit" TYPE = "text" VALUE = "1"><BR>
36         Volume [-10000 (low) to 0 (high)]
37         <INPUT NAME = "vol" TYPE = "text" VALUE = "0"><BR>
38         <INPUT TYPE = "button" VALUE = "Set Properties"
39                ONCLICK = "changeProperties()">
40      </P></FORM>
41   </BODY>
42
43   </HTML>
```

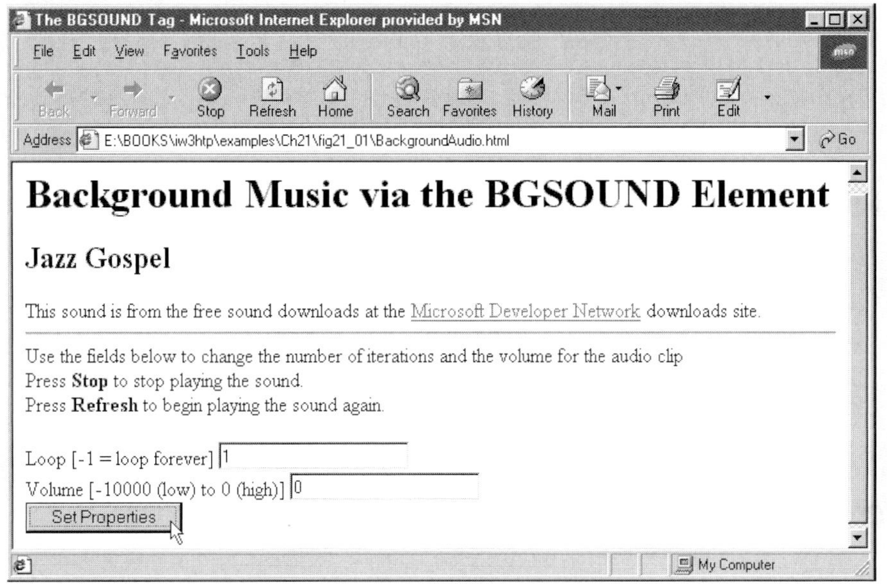

Fig. 21.1 Demonstrating background audio with **BGSOUND** (part 2 of 2).

Line 6

```
<BGSOUND ID = "audio" SRC = "jazzgos.mid" LOOP = "1"></BGSOUND>
```

specifies that the audio clip **jazzgos.mid** should exactly loop once. Because the **BALANCE** and **VOLUME** attributes are not specified, each will have the default **0** value.

Software Engineering Observation 21.5

*The ending **</BGSOUND>** tag is optional.*

Function **changeProperties** (line 9) is called when the user clicks the **Set Properties** button in the HTML form. Lines 11 and 12

```
var loop = parseInt( audioForm.loopit.value );
audio.loop = ( isNaN( loop ) ? 1 : loop );
```

read the new value for property **LOOP** from the form's **loopit** text field, convert the value to an integer and set the new property value by assigning a value to **audio.loop** (where **audio** is the **ID** of the **BGSOUND** element and **loop** is the scripting name of the property).

Lines 14 and 15

```
var vol = parseInt( audioForm.vol.value );
audio.volume = ( isNaN( vol ) ? 0 : vol );
```

read the new value for the **VOLUME** property from the form's **vol** text field, convert the value to an integer and set the new property value by assigning a value to **audio.volume** (where **volume** is the scripting name of the property).

21.3 Adding Video with the IMG Element's DYNSRC Property

You can tremendously enhance the multimedia presentations on your Web site by incorporating a variety of video formats in your Web pages. The **IMG** element (introduced in Chapter 3) enables both images and videos to be included in a Web page. The **SRC** property, shown previously, indicates that the source is an image. The ***DYNSRC*** (i.e., dynamic source) property indicates that the source is a video clip. The HTML document of Fig. 21.2 demonstrates the **IMG** element and its **DYNSRC** property.

Portability Tip 21.3

*The **DYNSRC** property of the **IMG** element is specific to Internet Explorer.*

```
<!DOCTYPE HTML PUBLIC "-//W3C//DTD HTML 4.0 Transitional//EN">
<HTML>
<!-- Fig. 21.2: DynamicIMG.html -->

<HEAD>
<TITLE>An Embedded Image Using the DYNSRC Property</TITLE>
<BGSOUND SRC = "newage.mid" LOOP = "-1">
</HEAD>

<BODY>
   <H1>An Embedded Video Using the IMG Element's
      DYNSRC Property</H1>
   <H2>Spinning Globe and New Age Music</H2>
   This video is from the
   <A HREF = "http://www.nasa.gov/gallery/">
     NASA Multimedia Gallery</A><BR>
   This sound is from the free sound downloads at the
   <A HREF = "http://msdn.microsoft.com/downloads/default.asp">
     Microsoft Developer Network</A> downloads site.
   <HR>
   <TABLE><TR>
   <TD><IMG DYNSRC = "pathfinder.mpeg" START = "mouseover"
            WIDTH = "180" HEIGHT = "135" LOOP = "-1"
            ALT = "A spinning image of the Earth"></TD>
   <TD>This page will play the audio clip and video in a
   loop.<BR>The video will not begin playing until you move
```

Fig. 21.2 Playing a video with the **IMG** element's **DYNSRC** property (part 1 of 2).

```
27       the mouse over the video.<BR>Press <B>Stop</B> to stop
28       playing the sound and the video.</TD></TR></TABLE>
29    </BODY>
30    </HTML>
```

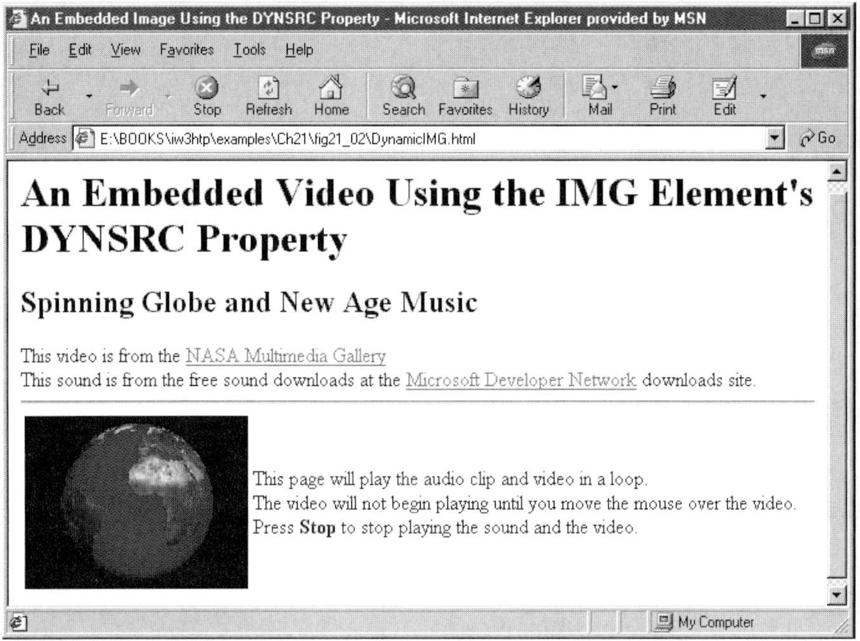

An Embedded Image Using the DYNSRC Property - Microsoft Internet Explorer provided by MSN
File Edit View Favorites Tools Help
Back Forward Stop Refresh Home Search Favorites History Mail Print Edit
Address E:\BOOKS\iw3htp\examples\Ch21\fig21_02\DynamicIMG.html
Go
An Embedded Video Using the IMG Element's DYNSRC Property
Spinning Globe and New Age Music
This video is from the NASA Multimedia Gallery
This sound is from the free sound downloads at the Microsoft Developer Network downloads site.
This page will play the audio clip and video in a loop.
The video will not begin playing until you move the mouse over the video.
Press Stop to stop playing the sound and the video.
My Computer

Fig. 21.2 Playing a video with the **IMG** element's **DYNSRC** property (part 2 of 2).

The **IMG** element in lines 22 through 24

```
<IMG DYNSRC = "pathfinder.mpeg" START = "mouseover"
     WIDTH = "180" HEIGHT = "135" LOOP = "-1"
     ALT = "A spinning image of the Earth"></TD>
```

uses the **DYNSRC** property to indicate that the video **pathfinder.mpeg** will be loaded and displayed. Property ***START*** indicates when the video should start playing. There are two possibilities—***fileopen*** indicates that the video should play as soon as it loads into the browser, and ***mouseover*** indicates that the video should play when the user first positions the mouse over the video.

The video used in this example is one of many videos that can be downloaded from the NASA Multimedia Gallery at

```
http://www.nasa.gov/gallery/
```

21.4 Adding Audio or Video with the EMBED Element

Previously, we used elements **BGSOUND** and **IMG** to embed audio and video in a Web page. In both cases, the user of the page is provided with little control over the media clip. In this section, we introduce the ***EMBED*** element, which embeds a media clip (audio or video) into a Web page. The **EMBED** element allows a graphical user interface to be displayed that gives the user direct control over the media clip. When the browser encounters a media clip in an **EMBED** element, the browser plays the clip with the player that is registered to handle that media type on the client computer. For example, if the media clip is a **.wav** file (i.e., a Windows Wave file), Internet Explorer will typically use the Windows Media Player ActiveX control to play the clip. The Windows Media Player has a GUI that enables the user to play, pause and stop the media clip. It also allows the user to control the volume of audio and to move forward and backward quickly through the clip. [*Note:* Section 21.5 discusses embedding the Windows Media Player ActiveX control in a Web page.]

The HTML document of Fig. 21.3 modifies the **wave** filter example from Chapter 17 by using an **EMBED** element to add audio to the Web page.

```
<!DOCTYPE HTML PUBLIC "-//W3C//DTD HTML 4.0 Transitional//EN">
<HTML>
<!-- Fig. 21.3: EmbeddedAudio.html -->

<HEAD>
<TITLE>Background Audio via the EMBED Element</TITLE>
<STYLE TYPE = "text/css">
   SPAN    { width: 600 }
   .big    { color: blue;
             font-family: sans-serif;
             font-size: 50pt;
             font-weight: bold }
</STYLE>

<SCRIPT LANGUAGE = "JavaScript">
   var TimerID;
   var updown  =  true;
   var str = 1;

   function start()
   {
      TimerID = window.setInterval( "wave()", 100 );
   }

   function wave()
   {
      if ( str > 20 || str < 1 )
         updown = !updown;

      if ( updown )
         str++;
      else
         str--;

      wft.filters( "wave" ).phase = str * 30;
      wft.filters( "wave" ).strength = str;
   }
</SCRIPT>
</HEAD>
```

Fig. 21.3 Embedding audio with the **EMBED** element (part 1 of 2).

```
40
41  <BODY ONLOAD = "start()">
42  <H1>Background Audio via the EMBED Element</H1>
43  <P>Click the text to stop the script.</P>
44
45  <SPAN ONCLICK = "window.clearInterval( TimerID )" ID = "wft"
46     STYLE =
47        "filter:wave(add=0, freq=3, light=0, phase=0, strength=5)">
48  <P CLASS = "big" ALIGN = "center">WAVE FILTER EFFECT</P></SPAN>
49
50  <P>These controls can be used to control the audio.</P>
51  <EMBED SRC = "humming.wav" HIDDEN = "false" LOOP = "true"></EMBED>
52  </BODY>
53  </HTML>
```

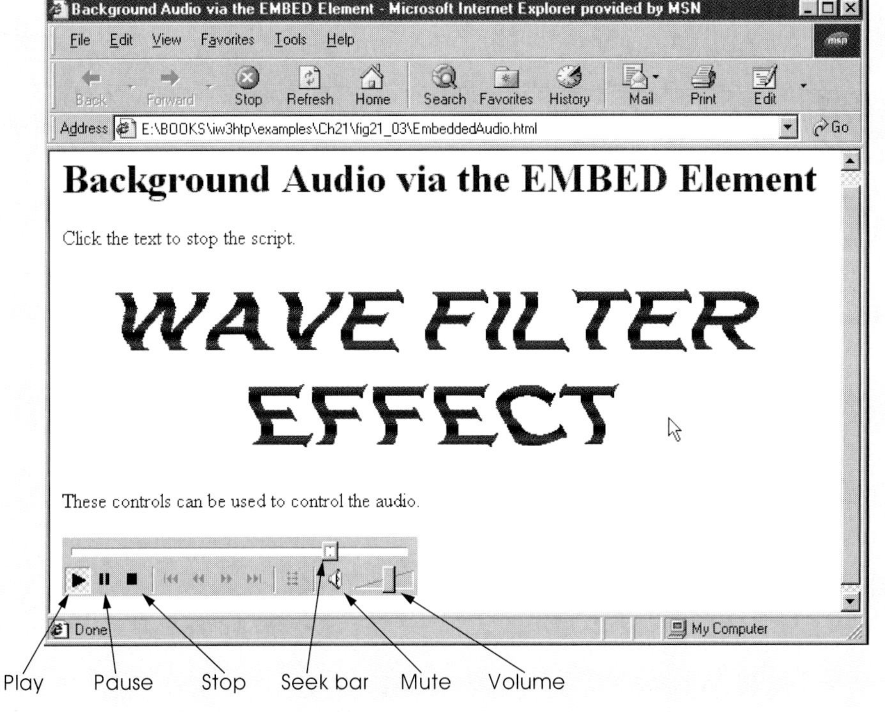

Fig. 21.3 Embedding audio with the **EMBED** element (part 2 of 2).

Line 51

```
<EMBED SRC = "humming.wav" LOOP = "true"></EMBED>
```

uses the **EMBED** element to specify that the audio file **humming.wav** should be embedded in the Web page. The ***LOOP*** property indicates that the media clip should loop forever. By default, the GUI for the media player is displayed. To prevent the GUI from appearing in the Web page, add the ***HIDDEN*** property to the **<EMBED>** element. If you want to script the element, specify a scripting name by adding the **ID** property to the **<EMBED>** element.

The **EMBED** element can specify video clips as well as audio clips. Figure 21.4 demonstrates an MPEG video from NASA's *Seaviewing Wide Field-of-view Sensor (SeaWiFS) Project*. The **EMBED** element that loads and plays the video is on iine 14. This video and several others, which together make up a two-minute animation, can be found at

http://seawifs.gsfc.nasa.gov/OCEAN_PLANET/HTML/ oceanography_flyby.html

This video is part of the NASA Multimedia Gallery.

Software Engineering Observation 21.6

*The **</EMBED>** tag is required to terminate an **<EMBED>** tag.*

21.5 Using the Windows Media Player ActiveX Control

One benefit of Microsoft ActiveX controls is that they can be embedded in Web pages that are to be displayed in Internet Explorer and enhance the functionality of those Web pages. In this section, we embed the *Windows Media Player ActiveX control* in Web pages. Doing so gives us access to the wide range of media formats supported by the Windows Media Player. The Windows Media Player and other ActiveX controls are embedded into Web pages with the ***OBJECT*** element.

```
1  <!DOCTYPE HTML PUBLIC "-//W3C//DTD HTML 4.0 Transitional//EN">
2  <HTML>
3  <!-- Fig. 21.4: EmbeddedVideo.html -->
4
5  <HEAD>
6  <TITLE>Video via the EMBED Element</TITLE>
7  </HEAD>
8
9  <BODY>
10    <H1>Displaying a Video via the EMBED Element</H1>
11    <H2>Earth Fly-By</H2>
12
13    <TABLE><TR>
14    <TD><EMBED SRC = "approach_1_337.mpeg" LOOP = "false"></EMBED>
15    </TD>
16
17    <TD><P>This video is part of the NASA Multimedia Archives.
18    You can find this video and six additional videos that
19    continue the animation at the <A HREF = "http://
seawifs.gsfc.nasa.gov/OCEAN_PLANET/HTML/oceanography_flyby.html">
20    Sea-viewing Wide Field-of-view Sensor(SeaWiFS) Project
21    </A> site.</P></TD></TABLE>
22    <HR>
23    This page will play the video once.<BR>
24    Use the controls on the embedded video player to play the
25    video again.
26 </BODY>
27 </HTML>
```

Fig. 21.4 Embedding video with the **EMBED** element (part 1 of 2).

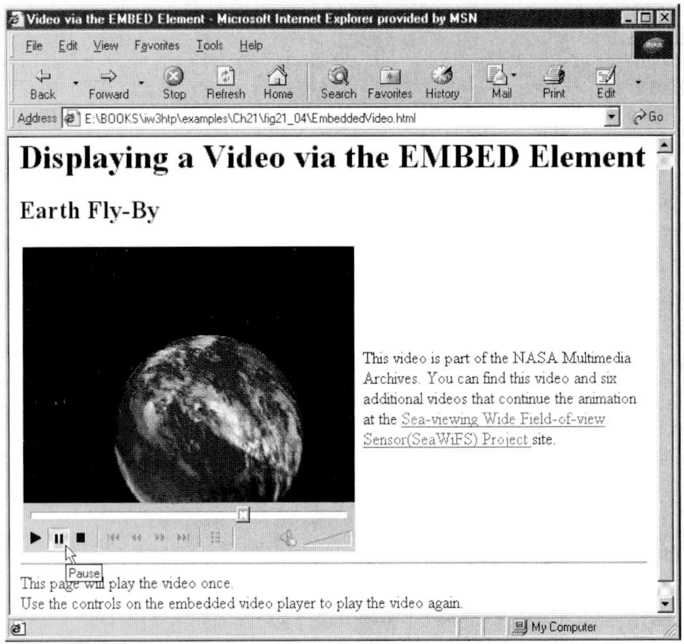

Fig. 21.4 Embedding video with the **EMBED** element (part 2 of 2).

The HTML document of Fig. 21.5 demonstrates using the **OBJECT** element to embed two Windows Media Player ActiveX controls in the Web page. One of the controls plays a video. The the other control plays an audio clip.

```
<!DOCTYPE HTML PUBLIC "-//W3C//DTD HTML 4.0 Transitional//EN">
<HTML>
<!-- Fig. 21.5: MediaPlayer.html -->

<HEAD><TITLE>Embedded Media Player Objects</TITLE>
<SCRIPT LANGUAGE = "JavaScript">
   var videoPlaying = true;

   function toggleVideo( b )
   {
      videoPlaying = !videoPlaying;
      b.value = videoPlaying ? "Pause Video" : "Play Video";
      videoPlaying ? VideoPlayer.Play() : VideoPlayer.Pause();
   }
</SCRIPT>
</HEAD>

<BODY>
<H1>Audio and video through embedded Media Player objects</H1>
```

Fig. 21.5 Using the **OBJECT** element to Embed the Windows Media Player ActiveX control in a Web page (part 1 of 2).

```
<HR>
<TABLE>
   <TR><TD VALIGN = "top" ALIGN = "center">
   <OBJECT ID = "VideoPlayer" WIDTH = 200 HEIGHT = 225
      CLASSID = "CLSID:22d6f312-b0f6-11d0-94ab-0080c74c7e95">
      <PARAM NAME = "FileName" VALUE = "pathfinder.mpeg">
      <PARAM NAME = "AutoStart" VALUE = "true">
      <PARAM NAME = "ShowControls" VALUE = "false">
      <PARAM NAME = "Loop" VALUE = "true">
   </OBJECT></TD>
   <TD VALIGN = "bottom" ALIGN = "center">
   <P>Use the controls below to control the audio clip.</P>
   <OBJECT ID = "AudioPlayer"
      CLASSID = "CLSID:22d6f312-b0f6-11d0-94ab-0080c74c7e95">
      <PARAM NAME = "FileName" VALUE = "newage.mid">
      <PARAM NAME = "AutoStart" VALUE = "true">
      <PARAM NAME = "Loop" VALUE = "true">
   </OBJECT></TD></TR>
   <TR><TD VALIGN = "top" ALIGN = "center">
      <INPUT NAME = "video" TYPE = "button" VALUE = "Pause Video"
            ONCLICK = "toggleVideo( this )"></TD>
</TABLE>
</BODY>
</HTML>
```

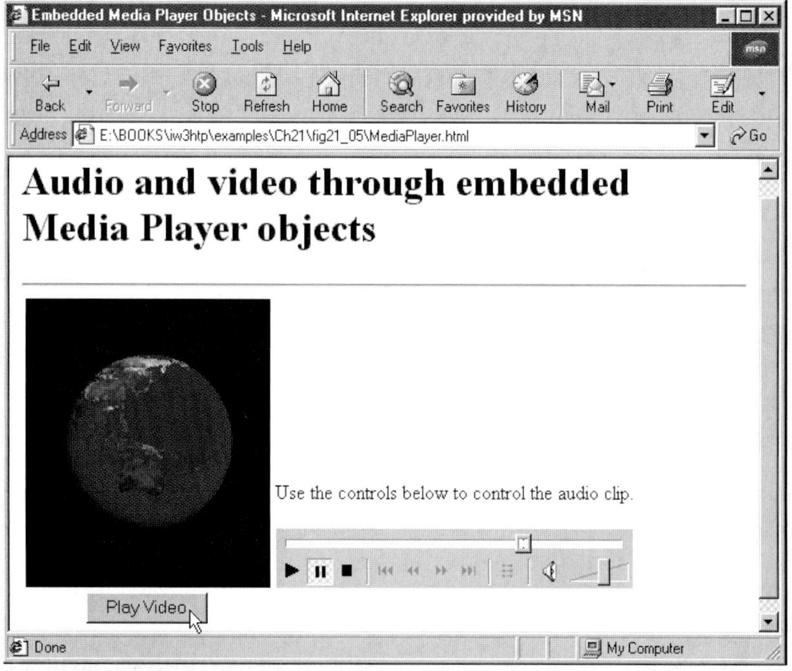

Fig. 21.5 Using the **OBJECT** element to Embed the Windows Media Player ActiveX control in a Web page (part 2 of 2).

When the **BODY** of this document loads, two instances of the Windows Media Player ActiveX control are created. The **OBJECT** element at lines 23 through 29

```
<OBJECT ID = "VideoPlayer" WIDTH = 200 HEIGHT = 225
   CLASSID = "CLSID:22d6f312-b0f6-11d0-94ab-0080c74c7e95">
   <PARAM NAME = "FileName" VALUE = "pathfinder.mpeg">
   <PARAM NAME = "AutoStart" VALUE = "true">
   <PARAM NAME = "ShowControls" VALUE = "false">
   <PARAM NAME = "Loop" VALUE = "true">
</OBJECT>
```

creates a Media Player object for the file **pathfinder.mpeg** (specified on line 25). Line 23 indicates the start of the embedded **OBJECT** definition. The ***ID*** property specifies the scripting name of the element (i.e., **VideoPlayer**). The ***WIDTH*** and ***HEIGHT*** properties specify the width and height in pixels that the control will occupy in the Web page. On line 24, property ***CLASSID*** specifies the unique ActiveX control ID for the Windows Media Player.

Software Engineering Observation 21.7

Most HTML authoring tools that support embedding ActiveX controls enable you to insert the ActiveX controls in a Web page by selecting from a list of available control names.

Lines 25 through 28 specify *parameters* that should be passed to the control when it is created in the Web page. Each parameter is specified with a ***PARAM*** element that contains a ***NAME*** property and a ***VALUE*** property. The ***FileName*** parameter specifies the file containing the media clip. The ***AutoStart*** parameter is a boolean value indicating whether the media clip should play automatically when it is loaded (**true** indicates it should; **false** indicates it should not). The ***ShowControls*** parameter is a boolean value indicating whether the Media Player controls should be displayed (**true** indicates they should; **false** indicates they should not). The ***Loop*** parameter is a boolean value indicating whether the Media Player should play the media clip in an infinite loop (**true** indicates it should; **false** indicates it should not).

The **OBJECT** element at lines 32 through 37

```
<OBJECT ID = "AudioPlayer"
   CLASSID = "CLSID:22d6f312-b0f6-11d0-94ab-0080c74c7e95">
   <PARAM NAME = "FileName" VALUE = "newage.mid">
   <PARAM NAME = "AutoStart" VALUE = "true">
   <PARAM NAME = "Loop" VALUE = "true">
</OBJECT>
```

embeds another Media Player object in the Web page. This Media Player plays the MIDI file **newage.mid** (specified with the **FileName** parameter), automatically starts playing the clip when it is loaded (specified with the **AutoStart** parameter) and infinitely loops the audio clip (specified with the **Loop** parameter).

The script at lines 6 through 15 shows that the Media Player can be controlled from a script. Function **toggleVideo** (line 9) is called when the user clicks the button below the video clip. The button is defined in the HTML form in lines 40 and 41

```
<INPUT NAME = "video" TYPE = "button" VALUE = "Pause Video"
      ONCLICK = "toggleVideo( this )"></TD>
```

The **ONLCLICK** event specifies that function **toggleVideo** is the event handler and **this** button should be passed as an argument to the function. This allows us to change the text on the button at line 12. Line 13

```
videoPlaying ? VideoPlayer.Play() : VideoPlayer.Pause();
```

uses the boolean variable **videoPlaying** to determine whether to call **VideoPlayer**'s **Play** or **Pause** methods to play or pause the video clip, respectively.

21.6 Microsoft Agent Control

Microsoft Agent is an exciting technology for *interactive animated characters* in a Windows application or World Wide Web page. The *Microsoft Agent control* provides access to four predefined characters—*Peedy the Parrot*, *Genie*, *Merlin* and *Robby the Robot*. These characters allow users of your application to interact with the application using more natural human communication techniques. The control accepts both mouse and keyboard interactions, speaks (if a compatible text-to-speech engine is installed) and also supports speech recognition (if a compatible speech recognition engine is installed). With these capabilities, your Web pages can speak to users and can actually respond to their voice commands. You can also create your own characters with the help of the *Microsoft Agent Character Editor* and the *Microsoft Linguistic Sound Editing Tool* (both downloadable from the Microsoft Agent web site).

In this section, we discuss some basic capabilities of the Microsoft Agent control. For complete details on downloading the Microsoft Agent control and taking advantage of the control's capabilities, visit the Microsoft Web site:

```
http://msdn.microsoft.com/workshop/imedia/agent
```

At this site you will find everything you need to use Microsoft Agent in your own Web pages, including the Microsoft Agent ActiveX control, the *Lernout and Hauspie TruVoice text-to-speech (TTS) engine* and the *Microsoft Speech Recognition Engine.*

In addition to the area of this Web site dedicated to Microsoft Agent, there are also discussions of several other multimedia technologies that are available for use in Windows applications and in Web pages. Simply visit

```
http://msdn.microsoft.com/workshop/imedia
```

for more information.

Figure 21.6 demonstrates the Microsoft Agent ActiveX control and the Lernout and Hauspie TruVoice text-to-speech engine (also an ActiveX control). The HTML document in Fig. 21.6 embeds each of these ActiveX controls into a Web page that acts as a tutorial for the various types of programming tips presented in this text. Peedy the Parrot will display and speak text that describes each of the programming tips. When the user clicks the icon for a programming tip, Peedy will fly to that tip and recite the appropriate text.

Performance Tip 21.2

The Microsoft Agent control and the Lernout and Hauspie TruVoice TTS engine will be downloaded automatically from the Microsoft Agent Web site if they are not already installed on your computer. You may want to download these controls in advance, to allow the Web page to use Microsoft Agent and the TTS engine immediately when the Web page is loaded.

Testing and Debugging Tip 21.1

The Microsoft Agent characters and animations are downloaded from the Microsoft Agent Web site. If you are not connected to the Internet, these will not be able to download. You can download the character information onto your local computer and modify the Microsoft Agent examples to load character data from the local computer for demonstration purposes.

```
<!DOCTYPE HTML PUBLIC "-//W3C//DTD HTML 4.0 Transitional//EN">
<HTML>
<!-- Fig. 21.6: tutorial.html -->

<HEAD>
<TITLE>Microsoft Agent and the text to speech engine</TITLE>

<!-- Microsoft Agent ActiveX Control -->
<OBJECT ID = "agent" WIDTH = "0" HEIGHT = "0"
   CLASSID = "CLSID:D45FD31B-5C6E-11D1-9EC1-00C04FD7081F"
   CODEBASE = "#VERSION = 2,0,0,0">
</OBJECT>

<!-- Lernout & Hauspie TruVoice text to speech engine -->
<OBJECT WIDTH = "0" HEIGHT = "0"
   CLASSID = "CLSID:B8F2846E-CE36-11D0-AC83-00C04FD97575"
   CODEBASE = "#VERSION = 6,0,0,0">
</OBJECT>

<SCRIPT LANGUAGE = "JavaScript">
   var parrot;
   var currentImage = null;
   var explanations = [
      // Good Programming Practice Text
      "Good Programming Practices highlight techniques for " +
      "writing programs that are clearer, more " +
      "understandable, more debuggable, and more " +
      "maintainable.",

      // Software Engineering Observation Text
      "Software Engineering Observations highlight " +
      "architectural and design issues that affect the " +
      "construction of complex software systems.",

      // Performance Tip Text
      "Performance Tips highlight opportunities for " +
      "improving program performance.",

      // Portability Tip Text
      "Portability Tips help students write portable code " +
      "that can execute in different Web browsers.",

      // Look-and-Feel Observation Text
      "Look-and-Feel Observations highlight graphical user " +
      "interface conventions. These observations help " +
```

Fig. 21.6 Demonstrating Microsoft Agent and the Lernout and Hauspie TruVoice text-to-speech (TTS) engine (part 1 of 5).

```
         "students design their own graphical user interfaces " +
         "in conformance with industry standards.",

         // Testing and Debugging Tip Text
         "Testing and Debugging Tips tell people how to test " +
         "and debug their programs. Many of the tips also " +
         "describe aspects of creating Web pages and scripts " +
         "that reduce the likelihood of 'bugs' and thus " +
         "simplify the testing and debugging process.",

         // Common Programming Error Text
         "Common Programming Errors focus the studentsí " +
         "attention on errors commonly made by beginning " +
         "programmers. This helps students avoid making the " +
         "same errors. It also helps reduce the long lines " +
         "outside instructorsí offices during office hours!" ];

      function loadAgent()
      {
         agent.Connected = true;
         agent.Characters.Load( "peedy",
            "http://agent.microsoft.com/agent2/" +
            "chars/peedy/peedy.acf" );
         parrot = agent.Characters.Character( "peedy" );
         parrot.LanguageID = 0x0409;

         // get states from server
         parrot.Get( "state", "Showing" );
         parrot.Get( "state", "Speaking" );
         parrot.Get( "state", "Hiding" );

         // get Greet animation and do Peedy introduction
         parrot.Get( "animation", "Greet" );
         parrot.MoveTo( screenLeft, screenTop - 100 );
         parrot.Show();
         parrot.Play( "Greet" );
         parrot.Speak( "Hello. My name is Peedy the Parrot. " +
            "Click a programming tip icon, and I will tell " +
            "you about it." );
         parrot.Play( "GreetReturn" );

         // get other animations
         parrot.Get( "animation", "Idling" );
         parrot.Get( "animation", "MoveDown" );
         parrot.Get( "animation", "MoveUp" );
         parrot.Get( "animation", "MoveLeft" );
         parrot.Get( "animation", "MoveRight" );
         parrot.Get( "animation", "GetAttention" );
      }

      function imageSelectTip( tip )
      {
```

Fig. 21.6 Demonstrating Microsoft Agent and the Lernout and Hauspie TruVoice text-to-speech (TTS) engine (part 2 of 5).

```
         parrot.Stop();
         for ( var i = 0; i < document.images.length; ++i )
            if ( document.images( i ) == tip )
               tellMeAboutIt( i );
      }

      function tellMeAboutIt( element )
      {
         currentImage = document.images( element );
         currentImage.style.background = "red";
         parrot.MoveTo( currentImage.offsetParent.offsetLeft,
            currentImage.offsetParent.offsetTop + 30 );
         parrot.Speak( explanations[ element ] );
      }
   </SCRIPT>

   <SCRIPT LANGUAGE="JavaScript" FOR = "agent" EVENT = "BalloonHide">
      if ( currentImage != null ) {
         currentImage.style.background = "lemonchiffon";
         currentImage = null;
      }
   </SCRIPT>

   <SCRIPT LANGUAGE = "JavaScript" FOR = "agent" EVENT = "Click">
      parrot.Stop();
      parrot.Play( "GetAttention" );
      parrot.Speak( "Stop poking me with that pointer!" );
   </SCRIPT>
   </HEAD>

   <BODY BGCOLOR = "lemonchiffon" ONLOAD = "loadAgent()">
   <TABLE BORDER = "0">
      <TH COLSPAN = "4"><H1 STYLE = "color: blue">
         Deitel & Deitel Programming Tips</H1></TH>
      <TR>
      <TD ALIGN = "CENTER" VALIGN = "top" WIDTH = "120">
         <IMG NAME = "gpp" SRC = "GPP_100h.gif"
              ALT = "Good Programming Practice" BORDER = "0"
              ONCLICK = "imageSelectTip( this )">
         <BR>Good Programming Practices</TD>
      <TD ALIGN = "CENTER" VALIGN = "top" WIDTH = "120">
         <IMG NAME = "seo" SRC = "SEO_100h.gif"
              ALT = "Software Engineering Observation" BORDER = "0"
              ONCLICK = "imageSelectTip( this )">
         <BR>Software Engineering Observations</TD>
      <TD ALIGN = "CENTER" VALIGN = "top" WIDTH = "120">
         <IMG NAME = "perf" SRC = "PERF_100h.gif"
              ALT = "Performance Tip" BORDER = "0"
              ONCLICK = "imageSelectTip( this )">
         <BR>Performance Tips</TD>
      <TD ALIGN = "CENTER" VALIGN = "top" WIDTH = "120">
         <IMG NAME = "port" SRC = "PORT_100h.gif"
```

Fig. 21.6 Demonstrating Microsoft Agent and the Lernout and Hauspie TruVoice text-to-speech (TTS) engine (part 3 of 5).

```
            ALT = "Portability Tip" BORDER = "0"
            ONCLICK = "imageSelectTip( this )">
      <BR>Portability Tips</TD>
   </TR>
   <TR>
   <TD ALIGN = "CENTER" VALIGN = "top" WIDTH = "120">
      <IMG NAME = "gui" SRC = "GUI_100h.gif"
            ALT = "Look-and-Feel Observation" BORDER = "0"
            ONCLICK = "imageSelectTip( this )">
      <BR>Look-and-Feel Observations</TD>
   <TD ALIGN = "CENTER" VALIGN = "top" WIDTH = "120">
      <IMG NAME = "dbt" SRC = "DBT_100h.gif"
            ALT = "Testing and Debugging Tip" BORDER = "0"
            ONCLICK = "imageSelectTip( this )">
      <BR>Testing and Debugging Tips</TD>
   <TD ALIGN = "CENTER" VALIGN = "top" WIDTH = "120">
      <IMG NAME = "cpe" SRC = "CPE_100h.gif"
            ALT = "Common Programming Error" BORDER = "0"
            ONCLICK = "imageSelectTip( this )">
      <BR>Common Programming Errors</TD>
   </TR>
</TABLE>
</BODY>
</HTML>
```

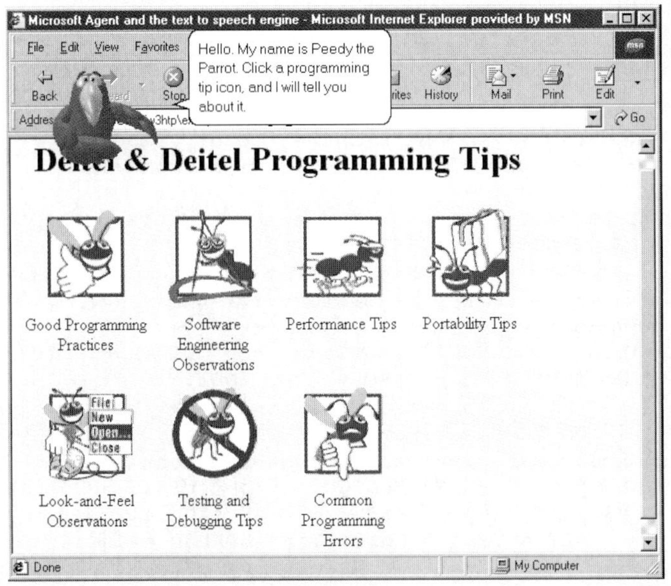

Fig. 21.6 Demonstrating Microsoft Agent and the Lernout and Hauspie TruVoice text-to-speech (TTS) engine (part 4 of 5).

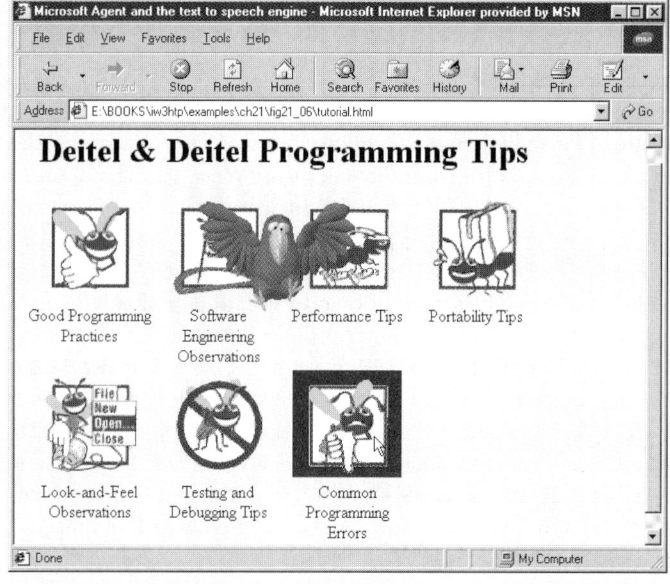

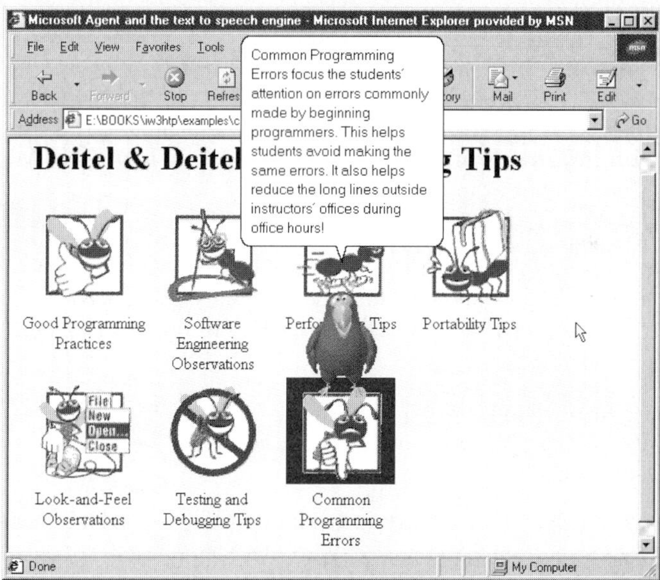

Fig. 21.6 Demonstrating Microsoft Agent and the Lernout and Hauspie TruVoice text-to-speech (TTS) engine (part 5 of 5).

The first screen capture illustrates Peedy finishing his introduction. The second screen capture shows Peedy flying toward the *Common Programming Error* icon. The last screen capture shows Peedy finishing his discussion of *Common Programming Errors.*

Before using Microsoft Agent or the Lernout and Hauspie TruVoice TTS engine in the Web page, they must both be loaded into the Web page via **OBJECT** elements. Lines 9 through 12 embed an instance of the Microsoft Agent ActiveX control into the Web page and give it the scripting name **agent** via the **ID** property. Similarly, lines 15 through 18 embed an instance of the Lernout and Hauspie TruVoice TTS engine into the Web page. This object is not scripted directly by the Web page. The TTS engine is used by the Microsoft Agent control to speak the text that Microsoft Agent displays. If either of these controls is not already installed on the computer browsing the Web page, the browser will attempt to download that control from the Microsoft Web site. The ***CODEBASE*** property (lines 11 and 17) specifies the URL from which to download the control and the version of the control to download (version 2 for the Microsoft Agent control and version 6 for the Lernout and Hauspie TruVoice TTS engine). The Microsoft Agent documentation discusses how to place these controls on your own server for download to your clients. [Note: Placing these controls on your own server requires a license from Microsoft.]

The **BODY** of the document (lines 128 through 172) defines a **TABLE** containing the seven programming tip icons. Each tip icon is given a scripting name via its **IMG** element's **NAME** property. This will be used to change the background color of the **IMG** element when the user clicks it to receive an explanation of that tip type. Each **IMG** element's **ONCLICK** event is registered as function **imageSelectTip**, defined at line 96. Each IMG element passes itself (i.e., **this**) to function **imageSelectTip** so the function can determine the particular image selected by the user.

The HTML document contains three separate **SCRIPT** elements. The **SCRIPT** element at lines 20 through 112 defines global variables used in all the **SCRIPT** elements and defines functions **loadAgent** (called in response to the **BODY** element's **ONLOAD** event), **imageSelectTip** (called when the user clicks an **IMG** element) and **tellMeAboutIt** (called by **imageSelectTip** to speak a few sentences about a tip).

Function **loadAgent** is particularly important, because it loads the Microsoft Agent character that is used in this example. Line 65

```
agent.Connected = true;
```

is provided mainly for backwards compatibility. This line may be needed to ensure that the Agent control executes properly in some older versions of Internet Explorer.

Lines 66 through 68

```
agent.Characters.Load( "peedy",
   "http://agent.microsoft.com/agent2/" +
   "chars/peedy/peedy.acf" );
```

use the Microsoft Agent control's ***Characters*** collection to load the character information for Peedy the Parrot from the Microsoft Web site. Method ***Load*** of the **Characters** collection takes two arguments—the first argument specifies a name for the character that can be used later to interact with that character, and the second argument specifies the URL of the character's data file (**peedy.acf** in this example).

Line 69

```
parrot = agent.Characters.Character( "peedy" );
```

assigns to global variable **parrot** a reference to the Peedy ***Character*** object. This object is used to interact with the character. Method ***Character*** of the **Characters** collection receives as its argument the name that was used to download the character data in lines 66 through 68. Line 70 sets the ***Character***'s ***LanguageID*** property to 0x0409 (English). Microsoft Agent can actually be used with several different languages. See the documentation for more information.

Lines 73 through 75

```
parrot.Get( "state", "Showing" );
parrot.Get( "state", "Speaking" );
parrot.Get( "state", "Hiding" );
```

use the **Character** object's ***Get*** method to download the ***Showing***, ***Speaking*** and ***Hiding*** states for the character. The method takes two arguments—the *type* of information to download (state in this case) and the *name* of the corresponding element (e.g., **Showing**). Each of these states has animation effects associated with it. When the character is displayed (i.e, the **Showing** state), its associated animation plays automatically (Peedy flies onto the screen). When the character is speaking (i.e, the **Speaking** state), the animations that make the character appear to be speaking are played. When the character hides (i.e, the **Hiding** state), the animations that make the character disappear are played (Peedy flies away).

Line 78

```
parrot.Get( "animation", "Greet" );
```

uses **Character** method **Get** to load an animation (**Greet**, in this example).

Lines 79 through 85

```
parrot.MoveTo( screenLeft, screenTop - 100 );
parrot.Show();
parrot.Play( "Greet" );
parrot.Speak( "Hello. My name is Peedy the Parrot. " +
   "Click a programming tip icon, and I will tell " +
   "you about it." );
parrot.Play( "GreetReturn" );
```

use a variety of **Character** methods to interact with Peedy. Line 79 uses the ***MoveTo*** method to specify Peedy's position on the screen. Line 80 uses method ***Show*** to display the character. When this occurs, the character goes into the **Showing** state, and its corresponding animation plays (i.e., Peedy flies onto the screen). Line 81 uses method ***Play*** to play the **Greet** animation (see the first screen capture). Lines 82 through 84 use method ***Speak*** to speak its string argument. If there is a compatible TTS engine installed, the character will display a bubble containing the text and will audibly speak the text as well. Finally, line 85 uses method **Play** to play the ***GreetReturn*** animation that returns the character to its normal standing state. Many animations have a "**Return**" animation that enables smooth transitions between different animations. The Microsoft Agent Web site contains complete lists of animations available for each character (some are standard to all characters, and others are specific to each character).

Lines 88 through 93 load several other animations. Line 88 loads the set of ***Idling*** animations that are used by Microsoft Agent when the user is not interacting with the character. When you run this example, be sure to leave Peedy alone for a while so you can see some of these animations. Lines 89 through 92 load the animations for moving the character up, down, left and right (***MoveUp***, ***MoveDown***, ***MoveLeft*** and ***MoveRight***, respectively).

Function **imageSelectTip** (lines 96 through 102) is called when the user clicks an image. The method first uses **Character** method ***Stop*** to terminate the current animation. Next, the **for** structure at lines 99 through 101 determines which image the user clicked. The condition at line 100

```
document.images( i ) == tip
```

uses the **document** object's ***images*** collection to determine the index of the clicked **IMG** element. If the current element of the collection is equal to **tip** (the clicked image), function **tellMeAboutIt** (defined at line 104) is called with the index of that **IMG** element.

Line 106 in function **tellMeAboutIt** assigns global variable **currentImage** a reference to the clicked **IMG** element. This will be used to change the background color of the **IMG** element the user clicked to highlight that image on the screen. Line 107 changes the background color of the image to red. Line 108 uses **Character** method **MoveTo** to position Peedy above the clicked image. When this statement executes, Peedy flies to the image. The **currentImage**'s ***offsetParent*** property determines the parent element that contains the image (in this example, the **TABLE** cell in which the image appears). The ***offsetLeft*** and ***offsetTop*** properties of the **TABLE** cell determine the location of the cell with respect to the upper-left corner of the browser window. Line 110 calls the **Character** object's **Speak** method to speak the text that is stored as strings in the array **explanations** for the selected tip.

The script for the **agent** control at lines 114 through 119 is invoked in response to the hiding of the text balloon. If the **currentImage** is not **null**, the background color of the image is changed to **lemonchiffon** (the document's background color) and variable **currentImage** is set to **null**.

The script for the **agent** control at lines 121 through 125 is invoked in response to the user's clicking the character. When this occurs, line 122 stops the current animation, line 123 plays the **GetAttention** animation and line 124 causes Peedy to speak the text "**Stop poking me with that pointer!**"

The HTML document of Fig. 21.7 enhances the example of Fig. 21.6 to include voice recognition. Most of the example is identical to Fig. 21.6, so here we discuss only the new features. The first screen capture illustrates Peedy finishing his introduction. The second screen capture shows Peedy after the user presses the *Scroll Lock* key to start issuing voice commands—this causes the voice recognition engine to initialize. The third screen capture shows Peedy ready to receive voice commands. The fourth screen capture shows Peedy after receiving a voice command (i.e., "Performance Tip"—this causes a ***Command*** event for the **agent** control). The last two screen captures show Peedy flying toward the Performance Tip icon and discussing Performance Tips, respectively.

To enable Microsoft Agent to recognize voice commands, a compatible voice recognition engine must be installed. Lines 21 through 24 use an **OBJECT** element to embed an instance of the Microsoft Speech Recognition Engine control in the Web page.

Next, the voice commands that the user can speak to interact with the Peedy must be registered in the **Character** object's ***Commands*** collection. The **for** structure at lines 118 through 120

```
for ( var i = 0; i < tips.length; ++i )
   parrot.Commands.Add( tips[ i ], tipNames[ i ],
      voiceTips[ i ], true, true );
```

uses the **Commands** collection's ***Add*** method to register each voice command. The method receives five arguments. The first argument is a string representing the command *name* (typically used in scripts that respond to voice commands). The second argument is a string that is displayed in a pop-up menu if you right-click the character or display the *Commands Window* (right-click the Microsoft Agent taskbar icon in the lower-right corner of your screen and select **Open Voice Commands Window**). The third argument is a string representing the words or phrases a user can speak for this command (stored in array **voiceTips** at lines 37 through 42). Optional words or phrases are enclosed in square brackets ([ ]). The last two arguments are boolean values indicating whether the command is currently enabled (i.e., the user can speak the command) and whether the command is currently visible in the pop-up menu and Commands Window for the character.

```
1  <!DOCTYPE HTML PUBLIC "-//W3C//DTD HTML 4.0 Transitional//EN">
2  <HTML>
3  <!-- Fig. 21.7: tutorial.html -->
4
5  <HEAD>
6  <TITLE>Speech Recognition</TITLE>
7
8  <!-- Microsoft Agent ActiveX Control -->
9  <OBJECT ID = "agent" WIDTH = "0" HEIGHT = "0"
10    CLASSID = "CLSID:D45FD31B-5C6E-11D1-9EC1-00C04FD7081F"
11    CODEBASE = "#VERSION = 2,0,0,0">
12 </OBJECT>
13
14 <!-- Lernout & Hauspie TruVoice text to speach engine -->
15 <OBJECT WIDTH = "0" HEIGHT = "0"
16    CLASSID = "CLSID:B8F2846E-CE36-11D0-AC83-00C04FD97575"
17    CODEBASE = "#VERSION = 6,0,0,0">
18 </OBJECT>
19
20 <!-- Microsoft Speech Recognition Engine -->
21 <OBJECT WIDTH = "0" HEIGHT = "0"
22    CLASSID = "CLSID:161FA781-A52C-11d0-8D7C-00A0C9034A7E"
23    CODEBASE = "#VERSION = 4,0,0,0">
24 </OBJECT>
25
26 <SCRIPT LANGUAGE = "JavaScript">
27    var parrot;
28    var currentImage = null;
29    var tips =
30       [ "gpp", "seo", "perf", "port", "gui", "dbt", "cpe" ];
31    var tipNames = [ "Good Programming Practice",
32                     "Software Engineering Observation",
33                     "Performance Tip", "Portability Tip",
34                     "Look-and-Feel Observation",
35                     "Testing and Debugging Tip",
36                     "Common Programming Error" ];
37    var voiceTips = [ "Good [Programming Practice]",
38                      "Software [Engineering Observation]",
```

Fig. 21.7 Microsoft Voice Recognition Engine and Microsoft Agent (part 1 of 8).

```
                        "Performance [Tip]", "Portability [Tip]",
                        "Look-and-Feel [Observation]",
                        "Testing [and Debugging Tip]",
                        "Common [Programming Error]" ];
   var explanations = [
      // Good Programming Practice Text
      "Good Programming Practices highlight techniques for " +
      "writing programs that are clearer, more " +
      "understandable, more debuggable, and more " +
      "maintainable.",

      // Software Engineering Observation Text
      "Software Engineering Observations highlight " +
      "architectural and design issues that affect the " +
      "construction of complex software systems.",

      // Performance Tip Text
      "Performance Tips highlight opportunities for " +
      "improving program performance.",

      // Portability Tip Text
      "Portability Tips help students write portable code " +
      "that can execute in different Web browsers.",

      // Look-and-Feel Observation Text
      "Look-and-Feel Observations highlight graphical user " +
      "interface conventions. These observations help " +
      "students design their own graphical user interfaces " +
      "in conformance with industry standards.",

      // Testing and Debugging Tip Text
      "Testing and Debugging Tips tell people how to test " +
      "and debug their programs. Many of the tips also " +
      "describe aspects of creating Web pages and scripts " +
      "that reduce the likelihood of 'bugs' and thus " +
      "simplify the testing and debugging process.",

      // Common Programming Error Text
      "Common Programming Errors focus the studentsí " +
      "attention on errors commonly made by beginning " +
      "programmers. This helps students avoid making the " +
      "same errors. It also helps reduce the long lines " +
      "outside instructorsí offices during office hours!" ];

   function loadAgent()
   {
      agent.Connected = true;
      agent.Characters.Load( "peedy",
         "http://agent.microsoft.com/agent2/" +
         "chars/peedy/peedy.acf" );
      parrot = agent.Characters.Character( "peedy" );
      parrot.LanguageID = 0x0409;  // needed in some conditions

```

Fig. 21.7 Microsoft Voice Recognition Engine and Microsoft Agent (part 2 of 8).

```
      // get states from server
      parrot.Get( "state", "Showing" );
      parrot.Get( "state", "Speaking" );
      parrot.Get( "state", "Hiding" );

      // get Greet animation and do Peedy introduction
      parrot.Get( "animation", "Greet" );
      parrot.MoveTo( screenLeft, screenTop - 100 );
      parrot.Show();
      parrot.Play( "Greet" );
      parrot.Speak( "Hello. My name is Peedy the Parrot. " +
         "If you would like me to tell you about a " +
         "programming tip, click its icon, or, press the " +
         "'Scroll Lock' key, and speak the name of the " +
         "tip, into your microphone." );
      parrot.Play( "GreetReturn" );

      // get other animations
      parrot.Get( "animation", "Idling" );
      parrot.Get( "animation", "MoveDown" );
      parrot.Get( "animation", "MoveUp" );
      parrot.Get( "animation", "MoveLeft" );
      parrot.Get( "animation", "MoveRight" );
      parrot.Get( "animation", "GetAttention" );

      // set up voice commands
      for ( var i = 0; i < tips.length; ++i )
         parrot.Commands.Add( tips[ i ], tipNames[ i ],
            voiceTips[ i ], true, true );

      parrot.Commands.Caption = "Programming Tips";
      parrot.Commands.Voice = "Programming Tips";
      parrot.Commands.Visible = true;
   }

   function imageSelectTip( tip )
   {
      for ( var i = 0; i < document.images.length; ++i )
         if ( document.images( i ) == tip )
            tellMeAboutIt( i );
   }

   function voiceSelectTip( cmd )
   {
      var found = false;

      for ( var i = 0; i < tips.length; ++i )
         if ( cmd.Name == tips[ i ] ) {
            found = true;
            break;
         }

```

Fig. 21.7 Microsoft Voice Recognition Engine and Microsoft Agent (part 3 of 8).

```
      if ( found )
         tellMeAboutIt( i );
   }

   function tellMeAboutIt( element )
   {
      currentImage = document.images( element );
      currentImage.style.background = "red";
      parrot.MoveTo( currentImage.offsetParent.offsetLeft,
         currentImage.offsetParent.offsetTop + 30 );
      parrot.Speak( explanations[ element ] );
   }
</SCRIPT>

<SCRIPT LANGUAGE = "JavaScript" FOR = "agent"
      EVENT = "Command( cmd )">
   voiceSelectTip( cmd );
</SCRIPT>

<SCRIPT LANGUAGE="JavaScript" FOR = "agent" EVENT = "BalloonHide">
   if ( currentImage != null ) {
      currentImage.style.background = "lemonchiffon";
      currentImage = null;
   }
</SCRIPT>

<SCRIPT LANGUAGE = "JavaScript" FOR = "agent" EVENT = "Click">
   parrot.Play( "GetAttention" );
   parrot.Speak( "Stop poking me with that pointer!" );
</SCRIPT>

</HEAD>

<BODY BGCOLOR = "lemonchiffon" ONLOAD = "loadAgent()">
<TABLE BORDER = "0">
   <TH COLSPAN = "4">
     <H1 STYLE="color: blue">Deitel & Deitel Programming Tips</H1>
   </TH>
   <TR>
   <TD ALIGN = "CENTER" VALIGN = "top" WIDTH = "120">
      <IMG NAME = "gpp" SRC = "GPP_100h.gif"
           ALT = "Good Programming Practice" BORDER = "0"
           ONCLICK = "imageSelectTip( this )">
      <BR>Good Programming Practices</TD>
   <TD ALIGN = "CENTER" VALIGN = "top" WIDTH = "120">
      <IMG NAME = "seo" SRC = "SEO_100h.gif"
           ALT = "Software Engineering Observation" BORDER = "0"
           ONCLICK = "imageSelectTip( this )">
      <BR>Software Engineering Observations</TD>
   <TD ALIGN = "CENTER" VALIGN = "top" WIDTH = "120">
      <IMG NAME = "perf" SRC = "PERF_100h.gif"
           ALT = "Performance Tip" BORDER = "0"
           ONCLICK = "imageSelectTip( this )">
```

Fig. 21.7 Microsoft Voice Recognition Engine and Microsoft Agent (part 4 of 8).

```
         <BR>Performance Tips</TD>
      <TD ALIGN = "CENTER" VALIGN = "top" WIDTH = "120">
         <IMG NAME = "port" SRC = "PORT_100h.gif"
              ALT = "Portability Tip" BORDER = "0"
              ONCLICK = "imageSelectTip( this )">
         <BR>Portability Tips</TD>
      </TR>
      <TR>
      <TD ALIGN = "CENTER" VALIGN = "top" WIDTH = "120">
         <IMG NAME = "gui" SRC = "GUI_100h.gif"
              ALT = "Look-and-Feel Observation" BORDER = "0"
              ONCLICK = "imageSelectTip( this )">
         <BR>Look-and-Feel Observations</TD>
      <TD ALIGN = "CENTER" VALIGN = "top" WIDTH = "120">
         <IMG NAME = "dbt" SRC = "DBT_100h.gif"
              ALT = "Testing and Debugging Tip" BORDER = "0"
              ONCLICK = "imageSelectTip( this )">
         <BR>Testing and Debugging Tips</TD>
      <TD ALIGN = "CENTER" VALIGN = "top" WIDTH = "120">
         <IMG NAME = "cpe" SRC = "CPE_100h.gif"
              ALT = "Common Programming Error" BORDER = "0"
              ONCLICK = "imageSelectTip(this)">
         <BR>Common Programming Errors</TD>
      </TR>
   </TABLE>
   </BODY>
   </HTML>
```

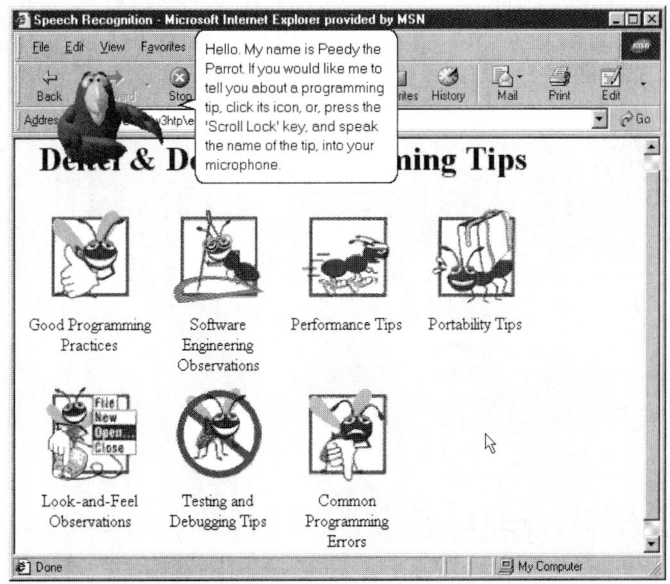

Fig. 21.7 Microsoft Voice Recognition Engine and Microsoft Agent (part 5 of 8).

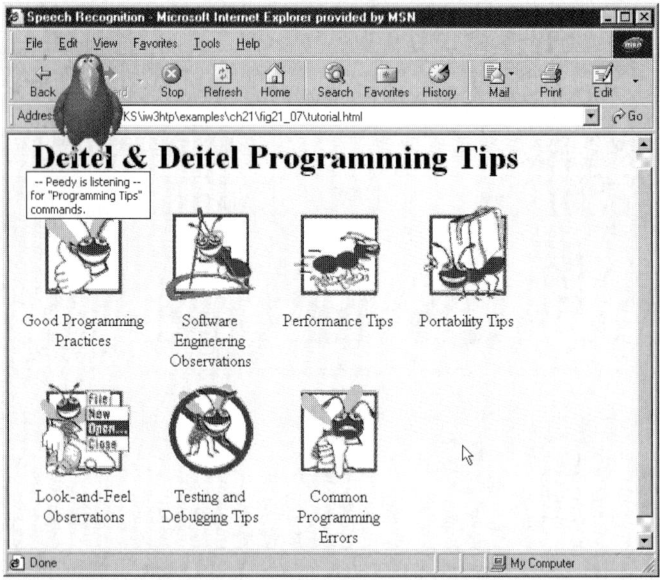

Fig. 21.7 Microsoft Voice Recognition Engine and Microsoft Agent (part 6 of 8).

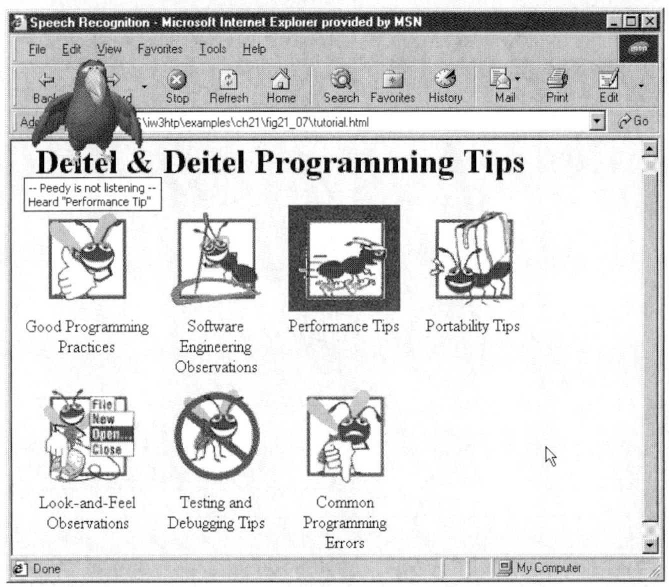

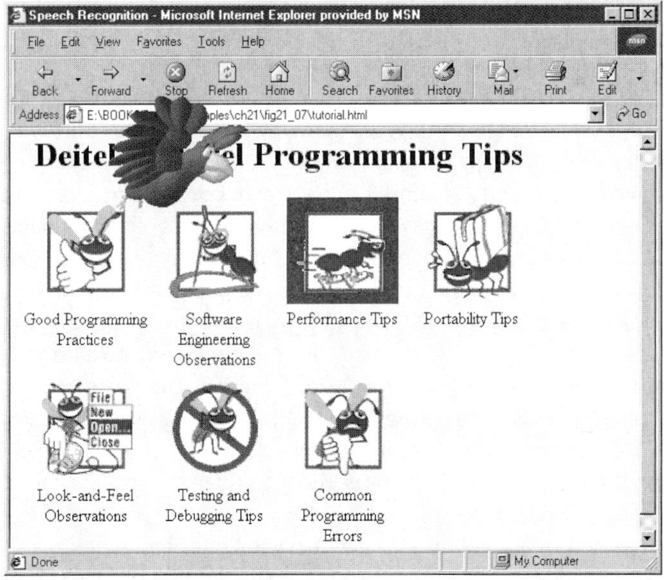

Fig. 21.7 Microsoft Voice Recognition Engine and Microsoft Agent (part 7 of 8).

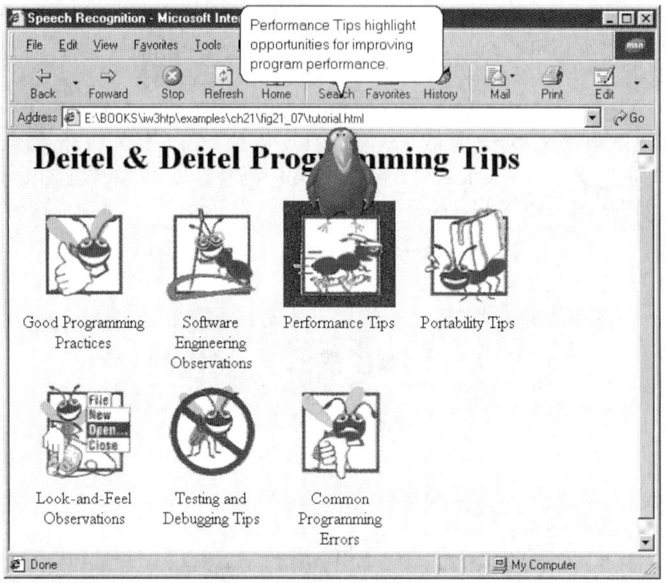

Fig. 21.7 Microsoft Voice Recognition Engine and Microsoft Agent (part 8 of 8).

Lines 122 through 124

```
parrot.Commands.Caption = "Programming Tips";
parrot.Commands.Voice = "Programming Tips";
parrot.Commands.Visible = true;
```

set the ***Caption***, ***Voice*** and ***Visible*** properties of the **Commands** object. The **Caption** property specifies text that describes the voice command set. This text appears in the small rectangular area that appears below the character when the user presses the *Scroll Lock* key. The **Voice** property is similar to the **Caption** property except that the specified text appears in the Commands Window with the set of voice commands the user can speak below it. The **Visible** property is a boolean value that specifies whether the commands of this **Commands** object should appear in the popup menu.

When a voice command is received, the **agent** control's **Command** event handler (lines 158 through 161) executes. This script calls function **voiceSelectTip** and passes it the name of the command that was received. Function **voiceSelectTip** (lines 134 through 146) uses the name of the command in the **for** structure (line 138) to determine the index of the command in the **Commands** object. This value is then passed to function **tellMeAboutIt** (line 148) which causes Peedy to fly to the specified tip and discuss the tip.

These two examples have shown you the basic features and functionality of Microsoft Agent. However, there are many more features available. Figure 21.8 shows several other Microsoft Agent events. For a complete listing of Microsoft Agent events, see the site

```
http://msdn.microsoft.com/workshop/imedia/agent/
progagentcontrol.asp#TOPIC8
```

Figure 21.9 shows some other properties and methods of the **Character** object. Remember that the **Character** object represents a character that is displayed on the screen and allows interaction with that character. For a complete listing of properties and methods, see the Microsoft Agent Web site.

Figure 21.10 shows some speech output tags that can customize speech output properties. These tags are inserted in the text string that will be spoken by the animated character. Speech output tags generally remain in effect from the time at which they are encountered until the end of the current **Speak** method call. For a complete listing of speech output tags, see

Event	Description
BalloonHide	Called when the text balloon for a character is hidden.
BalloonShow	Called when the text balloon for a character is shown.
Hide	Called when a character is hidden.
Move	Called when a character is moved on the screen.
Show	Called when a character is displayed on the screen.
Size	Called when a character's size is changed.

Fig. 21.8 Other events for the **Microsoft Agent** control.

Property or method	Description
Properties	
Height	The height of the character in pixels.
Left	The left edge of the character in pixels from the left of the screen.
Name	The default name for the character.
Speed	The speed of the character's speech.
Top	The top edge of the character in pixels from the top of the screen.
Width	The width of the character in pixels.
Methods	
Activate	Sets the currently active character when multiple characters appear on the screen.
GestureAt	Specifies that the character should gesture toward a location on the screen that is specified in pixel coordinates from the upper-left corner of the screen.
Interrupt	Interrupts the current animation. The next animation in the queue of animations for this character is then displayed.
StopAll	Stops all animations of a specified type for the character.

Fig. 21.9 Other properties and methods for the **Character** object.

http://msdn.microsoft.com/workshop/imedia/agent/speechoutputtags.asp

21.7 RealPlayer™ Activex Control

In Chapter 2, we discussed using RealPlayer for listening to streaming audio and video. Via the **EMBED** element, you can embed RealPlayer objects in your Web pages to add streaming audio and video to your pages. Figure 21.11 demonstrates streaming audio in a Web page by embedding a RealPlayer object in the page. The user can select from several different audio sources. When a new source is selected, a JavaScript calls RealPlayer methods to start playing the selected audio stream.

Tag	Description
\Chr=*string*****	Specifies the tone of the voice. Possible values for *string* are **Normal** (the default) for a normal tone of voice, **Monotone** for a monotone voice or **Whisper** for a whispered voice.
\Emp	Emphasizes the next spoken word.
\Lst	Repeats the last statement spoken by the character. This tag must be the only content of the string in the **Speak** method call.
\Pau=*number*****	Pauses speech for *number* milliseconds.
\Pit=*number*****	Changes the pitch of the character's voice. This value is specified in the range 50 to 400 hertz for the **Microsoft Agent** speech engine.
\Spd=*number*****	Changes the speech speed to a value in the range 50 to 250.
\Vol=*number*****	Changes the volume to a value in the range 0 (silent) to 65535 (maximum volume).

Fig. 21.10 Speech output tags .

```
<!DOCTYPE HTML PUBLIC "-//W3C//DTD HTML 4.0 Transitional//EN">
<HTML>

<!-- Fig 21.11: real.html                    -->
<!-- Embedding Realplayer into an HTML page -->

<HEAD>
<TITLE>Live Audio!</TITLE>

<SCRIPT LANGUAGE = "JavaScript">
   var locations =
      [ "http://kalx.berkeley.edu/kalx.ram",
        "http://wmbr.mit.edu/live.ram",
        "pnm://206.190.42.52/wfmu.ra" ]

```

Fig. 21.11 Embedding RealPlayer in a Web page (part 1 of 2).

```
16    function change( loc )
17    {
18       raControl.SetSource( locations[ loc ] );
19       raControl.DoPlayPause();
20    }
21
22 </SCRIPT>
23 </HEAD>
24
25 <BODY>
26
27 <P>
28 Pick from my favorite audio streams:
29
30 <SELECT ID = "streamSelect" ONCHANGE = "change( this.value )">
31    <OPTION VALUE = "">Select a station</OPTION>
32    <OPTION VALUE = "0">KALX</OPTION>
33    <OPTION VALUE = "1">WMBR</OPTION>
34    <OPTION VALUE = "2">WFMU</OPTION>
35 </SELECT>
36
37 <BR>
38 <EMBED ID = "raControl" SRC = ""
39    TYPE = "audio/x-pn-realaudio-plugin" WIDTH = "275"
40    HEIGHT = "125" CONTROLS = "Default" AUTOSTART = "false">
41
42 </BODY>
43 </HTML>
```

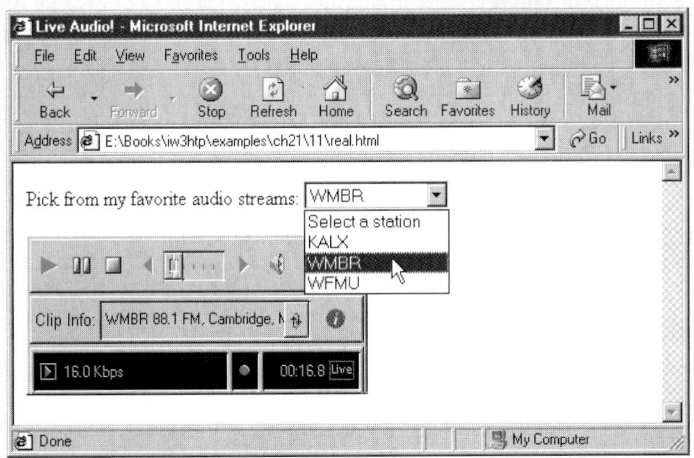

Fig. 21.11 Embedding RealPlayer in a Web page (part 2 of 2).

The **EMBED** element in lines 38 through 40

```
<EMBED ID = "raControl" SRC = ""
   TYPE = "audio/x-pn-realaudio-plugin" WIDTH = "275"
   HEIGHT = "125" CONTROLS = "Default" AUTOSTART = "false">
```

embeds the RealPlayer plug-in in your page. The ***TYPE*** *attribute* specifies the MIME type of the embedded file, which in this case is the MIME type for streaming audio. (Remember that MIME is a standard for specifying the format of content so the browser can determine how to handle the content). The ***WIDTH*** and ***HEIGHT*** *attributes* specify the dimensions the control will occupy on the page. The ***AUTOSTART*** *attribute* determines whether the audio should start playing when the page loads (here we set it to **false**). The ***CONTROLS*** *attribute* specifies which controls will be available to the user (i.e., *Play* button, *Pause* button, *volume control*, etc.). Setting **CONTROLS** to ***Default*** places the standard control buttons on screen. A list of the available controls can be found at the site

http://www.real.com/devzone/library/stream/plugtest/plugin.html

We do not set the ***SRC*** *attribute* of the **EMBED** element. Normally this would be the location of the streaming audio, but in this example we use JavaScript to change the source dynamically based on the user's selection.

Now that the player is embedded in the Web page, we use scripting to activate the streaming audio. The **SELECT** menu (line 30) lists three radio stations, corresponding to the three entries in the array **locations** (defined at line 11), which contains the actual URLs for the live audio of those stations. When the selection changes, function **change** (line 16) is called by the **ONCHANGE** event. This function calls methods ***SetSource*** and ***DoPlayPause*** of the RealPlayer object. Method **SetSource** sets the source URL of the audio stream to be played. Then, method **DoPlayPause** toggles between pausing and playing the stream. (In this case the stream is paused because it has not started playing yet, so it begins playing in response to the call to **DoPlayPause**.)

In this example, we only explore streaming audio. The latest versions of RealPlayer have the ability to receive streaming video as well. If you would like to view streaming video with RealPlayer, check out the following sites:

http://www.cnn.com/
http://www.msnbc.com/
http://www.broadcast.com/television/

If you'd like to learn more about programming with RealPlayer, visit the RealPlayer DevZone at

http://www.real.com/devzone/index.html

Broadcasting your own streaming audio and video requires a dedicated server and expensive software. As you see here however, embedding audio streams in your own pages is a simple way to enhance your page's look and feel.

21.8 Embedding VRML in a Web page

Another innovative technology for enhancing Web pages is *VRML*—the *Virtual Reality Modeling Language*. VRML is a markup language for specifying thee-dimensional (3D) objects and scenes. Like HTML, VRML is purely text and can be created by hand in text editors such as Notepad. In addition, many leading 3D modeling programs can save three-dimensional designs in VRML format.

Both Netscape and Internet Explorer have free, downloadable plug-ins that allow them to view VRML *worlds* (VRML files are known as worlds and end with the **.wrl** *file extension*). The Web page shown in Fig. 21.8 uses the **EMBED** element to place a **.wrl** file in the page—the default VRML plug-in for IE is used to view the file (the VRML plug-in is included with the full install of IE5 on your CD).

```
<HTML>

<!-- Fig 21.11: vrml.html                  -->
<!-- Embedding VRML into a Web page        -->

<HEAD>
<TITLE>Live VRML</TITLE>
</HEAD>

<BODY>

<EMBED SRC = "new.wrl" WIDTH = "400" HEIGHT = "400">

</BODY>
</HTML>
```

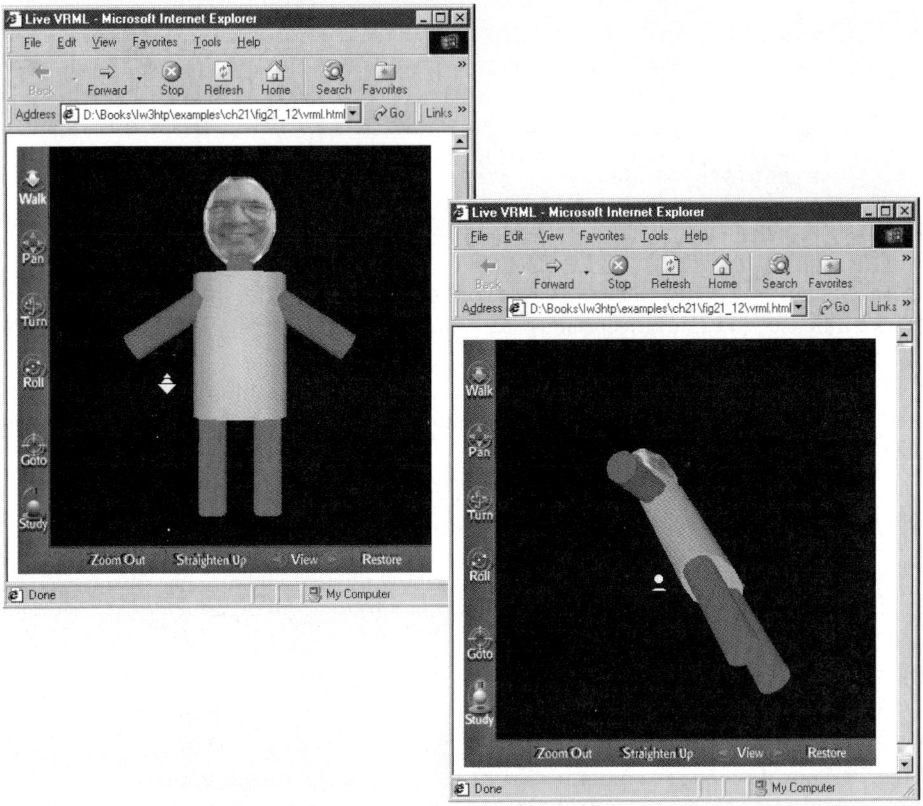

Fig. 21.12 Embedding VRML in a Web page (part 1 of 2).

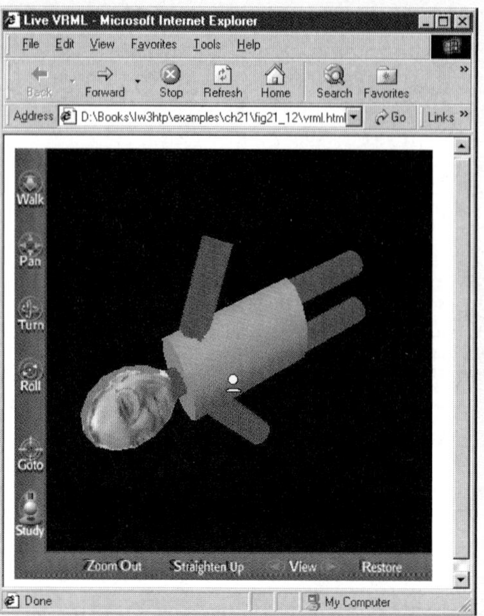

Fig. 21.12 Embedding VRML in a Web page (part 2 of 2).

Line 12

```
<EMBED SRC = "new.wrl" WIDTH = "400" HEIGHT = "400">
```

uses the **EMBED** element to embed the VRML world file **new.wrl** in the Web page, and specifies a width and height of 400 pixels for the viewing area. When the page loads and IE encounters the **EMBED** element, it sees that the file extension for the file specified in the SRC attribute is **.wrl**, and accordingly launches the VRML plug-in. The plug-in reads the **.wrl** file and renders the objects specified in the file on screen.

The controls on the left and bottom sides of the viewing area allow you to move around freely in the world—by clicking one of the controls and dragging the mouse in the viewing area, you can rotate the world, walk around or change which direction you are facing.

21.9 Internet and World Wide Web Resources

There are many multimedia-related resources on the Internet and World Wide Web. This section lists a variety of resources that can help you learn about multimedia programming and provides a brief description of each.

http://www.microsoft.com/windows/windowsmedia/

The *Windows Media* Web site contains information to help get you started with Microsoft's streaming media technologies. The site also links you to various software

http://www.microsoft.com/ntserver/basics/netshowservices

This is the *Windows NT Server site for Windows Media Technologies.* This site provides information for the serving of streaming media over the Internet.

http://msdn.microsoft.com/workshop/imedia/agent/default.asp
The *Microsoft Agent Home Page* provides you with everything you need to know about programming with Microsoft Agent.

http://msdn.microsoft.com/workshop/imedia/agent/agentdl.asp
The *Microsoft Agent downloads area* contains all the software downloads you need to build applications and Web pages that use Microsoft Agent.

http://msdn.microsoft.com/downloads/default.asp
The *Microsoft Developer Network Downloads* home page contains images, audio clips and other free downloads.

http://www.macromedia.com
This is the *Macromedia Home Page*. Macromedia specializes in tools for creating multimedia-rich Web sites. Check out this site for 30-day trial versions of their multimedia authoring tools.

http://www.shockwave.com/
The *Shockwave* web site contains a wide variety of Web-based games, cartoons and music. The site was created with Macromedia authoring tools.

http://xdude.com/
This site is an example of the power of the Macromedia Flash technology.

http://www.station.sony.com/
The Station is one of the most popular sites on the Internet today. It is loaded with games that use a variety of multimedia techniques.

http://www.broadcast.com
Broadcast.com is one of the leading Web sites for streaming media on the World Wide Web. From this site, you can access a variety of live and pre-recorded audio and video.

http://www.real.com/
The *RealNetworks* site is the home of RealPlayer—one of the most popular software products for receiving streaming media over the Web. Also, with their RealJukebox, you can download MP3 files and other digital music.

http://service.real.com/help/library/guides/extend/embed.htm
This site provides the details of embedding RealPlayer in a Web page. The site also provides a detailed listing of the methods and events of the RealPlayer.

http://www.nasa.gov/gallery/index.html
This site is *NASA's Multimedia Gallery*. You can view audio, video, and images from NASA's exploration of space and of our planet.

http://disney.go.com/disneyvideos/bvhevideo/index.html
This *Disney* site contains streaming video clips from several Disney movies.

http://www.space-tv.com/
This site contains streaming video from past NASA space missions and the Russian Mir space station.

http://www.w3.org/WAI/
The World Wide Web Consortium's *Web Accessibility Initiative (WAI)* site promotes design of universally accessible Web sites. This site will help you keep up-to-date with current guidelines and forthcoming standards for Web accessibility.

http://web.ukonline.co.uk/ddmc/software.html
This site provides links to software for people with disabilities.

http://www.hj.com/
Henter-Joyce, Inc. provides software for the blind and visually impaired.

`http://www.abledata.com/text2/icg_hear.htm`
This page contains a consumer guide that discusses technologies for the hearing impaired.

`http://www.washington.edu/doit/`
The University of Washingtion's *DO-IT (Disabilities, Opportunities, Internetworking and Technology) Program* Web site provides information and Web development resources for creating Web sites that are universally accessible.

`http://www.webable.com/`
The WebABLE site contains links to many disability-related Internet resources. The site is geared to development of technologies for people with disabilities.

`http://www.speech.cs.cmu.edu/comp.speech/SpeechLinks.html`
The *Speech Technology Hyperlinks Page* has over 500 links to sites related to computer-based speech and speech recognition.

`http://www.islandnet.com/~tslemko/`
The *Micro Consulting Limited* site contains shareware speech-synthesis software.

`http://www.chantinc.com/technology/`
The *Chant* Web site discusses what speech technology can do for you and how it works. Chant also provides speech-synthesis and speech-recognition software.

`http://www.dismusic.com/`
The *Disney Music Page* offers free Disney music in MIDI (**`.mid`**) format. MIDI format is particularly useful for embedding sound into a web page and having it play when someone enters onto the site.

`http://www.Tx-Marketeers.com/musicroom/`
The Music Room site has a great variety of MIDI format music.

`http://www.spinner.com/`
The *Spinner* site is an on-line radio station, with many genres from which to choose. Either download the player for your computer, or listen to the music through your browser with the RealPlayer plug-in.

`http://www.netradio.com/`
The *NetRadio* site is another on-line radio station that you can listen to with your browser and the RealPlayer plug-in.

`http://www.discjockey.com/`
The *DiscJockey.com* site is an on-line radio station with music from the 40s through the 90s. The music on this site can be played through RealPlayer or the Windows Media Player.

`http://www.mp3.com/`
The *mp3.com* site is an excellent resource for the MP3 audio format. The site offers files, info on the format, hardware info and software info.

`http://home.cnet.com/category/0-4004.html`
CNET is an Internet news group containing a variety of information about today's hottest computer and Internet topics. This page from the *CNET* web site discusses the MP3 format, MP3 encoders and streaming MP3 format audio over the Internet.

`http://www.mpeg.org/`
The *MPEG.org* site is the primary reference site for information on the MPEG video format.

`http://www.winamp.com/`
Winamp is probably the most popular and well-known player for the MP3 format. Winamp has capabilities of allowing you to stream MP3 over the Internet.

`http://www.shoutcast.com/`
SHOUTcast is a streaming audio system. Anyone that has Winamp and a fast Internet connection can broadcast their own net radio!

http://www.microsoft.com/windows/mediaplayer/default.asp
Here is the official site of the *Windows Media Player.* Go here to learn all about its capabilities, especially of streaming audio and video over the net.

SUMMARY

- **BGSOUND** is an Internet Explorer-specific element that adds background audio to a Web site. The **SRC** property specifies the URL of the audio clip to play. The **LOOP** property specifies the number of times the audio clip should play. The **BALANCE** property specifies the balance between the left and right speakers. The **VOLUME** property determines the volume of the audio clip. To change the property values via a script, assign a scripting name to the **ID** property.
- The **IMG** element enables both images and videos to be included in a Web page. The **SRC** property indicates that the source is an image. The **DYNSRC** (i.e., dynamic source) property indicates that the source is a video clip. Property **START** indicates when the video should start playing (specify **fileopen** to play when the clip is loaded or **mouseover** to play when the user first positions the mouse over the video).
- The **EMBED** element embeds a media clip in a Web page. A graphical user interface can be displayed to give the user control over the media clip. The GUI typically enables the user to play, pause and stop the media clip, to specify the volume and to move forward and backward quickly through the clip. The **LOOP** property indicates that the media clip should loop forever. To prevent the GUI from appearing in the Web page, add the **HIDDEN** property to the **<EMBED>** element. To script the element, specify a scripting name by adding the **ID** property to the **<EMBED>** element.
- A benefit of Microsoft's ActiveX controls is that they can be incorporated into Web pages that are to be displayed in Internet Explorer and enhance the functionality of those Web pages.
- The **OBJECT** element is used to embed ActiveX controls in Web pages. The **WIDTH** and **HEIGHT** properties specify the width and height in pixels that the control will occupy in the Web page. Property **CLASSID** specifies the unique ActiveX control ID for the ActiveX control.
- The ActiveX control ID for the Windows Media Player ActiveX control is

  CLSID:22d6f312-b0f6-11d0-94ab-0080c74c7e95

- Parameters can be passed to an ActiveX control by placing **PARAM** elements between the **OBJECT** element's **<OBJECT>** and **</OBJECT>** tags. Each parameter is specified with a **PARAM** element that contains a **NAME** property and a **VALUE** property.
- The Windows Media Player ActiveX control's **FileName** parameter specifies the file containing the media clip. Parameter **AutoStart** is a boolean value indicating whether the media clip should play automatically when it is loaded (**true** if so; **false** if not). The **ShowControls** parameter is a boolean value indicating whether the Media Player controls should be displayed (**true** if so; **false** if not). The **Loop** parameter is a boolean value indicating whether the Media Player should play the media clip in an infinite loop (**true** if so; **false** if not).
- The Windows Media Player ActiveX control's **Play** and **Pause** methods can be called to play or pause a media clip, respectively.
- Microsoft Agent is a technology for interactive animated characters in a Windows application or World Wide Web page. These characters allow users of your application to interact with the application by using more natural human communication techniques. The control accepts both mouse and keyboard interactions, speaks (if a compatible text-to-speech engine is installed) and also supports speech recognition (if a compatible speech-recognition engine is installed). With these capabilities, your Web pages can speak to users and can respond to their voice commands.

- The Microsoft Agent control provides four predefined characters—Peedy the Parrot, Genie, Merlin and Robby the Robot.
- The Lernout and Hauspie TruVoice Text to Speech (TTS) engine is used by the Microsoft Agent ActiveX control to speak the text that Microsoft Agent displays.
- The Microsoft Agent control's **Characters** collection stores information about the characters that are currently available for use in a program. Method **Load** of the **Characters** collection loads character data. The method takes two arguments—a name for the character that can be used later to interact with that character, and the URL of the character's data file.
- A **Character** object is used to interact with the character. Method **Character** of the **Characters** collection receives as its argument the name that was used to download the character data and returns the corresponding **Character** object.
- The **Character** object's **Get** method downloads character animations and states.
- Each state has animation effects associated with it. When the character enters a state (such as the **Showing** state), the state's associated animation plays automatically.
- **Character** method **MoveTo** moves the character to a new position on the screen.
- **Character** method **Show** displays the character.
- **Character** method **Play** plays the specified animation.
- **Character** method **Speak** speaks its string argument. If there is a compatible TTS engine installed, the character displays a bubble containing the text and audibly speaks the text as well.
- Many animations have a "**Return**" animation for smooth transitioning between animations.
- The **Idling** animations are displayed by Microsoft Agent when the user is not interacting with the character.
- **Character** method **Stop** terminates the current animation.
- To enable Microsoft Agent to recognize voice commands, a compatible voice-recognition engine, such as the Microsoft Speech Recognition Engine, must be installed.
- The voice commands that the user can speak to interact with a character must be registered in the **Character** object's **Commands** collection.
- The **Commands** collection's **Add** method registers each voice command. The method receives five arguments.
- The **Commands** object's **Caption** property specifies text that describes the voice command set. This text appears in the small rectangular area that appears below the character when the user presses the *Scroll Lock* key. The **Voice** property is similar to the **Caption** property, except that the specified text appears in the Commands Window with the set of voice commands the user can speak below it. The **Visible** property is a boolean value that specifies whether the commands of this **Commands** object should appear in the popup menu.
- When a voice command is received, the **agent** control's **Command** event handler executes.
- A RealPlayer object can be embedded (with the **EMBED** element) in a Web page to add streaming media to a Web page. The **TYPE** attribute specifies the MIME type of the embedded file. The **WIDTH** and **HEIGHT** attributes specify the dimensions the control will occupy on the page. The **AUTOSTART** attribute determines whether the audio should start playing when the page loads. The **CONTROLS** attribute specifies which controls will be available to the user. Setting **CONTROLS** to **Default** places the standard control buttons on screen. The **SRC** attribute specifies the location of the streaming audio.
- RealPlayer method **SetSource** sets the source URL of the audio stream to be played. Method **DoPlayPause** toggles between pausing and playing the stream.

- Both Netscape and Internet Explorer have free, downloadable plug-ins that allow them to view VRML worlds. The **EMBED** element can be used to place a **.wrl** file in a Web page.

TERMINOLOGY

ActiveX control
Add method of the **Commands** collection
animated characters
audio
audio format
AutoStart parameter of Windows Media Player
background sound
BALANCE property of the **BGSOUND** element
BGSOUND Element
Caption property of the **Commands** collection
CD-ROM
character data file
Character method of **Characters** collection
Character object (Microsoft Agent)
Characters collection of Microsoft Agent
CLASSID property of the **OBJECT** element
CODEBASE property of the **OBJECT** element
Command event for the Microsoft Agent control
Commands collection of the **Character** object
Commands Window
DoPlayPause method of RealPlayer
DVD
DYNSRC property of the **IMG** element
embed a media clip
EMBED element
FileName parameter of Windows Media Player
Genie
Get of the **Character** object
HEIGHT property of the **OBJECT** element
HIDDEN property of the **EMBED** element
Hiding state of a character
Idling animations
ID property of the **BGSOUND** element
ID property of the **EMBED** element
ID property of the **OBJECT** element
interactive animated character
Internet bandwidth
Lernout and Hauspie TruVoice TTS engine
load an animation
Load method of the **Characters** collection
Loop parameter of Windows Media Player
LOOP property of the **BGSOUND** element
LOOP property of the **EMBED** element
media clip
Merlin
Microsoft Agent
Microsoft Agent control
Microsoft Speech Recognition Engine
MoveTo method of **Character** object
multimedia
multimedia-based Web application
NAME property of the **PARAM** element
natural human communication techniques
OBJECT element
PARAM element
Pause method of Windows Media Player
Peedy the Parrot
Play method of **Character** object
Play method of Windows Media Player
"**Return**" animation
Robby the Robot
SetSource method of RealPlayer
ShowControls parameter
Showing state of a character
Show method of **Character** object
sound cards
Speaking state of a character
Speak method of **Character** object
speech recognition
SRC property of the **BGSOUND** element
START property of the **IMG** element
START property value **fileopen**
START property value **mouseover**
streaming audio
streaming technology
streaming video
text-to-speech (TTS) engine
three-dimensional (3D) object
VALUE property of the **PARAM** element
video
video clip
video format
Virtual Reality Modeling Language (VRML)
Visible property of the **Commands** collection
voice command
Voice property of the **Commands** collection
VOLUME property of the **BGSOUND** element
WIDTH property of the **OBJECT** element
Windows Media Player
Windows Media Player ActiveX control
world file (**.wrl**)
.wrl file extension

PERFORMANCE TIPS

21.1 Multimedia is performance intensive. Internet bandwidth and processor speed are still precious resources. Multimedia-based Web applications must be carefully designed to use resources wisely, or they may perform poorly.

21.2 The Microsoft Agent control and the Lernout and Hauspie TruVoice TTS engine will be downloaded automatically from the Microsoft Agent Web site if they are not already installed on your computer. You may want to download these controls in advance, to allow the Web page to use Microsoft Agent and the TTS engine immediately when the Web page is loaded.

PORTABILITY TIPS

21.1 The **BGSOUND** element is specific to Internet Explorer.

21.2 On most computers, the minimum audible volume for **BGSOUND** property **VOLUME** is a value much greater than **-10000**. This value will be machine dependent.

21.3 The **DYNSRC** property of the **IMG** element is specific to Internet Explorer.

SOFTWARE ENGINEERING OBSERVATIONS

21.1 The **BGSOUND** element should be placed in the **HEAD** section of the HTML document.

21.2 The audio clip specified with **BGSOUND**'s **SRC** property can be any type supported by Internet Explorer.

21.3 **BGSOUND** property **BALANCE** cannot be set via scripting.

21.4 The volume specified with **BGSOUND** property **VOLUME** is relative to the current volume setting on the client computer. If the client computer has sound turned off, the **VOLUME** property has no effect.

21.5 The ending **</BGSOUND>** tag is optional.

21.6 The **</EMBED>** tag is required to terminate an **<EMBED>** tag.

21.7 Most HTML authoring tools that support embedding ActiveX controls enable you to insert the ActiveX controls in a Web page by selecting from a list of available control names.

TESTING AND DEBUGGING TIP

21.1 The Microsoft Agent characters and animations are downloaded from the Microsoft Agent Web site. If you are not connected to the Internet, these will not be able to download. You can download the character information onto your local computer and modify the Microsoft Agent examples to load character data from the local computer for demonstration purposes.

SELF-REVIEW EXERCISES

21.1 Fill in the blanks in each of the following:

a) __________ is a technology for interactive animated characters.

b) The __________ element is used to play a background audio in Internet Explorer.

c) The __________ property of the **IMG** element specifies a video clip should appear in the **IMG** element's location in the Web page.

d) The __________ element can be used to embed an ActiveX control on a Web page.

e) The __________ element can be used to place an audio or video clip on a Web page.

f) The **IMG** element's __________ property has values **mouseover** and **fileopen**.

g) The __________ property of the **EMBED** element prevents a GUI containing media clip controls from being displayed with the media clip.

h) Microsoft Agent's _________ animations enable smooth transition between animations.
i) When set to **true**, the __________ parameter to the Windows Media Player specifies that a GUI should be displayed so the user can control a media clip.
j) When a compatible _________ engine is available to Microsoft Agent, characters have the ability to speak text.
k) The Microsoft Agent control's ________ collection keeps track of the information about each loaded character.

21.2 State whether each of the following is *true* or *false*. If *false*, explain why.
a) The **BGSOUND** element can be used with any browser.
b) The **IMG** element enables both images and videos to be included in a Web page.
c) **BGSOUND** property **BALANCE** cannot be set via scripting.
d) The **NAME** property of the **OBJECT** element specifies a scripting name for the element.
e) The Microsoft Agent **Character** object's **StopAnimation** method terminates the current animation for the character.

ANSWERS TO SELF-REVIEW EXERCISES

21.1 a) Microsoft Agent. b) **BGSOUND**. c) **DYNSRC**. d) **OBJECT**. e) **EMBED**. f) **START**. g) **HIDDEN**. h) "**Return**." i) **ShowControls**. j) text-to-speech. k) **Characters**.

21.2 a) False. The **BGSOUND** element is specific to Internet Explorer. b) True. c) True. d) False. The **ID** property of the **OBJECT** element specifies a scripting name. e) False. The **STOP** method terminates the current animation for the character.

EXERCISES

21.3 *(Story Teller)* Store a large number of nouns, verbs, articles, prepositions, etc. in arrays of strings. Then use random number generation to forms sentences and have your script speak the sentences with Microsoft Agent and the Lernout and Hauspie text-to-speech engine.

21.4 *(Limericks)* Modify the limerick-writing script you wrote in Exercise 13.8 to use a Microsoft Agent character and the Lernout and Hauspie text-to-speech engine to speak the limericks your program creates. Use the speech output tags in Fig. 21.10 to control the characteristics of the speech (i.e., emphasis on certain syllables, volume of the voice, pitch of the voice, etc.).

21.5 Modify the script of Exercise 21.4 to play character animations during pauses in the limerick.

21.6 *(Background Audio)* Write an HTML document and script that allows the user to choose from a list of the audio downloads available from the Microsoft Developer Network Downloads site

http://msdn.microsoft.com/downloads/default.asp

and listen to the chosen audio clip as background music with the **BGSOUND** element.

21.7 Modify Exercise 21.6 to use the **EMBED** element to play the audio clips.

21.8 Modify Exercise 21.6 to use the Windows Media Player ActiveX control to play the audio clips.

21.9 *(Video Browser)* Write an HTML document and script that allows the user to choose from a list of the videos available from the NASA Multimedia Gallery site

http://www.nasa.gov/gallery/

and view that video using the **EMBED** element.

21.10 Modify Exercise 21.7 to use the Windows Media Player ActiveX control to play the video clips.

21.11 Modify the program of Fig. 21.4 to download the other six videos from the SeaWiFs site and allow the user to select which video to play.

21.12 *(Text Flasher)* Create a script that repeatedly flashes text on the screen. Do this by interspersing the text with a plain background-color image. Allow the user to control the "blink speed" and the background color or pattern.

21.13 *(Image Flasher)* Create a script that repeatedly flashes an image on the screen. Do this by interspersing the image with a plain background-color image.

21.14 *(Towers of Hanoi)* Write an animated version of the Towers of Hanoi problem we presented in Exercise 11.35. As each disk is lifted off a peg or slid onto a peg, play a "whooshing" sound. As each disk lands on the pile, play a "clunking" sound. Play some appropriate background music.

21.15 *(Digital Clock)* Using features of this chapter and the previous Dynamic HTML chapters, implement an application that displays a digital clock in a Web page. You might add options to scale the clock; to display day, month and year; to issue an alarm; to play certain audios at designated times; and the like.

21.16 *(Analog Clock)* Create a script that displays an analog clock with hour, minute and second hands that move appropriately as the time changes. Use the Structured Graphics Control to create the graphics, and play a tick sound each time the second value changes. Play other sounds to mark every half-hour and hour.

21.17 *(Dynamic Audio and Graphical Kaleidoscope)* Develop a kaleidoscope that displays reflected graphics to simulate the popular children's toy. Incorporate audio effects that "mirror" your application's dynamically changing graphics.

21.18 *(One-Armed Bandit)* Develop a multimedia simulation of a one-armed bandit. Have three spinning wheels. Place various fruits and symbols on each wheel. Use true random-number generation to simulate the spinning of each wheel and the stopping of each wheel on a symbol.

21.19 *(Horse Race)* Create a simulation of a horse race. Have multiple contenders. Use audios for a race announcer. Play the appropriate audios to indicate the correct status of each of the contenders throughout the race. Use audios to announce the final results. You might try to simulate the kind of horse race games that are often played at carnivals. The players get turns at the mouse and have to perform some skill-oriented manipulation with the mouse to advance their horses.

21.20 *(Karaoke)* Create a Karaoke system that plays the music for a song and displays the words for your user to sing at the appropriate time.

21.21 *(Calling Attention to an Image)* If you want to emphasize an image, you might place a row of simulated light bulbs around your image. You can let the light bulbs flash in unison, or you can let them fire on and off in sequence, one after the other.

21.22 *(Physics Demo: Kinetics)* If you have taken physics, implement a Web page that will demo concepts like energy, inertia, momentum, velocity, acceleration, friction, coefficient of restitution, gravity and others. Create visual effects, and use audios where appropriate for emphasis and realism.

21.23 *(On-Line Product Catalog)* Companies are rapidly realizing the potential for doing business on the Web. Develop an on-line multimedia catalog from which your customers may select products to be shipped. Use the data binding features of Chapter 18 to load data into tables. Use Microsoft Agent to speak descriptions of a selected product.

21.24 Modify Exercise 21.23 to support voice commands that allow the user to speak a product name to receive a description of the product.

21.25 *(Reaction Time/Reaction Precision Tester)* Create a Web page that moves an image around the screen. The user moves the mouse to catch and click on the shape. The shape's speed and size can be varied. Keep statistics on how much time the user typically takes to catch a shape of a given size. The user will probably have more difficulty catching faster-moving, smaller shapes.

21.26 *(Animation)* Create a Web page that performs an animation by displaying a series of images that represent the frames in the animation. Allow the user to specify the speed at which the images are displayed.

21.27 *(Video Games)* Video games have become wildly popular. Develop your own Web page containing a video game script. Have a contest with your classmates to develop the best original video game.

21.28 *(Tortoise and the Hare)* Develop a multimedia version of the Tortoise and Hare simulation we presented in Exercise 12.41. You might record an announcer's voice calling the race, "The contenders are at the starting line." "And they're off!" "The Hare pulls out in front." "The Tortoise is coming on strong." and so forth. As the race proceeds, play the appropriate recorded audios. Play sounds to simulate the animals' running, and don't forget the crowd cheering! Do an animation of the animals racing up the side of the slippery mountain.

21.29 *(Knight's Tour Walker)* Develop multimedia-based versions of the Knight's Tour programs you wrote in Exercises 12.22 and 12.23.

21.30 *(Arithmetic Tutor)* Develop a multimedia version of the Computer-Assisted Instruction (CAI) systems you developed in Exercises 11.29, 11.30 and 11.31.

21.31 *(15 Puzzle)* Write a multimedia-based Web page that enables the user to play the game of 15. There is a 4-by-4 board for a total of 16 slots. One of the slots is empty. The other slots are occupied by 15 tiles, numbered 1 through 15. Any tile next to the currently empty slot can be moved into the currently empty slot by clicking on the tile. Your program should create the board with the tiles out of order. The goal is to arrange the tiles into sequential order row by row. Play sounds with the movement of the tiles.

21.32 *(Morse Code)* Modify your solution to Exercise 13.26 to output the morse code using audio clips. Use two different audio clips for the dot and dash characters in Morse code.

21.33 *(Calendar/Tickler File)* Create a general purpose calendar and "tickler" file. Use audio and images. For example, the application should sing "Happy Birthday" to you when you use it on your birthday. Have the application display images and play audios associated with important events. Have the application remind you in advance of important events. It would be nice, for example, to have the application give you a week's warning so you can pick up an appropriate greeting card for that special person. Store the calendar information in a file that can be used with the data-binding techniques of Chapter 18 to load the calendar information into a table in the Web page.

21.34 *(Multimedia-Based Simpletron Simulator)* Modify the Simpletron simulator that you developed in Exercises 12.42 through 12.44 to include multimedia features. Add computer-like sounds to indicate that the Simpletron is executing instructions. Add a breaking glass sound when a fatal error occurs. Use flashing lights to indicate which cells of memory and/or which registers are currently being manipulated. Use other multimedia techniques as appropriate to make your Simpletron simulator more valuable as an educational tool to its users.

22

Dynamic HTML: Client-Side Scripting with VBScript

Objectives

- To become familiar with the VBScript language.
- To use VBScript keywords, operators and functions to write client-side scripts.
- To be able to write **`Sub`** and **`Function`** procedures.
- To use VBScript arrays and regular expressions.
- To be able to write VBScript abstract data types called **`Class`**es.
- To be able to create objects from **`Class`**es.
- To be able to write **`Property Let`**, **`Property Get`** and **`Property Set`** procedures.

When they call the roll in the Senate, the senators do not know whether to answer "present" or "not guilty."
Theodore Roosevelt

While I nodded, nearly napping,
suddenly there came a tapping,
As of someone gently rapping, rapping at my chamber door.
Edgar Allan Poe

Basic research is what I am doing when I don't know what I am doing.
Wernher von Braun

A problem is a chance for you to do your best.
Duke Ellington

Everything comes to him who hustles while he waits.
Thomas Alva Edison

Outline

22.1 Introduction

Visual Basic Script (VBScript) is a subset of Microsoft Visual Basic® used in World Wide Web HTML documents to enhance the functionality of a Web page displayed in a Web browser. Microsoft's Internet Explorer Web browser contains a *VBScript scripting engine* (i.e., an interpreter) that executes VBScript code. In this chapter, we introduce client-side VBScript for use in HTML documents. Because JavaScript has become the de facto client-side scripting language in industry, you are not likely to use client-side VBScript.

Earlier in the text we used JavaScript to introduce fundamental computer programming concepts in the context of HTML documents and the World Wide Web. In this chapter, we overview VBScript, which provides capabilities similar to those of JavaScript. The material presented in this chapter is valuable for two reasons. First, company Intranets tend to standardize on a particular Web browser, and, if that browser is Internet Explorer, the VBScript techniques introduced in this chapter can readily be used on the client side to enhance HTML documents. Second, VBScript is particularly valuable when used with Microsoft Web servers to create *Active Server Pages* (*ASP*)—a technology that allows a server-side script to create dynamic content that is sent to the client's browser. Although other scripting languages can be used, VBScript is the de facto language for ASP. You will learn about ASP in Chapter 26.

22.2 Operators

VBScript is a case-insensitive language that provides arithmetic operators, logical operators, concatenation operators, comparison operators and relational operators. VBScript's arithmetic operators (Fig. 22.1) are similar to the JavaScript arithmetic operators. Two major differences are the *division operator*, \, which returns an integer result and the *exponentiation operator*, ^, which raises a value to a power. [Note: the precedence of operators is different in JavaScript. See Appendix B, "Operator Precedence Charts," for a list of VBScript operators and their precedences.]

VBScript operation	Arithmetic operator	Algebraic expression	VBScript expression
Addition	**+**	$x + y$	**x + y**
Subtraction	**-**	$z - 8$	**z – 8**
Multiplication	*****	yb	**y * b**
Division (floating-point)	**/**	$v \div u$ or $\frac{v}{u}$	**v / u**
Division (integer)	****	none	**v \\ u**
Exponentiation	**^**	q^p	**q ^ p**
Negation	**-**	$-e$	**—e**
Modulus	**Mod**	*q mod r*	**q Mod r**

Fig. 22.1 Arithmetic operators.

Figure 22.2 lists VBScript's comparison operators. Only the symbols for the equality operator and the inequality operator are different in JavaScript. In VBScript, these comparison operators may also be used to compare strings.

The VBScript logical operators are ***And*** (logical AND), ***Or*** (logical OR), ***Not*** (logical negation), ***Imp*** (logical implication), ***Xor*** (exclusive OR) and ***Eqv*** (logical equivalence). Figure 22.3 shows truth tables for these logical operators. Note: Despite the mixture of case in keywords, functions, etc., VBScript is not case-sensitive—uppercase and lowercase letters are treated the same, except, as we will see, in *character string constants* (also called *character string literals*).

Performance Tip 22.1

VBScript logical operators do not use "short-circuit" evaluation. Both conditions are always evaluated.

VBScript provides the *plus sign*, **+**, and *ampersand*, **&**, operators for string concatenation as follows:

```
s1 = "Pro"
s2 = "gram"
s3 = s1 & s2
```

or

```
s3 = s1 + s2
```

The ampersand is more formally called the *string concatenation operator*. The above statements would concatenate (or append) **s2** to the right of **s1** to create an entirely new string, **s3**, containing **"Program"**.

If both operands of the concatenation operator are strings, these two operators can be used interchangeably; however, if the **+** operator is used in an expression consisting of varying data types, there can be a problem. For example, consider the statement

```
s1 = "hello" + 22
```

Standard algebraic equality operator or relational operator	VBScript comparison operator	Example of VBScript condition	Meaning of VBScript condition
=	=	**d = g**	**d** is equal to **g**
≠	<>	**s <> r**	**s** is not equal to **r**
>	>	**y > x**	**y** is greater than **x**
<	<	**p < m**	**p** is less than **m**
≥	>=	**c >= z**	**c** is greater than or equal to **z**
≤	<=	**m <= s**	**m** is less than or equal to **s**

Fig. 22.2 Comparison operators.

Truth tables for VBScript Logical Operators

Logical And:
```
True And True = True
True And False = False
False And True = False
False And False = False
```

Logical Or:
```
True Or True = True
True Or False = True
False Or True = True
False Or False = False
```

Logical Imp:
```
True Imp True = True
True Imp False = False
False Imp True = True
False Imp False = True
```

Logical Eqv:
```
True Eqv True = True
True Eqv False = False
False Eqv True = False
False Eqv False = True
```

Logical Xor:
```
True Xor True = False
True Xor False = True
False Xor True = True
False Xor False = False
```

Logical Not:
```
Not True = False
Not False = True
```

Fig. 22.3 Truth tables for VBScript logical operators.

VBScript first tries to convert the string **"hello"** to a number, then add **22** to it. The string **"hello"** cannot be converted to a number, so a type mismatch error occurs at run time. For this reason, the **&** operator should be used for string concatenation.

Testing and Debugging Tip 22.1

*Always use the ampersand (**&**) operator for string concatenation.*

22.3 Data Types and Control Structures

VBScript has only one data type—*variant*—and it is capable of storing different types of data (e.g., strings, integers, floating-point numbers etc.). The data types (or *variant sub-*

types) a variant stores are listed in Fig. 22.4. VBScript interprets a variant in a manner that is suitable to the type of data it contains. For example, if a variant contains numeric information, it will be treated as a number; if it contains string information, it will be treated as a string.

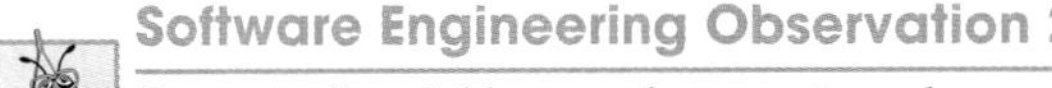

Software Engineering Observation 22.1

Because all variables are of type variant, the programmer does not specify a data type when declaring a variable in VBScript.

Variable names cannot be keywords and must begin with a letter. The maximum length of a variable name is 255 characters containing only letters, digits (0-9) and underscores. Variables can be declared simply by using their name in the VBScript code. The statement **`Option Explicit`** can be used to force all variables to be declared before they are used.

Common Programming Error 22.1

Attempting to declare a variable name that does not begin with a letter is an error.

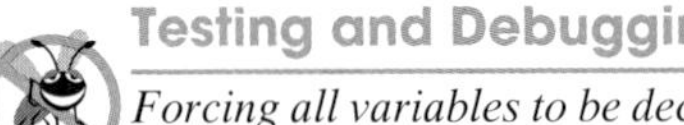

Testing and Debugging Tip 22.2

Forcing all variables to be declared, by using **`Option Explicit`**, *can help eliminate various kinds of subtle errors.*

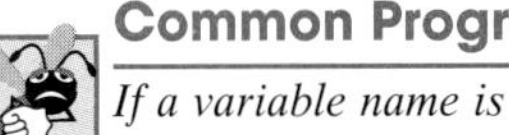

Common Programming Error 22.2

If a variable name is misspelled (when not using **`Option Explicit`**), *a new variable is declared, usually resulting in an error.*

Subtype	Range/Description
Boolean	**`True`** or **`False`**
Byte	Integer in the range 0 to 255
Currency	–922337203685477.5808 to 922337203685477.5807
Date/Time	1 January 100 to 31 December 9999 0:00:00 to 23:59:59.
Double	–1.79769313486232E308 to –4.94065645841247E–324 (negative) 1.79769313486232E308 to 4.94065645841247E–324 (positive)
Empty	Uninitialized. This value is 0 for numeric types (e.g., double), **`False`** for booleans and the *empty string* (i.e., " ") for strings.
Integer	–32768 to 32767
Long	–2147483648 to 2147483647
Object	Any object type.
Single	–3.402823E38 to –1.401298E–45 (negative) 3.402823E38 to 1.401298E–45 (positive)
String	0 to ~2000000000 characters.

Fig. 22.4 Some VBScript variant subtypes.

VBScript provides control structures (Fig. 22.5) for controlling program execution. Many of the control structures provide the same capabilities as their JavaScript counterparts. Syntactically, every VBScript control structure ends with one or more keywords (e.g., **End If**, **Loop** etc.). Keywords delimit a control structure's body—not curly braces (i.e., **{}**, as in JavaScript).

The **If**/**Then**/**End If** and **If**/**Then**/**Else**/**End If** control structures behave identically to their JavaScript counterparts. VBScript's multiple selection version of **If**/**Then**/**Else**/**End If** uses a different syntax from JavaScript's version because it includes keyword ***ElseIf*** (Fig. 22.6).

Common Programming Error 22.3

Writing an **If** *control structure that does not contain keyword* **Then** *is an error.*

Notice that VBScript does not use a statement terminator like the semicolon (**;**) in JavaScript. Unlike in JavaScript, placing parentheses around conditions in VBScript is optional. A condition evaluates to **True** if the variant subtype is boolean **True** or if the variant subtype is considered non-zero. A condition evaluates to **False** if the variant subtype is boolean **False** or if the variant subtype is considered to be 0.

JavaScript Control Structure	VBScript Control Structure Equivalent
sequence	sequence
if	**If**/**Then**/**End If**
if/**else**	**If**/**Then**/**Else**/**End If**
while	**While**/**Wend** or **Do While**/**Loop**
for	**For**/**Next**
do/**while**	**Do**/**Loop While**
switch	**Select Case**/**End Select**
none	**Do Until**/**Loop**
none	**Do**/**Loop Until**

Fig. 22.5 Comparing VBScript control structures to JavaScript control structures.

JavaScript

```
if ( s == t )
   u = s + t;
else if ( s > t )
   u = r;
else
   u = n;
```

VBScript

```
If s = t Then
   u = s + t
ElseIf s > t Then
   u = r
Else
   u = n
End If
```

Fig. 22.6 Comparing JavaScript's **if** structure to VBScript's **If** structure.

VBScript's ***Select Case/End Select*** structure provides all the functionality of JavaScript's **switch** structure, and more (Fig. 22.7).

Notice that the **Select Case/End Select** structure does not require the use of a statement like **break**. One **Case** cannot accidentally run into another. The VBScript **Select Case/End Select** structure is equivalent to VBScript's **If/Then/Else/End If** multiple selection structure. The only difference is syntax. Any variant subtype can be used with the **Select Case/End Select** structure.

VBScript's ***While/Wend*** repetition structure and ***Do While/Loop*** behave identically to JavaScript's **while** repetition structure. VBScript's ***Do/Loop While*** structure behaves identically to JavaScript's **do/while** repetition structure.

VBScript contains two additional repetition structures, ***Do Until/Loop*** and ***Do/Loop Until***, that do not have direct JavaScript equivalents. Figure 22.8 shows the closest comparison between VBScript's **Do Until/Loop** structure and JavaScript's **while** structure. The **Do Until/Loop** structure loops until its condition becomes **True**. In this example, the loop terminates when **x** becomes 10. We used the condition **!(x == 10)** in JavaScript here, so both control structures have a test to determine whether **x** is **10**. The JavaScript **while** structure loops while **x** is not equal to 10 (i.e., until **x** becomes 10).

Figure 22.9 shows the closest comparison between VBScript's **Do/Loop Until** structure and JavaScript's **do/while** structure. The **Do/Loop Until** structure loops until its condition becomes **True**. In this example, the loop terminates when **x** becomes 10. Once again, we used the condition **!(x == 10)** in JavaScript here so both control structures have a test to determine if **x** is **10**. The JavaScript **do/while** structure loops while **x** is not equal to 10 (i.e., until **x** becomes 10).

JavaScript

```
switch ( x ) {
   case 1:
      alert("1");
      break;
    case 2:
      alert("2");
      break;
   default:
      alert("?");
}
```

VBScript

```
Select Case x
   Case 1
      Call MsgBox("1")
   Case 2
      Call MsgBox("2")
   Case Else
      Call MsgBox("?")
End Select
```

Fig. 22.7 Comparing JavaScript's **switch** with VBScript's **Select Case**.

JavaScript

```
while ( !( x == 10 ) )
   ++x;
```

VBScript

```
Do Until x = 10
   x = x + 1
Loop
```

Fig. 22.8 Comparing JavaScript's **while** to VBScript's **Do Until**.

JavaScript

```
do {
   ++x;
} while ( !( x == 10 ) );
```

VBScript

```
Do
   x = x + 1
Loop Until x = 10
```

Fig. 22.9 Comparing JavaScript's **do/while** to VBScript's **Do Loop/Until**.

Notice that these **Do Until** repetition structures iterate until the condition becomes **True**. VBScript ***For*** repetition structure behaves differently from JavaScript's **for** repetition structure. Consider the side-by-side comparison in Fig. 22.10.

Unlike JavaScript's **for** repetition structures condition, VBScript's **For** repetition structure's condition cannot be changed during the loop's iteration. In the JavaScript **for**/VBScript **For** loop side-by-side code comparison, the JavaScript **for** loop would iterate exactly two times, because the condition is evaluated on each iteration. The VBScript **For** loop would iterate exactly eight times because the condition is fixed as **1 To 8**—even though the value of **x** is changing in the body. VBScript **For** loops may also use the optional **Step** keyword to indicate an increment or decrement. By default, **For** loops increment in units of 1. Figure 22.11 shows a **For** loop that begins at **2** and counts to **20** in **Step**s of **2**.

Common Programming Error 22.4

*Attempting to use a relational operator in a **For**/**Next** loop (e.g., **For x = 1 < 10**) is an error.*

The ***Exit Do*** statement, when executed in a **Do While**/**Loop**, **Do**/**Loop While**, **Do Until**/**Loop** or **Do**/**Loop Until**, causes immediate exit from that structure. The fact that a **Do While**/**Loop** may contain **Exit Do** is the only difference, other than syntax, between **Do While**/**Loop** and **While**/**Wend**. Statement ***Exit For*** causes immediate exit from the **For**/**Next** structure. With **Exit Do** and **Exit For**, program execution continues with the first statement after the exited repetition structure.

JavaScript

```
x = 8;
for ( y = 1; y < x; y++ )
   x /= 2;
```

VBScript

```
x = 8
For y = 1 To x
   x = x \ 2
Next
```

Fig. 22.10 Comparing JavaScript's **for** to VBScript's **For**.

```
' VBScript
For y = 2 To 20 Step 2
   Call MsgBox( "y = " & y )
Next
```

Fig. 22.11 Using keyword **Step** in VBScript's **For** repetition structure.

Common Programming Error 22.5

Attempting to use **`Exit Do`** *or* **`Exit For`** *to exit a* **`While`**/**`Wend`** *repetition structure is an error.*

Common Programming Error 22.6

Attempting to place the name of a **`For`** *repetition structures's control variable after* **`Next`** *is an error.*

22.4 VBScript Functions

VBScript provides several predefined functions, many of which are summarized in this section. We overview variant functions, math functions, functions for interacting with the user, formatting functions and functions for obtaining information about the interpreter.

Figure 22.12 summarizes several functions that allow the programmer to determine which subtype is currently stored in a variant. VBScript provides function ***`IsEmpty`*** to determine if the variant has ever been initialized by the programmer. If **`IsEmpty`** returns **`True`** the variant has not been initialized by the programmer.

VBScript math functions allow the programmer to perform common mathematical calculations. Figure 22.13 summarizes some VBScript math functions. Note that trigonometric functions such as **`Cos`**, **`Sin`**, etc. take arguments expressed in radians. To convert from degrees to radians use the formula: $radians = degrees \times \pi / 180$.

Function	Variant subtype returned	Description
`IsArray`	Boolean	Returns **`True`** if the variant subtype is an array and **`False`** otherwise.
`IsDate`	Boolean	Returns **`True`** if the variant subtype is a date or time and **`False`** otherwise.
`IsEmpty`	Boolean	Returns **`True`** if the variant subtype is **`Empty`** (i.e., has not been explicitly initialized by the programmer) and **`False`** otherwise.
`IsNumeric`	Boolean	Returns **`True`** if the variant subtype is numeric and **`False`** otherwise.
`IsObject`	Boolean	Returns **`True`** if the variant subtype is an object and **`False`** otherwise.
`TypeName`	String	Returns a string that provides subtype information. Some strings returned are **`"Byte"`**, **`"Integer"`**, **`"Long"`**, **`"Single"`**, **`"Double"`**, **`"Date"`**, **`"Currency"`**, **`"String"`**, **`"Boolean"`** and **`"Empty"`**.
`VarType`	Integer	Returns a value indicating the subtype (e.g., **`0`** for **`Empty`**, **`2`** for integer, **`3`** for long, **`4`** for single, **`5`** for double, **`6`** for currency, **`7`** for date/time, **`8`** for string, **`9`** for object etc.).

Fig. 22.12 Some variant functions.

Function	Description	Example
Abs(x)	Absolute value of **x**	**Abs(-7)** is **7** **Abs(0)** is **0** **Abs(76)** is **76**
Atn(x)	Trigonometric arctangent of **x** (in radians)	**Atn(1)*4** is **3.14159265358979**
Cos(x)	Trigonometric cosine of **x** (in radians)	**Cos(0)** is **1**
Exp(x)	Exponential function e^x	**Exp(1.0)** is **2.71828** **Exp(2.0)** is **7.38906**
Int(x)	Returns the whole-number part of **x**. **Int** rounds to the next smallest number.	**Int(-5.3)** is **–6** **Int(0.893)** is **0** **Int(76.45)** is **76**
Fix(x)	Returns the whole-number part of **x** (Note: **Fix** and **Int** are different. When **x** is negative, **Int** rounds to the next smallest number, while **Fix** rounds to the next-largest number.)	**Fix(-5.3)** is **–5** **Fix(0.893)** is **0** **Fix(76.45)** is **76**
Log(x)	Natural logarithm of **x** (base *e*)	**Log(2.718282)** is **1.0** **Log(7.389056)** is **2.0**
Rnd()	Returns a pseudo-random floating-point number in the range **0** ≤ **Rnd** < **1**. Call function ***Randomize*** once before calling **Rnd** to get a different sequence of random numbers each time the program is run.	**Call Randomize** **...** **z = Rnd()**
Round(x, y)	Rounds **x** to **y** decimal places. If **y** is omitted, **x** is returned as an **Integer**.	**Round(4.844)** is **5** **Round(5.7839, 2)** is **5.78**
Sgn(x)	Sign of **x**	**Sgn(-1988)** is **–1** **Sgn(0)** is **0** **Sgn(3.3)** is **1**
Sin(x)	Trigonometric sine of **x** (in radians)	**Sin(0)** is **0**
Sqr(x)	Square root of **x**	**Sqr(900.0)** is **30.0** **Sqr(9.0)** is **3.0**
Tan(x)	Trigonometric tangent of **x** (in radians)	**Tan(0)** is **0**

Fig. 22.13 VBScript math functions.

VBScript provides two functions, ***InputBox*** and ***MsgBox***, for interacting with the user. Function **InputBox** displays a dialog in which the user can input data. For example, the statement

```
intValue = InputBox( "Enter an integer", "Input Box", , _
                     1000, 1000 )
```

displays an *input dialog* (as shown in Fig. 22.15) containing the prompt (**"Enter an integer"**) and the caption (**"Input Box"**) at position *(1000, 1000)* on the screen. VBScript coordinates are measured in units of *twips* (1440 twips equal 1 inch). Position *(1000, 1000)* is relative to the upper-left corner of the screen, which is position *(0, 0)*. On the screen, *x* coordinates increase from left to right and *y* coordinates increase from top to bottom.

VBScript functions often take *optional arguments* (i.e., arguments that programmers can pass if they wish or that can be omitted). Notice, in the preceding call to **InputBox**, the consecutive commas (between **"Input Box"** and **1000**)—these indicate that an optional argument is being omitted. In this particular case, the optional argument corresponds to a file name for a help file—a feature we do not wish to use in this particular call to **InputBox**. Before using a VBScript function, check the VBScript documentation

```
http://msdn.microsoft.com/scripting/vbscript/doc
```

to determine whether the function allows for optional arguments.

The *underscore character*, _, is VBScript's *line-continuation character*. A statement cannot extend beyond the current line without using this character. A statement may use as many line-continuation characters as necessary.

Common Programming Error 22.7

Splitting a statement over several lines without the line-continuation character is an error.

Common Programming Error 22.8

Placing anything, including comments, after a line-continuation character is an error.

When called, function **MsgBox** displays a *message dialog* (a sample is shown in Fig. 22.15). For example, the statement

```
Call MsgBox( "VBScript is fun!", , "Results" )
```

displays a message dialog containing the string **"VBScript is fun!"** with **"Results"** in the title bar. Although not used here, the optional argument allows the programmer to customize the **MsgBox**'s buttons (e.g., **OK**, **Yes** etc.) and icon (e.g., question mark, exclamation point etc.)—see the VBScript documentation for more information on these features. The preceding statement could also have been written as

```
MsgBox "VBScript is fun!", , "Results"
```

which behaves identically to the version of the statement that explicitly uses **Call**. In VBScript, function calls that wrap arguments in parentheses must be preceded with keyword ***Call***—unless the function call is assigning a value to a variable, as in

```
a = Abs( z )
```

We prefer the more formal syntax that uses **Call** and parentheses to clearly indicate a function call.

VBScript provides formatting functions for currency values, dates, times, numbers and percentages. Figure 22.14 summarizes these formatting functions.

Although they are not discussed in this chapter, VBScript provides many functions for manipulating dates and times. Manipulations include adding dates, subtracting dates, parsing dates etc. Consult the VBScript documentation for a list of these functions.

Function	Description
FormatCurrency	Returns a string formatted according to the local machine's currency **Regional Settings** (in the **Control Panel**). For example, the call **FormatCurrency("-1234.789")** returns **"($1,234.78)"** and the call **FormatCurrency(123456.789)** returns **"$123,456.78"**. Note the truncation to the right of the decimal place.
FormatDateTime	Returns a string formatted according to the local machine's date/time **Regional Settings** (in the **Control Panel**). For example, the call **FormatDateTime(Now, vbLongDate)** returns the current date in the format **"Wednesday, September 01, 1999"** and the call **FormatDateTime(Now, vbShortTime)** returns the current time in the format **"17:26"**. Function ***Now*** returns the local machine's time and date. Constant ***vbLongDate*** indicates that the day of the week, month, day and year is displayed. Constant ***vbShortTime*** indicates that the time is displayed in 24-hour format. Consult the VBScript documentation for additional constants that specify other date and time formats.
FormatNumber	Returns a string formatted according to the number **Regional Settings** (in the **Control Panel**) on the local machine. For example, the call **FormatNumber("3472435")** returns **"3,472,435.00"** and the call **FormatNumber(-123456.789)** returns **"-123,456.79"**. Note the rounding to the right of the decimal place.
FormatPercent	Returns a string formatted as a percentage. For example the call **FormatPercent(".789")** returns **"78.90%"** and the call **FormatPercent(0.45)** returns **"45.00%"**.

Fig. 22.14 Some VBScript formatting functions.

VBScript also provides functions for getting information about the scripting engine (i.e., the VBScript interpreter). These functions are ***ScriptEngine*** (which returns "**JScript**", "**VBScript**" or "**VBA**"), ***ScriptEngineBuildVersion*** (which returns the current *build version*—i.e., the identification number for the current release), ***ScriptEngineMajorVersion*** (which returns the major version number for the script engine) and ***ScriptEngineMinorVersion*** (which returns the minor release number). For example, the expression

```
ScriptEngine() & ", " & ScriptEngineBuildVersion() & ", " _
& ScriptEngineMajorVersion() & ", " & _
ScriptEngineMajorVersion()
```

evaluates to **"VBScript, 3715, 5, 5"** (where the numbers are the build version, major version and minor version of the script engine at the time of this writing).

Testing and Debugging Tip 22.3

VBScript Functions ***ScriptEngine****,* ***ScriptEngineBuildVersion****,* ***ScriptEngineMajorVersion*** *and* ***ScriptEngineMinorVersion*** *are useful if you are experiencing difficulty with the scripting engine and need to report information about the scripting engine to Microsoft.*

Portability Tip 22.1

VBScript Functions **`ScriptEngine`**, **`ScriptEngineBuildVersion`**, **`ScriptEngineMajorVersion`** *and* **`ScriptEngineMinorVersion`** *can be used to determine whether the browser's script engine version is different from the script engine version you used to develop the page. Older script engines do not support the latest VBScript features.*

22.5 VBScript Example Programs

In this section, we present several complete VBScript "live-code" programs and show the screen inputs and outputs produced as the programs execute. The HTML document of Fig. 22.15 includes VBScript code that enables users to click a button to display an input dialog in which they can type an integer to be added into a running total. When the input dialog's **OK** button is clicked, a message dialog is displayed with a message indicating the number that was entered and the total of all the numbers entered so far.

```
<!DOCTYPE HTML PUBLIC "-//W3C//DTD HTML 4.0 Transitional//EN">
<HTML>
<!--Fig. 22.15: addition.html -->

<HEAD>
<TITLE>Our first VBScript</TITLE>

<SCRIPT LANGUAGE = "VBScript">
<!--
   Option Explicit
   Dim intTotal

   Sub cmdAdd_OnClick()
      Dim intValue

      intValue = InputBox("Enter an integer", "Input Box", , _
                          1000, 1000)
      intTotal = CInt( intTotal ) + CInt( intValue )
      Call MsgBox("You entered " & intValue & _
                  "; total so far is " & intTotal, , "Results")
   End Sub
-->
</SCRIPT>
</HEAD>

<BODY>
Click the button to add an integer to the total.
<HR>
<FORM>
<INPUT NAME = "cmdAdd" TYPE = "BUTTON"
       VALUE = "Click Here to Add to the Total">
</FORM>
</BODY>
</HTML>
```

Fig. 22.15 Adding integers on a Web page using VBScript (part 1 of 2).

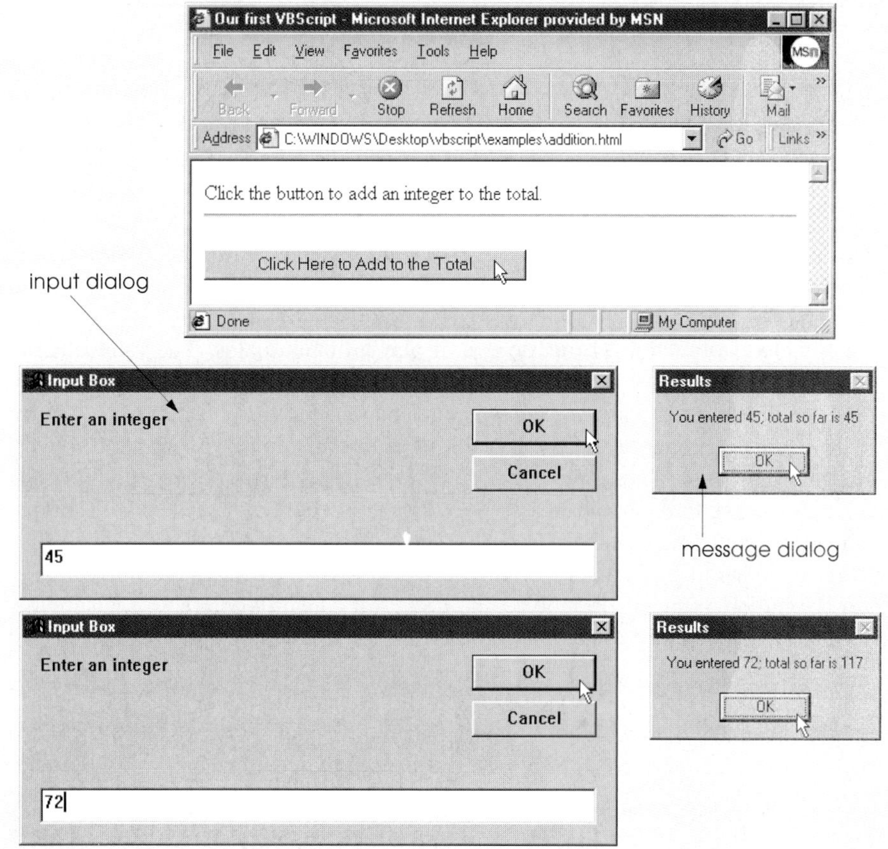

Fig. 22.15 Adding integers on a Web page using VBScript (part 2 of 2).

On Line 8, the HTML tag **SCRIPT** sets the **LANGUAGE** attribute to ***VBScript***. This tag tells the browser to use its built-in VBScript interpreter to interpret the script code. Notice the HTML comment tags on lines 9 and 22 which appear to "comment out" the VBScript code.

If the browser understands VBScript, these HTML comments are ignored, and the VBScript is interpreted. If the browser does not understand VBScript, the HTML comment prevents the VBScript code from being displayed as text.

Portability Tip 22.2

Always place client-side VBScript code inside HTML comments to prevent the code from being displayed as text in browsers that do not understand VBScript.

Line 10 uses the **Option Explicit** statement to force all variables in the VBScript code to be declared. Statement **Option Explicit**, if present, must be the first statement in the VBScript code. Line 11 declares variant variable **intTotal**, which is visible to all procedures within the script. Variables declared outside of procedures are called *script variables*.

Common Programming Error 22.9

Placing VBScript code before the **Option Explicit** *statement is an error.*

Lines 13 through 21 define a *procedure* (i.e., VBScript's equivalent of a function in JavaScript) called **OnClick** for the **cmdAdd** button. VBScript procedures that do not return a value begin with the keyword ***Sub*** (line 13) and end with the keywords ***End Sub*** (line 21). We will discuss VBScript procedures that return values later in this chapter. Line 14 declares the *local variable* **intValue**. Variables declared within a VBScript procedure are visible only within that procedure's body. Procedures that perform event handling (such as the **cmdAdd_OnClick** procedure in lines 13 through 21) are more properly called *event procedures*.

Line 16 calls the function **InputBox** to display an input dialog. The value entered into the input dialog is assigned to the **intValue** variable and is treated by VBScript as a string subtype. When using variants, conversion functions are often necessary to ensure that you are using the proper type. Line 18 calls VBScript function ***CInt*** twice to convert from the string subtype to the integer subtype. VBScript also provides conversion functions ***CBool*** for converting to the boolean subtype, ***CByte*** for converting to the byte subtype, ***CCur*** for converting to the currency subtype, ***CDate*** for converting to the date/time subtype, ***CDbl*** for converting to the double subtype, ***CLng*** for converting to the long subtype, ***CSng*** for converting to the single subtype and ***CStr*** for converting to the string subtype. Lines 19 and 20 display a message dialog indicating the last value input and the running total.

VBScript provides many predefined constants for use in your VBScript code. The constant categories include color constants, comparison constants (to specify how values are compared), date/time constants, date format constants, drive type constants, file attribute constants, file I/O constants, **MsgBox** constants, special folder constants, string constants, **VarType** constants (to help determine the type stored in a variable) and miscellaneous other constants. VBScript constants usually begin with the prefix ***vb***. For a list of VBScript constants, see the VBScript documentation. You can also create your own constants by using keyword ***Const***, as in

```
Const PI = 3.14159
```

Figure 22.16 provides another VBScript example. The HTML form provides a **SELECT** component, to allow the user to select a Web site from a list of sites. When the selection is made, the new Web site is displayed in the browser. Lines 30 through 35

```
<SCRIPT FOR = "SiteSelector" EVENT = "ONCHANGE"
        LANGUAGE = "VBScript">
<!--
   Document.Location = Document.Forms( 0 ).SiteSelector.Value
-->
</SCRIPT>
```

specify a VBScript. In such code, the **<SCRIPT>** tag's **FOR** attribute indicates the HTML component on which the script operates (**SiteSelector**), the **EVENT** attribute indicates the event to which the script responds (**OnChange**, which occurs when the user makes a selection) and the **LANGUAGE** attribute specifies the scripting language (**VBScript**).

```
<!DOCTYPE HTML PUBLIC "-//W3C//DTD HTML 4.0 Transitional//EN">
<HTML>
<!-- Fig. 22.16: site.html -->

<HEAD>
   <TITLE>Select a site to browse</TITLE>
</HEAD>

<BODY>
Select a site to browse<P>
<HR>
<FORM>
<SELECT NAME = "SiteSelector" SIZE = "1">

   <OPTION VALUE = "http://www.deitel.com">
       Deitel & Associates, Inc.
   </OPTION>

   <OPTION VALUE = "http://www.prenhall.com">
       Prentice Hall
   </OPTION>

   <OPTION VALUE = "http://www.phptr.com/phptrinteractive">
       Prentice Hall Interactive
   </OPTION>

</SELECT>

<!-- VBScript code -->
<SCRIPT FOR = "SiteSelector" EVENT = "ONCHANGE"
        LANGUAGE = "VBScript">
<!--
   Document.Location = Document.Forms( 0 ).SiteSelector.Value
-->
</SCRIPT>
</FORM>
</BODY>
</HTML>
```

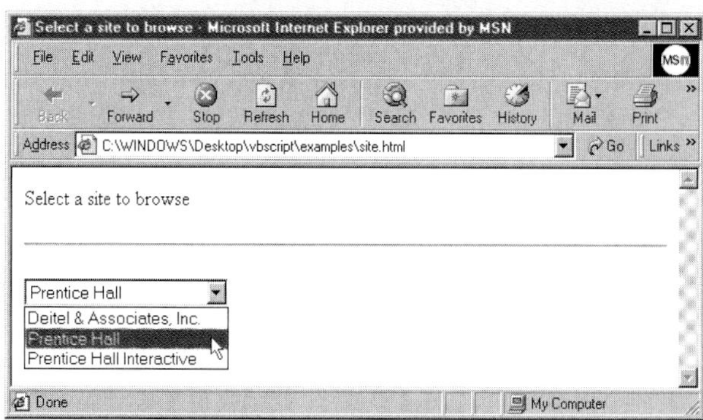

Fig. 22.16 Using VBScript code to respond to an event (part 1 of 2).

Fig. 22.16 Using VBScript code to respond to an event (part 2 of 2).

Line 33

```
Document.Location = Document.Forms( 0 ).SiteSelector.Value
```

causes the browser to change to the selected location. This line uses Internet Explorer's **Document** object to change the location. The **Document** object's ***Location*** *property* specifies the URL of the page to display. The expression **SiteSelector.Value** gets the **VALUE** of the selected **OPTION** in the **SELECT**. When the assignment is performed, Internet Explorer automatically loads and displays the Web page for the selected location.

Fig. 22.17 uses programmer-defined procedures: **Minimum**, to determine the smallest of three numbers; and **OddEven**, to determine whether the smallest number is odd or even.

```
<!DOCTYPE HTML PUBLIC "-//W3C//DTD HTML 4.0 Transitional//EN">
<HTML>
<!--Fig. 22.17: minimum.html -->

<HEAD>
<TITLE>Using VBScript Procedures</TITLE>

<SCRIPT LANGUAGE = "VBScript">
<!--
   Option Explicit

   ' Find the minimum value. Assume that first value is
   ' the smallest.
   Function Minimum( min, a, b )

      If a < min Then
         min = a
      End If

      If b < min Then
         min = b
      End If

```

Fig. 22.17 Program that determines the smallest of three numbers (part 1 of 2).

```
      Minimum = min      ' Return value
   End Function

   Sub OddEven( n )
      If n Mod 2 = 0 Then
         Call MsgBox( n & " is the smallest and is even" )
      Else
         Call MsgBox( n & " is the smallest and is odd" )
      End If
   End Sub

   Sub cmdButton_OnClick()
      Dim number1, number2, number3, smallest

      ' Convert each input to Long subtype
      number1 = CLng( Document.Forms( 0 ).txtBox1.Value )
      number2 = CLng( Document.Forms( 0 ).txtBox2.Value )
      number3 = CLng( Document.Forms( 0 ).txtBox3.Value )

      smallest = Minimum( number1, number2, number3 )
      Call OddEven( smallest )
   End Sub
-->
</SCRIPT>
</HEAD>

<BODY>
<FORM> Enter a number
<INPUT TYPE = "text" NAME = "txtBox1" SIZE = "5" VALUE = "0">
<P>Enter a number
<INPUT TYPE = "text" NAME = "txtBox2" SIZE = "5" VALUE = "0">
<P>Enter a number
<INPUT TYPE = "text" NAME = "txtBox3" SIZE = "5" VALUE = "0">
<P><INPUT TYPE = "BUTTON" NAME = "cmdButton" VALUE = "Enter">
</SCRIPT>
</FORM>
</BODY>
</HTML>
```

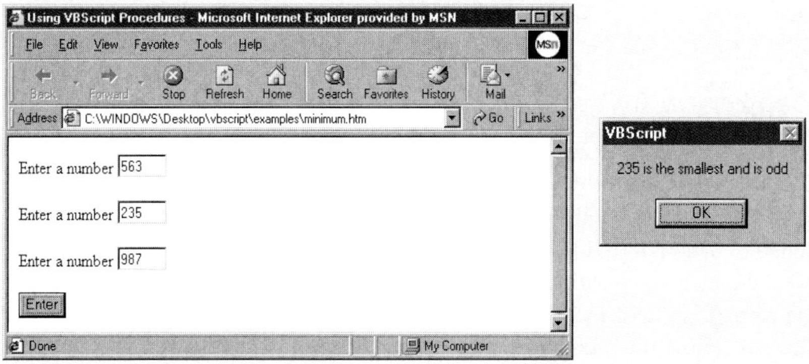

Fig. 22.17 Program that determines the smallest of three numbers (part 2 of 2).

Lines 12 and 13 are VBScript single-line comments. VBScript code is commented by either using a single quote (**'**) or the keyword ***Rem*** (for *remark*) before the comment. [Note: Keyword **Rem** can be used only at the beginning of line of VBScript code.]

Good Programming Practice 22.1

VBScript programmers use the single-quote character for comments. The use of **Rem** *is considered archaic.*

Lines 14 through 25 define the programmer-defined procedure **Minimum**. VBScript procedures that return a value are delimited with the keywords ***Function*** (line 14) and ***End Function*** (line 25). This procedure determines the smallest of its three arguments by using **If/Then/Else** structures. A value is returned from a **Function** procedure by assigning a value to the **Function** procedure name (line 24). A **Function** procedure can return only one value.

Procedure **OddEven** (lines 27 through 33) takes one argument and displays a message dialog indicating the smallest value and whether or not it is odd or even. The modulus operator **Mod** is used to determine whether the number is odd or even. Because the data stored in the variant variable can be viewed as a number, VBScript performs any conversions between subtypes implicitly before performing the modulus operation. The advantage of placing these procedures in the **HEAD** is that other VBScripts can call them.

Lines 35 through 45 define an event procedure for handling **cmdButton**'s **OnClick** event. The statement

```
smallest = Minimum( number1, number2, number3 )
```

calls **Minimum**, passing **number1**, **number2** and **number3** as arguments. Parameters **min**, **a** and **b** are declared in **Minimum** to receive the values of **number1**, **number2** and **number3**, respectively. Procedure **OddEven** is called with the smallest number, on line 44.

Common Programming Error 22.10

Declaring a variable in a procedure body with the same name as a parameter variable is an error.

One last word about procedures—VBScript provides statements **Exit Sub** and **Exit Function** for exiting **Sub** procedures and **Function** procedures, respectively. Control is returned to the caller and the next statement in sequence after the call is executed.

22.6 Arrays

Arrays are data structures consisting of related data items of the same type. A *fixed-size array*'s size does not change during program execution; a *dynamic array*'s size can change during execution. A dynamic array is also called a *redimmable array* (short for a "re-dimensionable" array). Individual array elements are referred to by giving the array name followed by the element position number in parentheses, **()**. The first array element is at position zero.

The position number contained within parentheses is more formally called an *index*. An index must be in the range 0 to 2,147,483,648 (any floating-point number is rounded to the nearest whole number).

The declaration

```
Dim numbers(2)
```

instructs the interpreter to reserve three elements for array **numbers**. The value **2** defines the *upper bound* (i.e., the highest valid index) of **numbers**. The *lower bound* (the lowest valid index) of **numbers** is **0**. When an upper bound is specified in the declaration, a fixed-size array is created.

Common Programming Error 22.11

Attempting to access an index that is less than the lower bound or greater than the upper bound is an error.

The programmer can explicitly initialize the array with assignment statements. For example, the lines

```
numbers(0) = 77
numbers(1) = 68
numbers(2) = 55
```

initialize **numbers**. Repetition statements can also be used to initialize arrays. For example, the statements

```
Dim h( 11 ), x, i
For x = 0 to 30 Step 3
   h(i) = CInt( x )
   i = CInt( i ) + 1
Next
```

initializes the elements of **h** to the values 0, 3, 6, 9, …, 30.

The program in Fig. 22.18 declares, initializes and prints three arrays. Two of the arrays are fixed-size arrays and one of the arrays is a dynamic array. The program introduces function ***UBound***, which returns the upper bound (i.e., the highest-numbered index). [Note: VBScript does provide function ***LBound*** for determining the lowest-numbered index. However, the current version of VBScript does not permit the lowest-numbered index to be non-zero.]

```
<!DOCTYPE HTML PUBLIC "-//W3C//DTD HTML 4.0 Transitional//EN">
<HTML>
<!--Fig. 22.18: arrays.html -->

<HEAD>
<TITLE>Using VBScript Arrays</TITLE>

<SCRIPT LANGUAGE = "VBScript">
<!--
   Option Explicit

   Public Sub DisplayArray( x, s )
      Dim j

      Document.Write( s & ": " )
```

Fig. 22.18 Using VBScript arrays (part 1 of 2).

```
         For j = 0 to UBound( x )
            Document.Write( x( j ) & " " )
         Next

         Document.Write( "<BR>" )
      End Sub

      Dim fixedSize( 3 ), fixedArray, dynamic(), k

      ReDim dynamic( 3 )   ' Dynamically size array
      fixedArray = Array( "A", "B", "C" )

      ' Populate arrays with values
      For k = 0 to UBound( fixedSize )
         fixedSize( k ) = 50 - k
         dynamic( k ) = Chr( 75 + k )
      Next

      ' Display contents of arrays
      Call DisplayArray( fixedSize, "fixedSize" )
      Call DisplayArray( fixedArray, "fixedArray" )
      Call DisplayArray( dynamic, "dynamic" )

      ' Resize dynamic, preserve current values
      ReDim Preserve dynamic( 5 )
      dynamic( 3 ) = 3.343
      dynamic( 4 ) = 77.37443

      Call DisplayArray( dynamic, _
                         "dynamic after ReDim Preserve" )
   -->
   </SCRIPT>
   </HEAD>
   </HTML>
```

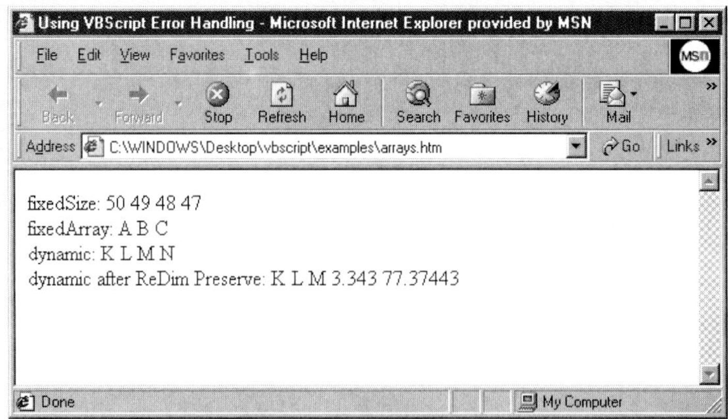

Fig. 22.18 Using VBScript arrays (part 2 of 2).

Testing and Debugging Tip 22.4

*Array upper bounds can vary. Use function **UBound** to ensure that each index is in range (i.e., within the bounds of the array).*

Lines 12 through 21 define **Sub** procedure **DisplayArray**. VBScript procedures are ***Public*** by default; therefore, they are accessible to scripts on other Web pages (as you will learn in Chapter 26 "Active Server Pages (ASP)"). Keyword ***Public*** can be used explicitly to indicate that a procedure is public. A procedure can be marked as ***Private*** to indicate that the procedure can be called only from the HTML document in which it is defined.

Procedure **DisplayArray** receives arguments **x** and **s** and declares local variable **j**. Parameter **x** receives an array and parameter **s** receives a string. The **For** header (line 16) calls function **UBound** to get the upper bound of **x**. The **Document** object's **Write** method is used to print each element of **x**.

The declaration at line 23

```
Dim fixedSize( 3 ), fixedArray, dynamic(), k
```

declares a four element fixed-sized array named **fixedSize** (the value in parentheses indicates the highest index in the array, and the array has a starting index of 0), variants **fixedArray** and **k**, and dynamic array **dynamic**.

Statement ***ReDim*** (line 25) allocates memory for array **dynamic** (four elements, in this example). All dynamic array memory must be allocated via **ReDim**. Dynamic arrays are more flexible than fixed-sized arrays, because they can be resized anytime by using **ReDim**, to accommodate new data.

Performance Tip 22.2

Dynamic arrays allow the programmer to manage memory more efficiently than do fixed-size arrays.

Performance Tip 22.3

Resizing dynamic arrays consumes processor time and can slow a program's execution speed.

Common Programming Error 22.12

*Attempting to use **ReDim** on a fixed-size array is an error.*

Line 26

```
fixedArray = Array( "A", "B", "C" )
```

creates an array containing three elements and assigns it to **fixedArray**. VBScript function ***Array*** takes any number of arguments and returns an array containing those arguments. Lines 35 through 37 pass the three arrays and three strings to **DisplayArray**. Line 40

```
ReDim Preserve dynamic( 5 )
```

reallocates **dynamic**'s memory to 5 elements. When keyword ***Preserve*** is used with **ReDim**, VBScript maintains the current values in the array; otherwise, all values in the array are lost when the **ReDim** operation occurs.

Common Programming Error 22.13

Using **ReDim** *without* **Preserve** *and assuming that the array still contains previous values is a logic error.*

Testing and Debugging Tip 22.5

Failure to **Preserve** *array data can result in unexpected loss of data at run time. Always double check every array* **ReDim** *to determine whether* **Preserve** *is needed.*

If **ReDim Preserve** creates a larger array, every element in the original array is preserved. If **ReDim Preserve** creates a smaller array, every element up to (and including) the new upper bound is preserved (e.g., if there were 10 elements in the original array and the new array contains five elements, the first five elements of the original array are preserved). Lines 41 and 42 assign values to the new elements. Procedure **DisplayArray** is called to display array **dynamic**.

Arrays can have multiple dimensions. VBScript supports at least 60 array dimensions, but most programmers will need to use only two- or three-dimensional arrays.

Common Programming Error 22.14

Referencing a two-dimensional array element **u(x, y)** *incorrectly as* **u(x)(y)** *is an error.*

A multidimensional array is declared much like a one-dimensional array. For example, consider the following declarations

```
Dim b(2, 2), tripleArray(100, 8, 15)
```

which declares **b** as a two-dimensional array and **tripleArray** as a three-dimensional array. Functions **UBound** and **LBound** can also be used with multidimensional arrays. When calling **UBound** or **LBound**, the dimension is passed as the second argument. Array dimensions always begin at one. If a dimension is not provided, the default dimension 1 is used. For example, the **For** header

```
For x = 0 To UBound(tripleArray, 3)
```

would increment **x** from the third dimension's lower bound, **0**, to the third dimension's upper bound, **15**.

Multidimensional arrays can also be created dynamically. Consider the declaration

```
Dim threeD()
```

which declares a dynamic array **threeD**. The number of dimensions is not set until the first time **ReDim** is used. Once the number of dimensions is set, the number of dimensions cannot be changed by **ReDim** (e.g., if the array is a two-dimensional array, it cannot become a three-dimensional array). The statement

```
ReDim threeD(11, 8, 1)
```

allocates memory for **threeD** and sets the number of dimensions at 3.

Common Programming Error 22.15

Attempting to change the total number of array dimensions using **ReDim** *is an error.*

Common Programming Error 22.16

Attempting to change the upper bound for any dimension except the last dimension in a dynamic-multidimensional array (when using **`ReDim Preserve`**) *is an error.*

Memory allocated for dynamic arrays can be *deallocated* (*released*) at run-time using the keyword ***`Erase`***. A dynamic array that has been deallocated must be redimensioned with **`ReDim`** before it can be used again. **`Erase`** can also be used with fixed-sized arrays to initialize all the array elements to the empty string. For example, the statement

```
Erase mDynamic
```

releases **`mDynamic`**'s memory.

Common Programming Error 22.17

Accessing a dynamic array that has been deallocated is an error.

22.7 String Manipulation

One of VBScript's most powerful features is its string-manipulation functions, some of which are summarized in Fig. 22.19. For a complete list consult the VBScript documentation. VBScript strings are case sensitive. The first character in a string has index 1 (as opposed to arrays which begin at index 0). [Note: Almost all VBScript string-manipulation functions do not modify their string argument(s); rather, they return new strings containing the results. Most VBScript string-manipulation functions take optional arguments.]

Function	Description
`Asc`	Returns the ASCII numeric value of a character. For example, **`Asc("x")`** returns **`120`**.
`Chr`	Returns the character representation for an ASCII value. For example the call **`Chr(120)`** returns "**`x`**." The argument passed must be in the range 0 to 255 inclusive, otherwise an error occurs.
`Instr`	Searches a string (i.e., the first argument) for a substring (i.e., the second argument). Searching is performed from left to right. If the substring is found, the index of the found substring in the search string is returned. For example, the call **`Instr("sparrow","arrow")`** returns **`3`** and the call **`Instr("japan","wax")`** returns **`0`**.
`Len`	Returns the number of characters in a string. For example, the call **`Len("hello")`** returns **`5`**.
`LCase`	Returns a lowercase string. For example, the call **`LCase("HELLO@97[")`** returns "**`hello@97[`**."
`UCase`	Returns an uppercase string. For example, the call **`UCase("hello@97[")`** returns "**`HELLO@97[`**."
`Left`	Returns a string containing characters from the left side of a string argument. For example, the call **`Left("Web",2)`** returns "**`We`**."

Fig. 22.19 Some string-manipulation functions (part 1 of 3).

Function	Description
Mid	Function **Mid** returns a string containing a range of characters from a string. For example, the call **Mid("abcd",2,3)** returns "**bcd**."
Right	Returns a string containing characters from the right side of a string argument. For example, the call **Right("Web",2)** returns "**eb**."
Space	Returns a string of spaces. For example, the call **Space(4)** returns a string containing four spaces.
StrComp	Compares two strings for equality. Returns **1** if the first string is greater than the second string, returns **-1** if the first string is less than the second string and returns **0** if the strings are equivalent. The default is a binary comparison (i.e., case-sensitive). An optional third argument of ***vbTextCompare*** indicates a case-insensitive comparison. For example the call **StrComp("bcd", "BCD")** returns **1**, the call **StrComp("BCD", "bcd")** returns **-1**, the call **StrComp("bcd", "bcd")** returns **0** and the call **StrComp("bcd", "BCD", vbTextCompare)** returns **0**.
String	Returns a string containing a repeated character. For example, the call **String(4,"u")** returns "**uuuu**."
Trim	Returns a string that does not contain leading or trailing space characters. For example the call **Trim(" hi ")** returns "**hi**."
LTrim	Returns a string that does not contain any leading space characters. For example, the call **LTrim(" yes")** returns "**yes**."
RTrim	Returns a string that does not contain any trailing space characters. For example, the call **RTrim("no ")** returns "**no**".
Filter	Returns an array of strings containing the result of the **Filter** operation. For example, the call **Filter(Array("A","S","D","F","G","D"),"D")** returns a two-element array containing **"D"** and **"D"**, and the call **Filter(Array("A","S","D","F","G","D"),"D",False)** returns an array containing **"A"** , **"S"**, **"F"** and **"G"**.

Fig. 22.19 Some string-manipulation functions (part 2 of 3).

We now present a VBScript program that converts a line of text into its pig Latin equivalent. Pig Latin is a form of coded language often used for amusement. Many variations exist in the methods used to form pig Latin phrases. For simplicity, we use the following algorithm:

> *To form a pig Latin phrase from an English language phrase, the translation proceeds one word at a time. To translate an English word into a pig Latin word, place the first letter of the English word (if it is not a vowel) at the end of the English word and add the letters "**ay**." If the first letter of the English word is a vowel place it at the end of the word and add "**y**." Thus, the word "**jump**" becomes "**umpjay**," the word "**the**" becomes "**hetay**," and the word "**ace**" becomes "**ceay**." Blanks between words remain as blanks. Make the following assumptions: the English phrase consists of words separated by blanks, there are no punctuation marks and all words have two or more letters.*

Function	Description
Join	Returns a string containing the concatenation of array elements separated by a delimiter. For example, the call **Join(Array("one","two","three"))** returns "**one two three**." The default delimiter is a space which can be changed by passing a delimiter string for the second argument. For example, the call **Join(Array("one","two","three"),"$^")** returns "**one$^two$^three**."
Replace	Returns a string containing the results of a **Replace** operation. Function **Replace** requires three string arguments: the string where characters will be replaced, the substring to search for and the replacement string. For example, **Replace("It's Sunday and the sun is out","sun","moon")** returns "**It's Sunday and the moon is out**." Note the case-sensitive replacement.
Split	Returns an array containing substrings. The default delimiter for **Split** is a space character. For example, the call **Split("I met a traveller")** returns an array containing elements **"I"**, **"met"**, **"a"** and **"traveller"** and **Split("red,white,and blue", ",")** returns an array containing elements **"red"**, **"white"** and **"and blue"**. The optional second argument changes the delimiter.
StrReverse	Returns a string in reverse order. For example, the call **StrReverse("deer")** returns "**reed**."
InStrRev	Searches a string (i.e., the first argument) for a substring (i.e., the second argument). Searching is performed from right to left. If the substring is found, the index of the found substring in the search string is returned. For example, the call **InstrRev("sparrow","arrow")** returns **3**, the call **InstrRev("japan","wax")** returns **0** and the call **InstrRev("to be or not to be","to be")** returns **14**.

Fig. 22.19 Some string-manipulation functions (part 3 of 3).

```
<!DOCTYPE HTML PUBLIC "-//W3C//DTD HTML 4.0 Transitional//EN">
<HTML>
<!--Fig. 22.20: piglatin.html -->

<HEAD>
<TITLE>Using VBScript String Functions</TITLE>

<SCRIPT LANGUAGE = "VBScript">
<!--
   Option Explicit

   Public Function TranslateToPigLatin( englishPhrase )
      Dim words         ' Stores each individual word
      Dim k, suffix

```

Fig. 22.20 Using VBScript string processing functions (part 1 of 3).

```
16        ' Get each word and store in words, the
17        ' default delimiter for Split is a space
18        words = Split( englishPhrase )
19
20        For k = 0 to UBound( words )
21           ' Check if first letter is a vowel
22           If InStr( 1, "aeiou", _
23                    LCase( Left( words( k ), 1 ) ) ) Then
24              suffix = "y"
25           Else
26              suffix = "ay"
27           End If
28
29           ' Convert the word to pig Latin
30           words( k ) = Right( words( k ), _
31                              Len( words( k ) ) - 1 ) & _
32                              Left( words( k ), 1 ) & suffix
33        Next
34
35        ' Return translated phrase, each word
36        ' is separated by spaces
37        TranslateToPigLatin = Join( words )
38     End Function
39
40     Sub cmdButton_OnClick()
41        Dim phrase
42
43        phrase = Document.Forms( 0 ).txtInput.Value
44
45        Document.forms( 0 ).txtPigLatin.Value = _
46           TranslateToPigLatin( phrase )
47     End Sub
48  -->
49  </SCRIPT>
50  </HEAD>
51
52  <BODY>
53  <FORM> Enter a sentence
54  <INPUT TYPE = "text" NAME = "txtInput" SIZE = "50"><P>
55  Pig Latin
56  <INPUT TYPE = "text" NAME = "txtPigLatin" SIZE = "70"><P>
57  <INPUT TYPE = "button" NAME = "cmdButton" VALUE = "Translate">
58  </SCRIPT>
59  </FORM>
60  </BODY>
61  </HTML>
```

Fig. 22.20 Using VBScript string processing functions (part 2 of 3).

Lines 12 through 38 define the **Function** procedure **TranslateToPigLatin** which translates the string input by the user from English to pig Latin. Line 18 calls function **Split** to extract each word in the sentence. By default, **Split** uses spaces as delimiters. The condition (line 22)

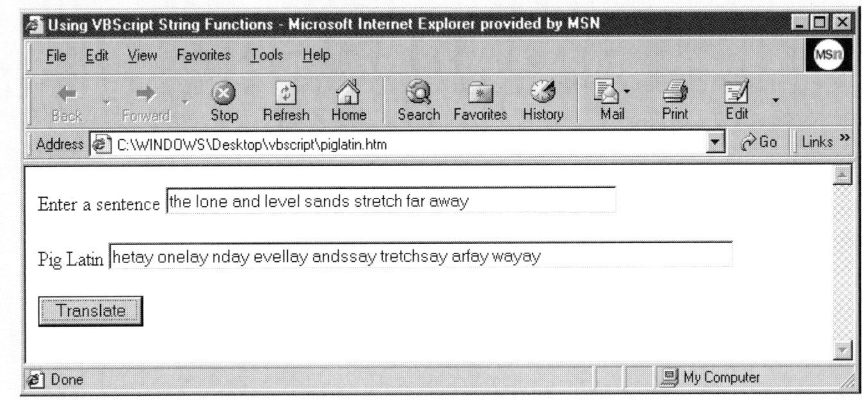

Fig. 22.20 Using VBScript string processing functions (part 3 of 3).

```
InStr( 1, "aeiou", _
       LCase( Left( words( k ), 1 ) ) )
```

calls functions **InStr**, **LCase** and **Left** to determine whether the first letter of a word is a vowel. Function **Left** is called to retrieve the first letter in **words(k)**—which is then converted to lowercase using **LCase**. Function **InStr** is called to search the string **"aeiou"** for the string returned by **LCase**. The starting index in every string is **1**, and this is where **Instr** begins searching.

Lines 30 through 33

```
words( k ) = Right( words( k ), _
                    Len( words( k ) ) - 1 ) & _
                    Left( words( k ), 1 ) & suffix
```

translate an individual word to pig Latin. Function **Len** is called to get the number of characters in **words(k)**. One is subtracted from the value returned by **Len**, to ensure that the first letter in **words(k)** is not included in the string returned by **Right**. Function **Left** is called to get the first letter of **words(k)**, which is then concatenated to the string returned by **Right**. Finally the contents of **suffix** (either **"ay"** or **"y"**) and a space are concatenated.

Lines 40 through 47 define an event procedure for **cmdButton**'s **OnClick** event. Line 46 calls function **TranslateToPigLatin**, passing the string input by the user. The pig Latin sentence returned by **TranslateToPigLatin** is displayed in a text box (line 45).

22.8 Classes and Objects

In this section, we introduce the concepts (i.e., "object think") and the terminology (i.e., "object speak") of object-oriented programming in VBScript. Objects *encapsulate* (i.e., wrap together) data (*attributes*) and methods (*behaviors*); the data and methods of an object are intimately related. Objects have the property of *information hiding*. This phrase means that, although objects may communicate with one another, objects do not know how other objects are implemented—implementation details are hidden within the objects themselves. Surely it is possible to drive a car effectively without knowing the details of how engines and transmissions work. Information hiding is crucial to good software engineering.

In VBScript, the unit of object-oriented programming is the **`Class`** from which objects are *instantiated* (i.e., created). *Methods* are VBScript procedures that are encapsulated with the data they process within the "walls" of classes.

VBScript programmers can create their own *user-defined types* called *classes*. Classes are also referred to as *programmer-defined types*. Each class contains data as well as the set of methods which manipulate that data. The data components of a class are called *instance variables*. Just as an instance of a variant is called a *variable*, an instance of a class is called an *object*. The focus of attention in object-oriented programming with VBScript is on classes rather than methods.

The *nouns* in a system-requirements document help the VBScript programmer determine an initial set of classes with which to begin the design process. These classes are then used to instantiate objects that will work together to implement the system. The *verbs* in a system-requirements document help the VBScript programmer determine what methods to associate with each class.

This section explains how to create and use objects, a subject we call *object-based programming (OBP)*. VBScript programmers craft new classes and reuse existing classes. Software is then constructed by combining new classes with existing, well-defined, carefully tested, well-documented, widely available components. This kind of *software reusability* speeds the development of powerful, high-quality software. *Rapid applications development (RAD)* is of great interest today.

Early versions of VBScript did not allow programmers to create their own classes, but VBScript programmers can now indeed develop their own classes, a powerful capability also offered by such object-oriented languages as C++ and Java.

Packaging software as classes out of which we make objects makes more significant portions of major software systems reusable. On the Windows platform, these classes have been packaged into class libraries, such as Microsoft's *MFC* (*Microsoft Foundation Classes*) that provide C++ programmers with reusable components for handling common programming tasks, such as the creating and manipulating of graphical user interfaces.

Objects are endowed with the capabilities to do everything they need to do. For example, employee objects are endowed with a behavior to pay themselves. Video game objects are endowed with the ability to draw themselves on the screen. This is like a car being endowed with the ability to "go faster" (if someone presses the accelerator pedal), "go slower" (if someone presses the brake pedal) and "turn left" or "turn right" (if someone turns the steering wheel in the appropriate direction). The blueprint for a car is like a class. Each car is like an instance of a class. Each car comes equipped with all the behaviors it needs, such as "go faster," "go slower" and so on, just as every instance of a class comes equipped with each of the behaviors instances of that class exhibit. We will discuss how to create classes and how to add properties and methods to those classes.

Software Engineering Observation 22.2

It is important to write programs that are understandable and easy to maintain. Change is the rule rather than the exception. Programmers should anticipate that their code will be modified. As we will see, using classes improves program modifiability.

Classes normally hide their implementation details from the *clients* (i.e., users) of the classes. This is called *information hiding.* As an example of information hiding, let us consider a data structure called a *stack.*

Think of a stack in terms of a pile of dishes. When a dish is placed on the pile, it is always placed at the top (referred to as *pushing* the dish onto the stack). When a dish is removed from the pile, it is always removed from the top (referred to as *popping* the dish off the stack). Stacks are known as *last-in, first-out (LIFO) data structures*—the last item *push*ed (inserted) on the stack is the first item *pop*ped (removed) from the stack. So if we push 1, then 2, then 3 onto a stack, the next three pop operations will return 3, then 2, then 1.

The programmer may create a stack class and hide from its clients the implementation of the stack. Stacks can be implemented with arrays and other techniques such as linked lists. A client of a stack class need not know how the stack is implemented. The client simply requires that when data items are placed in the stack with *push* operations, they will be recalled with *pop* operations in last-in, first-out order. Describing an object in terms of behaviors without concern for how those behaviors are actually implemented is called *data abstraction,* and VBScript classes define *abstract data types (ADTs).* Although users may happen to know how a class is implemented, users should not write code that depends on these details. This allows a class to be replaced with another version without affecting the rest of the system, as long as the **Public** interface of that class does not change (i.e. every method still has the same name, return type and parameter list in the new class definition).

Most programming languages emphasize actions. In these languages, data exists in support of the actions programs need to take. Data is "less interesting" than actions, anyway. Data is "crude." There are only a few built-in data types, and it is difficult for programmers to create their own new data types. VBScript elevates the importance of data. A primary activity in VBScript is creating new data types (i.e., *classes*) and expressing the interactions among *objects* of those classes.

An ADT actually captures two notions, a *data representation of the ADT* and the *operations allowed on the data of the ADT.* For example, subtype integer defines addition, subtraction, multiplication, division and other operations in VBScript, but division by zero is undefined. The allowed operations and the data representation of negative integers are clear, but the operation of taking the square root of a negative integer is undefined.

Software Engineering Observation 22.3

The programmer creates new types through the class mechanism. These new types may be designed to be used as conveniently as built-in types. Thus, VBScript is an extensible language. *Although it is easy to extend the language with these new types, the base language itself cannot be modified.*

Access to **Private** data should be carefully controlled by the class's methods. For example, to allow clients to read the value of **Private** data, the class can provide a *get method* (also called an *accessor* method or a *query* method).

To enable clients to modify **Private** data, the class can provide a *set* method (also called a *mutator* method). Such modification would seem to violate the notion of **Private** data. But a *set* method can provide data validation capabilities (such as range checking) to ensure that the data is set properly and to reject attempts to set data to invalid values. A *set* method can also translate between the form of the data used in the interface and the form used in the implementation. A *get* method need not expose the data in "raw" format; rather, the *get* method can edit the data and limit the view of the data the client will see.

Software Engineering Observation 22.4

The class designer need not provide set *and/or* get *methods for each* **`Private`** *data member; these capabilities should be provided only when it makes sense and after careful thought.*

Testing and Debugging Tip 22.6

Making the instance variables of a class **`Private`** *and the methods* **`Public`** *facilitates debugging because problems with data manipulations are localized to the class's methods.*

Classes often provide **`Public`** methods to allow clients of the class to *set* (i.e., assign values to) or *get* (i.e., obtain the values of) **`Private`** instance variables. These methods are special methods in VBScript called ***`Property Let`***, ***`Property Set`*** and ***`Property Get`*** (collectively these methods and the internal class data they manipulate are called *properties*). More specifically, a method that sets variable **`mInterestRate`** would be named **`Property Let InterestRate`** and a method that gets the **`InterestRate`** would be called **`Property Get InterestRate`**.

Procedures **`Property Let`** and **`Property Set`** differ in that **`Property Let`** is used for non-object subtypes (e.g., integer, string, byte, etc.) and **`Property Set`** is used for object subtypes.

Testing and Debugging Tip 22.7

`Property` *procedures should scrutinize every attempt to* set *the object's data and should reject invalid data to ensure that the object's data remains in a consistent state. This eliminates large numbers of bugs that have plagued systems development efforts.*

Software Engineering Observation 22.5

`Property Get` *procedures can control the appearance of data, possibly hiding implementation details.*

A **`Property Let Hour`** that stores the hour in universal time as 0 to 23 is shown in Fig. 22.21. Notice the change in the declaration of variable **`theHour`**—we are using keyword **`Private`** rather than **`Dim`**. In this case, **`Private`** restricts the scope of **`theHour`** to its class. If **`Dim`** or **`Public`** is used, the variable is accessible outside the class. Method definitions that are not preceded by **`Public`** or **`Private`** default to **`Public`**. Variables declared with **`Dim`** default to **`Public`**.

Good Programming Practice 22.2

Qualify all class members with either **`Public`** *or* **`Private`** *to clearly show their access.*

```
Private theHour

Public Property Let Hour( hr )
   If hr >= 0 And hr < 24 Then
      theHour = hr
   Else
      theHour = 0
   End If
End Property
```

Fig. 22.21 A simple **`Property Let`** procedure.

Suppose **Property Let Hour** is a member of class **CTime1** (we discuss how to create classes momentarily). An object of class **CTime1** is created with the following code

```
Dim wakeUp
Set wakeUp = New CTime1
```

When creating an object, VBScript keyword ***New*** is used and followed by the class name. When assigning the object to a variable, keyword ***Set*** must be used. When a variable (e.g., **wakeUp**) refers to an object, the variable is called a *reference*.

Common Programming Error 22.18

Attempting to call a method or access a property for a reference that does not refer to an object is an error.

Common Programming Error 22.19

Attempting to assign a reference a value without using ***Set*** *is an error.*

If we perform the assignments **wakeup.Hour = -6** or **wakeup.Hour = 27**, the **Property Let** procedure would reject these as invalid values and set **theHour** to 0. The **Property Get Hour** procedure is shown in Fig. 22.22.

Using **CTime1** class object **wakeUp**, we can store the value of **Hour** into variable **alarmClockHourValue**, as follows:

```
alarmClockHourValue = wakeup.Hour
```

which call **Property Get Hour** to get the value of **theHour**. The **Class** definition for **CTime1** is shown in Fig. 22.23. Keywords **Class** and **End Class** are used to encapsulate the class members.

```
Public Property Get Hour()
   Hour = theHour
End Property
```

Fig. 22.22 A simple **Property Get** procedure.

```
Class CTime1
   Private mHour

   Public Property Let Hour( hr )
      If hr >= 0 And hr < 24 Then
         theHour = hr
      Else
         theHour = 0
      End If
   End Property

   Public Property Get Hour()
      Hour = theHour
   End Property
End Class
```

Fig. 22.23 A simple **Class** definition.

Software Engineering Observation 22.6

To implement a read-only property, *simply provide a* **`Property Get`** *procedure but no* **`Property Let`** *(or* **`Property Set`***) procedure.*

Suppose we have a **`CEmployee`** class that contains an object **`mBirthDate`** of class **`CDate`**. We cannot use a **`Property Let`** to assign a value to an object. Instead, we must use a **`Property Set`**, as in each of the following **`Property`** procedures:

```
Public Property Set BirthDay(bDay)
   Set mBirthDate = bDay
End Property

Public Property Get BirthDay()
   Set BirthDay = mBirthDate
End Property
```

Any **`Property Get`**, **`Property Let`** or **`Property Set`** method may contain the ***`Exit Property`*** statement that causes an immediate exit from a **`Property`** procedure.

Access methods can read or display data. Another common use for access methods is to test the truth or falsity of conditions—such methods are often called *predicate methods.* An example of a predicate method would be an **`IsEmpty`** method for any container class—a class capable of holding multiple objects—such as a linked list or a stack. A program might test **`IsEmpty`** before attempting to remove another item from a container object. A program might test **`IsFull`** before attempting to insert another item into a container object.

It would seem that providing *set* and *get* capabilities is essentially the same as making the instance variables **`Public`**. This is another subtlety of VBScript that makes the language desirable for software engineering. If an instance variable is **`Public`**, it may be read or written at will by any method in the program. If an instance variable is **`Private`**, a **`Public`** *get* method certainly seems to allow other methods to read the data at will but the *get* method controls the formatting and display of the data. A **`Public`** *set* method can—and most likely will—carefully scrutinize attempts to modify the instance variable's value. This ensures that the new value is appropriate for that data item. For example, an attempt to *set* the day of the month to 37 would be rejected, an attempt to *set* a person's weight to a negative value would be rejected, and so on.

Software Engineering Observation 22.7

The benefits of data integrity are not automatic simply because instance variables are made **`Private`**. *Methods that set the values of* **`Private`** *data should verify that the intended new values are proper; if they are not, the* set *methods should place the* **`Private`** *instance variables into an appropriate consistent state.*

Software Engineering Observation 22.8

Every method that modifies the **`Private`** *instance variables of an object should ensure that the data remains in a consistent state.*

Figure 22.24 demonstrates using a VBScript **`Class`**. The Web page allows the user to enter a first name, age and social security number which are displayed in a message dialog. This example briefly introduces a VBScript feature for complex pattern matching called *regular expressions*. We use regular expressions to validate the format of the social security number. Client-side scripts often validate information before sending it to the server. In this example, we briefly introduce regular expressions in the context of client-side validation. In Chapter 27, "Perl/CGI," you will learn more about regular expressions.

Lines 12 through 65 define **Class Person**, which encapsulates **Private** data members, **Public Property** procedures and a **Private** method. Data members store the person's first name in **name**, the person's age in **yearsOld** and the person's social security number in **ssn**. Both **Property Let** and **Property Get** procedures are provided for the data members.

Procedure **Property Let SocialSecurityNumber** (lines 31 through 40) is the most interesting **Property** procedure. This **Property** procedure calls **Private** method **Validate** to verify the correct format for the social security number that was input. If **Validate** returns **True**, the social security number input is assigned to **ssn**; if **Validate** returns **False**, **ssn** is assigned the string **"000-00-0000"** and a message dialog is displayed.

```
1  <!DOCTYPE HTML PUBLIC "-//W3C//DTD HTML 4.0 Transitional//EN">
2  <HTML>
3  <!--Fig. 22.24: classes.html -->
4
5  <HEAD>
6  <TITLE>Using a VBScript Class</TITLE>
7
8  <SCRIPT LANGUAGE = "VBScript">
9  <!--
10    Option Explicit
11
12    Class Person
13       Private name, yearsOld, ssn
14
15       Public Property Let FirstName( fn )
16          name = fn
17       End Property
18
19       Public Property Get FirstName()
20          FirstName = name
21       End Property
22
23       Public Property Let Age( a )
24          yearsOld = a
25       End Property
26
27       Public Property Get Age()
28          Age = yearsOld
29       End Property
30
31       Public Property Let SocialSecurityNumber( n )
32
33          If Validate( n ) Then
34             ssn = n
35          Else
```

Fig. 22.24 Using VBScript classes and regular expressions (part 1 of 3).

```
            ssn = "000-00-0000"
            Call MsgBox( "Invalid Social Security Format" )
         End If

      End Property

      Public Property Get SocialSecurityNumber()
         SocialSecurityNumber = ssn
      End Property

      Private Function Validate( expression )
         Dim regularExpression
         Set regularExpression = New RegExp

         regularExpression.Pattern = "^\d{3}-\d{2}-\d{4}$"

         If regularExpression.Test( expression ) Then
            Validate = True
         Else
            Validate = False
         End If

      End Function

      Public Function ToString()
         ToString = name & Space( 3 ) & age & Space( 3 ) _
                     & ssn
      End Function

   End Class   ' Person

   Sub cmdButton_OnClick()
      Dim p                     ' Declare object reference
      Set p = New Person        ' Instantiate Person object

      With p
         .FirstName = Document.Forms(0).txtBox1.Value
         .Age = CInt( Document.Forms(0).txtBox2.Value )
         .SocialSecurityNumber = Document.Forms(0).txtBox3.Value
         Call MsgBox( .ToString() )
      End With

   End Sub
-->
</SCRIPT>
</HEAD>

<BODY>
<FORM>Enter first name
<INPUT TYPE = "text" NAME = "txtBox1" SIZE = "10">
<P>Enter age
<INPUT TYPE = "text" NAME = "txtBox2" SIZE = "5">
<P>Enter social security number
```

Fig. 22.24 Using VBScript classes and regular expressions (part 2 of 3).

```
89  <INPUT TYPE = "text" NAME = "txtBox3" SIZE = "10"> <P>
90  <INPUT TYPE = "button" NAME = "cmdButton" VALUE = "Enter">
91  </SCRIPT>
92  </FORM>
93  </BODY>
94  </HTML>
```

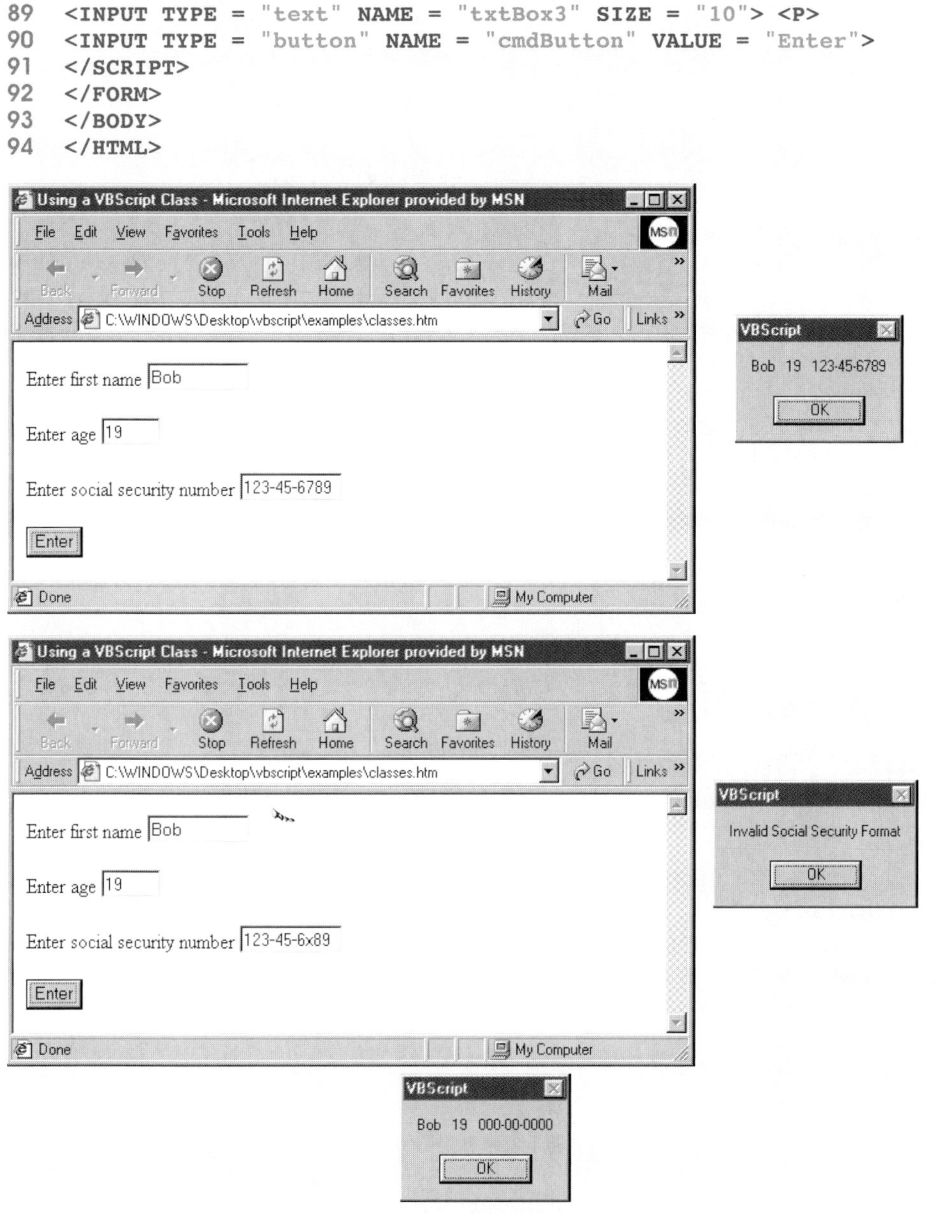

Fig. 22.24 Using VBScript classes and regular expressions (part 3 of 3).

Method **`Validate`** (line 46) checks the format of the social security number by using a so-called regular expression—a concept we explain in the next paragraph. Methods designated as **`Private`** are often called *utility* or *helper* methods. These methods are considered to be part of a class's implementation detail and therefore clients do not have access to them.

The statement

```
Set regularExpression = New RegExp
```

instantiates a regular expression object (i.e., an object of VBScript class ***RegExp***) and assigns it to reference **regularExpression**. Line 50

```
regularExpression.Pattern = "^\d{3}-\d{2}-\d{4}$"
```

sets the ***Pattern*** property to the pattern we wish to match—in this case a social security number which consists of three digits, a hyphen (i.e., **-**), two digits, a hyphen and four digits. This expression reads as follows: the beginning of the string should begin with exactly three digits followed by a hyphen, then two digits followed by a hyphen and end with exactly four digits. The *caret*, ^ indicates the beginning of the string and the **\d** indicates that any digit (i.e., 0 through 9) is a match. The **{3}**, **{2}** and **{4}** expressions indicate that exactly three occurrences of any digit, exactly two occurrences of any digit and exactly four occurrences of any digit, respectively, are a match. The *dollar sign*, **$** indicates the end of the string. The hyphens are treated as *literal characters* (i.e., a hyphen is not a special character used in a regular expression for pattern matching—so a hyphen literally is treated as a hyphen).

The **If**'s condition (line 52)

```
regularExpression.Test( expression )
```

calls function ***Test*** to determine whether the regular expression's pattern is a match for the string passed into **Test**. A successful match returns **True** and an unsuccessful match returns **False**. For more details on VBScript regular expressions, visit

```
http://msdn.microsoft.com/workshop/languages/clinic/
scripting051099.asp
```

Function **ToString** (line 60) returns a string containing the **name**, **age** and **ssn**. Function **Space** (line 61) is called to provide three spaces between words. Keywords ***End Class*** (line 65) designate the end of the class definition.

Lines 67 through 78 provide an event procedure for **cmdButton**'s **OnClick** event. Line 68 declares **p** as a variant—which can store object subtypes. The statement (line 69)

```
Set p = New Person
```

instantiates a **Person** object and assigns it to **p**. As mentioned earlier, VBScript requires the use of the **Set** keyword when assigning an object to a variable. To be more precise, we call **p** a reference, because it is used with an object. At any moment in time, a reference can refer to an object or **Nothing** (i.e., a special value that indicates the absence of an object).

Lines 71 through 76 use the ***With***/***End With*** statement to set several property values for **p** and to call **p**'s **ToString** method. The **With**/**End With** statement is provided for the convenience of the programmer, to minimize the number of times an object's name is written (when setting multiple properties or calling multiple methods). Note that lines 72 through 74 actually call the appropriate **Property Let** procedures—these lines are not directly accessing **p**'s data. Line 75

```
Call MsgBox( .ToString() )
```

calls **p**'s **ToString** method to get the string that the message dialog will display. Although the syntax may appear a bit strange, it is indeed correct.

22.9 Internet and World Wide Web Resources

Although the VBScript language contains far more features than can be presented in one chapter, there are many Web resources available that are related to VBScript. Visit the following sites for additional information.

http://msdn.microsoft.com/scripting/VBScript/doc/vbstutor.htm
The *VBScript tutorial* contains a short tutorial on VBScript.

http://msdn.microsoft.com/scripting/VBScript/doc/vbstoc.htm
The *VBScript language reference* contains links for constants, keywords, functions, etc.

http://www.msdn.microsoft.com/vbasic/technical/Documentation.asp
Visual Basic 6 documentation. Use the Visual Basic 6 documentation to get additional information on functions, constants etc. VBScript is a subset of Visual Basic.

http://msdn.microsoft.com/workshop/languages/clinic/scripting051099.asp
This is an article that discusses regular expressions in VBScript. One substantial example is provided at the end of the article.

SUMMARY

- Visual Basic Script (VBScript) is case-insensitive subset of Microsoft Visual Basic® used in World Wide Web HTML documents to enhance the functionality of a Web page displayed in a Web browser (such as Microsoft's Internet Explorer) that contains a VBScript scripting engine (i.e., interpreter) and used on servers to enhance the functionality of server-side applications.
- VBScript's arithmetic operators are similar to JavaScript arithmetic operators. Two major differences are the division operator, ****, which returns an integer result, and the exponentiation operator, **^**, which raises a value to a power. VBScript operator precedence differs from JavaScript operator precedence.
- VBScript's symbols for the equality operator and inequality operators are different from JavaScript's symbols. VBScript comparison operators may also be used to compare strings.
- VBScript provides the following logical operators: **And** (logical AND), **Or** (logical Or), **Not** (logical negation), **Imp** (logical implication), **Xor** (exclusive Or) and **Eqv** (logical equivalence).
- Despite the mixture of case in keywords, functions, etc., VBScript is not case-sensitive—uppercase and lowercase letters are treated the same.
- VBScript provides the plus sign, **+**, the and ampersand, **&**, operators for string concatenation. The ampersand is more formally called the string concatenation operator. If both operands of the concatenation operator are strings, these two operators can be used interchangeably. However, if the **+** operator is used in an expression consisting of varying data types, there can be a problem.
- VBScript code is commented either by using a single quote (**'**) or by keyword **Rem**. As with JavaScript's two forward slashes, **//**, VBScript comments are single-line comments.
- Like JavaScript, VBScript has only one data type—variant—and it is capable of storing different types of data (e.g., strings, integers, floating-point numbers, etc.). A variant is interpreted by VBScript in a manner that is suitable to the type of data it contains.
- Variable names cannot be keywords and must begin with a letter. The maximum length of a variable name is 255 characters containing only letters, numbers and underscores.Variables can be de-

clared simply by using their name in the VBScript code. Statement **Option Explicit** can be used to force all variables to be declared before they are used.

- VBScript provides nine control structures for controlling program execution. Many of the control structures provide the same capabilities as their JavaScript counterparts. Syntactically, every VBScript control structure ends with one or more keywords (e.g., **End If**, **Loop**, etc.). Keywords delimit a control structure's body—not curly braces (i.e., **{}**).
- The **If/Then/End If** and **If/Then/Else/End If** control structures behave identically to their JavaScript counterparts. VBScript's multiple selection version of **If/Then/Else/End If** uses a different syntax from JavaScript's version because it includes keyword **ElseIf**.
- VBScript does not use a statement terminator (e.g., a semicolon, **;**). Unlike JavaScript, placing parentheses around conditions in VBScript is optional. A condition evaluates to **True** if the variant subtype is boolean **True** or if the variant subtype is considered non-zero. A condition evaluates to **False** if the variant subtype is boolean **False** or if the variant subtype is considered to be 0.
- VBScript's **Select Case/End Select** structure provides the same functionality as JavaScript's **switch** structure and more. The **Select Case/End Select** structure does not require the use of a statement such as **break**. One **Case** cannot accidently run into another. The VBScript **Select Case/End Select** structure is equivalent to VBScript's **If/Then/Else/End If** multiple selection structure. The only difference is syntax. Any variant subtype can be used with the **Select Case/End Select** structure.
- VBScript's **While/Wend** repetition structure and **Do While/Loop** behave identically to JavaScript's **while** repetition structure. VBScript's **Do/Loop While** structure behaves identically to JavaScript's **do/while** repetition structure. VBScript contains two additional repetition structures, **Do Until/Loop** and **Do/Loop Until**, that do not have direct JavaScript equivalents. These **Do Until** repetition structures iterate until the condition becomes **True**.
- The **Exit Do** statement, when executed in a **Do While/Loop**, **Do/Loop While**, **Do Until/Loop** or **Do/Loop Until**, causes immediate exit from that structure and execution continues with the next statement in sequence. The fact that a **Do While/Loop** may contain **Exit Do** is the only difference, other than syntax, between **Do While/Loop** and **While/Wend**. Statement **Exit For** causes immediate exit from the **For/Next** structure.
- Function **IsEmpty** determines whether the variant has ever been initialized by the programmer. If **IsEmpty** returns **True**, the variant has not been initialized by the programmer.
- VBScript math functions allow the programmer to perform common mathematical calculations. Trigonometric functions such as **Cos**, **Sin**, etc. take arguments that are expressed in radians. To convert from degrees to radians use the formula: $radians = degrees \times \pi / 180$.
- Function **InputBox** displays a dialog in which the user can input data.
- VBScript coordinates are measured in units of twips (1440 twips equal 1 Inch). Coordinates are relative to the upper-left corner of the screen, which is position (0, 0). X coordinates increase from left to right and y coordinates increase from top to bottom.
- Many VBScript functions often take optional arguments.
- The underscore character, _ is VBScript's line continuation character. A statement cannot extend beyond the current line without using this character. A statement may use as many line continuation characters as necessary.
- Function **MsgBox** displays a message dialog.
- In VBScript, function calls that wrap arguments in parentheses must be preceded with keyword **Call**—unless the function call is assigning a value to a variable.
- VBScript provides functions for getting information about the scripting engine (i.e., the interpreter). These functions are **ScriptEngine**—which returns either **"JScript"**, **"VBScript"** or

"VBA", **ScriptEngineBuildVersion**—which returns the current build version, **ScriptEngineMajorVersion**—which returns the major version number for the script engine and **ScriptEngineMinorVersion**—which returns the minor release number.

- HTML comment tags comment out the VBScript code. If the browser understands VBScript, these tags are ignored and the VBScript is interpreted. If the browser does not understand VBScript, the HTML comment prevents the VBScript code from being displayed as text.
- Procedures that do not return a value begin with keyword **Sub** and end with keywords **End Sub**.
- Variables declared within a VBScript procedure are visible only within the procedure body. Procedures that perform event handling are more properly called event procedures.
- VBScript provides functions **CBool**, **CByte**, **CCur**, **CDate**, **CDbl**, **CInt**, **CLng**, **CSng** and **CStr** for converting between variant subtypes.
- Programmer-defined constants are created by using keyword **Const**.
- Because the **HEAD** section of an HTML document is decoded first by the browser, VBScript code is normally placed there, so it can be decoded before it is invoked in the document.
- VBScript procedures that return a value are delimited with keywords **Function** and **End Function**. A value is returned from a **Function** procedure by assigning a value to the **Function** procedure name. As in JavaScript, a **Function** procedure can return only one value at a time.
- VBScript provides statements **Exit Sub** and **Exit Function** for exiting **Sub** procedures and **Function** procedures, respectively. Control is returned to the caller, and the next statement in sequence after the call is executed.
- A fixed-size array's size does not change during program execution; a dynamic array's size can change during execution. A dynamic array is also called a redimmable array. Array elements may be referred to by giving the array name followed by the element position number in parentheses, **()**. The first array element is at index zero.
- Function **UBound** returns the upper bound (i.e., the highest-numbered index) and function **LBound** returns the lowest-numbered index (i.e., 0).
- Keyword **Public** explicitly indicates that a procedure is public. A procedure may also be marked as **Private**, to indicate that only scripts on the same Web page may call the procedure.
- Statement **ReDim** allocates memory for a dynamic array. All dynamic arrays must receive memory via **ReDim**. Dynamic arrays are more flexible than fixed-sized arrays, because they can be resized anytime using **ReDim** to accommodate new data.
- Function **Array** takes any number of arguments and returns an array containing those arguments.
- Keyword **Preserve** may be used with **ReDim** to maintain the current values in the array. When **ReDim** is executed without **Preserve**, all values contained in the array are lost.
- Arrays can have multiple dimensions. VBScript supports at least 60 array dimensions, but most programmers will need to use no more than two- or three-dimensional arrays. Multidimensional arrays can also be created dynamically.
- Memory allocated for dynamic arrays can be deallocated (released) at run-time using keyword **Erase**. A dynamic array that has been deallocated must be redimensioned with **ReDim** before it can be used again. **Erase** can also be used with fixed-sized arrays to initialize all the array elements to the empty string.
- VBScript strings are case sensitive and begin with an index of 1.
- Objects encapsulate data (attributes) and methods (behaviors); the data and methods of an object are intimately tied together. Objects have the property of information hiding. This means that although objects may communicate with one another, objects do not know how other objects are implemented—implementation details are hidden within the objects themselves.

- In VBScript, the unit of object-oriented programming is the **Class** from which objects are instantiated (i.e., created). Methods are VBScript procedures that are encapsulated with the data they process within the "walls" of classes.
- VBScript programmers can create their own user-defined types called classes. Classes are also referred to as programmer-defined types. Each class contains data as well as the set of methods which manipulate that data. The data components of a class are called instance variables. Just as an instance of a variant is called a variable, an instance of a class is called an object.
- Classes normally hide their implementation details from the clients (i.e., users) of the classes. This is called information hiding.
- Describing an object in terms of behaviors without concern for how those behaviors are actually implemented is called data abstraction, and VBScript classes define abstract data types (ADTs). Although users may happen to know how a class is implemented, users must not write code that depends on these details. This means that a class can be replaced with another version without affecting the rest of the system, as long as the **Public** interface of that class does not change (i.e. every method still has the same name, return type and parameter list in the new class definition).
- Access to **Private** data should be carefully controlled by the class's methods. For example, to allow clients to read the value of **Private** data, the class can provide a get method (also called an accessor method or a query method).
- To enable clients to modify **Private** data, the class can provide a set method (also called a mutator method). A set method can also translate between the form of the data used in the interface and the form used in the implementation. A get method need not expose the data in "raw" format; rather, the get method can edit the data and limit the view of the data the client will see.
- Classes often provide **Public** methods to allow clients of the class to set (i.e., assign values to) or get (i.e., obtain the values of) **Private** instance variables. These methods are special methods in VBScript called **Property Let**, **Property Set** and **Property Get** (collectively these methods and the internal class data they manipulate are called properties). Procedures **Property Let** and **Property Set** differ in that **Property Let** is used for non-object subtypes (e.g., integer, string, byte, etc.) and **Property Set** is used for object subtypes.
- Method definitions that are not preceded by **Public** or **Private** default to **Public**. Variables declared with **Dim** default to **Public**. Methods designated as **Private** are often called utility or helper methods. These methods are considered to be part of a class's implementation detail, and therefore clients do not have access to them.
- When creating an object, VBScript keyword **New** is used followed by the class name. When assigning the object to a variable, keyword **Set** must be used. When a variable (e.g., **wakeUp**) refers to an object, the variable is called a reference.
- Any **Property Get**, **Property Let** or **Property Set** method may contain the **Exit Property** statement that causes an immediate exit from a **Property** procedure.
- Class **RegExp** may be used to create a regular expression object. A **RegExp** object's **Pattern** property stores a regular expression. Function **Test** determines whether a regular expression's **Pattern** is a match for the string argument passed into it.

TERMINOLOGY

^
$
\d
Abs function
abstract data type (ADT)
accessor method
Active Server Pages (ASP)
addition operator, **+**
And logical operator
Array function

Asc function
Atn function
attribute
behavior
boolean subtype
build version
byte subtype
CBool function
CByte function
CCur function
CDate function
CDbl function
Chr function
CInt function
CLng function
Class keyword
client
comment character, **'**
comparison operator
Const keyword
Cos function
CStr function
currency subtype
date/time subtype
Dim keyword
Do Loop/**Until** control structure
Do Loop/**While** control structure
double subtype
Do Until/**Loop** control structure
Do While/**Loop** control structure
dynamic array
ElseIf keyword
empty string
empty subtype
encapsulation
End Class
End Function
End If
End Property
End Select
End Sub
End With
equality operator, **=**
Eqv logical operator
Erase statement
event procedure
Exit Do statement
Exit For statement
Exit Property statement
Exp function
exponentiation operator, **^**
False keyword
Filter function
Fix function
floating-point division operator, **/**
FormatCurrency function
FormateDateTime function
FormatNumber function
FormatPercent function
For/**Next** control structure
get method
greater-than operator, **>**
greater-than or equal-to operator, **>=**
If/**Then**/**End If** control structure
Imp logical operator
inequality operator, **<>**
information hiding
InputBox function
input dialog
instantiating an object
InStr function
InStrRev function
integer division operator, ****
integer subtype
Int function
Intranet
IsArray function
IsDate function
IsEmpty function
IsNumeric function
IsObject function
Join function
LBound function
LCase function
Left function
Len function
less-than operator, **<**
less-than or equal-to operator, **<=**
lexicographical comparison
line-continuation character, **_**
local variable
Log function
long subtype
Loop keyword
lower bound
LTrim function
method
MFC (Microsoft Foundation Classes)
Mid function
modulus operator, **Mod**

MsgBox function
multidimensional array
multiplication operator, *
mutator method
negation operator, -
New keyword
Next keyword
Not logical operator
noun
Now function
object
object-based programming (OBP)
object subtype
optional argument
Option Explicit
Or logical operator
parentheses, **()**
Pattern property
predicate method
Preserve keyword
Private keyword
procedure
programmer-defined type
Property Get method
Property keyword
Property Let method
Property Set method
Public keyword
query method
Randomize function
rapid application development (RAD)
read-only property
redimmable array
ReDim statement
reference
RegExp class
regular expressions
Rem keyword
Replace function
Right function
Rnd function
Round function
RTrim function
ScriptEngineBuildVersion function
ScriptEngine function
ScriptEngineMajorVersion function
ScriptEngineMinorVersion function
Set keyword
set method
Sgn function
Sin function
single subtype
software reusability
Space function
Split function
Sqr function
Step keyword
StrComp function
string concatenation operator, **&**
String function
string subtype
StrReverse function
subtraction operator, -
subtype of a variant
Tan function
Test function
To keyword
Trim function
True keyword
twip
TypeName function
UBound function
UCase function
upper bound
user-defined type
variant data type
variant subtype
VarType function
vbLongDate constant
VBScript (Visual Basic Scripting Edition)
VBScript language attribute
VBScript scripting engine
vbShortTime constant
vbTextCompare constant
verb
Wend keyword
While/Wend control structure
With keyword
x coordinate
XOr logical operator
y coordinate

COMMON PROGRAMMING ERRORS

22.1 Attempting to declare a variable name that does not begin with a letter is a syntax error.

22.2 If a variable name is misspelled (when not using **Option Explicit**), a new variable is declared, usually resulting in an error.

22.3 Writing an **If** control structure that does not contain keyword **Then** is an error.

22.4 Attempting to use a relational operator in a **For**/**Next** loop (e.g., **For x = 1 < 10**) is an error.

22.5 Attempting to use **Exit Do** or **Exit For** to exit a **While**/**Wend** repetition structure is an error.

22.6 Attempting to place the name of a **For** repetition structures's control variable after **Next** is an error.

22.7 Splitting a statement over several lines without the line-continuation character is a syntax error.

22.8 Placing anything, including comments, after a line-continuation character is a syntax error.

22.9 Placing VBScript code before **Option Explicit** is an error.

22.10 Declaring a variable in a procedure body with the same name as a parameter variable is an error.

22.11 Attempting to access an index that is less than the lower bound or greater than the upper bound is an error.

22.12 Attempting to use **ReDim** on a fixed-size array is a syntax error.

22.13 Using **ReDim** without **Preserve** and assuming that the array still contains previous values is a logic error.

22.14 Referencing a two-dimensional array element **u(x, y)** incorrectly as **u(x)(y)** is a syntax error.

22.15 Attempting to change the total number of array dimensions using **ReDim** is an error.

22.16 Attempting to change the upper bound for any dimension except the last dimension in a dynamic-multidimensional array (when using **ReDim Preserve**) is an error.

22.17 Accessing a dynamic array that has been deallocated is an error.

22.18 Attempting to call a method or access a property for a reference that does not refer to an object is an error.

22.19 Attempting to assign a reference a value without using **Set** is an error.

GOOD PROGRAMMING PRACTICES

22.1 VBScript programmers use the single-quote character for comments. The use of **Rem** is considered archaic.

22.2 Always place client-side VBScript code inside HTML comments to prevent the code from being displayed as text in browsers that do not understand VBScript.

22.3 Qualify all class members with either **Public** or **Private** to clearly show their access.

PERFORMANCE TIPS

22.1 VBScript logical operators do not use “short-circuit” evaluation. Both conditions are always evaluated.

22.2 Dynamic arrays allow the programmer to manage memory more efficiently than do fixed-size arrays.

22.3 Resizing dynamic arrays consumes processor time and can slow a program's execution speed.

PORTABILITY TIPS

22.1 VBScript Functions **ScriptEngine**, **ScriptEngineBuildVersion**, **ScriptEngineMajorVersion** and **ScriptEngineMinorVersion** can be used to determine whether the browser's script engine version is different from the script engine version you used to develop the page. Older script engines do not support the latest VBScript features.

22.2 Always place client-side VBScript code inside HTML comments to prevent the code from being displayed as text in browsers that do not understand VBScript.

SOFTWARE ENGINEERING OBSERVATIONS

22.1 Because all variables are of type variant, the programmer does not specify a data type when declaring a variable in VBScript.

22.2 It is important to write programs that are understandable and easy to maintain. Change is the rule rather than the exception. Programmers should anticipate that their code will be modified. As we will see, using classes improves program modifiability.

22.3 The programmer creates new types through the class mechanism. These new types may be designed to be used as conveniently as built-in types. Thus, VBScript is an extensible language. Although it is easy to extend the language with these new types, the base language itself cannot be modified.

22.4 The class designer need not provide set and/or get methods for each **Private** data member; these capabilities should be provided only when it makes sense and after careful thought.

22.5 **Property Get** procedures can control the appearance of data, possibly hiding implementation details.

22.6 To implement a read-only property, simply provide a **Property Get** procedure but no **Property Let** (or **Property Set**) procedure.

22.7 The benefits of data integrity are not automatic simply because instance variables are made **Private**. Methods that set the values of **Private** data should verify that the intended new values are proper; if they are not, the set methods should place the **Private** instance variables into an appropriate consistent state.

22.8 Every method that modifies the **Private** instance variables of an object should ensure that the data remains in a consistent state.

TESTING AND DEBUGGING TIPS

22.1 Always use the ampersand (**&**) operator for string concatenation.

22.2 Forcing all variables to be declared, by using **Option Explicit**, can help eliminate various kinds of subtle errors.

22.3 VBScript Functions **ScriptEngine**, **ScriptEngineBuildVersion**, **ScriptEngineMajorVersion** and **ScriptEngineMinorVersion** are useful if you are experiencing difficulty with the scripting engine and need to report information about the scripting engine to Microsoft.

22.4 Array upper bounds can vary. Use function **UBound** to ensure that each index is in range (i.e., within the bounds of the array).

22.5 Failure to **Preserve** array data can result in unexpected loss of data at run time. Always double check every array **ReDim** to determine whether **Preserve** is needed.

22.6 Making the instance variables of a class **Private** and the methods **Public** facilitates debugging because problems with data manipulations are localized to the class's methods.

22.7 **`Property`** procedures should scrutinize every attempt to set the object's data and should reject invalid data to ensure that the object's data remains in a consistent state. This eliminates large numbers of bugs that have plagued systems development efforts.

SELF-REVIEW EXERCISES

22.1 State whether the following are *true* or *false*. If the answer is *false*, explain why.
a) VBScript is case-sensitive.
b) **`Option Explicit`** forces all VBScript variables to be declared.
c) The single quote character indicates a VBScript comment.
d) The exponentiation operator's symbol is the caret, ^.
e) The starting index for an array may be set to either 0 or 1.
f) Array dimensions begin at 0.

22.2 Fill in the blanks in each of the following:
a) Keyword __________ is required when assigning an object to a reference.
b) Keyword __________ is required when instantiating an object.
c) VBScript variables are of type __________.
d) Function __________ returns a string containing characters from the left side of a string.
e) Class __________ defines a regular expression.
f) Function __________ returns an uppercase string.

22.3 Briefly explain the difference between a **`Function`** procedure and a **`Sub`** procedure.

22.4 Fill in the blanks in each of the following:
a) Keyword __________ is used to create a constant.
b) By default, script variables declared with **`Dim`** are __________.
c) Statement **`ReDim`** is used to allocate memory for a __________ array.
d) **`Property`** __________ returns a property's value.
e) __________ is the logical AND operator.
f) Function __________ returns the highest numbered array index.

ANSWERS TO SELF-REVIEW EXERCISES

22.1 a) False. VBScript is case-insensitive. b) True. c) True. d) True. e) False. An array's starting index is always 0. f) False. Array dimensions begin at 1.

22.2 a) **`Set`**. b) **`New`**. c) variant. d) **`Left`**. e) **`RegExp`**. f) **`UCase`**.

22.3 A **`Function`** procedure returns a value and a **`Sub`** procedure does not return a value.

22.4 a) **`Const`**. b) **`Public`**. c) dynamic. d) **`Get`**. e) **`And`**. f) **`UBound`**.

EXERCISES

22.5 *(Compound Interest Calculator)* Create an HTML document that enables the user to calculate compound interest. Provide several **`TEXT`** components in which the user can enter the *principal amount*, the yearly interest *rate* and the number of *years* (see the compound interest program of Fig. 10.6 for the calculation of interest). Provide a **`BUTTON`** to cause the VBScript to execute and calculate the interest. Display the result in another **`TEXT`** component. If any **`TEXT`** component is left empty, display a **`MsgBox`** indicating the error. Use a **`Function`** procedure to perform the calculation.

22.6 *(Monthly Compound Interest Calculator)* Modify Exercise 22.5 to calculate the compound interest on a monthly basis. Remember that you must divide the interest rate by 12 to get the monthly rate.

22.7 Write a VBScript that allows the user to enter a name, email address and phone number. Use regular expressions to perform the validation (e.g., names can only contain letters, email must be of the format *username@name.extension* and the phone number must have the format *(555) 555-5555*). Note: you should read the article on regular expression (listed in the Web Resources section) before attempting this exercise.

22.8 Modify the VBScript of Fig. 22.24 to use some of the string-related functions introduced in Section 22.7 to perform the validation instead of a regular expression. How does your new solution compare?

22.9 Write a VBScript that generates from the string "**abcdefghijklmnopqrstuvwxyz{**" the following:

```
              a
             bcb
            cdedc
           defgfed
          efghihgfe
         fghijkjihgf
        ghijklmlkjihg
       hijklmnonmlkjih
      ijklmnopqponmlkji
     jklmnopqrsrqponmlkj
    klmnopqrstutsrqponmlk
   lmnopqrstuvwvutsrqponml
  mnopqrstuvwxyxwvutsrqponm
 nopqrstuvwxyz{zyxwvutsrqpon
```

22.10 Law enforcement agencies often get partial descriptions of suspect license plate numbers and have to search for license plate numbers that match the description. Create a program that will allow a local law enforcement agency to determine how many license plate numbers match a partial description. Randomly create 500 6-character long license plate numbers and store them in an array. Allow the user to search for partial plate numbers of 3 or 4 digits. Note: License plate numbers can contain both digits and letters. The array should not contain any duplicates.

22.11 Write a program that reads a five-letter word from the user and produces all possible three-letter words that can be derived from the letters of the five-letter word. For example, the three-letter words produced from the word "bathe" include the commonly used words

```
ate    bat    bet    tab    hat    the    tea
```

22.12 Create a class called **CComplex** for performing arithmetic with complex numbers. Write a program to test your class.

Complex numbers have the form

```
realPart + imaginaryPart ∞ i
```

where *i* is

$$\sqrt{-1}$$

Use floating-point subtypes to represent the **Private** data of the class. Provide **Public** methods for each of the following:

a) Addition of two **CComplex** numbers: The real parts are added together and the imaginary parts are added together.

b) Subtraction of two **CComplex** numbers: The real part of the right operand is subtracted from the real part of the left operand and the imaginary part of the right operand is subtracted from the imaginary part of the left operand.
c) Printing **CComplex** numbers in the form **(A, B)**, where **A** is the real part and **B** is the imaginary part.

22.13 Create a class called **CRational** for performing arithmetic with fractions. Write a program to test your class.

Use integer variables to represent the **Private** instance variables of the class—**mNumerator** and **mDenominator**. The class should store the fraction in reduced form (i.e., the fraction

```
2/4
```

would be stored in the object as 1 in the **mNumerator** and 2 in the **mDenominator**). Provide **Public** methods for each of the following:

a) Addition of two **CRational** numbers. The result is stored in reduced form.
b) Subtraction of two **CRational** numbers. The result is stored in reduced form.
c) Multiplication of two **CRational** numbers. The result is stored in reduced form.
d) Division of two **CRational** numbers. The result is stored in reduced form.
e) Returning **CRational** numbers in the form **mNumerator/mDenominator** (i.e., a string with this format).
f) Returning **CRational** numbers in floating-point format. (Consider providing formatting capabilities that enable the user of the class to specify the number of digits of precision to the right of the decimal point.)

22.14 Use a two-dimensional array to solve the following problem. A company has four salespeople (with salesperson numbers 1 to 4) who sell five different products (with product numbers 1 to 5). Once a day, each salesperson passes in a slip for each different type of product sold. Each slip contains the following:

1. the salesperson number;
2. the product number;
3. the total dollar value of that product sold that day.

Write a program that reads this information and summarizes the total sales by salesperson by product. All totals should be stored in the two-dimensional array **sales**. After each input, print the results in tabular format, with each of the columns representing a particular salesperson and each of the rows representing a particular product. Cross-total each row to get the total sales of each product for last month; cross total each column to get the total sales by salesperson for last month. Your neat tabular printout should include these cross-totals to the right of the totaled rows and at the bottoms of the totaled columns. Use VBScript function **FormatCurrency** as part of your solution.

22.15 Use a one-dimensional array to solve the following problem. A company pays its salespeople on a commission basis. The salespeople receive $200 per week plus 9% of their gross sales for that week. For example, a salesperson who grosses $5000 in sales in a week receives $200 plus 9% of $5000, or a total of $650. Write a program (using an array of counters) that determines how many of the salespeople earned salaries in each of the following ranges (assume that each salesperson's salary is truncated to an integer amount):

1. $200-$299
2. $300-$399
3. $700-$799

4. $500-$599
5. $600-$699
6. $700-$799
7. $800-$899
8. $900-$999
9. $1000 and over

22.16 Use a one-dimensional dynamic array to solve the following problem. Read in 20 numbers, each of which is between 10 and 100, inclusive. As each number is input, print it only if it is not a duplicate of a number already input. Provide for the "worst case," in which all 20 numbers are different.

22.17 Write a Web page that allows the user to select one or more books by using check boxes. Display the name of each book and its price. Display the current total in a text box at the bottom of the page. When a book is selected (or unselected), update the total. Use VBScript to perform any arithmetic operations and to format the total.

22.18 *(VBScript Calculator)* Write a VBScript calculator that provides addition, subtraction, multiplication and division operations.

22.19 Modify your solution to Exercise 22.21 to include scientific features such as exponentiation, cosine, sine, etc. Use the Windows calculator as a guide.

22.20 In the chapter, we mentioned that VBScript contains various date/time manipulations. Study these date/time capabilities by visiting the resources listed in Section 22.9. Write a program that demonstrates as many of these capabilities as possible.

22.21 Write a **`Function`** procedure **`ToMorseCode`** that takes one string argument and returns a string containing the Morse code equivalent. Figure 22.25 lists the Morse code for letters and digits.

22.22 Write a program that plays the game of "guess the number," as follows: Your program chooses the number to be guessed by selecting an **`Integer`** at random in the range 1 to 1000. The program displays

```
I have a number between 1 and 1000.
Can you guess my number?
Please enter your first guess.
```

The player then types a first guess. The program responds with one of the following:

```
Excellent! You guessed the number!
Would you like to play again (y or n)?

Too low. Try again.

Too high. Try again.
```

If the player's guess is incorrect, your program should loop until the player finally gets the number right. Your program should keep telling the player "**`Too high`**" or "**`Too low`**" to help the player "zero in" on the correct answer.

Character	Code	Character	Code
A	.-	T	-
B	-...	U	..-
C	-.-.	V	...-
D	-..	W	.--
E	.	X	-..-
F	..-.	Y	-.--
G	--.	Z	--..
H	....		
I	..	Digits	
J	.---	1	.----
K	-.-	2	..---
L	.-..	3	...--
M	--	4	....-
N	-.	5	.....
O	---	6	-....
P	.--.	7	--...
Q	--.-	8	---..
R	.-.	9	----.
S	...	0	-----

Fig. 22.25 The letters of the alphabet as expressed in international Morse code.

23

Electronic Commerce and Security

Objectives

- To review the history of electronic commerce.
- To study popular e-business models, including those of Amazon, eBay, CyberCash and VeriSign.
- To understand the issues of billing, credit and cash transfers on the Internet.
- To understand Internet security technologies such as public-key/private-key cryptography, digital signatures and digital certificates.
- To understand the core technologies that underlie Internet Commerce.

O Gold! I still prefer thee unto paper,
Which makes bank credit like a bark of vapour.
Lord Byron

It is an immutable law in business that words are words, explanations are explanations, promises are promises—but only performance is reality.
Harold S. Green

My name is Sherlock Holmes. It is my business to know what other people don't know.
Sir Arthur Conan Doyle

When you stop talking, you've lost your customer.
Estée Lauder

So long as you are secure you will count many friends.
Ovid [Publius Ovidius Naso]

Outline

23.1 Introduction

In this chapter we introduce popular e-business models and the underlying technologies on which these models are based (such as database, Internet security and Web-based client/server computing). In the next several chapters, we build systems that employ several of these technologies. We will put additional historical and technical information about e-commerce on our Web site, **`http://www.deitel.com`**.

To conduct e-commerce, merchants need to organize an online catalog of products, take orders through their Web sites, accept payments in a secure environment, send merchandise to customers and manage customer data (such as customer profiles). They must also market their sites to potential customers. We present case studies of successful e-businesses and show the steps you can use to set up your own e-commerce Web sites by using popular approaches such as Yahoo! Store and Microsoft Site Server Commerce Edition.

Although the term e-commerce is fairly new, large corporations have been conducting e-commerce for decades, by networking systems together with those of business partners and clients. For example, the banking industry uses *Electronic Funds Transfer (EFT)* to transfer money between accounts. Many companies also use *Electronic Data Interchange (EDI),* in which business forms, such as purchase orders and invoices, are standardized so that companies can share information with customers, vendors and business partners electronically.

Until recently, e-commerce was feasible only for large companies. The Internet and the World Wide Web make it possible for even small businesses to compete with large companies. E-commerce allows companies to conduct business 24 hours a day, seven days a week, worldwide.

One problem with conducting business over the Web is that the Internet is an inherently insecure medium comprised of vast networks and millions of computers. It is important to secure the network transactions, to protect such private information as credit card numbers transferred between merchants and clients. We discuss several popular security protocols and demonstrate how such transactions as cash transfers and credit-card payments, are handled online.

The chapter includes an extensive Bibliography section listing many books and papers on e-commerce. We include a substantial collection of Internet and World Wide Web resources in Section 23.11.

23.2 Shopping-Cart Technology

One of the most common e-commerce models is the *shopping cart.* This order-processing technology allows customers to accumulate and store lists of items they wish to buy as they continue to shop. Supporting the shopping cart is the product catalog, which is hosted on the *merchant server* in the form of a *database.* The database is a collection of information. For example, a database for an online clothing retailer would typically include such product specifications as item description, size, availability, shipping information, stock levels and on-order information. Databases also store customer information, such as names, addresses, credit-card information and past purchases. Database programming is discussed in Chapter 25, and in additional case studies including Chapter 26, "Active Server Pages," Chapter 27, "Perl/CGI Programming" and Chapter 29, "Java Servlets."

23.2.1 Case Study: Amazon

Perhaps the most widely recognized example of an e-business that uses shopping cart technology is **`Amazon.com`** (Ha99) (Hi99). The company opened its "electronic doors" in 1994 and has rapidly grown to become one of the world's largest online retailers. Amazon offers millions of different products to more than 10 million customers.

In its first few years, **`Amazon.com`** served as a mail-order book retailer with a rather small inventory. **`Amazon.com`** has since expanded to include music, videos, DVDs, electronic cards, consumer electronics and toys. The online catalog allows you to navigate quickly among millions of product offerings. **`Amazon.com`** uses a sophisticated database on the server side that allows customers on the client side to search for millions of products in a variety of ways. This is an example of a *client/server application*.

The database that is used is a collection of product specifications, availability, shipping information, stock levels, on-order information and other data. Book titles, authors, prices, sales histories, publishers, reviews and in-depth descriptions are stored in the database. The database makes it possible to cross-reference products. For example, a novel may be listed under various categories, including fiction, best-sellers and recommended titles.

`Amazon.com` personalizes its site to service returning customers; this capability suggests that the database keeps a record of all previous transactions, including items purchased, shipping and credit-card information. Upon returning to the site, customers are greeted by name and a list of recommended titles is presented, based on the customer's previous purchases. The list of recommended titles suggests that Amazon searches the customer database for patterns and trends among its clientele. By monitoring such customer data, Amazon provides a service that would otherwise need to be handled by sales representatives. Amazon's computer system drives sales of additional items without human interaction.

Buying a product at Amazon is simple. You begin at the **`Amazon.com`** home page and decide the type of product you would like to purchase. For example, if you are looking for *C++ How to Program: Second Edition*, you can find the book by using the search box in the top-left corner of the home page. Select **Books** in the **Search Box**, then type the title of the book into the window. This takes you directly to the product page for the book. To purchase the item, select **Add to Shopping Cart** on the top right corner of the page. The shopping cart technology processes the information and displays a list of the products you have placed in the shopping cart. You then have the option to change the quantity of each item, remove an item from the shopping cart, check out or continue shopping.

When you are ready to place your order, you proceed to checkout. As a first-time visitor, you will be prompted to fill out a personal identification form including name, billing address, shipping address, shipping preference and credit-card information. You are also asked to enter a password that you will use to access your account data for all future transactions. Once you confirm your information, you proceed to place your order.

Customers returning to Amazon can use its *1-click^{SM} system*. This allows the customer to reuse previously entered payment and shipping information to place an order with just one click of the mouse. This is an excellent example of how an intelligently designed database application can make online business transactions faster and easier.

When your order is placed, Amazon sends a confirmation to you by email. A second email is sent to confirm when the order is shipped.

A database monitors the status of all shipments. You can track the status of your purchase until it leaves the **`Amazon.com`** shipping center by selecting the **Your Account** link at the bottom of the page and entering your password. This will bring you to an **Account Maintenance** page. You can cancel your order at any time before the product is shipped. Products are usually shipped within 24 hours.

`Amazon.com` operates on a secure server that protects your personal information. If you feel uncomfortable using your credit card on the Web, you can place your order through their Web site using the last five digits of your credit card, then you can call

Amazon's Customer Service Department to provide the remaining numbers to complete your order. But is using a telephone really any more secure than sending your information over the Web? Security is discussed in section 23.6.

In 1996, Amazon innovated a unique e-commerce marketing strategy to bring new customers to their Web site. Companies and individuals can create an income stream in exchange for posting Amazon links on their Web sites, thus sending their visitors to Amazon. This is known as the *Amazon.com Associates Program*. In industry, these programs are commonly called *affiliate programs*. Associates post links to **`Amazon.com`** from their Web sites. If a customer uses the link to click over to Amazon and then purchases a product, the associate receives a percentage of the sale as a referral fee. Higher referral fees may be paid for products sold through direct links to a specific item. **`Amazon.com`** sends weekly activity reports to associates, detailing click-throughs, sales and accrued referral fees.

This Associates Program is an example of how the Internet and the Web are profoundly changing the way business is done. Without the Internet and the Web, this type of program would not be feasible.

23.3 Online-Auction Case Study: eBay

I will buy with you, sell with you, talk with you, walk with you, and so following;...
William Shakespeare

Online auctions have become enormously successful on the Web. The leading company in this business is *eBay* (Pi99) (Hi99). At the time of publication, eBay was one of the most profitable e-businesses. The successful online auction house has its roots in a 50-year old novelty item—Pez® candy dispensers. Linda Omidyar, an avid collector of Pez® dispensers, came up with the idea of trading them over the Internet. When she expressed this idea to her boyfriend, Pierre Omidyar (now her husband), he was instantly struck with the soon-to-be-famous business concept. In 1995, the Omidyars created a company called AuctionWeb. The company was renamed eBay and it has become the premier online auction house (Fig. 23.1). The company posts as many as 2 million unique auctions and 250,000 new items each day.

The impact of eBay on e-business has been profound. The founders took a business model that was restrictive offline and brought it to the desktops of consumers worldwide. The business model is one of few that generates a profit on the World Wide Web. A recent article in *Business Week* (Hi99) states, "The bidding and close interaction between buyers and sellers promotes a sense of community—a near addiction that keeps them coming back." By implementing traditional marketing strategies and keeping the process simple, eBay has offered a clear alternative to storefront-style e-commerce.

On eBay, people can buy and sell just about anything. The company collects a submission fee plus a percentage of the sale amount. The final fee is multitiered. For example, if your product sells for $1500, then you would have a three-tiered final fee. As of this writing, you would be charged 5% on the first $25.00 of the selling price, 2.5% on the difference between $25 and $1000 and 1.25% on anything above $1000. Thus, if you were to sell a product for $1500, you would pay $31.86 in fees. The submission fee is based on the amount of exposure you want your item to receive. For instance, if you would like to be among the "featured auctions" in your specific product category, you can pay $14.95 for the auction period. For $99.95, your item will be listed on the eBay home page under **Featured Items**. This listing will not appear every time you go to the home page, but it will be shown on the site periodically. Another means of getting people to notice your auction is to publish the product listing in a bold-face font. This option costs $2.00.

eBay uses a database to manage the millions of auctions that it offers. The database evolves dynamically as sellers and buyers enter personal identification and product information. When a seller enters a product to be auctioned, the seller provides a description of the product, keywords, initial price, date, and personal information. This data is used to produce the product listings that the buyer sees (Fig. 23.2).

The auction process begins when the seller posts a description of the item for sale and fills in the appropriate registration information. The seller must specify a minimum opening bid. If potential buyers feel this price is too high, the item may not get any bids. In many cases, a *reserve price* is set. A reserve price is the lowest price that the seller will accept. Sellers can set the reserve price higher than the minimum bid. However, if no bid meets the reserve price, the auction is unsuccessful. For instance, if a classic automobile is auctioned with a starting bid of $15,000 and a reserve price of $20,000 and the highest bid reaches only $17,500, the auction is unsuccessful and the product is not sold. Therefore, it is best to set the reserve price at the same price as the minimum starting bid. Sellers might set the opening bid lower than the reserve price to generate bidding activity.

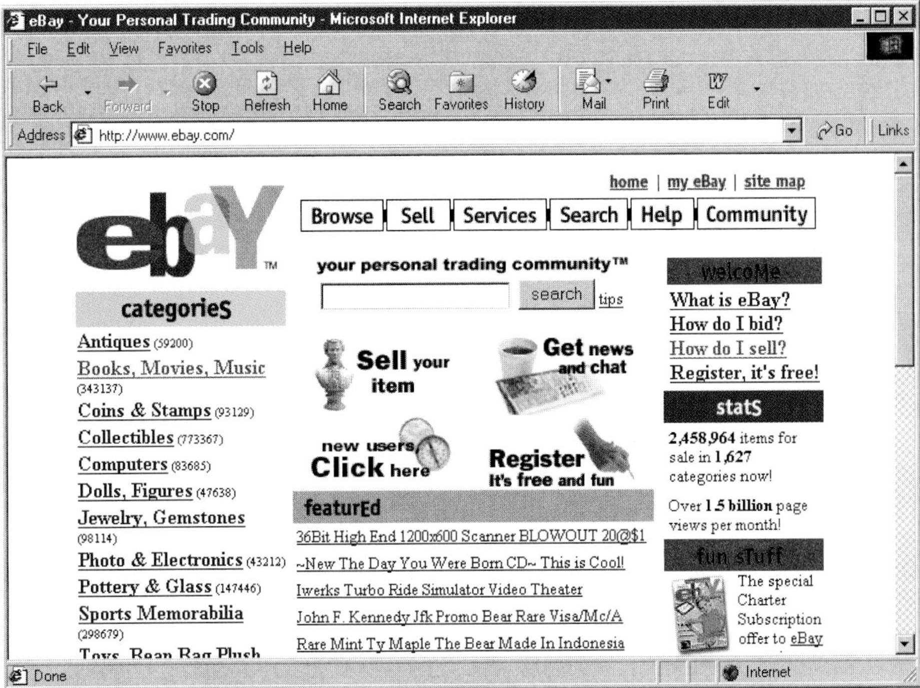

Fig. 23.1 eBay home page. (Courtesy of eBay.)

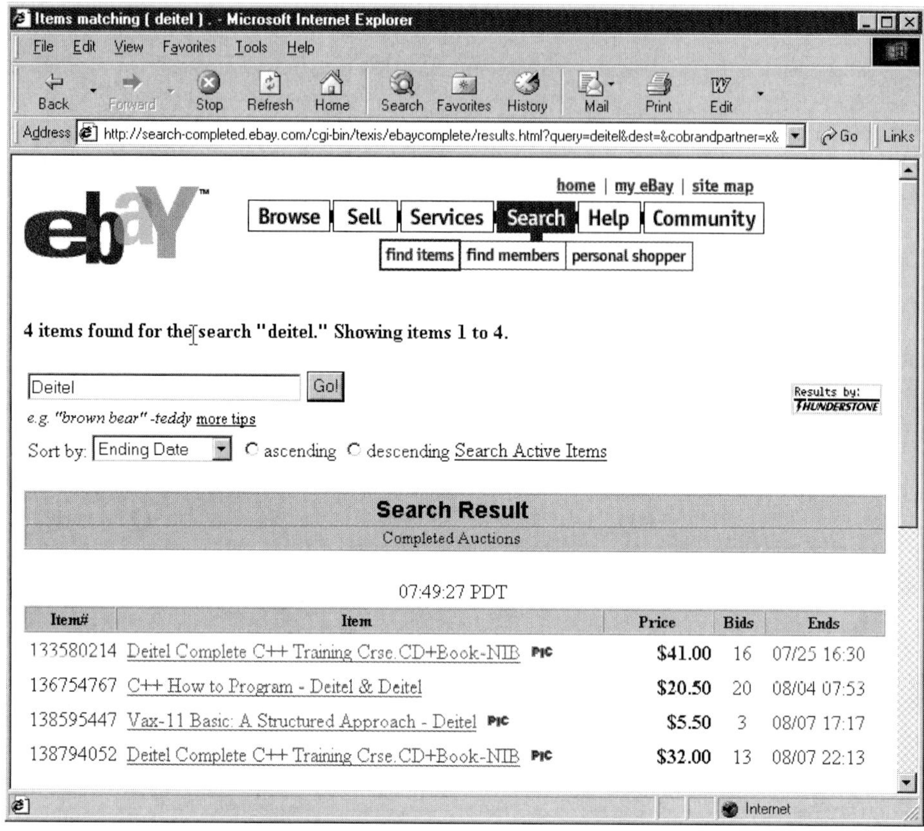

Fig. 23.2 Searching **`http://www.ebay.com`** for specific items up for auction. (Courtesy of eBay.)

If a successful bid is made, the seller and the buyer negotiate the shipping details, warranty and other particulars. eBay serves as a liaison between the parties—it is the interface through which sellers and buyers can conduct business. eBay does not maintain a costly physical inventory or deal with shipping, handling or other services that businesses such as Amazon and other retailers must provide.

eBay has spawned a number of new businesses that use the site as their means of selling products. These businesses depend on eBay to remain up and running continuously. To avoid down time, companies make investments in *high-availability computing* and *continuous-availability computing*. High-availability computing attempts to minimize down time; continuous-availability computing attempts to eliminate it completely. One key to such technologies is *fault-tolerant systems* that use *redundancy*. For example, every crucial piece of hardware—such as the processor, the disk and the communications channel—has one or more levels of backup, so, in a failure, the system simply shifts from a failed component to a backup component. The system keeps running while the failed component is fixed or replaced. The same is true of data. Companies cannot afford to lose their business data, so the data, too, is maintained redundantly.

Failure to keep businesses up and running can be costly, if not fatal. Companies such as Tandem and Stratus (and others) have based their businesses on continuous-availability and high-availability computing, respectively. For more information about these technologies, visit the Tandem Web site at **http://www.tandem.com** and the Stratus Web site at **http://www.stratus.com**.

There are several other online auction sites. A few of the largest auctions sites are Yahoo! Auctions at **http://auctions.yahoo.com**, Amazon Auctions at **http://www.amazon.com** and FairMarket, Inc. at **http://www.fairmarket.com**.

23.4 Online Trading

Another fast-growing area of e-commerce is online securities trading (Ho99) (We99). According to U.S. Bancorp Piper Jaffray, Company and Industry Sources (**http://www.piperjaffray.com/re/re_ne2.asp?id=188**), "online trading volumes accounted for 37 percent of all retail trades for the first half of 1999, up from 30 percent in the second half of 1998." The recent growth in online trading has put pressure on the major Wall Street firms to go online. Companies such as Charles Schwab, Merrill Lynch and many others have joined the online trading community.

Stock trades used to be handled only through brokers who were paid commissions for their services. Merrill Lynch, for example, has almost 15,000 brokers. As more people execute their trades on the Web without brokers, the number of brokers is likely to shrink dramatically. Online trading fees are nominal compared to traditional broker commissions.

For more information about e-commerce and online trading, check out the latest news reports and back issues of *Business Week* at **http://www.businessweek.com** and of *The Industry Standard* at **http://www.thestandard.com**.

23.4.1 Case Study: E*TRADE

One of the leaders in online trading is *E*TRADE* (Fig. 23.3). The company was founded in 1982 to offer online stock quotes to the nation's major investment firms. With the development of the Web, E*TRADE created a Web site (**http://www.etrade.com**) where individual investors could manage their own investments without the need for brokers.

Online trading is fast and cheap. Online trading companies such as E*TRADE and Ameritrade have made investing in stocks and options accessible to a larger audience.

At E*TRADE, you can buy, sell and research stocks, bonds and other securities. If you have little knowledge about buying and selling stocks, E*TRADE offers two games in which you use fake "game money" to carry out stock trades or stock and options trades. Each player is given $100,000 in virtual trading dollars to start. Game players have access to charts, graphs and recent news articles to help them choose their investments. There is no risk of losing real money, so the players can feel free to experiment with different trading strategies. Each trade takes approximately one minute to process. The goal of each game is, of course, to increase the value of your portfolio. The E*TRADE games are a friendly way for beginners to experiment with online trading. Players compete for real cash prizes. The two players with the highest-valued portfolios at the end of each trading game receive $1000 each. The trading games last one month. To play the E*TRADE games and to learn more about online trading, visit **http://www.etrade.com**. An exercise at the end of the chapter encourages the reader to play the E*TRADE game. If you win the prize, please let us know!

Fig. 23.3 E*TRADE[1] home page. (All images from **`http://www.etrade.com`** are copyright 1999 E*TRADE Securities, Inc. Used with permission. All rights reserved.)

23.5 Other E-Businesses

E-commerce is forcing traditional offline companies to transform into e-businesses or else they risk losing market share to competitors, including fast-moving Internet start-ups. One of the best e-business successes is *Dell Computer Corporation*. Dell took their thriving offline business and turned it into an e-business phenomenon, generating more than $30 million in sales through their Web site each day. Founded in 1984 as a mail-order catalog business, Dell's business model was to sell made-to-order computers directly to the customer. Their Web site is logically organized by customer category and easy to use. For more information about Dell, visit their Web site at **`http://www.dell.com`**.

Approximately two thirds of Dell's online sales are business-to-business transactions. Business-to-business e-commerce is growing exponentially. By one estimate, business-to-business transactions could reach $1 trillion by 2004. Manufacturers, service companies and wholesalers that sell their products to other businesses are finding tremendous success online. Established companies that delay shifting to e-commerce risk losing market share to fast-moving Internet start-up companies.

1. E*TRADE is a registered trademark of E*TRADE Securities, Inc. Other marks of E*TRADE that appear on its Web site are owned worldwide exclusively by E*TRADE Group, Inc. or its subsidiaries.

E-commerce is also creating opportunities for many new types of businesses. People are turning their hobbies into profitable businesses on the Web. There are companies, such as **ebates.com**, that do not even have a product. **ebates.com** is simply an affiliate of many online retailers. Here is how it works. **ebates.com** signs up with online merchants to be an affiliate, thus earning referral fees each time a customer clicks from **ebates.com** to the merchant's site and makes a purchase. Customers sign up to become members. Each member is given an **ebates.com** email address that they must use for purchases. When a customer follows a link from **ebates.com** to one of the affiliated merchant sites and makes a purchase, the merchant sends back an email confirming the amount of the purchase to the customer's **ebates.com** address. **ebates.com** uses the purchase information to update the customer's account with the amount of rebates owed. The company passes the referral fees it earns from its affiliates on to the individual consumer. **ebates.com** makes money by selling banner ads on their site. For more information, visit **http://www.ebates.com**.

The possibilities on the Web are vast. In the exercises at the end of this chapter, we encourage students to design your own e-business.

23.6 Security

Privacy issue: Would you want to transmit your credit-card number if you knew unauthorized parties might tap this information? *Integrity issue*: How can you determine whether information sent to you has been altered by a hacker? *Authentication issue*: How do you confirm that the company receiving your information is a reputable business? *Non-repudiation issue*: How do you legally prove that a message was sent? These questions address four of the fundamental requirements of a successful, secure transaction. In this section, we will discuss how these requirements are achieved by using various popular e-commerce security mechanisms.

Everyone using the Web for e-commerce needs to be concerned about the security of their personal information. There are several protocols that provide transaction security, such as *Secure Sockets Layer (SSL)* and *Secure Electronic Transfers™ (SET™)*. In the next several sections we will discuss these security protocols, plus *public-key cryptography*, *digital signatures* and *digital certificates*. We will also present case studies on companies such as VeriSign and CyberCash that employ these technologies to help e-businesses meet security challenges.

23.6.1 Public-Key Cryptography

The channels through which data passes over the Internet are not secure; therefore, any private information that is being passed must be protected (De90) (Di98) (Ko97). To secure information, data can be encrypted. *Cryptography* transforms data by using a *key* to make the data incomprehensible to all except its intended receivers. Unencrypted data is called *plaintext*; encrypted data is called *ciphertext*. Only the intended receivers should have the corresponding key to decrypt the ciphertext into plaintext.

In the past, organizations wishing to maintain a secure computing environment used *symmetric cryptography*, also known as *secret-key cryptography*, in which the same secret key is used both to encrypt and to decrypt a message. In this case, the sender encrypts a message using the secret key, then sends the encrypted message and the secret key to the intended recipient. There are flaws in this system. First, the privacy and integrity of the message could be compromised if the key is intercepted as it is passed between the sender and the receiver over insecure channels. Also, since both parties in the transaction use the same key to encipher and decipher a message, you cannot authenticate which party created the message. Finally, a different key is required for each person to whom messages are to be sent, so organizations could have huge numbers of secret keys to maintain.

A much higher degree of security is needed to make electronic commerce feasible. Public-key cryptography, which is *asymmetric*, is a more secure method. It uses two related keys—a *public key* and a *private key*. The private key is kept secret by its owner. The public key is freely distributed. If the public key is used to encrypt a message, only the corresponding private key can decrypt it, and vice versa. Each party in a transaction has both a public and a private key. To transmit a message securely, the sender uses the receiver's public key to encrypt the message. The receiver decrypts the message using the receiver's unique private key. No one else knows the private key, so the message cannot be read by anyone other than the intended receiver; this ensures the privacy of the message.

A digital signature, the electronic equivalent of a written signature, was developed to be used in public-key cryptography, to solve the problems of authentication and integrity. Authentication provides the receiver with proof of the sender's identity. A digital signature is legal proof of the sender's identity, and, like a written signature, it is difficult to forge. To create a digital signature, the sender takes the original plaintext message and runs it through a *hash function*, which is a mathematical calculation, to give the message a *hash value*. The hash function could be as simple as adding up all the 1s in a message, though it is usually more complex. The hash value is also known as a *message digest*. The chance that two different messages will have the same message digest is statistically insignificant. The sender uses its private key to encrypt the message digest, thus creating the digital signature and authenticating the sender, because only the owner of that private key could encrypt it. The original message encrypted with the receiver's public key, the digital signature and the hash function are sent to the receiver. The receiver uses the sender's public key to decipher the digital signature, and reveal the message digest. The receiver then uses its own private key to decipher the original message. Finally, the receiver applies the hash function to the original message. If the hash value of the original message matches the message digest included in the signature, then the message has integrity—it has not been altered in transmission.

One problem with public-key cryptography is that anyone with a set of keys could potentially pose as the sender. For example, say a customer wants to place an order with an online merchant. How does the customer know that the Web site being accessed, indeed belongs to that merchant and not to a third party that posted a site and is masquerading as that merchant to steal credit card information? *Public Key Infrastructure (PKI)* adds *digital certificates* to this process for authentication. A digital certificate is issued by a *certification authority (CA)* and signed using the CA's private key. A digital certificate includes the name of the subject (the company or individual being certified), the subject's public key, a serial number, an expiration date, the authorization of the trusted certification authority and any other relevant information (Fig. 23.4). A CA is a financial institution or other third party, such as *VeriSign*, that issues certificates to its customers to authenticate the subject's identity and bind the identity to a public key. The CA takes responsibility for authentication, so it must carefully check information before issuing a digital certificate. Digital certificates are publicly available and are held by the certification authority in certificate repositories.

VeriSign, Inc. is one of the leaders in online security. VeriSign develops PKI and digital certificate solutions. For more information about VeriSign, visit **http://www.verisign.com**. For a listing of other digital certificate vendors, please see the Internet and World Wide Web Resources section at the end of the chapter.

Many people still perceive e-commerce to be insecure. In fact, transactions using PKI and digital certificates are more secure than the exchanging of private information over phone lines, through the mail or even paying by credit card. The key algorithms used in most transactions are nearly impossible to compromise. By some estimates, the key algorithms used in public-key cryptography are so secure that even millions of computers working in parallel could not possibly break the code in a century.

RSA Security Inc. is the leader in online security. RSA was founded in 1982 by three MIT professors, Rivest, Shamir and Adleman, the inventors of the *RSA Public Key Cryptosystem*. Their encryption and authentication technologies are used by most Fortune 100 companies and leading e-commerce businesses. With the emergence of the Internet and the World Wide Web, their work related to security has become even more significant and plays a crucial role in e-commerce transactions. Their encryption products are built into more than 450 million copies of the most popular Internet applications, including Web browsers, commerce servers and email systems. Most secure e-commerce transactions and communication on the Internet use RSA products. For more information about RSA, cryptography and security, visit **http://www.rsasecurity.com**.

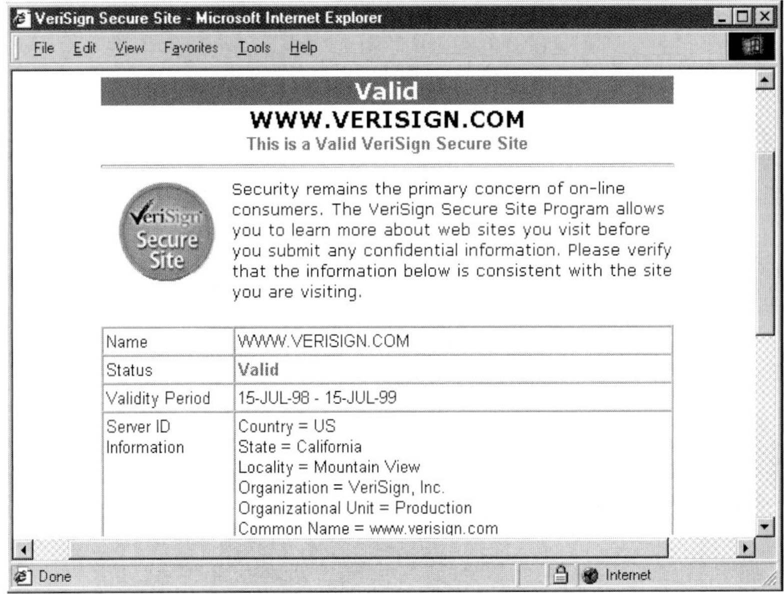

Fig. 23.4 VeriSign digital certificate. (Courtesy of VeriSign.)

23.6.2 Secure Sockets Layer (SSL)

The SSL protocol, developed by Netscape Communications, is a non-proprietary protocol commonly used to secure communication on the Internet and the Web (Ab99) (Ws99). SSL is built into many Web browsers, including Netscape Communicator, Microsoft Internet Explorer and numerous other software products. It operates at the network level, between the Internet's TCP/IP communications protocol and the application software.

In a standard correspondence over the Internet, a sender's message is passed to a socket that interprets the message to TCP/IP. TCP/IP (Transmission Control Protocol/Internet Protocol) is the standard set of protocols used for communication between computers on the Internet. Most Internet transmissions are sent as a (possibly large) set of individual message pieces, called *packets*. At the sending side, the packets of one (possibly long) message are numbered sequentially, and error-control information is attached. TCP routes packets to avoid traffic jams, so each packet might travel a different route over the Internet. At the receiving end, TCP makes sure that all of the packets have arrived, puts them in sequential order and determines if the packets have arrived with integrity and without alterations. If the packets have been altered, TCP/IP will re-transmit the packets. TCP/IP then passes the message to the socket at the receiver end. The socket translates the message back into a form that can be read by the receiver's application. In a transaction using SSL, the sockets are secured using public-key cryptography.

SSL uses public-key technology and digital certificates to authenticate the server in a transaction and to protect information as it passes from one party to another over the Internet. SSL transactions do not require client authentication. To begin, a client sends a message to a server. The server responds and sends its digital certificate for authentication. The client and server negotiate *session keys* to continue the transaction. Session keys are symmetric secret keys that are used for the duration of that particular transaction. Once the keys have been established, the communication proceeds between the client and the server by using the session keys and digital certificates.

Although SSL protects information as it is passed over the Internet, it does not protect private information, such as credit-card numbers, stored on the merchant's server. When a merchant receives credit-card information with an order, the information is often decrypted and stored on the merchant's server until the order is placed. If the server is not secure and the data is not encrypted, an unauthorized party could access the information.

For more information about SSL, check out the Netscape SSL tutorial at **http://developer.netscape.com/tech/security/ssl/protocol.html** and the Netscape Security Center Web site at **http://www.netscape.com/security/index.html**.

23.6.3 Secure Electronic Transaction™ (SET™)

Credit is a system whereby a person who can't pay gets another person who can't pay to guarantee that he can pay.
Charles Dickens

The Secure Electronic Transaction (SET) protocol, developed by Visa International and MasterCard, was designed specifically to protect e-commerce payment transactions (Ma98) (Me97) (Mk98). SET uses digital certificates to authenticate each party in an e-commerce transaction, including the customer, the merchant and the merchant's bank. Public-key cryptography is used to secure information as it is passed over the Web.

Merchants must have a digital certificate and special SET software to process transactions. Customers must have a digital certificate and *digital wallet* software. A digital wallet is similar to a real wallet. It stores credit (or debit) card information for multiple cards, as well as a digital certificate verifying the cardholders' identity. Digital wallets add convenience to online shopping; customers no longer need to re-enter their credit card information at each different site (An99).

Here is how an e-commerce transaction using SET works. When a customer is ready to place an order, the merchant's SET software sends the order information and the merchant's digital certificate to the customer's digital wallet, thus activating the wallet software. The customer selects the card for the transaction. The credit card and order information are encrypted by using the merchant's bank's public key and sent to the merchant along with the customer's digital certificate. The merchant then forwards the information to the merchant's bank to process the payment. Only the bank can decrypt the message. The merchant's bank then sends the amount of the purchase and its own digital certificate to the customer's bank to get approval to process the transaction. If the customer's charge is approved, the customer's bank sends an authorization back to the merchant's bank. The merchant's bank then sends a credit-card authorization to the merchant. Finally, the merchant sends a confirmation of the order to the customer.

In the SET protocol, the merchant never actually sees the client's proprietary information. Therefore, the client's credit-card number is not stored on the merchant's server, so this method reduces the risk of fraud.

Although SET is designed specifically for e-commerce transactions and provides a high level of security, it has yet to become the standard protocol used in the majority of transactions. Part of the problem is that SET requires special software on both the client and server side; that requirement creates additional costs. Also, the transactions are more time-consuming than transactions using other protocols, such as SSL.

SET Secure Electronic Transaction LLC is an organization formed by Visa and MasterCard to manage and promote the SET protocol. For more information about SET, visit these organizations online at **http://www.setco.org**, **http://www.visa.com** and **http://www.mastercard.com**. Visa has a demonstration of an online shopping transaction using SET at **http://www.visa.com/nt/ecomm/security/main.html**. GlobeSet, a digital-wallet software vendor, also offers a tutorial of a SET transaction that uses a digital wallet at **http://www.globeset.com/**.

23.6.4 Case Study: Microsoft Authenticode

How do you know the software you ordered online is safe and has not been altered? How can you be sure that you are not downloading a computer virus that could wipe out your computer? Do you trust the source of the software? With the emergence of e-commerce, software companies are offering their products online so that customers can download directly onto their computers. As a result, security is required to ensure that the downloaded software is trustworthy and has not been altered. *Microsoft Authenticode*, combined with VeriSign digital certificates (or *digital IDs*), authenticates the publisher of the software and detects whether the software has been altered (Mi96). Authenticode is a security feature built into Microsoft Internet Explorer.

Software publishers must obtain a digital certificate specifically designed for the purpose of publishing software. Certificates may be obtained through certificate authorities, such as VeriSign, as we described in section 23.6.1. To obtain a certificate, software publishers must provide their public key and identifying information and sign an agreement that they will not distribute harmful software. This gives customers legal recourse if any downloaded software from certified publishers causes harm.

Microsoft Authenticode uses digital-signature technology to sign software. Digital signatures are described in section 23.6.1. The signed software and the publisher's digital certificate provide proof that the software is safe and has not been altered.

When a customer attempts to download a file, a dialog box appears on the screen displaying the digital certificate and the name of the certificate authority. Links to the publisher and the certificate authority are provided, so that customers can learn more about each party before they agree to download the software. If Microsoft Authenticode determines that the software has been compromised, the transaction is terminated.

To learn more about Microsoft Authenticode and to read the white paper, visit **http://msdn.microsoft.com/workshop/security/authcode/authwp.asp**.

23.6.5 Online Payments; Case Study: CyberCash™

Ah, take the Cash, and let the Credit go,
Nor heed the rumble of a distant Drum!
Edward FitzGerald

No man's credit is as good as his money.
Edgar Watson Howe

To conduct e-commerce, businesses need to be able to accept payments through their Web sites a process that requires a high level of security and service. *CyberCash* is one of the leaders in secure-payment-processing solutions for e-businesses of all sizes (Fig. 23.5) (In99). In this section, we will outline a few of the payment-processing products.

CyberCash *CashRegister* enables e-businesses to accept credit-card payments. Businesses must first establish a *merchant account* with a financial institution. Once an account is in place, merchants can accept payments through their Web sites and transfer the funds directly into their merchant accounts. One of the benefits of using CashRegister is that CyberCash maintains all of the secure servers, so merchants are not responsible for storing customers' private credit-card information on their own servers. CashRegister uses the SSL and SET protocols to secure online transactions.

Digital wallets are making online shopping even more convenient for customers. There is no need to keep reentering your credit-card information at each site. *Instabuy*™ is the CyberCash digital wallet service. Customers can sign up for Instabuy and use their wallet at hundreds of participating merchant sites worldwide. Customers just click on the Instabuy logo at participating merchant sites and their order is placed. For more information about Instabuy, visit **http://www.instabuy.com**.

Throughout the chapter, we have commented on how e-commerce is changing the way business is done. Advancements in online payment systems are now making it possible for companies to send bills and collect payments over the Internet. CyberCash offers the

PayNow™ service, which gives merchants the ability to bill and collect payments online. Online billing can reduce costs for merchants by automating the billing process and eliminating the cost of postage. For more information about CyberCash products and services, visit **`http://www.cybercash.com`**.

23.7 XML and E-Commerce

We have studied HTML, which is a markup language used for publishing information on the Web. Content developers use a fixed set of HTML tags to describe the elements of online documents, such as headers, paragraphs, bold-face text, italicized text, etc.

XML (*Extensible Markup Language*) is not actually a markup language like HTML. Rather, it allows you to create customized tags unique to specific applications, so that you are not limited to using HTML's fixed set of publishing-industry-specific tags. For example, developers can make industry-specific (or even organization-specific) tags to categorize data more effectively within their communities. Some industries have already developed standardized XML tags for publishing documents online. For example, MathML (Math Markup Language) is a standardized XML-based language for marking up mathematical formulas in documents, and ChemML (Chemistry Markup Language) is a standardized XML-based language for marking up the molecular structure of chemicals.

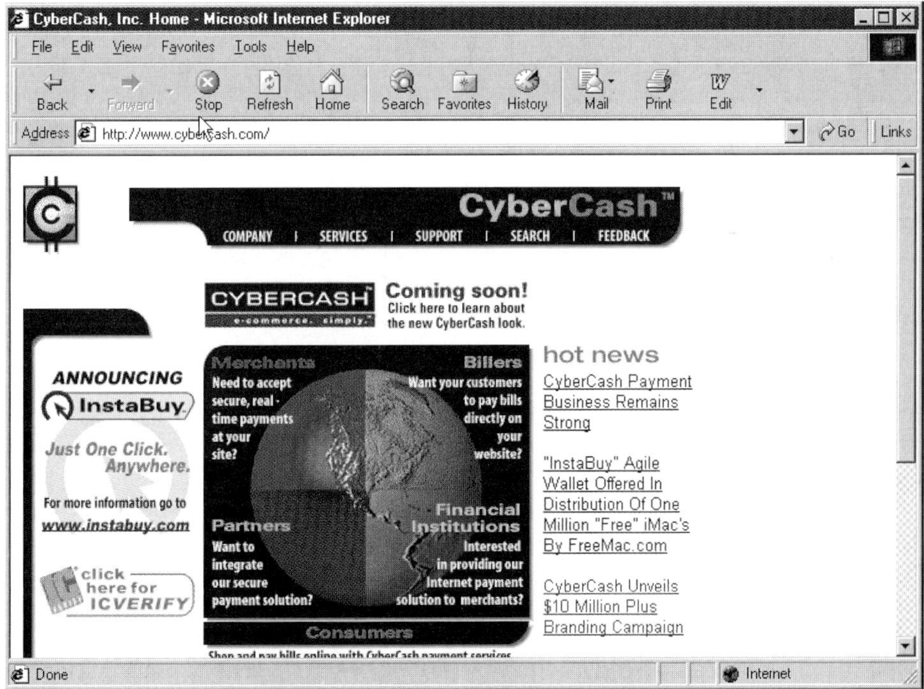

Fig. 23.5 CyberCash home page. (Copyright 1996-1999 CyberCash, Inc. Used with permission.)

The use of XML is growing quickly and is changing the way business is conducted over the Internet (Lv99) (Mr98) (Ud99) (Ba98). The ability to customize tags will allow business data to be used worldwide. For example, businesses could create XML tags specifically for invoices, electronic funds transfers or purchase orders. They could standardize tags for prices, the parties in the transaction, etc. XML will be used to define business transactions. In order to be used effectively, an industry's customized tags must be standardized across that industry.

Once tags are standardized, the browser must be able to recognize them. Either the tags can be built into the browser, or plug-ins could be downloaded. A customized XML tag could actually be used as a command for a browser to download the plug-in for the corresponding set of standardized tags.

The impact of XML on e-commerce is profound. XML gives online merchants a better means of tracking product information. By using standardized tags for data, bots and search engines are able to find products faster online.

Many industries are using XML to improve EDI. The health care industry, for example, uses XML to share patient information (even CAT scans) among health care-oriented applications. This helps doctors access information and make decisions faster, which can improve the care patients receive (Kw98).

The *Health Level Seven (HL7)* organization's *Application Protocol for Electronic Data Exchange in Healthcare Environments* uses XML. This standard enables health care-oriented applications to exchange data electronically by specifying the layout and order of information. Patient names, addresses, insurance providers, etc. are tagged so that they can be shared electronically among applications. Once a patient's identification information is entered, that information can be shared over the hospital's intranet with the labs and the accounting department, for example, thus eliminating the need to re-enter the same data. HL7 is a non-profit, ANSI (American National Standards Institute)-accredited Standards Developing Organization that focuses on clinical and administrative data. For more information on HL7, visit their Web site at **`http://www.HL7.org`**. The ANSI Web site is **`http://www.ansi.org`**.

The *XML Metadata Interchange Format (XMI)* is a standard that combines XML with UML (Unified Modeling Language). Software developers use UML to design object-oriented systems. XMI allows developers using object technology to tag design data. Using standardized XMI tags allows developers to exchange design data over the Internet and interact with multiple vendors using a variety of tools and applications. Thus, with XMI people worldwide can collaborate on the designs of object-oriented software systems. For more information about XMI, visit **`http://www-4.ibm.com/software/ad/features/xmi.html`**.

Software companies sell their products over the Web. The *Open Software Description Format* is an XML specification that enables the distribution of software over the Internet. Using OSD, developers tag the structure of an application and its files. The tags describe each component of the software and its relationship to the other components in the application. The ability to download software from the Web means vendors can save the time, resources and money previously required for creating boxed products and shipping them to customers.

Chapter 28 is a detailed introduction to XML. We have included many live-code examples to show you how XML is used to create customized markup languages.

23.8 Data Mining, Bots and Intelligent Agents

Searching through large amounts of data can be like searching for a needle in a haystack. *Data mining*, *shopping bots* and *intelligent agents* are tools that can help businesses and individuals dig through enormous amounts of information (Db95) (Id99) (Pa99). In this section, we describe how e-businesses and consumers benefit from these technologies.

Just as in mining for gold or rare gems, in data mining massive amounts of information are sifted through to find the few worthwhile "nuggets" or "gems" of information. Collected data is stored in a *data warehouse*. Information in a data warehouse may include sales data, customer profiles, demographic data or any other information a company needs to maintain.

Businesses are "data rich"; however, they often do not use their data to their best advantage. It would be extremely costly and time consuming to go through large amounts of data manually. Data mining uses a series of searches to find specific patterns and relationships within data. Businesses can use this information to analyze trends within their company or in the marketplace, information that in turn helps them market their products and run their businesses more effectively.

Data mining is expensive. The tools can cost millions of dollars. Despite the cost, data mining can often improve the bottom-line profitability of business. Bots make data mining even more effective. A bot allows you to make specific queries, thus eliminating the need for multiple searches. For example, individuals can use shopping bots to find specific products available through online retailers.

Intelligent agents are having a profound impact on e-commerce. Intelligent agents are smart bots that learn about customers over time by recording their preferences, actions and buying patterns. Intelligent agents enable e-businesses to offer a level of customer service similar to person-to-person interaction. For example, suppose a customer in Boston, Massachusetts is shopping for a new CD player and is looking at 5-disk CD players. In the past, this customer has bought a receiver and a dual-cassette player, both top-of-the-line. The customer has also bought a large number of CD-ROMs, including three different Rolling Stones CDs. An intelligent agent could recommend, based on the customer's buying history, a variety of top-of-the-line 5-disk CD players. It could also suggest a 100-disk CD changer that has just gone on sale and is now the same price as the 5-disk CD changer. Since the customer seems to be a Rolling Stones fan and the Stones have just announced they are playing in Boston in a few months, the intelligent agent could inform the customer and provide an option for buying tickets to the show.

Data mining provides a company with the information it needs to operate more effectively. Intelligent agents and bots allow the company to add a higher level of service and personalization to a Web site. These technologies can strongly differentiate a company from its competitors.

The following sections present case studies on some well known e-businesses using these technologies to change the way business is done. For more information on data mining, visit **`http://www.datamining.com/`**.

23.8.1 Case Study: `Priceline.com`

Employing the *name-your-price business model* has catapulted ***`Priceline.com`*** into the spotlight (Fig. 23.6). You can name-your-price by placing bids for airline tickets, hotel rooms, rental cars and mortgages. Their patented business mechanism, called the *demand-collection system*, is a shopping bot that takes customers' bids to the Priceline partners to see whether any of them will accept the price for the requested product or service.

The buying process is easy at **`Priceline.com`**. Let us use purchasing an airline ticket as an example. When looking for a domestic flight, you first enter your departure location, destination, bid price and the number of tickets you would like to purchase (Fig. 23.7). You then select the travel dates and airports in or near the departure or arrival cities (Fig. 23.8). The more flexible you are with your travel arrangements, the greater is your chance of winning a bid.

The **`Priceline.com`** bot presents the bid to the airlines and attempts to negotiate a fare below the customer's bid price. If the bid is accepted, **`Priceline.com`** retains the difference between the customer's bid and the actual fare price. The markup percentage varies with the price that is accepted by the airline. For domestic flights, the whole process takes one hour from the time the bid is placed.

`Priceline.com` is another excellent example of how the Internet and Web are profoundly changing the way business is conducted. In the case of airlines, hundreds of thousands of airline seats go empty each day. **`Priceline.com`** helps airlines sell these seats. **`Priceline.com`** sells the excess inventory at a discount, the airlines realize increased revenue and passengers save money.

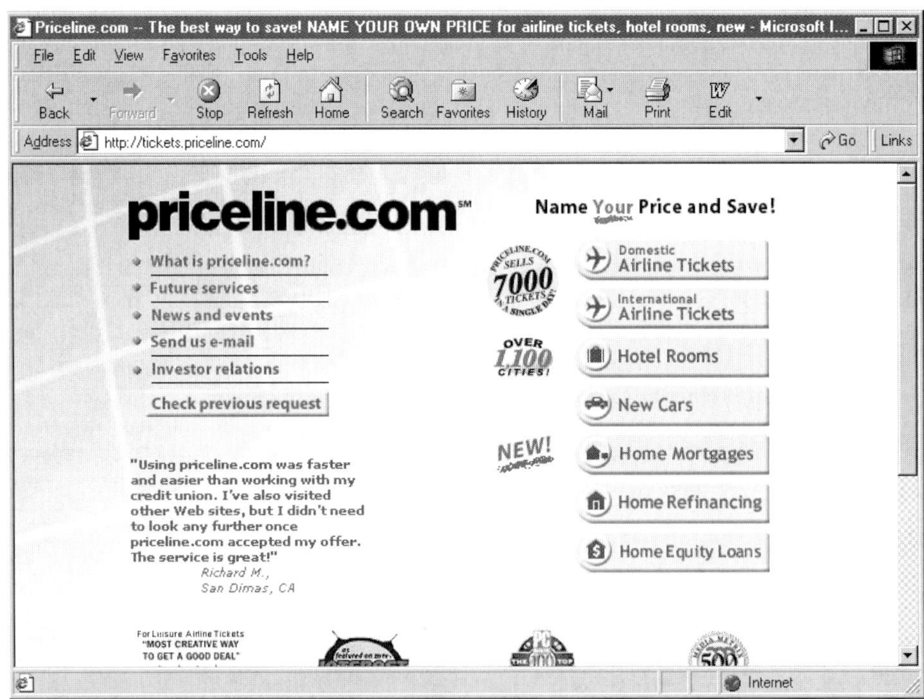

Fig. 23.6 **`Priceline.com`** home page. (Courtesy of **`Priceline.com`**.)

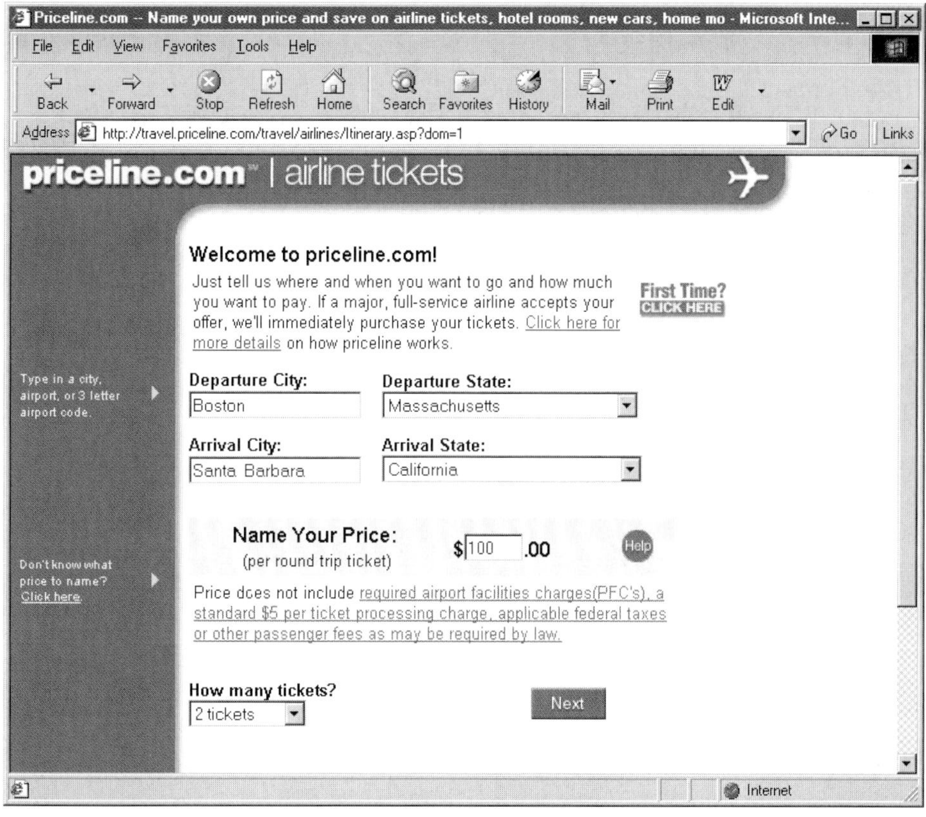

Fig. 23.7 Selecting a route and entering a bid for tickets with **Priceline.com**. (Courtesy of **Priceline.com**.)

23.8.2 Case Study: Travelocity.com

The travel service industry has achieved tremendous success on the Web in the past few years. Consumers are booking their travel itineraries online, often at lower prices than those available through travel agents. **Travelocity.com** is an online travel service that enables you to make all of your travel arrangements with a single visit to their Web site. You can book flights, rental cars, hotel rooms and vacation packages without involving a travel agent.

Travelocity.com also uses shopping-bot technology. For example, a customer who wishes to fly from New York to Los Angeles enters a time frame for the trip and airport codes to receive up-to-date fare information. The bot scans airline rate and scheduling databases for potential matches. The site then displays a list of flights that fit the submitted criteria, rate information and a ticket purchase option.

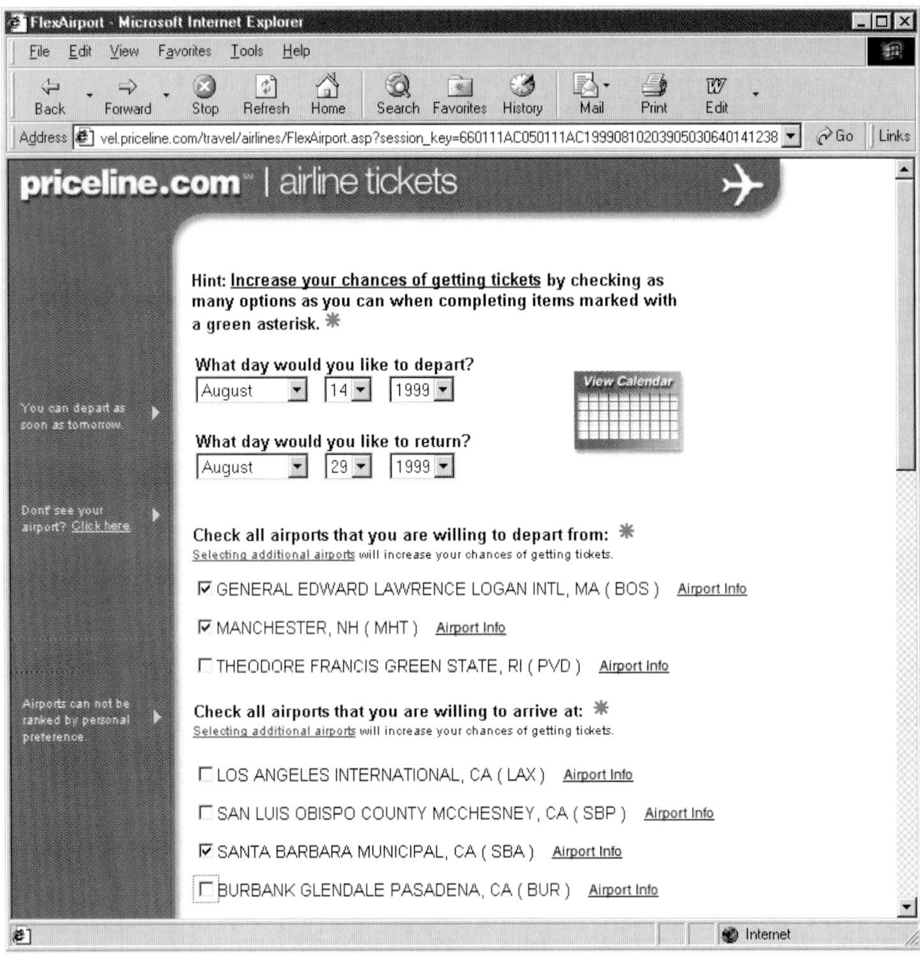

Fig. 23.8 Customers select multiple options to increase the chance of a successful bid on `Priceline.com`. (Courtesy of `Priceline.com`.)

23.8.3 Case Study: `Scour.net`

`Scour.net` uses bot technology to locate multimedia files on the Web. Users can find video clips, audio, images, live radio broadcasts and breaking news. In an instant, the bot "scours" the Web in search of the multimedia that the user specifies. **`Scour.net`** uses its SmartMatch intelligent agent to respond to customer queries, even if only partial names are entered and words are misspelled. It searches for specific file types, such as **`.mpg`** files for video and **`.au`** files for audio. Such searches would be difficult to conduct offline. Imagine trying to find multiple images of the Empire State building. Searching print resources or the Web would be time consuming. **`Scour.net`** automates the process and delivers the images you need in a matter of mouse clicks.

Currently, **`Scour.net`** (**`http://www.scour.net`**) is the most comprehensive multimedia search site available. Lycos offers a search for sounds and images within their search engine at **http://www.lycos.com**. Alta Vista also offers a multimedia search capability at **http://www.altavista.com**.

23.8.4 Case study: Bottomdollar.com

Have you ever gone comparison shopping to find the best price for a particular product? Chances are that you checked a few local stores or a handful of Web sites. Comparison shopping is time consuming, and customers are generally limited to a small number of resources. The Web gives customers access to a large number of stores worldwide. Shopping bots such as **Bottomdollar.com** can do comparison shopping for you (Mt99).

Bottomdollar.com uses intelligent-agent technology to search the Web to find the products you want at the best available prices. A customer can use **Bottomdollar.com** to search for a product or to browse the various categories on the site (Fig. 23.9). The service actually scans the catalogs of over 1000 online retailers to find the products you want at the best available prices. The search usually takes less than a minute. Imagine trying to visit 1000 different stores one-by-one to find the best price! **Bottomdollar.com** can save shoppers time and money.

Shopping bots and intelligent agents are changing the way people shop. Rather than going directly to the stores with established brand names, customers are using services like **Bottomdollar.com** to get the best available prices. Online retailers need to keep their prices competitive.

To check out **Bottomdollar.com**, visit **http://www.bottomdollar.com**. Similar shopping-bot services include **http://www.shopper.com**, **http://dealtime.com** and **http://www.mysimon.com**.

23.9 Case Study: Using Yahoo! Store to Set up an Online Store

Keep thy shop, and thy shop will keep thee.
George Chapman

There are many online *store-builder* solutions that allow merchants to set up online storefronts, complete with catalogs, shopping carts and order-processing capabilities. These fixed-price options are available to businesses of all sizes and are ideal for small businesses that cannot afford custom solutions or do not have secure merchant servers. *Yahoo! Store* is one of the most popular e-commerce store-builder solutions (Wi99) (Ne97). Yahoo! Store is available at **http://store.Yahoo.com** (Fig. 23.10).

Yahoo! Store charges a monthly fee based on the number of items you want to sell. This prepackaged product is designed to simplify setting up an online store. All of the features you need to set up a complete e-commerce site are included.

To set up your own demo store, go to **http://store.yahoo.com** and click the **Create a Store** link. Under **I'm a New User** click **Sign me up!** You will need to enter the address and name for your site. Click **Create**. You will be presented with the Yahoo! Store Merchant Service Agreement which you must accept before you can proceed to build your demo store. Your online demo store will be hosted for several days. Setting up a demo store is free, but you cannot accept orders through a demo store. After accepting the agreement, Yahoo! Store provides detailed directions to help merchants set up active online storefronts.

Fig. 23.9 `Bottomdollar.com` searches the Web for products and the best available prices. (Courtesy of WebCentric, Inc.—Owners and Operators of `Bottomdollar.com`.)

Yahoo! Store automatically sets up the front page with the name of your store. Then, you must create a name and a caption for the first product section of your store. Click **Update** when you are done. In Fig. 23.11, the name of the store is **The Deitel Book Shop**, the first product section is called **Books** and the caption appears below the section name.

After creating a product section, you may enter products to be listed in that section. First, click **Up** to get back to your home page, then click the **Books** product section button on the left side of the page. Click **New Item** to enter your first product. Each item must have a name, a product code, a price and any specific comments about the product. This information may be edited later. To add a picture to your product page, click **Image**. Select your own image from your computer and click **Send** to upload the image to your Yahoo! Store product page. The Web site in Fig. 23.12 is an example of a complete product page with an image. After all the products have been entered, you can click **Special** to feature any of the products on your home page. When your site is complete, click **Publish**.

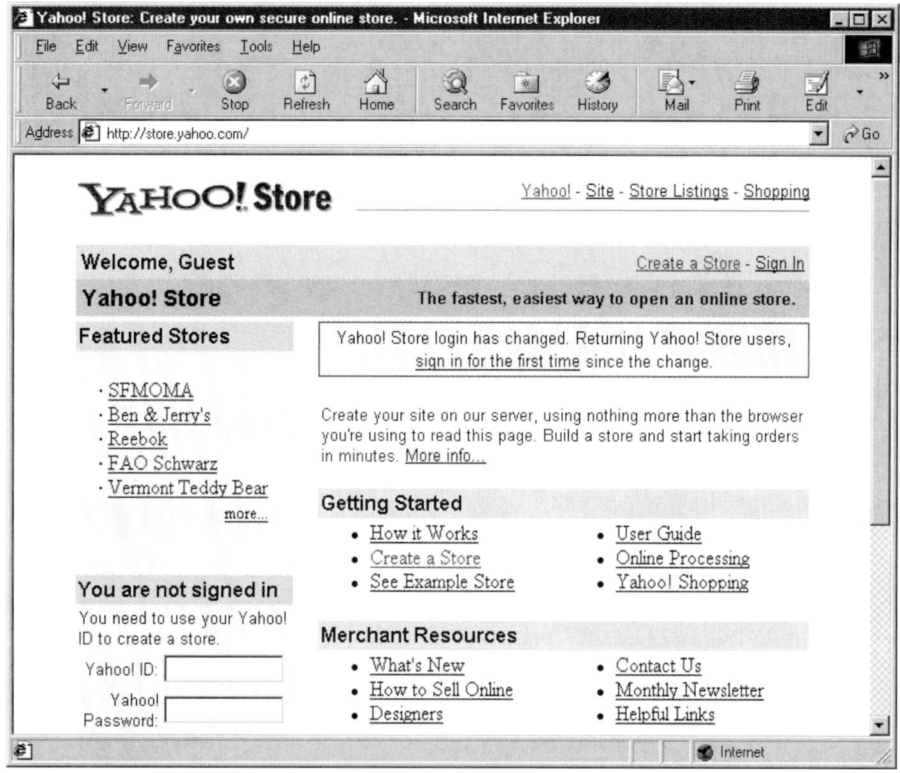

Fig. 23.10 Setting up an e-commerce site with Yahoo! Store. (Courtesy of Yahoo!)

You can change the style of your Web site by clicking on the **Look** button. There are several style templates. If you do not like the templates, you can select **Random** to change the colors and fonts. Yahoo! Store automatically sets up the shopping cart and secure order forms so customers can purchase products through your new Web site (Fig. 23.13).

To set up a working storefront where you can accept orders, you must sign on with Yahoo! Store and set up a merchant account, so that your site can accept credit-card payments. Generally, merchant banks and/or credit-card companies collect a small percentage of each transaction as their fee.

Yahoo! Store e-commerce sites are hosted on Yahoo! secure servers. Yahoo! maintains the servers on a *24-by-7 basis*—they keep your store up and running 24 hours per day and seven days per week. Yahoo! backs up all the information and provides SSL technology to encrypt all credit-card transactions handled through their stores.

There are many additional benefits to setting up a Yahoo! Store. Yahoo! Store merchants can track sales, see how customers are getting to their site, and use the Yahoo! wallet. Also, each Yahoo! Store is included in Yahoo! Shopping, so customers can access your store through a link at the Yahoo! Web site.

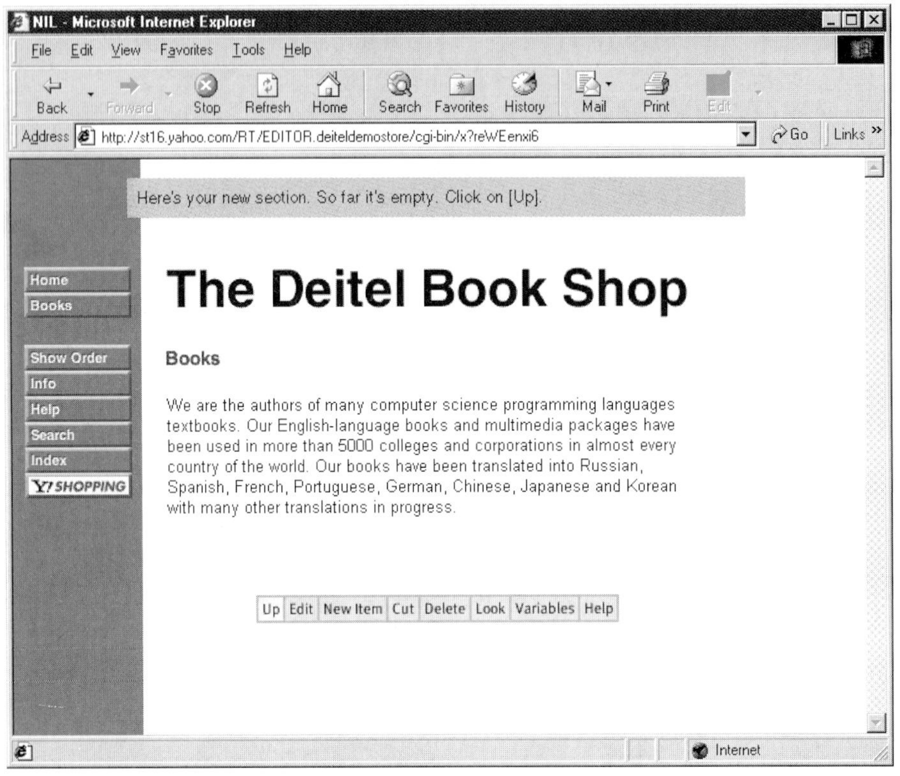

Fig. 23.11 Setting up the first product segment in our demo Yahoo! Store. (Courtesy of Yahoo!)

An exercise at the end of the chapter encourages you to set up a demo Yahoo! Store. There are several other store-builder solutions, such as SecureCC, Virtual Spin and iCat Web Store. **`Freemerchant.com`** is a free store-builder solution. They offer all the services you need to set up your own e-commerce site, including free hosting, Internet access, banking and a secure shopping cart. The free services are limited to basic functions. Most of the services they offer can be upgraded for a price. Other services are free for a trial period and can be purchased at a discount when the trial expires. For more information, visit **`http://www.freemerchant.com`**. URLs for additional information on store-builder solutions are listed in Section 23.14.

23.10 Commerce Server Case Study: Microsoft Site Server Commerce Edition

Large companies that need custom solutions can choose to build and maintain their own e-commerce sites. *Microsoft Site Server Commerce Edition* is a popular software package that allows companies to manage transactions, offer secure payment services using both the SSL and SET security protocols, support a large catalog of products, keep records of online transactions and even help design Web sites (Be98) (Dr98) (Sy98). Site Server Commerce Edition offers more options for an online business than pre-packaged e-commerce solutions such as Yahoo! Store or iCat Web Store. Site Server Commerce Edition is installed on a company's internal merchant servers.

Site Server Commerce Edition is designed for use with Microsoft Windows NT and Microsoft SQL Server. Microsoft Windows NT is an operating system that allows companies to build secure computer networks. Microsoft SQL Server is a powerful database product designed for large organizations. Microsoft SQL Server is a commercial-quality, business-critical database application that allows you to store massive amounts of such information as consumer profiles, employee information, etc. Microsoft Site Server Commerce Edition also includes Visual InterDev, which is Microsoft's high-end Web-site development software.

Microsoft Site Server Commerce Edition is more powerful than most of the prepackaged store-builder solutions, but is also more costly to license, manage and support. Initial licensing fees, at the time of publication, start at just under $5,000. Also, to run successful online stores, merchants must maintain their own 24-by-7 support. This is a tremendous commitment and is essential to e-commerce success.

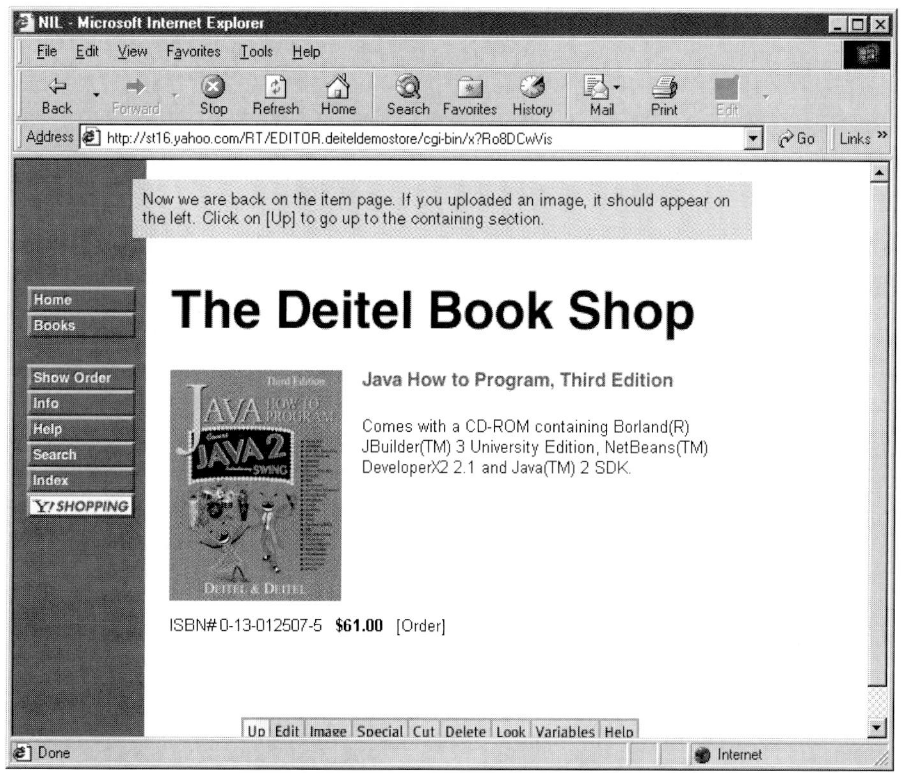

Fig. 23.12 A sample catalog page in our demo Yahoo! Store. (Courtesy of Yahoo!)

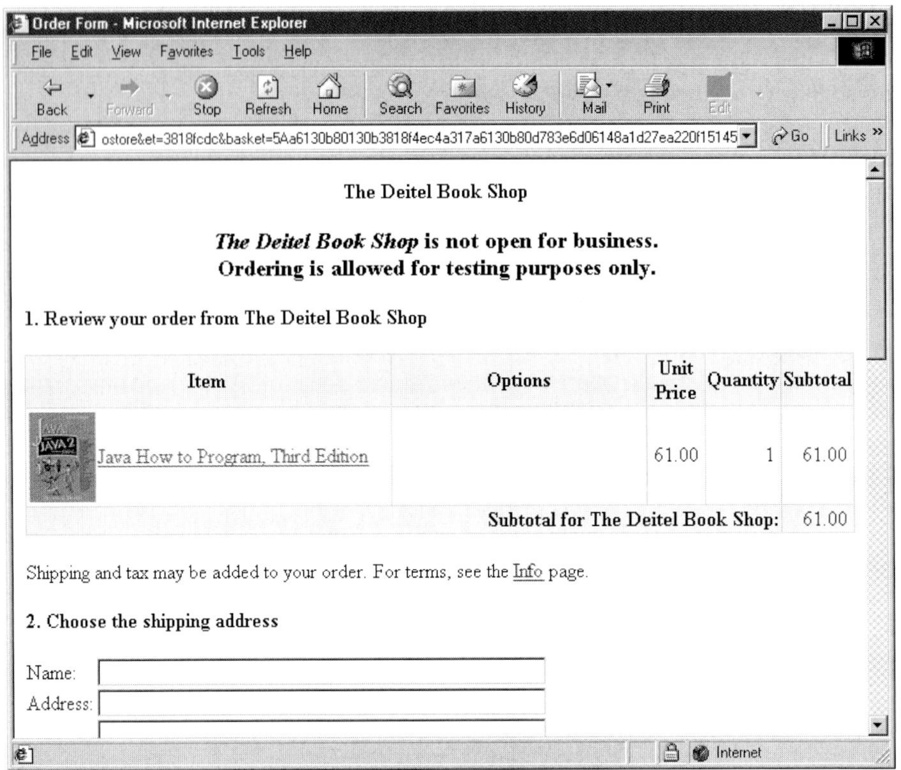

Fig. 23.13 Yahoo! Store shopping cart. (Courtesy of Yahoo!)

For more information, visit **`http://www.microsoft.com/siteserver/commerce/`**. Similar products include Netscape's CommerceXpert, available at **`http://home.netscape.com/commapps/solutions/index.html`**, IBM's Net.Commerce, available at **`http://www.software.ibm.com/commerce/net.commerce/`**, and Art Technology Group's Dynamo Commerce Server, available at **`http://www.atg.com/products/dcs/commerce_station.html`**.

23.11 E-Commerce Core Technologies

Time is the measure of business, as money is of wares.
Francis Bacon

In this section, we summarize the core technologies required to build e-commerce Web sites. We have mentioned how profoundly e-commerce is changing the way business is conducted. We have presented many case studies of well-known e-businesses, to familiarize you with their operation and their key business premises. Now, we focus our attention on enumerating the common technologies at the core of these businesses. In Chapters 24 through 29, we employ several of these technologies as we demonstrate how to implement several Web-based applications.

One of the most common e-commerce technologies is the shopping cart. Shopping-cart technology enables order-processing through a Web site. It is supported by the database of products that is hosted on the merchant server. We discuss databases in depth in Chapter 25 and then implement systems that use database technology in Chapters 26, 27 and 29.

Public-key cryptography ensures the privacy of messages transmitted over the Internet. It uses asymmetric key pairs to encrypt and decrypt messages, so that they may be read only by the intended receiver(s).

A digital signature, the electronic equivalent of a written signature, is used with public-key cryptography to solve the problem of authentication. A digital signature provides the receiver of a message with legal proof of the sender's identity. A digital signature is created by applying a hash function to a message to create a message digest and then encrypting the message digest with the sender's private key.

A digital certificate is issued by a certification authority (CA) and signed by using the CA's private key. A digital certificate typically includes the name of the subject (the company or individual being certified), the subject's public key, a serial number, an expiration date, the authorization of the trusted certification authority and any other relevant information. A CA is a financial institution or other third party that issues certificates to its customers to authenticate the subject's identity. Digital certificates are publicly available and are held by the certification authority in certificate repositories.

Secure Sockets Layer (SSL) uses public-key technology and digital certificates to authenticate the server in a transaction and to protect information as it passes from one party to another over the Internet. SSL transactions do not require client authentication. Once a secure connection is made, SSL uses symmetric secret keys (called session keys) to continue the transaction.

The Secure Electronic Transaction (SET) protocol uses digital certificates to authenticate each party in an e-commerce transaction, including the customer, the merchant and the merchant's bank. Public-key encryption is used to secure information as it is passed over the Web.

High-availability computing minimizes down time; continuous-availability computing attempts to eliminate down time completely. Redundant hardware, software, network connections and data are crucial to these kinds of computing.

Shopping bots and agents are giving consumers the ability to search the Web more effectively. Currently, bots and intelligent agents are commonly used for comparison shopping. In the future, more e-businesses will use intelligent agents to offer personalized customer service on the Web without human interaction with the customer. Intelligent agents are bots that learn about a customer over time by recording preferences, browsing patterns and purchases, to service the customer better in the future.

A popular way to customize Web pages is via *cookies* (En97). Cookies are small files sent from an e-business's server to a customer's client computer. Cookies store information on the user's computer for retrieval later in the same browsing session or in future browsing sessions. Cookies can be used, for example, in a shopping application, to indicate the client's identity, personal information and preferences. In a subsequent communication, the merchant can examine the cookie(s) it sent to the client in a previous communication, identify the client and the client's preferences and immediately display products of interest to the client. We discuss cookies in detail and show how to program with them in Chapters 26 and 27.

The *Unicode* standard can be used to encode the symbols of the world's "commercially viable" languages. Even third-world countries can now communicate more effectively with the rest of the world, and vice versa. Character sets for specific industries and specialized occupations have also been included in the standard. For instance, mathematicians now use specialized characters in their research documentation.

The Internet and advancements in e-commerce have made standard character-encoding methods even more important. As internationalization increases, Unicode will support the flow of information by providing a universal standard for character communication. For more information on the Unicode character set, visit the Web site **http://www.unicode.org**.

23.12 Future of E-Commerce

There are several key technology trends that will affect the future of e-business. Technology is evolving so rapidly that, literally every week, computer manufacturers advertise more powerful computers for less money. The physical size of memory has decreased so much that you can buy 12GB (i.e., 12 billion characters of memory) hard drives on notebook computers. Our ability to access bits is getting easier. The number of bits available on disks and in main memories is growing and the cost per bit is declining. Communication is getting faster and cheaper. Increased competition has prompted companies to provide greater bandwidth. As a result, we are able to transmit a larger number of bits per second and at a lower cost, than we could just a year ago.

The ability to transmit more information more cheaply will lead to increased ability to use the Internet for *streaming audio and video*, so that it will be easy to transmit sounds, voices, images, animations and videos. Also, advances in technology are making it possible for individuals to afford the computer power that was once available only to large organizations. This combination will make it possible for individuals to run their own radio and television stations right on the Web. Imagine the possibilities!

The Web is also making it worthwhile for companies to conduct smaller transactions—even micro-payments (measured in millicents—thousandths of a penny). For example, consider pay-per-view movies. Currently, many cable operators charge about $3.95 for a movie, which is generally several hours in length. But what about a four-minute music video? It probably is not worthwhile for cable companies to offer short videos because they could not charge more than a small fraction of the cost of a feature film; but with the Web and the increased bandwidth, streaming audio and video on demand to an individual will generate loads of new business based on smaller transactions. We can already see it happening with MP3. Now you can download a single song right off the Web, rather than going to your local music store to purchase the CD.

The Internet is creating opportunities for many new types of businesses. It is greatly impacting existing businesses. Egghead Software, for example, closed its retail stores in 1998 to become an Internet-only business. People are turning their lifelong hobbies into lucrative e-businesses by selling and trading goods over the Web. People are also creating businesses based on e-businesses that already exist. For example, there are people who are using eBay and other on-line auction sites as their Internet store fronts to sell or trade goods and services.

People are becoming more comfortable with purchasing over the Internet as the general public is becoming more Web-savvy. As the number of households with Internet access continues to grow significantly, experts predict that e-commerce will grow from under $10 billion in 1999 to over $100 billion by 2003. The Web is becoming the world's store front, and even small businesses are competing globally rather than just locally. Diverse cultures are doing business together. It is truly a small world, and the Web is making it even smaller.

23.13 Internet Marketing: Increasing Traffic at Your Web Site

How do you get people to visit your site? As the number of Web sites increases, marketing your site becomes more important. There are a number of inexpensive ways to increase traffic to your site. There are also several free Internet marketing resources available. We include URLs for Internet marketing resources in Section 23.14.

Traffic on Web sites is measured by hits. A *hit* is recorded for every file transfer from the server to the browser. For example, a Web page containing three images generates four hits—one for the text and one for each image. Therefore, you can only estimate the number of visitors to a site based on the number of hits. It is nearly impossible with current technology to get an exact count of visitors to a site.

Banner advertising is one means of marketing your site online. A banner ad is similar to the billboards you see along the side of the highway. Microsoft's LinkExchange, for example, posts your banner ad for free on thousands of Web sites, in exchange for your posting a LinkExchange banner on your own site. For more information on LinkExchange, visit **`http://www.linkexchange.com/`**.

Companies such as **`Adsmart.net`**, **`Valueclick.com`** and **`Doubleclick.com`** also offer banner-hosting services. Some companies charge you based on the number of times your banner ad is viewed on a page. Other companies charge you based on the number of click-throughs generated by your banner ad; you only pay when a viewer clicks on the banner ad and goes to your Web site. For more information, visit **`http://www.adsmart.net`**, **`http://www.valueclick.com`** and **`http://www.doubleclick.com`**.

You can help search engines by providing specific key information about your site in ***`META`*** *tags*. **`META`** tags are hidden tags on your Web site that allow you to specify keywords to describe your site. Using **`META`** tags correctly and effectively can help search engines find your site and categorize it properly. We described how to use **`META`** tags in Section 4.10.

Affiliate programs can also increase traffic at your site. We described the **`Amazon.com`** Associates Program is Section 23.2.1. Affiliates post links to your site in exchange for referral fees. Many affiliate programs offer a percentage of each sale or a fixed fee for click-throughs that result in sales. **`Befree.com`** is a fee-based service that helps you set up an affiliate program. For more information, visit **`http://www.befree.com`**.

Contests, promotional giveaways and games add value to a customer's browsing experience—these may keep people coming back to your site, though not always for the right reasons. You can also include an optional registration form on your Web site for people who are interested in receiving email newsletters about your e-business.

"Offline" marketing is an important and effective means of increasing traffic at your site, but it can be expensive. Companies use television, radio, newspaper and other "conventional" forms of advertising to create interest and awareness. Exhibiting at professional conferences and trade shows can help you meet potential customers, build mailing lists and create strategic alliances with other vendors.

23.14 E-Commerce Internet and World Wide Web Resources

Resources

`http://www.allec.com`
At the *All Electronic Commerce* Web site, you will find e-commerce news and general information. The site provides information on security, financial issues, reports, surveys, trends, corporate and product information, marketing news and links to other Web sites. They describe themselves as the "Navigational Hub of Electronic Commerce."

`http://ecommerce.internet.com/`
The *Electronic Commerce Guide* is a complete resource for e-commerce information including news, product reviews, an "Ask the Experts" section and library.

`http://www.cnet.com`
Cnet is an excellent source for technology news. You will find loads of articles, tutorials, resources and software reviews related to e-commerce.

`http://cism.bus.utexas.edu/`
The Center for Research in Electronic Commerce is a complete resource for e-commerce information. This site includes news, book lists, product information, FAQs, conferences, jobs and links to other e-commerce resources.

`http://www.tandem.com`
Visit the *Tandem* Web site for information on continuous-availability computing.

`http://www.stratus.com`
Visit the *Stratus* Web site for information on high-availability and continuous-availability computing.

`http://www.netscape.com/security/index.html`
The Netscape Security Center is an extensive resource for e-commerce security news, products and information.

Tutorials

`http://builder.cnet.com/Business/Tutorial/`
This on-line e-commerce tutorial walks you through the steps of creating an on-line store.

`http://developer.netscape.com/tech/security/ssl/protocol.html`
This is a tutorial on Secure Sockets Layer (SSL) from Netscape. There is also a FAQ with links to other SSL-related sites.

`http://webopedia.internet.com/Internet_and_Online_Services/Electronic_Commerce/`
Electronic Commerce from PCWebopedia is an encyclopedia of key e-commerce terms.

FAQs

`http://builder.cnet.com/Business/Ecommerce20/`
The *10 Questions on E-Commerce* site answers such key questions about E-commerce as "Are there any technology Standards for e-commerce?" and "What are the biggest barriers to e-commerce?"

Setting up an Online Store

`http://store.yahoo.com/`
Yahoo! Store is an easy way to set up your own online storefront.

http://www.freemerchant.com
Freemerchant.com offers a comprehensive, free e-commerce solution. Their free services include hosting, a secure shopping cart, a store-builder solution and auction tools.

http://www.securecc.com/
SecureCC is an e-commerce solution provider. Their software will allow you to set up a complete Internet storefront that uses the shopping-cart technology.

http://www.virtualspin.com/
Virtual Spin specializes in e-commerce software. Their Virtual Spin Internet Store™ allows you to set up your own storefront.

http://www.cybercash.com
CyberCash allows merchants to accept secure credit-card payments online.

http://www.2deg.com/
The Merchant Helper software helps you create Internet storefronts with shopping-cart technology.

http://www.clearcommerce.com/
ClearCommerce Merchant and Hosting Engine provides credit-card authorizations, order and payment processing, automated tax and shipping calculations, order tracking and Internet fraud detection.

http://www.microsoft.com/siteserver/commerce/default2.htm
The *Microsoft Site Server Commerce* site has the latest product information and downloads.

http://home.netscape.com/commapps/solutions/index.html
Visit *Netscape's Commerce Solutions* site for more information about CommerceXpert.

http://www.software.ibm.com/commerce/net.commerce/
IBM's Net.Commerce is a customizable solution that allows you to build secure e-commerce sites.

http://www.atg.com/products/dcs/commerce_station.html
The *Art Technology Group* Dynamo Commerce Server is a complete online storefront solution that allows you to build e-commerce sites.

SSL and SET

http://www.rsa.com/ssl/
Planet SSL, an RSA Data Security Web site, is an excellent resource for learning about SSL. You will find links to the latest news, FAQs and other SSL resources.

http://developer.netscape.com/tech/security/ssl/protocol.html
This Netscape page has a brief description of SSL, plus links to an SSL tutorial and FAQ.

http://www.netscape.com/security/index.html
The Netscape Security Center is an extensive resource for Internet and Web security. You will find news, tutorials, products and services.

http://psych.psy.uq.oz.au/~ftp/Crypto/
This FAQ has an extensive list of questions and answers about SSL technology.

http://www.setco.org/
The Secure Electronic Transaction LLC was formed through Visa and MasterCard to work on the SET specification. Visit this Web site to learn more about SET and the companies using SET in their products, and check out the brief FAQ and glossary.

http://www.visa.com/nt/ecomm/security/main.html
The *Visa International* security page includes information on SSL and SET. There is a demonstration of an online shopping transaction, which explains how SET works.

http://www.mastercard.com/shoponline/set/
The *MasterCard SET* Web site includes information about the SET protocol, a glossary of SET-related terms, the latest developments and a demonstration walking you through the steps of a purchase using SET technology.

Public-Key Cryptography

http://www.rsa.com/ie.html
RSA Data Security is a company that specializes in cryptography. Check out their detailed FAQ about cryptography.

http://www.entrust.com/
Entrust produces effective security software products using Public Key Infrastructure (PKI).

http://www.cse.dnd.ca/
The Communication Security Establishment has a short tutorial on Public Key Infrastructure (PKI) that defines PKI, public-key cryptography and digital signatures.

http://www.magnet.state.ma.us/itd/legal/pki.htm
The Commonwealth of Massachusetts Information Technology page has loads of links to sites related to PKI that contain information about standards, vendors, trade groups and government organizations.

Digital Signatures

http://www.ietf.org/html.charters/xmldsig-charter.html
The *XML Digital Signatures* site was created by a group working to develop digital signatures using XML. You can view the group's goals and drafts of their work.

http://www.elock.com/
E-Lock Technologies is a vendor of digital signature products used in Public Key Infrastructure. This site has a FAQ covering cryptography, keys, certificates and signatures.

http://www.digsigtrust.com
The Digital Signature Trust Co. is a vendor of Digital Signature and Public Key Infrastructure products. They have a tutorial titled "Digital Signatures and Public Key Infrastructure (PKI) 101."

Digital Certificates

http://www.verisign.com/
VeriSign creates digital IDs for individuals, small businesses and large corporations. Check out their Web site for product information, news and downloads.

http://www.thawte.com
Thawte Digital Certificate Services offers SSL certificates, developer certificates and personal certificates.

http://www.silanis.com/index.htm
Silanis Technology is a vendor of digital certificate software.

http://www.belsign.be/
Belsign issues digital certificates in Europe. They are the European authority for digital certificates.

http://www.certco.com/
Certco issues digital certificates to financial institutions.

Digital Wallets

http://www.globeset.com/
GlobeSet is a vendor of digital-wallet software. They have an animated tutorial demonstrating the use of an electronic wallet in an SET transaction.

http://www.trintech.com
Trintech digital wallets handle SSL and SET transactions.

http://wallet.yahoo.com
The *Yahoo! Wallet* is a digital wallet that can be used at thousands of Yahoo! Stores worldwide.

Data Mining

http://www.datamining.com/
Information Discovery, Inc. specializes in data-mining products. Check out their "Perspective on Data Mining" and the brief FAQ.

http://www.kdnuggets.com/
KDNuggets publishes a free biweekly newsletter for data mining. This site also has links to many data-mining tools, companies offering data-mining products, a list of related Web sites, a list of books, articles and other resources.

http://www.software.ibm.com/data/db2/
Visit this site for more information about IBM's DB2 data mining and data warehouse products.

Internet Marketing

http://www.adsmart.net
Adsmart sells online banner advertising. They post banner ads on hundreds of top Web sites. Advertisers can select from a variety of audiences to target specific markets.

http://www.valueclick.com
Value Click is a pay-per-click advertising solution. Advertisers pay for a fixed number of "click-throughs," where browsers click on the banner ad over the advertiser's Web site.

http://www.doubleclick.com
DoubleClick is a banner advertising network. Advertisers can select target audiences and run regional advertising campaigns.

http://www.linkexchange.com/
Microsoft's *LinkExchange* allows you to post your own banner ads in exchange for hosting LinkExchange banner ads on your Web site.

http://wwww.net-mercial.com
Net-mercial creates Internet commercials used to fill the time while a Web site is downloading or while a customer is browsing a site.

http://www.atWebsites.com/startaffiliate/index.html
This site is a step-by-step walkthrough explaining how to set up an affiliate program and to create your own affiliate program.

http://www.befree.com
beFree.com is an affiliate-program solution. Customers pay $5000 to set up a fully functional affiliate program. This site also has an explanation of affiliate marketing programs.

http://www.submiturl.com/metatags.htm
This site has a brief tutorial on **META** tags.

http://www.webdeveloper.com/html/html_metatags.html
The *Webdeveloper* **META** tag tutorial provides a detailed explanation of **META** tags.

http://companynewsletters.com/index.html
CompanyNewsletters.com will write your newsletter for you. Professional writers will research the topic, design the layout and write the newsletter. They specialize in both online and offline newsletters.

http://www.newsletters.com
This site is also a collection of newsletters. These newsletters are available on a 30-day free trial basis. You can publish your newsletters on Newsletter.com.

Organizations and Consortia

http://www.commerce.net/
CommerceNet is an international, non-profit organization supporting companies doing electronic commerce. This is an excellent resource for news, e-commerce resources, events and product listings.

http://icec.net/
The International Center for Electronic Commerce is a complete resource for e-commerce information.

http://www.crimson.com/market/
Dual-Use Marketplace is a forum for technologies and partnering ideas.

http://www.gbd.org/
Global Business Dialogue on Electronic Commerce is a collaboration among dozens of the world's top companies to promote more effective international e-commerce.

http://www.ecrc.ctc.com/
The Electronic Commerce Research Center site facilitates government efforts to become active in e-commerce. This organization offers training to the government in e-commerce strategy and technology. It offers links to e-commerce publications and to government Web sites focusing on e-commerce.

Online Magazines and News Sites

http://www.businessweek.com/ebiz/index.html
Check out the *Business Week* e.biz section for the latest news in online business. The e.biz section includes articles on the state of e-business, the leaders and key players in the industry and the hot (and not so hot) e-business stocks. It is an excellent resource for the latest news, and you can also read back issues to learn more about e-business as it has developed over the last few years.

http://www.thestandard.com
The Industry Standard is "the news magazine of the Internet economy." The site has an e-commerce section with the latest industry news, plus an archive of past articles. This is one of our favorite sources at Deitel & Associates, Inc.

http://www.ecommercetimes.com/
The E-Commerce Times is an excellent resource for e-commerce news. The site includes the latest headlines, success stories, product information, the "Small Business Advisor," job opportunities and links to related sites. The "Small Business Advisor" has information about starting up your own site, such as cost and selling strategies.

http://www.allec.com/Default.htm
At the *All Electronic Commerce* Web site, you will find e-commerce news and general information on the latest in e-commerce.

http://www.ecomworld.com/
Electronic Commerce World is a comprehensive online magazine featuring the latest e-commerce information.

http://www.internetnews.com/ec-news/
InternetNews online magazine has an e-commerce section with the latest e-commerce news stories.

http://www.internetworld.com/
Internet World magazine is a resource for Internet news. It has a section dedicated to e-commerce.

http://ecommerce.internet.com/opinions/merkow/
The *WebReference E-Commerce Watch* site provides recent news and past articles on e-commerce and technology.

http://www.iw.com/daily/stats/index.html
Internet World runs the *E-Commerce Statistics Toolbox* site, which offers statistical data on businesses and consumers participating in e-business. You will find statistics on anything from customers' perceptions of security in e-commerce to a forecast of the number of users who will be participating in e-commerce over the next few years.

http://www.arraydev.com/commerce/JIBC/
Journal of Internet Banking and Commerce is a free online journal dedicated to e-commerce news and information.

http://www.computerworld.com/home/emmerce.nsf/all/index
Computerworld E-Commerce is a biweekly publication dedicated to e-commerce.

http://www.online-commerce.com/
The eCommerce Guidebook site offers a step-by-step guide to help you set up your own e-commerce Web site. The site includes links to the vendors that provide e-commerce solutions.

http://www.eretail.net/
The *E-Retail Magazine* Web site includes news regarding online retailing.

http://www.techweb.com/netbiz/
The *NetBusiness* provides information you need to set up an e-commerce Web site. You will find helpful articles, links and even an ask-the-experts section.

SUMMARY

- To conduct e-commerce, merchants need to be able to organize an online catalog of products, take orders through their Web sites, accept payments in a secure environment and send merchandise to customers.
- The Internet and the World Wide Web have made it possible for even small businesses to compete with large companies.
- E-commerce allows companies to operate 24 hours a day, seven days a week, worldwide.
- One problem with conducting business over the Web is that the Internet is an inherently insecure medium.
- A shopping cart is an order-processing technology that allows customers to accumulate and store a list of items they wish to buy as they continue to shop.
- Supporting the shopping cart is the product catalog, which is hosted on the merchant server in the form of a database.
- Perhaps the most widely recognized example of an e-business using shopping cart technology is **Amazon.com**.
- The **Amazon.com** Associates Program, which is similar to what are commonly called affiliate programs in industry, allows Associates to post links to **Amazon.com** from their Web sites. If a customer uses the link to click over to Amazon and purchase a product, the associate receives a percentage of the sale as a referral fee.
- On-line auctions have become enormously successful on the Web. The leading company in this business is *eBay*, which at the time of publication was one of the most profitable e-businesses.
- eBay collects a percentage of the sale amount plus a small submission fee. The final fee is multi-tiered.

- eBay uses a database to manage the millions of auctions that it offers. The database evolves dynamically as sellers and buyers enter personal identification and product information.
- To avoid down time, companies make investments in high-availability computing and continuous-availability computing. The first attempts to minimize down time, the second attempts to eliminate it completely.
- Online trading is making it easier for people who might not otherwise buy and sell securities to do so at a low cost.
- One of the leaders in online trading is E*TRADE.
- The fundamental requirements of a successful, secure transaction are privacy, integrity, authentication and non-repudiation.
- Cryptography transforms data by using a key, which is a mathematical algorithm, to make the data incomprehensible to all except its intended receivers.
- In the past, corporations wishing to maintain a secure computing environment used symmetric cryptography, also known as secret-key cryptography, in which the same secret key is used both to encrypt and to decrypt a message.
- Public-key cryptography, which is asymmetric, uses two related keys—a public key and a private key. If the public key is used to encrypt a message, only the corresponding private key can decrypt it, and vice versa.
- A digital signature was developed to be used in public key cryptography to solve the problems of authentication and integrity.
- Authentication provides the receiver with proof of the sender's identity.
- To create a digital signature, the sender takes the original plaintext message and runs it through a hash function to give the message a hash value. The hash value is also known as a message digest. The sender uses its private key to encrypt the message digest, thus creating the digital signature and authenticating the sender since only to owner of that private key could encrypt it.
- Public Key Infrastructure (PKI) adds digital certificates to this process for authentication. A digital certificate is issued by a certification authority (CA) and signed using the CA's private key.
- A digital certificate includes the name of the subject (the company or individual being certified), the subject's public key, a serial number, an expiration date, the authorization of the trusted certification authority and any other relevant information.
- A CA is a financial institution or other third party, such as VeriSign, that issues certificates to its customers to authenticate the subject's identity and bind the identity to a public key.
- Digital certificates are publicly available and are held by the certification authority.
- Transactions using PKI and digital certificates are more secure than exchanging private information over phone lines, through the mail or even paying in person by credit card.
- The key algorithms used in most transactions are nearly impossible to compromise.
- RSA Security Inc. is the leader in online security. Most secure e-commerce transactions and communications on the Internet use RSA products.
- The SSL protocol, developed by Netscape Communications, is a non-proprietary protocol commonly used to secure communication on the Internet and the Web.
- SSL uses public-key technology and digital certificates to authenticate the server in a transaction and protect information as it passes from one party to another over the Internet.
- SSL transactions do not require client authentication.
- The client and server negotiate *session keys* to continue the transaction. Session keys are key pairs that are used for the duration of that particular transaction. Once the keys have been established,

the communication proceeds between the client and the server by using public-key cryptography and digital certificates.

- Although SSL protects information as it is passed over the Internet, it does not protect private information, such as credit card numbers, stored on the merchant's server.
- The Secure Electronic Transaction (SET) protocol, developed by Visa International and MasterCard, was designed specifically to protect e-commerce payment transactions.
- SET uses digital certificates to automatically authenticate each party in an e-commerce transaction, including the customer, the merchant and the merchant's bank. Public-key encryption is used to secure information as it is passed over the Web.
- Merchants must have a digital certificate and special SET software to process transactions. Customers must have a digital certificate and digital-wallet software.
- A digital wallet is similar to a real wallet. It stores credit (or debit) card information for multiple cards, as well as a digital certificate verifying the cardholder's identity.
- In the SET protocol, the merchant never actually sees the client's proprietary information. The client's credit card number is not stored on the merchant's server, so the risk of fraud is reduced.
- Although SET is designed specifically for e-commerce transactions and provides a high level of security, it has yet to become the standard protocol used in the majority of transactions.
- Microsoft Authenticode, combined with VeriSign digital certificates (or digital IDs), authenticates the publisher of the software and confirms whether the software has remained unaltered.
- Software publishers must obtain a digital certificate specifically designed for the purpose of publishing software.
- Microsoft Authenticode uses digital signature technology to sign software. The signed software and the publisher's digital certificate provide proof that the software is safe and has not been altered.
- To conduct e-commerce, businesses need to be able to accept payments through their Web sites, and that capability requires a high level of security and service.
- *CyberCash* is one of the leaders in secure-payment-processing solutions for e-businesses of all sizes.
- CyberCash CashRegister enables e-businesses to accept credit-card payments.
- A benefit of using CashRegister is that CyberCash maintains the secure servers, so merchants are not responsible for storing customers' private credit-card information on their own servers.
- *Instabuy* is the CyberCash digital wallet service. CyberCash offers the *PayNow* service, which gives merchants the ability to bill and collect payments online.
- Extensible Markup Language (XML) is a free, platform-independent, nonproprietary markup language extension used to develop customized forms and procedures for online documents.
- XML allows you to create customized tags unique to specific applications, so that you are not limited to using HTML's publishing-industry-specific tags.
- Data mining, shopping bots and intelligent agents are tools that can help businesses and individuals dig through the enormous amounts of information on the Internet.
- Data mining sifts through massive amounts of information to find the few worthwhile "nuggets" or "gems" of information.
- Collected data is stored in a data warehouse.
- Data mining is expensive. The tools can cost hundreds of thousands, even millions, of dollars.
- A bot allows you to make specific queries, thus eliminating the need for multiple searches.
- Intelligent agents are smart bots that learn about customers over time, by recording their preferences, actions and buying patterns.

- Intelligent agents and bots allow the company to add a higher level of service and personalization to a Web site.
- The **Priceline.com** bot presents the bid to the airlines and attempts to negotiate a fare below the customer's bid price. If the bid is accepted, **Priceline.com** retains the difference between the customer's bid and the actual fare price.
- **Travelocity.com** uses shopping-bot technology to search for flights, car rentals and hotel accommodations.
- **Scour.net** uses bot technology to locate multimedia files on the Web. Users can find video clips, audio, images, live radio broadcasts and breaking news.
- **Bottomdollar.com** uses intelligent-agent technology to search the Web to find the products you want at the best available prices.
- Yahoo! maintains the servers on a *24-by-7 basis*, backs up all the information and provides SSL technology to encrypt all credit-card transactions handled through their stores.
- *Microsoft Site Server Commerce Edition* is a popular software package that allows companies to manage transactions, offer secure payment services using both the SSL and SET security protocols, support a large catalog of products, keep records of online transactions and design Web sites.
- A popular way to customize Web pages is via *cookies*. Cookies are small files sent from an e-business's server to a customer's client computer.
- Cookies store information on the user's computer for retrieval later in the same browsing session or in future browsing sessions.
- The Unicode standard can be used to encode the symbols of the world's "commercially viable" languages.
- As internationalization increases, Unicode will support the flow of information by providing a universal standard for character communication.
- The ability to transmit more information more cheaply will lead to increased ability to use the Internet for *streaming audio and video*, so that it will be easy to transmit sounds, voices, images, animations and videos.
- The Web is also making it worthwhile for companies to conduct smaller transactions, even micropayments (measured in millicents—thousandths of a penny).
- As the number of households with Internet access continues to grow significantly, experts predict e-commerce will grow from under $10 billion in 1999 to over $100 billion by 2003.

TERMINOLOGY

1-click
24-by-7 support
affiliate programs
Amazon Associates Program
Amazon.com
asymmetric encryption
auctions online
authentication
authorization code
Bottomdollar.com
ciphertext
client
client/server computing
CommerceXpert products from Netscape
continuous-availability computing
cookies
CyberCash
database
data mining
data warehouse
decryption
Dell Computer Corporation
demand-collection system
digital certificates
digital IDs
digital signature

digital wallet
downtime
eBay
e-business
electronic funds transfer (EFT)
electronic data interchange (EDI)
elements
encryption
entities
E*TRADE
extensible markup language (XML)
fault-tolerant systems
Freemerchant.com
hash function
hash value
Health Level Seven (HL7)
high-availability computing
hit
integrity
intelligent agent
Instabuy
key
merchant account
merchant server
message digest
META tags
Microsoft Authenticode
Microsoft Site Server
name-your-price business model
non-repudiation
online auctions
online store builder
online trading
Open Software Description Format (OSD)
packets
PayNow
personalization
plaintext
Priceline.com
privacy
private key
public key
public-key cryptosystem
Public Key Infrastructure (PKI)
redundancy
reserve price in an eBay auction
RSA
RSA Public Key Cryptosystem
Scour.net
secret-key cryptography
secure electronic transaction (SET)
Secure Sockets Layer (SSL)
secure server
server
session keys
shopping bot
shopping cart
Site Server Commerce Edition (from Microsoft)
Standard Generalized Markup Language (SGML)
store-builder software
streaming audio and video
symmetric encryption
Travelocity.com
Unicode
VeriSign
wallet software
XML
XML Metadata Interchange Format (XMI)
Yahoo! Store

SELF-REVIEW EXERCISES

23.1 State whether the following are *true* or *false*. If the answer is *false*, explain why.

a) To conduct electronic commerce, a company must implement storefront technology.
b) Electronic Data Interchange (EDI) is the system that uses standardized electronic forms to facilitate transactions between businesses and their customers, suppliers, and distributors.
c) In continuous-availability computing, every crucial piece of hardware—such as the processor, the disk and the communications channel—has one or more levels of backup.
d) Down-time is one of the biggest threats to e-commerce.
e) In public-key technology, the same key is used to both encrypt and to decrypt a message.
f) A digital signature is created when a sender encrypts a message by using the sender's private key.

g) High-availability computing provides a higher level of service than continuous-availability computing.
h) Cryptography protects data being transferred over the Internet by transforming it to the point where it is incomprehensible to everyone but the intended user.
i) Secure Sockets Layer protects data stored on the merchant server.
j) Secure Electronic Transaction is another name for Secure Sockets Layer.
k) A digital signature is extremely difficult to alter or reproduce.
l) A merchant account gives companies the ability to accept a customer's credit card as payment for their products.
m) A shopping bot is a shopping cart that allows you to buy items from different stores, all at the same time.
n) A digital certificate is created by encrypting a digital signature.
o) XML allows developers to create unique tags to define specialized data.

23.2 Answer each of the following questions.
a) Customers are able to store products they wish to purchase in a ______ while they continue to browse the online catalog.
b) Public Key Encryption uses two types of keys of keys, the ______ and the ______.
c) ______ learn more about a customer over time.
d) Companies search large amounts of data using ______ technology in order to find patterns and correlation in the data.
e) The type of cryptography in which the message sender and receiver both hold an identical key is called ______.
f) A ______ is a document that authenticates the identity of the author of a specific piece of code or message.
g) A customer can store purchase information and multiple credit cards in an electronic purchasing and storage device called a ______.
h) Merchants using ______ within their e-commerce sites can automatically suggest items to their customers, on the basis of their past purchasing behavior.
i) A Yahoo! Store comes with core technologies built in. Customers can use the ______ to purchase products, while gaining security with the ______ protocol.
j) ______ and ______ are the two major security protocols of e-commerce. Both of these protocols use ______ encryption.
k) A ______ stores information such as product specifications and customer profiles.

ANSWERS TO SELF-REVIEW EXERCISES

23.1 a) False. Companies have many options when it comes to the design of their e-business. A storefront is a popular method, but it is not the only method. b) True. c) True. d) True. e) False. Separate, inversely related public and private keys are used. f) False. A digital signature is created when the sender encrypts the message digest using the sender's private key. g) False. Continuous-availability computing eliminates down-time. High-availability computing only minimizes down-time. h) True. i) False. Secure Sockets Layer is an Internet security protocol, which secures the transfer of information in electronic communication. It does not protect data stored on a merchant server. j) False. Secure Electronic Transaction is a Security protocol designed by Visa and MasterCard as a more secure alternative to Secure Sockets Layer. k) True. l) True. m) False. A shopping bot can be used to search multiple Web sites for the best available prices and availability. n) False. A digital certificate is issued by a certificate authority and includes information such as company name, the companies public key, a serial number and expiration date. o) True.

23.2 a) Shopping Cart. b) Public Key, Private Key. c) Intelligent Agents. d) Data Mining. e) Secret-key encryption. f) Digital certificate. g) Electronic Wallet. h) Intelligent Agents. i) Shopping Cart, SSL. j) SSL, SET, Public Key. k) Database.

EXERCISES

23.3 Use the Yahoo! Store demo at `http://store.yahoo.com` to build a mock e-commerce Web site. Complete each of the following tasks when using the demo. The demo is free for your use.

a) Create at least two product segments.
b) Create at least three products for each product segment.
c) Add a three-line description of your products.
d) Designate at least two of your products as "special."
e) Add a description of your store and the products you sell, to be included under the **Info** button.
f) Use the layout option to center the products in the store.
g) Use the **Look** option to change the design of your site.
h) Publish your Web site.
i) Place two products in the shopping cart.
j) Proceed with the order. (Note: your order will not be fully processed.)
k) Would you use Yahoo! Store or a similar product if you were to start an e-business? Why or why not?

23.4 E*Trade offers a stock and options trading simulation at `http://www.etrade.com`. Each player is allocated an initial $100,000 in order to be able to make his or her trades. As the round progresses, a player's stocks will gain or lose value, reflecting the actual stock market activity. Players compete to earn the greatest return on their investment (i.e., profits) for the round. Each new round begins on the first day of each month. At the end of the month, all portfolios are compared, and the two highest finishers each receive a $1000 prize! The E*TRADE game is free for your use and gives potential investors a chance to see how their stock picks would perform without actually putting their money at risk.

For this exercise, the class will be divided into teams. Each team should decide on a name and use it to register for the "stock trading only" version of the game. This exercise will let the teams compete over a period of three days, to see which can create the most valuable stock portfolio. Each team should begin the game on the same day. Teams should be aware that investing all of the available funds is not necessarily give you a more profitable portfolio. A market downturn could spell disaster for a fully invested team! (Note: E*TRADE automatically resets the game at the end of each month. Be sure to start this exercise at least three days prior to the end of the month, so that you do not lose your data.)

In order to begin trading, you should complete the following tasks. Good luck! Please let us know if you win the prize!

a) Create a written log of your stock choices.
b) Record the initial purchase value of each stock.
c) If a stock is sold, make a note of its sale in the log. How much was it sold for?
d) Record the value of your portfolio at least twice a day. Include the time it was recorded.
e) Record the final value of each stock and of the overall portfolio at the end of three days.
f) How did your stocks perform?
g) What rank did your portfolio achieve in the competition?

23.5 Create a spreadsheet listing the e-businesses from the chapter horizontally along the top of the page. Along the vertical axis, list the core e-commerce technologies. Fill in the spreadsheet by ranking the technologies in order of perceived importance to each company.

23.6 Visit each of the Web sites featured in the case studies. These Web sites should be ranked in terms of ease of use, design, products offered and business model. Students should also give suggestions, based on the specified criteria, on how they would improve these sites.

23.7 Have a brainstorming session to discuss potential e-business concepts. List the technologies that would be necessary in order to implement these concepts.

23.8 Define each of the following security terms and give an example of how it is used.
a) cryptography
b) public key
c) private key
d) digital signature
e) digital certificate
f) message digest
g) hash function
h) secret key
i) ciphertext
j) SSL

23.9 Define each of the following terms and give an example of how each is used.
a) database
b) auction
c) data mining
d) personalization
e) digital wallet
f) shopping bot
g) intelligent agent
h) XML
i) continuous-availability computing
j) cookies

23.10 Write a brief description of intelligent agents, giving examples of how they are currently used. Describe other ways in which intelligent agents can be used.

23.11 Many companies are using shopping bots to improve the service they provide to their customers. How do shopping bots help clients have more effective online shopping experiences? How do companies benefit from using shopping bots within their Web sites?

23.12 The Visa International Web site includes an interactive demonstration of the Secure Electronic Transaction (SET) protocol that uses animation to explain this complicated protocol in a way that most people will understand. Visit Visa at **http://www.visa.com/nt/sec/no_shock/intro_L.html** to view the demo. Write a short summary of SET. How does SET differ from SSL? Why are digital wallets important? How are they used? If you were asked to choose between the two protocols, which would you choose and why?

23.13 Zenexpress is an e-commerce demo that allows you to see what an online storefront should look like and how an order should be processed. Visit **http://gifts.zenexpress.com/** and complete the demo. How does this Web store differ from the Yahoo! Store (**http://store.yahoo.com**) and the iCat Web store (**http://www.icat.com/services/store**)? Which of these do you prefer?

23.14 In this chapter, we discussed cookies. How are cookies used? What is their purpose? Many people consider cookies to be an invasion of privacy. Do you agree? Discuss these privacy issues.

BIBLIOGRAPHY

(Ab99) Abbott, S., "The Debate for Secure E-Commerce," *Performance Computing,* February, 1999, pp. 37–42.

(An97) Andrews, W., "Shopping Agents: Promising Tool or Fad?", *WebWeek*, October 13, 1997, pp.12-14.

(An99) Andrews, W., "The Digital Wallet: A concept revolutionizing e-commerce," *Internet World*, October 15, 1999, pp.34-45.

(Ba98) Bradley, N., *The XML Companion*, Essex, United Kingdom: Addison Wesley Longman, 1998.

(Be98) Bethoney, H., and Repoza, J., "Microsoft Beta Bundles Basics for E-commerce," *PCWEEK Online*, January 26, 1998, **http://www.zdnet.com/pcweek/reviews/0126/26site.html**.

(Da99) Dalton, G., "Online Data's Fine Line—As the technology to gather customer data online gets more sophisticated, businesses walk a tightrope between use and abuse," *Information Week*, March 29, 1999, Issue 727.

(Db95) Dun & Bradstreet, "An Overview of Data Mining at Dunn & Bradstreet," Online document, **http://www3.shore.net/~kht/text/wp9501/wp9501.html**, 1995.

(De90) Deitel, H., *An Introduction to Operating Systems, Second Edition*, Reading, MA: Addison-Wesley, 1990.

(Di98) DiDio, L., "Private-key Nets Unlock E-Commerce," *Computerworld,* March 16, 1998, pp. 49–50.

(Di98a) DiDio, L., "Internet Boots Cryptography," *Computerworld,* March 16, 1998, p. 32.

(Dr98) Dragan, R., "Microsoft Site Server 3.0 Commerce Edition," *PC Magazine*, December 14, 1998, **http://www.zdnet.com/filters/printerfriendly/0,6061,374713-3,00.html**.

(En97) Enzer, M. and Wilson, B., "A Step-by-Step Guide To Using Cookies To Analyze User Activity & Create Custom Web Pages," *NetscapeWorld*, 1997, **http://www.netscape-world.com/netscapeworld/nw-01-1997/nw-02-cookiehowto.html**.

(Go99) Goncalves, M., "Consortium Aims for Standards for E-Business," *Mass High Tech,* August 28, 1999, p. 17.

(Ha99) Hayes, F., "Amazoned!" *Computerworld,* May 17, 1999, p. 116.

(Hi99) Himelstein, L. and Hof, R., "eBay vs. Amazon.com," *Business Week*, May, 1999, pp.128-132.

(Ho99) Hoffman, T., "Merrill Lynch Bows to Low-Cost Net Trading," *Computerworld*, Online News, June 1, 1999.

(Id99) Information Disco, Inc., "Perspective on Data Mining: Reaping Benefits from Your Data," online document, 1999, **http://www.datamining.com/datamine/dm-ka.htm**

(In99) InternetNews.com, "CyberCash Expands InstaBuy Service," *InternetNews.com,* July 21, 1999.

(Ko97) Kosiur, D., *Understanding Electronic Commerce*, Redmond, WA: Microsoft Press, 1997.

(Kw98) Kwon, R., Delivering Medical Records, Securely," *Internet World*, August 10, 1998, p. 23.

(Lv99) Levitt, J., "XML For the Masses," *Information Week,* August 9, 1999, p. 83.

(Ma98) Machlis, S., "IBM Hedges its Bets on SET," *Computerworld,* July 20, 1998, p. 4.

(Mc98) McFadden, M., "The Many Faces of Electronic Commerce," **http://www.entmag.com**, August 12, 1998, pp. 52--54.

(Mg98) McGee, M. K., and C. Wilder, "Computer Industry Aligns on E-Commerce Standards," *Information Week,* March 30, 1998, p. 28.

(Mi96) Microsoft Corp., "Microsoft Authenticode Technology," online document, **http://msdn.microsoft.com/workshop/security/authcode/authwp.asp**, October, 1996.

(Mk98) McKendrick, J., "Is Anyone SET for Secure Electronic Commerce?" *ENT,* March 4, 1998, pp. 44, 46.

(Mn97) McNamara, P., "Emerging Electronic Commerce Standard Passes First Big Test," *Network World,* October 6, 1997, p. 55.

(Mt99) Methvin, D. W., "How to Succeed in E-Business," *Windows Magazine,* August 1999, pp. 98–108.

(Mr98) Merrick, P., "XML: The Language of the World Wide Web," *Network World,* November 2, 1998, p. 41.

(Ne97) Nemzow, M., *Building CyberStores,* New York, NY: McGraw-Hill, 1997.

(Pa99) Palace, B., "Data Mining: What is Data Mining?", online document, 1996, **http://www.anderson.ucla.edu/faculty/jason.frand/teacher/technologies/palace/datamining.htm**

(Pi99) Price, D.L., *Online Auctions at* eBay*: Bid with Confidence, Sell with Success,* Rocklin, CA: PRIMA TECH (a Division of PRIMA Publishing), 1999.

(Sy98) Symoens, J., "Site Server is a fine set of tools for Web site building," *InfoWorld*, January 26, 1998, **http://www.infoworld.com**.

(Ud99) Udell, J., "XML Marks the Spot," *Computerworld,* April 12, 1999, pp. 84–85.

(Un96) Unicode Consortium, "The Unicode Standard A Technical Introduction," online document, **http://www.unicode.org/unicode/standards/principles.html**, 1996.

(We99) Weber, J., "World Wide Web Economy," *The Industry Standard,* June 21, 1999, p. 2.

(We99a) Weber, J., "Clicks and Mortar," *The Industry Standard,* August 2–9, 1999, p. 5.

(We99) Wilde, C., "Personal Business," *Information Week,* August 9, 1999, pp. 76, 78, 80.

(Wi99a) Wilder, C., "Online Ordering," *Information Week,* August 9, 1999, p. 73.

(Ws99) Wilson, T., "E-Biz Bucks Lost Under SSL Strain," *Internet Week,* May 24, 1999, pp. 1, 3.

24

Web Servers (PWS, IIS, Apache, Jigsaw)

Objectives

- To understand what a Web server does and what functionality it provides.
- To use the Microsoft Personal Web Server (PWS).
- To set up your Personal Web Server and your information for publishing Web pages.
- To install and use interactive applications on your Web server.
- To publish data by using an Open Database Connectivity (ODBC)-compliant data source.
- To provide a brief introduction to Microsoft Internet Information Server (IIS), Apache Web Server and Jigsaw Web Server.

In fact, a fundamental interdependence exists between the personal right to liberty and the personal right to property.
Potter Stewart

Stop abusing my verses, or publish some of your own.
Marcus Valerius Martialis

There are three difficulties in authorship: to write anything worth the publishing, to find honest men to publish it, and to get sensible men to read it.
Charles Caleb Colton

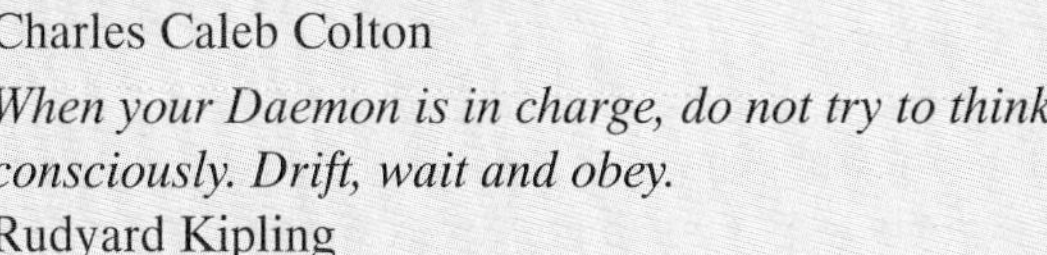

When your Daemon is in charge, do not try to think consciously. Drift, wait and obey.
Rudyard Kipling

Outline

24.1 Introduction

In this chapter, you will learn exactly what a Web server does and understand the basics of installing, configuring and administering several publicly available Web servers. We explore *Microsoft Personal Web Server (PWS)* in detail. We use PWS to publish HTML pages, run *CGI (Common Gateway Interface)* scripts (CGI is discussed in detail in Chapter 27), connect to ODBC data sources (database is discussed in Chapter 25), process *Active Server Pages (ASP)*—a technology discussed in Chapter 26, serve up Extensible Markup Language (XML) documents (discussed in Chapter 28) and more.

To understand what a Web server is used for, we first need to have a basic overview of Internet topology. A *network* allows two or more computers to communicate and share their resources. If we think of the Internet as a large network of computers, we can start to imagine the vast amount of information and computing resources the Internet has to offer. When a user is connected to the Internet, that user is actually a part of the Internet. Any network requires servers to manage access to files, folders, hardware and software. Thus a

Web server is a network server that manages access to files, folders and other resources over the Internet or a local Intranet via the platform-neutral *HTTP (HyperText Transfer Protocol)*.

In addition, Web servers possess unique Web networking characteristics. They handle permissions, execute programs, keep track of directories and files and communicate with client computers. These client computers make requests for files and actions from server computers using HTTP, an Internet protocol that enables the distribution of hypertext documents. Like other TCP/IP services, such as *File Transfer Protocol (FTP)*, *News Network Transfer Protocol (NNTP)* and *Simple Mail Transfer Protocol (SMTP)*, HTTP is a *client-server protocol*. Figure 24.1 illustrates a Web server and several HTTP clients.

Knowing how Web servers work can help Web site developers obtain a deeper understanding of Internet architecture and therefore become more proficient in what they do. Web servers allow you to serve content over the Internet using HTTP. The Web server accepts HTTP requests from browsers like Internet Explorer and Netscape Communicator and returns the appropriate HTML documents, images, Java applets, etc. A number of server-side technologies can be used to increase the power of the server beyond its ability to deliver standard HTML pages; these include CGI scripts (see Chapter 27) and server-side includes, SSL security (see Chapter 23), Java servlets (see Chapter 29), Active Server Pages (see Chapter 26), etc.

This chapter overviews four popular Web servers: *Microsoft Personal Web Server (PWS)*, *Microsoft Internet Information Server (IIS)*, *Apache* and *Jigsaw*. Apache and Microsoft IIS dominate the Web server market. W3C Jigsaw is an up-and-coming Web server that uses newer Internet technologies. PWS is an entry-level product that helps level the learning curve necessary for students and developers just beginning to work with Web server technology.

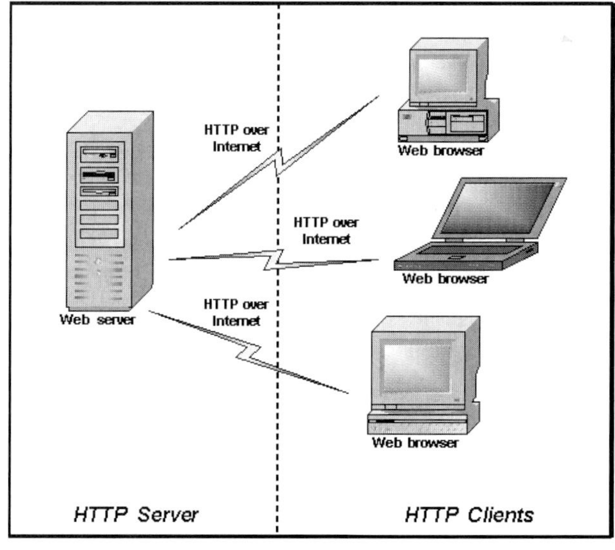

Fig. 24.1 A Web server communicating with several HTTP clients.

Web Server	PWS	IIS	Apache	Jigsaw
Version	4.0	4.0	1.3.9	2.0.3
Company	Microsoft Corporation	Microsoft Corporation	Apache Group	World Wide Web Consortium
Released	12/4/97	12/4/97	8/20/99	8/17/99
Platforms	Windows 95/98, Windows NT	Windows NT Server (Intel/Alpha)	UNIX, Windows NT, experimentally supports Windows 95/98.	Windows NT, Windows 95/98, UNIX (Solaris 2.x).
Brief description	Supports up to 10 concurrent connections; no longer supports FTP.	Latest release of the most popular Web server for Windows NT.	The most popular Web server currently in use on the Internet.	Java-based server that provides a blueprint for future Web development.
Features	A great entry-level Web server for publishing your own Web pages.	Updated versions of IIS, Index Server, Message Queue Server (MSMQ) and Transaction Server (MTS).	High performance, extremely reliable Web server.	Administration tools; completely object-oriented design; written entirely in Java.
Price	Freeware. Packaged with Microsoft IIS in NT 4.0 Option Pack, also included in Windows 98.	Free download (requires IE 4.01 or later). A CD-ROM version can be purchased.	Freeware.	Freely available under open-source license.

Fig. 24.2 Web servers discussed in this chapter.

24.2 Microsoft Personal Web Server Overview

You can connect to data sources using the *Internet Database Connector* (*IDC*), CGI (see Chapter 27) and ASP (see Chapter 26) with Microsoft PWS. PWS is a scaled-down version of Microsoft's Internet Information Server (IIS), the professional, commercial Web server found on many hosting services. PWS provides the following capabilities:

1. Allows *webs* to be published as a whole with a single command. A web is a set of files that comprise a particular Web site. Web servers can support multiple webs.
2. Allows publishing Web sites from the local computer to a remote computer, from a remote computer to the local computer (normally for an existing Web site that you want to develop and test on a local computer), or between remote Web sites.
3. Provides CGI, IDC, ASP and *Microsoft Internet Server Application Programming Interface* (*ISAPI*) programs, and the FrontPage WebBots on your local computer, so you can test your webs locally in your browser before making them public. All of these technologies require a server and/or FrontPage server extensions to run.
4. Provides "smart" web management. FrontPage uses special **`_vti`** files to keep track of what changes have been made, when and by whom. When you publish

using the "changed pages only" option, FrontPage knows which pages to publish. This can save a lot of time and trouble. FrontPage's tools can also help you identify any broken links. You can manage a remote Web site just as easily as a local one, even edit files as if they were on your computer. FrontPage treats local and remote webs the same, always communicating through the server.

5. Sets permissions and properties of webs and folders. FrontPage communicates with the server to do this. This is especially important if you want to use interactive technology, such as CGI, IDC or ASP.
6. Sets up virtual directories on the server.
7. You can browse your webs from another computer on the Internet, when you are logged on. This is handy for demonstrating your Web sites to clients, friends, etc.

The product home page address for PWS is

```
http://www.microsoft.com/windows/ie/pws/
```

The software download address for PWS is

```
http://www.microsoft.com/msdownload/ntoptionpack/askwiz.asp
```

24.3 Microsoft Personal Web Server Setup

The following section outlines the installation and configuration of PWS. PWS requires that Internet Explorer 4.0 or higher be installed on the system. Before proceeding, be certain that the latest version of Internet Explorer is installed.

In addition to the installation of the Microsoft Personal Web Server software, the *Personal Web Server Network Service* and Microsoft TCP/IP protocol will also need to be added to the system and configured correctly.

24.3.1 Verifying the Presence of the Microsoft TCP/IP Protocol

If the computer has a network adapter installed, then the TCP/IP protocol should have already been configured when Windows was installed. If the system does not have a network card installed, the following configuration is required for PWS to function properly:

To bind the TCP/IP protocol on Windows 95/98, add the **Dial-Up Adapter**. No further configuration is required. The following instructions allow you to install the TCP/IP protocol on Windows 95/98, which is required for a Web server to serve Web pages:

1. Click the **Start** button, select **Settings** and open the **Control Panel**.
2. In the **Control Panel** window, open the **Network** control panel.
3. If either **TCP/IP** or **TCP/IP -> Dial-Up Adapter** is listed here, make sure there are no two identical list items. If there are, highlight one (it does not matter which), and click **Remove**. If **TCP/IP** is not listed in either form, proceed with Step 4.
4. In the **Network** window, click the **Add...** button.
5. In the **Select Network Component Type** window, select **Protocol** and click the **Add** button.
6. In the **Select Network Protocol** window, choose **Microsoft** from the manufacturers list on the left side. From the available protocols list on the right side choose **TCP/IP** and click **OK**. **TCP/IP** now appears in your screen control panel.

7. In the **Network** window, set the **Primary Network Logon** to **Windows Logon**. Click **OK** to finish the installation. If you are asked for your Windows 95/98 CD-ROM or diskettes, insert the CD-ROM or appropriate diskette.
8. You will then be warned that your system configuration has been changed and that you should restart your computer. Click **Yes**.

The Microsoft TCP/IP protocol should now be installed. Normally, a host name (such as **`www.deitel.com`**) is used to access a Web server. The host name **`localhost`** is recognized by TCP/IP to reference the local system (**`http://localhost/`**) when a Web server is installed on that computer. You can also reference a computer on the Internet by its *Internet Protocol (IP) address*. Every host name corresponds to a numeric IP address. For **`localhost`**, the corresponding address is **`127.0.0.1`**, so you can reference the local Web server with (**`http://127.0.0.1/`**).

To access a Web server on the Windows NT platform, install the *MS Loopback Adapter* (if the computer is not already on a network). An IP address must be configured for the Loopback Adapter, preferably an IP address reserved for internal use (such as **`192.168.1.1`**). You must also specify a *subnet mask* (**`255.255.255.0`**). In large organizations, the subnet mask is used to identify a portion of the network. For example, in a world-wide corporation, two subnet masks could be used to identify computers as being from two different locations (such as Boston and Tokyo).

24.3.2 Installing the PWS Software

Double click the installation executable to display the licensing screen for **Windows NT 4.0 Option Pack** (Fig. 24.3). Although the window says **Windows NT**, the Option Pack contains components for Windows NT Server, Windows NT Workstation and Windows 95/98.

Read the license agreement and click **Yes**. This begins the installation process. Next, you will see the **Microsoft Personal Web Server Setup** dialog (Fig. 24.4). Follow the instructions on the screen and the software will install itself on your machine.

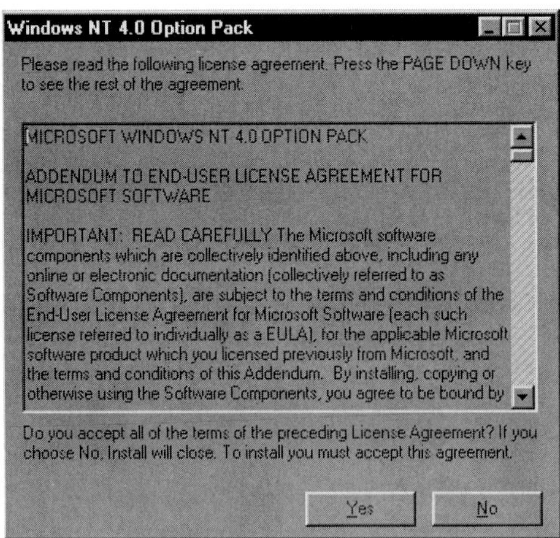

Fig. 24.3 **Windows NT 4.0 Option Pack** license agreement dialog.

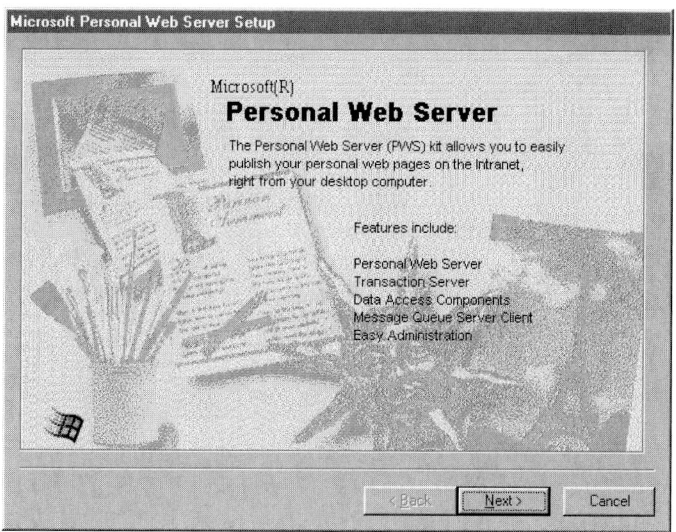

Fig. 24.4 **Microsoft Personal Web Server Setup** dialog.

24.3.3 Configuring the PWS Service (Windows 95 only)

Depending on how your machine is configured, you may need to go through the following steps as well:

Go to **Network** in the Windows **Control Panel** and click **Add...** to display the **Select Network Component Type** dialog (Fig. 24.5). Select **Service** and click **Add...** to display the **Select Network Service** dialog (Fig. 24.6).

Select **Microsoft** from the **Manufacturers** list, double click **Personal Web Server** and click **OK**:

The installation and configuration of PWS should now be complete. The next section shows how to launch PWS and verify that the setup was successful.

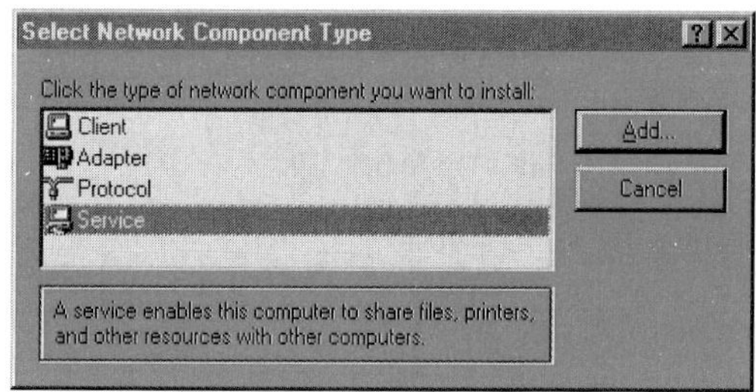

Fig. 24.5 **Select Network Component Type** dialog.

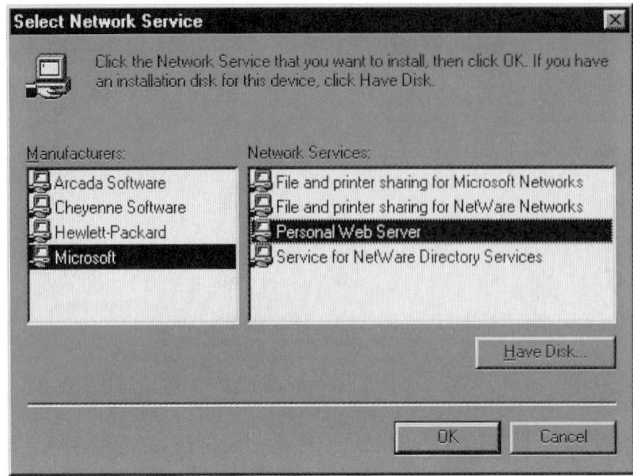

Fig. 24.6 **Select Network Service** dialog.

24.4 Getting Started with Microsoft Personal Web Server

In this section we discuss how to launch PWS, test that PWS was successfully installed, create a Web site, access PWS from a remote computer, prepare and publish information, publish dynamic content and publish data from a database.

24.4.1 Starting Personal Web Server

Launching PWS allows PWS to respond to clients' requests for Web pages and other data. There are several ways to launch PWS:

1. In the **Control Panel**, double click the Personal Web Server icon.
2. From the **Start** button, select the **Programs** menu, then **Microsoft Personal Web Server,** then **Personal Web Manager**. Once **Personal Web Manager** is open, click the **Start** button.
3. Right click the Personal Web Server icon in the system tray (i.e., the area of the taskbar where the time is displayed) and click **Start Service** (Fig. 24.7).
4. From the command prompt, type `pws /start`.

To have PWS start automatically when you restart your computer, select the check box labeled **Run The Web Server Automatically At Startup**.

24.4.2 Testing for a Successful Installation of PWS

To ensure that the installation was successful, and that PWS is capable of receiving Hyper-Text Transport Protocol (HTTP) requests and sending back HTTP responses, we need to use a Web browser capable of connecting to *port 80* on the server computer. Port 80 is the default port for HTTP and is the standard port used by most Internet Web servers.

The computer on which PWS is installed does not need to be connected to the Internet to serve HTTP requests. If the Microsoft TCP/IP protocol is correctly configured and PWS is installed (see in Section 24.3.1), clients can receive information from the Web server.

Fig. 24.7 The PWS icon highlighted in the system tray of the Windows taskbar.

Let us use Microsoft Internet Explorer to test the Web server. It is important to realize that any Web browser, including Microsoft Internet Explorer, Netscape Communicator, Opera, Lynx, etc., can request information from PWS. In turn, PWS will respond with information no matter what Web browser software the client computer is using. The HTTP address for our installation of PWS is

`http://127.0.0.1`

As described earlier, **`127.0.0.1`** is a special IP address used by TCP/IP for *loopback testing*. A *loopback address* is a virtual address that allows testing of a computer's TCP/IP stack (i.e., that computer's TCP/IP software) from that same computer. Other aliases may be used as well.

`http://localhost`
`http://`*ComputerName*

Open Internet Explorer and type **`http://127.0.0.1`** into the **Address** field. Press *Enter* or click **GO**. If everything is installed correctly, the default page for PWS is displayed (Fig. 24.8).

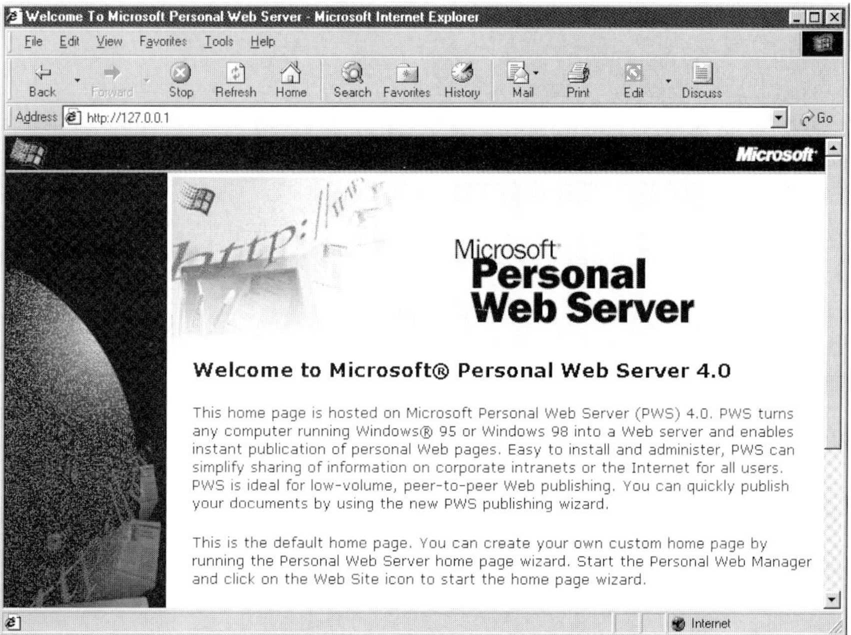

Fig. 24.8 Default Web site page for PWS.

To ensure that the ASP scripting engine is running correctly and is available for your site, we will need to run another test. The PWS documentation included with the PWS package employs ASP scripting technology. Viewing this documentation is a quick way of confirming that the ASP scripting engine is correctly configured. The PWS documentation can be run from the Windows **Start** menu. First select **Programs**, then **Personal Web Server**, then **Product Documentation** to confirm that ASP is running on the PWS server (Fig. 24.9). The ASP scripting engine is needed for the examples in Chapter 26.

24.4.3 Creating a Web Site on Your Own Computer

Following a successful installation of Personal Web Server, the steps below are required to create a *root web* and enable the execution of ASP script files. A root web is a web that is the top-level content directory of a Web server. It can have many levels of subdirectories, containing its content. There can be only one root web per installation of PWS. The root web points to a home directory that contains the files that will be displayed when a Web browser sends an HTTP request to the Web server.

By default, your home directory is **C:\Webshare\Wwwroot**. This is where all files sent to HTTP clients by PWS reside.

24.4.4 Accessing Personal Web Server from Other Computers

To test a Web server connected to the Internet, start Microsoft Internet Explorer or other Web browser on a computer that has an active connection to the Internet. If the computer does not have a direct Internet connection, you must connect to your Internet service provider (ISP) by using dial-up networking. We recommend that you use a different computer, if one is available, from the server you are testing.

Type the address of the computer running Personal Web Server into the **Address** field. In order to identify the computer's IP address, we can use a tool supplied by Microsoft called ***IP Configuration*** (Fig. 24.10).

To open this utility, select **Run** from the Windows **Start** menu and type **WINIPCFG** and click **OK**. Once the application is open, click **More Info >>**. Make certain to select **PPP Adapter** or your specific computer's Ethernet adapter from the pull-down menu.

The address is **http://** followed by the IP address of the server. (Note the forward slashes.) If your server was registered in the Domain Name System (DNS) as **www.company.com** and you want to view the file **home.htm** in the root of the home directory, you would type:

```
http://www.company.com/home.htm
```

Whereas Windows 95/98 has a utility called **WINIPCFG** that provides a graphical interface to display and reset TCP/IP settings, the Windows NT version is called ***WNTIPCFG***. Most Windows 95/98 and Windows NT platforms also have a command line utility called ***IPCONFIG***, which is a bit more archaic.

To test a Web server on an Intranet, first make certain the computer has an active network connection. To do this, double-click the **Network Neighborhood** icon, and make sure you can see other computers in the same workgroup.

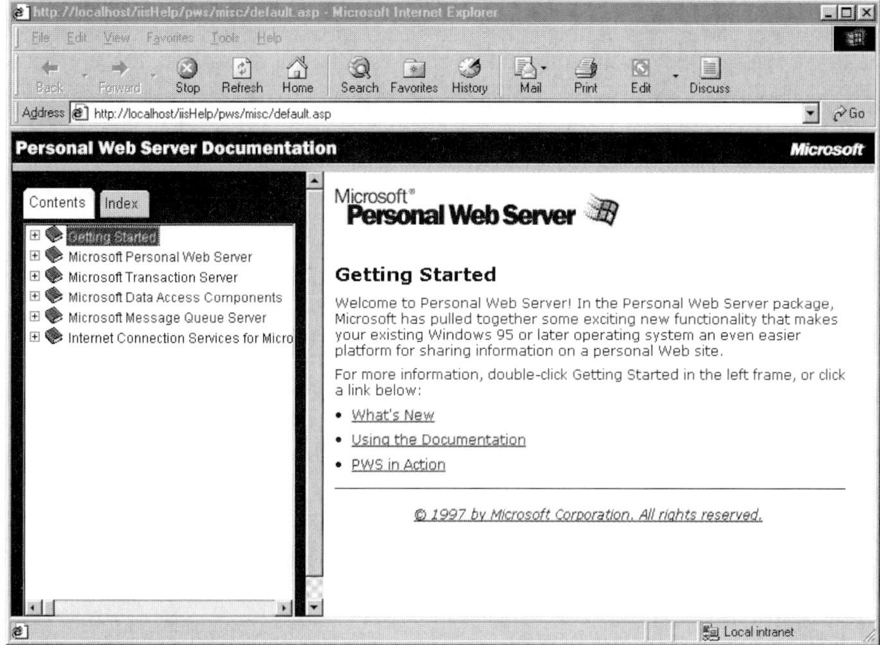

Fig. 24.9 PWS documentation employing use of the ASP scripting engine and the Web server.

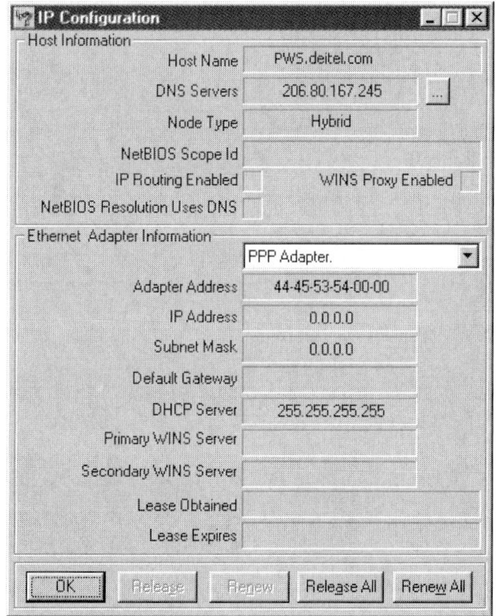

Fig. 24.10 Microsoft **IP Configuration** utility.

Next verify that the WINS server service (or other name-resolution method) is functioning. To do this, at a different computer on the network, click the **Start** menu, click the **Find** menu and select **Computer...**. Type the name of the computer running Personal Web Server and click **Find**. The computer should appear in the list.

Start a Web browser. Type the address for the home directory of your new server. The address is **`http://`** followed by the Windows networking name of your server and the file's path you want to view. For example, if your server is registered with the WINS server as **`Admin1`** and you want to view **`home.htm`** in the Web server's root directory, type

```
http://admin1/home.htm
```

and press *Enter* to load the page.

If the name of the computer is unknown, double-click the **Network** icon in the **Control Panel** and select the **Identification** tab (Fig. 24.11).

24.4.5 Publishing Information and Applications

Personal Web Server can publish both information and applications. This means your server can contain anything from static pages of information to interactive applications. You can also find and extract information from, and insert information into, databases.

24.4.6 Preparing Information for Publishing

Most Web pages are formatted in HTML. HTML specifications are changing constantly. You should regularly review the HTML specifications available at

```
http://www.w3c.org
```

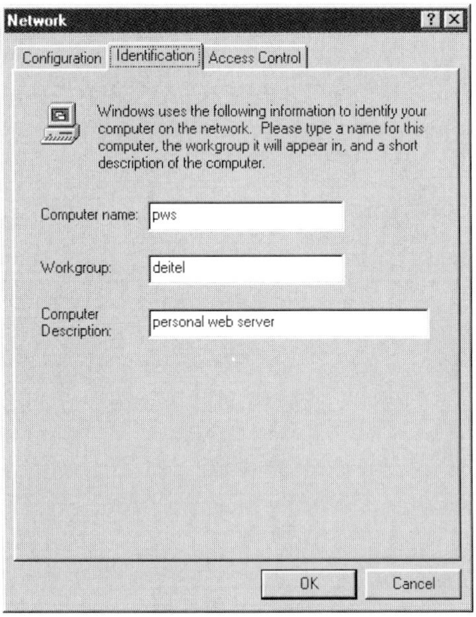

Fig. 24.11 **Network** dialog displaying the computer name.

You can use any text editor, such as Notepad, Wordpad or Windows Write, to create and edit your HTML files; but you will probably find an HTML editor, such as Internet Assistant for Microsoft Word, easier to use. If you want to include images or sounds, you will also need appropriate software (e.g., Paint Shop Pro) to create and edit those files.

Your files can include images and sounds. You can even create links to Microsoft Office files or to almost any other file format. Remote users must have the correct viewing application to view non-HTML files. For example, if you know that all remote users will have Microsoft Word, you can include links to Microsoft Word **`.doc`** files. The user can click the link and the document will appear in Word on the user's computer.

Once you have created your information in HTML or other formats, you can either copy the information to the default directory **`\Inetpub\Wwwroot`**, or you can change the default home directory to the directory containing your information.

24.4.7 Publishing Dynamic Applications

One of the most exciting features of Microsoft Personal Web Server is the ability to run applications or scripts that remote users start by clicking HTML links or by filling in and sending an HTML form. Using programming languages such as Perl (see Chapter 27) or C, you can create applications or scripts that generate HTML dynamically.

Interactive applications or scripts can be written in almost any 32-bit programming language, such as C or Perl, or as Windows batch files (**`.bat`** or **`.cmd`**). When you write your applications or scripts you can use one of two supported interfaces—the Common Gateway Interface (CGI), which is discussed in Chapter 27, or *ISAPI*.

Documentation for ISAPI is available from Microsoft via subscription to the *Microsoft Developer Network* (*MSDN*). You can also search the MSDN knowledge base at **`http://msdn.microsoft.com/`**. Documentation for CGI is available on the Internet (several sources are listed in the "Internet and Web Resources" section at the back of Chapter 27). Batch files can issue any command valid at the command prompt.

ISAPI for Windows NT can be used to write applications that Web users activate by filling out an HTML form or by clicking a hyperlink. The remote application can then take the user-supplied information and do almost anything with it that can be programmed, and return the results in an HTML page or post the information in a database.

ISAPI can be used to create applications that run as Dynamic Link Libraries (DLLs) on your Web server (DLLs are a Microsoft technology for shared code libraries). DLLs do not start a separate *process* (executing program), so they require less overhead than Common Gateway Interface (CGI) scripts, which each run in their own separate process from the Web server.

Performance Tip 24.1

Applications that use ISAPI are loaded by the Web service at startup. Because the programs are loaded into memory at server startup, ISAPI programs do not have the overhead of CGI applications when they are invoked by a client.

Portability Tip 24.1

ISAPI is a Microsoft-specific technology.

Another feature of ISAPI allows preprocessing of requests and postprocessing of responses, permitting site-specific handling of HyperText Transport Protocol (HTTP) requests and responses. ISAPI filters can be used for applications such as customized authentication, access or logging.

You can create complex sites by using both ISAPI filters and applications. ISAPI extensions can also be combined with the Internet Database Connector to create highly interactive sites. For complete information about programming with ISAPI, see the Microsoft BackOffice Software Development Kit (SDK) section titled, "Before You Begin," for further information about obtaining the ISAPI SDK.

The Common Gateway Interface (CGI) is a standard interface used to write applications that remote users can start by filling out an HTML form or clicking a hyperlink. As with ISAPI, the remote application can take the user-supplied information, process it and return the results of the application in an HTML page or post the information to a database. Because simple CGI applications are often written using scripting languages such as Perl, CGI applications are sometimes referred to as scripts. Microsoft Personal Web Server can use most Windows 95/98 32-bit applications that conform to the CGI specification.

After writing your application or script, place it in the `/Scripts` directory—a virtual directory for applications. This virtual directory has **Execute** and **Scripts** access.

You must also ensure that every process started by your application is running by using an account with adequate permissions. If your application interacts with other files, the account you assign to your program must have the right permissions to use those files. By default, applications run using the **`IUSR_`*`<computername>`*** account.

If your application does not require data from the user, create a link to your application in a simple HTML file. If your application does require data from the user, use an HTML form. In other instances, send a Uniform Resource Locator (URL) containing data parameters to invoke a program.

An HTML link to an application that does not require user input might look like this:

```
http://www.company.com/scripts/catalog.exe?
```

where `/scripts` is the virtual directory for interactive applications (`\Scripts` is the physical directory on the Web server's file system).

If you are creating an application that requires input from the user, you will need to understand both HTML forms and how to use the forms with ISAPI or CGI. This information is widely available on the Internet. HTML forms were discussed in Chapter 4 and CGI is discussed in Chapter 27.

Because you have the flexibility to create applications in almost any programming language, Personal Web Server uses the filename extension to determine which interpreter to invoke for each application. The default interpreter associations are listed Fig. 24.12. You can use the Registry Editor to create additional associations.

File Extension	Default Interpreter
`.exe`, `.com`, `.bat`, `.cmd`	`Cmd.exe`
`.idc`	`Httpodbc.dll`
`.asp`, `.asa`	`Asp.dll`

Fig. 24.12 PWS extension interpreters (Windows 95/98).

XML documents can be served by PWS once the **`text/xml`** MIME type has been registered on the server. Installing Microsoft Internet Explorer 5 on the server registers the **`text/xml`** MIME type and associates it with the **`.xml`** and **`.xsl`** file extensions. Alternatively, PWS can be updated to serve XML by downloading and running the following file

```
http://msdn.microsoft.com/xml/xslguide/register-xml.reg
```

on the server computer this file will update the server's registery with the appropriate XML MIME keys. PWS will now be able to deliver XML data to browsers that support XML.

In order to adjust virtual directory permissions, PWS comes with a simple administration utility called the **Personal Web Manager** (Fig. 24.13). The **Main** window of the **Personal Web Manager** provides basic start/stop tools and some usage statistics, including the number of current active connections to PWS, etc.

These statistics are located inside the **Monitoring** frame within the **Manager** and consist of

1. **Active Connections**: indicates how many connections are currently transferring data to or from the server.
2. **Started At**: indicates when the server was last started as a service.
3. **Visitors**: indicates number of unique addresses that have connected to the server since the **Started At** value.
4. **Requests**: indicates number of requests received since the **Started At** value.
5. **Bytes Served**: indicates how many bytes of information have been sent out since the **Started At** value.
6. **Most Concurrent Connections**: indicates the maximum number of simultaneous connections the server has handled since the **Started At** value.

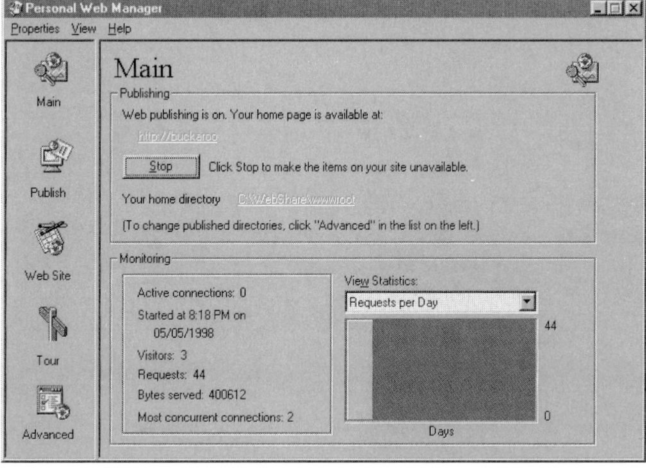

Fig. 24.13 **Personal Web Manager** dialog.

To display the **Personal Web Manager** dialog, right click the Personal Web Server icon on your Windows 95/98 taskbar and select **Properties** from the context menu.

The **Advanced Options** area of the **Personal Web Manager** enables you to reconfigure your Web site to accommodate new pages or to modify virtual directory permissions (Fig. 24.14).

When you allow remote users to run applications on your computer, you run the risk of hackers attempting to break into your system. Personal Web Server is not a highly secure Internet Web server. It is more of an educational tool.

One way that PWS limits security risks is through file and directory permissions. Virtual directories in PWS can be set to any or all **Read**, **Execute** and **Scripts** access using the **Personal Web Manager** (Fig. 24.15). The virtual directory `\Scripts` contains your applications and allows both **Read** and **Scripts** access. Thus, unauthorized users cannot copy a malicious application and run it on your computer.

Read allows visitors to read and download files stored in the home directory (`<Home>` inside of **Personal Web Manager**) or a virtual directory. If a directory's **Read** access is turned off, a browser is unable to download files from that directory and **Read** access is also turned off for all directories physically contained within the home directory. If you need to set directory access permissions on a directory-by-directory basis, virtual directories should be used. Directories containing Web content, such as HTML pages, only have **Read** access. However, **Read** access should be disallowed for directories containing Common Gateway Interface (CGI) applications, Internet Server Application Program Interfaces (ISAPI) and dynamic-link libraries (DLLs), which prevents these binary files form being downloaded. All directories created during setup have **Read** access enabled, by default.

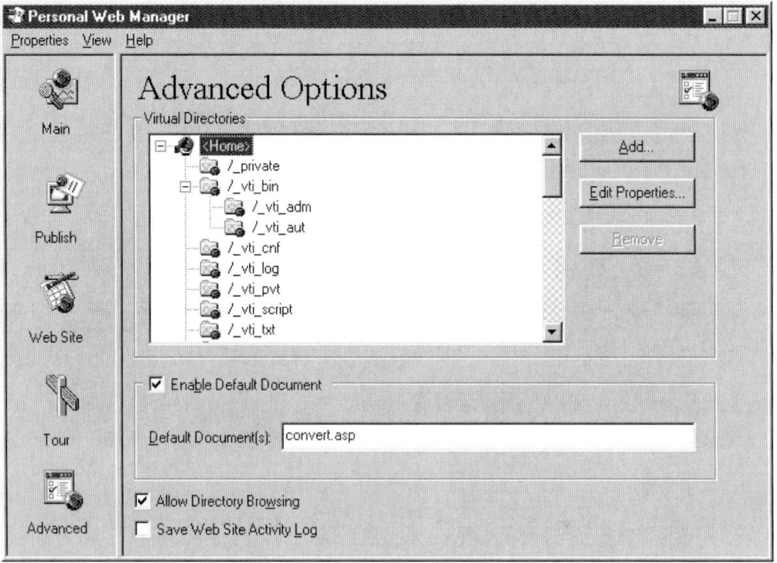

Fig. 24.14 **Advanced Options** area in the **Personal Web Manager** dialog.

Execute access allows an application to run in that directory. **Execute** access is not necessary for directories where only content files exist.

Scripts access allows scripts to be run in that directory. This occurs even without having **Execute** permission set. ASP scripts, Internet Database Connector (IDC) scripts, and other scripting file types can be executed without explicitly setting **Execute** access. **`Scripts`** access is safer than **`Execute`** access because it limits the applications that can be run in the directory. All directories created during setup have **Scripts** access enabled by default.

24.4.8 Publishing Information and Using a Database

With Personal Web Server and the Open Data Base Connectivity (ODBC) drivers, you can create Web pages from information contained in a database. These drivers also allow inserts, updates and deletes of the information in the database based on user input from a Web page and the execution of other Structured Query Language (SQL) commands. Database and SQL are discussed in Chapter 25.

Web browsers (such as Internet Explorer 5, or browsers from other companies such as Netscape and Opera Software) begin by submitting requests to the Web server via HTTP. The Web server responds with a document formatted in HTML. Access to databases is accomplished through Internet Database Connector (IDC) component of PWS, ***`Httpodbc.dll`***, which is an ISAPI DLL that uses ODBC to gain access to databases.

`Httpodbc.dll` uses two types of files to control how the database is accessed and how the Web page being output is constructed. These file types are Internet Database Connector (**`.idc`**) files and *HTML extension (**`.htx`**) files.*

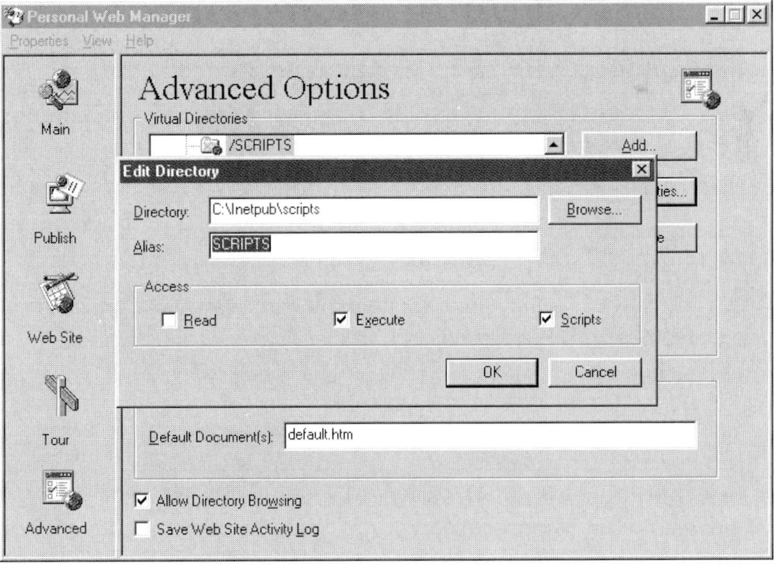

Fig. 24.15 Setting permissions in **Personal Web Manager**.

IDC files contain the necessary information to connect to the appropriate ODBC data source and execute the SQL statement. An IDC file also contains the name and location of the **.htx** file.

The **.htx** file is the template for the actual HTML document that will be returned to the Web browser after the database information has been merged into it by **Httpodbc.dll**. Whereas the IDC provides data retrieval details, the **.htx** file supplies the formatting. The **.htx** file contains **<% %>** placeholders for the fields, but is otherwise standard HTML. In order to configure PWS to be able to use the IDC, we first need to configure a system Data Source Name (DSN) and the FrontPage server extensions.

Before creating the DSN, which can be thought of as a handle that represents an ODBC connection to a database, we need a database. For this example, we will use the *Northwind database* that ships with Microsoft Access, Microsoft Visual Basic and other Microsoft products. If you do not already have the **Nwind.mdb** Microsoft Access database file on your system, you can download it from

http://officeupdate.microsoft.com/downloadDetails/nwind.htm

Once the location of the **Northwind.mdb** file has been determined or the file has been downloaded and extracted to a directory, we can create the system DSN which acts as the ODBC connection to the database. Follow these steps to create the system DSN:

1. Open the **Control Panel**.
2. Double-click the **ODBC Data Sources (32bit)** icon.

The **ODBC Data Sources** dialog appears. You may see other data sources in the list if you previously installed other ODBC drivers.

3. Click the **System DSN** tab to display the **System Data Sources** dialog. (Note: Be sure to click the **System DSN** tab. The Internet Database Connector works only with System DSNs.)
4. Click the **Add** button to display the **Add Data Source**.
5. Select **Microsoft Access Driver** from the list and click **OK** to display the **ODBC Microsoft Access Setup** dialog.
6. Enter **NWIND** for the **Data Source Name**.

The data source name is a logical name used by ODBC to refer to the Microsoft Access driver and the actual Microsoft Access database file.

7. Click the **Select** button and navigate to the directory where **Nwind.mdb** is located. Select **Nwind.mdb** and click **OK**.

The **System Data Sources** dialog is displayed again, but now it has the name of the data source displayed.

8. Click the **OK** button to complete the ODBC and DSN setup.

Start the **FrontPage Administrator** by clicking the **Start** button, select the **Programs** menu, then select **Microsoft Personal Web Server**, then select **FrontPage Server Administrator**. Next, you must uninstall the **FrontPage Server Extensions**.

9. Click **Uninstall** to uninstall the **FrontPage Server Extensions**. The installation program displays a confirmation dialog. To proceed, click **OK**.

10. Create an extension for PWS. Click **Install**. The installation program will display a list of available server extensions. Choose **Microsoft Personal Web Server**.
11. Select your Web server within the **Configure Server Type** dialog.

The installation program upgrades all your existing FrontPage webs to the new extension. After the upgrade is complete, PWS is the default server.

In order to provide access to the database specified in the System DSN from your Web page, you will need to create an Internet Database Connector file (`.idc`) and an HTML extension file (`.htx`). We are going to use these to dynamically display an HTML table created from customer names from the sample Northwind database.

We create two files that contain the code in Figs. 24.16 and 24.17. Name the files accordingly and save them to the root directory of PWS (e.g., `C:\Inetpub\Wwwroot`).

```
Datasource:NWIND
Template:Customers.htx
SQLStatement:SELECT * FROM [Customers]
Password:
Username:
```

Fig. 24.16 `customers.idc` file.

```
<!DOCTYPE html PUBLIC "-//W3C//DTD HTML 4.0 Transitional//EN">
<HTML>
<HEAD>
<META HTTP-EQUIV = "Content-Type"
CONTENT = "text/html; charset = windows-1252">
<TITLE>Customers</TITLE>
</HEAD>
<BODY>
<TABLE BORDER = 1 BGCOLOR = #ffffff CELLSPACING = 0 RULES = none>
<FONT FACE = "MS Sans Serif" COLOR = #000000><CAPTION>
<B>Customers</B></CAPTION>

<THEAD>
<TR>
<TH BGCOLOR = #c0c0c0 BORDERCOLOR = #000000><FONT SIZE = 2
FACE = "MS Sans Serif" COLOR = #000000>CustomerID</FONT></TH>
<TH BGCOLOR = #c0c0c0 BORDERCOLOR = #000000><FONT SIZE = 2
FACE = "MS Sans Serif" COLOR = #000000>CompanyName</FONT></TH>
<TH BGCOLOR = #c0c0c0 BORDERCOLOR = #000000><FONT SIZE = 2
FACE = "MS Sans Serif" COLOR = #000000>ContactName</FONT></TH>
<TH BGCOLOR = #c0c0c0 BORDERCOLOR = #000000><FONT SIZE = 2
FACE = "MS Sans Serif" COLOR = #000000>ContactTitle</FONT></TH>
<TH BGCOLOR = #c0c0c0 BORDERCOLOR = #000000><FONT SIZE = 2
FACE = "MS Sans Serif" COLOR = #000000>Address</FONT></TH>
<TH BGCOLOR = #c0c0c0 BORDERCOLOR = #000000><FONT SIZE = 2
FACE = "MS Sans Serif" COLOR = #000000>City</FONT></TH>
<TH BGCOLOR = #c0c0c0 BORDERCOLOR = #000000><FONT SIZE = 2
FACE = "MS Sans Serif" COLOR = #000000>Region</FONT></TH>
<TH BGCOLOR = #c0c0c0 BORDERCOLOR = #000000><FONT SIZE = 2
```

Fig. 24.17 `customers.htx` file.

```
FACE = "MS Sans Serif" COLOR = #000000>PostalCode</FONT></TH>
<TH BGCOLOR = #c0c0c0 BORDERCOLOR = #000000><FONT SIZE = 2
FACE = "MS Sans Serif" COLOR = #000000>Country</FONT></TH>
<TH BGCOLOR = #c0c0c0 BORDERCOLOR = #000000><FONT SIZE = 2
FACE = "MS Sans Serif" COLOR = #000000>Phone</FONT></TH>
<TH BGCOLOR = #c0c0c0 BORDERCOLOR = #000000><FONT SIZE = 2
FACE = "MS Sans Serif" COLOR = #000000>Fax</FONT></TH>

</TR>
</THEAD>
<TBODY>
<%BeginDetail%>
<TR VALIGN = TOP>
<TD BORDERCOLOR = #808080><FONT SIZE = 1 FACE = "MS Sans Serif"
COLOR = #800000><%CustomerID%><BR></FONT></TD>
<TD BORDERCOLOR = #808080><FONT SIZE = 1
FACE = "MS Sans Serif" COLOR = #800000><%CompanyName%><BR>
</FONT></TD>
<TD BORDERCOLOR = #808080><FONT SIZE = 1
FACE = "MS Sans Serif" COLOR = #800000><%ContactName%><BR>
</FONT></TD>
<TD BORDERCOLOR = #808080><FONT SIZE = 1
FACE = "MS Sans Serif"
COLOR = #800000><%ContactTitle%><BR></FONT></TD>
<TD BORDERCOLOR = #808080><FONT SIZE = 1
FACE = "MS Sans Serif" COLOR = #800000><%Address%><BR>
</FONT></TD>
<TD BORDERCOLOR = #808080><FONT SIZE = 1
FACE = "MS Sans Serif" COLOR = #800000><%City%><BR>
</FONT></TD>
<TD BORDERCOLOR = #808080><FONT SIZE = 1
FACE = "MS Sans Serif" COLOR = #800000><%Region%><BR>
</FONT></TD>
<TD BORDERCOLOR = #808080><FONT SIZE = 1
FACE = "MS Sans Serif" COLOR = #800000><%PostalCode%><BR>
</FONT></TD>
<TD BORDERCOLOR = #808080><FONT SIZE = 1
FACE = "MS Sans Serif" COLOR = #800000><%Country%><BR>
</FONT></TD>
<TD BORDERCOLOR = #808080><FONT SIZE = 1
FACE = "MS Sans Serif" COLOR = #800000><%Phone%><BR>
</FONT></TD>
<TD BORDERCOLOR = #808080><FONT SIZE = 1
FACE = "MS Sans Serif" COLOR = #800000><%Fax%><BR>
</FONT></TD>

</TR>
<%EndDetail%>
</TBODY>
<TFOOT></TFOOT>
</TABLE>
</BODY>
</HTML>
```

Fig. 24.17 **customers.htx** file.

We can execute the IDC by using a Web browser to send a request to the Web server for the IDC file. Since the file was saved to the root web in PWS, we can type

```
http://127.0.0.1/customers.idc?
```

The syntax is similar to that used in CGI scripting (which we discuss in Chapter 27). The question mark tells the server that the request can take parameters. In this case there are no parameters, but the question mark is still required. The browser should return an HTML page containing a table that was dynamically generated from the customer information in the **`Customers`** table of the Northwind database (Fig. 24.18).

24.5 Microsoft Internet Information Server (IIS)

Internet Information Server (IIS) extends Windows NT Server to the world of Intranets and the Internet. It works closely with NT services, security and monitoring. It adds World Wide Web Service, Gopher and FTP Service, Internet Service Manager (the IIS administration tool), Internet Database Connector (IDC) and Secure Sockets Layer (SSL) to a Windows NT server. IIS 2.0 is a part of Windows NT 4.0. You can install IIS when you install Windows NT 4.0 or later, after installing Windows NT 4.0. The latest version of the software, however, is IIS 4.0 and is included in Windows NT Option Pack 4.0 at no charge. We will cover the installation later in this chapter.

The product home page address for IIS is

```
http://www.microsoft.com/ntserver/Basics/WebServices/
default.asp
```

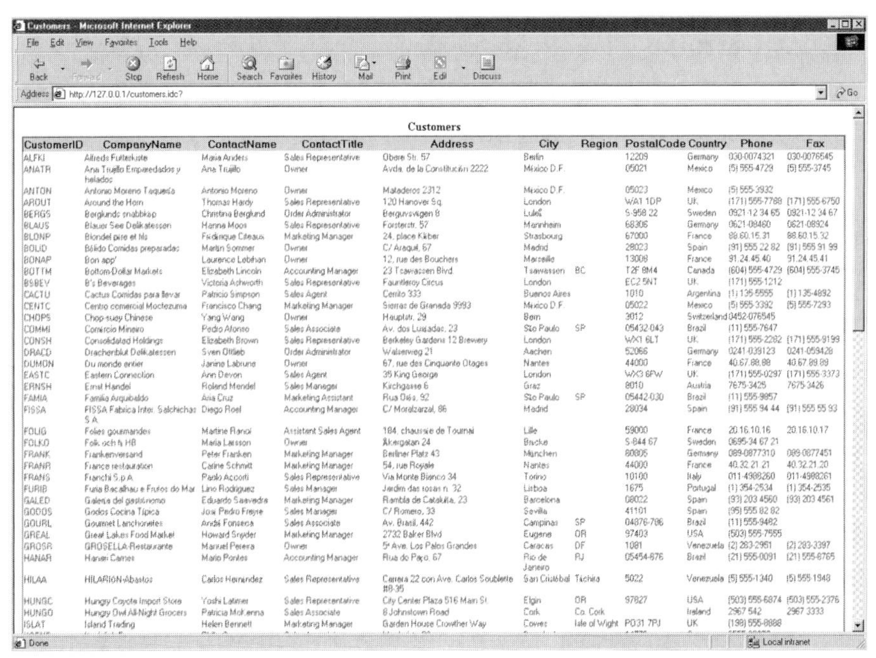

Fig. 24.18 **`customers.idc`** as requested and displayed in a Web browser.

The software download address for IIS is

`http://www.microsoft.com/ntserver/nts/downloads/recommended/NT4OptPk/default.asp`

IIS provides full Intranet and Internet Web capabilities, ranging from publishing information to complete access to data stored in various client/server databases. IIS supports CGI. But CGI creates a separate process for every request, which could mean more server resources, including memory. Microsoft's solution to this problem is the *Internet Server Application Programming Interface (ISAPI)*. You can write ISAPI applications as dynamic-link libraries which are loaded in the address space of the HTTP server. One DLL can handle all the user forms, data and programming logic. ISAPI also allows HTTP filters to be written that handle chosen events.

One of the most important and useful features for Intranets is the back-end database access and programming. IIS has IDC, which connects to back-end ODBC databases. The IDC capabilities include insert, update, delete, etc. Intranet interface to legacy and client/server databases is an essential part in the development of corporate information systems.

IIS is managed with a graphical user interface program called the *Internet Service Manager*. The Internet Service Manager uses the Windows NT DCE-compatible Remote Procedure Call (RPC) to securely administer the server and all the Web applications running on it. You can manage systems locally, over a local area network (LAN), and even over the Internet from a Windows NT Workstation.

In order to start the installation of IIS 4.0 on Windows NT 4.0, you will need

1. to install Windows NT Server 4.0 Service Pack 3 (or higher)
2. to install Microsoft Internet Explorer (IE 4.01 or higher)
3. 32 MB of RAM (at least 64 MB is recommended)
4. from 50 to 200 MB of free disk space, depending on the components you install
5. an Internet connection if you are publishing on the Internet, or a network adapter card if you are publishing on a local Intranet.

If you have not installed Service Pack 3 or at least IE 4.01, you will get a warning message (Fig. 24.19) and the setup process will abort.

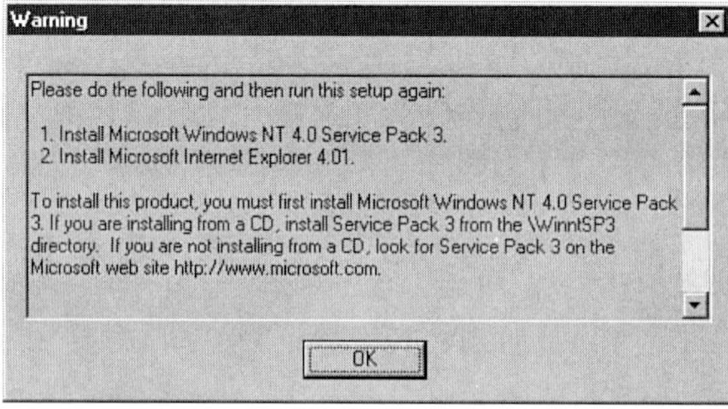

Fig. 24.19 IIS setup **Warning** dialog.

24.6 Apache Web Server

Apache is currently the leading UNIX Web server. It is a high-performance *httpd (HTTP daemon) server* that has its roots in UNIX. A *daemon* is a UNIX background process that implements the server side of a protocol. Also, httpd is the program you would run on a UNIX platform to launch a Web server. On other platforms, such as Microsoft Windows NT, the Web server is a background process implemented as a system service.

The Apache Web Server is a drop-in replacement for National Center for Supercomputing Applications (NCSA) HTTPd server. On a Web server already running NCSA, one can simply compile Apache and replace the HTTPd binary from NCSA with the new Apache binary. It is developed by the Apache Group and is available free of charge. Apache comes in source form and can be compiled on many platforms, such as AIX, HPUX, IRIX, Linux, SCO UNIX, SunOS, NeXT, BSDI, FreeBSD and Solaris. There are also versions of Apache for OS/2 and Windows NT.

The product home page address for Apache is

`http://www.apache.org/`

and the software download address for Apache is

`http://www.apache.org/dist/`

Binary distributions of Apache are available from

`http://www.apache.org/dist/binaries/`

There is an abundant array of server-side programming tools and languages available for the Apache Web Server platform. Included among these languages are included Perl, PHP3, Tcl and Python. *PHP3* is a scripting language that allows the embedding of scripting code into your HTML pages. Apache JServ is a Java servlet engine, which provides programmers with access to the Java Servlet API, an extremely powerful tool for building server-side component software. JavaServer Pages (JSP) embed java code within HTML templates to create dynamic pages which are processed entirely by the Web server.

Apache users can download modules that provide additional functionality. Programmers, webmasters and hobbyists can register and search for modules at

`http://modules.apache.org/`

This URL includes ***`mod_SSL`***—which provides strong cryptography for the Apache 1.3 Web server via the Secure Sockets Layer.

With ***`mod_perl`***, new Apache modules can be written entirely in Perl. Also, the persistent interpreter embedded in Apache eliminates the overhead of loading an external Perl interpreter every time a script is interpreted. Module **`mod_perl`** can be downloaded from

`http://perl.apache.org/dist/`

Future releases of the Apache Web Server will include a 100% Pure Java Servlet and JavaServer Pages implementation in the form of the JavaServer Web Development Kit. This project is known as *Jakarta* and is currently in the formative stages. *JServ* is an Apache module that implements Sun's Java Servlet API for running server-side Java code.

The installation of Apache varies depending on the platform. On most operating systems, the main Apache binary is compiled specifically for that environment during the installation. From the Apache download page, you can select the archive or binaries for the server platform of choice. Once the file is retrieved, read and follow the installation instructions included in the installation archive. Normally, the installation goes smoothly, and a simple batch install transfers all necessary files and configures all environment variables.

When run on Windows NT, the Apache Web Server can be run either as a console application or as a service. Running it as a console application (Fig. 24.20) means that stopping and starting the server is a manual process. Running it as a service means that Apache starts whenever the operating system starts.

The console window must remain open (or minimized) in order for Apache to serve Web requests. Figure 24.21 shows the default Web site page for the Apache Web Server.

24.7 W3C Jigsaw Web Server

W3C *Jigsaw* is a free Web server written entirely in Java. Two of its major design goals are portability and extensibility. Jigsaw runs on most machines that support Java environment, including Microsoft Windows 95/98/NT, Sun Microsystems' Solaris and Linux.

Fig. 24.20 Starting the Apache Web Server as a console application.

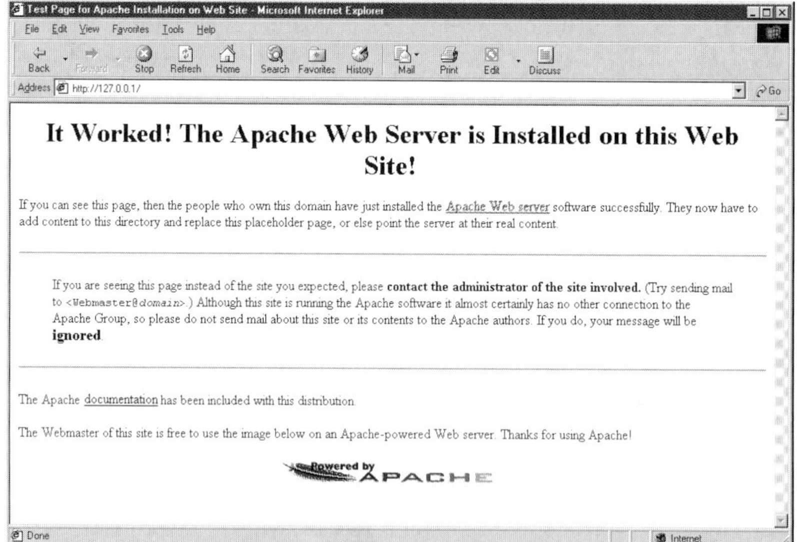

Fig. 24.21 Default Web site page for Apache Web Server.

Writing new resource objects in Java can extend the Jigsaw server's functionality. One possible extension would be a replacement for CGI scripts. Using this extension does not preclude the use of normal CGI scripts. The support for regular CGI scripts allows you to migrate existing CGI applications into Jigsaw. Portability adds tremendous value to the Jigsaw server when you select a hardware and software base for your Web applications.

Jigsaw is an object-oriented Web server. Each resource exported by the server is mapped to a Java object. Each resource can be configured independently and maintains its own state through a persistence mechanism provided by Jigsaw.

The major components of the Jigsaw server are the *daemon module* and the *resource module*. The daemon module deals with HTTP. It handles incoming connections, creates new client objects, decodes requests and sends replies. The resource module is responsible for managing the information space of the server.

Jigsaw's home page address is

http://www.w3.org/Jigsaw

The Jigsaw installation (Fig. 24.22) also requires that either the Sun Java 2 Runtime Environment or the entire Java 2 SDK (previously termed the JDK) be installed on the system prior to either launching the Web server or the administration tools. Although Jigsaw functions with earlier versions, Java 2 (which is actually version 1.2 of the Sun Java software distribution) is highly recommended. The Java 2 Runtime Environment can be downloaded from

http://java.sun.com/products/jdk/1.2/jre/index.html

The Java 2 SDK, Standard Edition can be downloaded from

http://java.sun.com/products/jdk/1.2/

Figure 24.23 shows the default Web site page for the Jigsaw Web server.

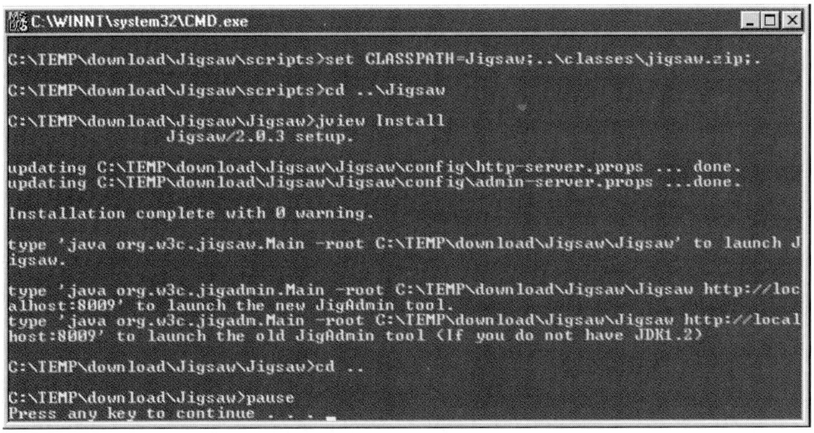

```
C:\WINNT\system32\CMD.exe

C:\TEMP\download\Jigsaw\scripts>set CLASSPATH=Jigsaw;..\classes\jigsaw.zip;.

C:\TEMP\download\Jigsaw\scripts>cd ..\Jigsaw

C:\TEMP\download\Jigsaw\Jigsaw>jview Install
                Jigsaw/2.0.3 setup.

updating C:\TEMP\download\Jigsaw\Jigsaw\config\http-server.props ... done.
updating C:\TEMP\download\Jigsaw\Jigsaw\config\admin-server.props ...done.

Installation complete with 0 warning.

type 'java org.w3c.jigsaw.Main -root C:\TEMP\download\Jigsaw\Jigsaw' to launch J
igsaw.

type 'java org.w3c.jigadmin.Main -root C:\TEMP\download\Jigsaw\Jigsaw http://loc
alhost:8009' to launch the new JigAdmin tool.
type 'java org.w3c.jigadm.Main -root C:\TEMP\download\Jigsaw\Jigsaw http://local
host:8009' to launch the old JigAdmin tool (If you do not have JDK1.2)

C:\TEMP\download\Jigsaw\Jigsaw>cd ..

C:\TEMP\download\Jigsaw>pause
Press any key to continue . . .
```

Fig. 24.22 Jigsaw batch installation process.

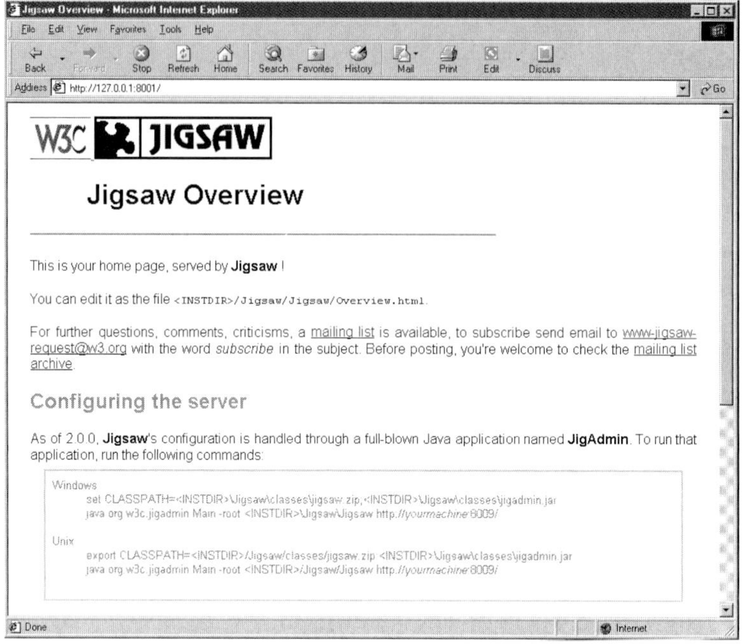

Fig. 24.23 Default Web site page for the Jigsaw Web server.

The main command to start **JigAdmin** is

```
java org.w3c.jigadm.Main -root INSTDIR/Jigsaw/Jigsaw
```

(Note: Change the "**/**" to "****" for Windows servers.)

Upon executing the above command, the **Authorization for JigAdmin** dialog (Fig. 24.24) is displayed. By default, Jigsaw comes with predefined **User name** and **Password** (**admin**/**admin**) for the administration server, and no protection on the **Admin** directory of the HTTP server.

Upon successful login, the **JigAdmin** dialog is displayed (Fig. 24.25 and Fig. 24.26). This dialog provides a graphical user interface for managing the Web server.

Fig. 24.24 **JigAdmin** (Jigsaw Administration tool) authorization dialog.

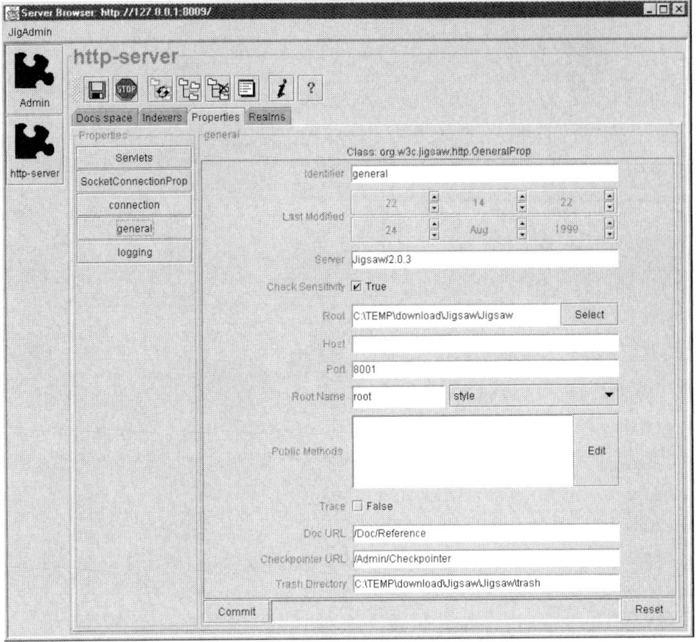

Fig. 24.25 **JigAdmin** general properties page.

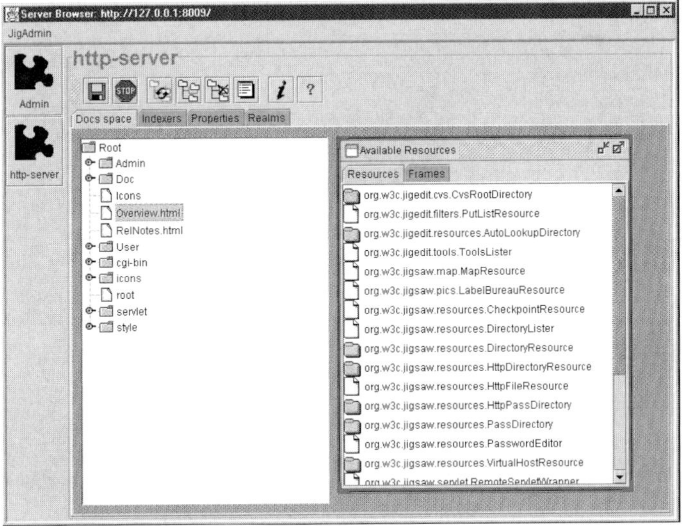

Fig. 24.26 **JigAdmin** Web configuration page.

24.8 Web Server Error Codes

The W3C's HTTP specification identifies specific errors that can be returned in the Web server's response to HTTP requests. All HTTP-compliant Web servers support these as well as HTTP status codes that identify redirected and successful transactions. Values of the more common numeric error status codes are listed in Fig. 24.27.

24.9 Internet and World Wide Web Resources

There are many Web server resources available on the Web. This section lists several URLs where Web servers, Option Packs, etc. can be downloaded. Other URLs related to this chapter are listed as well.

http://www.microsoft.com/Windows/ie/pws/
Home page URL for PWS.

http://www.microsoft.com/msdownload/ntoptionpack/askwiz.asp
Download URL for Windows NT Option Pack.

http://www.microsoft.com/data/
Microsoft Universal Data Access (UDA) Web site.

http://msdn.microsoft.com/xml/xslguide/register-xml.reg
XML registry update file for PWS.

http://www.microsoft.com/ntserver/Basics/WebServices/default.asp
Product home page URL for IIS.

http://www.apache.org/
Product home page URL for Apache.

http://www.apache.org/dist/
Apache download URL.

Error Code	Description
Bad Request 400	Error in request syntax.
Unauthorized 401	Request requires an Authorization: field, and the client did not provide one. This response is accompanied by a list of acceptable authorization schemes use WWW-Authenticate response headers. Error 401 can be part of a client/server dialogue to negotiate encryption and user-authentication schemes.
Payment Required 402	The requested operation costs money, and the client did not specify a valid **ChargeTo** field.
Forbidden 403	Request for forbidden resource denied.
Not found 404	Requested resource not found.
Internal Error 500	The server has encountered an internal error and cannot continue processing the request.
Not implemented 501	Request acceptable but denied because server does not support this transaction method.

Fig. 24.27 Common numeric error status codes.

http://www.avenida.co.uk/products/aws/index.html
Product home page URL for Avenida Web server.

http://www.w3.org/Jigsaw
Jigsaw download URL.

http://java.sun.com/products/jdk/1.2/jre/index.html
The Java 2 Runtime Environment download URL.

http://java.sun.com/products/jdk/1.2/
The Java 2 SDK, Standard Edition download URL.

http://msdn.microsoft.com
Microsoft Developer Network (MSDN) URL which contains documentation and examples.

http://www.w3.org/MarkUp/
W3C HTML specification URL.

http://www.w3.org/Protocols/
W3C HTTP specification URL.

SUMMARY

- A network allows two or more computers to share their resources. Any network requires servers to manage access to files, folders, hardware and software. Thus a Web server is a network server that manages access to files, folders and other resources over the Internet or a local Intranet.
- Web servers possess unique Web networking characteristics. They handle permissions, execute programs, keep track of directories and files, and communicate with client computers. These client computers make requests for files and actions from server computers using HTTP (HyperText Transfer Protocol), an Internet protocol that enables the distribution of hypertext documents. HTTP is a client/server protocol.
- Web servers allow you to serve content over the Internet using HTML. The Web server accepts requests from browsers like Internet Explorer and Netscape Communicator then returns the appropriate HTML documents.
- A number of server-side technologies can be used to increase the power of the server beyond its ability to deliver standard HTML pages; these include CGI scripts and server-side includes, SSL security and Active Server Pages.
- You can connect to data sources using the Internet Database Connector (IDC), CGI and ASP with Microsoft PWS. PWS is a scaled-down version of Microsoft's Internet Information Server (IIS), the professional, commercial Web server found on many hosting services. PWS requires that Internet Explorer 4.0 or higher be installed on the system.
- PWS must be running to respond to clients' requests for Web pages and other data. Port 80 is the default port for PWS networking and is the standard port used by most Internet Web servers.
- The computer on which PWS is installed does not need to be connected to the Internet in order to serve HTTP requests. If the Microsoft TCP/IP protocol is correctly configured and PWS is installed clients can receive information from the Web server.
- It is important to realize that any Web browser, including Microsoft Internet Explorer, Netscape Communicator, Opera, Lynx, etc. can request information from PWS.
- A loopback address is a virtual address that allows testing of a computer's TCP/IP stack (i.e., that computer's TCP/IP software) from that same computer.
- A root web is a web that is the top-level content directory of a Web server. It can have many levels of subdirectories, containing content. There can be only one root web per installation of PWS. The

root web points to a home directory that contains the files that are displayed when a Web browser sends HTTP request to the Web server. By default, the home directory is **C:\Webshare\Wwwroot**. This is where all files sent to HTTP clients by PWS reside.

- Personal Web Server can publish both information and applications. This means your server can contain anything from static pages of information to interactive applications. You can also find and extract information from, and insert information into, databases.
- You can use any text editor, such as Notepad, Wordpad or Windows Write, to create and edit your HTML files; but you will probably find an HTML editor, such as Internet Assistant for Microsoft Word, easier to use. If you want to include images or sounds, you will also need appropriate software (e.g., PaintShop Pro) to create and edit those files.
- Your files can include images and sounds. You can even create links to Microsoft Office files or to almost any other file format. Remote users must have the correct viewing application to view non-HTML files.
- One of the most exciting features of Microsoft Personal Web Server is the ability to run applications or scripts that remote users start by clicking HTML links or by filling in and sending an HTML form. Using programming languages such as C or Perl, you can create applications or scripts that communicate with the user in HTML pages created dynamically.
- Interactive applications or scripts can be written in almost any 32-bit programming language, such as C or Perl, or as Windows batch files (**.bat** or **.cmd**). When you write your applications or scripts you can use one of two supported interfaces, the Microsoft Internet Server Application Programming Interface (ISAPI) or the Common Gateway Interface (CGI). Batch files can issue any command valid at the command prompt.
- ISAPI for Windows NT can be used to write applications that Web users activate by filling out an HTML form or by clicking a hyperlink. The remote application can then take the user-supplied information and do almost anything with it that can be programmed, and return the results in an HTML page or post the information in a database.
- ISAPI can be used to create applications that run as Dynamic link Libraries (DLLs) on your Web server. A DLL requires less overhead because each request does not start a separate process, unlike Common Gateway Interface (CGI) scripts which each run in their own separate process.
- ISAPI allows pre-processing of requests and post-processing of responses, permitting site-specific handling of HyperText Transport Protocol (HTTP) requests and responses. ISAPI filters can be used for applications such as customized authentication, access or logging. You can create complex sites by using both ISAPI filters and applications. ISAPI extensions can also be combined with the Internet Database Connector to create highly interactive sites.
- The Common Gateway Interface (CGI) is a standard interface used to write applications that remote users can start by filling out an HTML form or clicking a hyperlink. As with ISAPI, the remote application can then take the user-supplied information, process it, then return the results of the application in an HTML page or post the information to a database. Because simple CGI applications are often written using scripting languages such as Perl, CGI applications are sometimes referred to as scripts. Microsoft Personal Web Server can use most Windows 95/98 32-bit applications that conform to the CGI specification.
- Because you have the flexibility to create applications in almost any programming language, Personal Web Server uses the filename extension to determine which interpreter to invoke for each application. You can use the Registry Editor to create additional associations.
- XML documents can be served by PWS once the **text/xml** MIME type has been registered on the server. Installing Microsoft Internet Explorer 5 on the server registers the **text/xml** MIME type and associates it with the **.xml** and **.xsl** file extensions.

- In order to adjust virtual directory permissions, PWS comes with a simple administration utility called the **Personal Web Manager**. The **Main** window of the **Personal Web Manager** provides basic start/stop tools and some usage statistics including the number of current active connections to PWS, etc.
- The **Advanced Options** area of the **Personal Web Manager** enables you to reconfigure your Web site to accommodate new pages or to modify virtual directory permissions.
- When you allow remote users to run applications on your computer, you run the risk of hackers attempting to break into your system. PWS is not a highly secure Internet Web server. It is more of an educational tool.
- One way that PWS limits security risks is through file and directory permissions. Virtual directories in PWS can be set to any or all **Read**, **Execute** and **Script** permissions. The virtual directory **`\Scripts`** contains your applications and allows both **Read** and **Script** access. Unauthorized users cannot copy a malicious application and run it on your computer without first gaining access.
- With Personal Web Server and the Open Data Base Connectivity (ODBC) drivers, you can create Web pages from information contained in a database. Access to databases is accomplished through Internet Database Connector (IDC) component of PWS. **`Httpodbc.dll`** is an ISAPI DLL that uses ODBC to gain access to databases.
- **`Httpodbc.dll`** uses two types of files to control how the database is accessed and how the Web page being output is constructed. These file types are Internet Database Connector (**`.idc`**) files and HTML extension (**`.htx`**) files.
- The **`.htx`** file is the template for the actual HTML document that will be returned to the Web browser after the database information has been merged into it by **`Httpodbc.dll`**.
- A system DSN acts as the ODBC connection to a database. The data source name is a logical name used by ODBC to refer to the Microsoft Access driver and the Microsoft Access database file.
- To provide access to the database specified in the System DSN from your Web page, you will need to create an Internet Database Connector file (**`.idc`**) and an HTML extension file (**`.htx`**).
- Internet Information Server (IIS) extends Windows NT Server to the world of Intranets and the Internet. It works closely with NT services, security and monitoring. It adds World Wide Web Service, Gopher and FTP Service, Internet Service Manager (the IIS administration tool), Internet Database Connector (IDC) and Secure Sockets Layer (SSL) to a Windows NT server. IIS 2.0 is a part of Windows NT 4.0. You can install IIS when you install Windows NT 4.0 or later, after installing Windows NT 4.0. The latest version of the software, however, is IIS 4.0 and is included in Windows NT Option Pack 4.0 at no charge.
- IIS provides full Intranet and Internet Web capabilities ranging, from publishing information, to complete access to data stored in various client/server databases. IIS supports CGI.
- One of the most important and useful features for Intranets is the back-end database access and programming. IIS has IDC, which connects to back-end ODBC databases. The IDC capabilities include insert, update, delete, etc.
- IIS is managed with a graphical user interface program called the Internet Service Manager which uses the Windows NT DCE-compatible Remote Procedure Call (RPC) to securely administer the server and all the Web applications running on it. You can manage systems locally, over a local area network (LAN) and even over the Internet from a Windows NT Workstation.
- Apache is currently the leading UNIX Web server. It is a high performance httpd (HTTP daemon) server, which has its roots in UNIX. A daemon is a UNIX background process that implements the server side of a protocol. The httpd command is executed on a UNIX platform to launch a Web server. On other platforms, such as Microsoft Windows NT, the Web server is a background process implemented as a system service.

- The Apache Web Server is a drop-in replacement for National Center for Supercomputing Applications (NCSA) HTTPd server. Apache comes in source form and can be compiled on many platforms such as, AIX, HPUX, IRIX, Linux, SCO UNIX, SunOS, NeXT, BSDI, FreeBSD and Solaris. There are also versions of Apache for OS/2 and Windows NT.
- The installation of Apache varies depending on the platform. On most operating systems, the main Apache binary is compiled specifically for that environment during the installation.
- When run on Windows NT, the Apache Web Server can be run either as a console application or as a service. Running it as a console application means that stopping and starting the server is a manual process. Running it as a service means that Apache starts whenever the operating system starts.
- W3C Jigsaw is the first Web server written entirely in Java. Jigsaw is a free Web server that is available for download from the W3C Web site. Two of its major design goals are portability and extensibility. The Jigsaw server runs on most machines for which a Java environment is available, including Microsoft Windows 95/98/NT, Sun Microsystems' Solaris and Linux.
- Portability adds tremendous value to the Jigsaw server when you select a hardware and software base for your Web applications.
- Jigsaw is an object-oriented Web server. Each resource exported by the server is mapped to a Java object. Each resource can be configured independently and maintains its own state through a persistence mechanism provided by Jigsaw.
- The major components of the Jigsaw server are the daemon module and the resource module. The daemon module deals with HTTP. It handles incoming connections, creates new client objects, decodes requests and sends replies. The resource module is responsible for managing the information space of the server.
- The Jigsaw installation also requires that either the Sun Java 2 Runtime Environment or the entire Java 2 SDK (previously termed the JDK) be installed on the system prior to either launching the Web server or the administration tools.
- The W3C's HTTP specification identifies specific errors that can be returned in the Web server's response to HTTP requests. All HTTP-compliant Web servers support these as well as HTTP status codes that identify redirected and successful transactions.

TERMINOLOGY

active connection
Add Data Source dialog
Apache Group
Apache SSL patch
Apache Web Server
application directory
.asa file
ASP scripting engine
ASP scripting technology
.bat file
C:\Webshare\Wwwroot
client/server protocol
cmd.exe
.cmd file
Common Gateway Interface (CGI)
daemon module
domain server name (DNS)
dynamic-link library (DLL)
Execute access
FrontPage Server Extensions
FrontPage WebBots
HTML extension (.htx) files
HTTP client
httpd
http://localhost
httpodbc.dll
http://127.0.0.1
.htx (HTML extension) files
.idc file
Internet Assistant for Microsoft Word
Internet Database Connector (IDC)
Internet Protocol (IP) address
Internet Server Application Programming Interface (ISAPI)

Internet Service Manager
ISAPI DLL
ISAPI extension
ISAPI filter
ISAPI SDK
Jakarta
JigAdmin Web configuration page
Jigsaw run time
Jigsaw Web server
JServ
loopback address
loopback testing
Lynx Web browser
Microsoft Developer Network (MSDN)
Microsoft Internet Explorer
Microsoft Internet Information Server (IIS)
Microsoft Internet Server Application Programming Interface (ISAPI)
Microsoft IP Configuration Utility
Microsoft loopback adapter
Microsoft Personal Web Server (PWS)
Microsoft Personal Web Server Setup dialog
Microsoft TCP/IP protocol
mod_perl
mod_SSL
Multipurpose Internet Mail Extension (MIME)
NCSA
network
network adapter
network card
Network Identification Panel
Northwind database
ODBC-compliant data source
ODBC Data Sources dialog
Open Database Connectivity (ODBC)
Open Database Connectivity driver
Opera Web browser
peer-to-peer network
Personal Web Manager
Personal Web Server (PWS)
Personal Web Server Network Service
PHP3
port 80
Read access
resource module
root web
Run The Web Server Automatically At Startup check box
Scripts access
/Scripts directory
Secure Socket Layer (SSL)
Select Network Component Type dialog
Select Network Service dialog
Structured Query Language (SQL)
System Data Sources dialog
text/xml MIME type
Uniform Resource Locator (URL)
virtual directory
_vti files
Web server
webs
Windows NT File System (NTFS)
Windows NT 4.0 Option Pack dialog
WINIPCFG utility
WINS server service
WWW networking characteristic

PERFORMANCE TIP

24.1 Applications that use ISAPI are loaded by the Web service at startup. Because the programs are loaded into memory at server startup, ISAPI programs do not have the overhead of CGI applications when they are invoked by a client.

PORTABILITY TIP

24.1 ISAPI is a Microsoft-specific technology.

SELF-REVIEW EXERCISES

24.1 Fill in the blanks for each of the following:

a) A Web browser sends a __________ request using the TCP layer to a Web server when retrieving information over the Internet.

b) When using a Web browser to request data from a Web server that is running on the same machine, use the local machine address of __________. This is often referred to as the loopback address.
c) The default root directory for Personal Web Server is __________.
d) The __________ is an ISAPI DLL that uses ODBC to gain access to databases.
e) __________ is a Web server written entirely in Java.
f) __________ applications require less overhead than Common Gateway Interface (CGI) scripts because each request does not start a separate process, and runs within the process space of the Web server.
g) A __________ directory is not physically contained within the root directory.
h) The __________ directory is the "home" directory of the Web server.
i) __________ is Microsoft's commercial Intranet and Internet Web server.
j) Both Personal Web Server and Internet Information Server support __________. Files of this type employ a Microsoft scripting technology that allows the dynamic creation of Web pages by the Web server.

24.2 State whether each of the following is *true* or *false*. If *false*, explain why.
a) A computer must be connected to the Internet before running a Web server on it.
b) Once configured properly, Personal Web Server is capable of serving XML.
c) Web servers use the FTP protocol to send data over the Internet.
d) Microsoft Personal Web server is a fully scalable Internet Web server able to support easily a large number of commercial users.
e) Both Active Server Pages using ADO and the Internet Database Connector (IDC) can be used to connect a Web server to information within databases.
f) A Web browser running on Windows is unable to access Web pages that are located on a UNIX Web server because of the difference in operating systems.
g) The Apache Web Server is only supported on UNIX operating systems.
h) An IP address is a unique address for an Internet host such as a Web server.
i) Personal Web Server does not support ISAPI extensions.
j) Windows 95/98 has no built-in user authentication, and therefore Personal Web Server is not a good choice for Web sites where high security is a concern.
k) Internet Explorer is a Windows utility that can be used to determine a Web server's IP address.
l) Web pages are always composed of files ending with the **`.htm`** or **`.html`** extensions.
m) Active Server Pages are a type of CGI script.

ANSWERS TO SELF-REVIEW EXERCISES

24.1 a) HTTP. b) **`127.0.0.1`**. c) **`C:\Inetpub\Wwwroot`**. d) Internet Database Connector (IDC). e) W3C Jigsaw (Jigsaw). f) Internet Server Application Programming Interface (ISAPI). g) virtual. h) root. i) Internet Information Server (IIS). j) Active Server Pages (ASP).

24.2 a) False. A computer running a Web server can serve HTTP requests from a local Web browser client running on the same computer or other clients that are on the same local area network. b) True. c) False. Web servers use HTTP to transmit data across the Internet. d) False. PWS only supports 10 concurrent HTTP connections and is not recommended as a commercial Internet Web server solution. Given these requirements, Microsoft Internet Information Server running on Windows NT Server would be the recommended Web server solution. e) True. f) False. The HTTP protocol is a platform-neutral protocol, which allows data to be exchanged between all operating systems that support TCP and a Web browser. g) False. There are Apache versions for many operating systems, including Windows and OS/2. h) True. i) False. Personal Web Server does support ISAPI extensions. j) True. k) False. Internet Explorer is a Web browser and must rely on DNS for resolving Web server IP addressing. WINIPCFG, WNTIPCFG and IPCONFIG are all utilities that can run on the same computer as the Web server in order to determine that computer's IP address. l) False. As long as a file's MIME type is registered with the Web server, that file can be processed and transmitted to Web browser clients. m) False. ASP and CGI are two entirely different technologies. The primary difference is that ASPs run within the process space of the Web server, whereas CGI spawns separate running processes for each CGI request.

25

Database: SQL, ADO and RDS

Objectives

- To understand the relational database model.
- To be able to write database queries using Structured Query Language (SQL).
- To understand Microsoft's ActiveX Data Object (ADO) Technology.
- To understand Microsoft's Remote Data Services (RDS) Technology.
- To be able to implement a client-side RDS program.

It is a capital mistake to theorize before one has data.
Arthur Conan Doyle

Now go, write it before them in a table, and note it in a book, that it may be for the time to come for ever and ever.
The Holy Bible: The Old Testament

Let's look at the record.
Alfred Emanuel Smith

True art selects and paraphrases, but seldom gives a verbatim translation.
Thomas Bailey Aldrich

Get your facts first, and then you can distort them as much as you please.
Mark Twain

I like two kinds of men: domestic and foreign.
Mae West

Outline

25.1 Introduction[1]

A *database* is an integrated collection of data. A *database management system (DBMS)* involves the data itself and the software that controls the storage and retrieval of data. Database management systems provide mechanisms for storing and organizing data in a manner that facilitates satisfying sophisticated queries and manipulations of the data.

The most popular database systems in use today are *relational databases*. A language called *Structured Query Language* (*SQL*—pronounced "sequel") is almost universally used with relational database systems to make *queries* (i.e., to request information that satisfies given criteria) and manipulate data. Some popular enterprise-level relational database systems include Microsoft SQL Server, Oracle, Sybase, DB2 and Informix. A popular personal relational database is Microsoft Access (which we use for simplicity in our examples).

In this chapter, we present basic SQL queries using a database containing many of our books. We also introduce two Microsoft technologies that provide access to database contents—*ActiveX Data Objects (ADO)* and *Remote Data Services (RDS)*. Together, these two technologies enable a client Web browser to retrieve information from a database on a Web server, process that information on the client computer and return modifications of the data to the Web server so that data can be updated in the database. The manipulation of the data on the client increases the performance of Web-based database applications because every

1. Portions of Sections 25.1 and 25.2 are based on Deitel, H. M., *Operating Systems, 2/E*, pp. 404–409. Reading, MA: Addison-Wesley, Copyright 1990.

interaction with the data (e.g., sorting the data differently) does not require a new request to the server containing the database. Accordingly, this reduces the number of times that results must be sent to the client from the server (and possibly back to the server again). Manipulating data on the client also reduces the overall load on the server computer. Fewer interactions over the network and reduced server loads generally result in higher distributed application performance—a key aspect in designing today's distributed applications.

25.2 Relational Database Model

The *relational database model* is a logical representation of the data that allows the relationships between the data to be considered without concerning oneself with the physical implementation of the data structures.

A relational database is composed of *tables*. Figure 25.1 illustrates a sample table that might be used in a personnel system. The name of the table is **Employee** and its primary purpose is to illustrate the attributes of an employee and how they are related to a specific employee. Any particular row of the table is called a *record* (or *row*). This table consists of six records. The **Employee** table's **Number** field of each record in this table is used as the *primary key* for referencing data in the table. The records of Fig. 25.1 are *ordered* by primary key. Tables in a database normally have primary keys. Primary key fields in a table cannot contain duplicate values.

Each column of the table represents a different *field* (or *column* or *attribute*). Records are normally unique (by primary key) within a table, but particular field values may be duplicated between records. For example, three different records in the **Employee** table's **Department** field contain number 413. The primary key can be composed of more than one column (or field) in the database.

Different users of a database are often interested in different data and different relationships between those data. Some users want only certain subsets of the table columns. To obtain table subsets, we use SQL statements to specify the data to *select* from the table. SQL provides a complete set of keywords (including **SELECT**) that enable programmers to define complex queries that select data from a table. The results of a query are commonly called *result sets* (or *record sets*). Other users of a database wish to combine smaller tables into larger ones to produce more complex result sets. The combination operation is called *join* (specified with **INNER JOIN** in SQL). SQL queries are discussed in Section 25.4.

For example, we might select data from the table in Fig. 25.1 to create a new result set whose purpose is to show where departments are located. This result set is shown in Fig. 25.2.

25.3 Relational Database Overview: Books.mdb

In this section, we overview Structured Query Language (SQL) in the context of a sample database we created for this chapter. Before we discuss SQL, we overview the tables of the **Books.mdb** database. We use this database throughout the chapter to introduce various database concepts, including the use of SQL to obtain useful information from the database and to manipulate the database. The database can be found with the examples for this book.

The database consists of four tables—**Authors**, **Publishers**, **AuthorISBN** and **Titles**. [*Note:* The primary key field for each table is shown in italics in both the figures containing the descriptions of the columns of the table and in the figures showing the contents of the tables.]

Table: **Employee**

	Number	**Name**	**Department**	**Salary**	**Location**
	23603	JONES, A.	413	1100	NEW JERSEY
	24568	KERWIN, R.	413	2000	NEW JERSEY
A record	34589	LARSON, P.	642	1800	LOS ANGELES
	35761	MYERS, B.	611	1400	ORLANDO
	47132	NEUMANN, C.	413	9000	NEW JERSEY
	78321	STEPHENS, T.	611	8500	ORLANDO
	Primary key		A column		

Fig. 25.1 Relational database structure.

Department	**Location**
413	NEW JERSEY
611	ORLANDO
642	LOS ANGELES

Fig. 25.2 A result set formed by selecting data from a table.

The **Authors** table (shown in Fig. 25.3) consists of four fields that maintain each author's unique ID number in the database, first name, last name and the year in which the author was born. Figure 25.4 contains the data from the **Authors** table of the **Books.mdb** database.

Field	Description
AuthorID	An integer representing the author's ID number in the database. This is the primary key field for this table.
FirstName	A string representing the author's first name.
LastName	A string representing the author's last name.
YearBorn	A string representing the author's year of birth.

Fig. 25.3 **Authors** table from **Books.mdb**.

AuthorID	**FirstName**	**LastName**	**YearBorn**
1	Harvey	Deitel	1946
2	Paul	Deitel	1968
3	Tem	Nieto	1969

Fig. 25.4 Data from the **Authors** table of **Books.mdb**.

The **Publishers** table (shown in Fig. 25.5) consists of two fields representing each publisher's unique ID and name. Figure 25.6 contains the data from the **Publishers** table of the **Books.mdb** database.

The **AuthorISBN** table (Fig. 25.7) consists of two fields that maintain each ISBN number and its corresponding author's ID number. This table will help link the names of the authors with the titles of their books. Figure 25.8 contains the data from the **AuthorISBN** table of the **Biblio.mdb** database.

Field	Description
PublisherID	An integer representing the publisher's ID number in the database. This is the primary key field for this table.
PublisherName	A string representing the abbreviated name for the publisher.

Fig. 25.5 **Publishers** table from **Books.mdb**.

PublisherID	**PublisherName**
1	Prentice Hall
2	Prentice Hall PTR

Fig. 25.6 Data from the **Publishers** table of **Books.mdb**.

Field	Description
ISBN	A string representing the ISBN number for a book.
AuthorID	An integer representing the author's ID number, which allows the database to connect each book to a specific author. The ID number in this field must also appear in the **Authors** table.

Fig. 25.7 **AuthorISBN** table from **Books.mdb**.

ISBN	AuthorID	ISBN	AuthorID
0-13-010671-2	1	*(continued from bottom left of this table)*	
0-13-010671-2	2	0-13-020522-2	3
0-13-020522-2	1	0-13-082714-2	1
0-13-020522-2	2	0-13-082714-2	2
(continued on top right of this table)		0-13-082925-0	1

Fig. 25.8 Data from the **AuthorISBN** table of **Books.mdb** (part 1 of 2).

ISBN	AuthorID	ISBN	AuthorID
(continued from previous page)		*(continued from bottom left of this table)*	
0-13-082925-0	2	0-13-565912-4	2
0-13-082927-7	1	0-13-565912-4	3
0-13-082927-7	2	0-13-899394-7	1
0-13-082928-5	1	0-13-899394-7	2
0-13-082928-5	2	0-13-904947-9	1
0-13-082928-5	3	0-13-904947-9	2
0-13-083054-2	1	0-13-904947-9	3
0-13-083054-2	2	0-13-013249-7	1
0-13-083055-0	1	0-13-013249-7	2
0-13-083055-0	2	0-13-085609-6	1
0-13-118043-6	1	0-13-085609-6	2
0-13-118043-6	2	0-13-085609-6	3
0-13-226119-7	1	0-13-016143-8	1
0-13-226119-7	2	0-13-016143-8	2
0-13-271974-6	1	0-13-016143-8	3
0-13-271974-6	2	0-13-015870-4	1
0-13-456955-5	1	0-13-015870-4	2
0-13-456955-5	2	0-13-015870-4	3
0-13-456955-5	3	0-13-012507-5	1
0-13-528910-6	1	0-13-012507-5	2
0-13-528910-6	2	0-13-085248-1	1
0-13-565912-4	1	0-13-085248-1	2
(continued on top right of this table)			

Fig. 25.8 Data from the **AuthorISBN** table of **Books.mdb** (part 2 of 2).

The **Titles** table (Fig. 25.9) consists of six fields that maintain general information about each book in the database including the ISBN number, title, edition number, year published, a description of the book and the publisher's ID number. Figure 25.10 contains the data from the **Titles** table. [*Note:* We did not have room to show the **Description** field of the **Titles** table in Fig. 25.10.

Figure 25.11 illustrates the relationships among the tables in the **Books.mdb** database (this diagram was produced in Microsoft Access when we originally designed the database). A field name in bold in a table is that table's *primary key*. A table's primary key uniquely identifies each record in the table. Every record must have a value in the primary key field and the value must be unique. This is known as the *Rule of Entity Integrity*.

Field	Description
ISBN	A string representing the ISBN number of the book.
Title	A string representing the title of the book.
EditionNumber	A string representing the edition number of the book.
YearPublished	A string representing the year in which the book was published.
Description	A string representing the description of the book.
PublisherID	An integer representing the publisher's ID number. This value must correspond to an ID number in the **Publishers** table.

Fig. 25.9 **Titles** table from **Books.mdb**.

ISBN	**Title**	**Edition Number**	**Year Published**	**Publisher ID**
0-13-226119-7	C How to Program	2	1994	1
0-13-528910-6	C++ How to Program	2	1997	1
0-13-899394-7	Java How to Program	2	1997	1
0-13-012507-5	Java How to Program	3	1999	1
0-13-456955-5	Visual Basic 6 How to Program	1	1998	1
0-13-016143-8	Internet and World Wide Web How to Program	1	1999	1
0-13-013249-7	Getting Started with Visual C++ 6 with an Introduction to MFC	1	1999	1
0-13-565912-4	C++ How to Program Instructor's Manual with Solutions Disk	2	1998	1
0-13-904947-9	Java How to Program Instructor's Manual with Solution Disk	2	1997	1
0-13-020522-2	Visual Basic 6 How to Program Instructor's Manual with Solution Disk	1	1999	1
0-13-015870-4	Internet and World Wide Web How to Program Instructor's Manual with Solutions Disk	1	1999	1
0-13-082925-0	The Complete C++ Training Course	2	1998	2
0-13-082927-7	The Complete Java Training Course	2	1997	2
0-13-082928-5	The Complete Visual Basic 6 Training Course	1	1999	2
0-13-085248-1	The Complete Java Training Course	3	1999	2

Fig. 25.10 Data from the **Titles** table of **Books.mdb** (part 1 of 2).

ISBN	Title	Edition Number	Year Published	Publisher ID
0-13-085609-6	The Internet and World Wide Web How to Program Complete Training Course	1	1999	2
0-13-082714-2	C++ How to Program 2/e and Getting Started with Visual C++ 5.0 Tutorial	2	1998	1
0-13-010671-2	Java How to Program 2/e and Getting Started with Visual J++ 1.1 Tutorial	2	1998	1
0-13-083054-2	The Complete C++ Training Course 2/e and Getting Started with Visual C++ 5.0 Tutorial	2	1998	1
0-13-083055-0	The Complete Java Training Course 2/e and Getting Started with Visual J++ 1.1 Tutorial	2	1998	1
0-13-118043-6	C How to Program	1	1992	1
0-13-271974-6	Java Multimedia Cyber Classroom	1	1996	2

Fig. 25.10 Data from the **Titles** table of **Books.mdb** (part 2 of 2).

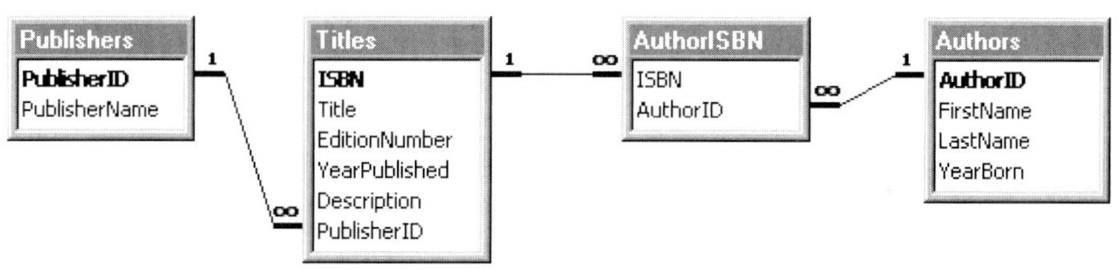

Fig. 25.11 Table relationships in **Books.mdb**.

The lines between the tables represent the relationships. Consider the line between the **Publishers** and **Titles** tables. On the **Publishers** end of the line there is a **1** and on the **Titles** end there is an infinity symbol. This indicates that every publisher in the **Publishers** table can have an arbitrary number of books in the **Titles** table—a *one-to-many relationship.*

The **Publishers** table and the **Titles** table are linked by their **PublisherID** fields. The **PublisherID** field in the **Titles** table is the *foreign key* of the **PublisherID** field in the **Publishers** table. A foreign key field in one table corresponds to the primary key field in a different table. There is a one-to-many relationship between a primary key and its corresponding foreign key. The foreign key helps maintain the *Rule of Referential Integrity*—every foreign key field value must reference a unique primary key value in another table. It is not possible to publish a book without a publisher for the book. Therefore, in the **Books.mdb** database, it is not possible to place an entry in the **Titles** table for a book without a corresponding publisher in the **Publishers** table. Referential integrity is normally maintained by the application manipulating the database and by the database management system. In our example, Microsoft Access ensures that every record in the **Titles** table refers to one record in the **Publishers** table (this was configured when we first created the database in Access). Foreign keys also enable information from multiple tables to be joined together to create temporary tables for analysis purposes.

Common Programming Error 25.1

When a field is specified as the primary key field, not providing a value for that field in every record breaks the Rule of Entity Integrity and is an error.

Common Programming Error 25.2

When a field is specified as the primary key field, providing duplicate values for multiple records is an error.

The line between the **AuthorISBN** and **Authors** tables indicates that for each author in the **Authors** table there can be an infinite number of ISBNs for books that author wrote in the **AuthorISBN** table. The **AuthorID** field in the **AuthorISBN** table is a foreign key of the **AuthorID** field (the primary key) of the **Authors** table. The **AuthorID** table is used to link information in the **Titles** and **Authors** tables.

Finally, the line between the **Titles** and **AuthorISBN** tables illustrates a one-to-many relationship—a title can be written by any number of authors.

25.4 Structured Query Language

In this section we provide an overview of Structured Query Language (SQL) in the context of the **Books.mdb** sample database we provided for this chapter. You will be able to use the SQL queries discussed here in the examples later in the chapter.

The SQL keywords (Fig. 25.12) for querying a database, inserting records into a database and updating existing records in a database are discussed in the context of complete SQL queries in the next several sections. Note that there are other SQL keywords that are beyond the scope of this text. (*Note:* For more information on SQL, please refer to the bibliography at the end of this chapter and to Section 25.8, "Internet and World Wide Web Resources.")

SQL keyword	Description
SELECT	Select (retrieve) fields from one or more tables.
FROM	Tables from which to get fields. Required in every **SELECT**.
WHERE	Criteria for selection that determine the rows to be retrieved.
ORDER BY	Criteria for ordering (sorting) of records.
INSERT INTO	Insert values into one or more tables. [*Note:* Some databases do not require the SQL keyword **INTO**.]
UPDATE	Update existing data in one or more tables.

Fig. 25.12 SQL query keywords.

25.4.1 Basic SELECT Query

Let us consider several SQL queries that extract information from the **Books.mdb** database. A typical SQL query selects information from one or more tables in a database. Such selections are performed by ***SELECT** queries*. The simplest form of a **SELECT** query is

```
SELECT * FROM TableName
```

In the preceding query, the asterisk (*****) indicates that all rows and columns (fields) from *TableName* should be selected and *TableName* specifies the table in the database from which the data will be selected. For example, to select the entire contents of the **Authors** table (i.e., all the data in Fig. 25.4), use the query

```
SELECT * FROM Authors
```

To select specific fields from a table, replace the asterisk (*****) with a comma-separated list of the field names to select. For example, to select only the fields **AuthorID** and **LastName** for all rows in the **Authors** table use the query

```
SELECT AuthorID, LastName FROM Authors
```

The preceding query selects the data shown in Fig. 25.13.

Software Engineering Observation 25.1

*For most SQL statements, the asterisk (*****) should not be used to specify field names to select from a table (or several tables). In general, programmers process result sets by knowing in advance the order of the fields in the result set. For example, selecting **AuthorID** and **LastName** from the **Authors** table guarantees that the fields will appear in the result set in the same order (**AuthorID** as the first field and **LastName** as the second field). The fields in the result set are processed by specifying the column number in the result set (column numbers typically start at 1 for the first field in the result set).*

Software Engineering Observation 25.2

Specifying the actual field names to select from a table (or several tables) guarantees that the fields are always returned in the same order even if the actual order of the fields in the database table(s) changes.

Common Programming Error 25.3

When performing an SQL statement using the asterisk (*****) to select fields, assuming that the fields in the result set of the query are always returned in the same order may result in incorrect processing of the data in the application receiving the result set. If the order of the fields in the database table(s) changes, the order of the fields in the result set would change accordingly.

AuthorID	**LastName**
1	Deitel
2	Deitel
3	Nieto

Fig. 25.13 **AuthorID** and **LastName** from the **Authors** table.

Performance Tip 25.1

Specifying the actual field names to select from a table allows the result set to be processed more efficiently by the application receiving the result set. This technique allows the fields to be processed by column number which is typically more efficient than processing the fields by field name.

Software Engineering Observation 25.3

*If a field name contains spaces, it must be enclosed in square brackets (**`[]`**) in the query. For example, if the field name is **`First Name`**, the field name would appear in the query as **`[First Name]`**.*

Common Programming Error 25.4

*In a query, forgetting to enclose a field name containing spaces in square brackets (**`[]`**) is an error.*

Good Programming Practice 25.1

Avoid field names containing spaces when designing database tables.

25.4.2 WHERE Clause

In most cases, it is necessary to locate records in a database that satisfy certain *selection criteria*. Only records that match the selection criteria are selected. SQL uses the optional ***`WHERE`*** *clause* in a **`SELECT`** query to specify the selection criteria for the query. The simplest form of a **`SELECT`** query with selection criteria is

`SELECT` *fieldName1*, *fieldName2*, ... **`FROM`** *TableName* **`WHERE`** *criteria*

For example, to select all fields from the **`Authors`** table where the author's **`YearBorn`** is greater than **`1960`**, use the query

```
SELECT AuthorID, FirstName, LastName, YearBorn
   FROM Authors
   WHERE YearBorn > 1960
```

Our database contains only three authors in the **`Authors`** table. Two of the authors were born after 1960, so the two records selected by the preceding query are shown in Fig. 25.14.

Performance Tip 25.2

Using selection criteria improves performance by selecting a portion of the database that is normally smaller than the entire database. Working with a smaller portion of the data is easier and faster than working with the entire set of data stored in the database.

AuthorID	FirstName	LastName	YearBorn
2	Paul	Deitel	1968
3	Tem	Nieto	1969

Fig. 25.14 Authors born after 1960 from the **`Authors`** table.

The **WHERE** clause condition can contain operators such as **<**, **>**, **<=**, **>=**, **=**, **<>** and **LIKE**. Operator **LIKE** is used for *pattern matching* with wildcard characters *asterisk* (*****) and *question mark* (**?**). Pattern matching allows SQL to search for similar strings that "match a pattern." An asterisk (*****) in the pattern indicates any number of (i.e., zero or more) characters in a row at the asterisk's location in the pattern. [*Note:* Many databases use the **%** character in place of the ***** in a **LIKE** expression.] For example, the following query locates the records of all the authors whose last names start with the letter **d**:

```
SELECT AuthorID, FirstName, LastName, YearBorn
   FROM Authors
   WHERE LastName LIKE 'd*'
```

Notice that the pattern string is surrounded by single-quote characters. The preceding query selects the two records shown in Fig. 25.15 because two of the three authors in our database have last names starting with the letter **d** (followed by zero or more characters). Do not confuse the of ***** in the preceding query with the use of ***** to specify the fields to select. The ***** in the **WHERE** clause's **Like** pattern indicates that any number of characters can appear after the letter **d** in the **LastName** field.

Portability Tip 25.1

SQL is case sensitive on some database systems. See your database system documentation to determine if SQL is case sensitive on your database system and to determine the syntax that should be used for SQL keywords (i.e., should they be all uppercase letters, all lowercase letters or some combination of the two?).

Portability Tip 25.2

Not all database systems support the **LIKE** *operator, so be sure to read your database system's documentation carefully.*

Good Programming Practice 25.2

By convention, SQL keywords should use all uppercase letters on systems that are not case sensitive to emphasize the SQL keywords in an SQL statement.

Good Programming Practice 25.3

In database systems that support uppercase and lowercase letters for table names and field names, use an uppercase first letter for every word in a table name or field name (e.g., **LastName***) to make SQL statements more readable.*

A question mark (**?**) in the pattern string indicates a single character at that position in the pattern. For example, the following query locates the records of all the authors whose last names start with any character (specified with **?**) followed by the letter **i** followed by any number of additional characters (specified with *****):

AuthorID	FirstName	LastName	YearBorn
1	Harvey	Deitel	1946
2	Paul	Deitel	1968

Fig. 25.15 Authors whose last names start with **d** from the **Authors** table.

```
SELECT AuthorID, FirstName, LastName, YearBorn
   FROM Authors
   WHERE LastName LIKE '?i*'
```

The preceding query produces the record in Fig. 25.16 because only one author in our database has a last name that contains the letter **i** as its second letter.

A query can be specialized to allow any character in a range of characters in one position of the pattern string. A range of characters can be specified as follows:

[*startValue***-***endValue***]**

where *startValue* is the first character in the range and *endValue* is the last value in the range. For example, the following query locates the records of all the authors whose last names start with any letter (specified with the **?**) followed by any letter in the range **a** to **i** (specified with **[a-i]**) followed by any number of additional characters (specified with *****):

```
SELECT AuthorID, FirstName, LastName, YearBorn
   FROM Authors
   WHERE LastName LIKE '?[a-i]*'
```

The preceding query selects all the records of the **Authors** table (Fig. 25.4) because every author in the table has a last name that contains a second letter in the range **a** to **i**.

25.4.3 ORDER BY Clause

The results of a query can be sorted into ascending or descending order using the optional ***ORDER BY*** *clause*. The simplest forms of an **ORDER BY** clause are

SELECT *fieldName1***,** *fieldName2***,** ... **FROM** *TableName* **ORDER BY** *fieldName* **ASC**
SELECT *fieldName1***,** *fieldName2***,** ... **FROM** *TableName* **ORDER BY** *fieldName* **DESC**

where **ASC** specifies ascending (lowest to highest) order, **DESC** specifies descending (highest to lowest) order and *fieldName* represents the field (the column of the table) that is used for sorting purposes.

For example, to obtain the list of authors in ascending order by last name (Fig. 25.17), use the query

```
SELECT AuthorID, FirstName, LastName, YearBorn
   FROM Authors
   ORDER BY LastName ASC
```

Note that the default sorting order is ascending, so **ASC** is optional.

To obtain the same list of authors in descending order by last name (Fig. 25.18), use the query

```
SELECT AuthorID, FirstName, LastName, YearBorn
   FROM Authors
   ORDER BY LastName DESC
```

Multiple fields can be used for ordering purposes with an **ORDER BY** clause of the form

ORDER BY *field1 SortingOrder***,** *field2 SortingOrder***, ...**

where *SortingOrder* is either **ASC** or **DESC**. Note that the *SortingOrder* does not have to be identical for each field. The query

```
SELECT AuthorID, FirstName, LastName, YearBorn
   FROM Authors
   ORDER BY LastName, FirstName
```

sorts in ascending order all the authors by last name, then by first name. In the set of selected records, the records for authors with the same last name are sorted in ascending order by their first name (Fig. 25.19).

AuthorID	**FirstName**	**LastName**	**YearBorn**
3	Tem	Nieto	1969

Fig. 25.16 Authors from the **Authors** table whose last names contain **i** as the second letter.

AuthorID	**FirstName**	**LastName**	**YearBorn**
2	Paul	Deitel	1968
1	Harvey	Deitel	1946
3	Tem	Nieto	1969

Fig. 25.17 Authors from the **Authors** table in ascending order by **LastName**.

AuthorID	**FirstName**	**LastName**	**YearBorn**
3	Tem	Nieto	1969
2	Paul	Deitel	1968
1	Harvey	Deitel	1946

Fig. 25.18 Authors from the **Authors** table in descending order by **LastName**.

AuthorID	**FirstName**	**LastName**	**YearBorn**
1	Harvey	Deitel	1946
2	Paul	Deitel	1968
3	Tem	Nieto	1969

Fig. 25.19 Authors from the **Authors** table in ascending order by **LastName** and by **FirstName**.

The **WHERE** and **ORDER BY** clauses can be combined in one query. The query

```
SELECT ISBN, Title, EditionNumber,
       YearPublished, PublisherID
   FROM Titles
   WHERE Title LIKE '*How to Program'
   ORDER BY Title ASC
```

selects all records from the **Titles** table that have a **Title** ending with "**How to Program**" and orders them in ascending order by **Title**. The results of the query are shown in Fig. 25.20 (we did not have room to show the **Description** field). [*Note:* When we construct a query we will simply create one long string containing the entire query. When we display queries in the text, we often use multiple lines and indentation for readability.]

25.4.4 Using INNER JOIN to Merge Data from Multiple Tables

Often it is necessary to merge data from multiple tables into a single view for analysis purposes. This is referred to as *joining* the tables and is accomplished using the ***INNER JOIN*** operation in the **FROM** clause of a **SELECT** query. An **INNER JOIN** merges records from two or more tables by testing for matching values in a field common to both tables. The simplest form of an **INNER JOIN** clause is

```
SELECT fieldName1, fieldName2, ...
   FROM Table1 INNER JOIN Table2 ON Table1.field = Table2.field
```

The **ON** part of the **INNER JOIN** clause specifies the fields from each table that should be compared to determine which records will be selected. For example, to merge the **FirstName** and **LastName** fields from the **Authors** table with the **ISBN** field from the **AuthorISBN** table in ascending order by **LastName** and **FirstName** so you can see the ISBN numbers for the books that each author wrote, use the query

```
SELECT FirstName, LastName, ISBN
   FROM Authors INNER JOIN AuthorISBN
      ON Authors.AuthorID = AuthorISBN.AuthorID
   ORDER BY LastName, FirstName
```

ISBN	**Title**	**Edition Number**	**Year Published**	**Publisher ID**
0-13-118043-6	C How to Program	1	1992	1
0-13-226119-7	C How to Program	2	1994	1
0-13-528910-6	C++ How to Program	2	1997	1
0-13-016143-8	Internet and World Wide Web How to Program	1	1999	1
0-13-012507-5	Java How to Program	3	1999	1
0-13-899394-7	Java How to Program	2	1997	1
0-13-456955-5	Visual Basic 6 How to Program	1	1998	1

Fig. 25.20 Books from the **Titles** table whose titles end with **How to Program** in ascending order by **Title**.

Notice the use of the syntax *TableName***.***FieldName* in the **ON** clause of the **INNER JOIN**. This syntax (called a *fully-qualified name*) specifies the fields from each table that should be compared to join the tables. The "*TableName***.**" syntax is required if the fields have the same name in both tables. The same syntax can be used in a query any time it is necessary to distinguish between fields in different tables that happen to have the same name. Fully qualified names that include the database name can be used to perform cross-database queries.

Software Engineering Observation 25.4

*If an SQL statement uses fields with the same name from multiple tables, the field name must be fully qualified with its table name and a dot operator (***.***) as in* **Authors.AuthorID***.*

Common Programming Error 25.5

In a query, not providing fully-qualified names for fields with the same name from two or more tables is an error.

As always, the **FROM** clause (including the **INNER JOIN**) can be followed by **WHERE** and **ORDER BY** clauses. Figure 25.21 shows the results of the preceding query. [*Note:* To save vertical space, we split the results of the query into two columns each containing the **FirstName**, **LastName** and **ISBN** fields.]

FirstName	**LastName**	**ISBN**	**FirstName**	**LastName**	**ISBN**
Harvey	Deitel	0-13-013249-7	*(continued from bottom left of this table)*		
Harvey	Deitel	0-13-271974-6	Harvey	Deitel	0-13-010671-2
Harvey	Deitel	0-13-528910-6	Harvey	Deitel	0-13-118043-6
Harvey	Deitel	0-13-083055-0	Paul	Deitel	0-13-082928-5
Harvey	Deitel	0-13-565912-4	Paul	Deitel	0-13-082925-0
Harvey	Deitel	0-13-083054-2	Paul	Deitel	0-13-020522-2
Harvey	Deitel	0-13-899394-7	Paul	Deitel	0-13-904947-9
Harvey	Deitel	0-13-904947-9	Paul	Deitel	0-13-012507-5
Harvey	Deitel	0-13-226119-7	Paul	Deitel	0-13-015870-4
Harvey	Deitel	0-13-082928-5	Paul	Deitel	0-13-016143-8
Harvey	Deitel	0-13-456955-5	Paul	Deitel	0-13-085609-6
Harvey	Deitel	0-13-015870-4	Paul	Deitel	0-13-013249-7
Harvey	Deitel	0-13-085609-6	Paul	Deitel	0-13-226119-7
Harvey	Deitel	0-13-085248-1	Paul	Deitel	0-13-899394-7
Harvey	Deitel	0-13-082925-0	Paul	Deitel	0-13-565912-4
Harvey	Deitel	0-13-016143-8	Paul	Deitel	0-13-528910-6
Harvey	Deitel	0-13-082714-2	Paul	Deitel	0-13-085248-1
(continued on top right of this table)			*(continued on next page)*		

Fig. 25.21 Authors and the ISBN numbers for the books they have written in ascending order by **LastName** and **FirstName** (part 1 of 2).

(continued from previous page)

FirstName	LastName	ISBN
Harvey	Deitel	0-13-082927-7
Harvey	Deitel	0-13-012507-5
Harvey	Deitel	0-13-020522-2
Paul	Deitel	0-13-118043-6
Paul	Deitel	0-13-010671-2
Paul	Deitel	0-13-083055-0
Paul	Deitel	0-13-082927-7
Paul	Deitel	0-13-083054-2
Paul	Deitel	0-13-082714-2
Paul	Deitel	0-13-456955-5
Paul	Deitel	0-13-271974-6
Tem	Nieto	0-13-082928-5
Tem	Nieto	0-13-565912-4
Tem	Nieto	0-13-456955-5
Tem	Nieto	0-13-085609-6
Tem	Nieto	0-13-016143-8
Tem	Nieto	0-13-020522-2
Tem	Nieto	0-13-015870-4
Tem	Nieto	0-13-904947-9

(continued on top right of this table) / *(continued from bottom left of this table)*

Fig. 25.21 Authors and the ISBN numbers for the books they have written in ascending order by **LastName** and **FirstName** (part 2 of 2).

25.4.5 TitleAuthor Query from Books.mdb

The **Books.mdb** database contains one predefined query (**TitleAuthor**) that produces a table (as in Fig. 25.23) containing the book title, ISBN number, author's first name, author's last name, book's year published and publisher's name for each book in the database. For books with multiple authors, the query produces a separate composite record for each author. The **TitleAuthor** query is shown in Fig. 25.22. A portion of the query results are shown in Fig. 25.23.

The indentation in the preceding query is simply to make the query more readable. This indentation is for the benefit of the reader and is ignored by SQL. For the purpose of this query, we fully qualified each field name with its table name (e.g., **Titles.ISBN**).

Good Programming Practice 25.4

Use spacing and indentation in a SQL query to make the query more readable.

Good Programming Practice 25.5

Fully qualify the names of the fields used in a SQL query to ensure that the query references fields from the proper tables.

Software Engineering Observation 25.5

Many database programs that automatically generate SQL statements use fully-qualified field names for every field reference.

Let us now break down the query of Fig. 25.22 into its various parts. Lines 1 through 3 indicate the fields to select in the query and their order in the temporary result set from left to right. This query selects the **Title** and **ISBN** fields from the **Titles** table, the **FirstName** and **LastName** fields from the **Authors** table, the **YearPublished** field from the **Titles** table and the **PublisherName** field from the **Publishers** table.

```
SELECT Titles.Title, Titles.ISBN, Authors.FirstName,
       Authors.LastName, Titles.YearPublished,
       Publishers.PublisherName
   FROM
      ( Publishers INNER JOIN Titles
          ON Publishers.PublisherID = Titles.PublisherID )
      INNER JOIN
      ( Authors INNER JOIN AuthorISBN
          ON Authors.AuthorID = AuthorISBN.AuthorID )
      ON Titles.ISBN = AuthorISBN.ISBN
   ORDER BY Titles.Title
```

Fig. 25.22 The **TitleAuthor** query from the **Books.mdb** database.

Title	**ISBN**	**First Name**	**Last Name**	**Year Published**	**Publisher Name**
C How to Program	0-13-226119-7	Paul	Deitel	1994	Prentice Hall
C How to Program	0-13-118043-6	Paul	Deitel	1992	Prentice Hall
C How to Program	0-13-118043-6	Harvey	Deitel	1992	Prentice Hall
C How to Program	0-13-226119-7	Harvey	Deitel	1994	Prentice Hall
C++ How to Program	0-13-528910-6	Harvey	Deitel	1997	Prentice Hall
C++ How to Program	0-13-528910-6	Paul	Deitel	1997	Prentice Hall
...					
Internet and World Wide Web How to Program	0-13-016143-8	Paul	Deitel	1999	Prentice Hall
Internet and World Wide Web How to Program	0-13-016143-8	Harvey	Deitel	1999	Prentice Hall
Internet and World Wide Web How to Program	0-13-016143-8	Tem	Nieto	1999	Prentice Hall
...					
Java How to Program	0-13-012507-5	Harvey	Deitel	1999	Prentice Hall
Java How to Program	0-13-899394-7	Paul	Deitel	1997	Prentice Hall
Java How to Program	0-13-899394-7	Harvey	Deitel	1997	Prentice Hall
Java How to Program	0-13-012507-5	Paul	Deitel	1999	Prentice Hall
...					
Visual Basic 6 How to Program	0-13-456955-5	Harvey	Deitel	1998	Prentice Hall
Visual Basic 6 How to Program	0-13-456955-5	Paul	Deitel	1998	Prentice Hall
Visual Basic 6 How to Program	0-13-456955-5	Tem	Nieto	1998	Prentice Hall

Fig. 25.23 A portion of the query results from the **TitleAuthor** query.

Lines 4 through 11 specify the **INNER JOIN** operations that will combine information from the tables. Notice that there are three **INNER JOIN** operations. Remember that an **INNER JOIN** is performed on two tables. It is important to note that either of those two tables can be the result of another query or another **INNER JOIN**. Parentheses are used to nest the **INNER JOIN** operations and the parentheses are always evaluated from the innermost set of parentheses first. So, we begin with the **INNER JOIN** of lines 5 and 6

```
( Publishers INNER JOIN Titles
    ON Publishers.PublisherID = Titles.PublisherID )
```

which specifies that the **Publishers** table and the **Titles** table should be joined **ON** the condition that the **PublisherID** number in each table matches. The temporary result set from this operation contains all the information about each book and the publisher that published it.

Moving to the other nested set of parentheses, lines 8 and 9

```
( Authors INNER JOIN AuthorISBN
    ON Authors.AuthorID = AuthorISBN.AuthorID )
```

perform an **INNER JOIN** on the **Authors** table and the **AuthorISBN** table. This **INNER JOIN** joins the tables **ON** the condition that the **AuthorID** field in the **Authors** table matches the **AuthorID** field from the **AuthorISBN** table. Remember that the table **AuthorISBN** may have multiple entries for each **ISBN** number if there is more than one author for that book.

Next, the results of the two preceding **INNER JOIN** operation are combined with the **INNER JOIN** in lines 5 through 10

```
( Publishers INNER JOIN Titles
    ON Publishers.PublisherID = Titles.PublisherID )
INNER JOIN
( Authors INNER JOIN AuthorISBN
    ON Authors.AuthorID = AuthorISBN.AuthorID )
ON Titles.ISBN = AuthorISBN.ISBN
```

which combines the two temporary result sets **ON** the condition that the **Titles.ISBN** field in the first temporary table matches the **AuthorISBN.ISBN** field in the second temporary table. The result of all these **INNER JOIN** operations is a temporary table from which the appropriate fields are selected for the results of this query.

Finally, line 11 of the query

```
ORDER BY Titles.Title
```

indicates that all the titles should be sorted in ascending order (the default).

25.4.6 Inserting a Record

Often it is necessary to insert data into a table (e.g., add a new record). This is accomplished using an ***INSERT INTO*** operation. The simplest form for an **INSERT INTO** statement is

```
INSERT INTO TableName ( fieldName1, fieldName2, ..., fieldNameN )
   VALUES ( value1, value2, ..., valueN )
```

where *TableName* is the table into which the record will be inserted. The *TableName* is followed by a comma-separated list of field names in parentheses (this list is not required if the **INSERT INTO** operation fills a complete row in the table). The list of field names is followed by the SQL keyword **VALUES** and a comma-separated list of values in parentheses. The values specified here should match the field names specified after the table name in order and type (i.e., if *fieldName1* is supposed to be the **FirstName** field, then *value1* should be a string in single quotes representing the first name). The **INSERT INTO** statement

```
INSERT INTO Authors ( FirstName, LastName, YearBorn )
   VALUES ( 'Sue', 'Smith', 1960 )
```

inserts a record into the **Authors** table. The statement indicates that values will be inserted for the **FirstName**, **LastName** and **YearBorn** fields. The corresponding values to insert are **'Sue'**, **'Smith'** and **1960**. *Note:* We do not specify an **AuthorID** in this example, because the **AuthorID** field is set up in the Microsoft Access database as an *auto-numbered* field. Every new record added to this table will automatically be assigned a unique **AuthorID** which is the next value in the auto-numbered sequence (i.e., 1, 2, 3, etc.). In this case, Sue Smith would be assigned **AuthorID** number 4. Figure 25.24 shows the **Authors** table after the **INSERT INTO** operation.

Common Programming Error 25.6

The single quote (') character is used as a delimiter for strings being inserted in the database. Therefore, to insert a name containing quotes (such as O'Malley) into a database, the name must two single quotes in the position where the quote character appears in the name (e.g., **'O''Malley'***).*

25.4.7 Updating a Record

Often it is necessary to modify data in a table (e.g., update a record). This is accomplished using an ***UPDATE*** operation. The simplest form for an **UPDATE** statement is

```
UPDATE TableName
   SET fieldName1 = value1, fieldName2 = value2, ..., fieldNameN = valueN
   WHERE criteria
```

where *TableName* is the table in which the record will be updated. The *TableName* is followed by the ***SET*** keyword and a comma-separated list of field name/value pairs in the format *fieldName = value*. The **WHERE** clause specifies the criteria used to determine which record(s) to update. The **UPDATE** statement

AuthorID	FirstName	LastName	YearBorn
1	Harvey	Deitel	1946
2	Paul	Deitel	1968
3	Tem	Nieto	1969
4	Sue	Smith	1960

Fig. 25.24 **Authors** table after an **INSERT INTO** operation to add a record.

```
UPDATE Authors
   SET YearBorn = '1969'
   WHERE LastName = 'Deitel' AND FirstName = 'Paul'
```

updates a record in the **Authors** table. The statement indicates that the **YearBorn** field will be assigned the value 1969 for the record in which **LastName** is equal to **Deitel** and **FirstName** is equal to **Paul**. *Note:* If we know the **AuthorID** in advance of the **UPDATE** operation (possibly because we searched for the record previously), the **WHERE** clause could be simplified as follows:

```
WHERE AuthorID = 2
```

Figure 25.25 shows the **Authors** table after the **UPDATE** operation.

25.5 Registering Books.mdb as an ODBC Data Source

To execute an SQL query, a program must be able to access a database. Many different database vendors exist—with each one potentially providing different database manipulation methods. Microsoft developed the *Open Database Connectivity (ODBC) Application Programming Interface (API)* to allow Windows applications to communicate in a uniform manner with disparate relational databases. Database vendors write a piece of software—called an *ODBC driver*—using the ODBC API to provides uniform access to the database (i.e., database programmers do not have to learn vendor-specific database implementations).

In this section, we discuss the steps necessary to register a Microsoft Access database as an ODBC source. [*Note:* The computer must have Microsoft Access installed.] Once the database has been registered, we can access it through Active Server Pages (see Chapter 26), Perl (see Chapter 27), etc. The steps outlined in this section are the same ones we use for registering all databases used in this book.

Before accessing an Access database from the Web, the database must be given a *System Data Source Name* (*DSN*) on the server. A DSN specifies a database's name, location and driver.

The first step in registering an ODBC data source is to double-click the **ODBC Data Sources (32bit)** icon (Fig. 25.26) in the Windows **Control Panel** to display the ***ODBC Data Source Administrator*** dialog (Fig. 25.27).

Click the ***System DSN*** tab to view a list of all system DSNs. Select the name to the right of **Microsoft Access Driver (*.mdb)** from the list. [*Note:* The name that appears under the **Name** column may be different on your machine.] Click **Add...** to display the ***Create New Data Source*** dialog (Fig. 25.28).

AuthorID	FirstName	LastName	YearBorn
1	Harvey	Deitel	1946
2	Paul	Deitel	1969
3	Tem	Nieto	1969
4	Sue	Smith	1960

Fig. 25.25 **Authors** table after an **UPDATE** operation to modify a record.

Fig. 25.26 **ODBC Data Sources (32bit)** control panel icon.

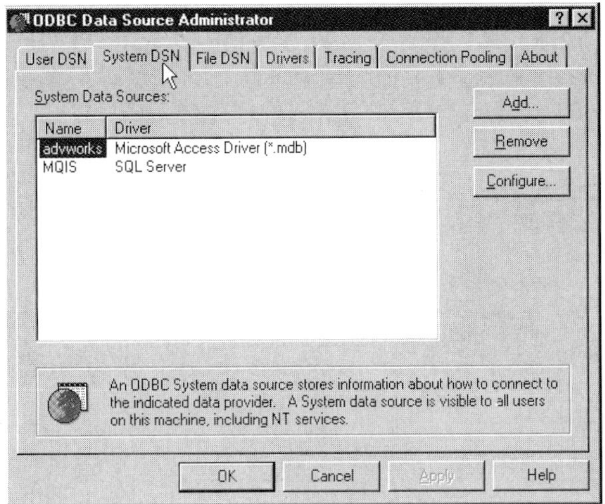

Fig. 25.27 **ODBC Data Source Administrator** dialog.

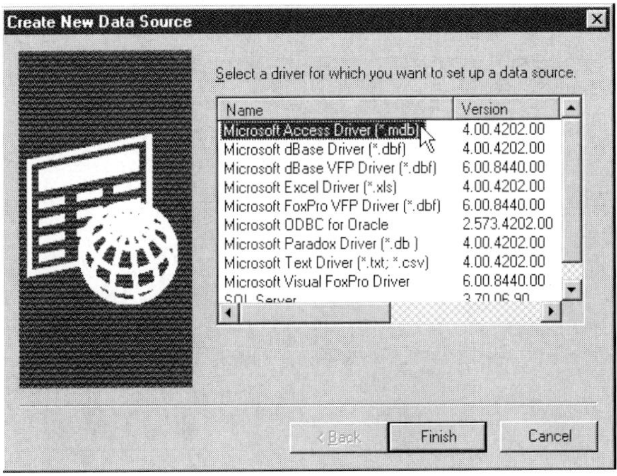

Fig. 25.28 **Create New Data Source** dialog.

In the **Create New Data Source** dialog, select **Microsoft Access Driver (*.mdb)** and click **Finish** to display the ***ODBC Microsoft Access Setup*** dialog (Fig. 25.29). [*Note:* Click the ***Advanced...*** button to display the ***Set Advanced Options*** dialog in which a user name and the password can be specified to control access to the database.]

The next example uses an Access database we created named **`books.mdb`**. In the **Data Source Name** field we enter **Books**. The DSN can be whatever you like as long as it does not conflict with other DSNs. The **Description** field allows the user to describe the DSN. Click the ***Select...*** button to display the ***Select Database*** dialog (Fig. 25.30).

In the **Select Database** dialog, locate the database. If the database resides on the network then click ***Network...***. Click **OK** to return to the **ODBC Microsoft Access Setup** dialog. Click the **ODBC Microsoft Access Setup** dialog's **OK** button to return to the **ODBC Data Source Administrator** dialog (Fig. 25.31). The **`Books`** DSN is now listed. Click **OK** to close this dialog.

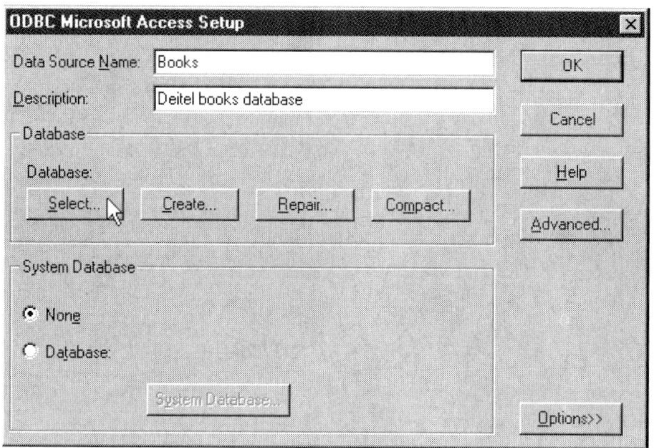

Fig. 25.29 **ODBC Microsoft Access Setup** dialog.

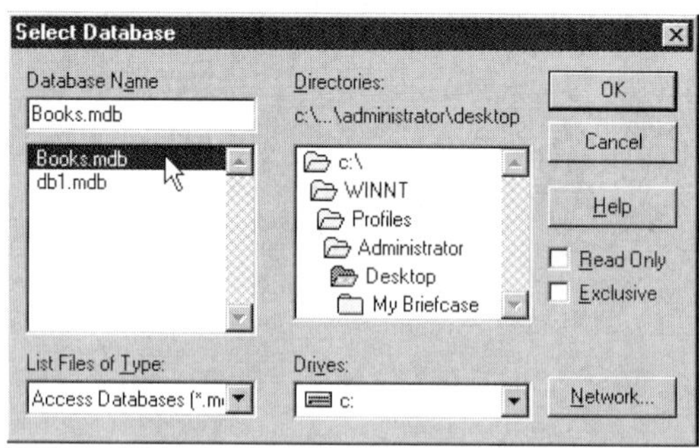

Fig. 25.30 **Select Database** dialog.

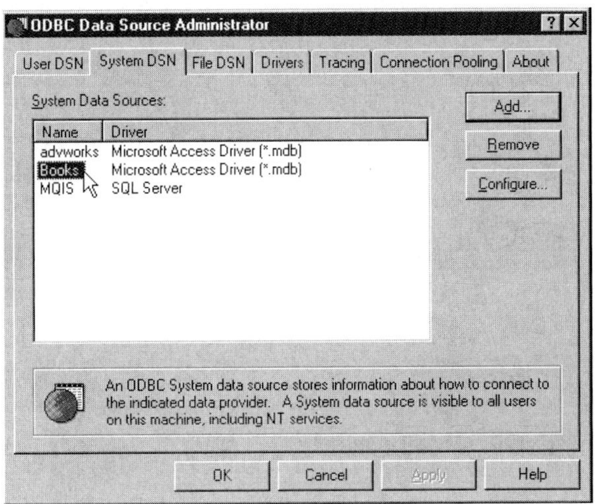

Fig. 25.31 **ODBC Data Source Administrator** dialog showing successful registration.

25.6 ActiveX Data Objects (ADO)

Microsoft *Universal Data Access* (*UDA*) is an architecture that is designed for high-performance data access to relational data sources, non-relational data sources and mainframe/legacy data sources. The UDA architecture (Fig. 25.32) consists of three primary components: *OLE DB*—the core of the UDA architecture that provides low-level access to any data source, Open Database Connectivity (ODBC)—a C programming language library that uses SQL to access data, and *ActiveX Data Objects* (*ADO*)—a simple object model (Fig. 25.33) that provides uniform access to any data source by interacting with OLE DB. (*Note:* OLE DB is required to implement a minimum set of data access services that can be used by ADO.)

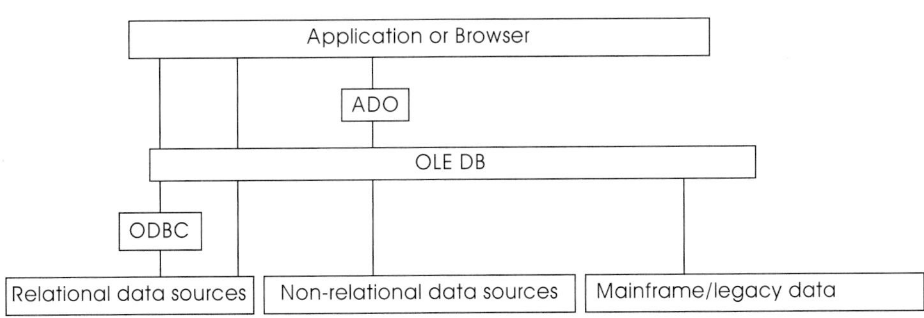

Fig. 25.32 Microsoft's UDA architecture.

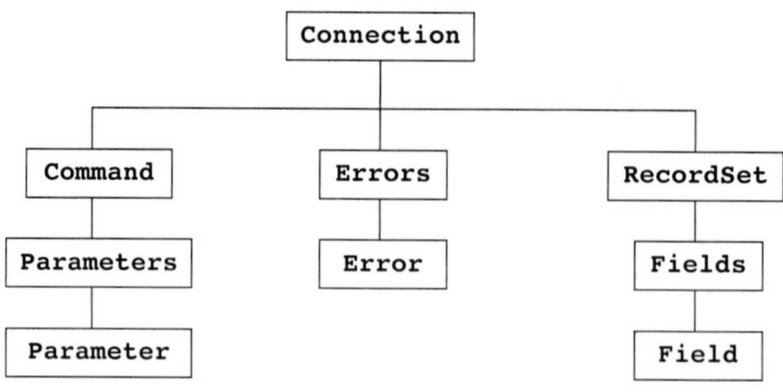

Fig. 25.33 A portion of the ADO object model.

More specifically, the *ADO object model* provides objects and *collections* (i.e., containers that hold one or more objects of a specific type). Figure 25.34 briefly describes some ADO objects and collections. Visit

`http://www.microsoft.com/data/ado/adords15/`

to access the ADO documentation and view a complete list of methods, properties and events for these ADO objects. In the next section and in Chapter 26 "Active Server Pages," we show live-code examples using ADO and VBScript to access a database.

In the next section, we discuss a new Microsoft client-side technology called *Remote Data Services* (*RDS*). The RDS ActiveX control in Internet Explorer 5 transparently uses ADO to remotely access and manipulate database contents over the Internet (or intranet). It allows a client Web browser to download a **`Recordset`**, manipulate the records and return data to the server for update in the physical database.

Object/Collection	Description
`Connection` object	The connection to the data source.
`Command` object	Contains the query that will interact with the database (the *data source*) to manipulate data.
`Parameter` object	Contains information needed by a **`Command`** object to query the data source.
`Parameters` collection	Contains one or more **`Parameter`** objects.
`Error` object	Created when an error occurs while accessing data.
`Errors` collection	Contains one or more **`Error`** objects.
`Recordset` object	Contains zero or more records that match the database query. Collectively this group of records is called a *recordset*.
`Field` object	Contains the value (and other attributes) of one data source field.
`Fields` collection	Contains one or more **`Field`** objects.

Fig. 25.34 ADO object and collection types.

25.7 Remote Data Services (RDS)

Remote Data Services (*RDS*) is an emerging Microsoft technology for client-side database manipulation across the Internet. Figure 25.35 illustrates the RDS architecture. Recordsets are retrieved on the server using ADO and sent to the client browser. Because a connection is not maintained between the the data source and the client, the recordset stored on the client is called a *disconnected recordset*. The client can execute queries against the recordset (similar to using the Tabular Data control presented in Chapter 18, "Data Binding"). The most significant difference between RDS and the Tabular Data control is that RDS provides a mechanism for sending updated records to the Web server and the Tabular Data control does not. [*Note:* As of this writing, RDS does not work with Personal Web Server. This will be fixed in a future release of RDS. RDS currently works with IIS running on Windows NT Server.]

[Note: RDS is a developing, feature-rich technology. In this section, our primary objective is to provide an introduction to RDS to illustrate that the technology works. We show only the client side of this client/server relationship. We do not discuss the server-side setup which is complex, developing rapidly and involves security issues that are beyond the scope of this book. To learn more about RDS, visit the sites listed in Section 25.8.]

RDS is implemented as a client-side ActiveX control (included with IE5) named ***RDS.Datacontrol***. As of this writing, the current version of the **RDS.Datacontrol** is version 2.1 (**CLASSID** of **BD96C556-65A3-11D0-983A-00C04FC29E33**). Figure 25.36 describes some of the **RDS.Datacontrol** properties and Fig. 25.37 describes some of the **RDS.Datacontrol** methods.

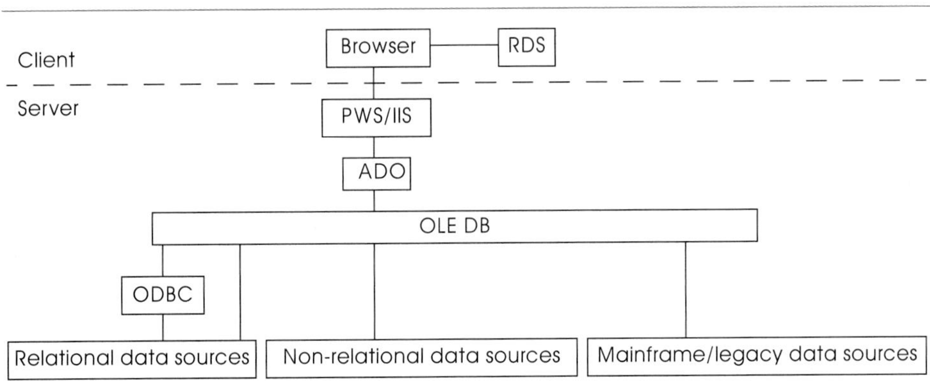

Fig. 25.35 RDS architecture.

Property	Description
Connect	The data source name (DSN) of a Web server's database.
Sql	The actual query to execute against the database.
Server	Indicates the Web server to which the **RDS.Datacontrol** connects.
Recordset	The actual recordset downloaded from the Web server.

Fig. 25.36 Some **RDS.Datacontrol** properties.

Method	Description
Refresh	Executes a query against the database. Also forces any records that have not been uploaded to the server to upload.
SubmitChanges	Sends updated records to the Web server.
CancelUpdate	Cancels all records that were updated (but not sent to the server) and reverts them back to their original values.

Fig. 25.37 Some **RDS.Datacontrol** methods.

We now present an example (Fig. 25.38) that uses RDS to update a book's title in the **Books.mdb** database. The example assumes that a database—with the data source name (DSN) **books**—is located at a valid HTTP IP address. Because the database is physically located on a different machine, it is often referred to as a *remote database*. The example allows the user to get a book's title using the book's ISBN number, edit the title and send the updated title to the server. In this example, we use client-side VBScript (see Chapter 22). [*Note:* Normally, we use JavaScript/JScript on the client side in an effort to create a universal client. RDS is a Microsoft Internet Explorer 5 technology, so anyone using it from the client side will have a VBScript interpreter built into their browser. Therefore, this example gives us a nice teaching opportunity to demonstrate client-side scripting with VBScript.]

For security reasons, we do not show the server's IP address used in this example. Visit

http://www.microsoft.com/security/bulletins/ms99-025.asp

to learn more about RDS security issues. To execute this example, you must replace **xxx.xxx.xxx.xxx** with the HTTP IP address of the server. To setup the server visit

http://www.microsoft.com/data/ado/adords15/

and read "getting started with RDS" and "the RDS tutorial" topics.

```
<!DOCTYPE HTML PUBLIC "-//W3C//DTD HTML 4.0 Transitional//EN">
<HTML>
<!--Fig. 25.38: rds.html -->

<!--Creates an instance of the RDS.Datacontrol-->
<OBJECT CLASSID = "clsid:BD96C556-65A3-11D0-983A-00C04FC29E33"
        ID = deitelDC WIDTH = 0 HEIGHT = 0>
</OBJECT>

<SCRIPT LANGUAGE = VBScript>
<!--
Option Explicit

<!-- Microsoft predefined constants -->
Const adcReadyStateLoaded = 2
```

Fig. 25.38 Updating a remote database using RDS (part 1 of 7).

```
Const adcReadyStateInteractive = 3
Const adcReadyStateComplete = 4

Dim state

Public Sub window_OnLoad()
   ' Set the state machine at the first state
   StatusText.Value = "Click Find."
   state = 0
End Sub

Public Sub deitelDC_OnReadyStateChange()
   If state = 1 Then
      Select Case deitelDC.ReadyState
         ' Just started downloading, there is no
         ' data to look at.
         Case adcReadyStateLoaded
            StatusText.Value = "Downloading..."

         ' Partially downloaded the data,
         ' there is more to come.
         Case adcReadyStateInteractive
            StatusText.Value = "Still downloading..."

         ' Completely downloaded the data,
         ' there's no more coming.
         Case adcReadyStateComplete

            ' Fill in the fields for updating
            ' Get ISBN field to prove we got the right one
            FoundISBN.Value = deitelDC.Recordset( "ISBN" )

            ' The title we want to modify
            FoundTitle.Value = deitelDC.Recordset( "Title" )

            ' OK for updating. Everything worked.
            StatusText.Value = "Finished downloading."
            state = 2
      End Select

   ElseIf state = 2 Then

      Select Case deitelDC.ReadyState
         ' Started uploading, there is no data sent.
         Case adcReadyStateLoaded
            ' OK for updating. Everything worked.
            StatusText.Value = "Uploading..."

         ' Partially uploaded the data, there is more to send.
         Case adcReadyStateInteractive
            ' OK for updating. Everything worked.
            StatusText.value = "Still Uploading..."

```

Fig. 25.38 Updating a remote database using RDS (part 2 of 7).

```
         ' Completely downloaded the data,
         ' there is no more coming.
         ' Goto readystate = complete if it works
         Case adcReadyStateComplete
            ' OK for updating. Everything worked.
            StatusText.value = "Finished updating."
            state = 0
      End Select
   End If
End Sub

Public Sub Find_OnClick()
   ' Validate the input values. Never assume valid
   ' data is in the text boxes.

   ' Server.Value will be used to designate the
   ' server with the database
   If Server.Value = "" Then
      Call Msgbox( "Please specify a web server. " & _
                   "Suggest: http://xxx.xxx.xxx.xxx" )

   ' ISBN.Value is the record we want to search for
   ElseIf ISBN.value = "" Then
      Call MsgBox( "Please specify an ISBN to examine. " & _
                   "Suggest: 0-13-226119-7" )

   ' All data is probably valid so begin the data download.
   Else
      ' Request the data from.
      deitelDC.Server = Server.Value

      ' Set the SQL query.
      deitelDC.SQL = "SELECT ISBN, " & _
         "Title FROM Titles WHERE ISBN = '" & ISBN.Value & "'"

      ' Set the DSN to fetch the data.
      deitelDC.Connect = "DSN=Books;"

      ' Tell the server to begin sending the data to us.
      Call deitelDC.Refresh()
      state = 1
   End If
End Sub

Public Sub Update_OnClick()
   ' If everything worked above, we can change
   ' the record in the database
   If state = 2 Then
      ' We are only updating this field in the database.
      ' so we fetch the value from the text box and set it to go
      ' back to the server for update
      deitelDC.Recordset( "Title" ) = FoundTitle.Value

```

Fig. 25.38 Updating a remote database using RDS (part 3 of 7).

```
        ' Save these changes
        Call deitelDC.SubmitChanges()

        ' Refresh after submit operation
        Call deitelDC.Refresh()
    End If
End Sub
-->
</SCRIPT>

<HEAD>
<META NAME = VI60_defaultClientScript CONTENT = VBScript>
</HEAD>

<BODY>
RDS Example--Correct titles in a remote database<BR>
Record to Find<BR>
<TABLE BORDER = "0" CELLPADDING = "0">
<TR>
<TD>Server:</TD>
<TD><INPUT ID= server NAME= server VALUE= "http://xxx.xxx.xxx.xxx"
           TYPE = "text" SIZE = 60></TD>
</TR>
<TR>
<TD>ISBN:</TD>
<TD><INPUT ID = ISBN NAME = ISBN VALUE = "0-13-226119-7"
           TYPE = "text"></TD>
</TR>
</TABLE>
<INPUT TYPE = "button" ID = "Find" NAME = "Find" VALUE= "Find"><BR>
<BR>
Results<BR>
<TABLE BORDER = "0" CELLPADDING = "0">
<TR>
<TD>Found ISBN( readonly ):</TD>
<TD><INPUT ID = FoundISBN READONLY NAME = FoundISBN TYPE = "text">
</TD>
</TR>
<TR>
<TD>Found Title:</TD>
<TD><INPUT ID = FoundTitle NAME = FoundTitle TYPE = "text"></TD>
</TR>
</TABLE>
<INPUT TYPE = "button" ID = "Update" NAME = "Update"
       VALUE = "Update Title"><BR>
<BR>
Status:<INPUT TYPE = "text" ID = "StatusText" NAME = "StatusText"
              SIZE = 30 READONLY VALUE = "Click Find."><BR>
</BODY>
</HTML>
```

Fig. 25.38 Updating a remote database using RDS (part 4 of 7).

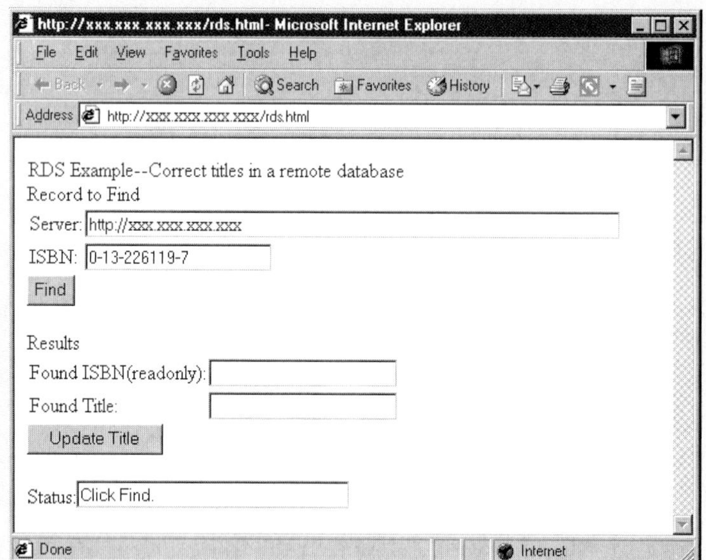

The page is loaded.

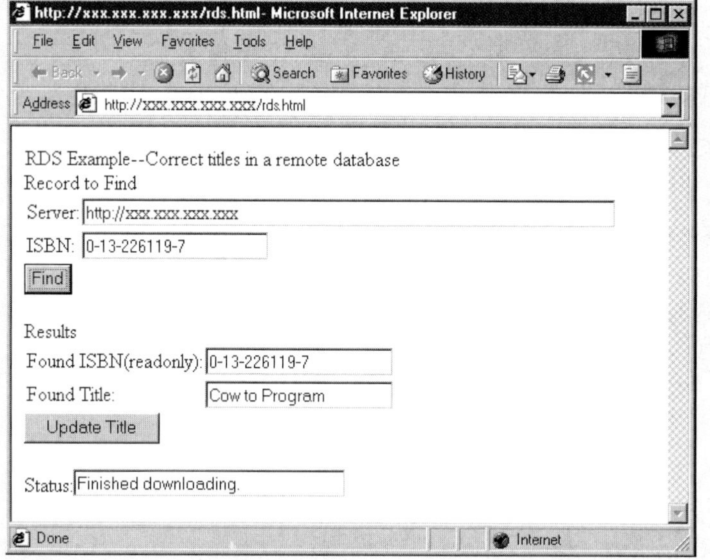

The user has clicked the **Find** button which results in the **Found ISBN** and **Found Title** fields being populated.

Fig. 25.38 Updating a remote database using RDS (part 5 of 7).

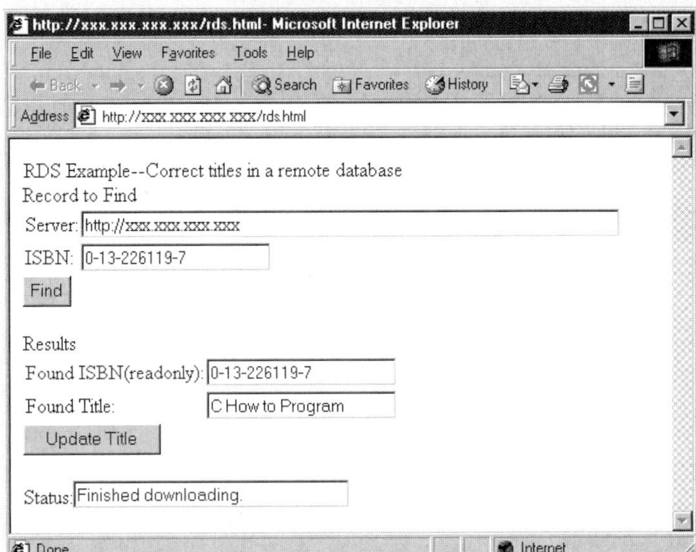

User has edited the **Found Title** field.

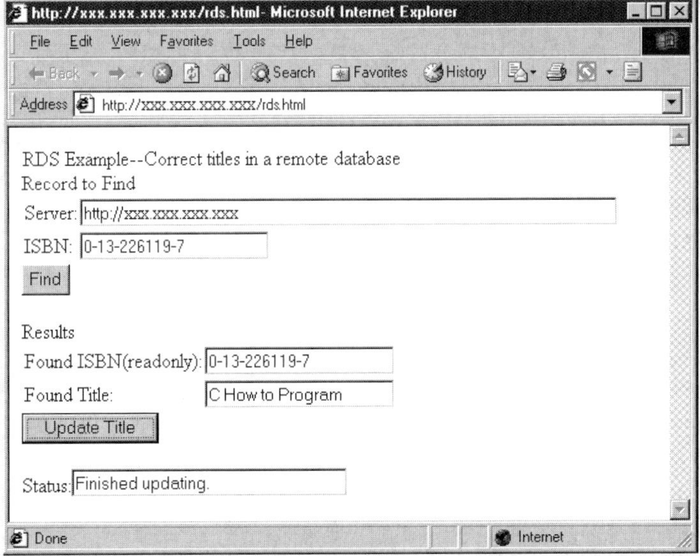

User has clicked **Update Title**.

Fig. 25.38 Updating a remote database using RDS (part 6 of 7).

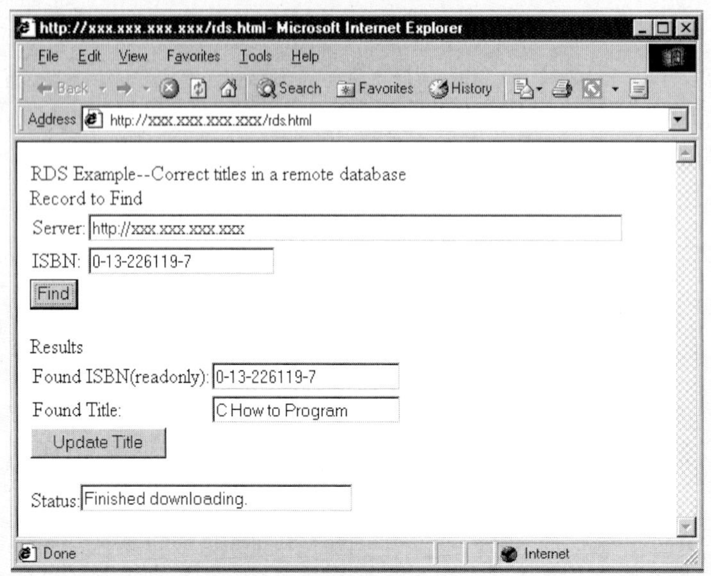

User has clicked **Find**.

Fig. 25.38 Updating a remote database using RDS (part 7 of 7).

Lines 6 through 8 use an **<OBJECT>** tag to create an **RDS.Datacontrol** object with **ID deitelDC**. Because the **RDS.Datacontrol** does not have a graphical user interface, we set both the **WIDTH** and **HEIGHT** to **0**.

Lines 15 through 17 declare constants ***adcReadyStateLoaded***, ***adcReady-StateInteractive*** and ***adcReadyStateComplete*** that represent the three **RDS.Datacontrol** states used in this program. These constants are summarized in Fig. 25.39.

By default, the **RDS.Datacontrol** transfers data *asynchronously* (i.e., the data transfer occurs in parallel with other executing code). The **RDS.Datacontrol**'s ***ReadyState*** *property* stores the control's current state. When the **ReadyState** property's value changes asynchronously, event procedure ***OnReadyStateChange*** (line 27) executes.

State	Description
adcReadyStateLoaded	The recordset does not contain any data because the query has not completed executing.
adcReadyStateInteractive	Some records in the recordset are available, but others are still being downloaded (or uploaded).
adcReadyStateComplete	All recordset records are available. The download (or upload) is complete.

Fig. 25.39 Constants representing several **RDS.Datacontrol** states.

On line 19 we declare variable **state** to allow us to coordinate user interaction with the **RDS.Datacontrol**'s asynchronous behavior. Throughout the code we give **state** one of three values—**0** to indicate that there is no user activity, **1** to indicate a download state (occurs when the user clicks **Find** to locate a specific book) and **2** to indicate an upload state (occurs when the user clicks **Update** to change a book title). In the **OnLoad** event procedure (line 21), we set **state** to **0** to indicate that we are neither downloading nor uploading because the Web page was just loaded.

Using an **If** structure (line 28), we divide **OnReadyStateChange** into two parts—one corresponding to downloading the recordset and the other to uploading the recordset. If **state** is **1** a download is occurring; if **state** is **2** an upload is occurring.

On line 29, we use a **Select Case** structure to get the status of the download by accessing the **RDS.Datacontrol**'s **ReadyState** property. As mentioned earlier, this property can have one of three values (i.e., **adcReadyStateLoaded**, **adcReadyStateInteractive** and **adcReadyStateComplete**). We provide a **Case** for each. The **Case** (line 4) we are primarily interested in is **adcReadyStateComplete**.

Line 46

```
FoundISBN.Value = deitelDC.Recordset( "ISBN" )
```

uses the **RecordSet** property to retrieve the **ISBN** field's value and assign it to the HTML text field **FoundISBN**. The value in parentheses is the field name for which a value should be returned from the current record in the **Recordset**. A similar statement (line 49) retrieves the value of the recordset's **Title** field and assigns it to the HTML text field **FoundTitle**. Because the download is complete, we set the value of **state** to 2 (line 53) to permit other updates. The upload **Case**s in the **Select Case** structure at lines 58 through 76 are similar to the download **Case**s.

Procedure **Find_OnClick** (line 80) executes when the user clicks **Find** in the HTML form. The procedure performs simple validation to ensure that the user entered data in the **Server** HTML text field and the **ISBN** HTML text field. Line 98 assigns the value in the **Server** HTML text field to the **RDS.Datacontrol**'s **Server** property. The **RDS.Datacontrol** will attempt to connect to the server specified in property **Server**.

We specify the SQL query on lines 101 and 102, and assign the query to the **RDS.Datacontrol**'s **Sql** property. The **RDS.Datacontrol** will attempt to query to the server's database with the query set in property **Sql**. Line 105 assigns the data source name of the database (e.g., **books** in this particular example) to the **Connect** property of the **RDS.Datacontrol**. The **RDS.Datacontrol** will attempt to query this data source on the server. Line 108 calls the **RDS.Datacontrol**'s method **Refresh** to execute the query against the database. We then set **state** to **1** to indicate that a download is occurring.

Event procedure **Update_OnClick** (line 113) executes when the user clicks **Update** in the HTML form. The **If** structure on line 116 tests if **state** is **2** (an upload is allowed). If **state** is not **2** then the download has not completed. Line 120 assigns the updated title in the **FoundTitle** text field to the **RecordSet**'s **Title** field. Line 123

```
Call deitelDC.SubmitChanges()
```

calls the **RDS.Datacontrol**'s method **SubmitChanges** to send the updated record to the server so the database on the server can store the updated values. We then call **Refresh** to ensure that all updates have been made.

Performance Tip 25.3

When **`SubmitChanges`** *is called, only the modified records in the* **`Resultset`** *(not the entire* **`Resultset`***) are sent to the server.*

In this chapter we introduced databases and the fundamentals of database processing with SQL, and two key Microsoft technologies—ADO and RDS. Our discussion of ADO introduced only basic concepts. We continue our discussion of server-side programming in the next chapter, in which we discuss Microsoft's Active Server Pages (ASP) technology. We present several substantial ASP examples that include database access via ADO.

25.8 Internet and World Wide Web Resources

There are many database-related resources on the Internet and World Wide Web. This section lists a variety of database, SQL, ADO, RDS and ODBC resources available on the Internet and provides a brief description of each.

`http://www.microsoft.com/data/`

Microsoft's *Universal Data Access Web Site* provides helpful information on Microsoft's database technologies with references for ADO, RDS, OLE DB and ODBC, technical information and software downloads.

`http://www.microsoft.com/data/related.htm`

This area of Microsoft's *Universal Data Access Web Site* contains links to Web sites for a variety of database-related technologies.

`http://www.microsoft.com/data/download.htm`

This area of Microsoft's *Universal Data Access Web Site* contains links to downloads related to Universal Data Access.

`http://msdn.microsoft.com/workshop/c-frame.htm#/workshop/database/default.asp`

This is the *Microsoft Developer Network (MSDN) Online Web Workshop* on Data Access and Databases. This page is an excellent starting point for information from Microsoft on databases, focusing on ADO/RDS, ODBC, OLE DB, SQL, data binding and the Tabular Data Control.

`http://www.microsoft.com/data/ado/adords15`

This site contains the *Microsoft Remote Data Services documentation.* This is an excellent place to learn about RDS. The site contains tutorials, a developer's guide and demos of RDS applications.

`http://www.microsoft.com/sql/`

The *Microsoft SQL Server 7.0 Web Site* contains product information, technical support, SQL news and tips on using the SQL Server to solve business problems.

`http://www.microsoft.com/backoffice/downloads.htm#SQL`

This download page offers tools for use with *Microsoft's SQL Server.*

`http://www.microsoft.com/data/ado/workshop/wshp_arch.htm`

The *Microsoft ADO Workshop Archive* contains past ADO workshops.

`http://www.microsoft.com/data/odbc/?RLD=17`

This section of Microsoft's *Universal Data Access Web Site* contains articles related to ODBC.

`http://www.deja.com`

`Deja.com` is a news group search engine that indexes the Microsoft news group servers (e.g., **`msnews.microsoft.com`**) and other public news group servers. Typing error messages into the search engine may help you find information about how to solve a variety of programming problems.

http://support.microsoft.com/support/kb/articles/Q181/0/92.ASP
This *Remote Data Services FAQ* answers several frequently asked RDS questions.

http://msdn.microsoft.com/isapi/msdnlib.idc?theURL=/library/sdkdoc/dasdk/sdko3sc7.htm
The *Microsoft Data Access Components (MDAC) SDK Overview* site provides references for version 2.x of RDS, ADO, ODBC and other database-related technologies.

http://w3.one.net/~jhoffman/sqltut.htm
This is a *tutorial* that teaches data manipulation using standard SQL. The tutorial contains explanations of SQL statements with code examples.

http://clubs.yahoo.com/clubs/structuredquerylanguage
The *Yahoo SQL Club* is an online forum for SQL discussion with a chat room, a message board, SQL news and links to SQL information sites.

http://www.sqlmag.com
SQL Server Magazine is an excellent SQL resource for those who subscribe. Subscribers receive monthly issues filled with articles on SQL design and information on current developments involving SQL. Certain articles are also available free at the Web site.

SUMMARY

- Database systems provide file-processing capabilities but organize data in a manner to facilitate satisfying sophisticated queries.
- The most popular style of database system on personal computers is the relational database.
- Structured Query Language (SQL) is almost universally used to make relational database queries.
- A database is an integrated collection of data which is centrally controlled.
- A database management system (DBMS) controls the storage and retrieval of data in a database.
- A distributed database is a database that is spread throughout the computer systems of a network.
- A relational database is composed of tables that can be manipulated as a recordset.
- Any particular row of the table is called a record or a row.
- Each column of the table represents a different field.
- Subsets of a table can be created by selecting data from the table (**SELECT** in SQL). Table data can be combined with join operations (**INNER JOIN** in SQL).
- A table's primary key uniquely identifies each record in the table. Every record must have a value in the primary key field—Rule of Entity Integrity—and the value must be unique.
- A foreign key is a field in a table for which every entry has a unique value in another table and where the field in the other table is the primary key for that table. The foreign key helps maintain the Rule of Referential Integrity—every value in a foreign key field must appear in another table's primary key field. Foreign keys enable information from multiple tables to be joined and presented to the user.
- A typical SQL query "selects" information from one or more tables in a database. Such selections are performed by **SELECT** queries. The simplest form of a **SELECT** query is

  SELECT * FROM *TableName*

  where the asterisk (*) indicates that all fields from *TableName* should be selected and *TableName* specifies the table in the database from which the fields will be selected. To select specific fields from a table, replace the asterisk (*) with a comma-separated list of the field names to select.

- SQL uses the optional **WHERE** clause to specify the selection criteria for the query. The simplest form of a **SELECT** query with selection criteria is

  SELECT * FROM *TableName* **WHERE** *criteria*

  The condition in the **WHERE** clause can contain operators **<**, **>**, **<=**, **>=**, **=**, **<>** and **LIKE**. Operator **LIKE** is used for pattern matching with the wildcard characters asterisk (*****) and question mark (**?**).
- The results of a query can be arranged in ascending or descending order using the optional **ORDER BY** clause. The simplest form of an **ORDER BY** clause is

  SELECT * FROM *TableName* **ORDER BY** *field* **ASC**
  SELECT * FROM *TableName* **ORDER BY** *field* **DESC**

  where **ASC** specifies ascending (lowest to highest) order, **DESC** specifies descending (highest to lowest) order and *field* represents the field that is used for sorting purposes.
- Multiple fields can be used for ordering purposes with an **ORDER BY** clause of the form

  ORDER BY *field1 SortingOrder***,** *field2 SortingOrder***, ...**

  where *SortingOrder* is either **ASC** or **DESC**.
- The **WHERE** and **ORDER BY** clauses can be combined in one query.
- An **INNER JOIN** merges records from two tables by testing for matching values in a field that is common to both tables. The simplest form of an **INNER JOIN** clause is

  SELECT * FROM *Table1* **INNER JOIN** *Table2* **ON** *Table1.field* **=** *Table2.field*

  The **ON** part of the **INNER JOIN** clause specifies the fields from each table that should be compared to determine which records will be selected.
- The syntax *TableName.FieldName* is used in a query to distinguish between fields in different tables that have the same name.
- To connect to an *ODBC data source* the database must be registered with the system through the ***ODBC Data Sources*** option in the Windows **Control Panel**.
- The basic form of an **INSERT INTO** SQL statement is

  INSERT INTO *tableName* **(** *fieldName1***,** *fieldName2***, ...)**
  VALUES ('*value1***', '***value2***', ...)**

  where *tableName* is the table in which the data will be inserted. Each field name to be updated is specified in a comma-separated list in parentheses. The value for each field is specified after the SQL keyword **VALUES** in another comma-separated list in parentheses.
- A basic **UPDATE** SQL statement has the form

  UPDATE *tableName*
  SET *fieldName1* = *value1***,** *fieldName2* = *value2***, ...**
  WHERE *criteria*

  where *tableName* is the table to update, the individual fields to update are specified (followed by an equal sign an a new value in single quotes) after the SQL **SET** keyword and the **WHERE** clause determines a single record to update.
- Microsoft *Universal Data Access* (*UDA*) is an architecture that is designed for high-performance data access to both relational data sources, non-relational data sources and mainframe/legacy data

sources. The UDA architecture is comprised of three primary components: *OLE DB*—the core of the UDA architecture that provides uniform access to any data source, *Open Database Connectivity* (*ODBC*)—a C programming language library that uses SQL to access data and *ActiveX Data Objects* (*ADO*)—a simple object model that exposes the capabilities of OLE DB.

- The ADO object model provides objects and *collections. A collection* is a type that contains one or more objects of a specific type.
- ADO provides the **Connection** object for connecting to a data source, the **Command** object for querying a data source, the **Parameter** object for providing additional information a **Command** object needs, the **Error** object for debugging, the **RecordSet** object for storing one or more records and the **Field** object for accessing a field.
- ADO provides collections **Parameters**, **Errors** and **Fields**.
- *Remote Data Services* (*RDS*) is an emerging Microsoft technology designed for database manipulation across the Internet. Recordsets are retrieved on the server using ADO and sent to the client. Because a connection is not maintained to the data source by the client, the recordset stored on the client is more properly called a *disconnected recordset.* The client may then execute queries against the recordset—which is similar to the Tabular Data control. The most significant difference between RDS and the Tabular Data control is that RDS provides a mechanism for sending updated records to the Web server and the Tabular Data control does not.
- RDS is implemented as a client-side ActiveX control (which is included with Internet Explorer 5) named **RDS.Datacontrol**.
- RDS property **Connect** stores the data source name (DSN) of a Web server's database, property **Sql** stores the query to execute against the database, property **Server** indicates the Web server to which the **RDS.Datacontrol** connects and **RecordSet** stores the recordset downloaded from the Web server.
- RDS method **Refresh** forces a query to execute against the database and forces any records that have not been uploaded to the server to upload, **SubmitChanges** sends updated records to the Web server and method **CancelUpdate** cancels all records that were updated (but not sent to the server) and reverts them back to their original values.
- A database that is physically located on a different machine is often referred to as a *remote database*.
- Constants **adcReadyStateLoaded** (i.e., the recordset does not contain any data because the query has not completed executing), **adcReadyStateInteractive** (i.e., some records in the recordset are available, but others are still being downloaded or uploaded) and **adcReadyStateComplete** (i.e., all recordset records are available because the download or upload is complete) represent the three **RDS.Datacontrol** states.
- By default, the **RDS.Datacontrol** transfers data *asynchronously* (i.e., the data transfer occurs in parallel with other executing code). The **RDS.Datacontrol**'s **ReadyState** property stores the control's current state. When the **ReadyState** property's value changes asynchronously, event procedure **OnReadyStateChange** is executed.

TERMINOLOGY

ActiveX Data Objects (ADO)
adcReadyStateComplete RDS constant
adcReadyStateInteractive RDS constant
adcReadyStateLoaded constant in RDS
ADO object model
ASC (ascending order) in SQL **ORDER BY** clause
asterisk (*) wildcard character in SQL queries
asynchronous data transfer in RDS
CancelUpdate method
collections
Command object
Connection object

Connect property of **RDS.DataControl**
criteria clause
database
database file
database management system (DBMS)
DESC (descending order) in **ORDER BY** clause
disconnected recordset
Error object
Errors collection
field
field as column of table in relational database
Field object
Fields collection
foreign key
FROM SQL keyword
INNER JOIN clause of **SELECT** statement
INNER JOIN … **ON** …
INSERT INTO SQL keywords
join two relational database tables
LIKE operator in a criteria clause
Microsoft Access
Microsoft SQL Server
ODBC data source
ODBC driver
OLE DB
OnReadyStateChange RDS event procedure
Open Database Connectivity (ODBC)
ORDER BY … **ASC** clause
ORDER BY … **DESC** clause
Parameter object
Parameters collection
primary key field of a record in a table
question mark (**?**) wildcard character
RDS (Remote Data Services)
RDS.DataControl
ReadyState property of **RDS.DataControl**
record as row of a table in relational database
recordset
RecordSet object
RecordSet property
Refresh method
relational database
Remote Data Services (RDS)
remote database
row of a table (record)
Rule of Entity Integrity
Rule of Referential Integrity
SELECT … **FROM** …
SELECT … **FROM** … **WHERE** … **ORDER BY** …
Server property of **RDS.DataControl**
square brackets (**[ ]**)
SQL (Structured Query Language)
Sql property of the **RDS.DataControl**
SubmitChanges method
table in a database
Universal Data Access (UDA)
UPDATE SQL statement
view in a relational database
WHERE clause of **SELECT** statement
wildcard characters

COMMON PROGRAMMING ERRORS

25.1 When a field is specified as the primary key field, not providing a value for that field in every record breaks the Rule of Entity Integrity and is an error.

25.2 When a field is specified as the primary key field, providing duplicate values for multiple records is an error.

25.3 When performing an SQL statement using the asterisk (*) to select fields, assuming that the fields in the result set of the query are always returned in the same order may result in incorrect processing of the data in the application receiving the result set. If the order of the fields in the database table(s) changes, the order of the fields in the result set would change accordingly.

25.4 In a query, forgetting to enclose a field name containing spaces in square brackets (**[ ]**) is an error.

25.5 In a query, not providing fully-qualified names for fields with the same name from two or more tables is an error.

25.6 The single quote (**'**) character is used as a delimiter for strings being inserted in the database. Therefore, to insert a name containing quotes (such as O'Malley) into a database, the name must two single quotes in the position where the quote character appears in the name (e.g., ***'O''Malley'***).

GOOD PROGRAMMING PRACTICES

25.1 Avoid field names containing spaces when designing database tables.

25.2 By convention, SQL keywords should use all uppercase letters on systems that are not case sensitive to emphasize the SQL keywords in an SQL query.

25.3 In database systems that support uppercase and lowercase letters for table names and field names, use an uppercase first letter for every word in a table name or field name (e.g., **LastName**) to make SQL statements more readable.

25.4 Use spacing and indentation in a SQL query to make the query more readable.

25.5 Fully qualify the names of the fields used in a SQL query to ensure that the query references fields from the proper tables.

PERFORMANCE TIPS

25.1 Using selection criteria improves performance by selecting a portion of the database that is normally smaller than the entire database. Working with a smaller portion of the data is easier and faster than working with the entire set of data stored in the database.

25.2 When **SubmitChanges** is called, only the modified records in the **Resultset** (not the entire **Resultset**) are sent to the server.

PORTABILITY TIPS

25.1 SQL is case sensitive on some database systems. See your database system documentation to determine if SQL is case sensitive on your database system and to determine the syntax that should be used for SQL keywords (i.e., should they be all uppercase letters, all lowercase letters or some combination of the two?).

25.2 Not all database systems support the **LIKE** operator, so be sure to read your database system's documentation carefully.

SOFTWARE ENGINEERING OBSERVATIONS

25.1 For most SQL statements, the asterisk (*) should not be used to specify field names to select from a table (or several tables). In general, programmers process result sets by knowing in advance the order of the fields in the result set. For example, selecting **AuthorID** and **LastName** from the **Authors** table guarantees that the fields will appear in the result set in the same order (**AuthorID** as the first field and **LastName** as the second field). The fields in the result set are processed by specifying the column number in the result set (column numbers typically start at 1 for the first field in the result set).

25.2 Specifying the actual field names to select from a table (or several tables) guarantees that the fields are always returned in the same order even if the actual order of the fields in the database table(s) changes.

25.3 If a field name contains spaces, it must be enclosed in square brackets (**[ ]**) in the query. For example, if the field name is **First Name**, the field name would appear in the query as **[First Name]**.

25.4 If an SQL statement uses fields with the same name from multiple tables, the field name must be fully qualified with its table name and a dot operator (**.**) as in **Authors.AuthorID**.

25.5 Many database programs that automatically generate SQL statements use fully-qualified field names for every field reference.

SELF-REVIEW EXERCISES

25.1 Fill in the blanks in each of the following:

a) The most popular database query language is ________.
b) A table in a database consists of ________ and ________.
c) A ________ is a field in a table for which every entry has a unique value in another table and where the field in the other table is the primary key for that table.
d) The ________ uniquely identifies each record in a table.
e) SQL keyword ________ is followed by the selection criteria that specify the records to select in a query.
f) SQL keyword ________ specifies the order in which records are sorted in a query.
g) SQL keyword ________ is used to merge data from two or more tables.
h) A ________ is an integrated collection of data which is centrally controlled.

ANSWERS TO SELF-REVIEW EXERCISES

25.1 a) SQL. b) rows, columns. c) foreign key. d) primary key. e) **WHERE**. f) **ORDER BY**. g) **INNER JOIN**. h) database.

EXERCISES

25.2 Write SQL queries for the **Books.mdb** database (discussed in Section 25.3) that perform each of the following tasks:

a) Select all authors from the **Authors** table.
b) Select all publishers from the **Publishers** table.
c) Select a specific author and list all books for that author. Include the title, year and ISBN number. Order the information alphabetically by title.
d) Select a specific publisher and list all books published by that publisher. Include the title, year and ISBN number. Order the information alphabetically by title.

25.3 Write SQL statements for the **Books.mdb** database (discussed in Section 25.3) that perform each of the following tasks:

a) Add a new author to the **Authors** table.
b) Add a new title for an author (remember that the book must have an entry in the **AuthorISBN** table). Be sure to specify the publisher of the title.
c) Add a new publisher.

25.4 Fill in the blanks in each of the following:

a) ADO is an acronym for ________.
b) RDS is an acronym for ________.
c) UDA is an acronym for ________.
d) ADO provides objects and ________.

25.5 Fill in the blanks in each of the following:

a) ADO object ________ represents the connection to the data source.
b) ADO object ________ stores an SQL query.
c) **RDS.Datacontrol** property ________ stores an SQL query.
d) A database that is physically located on different machine is called a ________ database.

25.6 What is the primary difference between the **RDS.DataControl** and the Tabular Data Control?

25.7 Modify the **`Find_OnClick`** procedure of Fig. 25.36 to validate the format of the ISBN number input. Use VBScript regular expressions (see Chapter 22 for more on regular expressions).

25.8 Modify Fig. 25.36 to allow the **`PublisherID`** to be updated in addition to the **`Title`**.

BIBLIOGRAPHY

(Bl88) Blaha, M. R.; W. J. Premerlani; and J. E. Rumbaugh, "Relational Database Design Using an Object-Oriented Methodology," *Communications of the ACM*, Vol. 31, No. 4, April 1988, pp. 414–427.

(Co70) Codd, E. F., "A Relational Model of Data for Large Shared Data Banks," *Communications of the ACM*, June 1970.

(Co72) Codd, E. F., "Further Normalization of the Data Base Relational Model," in *Courant Computer Science Symposia*, Vol. 6, *Data Base Systems*. Upper Saddle River, NJ: Prentice Hall, 1972.

(Co88) Codd, E. F., "Fatal Flaws in SQL," *Datamation*, Vol. 34, No. 16, August 15, 1988, pp. 45–48.

(De90) Deitel, H. M., *Operating Systems, Second Edition*. Reading, MA: Addison-Wesley Publishing, 1990.

(Da81) Date, C. J., *An Introduction to Database Systems*. Reading, MA: Addison-Wesley Publishing, 1981.

(Re88) Relational Technology, *INGRES Overview*. Alameda, CA: Relational Technology, 1988.

(St81) Stonebraker, M., "Operating System Support for Database Management," *Communications of the ACM*, Vol. 24, No. 7, July 1981, pp. 412–418.

(Wi88) Winston, A., "A Distributed Database Primer," *UNIX World*, April 1988, pp. 54–63.

26

Active Server Pages (ASP)

Objectives

- To be able to program Active Server Pages using VBScript.
- To understand how Active Server Pages work.
- To understand the differences between client-side scripting and server-side scripting.
- To be able to pass data between Web pages.
- To be able to use server-side includes.
- To be able to use server-side ActiveX components.
- To be able to create sessions.
- To be able to use cookies.
- To be able to use ActiveX Data Objects (ADO) to access a database.

A client is to me a mere unit, a factor in a problem.
Sir Arthur Conan Doyle

Rule One: Our client is always right.
Rule Two: If you think our client is wrong, see Rule One.
Anonymous

Protocol is everything.
Francoise Giuliani

You will come here and get books that will open your eyes, and your ears, and your curiosity, and turn you inside out or outside in.
Ralph Waldo Emerson

Outline

26.1 Introduction

In this chapter, we introduce server-side text files called *Active Server Pages* (*ASP*) that are processed in response to a client (e.g., browser) request. An ASP file—which has file extension **.asp**—contains HTML and scripting code. Although other languages such as JavaScript can be used for ASP scripting, VBScript is the de facto language for ASP scripting. If you are not familiar with VBScript, you should read Chapter 22, "VBScript," before reading this chapter.

Software Engineering Observation 26.1

Some independent software vendors (ISVs) provide scripting engines for use with ASP that support languages other than VBScript and JavaScript.

ASP is a Microsoft-developed technology for sending dynamic Web content—which includes HTML, Dynamic HTML, ActiveX controls, client-side scripts and *Java applets* (i.e., client-side Java programs that are embedded in a Web page)—to the client.

26.2 How Active Server Pages Work

The Active Server Pages in this chapter demonstrate communication between clients and servers via the HTTP protocol of the World Wide Web. When a client sends an HTTP request to the server, the server receives the request and directs it to be processed by the appropriate Active Server Page. The Active Server Page does its processing (which often includes interacting with a database), then returns its result to the client—normally in the form of a HTML document to display in a browser, but other data formats, such as images and binary data, can be returned.

The two most common HTTP *request types* (also known as *request methods*) are ***GET*** and ***POST***. A **GET** request *gets* (or *retrieves*) information from the server. Common uses of

GET requests are to retrieve an HTML document or an image. A **POST** request *posts* (or *sends*) data to the server. Common uses of **POST** requests are to send to a server information from an HTML form in which the client has entered data, to send to the server information so it can search the Internet or query a database for the client, to send authentication information to the server, etc.

An HTTP **POST** request is often used to post data from an HTML form to a server-side form handler that processes the data. For example, when you respond to a Web-based survey, a **POST** request normally sends to a Web server the information specified in an HTML form.

Browsers often *cache* (save on disk) Web pages so they can quickly reload the pages, because there are no differences between the last version stored in the cache and the current version on the Web. This helps speed up your browsing experience by minimizing the amount of data that must be downloaded for you to view a Web page. Browsers typically do not cache the server's response to a **POST** request because the next **POST** request from the client may not return the same result. For example, in a survey, many users could visit the same Web page and respond to a question. The survey results could then be displayed for the user. Each new response changes the overall results of the survey.

When you use a Web-based search engine, a **GET** request normally supplies the information you specify in the HTML form to the search engine. The search engine performs the search, then returns the results to you as a Web page. Such pages are often cached in case you perform the same search again. As with **POST** requests, **GET** requests can supply parameters as part of the request to the Web server.

When a client requests an ASP file, the ASP file is parsed (top to bottom) by an *ActiveX component* (i.e., a server-side ActiveX control that usually does not have a graphical user interface) named ***asp.dll***. Scripting code is executed as it is encountered. The ***@LANGUAGE*** statement is used by the programmer to specify which scripting engine is needed to interpret the scripting code. If **@LANGUAGE** is not used, VBScript is assumed to be the default. As the script is interpreted, HTML (plus any client-side scripts) is sent to the client. We will see exactly how the **@LANGUAGE** statement is used momentarily.

Good Programming Practice 26.1

When using VBScript code in an Active Server Page, use the **@Language** *statement for clarity.*

Portability Tip 26.1

Because browsers are capable of rendering HTML, an ASP page that generates pure HTML can be rendered on any client browser—regardless of the fact that the page requested ends in **.asp**.

Software Engineering Observation 26.2

An Active Server Page file is parsed each time a request is made for it. This allows the Web developer to conveniently modify ASP files and have the updated ASP file available for the next request.

Software Engineering Observation 26.3

In order to take advantage of Active Server Page technology, a Web server must support ASP by providing a component such as **asp.dll**.

26.3 Client-side Scripting versus Server-side Scripting

In the first 22 chapters, we focused on client-side scripting with JavaScript and VBScript. Client-side scripting is often used for validation, interactivity, enhancing a Web page with ActiveX controls, Dynamic HTML and Java applets and for accessing the browser. Validation is important for reducing the number of trips to the server and for reducing the amount of work the server must perform. Interactivity allows the user to make decisions, click buttons, play games, etc.—which is often more interesting than just reading text. ActiveX controls, Dynamic HTML and Java applets enhance a Web page's appearance by providing richer functionality than HTML. Client-side scripts can access the browser and use features specific to that browser as well as manipulate browser documents.

Client-side scripting does have limitations. Client-side scripting is browser dependent—the scripting language must be supported by the browser or *scripting host*. Because Microsoft Internet Explorer and Netscape Communicator both support JavaScript, JavaScript has become the de facto scripting language on the client. Another limitation is that client-side scripts are viewable (e.g., using the ***View*** menu's ***Source*** command in Internet Explorer) on the client—protecting source code, especially if it is proprietary—is difficult.

Performance Tip 26.1

Perform as much processing on the client as possible to conserve server resources.

Because server-side scripts reside on the server, programmers have greater flexibility—especially with database access. Scripts executed on the server usually generate custom responses for clients. For example, a client might connect to an airline's Web server and request a list of all flights from Boston to Dallas between September 18th and November 5th. The script queries the database and dynamically generates HTML containing the list and sends it to the client. Clients connecting to the airline's Web server always get the most current database information.

Server-side scripts also have access to *ActiveX server components*—which extend scripting language functionality. We discuss some of these components later in the chapter.

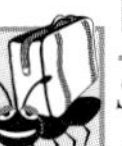

Portability Tip 26.2

Server-side scripts run exclusively on the server and therefore cross-platform issues are not a concern.

Software Engineering Observation 26.4

Server-side scripts are not visible to the client—only HTML (plus any client-side scripts) are sent to the client.

26.4 Using Personal Web Server or Internet Information Server

This chapter contains seven examples that require Personal Web Server (PWS) 4.0 or Internet Information Server (IIS) 4.0 or higher to execute. Before attempting to execute any example, you should make sure PWS or IIS is running. For help installing or running PWS/IIS, see Chapter 24, "Web Servers."

Although we used a specific directory structure for the chapter examples, we recommend that you create a subdirectory beneath **`C:\Webshare\Wwwroot`** named **`Deitel_Iw3htp`**. In this directory, copy all the **`.asp`** files. Create two other directories beneath **`C:\Webshare\Wwwroot`** named **`includes`** and **`images`**. Copy all **`.inc`** files to **includes** and all **.gif** files to **images**. [*Note*: you will have to modify most of the paths in the **.asp** files to reflect these directories.]

To execute a particular example, type **http://***machineName***/Deitel_Iw3htp/***name***.asp** into the Web browser's **Address** field and press *Enter*. For example, to execute **clock.asp** on a machine named **thunder** type

http://thunder/Deitel_Iw3htp/clock.asp

into the Web browser's **Address** field and press *Enter*. If you do not know the name of your machine, right-click **Network Neighborhood** and select ***Properties*** from the context menu to display the **Network** dialog. In the **Network** dialog, click the ***Identification*** tab. The computer name is displayed in the **Computer name:** field. Click **Cancel** to close the **Network** dialog.

Some examples access a database. The database files (e.g., **.mdb** files) can be copied into any directory on your system. Before executing these examples, you must set up a Data Source Name (DSN). See Section 25.5 for instructions on setting up a DSN for the databases used in the examples.

26.5 A Simple ASP Example

In this section we present a simple ASP example (Fig. 26.1) that generates an HTML page that represents a clock. Every 60 seconds the page is updated with the server's current time. After the program listing we discuss the program code.

```
<% @LANGUAGE = VBScript %>
<% Option Explicit %>
<!DOCTYPE HTML PUBLIC "-//W3C//DTD HTML 4.0 Transitional//EN">
<% ' Fig. 26.1 : clock.asp %>

<HTML>
<HEAD>
<TITLE>A Simple ASP Example</TITLE>
<META HTTP-EQUIV = "REFRESH" CONTENT = "60; URL = CLOCK.ASP">
</HEAD>
<BODY>

<FONT FACE = ARIAL SIZE = 4><STRONG>Simple ASP Example<STRONG>
</FONT><P>
   <TABLE BORDER = "6">
   <TR>
   <TD BGCOLOR = "#000000">
      <FONT FACE = Arial COLOR = "#00FF00" SIZE = 4>
         <% =Time() %>
      </FONT>
   </TD>
   </TR>
   </TABLE>
</BODY>
</HTML>
```

Fig. 26.1 Output from a simple Active Server Page (part 1 of 2).

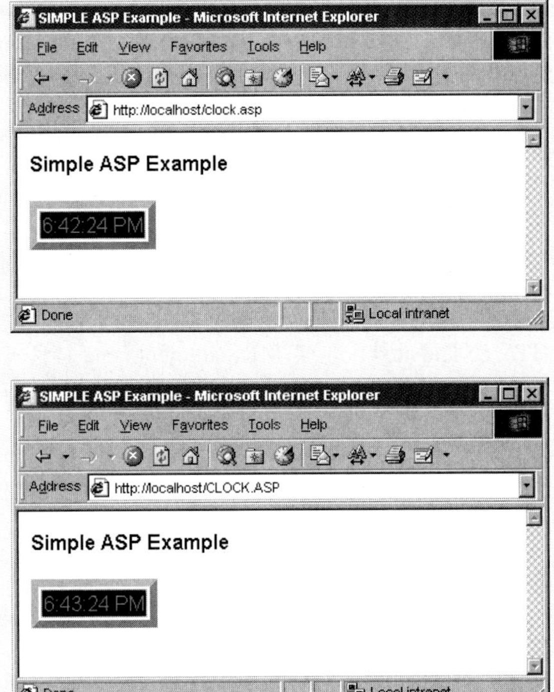

Fig. 26.1 Output from a simple Active Server Page (part 2 of 2).

When looking at the ASP file, you may have noticed the *scripting delimiters* **<%** and **%>** wrapped around the VBScript code. These scripting delimiters indicate that the scripting code is to be executed on the server—not the client. Scripting code enclosed in a scripting delimiter is never sent to the client.

Common Programming Error 26.1

Missing the opening delimiter, **<%***, or closing delimiter,* **%>***, or both for a server-side scripting statement is an error.*

Line 1

```
<% @LANGUAGE = "VBScript" %>
```

uses the **@LANGUAGE** processing directive to specify VBScript as the scripting language. In this chapter, we use VBScript exclusively to develop our Active Server Pages although other scripting languages can be used.

Common Programming Error 26.2

When using the **@LANGUAGE** *tag, not placing it as the first statement in an ASP file is an error.*

Line 2 uses **Option Explicit** to indicate that all VBScript variables be explicitly declared by the programmer. Remember that VBScript allows variables to be declared implicitly by simply mentioning a new name, which can lead to subtle errors. When used, statement **Option Explicit** must be the first VBScript scripting statement. In this particular example we do not declare any variables, but include **Option Explicit** as a good programming practice.

Testing and Debugging Tip 26.1

Always include **Option Explicit** *even if you are not declaring any VBScript variables. As a script evolves over time, you may need to declare variables and the presence of* **Option Explicit** *can help eliminate subtle errors.*

We use the **META** tag on line 9 to set the refresh interval for the page. The **CONTENT** attribute specifies the number of seconds until the **URL** attribute's value **clock.asp** is requested. Refreshing occurs every minute. Remember that Active Server Pages contain scripting code and HTML. The next non-HTML statement (line 19)

```
<% =Time() %>
```

calls VBScript function ***Time*** to get the current time on the server and write it to the client. Function ***Time*** returns the time in the format, *hh:mm:ss*. This statement is short for

```
<% Call Response.Write( Time() ) %>
```

which calls the ***Response*** *object* method ***Write***. The **Response** object provides functionality for sending information to the client. You will learn more about the **Response** object later in the chapter.

Each time the page is refreshed, the server loads the Active Server Page, interprets it using the VBScript scripting engine to process anything within the script delimiter tags, and sends HTML to the client.

26.6 Server-side ActiveX Components

Server-side script functionality is extended with server-side ActiveX components—ActiveX controls that typically do not have a graphical user interface that resides on the Web server. These components make powerful features accessible to the ASP author. Figure 26.2 summarizes some of the ActiveX components included with Internet Information Server (IIS) and Personal Web Server (PWS).

Software Engineering Observation 26.5

If the scripting language you are using in an Active Server Page does not support a certain feature, an ActiveX Server component can be created using Visual C++, Visual Basic, Delphi, etc., to provide that feature.

Performance Tip 26.2

Server-side ActiveX components usually execute faster than their scripting language equivalents.

Many Web sites sell advertising space—especially Web sites with large numbers of hits. In Fig. 26.3, we demonstrate the *AdRotator ActiveX component* for rotating advertisements on a Web page. Each time a client requests this Active Server Page the AdRotator component displays one of several advertisements—in this particular example, one of five flag images. When a country's flag image is clicked, the corresponding Central Intelligence Agency (CIA) Factbook Web page for that country is displayed.

Line 19

```
Set flagChanger = Server.CreateObject( "MSWC.AdRotator" )
```

creates an instance of an AdRotator component and assigns it to reference **flagChanger**. Server-side ActiveX components are instantiated by passing the name of the component as a string to **Server** object method ***CreateObject***. The ***Server*** object represents the Web server. You will learn more about the **Server** object later in the chapter.

Line 22

```
Call Response.Write( _
   flagChanger.GetAdvertisement( "config.txt" ) )
```

calls the **Response** object's **Write** method to send the advertisement to the client. Method ***GetAdvertisement*** is called from reference **flagChanger** to get the advertisement from the file **config.txt**.

Software Engineering Observation 26.6

The AdRotator ActiveX component allows the page author to minimize the amount of space on a Web page committed to advertisements, while at the same time maximizing the number of advertisements to display.

Portability Tip 26.3

Because the AdRotator ActiveX component is executed on the server, clients do not directly interact with it and therefore do not have to support ActiveX technologies.

Component Name	Description
MSWC.BrowserType	ActiveX component for gathering information (e.g., type, version, etc.) about the client's browser.
MSWC.AdRotator	ActiveX component for rotating advertisements on a Web Page.
MSWC.NextLink	ActiveX component for linking together Web pages.
MSWC.ContentRotator	ActiveX component for rotating HTML content on a Web page.
MSWC.PageCounter	ActiveX component for storing the number of times a Web page has been requested.
MSWC.Counters	ActiveX components that provides general-purpose persistent counters.
MSWC.MyInfo	ActiveX component that provides information (e.g., owner name, owner address, etc.) about a Web site.
Scripting.FileSystemObject	ActiveX component that provide an object library for accessing files on the server or on the server's network.
ActiveX Data Objects (ADO) Data Access Components	ActiveX components that provide an object library for accessing databases.

Fig. 26.2 Some server-side ActiveX components included with IIS and PWS.

```
<% @LANGUAGE = VBScript %>
<% Option Explicit %>
<% ' Fig. 26.3 : rotate.asp %>

<!DOCTYPE HTML PUBLIC "-//W3C//DTD HTML 4.0 Transitional//EN">
<HTML>
<HEAD>
<TITLE>AdRotator Example</TITLE>
</HEAD>

<BODY>
<FONT FACE = "Arial" SIZE = 4><STRONG>AdRotator Example<STRONG>
</FONT><P>
<%
   ' Declare flagChanger
   Dim flagChanger

   ' Create an AdRotator object
   Set flagChanger = Server.CreateObject( "MSWC.AdRotator" )

   ' Use config.txt to send an advertisement to the client
   Call Response.Write( _
      flagChanger.GetAdvertisement( "config.txt" ) )
%>
</BODY>
</HTML>
```

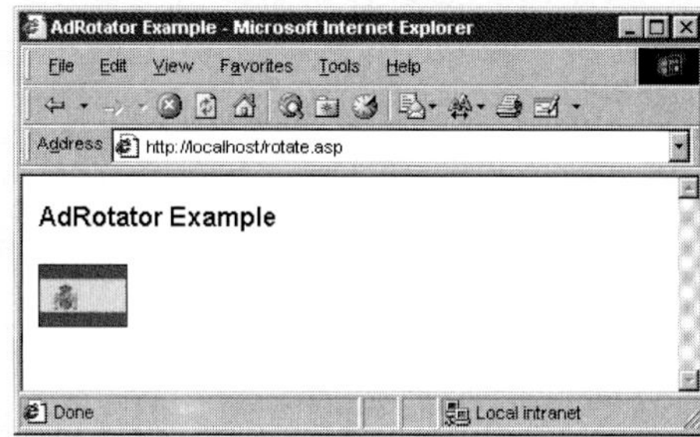

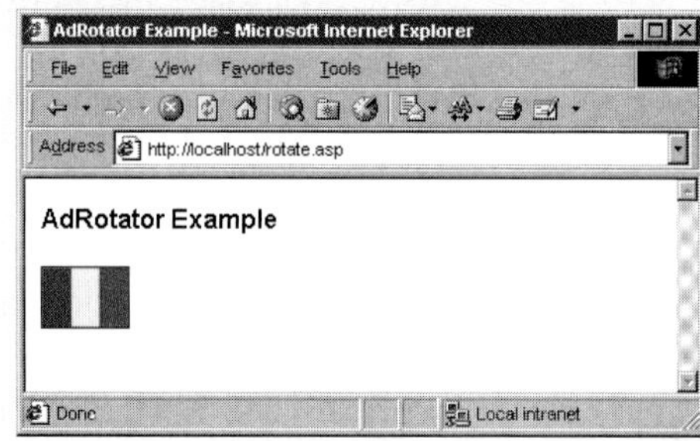

Fig. 26.3 Demonstrating the AdRotator ActiveX component (part 1 of 2).

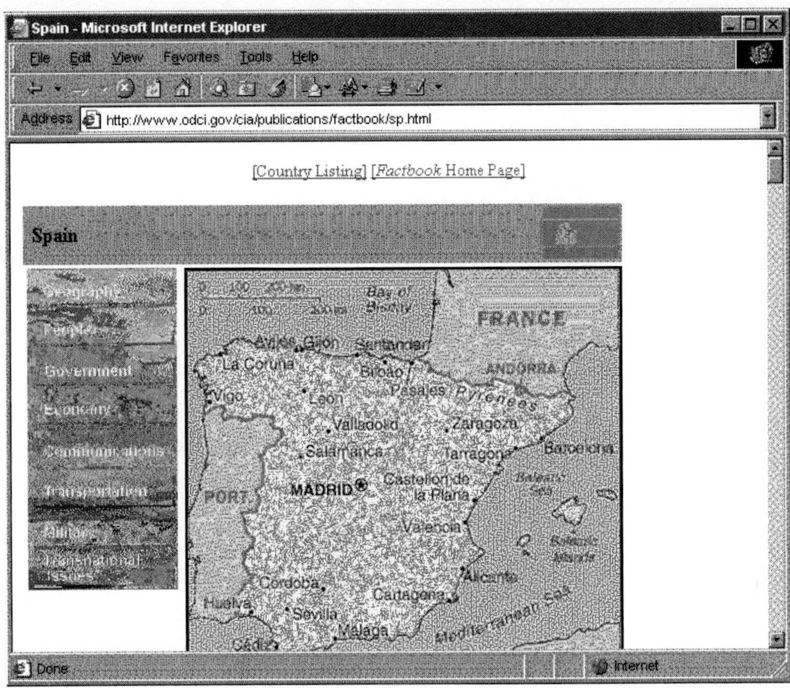

Fig. 26.3 Demonstrating the AdRotator ActiveX component (part 2 of 2).

File **config.txt** is listed in Fig. 26.4. This file is created by the programmer and does not have to be named **config.txt**. This file is located on the server and never is sent to the client. [*Note:* This is the first of several examples that consist of multiple files. When a file is part of the same example, we continue the line numbers relative to the last line number in the last listing. We do this for discussion purposes and to tie together one program.]

The file's header (lines 27 through 29) includes the image **HEIGHT**, image **WIDTH** and image **BORDER** width. The asterisk (line 30) separates the header from the advertisements. Lines 31 through 34

```
images/us.gif
http://www.odci.gov/cia/publications/factbook/us.html
United States Information
20
```

describes the first advertisement by providing the image URL—the image's location, the destination URL, a value for the **ALT** tag—browsers that cannot display graphics display the specified text and a number representing the percentage of time this particular image appears. The percentages do not have to add up to 100. Lines 35 through 50 list four other advertisements. [*Note*: If you are running this example, copy **config.txt** to the **Deitel_Iw3htp** directory (you created this directory in Section 26.4).]

```
WIDTH 54
HEIGHT 36
BORDER 1
*
/images/us.gif
http://www.odci.gov/cia/publications/factbook/us.html
United States Information
20
/images/france.gif
http://www.odci.gov/cia/publications/factbook/fr.html
France Information
20
/images/germany.gif
http://www.odci.gov/cia/publications/factbook/gm.html
Germany Information
20
/images/italy.gif
http://www.odci.gov/cia/publications/factbook/it.html
Italy Information
20
/images/spain.gif
http://www.odci.gov/cia/publications/factbook/sp.html
Spain Information
20
```

Fig. 26.4 File **config.txt** that describes the advertisements for Fig. 26.3.

26.7 File System Objects

File System Objects (*FSOs*) provide the programmer with the ability to manipulate files, directories and drives. FSOs also allow the programmer to read and write text. FSOs are an essential element for Active Server Pages with persistent data. We first overview FSO features and then provide a "live-code" example that uses FSOs.

FSOs are objects in the *Microsoft Scripting Runtime Library*. Five FSO types exist: ***FileSystemObject***, ***File***, ***Folder***, ***Drive*** and ***TextStream***. Each type is summarized in Fig. 26.5.

Object type	Description
FileSystemObject	Allows the programmer to interact with **File**s, **Folder**s and **Drive**s.
File	Allows the programmer to manipulate **File**s of any type.
Folder	Allows the programmer to manipulate **Folder**s (i.e., directories).
Drive	Allows the programmer to gather information about **Drive**s (hard disks, RAM disks—computer memory used as a substitute for hard disks to allow high-speed file operations, CD-ROMs, etc.). **Drive**s can be local or remote.
TextStream	Allows the programmer to read and write text files.

Fig. 26.5 File System Objects (FSOs).

Type **FileSystemObject** allows the programmer to interact with **File**s, **Folder**s and **Drive**s. The programmer can use **FileSystemObject**s to create directories, move files, determine whether or not a **Drive** exists, etc. Some common methods of **FileSystemObject** are summarized in Fig. 26.6.

Files allow the programmer to gather information about files, manipulate files and open files. Figure 26.7 lists some common **File** properties and methods.

Methods	Description
CopyFile	Copies an existing **File**.
CopyFolder	Copies an existing **Folder**.
CreateFolder	Creates and returns a **Folder**.
CreateTextFile	Creates and returns a text **File**.
DeleteFile	Deletes a **File**.
DeleteFolder	Deletes a **Folder**.
DriveExists	Tests whether or not a **Drive** exists.
FileExists	Tests whether or not a **File** exists. Returns boolean.
FolderExists	Tests whether or not a **Folder** exists. Returns boolean.
GetAbsolutePathName	Returns the absolute path as a string.
GetDrive	Returns the specified **Drive**.
GetDriveName	Returns the **Drive** drive name.
GetFile	Returns the specified **File**.
GetFileName	Returns the **File** file name.
GetFolder	Returns the specified **Folder**.
GetParentFolderName	Returns a string representing the parent folder name.
GetTempName	Creates and returns a string representing a file name.
MoveFile	Moves a **File**.
MoveFolder	Moves a **Folder**.
OpenTextFile	Opens an existing text **File**. Returns a **TextStream**.

Fig. 26.6 **FileSystemObject** methods.

Property/method	Description
Properties	
DateCreated	Date. The date the **File** was created.
DateLastAccessed	Date. The date the **File** was last accessed.
DateLastModified	Date. The date the **File** was last modified.
Drive	Drive. The **Drive** where the file is located.

Fig. 26.7 Some common **File** properties and methods (part 1 of 2).

Property/method	Description
Name	String. The **File** name.
ParentFolder	String. The **File**'s parent folder name.
Path	String. The **File**'s path.
ShortName	String. The **File**'s name expressed as a short name.
Size	The size of the **File** in bytes.
Methods	
Copy	Copy the **File**. Same as **CopyFile** of **FileSystemObject**.
Delete	Delete the **File**. Same as **DeleteFile** of **FileSystemObject**.
Move	Move the **File**. Same as **MoveFile** of **FileSystemObject**.
OpenAsTextStream	Opens an existing **File** as a text **File**. Returns **TextStream**.

Fig. 26.7 Some common **File** properties and methods (part 2 of 2).

Property **Path** contains the **File**'s path in *long name format* (the operating system does not abbreviate the name when it exceeds the 8.3 format). Property **ShortName** contains, if applicable, the file name in *short name format* (a file name exceeding the 8.3 format is abbreviated). For example, a file name in long name format might be "**ABCD EFG HIJ.doc**." That same file name in short name format might be "**ABCDEF~1.doc**."

Folder objects allow the programmer to gather information about directories and to manipulate directories. Figure 26.8 lists some common **Folder** properties and methods.

Property/method	Description
Properties	
Attributes	Integer. Value indicating **Folder**'s attributes (read only, hidden, etc.)
DateCreated	Date. The date the folder was created.
DateLastAccessed	Date. The date the folder was last accessed.
DateLastModified	Date. The date the folder was last modified.
Drive	Drive. The **Drive** where the folder is located.
IsRootFolder	Boolean. Indicates whether or not a **Folder** is the root folder.
Name	String. The **Folder**'s name.
ParentFolder	String. The **Folder**'s parent folder name.
Path	String. The **Folder**'s path.
ShortName	String. The **Folder**'s name expressed as a short name.
ShortPath	String. The **Folder**'s path expressed as a short path.
Size	Variant. The total size in bytes of all subfolders and files.
Type	String. The **Folder** type.

Fig. 26.8 Some **Folder** properties and methods (part 1 of 2).

Property/method	Description
Methods	
Delete	Delete the **Folder**. Same as **DeleteFolder** of **FileSystemObject**.
Move	Move the **Folder**. Same as **MoveFolder** of **FileSystemObject**.
Copy	Copy the **Folder**. Same as **CopyFolder** of **FileSystemObject**.

Fig. 26.8 Some **Folder** properties and methods (part 2 of 2).

Property **IsRootFolder** indicates whether or not the folder is the *root folder* for the **Drive**—i.e., the folder that contains everything on the drive. If the folder is not the root folder, method **ParentFolder** is called to print the folder's *parent folder* (i.e., the folder in which the selected folder is contained). Method **Size** is called to print the total number of bytes the folder contains. The size includes *subfolders* (i.e., the folders inside the selected folder) and files.

Drive objects allow the programmer to gather information about drives. Figure 26.9 lists some common **Drive** properties.

Property **DriveLetter** contains the **Drive**'s letter. Property **SerialNumber** contains the **Drive**'s serial number. Property **FreeSpace** contains the number of bytes available.

Figure 26.10 is an Active Server Page for a *guest book* that allows the visitor to enter their name, email and comments. File system objects are used to write the visitor information to disk on the server.

Property	Description
AvailableSpace	Variant. The amount of available **Drive** space in bytes.
DriveLetter	String. The letter assigned the **Drive** (e.g., "C").
DriveType	Integer. The **Drive** type. Constants **Unknown**, **Removable**, **Fixed**, **Remote**, **CDRom** and **RamDisk** represent **Drive** types and have the values 0–5, respectively.
FileSystem	String. The file system **Drive** description (FAT, FAT32, NTFS, etc.).
FreeSpace	Variant. Same as **AvailableSpace**.
IsReady	Boolean. Indicates whether or not a **Drive** is ready for use.
Path	String. The **Drive**'s path.
RootFolder	Folder. The **Drive**'s root **Folder**.
SerialNumber	Long. The **Drive** serial number.
TotalSize	Variant. The total **Drive** size in bytes.
VolumeName	String. The **Drive** volume name.

Fig. 26.9 **Drive** properties.

```
<% @LANGUAGE = VBScript %>
<% Option Explicit %>

<% ' Fig. 26.10 : guestbook.asp %>
<%
   Dim fso, tso, guestBook, mailtoUrl

   If Request( "entry" ) = "true" Then

      ' Instantiate a FileSystem Object
      Set fso = CreateObject( "Scripting.FileSystemObject" )

      ' Guestbook must be open for write by all!
      ' guestbook path must be modified to reflect the file
      ' structure of the server
      guestBook = "c:\webshare\wwwroot\deitel_iw3htp\" & _
                  "guestbook.txt"

      ' Check if the file exists, if not create it
      If fso.FileExists( guestbook ) <> True Then
         Call fso.CreateTextFile( guestBook )
      End If

      ' Open the guestbook and create the entry
      Set tso = fso.OpenTextFile( guestbook, 8, True )

      ' Build the mailtoUrl
      mailtoUrl = Request( "pubdate" ) & " <A HREF=" & Chr( 34 )
      mailtoUrl = mailtoUrl & "mailto:" & Request( "email" )
      mailtoUrl = mailtoUrl & Chr( 34 ) & ">" & Request( "name" )
      mailtoUrl = mailtoUrl & "</A>:  "

      ' Send the information to guestbook.txt
      Call tso.WriteLine( "<HR COLOR = BLUE SIZE = 1>" )
      Call tso.WriteLine( mailtoUrl )
      Call tso.WriteLine( Request( "comment" ) )
      Call tso.Close()
   End If
%>
<!DOCTYPE HTML PUBLIC "-//W3C//DTD HTML 4.0 Transitional//EN">
<HTML>
<HEAD>
<TITLE> GuestBook Example</TITLE>

<BODY>
<FONT SIZE = 2 FACE = "arial">
<FONT SIZE = 4 COLOR = "blue">

<%
   ' Print a thank you if they have made a request
   If Request( "entry" ) = "true" Then
%>

```

Fig. 26.10 Guest book Active Server Page (part 1 of 4).

```
Thanks for your entry!<P>
<% Else %>
Please leave a message in our guestbook.<P>
<% End If %>
</FONT>
<FORM ACTION = "guestbook.asp?entry=true" METHOD = "POST">
<CENTER>
<INPUT TYPE = "hidden" NAME = "pubdate" VALUE = "<% =Date() %>">
<TABLE>
<TR>
<TD><FONT FACE = "arial" SIZE = "2">Your Name:  </FONT><BR></TD>
<TD><INPUT TYPE = "text" FACE = ARIAL
    SIZE = "60" NAME = "name"><BR></TD>
</TR>
<TR>
<TD><FONT FACE = "arial" SIZE = "2">Your email address:
</FONT><BR></TD>
<TD><INPUT TYPE = "text" FACE = "arial" SIZE = "60" NAME = "email"
VALUE = "user@isp.com"><BR></TD>
</TR>
<TR>
<TD><FONT FACE = "arial" SIZE = "2">Tell the world:  </FONT>
<BR></TD>
<TD><TEXTAREA NAME = "comment" ROWS = "3" COLS = "50">
Replace this text with the information
you would like to post.
</TEXTAREA><BR></TD>
</TR>
</TABLE>
<INPUT TYPE = "submit" VALUE = "SUBMIT">
<INPUT TYPE = "reset" VALUE = "CLEAR">
</CENTER>
</FORM>
<%
   Dim fso2, tso2
   ' Instantiate a FileSystem Object
   Set fso2 = Server.CreateObject( _
      "Scripting.FileSystemObject" )
   ' Guestbook must be open for write by all!
   ' Guestbook path must be modified to reflect
   ' the file structure of the server
   guestBook = "c:\webshare\wwwroot\deitel_iw3htp\" & _
               "guestbook.txt"
   ' Check if the file exists, if not create it
   If fso2.FileExists( guestBook ) = True Then
```

Fig. 26.10 Guest book Active Server Page (part 2 of 4).

```
         ' Open the guestbook, "1" is for reading
         Set tso2 = fso2.OpenTextFile( guestbook, 1 )

         ' Read the entries
         Call Response.Write( "Guestbook Entries:<BR>" )
         Call Response.Write( tso2.ReadAll() )
         Call tso2.Close()
      End If
%>

</BODY>

</HTML>
```

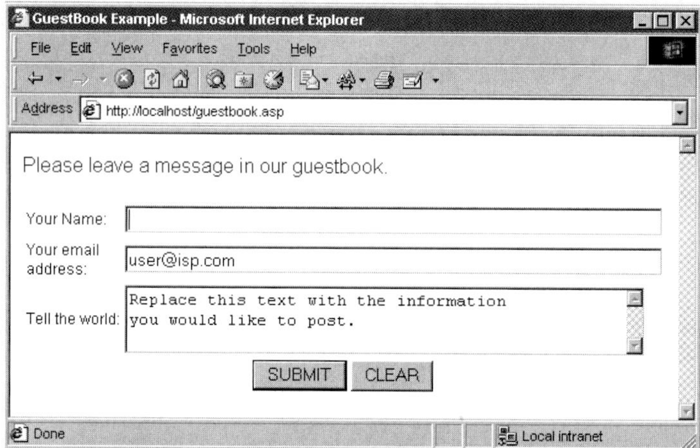

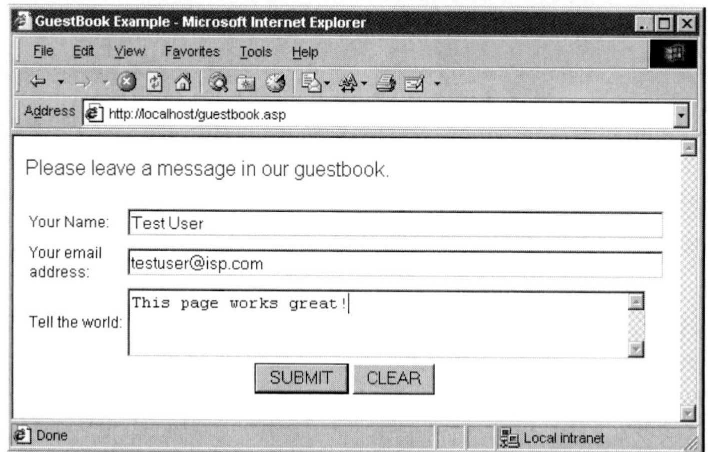

Fig. 26.10 Guest book Active Server Page (part 3 of 4).

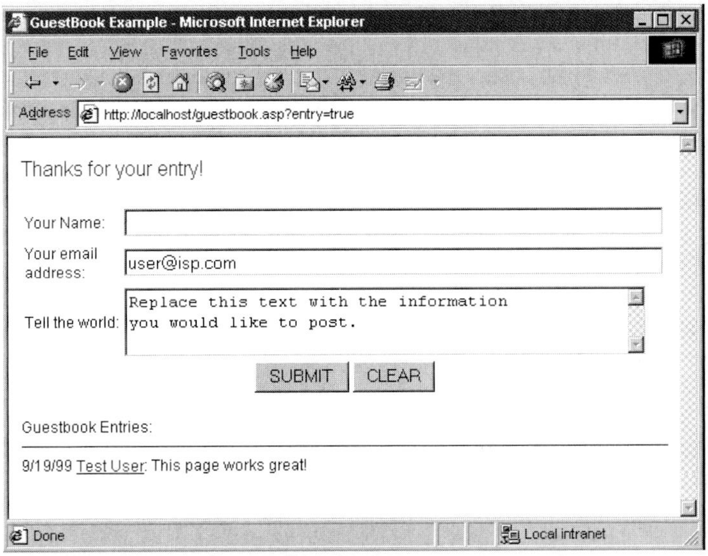

Fig. 26.10 Guest book Active Server Page (part 4 of 4).

The **If** condition (line 8)

```
Request( "entry" ) = "true"
```

uses the **Request** object to get the value of the **entry** variable passed to this Active Server Page and test it against **"true"**. When this page is first requested, **entry** has the value **""**. So lines 9 through 38 are not executed. Variable **entry** is passed a **"true"** value during the **POST** operation (line 60)—which requests **guessbook.asp** be reloaded. Because entry is now **"true"**, lines 9 through 38 are executed.

Line 11

```
Set fso = Server.CreateObject( "Scripting.FileSystemObject" )
```

creates an FSO instance (i.e., an object) and assigns it to reference **fso**. When assigning an object to a reference in VBScript, keyword **Set** must be used. We specify the location of the file (e.g., **guestbook.txt**) that stores guest book information on line 16. You may need to modify this path to conform to the directory structure on your machine.

Before writing data to the guest book, we call **FileExists** on line 20 to determine if **guestbook.txt** exists. If the file does not exist, method **CreateTextFile** is called to create the file.

Line 25

```
Set tso = fso.OpenTextFile( guestbook, 8, True )
```

calls method **OpenTextFile** to get a **TextStream** object for accessing the text file **guestbook.txt**. The constant value **8** indicates that the file will be opened for *appending* (writing to the end of the file) and **True** indicates that the file will be created if it does not exist. Opening for read or write is specified with constant values **1** and **2**, respectively.

The user's submitted name and email are combined with some HTML formatting and assigned to string **mailtoUrl** (lines 28 through 31). This string, when displayed in the browser, shows the submitted name as a *mailto link* (clicking this link opens an email message editor with the person's name in the **To:** field). The **Request** object is used to get the values in the **pubdate** text box (line 28), **email** text box (line 29) and **name** text box (line 29). Text box **pubdate** (line 63) is not visible to the user (i.e., it is **HIDDEN**) and contains the current date—which is retrieved using VBScript function ***Date***. VBScript function **Chr** is passed **34** to get a double quote (**"**) character.

Lines 34 through 36 write HTML as text to **guestbook.txt** using **TextStream** method **WriteLine**. **TextStream** method **Close** is called on line 37 to close the file.

Lines 49 through 57 determine if the user has submitted an entry. Either "**Thanks for your entry!**" or "**Please leave a message in our guestbook.**" is sent to the client.

Line 60

```
<FORM ACTION = "guestbook.asp?entry=true" METHOD = "POST">
```

specifies that a **POST** operation to the server occurs and that the **guestbook.asp** file is requested. Variable **entry** is created and given a value of **true**. Remember that when this page is requested, all server-side scripts are executed as they are encountered. HTML is sent to the client as the page is processed. If **entry** is **""**, certain blocks of scripting code are not executed. When the user fills in the form and submits it, **guestbook.asp** is loaded and passed variable **entry**—which is given a **"true"** value to allow scripting code inside certain **If** blocks (lines 8 and 51) to execute. HTML is sent to the client as the page is processed.

Each time this Active Server Page is loaded, lines 91 through 115 are executed. This block of VBScript code simply provides a list of all the users who have made guest book entries. If the **guestbook.txt** file exists, it is opened for reading on line 108. Lines 111 and 112 write HTML/text to the client. **TextStream** method **ReadAll** is called to read the entire contents of **guestbook.txt**.

26.8 Session Tracking and Cookies

Many Web sites today provide custom Web pages and/or functionality on a client-by-client basis. For example, some Web sites allow you to customize their home page to suit your needs. An excellent example of this is the *Yahoo!* Web site. If you go to the site

```
http://my.yahoo.com/
```

you can customize how the Yahoo! site appears to you when you revisit the site. [*Note:* You need to get a free Yahoo! ID to do this.] The HTTP protocol does not support persistent information that could help a Web server determine that a request is from a particular client. As far as a Web server is concerned, every request could be from the same client or every request could be from a different client.

Another example of a service that is customized on a client-by-client basis is a *shopping cart* for shopping on the Web (see Chapter 23). Obviously, the server must distinguish between clients so the company can determine the proper items and charge the proper amount for each client.

A third purpose of customizing on a client-by-client basis is marketing. Companies often track the pages you visit throughout a site so they can display advertisements that are targeted to your browsing trends. A problem with tracking is that many people consider it to be an invasion of their privacy, an increasingly sensitive issue in our information-based society.

To help the server distinguish between clients, each client must identify itself to the server. There are a number of popular techniques for distinguishing between clients. For the purpose of this chapter, we introduce two techniques to track clients individually—*session tracking* and *cookies*.

Session tracking is handled by the server. The first time a client connects to the server, it is assigned a unique *session ID* by the server. When the client makes additional requests, the client's session ID is compared against the session IDs stored in the server's memory. Active Server Pages use the ***Session*** object to manage sessions. The **Session** object's ***Timeout*** property specifies the number of minutes that a session exists before it expires. The default value for property **Timeout** is 20 minutes. An individual session can also be terminated by calling **Session** method ***Abandon***.

Another popular way to customize Web pages is via *cookies*. Cookies can store information on the client's computer for retrieval later in the same browsing session or in future browsing sessions. For example, cookies could be used in a shopping application to indicate the client's preferences. When the Active Server Page receives the client's next communication, the Active Server Page can examine the cookie(s) it sent to the client in a previous communication, identify the client's preferences and immediately display products of interest to the client.

Cookies are small files that are sent by an Active Server Page (or another similar technology such as Perl/CGI and Java Servlets discussed in Chapters 27 and 29, respectively) as part of a response to a client. Every HTTP-based interaction between a client and a server includes a *header* that contains information about the request (when the communication is from the client to the server) or information about the response (when the communication is from the server to the client). When an Active Server Page receives a request, the header includes information such as the request type (e.g., **GET** or **POST**) and cookies stored on the client machine by the server. When the server formulates its response, the header information includes any cookies the server wants to store on the client computer.

Software Engineering Observation 26.7

Some clients do not allow cookies to be written on those clients. When a client declines a cookie the client is normally informed that such a refusal may prevent browsing the site.

Depending on the *maximum age* of a cookie, the Web browser either maintains the cookie for the duration of the browsing session (i.e., until the user closes the Web browser) or stores the cookies on the client computer for future use. When the browser makes a request of a server, cookies previously sent to the client by that server are returned to the server (if they have not expired) as part of the request formulated by the browser. Cookies are automatically deleted when they *expire* (i.e., reach their maximum age). We use cookies in Section 26.10 to store user IDs on clients.

We are now ready to present an example that uses session tracking. Figure 26.11 is a quick and efficient HTML page generator. This example consists of two Active Server Pages linked to each other through HTTP **POST** requests. Multiple Active Server Pages connected in this manner are sometimes called an *ASP application*. A user who is not familiar with HTML/ASP can input their information into a form, submit the form and the ASP application does all the work of generating an ASP page. We use session tracking in this example to maintain a state between the two ASP pages.

```
<% @LANGUAGE = VBScript %>
<% Option Explicit %>

<% ' Fig. 26.11 : instantpage.asp %>

<!DOCTYPE HTML PUBLIC "-//W3C//DTD HTML 4.0 Transitional//EN">
<HTML>
<HEAD>
<TITLE>Instant Page Content Builder</TITLE>
</HEAD>

<BODY>

<!-- include header goes here-->
<!-- #include virtual="/includes/mgtheader.inc" -->

<FONT FACE = "ARIAL" SIZE = "2">
<H2>Instant Page Content Builder</H2>

<%
   ' If there is a value from process.asp, show it here
   Call Response.Write( Session( "fileNameString" ) & "<BR>" )

   ' Begin the form
%>
<FORM ACTION = "process.asp" METHOD = "POST">

<CENTER>
<INPUT TYPE = "hidden" NAME = "pubdate" VALUE = "<% =Date() %>">
<TABLE>
<TR>
<TD><FONT FACE = "arial" SIZE = "2">Your Name:
</FONT><BR></TD>
<TD><INPUT TYPE = "text" FACE = "arial" SIZE = "60"
           NAME = "name"><BR></TD>
</TR>
<TR>
<TD><FONT FACE = "arial" SIZE = "2"> Enter the Filename:
</FONT><BR></TD>
<TD><INPUT TYPE = "text" FACE = "arial" SIZE = "60"
          NAME = "filename" VALUE = "YourFileName.asp"><BR></TD>
</TR>
<TR>
<TD><FONT FACE = "arial" SIZE = "2">Enter the Title:
</FONT><BR></TD>
<TD><INPUT TYPE = "text" FACE = "arial" SIZE = "60"
           NAME = "doctitle" VALUE = "Document Title"><BR></TD>
</TR>
```

Fig. 26.11 Creating Web pages using an Active Server Page (part 1 of 2).

```
<TR>
<TD><FONT FACE = "arial" SIZE = "2">Enter the Content:
</FONT><BR></TD>
<TD><TEXTAREA NAME = "content" ROWS = "3" COLS = "50">
Replace this text with the
information you would like to post.
</TEXTAREA><BR></TD>
</TR>
</TABLE>
<INPUT TYPE = "submit" VALUE = "SUBMIT">
<INPUT TYPE = "reset" VALUE = "CLEAR">
</CENTER>
</FORM>

<!-- #include virtual="/includes/mgtfooter.inc" -->

</BODY>
</HTML>
```

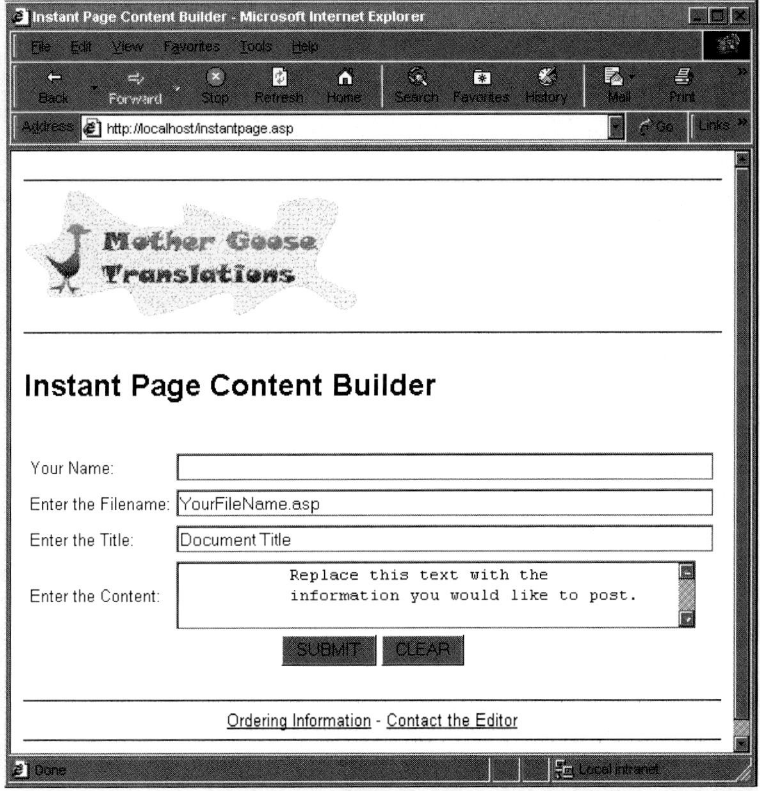

Fig. 26.11 Creating Web pages using an Active Server Page (part 2 of 2).

Line 15

```
<!-- #include virtual="/includes/mgtheader.inc" -->
```

uses a *server side include* (*SSI*) statement to incorporate the contents **mgtheader.inc** (Fig. 26.12) into the ASP file. The SSI statement is literally replaced with the contents of the file **mgtheader.inc**. SSI statements always execute before any scripting code executes. We also use an SSI on line 63 to include **mgtfooter.inc** (Fig. 26.13). The word ***virtual*** in the SSI refers to the include file's path as it appears below the server root directory. This is often referred to as a *virtual path*. SSIs can also use **file** instead of **virtual** to indicate a *physical path* on the server. For example, line 15 could be rewritten as

```
<!--#include file="c:/webshare/wwwroot/includes/
mgtheader.inc"-->
```

which assumes that **mgtheader.inc** is in the directory **c:/webshare/wwwroot/includes** on the server.

Software Engineering Observation 26.8

Virtual paths hide the server's internal file structure.

Line 22

```
Call Response.Write( Session( "fileNameString" ) & "<BR>" )
```

retrieves the value of session variable **fileNameString** using the **Session** object and writes the session variable's value to the client. As we will see momentarily, the value of session variable **fileNameString** is set in **process.asp** (Fig. 26.14) to HTML formatted text that either indicates that the file name entered in the **Enter the Filename:** field is not unique or welcomes the current session's user back to **instantpage.asp**.

Line 26

```
<FORM ACTION = "process.asp" METHOD = "POST">
```

specifies that Active Server Page **process.asp** is loaded on a **POST**. The remainder of **instantpage.asp** is HTML code.

```
<HR SIZE = 1 COLOR = BLUE>
<IMG HEIGHT = 100 SRC = "/images/mgheader.gif">
<HR SIZE = 1 COLOR = BLUE>
```

Fig. 26.12 File listing for **mgtheader.inc**.

```
<HR COLOR = BLUE SIZE = 1>
<CENTER>
<A HREF = "mailto:orders">Ordering Information</A> -
<A HREF = "mailto:editor">Contact the Editor</A><BR>
<HR COLOR = BLUE SIZE = 1>
</CENTER>
</FONT>
```

Fig. 26.13 File listing for **mgtfooter.inc**.

Software Engineering Observation 26.9

Server-side includes may include any type of information. Text files and HTML files are two of the most common server-side include files.

Software Engineering Observation 26.10

Server-side includes are performed before any scripting code is interpreted. Therefore, an Active Server Page cannot dynamically decide which server-side includes are included and which are not. Through scripting, an ASP can determine which SSI block is sent to the client.

Testing and Debugging Tip 26.2

Server-side includes that contain scripting code should enclose the scripting code in **<SCRIPT>** *tags or in* **<% %>** *delimiters to prevent one block of scripting code from running into another block of scripting code.*

Software Engineering Observation 26.11

By convention, server-side include (SSI) files end with the **.inc** *extension.*

Software Engineering Observation 26.12

Server-side includes are an excellent technique for reusing HTML, Dynamic HTML, scripts and other programming elements.

Figure 26.14 (i.e., **process.asp**) creates the ASP file for the user and presents a link to the page for the user to review or download. This page is loaded in response to a **POST** request from **instantpage.asp** (line 26).

Lines 88 through 100 create the first one-third of the user's ASP page and assigns the HTML to string **header**. VBScript constant ***vbCrLf*** is used to insert a carriage-return line-feed combination. The **Request** object is used to retrieve the values from the posted form. Lines 104 through 109 create the last one-third of the ASP page and assign the HTML to variable **footer**.

An FSO object is created on line 112 and assigned to reference **fso**. Line 117 specifies the path on the server where the HTML file will eventually be written. You may need to modify this path on your machine.

Lines 120 through 126 validate the contents of text box **Enter the Filename** to determine if it contains the default string **YourFileName.asp**. If so, the statement

```
Session( "filenamestring" )= _
   "<FONT COLOR=" & Chr( 34 ) & "red" _
   & Chr( 34 ) & "SIZE=4>" _
   & "Please enter a unique filename.</FONT>"
```

assigns HTML to **Session** variable **filenamestring**. This HTML is eventually written to the client using **Response** method **Write** in **instantpage.asp** (line 22).

The statement (line 125)

```
Call Response.Redirect( "instantpage.asp" )
```

calls **Response** method ***Redirect*** to redirect the browser back to **instantpage.asp** because the file name conflicts with an existing file name. Because a different Active Server Page is loaded, state is preserved through the use of session variable **filenamestring**.

```
<% @LANGUAGE = VBScript %>
<% Option Explicit %>

<% ' Fig. 26.14 : process.asp %>
<%
   Dim header, footer, directoryPath, filePathname, fileName
   Dim fileNameString, newTitle, fso, tso

   ' Build the header
   ' vbCrLf inserts a carriage return/linefeed into the text
   ' string which makes the HTML code more legible
   header = "<HTML>" & vbCrLf & "<HEAD>" & vbCrLf _
     & "<META NAME= " & Chr( 34 ) & "author" & Chr( 34 ) _
     & " CONTENT = "  & Chr( 34 ) & Request( "name" ) _
     & Chr( 34 ) & ">" & vbCrLf & "<META NAME= " & Chr( 34 ) _
     & "pubdate" & Chr( 34 )  & " CONTENT = " & Chr( 34 ) _
     & request( "pubdate" ) & Chr( 34 ) & ">" & vbCrLf _
     & "<TITLE>" & request( "doctitle" ) & "</TITLE>" _
     & vbCrLf & "</HEAD>" & vbCrLf & "<BODY>" _
     & vbCrLf & "<FONT FACE=" & Chr( 34 ) & "arial" _
     &  Chr( 34 ) & " SIZE=2>" & vbCrLf _
     & "<!-- #include virtual=" & Chr( 34 ) _
     & "/includes/mgtheader.inc" & Chr( 34 ) & " -->" _
     & vbCrLf & "<H1>" & Request("doctitle") & "</H1>" & vbCrLf

   ' Build the footer using a different method for
   ' building the string
   footer = "<!-- #include virtual=" & Chr( 34 )
   footer = footer & "/includes/mgtfooter.inc"
   footer = footer & Chr( 34 ) & " -->" & vbCrLf
   footer = footer & "</FONT>" & vbCrLf
   footer = footer & "</BODY>" & vbCrLf
   footer = footer & "</HTML>" & vbCrLf

   ' Creates a FileSystem Object
   Set fso = Server.CreateObject( "Scripting.FileSystemObject" )

   ' Directory must be open for write by all!
   ' directoryPath must be modified to reflect the file structure
   ' of the server
   directoryPath = "c:\webshare\wwwroot\temp\"

   'check to make sure that the filename is not empty
   If Request( "filename" ) = "YourFileName.asp" Then
      Session( "filenamestring" )= _
         "<FONT COLOR=" & Chr( 34 ) & "red" _
         & Chr( 34 ) & "SIZE=4>" _
         & "Please enter a unique filename.</FONT>"
      Call Response.Redirect( "instantpage.asp" )
   End If

   ' Builds path for text file
   filePathname = directoryPath & Request( "filename" )
```

Fig. 26.14 ASP file that creates an ASP file for the user (part 1 of 3).

```
   ' See if the directory exists
   If fso.FolderExists( directoryPath ) <> True Then
      Call fso.CreateFolder( directoryPath )
   End If

   ' Check if the filename already exists
   If fso.FileExists( filePathname ) = True Then
      Session( "filenamestring" ) = "<FONT COLOR=" _
         & Chr( 34 ) & "red" & Chr( 34 ) & "SIZE=" _
         & Chr( 34 ) & "4" & Chr( 34 ) & ">" _
         & "That filename is being used." _
         & "Please enter a unique filename.</FONT>"
      Call Response.Redirect( "instantpage.asp" )
   End If

   ' If fileNameString does not get set by an error,
   ' give it a friendly value so that
   ' when the user repeats the process,
   ' fileNameString is initialized
   Session( "filenamestring" ) = "<FONT COLOR=" _
      & Chr( 34 ) & "blue"  & Chr( 34 ) & "SIZE =" _
      & Chr( 34 ) & "4" & Chr( 34 ) & ">" _
      & "Welcome Back " & Request( "name" ) & "!</FONT>"

   ' Create the html file
   Set tso = fso.CreateTextFile( filePathName, False )
   Call tso.WriteLine( header )
   Call tso.WriteLine( Request( "content" ) )
   Call tso.WriteLine( footer )
   Call tso.Close

   ' Create the results page
%>
<!DOCTYPE HTML PUBLIC "-//W3C//DTD HTML 4.0 Transitional//EN">
<HTML>
<HEAD>

<% ' Use the title given by the user %>
<TITLE>File Generated: <% =Request( "doctitle" ) %></TITLE>
</HEAD>

<BODY>
<!-- #include virtual="/includes/mgtheader.inc" -->
<FONT FACE = "arial" SIZE = "2">
<H1>File Generated: <% =Request( "doctitle" ) %></H1>

<% ' Provide a link to the generated page %>
Your file is ready:
<A HREF = "/temp/<% =Request( "filename" ) %>">
<% =Request( "doctitle" ) %></A>
<P>
<!-- #include virtual = "/includes/mgtfooter.inc" -->
```

Fig. 26.14 ASP file that creates an ASP file for the user (part 2 of 3).

```
183 </FONT>
184 </BODY>
185 </HTML>
```

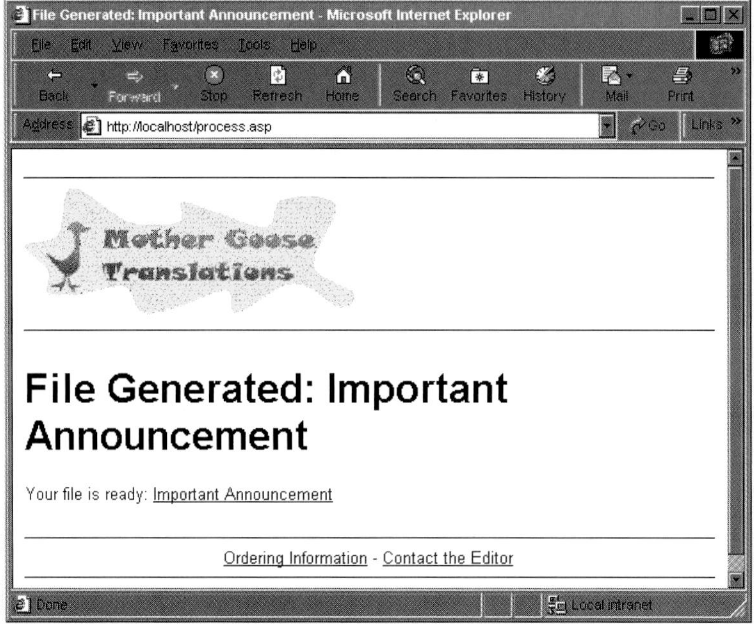

Fig. 26.14 ASP file that creates an ASP file for the user (part 3 of 3).

Line 132 calls FSO method **FolderExists** to determine if the path created on line 129 exists. If the path does not exist, FSO method **CreateFolder** is called to create it.

FSO method **FileExists** determines if the file exists (line 137). If so, the user is redirected back to **instantpage.asp** by calling **Redirect**.

Line 150

```
Session( "filenamestring" )= "<FONT COLOR=" _
   & Chr( 34 ) & "blue"  & Chr( 34 ) & "SIZE =" _
   & Chr( 34 ) & "4" & Chr( 34 ) & ">" _
   & "Welcome Back " & Request( "name" ) & "!</FONT>"
```

assigns a string containing HTML to session variable **filenamestring** before redirecting the client back to **instantpage.asp**—which results in **instantpage.asp**'s line 22 displaying text that welcomes the user back.

Lines 157 through 159 write **header**, text area **content**'s text and **footer** to a text file. Lines 164 through 185 send HTML to the client with a link to the created page. Figure 26.15 lists a sample ASP file—named **announcement.asp**—created by Active Server Page **process.asp**.

```
<HTML>
<HEAD>
<META NAME = "author" CONTENT = "J Smith">
<META NAME = "pubdate" CONTENT = "9/19/99">
<TITLE>Important Announcement</TITLE>
</HEAD>
<BODY>
<FONT FACE = "arial" SIZE = 2>
<!-- #include virtual = "/includes/mgtheader.inc" -->
<H1>Important Announcement</H1>
Instant Page Builder is ready!
<!-- #include virtual = "/includes/mgtfooter.inc" -->
</FONT>
</BODY>
</HTML>
```

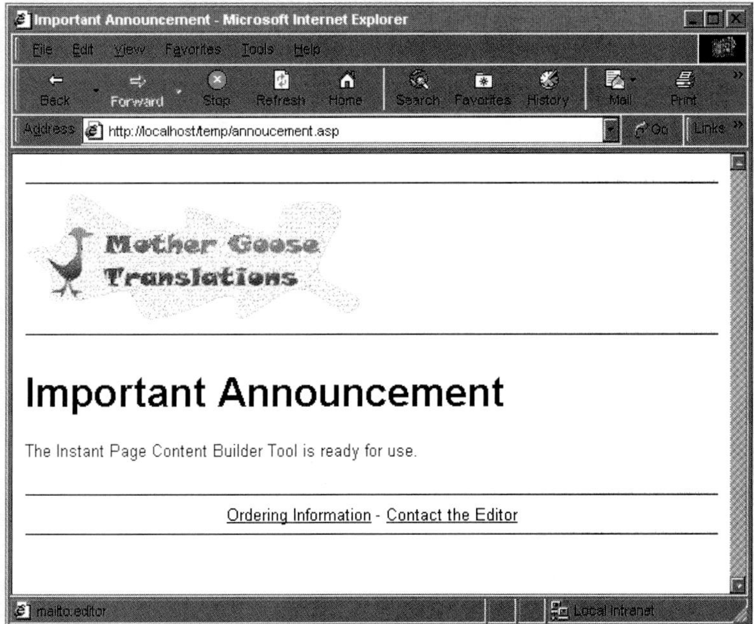

Fig. 26.15 Sample page generated by **instantpage.asp**.

26.9 Accessing a Database from an Active Server Page

Active Server Pages can communicate with databases via ADO (ActiveX Data Objects). As we discussed in Chapter 25, ADO provides a uniform way for a program to connect with a variety of databases in a general manner without having to deal with the specifics of those database systems.

Web applications are typically *three-tier distributed applications,* consisting of a *user interface*, *business logic* and *database access*. The user interface in such an application is often created using HTML (as shown in this chapter), Dynamic HTML or XML (see

Chapter 28). The user interface can of course contain ActiveX controls and client-side scripts. In some cases, Java applets are also used for this tier. HTML is the preferred mechanism for representing the user interface in systems where portability is a concern. Because HTML is supported by all browsers, designing the user interface to be accessed through a Web browser guarantees portability across all platforms that have browsers. Using the networking provided automatically by the browser, the user interface can communicate with the middle-tier business logic. The middle tier can then access the database to manipulate the data. All three tiers may reside on separate computers that are connected to a network or all three tiers may reside on a single machine.

In multitier architectures, Web servers are increasingly used to build the middle tier. They provide the business logic that manipulates data from databases and that communicates with client Web browsers. Active Server Pages, through ADO, can interact with popular database systems. Developers do not need to be familiar with the specifics of each database system. Rather, developers use SQL-based queries and ADO handles the specifics of interacting with each database system through OLE DB.

Figure 26.11 (**instantpage.asp**) puts the power of Web page creation into the hands of individuals who are not familiar with HTML, but we may want only a certain subset of preapproved users to be able to access **instantpage.asp**. To restrict access, we can use password protection. In Fig. 26.16, we provide an Active Server Page named **login.asp** that forces the user to provide a login name and password to access **instantpage.asp**. Login IDs are retrieved from an Access database and from cookies.

```
<% @LANGUAGE = VBScript %>
<% Option Explicit %>

<% ' Fig. 26.16 : login.asp %>

<%
   ' Set up the variables for this page
   Dim dbConn, dbQuery, loginRS, loginFound

   ' Check to see if there is an existing connection to
   ' the Database. If not, create one
   If IsObject( Session( "mothergoose_dbConn" ) ) Then
      Set dbConn = Session( "mothergoose_dbConn" )
   Else
      Set dbConn = Server.CreateObject( "ADODB.Connection" )
      Call dbConn.Open( "mothergoose", "", "" )
      Set Session( "mothergoose_dbConn" ) = dbConn
   End If

   ' Create the SQL query
   dbQuery = "SELECT * FROM users"

   ' Create the recordset
   Set loginRS = Server.CreateObject( "ADODB.Recordset" )
   Call loginRS.Open( dbQuery, dbConn )

```

Fig. 26.16 Code listing for **login.asp** (part 1 of 3).

```
   On Error Resume Next ' If an error occurs, ignore it

   ' Move to the first record in the recordset
   Call loginRS.MoveFirst()
%>

<!DOCTYPE HTML PUBLIC "-//W3C//DTD HTML 4.0 Transitional//EN">
<HTML>
<HEAD><TITLE>Login Page</TITLE></HEAD>

<BODY>
<!-- include header goes here-->
<!-- #include virtual = "/includes/mgtheader.inc" -->

<%
   ' If this is a return after a failed attempt, print an error
   If Session( "loginFailure" ) = True Then %>
<FONT SIZE = 4 COLOR = "red"> Login attempt failed,
please try again <P></FONT>
   <% End If %>

<% ' Begin the form %>
<FONT FACE = "arial" SIZE = 2>
Please select your name and enter
your password to login:<BR>
</FONT>
<FORM NAME = sublogform ACTION = "submitlogin.asp" METHOD = POST>

<% ' Format the form using a table %>
<TABLE BORDER = 0>
<TR>
<TD><FONT FACE = "arial" SIZE = 2>Name:</FONT></TD>
<TD><SELECT NAME = "LOGINID">
<OPTION VALUE = "000">Select your name
<%
   ' Pull user names from the query to populate the dropdown
   While Not loginRS.EOF

      ' If there is a session loginid, reuse it
      If Session( "loginid" ) = loginRS( "loginid" ) Then
         loginFound = "selected "
      End If

      ' If a login cookie was found, reuse it
      If Request.Cookies( "loginid" ) = loginRS( "loginid" ) Then
         loginfound = "selected "
      End If

      ' Create each dropdown entry %>
<OPTION <% =loginFound %>
VALUE = "<% =loginRS( "loginid" ) %>">
<% =loginRS( "loginid" ) %>
<% loginfound = " " %>
```

Fig. 26.16 Code listing for **login.asp** (part 2 of 3).

```
<%
      Call loginRS.MoveNext()
   Wend
%>
</SELECT>
</TD>
</TR>

<TR>
<TD><FONT FACE = "arial" SIZE = "2">Password:</FONT></TD>
<TD><INPUT TYPE = "password" NAME = "SUBMIT_LOGIN"></TD>
</TR>
<TR>
<TD> </TD>
<TD ALIGN = "LEFT"><INPUT TYPE = "submit" VALUE = "Log Me In"
ID = "login1" NAME = "login1"></TD>
</TR>
</TABLE>
</FORM>
</FONT>

<!-- #include virtual = "/includes/mgtfooter.inc" -->

</BODY>

</HTML>
```

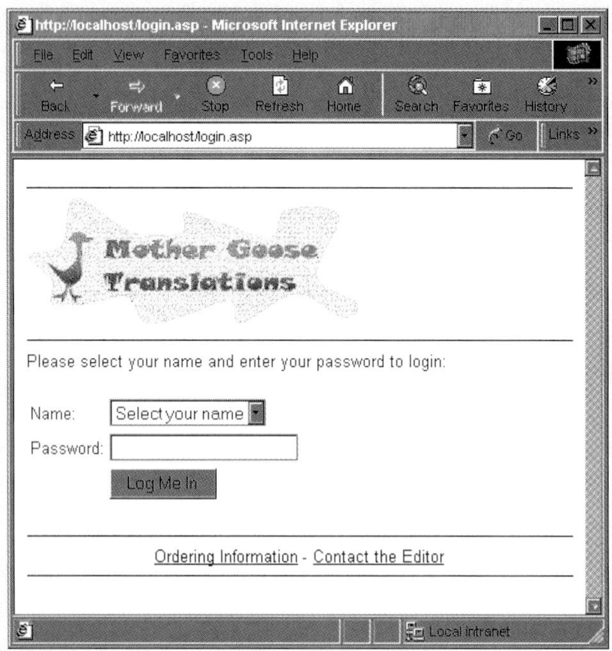

Fig. 26.16 Code listing for **login.asp** (part 3 of 3).

The condition (line 12)

```
IsObject( Session( "mothergoose_dbConn" ) )
```

tests if the session variable **mothergoose_dbConn** is storing an object. If it is, reference **dbConn** is assigned the object referenced by **mothergoose_dbConn**.

If line 12's condition is **False**, the statements

```
Set dbConn = Server.CreateObject( "ADODB.Connection" )
Call dbConn.Open( "mothergoose", "", "" )
Set Session( "mothergoose_dbConn" ) = dbConn
```

are executed. **Server** method **CreateObject** is called to create an **ADODB.Connection** object that is **Set** to reference **dbConn**. The **ADODB.Connection** object encapsulates the functionality necessary to connect to a data source. Method ***Open*** is called to open the specified DSN (e.g., **mothergoose**). Because the database does not have password protection, we need only pass an empty string, **""**, for both the user ID (i.e., the third argument) and the password (i.e., the last argument), respectively. Session variable **mothergoose_dbConn** is assigned the **ADODB.Connection** object referenced by **dbConn**. Session variable **mothergoose_dbConn** does not reference an object the first time this page is requested—so the **Else**'s body is executed. When a login attempt fails this page is reloaded and the session variable **mothergoose_dbConn** maintains its state—so the **If**'s body is executed. A second ASP named **submitlogin.asp** (Fig. 26.17) validates the login and either redirects the client back to **login.asp** for an invalid login or directs the client to **instantpage.asp** for a successful login. We will discuss **submitlogin.asp** in detail momentarily.

Lines 24 and 25

```
Set loginRS = Server.CreateObject( "ADODB.Recordset" )
Call loginRS.Open( dbQuery, dbConn )
```

Set reference **loginRS** to an **ADODB.Recordset** object and call method **Open** to open a connection to the data source. Method **Open** is passed the SQL query (line 21) and the **ADODB.Connection** object that **dbConn** references. When **Open** finishes executing, the **ADODB.Recordset** object referenced by **loginRS** contains all records that match the SQL query.

If any errors occur while the records are being retrieved, we choose to ignore them. The statement (line 27)

```
On Error Resume Next
```

specifies that if any error is raised by a statement on subsequent lines, control is transferred to the next statement immediately following the one that raised the error.

Line 30

```
Call loginRS.MoveFirst()
```

calls **ADODB.Recordset** method ***MoveFirst*** to move to the first record in the recordset.

Lines 43 through 46 test if session variable **loginFailure** is **True**. If so, the client is informed that the login attempt failed. Session variable **loginFailure** is given a **True** value by **submitlogin.asp** when an invalid login attempt occurs. When the client is redirected back to **login.asp** this **If**'s body is executed.

When the user **POST**s the **sublogform** to the server, ASP file **submitlogin.asp** (Fig. 26.17 that we will discuss momentarily) is loaded. This behavior is specified on line 53.

The **While** loop (lines 63 through 82) populates a **SELECT** control with login information by searching a recordset and by checking for cookies on the client machine. The first **If** condition (line 66) compares the value of session variable **loginid** against the current recordset's **loginid** field for equality. The second **If** condition (line 71) compares any cookie named **loginid** against the recordset **loginid** field for equality. ASP **submitlogin.asp** is responsible for writing this cookie. As long as we have not read past the recordset's end-of-file—represented by **RecordSet** constant ***EOF***—the **While** loop iterates. The next record in the recordset is accessed by calling **RecordSet** method **MoveNext**. When the user **POST**s the form, **submitlogin.asp** is requested (line 53). [*Note*: For this particular example, all users have the same password (**password**).]

Active Server Page **submitlogin.asp** (Fig. 26.17) takes the values passed to it by **login.asp** and checks them against the user's table in the database. If a match is found, **instantpage.asp** is presented. If the login fails, the user is redirected back to **login.asp**. In fact, the user never sees, or knows about **submitlogin.asp**.

```
<% @LANGUAGE = VBScript %>
<% Option Explicit %>

<% ' Fig. 26.17 : submitlogin.asp %>
<%
   ' Set up the variables for this page
   Dim dbConn, dbQuery, loginRS

   ' Check to see if there is an existing connection to
   ' the Database.  If not, create one
   If IsObject( Session( "mothergoose_dbConn" ) ) Then
      Set dbConn = Session( "mothergoose_dbConn" )
   Else
      Set dbConn = Server.CreateObject( "ADODB.Connection" )
      Call dbConn.Open( "mothergoose", "", "" )
      Set Session( "mothergoose_dbConn" ) = dbConn
   End If

   ' Create the SQL query
   dbQuery = "SELECT * FROM users"

   ' Create the recordset
   Set loginRS = Server.CreateObject( "ADODB.Recordset" )
   Call loginRS.Open( dbQuery, dbConn )

   On Error Resume Next   ' If an error occurs, ignore it

   ' Move to the first record in the recordset
   Call loginRS.MoveFirst()

```

Fig. 26.17 Code listing for **submitlogin.asp** (part 1 of 2).

```
136    ' If the loginid is not empty then
137    If Request( "loginid" ) <> "" Then
138       While Not loginRS.EOF
139          If Request( "loginid" ) = loginRS( "loginid" ) AND _
140            Request( "submit_login" ) = loginRS( "password" ) Then
141
142             ' Password and loginid are OK set a Session variable
143             Session( "loginfailure" ) = False
144
145             ' Set a cookie to recognize them the next time they
146             ' go to login.asp
147             Response.Cookies( "loginid" ) = Request( "loginid" )
148
149             ' Send them on to the next page
150             Call Response.Redirect( "instantpage.asp" )
151          End If
152
153          Call loginRS.MoveNext()      ' Move on to the next record
154       Wend
155    End If
156
157    ' If loginid is empty, or no match was found
158    Session( "loginFailure" ) = True   ' Set loginFailure to true
159
160    ' Return to the login page
161    Call Response.Redirect( "login.asp" )
162 %>
```

Fig. 26.17 Code listing for **submitlogin.asp** (part 2 of 2).

The **If** condition (line 116) calls VBScript method **IsObject** to determine if the session variable **mothergoose_dbconn** refers to an object—in this particular example an **ADODB.Connection** object. If **True**, reference **dbConn** is **Set** to the object on line 117. If **False**, a new **ADODB.Connection** object is created and **Set** to **dbConn**, method **Open** is called to open a connection to DSN **mothergoose** and session variable **mothergoose_dbconn** is assigned the object **dbConn** references.

Lines 128 and 129 **Set** an **ADODB.Recordset** object to reference **loginRS** and call method **Open** to populate the recordset with records that match query **dbQuery**. Method **MoveFirst** is called on line 134 to move to the first recordset.

The **While** loop (line 138) is executed when the submitted form's **loginid** value is not the empty string. The **If** condition (line 139)

```
Request( "loginid" ) = loginRS( "loginid" ) And _
Request( "submit_login" ) = loginRS( "password" )
```

takes the form's **loginid** value and compares it to the current record's **loginid** field, **And** compares the form's **submit_login** value to the current record's **password** field. If this condition is **True**, a successful login has occurred that results in line 143 setting session variable **loginfailure** to **False**. Line 147

```
Response.Cookies( "loginid" ) = Request( "loginid" )
```

writes the form's **loginid** value as a cookie on the client. The cookie is given the name **loginid**—we of course could have named this anything we wanted. Method **Redirect** sends the client to **instapage.asp** on line 150.

Unsuccessful login results in session variable **loginfailure** being set to **True** (line 158) and the client is redirected back to **login.asp** (line 161).

Figure 26.18 (**translation.asp**) presents a second example that uses ADO to access a database. The Web page maintains a list of nursery rhymes and the languages into which these nursery rhymes have been translated. This ASP retrieves the nursery rhyme name and image name(s) from the **mothergoose.mdb** database.

```
<% @LANGUAGE = VBScript %>
<% Option Explicit %>

<% ' Fig. 26.18 : translation.asp %>

<!DOCTYPE HTML PUBLIC "-//W3C//DTD HTML 4.0 Transitional//EN">
<HTML>
<HEAD>
<META HTTP-EQUIV = "CONTENT-TYPE"
      CONTENT = "TEXT/HTML;CHARSET = WINDOWS-1252">
<TITLE>Mother Goose Translations</TITLE>
</HEAD>

<BODY>
<% ' Use the mothergoose header %>
<!--#include virtual = "/includes/mgtheader.inc"-->

<%
   Dim conn, sql, rs, titleTest, image

   ' Check if there is a mothergoose database connection open
   If IsObject( Session( "mothergoose_conn" ) ) Then
      Set conn = Session( "mothergoose_conn" )
   Else     ' If not open one
      Set conn = Server.CreateObject( "ADODB.Connection" )
      Call conn.Open( "mothergoose", "", "" )
      Set Session( "mothergoose_conn" ) = conn
   End If

   ' Prepare the SQL statement that collects all
   ' the information for this page
   sql = "SELECT product.title, language.language " & _
         "FROM language " & _
         "INNER JOIN (product INNER JOIN translations ON " _
         & "product.productID = translations.ProductID) ON " _
         & "language.languageid = translations.languageID " _
         & "ORDER BY translations.ProductID, " & _
         " translations.languageID"
```

Fig. 26.18 Web browser showing the page **translation.asp** (part 1 of 3).

```
   Set rs = Server.CreateObject( "ADODB.Recordset" )
   Call rs.Open( sql, conn )

   titleTest = "nothing"      ' Initialize titleTest
   On Error Resume Next       ' Ignore errors
   Call rs.MoveFirst()        ' Goto first record

   ' Cycle through the records as long as there are more records
   Do While Not rs.EOF
      ' Check to see if we have printed this title before
      If rs.Fields( "title" ).Value <> titleTest Then
         ' If we have not seen the title before, print it out
%>
<P><FONT FACE = "arial" SIZE = "4">
<% =rs.Fields( "title" ).Value %></FONT>
<FONT FACE = "arial" SIZE = "1"><BR>
Available in: </FONT>
<%
      End If

      ' Check the value of the language field and
      ' match it with the appropriate flag
      Select Case rs.Fields( "language" ).Value
         Case "English"
            image = "/images/us.gif"
         Case "French"
            image = "/images/france.gif"
         Case "Italian"
            image = "/images/italy.gif"
         Case "German"
            image = "/images/germany.gif"
         Case "Spanish"
            image = "/images/spain.gif"
      End Select

      ' Now print the image using the value of the
      ' language field to provide an alt tag value
%>
<IMG SRC = "<% =image %>"
ALT = "<% =rs.Fields( "language" ).Value %>"
HEIGHT = "25">
<%
      ' set titleTest to the current title
      titleTest = rs.Fields( "title" ).Value

      Call rs.MoveNext()    'move to the next record
   Loop

   ' Add in the footer and end the page
%>
<!--#include virtual = "/includes/mgtfooter.inc"--></P>
</BODY>
</HTML>
```

Fig. 26.18 Web browser showing the page **translation.asp** (part 2 of 3).

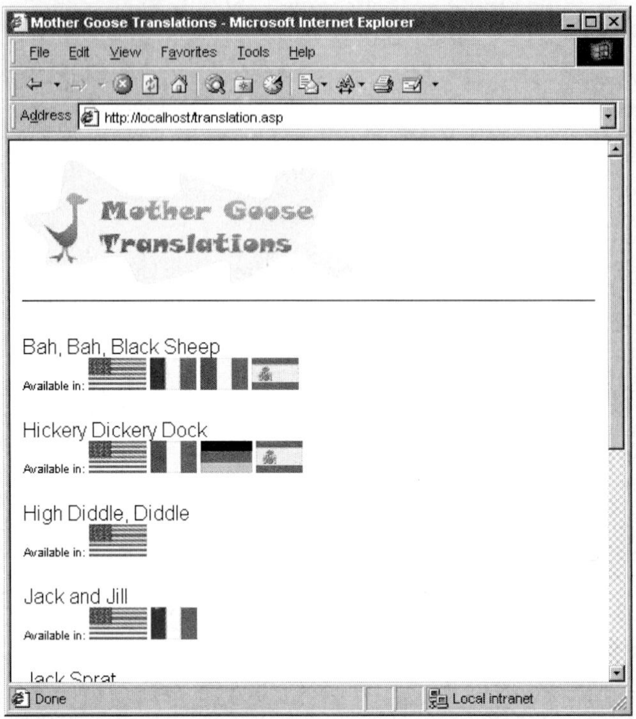

Fig. 26.18 Web browser showing the page **translation.asp** (part 3 of 3).

Lines 22 through 28 ensure that a connection to the database **mothergoose.mdb** using the same techniques presented in the last example. Line 32 creates the SQL query used to query the database. This SQL query joins two tables from the database and orders the information by product ID and by language ID. Line 39 creates an **ADODB.Recordset** object and assigns it to reference **rs**. Line 40 calls method **Open** to get the recordset corresponding to the SQL query.

The **Do/While** loop (line 47) contains the code that reads the recordset's **title** field and **language** field and sends them to the client. The **If** condition (line 49)

```
rs.Fields( "title" ).Value <> titleTest
```

retrieves the recordset's **title** ***Value*** using the ***Fields*** collection and compares it against **titleTest** for inequality. Each recordset field can be accessed through the **Fields** collection—which contains each field as an individual ***Field*** object. Each **Field**'s value is accessed using the **Value** property. If you are unclear on the relationship between these ADO objects, see Chapter 25 "Database: SQL, ADO, RDS," Section 25.6.

Before entering the loop, **titleTest**'s value was initialized on line 42 to **"nothing"**. Variable **titleTest** is used to determine if we are still processing the same **title**. Because a **title** may contain one or more translations, we do not want to write the **title** more than once to the client. When the **If** condition on line 49 is **True**, a new **title** has been encountered and the VBScript on line 53

```
<% =rs.Fields( "title" ).Value %>
```

is executed to write the **title** field's **Value** to the client.

Because we know all the possible values for **language**s (i.e., the database uses the same five languages used in Fig. 26.3's **rotate.asp**), we use a **Select Case** structure (line 61) to determine the **Value** of the current recordset's **language Field**. In the **Select Case**'s body, variable **image** is assigned the relative path for the appropriate image. Line 77 writes **image**'s value to the **IMG SRC** attribute and line 78 writes the **language** field's **Value** to the **ALT** attribute. Line 82 assigns **titleTest** the current **Field**'s **title** and line 84 moves to the next recordset.

26.10 Case Study: A Product Catalog

In this section, we present a substantial application that uses three Active Server Pages to display a catalog of Deitel textbooks. To accomplish this, each page queries **catalog.mdb** (which must be registered as a DSN on the server).

Each of the Active Server Pages uses server-side includes to provided a consistent look and feel. The major difference between these three Active Server Pages is the title and the information presented in the center of the page.

Active Server Page **catalog.asp** is shown in Fig. 26.19. This page creates a hyperlinked list of programming languages covered in Deitel books. Clicking a hyperlink sends the user to **titles.asp** that presents a hyperlink list of the textbooks related to the selected programming language.

```
<% @LANGUAGE = VBScript %>
<% Option Explicit %>

<% ' Fig. 26.19 : catalog.asp %>

<!DOCTYPE HTML PUBLIC "-//W3C//DTD HTML 4.0 Transitional//EN">
<HTML>
<HEAD>
<TITLE>Textbook Information Center: Technology</TITLE>
</HEAD>

<!-- #include virtual = "/includes/header.inc" -->

<CENTER>
<H2>
<FONT COLOR = "brown">
Welcome to the Textbook Information Center</FONT>
</H2>
</CENTER>

<TABLE BORDER = 0 WIDTH = 100% CELLPADDING = 0 CELLSPACING = 0>
<TR>
<TD WIDTH = 25%> </TD>
```

Fig. 26.19 Code listing for **catalog.asp** (part 1 of 3).

```
<TD BGCOLOR = "#008080" WIDTH = 10%> </TD>
<TD BGCOLOR = "#008080" WIDTH = 40%>
<FONT COLOR = "yellow" SIZE = 2>To view available titles
for a technology<BR>
select a link from this list:</FONT><P>

<%
   Dim dbConn, dbQuery, techRS

   ' Check for an active connection, if not open one
   If IsObject( Session( "catalog_dbConn" ) ) Then
      Set dbConn = Session( "catalog_dbConn" )
   Else
      Set dbConn = Server.CreateObject( "ADODB.Connection" )
      Call dbConn.Open( "catalog", "", "" )
      Set Session( "catalog_dbConn" ) = dbConn
   End If

   ' Create the SQL query and create the recordset
   dbQuery = "SELECT * FROM tech"
   Set techRS = Server.CreateObject( "ADODB.Recordset" )
   Call techRS.Open( dbQuery, dbConn )

   On Error Resume Next       ' If an error occurs, ignore it

   ' Move to the first record of the recordset
   Call techRS.MoveFirst()

   ' Begin a Do/While loop that will continue to
   ' iterate as long as there are records
   Do While Not techRS.EOF
      ' Create a HREF that passes the techid number to the
      ' next page and use the text value of technology to
      ' label the link
%>

<LI><A HREF = "titles.asp?techid = <% =techRS( "techID" ) %>">
<FONT COLOR = "yellow" SIZE = 2>
<% =techRS( "technology" ) %>
</FONT></A>
<%
      ' Move to the next record in the recordset
      Call techRS.MoveNext()
   Loop
%>
</FONT><P>
</TD>
<TD WIDTH = 25%> </TD>
</TR>
</TABLE>
<!-- #include virtual = "/includes/footer.inc" -->
</HTML>
```

Fig. 26.19 Code listing for **catalog.asp** (part 2 of 3).

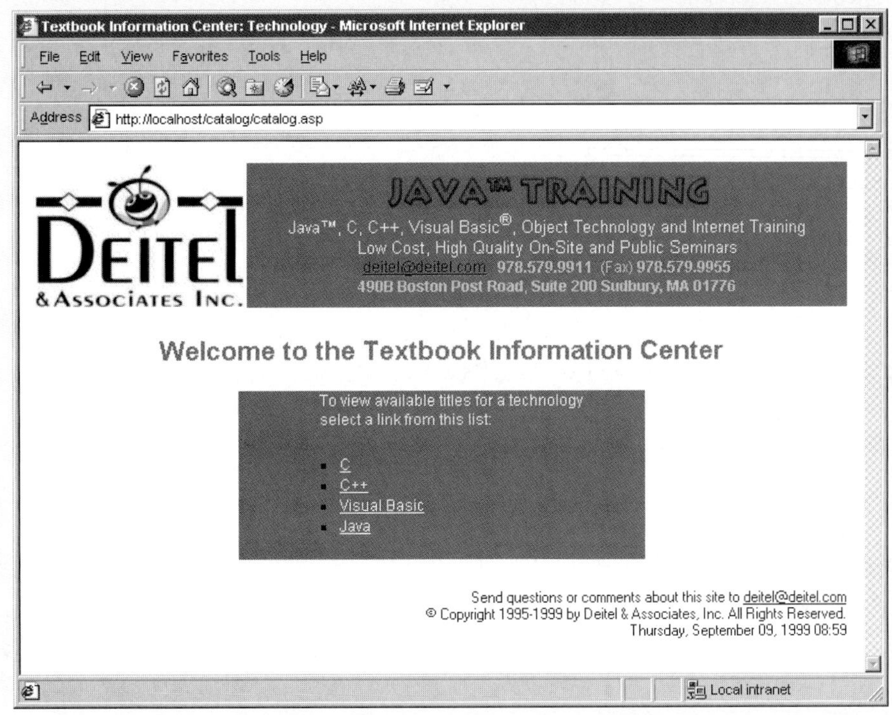

Fig. 26.19 Code listing for **catalog.asp** (part 3 of 3).

The **If** condition (line 34) calls method **IsObject** to determine if the session variable **catalog_dbConn** refers to an object—in this particular example an **ADODB.Connection** object. If **True**, reference **dbConn** is **Set** to the object on line 35. If **False**, a new **ADODB.Connection** object is created and **Set** to **dbConn**, method **Open** is called to open a connection to DSN **catalog** and session variable **catalog_dbConn** is assigned the object **dbConn** references.

Lines 44 and 45 **Set** an **ADODB.Recordset** object to reference **techRS** and call method **Open** to populate the recordset with records that match query **dbQuery**. Method **MoveFirst** is called on line 50 to move to the first recordset.

For each record's **techID** field, a list-item hyperlink is created on line 60. The hyperlink connects to **titles.asp** (Fig. 26.22—which we will discuss momentarily). To pass data via a URL, we must use the question mark (**?**), followed by a variable name for the data, then an equal sign (**=**) followed by the content. Here **techid** is the variable name. Line 60 uses the (**=**) abbreviation for **Response** method **Write** to send the contents of **techid** to the URL. Line 62 sends the value of the **technology** field to the browser to label the link.

The Active Server Page uses two server-side includes—**header.inc** (Fig. 26.20) and **footer.inc** (Fig. 26.21). These SSI files provide the Deitel image, training banner and copyright information.

```
<BODY BGCOLOR = "#ffffff">
<TABLE BORDER = "0" WIDTH = "600">
<TR>
<TD><A HREF = "http://www.deitel.com"><IMG
   SRC = "/images/logotiny.gif" BORDER = 0></A></TD>
<TD BGCOLOR = "#008080">
<P ALIGN = "center">
<SPAN STYLE = "font-family: Arial, Helvetica, sans-serif">
<IMG SRC = "/images/banneranim.gif"
ALT = "banneranim.gif (185545 bytes)" WIDTH = "481"
   HEIGHT = "28"><BR>
<FONT COLOR = "#FFFF00">Java&#153;, C, C++, Visual
Basic<SUP>&#174;</SUP>,
Object Technology and Internet Training<BR>
Low Cost, High Quality On-Site and Public Seminars<BR>
<SMALL><A HREF = "mailto:deitel@deitel.com">deitel@deitel.com
</A>
</FONT> 
<FONT COLOR = "#80FFFF"><STRONG>978.579.9911</STRONG> 
(Fax) <STRONG>978.579.9955</STRONG><BR>
<STRONG>490B Boston Post Road</STRONG>,
<STRONG>Suite 200 Sudbury, MA 01776</STRONG></FONT>
</SMALL></SPAN></P>
</TD>
</TR>
<TR><TD COLSPAN = 2> </TD></TR>
<TR>
<TD COLSPAN = 2>
<FONT FACE = "arial" SIZE = 2>
```

Fig. 26.20 Listing for **header.inc**.

```
</FONT>
</TD></TR>
<TR><TD COLSPAN = 2> </TD></TR>
<TR><TD COLSPAN = 2 ALIGN = right>

<SPAN STYLE = "font-family: sans-serif, Helvetica, Arial;
font-size: 8pt">
Send questions or comments about this site to
<A HREF = "mailto:deitel@deitel.com">deitel@deitel.com</A><BR>
&copy; Copyright 1995-1999 by Deitel &amp; Associates, Inc.
All Rights Reserved.<BR>
Thursday, September 09, 1999 08:59<BR>
</SPAN>
</TD></TR>
</TABLE>
</BODY>
</HTML>
```

Fig. 26.21 Listing for **footer.inc**.

When the user clicks a programming language link on **catalog.asp**, **titles.asp** is loaded and passed the value of **techid**. Page **titles.asp** displays one or more book links related to the selected programming language. Figure 26.22 lists the **titles.asp**'s code.

The **If** condition (line 150) calls method **IsObject** to determine if the session variable **catalog_dbConn** refers to an object—in this particular example an **ADODB.Connection** object. If **True**, reference **dbConn** is **Set** to the object on line 151. If **False**, a new **ADODB.Connection** object is created and **Set** to **dbConn**, method **Open** is called to open a connection to DSN **catalog** and session variable **catalog_dbConn** is assigned the object **dbConn** references.

Lines 161 and 162 **Set** an **ADODB.Recordset** object to reference **titleRS** and call method **Open** to populate the recordset with records that match query **dbQuery**. Notice that the SQL query (line 160) uses the **techID** passed to the page. Method **MoveFirst** is called on line 167 to move to the first recordset.

```
122 <% @LANGUAGE = VBScript %>
123 <% Option Explicit %>
124
125 <% ' Fig. 26.22 : titles.asp %>
126
127 <!DOCTYPE HTML PUBLIC "-//W3C//DTD HTML 4.0 Transitional//EN">
128 <HTML>
129 <HEAD>
130 <TITLE>Textbook Information Center: Titles</TITLE>
131 </HEAD>
132 <!-- #include virtual = "/includes/header.inc" -->
133
134 <CENTER>
135 <H2><FONT COLOR = "brown">Welcome to the Textbook Information
136 Center</FONT></H2>
137 </CENTER>
138 <TABLE BORDER = 0 WIDTH = 100% CELLPADDING = 0 CELLSPACING = 0>
139 <TR>
140 <TD WIDTH = 15%> </TD>
141 <TD BGCOLOR = "#008080" WIDTH = 5%> </TD>
142 <TD BGCOLOR = "#008080" WIDTH = 60%>
143 <FONT COLOR ="yellow" SIZE = 2>Select a title from the list below:
144 </FONT><P>
145 <UL>
146 <%
147    Dim dbConn, dbQuery, titleRS
148
149    ' Check for an active connection, if not open one
150    If IsObject( Session( "catalog_dbConn" ) ) Then
151       Set dbConn = Session( "catalog_dbConn" )
152    Else
153       Set dbConn = Server.CreateObject( "ADODB.Connection" )
154       Call dbConn.Open( "catalog", "", "" )
155       Set Session( "catalog_dbConn" ) = dbConn
156    End If
```

Fig. 26.22 Code listing for **titles.asp** (part 1 of 3).

```

   ' Create the SQL query and create the recordset
   dbQuery = "SELECT * FROM products WHERE techid="
   dbQuery = dbQuery & Request( "techid" )
   Set titleRS = Server.CreateObject( "ADODB.Recordset" )
   Call titleRS.Open( dbQuery, dbConn )

   On Error Resume Next    ' If an error occurs, ignore it

   ' Move to the first record of the recordset
   Call titleRS.MoveFirst()

   ' Begin a do while loop that will continue to
   ' iterate as long as there are records
   Do While Not titleRS.EOF

      ' Create a HREF that passes the productid number to the
      ' next page and use the title and the edition to label
      ' the link
%>

<LI><A HREF = "description.asp?productid=<%
=titleRS( "productID" ) %>">
<FONT COLOR = "yellow" SIZE = 2>
<% =titleRS( "title" ) %>
</FONT></A>
<FONT COLOR = "yellow" SIZE = 2>   Edition
<% =titleRS( "edition" ) %>
</FONT>

<%
      Call titleRS.MoveNext()    ' Move to the next record
   Loop
%>

</UL>
</FONT><P>
</TD>

<TD BGCOLOR = "#008080" WIDTH = 5%> </TD>

<TD WIDTH = 15%></TD>
</TR>
</TABLE>

<% ' Provide a link back to the previous page %>
<P ALIGN = CENTER>
Back to the <STRONG>
<A HREF = "catalog.asp">Technology List</A><STRONG></P>

<!-- #include virtual = "/includes/footer.inc" -->
</HTML>
```

Fig. 26.22 Code listing for **titles.asp** (part 2 of 3).

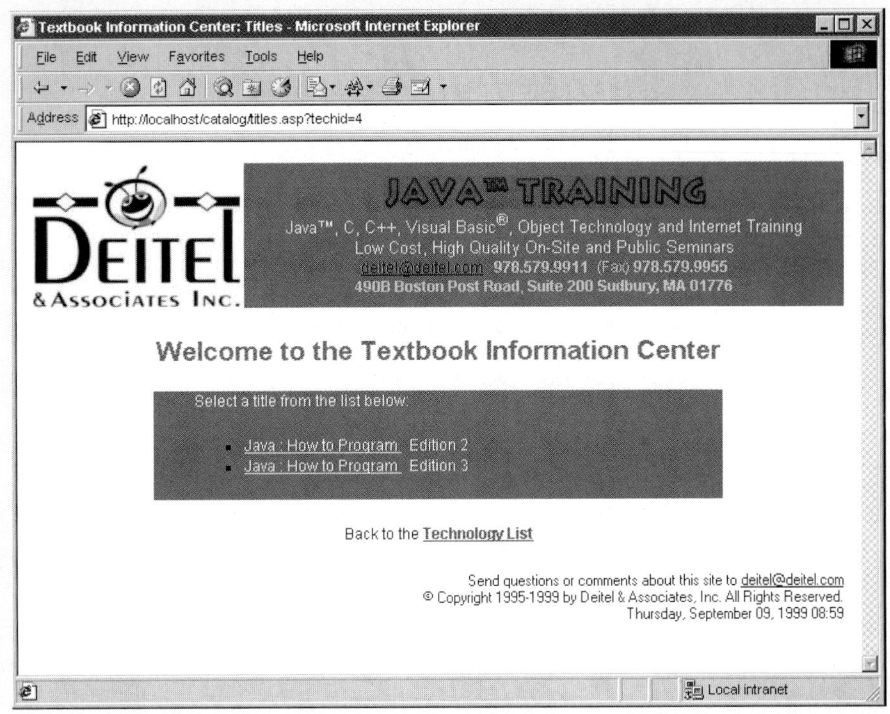

Fig. 26.22 Code listing for **titles.asp** (part 3 of 3).

As before in **catalog.asp**, **titles.asp** iterates through the recordset row by row. Lines 178 through 182 build the hyperlink to **description.asp** (Fig. 26.23—which we will discuss momentarily). This time, the **productid** from the recordset is appended to the URL string. The **productid** is used by **description.asp** to return a recordset containing some information about the textbook and a link to the book cover image.

When the user clicks one of the book links on **titles.asp**, **description.asp** is loaded and passed the value of **productid**. Page **description.asp** displays the specified book's front cover, the book's information and a link to **www.amazon.com**. Figure 26.23 lists **description.asp**'s code.

```
<% @LANGUAGE = VBScript %>
<% Option Explicit %>

<% ' Fig. 26.23 : description.asp %>

<!DOCTYPE HTML PUBLIC "-//W3C//DTD HTML 4.0 Transitional//EN">
<HTML>
<HEAD>
```

Fig. 26.23 **description.asp** displays the text information (part 1 of 3).

```
<TITLE>Textbook Information Center: Description
</TITLE>
</HEAD>
<!-- #include virtual = "/includes/header.inc" -->

<%
   Dim dbConn, dbQuery, productRS, isbnString

   ' Check for an active connection, if not open one
   If IsObject( Session( "catalog_dbConn" ) ) Then
      Set dbConn = Session( "catalog_dbConn" )
   Else
      Set dbConn = Server.CreateObject( "ADODB.Connection" )
      Call dbConn.Open( "catalog", "", "" )
      Set Session( "catalog_dbConn" ) = dbConn
   End If

   ' Create the SQL query and create the recordset
   dbQuery = "SELECT * FROM products WHERE productid="
   dbQuery = dbQuery & Request( "productid" )
   Set productRS = Server.CreateObject( "ADODB.Recordset" )
   Call productRS.Open( dbQuery, dbConn )
%>

<CENTER>
<H2>
<FONT COLOR = "brown">
<% =productRS( "title" ) %>
</FONT>
</H2>
</CENTER>

<TABLE BORDER = 0 WIDTH = 100% CELLPADDING = 0 CELLSPACING = 0>
<TR>
<TD WIDTH = 25%> </TD>
<TD BGCOLOR = "#008080" WIDTH = 10%>
<% ' Display the image from the database %>
<IMG SRC = "/images/<% =productRS( "coverart" ) %>">
</TD>

<TD BGCOLOR = "#008080" WIDTH = 40%>
<FONT COLOR = "yellow" SIZE = 2>

<% ' Display the values from the database %>
<DD>Published in <% =productRS( "pubdate" ) %><BR>
<DD>ISBN:<% =productRS( "ISBN" ) %><BR>
<DD>EDITION <% =productRS( "edition" ) %><BR>
</FONT>

<P ALIGN = CENTER>
<FONT SIZE = 4 COLOR = "red">
<STRONG>Buy this book now!</STRONG></FONT><BR>

```

Fig. 26.23 **description.asp** displays the text information (part 2 of 3).

```
<%
   ' Remove the dashes from the ISBN string
   isbnString = Replace( productRS( "ISBN" ), "-", "" )

   ' Use the isbn from the database to create a link directly
   ' to the book at amazon.com
%>
<A HREF = "http://www.amazon.com/exec/obidos/ASIN/<%
   =isbnString %>/deitelassociatin">
<IMG SRC = "/images/amazonw.gif" ALT = "amazonw.gif (1557 bytes)"
    WIDTH = "90" HEIGHT = "29"></A>
</P>
</FONT><P>
</TD>

<TD WIDTH = 25%> </TD>

</TR>
</TABLE>

<P ALIGN = CENTER>Back to the <STRONG>
<A HREF = "titles.asp?techid=<% =productRS( "techID" ) %>">Titles
</A></STRONG>

<!-- #include virtual = "/includes/footer.inc" -->
</HTML>
```

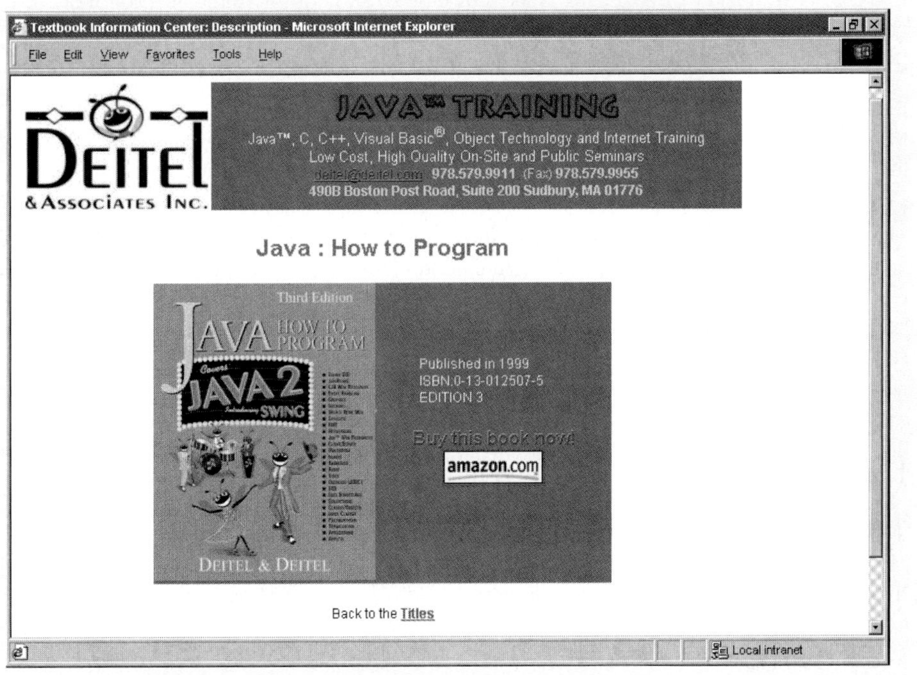

Fig. 26.23 **`description.asp`** displays the text information (part 3 of 3).

The **If** condition (line 226) calls method **IsObject** to determine if the session variable **catalog_dbConn** refers to an object—in this particular example an **ADODB.Connection** object. If **True**, reference **dbConn** is **Set** to the object on line 227. If **False**, a new **ADODB.Connection** object is created and **Set** to **dbConn**, method **Open** is called to open a connection to DSN **catalog** and session variable **catalog_dbConn** is assigned the object **dbConn** references.

Lines 235 and 236 build the query that selects the rows from the **products** table that have the same **techid** that the user selected on the previous page (i.e., **titles.asp**). The content of **productid** limits the records returned to the textbook selected in **titles.asp**. The textbook title returned by the recordset is used in line 244 as a header for the page.

The left cell of the table contains an image reference that is defined on line 254. The file name of the cover image is stored in the **coverart** column of the database, and the value of that cell is used as the end of the image URL.

Lines 261 through 263 insert the publication date (i.e., **pubdate**), the ISBN and the edition number of the book into the right table cell.

We have included a direct link to **Amazon.com** so that the user can purchase a copy of the selected book. Because we know that **Amazon.com** uses a URL of the form

www.amazon.com/exec/obidos/ASIN/*ISBN#***/***referrer*

where *ISBN#* is the book's ISBN and *referrer* is **Amazon.com**'s code for the referring site, we can generate a URL for each book in the **product** table. Because the ISBN in the URL must be numeric, we replace the dashes with an empty string using function **Replace** on line 272. Variable **isbnString** is used on line 278 to complete the amazon link.

26.11 Internet and World Wide Web Resources

http://www.microsoft.com/
Microsoft's home page. Provides a link to searching Microsoft's entire Web-based information structure. Check this site first for answers. Some information is provided on a subscriber-only basis.

http://www.tcp-ip.com/
The *ASP Toolbox* home page is an excellent source for ASP information and resources. The site contains numerous links to free components and other resources helpful in Web development using Active Server Pages. The site tutorials includes an overview of Active Server technology as well as helpful hints and demos with source code provided. Other features of this page include ASP discussion forums and resources.

http://www.15seconds.com/listserv.htm
The *Fifteen Seconds* page focuses on Active Server Pages using Microsoft products, providing up-to-date information on Microsoft Internet Information Server (IIS) and articles on both IIS and ASP. Fifteen Seconds also provides mailing lists, FAQ and resource archives.

http://www.asphole.com/asphole/default.asp
ASP Hole is a resource page containing links to ASP components, tutorials, news groups and FAQs.

http://www.4guysfromrolla.com/webtech/index_asp.shtml
Contains FAQs, ASP-related articles, coding tips, message boards, etc.

http://www.aspin.com/index/
Contains ASP resources including applications, books, forums, references, examples and tutorials, links, etc.

`http://www.kamath.com/default.asp`
Contains downloads, FAQs, tutorials, book excerpts, columns, etc.

`http://www.aspwatch.com/`
Contains ASP-related articles and code examples.

`http://www.developer.com/`
Great source of information for developers. The ASP section contains working code, troubleshooting techniques and advice.

`http://www.xbuilder.net/`
Home of a tool that can convert an ASP-generated Web structure into HTML files for publishing on a non-Microsoft server, or onto a CD-ROM.

`http://www.paessler.com/tools/ASPBeautify/`
Home of a tool that formats ASP pages for readability.

SUMMARY

- Active Server Pages (ASP) are processed in response to a client (e.g., browser) request. An ASP file—which has file extension **`.asp`**—contains HTML and scripting code. Although other languages such as JavaScript can be used for ASP scripting, VBScript is the de facto language for ASP scripting.
- ASP is a Microsoft-developed technology for generating dynamic Web content—which includes HTML, Dynamic HTML, ActiveX controls, client-side scripts and Java applets (i.e., client-side Java programs that are embedded in a Web page).
- The two most common HTTP request types (also known as request methods) are **`GET`** and **`POST`**. A **`GET`** request gets (or retrieves) information from the server. A **`POST`** request posts (or sends) data to the server. An HTTP **`POST`** request is often used to post data from an HTML form to a server-side form handler that processes the data.
- Browsers often cache (save on disk) Web pages so they can quickly reload the pages. There are no changes between the last version stored in the cache and the current version on the Web. Browsers typically do not cache the server's response to a **`POST`** request because the next **`POST`** may not return the same result.
- When a client requests an ASP file, the ASP file is parsed (top to bottom) by an ActiveX component (i.e., a server-side ActiveX control that usually does not have a graphical user interface) named **`asp.dll`**. Scripting code is executed as it is encountered.
- The **`@LANGUAGE`** statement is used by the programmer to specify which scripting engine is needed to interpret the scripting code. If **`@LANGUAGE`** is not used, VBScript is assumed to be the default. As the script is interpreted, HTML (plus any client-side scripts) is sent to the client.
- Client-side scripting is often used for validation, interactivity, enhancing a Web page with ActiveX controls, Dynamic HTML and Java applets and for accessing the browser.
- Client-side scripting is browser dependent—the scripting language must be supported by the browser or scripting host. Because Microsoft Internet Explorer and Netscape Communicator both support JavaScript, JavaScript has become the de facto scripting language on the client.
- Because server-side scripts reside on the server, programmers have greater flexibility—especially with database access. Scripts executed on the server usually generate custom responses for clients.
- Server-side scripts have access to ActiveX server components—which extend scripting language functionality. Server-side ActiveX components typically do not have a graphical user interface. Many ActiveX components are included with Internet Information Server (IIS) and Personal Web Server (PWS).

- Scripting delimiters **<%** and **%>** indicate that the scripting code is to be executed on the server—not the client. Scripting code enclosed in a scripting delimiter is never sent to the client.
- Function **Time** to returns the server's current time in the format, *hh:mm:ss.*
- The **Response** object provides functionality for sending information to the client.
- The AdRotator ActiveX component rotates advertisements on a Web page.
- Server-side ActiveX components are instantiated by passing the name of the component as a string to **Server** object method **CreateObject**. The **Server** object represents the Web server.
- **Response** object method **Write** writes text to the client.
- File System Objects (FSOs) provide the programmer with the ability to manipulate files, directories and drives. FSOs also allow the programmer to read and write text to sequential files. FSOs are an essential element for Active Server Pages with persistent data.
- FSOs are objects in the Microsoft Scripting Runtime Library. Five FSO types exist: **FileSystemObject**, **File**, **Folder**, **Drive** and **TextStream**.
- Type **FileSystemObject** allows the programmer to interact with **File**s, **Folder**s and **Drive**s. The programmer can use **FileSystemObject**s to create directories, move files, determine whether or not a **Drive** exists, etc. **File**s allow the programmer to gather information about files, manipulate files and open files. **Folder** objects allow the programmer to gather information about directories and to manipulate directories. **Drive** objects allow the programmer to gather information about drives.
- Many Web sites today provide custom Web pages and/or functionality on a client-by-client basis. The HTTP protocol does not support persistent information that could help a Web server determine that a request is from a particular client. As far as a Web server is concerned, every request could be from the same client or every request could be from a different client.
- Session tracking is handled by the server. The first time a client connects to the server, it is assigned a unique session ID by the server. When the client makes additional requests, the client's session ID is compared against the session IDs stored in the server's memory. Active Server Pages use the **Session** object to manage sessions. The **Session** object's **Timeout** property specifies the number of minutes a session exists for before it expires. The default value for property **Timeout** is 20 minutes. An individual session can also be terminated by calling **Session** method **Abandon**.
- Cookies can store information on the client's computer for retrieval later in the same browsing session or in future browsing sessions. Cookies are files that are sent by an Active Server Page as part of a response to a client. Every HTTP-based interaction between a client and a server includes a header that contains information about the request or information about the response. When an Active Server Page receives a request, the header includes information such as the request type and cookies stored on the client machine by the server. When the server formulates its response, the header information includes any cookies the server wants to store on the client computer.
- Server-side include (SSI) statements are always executed before any scripting code is executed. The word **virtual** in the SSI refers to the include file's path as it appears below the server root directory. This is often referred to as a virtual path. SSIs can also use **file** instead of **virtual** to indicate a physical path on the server.
- VBScript constant **vbCrLf** is used to insert a carriage-return line-feed combination.
- Method **Redirect** redirects the client to another Web page.
- Web applications are three-tier distributed applications, consisting of a user interface (UI), business logic and database access. The UI in such an application is often created using HTML, Dynamic HTML or XML. The UI can contain ActiveX controls and client-side scripts. Using the

browser's networking, the UI can communicate with the middle-tier business logic. The middle tier can then access the database to manipulate the data. All three tiers may reside on separate computers that are connected to a network or all three tiers may reside on a single machine.

- In multitier architectures, Web servers are increasingly used to build the middle tier. They provide the business logic that manipulates data from databases and that communicates with client Web browsers. Active Server Pages, through ADO, can interact with popular database systems. Developers use SQL-based queries and ADO handles the specifics of interacting with each database system through OLE DB.
- Method **Open** opens a connection to the data source.
- Method **Execute** executes a query against the data source.
- **On Error Resume Next** specifies that if any error is raised by a statement on subsequent lines, control is transferred to the statement immediately following the statement that raised the error.
- **ADODB.Recordset** method **MoveFirst** moves to the first record in a recordset.
- **ADODB.RecordSet** constant **EOF** represents a recordset's end-of-file.
- Each recordset field can be accessed through the **Fields** collection—which contains each field as an individual **Field** object. Each **Field**'s value is accessed using the **Value** property.

TERMINOLOGY

<% opening scripting delimiter
%> closing scripting delimiter
Abandon method of **Session**
ActiveConnection property
ADODB.Command object
ADODB.Connection object
ADODB.RecordSet object
AdRotator ActiveX Control
appending to a file
ASP (Active Server Pages)
ASP application
asp.dll
.ASP file
business logic
cache Web pages
Chr method
client-side scripting
Close method
CommandText property
CommandType property
configuration file
cookie
cookie expiration
CreateObject method
CreateTextFile method
database access
Drive
EOF constant
Execute method
expiration of a cookie
Fields collection
File
FileExists method
file system object
FileSystemObject
Folder
GetAdvertisement method
GET HTTP request
guest book application
header
.inc file
#include
@LANGUAGE directive
mailto link
maximum age of a cookie
.mdb file
MoveFirst method
MoveNext method
On Error Resume Next statement
Open method
OpenTextFile method
Option Explicit statement
physical path
POST HTTP request
ReadAll method
Redirect method of **Response**
Request object
Response object
script engine
script host

Server object
server-side ActiveX component
server-side include (SSI)
server-side scripting
session
session ID
Session object
session tracking
Set keyword
shopping cart application
short name format
TextStream
three-tier distributed application
Timeout property of **Session**
user interface
virtual path
vbCrLf constant
VBScript
Write method
WriteLine method

COMMON PROGRAMMING ERRORS

26.1 Missing the opening delimiter, **<%**, or closing delimiter, **%>**, for a server-side scripting statement is an error.

26.2 When using the **@LANGUAGE** tag, not placing it as the first statement in an ASP file is an error.

GOOD PROGRAMMING PRACTICE

26.1 When using VBScript code in an Active Server Page, use the **@Language** statement for clarity.

PERFORMANCE TIPS

26.1 Perform as much processing on the client as possible to conserve server resources.

26.2 Server-side ActiveX components usually execute faster than their scripting language equivalents.

PORTABILITY TIPS

26.1 Because browsers are capable of rendering HTML, an ASP page that generates pure HTML can be rendered on any client browser—regardless of the fact that the page requested ends in **.asp**.

26.2 Server-side scripts run exclusively on the server and therefore cross-platform issues are not a concern.

26.3 Because the AdRotator ActiveX component is executed on the server, clients do not directly interact with it and therefore do not have to support ActiveX technologies.

SOFTWARE ENGINEERING OBSERVATIONS

26.1 Some Independent Software Vendors (ISVs) provide scripting engines for use with ASP that support languages other than VBScript and JavaScript.

26.2 An Active Server Page file is parsed each time a request is made for it. This allows the Web developer to conveniently modify ASP files and have the updated ASP file available for the next request.

26.3 In order to take advantage of Active Server Page technology, a Web server must support ASP by providing a component such as **asp.dll**.

26.4 Server-side scripts are not visible to the client—only HTML (plus any client-side scripts) are sent to the client.

26.5 If the scripting language you are using in an Active Server Page does not support a certain feature, an ActiveX server component can be created using Visual C++, Visual Basic, Delphi, etc., to provide that feature.

26.6 The AdRotator ActiveX component allows the page author to minimize the amount of space on a Web page committed to advertisements, while at the same time maximizing the number of advertisements to display.

26.7 Some clients do not allow cookies to be written on them. When a client declines a cookie the client is normally informed that such a refusal may prevent browsing the site.

26.8 Virtual paths hide the server's internal file structure.

26.9 Server-side includes may include any type of information. Text files and HTML files are two of the most common server-side include files.

26.10 Server-side includes are performed before any scripting code is interpreted. Therefore, an Active Server Page cannot dynamically decide which server-side includes are included and which are not. Through scripting, an ASP can determine which SSI block is sent to the client.

26.11 By convention, server-side include (SSI) files end with the **.inc** extension.

26.12 Server-side includes are an excellent technique for reusing HTML, Dynamic HTML, scripts and other programming elements.

TESTING AND DEBUGGING TIPS

26.1 Always include **Option Explicit** even if you are not declaring any VBScript variables. As a script evolves over time, you may need to declare variables and the presence of **Option Explicit** can help eliminate subtle errors.

26.2 Server-side includes that contain scripting code should enclose the scripting code in **<SCRIPT>** tags or in **<% %>** delimiters to prevent one block of scripting code from running into another block of scripting code.

SELF-REVIEW EXERCISES

26.1 State whether each of the following is *true* or *false*. If *false*, explain why.

a) VBScript is the only language that can be used in an Active Server Page.
b) Active Server Page file names typically end in **.asp**.
c) Only Microsoft Internet Explorer can render an Active Server Page.
d) The **<% Option Explicit %>** statement is optional.
e) ActiveX components execute on the server—not the client.
f) Variables can be passed from one Active Server Page to another without using a form.
g) VBScript statements cannot be present in a server-side include file.
h) Server-side ActiveX components typically do not have graphical user interfaces.
i) AdRotator is a client-side Activex control.
j) Server-side include files end in **.ssi** by convention.

26.2 Fill in the blanks for each of the following:

a) Processing directive __________ informs **asp.dll** that scripting language is used.
b) Passing an integer value of __________ to function **Chr** returns the double quote (") character.
c) Session variables retain their value during the duration of the __________.
d) Cookies are files placed on the __________ machine.
e) Constant __________ represents a carriage-return line-feed combination.
f) ASP is an acronym for __________.

g) Method __________ moves to the first record in a recordset.
h) **`Server`** method __________ is called to create an object.
i) A recordset's **`Fields`** collection contains a series of __________ objects.
j) A __________ contains a database's name, location and driver.

ANSWERS TO SELF-REVIEW EXERCISES

26.1 a) False. Any scripting language recognized by the server can be used. b) True. c) False. Most browsers can render HTML returned by an Active Server Page. d) True. e) True. f) True. Variables can be embedded in a URL (e.g., **`http://localhost/page.asp?var=true`**). g) False. A server-side include can contain scripting code, HTML, text, etc. h) True. i) False. AdRotator is a server-side ActiveX component. j) False. Server-side include files end in **`.inc`** by convention.

26.2 a) **`@LANGUAGE`**. b) **`Chr(34)`**. c) session. d) client. e) **`vbCrLf`**. f) data source name. g) **`MoveFirst`**. h) **`CreateObject`**. i) **`Field`**. j) Active Server Page (ASP).

EXERCISES

26.3 Create a server-side include file containing the AdRotator code listed in Fig. 26.3. Write an Active Server Page that uses this server-side include file.

26.4 Modify Fig. 26.1's **`clock.asp`** to also display Pacific time.

26.5 Modify Fig. 26.10's **`guestbook.asp`** to read and write to a database rather than a text file. This exercise requires the use of a database development tool such as Microsoft Access.

26.6 Modify Fig. 26.19's **`catalog.asp`** such that a client can also get a list of publications by author.

26.7 Using the same techniques as Fig. 26.10 (**`guestbook.asp`**) develop an ASP application for a discussion group. Allow new links to be created for new topics.

26.8 Modify Fig. 26.16's **`login.asp`** to read and write to a text file rather than a database.

26.9 Modify Fig. 26.18's **`translation.asp`** to provide a text box that allows the user to enter SQL statements to query the database. Provide a submit button.

26.10 Create an ASP application that allows the user to customize a Web page. The application should consist of three ASP files: one that asks the user to login and reads from a text file to determine if the user is known. If the user is not known, a second ASP file is loaded asking the user to choose their preference for foreground color, background color and image. Write the new user name and preferences to the text file. Next display the page customized according to the preferences selected. If the user is known at login, the customized page should be displayed.

27

CGI (Common Gateway Interface) and Perl 5

Objectives

- To understand the Common Gateway Interface.
- To understand string processing and regular expressions in Perl.
- To be able to read and write client data using cookies.
- To construct programs that interact with databases.
- To be able to implement a Web search engine.

This is the common air that bathes the globe.
Walt Whitman

The longest part of the journey is said to be the passing of the gate.
Marcus Terentius Varro

Railway termini... are our gates to the glorious and unknown. Through them we pass out into adventure and sunshine, to them, alas! we return.
E.M. Forster

There comes a time in a man's life when to get where he has to go—if there are no doors or windows—he walks through a wall.
Bernard Malamud

You ought to be able to show that you can do it a good deal better than anyone else with the regular tools before you have a license to bring in your own improvements.
Ernest Hemingway

Outline

27.1 Common Gateway Interface (CGI)

Much of the book has focused on client-side programming. HTML documents are downloaded from servers and viewed in Web browsers. In this section of the book we concentrate on *server-side programming*, i.e., processing data on the server to increase communication between *clients* and *servers*, thus creating interactive applications. With scripting languages such as JavaScript and VBScript used with Dynamic HTML (Chapters 8–22), we showed how to reduce the load on the server (and on the Internet, for that matter). This chapter shows that client-side scripting is not always sufficient when building truly interactive Web-based applications.

Hypertext Transfer Protocol (*HTTP*) is used by Web browsers and Web servers to communicate with one another. *Universal Resource Locators* (*URL*s) are used by Web browsers (clients) to indicate the name of the Web server from which to request information and what information to retrieve from that server. By issuing the HTTP **`GET`** command, the Web browser directs the server to send specific data such as text, images or other types of data to the Web browser. The term *client* refers to a Web browser throughout this chapter.

This is where the *Common Gateway Interface (CGI)* comes into action. CGI lets HTTP clients interact with programs across a network through a Web server. CGI is a standard for interfacing applications with a Web server. These CGI applications can be written in many different programming languages. Permission is granted within the Web server by a *Web master* (or the author of the Web site) to allow specific programs to be executed on the Web server. Typically, CGI applications reside in the *directory* **`/cgi-bin`**.

A Web browser takes information from a user (usually by means of an HTML form) and sends it, using HTTP, to a Web server. This information might be anything from credit-card data to a person's height. A server-side CGI program is then executed, perhaps verifying credit-card information, and sends back information, such as whether a credit purchase is accepted or rejected, to the client. The information sent to the client is typically an HTML Web page, but may contain images, streaming audio, Macromedia flash files or even XML (see Chapter 28). Because CGI is an interface, it cannot be directly programmed—a script or executable program must be used to interact with it. Figure 27.1 illustrates a typical interaction that occurs when a client requests a page that contains a CGI script.

Applications written in many of today's popular programming languages use *standard input* (typically the keyboard) and *standard output* (typically the screen) to interact with users. Standard input is the stream of information input either by a user, from a text file or from another input device. Standard output is the information stream presented to the user by an application—which is typically displayed on the screen but may be printed on a printer, written to a file, etc.

The standard output from server-side applications or scripts is redirected, or *piped*, to the Common Gateway Interface and then sent over the Internet to a Web browser for rendering.

27.2 Introduction to Perl

Perl (Practical Extraction and Report Language) is a high-level programming language developed by Larry Wall in 1987 while working at Unisys; he now works at O'Reilly & Associates as a developer and researcher for the Perl programming language. Wall's initial intent was to create a programming language to monitor large software projects and generate reports. Perl has particularly rich, easy-to-use text-processing capabilities. Perl is an alternative to the terse and strict C programming language and a powerful alternative to UNIX shell scripts. In this chapter, we discuss Perl 5.

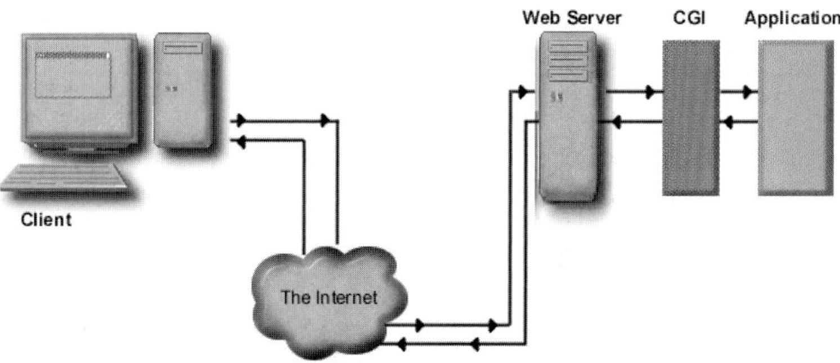

Fig. 27.1 Data path of a typical CGI-based application.

With the advent of the World Wide Web and Web browsers, the Internet gained tremendous popularity. This greatly increased the volume of requests users made for information from Web servers. As the Web increased in popularity, it became evident that the ability for the user to interact with the server would be crucial. The true power of the Web lay not only in serving content but also in responding to requests from users and generating dynamic content. The framework for such communication already existed through CGI. Because most of the information users send to servers is text—such as user names, passwords and email addresses—Perl was the logical choice for programming the server side of interactive Web-based applications and is the most popular language for doing so today. The Perl community continuously corrects problems that appear and evolves the language to keep it competitive with newer server-side technologies such as Microsoft's Active Server Pages (see Chapter 26) and Sun Microsystem's Java Servlets (see Chapter 29, which is a bonus chapter included for programmers who already know Java).

While Perl was initially developed on the UNIX platform, it was always intended to be a cross-platform computer language. *ActivePerl* is the version of Perl for Windows. The latest version of ActivePerl, the Perl 5 implementation for Windows, can be downloaded free of charge from **`http://www.activestate.com`**. Once you have downloaded the executable program, you can install the package by double clicking the filename (e.g., **`Api519.exe)`**. This filename will change with subsequent versions of ActivePerl, to reflect the current version number. The ActivePerl installation begins with the **Welcome** dialog of Fig. 27.2.

This installation includes the *core Perl package*—predefined functionality that is expected to behave the same across platforms. During installation the Perl interpreter, ***`perl.exe`***, is placed in the **`bin`** directory, one level below the **`Perl`** installation directory. The Perl interpreter is loaded into memory each time a Perl program is invoked. [*Note:* **`mod_perl`** for the Apache Web Server alters this behavior by loading the interpreter only once—see Chapter 24, "Web Servers," for more on Apache and **`mod_perl`**.] This feature allows programmers to quickly edit programs and execute them without explicitly compiling and linking the source code. The extension for Perl programs is ***`.pl`*** and is, by default, associated with the Perl interpreter. In Windows, a user may execute a Perl script by double clicking a **`.pl`** file. A Perl program may also be executed by typing **`perl`** followed by the filename of the Perl source code at the command line (e.g., a DOS command prompt in Windows, etc.). For example,

```
perl myperl.pl
```

invokes the **`perl`** interpreter on the file **`myperl.pl`**.

Figure 27.3 lists some of the command-line switches that can be passed to the Perl interpreter. Like Perl, these command-line switches are case-sensitive.

Testing and Debugging Tip 27.1

When running a Perl script from the command line, always use the **`-w`** *option. The program may seem to execute correctly when there is actually something wrong with the source code. The* **`-w`** *option displays warnings encountered while executing a Perl program.*

Testing and Debugging Tip 27.2

Function **`print`** *can be used to display the value of a variable at a particular point during a program's execution. This is often helpful in debugging a program.*

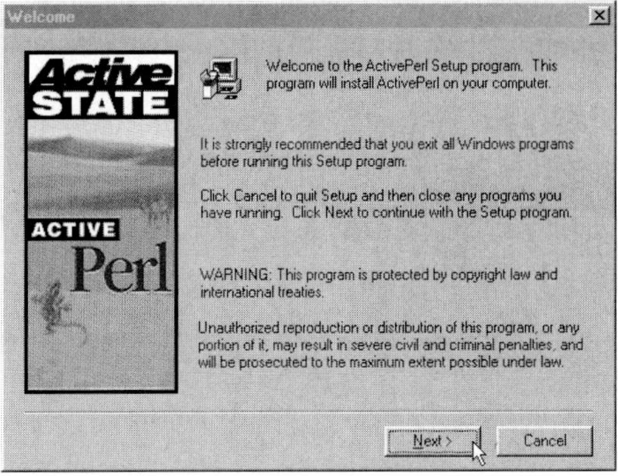

Fig. 27.2 ActivePerl installation **Welcome** dialog.

Command-line switch	Description
-e 'command'	Interpret one line of Perl code.
-S	Search for the specified script using the **PATH** environment variable.
-U	Allow unsafe operations to be executed.
-v	Print the version of Perl.
-w	Allow warnings to be displayed on compilation of the script.
-h	Display all options for **perl.exe**.

Fig. 27.3 Some of the common command-line switches used with **perl.exe**.

Common Programming Error 27.1

Forgetting to terminate a statement with a **;** *is a syntax error.*

Figure 27.4 presents a simple Perl program that prints the text **"Welcome to Perl!"** to the screen. Lines 1 and 2 contain the Perl *comment character*, (**#**)—which instructs the Perl interpreter to ignore everything after the **#** character to the end of the line. Line 4 calls function ***print*** to send text to the screen. *Escape sequence* **\n** moves the cursor to the next line. This is the blank line beneath the output **"Welcome to Perl"**. Semicolons (**;**) are used to terminate statements—except where *braces* (**{}**) are used to denote a block of code.

```
1  # Fig. 27.4: first.pl
2  # A first program in Perl.
3
4  print "Welcome to Perl!\n";
```

```
Welcome to Perl!
```

Fig. 27.4 A first program in Perl and its output.

Like other scripting languages discussed in this book, Perl contains a set of data types (Fig. 27.5) that represent different kinds of information (e.g., strings, integers and arrays). Notice that each variable name has a special character (i.e., **$**, **@** and **%**) preceding it. The **$** character specifies that the variable contains a scalar value (i.e., strings, integer numbers and floating-point numbers). Variables do not need to be explicitly initialized by the programmer before being used. We will discuss the **@** and **%** characters momentarily. Figure 27.6 declares, initializes and displays scalar variables.

Common Programming Error 27.2

*Failure to place a preceding **$** character before a scalar variable name is an error.*

Data type	Format for variable names of this type	Description
Scalar variable	**$***varname*	Scalar variables are used to contain strings, integer numbers and floating-point numbers.
Indexed array	**@***arrayname*	An indexed array uses an integer (called an index) to reference individual array elements.
Hash	**%***hashname*	A hash uses keys that are strings to reference individual array elements.

Fig. 27.5 Perl data types.

```
# Fig. 27.6: variable.pl
# Program to illustrate the use of scalar variables.

# using a variable in the context of a string
print "Using a variable before initializing: $var\n";

# using a variable in a numeric context
$test = $num + 5;
print "Adding uninitialized variable num to 5 yields: $test.\n";

$a = 5;
print "The value of variable a is: $a\n";

$a = $a + 5;
print "Variable a after adding 5 is $a.\n";

$b = "A string value";
$a = $a + $b;

print "Adding a string to an integer yields: $a\n";

$number = 7;
$b = $b + $number;

print "Adding an integer to a string yields: $b\n";
```

Fig. 27.6 Using scalar variables (part 1 of 2).

```
Using a variable before initializing:
Adding uninitialized variable num to 5 yields: 5.
The value of variable a is: 5
Variable a after adding 5 is 10.
Adding a string to an integer yields: 10
Adding an integer to a string yields: 7
```

Fig. 27.6 Using scalar variables (part 2 of 2).

Line 5 calls function **`print`** to print the contents of **`$var`**. Notice that **`$var`** is placed within the double quotes of the string—the variable name serves as a place-holder for the actual value (i.e., the Perl interpreter replaces the variable name with the variable's actual value). Variables, such as **`$var`**, not declared prior to their first use are implicitly declared. Because **`$var`** is inferred to be a string variable, it is set to *null* (i.e., an empty value). Notice that, in the output, there is no text output from the variable **`$var`**.

Line 8 assigns **`$test`** the result of adding **`$num`** to **`5`**. Because **`$num`** is used in a numeric context, it is inferred by the interpreter to be a number, so it is set to **0** rather than null.

Line 11 assigns variable **`$a`** the value **`5`**. Line 14 adds **`5`** to the value of **`$a`**. Line 18 attempts to add a string value, **`$b`**, to an integer value. The result is output on line 20. Line 23 attempts to add an integer to a string. Because there is no logical way to do this operation mathematically, the string value is ignored.

Common Programming Error 27.3

Using an uninitialized variable might make a numerical calculation incorrect. Consider multiplying a number by an uninitialized variable. The result is **0**.

Testing and Debugging Tip 27.3

While it is not always necessary to initialize variables before using them, doing so can avoid errors.

Perl has the ability to store data in arrays. Arrays are divided into *elements* that can each contain an individual scalar variable. Figure 27.7 uses arrays to store a possible list of user names and displays the user names on the screen.

```
# Fig. 27.7: arrays.pl
# Program to demonstrate arrays in Perl

@array = ("Bill", "Bobby", "Sue", "Michelle");

print "The array contains:\n\n";
print "@array \n\n";
print "Third element: $array[2]\n\n";

@array2 = (A..Z);

print "The range operator is used to store all\n";
print "letters from capital A to Z:\n\n";
print "@array2 \n";
```

Fig. 27.7 Using arrays (part 1 of 2).

```
The array contains:

Bill Bobby Sue Michelle

Third element: Sue

The range operator is used to store all
letters from capital A to Z:

A B C D E F G H I J K L M N O P Q R S T U V W X Y Z
```

Fig. 27.7 Using arrays (part 2 of 2).

Line 4 initializes array **`@array`** to contain four strings, namely **`"Bill"`**, **`"Bobby"`**, **`"Sue"`** and **`"Michelle"`**. Parentheses, **`()`**, are used to group the strings. Each name is placed into an individual array element. The entire contents of **`@array`** is **`print`**ed on line 7. Line 8 displays one element using subscript notation, **`[2]`**. This notation actually prints the third array element because elements are numbered starting with **`0`**. Notice that while the **`@`** character is used to reference the array as a whole, the **`$`** character is used to reference one individual array element. An individual element is considered to be a scalar value and therefore the **`$`** notation is required.

Line 10 initializes array **`@array2`** to contain all letters from **`A`** to **`Z`**. The *range operator*, **`..`**, specifies that all values between uppercase **`A`** and **`Z`** inclusive should be placed in the array. Parentheses are required to group the values. Line 14 **`print`**s the values contained in **`@array2`**—all 26 values from **`A`** to **`Z`**.

In addition to the core Perl package, add-ons called *packages* provide additional functionality. Packages often provide platform-specific features and are available free of charge from **`http://www.activestate.com/packages`**. Figure 27.8 lists some of the packages available and the functionality provided by them. Several of these packages are used to enhance the functionality of Perl in this chapter—specifically, ODBC for database access, and Internet connectivity enhancements with the ***`libwww-perl.ppd`*** package. A package is downloaded in compressed format (e.g., **`.zip`**) and usually contains a **`readme`** text file with instructions on how to install the package. Typically the zip file contains a ***`.ppd`*** file that must be extracted to Perl's installation directory. To install a package, ActivePerl's *Perl Package Manager* must be invoked. For example, the command

```
ppm install libwww-perl.ppd
```

installs the **`libwww-perl`** package.

The installation asks a series of questions regarding the Internet settings for your server. Pressing *Enter* uses the default settings. [*Note:* When prompted, you must enter a valid Internet domain name for the examples in this chapter to work correctly.]

ActivePerl installs HTML documentation onto your computer that may be accessed through the **Start** menu. Additional support for the Perl programming language can be found at the *Comprehensive Perl Archive Network, CPAN*. The CPAN contains searchable documentation, sample scripts and Frequently Asked Questions; and is located at

```
http://www.perl.com/CPAN/
```

Software Engineering Observation 27.1

Using packages, pre-defined portions of reusable code, greatly reduces the time required to develop applications.

27.3 Configuring Personal Web Server (PWS) for Perl/CGI

To run CGI scripts with Personal Web Server (PWS), which you learned how to install in Chapter 24, you must make several modifications to the *Windows Registry*. By default, PWS cannot execute Perl scripts or associate an executable file with the **.pl** file extension. To enable PWS to execute Perl scripts, you must add an entry to the Windows Registry.

1. To add an entry to the Windows Registry, select **Run** from the **Start** menu, type **regedit** in the **Open:** text field and click **Run** (Fig. 27.9). This launches (i.e., executes) the Microsoft **Registry Editor** application. [*Note:* that the Registry should be backed up before making any changes. This is done by selecting **Export Registry File** from the **File** menu. *Caution: editing Registry settings is dangerous. If the editing is not done correctly, your machine may not start properly. Edit the Registry at your own risk.*]
2. Figure 27.10 shows the **Registry Editor**. In the left pane of the window, a series of *keys* (i.e., configuration data used by Windows) is displayed. Select key ***HKEY_LOCAL_MACHINE***—which contains configuration data for hardware, the operating system and installed applications—and expand it (by clicking the **+** to its left) to see its child keys. Expand the tree further by selecting **System**, **CurrentControlSet**, **Services**, **W3Svc**, **Parameters** and finally ***Script Map***. This key is responsible for file extensions and their executable associations in PWS.

Package	Functionality
libwww-perl	Increases network programming functionality.
Win32-API	Enables Perl programs to make Windows system calls.
Win32-ODBC	Enables ODBC connectivity within Perl programs.
Win32-Registry	Allows Perl programs to read and write to the *Windows Registry* (i.e., a database containing hardware and software information about your computer system).
XML-Parser	Allows Perl programs to parse XML documents (see Chapter 28).

Fig. 27.8 Some packages available from ActiveState's Perl package repository.

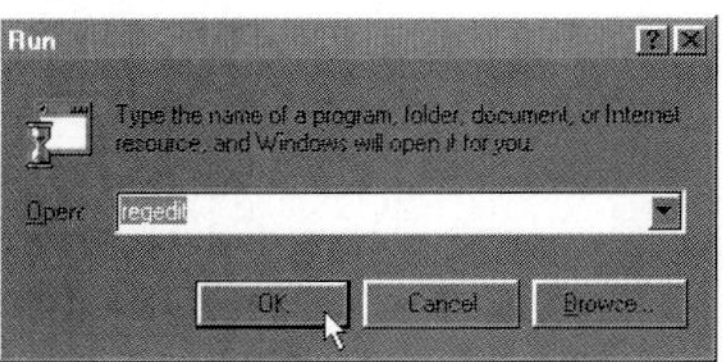

Fig. 27.9 Launching the **Registry Editor** from the **Run** dialog.

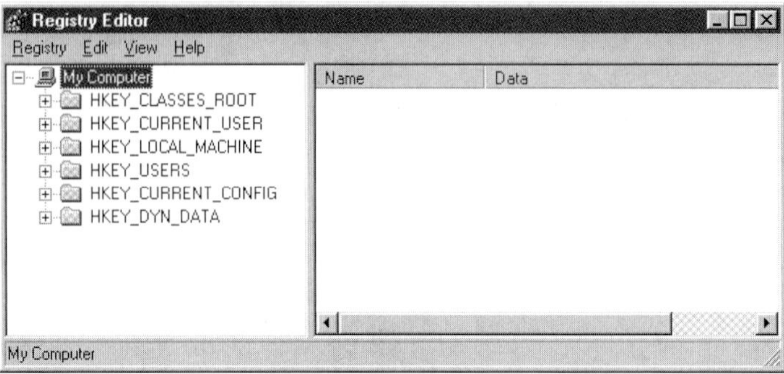

Fig. 27.10 Registry Editor application.

3. Select this key by clicking **Script Map**. The right pane reads **(Default) (value not set)** and is shown in Fig. 27.11. Click the right mouse button in the right pane and select **New**, then **String Value** from the context menu. In the editable field, type `.pl` to indicate the Perl file extension. Once you have entered the text, press *Enter* to confirm the extension. Double click the `.pl` entry you created to modify its value. The value associates the file extension with the executable application for which it is intended.

4. In the **Edit String** dialog (Fig. 27.12), type the absolute path for the Perl interpreter. The default path is usually `C:\Perl\bin\perl.exe %s %s`, but this can vary depending on where ActivePerl was installed. Exit the **Registry Editor** by selecting **Exit** from the **Registry** menu.

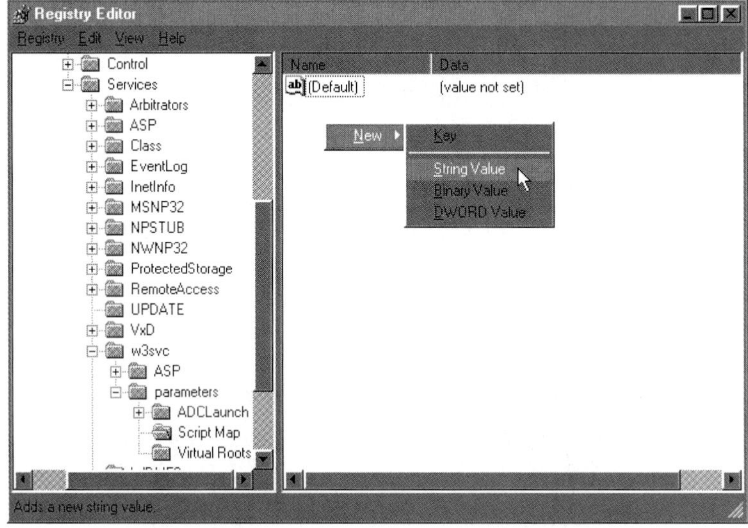

Fig. 27.11 Adding a new association to the **Script Map** key.

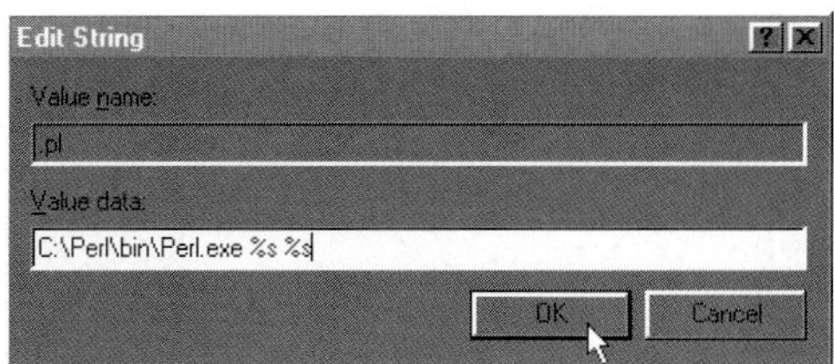

Fig. 27.12 Modifying the path information for the **`.pl`** file extension.

Now that the Registry settings have been saved, run PWS and click the **Advanced** icon in the left pane (Fig. 27.13). The **Advanced Options** dialog is displayed in the right pane (Fig. 27.14). This dialog sets permissions for directories, including ***`cgi-bin`***—which is where Perl scripts are typically located. Permissions must be set properly in order to run CGI programs on the Web server. Clicking the **Edit Properties** button displays the **Edit Directory** dialog. The directory listed is the path where your CGI scripts are located. Usually, this directory is **`C:\Inetpub\wwwroot\cgi-bin`**. [*Note:* You may need to create the **`cgi-bin`** directory]. Select the **Read**, **Execute** and **Scripts** check boxes in the **Access** field and click **OK** (Fig. 27.15). PWS is now configured to run CGI scripts.

27.4 String Processing and Regular Expressions

One of Perl's most powerful capabilities is processing textual data easily and efficiently. Perl text manipulation is usually done through the use of *regular expressions*—patterns of characters used to search through text files and databases. This feature allows large amounts of text to be searched, using relatively simple expressions.

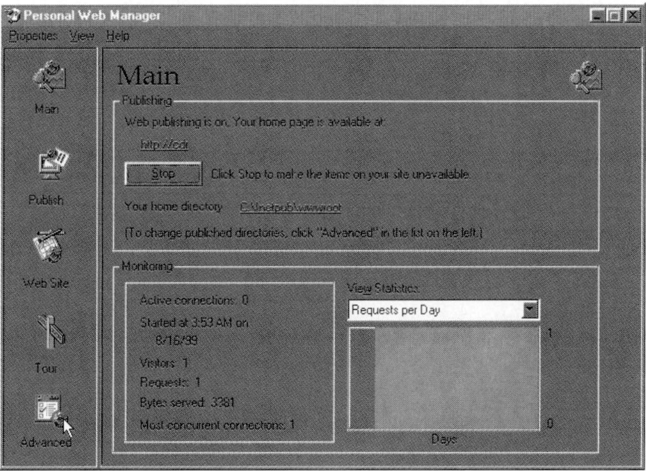

Fig. 27.13 `Advanced` icon in PWS.

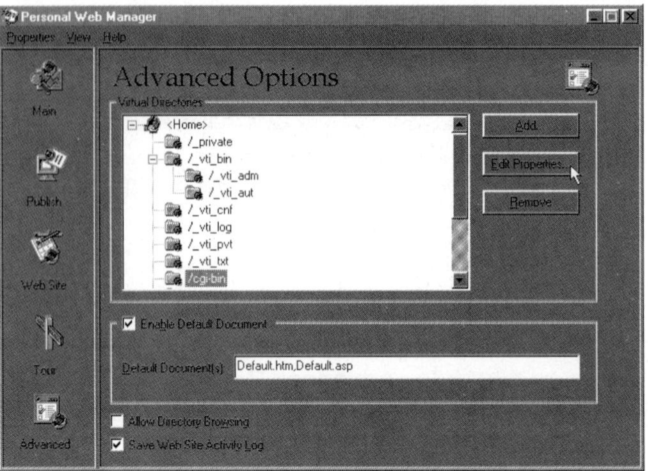

Fig. 27.14 Configuring the **`cgi-bin`** directory in PWS.

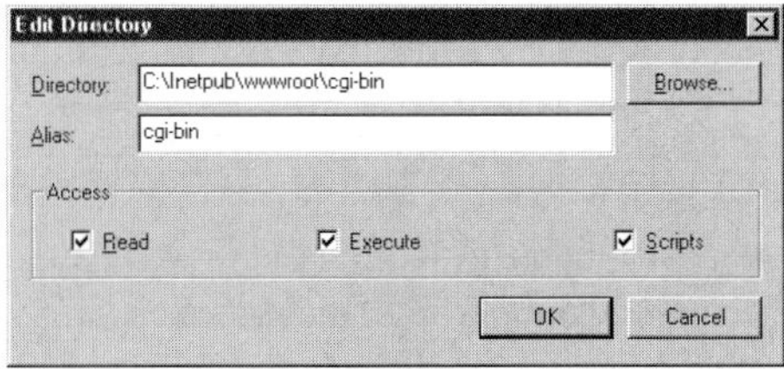

Fig. 27.15 Setting permissions for the **`cgi-bin`** directory.

One of the most important capabilities in any language is to be able to test equality on textual data or strings. Perl operator **`eq`** tests whether two strings are equivalent. Figure 27.16 uses operator **`eq`** to determine if two strings are equivalent.

```
# Fig. 27.16: equals.pl
# Program to demonstrate the eq operator

my $stringa = "Test";
my $stringb = "Testing";

if ($stringa eq "Test")
{
   print "$stringa matches Test.\n";
}
else
{
   print "$stringa does not match Test.\n";
}

```

Fig. 27.16 Using the **`eq`** operator (part 1 of 2).

```
1  if ($stringb eq "Test")
2  {
3     print "$stringb matches Test.\n";
4  }
5  else
6  {
7     print "$stringb does not match Test.\n";
8  }
```

```
Test matches Test.
Testing does not match Test.
```

Fig. 27.16 Using the **eq** operator (part 2 of 2).

Line 4 declares scalar variable **$stringa** and assigns it string **"Test"**. Perl 5 *keyword* **my** indicates that the variable is only valid for the block of code in which it is declared. Line 5 declares scalar variable **$stringb** and assigns it the value **"Testing"**. Line 7 introduces the **if** statement. Parentheses are required in an **if** statement to surround the condition being tested. Scalar variable **$stringa** is being compared to string value **"Test"** with **eq**. Unlike other Perl statements, an **if** statement does not terminate with a semicolon. The **if** statement uses curly braces **{** and **}** to mark the beginning and the end of a block of code. In this case, the condition is true, and line 9 is executed, printing the value of **$stringa** and a brief message.

Because operator **eq** cannot be used to search though an entire document (or even through a series of words), Perl provides a *matching operator* (**=~**) that tests whether a match for a string is found within a single string or a series of words. Figure 27.17 uses the matching operator to determine if a string is a substring within another string.

```
# Fig 27.17: expression1.pl
# searches using the matching operator and regular expressions

$search = "Testing pattern matches";

if ( $search =~ /Test/ )
{
   print "Test was found.\n";
}

if ( $search =~ /^Test/ )
{
   print "Test was found at the beginning of the line.\n";
}

if ( $search =~ /Test$/ )
{
   print "Test was found at the end of the line.\n";
}

```

Fig. 27.17 Using the matching operator **=~** (part 1 of 2).

```
1  if ( $search =~ / \b ( \w+ es ) \b /x )
2  {
3     print "Word ending in es: $1 \n";
4  }
```

```
Test was found.
Test was found at the beginning of the line.
Word ending in es: matches
```

Fig. 27.17 Using the matching operator =~ (part 2 of 2).

We begin in line 4 by assigning the string **"Testing pattern matches"** to variable **$search**. The **if**'s condition (line 6)

```
$search =~ /Test/
```

searches for the pattern **Test** inside variable **$search**. Because the pattern **Test** is found in the string **"Testing pattern matches"**, the matching operator returns true.

Our next condition

```
$search =~ /^Test/
```

uses the character **^**, which matches the beginning of a line. Because this pattern also matches our string in **$search**, the search is successful.

The counterpart to **^** is **$**, which matches the end of a line. Line 16's **if** condition uses the matching operator to search for the pattern **Test$**, and because **Test** is not found at the end of the line, the search is unsuccessful.

In our last condition (line 21),

```
$search =~ / \b ( \w+ es ) \b /x
```

we search for a word ending with the letters **es**. All characters preceded by backslashes have special significance. The two **\b** characters each signify a *word boundary*, i.e., a space or a newline character. Between the two word boundaries are two parentheses—these will be explained momentarily. Inside those parentheses, we search for **\w+** followed by **es**. The first part, **\w+**, is a combination of **\w**, which matches any *alphanumeric character* (**0**–**9**, **a**–**z**, **A**–**Z**, and the underscore character, **_**), and the **+** modifier, which instructs Perl to match the preceding character one or more times. Thus, **\w+** searches for one or more alphanumeric characters. Characters **es** are *literal characters* (i.e., the regular expression matches the actual characters **es** in a string).

Because we add the **/x** modifying character to the end of the regular expression, whitespace characters are ignored. This allows programmers to add space characters to their regular expressions for readability. Other modifying characters besides **/x** are listed in Fig. 27.18.

Line 23

```
print "Word ending in es: $1 \n";
```

prints the matched word. Variable ***$1*** is assigned a value equal to the pattern matched inside the parentheses we saw earlier. In line 21, the pattern **\w+ es** is enclosed in parentheses (**\w+ es** is the part of the regular expression that matched the actual word ending in **es**), and so that matched pattern is assigned to **$1** by the Perl interpreter. Perl provides for up to nine of these parenthetical matches in a single regular expression, assigning matches to Perl variables **$1** through **$9**.

Metacharacters enhance the searching capabilities of regular expressions. They give search strings different meanings and allow programmers to search for substrings or for specific characteristics of strings.

Built-in metacharacters include *modifying characters*—which allow programmers to modify the search string to look for specific, or multiple, instances of characters within the text being searched. Some modifying characters are listed in Fig. 27.18.

To use modifying characters in a regular expression, they are placed to the right of the forward slashes which delimit the regular expression. For example, the regular expression

```
/computer/i
```

matches **computer**, **COMPUTER**, **Computer**, **CoMputER**, etc. because the modifying character **i** instructs the regular expression to ignore case.

27.5 Viewing Client/Server Environment Variables

Knowing information about a client can be extremely useful to administrators. *CGI environment variables* contain such information as the type of Web browser being used, the version of CGI that the server is running, the HTTP host, the HTTP connection, etc. A server might send one Web page to Microsoft Internet Explorer 5 and an entirely different Web page to Netscape Communicator. Figure 27.19 displays all the CGI environment variables and the values for each.

Line 3 introduces the ***use*** *statement*—which allows Perl programs to include the contents of predefined packages called *libraries*. The ***CGI*** *library* is included to provide functionality that makes it easier to write the HTML sent to the Web browser. Specifically, the **CGI** library contains keywords that represent HTML tags. Line 5 directs the Perl program to **print** a valid *HTTP header,* using function **header** from the **CGI** library. Browsers use headers to determine how to handle the incoming data.

Modifying Character	Purpose
/g	Search everywhere for the expression (global search).
/i	Ignores the case of the search string.
/m	The string is evaluated as if it had multiple lines (i.e., contains multiple newline characters) of text.
/s	Ignore the newline character and treat it as whitespace. The text is seen as a single line.
/x	All whitespace characters are ignored when searching the string.

Fig. 27.18 Some of Perl's modifying characters.

```
# Fig. 27.19: environment.pl
# Program to display CGI environment variables
use CGI qw/:standard/;

print header;
print "<HTML>";
print "   <HEAD>";
print "      <TITLE>Environment Variables...</TITLE>";
print "   </HEAD>";
print "   <BODY TEXT = BLACK BGCOLOR = WHITE>";
print "   <BASEFONT FACE = \"ARIAL,SANS-SERIF\" SIZE = 2>";
print "   <TABLE BORDER = 0 CELLPADDING = 2 CELLSPACING = 0";
print "    WIDTH = 100%>";

foreach $key (sort keys %ENV)
{
   print "<TR>";
   print "<TD BGCOLOR = #11BBFF><STRONG>$key</STRONG></TD>";
   print "<TD><FONT COLOR = BLACK SIZE = 2>$ENV{$key}";
   print "</Font></TD>";
   print "</TR>";
}

print "      </TABLE>";
print "   </BODY>";
print "</HTML>";
```

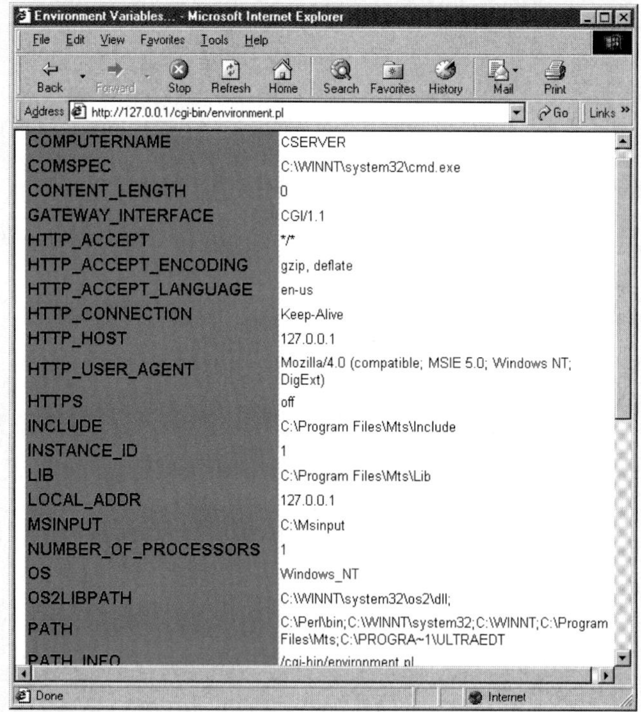

Fig. 27.19 Displaying CGI environment variables.

A valid HTTP header must be sent to ensure that the browser displays the information correctly. The header produced by calling function **print** on line 5 is

```
Content-type: text/html
```

The **text/html** portion of the header indicates that the browser must display the returned information as an HTML document. Function **print** sends HTML to the standard output, which is then sent to the Web browser through CGI. Lines 6 through 13 write HTML to the client. An HTML **TABLE** (line 12) is used in this example to produce an organized view of the environment variables.

The ***foreach*** *loop*, line 15, iterates through the keys in the ***%ENV*** *hashtable*, a built-in table in Perl that contains the names and values of all CGI environment variables. Each CGI environment variable has a key and a value in the **%ENV** hashtable. Perl function **sort** returns a list of the hashtable keys in alphabetical order. The **foreach** loop iterates sequentially through the list returned by function **sort**, assigning the current key to **$key**. Keys are discussed in greater detail in Section 27.10, "Using ODBC to Connect to a Database".

27.6 Form Processing and Business Logic

HTML **FORM**s allow users to enter data that is sent to a Web server for processing. Once the form is received by a server, a program processes the data. Such a program could help people to purchase products, send and receive Web-based email, take a political poll, perform online paging, etc. These types of Web applications allow users to interact with the server. This technology, is vital to electronic commerce (see Chapter 23).

Figure 27.20 uses an HTML **FORM** to allow users to input personal information for a mailing list. This type of registration form might be used to store user information in a database for a software company before allowing the user to download the software.

```
<!DOCTYPE html PUBLIC "-//W3C//DTD HTML 4.0 Transitional//EN">
<!-- Fig. 27.20: form.html -->

<HTML>
<HEAD>
<TITLE>Sample FORM to take user input in HTML</TITLE>
</HEAD>

<BODY BACKGROUND = "images/back.gif">
<BASEFONT FACE = "ARIAL,SANS-SERIF" SIZE = 2>

   <FONT SIZE = +2>
      <STRONG>This is a sample registation form.</STRONG>
   </FONT><BR>
   Please fill in all fields and click Register.

```

Fig. 27.20 User entering a valid phone number (part 1 of 3).

```
   <FORM METHOD = "POST" ACTION = "/cgi-bin/form.pl">
      <IMG SRC = "images/user.gif"><BR>
      <FONT COLOR = BLUE>
         Please fill out the fields below.<BR>
      </FONT>

      <IMG SRC = "images/fname.gif">
      <INPUT TYPE = "TEXT" NAME = "FNAME"><BR>
      <IMG SRC = "images/lname.gif">
      <INPUT TYPE = "TEXT" NAME = "LNAME"><BR>
      <IMG SRC = "images/email.gif">
      <INPUT TYPE = "TEXT" NAME = "EMAIL"><BR>
      <IMG SRC = "images/phone.gif">
      <INPUT TYPE = "TEXT" NAME = "PHONE"><BR>

      <FONT SIZE=-2>
         Must be in the form (555)555-5555<BR><BR>
      </FONT>

      <IMG SRC = "images/downloads.gif"><BR>
      <FONT COLOR = BLUE>
         Which book would you like information about?<BR>
      </FONT>

      <SELECT NAME = "BOOK">
         <OPTION>Internet and WWW How to Program
         <OPTION>C++ How to Program 2e
         <OPTION>Java How to Program 3e
         <OPTION>Visual Basic How to Program 1e
      </SELECT>
      <BR><BR>

      <IMG SRC = "images/os.gif"><BR>
      <FONT COLOR = BLUE>
         Which operating system are you
         currently using?<BR>
      </FONT>

      <INPUT TYPE = "RADIO" NAME = "OS" VALUE = "Windows NT"
      CHECKED>
      Windows NT
      <INPUT TYPE = "RADIO" NAME = "OS" VALUE = "Windows 95">
      Windows 95
      <INPUT TYPE = "RADIO" NAME = "OS" VALUE = "Windows 98">
      Windows 98<BR>
      <INPUT TYPE = "RADIO" NAME = "OS" VALUE = "Linux">
      Linux
      <INPUT TYPE = "RADIO" NAME = "OS" VALUE = "Other">
      Other<BR>
      <INPUT TYPE = "SUBMIT" VALUE = "Register">
   </FORM>
</BODY>
</HTML>
```

Fig. 27.20 User entering a valid phone number (part 2 of 3).

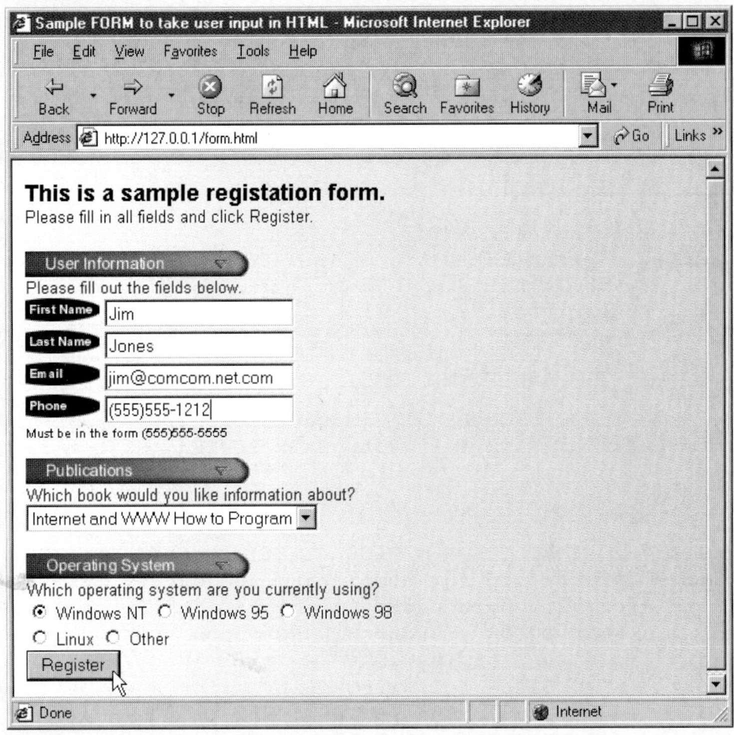

Fig. 27.20 User entering a valid phone number (part 3 of 3).

HTML element **FORM** (line 17) indicates that, when the user clicks **Register**, an action should occur. The first attribute, **METHOD = "POST"**, directs the browser to send the information to the server. The second attribute, **ACTION = "cgi-bin/form.pl"**, directs the server to execute the **form.pl** Perl script. The names given to the input items (e.g., **FNAME**) in the Web page are important when the Perl script is executed on the server. These names allow the script to refer to the individual pieces of data being submitted.

Figure 27.21 (**form.pl**) takes user information from the **form.html** Web page of Fig. 27.20, and sends a Web page to the client indicating that the information was received.

Good Programming Practice 27.1

Using business logic ensures that invalid information is not stored into databases.

Good Programming Practice 27.2

*Use meaningful HTML object names for input fields. This makes Perl programs easier to understand when retrieving **FORM** data.*

On line 7, the variable **$os** gets assigned the value of **param(OS)**. The ***param* method** is part of the Perl 5 **CGI** module and is responsible for retrieving form data—in this instance, the **INPUT** field named **OS**. Method **param** is called on lines 8 through 12 to get the values of the remaining HTML tags from the Web page and assigns them to variables **$firstname**, **$lastname**, **$email**, **$phone** and **$book**, respectively.

```
# Fig. 27.21: form.pl
# Program to read information sent to the server
# from the FORM in the form.html document.

use CGI qw/:standard/;

$os = param(OS);
$firstname  = param(FNAME);
$lastname  = param(LNAME);
$email  = param(EMAIL);
$phone  = param(PHONE);
$book  = param(BOOK);

print header;
print "<BODY BACKGROUND = \"/images/back.gif\">";
print "<BASEFONT FACE = \"ARIAL,SANS-SERIF\" SIZE = 3>";

if ( $phone =~ / \( \d{3} \) \d{3} - \d{3} /x )
{
   print "Hi <FONT COLOR = BLUE><B>$firstname</B></FONT>";
   print ". Thank you for completing the survey.<BR>";
   print "You have been added to the ";
   print "<FONT COLOR = BLUE><STRONG>$book </STRONG></FONT>";
   print "mailing list.<BR><BR>";
   print "<STRONG>The following information has been saved ";
   print "in our database:</STRONG><BR>";
   print "<TABLE BORDER = 0 CELLPADDING = 0";
   print "       CELLSPACING = 10>";
   print "<TR><TD BGCOLOR = #FFFFAA>Name </TD>";
   print "    <TD BGCOLOR = #FFFFBB>Email</TD>";
   print "    <TD BGCOLOR = #FFFFCC>Phone</TD>";
   print "    <TD BGCOLOR = #FFFFDD>OS</TD></TR>";
   print "<TR><TD>$firstname $lastname</TD><TD>$email</TD>";
   print "<TD>$phone</TD><TD>$os</TD></TR>";
   print "</TABLE>";
   print "<BR><BR><BR>";
   print "<CENTER><FONT SIZE = -3>";
   print "This is only a sample form. ";
   print "You have not been added to a mailing list.";
   print "</FONT></CENTER>";
}
else
{
   print "<FONT COLOR = RED SIZE = +2>";
   print "INVALID PHONE NUMBER</FONT><BR>";
   print " A valid phone number must be in the form";
   print "<STRONG>(555)555-5555</STRONG>";
   print "<FONT COLOR = BLUE> Click the Back button, ";
   print "enter a valid phone number and resubmit.<BR><BR>";
   print "Thank You.";
}
```

Fig. 27.21 Script to process user data from **`form.html`** (part 1 of 2).

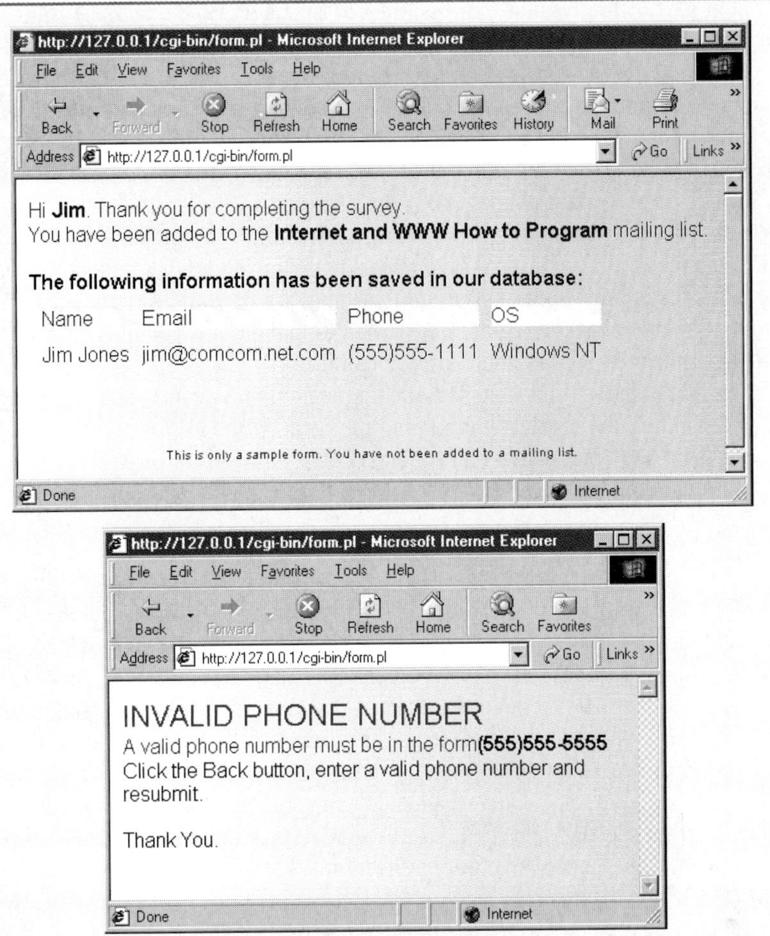

Fig. 27.21 Script to process user data from **`form.html`** (part 2 of 2).

The program tests to determine if the phone number is valid, i.e., consistent with the format *(555) 555-5555*. Validating this information is often crucial when you are maintaining a large database or a mailing list. Validation ensures that valid data is stored in the proper format in a database, that credit card numbers contain the proper number of digits before encrypting it and submitting it to a merchant, etc. The processes or algorithms designed to verify this information are known as *business logic* (also called *business rules*). Business logic can be as simple as verifying a password or a credit card number.

Line 18's **`if`** condition

```
$phone =~ / \( \d{3} \) \d{3} - \d{3} /x
```

uses a regular expression to validate the phone number. The first part of the regular expression, `\(`, matches the opening parenthesis of the phone number. The `\` character is needed to escape the `(` character because it is a special character in regular expressions.

The next part of the regular expression, **\d{3}**, checks for exactly **3** digits. The **\d** character matches any digit, and the **{3}** indicates that whatever preceded it must be matched exactly **3** times. The **{*x*}** syntax can be expanded to a minimum or maximum number of characters matched—for example, to match at least **3** and at most **5** of the preceding character, we would use the syntax **{3, 5}**. Other modifiers are **+** (one or more of the preceding character), ***** (any number of the preceding character, including zero) and **?** (zero or one of the preceding character).

The next part of our regular expression, **\)**, matches the closing parenthesis. Then **\d{3}** then matches **3** more digits, **-** matches a hyphen, and **\d{3}** matches **4** digits. Perl ignores the spaces in our regular expression, because we used the **/x** modifier. This modifier allows us to space out the regular expression to make it as readable as possible. If you want to match an actual space character, you can use **\s**.

If the regular expression is matched, the phone number is valid and a Web page is sent to the client thanking the user for completing the form. If the user enters an invalid phone number into the **FORM**, the **else** clause is executed, lines 42 through 51, instructing the user to enter a valid phone number.

27.7 Server-Side Includes

The Web offers the ability to track where a client is coming from and what the client views on your Web site and in some cases where the client is going after they leave your site. Tracking Web data is important to any business because it allows Web masters to know which sites are visited most frequently and how effective advertisements and products are. The use of banners, or paid advertisements, has dramatically increased over the past few years because of this technology.

Server-side includes (SSIs) are commands embedded in HTML documents to provide for content creation. Server-side includes allow Web masters to include the current time, the date or even the contents of an entirely different HTML document. *SSI commands* (e.g., ***DATE_LOCAL*** which displays the machine's date, etc.) execute CGI scripts on a server and are even capable of connecting to an ODBC data source. This capability can be used to create customized Web pages depending on the time of day or on whether an entry in a database has changed. The document containing these SSI commands typically has the ***.SHTML*** file extension.

Performance Tip 27.1

Parsing HTML documents on a server can dramatically increase the load on that server. To increase the performance of a heavily loaded server try to limit the use of Server-Side Includes.

Figure 27.22 implements a *Web-page hit counter*. Each time a client requests the document, the counter is incremented by one. Perl script **counter.pl** (Fig. 27.23) manipulates the counter.

Line 14 of **counter.shtml** calls the **counter.pl** script. Before the HTML document is sent to the client, the SSI command is issued and replaced by HTML code and sent to the client. This is true only when the command generates HTML. This technique can increase the load on the server tremendously, depending on how many times the script has to be parsed. The ***EXEC CGI*** *command* is issued to execute the **counter.pl** Perl script, before the document is sent to the client.

```
<!DOCTYPE html PUBLIC "-//W3C//DTD HTML 4.0 Transitional//EN">
<!-- Fig. 27.22 counter.shtml -->

<HTML>
   <HEAD>
      <TITLE>Using Server Side Includes</TITLE>
   </HEAD>

<BODY>
   <CENTER>
      <H3> Using Server Side Includes</H3>
   </CENTER>

   <!-- #EXEC CGI="/cgi-bin/counter.pl" --><BR>
   The Greenwich Mean Time is
   <FONT COLOR = BLUE>

   <!-- #ECHO VAR="DATE_GMT" -->.
   </FONT><BR>
   The name of this document is
   <FONT COLOR = BLUE>

   <!-- #ECHO VAR="DOCUMENT_NAME" -->
   </FONT><BR>
   The local date is
   <FONT COLOR = BLUE>

   <!-- #ECHO VAR="DATE_LOCAL" -->
   </FONT><BR>
   This document was last modified on
   <FONT COLOR = BLUE>

   <!-- #ECHO VAR="LAST_MODIFIED" -->
   </FONT><BR>
   Your current IP Address is
   <FONT COLOR = BLUE>

   <!-- #ECHO VAR="REMOTE_ADDR" -->
   </FONT><BR>
   My server name is
   <FONT COLOR = BLUE>

   <!-- #ECHO VAR="SERVER_NAME" -->
   </FONT><BR>
   And I am using the
   <FONT COLOR = BLUE>

   <!-- #ECHO VAR="SERVER_SOFTWARE" -->
   Web Server.</FONT><BR>
   You are using
   <FONT COLOR = BLUE>

```

Fig. 27.22 Incorporating a Web-page hit counter and displaying environment variables (part 1 of 2).

```
53       <!-- #ECHO VAR="HTTP_USER_AGENT" -->.
54       </FONT><BR>
55       This server is using <FONT COLOR = BLUE>
56
57       <!-- #ECHO VAR="GATEWAY_INTERFACE" -->.
58       </FONT><BR>
59       <BR><BR>
60       <CENTER>
61       <HR>
62       <FONT SIZE = -5>This document was last modified on
63
64       <!-- #ECHO VAR="LAST_MODIFIED" --></FONT>
65
66       </CENTER>
67    </BODY>
68    </HTML>
```

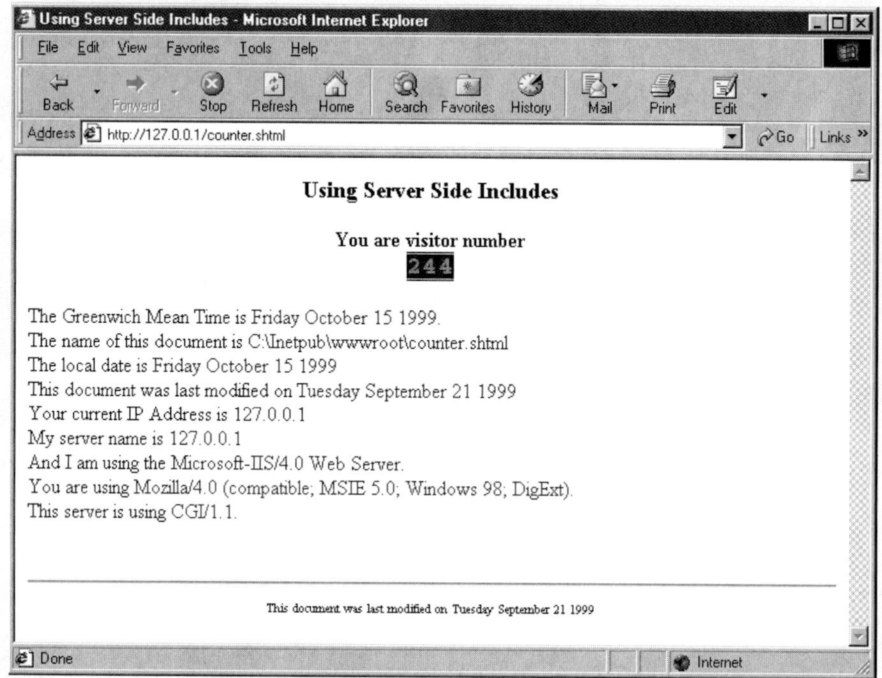

Fig. 27.22 Incorporating a Web-page hit counter and displaying environment variables (part 2 of 2).

Line 18 uses the ***ECHO*** *command* to display variable information. The **ECHO** command is followed by the *keyword* ***VAR*** and the variable's constant name.

Variable ***DATE_GMT*** contains the current Greenwich Mean Time. On line 23, the name of the current document is included in the HTML page with the ***DOCUMENT_NAME*** *variable*. On line 28, the ***DATE_LOCAL*** *variable* inserts the date (in local format—different formats are used around the world) for the user. Notice, in the output of this program, that the Greenwich Mean Time shows a different date from the local date.

```
1   # Counter.pl
2   # Program to track the number of times a web page
3   # has been accessed.
4
5   open(COUNTREAD, "counter.dat");
6      my $data = <COUNTREAD>;
7      $data++;
8   close(COUNTREAD);
9
10  open(COUNTWRITE, ">counter.dat");
11     print COUNTWRITE $data;
12  close(COUNTWRITE);
13
14  print "<CENTER>";
15  print "<STRONG>You are visitor number</STRONG><BR>";
16
17  for ($count = 0; $count < length($data);$count++)
18  {
19     $number = substr( $data, $count, 1 );
20     print "<IMG SRC=\"images/counter/$number.jpg\">";
21  }
22
23  print "</CENTER>";
```

Fig. 27.23 Perl script for counting Web page hits.

Line 5 opens the file **counter.dat**, which contains a number that represents the number of hits on that page. The next two lines assign the file's contents the variable **$data** and increment **$data** by one with the unary **++** *operator*.

Now that our counter has been incremented for this hit, we write the counter back to our **counter.dat** file.

In line 10,

```
open(COUNTWRITE, ">counter.dat");
```

we open the **counter.dat** file for writing—this is done by preceding the file name with a **>** *character*. This immediately truncates (i.e., discards) any data in that file. If the file does not exist, Perl creates a new file with the specified name. In addition to read and write modes, Perl provides an *append* mode, indicated by preceding the file name with characters **>>**. Any output to the file is written to the end of the file.

Now that we have **counter.dat** open for writing, we can write to it. This is done in line 11, with the **print** function call

```
print COUNTWRITE $data;
```

which redirects output to the file that filehandle **COUNTWRITE** refers.

Lines 17 through 21

```
for ( $count = 0; $count < length($data); $count++ )
{
   $number = substr( $data, $count, 1 ) ;
   print "<IMG SRC=\"images/counter/$number.jpg\">";
}
```

use a `for` loop to iterate through the characters contained in `$data`. We loop from `0` until `length( $data )`—*function* `length` returns the length of a string.

On each iteration, we obtain the current digit by calling *function* `substr` (this is similar to JavaScript's `substr` function). The first argument of function `substr` specifies the string from which to take a substring, the second argument specifies the offset, in characters, from the beginning of the string, and the third argument specifies the length of the substring.

In our loop, each digit is read into `$number`, and then an HTML **IMG** tag is `print`ed. The **SRC** of the **IMG** tag is based on the value of `$number`. This allows us to display each digit as an image instead of text.

27.8 Verifying a username and password

It is often desirable to have a *private Web site*—one that is visible to only certain people. Implementing privacy typically involves username and password verification; sometimes an email address is also required. Web sites for developers often employ this type of authentication to allow access to developers but not to the general public. Figure 27.24 authenticates a username and a password sent to the server. For simplicity, this example does not encrypt the data sent to the server.

```
<!DOCTYPE html PUBLIC "-//W3C//DTD HTML 4.0 Transitional//EN">
<!-- Fig. 27.24: verify.html -->

<HTML>
<HEAD>
<TITLE>Verifying a username and a password.</TITLE>
</HEAD>

<BODY BACKGROUND = "images/back.gif">
   <P>
      <FONT FACE = Arial>
      Type in your username and password below.
      </FONT><BR>
      <FONT COLOR = #0000FF FACE = Arial SIZE = 1>
      <STRONG>
      Note that password will be sent as plain text
      </STRONG>
      </FONT>
   </P>

   <FORM ACTION = "/cgi-bin/password.pl" METHOD = "post">
   <BR>

   <TABLE BORDER = "0" CELLSPACING = "0" STYLE = "HEIGHT: 90px;
         WIDTH: 123px" CELLPADING = "0">
      <TR>
         <TD BGCOLOR = #DDDDDD COLSPAN = 3>
         <FONT FACE = Arial SIZE = 2>
```

Fig. 27.24 Entering a username and a password (part 1 of 3).

```
            <STRONG>Username:</STRONG>
            </FONT>
            </TD>
         </TR>
         <TR>
            <TD BGCOLOR = #DDDDDD COLSPAN = 3>
            <INPUT SIZE = "40" NAME = "USERNAME"
                   STYLE = "HEIGHT: 22px; WIDTH: 115px">
            </TD>
         </TR>
         <TR>
            <TD BGCOLOR = #DDDDDD COLSPAN = 3>
            <FONT FACE = Arial SIZE = 2>
            <STRONG>Password:</STRONG>
            </FONT></TD>
         </TR>
         <TR>
            <TD BGCOLOR = #DDDDDD COLSPAN = 3>
            <INPUT SIZE = "40" NAME = "PASSWORD"
                   STYLE = "HEIGHT: 22px; WIDTH: 115px"
                   TYPE = PASSWORD>
            <BR></TD>
         </TR>
         <TR>
            <TD COLSPAN = 3>
            <INPUT TYPE = "submit" VALUE = "Enter"
                   STYLE = "HEIGHT: 23px; WIDTH: 47px">
            </TD>
         </TR>
      </TABLE>
      </FORM>
   </BODY>
   </HTML>
```

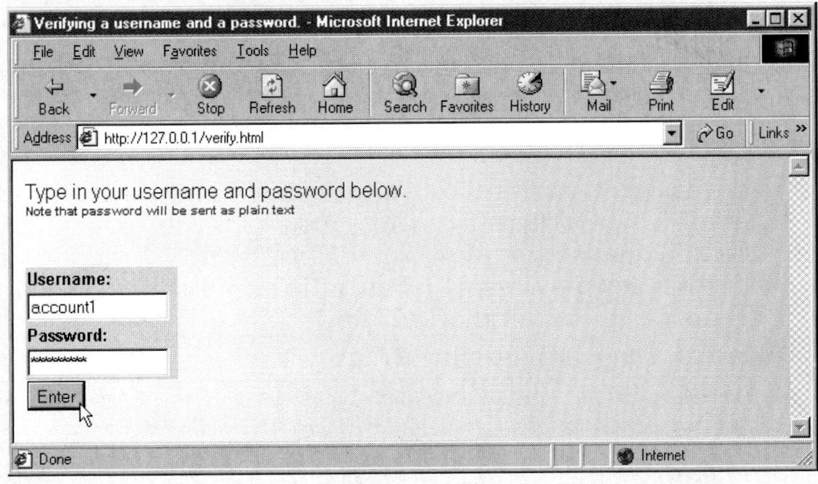

Fig. 27.24 Entering a username and a password (part 2 of 3).

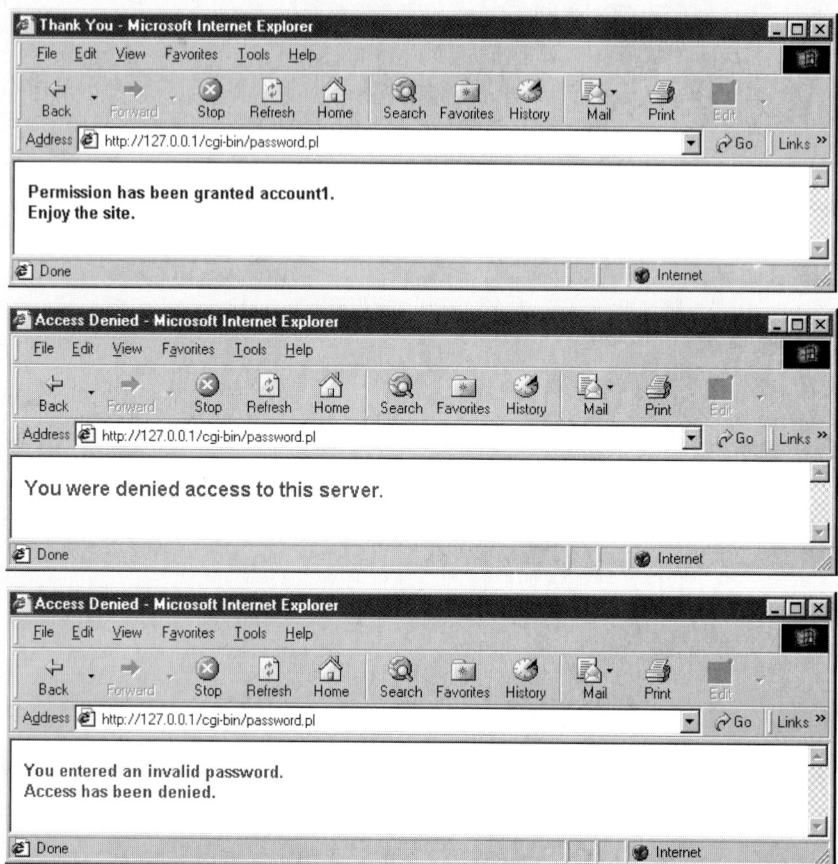

Fig. 27.24 Entering a username and a password (part 3 of 3).

The fields allow the client to enter a username and password and gain access to an otherwise restricted portion of a Web site. Lines 35 and 36 add a text **`INPUT`** box and name the field **`USERNAME`**. Lines 47 through 49 use another **`INPUT`** box to allow the client to enter a password.

Perl script **`password.pl`** (Fig. 27.24) is responsible for verifying information sent from the client to the server. In this program, the information sent is the username and password of the client. The **`password.pl`** script verifies that the entered username exists in the database and that the password entered is correct. The list of valid users and their passwords is located in text file **`data.txt`** (Fig. 27.25).

Good Programming Practice 27.3

When opening a text file to read its contents, open the file in read-only mode. Opening the file in other modes allows for the possibility of data to accidentally be overwritten.

Good Programming Practice 27.4

Always close files as soon as you are finished with them.

```
# Fig. 27.25: password.pl
# Program to search a database for usernames and passwords.
use CGI qw/:standard/;

my $username = param(USERNAME);
my $password = param(PASSWORD);

open(FILE, "data.txt") ||
   die "The database could not be opened";

   while(<FILE>)
   {
      @data = split(/\n/);

      foreach $entry (@data)
      {
         ($name, $pass) = split(/,/, $entry);

         if($name eq "$username")
         {
            $userverified = 1;
            if ($pass eq "$password")
            {
               $passwordverified = 1;
            }
         }
      }
   }

   close(FILE);

   if ($userverified && $passwordverified)
   {
      &accessgranted;
   }
   elsif ($userverified && !$passwordverified)
   {
      &wrongpassword;
   }
   else
   {
      &accessdenied;
   }

sub accessgranted
{
   print header;
   print "<TITLE>Thank You</TITLE>";
   print "<FONT FACE = Arial SIZE = 2 COLOR = BLUE>";
   print "<STRONG>Permission has been granted $username.";
   print "<BR> Enjoy the site.</STRONG></FONT>";
}

```

Fig. 27.25 Contents of `password.pl` Perl script (part 1 of 2).

```
54   sub wrongpassword
55   {
56      print header;
57      print "<TITLE>Access Denied</TITLE>";
58      print "<FONT FACE=Arial SIZE=2 COLOR=Red><STRONG>";
59      print "You entered an invalid password.<br> ";
60      print "Access has been denied.</STRONG></FONT>";
61      exit;
62
63   }
64
65   sub accessdenied
66   {
67      print header;
68      print "<TITLE>Access Denied</TITLE>";
69      print "<FONT FACE=Arial SIZE=3 COLOR=Red><STRONG>";
70      print "You were denied access to this server.";
71      print "</STRONG></FONT>";
72      exit;
73   }
```

Fig. 27.25 Contents of **password.pl** Perl script (part 2 of 2).

```
account1,password1
account2,password2
account3,password3
account4,password4
account5,password5
account6,password6
account7,password7
account8,password8
account9,password9
account10,password10
```

Fig. 27.26 Database **data.txt** containing user names and passwords.

Line 8 ***opens*** the file **data.txt** for reading. The file is given a name (**FILE**) that is used to reference the file, typically called a *file-handle*. The *logical OR operator* (**||**) is used to test whether the file **open**ed properly. If not, function **die** is called to exit the program with the message "**The database could not be opened**".

Line 11 directs the program to repeat while there is still information in the file. Line 13 reads the entire contents of **FILE** into array **@data**, using *function* ***split*** to create a new array entry after every occurrence of the newline character, **\n**. Each username and password is an element in the **@data** array. Line 15 iterates for each ***$entry*** in the array. Function **split** is again called on line 17 to split each individual **$entry** into its two parts. Variables **$name** and **$pass** are grouped by parentheses and separated by a comma. The first value returned by function **split** is the first entry found before the comma in the array—the username; the second entry is the password.

If the condition is true (line 19), the username entered in the Web page was found in the array and the **$userverified** variable is set to **1**. Next, the value of **$pass** is tested against the value in **$password**. If the password entered by the client in the Web browser matches the password for the entered username, the **$passwordverified** variable is set to **1**.

The file is closed on line 30 by calling function **close** with the file handle, **FILE**, as the parameter. Line 32 tests to see whether both the username and password are verified. In order to do this, the Perl *logical AND operator* is required, **&&**. If both conditions are true, the function **accessgranted** is called and a Web page is sent to the client indicating a successful logon. Line 36 tests if a correct username was entered but its valid password was not entered. The user may have forgotten the password or simply mistyped it. The **!**, *logical negation operator*, is used in this instance to negate the value of **$passwordverified**. Function **wrongpassword** is called, indicating that an incorrect password was entered. The **elsif** statement indicates an alternate course of action if the initial **if** statement fails. The last situation that might occur for such a program is when the user enters an invalid username. In this case, function **accessdenied** is called, and a message indicating that permission has been denied is sent to the client and the script is ***exit***ed (line 61).

Perl allows programmers to define their own functions. Keyword ***sub*** begins a function definition and curly braces delimit the function body. To call a function, precede the function call with an ampersand (line 34).

27.9 Sending E-Mail From a Web Browser

One of the most frequently used capabilities of the Internet is email. Many Web sites can email an article or allow a person to check email from anywhere in the world. *Microsoft's Hotmail* service has become tremendously popular, because it allows people to have email addresses at no charge. Hotmail also allows its users to check their mail from most Web browsers. In the example of Fig. 27.27, a Web page is built, using an HTML **FORM**, to allow a user to type and send email.

```
<!DOCTYPE html PUBLIC "-//W3C//DTD HTML 4.0 Transitional//EN">
<!-- Fig. 27.27: email.html -->
<HTML>
<HEAD>
   <TITLE>Web-based email interface.</TITLE>
</HEAD>

<BODY BACKGROUND = "images/back.gif">
   <FORM ACTION = "cgi-bin/mail.pl" METHOD = "POST">
   <TABLE BORDER = "0" CELLSPACING = "0" CELLPADING = "0">

      <TR>
         <TD BGCOLOR = #DDDDDD COLSPAN = 3>
         <INPUT SRC = "images/send.gif" TYPE = "IMAGE">
         <IMG SRC = "images/bar.gif">
         </TD>
      </TR>

```

Fig. 27.27 HTML to display Web-based email **FORM** (part 1 of 3).

```
        <TR>
           <TD BGCOLOR = #DDDDDD WIDTH = "10%"><STRONG>
           <FONT FACE = "Arial" SIZE = "2">To: </FONT>
           </STRONG>
           </TD>
           <TD BGCOLOR = #DDDDDD><INPUT NAME = "TO">
           </TD>
        </TR>

        <TR>
           <TD BGCOLOR = #DDDDDD>
           <P><FONT FACE = Arial SIZE = 2>
           <STRONG>From:</STRONG>
           </FONT></P>
           </TD>
           <TD BGCOLOR = #DDDDDD><INPUT NAME = "FROM">
           </TD>
        </TR>

        <TR>
           <TD BGCOLOR = #DDDDDD>
           <P><FONT FACE = Arial SIZE = 2>
           <STRONG>Subject:</STRONG>
           </FONT></P>
           </TD>
           <TD BGCOLOR = #DDDDDD><INPUT NAME = "SUBJECT">
           </TD>
        </TR>

        <TR>
           <TD BGCOLOR = #DDDDDD>
           <P><FONT FACE = "Arial" SIZE = 2><STRONG><EM>Mail
           Server:</EM></STRONG></FONT></P>
           </TD>
           <TD BGCOLOR = #DDDDDD><INPUT NAME = "MAILSERVER">
           </TD>
        </TR>

        <TR>
           <TD BGCOLOR = #DDDDDD COLSPAN = 3>
           <P>
           <STRONG><FONT FACE = "Arial" SIZE = "2"><BR>Message:
           </FONT>
           </STRONG><BR>
           <TEXTAREA COLS = 50 NAME = "MESSAGE" ROWS = 6
           STYLE = "HEIGHT: 170px; WIDTH: 538px"></TEXTAREA>
           </P><P> </P>
           </TD>
        </TR>

     </TABLE>
     </FORM>
  </HTML>
```

Fig. 27.27 HTML to display Web-based email **FORM** (part 2 of 3).

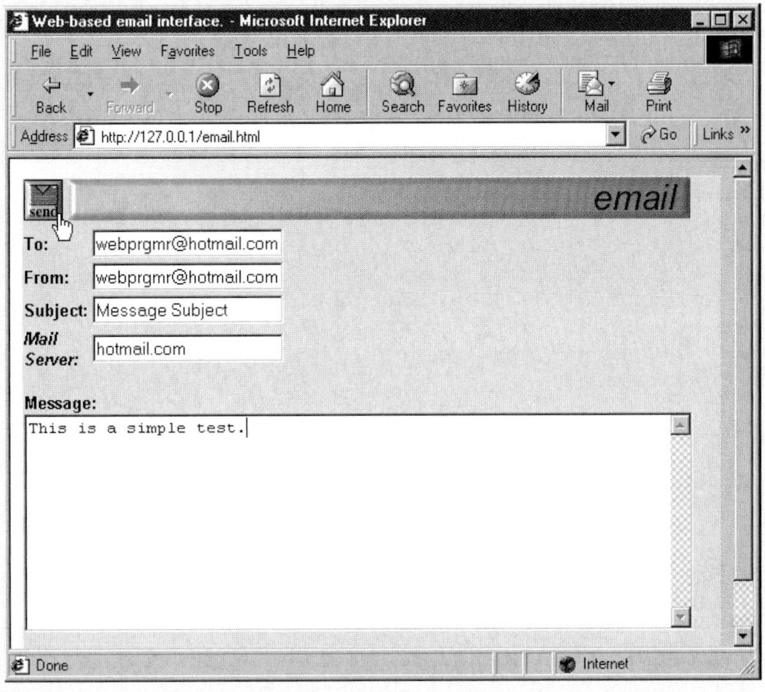

Fig. 27.27 HTML to display Web-based email **FORM** (part 3 of 3).

Software Engineering Observation 27.2

Typically the domain name of the email server should be programmed directly into the Perl program. This allows users to simply type in a message without being concerned about an appropriate mail server.

Figure 27.28 is the Perl script (**`mail.pl`**) that sends email. The email sent contains information that was **`POST`**ed to the server by the Fig. 27.27's Web page. [*Note:* this script and the next use object-based programming techniques. You may want to review Chapter 13 and Section 22.8 before proceeding.]

```
# Fig. 27.28: mail.pl
# Program to send email from a Web-based form.

use Net::SMTP;
use CGI qw/:standard/;

my $to = param("TO");
my $from  = param("FROM");
my $subject  = param("SUBJECT");
my $message  = param("MESSAGE");
my $mailserver = param("MAILSERVER");

```

Fig. 27.28 Results of **`email.html`** after user clicks **send** in Fig. 27.27 (part 1 of 2).

```
13 print header;
14 print "<H3>The request has been Processed. ";
15 print "Thank You $from</H3>";
16
17 $smtp = Net::SMTP->new($mailserver);
18
19 $smtp->mail($ENV{USER});
20 $smtp->to("$to");
21 $smtp->data();
22 $smtp->datasend("To: $to \n");
23 $smtp->datasend("From: $from \n");
24 $smtp->datasend("Subject: $subject \n");
25 $smtp->datasend("\n");
26 $smtp->datasend("$message \n");
27 $smtp->dataend();
28
29 $smtp->quit;
```

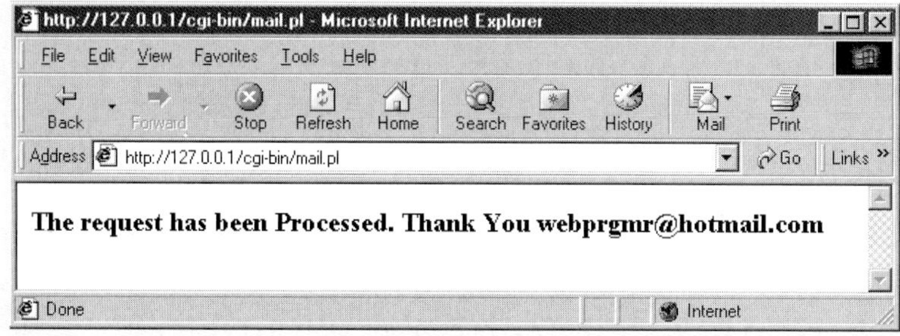

Fig. 27.28 Results of **`email.html`** after user clicks **send** in Fig. 27.27 (part 2 of 2).

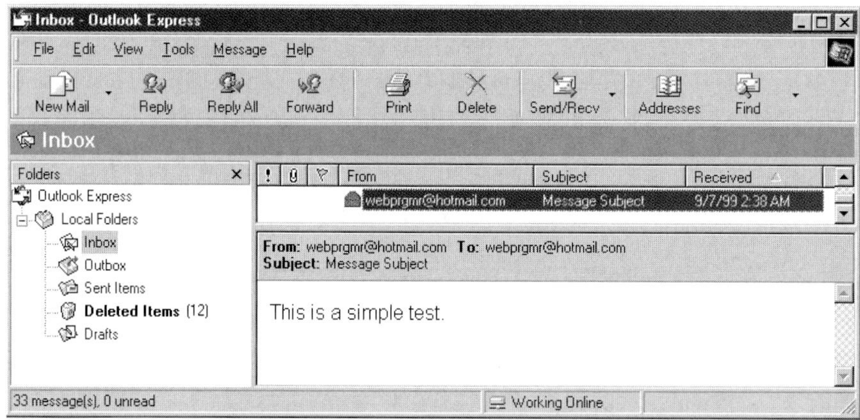

Fig. 27.29 Inbox of Microsoft **Outlook Express** showing a new message.

Line 4 uses keyword **`use`** to include the **`Net`** *package*'s *Simple Mail Transfer Protocol* (**`SMTP`**) functionality. **`SMTP`** is used in this example to send email. Notice, on lines 7 through 11, that the user's data is retrieved and stored in variables with function **`param`**.

Line 17 creates a ***new*** *instance* of a mail server object and passes it the **`$mailserver`** variable. The **`->`** is Perl's *scope operator*, which is equivalent to **`.`** in JavaScript.

Email cannot be sent without a valid **`SMTP`** server. [Note: When using this example, you should use your own mail server to send mail. The mail server that a client usually uses is the domain name after the **`@`** symbol in an email address (e.g., **`hotmail.com`**). Hotmail is not a valid server to use for this program but is used in this example to demonstrate the process.]

Line 20 calls function ***to*** to indicate the email address of the recipient. Line 23 calls function ***datasend*** to tell the mail server that a command is being issued. Line 23 indicates who the message is being sent from by specifying **`From: $from`**. The subject of the message is sent on line 24, again by using function ***datasend***. Line 26 sends the contents of the message, using function **`datasend`** and the parameter **`$message`**—the message input by the user in the HTML **`FORM`**. Line 29 closes the connection to the **`SMTP`** server by calling function ***quit***.

27.10 Using ODBC to Connect to a Database

Database connectivity allows system administrators to maintain such things as user accounts, passwords, credit-card information, mailing lists and product inventory information. Databases allow companies to enter the world of electronic commerce and maintain crucial data. The demands of companies shifting from real-world to cyberspace forced programming languages to support database integration. The Perl package ***Win32-ODBC*** enables Perl programs to connect to ODBC (Open Database Connectivity) data sources. To do database processing, a data source must first be defined by using the Data Source Administrator in Microsoft Windows (see Section 25.5). From a Web browser, the client enters an SQL query string that is sent to the Web server. The Perl script is then executed, querying the database and then sending a record set in the form of an HTML document back to the client.

Figure 27.30 (**`data.html`**) is a Web page that **`POST`**s a form containing an SQL query to the server. Perl script **`data.pl`** (Fig. 27.31) is requested.

```
<!DOCTYPE html PUBLIC "-//W3C//DTD HTML 4.0 Transitional//EN">
<!-- Fig. 27.30: data.html -->

<HTML>
<HEAD>
<TITLE>Sample Database Query</TITLE>
</HEAD>

<BODY BACKGROUND = "images/back.gif">
<BASEFONT FACE = "ARIAL,SANS-SERIF" SIZE = 2>

   <FONT SIZE = +2>
      <STRONG>Querying an ODBC database.</STRONG>
   </FONT><BR>

   <FORM METHOD = "POST" ACTION = "cgi-bin/data.pl">
      <INPUT TYPE = "TEXT" NAME = "QUERY" SIZE = 40
             VALUE = "SELECT * FROM AUTHORS"><BR><BR>
```

Fig. 27.30 Source code and output of the **`data.html`** document (part 1 of 2).

```
19          <INPUT TYPE = "SUBMIT" VALUE = "Send Query">
20       </FORM>
21    </BODY>
22    </HTML>
```

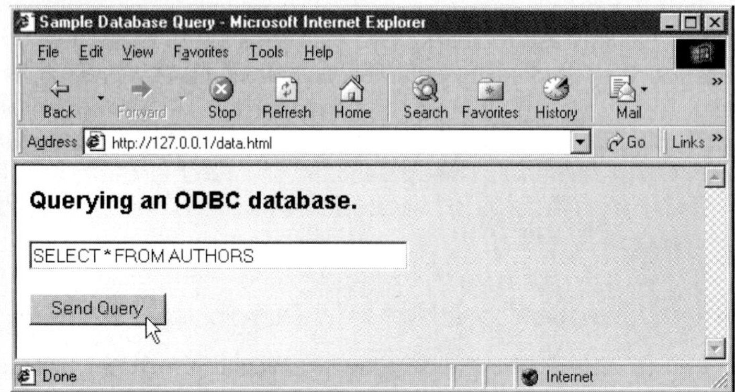

Fig. 27.30 Source code and output of the **data.html** document (part 2 of 2).

Line 16 creates an HTML **FORM** which is used to specify that the data submitted from the **FORM** will be **POST**ed to the Web server and the **ACTION** to occur will be the execution of the **data.pl** Perl script (Fig. 27.31). Line 17 adds a text field to the **FORM** and set its name to **QUERY** and sets the **Value** to an SQL query string. This query specifies that all records (**SELECT ***) are to be retrieved from the **AUTHORS** table inside the **deitel.mdb** database.

Look-and-Feel Observation 27.1

Using tables to output fields in a database organizes information nicely into rows and columns.

The **data.pl** program is responsible for taking the query string and sending the actual SQL statement to the database management system. Line 5 **use**s the ***Win32::ODBC*** package to provide functionality interacting with databases. The **param** function is passed value **QUERY**, the HTML name of the text field. The function returns the string input by the user and assigns it to scalar variable **$querystring**. Line 9 creates scalar variable **$DSN** and assigns it the string **"Products"**. [See Chapter 25 for registering a database as an ODBC data source.] The database used in this example is **deitel.mdb**, which is located in the Chapter 27 examples directory.

```
1   # Fig. 27.31: data.pl
2   # Program to query a database and send
3   # results to the client.
4
5   use Win32::ODBC;
6   use CGI qw/:standard/;
7
```

Fig. 27.31 Data returned by the database query (part 1 of 3).

```
my $querystring = param(QUERY);
$DSN = "Products";

print header;

if (!($Data = new Win32::ODBC($DSN)))
{
   print "Error connecting to $DSN\n";
   print "Error: " . Win32::ODBC::Error() . "\n";
   exit;
}

if ($Data->Sql($querystring))
{
   print "SQL failed.\n";
   print "Error: " . $Data->Error() . "\n";
   $Data->Close();
   exit;
}

print "<BODY BACKGROUND = \"/images/back.gif\">";
print "<BASEFONT FACE = \"ARIAL,SANS-SERIF\" SIZE = 3>";
print "<FONT COLOR = BLUE SIZE = 4> Search Results </FONT>";

$counter = 0;

print "<TABLE BORDER = 0 CELLPADDING = 5 CELLSPACING = 0>";

while($Data->FetchRow())
{

   %Data = $Data->DataHash();
   @key_entries = keys(%Data);

   print "<TR>";

   foreach $key( keys( %Data ) )
   {
      print "<TD BGCOLOR = #9999CC>$Data{$key}</TD>";
   }
   print "</TR>";
   $counter++;
}
print "</TABLE>";
print "<BR>Your search yielded <B>$counter</B> results.";
print "<BR><BR>";
print "<FONT SIZE = 2>";
print "Please email comments to ";
print "<A href = \"mailto:deitel\@deitel.com\">Deitel ";
print "and Associates, Inc.</A>.";
print end_html;

$Data->Close();
```

Fig. 27.31 Data returned by the database query (part 2 of 3).

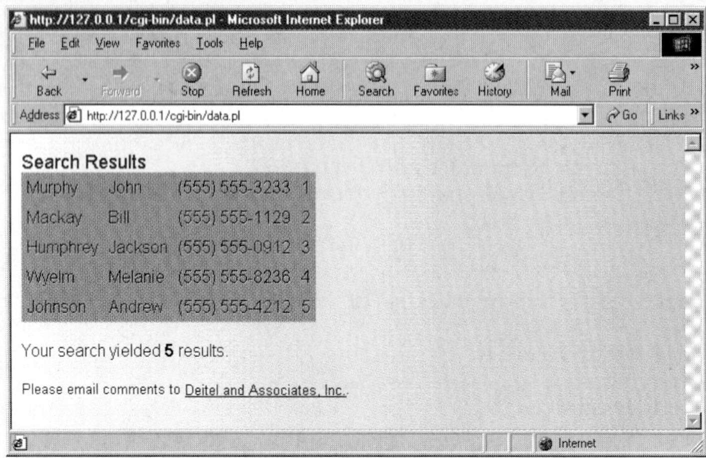

Fig. 27.31 Data returned by the database query (part 3 of 3).

Line 13 connects to the ODBC Data source by passing the Data Source Name, **`$DSN`**, to the constructor for the **`Win32::ODBC`** object. The **`new`** keyword specifies that a new instance of the object is to be created. Variable **`$Data`** is used to query the database. If the condition is false on line 13, lines 15 through 17 are executed. Line 15 reports an error in connecting to the database, and line 16 calls method ***`Win32::ODBC::Error`***, which returns the error that occurred. Line 20 sends the query string to the database. The record set generated by the SQL statement is now contained in variable **`$Data`**. Notice that, if the statement is true, it is perceived to be an error. If an error occurred, lines 22 through 25 are executed. The connection to the database is **`Close`**d on line 24.

Line 32 creates the scalar variable **`$counter`** to store the total number of records in the record set. This technique might be used in a search engine, to report the total number of matches retrieved during a search. Line 36 iterates using the **`while`** statement as long as there is data returned from method ***`FetchRow`***. Line 39 uses method **`DataHash`** to retrieve the fields in a row from the record set. The data is then placed in variable **`%Data`**. Line 40 creates an array of **`key`** values. A **`key`** is associated with a value in an array that is used to specify a particular element of an array. Function **`keys`** is passed the variable **`%Data`** and returns all the keys associated with the hash.

The **`foreach`** loop, line 44, iterates through one row of the record set and divides it according to each field name—every key that exists for **`%Data`**, as specified in the **`deitel.mdb`** database file. Line 46 indicates the start of a new field in the **`TABLE`**. After all fields have been displayed for the current row, the **`foreach`** loop fails and line 48 closes the current row of the table. Line 49 increments the value of **`$counter`**, the total number of results, by one. After all rows of the record set have been displayed, the condition for the **`while`** loop (line 36) fails and the **`TABLE`** is closed (line 51). The number of results is contained in **`$counter`** is sent to the client. Line 58 uses ***`end_html`*** from the **`CGI`** library in place of the closing HTML tag. Line 60 closes the connection to the database by calling method **`Close`**.

27.11 Cookies and Perl

Cookies are used to maintain *state* information for a particular client that uses a Web browser. State information may contain a username, password or specific information that might be helpful when a user returns to the same Web site. Many Web sites use cookies to store a client's postal zip code. The zip code is used when the client requests a Web page from the same server. The server may send the current weather information or news updates for the client's region.

Cookies are small text files saved on the client's machine, containing information that may be useful the next time the client visits the Web site. The cookie is sent back to the Web server whenever the user requests a Web page.

Figure 27.32 uses a script to write a cookie to the client's machine. The **cookies.html** file is used to display an HTML **FORM** that allows a user to enter a name, height and favorite color. When the user clicks the **Write Cookie** button, the **cookies.pl** script (Fig. 27.33) is executed.

Good Programming Practice 27.5

Critical information such as credit card or password information should not be stored using cookies. Cookies cannot be used to retrieve information from a client's computer such as email addresses or data on the hard drive.

```
<!DOCTYPE html PUBLIC "-//W3C//DTD HTML 4.0 Transitional//EN">
<!-- Fig. 27.32: cookies.html -->

<HTML>
   <HEAD>
      <TITLE>Writing a cookie to the client computer</TITLE>
   </HEAD>

<BODY BACKGROUND = "images/back.gif">
<BASEFONT FACE = "ARIAL,SANS-SERIF" SIZE = 2>

   <FONT SIZE = +2>
      <B>Click Write Cookie to save your cookie data.</B>
   </FONT><BR>

   <FORM METHOD = "POST" ACTION = "cgi-bin/cookies.pl">
      <STRONG>Name:</STRONG><BR>
      <INPUT TYPE = "TEXT" NAME = "NAME"><BR>
      <STRONG>Height:</STRONG><BR>
      <INPUT TYPE = "TEXT" NAME = "HEIGHT"><BR>
      <STRONG>Favorite Color</STRONG><BR>
      <INPUT TYPE = "TEXT" NAME = "COLOR"><BR>
      <INPUT TYPE = "SUBMIT" VALUE = "Write Cookie">
   </FORM>
</BODY>
</HTML>
```

Fig. 27.32 Source for **cookies.html** Web page (part 1 of 2).

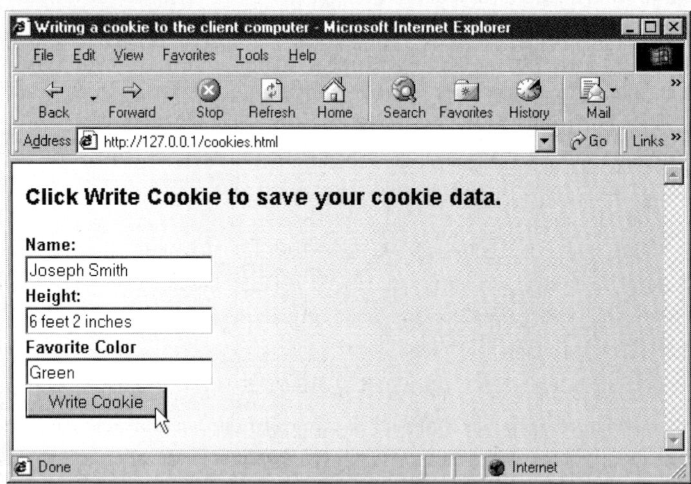

Fig. 27.32 Source for **cookies.html** Web page (part 2 of 2).

```
# Fig. 27.33: cookies.pl
# Program to write a cookie to a client's machine

use CGI qw/:standard/;

my $name = param(NAME);
my $height = param(HEIGHT);
my $color = param(COLOR);

$expires = "Monday, 20-Dec-99 16:00:00 GMT";
$path = "";
$server_domain = "127.0.0.1";

print "Set-Cookie: ";
print "Name", "=", $name, "; expires=", $expires,
      "; path=", $path, "; domain=", $server_domain, "\n";

print "Set-Cookie: ";
print "Height", "=", $height, "; expires=", $expires,
      "; path=", $path, "; domain=", $server_domain, "\n";

print "Set-Cookie: ";
print "Color", "=", $color, "; expires=", $expires,
      "; path=", $path, "; domain=", $server_domain, "\n";
```

Fig. 27.33 Writing a cookie to the client (part 1 of 2).

```
25
26 print header;
27 print "<BODY BACKGROUND = \"/images/back.gif\">";
28 print "<BASEFONT FACE = \"ARIAL,SANS-SERIF\" SIZE = 3>";
29 print "The cookie has been set with the folowing data:";
30 print "<BR><BR>";
31 print "<FONT COLOR=BLUE>Name:</FONT> $name <BR>";
32 print "<FONT COLOR = BLUE>Height:</FONT> $height<BR>";
33 print "<FONT COLOR = BLUE>Favorite Color:</FONT> ";
34 print "<FONT COLOR = $color> $color<BR>";
```

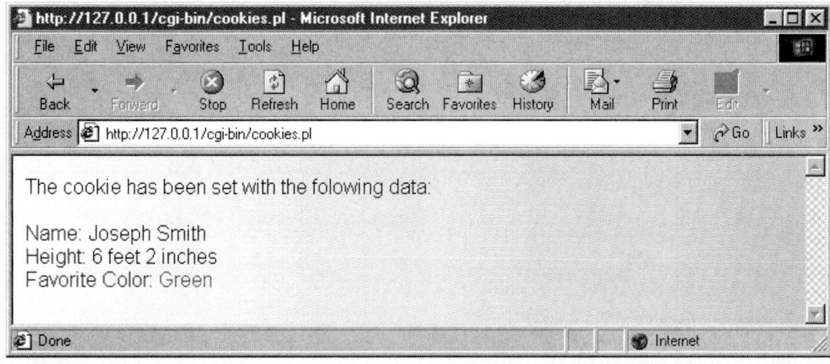

Fig. 27.33 Writing a cookie to the client (part 2 of 2).

The **`cookies.pl`** script reads the data sent from the client on lines 6 through 8. Line 10 declares and initializes variable **`$expires`** to contain the *expiration date of the cookie*. A cookie is deleted by the browser after it expires. Line 12 specifies the domain name of the server, **`127.0.0.1`**, and stores it in variable **`$server_domain`**. When deploying such a cookie on a Web site, this variable should be replaced with your domain name. Line 14 uses the ***`Set-Cookie:`*** *directive* to indicate that the browser should store the incoming data in a cookie. A cookie is sent by the server in an HTTP *response*. Line 15 calls function **`print`** to output a string to save in a cookie on the client's machine. Lines 26 through 34 send a Web page indicating that the cookie has been written to the client.

If the client is Internet Explorer, cookies are stored in the **Temporary Internet Files** directory on the client's machine. Figure 27.34 shows the contents of this directory prior to the execution of **`cookies.pl`**. After the cookie is written, a text file is added to this list. The file **`Cookie:administrator@127.0.0.1`** can be seen in the **Temporary Internet Files** directory in Fig. 27.35.

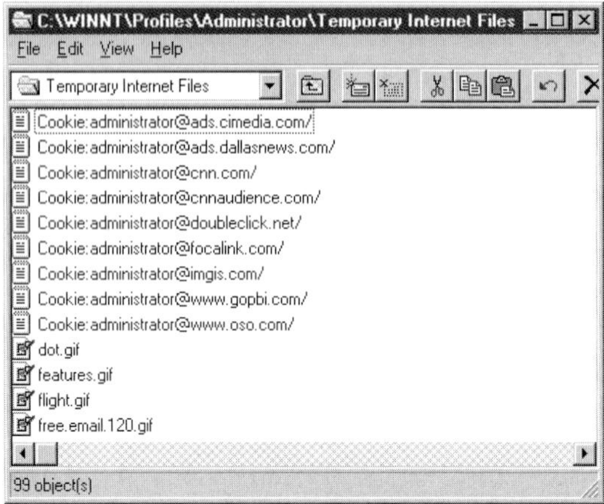

Fig. 27.34 **Temporary Internet Files** directory before a cookie is written.

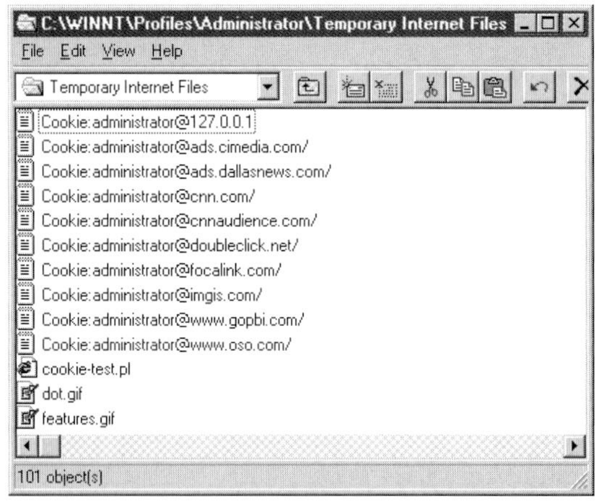

Fig. 27.35 **Temporary Internet Files** directory after a cookie is written.

Figure 27.36 (**read_cookies.pl**) reads the cookie written in Fig. 27.33 and displays the information in a table.

```
# Fig. 27.36: read_cookies.pl
# Program to read cookies from the client's computer

use CGI qw/:standard/;

print header;
print "<BODY BACKGROUND = \"/images/back.gif\">";
print "<BASEFONT FACE = \"ARIAL,SANS-SERIF\" SIZE = 3>";
print "<STRONG>The folowing data is saved in a cookie on your ";
```

Fig. 27.36 Output displaying the cookie's content (part 1 of 2).

```
10  print "computer.<STRONG><BR><BR>";
11
12  my %cookie = &readCookies;
13
14  print ("<TABLE ",
15         "BORDER = \"5\" ",
16         "CELLSPACING = \"0\" ",
17         "CELLPADDING = \"10\">");
18
19  foreach $cookie_name (keys %cookie)
20  {
21     print "<TR>";
22     print "   <TD BGCOLOR=#AAAAFF>$cookie_name</TD>";
23     print "   <TD BGCOLOR=#AAAAAA>$cookie{$cookie_name}</TD>";
24     print "</TR>";
25  }
26  print "</TABLE>";
27
28  sub readCookies
29  {
30     my @cookie_values = split (/; /,$ENV{'HTTP_COOKIE'});
31
32     foreach (@cookie_values)
33     {
34        my ($cookie_name, $cookie_value) = split ( /=/, $_ );
35        $cookies{$cookie_name} = $cookie_value;
36     }
37
38     return %cookies;
39  }
```

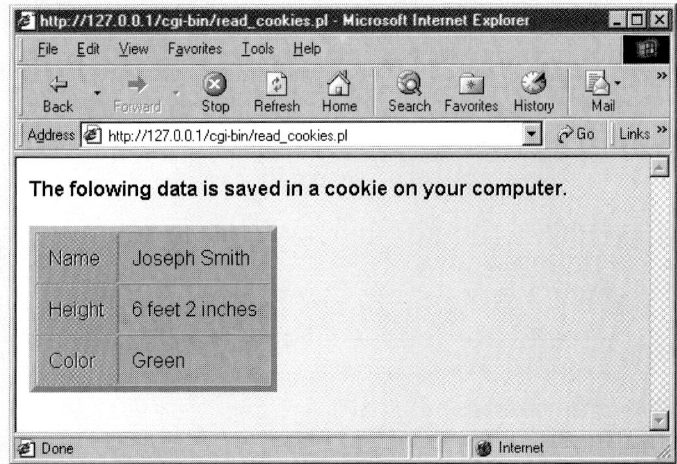

Fig. 27.36 Output displaying the cookie's content (part 2 of 2).

The environment variable contains the cookies sent from the client. Line 12 calls **readCookies** and places the returned information into hash **%cookie**. The **foreach** loop (line 19) iterates through every key in the hash. Line 22 **print**s the name of each cookie, **$cookie_name**, in a cell within an HTML **TABLE**. Line 23 creates an additional cell in the **TABLE** and displays the value for the cookie—**$cookie{$cookie_name}**.

27.12 Case Study: Building a Search Engine

Search engines allow clients to search through catalogs of information for particular data. Typically, a search string is entered by a client using a Web browser, and a program is executed on a Web server that searches through a database. This database typically contains URLs to specific Web sites and descriptions of what these sites offer. This information is sometimes entered by Web administrators but may also be gathered by programs running on the Web server. In the following example, a Web page is designed to allow a user to enter a search string (Fig. 27.37). The string is then used by a Perl script to search through a database to find a description containing the string.

```
<!DOCTYPE html PUBLIC "-//W3C//DTD HTML 4.0 Transitional//EN">
<!-- Fig. 27.37: search.html -->

<HTML>
   <HEAD>
      <TITLE>A Simple Search Engine</TITLE>
   </HEAD>

<BODY BACKGROUND = "images/back.gif">
<BASEFONT FACE = "ARIAL,SANS-SERIF" SIZE = 2>

   <FONT SIZE = +2>
      <STRONG>Enter a search string and click Find.</STRONG>
   </FONT><BR>

   <FORM METHOD = "POST" ACTION = "cgi-bin/search.pl">
      <INPUT TYPE = "TEXT" NAME = "SEARCH"><BR>
      <INPUT TYPE = "SUBMIT" VALUE = "Find">
   </FORM>
</BODY>
</HTML>
```

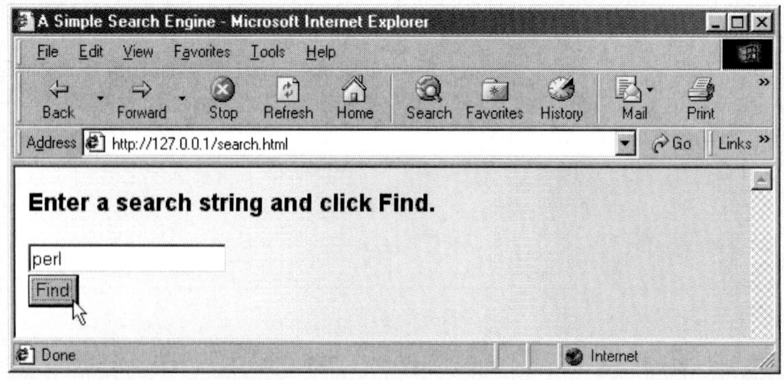

Fig. 27.37 Web site used to enter text to search for with the search engine.

The program searches through a database (Fig. 27.39) to find an instance of the search string sent from the client. Line 6 retrieves the search string by using method **param**, and the value is stored in variable **$search**. The first time that a match is found, a message indicating that a result was found is displayed. Line 12 calls function **open** to set a file handle, **FILE**, for the database, **urls.txt**. Line 17 calls function **split** to separate each line of the file according to the newline character, **\n**, and stores each line as an element in the **@data** array. On line 19, the **foreach** loop is executed for each individual line in the database. Each of these lines is stored in **$entry**.

```
1  # Fig. 27.38: search.pl
2  # Program to search for Web pages
3
4  use CGI qw/:standard/;
5
6  my $search = param(SEARCH);
7  my $counter = 0;
8
9  print header;
10 print "<BASEFONT FACE = \"ARIAL,SANS-SERIF\" SIZE = 3>";
11
12 open(FILE, "urls.txt") ||
13    die "The URL database could not be opened";
14
15 while(<FILE>)
16 {
17    my @data = split(/\n/);
18
19    foreach $entry (@data)
20    {
21       my ($data, $url) = split(/;/, $entry);
22
23       if ($data =~ /$search/i)
24       {
25          if ($counter == 0)
26          {
27             print "<STRONG>Search Results:<BR><BR></STRONG>";
28          }
29
30          print "<A HREF=\"http://$url/\">";
31          print "http://$url/";
32          print "</A>";
33          print "<BR>$data<BR><BR>";
34          $counter++;
35       }
36    }
37 }
38 close FILE;
39
40 if ($counter == 0)
41 {
42    print "<B>Sorry, no results were found matching </B>";
```

Fig. 27.38 Perl program to implement a simple search engine (part 1 of 2).

```
43      print "<FONT COLOR = BLUE>$search</FONT>. ";
44   }
45   else
46   {
47      print "<STRONG>$counter matches found for </STRONG>";
48      print "<FONT COLOR = BLUE>$search</FONT>";
49   }
```

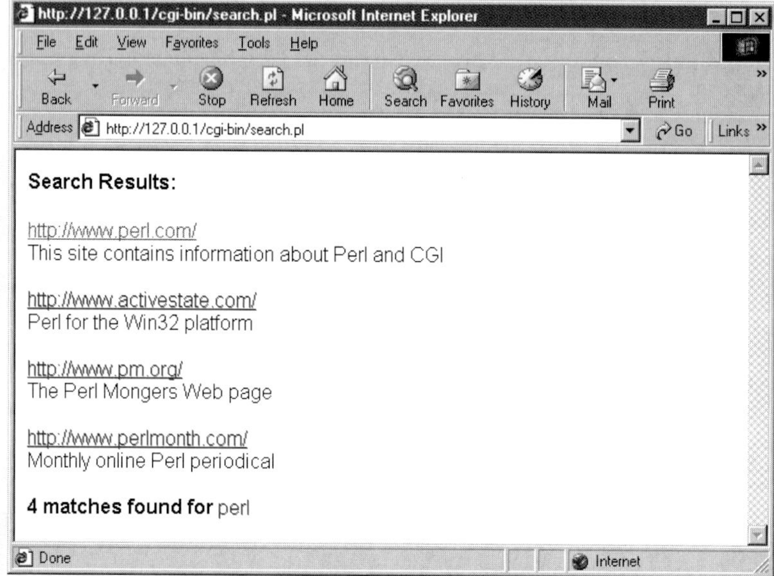

Fig. 27.38 Perl program to implement a simple search engine (part 2 of 2).

```
This site contains information about Perl and CGI;www.perl.com
The Deitel and Deitel Web Site;www.deitel.com
Purchase books on this web site;www.amazon.com
Perl for the Win32 platform;www.activestate.com
The Perl Mongers Web page;www.pm.org
Monthly online Perl periodical;www.perlmonth.com
```

Fig. 27.39 Database (**`urls.txt`**) containing URLs and brief descriptions of the Web sites.

The database is separated into two fields by using a semicolon delimiter. The first field of the database contains a brief description of a Web site, while the second contains the link, or URL, to the site. Line 21 **`split`**s the individual line using the semicolon delimiter (**`;`**). The value of the first field is placed in **`$data`**, and the URL is placed in **`$url`**. On Line 23, the matching operator, **`=~`**, checks if the regular expression, **`/$search/i`**, is found within the Web site description, **`$data`**. The **`/i`** indicates that the case of the string should be ignored when matching. If a match is found, line 25 tests to see whether this is the first time. If this is the first match, a message is displayed. Lines 30 through 32 output the text for the link and set a hyperlink to the actual URL. Line 33 displays the data associated with the URL, as can be seen in the output (Fig. 27.40). For each match, **`$counter`** is incremented by **`1`**.

This counter provides the user with a total number of matches found for the request. If no matches were found for the search, lines 42 and 43 are executed, indicating that no results were found. If a match was found, line 47 displays the total number of results.

27.13 Internet and World Wide Web Resources

`http://www.perl.com/`
`Perl.com` is the first place to look for information about Perl. The homepage provides up-to-date news on Perl, answers to common questions about Perl, and an impressive collection of links to Perl resources of all kinds on the Internet. It includes sites for Perl software, tutorials, user groups and demos.

`http://www.activestate.com/`
From this site you can download ActivePerl—the Perl 5 implementation for Windows.

`http://www.activestate.com/packages/`
From this site you can download various Perl packages.

`http://www.perl.com/CPAN/README.html`
The "Comprehensive Perl Archive Network" is exactly what the name suggests. Here you will find an extensive listing of Perl related information.

`http://www.perl.com/CPAN/scripts/index.html`
This is the scripts index from the CPAN archive. Here you will find a wealth of scripts written in Perl.

`http://www.pm.org/`
This is the homepage of Perl Mongers, a group dedicated to supporting the Perl community. This site is helpful in finding others in the Perl community to converse with; Perl Mongers has established Perl user groups around the globe.

`http://www.speakeasy.org/~cgires/`
This is a collection of tutorials and scripts that can provide a thorough understanding of CGI and of how it is used.

`http://www.cgi101.com/`
CGI 101 is a site for those looking to improve their programming ability through familiarity with CGI. The site contains a six-chapter class outlining techniques for CGI programming in the Perl language. The class includes both basics and more sophisticated scripts, with working examples. Also included in the site are script libraries and links to other helpful sources.

`http://www.jmarshall.com/easy/cgi/`
A good, brief explanation of CGI for those with programming experience.

`http://wdvl.internet.com/Authoring/Languages/Perl/Resources.html`
This site contains many links to Perl resources.

`http://wdvl.internet.com/Authoring/CGI/`
The Web Developer's Virtual Library provides tutorials for learning both CGI and Perl, the language most commonly used in developing CGIs.

`http://www.perlmonth.com`
Perlmonth is a monthly online periodical devoted to Perl, with featured articles from professional programmers. This is a good source for those who use Perl frequently and wish to keep up on the latest developments involving Perl.

http://www.itknowledge.com/tpj/
The Perl Journal is a large magazine dedicated to Perl. Subscribers are provided with up-to-date Perl news and articles, on the Internet as well as in printed form.

http://home.t-online.de/home/wahls/perlnet.html
This page provides a brief tutorial on Perl network programming for those who already know the language. The tutorial uses code examples to explain the basics of network communication.

http://www.w3.org/CGI/
The World Wide Web Consortium page on CGI is concerned with security issues involving the Common Gateway Interface. This page provides links concerning CGI specifications, as indicated by the National Center for Supercomputing Applications (NCSA).

SUMMARY

- CGI allows for programs running externally—such as Web browsers—to interface with programs running on a Web server.
- Permission is granted within the Web server by a Web master, or author of the Web site to allow specific programs to be executed on the Web server.
- Typically all CGI programs reside in directory **/cgi-bin**.
- Since CGI is an interface, it cannot be directly programmed—a script or executable program must be used to interact with it.
- The standard output from server-side applications or scripts is redirected, or piped, to the Common Gateway Interface and then sent over the Internet to the Web browser to be displayed.
- Perl (Practical Extraction and Report Language) is a high-level programming language developed by Larry Wall while working at Unisys; he now works at O'Reilly & Associates as a developer and researcher for the Perl programming language.
- Perl has particularly rich, easy-to-use, text-processing capabilities.
- While Perl was initially developed on the UNIX platform, it was always intended to be a cross-platform computer language.
- ActivePerl is the version of Perl for the Windows platform.
- The extension for Perl programs is **.pl** and is, by default, associated with the Perl interpreter.
- The **#** character indicates that the remainder of the line is a comment.
- The **\n** escape sequence is used to move the cursor to the next line for printing.
- Semicolons are used to terminate statements in Perl.
- The **$** character specifies that a variable contains a scalar value.
- A scalar variable holds information such as strings, integer numbers and floating point numbers.
- The range operator (**..**) specifies a range of values.
- In addition to the core implementation of Perl, add-ons known as packages can be used to provide additional functionality.
- Packages provide programmers with extensions to core Perl and are often designed for platform-specific reasons.
- To run CGI scripts with PWS several modifications must be made to the Windows Registry.
- Perl text manipulation is usually done through the use of regular expressions—patterns of characters used to search through text files and databases.

- Operator **eq** tests if two strings are equal.
- The Perl 5 keyword **my** is used to indicate that the variable is only valid for the block of code in which it was defined.
- Perl contains a built-in matching operator (**=~**) that tests if a match for a string is found within a variable.
- CGI environment variables contain such information as the type of Web browser the client is using, the version of CGI that the server is running, the HTTP host, HTTP connection, etc.
- The **use** statement allows Perl programs to include the contents of predefined packages.
- Packages contain Perl code known as libraries.
- The **param** method is part of the Perl 5 **CGI** module and is responsible for getting the value of an HTML tag.
- Server-side includes (SSIs) are commands embedded in HTML documents to provide for content creation.
- Server-side includes allow Web masters to include such things as the current time, date, or even the contents of an entirely different HTML document.
- Server-side includes are coded by embedding commands within an HTML document.
- The **!**, logical negation operator, is used to negate the value of an expression.
- The Perl package **Win32-ODBC** enables Perl programs to connect to ODBC (Open Database Connectivity) data sources.
- A Data Source Name is used by the Perl program, or any other language allowing ODBC connectivity, to refer to a database.
- Cookies are used to maintain state information for a particular client using a Web browser.
- Cookies are small text files saved on the client's machine containing information that may be useful the next time the client visits the Web site.
- The cookie is sent back to the Web server whenever the user requests a Web page.
- A cookie is set by the server in an HTTP response.
- Search engines allow clients to search through catalogs of information for particular data.
- Typically a search string is entered by a client using a Web browser and a program is executed on a Web server that searches through a database. This database typically contains URLs to specific Web sites and descriptions of what these sites offer.

TERMINOLOGY

comment character
=~ matching operator
$_ variable in Perl
* mask character
== numerical equality operator in Perl
&& logical and operator in Perl
! logical negation operator
\n newline character
{} braces denoting a block of code
.pl
ActivePerl
Advanced Options icon in PWS
Apache Web Server
business logic
business rules
cgi-bin directory
CGI environment variables
CGI library
client
command-line switches in Perl
Common Gateway Interface (CGI)
CONFIG command
cookies
CPAN (Comprehensive Perl Archive Network)
Data Source Administrator (Microsoft Windows)
Data Source Name (DSN)

DATE_GMT variable
DATE_LOCAL variable
DOCUMENT_NAME variable
ECHO command
end_html keyword from **CGI** library
%ENV table in Perl
eq operator in Perl
EXEC SSI command
exit function
expiration date of a cookie
FLASTMOD SSI command
foreach statement in Perl
for statement in Perl
FSIZE command
GATEWAY_INTERFACE variable
GET command HTTP
hit counter (for a Web page)
HKEY_LOCAL_MACHINE
Hotmail
HTML
HTTP **GET** command
HTTP header
HTTP_USER_AGENT variable
HyperText Transfer Protocol (HTTP)
if statement in Perl
indexed array
Internet
interpreter
LAST_MODIFIED
libraries
libwww-perl.ppd package
Logical AND operator, **&&**
logical negation operator, **!**
logical OR operator, **||**
mask character (*****)
matching operator (**=~**)
metacharacters in regular expressions
Microsoft **Registry Editor**
MIME types
modifying characters
modules
my function
packages in Perl
param method of Perl5 **CGI** module
Perl
perl.exe
Perl interpreter
Perl Package Manager
Personal Web Server (PWS)
.pl extension for Perl programs
POST command in HTTP
ppm
Practical Extraction and Report Language (Perl)
print function in Perl
PWS (Personal Web Server)
range operator (**..**)
regedit
Registry
Registry Editor
Registry menu
regular expressions
REMOTE_ADDR variable
scalar variable
script
search engine
server
SERVER_NAME variable
server-side include (SSI) in Perl
SERVER_SOFTWARE variable
.SHTML file extension
SMTP (Simple Mail Transfer Protocol)
sort function in Perl
split function
SSI (Server-Side Include)
standard input
standard output
string processing
use statement in Perl
Wall, Larry
Web client
Web page hit counter
Web search engine
Web server
while statement in Perl
Win32-API Perl package
Win32-ODBC Perl package
XML-Parser Perl package

COMMON PROGRAMMING ERRORS

27.1 Forgetting to terminate a statement with a **;** is a syntax error.

27.2 Failure to place a preceding **$** character before a scalar variable name is an error.

27.3 Using an uninitialized variable might make a numerical calculation incorrect. Consider multiplying a number by an uninitialized variable. The result is **0**.

GOOD PROGRAMMING PRACTICES

27.1 Using business logic ensures that invalid information is not stored into databases.

27.2 Use meaningful HTML object names for input fields. This makes Perl programs easier to understand when retrieving **FORM** data.

27.3 When opening a text file to read its contents, open the file in read-only mode. Opening the file in other modes allows for the possibility of data to accidentally be overwritten.

27.4 Always close files as soon as you are finished with them.

27.5 Critical information such as credit card or password information should not be stored using cookies. Cookies cannot be used to retrieve information from a client's computer such as email addresses or data on the hard drive.

LOOK-AND-FEEL OBSERVATION

27.1 Using tables to output fields in a database organizes information nicely into rows and columns.

PERFORMANCE TIP

27.1 Parsing HTML documents on a server can dramatically increase the load on that server. To increase the performance of a heavily loaded server try to limit the use of Server-Side Includes.

SOFTWARE ENGINEERING OBSERVATIONS

27.1 Using packages, pre-defined portions of reusable code, greatly reduces the time required to develop applications.

27.2 Typically the domain name of the email server should be programmed directly into the Perl program. This allows users to simply type in a message without being concerned about an appropriate mail server.

TESTING AND DEBUGGING TIPS

27.1 When running a Perl script from the command line, always use the *-w* option. The program may seem to execute correctly when there is actually something wrong with the source code. The **-w** option displays warnings encountered while executing a Perl program.

27.2 Function **print** can be used to display the value of a variable at a particular point during a program's execution. This is often helpful in debugging a program.

27.3 While it is not always necessary to initialize variables before using them, doing so can avoid errors.

SELF-REVIEW EXERCISES

27.1 Answer each of the following:

a) The _______ Protocol is used by Web browsers and Web servers to communicate with each other.

b) Typically all CGI programs reside in directory _______.

c) To output warnings as a Perl program executes, the _______ command-line switch should be used.
d) The three data types in Perl are _______, _______ and _______.
e) _______ are divided into individual elements that can each contain an individual scalar variable.
f) To test the equality of two strings operator _______ should be used.
g) Business _______ is used to ensure that invalid data is not entered into a database.
h) _______ includes allow Web masters to include such things as the current time, date, or even the contents of an entirely different HTML document.

27.2 State whether the following are *true* or *false*. If *false*, explain why.
a) Documents containing Server Side Includes must have a file extension of **.SSI** in order to be parsed by the server.
b) A valid HTTP header must be sent to the client to ensure that the browser displays the information correctly.
c) The numerical equality operator, **eq**, is used to determine if two numbers are equal.
d) Perl keyword **my** is used to indicate that a variable is only valid for the block of code in which it was defined.
e) Perl has a built-in matching operator, =, that tests if a matching string is found within a variable.
f) Cookies can read information from a client's hard drive such as email addresses and personal files.
g) An example of a valid HTTP header is: **Content-type text\html**.
h) CGI environment variables contain such information as the type of Web browser the client is running.

ANSWERS TO SELF-REVIEW EXERCISES

27.1 a) Hypertext Transfer. b) **/cgi-bin**. c) **-w**. d) scalar variable, indexed array and hash. e) Arrays. f) **eq**. g) logic. h) Server-side.

27.2 a) False. Documents containing Server Side Includes must have a file extension of **.SHTML**. b) True. c) False. The numerical equality operator is ==. d) True. e) False. The built-in matching operator is, =~. f) False. Cookies do not have access to private information such as email addresses or private data stored on the hard drive. g) False. A valid HTTP header might be: **Content-type: text/html**. h) True.

EXERCISES

27.3 How can a Perl program determine the type of browser a Web client is using?

27.4 Describe how input from an HTML **FORM** is retrieved in a Perl program.

27.5 How does a Web browser determine how to handle or display incoming data?

27.6 What is the terminology for a command that is embedded in an HTML document and parsed by a server prior to being sent?

27.7 Describe how an email message can be sent from a Perl program.

27.8 In the text we presented CGI environment variables. Develop a program that determines whether or not the client is using Internet Explorer. If so, determine the version number and send that information back to the client.

27.9 Modify the program of Fig. 27.25 to save information sent to the server into a text file.

27.10 Write a Perl program that tests whether an email addresses is input correctly. A valid email address contains a series of characters followed by the **`@`** character and a domain name.

27.11 Using CGI environment variables, write a program that logs the addresses (obtained with the **`REMOTE_ADDR`** CGI environment variable) that request information from the Web server.

27.12 Write a Perl program that stores URL information into a database using **`Win32::ODBC`**. The first field of the database should contain an actual URL and the second should contain a description of that URL.

27.13 Modify the program of Exercise 27.12 to query the database and return the results to the client.

28

XML (Extensible Markup Language)

Objectives

- To understand what XML is.
- To understand the relationship between HTML and XML.
- To understand how to create new markup tags.
- To be able to parse XML tags on a Web client.
- To understand the relationship between a DTD and an XML document.
- To understand the concept of schema.
- To be able to create style sheets using XSL.
- To understand the role of XHTML in Web publishing.

It is the huge buildings of commerce and trade which now align the people to attention.
Sean O'Casey

If you describe things as better than they are, you are considered to be romantic; if you describe things as worse than they are, you will be called a realist; and if you describe things exactly as they are, you will be thought of as a satirist.
Quentin Crisp

Like everything metaphysical, the harmony between thought and reality is to be found in the grammar of the language.
Ludwig Wittgenstein

Oh! what a snug little Island, A right little, tight little Island!
Thomas Dibdin

Outline

28.1 Introduction[1]

In Chapter 23, we discussed XML (Extensible Markup Language) in the context of electronic commerce. In this chapter, we discuss creating and manipulating XML documents.

We have covered HTML, which is structured and concrete. HTML markup is for displaying information, while XML markup is for describing data of virtually any type. Actually, HTML is a markup language, whereas XML is a markup language and a language for creating markup languages. HTML is a markup language for marking up documents with such book-like elements as headings and paragraphs. XML enables the creation of new markup languages to markup anything imaginable (such as mathematical formulas, the molecular structure of chemicals, music, recipes, etc.).

HTML limits you to a fixed collection of tags. These tags are used primarily to describe how content is displayed, such as by making text bold or italic or making headings large or small. With XML, you can create new tags. If we have a database of books, you can have tags specifying book titles, prices, ISBN numbers or anything else you would like.

XML derives from *SGML* (*Standard Generalized Markup Language*), which was established in 1986 as an electronic document exchange standard. SGML is for structuring documents. Using the structure of a document, you can then apply formatting or decide the layout. For example, a newspaper article is structured into headlines, images and text. Within each of these elements may be other information, such as quotes. Given a markup, deciding how to display the information is arbitrary, since it is the content that truly matters.

With XML, you store information in a structured manner. The difference between SGML and XML is that XML is interoperable with both HTML and SGML. This is done so the data can be displayed (e.g., using HTML) or be integrated with SGML documents.

---

1. Deitel & Associates, Inc. is currently writing *XML How to Program*. We will be putting historical and technical information about XML on our Web site (**`http://www.deitel.com/`**).

Portability Tip 28.1

XML is defined by the World Wide Web Consortium (W3C) to be application and vender neutral—which ensures maximum portability.

28.2 Structuring Data

In this section and throughout this chapter, we will create our own custom XML markup. With XML, element types can be declared to describe data structure. This allows the programmer an incredible amount of flexibility in describing data. Tags are used to show the beginning and end of elements (or in the case of empty elements, the complete element).

Figure 28.1 shows how we can format a simple news article using XML. The creator of this document simply uses the tags—once they are familiar with them—the same way HTML tags are used.

Common Programming Error 28.1

XML is case sensitive. Using the wrong case for an XML tag is a syntax error.

We begin by defining the document with *XML declaration* **`xml`** (line 1). This lets a *parser* (i.e., a program responsible for processing an XML document—we will say more about parsers in Section 28.5) know that a specific ***`version`*** of XML is being used. Version **`1.0`** of the XML specification is complete and will not change. New versions of XML will be released as XML evolves to meet the requirements of many fields, especially electronic commerce (see Chapter 23).

```
1   <?xml version = "1.0"?>
2
3   <!-- Fig. 28.1: article.xml         -->
4   <!-- Article formatted with XML     -->
5
6   <article>
7
8      <title>Simple XML</title>
9
10     <date>September 6, 1999</date>
11
12     <author>
13        <fname>Tem</fname>
14        <lname>Nieto</lname>
15     </author>
16
17     <summary>XML is pretty easy.</summary>
18
19     <content>Once you have mastered HTML, XML is easily
20        learned. You must remember that XML is not for
21        displaying information but for managing information.
22     </content>
23
24  </article>
```

Fig. 28.1 An article formatted with XML.

We start the document by writing the *root element*, **`article`** (line 6). A root element contains all other elements (e.g., **`title`**, **`date`**, **`author`** etc.) in the document. Lines preceding the root element are collectively called the *prolog*.

Common Programming Error 28.2

Attempting to create more than one root element is a syntax error.

Because the article we are defining has a title, author, date, summary and content, we create *sub-elements* (also called *children*) for each one of these within the **`article`** element. The **`title`** element (line 8) contains the text for the title of the article. Similarly the **`date`** (line 10), **`summary`** (line 17) and **`content`** (line 19) elements contain the text appropriate for their tags.

The **`author`** element is a *container element*, because it contains sub-elements: **`fname`** (line 13) and **`lname`** (line 14). These elements contain the author's first name and last name, respectively.

Now that we have seen a simple XML document, let us examine a slightly more complex XML document that represents a business letter (Fig. 28.2).

```
<?xml version = "1.0"?>

<!-- Fig. 28.2: letter.xml                      -->
<!-- Business letter formatted with XML         -->

<!DOCTYPE letter SYSTEM "letter.dtd">

<letter>

   <contact type = "from">
      <name>John Doe</name>
      <address1>123 Main St.</address1>
      <address2></address2>
      <city>Anytown</city>
      <state>Anystate</state>
      <zip>12345</zip>
      <phone>555-1234</phone>
      <flag id = "P"/>
   </contact>

   <contact type = "to">
      <name>Joe Schmoe</name>
      <address1>Box 12345</address1>
      <address2>15 Any Ave.</address2>
      <city>Othertown</city>
      <state>Otherstate</state>
      <zip>67890</zip>
      <phone>555-4321</phone>
      <flag id = "B"/>
   </contact>

   <paragraph>Dear Sir,</paragraph>
```

Fig. 28.2 A business letter formatted with XML (part 1 of 2).

```
33
34      <paragraph>It is our privilege to inform you about our new
35         database managed with XML. This new system will allow
36         you to reduce the load of your inventory list server by
37         having the client machine perform the work of sorting
38         and filtering the data.</paragraph>
39      <paragraph>Sincerely, Mr. Doe</paragraph>
40
41   </letter>
```

Fig. 28.2 A business letter formatted with XML (part 2 of 2).

As with the previous example, we begin the document's definition with the **xml** declaration (line 1). Line 6

```
<!DOCTYPE letter SYSTEM "letter.dtd">
```

specifies the *document type definition (DTD)* file for the business letter. Document type definition files define the grammatical rules for the document. This tag contains three items: the name of the root element to which the DTD is applied, the ***SYSTEM*** flag (which denotes an external DTD), and the DTD's name and location (i.e., "**letter.dtd**"). By convention, XML documents end in the ***.xml*** extension and DTD documents in the ***.dtd*** extension. We discuss document type definition files in greater detail in the next section.

The root element is **letter**, which contains the sub-elements **contact** and **paragraph**. The first **contact** element (line 10) contains a ***type*** attribute with value "**from**" that identifies the letter's sender. The second **contact** element (line 21) has **type "to"**, which identifies the letter's recipient. In the **contact** element, we store the contact's name, address and phone number. The **paragraph** elements contain the letter's body text.

On line 18, we introduce a *empty element*, ***flag***—which does not have a matching end tag. For example, the **<IMG>** tag is an HTML empty element. In XML, empty elements must be terminated with a *forward slash* (**/**). We use this empty element to indicate whether the contact is primarily a business contact (i.e., "**B**") or a personal contact (i.e., "**P**").

Common Programming Error 28.3

Not terminating an empty element with a forward slash (/) is a syntax error.

Common Programming Error 28.4

Omitting a closing XML tag is a syntax error.

Common Programming Error 28.5

Omitting quotes (either single or double) around an XML attribute's value is a syntax error.

28.3 Document Type Definitions (DTDs)

In Fig. 28.2, we presented a simple business letter formatted with XML. The business letter's list of element types, attributes and their relationships to each other are specified using a document type definition (*DTD*). A DTD is not required for an XML document but is recommended for document conformity. It provides a method to type check an XML document, thus verifying its *validity* (e.g., tags are closed, tags contain the proper attributes etc.). Specifying the set of rules that structure a document is done with *EBNF* (*Extended Backus-Naur Form*) *grammar*—which sometimes uses a regular expression syntax. Let us define in Fig. 28.3 the set of rules (i.e., the grammar) for structuring the business letter document of Fig. 28.2. This DTD file is the one specified on line 6 in Fig. 28.2.

Line 1's ***!ELEMENT*** *element type declaration* specifies that an element is being created. In this case, this element contains one or more **contact** elements and one or more **paragraph** elements, in that order. The *plus sign* (**+**) *operator* indicates one or more occurrences. Other operators include the *asterisk* (*****), which indicates any number of occurrences and the *question mark* (**?**), which indicates either zero occurrences or exactly one occurrence. If an operator is omitted, exactly one occurrence is assumed.

The **contact** element definition on line 3 specifies that it contains ***name***, ***address1***, ***address2***, ***city***, ***state***, ***zip***, ***phone*** and ***flag*** elements—in that order. Exactly one occurrence of each is expected.

Line 5

```
<!ATTLIST contact type CDATA #IMPLIED>
```

uses the ***!ATTLIST*** element type declaration to define an attribute (i.e., **type**) for the **contact** element type. Flag ***#IMPLIED*** indicates that the attribute is unspecified—the system gives it a value. Flag ***CDATA*** defines that this attribute contains a string.

Flag ***#PCDATA*** (line 7) specifies that this element can store *parsed character data* (i.e., text). Line 14

```
<!ELEMENT flag (EMPTY)>
```

creates an empty element named **flag**. Keyword ***EMPTY*** specifies that the element does not contain content. Empty elements are commonly used for their attributes.

Portability Tip 28.2

DTDs ensure that XML documents created by different programs are consistent.

```
1  <!ELEMENT letter (contact+, paragraph+)>
2
3  <!ELEMENT contact (name, address1, address2, city, state,
4     zip, phone, flag)>
5  <!ATTLIST contact type CDATA #IMPLIED>
6
7  <!ELEMENT name (#PCDATA)>
8  <!ELEMENT address1 (#PCDATA)>
9  <!ELEMENT address2 (#PCDATA)>
10 <!ELEMENT city (#PCDATA)>
11 <!ELEMENT state (#PCDATA)>
12 <!ELEMENT zip (#PCDATA)>
13 <!ELEMENT phone (#PCDATA)>
14 <!ELEMENT flag (EMPTY)>
15 <!ATTLIST flag id CDATA #IMPLIED>
16
17 <!ELEMENT paragraph (#PCDATA)>
```

Fig. 28.3 Business letter DTD.

Common Programming Error 28.6

Any element, attribute, tag or relationship not explicitly defined by a DTD is an error.

28.4 Customized Markup Languages

Many applications for XML have been created for structuring data in various fields. In the mathematics field, *MathML (Mathematical Markup Language)* has been developed for describing mathematical notation. Up to this point in time, mathematical expressions have always been displayed by using images or special software packages such as TeX and LaTeX, which do not describe the information in a meaningful manner. So MathML creates a method for describing mathematical expressions on the Web.

Some other examples of XML applications are: *Chemical Markup Language (CML)*, *Speech Markup Language (SpeechML)*, *Extensible Financial Reporting Markup Language (XFRML)*, *Synchronized Multimedia Interface Language (SMIL)* and *Product Data Markup Language (PDML)*.

An application that can render MathML is the *Amaya* editor from the W3C, which can be downloaded at **`http://www.w3.org/Amaya/`**. Amaya is W3C's browser and editing tool for HTML and XML. At the W3 Web site, you will find a link to **Amaya 2.1public release**:

`http://www.w3.org/Amaya/User/BinDist.html`

On this page, there are several download links for Amaya. Download versions include Windows 95/98/NT, Linux and Solaris. Amaya documentation and installation notes are also available at the W3 Web site.

MathML markup is used as a simple method of describing mathematical expressions for display. Figure 28.4 uses MathML to mark up a simple expression.

```
<!DOCTYPE HTML PUBLIC "-//W3C//DTD HTML 4.0 Transitional//EN">
<HTML>

<!-- Fig. 28.4: mathml1.html -->
<!-- Simple MathML            -->

<BODY>

<MATH>
   <mrow>
      <mn>2</mn>
      <mo>+</mo>
      <mn>3</mn>
      <mo>=</mo>
      <mn>5</mn>
   </mrow>
</MATH>

</BODY>
</HTML>
```

Fig. 28.4 An expression marked up with MathML (part 1 of 2).

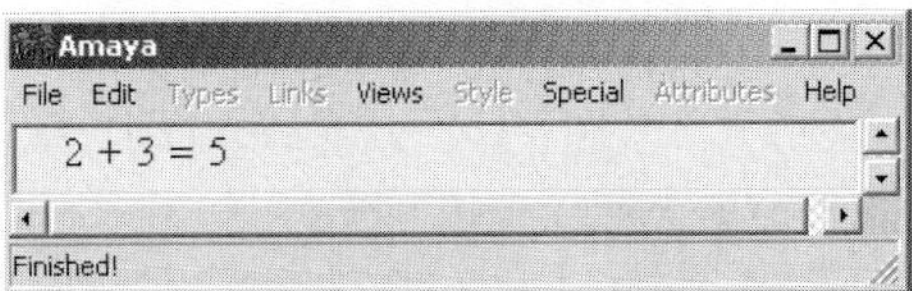

Fig. 28.4 An expression marked up with MathML (part 2 of 2).

We embed the MathML content into an HTML file by using the HTML ***MATH*** element (line 9). Inside the **MATH** element, we embed MathML.

The ***mrow*** *element* (line 10) is a container element for expressions containing more than one element. In this case, it contains five elements. The ***mn*** *element* (line 11) is used to mark up a number. The ***mo*** *element* (line 12) is used to markup an operator (i.e., **+**). By using this markup, we define the expression: *2+3=5*, which could be input into a math software program that supported MathML.

Let us now consider using MathML to mark up an algebraic equation (Fig. 28.5) that uses exponents and arithmetic operators.

```
<!DOCTYPE HTML PUBLIC "-//W3C//DTD HTML 4.0 Transitional//EN">
<HTML>

<!-- Fig. 28.5: mathml2.html -->
<!-- Simple MathML           -->

<BODY>

<MATH>
   <mrow>

      <mrow>
         <mn>3</mn>
         <mo>&InvisibleTimes;</mo>
         <msup>
            <mi>x</mi>
            <mn>2</mn>
         </msup>
      </mrow>

      <mo>+</mo>
      <mi>x</mi>
      <mo>-</mo>
      <mfrac>
         <mn>2</mn>
         <mi>x</mi>
      </mfrac>
      <mo>=</mo>
      <mn>0</mn>
   </mrow>
</MATH>
```

Fig. 28.5 An algebraic equation marked up with MathML (part 1 of 2).

```
32
33 </BODY>
34 </HTML>
```

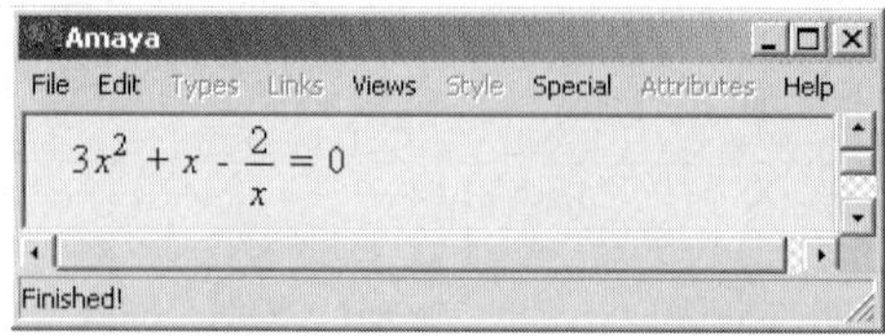

Fig. 28.5 An algebraic equation marked up with MathML (part 2 of 2).

Element **mrow** behaves like parentheses. This allows the document's author to properly group together related elements. Line 14 uses entity reference ***⁢*** to indicate a multiplication operation without a *symbolic representation* (i.e., the multiplication symbol does not appear between the **3** and **x**). To do exponentiation, we use the ***msup*** element (line 15). This superscripting element has two subelements: the expression to be superscripted (i.e., the base) and the superscript (i.e., the exponent). Each argument is only one element, so no additional **mrow** element is needed. Correspondingly, there is the ***msub*** element, which defines a subscript. To display variables such as **x**, we use identifier element ***mi*** (line 16).

To display a fraction, we use element ***mfrac*** (line 24). Between the **mfrac** tags, we specify the numerator and the denominator, respectively. If either the numerator or the denominator contains more than one element, it must be enclosed in **mrow** elements.

Let us take a more substantial calculus expression and mark it up using MathML. Figure 28.6 shows how to mark up a calculus expression that uses an integral symbol and a square-root symbol.

```
<!DOCTYPE HTML PUBLIC "-//W3C//DTD HTML 4.0 Transitional//EN">
<HTML>

<!-- Fig. 28.6: mathml3.html -->
<!-- Complex MathML          -->

<BODY>

<MATH>
   <mrow>
      <msubsup>
         <mo>&Integral;</mo>
         <mn>0</mn>
         <mrow>
            <mn>1</mn>
            <mo>-</mo>
            <mi>x</mi>
         </mrow>
      </msubsup>

```

Fig. 28.6 A calculus expression marked up with MathML (part 1 of 2).

```
21        <msqrt>
22           <mrow>
23              <mn>4</mn>
24              <mo>&InvisibleTimes;</mo>
25              <msup>
26                 <mi>x</mi>
27                 <mn>2</mn>
28              </msup>
29              <mo>+</mo>
30              <mi>y</mi>
31           </mrow>
32        </msqrt>
33
34        <mi>&delta;</mi>
35        <mi>x</mi>
36     </mrow>
37  </MATH>
38  </BODY>
39  </HTML>
```

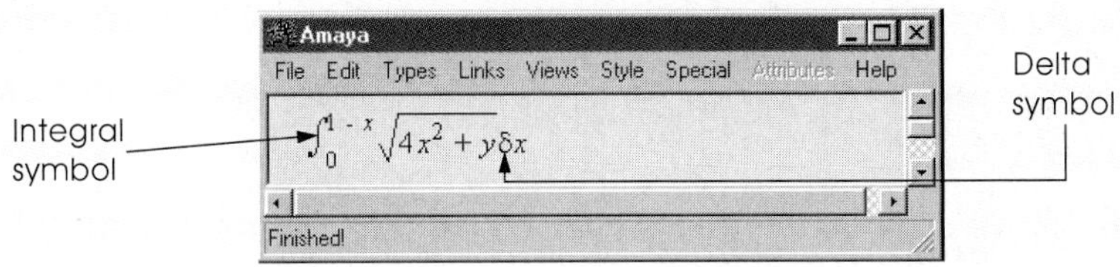

Fig. 28.6 A calculus expression marked up with MathML (part 2 of 2).

To create the integral expression, we use an integral operator, which contains superscripted and subscripted expressions. The integral symbol is defined by ***∫*** (line 12), and the superscript and subscript markup is defined using ***msubsup*** (line 11). The **msubsup** element requires three subelements, the item to be scripted (line 12), the subscript (line 13) and finally the superscript (lines 14 through 18). To display the square root symbol, we use the ***msqrt*** element (line 21), which takes one element, so an **mrow** element must be used to contain the inner expression. The delta symbol is defined by ***δ*** (line 34).

Using the tags from the previous examples, we can start defining even more complex equations. To see what other operations and symbols can be used, see the MathML definition at **http://www.w3.org/Math/**.

Some algebraic equations are often expressed using special tables called *matrices*. Each matrix consists of n rows and m columns. Figure 28.7 shows the markup for a 5-by-5 matrix. Creating a matrix in XML is similar to creating a **TABLE** in HTML.

To define a matrix, we create a table using element ***mtable*** (line 10). To create the matrix rows, we use element ***mtr*** (line 12). Each row contains ***mtd*** element (line 13) columns.

```
<!DOCTYPE HTML PUBLIC "-//W3C//DTD HTML 4.0 Transitional//EN">
<HTML>

<!-- Fig. 28.7: mathml4.html -->
<!-- Matrix MathML           -->

<BODY>

<MATH>
   <mtable>

      <mtr>
         <mtd>2</mtd>
         <mtd>5</mtd>
         <mtd>8</mtd>
         <mtd>3</mtd>
         <mtd>0</mtd>
      </mtr>

      <mtr>
         <mtd>1</mtd>
         <mtd>-5</mtd>
         <mtd>3</mtd>
         <mtd>0</mtd>
         <mtd>y</mtd>
      </mtr>

      <mtr>
         <mtd>15</mtd>
         <mtd>2</mtd>
         <mtd>1</mtd>
         <mtd>1</mtd>
         <mtd>-2</mtd>
      </mtr>

      <mtr>
         <mtd>-2</mtd>
         <mtd>x</mtd>
         <mtd>8</mtd>
         <mtd>12</mtd>
         <mtd>22</mtd>
      </mtr>

      <mtr>
         <mtd>-2</mtd>
         <mtd>0</mtd>
         <mtd>0</mtd>
         <mtd>3</mtd>
         <mtd>7</mtd>
      </mtr>

   </mtable>
</MATH>
```

Fig. 28.7 A matrix marked up using MathML and rendered with Amaya (part 1 of 2).

```
</BODY>
</HTML>
```

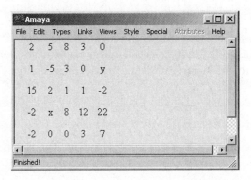

Fig. 28.7 A matrix marked up using MathML and rendered with Amaya (part 2 of 2).

28.5 XML Parsers

An *XML parser* (also called an *XML processor*) determines the content and structure of an XML document by combining an XML document and its DTD (if one is present). Figure 28.8 shows a simple relationship between XML documents, DTDs, parsers and applications. Although many XML parsers exist, we discuss only Microsoft's parser used by Internet Explorer and the W3C's parser that Amaya uses.

Software Engineering Observation 28.1

Several Independent Software Vendors (ISVs) have written XML parsers. Some of these parsers can be found at **`http://www.xml.com/xml/pub/Guide/XML_Parsers`**.

Internet Explorer 5 has a built-in XML parser (i.e., **`msxml`**). This provides a means of integrating XML information into Web documents. Microsoft also provides a collection of tools for editing and validating XML documents, which can be obtained through the MSDN Web site (i.e., **`http://www.msdn.microsoft.com`**).

Amaya is an open-source editor and viewer of XML and HTML documents. Amaya uses the *W3C XML parser*. At the time of this writing, many of Amaya's planned features are not implemented.

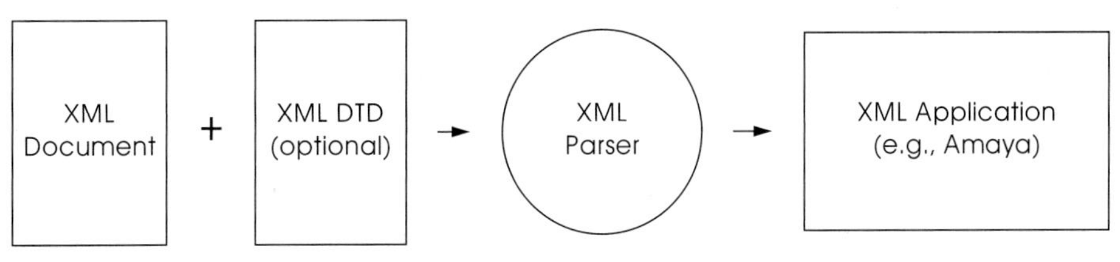

Fig. 28.8 XML documents and their corresponding DTDs are parsed and sent to an application.

XML parsers build *tree structures* (i.e., data structures) from XML documents. For example, an XML parser would build the tree structure shown in Fig. 28.9 for **article.xml** (Fig. 28.1). If this tree structure is created successfully *without* using a DTD, the XML document is considered *well-formed.* If the tree structure is created successfully and a DTD is used, the XML document is considered *valid* (or *type valid*). By definition, a valid XML document is also a well-formed XML document. XML parsers exist in two varieties: *validating* (i.e., enforces DTD rules) and *nonvalidating* (i.e., ignores DTD rules). [*Note:* a nonvalidating parser must still check certain entity declarations, despite the fact that it ignores DTDs.]

28.6 Using XML with HTML

Because an XML document is primarily concerned with data, XML documents are a data source. Internet Explorer 5 allows XML documents to be embedded into an HTML document using the ***XML*** *tag*. An XML document that exists within an HTML page is called a *data island.* Figure 28.10 uses a data island as a data source for an HTML table.

Portability Tip 28.3

The ***XML*** *tag is Microsoft-specific.*

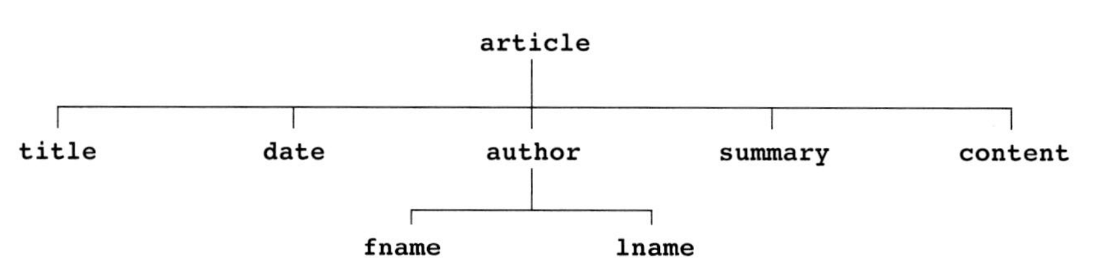

Fig. 28.9 Tree structure for **article.xml**.

```
<!DOCTYPE HTML PUBLIC "-//W3C//DTD HTML 4.0 Transitional//EN">
<HTML>

<!-- Fig. 28.10: simple_contact.html  -->
<!-- A Simple Contact List Database   -->

<BODY>

<XML ID = "xmlDoc">
   <contacts>

      <contact>
         <LastName>Deitel</LastName>
         <FirstName>Harvey</FirstName>
      </contact>

```

Fig. 28.10 A simple contact list (part 1 of 2).

```
17          <contact>
18             <LastName>Deitel</LastName>
19             <FirstName>Paul</FirstName>
20          </contact>
21
22          <contact>
23             <LastName>Nieto</LastName>
24             <FirstName>Tem</FirstName>
25          </contact>
26
27       </contacts>
28    </XML>
29
30    <TABLE BORDER = "1" DATASRC = "#xmlDoc">
31       <THEAD>
32       <TR>
33          <TH>Last Name</TH>
34          <TH>First Name</TH>
35       </TR>
36       </THEAD>
37
38       <TR>
39          <TD><SPAN DATAFLD = "LastName"></SPAN></TD>
40          <TD><SPAN DATAFLD = "FirstName"></SPAN></TD>
41       </TR>
42    </TABLE>
43
44    </BODY>
45    </HTML>
```

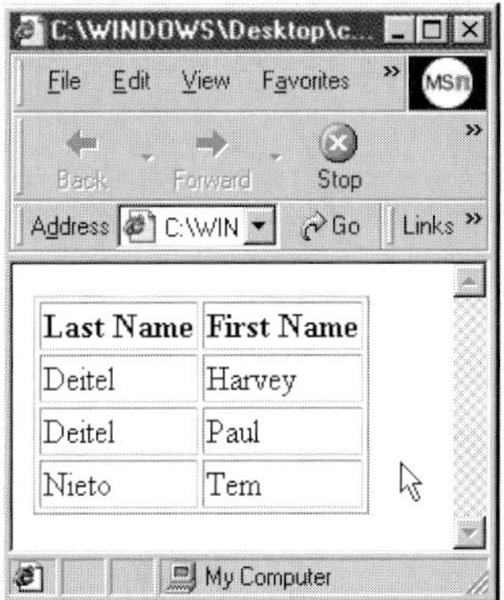

Fig. 28.10 A simple contact list (part 2 of 2).

Line 9

```
<XML ID = "xmlDoc">
```

uses the **<XML>** tag to mark the beginning of the data island, and line 28 uses the closing **</XML>** tag to mark the end of the data island. Attribute **ID** is set to **"xmlDoc"**—the name used by the programmer to reference this data island. This attribute's value is a programmer-defined name.

The data island contains a root-level **contacts** element (line 10) with three **contact** elements. Each **contact** element contains a **LastName** and **FirstName** element representing the **contact**'s last name and first name, respectively (as in lines 13 and 14).

In the HTML file, we add a **DATASRC** attribute (line 30) to the **TABLE** element's start-tag to bind the data island (**xmlDoc**) to the table. To use bound data, we use a **SPAN** element with a **DATAFLD** attribute (line 39).

With data islands, binding data to a table requires minimal effort. Internet Explorer 5 can handle many different data sources (e.g., XML, comma-delimited lists, ADO etc.) by using this system. Subsequent examples show more data-island features.

28.7 Extensible Style Language (XSL)

Extensible style language (*XSL*) defines the layout of an XML document much like CSS defines the layout of an HTML document—although XSL is much more powerful. An *XSL style sheet* provides the rules for displaying or organizing an XML document's data. XSL also provides elements that define rules for how one XML document is transformed into another XML document. For example, an XML document can be transformed into a *well-formed HTML document* (i.e., an XML document that uses only HTML elements and attributes). This part of XSL concerned with transformations is called *XSL Transformations (XSLT)*. In this section, we use XSLT and in the next section we use XSL style sheets.

Software Engineering Observation 28.2

XSL allows data presentation to be separated from data description.

Figure 28.11 enhances Fig. 28.10 by adding the ability to sort and filter data. We use XSLT to perform the sorting and filtering of data.

```
<?xml version = "1.0"?>

<!-- Fig. 28.11: contact.xml -->

<contacts>

   <contact>
      <LastName>Deitel</LastName>
      <FirstName>Harvey</FirstName>
   </contact>

   <contact>
      <LastName>Deitel</LastName>
      <FirstName>Paul</FirstName>
   </contact>

   <contact>
      <LastName>Nieto</LastName>
      <FirstName>Tem</FirstName>
   </contact>

</contacts>
```

Fig. 28.11 A contact list database in XML.

```
<!DOCTYPE HTML PUBLIC "-//W3C//DTD HTML 4.0 Transitional//EN">
<HTML>

<!-- Fig. 28.12: contact_list.html -->

<BODY>

<XML ID = "xmlData" src = "contact.xml"></XML>

<XML ID = "xmlSortLastName">
   <contacts>
      <xsl:for-each order-by = "+LastName;+FirstName"
         select = "contact"
         xmlns:xsl = "http://www.w3.org/TR/WD-xsl">
         <contact>
            <LastName><xsl:value-of select = "LastName"/>
               </LastName>
            <FirstName><xsl:value-of select = "FirstName"/>
               </FirstName>
         </contact>
      </xsl:for-each>
   </contacts>
</XML>

<XML ID = "xmlSortFirstName">
   <contacts>
      <xsl:for-each order-by = "+FirstName;+LastName"
         select = "contact"
         xmlns:xsl = "http://www.w3.org/TR/WD-xsl">
         <contact>
            <LastName><xsl:value-of select = "LastName"/>
               </LastName>
            <FirstName><xsl:value-of select = "FirstName"/>
               </FirstName>
         </contact>
      </xsl:for-each>
   </contacts>
</XML>

<XML ID = "xmlRevertOrder">
   <contacts>
      <xsl:for-each select = "contact"
         xmlns:xsl = "http://www.w3.org/TR/WD-xsl">
         <contact>
            <LastName><xsl:value-of select = "lastName"/>
               </LastName>
            <FirstName><xsl:value-of select = "firstName"/>
               </FirstName>
         </contact>
      </xsl:for-each>
   </contacts>
</XML>

```

Fig. 28.12 Using XSL style sheets (part 1 of 3).

```
<XML ID = "xmlFilterLastName">
   <contacts>
      <xsl:for-each select = "contact[LastName='Nieto']"
         xmlns:xsl = "http://www.w3.org/TR/WD-xsl">
         <contact>
            <LastName><xsl:value-of select = "LastName"/>
               </LastName>
            <FirstName><xsl:value-of select = "FirstName"/>
               </FirstName>
         </contact>
      </xsl:for-each>
   </contacts>
</XML>

<SCRIPT LANGUAGE = "Javascript">
   var xmldoc = xmlData.cloneNode( true );

   function sort( xsldoc ) {
      xmldoc.documentElement.transformNodeToObject(
         xsldoc.documentElement, xmlData.XMLDocument );
   }
</SCRIPT>

<TABLE BORDER = "1" DATASRC = "#xmlData" DATAPAGESIZE = "2"
   ID = "tbl">
   <THEAD>
   <TR>
      <TH>Last Name</TH>
      <TH>First Name</TH>
   </TR>
   </THEAD>

   <TR>
      <TD><SPAN DATAFLD = "LastName"></SPAN></TD>
      <TD><SPAN DATAFLD = "FirstName"></SPAN></TD>
   </TR>
</TABLE>

<INPUT TYPE = "button" VALUE = "Sort By Last Name"
   ONCLICK = "sort(xmlSortLastName.XMLDocument);">
<INPUT TYPE = "button" VALUE = "Sort By First Name"
   ONCLICK = "sort(xmlSortFirstName.XMLDocument);">
<INPUT TYPE = "button" VALUE = "Revert"
   ONCLICK = "sort(xmlRevertOrder.XMLDocument);">
<BR>
<INPUT TYPE = "button" VALUE = "Filter for Nieto"
   ONCLICK = "sort(xmlFilterLastName.XMLDocument);">
<BR>
<INPUT TYPE = "button" VALUE = "|<" ONCLICK = "tbl.firstPage();">
<INPUT TYPE = "button" VALUE = "<" ONCLICK ="tbl.previousPage();">
<INPUT TYPE = "button" VALUE = ">" ONCLICK = "tbl.nextPage();">
<INPUT TYPE = "button" VALUE = ">|" ONCLICK = "tbl.lastPage();">
```

Fig. 28.12 Using XSL style sheets (part 2 of 3).

```
129 </BODY>
130 </HTML>
```

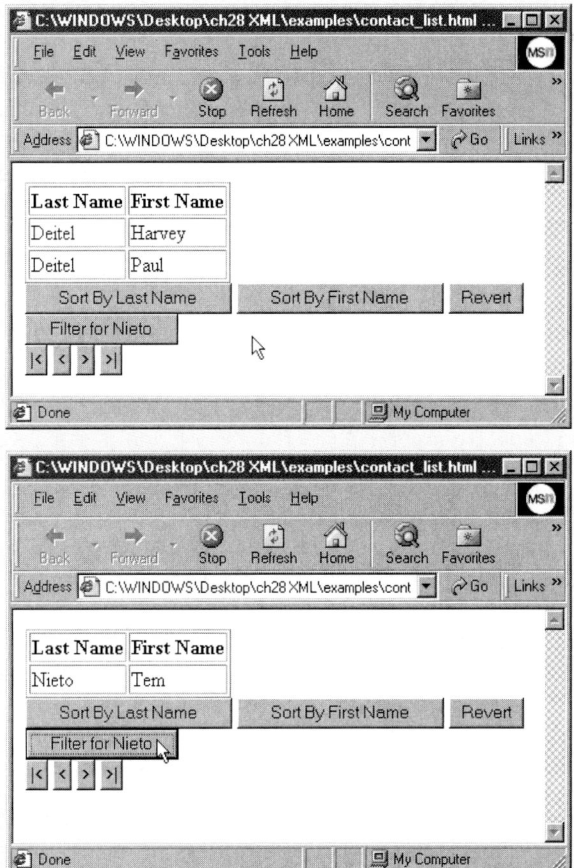

Fig. 28.12 Using XSL style sheets (part 3 of 3).

Instead of physically embedding the XML document in the HTML file, as we did in the last example, we place the XML document in its own file—**contact.xml** (lines 1 through 22).

Line 30 in **contactList.html**

```
<XML ID = "xmlData" SRC = "contact.xml"></XML>
```

uses the **SRC** attribute to reference the data island.

We add four XML elements that contain our XSL style sheets: **xmlSortLastName** (line 32)—which encloses an XSL element to sort the data by **LastName**, **xmlSortFirstName** (line 47)—which encloses an XSL element to sort the data by **FirstName**, **xmlRevertOrder** (line 62)—which encloses an XSL element to revert the data to its original order and **xmlFilterLastName** (line 76)—which filters for data matching a particular criteria.

The statement in lines 34 through 36

```
<xsl:for-each order-by = "+LastName;+FirstName"
   select = "contact"
   xmlns:xsl = "http://www.w3.org/TR/WD-xsl">
```

uses the ***xsl:for-each*** element to iterate over items in the **contact.xml** document. Attribute ***order-by*** specifies what is sorted. A *plus sign* (**+**) indicates ascending order; a *minus sign* (**-**) indicates descending order. When more than one item is to be sorted, a *semicolon* (***;***) separates them. Attribute ***select*** defines which elements are selected. In this case, we select all **contact** elements. Attribute ***xmlns:xsl*** indicates where the specification for this element is located.

Attribute ***xmlns*** defines an *XML namespace*. Namespaces identify collections of element type declarations so that they do not conflict with other element type declarations with the same name created by other programmers. Two predefined XML namespaces are ***xml*** and ***xsl***. Programmers can create their own namespaces. For example,

```
<subject>English</subject>
```

and

```
<subject>Thrombosis</subject>
```

can be differentiated by using namespaces, as in

```
<school:subject>English</school:subject>
<medical:subject>Thrombosis</medical:subject>
```

Line 38

```
<LastName><xsl:value-of select = "LastName"/>
```

uses element ***xsl:value-of*** to retrieve the data specified in attribute **select**. The data returned by this element replaces element **xsl:value-of**. Because this is an empty element, it ends in a forward slash.

Performance Tip 28.1

Because XSL style sheets are interpreted on the client, server resources are conserved.

ID xmlFilterLastName (line 76) encloses an XSL element for filtering the **LastName**. The formatting is similar to sorting, except that we have modified the **select** attribute. The attribute value **"contact[LastName='Nieto']"** indicates that only **LastName**s equal to **Nieto** should be selected. The brackets (***[]***) specify an *XSL conditional statement.*

XML includes an *XML Document Object Model* (*DOM*) that allows dynamic content to be generated from an XML document by using scripting. Some vendors, such as Microsoft, have extended the DOM to add additional features for use with Internet Explorer 5. We use the Microsoft XML DOM in this example and later in the chapter. For more information about Microsoft's XML DOM visit

http://msdn.microsoft.com/xml/reference/xmldom/start.asp

On line 91, we call method ***cloneNode*** to copy the **xmlData** object and assign it to JavaScript variable **xmldoc** object. This provides us with a backup of the data so when we write to **xmlData**, we do not lose the original data. Passing **true** as an argument allows the results in all sub-nodes and their attribute values in **xmlData** to be copied. If **false** is passed, only the node and its attribute value is copied.

Microsoft XML DOM method ***transformNodeToObject*** is called by function **sort** (defined on line 93) to apply a specified XSL style sheet to the data contained in the parent object. So, in lines 94 and 95, we apply **xsldoc** to **xmldoc** and write to **xmldata**. Property ***documentElement*** is used to get the root element of **xmldoc** and **xsldoc**, respectively. Property ***XMLDocument*** is used to access the XML document to which **xmlData** refers.

The **TABLE** (line 99) specifies the number of data records to display with attribute ***DATAPAGESIZE***. We also provide buttons to sort, filter and navigate the data.

The navigation button **OnClick** event handlers (lines 124 through 127) call methods ***firstPage***—to move to the first record, ***previousPage***—to move to the previous record, ***nextPage***—to move to the next record and ***lastPage***—to move to the last record. The sort/filter buttons each call function **sort** and pass it an **XMLDocument** (i.e., the document that represents **xmlSortLastName**, **xmlSortFirstName** etc. that can be used within the **SCRIPT** tag).

28.8 Microsoft Schema

A *schema* is Microsoft's expansion of the DTD. Because a DTD is written in a format dissimilar to the format of XML, Microsoft developed a schema to create document definitions using the syntax of XML. This schema is called *XML-Data*. Either schemas or DTDs may be used to specify a document's grammar, though DTDs may be preferred because Microsoft's schema language is a proprietary technology. The W3C is currently developing a schema format called *Document Content Description (DCD)*.

Figure 28.13 uses XML, XSL and schemas to display data. In this example, we do not use an HTML file. This example consists of three XML documents: **books.xml**, **books-schema.xml**, and **books.xsl**—which define the database, the element grammar and the rendering style, respectively.

```
<?xml version = "1.0"?>
<?xml:stylesheet type = "text/xsl" href = "books.xsl"?>
<!-- Fig. 28.13: books.xml -->

<database xmlns = "x-schema:books-schema.xml">
   <author>Deitel Associates</author>

   <book>
      <title>C++ How to Program, Second Edition</title>
      <isbn>0-13-528910-6</isbn>
      <pages>1130</pages>
      <description>For CS1 and other courses on programming in
         C++. This comprehensive text, aimed at students with
```

Fig. 28.13 Book list database document in XML (part 1 of 4).

```
         little or no programming experience, teaches
         programming "the right way" from the start by placing
         emphasis on achieving program clarity through
         structured and object-oriented programming.
         </description>
      <image>cplus.jpg</image>
   </book>

   <book>
      <title>The Complete C++ Training Course, Second
         Edition</title>
      <isbn>0-13-916305-0</isbn>
      <pages>Boxed</pages>
      <description>For any course teaching C++ programming.
         The ultimate C++ programming package. The Complete
         C++ Training Course, 2/e features Harvey and Paul
         Deitel's best-selling C++ How to Program, 2/e text
         along with a fully-interactive CD-ROM - The C++
         Multimedia Cyber Classroom CD-ROM, 2/e - provides
         students and programmers with the ideal medium for
         learning how to program with C++. It's a proven fact
         that the more involved students are, the more they
         learn. That's what the C++ Multimedia Cyber Classroom
         is all about - helping students learn in every way
         possible.</description>
      <image>cplustrain.jpg</image>
   </book>

   <book>
      <title>Getting Started with Microsoft's Visual C++ 6
         with an Introduction to MFC</title>
      <isbn>0-13-016147-0</isbn>
      <pages></pages>
      <description></description>
      <image></image>
   </book>

   <book>
      <title>Java How to Program, Third Edition</title>
      <isbn>0-13-012507-5</isbn>
      <pages>1200</pages>
      <description>For CS1 and other courses on programming in
         Java. Written by the authors of the world's
         best-selling introductory C and C++ texts, this
         state-of-the-art guide examines one of today's
         hottest computer languages - Java; the first
         general-purpose, object-oriented language that is
         truly platform-independent. The latest Java 2
         features are incorporated throughout this
         edition.</description>
      <image></image>
   </book>

```

Fig. 28.13 Book list database document in XML (part 2 of 4).

```
   <book>
      <title>Java How to Program, Second Edition</title>
      <isbn>0-13-899394-7</isbn>
      <pages></pages>
      <description></description>
      <image></image>
   </book>

   <book>
      <title>The Complete Java Training Course, Second
         Edition</title>
      <isbn>0-13-790569-6</isbn>
      <pages>Boxed</pages>
      <description>For any course teaching Java programming.
         The ultimate Java programming package. The Complete
         Java Training Course, 2/e features Harvey and Paul
         Deitel's best-selling Java How to Program, 2/e text
         along with a fully-interactive CD-ROM - The Java
         Multimedia Cyber Classroom - which provides students
         and programmers with the ideal medium for learning
         how to program with Java. It's a proven fact that the
         more involved students are, the more they learn.
         That's what the Java Multimedia Cyber Classroom is
         all about - helping students learn in every way
         possible.</description>
      <image></image>
   </book>

   <book>
      <title>Visual Basic 6 How to Program</title>
      <isbn>0-13-456955-5</isbn>
      <pages>1015</pages>
      <description>For introductory through advanced level
         courses in Visual Basic. The latest book in the
         Deitels' How to Program Series of worldwide
         programming language bestsellers, this is one of the
         first books on the newest version of Microsoft's
         Visual Basic - Visual Basic 6. Designed for beginning
         through experienced programmers, it includes hundreds
         of complete working programs - totaling more than
         10,000 lines of code - numerous valuable programming
         tips, and hundreds of interesting and challenging
         exercises.</description>
      <image>vb.jpg</image>
   </book>

   <book>
      <title>The Complete Visual Basic 6 Course</title>
      <isbn>0-13-082929-3</isbn>
      <pages>Boxed</pages>
      <description>For any course teaching Visual Basic 6
         programming. The ultimate Visual Basic programming
         package, The Complete Visual Basic Training Course,
```

Fig. 28.13 Book list database document in XML (part 3 of 4).

```
            features Harvey and Paul Deitel's Visual Basic 6 How
            to Program text along with a fully-interactive CD-ROM
            - The Visual Basic Multimedia Cyber Classroom CD-ROM
            - which provides students and programmers with the
            ideal medium for learning how to program with Visual
            Basic. It's a proven fact that the more involved
            students are, the
            more they learn. That's what the Visual Basic
            Multimedia Cyber Classroom is all about - helping
            students learn in every way possible.</description>
         <image>vbtrain.jpg</image>
      </book>

      <book>
         <title>C How to Program, Second Edition</title>
         <isbn>0-13-226119-7</isbn>
         <pages>926</pages>
         <description>This text is especially appropriate for
            students learning programming for the first time.
            Highly practical in approach, it introduces
            fundamental notions of structured programming, gets
            up to speed quickly, and covers not only the full C
            language, but includes a review of library functions
            and a solid introduction C++ and object- oriented
            programming.</description>
         <image>c.gif</image>
      </book>

   </database>
```

Fig. 28.13 Book list database document in XML (part 4 of 4).

```
<?xml version = "1.0"?>

<!-- Fig. 28.14: books-schema.xml -->

<Schema xmlns = "urn:schemas-microsoft-com:xml-data"
   xmlns:dt = "urn:schemas-microsoft-com:datatypes">

   <ElementType name = "author"/>

   <ElementType name = "image"/>
   <ElementType name = "title"/>
   <ElementType name = "isbn"/>
   <ElementType name = "pages"/>
   <ElementType name = "description"/>

   <ElementType name = "database" content = "eltOnly">
      <group minOccurs = "0" maxOccurs = "1">
         <element type = "author"/>
      </group>
```

Fig. 28.14 XML schema for the database document type (part 1 of 2).

```
      <group minOccurs = "1" maxOccurs = "*">
         <element type = "book"/>
      </group>
   </ElementType>

   <ElementType name = "book" content = "eltOnly">
      <element type = "image"/>
      <element type = "title"/>
      <element type = "isbn"/>
      <element type = "pages"/>
      <element type = "description"/>
   </ElementType>

</Schema>
```

Fig. 28.14 XML schema for the database document type (part 2 of 2).

```
<?xml version = "1.0"?>

<!-- Fig. 28.15: books.xsl -->

<xsl:stylesheet xmlns:xsl = "http://www.w3.org/TR/WD-xsl">
   <xsl:template match = "/">
      <HTML>
      <HEAD>
         <TITLE>
            <xsl:value-of select = "database/author"/>
         </TITLE>
         <STYLE>
            .head1 {font: bold}
            .head2 {font: bold; cursor: hand}
         </STYLE>
      </HEAD>

      <SCRIPT><xsl:comment><![CDATA[
         var sortBy;
         var source;
         var stylesheet;

         function sort( data )
         {
            sortBy.value  =  data;
            list.innerHTML =
               source.documentElement.transformNode(
                  stylesheet );
         }
      ]]></xsl:comment></SCRIPT>

      <SCRIPT FOR = "window" EVENT = "ONLOAD">
         <xsl:comment><![CDATA[
            stylesheet = document.XSLDocument;
            source = document.XMLDocument;
```

Fig. 28.15 XSL specification for the book database (part 1 of 4).

```
               sortBy = document.XSLDocument.selectSingleNode(
                  "//@order-by" );
         ]]></xsl:comment>
      </SCRIPT>

      <BODY>
         <H1>
            <CENTER>
               <xsl:value-of select = "database/author"/>
            </CENTER>
         </H1>

         <DIV ID = "list">
           <xsl:apply-templates match = "database"/>
         </DIV>
      </BODY>
      </HTML>
   </xsl:template>

   <xsl:template match = "database">
      <TABLE WIDTH = "100%" CELLSPACING = "0" BORDER = "1">
         <THEAD>
            <TD WIDTH = "200" ALIGN = "center">
               <DIV CLASS = "head1">Image</DIV>
            </TD>
            <TD WIDTH = "25%" ALIGN = "center">
               <DIV ONCLICK = "sort('title;isbn')"
                  CLASS = "head2">Title</DIV>
            </TD>
            <TD WIDTH = "10%" ALIGN = "center">
               <DIV ONCLICK = "sort('isbn;title')"
                  CLASS = "head2">ISBN</DIV>
            </TD>
            <TD WIDTH = "5%" ALIGN = "center">
               <DIV ONCLICK = "sort('pages;title')"
                  CLASS = "head2">Pages</DIV>
            </TD>
            <TD WIDTH = "60%" ALIGN = "center">
               <DIV CLASS = "head1">Description</DIV>
            </TD>
         </THEAD>

         <xsl:for-each select = "book" order-by = "title">
            <TR>
               <TD WIDTH = "200" ALIGN = "center" VALIGN = "top">
                  <xsl:choose>
                     <xsl:when test = "image[.!='']">
                        <xsl:element name = "IMG">
                           <xsl:attribute name = "SRC">
                              <xsl:value-of select = "image"/>
                           </xsl:attribute>
                        </xsl:element>
                     </xsl:when>
```

Fig. 28.15 XSL specification for the book database (part 2 of 4).

```
                  <xsl:otherwise>
                     n/a
                  </xsl:otherwise>
               </xsl:choose>
            </TD>

            <TD WIDTH = "25%" ALIGN = "LEFT" VALIGN = "top">
               <xsl:choose>
                  <xsl:when test = "title[.!='']">
                     <xsl:value-of select = "title"/>
                  </xsl:when>
                  <xsl:otherwise>
                     n/a
                  </xsl:otherwise>
               </xsl:choose>
            </TD>

            <TD WIDTH = "10%" ALIGN = "center" VALIGN = "top">
               <xsl:choose>
                  <xsl:when test = "isbn[.!='']">
                     <xsl:value-of select = "isbn"/>
                  </xsl:when>
                  <xsl:otherwise>
                     n/a
                  </xsl:otherwise>
               </xsl:choose>
            </TD>

            <TD WIDTH = "5%" ALIGN = "center" VALIGN = "top">
               <xsl:choose>
                  <xsl:when test = "pages[.!='']">
                     <xsl:value-of select = "pages"/>
                  </xsl:when>
                  <xsl:otherwise>
                     n/a
                  </xsl:otherwise>
               </xsl:choose>
            </TD>

            <TD WIDTH = "60%" ALIGN = "LEFT" VALIGN = "top">
               <xsl:choose>
                  <xsl:when test = "description[.!='']">
                     <xsl:value-of select = "description"/>
                  </xsl:when>
                  <xsl:otherwise>
                     n/a
                  </xsl:otherwise>
               </xsl:choose>
            </TD>

         </TR>
      </xsl:for-each>
   </TABLE>
```

Fig. 28.15 XSL specification for the book database (part 3 of 4).

```
323     </xsl:template>
324 </xsl:stylesheet>
```

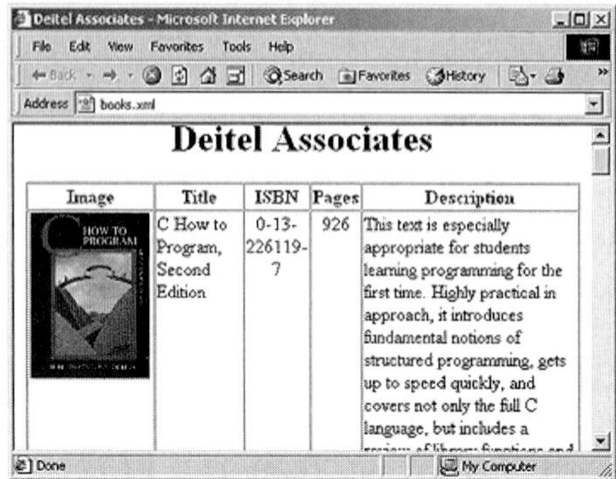

Fig. 28.15 XSL specification for the book database (part 4 of 4).

The book database (i.e., **books.xml**) is straightforward. We have a **database** root-level element, which contains an **author** element and many **book** elements. Each **book** element contains the **title**, ISBN number (i.e., **isbn**), page count (i.e., **pages**), **image** and **description**.

Line 2

```
<?xml:stylesheet type = "text/xsl" href = "books.xsl"?>
```

uses an ***xml:stylesheet*** *processing instruction* to indicate that the XML document uses style sheet **books.xsl**. By convention, XSL documents end in the ***.xsl*** extension. Line 5

```
<database xmlns = "x-schema:books-schema.xml">
```

defines the **database** element as using the **books-schema.xml** file as a schema.

Line 153

```
<Schema xmlns = "urn:schemas-microsoft-com:xml-data"
   xmlns:dt = "urn:schemas-microsoft-com:datatypes">
```

uses element ***Schema*** to describe **"urn:schemas-microsoft-com:xml-data"** and **"urn:schemas-microsoft-com:datatypes"** as the schema used.

First, we declare our element types. This is done by using element ***ElementType*** (line 156). *Attribute* ***name****'s* value defines the name of our element. Attribute ***content*** (line 164) defines the element's contents. In this case, ***eltOnly*** specifies that this element can only contain other elements.

Element ***group*** (line 165) defines the number of times an element is allowed to occur. Attribute ***minOccurs*** defines an element's minimum number of occurrences. Assigning a value of **0** to **minOccurs** sets the element as optional, and assigning a value of **1** to **minOccurs** sets the element as occurring at least once. Attribute ***maxOccurs*** defines an element's maximum number of occurrences. A value of **1** sets the element as occurring at most once and an asterisk (*****) sets the element as occurring any number of times.

Element ***element*** (line 166) references an element type that can appear as part of the enclosing **ElementType** element's content model. In this case, the **author** element can occur at most once and the **book** element can occur one or more times.

On lines 182 through 324, we define XSL stylesheet **books.xsl**, which describes how to render an XML document.

We start by using the **xsl:stylesheet** processing instruction (line 186)—the *style sheet definition*. We use element ***xsl:template*** (line 187) to define a *template rule*. Attribute ***match*** selects the nodes (i.e., elements) to which the **xsl:template** is applied. In this case, a value of **"/"** defines that this template applies to the root element.

To preserve the text in a section (i.e., have the XML parser not process the text), we use the optional ***<![CDATA[*** *sections* (line 199). Any material between the opening **<![CDATA[** and the closing ***]]>*** (line 211) is not processed by the style sheet and is rendered exactly as it appears within the tags. To ensure that our scripting code does not conflict with the XSL style sheet, we enclose the scripting code in ***xsl:comment***s.

On line 217, we call method ***selectSingleNode*** to return the first node in the XSL style sheet that has an **order-by** attribute. By doing this, we can dynamically set the value of attribute **order-by** in the **xsl:for-each** element on line 259. We use the ***XSLDocument*** property to access the **document**'s XSL style sheet.

On line 204, we define function **sort**, which sorts the XML document according to the passed argument. We set variable **sortBy**'s value to **data**'s value and call method ***transformNode*** (line 208) to send the XML data through the **stylesheet**. The only data that is processed are the elements in the **database** element.

To embed another template section, we use the ***xsl:apply-templates*** *element* (line 230). This element applies the specified template at the position of the tag. In this case, we apply the **database** template (defined on line 236) here.

To perform conditional tests, we have the ***xsl:choose*** *element* (line 262) which is composed of one or more ***xsl:when*** *elements* and an optional ***xsl:otherwise*** *element*. The ***xsl:when*** element (line 263) is a conditional statement, with the conditional placed in the ***test*** attribute. In this case, we test whether the ***image*** record item is not equal to an empty string. Finally, the ***xsl:otherwise*** element (line 270) is used to define the default case.

The ***xsl:element*** *element* (line 264) generates the markup for an element of the specified name (i.e., **IMG**). To add an attribute to a markup, we use the ***xsl:attribute*** *element* (line 265). This tag generates an attribute of an ***xsl:element***.

28.9 Case Study: A Chess Example

In this section, we use XML in a chess example. The example consist of images that represent the chess board and its pieces, a **Start** button, a table that displays the last move and a field that displays the name of the XML file the example uses. When the user clicks the **Start** button, a series of predefined moves is executed—this example does not allow the user to move individual chess pieces. While the moves are being made, the button's face displays **Stop**. Instead of embedding the XML data directly into the HTML file, we use the **msxml** parser—an ActiveX object—to retrieve the data. Figure 28.16 lists the **chess.html** file that graphically displays the chess board and its pieces, and Fig. 28.17 lists the **scholarmate.xml** file that provides the markup describing the moves.

```
<!DOCTYPE HTML PUBLIC "-//W3C//DTD HTML 4.0 Transitional//EN">
<HTML>

<!-- Fig. 28.16: chess.html -->

<HEAD>
<TITLE>Chess</TITLE>

<SCRIPT LANGUAGE = "JavaScript">
<!--
   // variables for display of captured pieces
   var captureWhite = 0;
   var captureBlack = 0;

   // variables for going through the xml data
   var i = 0;
   var timer;

   // variables for the xml data
   var xml = new ActiveXObject( "msxml" );
   var gameInfo;
   var gameMoves;

   // temporary data variables
   var move;
   var info;
   var pieceSrc1;
   var pieceSrc2;

   // displays a single move
   function display()
   {

      if ( i >= gameMoves.length ) {
         clearInterval( timer );
         window.button.value = "Reset";
         return;
      }

      move = gameMoves.item( i );

      if ( parseInt( i/2 + 1 ) != move.getAttribute( "turn" ) ) {
         alert( "The XML data set is invalid" );
         clearInterval( timer );
         window.button.value = "Reset";
         return;
      }

      // determine the turn data.
      window.infoTurn.innerText = move.getAttribute( "turn" );

      if ( move.getAttribute( "player" ) == "white" )
         window.infoTurn.innerText += "w";
```

Fig. 28.16 Chess example with the **ScholarMate.xml** file (part 1 of 14).

```
         else
            window.infoTurn.innerText += "b";

         // determine which piece is moved.
         window.infoPiece.innerText = move.getAttribute( "piece" );

         if ( window.infoPiece.innerText == "" )
            window.infoPiece.innerText = " ";

         // determine where to move from.
         info = move.children.item( "from" );
         window.infoFrom.innerText = info.getAttribute( "x" ) +
            info.getAttribute( "y" );

         if ( window.infoFrom.innerText != "" ) {
            pieceSrc1 = window.document.images( "image" +
               window.infoFrom.innerText ).src;
            window.document.images( "image" +
               window.infoFrom.innerText ).src = "blank.gif";

            if ( pieceSrc1.indexOf( "blank.gif" ) != -1 ) {
               alert( "The XML data set is invalid" );
               clearInterval( timer );
               window.button.value = "Reset";
               return;
            }
         }
         else
            window.infoFrom.innerText = " ";

         // determine where to move to.
         info = move.children.item( "to" );
         window.infoTo.innerText = info.getAttribute( "x" ) +
            info.getAttribute( "y" );

         if ( window.infoTo.innerText != "" ) {
            pieceSrc2 = window.document.images( "image" +
               window.infoTo.innerText ).src;
            window.document.images( "image" +
               window.infoTo.innerText ).src = pieceSrc1;
         }
         else
            window.infoTo.innerText = " ";

         // determine if there are any special flags.
         info = move.children.item( "flag" );
         window.infoFlag.innerText = info.text;

         // no flags
         if ( info.text == "" )
            window.infoFlag.innerText = " ";

```

Fig. 28.16 Chess example with the **ScholarMate.xml** file (part 2 of 14).

```
      // capture flag
      if ( info.text.indexOf( "x" ) != -1 ) {
         window.infoFlag.innerText = info.text;

         if ( move.getAttribute( "player" ) == "white" ) {
            window.document.images( "black" +
               captureBlack ).src = pieceSrc2;
            captureBlack++;
         }
         else {
            window.document.images( "white" +
               captureWhite ).src = pieceSrc2;
            captureWhite++;
         }
      }

      // king-side castle flag
      if ( info.text.indexOf( "0-0" ) != -1 ) {
         if ( move.getAttribute( "player" ) == "white" ) {
            window.document.images( "imageg1" ).src =
               "whiteking.gif";
            window.document.images( "imagee1" ).src =
               "blank.gif";
            window.document.images( "imagef1" ).src =
               "whiterook.gif";
            window.document.images( "imageh1" ).src =
               "blank.gif";
         }
         else {
            window.document.images( "imageg8" ).src =
               "blackking.gif";
            window.document.images( "imagee8 ").src =
               "blank.gif";
            window.document.images( "imagef8" ).src =
               "blackrook.gif";
            window.document.images( "imageh8" ).src =
               "blank.gif";
         }
      }

      // queen-side castle flag
      if ( info.text.indexOf("0-0-0") != -1 ) {
         if ( move.getAttribute( "player" ) == "white" ) {
            window.document.images( "imagec1" ).src =
               "whiteking.gif";
            window.document.images( "imagee1" ).src =
               "blank.gif";
            window.document.images( "imaged1" ).src =
               "whiterook.gif";
            window.document.images( "imagea1" ).src =
               "blank.gif";
         }
```

Fig. 28.16 Chess example with the **ScholarMate.xml** file (part 3 of 14).

```
            else {
               window.document.images( "imagec8" ).src =
                  "blackking.gif";
               window.document.images( "imagee8 ").src =
                  "blank.gif";
               window.document.images( "imaged8" ).src =
                  "blackrook.gif";
               window.document.images( "imagea8" ).src =
                  "blank.gif";
            }
         }

         i++;
      }

      // controls the display function
      function main()
      {
         if ( window.button.value == "Start" ) {
            window.button.value = "Stop";
            timer = setInterval( "display()", 1500 );
         }
         else if ( window.button.value == "Stop" ) {
            window.button.value = "Start";
            clearInterval( timer );
         }
         else if ( window.button.value == "Reset" ) {
            xml.url = window.xmlfile.value;
            gameInfo = xml.root.children.item( 0 ).text;
            gameMoves = xml.root.children.item( 1 ).children;

            window.gameTitle.innerText = gameInfo;

            i = 0;
            captureBlack = 0;
            captureWhite = 0;

            window.button.value = "Start";
            resetPieces();
         }
      }

      // resets the location of the chess pieces
      function resetPieces()
      {
         window.document.images("imagea1").src = "whiterook.gif";
         window.document.images("imageb1").src =
            "whiteknight.gif";
         window.document.images("imagec1").src =
            "whitebishop.gif";
         window.document.images("imaged1").src =
            "whitequeen.gif";
         window.document.images("imagee1").src = "whiteking.gif";
```

Fig. 28.16 Chess example with the **ScholarMate.xml** file (part 4 of 14).

```
         window.document.images("imagef1").src =
            "whitebishop.gif";
         window.document.images("imageg1").src =
            "whiteknight.gif";
         window.document.images("imageh1").src = "whiterook.gif";

         window.document.images("imagea2").src = "whitepawn.gif";
         window.document.images("imageb2").src = "whitepawn.gif";
         window.document.images("imagec2").src = "whitepawn.gif";
         window.document.images("imaged2").src = "whitepawn.gif";
         window.document.images("imagee2").src = "whitepawn.gif";
         window.document.images("imagef2").src = "whitepawn.gif";
         window.document.images("imageg2").src = "whitepawn.gif";
         window.document.images("imageh2").src = "whitepawn.gif";

         window.document.images("imagea8").src = "blackrook.gif";
         window.document.images("imageb8").src =
            "blackknight.gif";
         window.document.images("imagec8").src =
            "blackbishop.gif";
         window.document.images("imaged8").src =
            "blackqueen.gif";
         window.document.images("imagee8").src = "blackking.gif";
         window.document.images("imagef8").src =
            "blackbishop.gif";
         window.document.images("imageg8").src =
            "blackknight.gif";
         window.document.images("imageh8").src = "blackrook.gif";

         window.document.images("imagea7").src = "blackpawn.gif";
         window.document.images("imageb7").src = "blackpawn.gif";
         window.document.images("imagec7").src = "blackpawn.gif";
         window.document.images("imaged7").src = "blackpawn.gif";
         window.document.images("imagee7").src = "blackpawn.gif";
         window.document.images("imagef7").src = "blackpawn.gif";
         window.document.images("imageg7").src = "blackpawn.gif";
         window.document.images("imageh7").src = "blackpawn.gif";

         for ( var a = 97; a <= 104; a++ ) {
            for ( var b = 3; b <= 6; b++ ) {
               window.document.images( "image" +
                  String.fromCharCode( a ) + b ).src = "blank.gif";
            }
         }

         for ( var a = 0; a <= 15; a++ ) {
            window.document.images( "white" + a ).src =
               "blank.gif";
            window.document.images( "black" + a ).src =
               "blank.gif";
         }

```

Fig. 28.16 Chess example with the **ScholarMate.xml** file (part 5 of 14).

```
         window.infoFlag.innerText = " ";
         window.infoFrom.innerText = " ";
         window.infoPiece.innerText = " ";
         window.infoTo.innerText = " ";
         window.infoTurn.innerText = " ";
      }
// -->
</SCRIPT>
</HEAD>

<BODY BGCOLOR = "#ffffe1">
<FONT FACE = "Arial" SIZE = "2">

<DIV ALIGN = "center">
   <TABLE BORDER = "1" WIDTH = "75%">
      <TR>
         <TD WIDTH = "100%" ALIGN = "middle" ID = "gameTitle">
             </TD>
      </TR>
   </TABLE>
</DIV>

<BR>

<DIV ALIGN = "center">
   <TABLE BORDER = "0" CELLSPACING = "0" CELLPADDING = "0"
      HEIGHT = "200">

      <TR>
         <TD WIDTH = "25" HEIGHT = "25" BGCOLOR = "#eeeeaa">
            <IMG HEIGHT = "25" NAME = "white0" SRC = "blank.gif"
               WIDTH = "25"></TD>
         <TD WIDTH = "25" HEIGHT = "25" BGCOLOR = "#eeeeaa">
            <IMG HEIGHT = "25" NAME = "white1" SRC = "blank.gif"
               WIDTH = "25"></TD>
         <TD WIDTH = "50" HEIGHT = "25"></TD>
         <TD VALIGN = "center" ALIGN = "right" WIDTH = "25"
            HEIGHT = "25">8 </TD>
         <TD WIDTH = "25" HEIGHT = "25" BGCOLOR = "#eeeeaa">
            <IMG HEIGHT = "25" NAME = "imagea8"
               SRC = "blackrook.gif" WIDTH = "25"></TD>
         <TD WIDTH = "25" HEIGHT = "25" BGCOLOR = "#d26900">
            <IMG HEIGHT = "25" NAME = "imageb8"
               SRC = "blackknight.gif" WIDTH = "25"></TD>
         <TD WIDTH = "25" HEIGHT = "25" BGCOLOR = "#eeeeaa">
            <IMG HEIGHT = "25" NAME = "imagec8"
               SRC = "blackbishop.gif" WIDTH = "25"></TD>
         <TD WIDTH = "25" HEIGHT = "25" BGCOLOR = "#d26900">
            <IMG HEIGHT = "25" NAME = "imaged8"
               SRC = "blackqueen.gif" WIDTH = "25"></TD>
         <TD WIDTH = "25" HEIGHT = "25" BGCOLOR = "#eeeeaa">
            <IMG HEIGHT = "25" NAME = "imagee8"
               SRC = "blackking.gif" WIDTH = "25"></TD>
```

Fig. 28.16 Chess example with the **ScholarMate.xml** file (part 6 of 14).

```
            <TD WIDTH = "25" HEIGHT = "25" BGCOLOR = "#d26900">
               <IMG HEIGHT = "25" NAME = "imagef8"
                  SRC = "blackbishop.gif" WIDTH = "25"></TD>
            <TD WIDTH = "25" HEIGHT = "25" BGCOLOR = "#eeeeaa">
               <IMG HEIGHT = "25" NAME = "imageg8"
                  SRC = "blackknight.gif" WIDTH = "25"></TD>
            <TD WIDTH = "25" HEIGHT = "25" BGCOLOR = "#d26900">
               <IMG HEIGHT = "25" NAME = "imageh8"
                  SRC = "blackrook.gif" WIDTH = "25"></TD>
            <TD WIDTH = "50" HEIGHT = "25"></TD>
            <TD WIDTH = "25" HEIGHT = "25" BGCOLOR = "#d26900">
               <IMG HEIGHT = "25" NAME = "black0" SRC = "blank.gif"
                  WIDTH = "25"></TD>
            <TD WIDTH = "25" HEIGHT = "25" BGCOLOR = "#d26900">
               <IMG HEIGHT = "25" NAME = "black1" SRC = "blank.gif"
                  WIDTH = "25"></TD>
         </TR>

         <TR>
            <TD WIDTH = "25" HEIGHT = "25" BGCOLOR = "#eeeeaa">
               <IMG HEIGHT = "25" NAME = "white2" SRC = "blank.gif"
                  WIDTH = "25"></TD>
            <TD WIDTH = "25" HEIGHT = "25" BGCOLOR = "#eeeeaa">
               <IMG HEIGHT = "25" NAME = "white3" SRC = "blank.gif"
                  WIDTH = "25"></TD>
            <TD WIDTH = "50" HEIGHT = "25"></TD>
            <TD VALIGN = "center" ALIGN = "right" WIDTH = "25"
               HEIGHT = "25">7 </TD>
            <TD WIDTH = "25" HEIGHT = "25" BGCOLOR = "#d26900">
               <IMG HEIGHT = "25" NAME = "imagea7"
                  SRC = "blackpawn.gif" WIDTH = "25"></TD>
            <TD WIDTH = "25" HEIGHT = "25" BGCOLOR = "#eeeeaa">
               <IMG HEIGHT = "25" NAME = "imageb7"
                  SRC = "blackpawn.gif" WIDTH = "25"></TD>
            <TD WIDTH = "25" HEIGHT = "25" BGCOLOR = "#d26900">
               <IMG HEIGHT = "25" NAME = "imagec7"
                  SRC = "blackpawn.gif" WIDTH = "25"></TD>
            <TD WIDTH = "25" HEIGHT = "25" BGCOLOR = "#eeeeaa">
               <IMG HEIGHT = "25" NAME = "imaged7"
                  SRC = "blackpawn.gif" WIDTH = "25"></TD>
            <TD WIDTH = "25" HEIGHT = "25" BGCOLOR = "#d26900">
               <IMG HEIGHT = "25" NAME = "imagee7"
                  SRC = "blackpawn.gif" WIDTH = "25"></TD>
            <TD WIDTH = "25" HEIGHT = "25" BGCOLOR = "#eeeeaa">
               <IMG HEIGHT = "25" NAME = "imagef7"
                  SRC = "blackpawn.gif" WIDTH = "25"></TD>
            <TD WIDTH = "25" HEIGHT = "25" BGCOLOR = "#d26900">
               <IMG HEIGHT = "25" NAME = "imageg7"
                  SRC = "blackpawn.gif" WIDTH = "25"></TD>
            <TD WIDTH = "25" HEIGHT = "25" BGCOLOR = "#eeeeaa">
               <IMG HEIGHT = "25" NAME = "imageh7"
               SRC = "blackpawn.gif" WIDTH = "25"></TD>
            <TD WIDTH = "50" HEIGHT = "25"></TD>
```

Fig. 28.16 Chess example with the **ScholarMate.xml** file (part 7 of 14).

```
      <TD WIDTH = "25" HEIGHT = "25" BGCOLOR = "#d26900">
         <IMG HEIGHT = "25" NAME = "black2" SRC = "blank.gif"
            WIDTH = "25"></TD>
      <TD WIDTH = "25" HEIGHT = "25" BGCOLOR = "#d26900">
         <IMG HEIGHT = "25" NAME = "black3" SRC = "blank.gif"
            WIDTH = "25"></TD>
   </TR>

   <TR>
      <TD WIDTH = "25" HEIGHT = "25" BGCOLOR = "#eeeeaa">
         <IMG HEIGHT = "25" NAME = "white4" SRC = "blank.gif"
            WIDTH = "25"></TD>
      <TD WIDTH = "25" HEIGHT = "25" BGCOLOR = "#eeeeaa">
         <IMG HEIGHT = "25" NAME = "white5" SRC = "blank.gif"
            WIDTH = "25"></TD>
      <TD WIDTH = "50" HEIGHT = "25"></TD>
      <TD VALIGN = "center" ALIGN = "right" WIDTH = "25"
         HEIGHT = "25">6 </TD>
      <TD WIDTH = "25" HEIGHT = "25" BGCOLOR = "#eeeeaa">
         <IMG HEIGHT = "25" NAME = "imagea6" SRC = "blank.gif"
            WIDTH = "25"></TD>
      <TD WIDTH = "25" HEIGHT = "25" BGCOLOR = "#d26900">
         <IMG HEIGHT = "25" NAME = "imageb6" SRC = "blank.gif"
            WIDTH = "25"></TD>
      <TD WIDTH = "25" HEIGHT = "25" BGCOLOR = "#eeeeaa">
         <IMG HEIGHT = "25" NAME = "imagec6" SRC = "blank.gif"
            WIDTH = "25"></TD>
      <TD WIDTH = "25" HEIGHT = "25" BGCOLOR = "#d26900">
         <IMG HEIGHT = "25" NAME = "imaged6" SRC = "blank.gif"
            WIDTH = "25"></TD>
      <TD WIDTH = "25" HEIGHT = "25" BGCOLOR = "#eeeeaa">
         <IMG HEIGHT = "25" NAME = "imagee6" SRC = "blank.gif"
            WIDTH = "25"></TD>
      <TD WIDTH = "25" HEIGHT = "25" BGCOLOR = "#d26900">
         <IMG HEIGHT = "25" NAME = "imagef6" SRC = "blank.gif"
            WIDTH = "25"></TD>
      <TD WIDTH = "25" HEIGHT = "25" BGCOLOR = "#eeeeaa">
         <IMG HEIGHT = "25" NAME = "imageg6" SRC = "blank.gif"
            WIDTH = "25"></TD>
      <TD WIDTH = "25" HEIGHT = "25" BGCOLOR = "#d26900">
         <IMG HEIGHT = "25" NAME = "imageh6" SRC = "blank.gif"
            WIDTH = "25"></TD>
      <TD WIDTH = "50" HEIGHT = "25"></TD>
      <TD WIDTH = "25" HEIGHT = "25" BGCOLOR = "#d26900">
         <IMG HEIGHT = "25" NAME = "black4" SRC = "blank.gif"
            WIDTH = "25"></TD>
      <TD WIDTH = "25" HEIGHT = "25" BGCOLOR = "#d26900">
         <IMG HEIGHT = "25" NAME = "black5" SRC = "blank.gif"
            WIDTH = "25"></TD>
   </TR>

   <TR>
      <TD WIDTH = "25" HEIGHT = "25" BGCOLOR = "#eeeeaa">
```

Fig. 28.16 Chess example with the **ScholarMate.xml** file (part 8 of 14).

```
            <IMG HEIGHT = "25" NAME = "white6" SRC = "blank.gif"
               WIDTH = "25"></TD>
         <TD WIDTH = "25" HEIGHT = "25" BGCOLOR = "#eeeeaa">
            <IMG HEIGHT = "25" NAME = "white7" SRC = "blank.gif"
               WIDTH = "25"></TD>
         <TD WIDTH = "50" HEIGHT = "25"></TD>
         <TD VALIGN = "center" ALIGN = "right" WIDTH = "25"
            HEIGHT = "25">5 </TD>
         <TD WIDTH = "25" HEIGHT = "25" BGCOLOR = "#d26900">
            <IMG HEIGHT = "25" NAME = "imagea5" SRC = "blank.gif"
               WIDTH = "25"></TD>
         <TD WIDTH = "25" HEIGHT = "25" BGCOLOR = "#eeeeaa">
            <IMG HEIGHT = "25" NAME = "imageb5" SRC = "blank.gif"
               WIDTH = "25"></TD>
         <TD WIDTH = "25" HEIGHT = "25" BGCOLOR = "#d26900">
            <IMG HEIGHT = "25" NAME = "imagec5" SRC = "blank.gif"
               WIDTH = "25"></TD>
         <TD WIDTH = "25" HEIGHT = "25" BGCOLOR = "#eeeeaa">
            <IMG HEIGHT = "25" NAME = "imaged5" SRC = "blank.gif"
               WIDTH = "25"></TD>
         <TD WIDTH = "25" HEIGHT = "25" BGCOLOR = "#d26900">
            <IMG HEIGHT = "25" NAME = "imagee5" SRC = "blank.gif"
               WIDTH = "25"></TD>
         <TD WIDTH = "25" HEIGHT = "25" BGCOLOR = "#eeeeaa">
            <IMG HEIGHT = "25" NAME = "imagef5" SRC = "blank.gif"
               WIDTH = "25"></TD>
         <TD WIDTH = "25" HEIGHT = "25" BGCOLOR = "#d26900">
            <IMG HEIGHT = "25" NAME = "imageg5" SRC = "blank.gif"
               WIDTH = "25"></TD>
         <TD WIDTH = "25" HEIGHT = "25" BGCOLOR = "#eeeeaa">
            <IMG HEIGHT = "25" NAME = "imageh5" SRC = "blank.gif"
               WIDTH = "25"></TD>
         <TD WIDTH = "50" HEIGHT = "25"></TD>
         <TD WIDTH = "25" HEIGHT = "25" BGCOLOR = "#d26900">
            <IMG HEIGHT = "25" NAME = "black6" SRC = "blank.gif"
               WIDTH = "25"></TD>
         <TD WIDTH = "25" HEIGHT = "25" BGCOLOR = "#d26900">
            <IMG HEIGHT = "25" NAME = "black7" SRC = "blank.gif"
               WIDTH = "25"></TD>
      </TR>

      <TR>
         <TD WIDTH = "25" HEIGHT = "25" BGCOLOR = "#eeeeaa">
            <IMG HEIGHT = "25" NAME = "white8" SRC = "blank.gif"
               WIDTH = "25"></TD>
         <TD WIDTH = "25" HEIGHT = "25" BGCOLOR = "#eeeeaa">
            <IMG HEIGHT = "25" NAME = "white9" SRC = "blank.gif"
               WIDTH = "25"></TD>
         <TD WIDTH = "50" HEIGHT = "25"></TD>
         <TD VALIGN = "center" ALIGN = "right" WIDTH = "25"
            HEIGHT = "25">4 </TD>
         <TD WIDTH = "25" HEIGHT = "25" BGCOLOR = "#eeeeaa">
```

Fig. 28.16 Chess example with the **ScholarMate.xml** file (part 9 of 14).

```
            <IMG HEIGHT = "25" NAME = "imagea4" SRC = "blank.gif"
               WIDTH = "25"></TD>
         <TD WIDTH = "25" HEIGHT = "25" BGCOLOR = "#d26900">
            <IMG HEIGHT = "25" NAME = "imageb4" SRC = "blank.gif"
               WIDTH = "25"></TD>
         <TD WIDTH = "25" HEIGHT = "25" BGCOLOR = "#eeeeaa">
            <IMG HEIGHT = "25" NAME = "imagec4" SRC = "blank.gif"
               WIDTH = "25"></TD>
         <TD WIDTH = "25" HEIGHT = "25" BGCOLOR = "#d26900">
            <IMG HEIGHT = "25" NAME = "imaged4" SRC = "blank.gif"
               WIDTH = "25"></TD>
         <TD WIDTH = "25" HEIGHT = "25" BGCOLOR = "#eeeeaa">
            <IMG HEIGHT = "25" NAME = "imagee4" SRC = "blank.gif"
               WIDTH = "25"></TD>
         <TD WIDTH = "25" HEIGHT = "25" BGCOLOR = "#d26900">
            <IMG HEIGHT = "25" NAME = "imagef4" SRC = "blank.gif"
               WIDTH = "25"></TD>
         <TD WIDTH = "25" HEIGHT = "25" BGCOLOR = "#eeeeaa">
            <IMG HEIGHT = "25" NAME = "imageg4" SRC = "blank.gif"
               WIDTH = "25"></TD>
         <TD WIDTH = "25" HEIGHT = "25" BGCOLOR = "#d26900">
            <IMG HEIGHT = "25" NAME = "imageh4" SRC = "blank.gif"
               WIDTH = "25"></TD>
         <TD WIDTH = "50" HEIGHT = "25"></TD>
         <TD WIDTH = "25" HEIGHT = "25" BGCOLOR = "#d26900">
            <IMG HEIGHT = "25" NAME = "black8" SRC = "blank.gif"
               WIDTH = "25"></TD>
         <TD WIDTH = "25" HEIGHT = "25" BGCOLOR = "#d26900">
            <IMG HEIGHT = "25" NAME = "black9" SRC = "blank.gif"
               WIDTH = "25"></TD>
      </TR>

      <TR>
         <TD WIDTH = "25" HEIGHT = "25" BGCOLOR = "#eeeeaa">
            <IMG HEIGHT = "25" NAME = "white10" SRC = "blank.gif"
               WIDTH = "25"></TD>
         <TD WIDTH = "25" HEIGHT = "25" BGCOLOR = "#eeeeaa">
            <IMG HEIGHT = "25" NAME = "white11" SRC = "blank.gif"
               WIDTH = "25"></TD>
         <TD WIDTH = "50" HEIGHT = "25"></TD>
         <TD VALIGN = "center" ALIGN = "right" WIDTH = "25"
            HEIGHT = "25">3 </TD>
         <TD WIDTH = "25" HEIGHT = "25" BGCOLOR = "#d26900">
            <IMG HEIGHT = "25" NAME = "imagea3" SRC = "blank.gif"
               WIDTH = "25"></TD>
         <TD WIDTH = "25" HEIGHT = "25" BGCOLOR = "#eeeeaa">
            <IMG HEIGHT = "25" NAME = "imageb3" SRC = "blank.gif"
               WIDTH = "25"></TD>
         <TD WIDTH = "25" HEIGHT = "25" BGCOLOR = "#d26900">
            <IMG HEIGHT = "25" NAME = "imagec3" SRC = "blank.gif"
               WIDTH = "25"></TD>
         <TD WIDTH = "25" HEIGHT = "25" BGCOLOR = "#eeeeaa">
```

Fig. 28.16 Chess example with the **ScholarMate.xml** file (part 10 of 14).

```
               <IMG HEIGHT = "25" NAME = "imaged3" SRC = "blank.gif"
                  WIDTH = "25"></TD>
            <TD WIDTH = "25" HEIGHT = "25" BGCOLOR = "#d26900">
               <IMG HEIGHT = "25" NAME = "imagee3" SRC = "blank.gif"
                  WIDTH = "25"></TD>
            <TD WIDTH = "25" HEIGHT = "25" BGCOLOR = "#eeeeaa">
               <IMG HEIGHT = "25" NAME = "imagef3" SRC = "blank.gif"
                  WIDTH = "25"></TD>
            <TD WIDTH = "25" HEIGHT = "25" BGCOLOR = "#d26900">
               <IMG HEIGHT = "25" NAME = "imageg3" SRC = "blank.gif"
                  WIDTH = "25"></TD>
            <TD WIDTH = "25" HEIGHT = "25" BGCOLOR = "#eeeeaa">
               <IMG HEIGHT = "25" NAME = "imageh3" SRC = "blank.gif"
                  WIDTH = "25"></TD>
            <TD WIDTH = "50" HEIGHT = "25"></TD>
            <TD WIDTH = "25" HEIGHT = "25" BGCOLOR = "#d26900">
               <IMG HEIGHT = "25" NAME = "black10" SRC = "blank.gif"
                  WIDTH = "25"></TD>
            <TD WIDTH = "25" HEIGHT = "25" BGCOLOR = "#d26900">
               <IMG HEIGHT = "25" NAME = "black11" SRC = "blank.gif"
                  WIDTH = "25"></TD>
         </TR>

         <TR>
            <TD WIDTH = "25" HEIGHT = "25" BGCOLOR = "#eeeeaa">
               <IMG HEIGHT = "25" NAME = "white12" SRC = "blank.gif"
                  WIDTH = "25"></TD>
            <TD WIDTH = "25" HEIGHT = "25" BGCOLOR = "#eeeeaa">
               <IMG HEIGHT = "25" NAME = "white13" SRC = "blank.gif"
                  WIDTH = "25"></TD>
            <TD WIDTH = "50" HEIGHT = "25"></TD>
            <TD VALIGN = "center" ALIGN = "right" WIDTH = "25"
               HEIGHT = "25">2 </TD>
            <TD WIDTH = "25" HEIGHT = "25" BGCOLOR = "#eeeeaa">
               <IMG HEIGHT = "25" NAME = "imagea2"
                  SRC = "whitepawn.gif" WIDTH = "25"></TD>
            <TD WIDTH = "25" HEIGHT = "25" BGCOLOR = "#d26900">
               <IMG HEIGHT = "25" NAME = "imageb2"
                  SRC = "whitepawn.gif" WIDTH = "25"></TD>
            <TD WIDTH = "25" HEIGHT = "25" BGCOLOR = "#eeeeaa">
               <IMG HEIGHT = "25" NAME = "imagec2"
                  SRC = "whitepawn.gif" WIDTH = "25"></TD>
            <TD WIDTH = "25" HEIGHT = "25" BGCOLOR = "#d26900">
               <IMG HEIGHT = "25" NAME = "imaged2"
                  SRC = "whitepawn.gif" WIDTH = "25"></TD>
            <TD WIDTH = "25" HEIGHT = "25" BGCOLOR = "#eeeeaa">
               <IMG HEIGHT = "25" NAME = "imagee2"
                  SRC = "whitepawn.gif" WIDTH = "25"></TD>
            <TD WIDTH = "25" HEIGHT = "25" BGCOLOR = "#d26900">
               <IMG HEIGHT = "25" NAME = "imagef2"
                  SRC = "whitepawn.gif" WIDTH = "25"></TD>
            <TD WIDTH = "25" HEIGHT = "25" BGCOLOR = "#eeeeaa">
```

Fig. 28.16 Chess example with the **ScholarMate.xml** file (part 11 of 14).

```
               <IMG HEIGHT = "25" NAME = "imageg2"
                  SRC = "whitepawn.gif" WIDTH = "25"></TD>
            <TD WIDTH = "25" HEIGHT = "25" BGCOLOR = "#d26900">
               <IMG HEIGHT = "25" NAME = "imageh2"
                  SRC = "whitepawn.gif" WIDTH = "25"></TD>
            <TD WIDTH = "50" HEIGHT = "25"></TD>
            <TD WIDTH = "25" HEIGHT = "25" BGCOLOR = "#d26900">
               <IMG HEIGHT = "25" NAME = "black12" SRC = "blank.gif"
                  WIDTH = "25"></TD>
            <TD WIDTH = "25" HEIGHT = "25" BGCOLOR = "#d26900">
               <IMG HEIGHT = "25" NAME = "black13" SRC = "blank.gif"
                  WIDTH = "25"></TD>
         </TR>

         <TR>
            <TD WIDTH = "25" HEIGHT = "25" BGCOLOR = "#eeeeaa">
               <IMG HEIGHT = "25" NAME = "white14" SRC = "blank.gif"
                  WIDTH = "25"></TD>
            <TD WIDTH = "25" HEIGHT = "25" BGCOLOR = "#eeeeaa">
               <IMG HEIGHT = "25" NAME = "white15" SRC = "blank.gif"
                  WIDTH = "25"></TD>
            <TD WIDTH = "50" HEIGHT = "25"></TD>
            <TD VALIGN = "center" ALIGN = "right" WIDTH = "25"
               HEIGHT = "25">1 </TD>
            <TD WIDTH = "25" HEIGHT = "25" BGCOLOR = "#d26900">
               <IMG HEIGHT = "25" NAME = "imagea1"
                  SRC = "whiterook.gif" WIDTH = "25" ></TD>
            <TD WIDTH = "25" HEIGHT = "25" BGCOLOR = "#eeeeaa">
               <IMG HEIGHT = "25" NAME = "imageb1"
                   SRC = "whiteknight.gif" WIDTH = "25"></TD>
            <TD WIDTH = "25" HEIGHT = "25" BGCOLOR = "#d26900">
               <IMG HEIGHT = "25" NAME = "imagec1"
                  SRC = "whitebishop.gif" WIDTH = "25"></TD>
            <TD WIDTH = "25" HEIGHT = "25" BGCOLOR = "#eeeeaa">
               <IMG HEIGHT = "25" NAME = "imaged1"
                  SRC = "whitequeen.gif" WIDTH = "25"></TD>
            <TD WIDTH = "25" HEIGHT = "25" BGCOLOR = "#d26900">
               <IMG HEIGHT = "25" NAME = "imagee1"
                  SRC = "whiteking.gif" WIDTH = "25"></TD>
            <TD WIDTH = "25" HEIGHT = "25" BGCOLOR = "#eeeeaa">
               <IMG HEIGHT = "25" NAME = "imagef1"
                  SRC = "whitebishop.gif" WIDTH = "25"></TD>
            <TD WIDTH = "25" HEIGHT = "25" BGCOLOR = "#d26900">
              <IMG HEIGHT = "25" NAME = "imageg1"
                  SRC = "whiteknight.gif" WIDTH = "25"></TD>
            <TD WIDTH = "25" HEIGHT = "25" BGCOLOR = "#eeeeaa">
               <IMG HEIGHT = "25" NAME = "imageh1"
                  SRC = "whiterook.gif" WIDTH = "25"></TD>
            <TD WIDTH = "50" HEIGHT = "25"></TD>
            <TD WIDTH = "25" HEIGHT = "25" BGCOLOR = "#d26900">
               <IMG HEIGHT = "25" NAME = "black14" SRC = "blank.gif"
                  WIDTH = "25"></TD>
            <TD WIDTH = "25" HEIGHT = "25" BGCOLOR = "#d26900">
```

Fig. 28.16 Chess example with the **ScholarMate.xml** file (part 12 of 14).

```
                <IMG HEIGHT = "25" NAME = "black15" SRC = "blank.gif"
                   WIDTH = "25"></TD>
         </TR>

         <TR>
            <TD WIDTH = "25" HEIGHT = "25"></TD>
            <TD WIDTH = "25" HEIGHT = "25"></TD>
            <TD WIDTH = "50" HEIGHT = "25"></TD>
            <TD VALIGN = "top" ALIGN = "middle" WIDTH = "25"
               HEIGHT = "25"></TD>
            <TD WIDTH = "25" HEIGHT = "25" VALIGN = "top"
               ALIGN = "middle">a</TD>
            <TD WIDTH = "25" HEIGHT = "25" VALIGN = "top"
               ALIGN = "middle">b</TD>
            <TD WIDTH = "25" HEIGHT = "25" VALIGN = "top"
               ALIGN = "middle">c</TD>
            <TD WIDTH = "25" HEIGHT = "25" VALIGN = "top"
               ALIGN = "middle">d</TD>
            <TD WIDTH = "25" HEIGHT = "25" VALIGN = "top"
               ALIGN = "middle">e</TD>
            <TD WIDTH = "25" HEIGHT = "25" VALIGN = "top"
               ALIGN = "middle">f</TD>
            <TD WIDTH = "25" HEIGHT = "25" VALIGN = "top"
               ALIGN = "middle">g</TD>
            <TD WIDTH = "25" HEIGHT = "25" VALIGN = "top"
               ALIGN = "middle">h</TD>
            <TD WIDTH = "50" HEIGHT = "25"></TD>
            <TD WIDTH = "25" HEIGHT = "25"></TD>
            <TD WIDTH = "25" HEIGHT = "25"></TD>
         </TR>

      </TABLE>
   </DIV>

   <BR>

   <DIV ALIGN = "center">
      <TABLE BORDER = "1" CELLSPACING = "0" CELLPADDING = "2">
         <TR>
            <TD WIDTH = "50" ALIGN = "middle"><B><FONT SIZE = "2">
               Turn</FONT></B></TD>
            <TD WIDTH = "50" ALIGN = "middle"><B><FONT SIZE = "2">
               Piece</FONT></B></TD>
            <TD WIDTH = "50" ALIGN = "middle"><B><FONT SIZE = "2">
               From</FONT></B></TD>
            <TD WIDTH = "50" ALIGN = "middle"><B><FONT SIZE = "2">
               To</FONT></B></TD>
            <TD WIDTH = "50" ALIGN = "middle"><B><FONT SIZE = "2">
               Flag</FONT></B></TD>
         </TR>

         <TR>
            <TD WIDTH = "50" ALIGN = "middle" ID = "infoTurn">
```

Fig. 28.16 Chess example with the **ScholarMate.xml** file (part 13 of 14).

```
                 </TD>
            <TD WIDTH = "50" ALIGN = "middle" ID = "infoPiece">
                 </TD>
            <TD WIDTH = "50" ALIGN = "middle" ID = "infoFrom">
                 </TD>
            <TD WIDTH = "50" ALIGN = "middle" ID = "infoTo">
                 </TD>
            <TD WIDTH = "50" ALIGN = "middle" ID = "infoFlag">
                 </TD>
        </TR>

    </TABLE>
</DIV>

<BR>

<CENTER>
    <INPUT TYPE = "button" VALUE = "Reset" ID = "button"
        ONCLICK = "main();"><BR>
    <INPUT TYPE = "textbox" VALUE ="ScholarMate.xml" ID ="xmlfile">
</CENTER>

</FONT>
</BODY>

</HTML>
```

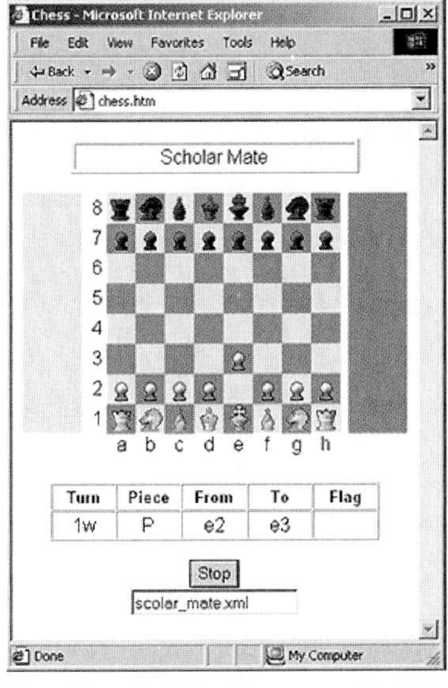

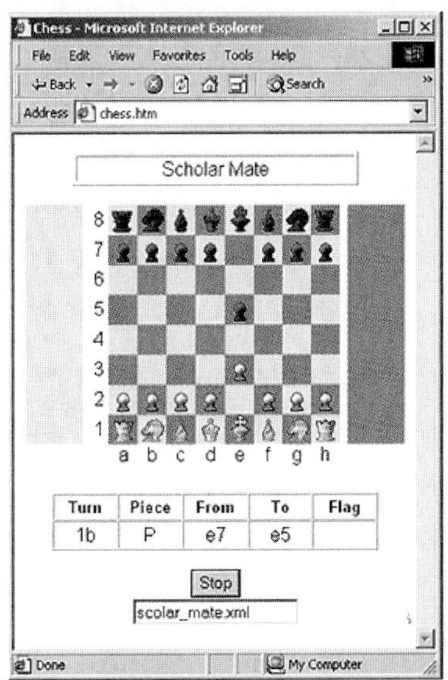

Fig. 28.16 Chess example with the **ScholarMate.xml** file (part 14 of 14).

```
<?xml version = "1.0"?>

<!-- Fig. 28.17: ScholarMate.xml -->

<game>
   <info>Scholar Mate</info>
   <moves>

      <move turn = "1" player = "white" piece = "P">
         <from x = "e" y = "2"/>
         <to x = "e" y = "3"/>
         <flag></flag>
      </move>

      <move turn = "1" player = "black" piece = "P">
         <from x = "e" y = "7"/>
         <to x = "e" y = "5"/>
         <flag></flag>
      </move>

      <move turn = "2" player = "white" piece = "B">
         <from x = "f" y = "1"/>
         <to x = "c" y = "4"/>
         <flag></flag>
      </move>

      <move turn = "2" player = "back" piece = "P">
         <from x = "h" y = "7"/>
         <to x = "h" y = "6"/>
         <flag>?</flag>
      </move>

      <move turn = "3" player = "white" piece = "Q">
         <from x = "d" y = "1"/>
         <to x = "h" y = "5"/>
         <flag></flag>
      </move>

      <move turn = "3" player = "black" piece = "P">
         <from x = "a" y = "7"/>
         <to x = "a" y = "5"/>
         <flag>??</flag>
      </move>

      <move turn = "4" player = "white" piece = "Q">
         <from x = "h" y = "5"/>
         <to x = "f" y = "7"/>
         <flag>x#</flag>
      </move>

   </moves>
</game>
```

Fig. 28.17 XML file that describes a sequence of chess moves.

In this example, we use JavaScript to access the XML document. We create an XML interface by declaring a new **msxml** ActiveX object (line 20). By setting the **url** property (line 185) of the object we can link to an XML document.

Once we have the XML data, we must use it correctly. First, we define the variables needed for the page. The **captureWhite** and **captureBlack** variables (lines 12 and 13) store the index of captured pieces. Variable **i** (line 16) keeps track of the location in the XML document containing the list of moves. Variable **timer** (line 17) is used for calling a function at set intervals. Variables **gameInfo** and **gameMoves** (lines 21 and 22) reference parts of the XML document. Variables **move**, **info**, **pieceSrc1** and **pieceSrc2** (lines 25 through 28) are temporary variables that store move information.

While the game is in progress, a move occurs every 1.5 seconds. We call method ***setInterval*** (line 178) to specify that **display** should be called every **1500** milliseconds. We call method ***clearInterval*** (line 182) to disable the automatic calling of **display**—which occurs when a game is finished.

Function **display** (line 31) displays a single move. First, we check on whether we have finished the game (lines 34 through 38). If we have, then we terminate the **timer** and reset the game. Next, we retrieve the element that has the information on the move (line 40) via **gameMoves** method **item**. We then parse the information (lines 50 through 170) to generate the output. Throughout this function, we call method ***innerText*** to get text embedded between element tags. On line 42, we use method ***getAttribute*** to retrieve an attribute's value.

On lines 174 through 198, we define function **main**, which controls the application. If we are in a "start" state, we start the **timer**, which calls function **display** every 1.5 seconds. If we are in a "stop" state, we reset to a "start" state and reset the **timer**. If we are in a "reset" state, we initialize the XML document and JavaScript variables.

We set the location of the XML document on line 185, and, using that document, we define variables **gameInfo** and **gameMoves** to reference the ***root*** element's first element (i.e., **info**) and the **root** element's second element (i.e., **moves**), respectively. We call method ***text*** to get the first element's text. To get a specific element, we use the ***children*** property. To determine how many children an element has, we use the ***length*** property (line 34).

Lines 201 through 268 define function **resetPieces**, which initializes the HTML chess board. The chess board is created by using an 8-by-8 **TABLE**, with alternating background colors **#eeeeaa** and **#d26900**. We also have two side **TABLE**s, which display captured pieces. The chess pieces images are transparent **gif**s—which are included in the Chapter 28 examples directory's **Chess** folder.

When clicked, the **reset** button (line 701) calls function **main**. We also have a text box (line 703), which provides a means to access various data sources. We provide data source **Scholar.xml**—which contains a classic 4-move checkmate match. Four moves is the minimum number of moves a player can make for checkmate.

Within the **game** root element (line 714), we have two sub-elements—**info** and **moves**. Element **info** stores information about the game, while element **moves** stores the series of **move** elements.

Each **move** element contains the turn number, player, piece moved, initial piece coordinates, ending piece coordinates and special flags. These flags contain symbols that are used to represent capture, check, checkmate and so on.

28.10 Extensible Hypertext Markup Language (XHTML)

This section provides a brief introduction to an XML-related technology called *Extensible Hypertext Markup Language (XHTML)*. XHTML includes HTML 4 and XML, and is the proposed successor to HTML 4. XHTML allows complex documents to be created by combining HTML elements with XML's extensibility (e.g., the ability to create new elements). For example, an XHTML document might contain HTML elements for images, MathML elements for mathematical expressions, CML elements for chemical notations, etc.

XHTML contains the HTML 4 tag set for backwards compatibility—which allows existing HTML documents to be conveniently converted to XHTML documents. XHTML uses XML syntax (e.g., all tags are lowercase and closed). XHTML documents are well-formed documents (i.e., each XHTML document is validated using DTDs). These XML features provide the structure HTML is lacking.

Some HTML authoring tools (e.g., XML Spy 2.0—**`http://www.xmlspy.com`**) already include support for XHTML. This trend will continue to grow as XHTML increases in popularity. For more information on XHTML visit

`http://www.w3.org/TR/xhtml1/`

and

`http://wdvl.com/Authoring/Languages/XML/XHTML`

28.11 Internet and World Wide Web Resources

`http://www.xml.org`
`XML.org` is a reference for XML, DTDs, schemas and namespaces.

`http://www.w3.org/style/XSL`
Provides information on XSL which includes the topics on what is new in XSL, learning XSL, XSL-enabled tools, XSL specification, FAQs, XSL history, etc.

`http://www.w3.org/TR`
W3C technical reports and publications page. Contains links to working drafts, proposed recommendations, recommendations, etc.

`http://www.xmlbooks.com`
Contains a list of recommended XML books by Charles GoldFarb—one of the original designers of GML (General Markup Language) from which SGML was derived.

`http://www.xmlsoftware.com`
Contains links for downloading XML-related software. Download links include XML browsers, conversion tools, database systems, DTD editors, XML editors, etc.

`http://www.xml-zone.com/`
The Development Exchange XML Zone is a complete resource for XML information. This site includes a FAQ, news, articles, links to other XML site and newsgroups.

`http://wdvl.internet.com/Authoring/Languages/XML/`
Web Developer's Virtual Library XML site includes tutorials, a FAQ, the latest news and extensive links to XML sites and software downloads.

`http://www.xml.com/`
Visit **`XML.com`** for the latest news and information about XML, conference listings, links to XML Web resources organized by topic, tools and more.

http://msdn.microsoft.com/xml/default.asp
The MSDN Online XML Development Center features articles on XML, Ask the Experts chat sessions, samples and demos, newsgroups and other helpful information.

http://www.w3.org/xml/
The W3C (World Wide Web Consortium) works to develop common protocols to ensure interoperability on the Web. Their XML page includes information about upcoming events, publications, software and discussion groups. Visit this site to read about the latest developments in XML.

http://www.oasis-open.org/cover/xml.html
The SGML/XML Web Page is an extensive resource that includes links to several FAQs, online resources, industry initiatives, demos, conferences and tutorials.

http://www.gca.org/conf/xml/xml_what.htm
The GCA site has an XML glossary, list of books, brief descriptions of the draft standards for XML and links to online drafts.

http://www.xmlinfo.com/
XMLINFO is a resource site with tutorials, a list of recommended books, documentation, discussion forums and more.

http://xdev.datachannel.com/
The title of this site is xDev: The Definitive Site for Serious XML Developers. This Web site includes several short tutorials with code examples, toolkits downloads and a reference library.

http://www.ibm.com/developer/xml/
The IBM XML Zone site is a great resource for developers. You will find news, tools, a library, case studies, events and information about standards.

http://developer.netscape.com/tech/metadata/index.html
The XML and Metadata Developer Central site has demos, technical notes and news articles related to XML.

http://www.projectcool.com/developer/xmlz/
The Project Cool Developerzone site includes several tutorials covering introductory through advanced XML.

http://www.poet.com/products/cms/xml_library/xml_lib.html
POET XML Resource Library includes links to XML white papers, tools, news, publications and Web links.

http://www.bluestone.com/xml/
Bluestone XML Suite software products allow you to develop e-commerce applications and integrate applications. This site also has free downloads and XML resources, such as links to white papers, standards, a FAQ and a glossary.

http://www.ucc.ie/xml/
This site is a detailed XML FAQ. Check out responses to some popular questions or submit your own questions through the site.

http://www.bell-labs.com/project/tts/sable.html
The Sable Markup Language is designed to markup text for input into speech synthesizers.

http://www.xml-cml.org/
This site is a resource for the Chemical Markup Language (CML). It includes a FAQ list, documentation, software and XML links.

http://www.tcf.nl/3.0/musicml/index.html
MusicML is a DTD for sheet music. Visit this site for examples and the specification.

http://www.hr-xml.org/
The HR-XML Consortium is a nonprofit organization working to set standardized XML tags for use in Human Resources.

http://www.textuality.com/xml/
Contains FAQ and the Lark non-validating XML parser.

SUMMARY

- XML markup is for describing data of virtually any type. XML is a language for creating mark up languages. XML enables the creation of new markup languages to mark up anything imaginable.
- With XML, you can create new element types.
- XML is derived from SGML (Standard Generalized Markup Language), which was established in 1986 as a standard for electronic document exchange. SGML is for structuring documents. Using the structure of a document, you can then apply formatting or decide the layout. Given the markup of a well-designed document type, deciding how to display the information is arbitrary, because it is the content that truly matters.
- With XML, you generate a method for storing information in a structured manner. The difference between SGML and XML is that XML is interoperable with both HTML and SGML. This is done so the data can be displayed (using HTML) or be integrated with available SGML records.
- Version 1.0 of the XML specification is complete and will not change. New versions of XML will be released as XML evolves to meet the requirements of many fields, especially e-commerce.
- A root element contains all other elements in the document.
- A container element contains sub-elements.
- By convention, XML documents end in the **.xml** extension and Document type definition (DTD) documents in the **.dtd** extension.
- Empty elements do not have matching end tags. In XML, empty elements must be terminated with a forward slash (**/**).
- DTD files define the grammatical rules for the document. A DTD is not required for an XML document but is recommended for document conformity. DTDs provide a method for type-checking an XML document, thus verifying its validity. Specifying the set of rules that structure a document is done with EBNF (Extended Backus-Naur Form) grammar.
- Element type declaration **!ELEMENT** specifies that an element is being created. The plus sign (**+**) operator indicates one or more occurrences. Other operators include the asterisk (*****), which indicates any number of occurrences, and the question mark (**?**), which indicates either zero occurrences or exactly one occurrence. If an operator is omitted, exactly one occurrence is assumed.
- Element type declaration **!ATTLIST** defines an attribute. The flag **#IMPLIED** indicates that an attribute does not have a default value. Flag **CDATA** defines that an attribute contains a string.
- Flag **#PCDATA** specifies that an element can store parsed character data. Keyword **EMPTY** specifies that the element does not contain content.
- Many applications for XML have been created for structuring data in various fields. In the mathematics field, MathML (Mathematical Markup Language) has been developed for describing mathematical notation on the Web. Other examples of XML applications are Chemical Markup Language (CML), Speech Markup Language (SpeechML), Extensible Financial Reporting Markup Language (XFRML) and Product Data Markup Language (PDML).
- One application that can render MathML is the Amaya editor from the W3C.
- MathML content is embedded into an HTML file by using the HTML **MATH** element.

- MathML element **mrow** is a container element for expressions containing more than one element. Element **mn** marks up a number. Element **mo** marks up an operator.
- MathML entity reference **⁢** represents a multiplication operation without a symbolic representation. Element **msup** is a superscripting element. Element **msub** defines a subscript element. Element **mi** displays variables. Element **mfrac** displays a fraction. The integral symbol is defined by **∫** and the superscript and subscript markup is defined using **msubsup**. Element **msqrt** displays the square-root symbol. The delta symbol is defined by **δ**. Element **mtable** defines a matrix. To create the matrix rows, use element **mtr**. Each row contains **mtd** element columns.
- An XML parser (also called an XML processor) determines the content and structure of an XML document by combining an XML document and its DTD (if one is present). Internet Explorer 5 has a built-in XML parser (**msxml**).
- XML parsers build tree structures from XML documents. If this tree structure is created successfully without using a DTD, the XML document is considered well-formed. If the tree structure is created successfully and a DTD is used, the XML document is considered valid (or type valid). By definition a valid XML document is also a well-formed XML document. XML parsers exist in two varieties: validating (i.e., enforces DTD rules) and nonvalidating (i.e., ignores DTD rules).
- Because an XML document is primarily concerned with data, XML documents are a data source. Internet Explorer 5 allows XML documents to be embedded into an HTML document by using the **XML** element. An XML document that exists within an HTML page is called a data island.
- With data islands, binding data to a table requires minimal effort. Internet Explorer 5 can handle many different data sources (e.g., XML, comma-delimited lists, ADO, etc.) using this system.
- Extensible Style Language (XSL) defines the layout of an XML document. An XSL style sheet provides the rules for displaying or organizing an XML document's data. XSL Transformations (XSLT) is the part of XSL that transforms one XML document into another XML document.
- Element **xsl:for-each** iterates over items. Attribute **order-by** specifies what is sorted. A plus sign (**+**) indicates ascending order; a minus sign (**-**) indicates descending order. When more than one element is to be sorted, a semicolon (**;**) separates them. Attribute **select** defines which elements are selected. Attribute **xmlns:xsl** indicates where the specification for an element is located.
- Attribute **xmlns** defines an XML namespace. Namespaces identify collections of elements type declarations so that they do not conflict with other element type declarations with the same name created by other programmers. Two predefined XML namespaces are **xml** and **xsl**. Programmers can create their own namespaces.
- Element **xsl:value-of** retrieves the data specified in attribute **select**. The data returned by this element replaces element **xsl:value-of**.
- Brackets (**[ ]**) specify an XSL conditional statement.
- XML includes an XML Document Object Model (DOM) that allows dynamic content to be generated from an XML document using scripting. Some vendors, such as Microsoft, have extended the DOM to add additional features for use with Internet Explorer 5.
- Method **cloneNode** copies nodes. Passing **true** as an argument allows all sub-nodes and their attribute values to be copied. If **false** is passed, only the node and its attribute value are copied.
- Microsoft XML DOM method **transformNodeToObject** applies a specified XSL style sheet to the data contained in the parent object and outputs it to a new XML document. Property **documentElement** returns the root element. Property **XMLDocument** returns an XML document.
- Methods **firstPage**—which moves to the first record, **previousPage**—which moves to the previous record, **nextPage**—which moves to the next record and **lastPage**—which moves to the last record are Microsoft XML DOM methods.

- Because a DTD is written in a format dissimilar to the format of XML, Microsoft developed a schema to create document definitions using the style of XML. This schema is called XML-Data.
- Element **xml:stylesheet** specifies the XSL style sheet an XML document uses. This tag is the root-level element of a style sheet definition.
- Element **ElementType** declares an element type. Attribute **name**'s value defines the element's name. Attribute **content** defines the element's contents—**eltOnly** specifies that this element can only contain other elements.
- Element **group** defines the number of times an element is allowed to occur. Attribute **minOccurs** defines an element's minimum number of occurrences. Attribute **maxOccurs** defines an element's maximum number of occurrences. Element **element** defines the declared element type that can occur.
- Element **xsl:template** defines a style. Attribute **match** defines what the template matches.
- Any material between the opening **<![CDATA[** section and the closing **]]>** is not processed by the style sheet and is rendered exactly as it appears. To ensure that scripting code does not conflict with an XSL style sheet, the scripting code is often enclosed in **xsl:comment**s.
- Method **selectSingleNode** returns the first node in an XSL style sheet that has an attribute named **order-by**. The **XSLDocument** property returns the **document**'s XSL style sheet.
- Method **transformNode** sends XML data through a **stylesheet**.
- To embed another template section, use element **xsl:apply-templates**. This tag applies the specified template at the position of the tag.
- To perform conditional tests, use the **xsl:choose** element. An **xsl:choose** element is composed of one or more **xsl:when** elements and an optional **xsl:otherwise** element. The **xsl:when** element is a conditional statement, with the conditional placed in the **test** attribute. Element **xsl:otherwise** defines the default case.
- Element **xsl:element** generates a markup of a specified name. To add an attribute to a markup, use element **xsl:attribute**. This tag generates an attribute of an **xsl:element**.
- Use property **length** to determine the number of children for an element.
- Method **getAttribute** returns the element's attribute. To get the text inside an element, use the **text** property.
- Extensible Hypertext Markup Language (XHTML) combines HTML 4 and XML, and is the proposed successor to HTML 4. XHTML allows complex documents to be created by combining well-known HTML elements with XML's extensibility. XHTML contains the HTML 4 tag set for backwards compatibility—which allows existing HTML documents to be conveniently converted to XHTML documents. XHTML uses XML syntax. XHTML documents are well-formed documents (i.e., each XHTML document is validated using DTDs).

TERMINOLOGY

Amaya editor from W3C
asterisk, * (any number of occurrences)
!ATTLIST element type declaration
attributes
brackets, [] (XSL condition statement)
case sensitive
CDATA section
Chemical Markup Language (CML)
closing tag
CML (Chemical Markup Language)
container element
customized markup languages
data island
&delta in MathML
describing data
displaying data
document
Document Content Description (DCD)

document type definition (DTD)
.dtd extension
EBNF (Extended Backus-Naur Form) grammar
!ELEMENT element type declaration
ELEMENTTYPE
EMPTY
empty element
entities
Extended Backus-Naur Form (EBNF) grammar
Extensible Financial Reporting Markup Language
Extensible Style Language (XSL)
forward slash, **/**
HTML
#IMPLIED flag
∫ in MathML
&Invisible Times; in MathML
MATH element in HTML
MathML (Mathematical Markup Language)
metadata
mfrac element in MathML
mi element in MathML
mn element in MathML
mo element in MathML
mrow element in MathML
msqrt element in MathML
msub element in MathML
msubsup element in MathML
msup element in MathML
msxml (Internet Explorer 5 XML parser)
mtable element in MathML
mtr element in MathML
mtd element in MathML
namespace
objects in XML
opening tag
parsed character data (**#PCDATA**)
parser
#PCDATA (parsed character data)
PDML (Product Data Markup Language)
plus sign (**+**) operator (one or more occurrences)
processing instruction
processor
Product Data Markup Language (PDML)
prolog
question mark (**?**) for zero or one occurrence
root element
Schema element
semicolon (**;**)
SGML (Standard Generalized Markup Language)
slash (**/**)
Speech Markup Language (SpeechML)
SpeechML
style sheet
sub-element
Synchronized Multimedia Interface Language
tag
tag set
type attribute
valid document
Web Collection
well-formed document
W3C XML working group
XFRML (Extensible Financial Reporting ML)
XHTML (Extensible Hypertext Markup Language)
XML editor
XML (Extensible Markup Language)
.xml extension
xml namespace (**xmlns**)
xmlns (XML namespace)
XML Developers Group
XML Document Object Model (DOM)
XML parser
XML specification
XML tag
XML-Data
.xsl extension
xsl namespace
xsl:apply-templates element
xsl:attribute element
xsl:choose element
XSL conditional statement
xsl:element element
xsl:for-each element
XSL (Extensible Style Language)
XSLT (XSL Transformations)
xsl:otherwise element
xsl:stylesheet element
xsl:template element
xsl:value-of element
xsl:when element

COMMON PROGRAMMING ERRORS

28.1 XML is case sensitive. Using the wrong case for an XML tag is a syntax error.

28.2 Attempting to create more than one root element is a syntax error.

28.3 Not terminating an empty element with a forward slash (**/**) is a syntax error.

28.4 Omitting a closing XML tag is a syntax error.

28.5 Omitting quotes (either single or double) around an XML attribute's value is a syntax error.

28.6 Any element, attribute, tag or relationship not explicitly defined by a DTD is an error.

PERFORMANCE TIP

28.1 Because XSL style sheets are interpreted on the client, server resources are conserved.

PORTABILITY TIPS

28.1 XML is defined by the World Wide Web Consortium (W3C) to be application and vendor neutral—which ensures maximum portability.

28.2 DTDs ensure that XML documents created by different programs are consistent.

28.3 The **XML** tag is Microsoft-specific.

SOFTWARE ENGINEERING OBSERVATIONS

28.1 Several Independent Software Vendors (ISVs) have written XML parsers. Some of these parsers can be found at **http://www.xml.com/xml/pub/Guide/XML_Parsers**.

28.2 XSL allows data presentation to be separated from data description.

SELF-REVIEW EXERCISES

28.7 Fill in the blanks for each of the following:

a) Element _________ defines a mathematical operator.
b) A data island uses attribute _________ to bind to a data source.
c) To embed an XML document into an HTML file requires the _________ tag.
d) ActiveX object _________ binds XML to HTML documents.
e) Element _________ generates a markup tag in an HTML document.
f) We use the _________ property to get the contents of an element in JavaScript.
g) MathML symbol **∫** is an example of _________.
h) To define a DTD element attribute, you use the _________ tag.
i) Element _________ defines an XML stylesheet.
j) Element _________ selects specific XML elements.

28.8 State which of the following statements are *true* and which are *false*. If *false*, explain why.

a) XML is not case sensitive.
b) There can be only one root-level element.
c) XML is used to display information.
d) A DTD/Schema is used to define the style of a XML document.
e) Schema **group** element with a **maxOccurs** attribute value of **2** specifies two occurrences of an element.
f) MathML is a subset of XML.
g) Data placed between **<![CDATA[** and **]]>** is not parsed by the XML parser.
h) Element **xsl:otherwise** is used within an **xsl:when** element.
i) The **<!ELEMENT list (item*)>** tag defines a list element containing one or more **item** elements.
j) Element **MATH** is an XML element.

28.9 Find the error(s) in each of the following and explain how to correct it (them).

a) **<job>**

```
        <title>Manager</title>
        <task number = "42">
    </job>
```

b)
```
    <mfrac>
        <mi>x</mi>
        <mo>+</mo>
        <mn>4</mn>
        <mi>y</mi>
    </mfrac>
```

28.10 In Fig 28.1 we subdivided the **author** element into more detailed pieces. How would you subdivide the **date** element?

28.11 What is the **#PCDATA** flag used for?

28.12 In Fig. 28.15, how would you design an XSLT to filter for the first name, "**Paul**"?

28.13 What is the difference between HTML and XML?

ANSWERS TO SELF-REVIEW EXERCISES

28.1 a) **mo**. b) **DATASRC**. c) **XML**. d) **msxml**. e) **xsl:element**. f) **text**. g) an operator (**mo**). h) **!ATTLIST**. i) **xsl:stylesheet**. j) **xsl:for-each**.

28.2 a) False. XML is case sensitive. b) True. c) False. XML is used to organize material in a structured manner. d) False. A DTD/schema is used to define the grammar of an XML document. e) False. This is an invalid syntax. A **maxOccurs** attribute can only have a value of **1** or *****. f) True. g) True. h) False. Element **xsl:otherwise** is used within element **xsl:choose**. i) False. **(item*)** defines a **list** element containing any number of **item** elements. j) False. Element **MATH** is an HTML tag.

28.3 a) A **/** in the empty element is missing:

```
<task number = "42"/>
```

b) **<mrow>** element is needed to contain $x + 2$

28.4
```
<date>
    <month>September</month>
    <day>9</day>
    <year>1999</year>
</date>
```

28.5 The **#PCDATA** flag denotes that parsed character data can be contained by the element.

28.6 Use the **select** attribute value of **contact[FirstName='Paul']**.

28.7 Simply, the difference between HTML and XML is that HTML is a method for displaying data, while XML is a method for storing data.

EXERCISES

28.8 In Fig 28.3 we defined a DTD for the business letter document. What would be a valid DTD for Fig 28.1?

28.9 Using Amaya and MathML, generate the following:

a) $\int_{-\frac{1}{2}}^{0} 5y\delta x$

b) $\begin{bmatrix} 1 & -9 & 3 \\ 5 & 0 & -1 \\ 7 & 7 & 7 \end{bmatrix}$

c) $x = \sqrt{(2y^{-3})} - 8y + \frac{\sqrt{y}}{3}$

28.10 Write an XML document that stores the following information:

Name	Job	Department	Cubicle
Joe	Programmer	Engineering	5E
Mary	Designer	Marketing	9M
Elaine	Designer	Human Resources	8H
Tim	Administrator	Engineering	4E
Peter	Project Coordinator	Marketing	3M
Bill	Programmer	Engineering	12E
Mark	Salesperson	Marketing	17M
Karin	Programmer	Technical Support	19T

28.11 Write a DTD for the XML document in Exercise 28.10.

28.12 Write an XSL that displays the XML document in Exercise 28.11.

28.13 Write an HTML page that displays the XML data in Exercise 28.10, using data islands.

28.14 Create an Active Server Page that creates an XML document from the following database:

Product ID	Product
152341	Acme Anvil
015832	Big Bug
951324	Candy Crab
765421	Distorted Dinosaur
235231	Easy Exercise
882312	Foggy Freeway
441221	Green Grass
722345	Happy Heifer
523119	Icky Illness
612214	Jumpy Jellybeans

28.15 Write the DTD for Fig. 28.16.

28.16 Write an Active Server Page that dynamically creates an XML data island as part of the HTML page sent to the client.

29

Servlets: Bonus for Java™ Developers

Objectives

- To write servlets and execute them with the JavaServer™ Web Development Kit WebServer.
- To be able to respond to HTTP **GET** and **POST** requests from an **HttpServlet**.
- To be able to use cookies to store client information during a browsing session.
- To be able to use session tracking from a servlet.
- To be able to read and write files from a servlet.
- To be able to access a database from a servlet.

A fair request should be followed by the deed in silence.
Dante Alighieri

The longest part of the journey is said to be the passing of the gate.
Marcus Terentius Varro

Friends share all things.
Pythagorus

If at first you don't succeed, destroy all evidence that you tried.
Newt Heilscher

If nominated, I will not accept; if elected, I will not serve.
General William T. Sherman

Me want cookie!
The Cookie Monster, Sesame Street

That's the way the cookie crumbles.
Anonymous

Outline

29.1 Introduction[1]

There is much excitement over the Internet and the World Wide Web. The Internet ties the "information world" together. The World Wide Web makes the Internet easy to use and gives it the flair and sizzle of multimedia. Organizations see the Internet and the Web as crucial to their information systems strategies. Java provides a number of built-in networking capabilities that make it easy to develop Internet-based and Web-based applications. Java can enable programs to search the world for information and to collaborate with programs running on the Internet or in an intranet. Java can even enable applets and applications running on the same computer to communicate with one another, subject to security constraints. Java provides a rich complement of networking capabilities and will likely be used as an implementation vehicle in computer networking courses. In *Java How to Program, Third Edition* we introduce a wide variety of Java networking concepts and capabilities.

Java has several networking capabilities. The fundamental networking capabilities are defined by classes and interfaces of package ***`java.net`***, through which Java offers *socket-based communications* that enable applications to view networking as streams of data—a program can read from a *socket* or write to a socket as simply as reading from a file

1. This chapter is provided as a bonus for established Java developers who are interested in learning Java servlets. This chapter assumes that the reader is already familiar with Java programming. Also note that JavaScript and JScript are not Java. For more information on the Java programming language, please see our book, "Java How to Program, Third Edition."

or writing to a file. The classes and interfaces of package **java.net** also offer *packet-based communications* that enable individual *packets* of information to be transmitted—commonly used to transmit audio and video over the Internet.

Higher-level views of networking are provided by classes and interfaces in the ***java.rmi*** packages (five packages) for *Remote Method Invocation (RMI)* and ***org.omg*** packages (seven packages) for *Common Object Request Broker Architecture (CORBA)* that are part of the Java 2 Applications Programming Interface (API). The RMI packages allow Java objects running on separate Java Virtual Machines (normally on separate computers) to communicate via remote method calls. Such method calls appear to be to an object in the same program, but actually have built-in networking (based on the capabilities of package **java.net**) that communicates the method calls to another object in the same program, in another program on the same computer or on a separate computer. The CORBA packages provide similar functionality to the RMI packages. A key difference between RMI and CORBA is that RMI can only be used between Java objects, whereas CORBA can be used between any two applications that understand CORBA—including applications written in other programming languages.

Our discussion of networking focuses on both sides of a *client-server relationship*. The *client* requests that some action be performed and the *server* performs the action and responds to the client. This *request-response model* of communication is the foundation for Java *servlets*. A servlet extends the functionality of a server. The ***javax.servlet*** package and the ***javax.servlet.http*** package provide the classes and interfaces to define servlets.

A common implementation of the request-response model is between World Wide Web browsers and World Wide Web servers (as shown previously in Chapter 26, "Active Server Pages," and in Chapter 27, "Perl/CGI"). When a user selects a Web site to browse through his or her browser (the client application), a request is sent to the appropriate Web server (the server application). The server normally responds to the client by sending the appropriate HTML Web page or other content.

This chapter discusses *servlets* that enhance the functionality of World Wide Web servers—the most common form of servlet today. Servlet technology today is primarily designed for use with the HTTP protocol of the World Wide Web, but servlets are being developed for other technologies. Servlets are effective for developing Web-based solutions that help provide secure access to a Web site, that interact with databases on behalf of a client, that dynamically generate custom HTML documents to be displayed by browsers and that maintain unique session information for each client.

Many developers feel that servlets are the right solution for database-intensive applications that communicate with so-called *thin clients*—applications that require minimal client-side support. The server is responsible for the database access. Clients connect to the server using standard protocols available on all client platforms. Thus, the logic code can be written once and reside on the server for access by clients.

Our servlet examples will make use of Java's input/output streams facilities (for reading and writing files) and the Java Database Connectivity (JDBC) facilities discussed in Chapters 17 and 18 of *Java How to Program, Third Edition*. Using servlets, input/output streams and JDBC, we can build multitier client-server applications that access databases. [*Note:* You will need to install the Java 2 Software Development Kit from Sun Microsystems (**http://java.sun.com/**) to execute the examples in this chapter.]

29.2 Overview of Servlet Technology

In this section we present an overview of Java servlet technology. We discuss at a high level the servlet-related classes, methods and exceptions. The next several sections present live-code examples in which we build multitier client-server systems using servlet and JDBC technology.

The Internet offers many *protocols*. The *HTTP protocol (HyperText Transfer Protocol)* that forms the basis of the World Wide Web uses URLs (*Uniform Resource Locators*, also called *Universal Resource Locators*) to locate data on the Internet. Common URLs reference files or directories but can also reference complex tasks such as database lookups and Internet searches. For more information on URL formats visit

`http://www.ncsa.uiuc.edu/demoweb/url-primer.html`

For more information on the *HTTP* protocol visit

`http://www.w3.org/Protocols/HTTP/`

For general information on a variety of World Wide Web topics visit

`http://www.w3.org/`

Servlets are the analog on the server side to applets on the client side and are similar to ASP (discussed in Chapter 26) and CGI (discussed in Chapter 27). Servlets are normally executed as part of a Web server (see Chapter 24 for more information on Web servers). In fact, servlets have become so popular that they are now supported by most major Web servers, including Microsoft's *Internet Information Server* (through a Web server plug-in such as *Allaire Corporations JRun*), the Netscape Web servers, the World Wide Web Consortium's Java-based Jigsaw Web server, Sun Microsystems' Java Web Server and the popular Apache Web server.

The servlets in this chapter demonstrate communication between clients and servers via the HTTP protocol of the World Wide Web. A client sends an HTTP request to the server. The server receives the request and directs it to be processed by appropriate servlets. The servlets do their processing (which often includes interacting with a database), then return their results to the client—normally in the form of HTML documents to display in a browser, but other data formats, such as images, binary data and XML, can be returned.

29.2.1 `Servlet` Interface

Architecturally, all servlets must implement the ***`Servlet`*** interface. This enables a servlet to reside in the framework provided by the Web server that will call the servlet's methods. As with many key applet methods, the methods of interface **`Servlet`** are invoked automatically (by the server on which the servlet is installed). This interface defines five methods described in Fig. 29.1.

Software Engineering Observation 29.1

All servlets must implement the **`javax.servlet.Servlet`** *interface.*

Method	Description
`void init( ServletConfig config )`	
	This method is automatically called once during a servlet's execution cycle to initialize the servlet. The **`ServletConfig`** argument is supplied automatically by the server that executes the servlet.
`ServletConfig getServletConfig()`	
	This method returns a reference to an object that implements interface **`ServletConfig`**. This object provides access to the servlet's configuration information, such as initialization parameters, and the servlet's **`ServletContext`**, which provides the servlet with access to its environment (i.e., the server in which the servlet is executing).
`void service( ServletRequest request, ServletResponse response )`	
	This is the first method called on every servlet to respond to a client request.
`String getServletInfo()`	
	This method is defined by a servlet programmer to return a **`String`** containing servlet information such as the servlet's author and version.
`void destroy()`	
	This "cleanup" method is called when a servlet is terminated by the server on which it is executing. This is a good method to use to deallocate a resource used by the servlet (such as an open file or an open database connection).

Fig. 29.1 Methods of interface **`Servlet`**.

The servlet packages define two **`abstract`** classes that implement the interface **`Servlet`**—class ***`GenericServlet`*** (from the package **`javax.servlet`**) and class ***`HttpServlet`*** (from the package **`javax.servlet.http`**). These classes provide default implementations of all the **`Servlet`** methods. Most servlets extend either **`GenericServlet`** or **`HttpServlet`** and override some or all of their methods with appropriate customized behaviors.

The examples in this chapter all extend class **`HttpServlet`**, which defines enhanced processing capabilities for servlets that extend the functionality of a Web server. The key method in every servlet is method **`service`**, which receives both a ***`ServletRequest`*** object and a ***`ServletResponse`*** object. These objects provide access to input and output streams that allow the servlet to read data from the client and send data to the client. These streams can be either byte-based binary streams or character-based text streams. If problems occur during the execution of a servlet, either **`ServletException`**s or **`IOException`**s are thrown to indicate the problem.

29.2.2 `HttpServlet` Class

Web-based servlets typically extend class **`HttpServlet`**. Class **`HttpServlet`** overrides method **`service`** to distinguish between the typical requests received from a client Web browser. The two most common HTTP *request types* (also known as *request methods*) are ***`GET`*** and ***`POST`***. A **`GET`** request *gets* information from the server. Common uses of **`GET`** requests are to retrieve content from a Web server such as an HTML document or an image. A **POST** request also gets information from the server, but normally the results of a **POST** request are not cached (i.e., stored) on the local computer (cached Web pages can be loaded from the local computer's disk to avoid the overhead of retrieving the page the next time you visit the site). Common uses of **POST** requests are to send the server information from an *HTML form* in which the client enters data, to send the server information so it can search the Internet or query a database for the client, to send authentication information to the server, etc. Note that both **GET** and **POST** requests can send data to the server; however, **GET** requests only include that data as part of the URL. **POST** requests have a separate message body in which data is placed.

Class **HttpServlet** defines methods ***doGet*** and ***doPost*** to respond to **GET** and **POST** requests from a client, respectively. These methods are called by the **HttpServlet** class's **service** method, which is called when a request arrives at the server. Method **service** first determines the request type, then calls the appropriate method. Other less common request types are available, but these are beyond the scope of this book. For more information on the HTTP protocol visit the site

http://www.w3.org/Protocols/

Methods of class **HttpServlet** that respond to the other request types are shown in Fig. 29.2 (all receive parameters of type ***HttpServletRequest*** and ***HttpServletResponse*** and return **void**). The methods of Fig. 29.2 are not frequently used.

Methods **doGet** and **doPost** receive as arguments an **HttpServletRequest** object and an **HttpServletResponse** object that enable interaction between the client and the server. The methods of **HttpServletRequest** make it easy to access the data supplied as part of the request. The **HttpServletResponse** methods make it easy to return the servlet's results in HTML format to the Web client. Interfaces **HttpServletRequest** and **HttpServletResponse** are discussed in the next two sections.

Method	Description
doDelete	Called in response to an HTTP ***DELETE*** request. Such a request is normally used to delete a file from the server. This may not be available on some servers because of its inherent security risks.
doOptions	Called in response to an HTTP ***OPTIONS*** request. This returns information to the client indicating the HTTP options supported by the server.
doPut	Called in response to an HTTP ***PUT*** request. Such a request is normally used to store a file on the server. This may not be available on some servers because of its inherent security risks.
doTrace	Called in response to an HTTP ***TRACE*** request. Such a request is normally used for debugging. The implementation of this method automatically returns an HTML document to the client containing the request header information (data sent by the browser as part of the request).

Fig. 29.2 Other methods of class **HttpServlet**.

29.2.3 HttpServletRequest Interface

Every call to **doGet** or **doPost** for an **HttpServlet** receives an object that implements interface **HttpServletRequest**. The Web server that executes the servlet creates an **HttpServletRequest** object and passes this to the servlet's **service** method (which, in turn, passes it to **doGet** or **doPost**). This object contains the request from the client. A variety of methods are provided to enable the servlet to process the client's request. Some of these methods are from interface ***ServletRequest***—the interface that **HttpServletRequest** extends. A few key methods used in this chapter are presented in Fig 29.3.

29.2.4 HttpServletResponse Interface

Every call to **doGet** or **doPost** for an **HttpServlet** receives an object that implements interface **HttpServletResponse**. The Web server that executes the servlet creates an **HttpServletResponse** object and passes this to the servlet's **service** method (which, in turn, passes it to **doGet** or **doPost**). This object contains the response to the client. A variety of methods are provided to enable the servlet to formulate the response to the client. Some of these methods are from interface ***ServletResponse***—the interface that **HttpServletResponse** extends. A few key methods used in this chapter are presented in Fig 29.4.

Method	Description
String getParameter(String name)	Returns the value associated with a parameter sent to the servlet as part of a **GET** or **POST** request. The **name** argument represents the parameter name.
Enumeration getParameterNames()	Returns the names of all the parameters sent to the servlet as part of a request.
String[] getParameterValues(String name)	Returns an array of **String**s containing the values for a specified servlet parameter.
Cookie[] getCookies()	Returns an array of **Cookie** objects stored on the client by the server. **Cookie**s can be used to uniquely identify clients to the servlet.
HttpSession getSession(boolean create)	Returns an **HttpSession** object associated with the client's current browsing session. An **HttpSession** object can be created by this method (**true** argument) if an **HttpSession** object does not already exist for the client. **HttpSession** objects can be used in similar ways to **Cookie**s for uniquely identifying clients.

Fig. 29.3 Important methods of interface **HttpServletRequest**.

Method	Description
`void addCookie( Cookie cookie )`	
	Used to add a **`Cookie`** to the header of the response to the client. The **`Cookie`**'s maximum age and whether the client allows **`Cookie`**s to be saved determine whether or not **`Cookie`**s will be stored on the client.
`ServletOutputStream getOutputStream()`	
	Obtains a byte-based output stream that enables binary data to be sent to the client.
`PrintWriter getWriter()`	
	Obtains a character-based output stream that enables text data to be sent to the client.
`void setContentType( String type )`	
	Specifies the MIME type of the response to the browser. The MIME type helps the browser determine how to display the data (or possibly what other application to execute to process the data). For example, MIME type **`"text/html"`** indicates that the response is an HTML document, so the browser displays the HTML page.

Fig. 29.4 Important methods of **`HttpServletResponse`**.

29.3 Downloading the JavaServer™ Web Development Kit (JSWDK)

Before you can program with servlets, you must download and install the *JavaServer Web Development Kit (JSWDK)* so you can build and test your servlets. The JSWDK was formerly known as the *Java Servlet Development Kit (JSDK)*. You may download the JSWDK at no charge from Sun Microsystems at the Web site

`http://java.sun.com/products/servlet/index.html`

The download is accessible near the bottom of this page. Sun provides download for Windows and UNIX platforms. At the time of this publication, the current version of the JSWDK (version 1.0.1) was based on the Java Servlet Specification version 2.1.

After downloading the JSWDK, install it on your system and carefully read the **`README.txt`** file supplied in the installation directory. It explains how to set up the JSWDK and discusses how to start the *server* that can be used to test servlets if you do not have a Web server that supports servlets. To develop servlets, you also need to copy the ***`servlet.jar`*** file containing the JSWDK class files from the **`lib`** subdirectory in the JSWDK's installation directory (**`jswdk-1.0.1`**) to your Java 2 Software Development Kit (J2SDK) extensions directory—the directory **`c:\jdk1.2.2\jre\lib\ext`** on Windows or the directory **`~/jdk1.2.2/jre/lib/ext`** on UNIX. *Note:* We assume here that you have J2SDK version 1.2.2 installed. If you have a different version of the J2SDK installed, you will need to copy **`servlet.jar`** into the appropriate directory structure.

If you would like to test your servlets with an industrial Web server that supports servlets, you can try the *World Wide Web Consortium's (W3C)* free Java-based *Jigsaw* Web server. The W3C is a multinational organization dedicated to developing common protocols for the World Wide Web that "promote its evolution and ensure its interoperability." To that end, W3C provides *Open Source software*—a main benefit of such software is that it is free for anyone to use. W3C provides Jigsaw through its Open Source license. Jigsaw and its documentation can be downloaded from

http://www.w3.org/Jigsaw/

For more information on the Open Source license, visit the site

http://www.opensource.org/

29.4 Handling HTTP GET Requests

The primary purpose of an HTTP **GET** request is to retrieve the content of a specified URL—normally the content is an HTML document (e.g., a Web page or an image). The servlet of Fig. 29.5 and the HTML document of Fig. 29.6 demonstrate a servlet that handles HTTP **GET** requests. When the user clicks the **Get Page** button in the HTML document (Fig. 29.6), a **GET** request is sent to the servlet **HTTPGetServlet** (Fig. 29.5). The servlet responds to the request by dynamically generating an HTML document for the client that displays "Welcome to Servlets!" Figure 29.5 shows the **HTTPGetServlet.java** source code. Figure 29.6 shows the HTML document the client loads to access the servlet and shows screen captures of the client's browser window before and after the interaction with the servlet. The HTML document in this example was displayed using Microsoft's Internet Explorer 5 browser; however, the example should work from any browser.

```
// Fig. 29.5: HTTPGetServlet.java
// Creating and sending a page to the client
import javax.servlet.*;
import javax.servlet.http.*;
import java.io.*;

public class HTTPGetServlet extends HttpServlet {
   public void doGet( HttpServletRequest request,
                      HttpServletResponse response )
      throws ServletException, IOException
   {
      PrintWriter output;

      response.setContentType( "text/html" );  // content type
      output = response.getWriter();           // get writer

      // create and send HTML page to client
      StringBuffer buf = new StringBuffer();
      buf.append( "<HTML><HEAD><TITLE>\n" );
      buf.append( "A Simple Servlet Example\n" );
      buf.append( "</TITLE></HEAD><BODY>\n" );
```

Fig. 29.5 The **HTTPGetServlet**, which processes an HTTP **GET** request (part 1 of 2).

```
22          buf.append( "<H1>Welcome to Servlets!</H1>\n" );
23          buf.append( "</BODY></HTML>" );
24          output.println( buf.toString() );
25          output.close();     // close PrintWriter stream
26       }
27    }
```

Fig. 29.5 The **HTTPGetServlet**, which processes an HTTP **GET** request (part 2 of 2).

Lines 3 and 4 import the **javax.servlet** and **javax.servlet.http** packages. We use several data types from these packages in the example.

For servlets that handle HTTP **GET** and **POST** requests, the JSWDK provides superclass **HttpServlet** (from package **javax.servlet.http**). This class implements the **javax.servlet.Servlet** interface and adds methods that support HTTP protocol requests. Class **HTTPGetServlet** extends **HttpServlet** (line 7) for this reason.

Superclass **HttpServlet** provides method **doGet** to respond to **GET** requests. Its default functionality is to indicate a **BAD_REQUEST** error. (Typically this error is indicated in the browser with a Web page that displays an error message). We override method **doGet** (lines 8 through 26) to provide custom **GET** request processing. Method **doGet** receives two arguments—an object that implements **javax.servlet.http.HttpServletRequest** and an object that implements **javax.servlet.http.HttpServletResponse**. The **HttpServletRequest** object represents the client's request and the **HttpServletResponse** object represents the server's response. If **doGet** is unable to handle a client's request, it throws a **javax.servlet.ServletException**. If **doGet** encounters an error during stream processing (reading from the client or writing to the client), it throws a **java.io.IOException**.

To demonstrate a response to a **GET** request, our servlet creates a small HTML document containing the text "**Welcome to Servlets!**" The text of the HTML document is the response to the client. The response is sent to the client through the **PrintWriter** object that it accessed through the **HttpServletResponse** object. Line 12 declares **output** as a **PrintWriter**.

Line 14 uses method ***setContentType*** of the **HTTPServletResponse** object **response** to indicate the content type for the response to the client. This enables the client browser to understand and handle the content. In this example, we specify content type ***text/html*** to indicate to the browser that the response is an HTML text file. The browser knows that it must read the HTML tags in the HTML file, format the document according to the tags and display the document in the browser window for the user to see.

Line 15 uses method ***getWriter*** of **HTTPServletResponse** object **response** to obtain a reference to the **PrintWriter** object that sends the text of the HTML document to the client. (*Note:* If the response is binary data such as an image, method **getOutputStream** is used to obtain a reference to a **ServletOutputStream** object.)

Lines 19 through 23

```
buf.append( "<HTML><HEAD><TITLE>\n" );
buf.append( "A Simple Servlet Example\n" );
buf.append( "</TITLE></HEAD><BODY>\n" );
buf.append( "<H1>Welcome to Servlets!</H1>\n" );
buf.append( "</BODY></HTML>" );
```

create the HTML document by appending strings to **StringBuffer buf**. Line 24

```
output.println( buf.toString() );
```

sends the response (the contents of the **StringBuffer**) to the client. Line 25 closes the **output PrintWriter** output stream. This flushes the output buffer and sends the information to the client.

The client can only access the servlet if the servlet is running on a server. Web servers that support servlets (such as Sun Microsystems' Java Web Server, the World Wide Web Consortium's Jigsaw Web server or the Apache Group's Apache HTTP server) normally have an installation procedure for servlets. If you intend to execute your servlet as part of a Web server, please refer to your Web server's documentation on how to install a servlet. For our examples, we demonstrate servlets with the JSWDK server.

The JSWDK comes with the *JSWDK WebServer* so you can test your servlets. The JSWDK WebServer assumes that the servlet **.class** files are *installed* in the subdirectory

```
webpages\WEB-INF\servlets
```

of the JSWDK install directory on Windows or

```
webpages/WEB-INF/servlets
```

on UNIX. To install a servlet, first compile the servlet with **javac** as you normally would any other Java source code file. Next, place the **.class** file containing the compiled servlet class in the **servlets** directory (in the proper subdirectory structure if your servlet is in a Java package). This installs the servlet on the JSWDK WebServer.

In the JSWDK install directory are a Windows batch file (***startserver.bat***) and a UNIX shell script (***startserver***) that can be used to start the JSWDK WebServer on Windows and UNIX, respectively. (*Note:* The JSWDK also provides ***stopserver.bat*** and ***stopserver*** to terminate the JSWDK WebServer on Windows and UNIX, respectively.) Type the appropriate command for your platform in a command window. When the server starts executing it displays the following command line output (the **...** indicates that other text is displayed, but not shown here to save space):

```
JSDK WebServer Version 2.1
Loaded configuration from file:D:\jswdk-1.0.1\webserver.xml
   ...
endpoint created: localhost/127.0.0.1:8080
```

indicating that the JSWDK WebServer is waiting for requests on this computer's *port number* 8080. (*Note:* Ports in this case are not physical hardware ports to which you attach cables; rather, they are integers representing TCP ports that allow clients to request different services on the same server.) The port number specifies where a server waits for and receives connections from clients—this is frequently called the *handshake point*. When a client connects to a server to request a service, the client must specify the proper port number; otherwise, the client request cannot be processed. Port numbers are positive integers with values up to 65535. Many operating systems reserve port numbers below 1024 for system services (such as email and World Wide Web servers). Generally, these ports should not be specified as connection ports in user programs. In fact, some operating systems require special access privileges to use port numbers below 1024.

Testing and Debugging Tip 29.1

On Windows 95 and Windows 98 computers, executing startserver.bat or stopserver.bat may result in an "Out of environment space" message. See the **README.txt** *file in the JSWDK install directory for directions on correcting this problem.*

With so many ports from which to choose, how does a client know which port to use when requesting a service? You will often hear the term *well-known port number* used when describing popular Internet services such as Web servers and email servers. For example, a Web server waits for clients to make requests at port 80 by default. All Web browsers know this number as the well-known port on a Web server where HTTP URL requests are made. So when you type an HTTP URL into a Web browser, the browser normally connects to port 80 on the server. Similarly, the JSWDK WebServer uses port 8080 as its port number. You can specify a different port for the JSWDK WebServer by editing the file **webserver.xml** in the JSWDK install directory. At the bottom of the file, change the line

```
port="8080"
```

to specify the port on which you would like the JSWDK WebServer to await requests.

Once the JSWDK WebServer is running, you can load the HTML document **HTTPGetServlet.html** (Fig. 29.6) into a browser (see the first screen capture).

```
<!DOCTYPE HTML PUBLIC "-//W3C//DTD HTML 4.0 Transitional//EN">
<HTML>
<!-- Fig. 29.6: HTTPGetServlet.html -->

<HEAD>
<TITLE>Servlet HTTP GET Example</TITLE>
</HEAD>

<BODY>
<FORM ACTION = "http://localhost:8080/servlet/HTTPGetServlet"
      METHOD = "GET">
   <P>Click the button to have the servlet send
      an HTML document</P>
   <INPUT TYPE = "submit" VALUE = "Get HTML Document">
</FORM>
</BODY>
</HTML>
```

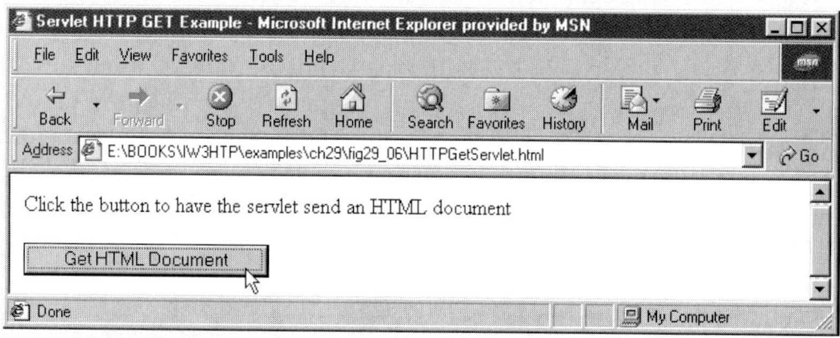

Fig. 29.6 HTML document to issue a **GET** request to **HTTPGetServlet** (part 1 of 2).

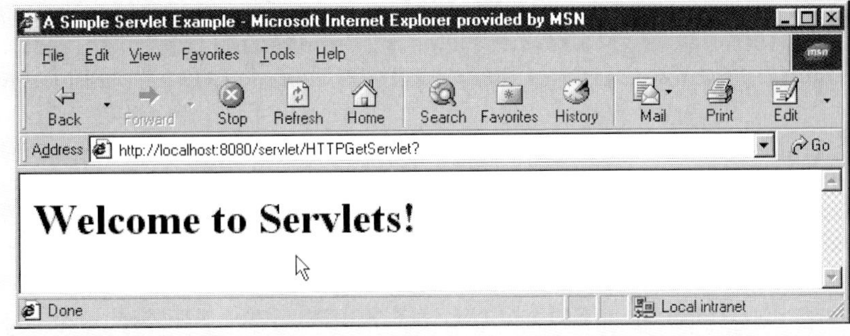

Fig. 29.6 HTML document to issue a **GET** request to **HTTPGetServlet** (part 2 of 2).

The important part of the HTML document for this example is the *form* specified at lines 10 through 15

```
<FORM ACTION = "http://localhost:8080/servlet/HTTPGetServlet"
      METHOD = "GET">
   <P>Click the button to have the servlet send
      an HTML document</P>
   <INPUT TYPE = "submit" VALUE = "Get HTML Document">
</FORM>
```

The first two lines indicate that the **ACTION** for this form is

```
"http://localhost:8080/servlet/HTTPGetServlet"
```

and the **METHOD** is **"GET"**. The **ACTION** specifies the server-side *form handler*—in this case, the servlet **HTTPGetServlet**. The **METHOD** is the *request type* that the server uses to decide how to handle the request and possibly causes the browser to attach arguments to the end of the URL specified in the **ACTION**.

Let us take a closer look at the **ACTION**'s URL. The server ***localhost*** is a well-known server host name on most computers that support TCP/IP-based networking protocols such as HTTP. The server ***localhost*** refers to your own computer. We often use **localhost** in this book to demonstrate networking programs on one computer so students without a network connection can still learn network programming concepts. In this example, **localhost** indicates that the server on which the servlet is installed is running on the local machine. The server host name is followed by "**:8080**", specifying the port number at which the JSWDK WebServer is awaiting requests from clients. Remember, Web browsers assume port 80 by default as the server port at which clients make HTTP requests, but the JSWDK WebServer awaits client requests at port 8080. If we do not explicitly specify the port number in the URL, the servlet will not receive our request and an error message will display in the browser. Notice that the URL contains **/servlet**. This is known as a *URL prefix*—it is used by the JSWDK WebServer to distinguish a servlet request from a standard HTTP URL request for other content. This is similar to the prefix **cgi-bin** used with CGI. Most Web servers have a specific directory in which a servlet's class file is placed to install the servlet on the server. Often this directory is called **servlet** or **servlets**. The JSWDK WebServer simulates this by making it appear to the client that servlet **HTTPGetServlet** is in the **servlet** directory on the server. Any servlet that executes through the JSWDK WebServer must be accessed in this manner.

When the user presses the **submit** button in a form (button **Get HTML Document** in this example), the form performs its **ACTION**—the browser connects to the specified server at the specified port number (port 80 if no port is supplied for HTTP protocol) and requests the service (**HTTPGetServlet**). In this example, the browser contacts the JSWDK WebServer and servlet (i.e., the form handler) specified in the **ACTION**, and indicates that the **METHOD** is **GET**. The JSWDK WebServer invokes the servlet's **service** method and passes it an **HTTPServletRequest** object that contains the **METHOD** (**GET**) specified by the client and an **HTTPServletResponse** object. The **service** method determines the request type (**GET**) and responds with a call to its **doGet** method, which returns the Web page shown in the second screen capture of Fig. 29.6.

In the second screen capture, notice that the **Address** field of the browser contains the URL specified as our **ACTION** in the HTML document. Also notice the "**?**" at the end of the URL. If there are any parameters to pass to the server-side form handler, the "**?**" character separates the URL and the arguments.

You can also see the affect of this servlet by simply typing the URL

```
http://localhost:8080/servlet/HTTPGetServlet
```

as the Web page for the browser to display. The default action for the Web browser is to issue a **GET** request to the server—in this case the **HTTPGetServlet**.

29.5 Handling HTTP POST Requests

An HTTP **POST** request is often used to post data from an HTML form to a server-side form handler that processes the data. For example, when you respond to a Web-based survey a **POST** request normally supplies the information you specify in the HTML form to the Web server.

Browsers often *cache* (save on disk) Web pages so they can quickly reload the pages. Frequently, there are no changes between the last version stored in the cache and the current version on the Web. This helps speed up your browsing experience by minimizing the amount of data that must be downloaded for you to view a Web page. Browsers do not cache the server's response to a **POST** request because the next **POST** may not return the same result. For example, in a survey, many users could visit the same Web page and respond to a question. The survey results could then be displayed for the user. Each new response changes the overall results of the survey.

When you use a Web-based search engine, a **GET** request normally supplies the information you specify in the HTML form to the search engine. The search engine performs the search, then returns the results to you as a Web page. Such pages are often cached in case you perform the same search again. As with **POST** requests, **GET** requests can supply parameters as part of the request to the Web server, but only as part of the URL.

The servlet of Fig. 29.7 stores the results of a survey about favorite pets in a file on the server. When a user responds to the survey, the servlet **HTTPPostServlet** sends an HTML document to the client summarizing the results of the survey to this point. The user selects a radio button on the Web page (Fig. 29.8) indicating his or her favorite pet and presses **Submit**. The browser sends an HTTP **POST** request to the servlet. The servlet responds by reading the previous survey results from a file on the server, updating the survey results, writing the survey results back to the file on the server and sending a Web page to the client indicating the cumulative results of the survey. For the purpose of this example, we loaded the HTML document in the Netscape Communicator 4.61 browser.

```
// Fig. 29.7: HTTPPostServlet.java
// A simple survey servlet
// This servlet writes data to a file on the Web server.
import javax.servlet.*;
import javax.servlet.http.*;
import java.text.*;
import java.io.*;

public class HTTPPostServlet extends HttpServlet {
   private String animalNames[] =
      { "dog", "cat", "bird", "snake", "none" };

   public void doPost( HttpServletRequest request,
                       HttpServletResponse response )
      throws ServletException, IOException
   {
      int animals[] = null, total = 0;
      File f = new File( "survey.dat" );

      if ( f.exists() ) {
         // Determine # of survey responses so far
         try {
            ObjectInputStream input = new ObjectInputStream(
               new FileInputStream( f ) );

            animals = (int []) input.readObject();
            input.close();    // close stream

            for ( int i = 0; i < animals.length; ++i )
               total += animals[ i ];
         }
         catch( ClassNotFoundException cnfe ) {
            cnfe.printStackTrace();
         }
      }
      else
         animals = new int[ 5 ];

      // read current survey response
      String value =
         request.getParameter( "animal" );
      ++total;    // update total of all responses

      // determine which was selected and update its total
      for ( int i = 0; i < animalNames.length; ++i )
         if ( value.equals( animalNames[ i ] ) )
            ++animals[ i ];

```

Fig. 29.7 `HTTPPostServlet` that processes an HTTP **`POST`** request (part 1 of 2).

```
49          // write updated totals out to disk
50          ObjectOutputStream output = new ObjectOutputStream(
51             new FileOutputStream( f ) );
52
53          output.writeObject( animals );
54          output.flush();
55          output.close();
56
57          // Calculate percentages
58          double percentages[] = new double[ animals.length ];
59
60          for ( int i = 0; i < percentages.length; ++i )
61             percentages[ i ] = 100.0 * animals[ i ] / total;
62
63          // send a thank you message to client
64          response.setContentType( "text/html" ); // content type
65
66          PrintWriter responseOutput = response.getWriter();
67          StringBuffer buf = new StringBuffer();
68          buf.append( "<html>\n" );
69          buf.append( "<title>Thank you!</title>\n" );
70          buf.append( "Thank you for participating.\n" );
71          buf.append( "<BR>Results:\n<PRE>" );
72
73          DecimalFormat twoDigits = new DecimalFormat( "#0.00" );
74          for ( int i = 0; i < percentages.length; ++i ) {
75             buf.append( "<BR>" );
76             buf.append( animalNames[ i ] );
77             buf.append( ": " );
78             buf.append( twoDigits.format( percentages[ i ] ) );
79             buf.append( "%  responses: " );
80             buf.append( animals[ i ] );
81             buf.append( "\n" );
82          }
83
84          buf.append( "\n<BR><BR>Total responses: " );
85          buf.append( total );
86          buf.append( "</PRE>\n</html>" );
87
88          responseOutput.println( buf.toString() );
89          responseOutput.close();
90       }
91    }
```

Fig. 29.7 **HTTPPostServlet** that processes an HTTP **POST** request (part 2 of 2).

As in Fig. 29.5, **HTTPPostServlet** extends **HttpServlet** at line 9 so that each **HTTPPostServlet** is capable of handling HTTP **GET** and **POST** requests (although this servlet only overrides **doPost**). Lines 10 and 11 define **String** array **animalNames** to contain the names of the animals in the survey. These are used to determine the response to the survey and update the counter for the appropriate animal.

Method ***doPost*** (lines 13 through 90) responds to **POST** requests. Its default functionality is to indicate a **BAD_REQUEST** error. We override this method to provide **POST** request processing. Method **doPost** receives the same two arguments as **doGet**—an object that implements **javax.servlet.http.HttpServletRequest** and an object that implements **javax.servlet.http.HttpServletResponse** to represent the client's request and the servlet's response, respectively. Method **doPost** throws a ***javax.servlet.ServletException*** if it is unable to handle a client's request and throws an **IOException** if a problem occurs during stream processing.

Method **doPost** begins by determining if the file **survey.dat** exists on the server. Line 18 defines a **File** object **f** for this purpose. The program does not provide a location for the file. By default, files that are created by a servlet executed with the JSWDK Web-Server are stored in the JSWDK installation directory (**jswdk-1.0.1**). You can specify the storage location for the file as part of creating the **File** object. At line 20, if the file exists, the contents of that file will be read into the servlet so the survey results can be updated and returned to the current client. If the file does not exist (i.e., the current request is the first survey response), method **doPost** creates the file later in the method.

Integer array **animals** stores the number of responses for each type of animal. If the file containing the previous survey results exists, lines 23 through 30 open an **ObjectInputStream** to read the integer array **animals** and total the number of responses that have been received to this point. When the servlet creates the file and stores the integer array, it uses an **ObjectOutputStream** to write the file.

Lines 40 and 41

```
String value =
      request.getParameter( "animal" );
```

use method **getParameter** of interface **javax.servlet.ServletRequest** to retrieve the survey response **POST**ed by the client. This method receives as its argument the name of the parameter (**"animal"**) as specified in the HTML document of Fig. 29.8, which we will discuss shortly. The method returns a **String** containing the value of the parameter or **null** if the parameter is not found. The HTML file (Fig. 29.8) that uses this servlet as a form handler contains five radio buttons, each of which is named **animal** (lines 13 through 17 of Fig. 29.8). Because only one radio button can be selected, the **String** returned by **getParameter** represents the one radio button selected by the user. The value for each radio button is one of the strings in the **animalNames** array in the servlet. (*Note:* If we were processing a form that could return many values for a particular parameter, method **getParameterValues** would be used here instead to obtain a **String** array containing the values.)

Line 42 increments the **total** to indicate one more survey response. Lines 45 through 47 determine the animal selected by the client and update the appropriate animal's total. Lines 50 through 55 open an **ObjectOutputStream** to store the updated survey results to the file **survey.dat**. This file ensures that even if the servlet is stopped and restarted, the survey results will persist on disk.

Lines 58 through 61 prepare for each animal the percentage of the **total** votes that represent each animal. These results are returned to the user as part of the **HttpServletResponse**. We prepare the response beginning at line 64, where **ServletResponse** method **setContentType** specifies that the content will be an HTML document (**text/html**).

Line 66 uses **ServletResponse** method **getWriter** to obtain a reference to a **PrintWriter** object and assigns it to **responseOutput**. This reference is used to send the response to the client. **StringBuffer buf** (line 67) stores the content of the response as the servlet prepares the HTML. Lines 68 through 86 prepare the content with a series of calls to **StringBuffer** method **append**. Lines 71 and 86 append the HTML tags **<PRE>** and **</PRE>** to specify that the text between them is preformatted text. Preformatted text is normally displayed in a fixed-width font. Several lines also insert the **
** tag to indicate a *break*—the browser should start a new line of text. Line 88

```
responseOutput.println( buf.toString() );
```

sends the content of **buf** to the client. Line 89 closes the **responseOutput** stream.

Once the servlet is running, you can load the HTML document **HTTPPost-Servlet.html** (Fig. 29.8) into a browser (see the first screen capture).

```
<!DOCTYPE HTML PUBLIC "-//W3C//DTD HTML 4.0 Transitional//EN">
<HTML>
<!-- Fig. 29.8: HTTPPostServlet.html -->

<HEAD>
<TITLE>Servlet HTTP Post Example</TITLE>
</HEAD>

<BODY>
<FORM ACTION = "http://localhost:8080/servlet/HTTPPostServlet"
      METHOD = "POST">
   What is your favorite pet?<BR><BR>
   <INPUT TYPE = "radio" NAME = "animal" VALUE = "dog">Dog<BR>
   <INPUT TYPE = "radio" NAME = "animal" VALUE = "cat">Cat<BR>
   <INPUT TYPE = "radio" NAME = "animal" VALUE = "bird">Bird<BR>
   <INPUT TYPE = "radio" NAME = "animal" VALUE = "snake">Snake<BR>
   <INPUT TYPE = "radio" NAME = "animal" VALUE = "none"
         CHECKED>None
   <BR><BR><INPUT TYPE = "submit" VALUE = "Submit">
   <INPUT TYPE = "reset">
</FORM>
</BODY>
</HTML>
```

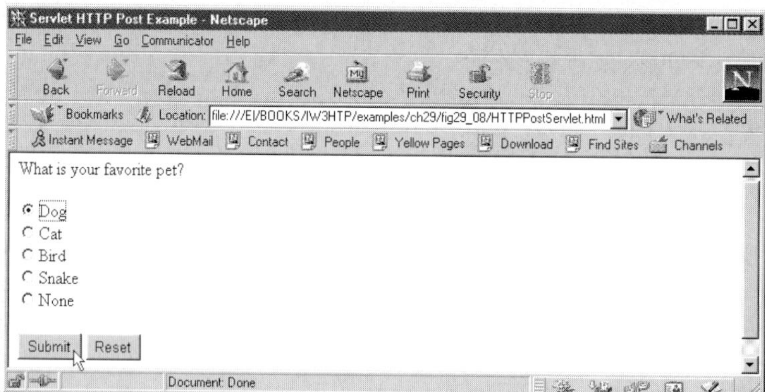

Fig. 29.8 Issuing a **POST** request to **HTTPPostServlet** (part 1 of 2).

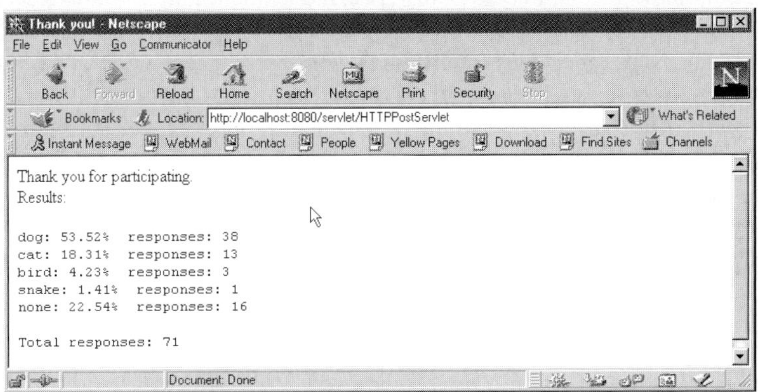

Fig. 29.8 Issuing a **POST** request to **HTTPPostServlet** (part 2 of 2).

The important part of the HTML document for this example is the form specified at lines 10 through 21.

```
<FORM ACTION = "http://localhost:8080/servlet/HTTPPostServlet"
      METHOD = "POST">
  What is your favorite pet?<BR><BR>
  <INPUT TYPE = "radio" NAME = "animal" VALUE = "dog">Dog<BR>
  <INPUT TYPE = "radio" NAME = "animal" VALUE = "cat">Cat<BR>
  <INPUT TYPE = "radio" NAME = "animal" VALUE = "bird">Bird<BR>
  <INPUT TYPE = "radio" NAME = "animal" VALUE="snake">Snake<BR>
  <INPUT TYPE = "radio" NAME = "animal" VALUE = "none"
         CHECKED>None
  <BR><BR><INPUT TYPE = "submit" VALUE = "Submit">
  <INPUT TYPE = "reset">
</FORM>
```

Line 10 indicates that the **ACTION** is

```
"http://localhost:8080/servlet/HTTPPostServlet"
```

and the ***METHOD*** for this form is **"POST"**. The **ACTION** specifies the server-side form handler—**HTTPPostServlet**. The **METHOD** helps the server understand the request type, decide how to handle the request and possibly causes the browser to attach arguments to the end of the URL specified in the **ACTION**.

Lines 13 through 18 specify the radio buttons form components. The **NAME** of each **radio** button is **animal** (these **radio** buttons are in the same group and only one can be selected at a time) and the **VALUE** of each is the string to post when the form contents are sent to the servlet (**POST**ed). Initially, the radio button defined on line 17 is **CHECKED** (i.e., selected). Line 19 defines the **submit** button that causes the form's **ACTION** to execute (i.e., post the form data to the servlet). When the user clicks the button, the browser sends a **POST** request to the servlet specified in the **ACTION**. Because the **METHOD** is **POST**, the browser also attaches to the request the **value**s associated with each HTML form component. For the radio button group, the selected radio button's value is attached to the request. The servlet reads the values submitted as part of the request using method **getParameter** of interface **javax.servlet.ServletRequest**. If the user clicks the **Reset** button (defined at line 20 in the HTML document), the browser resets the form to its initial state with the option **None** selected.

Notice that as you repeatedly submit votes, the servlet keeps track of all votes tallied so far (even if you terminate the servlet and run it again). You can repeatedly submit votes by pressing **Submit** to submit a vote, pressing the **Back** button in your browser to go back to the survey page, selecting a new animal (or the same animal) and pressing **Submit** again. You can also reload the **`HTTPPostServlet.html`** file into the browser repeatedly. We do not synchronize access to the file in this example. It is possible that two clients could access the survey at the same time and two (or more) separate server threads may attempt to modify the file at the same time. This problem can be fixed by implementing the tagging interface **`javax.servlet.SingleThreadModel`**. This interface indicates that the implementing servlet should handle only one client request at a time.

29.6 Session Tracking

Many Web sites today provide custom Web pages and/or functionality on a client-by-client basis. For example, some Web sites allow you to customize their home page to suit your needs. An excellent example of this is the *Yahoo!* Web site. If you go to the site

`http://my.yahoo.com/`

you can customize how the Yahoo! site appears to you in the future when you revisit the site. (*Note:* You need to get a free Yahoo! ID to do this.) The HTTP protocol does not support persistent information that could help a Web server determine that a request is from a particular client. As far as a Web server is concerned, every request could be from the same client or every request could be from a different client.

Another example of a service that is customized on a client-by-client basis is a shopping cart for shopping on the Web. Obviously, the server must distinguish between clients so the company can determine the proper items and charge the proper amount for each client.

A third purpose of customizing on a client-by-client basis is marketing. Companies often track the pages you visit throughout a site so they can display advertisements that are targeted to your browsing trends. A problem with tracking is that many people consider it to be an invasion of their privacy, an increasingly sensitive issue in our information society.

To help the server distinguish between clients, each client must identify itself to the server. There are a number of popular techniques for distinguishing between clients. For the purpose of this chapter, we introduce two techniques to track clients individually—*cookies* (Section 29.6.1) and *session tracking* using the Java Servlet API's **`HttpSession`** class (Section 29.6.2).

29.6.1 Cookies

A popular way to customize Web pages is via *cookies*. Cookies can store information on the user's computer for retrieval later in the same browsing session or in future browsing sessions. For example, cookies could be used in a shopping application to indicate the client's preferences. When the servlet receives the client's next communication, the servlet can examine the cookie(s) it sent to the client in a previous communication, identify the client's preferences and immediately display products of interest to the client.

Cookies are strings that are sent by a servlet (or another similar technology such as ASP or CGI) as part of a response to a client. Every HTTP-based interaction between a client and a server includes a *header* that contains information about the request (when the communication is from the client to the server) or information about the response (when the communication is from the server to the client). When an **HttpServlet** receives a request, the header includes information such as the request type (e.g., **GET** or **POST**) and cookies stored on the client machine by the server. When the server formulates its response, the header information includes any cookies the server wants to store on the client computer.

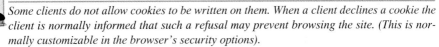

Software Engineering Observation 29.2

Some clients do not allow cookies to be written on them. When a client declines a cookie the client is normally informed that such a refusal may prevent browsing the site. (This is normally customizable in the browser's security options).

Depending on the *maximum age* of a cookie, the Web browser either maintains the cookie for the duration of the browsing session (i.e., until the user closes the Web browser) or stores the cookies on the client computer for future use. When the browser makes a request of a server, cookies previously sent to the client by that server are returned to the server (if they have not expired) as part of the request formulated by the browser. Cookies are automatically deleted when they *expire* (i.e., reach their maximum age).

The next example demonstrates cookies. The servlet (Fig. 29.9) handles both **GET** and **POST** requests. The HTML document of Fig. 29.10 contains four radio buttons (**C**, **C++**, **Java** and **Visual Basic 6**) and two buttons **Submit** and **Reset**. When the user presses **Submit**, the servlet is invoked with a **POST** request. The servlet responds by adding a cookie containing the selected language to the response header and sends an HTML page to the client. Each time the user clicks **Submit**, a cookie is sent to the client. This example does not allow duplicate cookies to be written. The HTML document of Fig. 29.11 presents users with a button he or she can press to get a book recommendation based on their programming language selection from the previous HTML document. When the user presses the button **Recommend Books**, the servlet in Fig. 29.9 is invoked with a **GET** request. The browser sends any cookies previously received from the servlet back to the servlet. The servlet responds by getting the cookies from the request header and creating an HTML document that recommends a book for each language the user selected from the HTML document of Fig. 29.10. We discuss the servlet followed by the two HTML documents.

```
// Fig. 29.9: CookieExample.java
// Using cookies.
import javax.servlet.*;
import javax.servlet.http.*;
import java.io.*;

public class CookieExample extends HttpServlet {
   private final static String names[] = { "C", "C++", "Java",
                                           "Visual Basic 6" };
   private final static String isbn[] = {
      "0-13-226119-7", "0-13-528910-6",
      "0-13-012507-5", "0-13-456955-5" };
```

Fig. 29.9 Demonstrating **Cookie**s (part 1 of 3).

```

   public void doPost( HttpServletRequest request,
                       HttpServletResponse response )
      throws ServletException, IOException
   {
      PrintWriter output;
      String language = request.getParameter( "lang" );

      Cookie c = new Cookie( language, getISBN( language ) );
      c.setMaxAge( 120 );  // seconds until cookie removed
      response.addCookie( c );  // must precede getWriter

      response.setContentType( "text/html" );
      output = response.getWriter();

      // send HTML page to client
      output.println( "<HTML><HEAD><TITLE>" );
      output.println( "Cookies" );
      output.println( "</TITLE></HEAD><BODY>" );
      output.println( "<P>Welcome to Cookies!<BR>" );
      output.println( "<P>" );
      output.println( language );
      output.println( " is a great language." );
      output.println( "</BODY></HTML>" );

      output.close();    // close stream
   }

   public void doGet( HttpServletRequest request,
                      HttpServletResponse response )
                      throws ServletException, IOException
   {
      PrintWriter output;
      Cookie cookies[];

      cookies = request.getCookies(); // get client's cookies

      response.setContentType( "text/html" );
      output = response.getWriter();

      output.println( "<HTML><HEAD><TITLE>" );
      output.println( "Cookies II" );
      output.println( "</TITLE></HEAD><BODY>" );

      if ( cookies != null && cookies.length != 0 ) {
         output.println( "<H1>Recommendations</H1>" );

         // get the name of each cookie
         for ( int i = 0; i < cookies.length; i++ )
            output.println(
               cookies[ i ].getName() + " How to Program. " +
               "ISBN#: " + cookies[ i ].getValue() + "<BR>" );
      }
```

Fig. 29.9 Demonstrating **Cookie**s (part 2 of 3).

```
66          else {
67             output.println( "<H1>No Recommendations</H1>" );
68             output.println( "You did not select a language or" );
69             output.println( "the cookies have expired." );
70          }
71
72          output.println( "</BODY></HTML>" );
73          output.close();    // close stream
74       }
75
76       private String getISBN( String lang )
77       {
78          for ( int i = 0; i < names.length; ++i )
79             if ( lang.equals( names[ i ] ) )
80                return isbn[ i ];
81
82          return "";  // no matching string found
83       }
84    }
```

Fig. 29.9 Demonstrating **Cookie**s (part 3 of 3).

Lines 8 and 10 declare **String** arrays that store the programming language names and ISBN numbers for the books that will be recommended, respectively. (*Note:* ISBN is an abbreviation for "International Standard Book Number"—a numbering scheme publishers worldwide use to give each different book title a unique identification number.) Method **doPost** (line 14) is invoked in response to the **POST** request from the HTML document of Fig. 29.10. Line 19 gets the user's **language** selection (the value of the selected radio button on the Web page) with method **getParameter**.

Line 21 passes the **language** value to the ***javax.servlet.http.Cookie*** class constructor in the statement

```
Cookie c = new Cookie( language, getISBN( language ) );
```

The first constructor argument specifies the *cookie name* (the **language**) and the second constructor argument specifies the *cookie value*. The cookie name identifies the cookie and the cookie value is the information associated with the cookie. As the **Cookie**'s value in this example, we use the ISBN number for a book that will be recommended to the user when the servlet receives a **GET** request. Note that the user of a browser can turn off cookies, so this example may not function properly on certain users' computers (no errors are reported if cookies are disabled). A minimum of 20 cookies per Web site and 300 cookies per user are supported by browsers that support cookies. Browsers may limit the cookie size to 4K (4096 bytes). Cookies can be used only by the server that created the cookie. Line 22

```
c.setMaxAge( 120 );  // seconds until cookie removed
```

sets the maximum age for the cookie. In this example, the cookie exists for 120 seconds (2 minutes). The argument to **setMaxAge** is an integer value. This allows a cookie to have a maximum age of up to 2,147,483,647 (or approximately 24,855 days). We set the maximum age of the **Cookie** in this example to emphasize that cookies are automatically deleted when they expire.

Software Engineering Observation 29.3

By default cookies only exist for the current browsing session (until the user closes the browser). To make cookies persist beyond the current session, call **`Cookie`** *method* **`setMaxAge`** *to indicate the number of seconds until the cookie expires.*

Line 23

```
response.addCookie( c );   // must precede getWriter
```

adds the cookie to the client response. Cookies are sent to the client as part of the HTTP header (i.e., information such as the request type, the request's status, etc.). The header information is always provided to the client first, so the cookies should be added to the **`response`** with **`addCookie`** before any other information.

Software Engineering Observation 29.4

Call method **`addCookie`** *to add a cookie to the* **`HTTPServletResponse`** *before writing any other information to the client.*

After the cookie is added, the servlet sends an HTML document to the client (see the second screen capture of Fig. 29.10).

Method **`doGet`** (line 41) is invoked in response to the **`GET`** request from the HTML document of Fig. 29.11. The method reads any **`Cookie`**s that were written to the client in **`doPost`**. For each **`Cookie`** written, the servlet recommends a Deitel book on the subject. Up to four books are displayed on the Web page created by the servlet. Line 48

```
cookies = request.getCookies(); // get client's cookies
```

retrieves the cookies from the client with **`HttpServletRequest`** method ***`getCookies`***, which returns an array of **`Cookies`**. When a **`GET`** or **`POST`** operation is performed to invoke the servlet, the cookies associated with that server are automatically sent to the servlet.

If the condition at line 57 is true (i.e., there are cookies to process), the **`for`** structure at line 61 retrieves the name of each **`Cookie`** using **`Cookie`** method **`getName`**, retrieves the value of each **`Cookie`** (i.e., the ISBN number) using **`Cookie`** method **`getValue`** and writes a line to the client indicating the name of a recommended book and the ISBN number for the book.

Figure 29.10 shows the HTML document the user loads to select a language. Lines 10 and 11 specify that the **`ACTION`** of the form is to **`POST`** information to the **`CookieExample`** servlet.

```
1  <!DOCTYPE HTML PUBLIC "-//W3C//DTD HTML 4.0 Transitional//EN">
2  <HTML>
3  <!-- Fig. 29.10: SelectLanguage.html -->
4
5  <HEAD>
6  <TITLE>Cookies</TITLE>
7  </HEAD>
8
```

Fig. 29.10 HTML document that invokes the cookie servlet with a **POST** request and passes the user's language selection as an argument (part 1 of 2).

```
<BODY>
<FORM ACTION = "http://localhost:8080/servlet/CookieExample"
      METHOD = "POST">
   <STRONG>Select a programming language:</STRONG><BR>
   <INPUT TYPE = "radio" NAME = "lang" VALUE = "C">C<BR>
   <INPUT TYPE = "radio" NAME = "lang" VALUE = "C++">C++<BR>
   <INPUT TYPE = "radio" NAME = "lang" VALUE = "Java" CHECKED>
   Java<BR>
   <INPUT TYPE = "radio" NAME = "lang" VALUE = "Visual Basic 6">
   Visual Basic 6
   <P><INPUT TYPE = "submit" VALUE = "Submit">
   <INPUT TYPE = "reset"> </P>
</FORM>
</BODY>
</HTML>
```

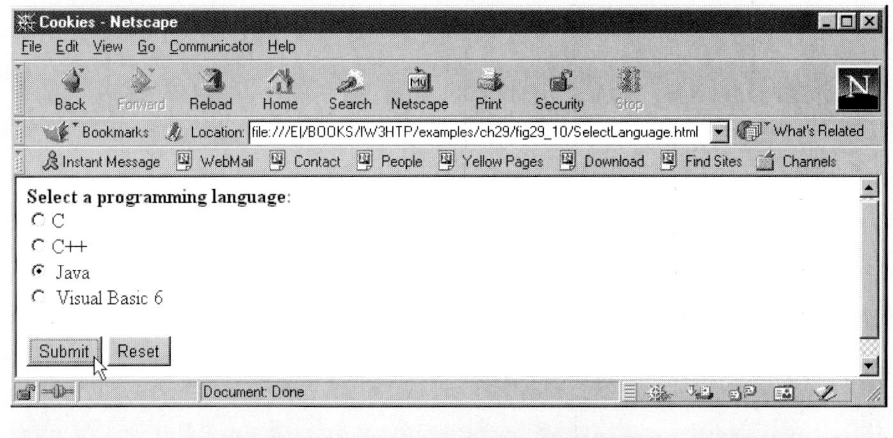

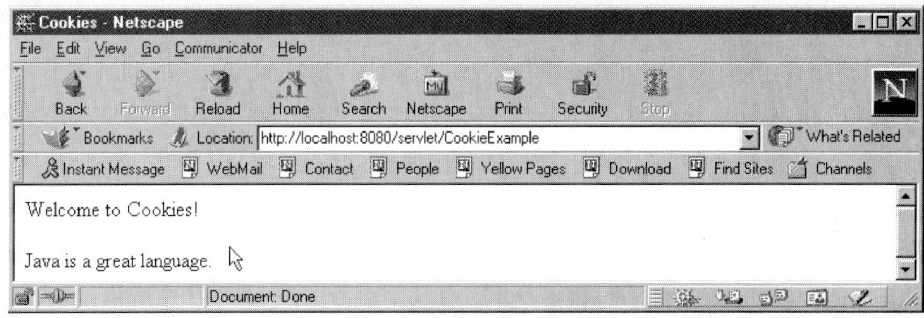

Fig. 29.10 HTML document that invokes the cookie servlet with a **POST** request and passes the user's language selection as an argument (part 2 of 2).

The HTML document in Fig. 29.11 invokes the servlet in response to a button press. Lines 10 and 11 specify that the form's **ACTION** is to **GET** information from the **CookieExample** servlet. Because we set the cookie's maximum age to 2 minutes, you must load this HTML document and press **Recommend Books** within 2 minutes of your interaction with the servlet from the HTML document of Fig. 29.10. Otherwise, the cookie will expire before you can receive a recommendation. (*Note:* Not all Web browsers adhere to the expiration date of a cookie. For the purpose of this example, we use Netscape's Communicator browser because it supports cookie expiration.) Normally, a cookie's lifetime is set to a larger value. Remember, we intentionally set a small value to demonstrate that cookies are automatically deleted when they expire. After receiving your book recommendation, wait 2 minutes to ensure that the cookie expires. Then, go back to the HTML document of Fig. 29.11 and press **Recommend Books** again. The third screen capture in Fig. 29.11 shows the returned HTML document when there are no cookies as part of the request from the client.

```
<!DOCTYPE HTML PUBLIC "-//W3C//DTD HTML 4.0 Transitional//EN">
<HTML>
<!-- Fig. 29.11: BookRecommendation.html -->

<HEAD>
<TITLE>Cookies</TITLE>
</HEAD>

<BODY>
<FORM ACTION = "http://localhost:8080/servlet/CookieExample"
      METHOD = "GET">
   Press "Recommend books" for a list of books.
   <INPUT TYPE = submit VALUE = "Recommend books">
</FORM>
</BODY>
</HTML>
```

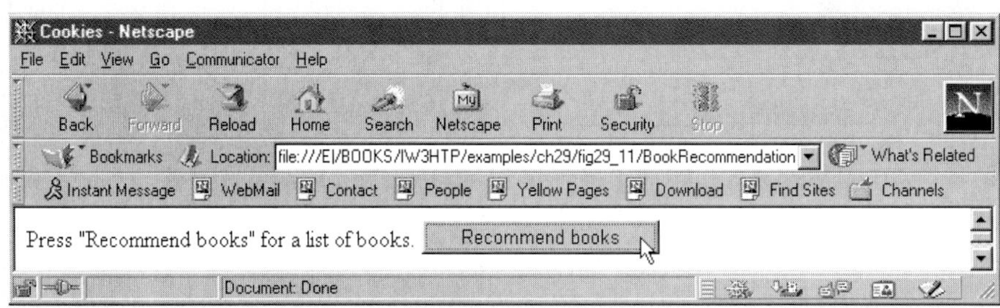

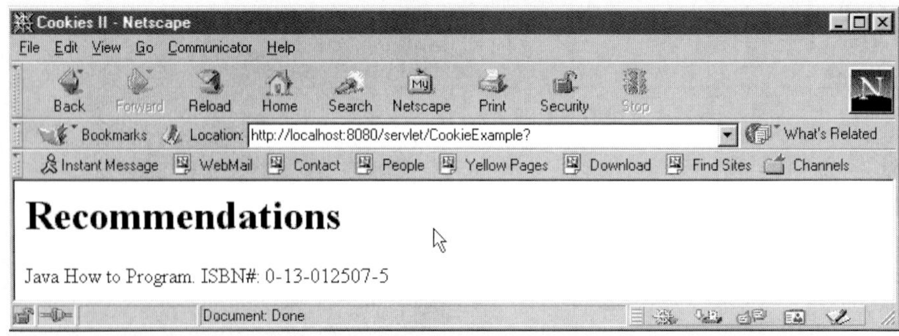

Fig. 29.11 HTML document for a servlet that reads a client's cookies (part 1 of 2).

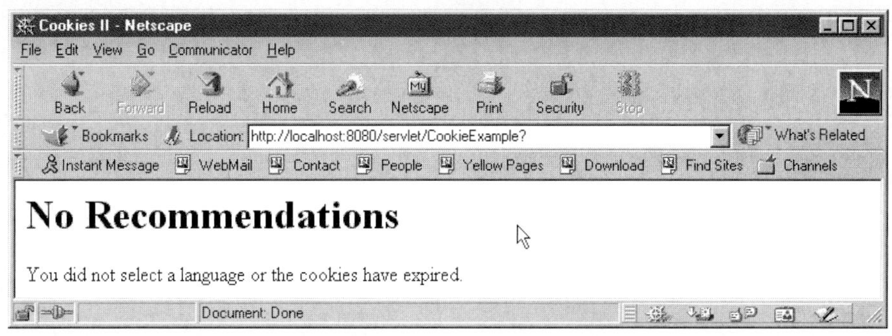

Fig. 29.11 HTML document for a servlet that reads a client's cookies (part 2 of 2).

Various **Cookie** methods are provided to manipulate the members of a **Cookie**. Some of these methods are listed in Fig. 29.12.

Method	Description
getComment()	Returns a **String** describing the purpose of the cookie (**null** if no comment has been set with **setComment**).
getDomain()	Returns a **String** containing the cookie's domain. This determines which servers can receive the cookie. By default cookies are sent to the server that originally sent the cookie to the client.
getMaxAge()	Returns an **int** representing the maximum age of the cookie in seconds.
getName()	Returns a **String** containing the name of the cookie as set by the constructor.
getPath()	Returns a **String** containing the URL prefix for the cookie. Cookies can be "targeted" to specific URLs that include directories on the Web server. By default a cookie is returned to services operating in the same directory as the service that sent the cookie or a subdirectory of that directory.
getSecure()	Returns a **boolean** value indicating if the cookie should be transmitted using a secure protocol (**true** if so).
getValue()	Returns a **String** containing the value of the cookie as set with **setValue** or the constructor.
getVersion()	Returns an **int** containing the version of the cookie protocol used to create the cookie. Cookies are currently undergoing standardization. A value of 0 (the default) indicates the original cookie protocol as defined by Netscape. A value of 1 indicates the version currently undergoing standardization.

Fig. 29.12 Important methods of class **Cookie** (part 1 of 2).

Method	Description
`setComment( String )`	The comment describing the purpose of the cookie that is presented by the browser to the user (some browsers allow the user to accept cookies on a per-cookie basis).
`setDomain( String )`	This determines which servers can receive the cookie. By default cookies are sent to the server that originally sent the cookie to the client. The domain is specified in the form **`".deitel.com"`**, indicating that all servers ending with **`.deitel.com`** can receive this cookie.
`setMaxAge( int )`	Sets the maximum age of the cookie in seconds.
`setPath( String )`	Sets the "target" URL indicating the directories on the server that lead to the services that can receive this cookie.
`setSecure( boolean )`	A **`true`** value indicates that the cookie should only be sent using a secure protocol.
`setValue( String )`	Sets the value of a cookie.
`setVersion( int )`	Sets the cookie protocol for this cookie.

Fig. 29.12 Important methods of class **`Cookie`** (part 2 of 2).

29.6.2 Session Tracking with `HttpSession`

An alternative approach to cookies is to track a session with the JSWDK's interfaces and classes from package **`javax.servlet.http`** that support session tracking. To demonstrate basic session tracking techniques, we modified the servlet from Fig. 29.9 that demonstrated **`Cookie`**s to use objects that implement interface **`HttpSession`** (Fig. 29.13). Once again the servlet handles both **`GET`** and **`POST`** requests. The HTML document of Fig. 29.14 contains four radio buttons (**C**, **C++**, **Java** and **Visual Basic 6**) and two buttons, **Submit** and **Reset**. When the user presses **Submit**, the servlet (Fig. 29.13) is invoked with a **`POST`** request. The servlet responds by creating a session for the client (or using an existing session for the client) and adds the selected language and an ISBN number for the recommended book to the **`HttpSession`** object, then sends an HTML page to the client. Each time the user clicks **Submit**, a new language/ISBN pair is added to the **`HttpSession`** object. If the language was already added to the **`HttpSession`** object, it is simply replaced with the new pair of values. The HTML document of Fig. 29.15 presents users with a button they can press to get a book recommendation based on their programming language selection from the previous HTML document. When the user presses the button **Recommend Books**, the servlet in Fig. 29.13 is invoked with a **`GET`** request. The servlet responds by getting the value names (i.e., the languages) from the **`HttpSession`** object and creating an HTML document that recommends a book for each language the user selected from the HTML document of Fig. 29.14.

```
// Fig. 29.13: SessionExample.java
// Using sessions.
import javax.servlet.*;
import javax.servlet.http.*;
import java.io.*;

public class SessionExample extends HttpServlet {
   private final static String names[] =
      { "C", "C++", "Java", "Visual Basic 6" };
   private final static String isbn[] = {
      "0-13-226119-7", "0-13-528910-6",
      "0-13-012507-5", "0-13-456955-5" };

   public void doPost( HttpServletRequest request,
                       HttpServletResponse response )
      throws ServletException, IOException
   {
      PrintWriter output;
      String language = request.getParameter( "lang" );

      // Get the user's session object.
      // Create a session (true) if one does not exist.
      HttpSession session = request.getSession( true );

      // add a value for user's choice to session
      session.putValue( language, getISBN( language ) );

      response.setContentType( "text/html" );
      output = response.getWriter();

      // send HTML page to client
      output.println( "<HTML><HEAD><TITLE>" );
      output.println( "Sessions" );
      output.println( "</TITLE></HEAD><BODY>" );
      output.println( "<P>Welcome to Sessions!<BR>" );
      output.println( "<P>" );
      output.println( language );
      output.println( " is a great language." );
      output.println( "</BODY></HTML>" );

      output.close();    // close stream
   }

   public void doGet( HttpServletRequest request,
                      HttpServletResponse response )
                      throws ServletException, IOException
   {
      PrintWriter output;

      // Get the user's session object.
      // Don't create a session (false) if one does not exist.
      HttpSession session = request.getSession( false );

```

Fig. 29.13 Session tracking example (part 1 of 2).

```
54          // get names of session object's values
55          String valueNames[];
56
57          if ( session != null )
58             valueNames = session.getValueNames();
59          else
60             valueNames = null;
61
62          response.setContentType( "text/html" );
63          output = response.getWriter();
64
65          output.println( "<HTML><HEAD><TITLE>" );
66          output.println( "Sessions II" );
67          output.println( "</TITLE></HEAD><BODY>" );
68
69          if ( valueNames != null && valueNames.length != 0 ) {
70             output.println( "<H1>Recommendations</H1>" );
71
72             // get value for each name in valueNames
73             for ( int i = 0; i < valueNames.length; i++ ) {
74                String value =
75                   (String) session.getValue( valueNames[ i ] );
76
77                output.println(
78                   valueNames[ i ] + " How to Program. " +
79                   "ISBN#: " + value + "<BR>" );
80             }
81          }
82          else {
83             output.println( "<H1>No Recommendations</H1>" );
84             output.println( "You did not select a language" );
85          }
86
87          output.println( "</BODY></HTML>" );
88          output.close();    // close stream
89       }
90
91       private String getISBN( String lang )
92       {
93          for ( int i = 0; i < names.length; ++i )
94             if ( lang.equals( names[ i ] ) )
95                return isbn[ i ];
96
97          return "";  // no matching string found
98       }
99    }
```

Fig. 29.13 Session tracking example (part 2 of 2).

Lines 8 and 10 declare **String** arrays that store the programming language names and ISBN numbers for the books that will be recommended, respectively. Method **doPost** (line 14) is invoked in response to the **POST** request from the HTML document of Fig. 29.14. Line 19 gets the user's **language** selection (the value of the selected radio button on the Web page) with method **getParameter**.

Line 23

```
HttpSession session = request.getSession( true );
```

obtains the **HttpSession** object for the client with **HttpServletRequest** method ***getSession***. If the client already has an **HttpSession** object from a previous request during the client's browsing session, method **getSession** returns that **HttpSession** object. Otherwise, the **true** argument indicates that the servlet should create a unique **HttpSession** object for the client (a **false** argument would cause method **getSession** to return **null** if the **HttpSession** object for the client did not already exist).

Line 26

```
session.putValue( language, getISBN( language ) );
```

puts the language and the corresponding recommended book's ISBN number into the **HttpSession** object.

Software Engineering Observation 29.5

*Name/value pairs added to an **HttpSession** object with **putValue** remain available until the client's current browsing session ends or until the session is explicitly invalidated by a call to the **HttpSession** object's **invalidate** method.*

After the values are added to the **HttpSession** object, the servlet sends an HTML document to the client (see the second screen capture of Fig. 29.14).

Method **doGet** (line 44) is invoked in response to the **GET** request from the HTML document of Fig. 29.15. The method obtains the **HttpSession** object for the client, reads the data stored in the object and, for each value stored in the session, recommends a book on the subject. Up to four books are displayed in the Web page created by the servlet.

Line 52

```
HttpSession session = request.getSession( false );
```

retrieves the **HttpSession** object for the client using **HttpServletRequest** method **getSession**. If an **HttpSession** object does not exist for the client, the **false** argument indicates that the servlet should not create one.

If method **getSession** does not return **null** (i.e., there is an **HttpSession** object for the client), line 58

```
valueNames = session.getValueNames();
```

uses **HttpSession** method **getValueNames** to retrieve the value names (i.e., names used as the first argument to **HttpSession** method **putValue**) and assigns the array of **String**s to **valueNames**. Each name is used to retrieve the ISBN of a book from the **HttpSession** object. The **for** structure at lines 73 through 80 uses the statement

```
String value =
   (String) session.getValue( valueNames[ i ] );
```

to get the value associated with each name in **valueNames**. Method **getValue** receives the name and returns an **Object** reference to the corresponding value. The cast operator allows the program to use the returned reference as a **String** reference. Next, a line is written in the response to the client containing the title of the recommended book and that book's ISBN.

Figure 29.14 shows the HTML document the user loads to select a language. Lines 10 and 11 specify that the **ACTION** of the form is to **POST** information to the **SessionExample** servlet.

The HTML document in Fig. 29.15 invokes the servlet in response to a button press. Lines 10 and 11 specify that the **ACTION** of the form is to **GET** information from the servlet **SessionExample**. The third screen capture in Fig. 29.15 shows the returned HTML document when there is no **HttpSession** object for the client or there are no name/value pairs stored in the **HttpSession** object.

```
1  <!DOCTYPE HTML PUBLIC "-//W3C//DTD HTML 4.0 Transitional//EN">
2  <HTML>
3  <!-- Fig. 29.14: SelectLanguage.html -->
4
5  <HEAD>
6  <TITLE>Sessions</TITLE>
7  </HEAD>
8
9  <BODY>
10 <FORM ACTION = "http://localhost:8080/servlet/SessionExample"
11       METHOD = "POST">
12    <STRONG>Select a programming language:</STRONG><BR>
13    <INPUT TYPE = "radio" NAME = "lang" VALUE = "C">C<BR>
14    <INPUT TYPE = "radio" NAME = "lang" VALUE = "C++">C++<BR>
15    <INPUT TYPE = "radio" NAME = "lang" VALUE = "Java" CHECKED>
16    Java<BR>
17    <INPUT TYPE = "radio" NAME = "lang" VALUE = "Visual Basic 6">
18    Visual Basic 6
19    <P><INPUT TYPE = "submit" VALUE = "Submit">
20    <INPUT TYPE = "reset"> </P>
21 </FORM>
22 </BODY>
23 </HTML>
```

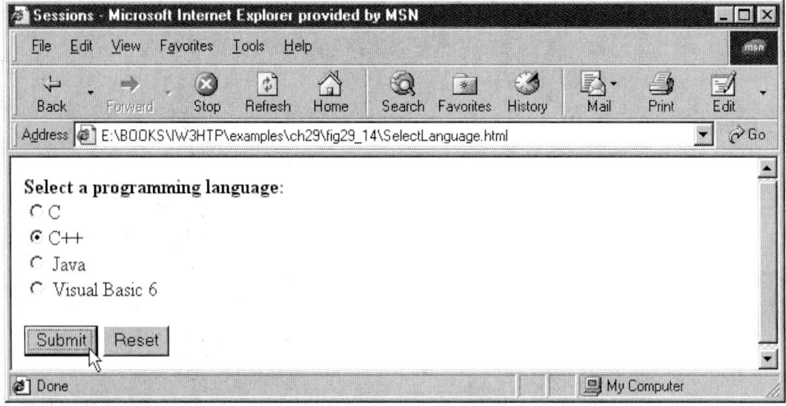

Fig. 29.14 HTML document that invokes the session tracking servlet with a **POST** request and passes the language selection as an argument (part 1 of 2).

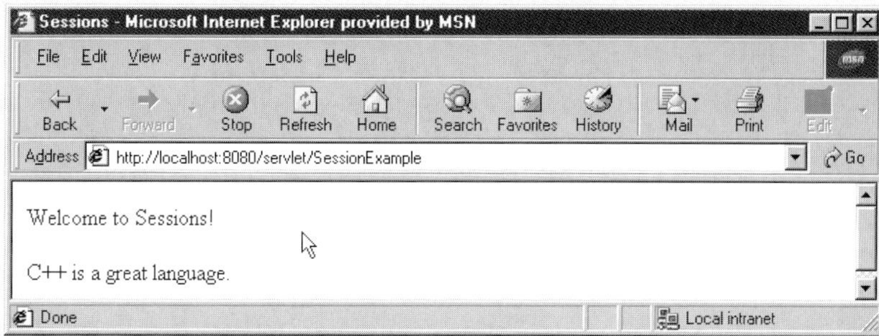

Fig. 29.14 HTML document that invokes the session tracking servlet with a **POST** request and passes the language selection as an argument (part 2 of 2).

```
<!DOCTYPE HTML PUBLIC "-//W3C//DTD HTML 4.0 Transitional//EN">
<HTML>
<!-- Fig. 29.15: BookRecommendation.html -->

<HEAD>
<TITLE>Sessions</TITLE>
</HEAD>

<BODY>
<FORM ACTION = "http://localhost:8080/servlet/SessionExample"
      METHOD = "GET">
   Press "Recommend books" for a list of books.
   <INPUT TYPE = submit VALUE = "Recommend books">
</FORM>
</BODY>
</HTML>
```

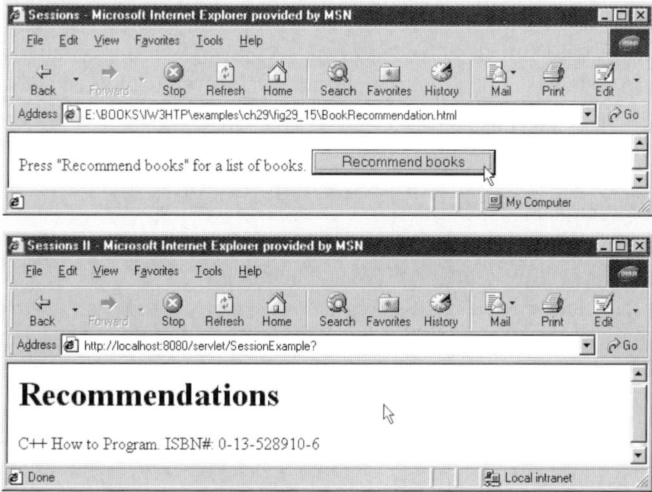

Fig. 29.15 HTML that interacts with the session tracking servlet to read the session information and return book recommendations to the user (part 1 of 2).

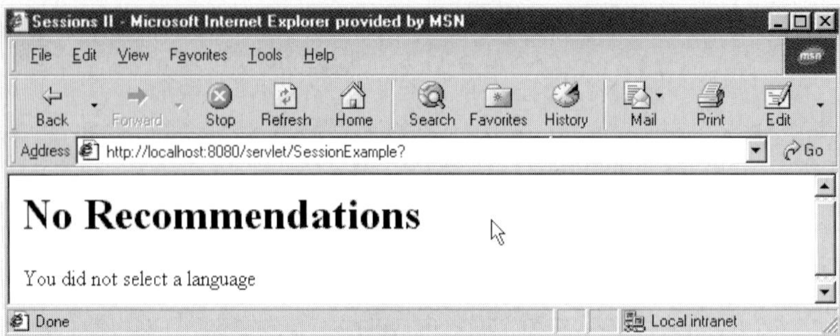

Fig. 29.15 HTML that interacts with the session tracking servlet to read the session information and return book recommendations to the user (part 2 of 2).

29.7 Multitier Applications: Using JDBC from a Servlet

Servlets can communicate with databases via JDBC (Java Database Connectivity). As we discussed in Chapter 18 of *Java How to Program, Third Edition*, JDBC provides a uniform way for a Java program to connect to a variety of databases in a general manner without having to deal with the specifics of those database systems.

Many of today's applications are *three-tier distributed applications,* consisting of a *user interface*, *business logic* and *database access*. The user interface in such an application is often created using HTML (as shown in this chapter) or Dynamic HTML. In some cases, Java applets are also used for this tier. HTML is the preferred mechanism for representing the user interface in systems where portability is a concern. Because HTML is supported by all browsers, designing the user interface to be accessed through a Web browser guarantees portability across all platforms that have browsers. Using the networking provided automatically by the browser, the user interface can communicate with the middle-tier business logic. The middle tier can then access the database to manipulate the data. All three tiers may reside on separate computers that are connected to a network.

In multitier architectures, Web servers are increasingly used to build the middle tier. They provide the business logic that manipulates data from databases and that communicates with client Web browsers. Servlets, through JDBC, can interact with popular database systems. Developers do not need to be familiar with the specifics of each database system. Rather, developers use SQL-based queries and the JDBC driver handles the specifics of interacting with each database system.

Figures 29.16 and 29.17 demonstrate a three-tier distributed application that displays the user interface in a browser using HTML. The middle tier is a Java servlet that handles requests from the client browser and provides access to the third tier—a Microsoft Access database (set up as an ODBC data source) accessed via JDBC (in this example). The servlet in this example is a guest book servlet that allows the user to register for several different mailing lists. When the servlet receives a **POST** request from the HTML document of Fig. 29.17, it ensures that the required data fields are present, then stores the data in the database and sends a confirmation page to the client. (*Note:* This example assumes that the database **GuestBook.mdb** provided with the example is already registered as an ODBC data source named **GuestBook**. See Chapter 25 for more information on creating an ODBC data source name.)

```
// Fig. 29.16: GuestBookServlet.java
// Three-Tier Example
import java.io.*;
import javax.servlet.*;
import javax.servlet.http.*;
import java.util.*;
import java.sql.*;

public class GuestBookServlet extends HttpServlet {
   private Statement statement = null;
   private Connection connection = null;
   private String URL = "jdbc:odbc:GuestBook";

   public void init( ServletConfig config )
      throws ServletException
   {
      super.init( config );

      try {
         Class.forName( "sun.jdbc.odbc.JdbcOdbcDriver" );
         connection =
            DriverManager.getConnection( URL, "", "" );
      }
      catch ( Exception e ) {
         e.printStackTrace();
         connection = null;
      }
   }

   public void doPost( HttpServletRequest req,
                       HttpServletResponse res )
      throws ServletException, IOException
   {
      String email, firstName, lastName, company,
             snailmailList, cppList, javaList, vbList,
             iwwwList;

      email = req.getParameter( "Email" );
      firstName = req.getParameter( "FirstName" );
      lastName = req.getParameter( "LastName" );
      company = req.getParameter( "Company" );
      snailmailList = req.getParameter( "mail" );
      cppList = req.getParameter( "c_cpp" );
      javaList = req.getParameter( "java" );
      vbList = req.getParameter( "vb" );
      iwwwList = req.getParameter( "iwww" );

      res.setContentType( "text/html" );
      PrintWriter output = res.getWriter();

      if ( email.equals( "" ) ||
           firstName.equals( "" ) ||
           lastName.equals( "" ) ) {
```

Fig. 29.16 `GuestBookServlet` for mailing list registration (part 1 of 3).

```
            output.println( "<H3> Please click the back " +
                            "button and fill in all " +
                            "fields.</H3>" );
            output.close();
            return;
         }

         /* Note: The GuestBook database actually contains fields
          * Address1, Address2, City, State and Zip that are not
          * used in this example. However, the insert into the
          * database must still account for these fields. */
         boolean success = insertIntoDB(
            "'" + email + "','" + firstName + "','" + lastName +
            "','" + company + "','','','','','" +
            ( snailmailList != null ? "yes" : "no" ) + "','" +
            ( cppList != null ? "yes" : "no"  ) + "','" +
            ( javaList != null ? "yes" : "no"  ) + "','" +
            ( vbList != null ? "yes" : "no"  ) + "','" +
            ( iwwwList != null ? "yes" : "no"  ) + "'" );

         if ( success )
            output.print( "<H2>Thank you " + firstName +
                          " for registering.</H2>" );
         else
            output.print( "<H2>An error occurred. " +
                          "Please try again later.</H2>" );

         output.close();
      }

      private boolean insertIntoDB( String stringtoinsert )
      {
         try {
            statement = connection.createStatement();
            statement.execute(
               "INSERT INTO GuestBook values (" +
               stringtoinsert + ");" );
            statement.close();
         }
         catch ( Exception e ) {
            System.err.println(
               "ERROR: Problems with adding new entry" );
            e.printStackTrace();
            return false;
         }

         return true;
      }

      public void destroy()
      {
         try {
            connection.close();
```

Fig. 29.16 `GuestBookServlet` for mailing list registration (part 2 of 3).

```
107         }
108         catch( Exception e ) {
109            System.err.println( "Problem closing the database" );
110         }
111      }
112 }
```

Fig. 29.16 **`GuestBookServlet`** for mailing list registration (part 3 of 3).

Class **`GuestBookServlet`** extends class **`HttpServlet`** (line 9) so it is capable of responding to **`GET`** and **`POST`** requests. Servlets are initialized by overriding method ***`init`*** (line 14). Method **`init`** is called exactly once in a servlet's lifetime and is guaranteed to complete before any client requests are accepted. Method **`init`** takes a ***`ServletConfig`*** argument and throws a **`ServletException`**. The argument provides the servlet with information about its *initialization parameters* (i.e., parameters not associated with a request, but passed to the servlet for initializing servlet variables). These parameters can be specified in a file that is normally called **`servlets.properties`** and resides in the subdirectory **`webpages\WEB-INF`** in the JSWDK install directory (other Web servers may name this file differently (or not use a file at all) and may store it in a directory specific to the Web server). The most common properties that are typically specified are *servletname*.**`code`** and *servletname*.**`initparams`**, where *servletname* is any name you want to specify as your servlet's name. This name might be used in the invocation of the servlet from a Web page. For a sample **`servlets.properties`** file, see the one provided with the JSWDK in the subdirectory **`webpages\WEB-INF`** in the JSWDK install directory.

In this example, the servlet's **`init`** method performs the connection to the Microsoft Access database. The method loads the **`JdbcOdbcDriver`** at line 20 with

```
Class.forName( "sun.jdbc.odbc.JdbcOdbcDriver" );
```

Lines 21 and 22 attempt to open a connection to the **`GuestBook`** database. When method **`insertIntoDB`** (line 84) is called by the servlet (line 65 of **`doPost`**), lines 87 through 91

```
statement = connection.createStatement();
statement.execute(
   "INSERT INTO GuestBook values (" +
   stringtoinsert + ");" );
statement.close();
```

create **`statement`** to perform the next insert into the database, call **`statement.execute`** to execute an **`INSERT INTO`** statement (**`stringtoinsert`** is the **`String`** passed into **`insertIntoDB`**) and close the **`statement`** to ensure that the insert operation is committed to the database.

When a **`POST`** request is received from the HTML document in Fig. 29.17, method **`doPost`** (line 30) responds by reading the HTML form field values from the **`POST`** request, formatting the field values into a **`String`** for use in an **`INSERT INTO`** operation on the database and sending the **`String`** to method **`insertIntoDB`** (line 84) to perform the insert operation. Each form field's value is retrieved in lines 38 through 46.

The **if** structure at lines 51 through 59 determines if the email, first name or last name parameters are empty **String**s. If so, the servlet response asks the user to return to the HTML form and enter those fields.

Lines 65 through 72 formulate the call to **insertIntoDB**. The method returns a **boolean** value indicating whether the insert into the database was successful.

Line 103 defines method **destroy** to ensure that the database connection is closed before the servlet terminates.

Figure 29.17 defines the HTML document that presents the guest book form to the user and **POST**s the information to the servlet of Fig. 29.16.

Lines 11 and 12 specify that the form's **ACTION** is to **POST** information to the **GuestBookServlet**. The screen captures show the form filled with one set of information (the first screen) and the confirmation Web page that was sent back to the client as the response to the **POST** request. This confirmation is displayed only if the insert into the database is successful; otherwise, an error message is displayed.

```
1  <!DOCTYPE HTML PUBLIC "-//W3C//DTD HTML 4.0 Transitional//EN">
2  <HTML>
3  <!-- Fig. 29.17: GuestBookForm.html -->
4
5  <HEAD>
6  <TITLE>Deitel Guest Book Form</TITLE>
7  </HEAD>
8
9  <BODY>
10 <H1>Guest Book</H1>
11 <FORM ACTION = "http://localhost:8080/servlet/GuestBookServlet"
12       METHOD = "POST"><PRE>
13 Email address (*): <INPUT TYPE = text NAME = Email>
14    First Name (*): <INPUT TYPE = text NAME = FirstName>
15     Last name (*): <INPUT TYPE = text NAME = LastName>
16          Company: <INPUT TYPE = text NAME = Company>
17
18                   NOTE: (*) fields are required</PRE>
19    <P>Select mailing lists from which you want
20       to receive information<BR>
21    <INPUT TYPE = "checkbox" NAME = "mail" VALUE = "mail">
22    Snail Mail<BR>
23    <INPUT TYPE = "checkbox" NAME = "c_cpp" VALUE = "c_cpp">
24    <I>C++ How to Program & C How to Program</I><BR>
25    <INPUT TYPE = "checkbox" NAME = "java" VALUE = "java">
26    <I>Java How to Program</I><BR>
27    <INPUT TYPE = "checkbox" NAME = "vb" VALUE = "vb">
28    <I>Visual Basic How to Program</I><BR>
29    <INPUT TYPE = "checkbox" NAME = "iwww" VALUE = "iwww">
30    <I>Internet and World Wide Web How to Program</I><BR></P>
31    <INPUT TYPE = "SUBMIT" VALUE = "Submit">
32 </FORM>
33 </BODY>
34 </HTML>
```

Fig. 29.17 Web page that invokes the **GuestBookServlet**.

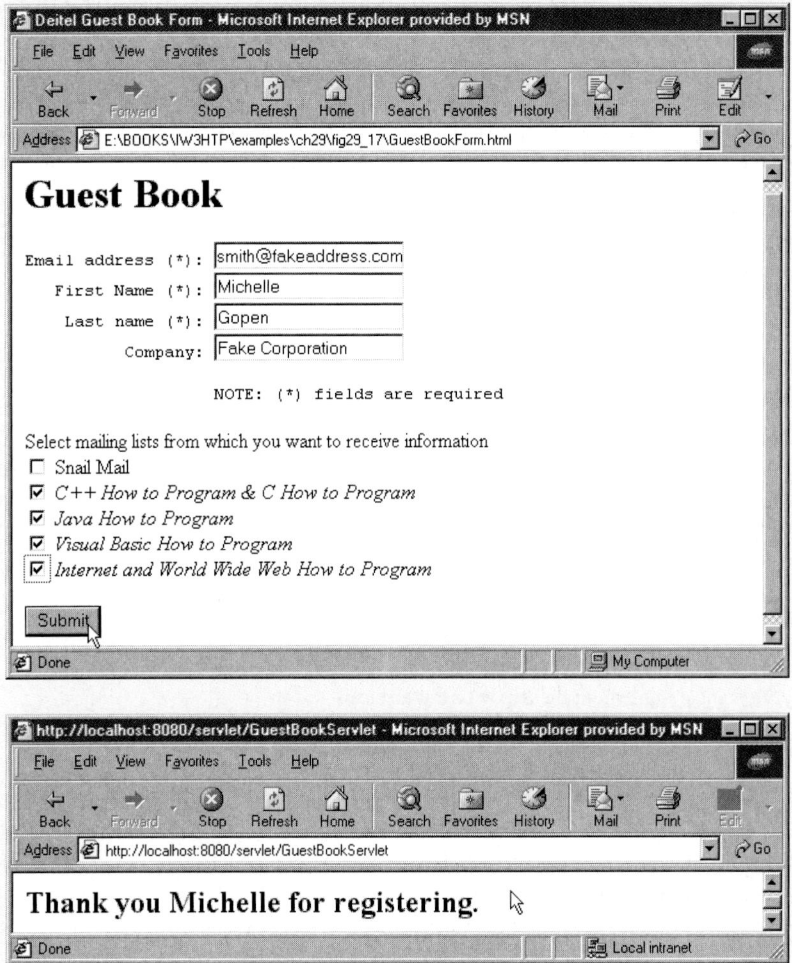

Fig. 29.17 Web page that invokes the **`GuestBookServlet`**.

29.8 Servlet Internet and World Wide Web Resources

This section lists a variety of servlet resources available on the Internet and provides a brief description of each. For other Java Internet resources, see the appendix "Internet and World Wide Web Resources."

`http://java.sun.com/products/servlet/index.html`

The servlet page at the *Sun Microsystems, Inc. Java* Web site provides access to the latest servlet information, servlet resources and the *JavaServer Web Development Kit (JSWDK)*. You can also download previous versions of the *Java Servlet Development Kit (JSDK)* from this site.

`http://www.servlets.com/`

This is the Web site for the book *Java Servlet Programming* published by O'Reilly. The book provides a variety of resources and is an excellent resource for programmers who are learning servlets.

http://www.servletcentral.com/
Servlet Central is an online magazine for Java programmers interested in servlets. This includes technical articles and columns, news and "Ask the Experts." Resources include books, servlet documentation links on the Web, a servlet archive, a list of servlet-enabled applications and servers and servlet development tools.

http://www.servletsource.com/
ServletSource.com is a general servlet resource site containing code, tips, tutorials and links to many other Web sites with information on servlets.

http://www.cookiecentral.com/
A good all-around resource site for cookies.

SUMMARY

- Often, networking is a client-server relationship. The client requests that some action be performed and the server performs the action and responds to the client.
- A common use of the request-response model is between World Wide Web browsers and World Wide Web servers. When a user selects a Web site to browse through a Web browser (the client application), a request is sent to the appropriate Web server (the server application), which normally responds to the client by sending the appropriate HTML Web page.
- A servlet extends the functionality of a server. Most servlets enhance the functionality of World Wide Web servers.
- The Internet offers many protocols, the most common being the HTTP protocol (HyperText Transfer Protocol), which forms the basis of the World Wide Web.
- All servlets must implement the **Servlet** interface.
- As with many key applet methods, the methods of interface **Servlet** are invoked automatically (by the server on which the servlet is installed).
- **Servlet** method **init** takes one **ServletConfig** argument and throws a **ServletException**. The **ServletConfig** argument provides the servlet with information about its initialization parameters (i.e., parameters not associated with a request, but passed to the servlet for initializing servlet variables).
- **Servlet** method **getServletConfig** returns a reference to an object that implements interface **ServletConfig**. This object provides access to the servlet's configuration information, such as initialization parameters, and the servlet's **ServletContext**.
- The servlet packages define two abstract classes that implement interface **Servlet**—**GenericServlet** and **HttpServlet**. These classes provide default implementations of all methods of interface **Servlet**. Most servlets extend one of these classes and override some or all of their methods with appropriate customized behaviors.
- The key method in every servlet is method **service**, which receives both a **ServletRequest** object and a **ServletResponse** object. These objects provide access to input and output streams that allow the servlet to read data from the client and send data to the client.
- Web-based servlets typically extend class **HttpServlet**. Class **HttpServlet** overrides method **service** to distinguish between the typical requests received from a client Web browser.
- The two most common HTTP request types (also known as request methods) are **GET** and **POST**.
- Class **HttpServlet** defines methods **doGet** and **doPost** to respond to **GET** and **POST** requests from a client, respectively. These methods are called by the **HttpServlet** class's service method, which first determines the request type, then calls the appropriate method.

- Methods **doGet** and **doPost** each receive as arguments an **HttpServletRequest** object and an **HttpServletResponse** object that enable interaction between the client and the server. The **HttpServletRequest** object represents the client's request and the **HttpServlet-Response** object represents the server's response.
- The method **getParameter** of interface **ServletRequest** retrieves the survey response **POST**ed by the client. The method returns a **String** containing the value of the parameter or **null** if the parameter is not found.
- The method **getParameterNames** of interface **ServletRequest** returns an **Enumeration** of **String** names of all the parameters **POST**ed by the client.
- **HttpServletResponse** method **getOutputStream** obtains a byte-based output stream that enables binary data to be sent to the client.
- **HttpServletResponse** method **getWriter** obtains a character-based output stream that enables text data to be sent to the client.
- **HttpServletResponse** method **setContentType** specifies the MIME type of the response to the browser. The MIME type helps the browser determine how to display the data (or possibly what other application to execute to process the data). For example, type **"text/html"** indicates that the response is an HTML document, so the browser displays the HTML page.
- If **doGet** or **doPut** is unable to handle a client's request, it throws a **javax.servlet.ServletException**. If **doGet** encounters an error during stream processing (reading from the client or writing to the client), it throws a **java.io.IOException**.
- The client can only access a servlet if the servlet is running on a server. The JSWDK WebServer can be used to test servlets.
- When a client connects to a server to request a service, the client must specify the proper port number; otherwise, the client request cannot be processed (unless the default port is the correct port).
- The term *well-known port number* is used to describe the default port for many Internet services. For example, a Web server waits for clients to make requests at well-known port 80 by default.
- The JSWDK WebServer uses port 8080 as test port.
- The server **localhost** is a well-known server name on all computers that support TCP/IP-based networking protocols such as HTTP. The server **localhost** refers to your own computer.
- Browsers often cache (save on disk) Web pages so they can quickly reload the pages. However, browsers typically do not cache the server's response to a **POST** request because the next **POST** may not return the same result.
- Many Web sites keep track of individual clients as they browse in order to have specific information about a particular user. This is often done to provide customized content and/or to gather data on browsing habits.
- Two common techniques used to track clients individually are cookies and session tracking.
- Cookies are small strings that are sent by a servlet (or another similar technology such as ASP or CGI) as part of the HTTP header and can store information on the user's computer for retrieval later in the same or in future browsing sessions.
- When the browser makes a request of a server, cookies previously sent to the client by that server are returned to the server (if they have not expired) as part of the request formulated by the browser. Cookies are automatically deleted when they expire (i.e., reach their maximum age).
- The method **setMaxAge** of class **Cookie** sets the maximum age for the cookie. The method **getMaxAge** of class **Cookie** returns the maximum age for the cookie.
- The user of a browser can turn off cookies.

- **HttpServletRequest** method **getCookies**, which returns an array of **Cookie**s, retrieves the cookies from the client. **HttpServletResponse** method **addCookie** adds a **Cookie** to the header of the response.
- The method **getName** of class **Cookie** returns a **String** containing the name of the cookie as set with **setName** or the constructor.
- The method **getValue** of class **Cookie** returns a **String** containing the name of the cookie as set with **setValue** or the constructor.
- Session tracking uses **HttpSession** objects.
- The **HttpServletRequest** method **getSession** returns an **HttpSession** objects for the client. Supplying the boolean **true** as an argument to this function will cause a session to be created if there is not one already.
- The **HttpSession** method **getValue** returns the object that was associated with a particular name using **putValue**.
- The **HttpSession** method **getValueNames** returns a list of names of the values already set.
- Servlets can communicate with databases via JDBC (Java Database Connectivity).
- Many of today's applications are three-tier distributed applications, consisting of a user interface, business logic and database access. The user interface in such an application is often created using HTML or Dynamic HTML. Java applets are also used for this tier.
- In multitier architectures, Web servers are increasingly used to build the middle tier. They provide the business logic that manipulates data from databases and that communicates with client Web browsers.

TERMINOLOGY

addCookie method
BAD_REQUEST error
business logic
class **Cookie**
class **GenericServlet**
class **HttpServlet**
client-server relationship
destroy method of **Servlet** interface
doDelete method of **HttpServlet** class
doGet method of **HttpServlet** class
doOptions method of **HttpServlet** class
doPost method of **HttpServlet** class
doPut method of **HttpServlet** class
doTrace method of **HttpServlet** class
Dynamic **HTML**
GET request
getComment method of class **Cookie**
getCookies method
getDomain method of class **Cookie**
getMaxAge method of class **Cookie**
getName method of class **Cookie**
getOutputStream method
getParameter method
getParameterNames method
getPath method of class **Cookie**
getSecure method of class **Cookie**
getServletConfig method of **Servlet**
getServletInfo method of **Servlet**
getSession method
getValue method of class **Cookie**
getValue method of interface **HttpSession**
getValueNames method of **HttpSession**
getVersion method of class **Cookie**
getWriter method
handshake point
header
HTTP protocol
init method of **Servlet** interface
interface **HttpServletRequest**
interface **HttpServletResponse**
interface **HttpSession**
JavaServer Web Development Kit (JSWDK)
java.*servletname***.code** argument
java.*servletname***.initargs** argument
javax.servlet.http package
javax.servlet package
JSWDK WebServer
localhost

putValue method of interface **HttpSession**
request-response model
request types / request methods
service method of **Servlet** interface
ServletConfig class
ServletException
Servlet interface
ServletRequest object
ServletResponse object
servlets
setComment method of class **Cookie**
setContentType method
setDomain method of class **Cookie**
setMaxAge method of class **Cookie**
setPath method of class **Cookie**
setSecure method of class **Cookie**
setValue method of class **Cookie**
setVersion method of class **Cookie**
socket-based communications
startserver
startserver.bat
"**submit**" **INPUT** type
thin clients
three-tier distributed applications
well-known port number

SOFTWARE ENGINEERING OBSERVATIONS

29.1 All servlets must implement the **javax.servlet.Servlet** interface.

29.2 Some clients do not allow cookies to be written on them. When a client declines a cookie the client is normally informed that such a refusal may prevent browsing the site. (This is normally customizable in the browser's security options).

29.3 By default cookies only exist for the current browsing session (until the user closes the browser). To make cookies persist beyond the current session, call **Cookie** method **setMaxAge** to indicate the number of seconds until the cookie expires.

29.4 Call method **addCookie** to add a cookie to the **HTTPServletResponse** before writing any other information to the client.

29.5 Name/value pairs added to an **HttpSession** object with **putValue** remain available until the client's current browsing session ends or until the session is explicitly invalidated by a call to the **HttpSession** object's **invalidate** methods.

TESTING AND DEBUGGING TIP

29.1 On Windows 95 and Windows 98 computers, executing **startserver.bat** or **stopserver.bat** may result in an "Out of environment space" message. See the **README.txt** file in the JSWDK install directory for directions on correcting this problem.

SELF-REVIEW EXERCISES

29.1 Fill in the blanks in each of the following:

d) Classes **HttpServlet** and **GenericServlet** implement the ________ interface.
e) Class **HttpServlet** defines the methods __________ and __________ to respond to **GET** and **POST** requests from a client.
f) **HttpServletResponse** method ________ obtains a character-based output stream that enables text data to be sent to the client.
g) **FORM** attribute __________ specifies the server-side *form handler* (i.e., the service that will handle the request).
h) _________ is the well-known server name that refers to your own computer.
i) **Cookie** method _________ returns a **String** containing the name of the cookie as set with _________ or the constructor.
j) **HttpServletRequest** method **getSession** returns an _________ object for the client.

29.2 State whether each of the following is *true* or *false*. If *false*, explain why.

a) Servlets usually are used on the client side of a networking application.
b) Servlet methods are executed automatically.
c) The two most common **HTTP** requests are **GET** and **PUT**.
d) The well-known port number for HTTP requests is 55.
e) **Cookie**s never expire.
f) **HttpSession**s expire only when the browsing session ends or when the **invalidate** method is called.
g) The **HttpSession** method **getValue** returns the object associated with a particular name.

ANSWERS TO SELF-REVIEW EXERCISES

29.1 a) **Servlet**. b) **doGet**, **doPost**. c) **getWriter**. d) **ACTION**. e) **localhost**. f) **getName**, **setName**. g) **HttpSession**.

29.2 a) False. Servlets are used on the server side.
b) True.
c) False. The two most common HTTP requests are **GET** and **POST**.
d) False. The well-known port number for HTTP requests is 80.
e) False. **Cookie**s expire when they reach their maximum age.
f) True.
g) True.

EXERCISES

29.3 Modify the **Cookie** example in Figs. 29.9 through 29.11 to have the book recommendation list prices for each book. Also, allow the user to select some or all of the recommended books and "order" them.

29.4 Modify the **HttpSession** example in Figs. 29.13 through 29.15 to have the book recommendation list prices for each book. Also, allow the user to select some or all of the recommended books and "order" them.

29.5 Modify the **GuestBook** example in Figs. 29.16 and 29.17 to implement the fields **Address1**, **Address2**, **City**, **State** and **Zip**. Modify it further to look up a guest by name or email address and return an HTML page with all of the guest's information.

29.6 Modify the servlet of Fig. 29.7 to synchronize access to the **survey.dat** file by having the **HTTPPostServlet** class implement **javax.servlet.SingleThreadModel**.

29.7 *(Project: Auction Servlet)* Create your own auction servlet. Create a database of several items that are being auctioned. Make a Web page that allows users to select an item on which to place a bid. When users place the bid they should be notified if the bid is lower than the previous high bid and asked to submit their bid again. Allow users to return to the servlet and query it to determine if they won the auction.

29.8 Modify Exercise 29.7 to use session tracking such that when the client connects to the servlet again, the client is automatically sent a Web page indicating the status of the bidding on the items for which he or she have previously bid.

HTML Special Characers

The table of Fig. A.1 shows many commonly used HTML special characters—called *character entity references* by the World Wide Web Consortium. For a complete list of character entity references, see the site

`http://www.w3.org/TR/REC-html40/sgml/entities.html`

Character	HTML encoding	Character	HTML encoding
non-breaking space	` `	ê	`ê`
§	`§`	ì	`ì`
©	`©`	í	`í`
®	`®`	î	`î`
π	`¼`	ñ	`ñ`
∫	`½`	ò	`ò`
Ω	`¾`	ó	`ó`
à	`à`	ô	`ô`
á	`á`	õ	`õ`
â	`â`	÷	`÷`
ã	`ã`	ù	`ù`
å	`å`	ú	`ú`
ç	`ç`	û	`û`
è	`è`	•	`•`
é	`é`	™	`™`

Fig. A.1 HTML special characters.

Operator Precedence Charts

This appendix contains the operator precedence charts for JavaScript/JScript/ECMA-Script (Fig. B.1), VBScript (Fig. B.2) and Perl (Fig. B.3). In each figure, the operators are shown in decreasing order of precedence from top to bottom.

Operator	Type	Associativity
`.`	member access	left to right
`[]`	array indexing	
`()`	function calls	
`++`	increment	right to left
`--`	decrement	
`-`	unary minus	
`~`	bitwise complement	
`!`	logical NOT	
`delete`	delete an array element or object property	
`new`	create a new object	
`typeof`	returns the data type of its argument	
`void`	prevents an expression from returning a value	
`*`	multiplication	left to right
`/`	division	
`%`	modulus	
`+`	addition	left to right
`-`	subtraction	
`+`	string concatenation	

Fig. B.1 JavaScript/JScript/ECMAScript operator precedence and associativity (part 1 of 2).

<table>
<tr><th>Operator</th><th>Type</th><th>Associativity</th></tr>
<tr><td><<</td><td>left shift</td><td>left to right</td></tr>
<tr><td>>></td><td>right shift with sign extension</td><td></td></tr>
<tr><td>>>></td><td>right shift with zero extension</td><td></td></tr>
<tr><td><</td><td>less than</td><td>left to right</td></tr>
<tr><td><=</td><td>less than or equal</td><td></td></tr>
<tr><td>></td><td>greater than</td><td></td></tr>
<tr><td>>=</td><td>greater than or equal</td><td></td></tr>
<tr><td>instanceof</td><td>type comparison</td><td></td></tr>
<tr><td>==</td><td>equality</td><td>left to right</td></tr>
<tr><td>!=</td><td>inequality</td><td></td></tr>
<tr><td>===</td><td>identity</td><td></td></tr>
<tr><td>!==</td><td>nonidentity</td><td></td></tr>
<tr><td>&</td><td>bitwise AND</td><td>left to right</td></tr>
<tr><td>^</td><td>bitwise XOR</td><td>left to right</td></tr>
<tr><td>|</td><td>bitwise OR</td><td>left to right</td></tr>
<tr><td>&&</td><td>logical AND</td><td>left to right</td></tr>
<tr><td>||</td><td>logical OR</td><td>left to right</td></tr>
<tr><td>?:</td><td>conditional</td><td>left to right</td></tr>
<tr><td>=</td><td>assignment</td><td>right to left</td></tr>
<tr><td>+=</td><td>addition assignment</td><td></td></tr>
<tr><td>-=</td><td>subtraction assignment</td><td></td></tr>
<tr><td>*=</td><td>multiplication assignment</td><td></td></tr>
<tr><td>/=</td><td>division assignment</td><td></td></tr>
<tr><td>%=</td><td>modulus assignment</td><td></td></tr>
<tr><td>&=</td><td>bitwise AND assignment</td><td></td></tr>
<tr><td>^=</td><td>bitwise exclusive OR assignment</td><td></td></tr>
<tr><td>|=</td><td>bitwise inclusive OR assignment</td><td></td></tr>
<tr><td><<=</td><td>bitwise left shift assignment</td><td></td></tr>
<tr><td>>>=</td><td>bitwise right shift with sign extension assignment</td><td></td></tr>
<tr><td>>>>=</td><td>bitwise right shift with zero extension assignment</td><td></td></tr>
</table>

Fig. B.1 JavaScript/JScript/ECMAScript operator precedence and associativity (part 2 of 2).

Operator	Type	Associativity
`()`	parentheses	left to right
`^`	exponentiation	left to right
`-`	unary minus	left to right

`*`
`/`
`\`
	multiplication
	division
	integer division
		left to right

`Mod`	modulus	left to right
`+` `-`	addition subtraction	left to right
`&`	string concatenation	left to right

`=`
`<>`
`<`
`<=`
`>`
`>=`
`Is`
	equality
	inequality
	less than
	less than or equal
	greater than
	greater than or equal
	object equivalence
		left to right

`Not`	logical NOT	left to right
`And`	logical AND	left to right
`Or`	logical OR	left to right
`Xor`	logical exclusive OR	left to right
`Eqv`	logical equivalence	left to right
`Imp`	logical implication	left to right

Fig. B.2 VBScript operator precedence chart .

Operator	Type	Associativity
terms and list operators	**print @array** or **sort (4, 2, 7)**	left to right
->	member access	left to right
++ **--**	increment decrement	none
**	exponentiation	right to left
! **~** **** **+** **-**	logical NOT bitwise one's complement reference unary plus unary minus	right to left
=~ **!~**	matching negated match	left to right
* **/** **%** **x**	multiplication division modulus repetition	left to right
+ **-** **.**	addition subtraction string concatenation	left to right
<< **>>**	left shift right shift	left to right
named unary operators	unary operators, e.g. **-e** (filetest)	none
< **>** **<=** **>=** **lt** **gt** **le** **ge**	numerical less than numerical greater than numerical less than or equal numerical greater than or equal string less than string greater than string less than or equal string greater than or equal	none
== **!=** **<=>** **eq** **ne** **cmp**	numerical equality numerical inequality numerical comparison (returns -1, 0 or 1) string equality string inequality string comparison (returns -1, 0 or 1)	none
&	bitwise AND	left to right

Fig. B.3 Perl operator precedence chart (part 1 of 2).

Operator	Type	Associativity
`|` `^`	bitwise inclusive OR bitwise exclusive OR	left to right
`&&`	logical AND	left to right
`||`	logical OR	left to right
`..`	range operator	none
`?:`	conditional operator	right to left

`=`
`+=`
`-=`
`*=`
`/=`
`%=`
`**=`
`.=`
`x=`
`&=`
`|=`
`^=`
`<<=`
`>>=`
`&&=`
`||=`
	assignment
	addition assignment
	subtraction assignment
	multplication assignment
	division assignment
	modulus assignment
	exponentiation assignment
	string concatenation assignment
	repetition assignment [***]
	bitwise AND assignment
	bitwise inclusive OR assignment
	bitwise exclusive OR assignment
	left shift assignment
	right shift assignment
	logical AND assignment
	logical OR assignment
		right to left

`,` `=>`	expression separator; returns value of last expression expression separator; groups two expressions	left to right
not	logical NOT	right to left
and	logical AND	left to right
or **xor**	logical OR logical exclusive OR	left to right

Fig. B.3 Perl operator precedence chart (part 2 of 2).

ASCII Character Set

ASCII character set

	0	1	2	3	4	5	6	7	8	9
0	nul	soh	stx	etx	eot	enq	ack	bel	bs	ht
1	nl	vt	ff	cr	so	si	dle	dc1	dc2	dc3
2	dc4	nak	syn	etb	can	em	sub	esc	fs	gs
3	rs	us	sp	!	"	#	$	%	&	'
4	(	)	*	+	,	-	.	/	0	1
5	2	3	4	5	6	7	8	9	:	;
6	<	=	>	?	@	A	B	C	D	E
7	F	G	H	I	J	K	L	M	N	O
8	P	Q	R	S	T	U	V	W	X	Y
9	Z	[	\	]	^	_	`	a	b	c
10	d	e	f	g	h	i	j	k	l	m
11	n	o	p	q	r	s	t	u	v	w
12	x	y	z	{	|	}	~	del		

Fig. C.1 ASCII Character Set.

The digits at the left of the table are the left digits of the decimal equivalent (0-127) of the character code, and the digits at the top of the table are the right digits of the character code. For example, the character code for "F" is 70, and the character code for "&" is 38.

Note: Most users of this book are interested in the ASCII character set used to represent English characters on many computers. The ASCII character set is a subset of the Unicode character set used by Java to represent characters from most of the world's languages. For more information on the Unicode character set, visit the World Wide Web site **http://unicode.org/**.

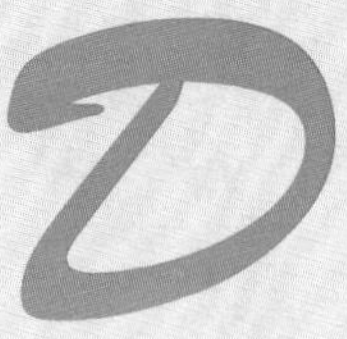

Number Systems

Objectives

- To understand basic number systems concepts such as base, positional value, and symbol value.
- To understand how to work with numbers represented in the binary, octal, and hexadecimal number systems
- To be able to abbreviate binary numbers as octal numbers or hexadecimal numbers.
- To be able to convert octal numbers and hexadecimal numbers to binary numbers.
- To be able to covert back and forth between decimal numbers and their binary, octal, and hexadecimal equivalents.
- To understand binary arithmetic, and how negative binary numbers are represented using two's complement notation.

Here are only numbers ratified.
William Shakespeare

Nature has some sort of arithmetic-geometrical coordinate system, because nature has all kinds of models. What we experience of nature is in models, and all of nature's models are so beautiful.
It struck me that nature's system must be a real beauty, because in chemistry we find that the associations are always in beautiful whole numbers—there are no fractions.
Richard Buckminster Fuller

Outline

D.1 Introduction

In this appendix, we introduce the key number systems that programmers use, especially when they are working on software projects that require close interaction with "machine-level" hardware. Projects like this include operating systems, computer networking software, compilers, database systems, and applications requiring high performance.

When we write an integer such as 227 or -63 in a program, the number is assumed to be in the *decimal (base 10) number system*. The *digits* in the decimal number system are 0, 1, 2, 3, 4, 5, 6, 7, 8, and 9. The lowest digit is 0 and the highest digit is 9—one less than the *base* of 10. Internally, computers use the *binary (base 2) number system*. The binary number system has only two digits, namely 0 and 1. Its lowest digit is 0 and its highest digit is 1—one less than the base of 2. Figure D.1 summarizes the digits used in the binary, octal, decimal and hexadecimal number systems.

As we will see, binary numbers tend to be much longer than their decimal equivalents. Programmers who work in assembly languages and in high-level languages that enable programmers to reach down to the "machine level," find it cumbersome to work with binary numbers. So two other number systems the *octal number system (base 8)* and the *hexadecimal number system (base 16)*—are popular primarily because they make it convenient to abbreviate binary numbers.

In the octal number system, the digits range from 0 to 7. Because both the binary number system and the octal number system have fewer digits than the decimal number system, their digits are the same as the corresponding digits in decimal.

The hexadecimal number system poses a problem because it requires sixteen digits—a lowest digit of 0 and a highest digit with a value equivalent to decimal 15 (one less than the base of 16). By convention, we use the letters A through F to represent the hexadecimal digits corresponding to decimal values 10 through 15. Thus in hexadecimal we can have numbers like 876 consisting solely of decimal-like digits, numbers like 8A55F consisting of digits and letters, and numbers like FFE consisting solely of letters. Occasionally, a hexadecimal number spells a common word such as FACE or FEED—this can appear strange to programmers accustomed to working with numbers. Figure D.2 summarizes each of the number systems.

Each of these number systems uses *positional notation*—each position in which a digit is written has a different *positional value*. For example, in the decimal number 937 (the 9, the 3, and the 7 are referred to as *symbol values*), we say that the 7 is written in the *ones position*, the 3 is written in the *tens position*, and the 9 is written in the *hundreds position*. Notice that each of these positions is a power of the base (base 10), and that these powers begin at 0 and increase by 1 as we move left in the number (Fig. D.3).

Binary digit	Octal digit	Decimal digit	Hexadecimal digit
0	0	0	0
1	1	1	1
	2	2	2
	3	3	3
	4	4	4
	5	5	5
	6	6	6
	7	7	7
		8	8
		9	9
			A (decimal value of 10)
			B (decimal value of 11)
			C (decimal value of 12)
			D (decimal value of 13)
			E (decimal value of 14)
			F (decimal value of 15)

Fig. D.2 Digits of the binary, octal, decimal and hexadecimal number systems.

Attribute	Binary	Octal	Decimal	Hexadecimal
Base	2	8	10	16
Lowest digit	0	0	0	0
Highest digit	1	7	9	F

Fig. D.3 Comparison of the binary, octal, decimal and hexadecimal number systems.

Positional values in the decimal number system			
Decimal digit	9	3	7
Position name	Hundreds	Tens	Ones
Positional value	100	10	1
Positional value as a power of the base (10)	10^2	10^1	10^0

Fig. D.4 Positional values in the decimal number system.

For longer decimal numbers, the next positions to the left would be the *thousands position* (10 to the 3rd power), the *ten-thousands position* (10 to the 4th power), the *hundred-thousands position* (10 to the 5th power), the *millions position* (10 to the 6th power), the *ten-millions position* (10 to the 7th power), and so on.

In the binary number 101, we say that the rightmost 1 is written in the *ones position*, the 0 is written in the *twos position*, and the leftmost 1 is written in the *fours position*. Notice that each of these positions is a power of the base (base 2), and that these powers begin at 0 and increase by 1 as we move left in the number (Fig D.4).

For longer binary numbers, the next positions to the left would be the *eights position* (2 to the 3rd power), the *sixteens position* (2 to the 4th power), the *thirty-twos position* (2 to the 5th power), the *sixty-fours position* (2 to the 6th power), and so on.

In the octal number 425, we say that the 5 is written in the *ones position*, the 2 is written in the *eights position*, and the 4 is written in the *sixty-fours position*. Notice that each of these positions is a power of the base (base 8), and that these powers begin at 0 and increase by 1 as we move left in the number (Fig. D.5).

For longer octal numbers, the next positions to the left would be the *five-hundred-and-twelves position* (8 to the 3rd power), the *four-thousand-and-ninety-sixes position* (8 to the 4th power), the *thirty-two-thousand-seven-hundred-and-sixty eights position* (8 to the 5th power), and so on.

In the hexadecimal number 3DA, we say that the A is written in the *ones position*, the D is written in the *sixteens position*, and the 3 is written in the *two-hundred-and-fifty-sixes position*. Notice that each of these positions is a power of the base (base 16), and that these powers begin at 0 and increase by 1 as we move left in the number (Fig. D.6).

For longer hexadecimal numbers, the next positions to the left would be the *four-thousand-and-ninety-sixes position* (16 to the 3rd power), the *sixty-five-thousand-five-hundred-and-thirty-six position* (16 to the 4th power), and so on.

Positional values in the binary number system

Binary digit	1	0	1
Position name	Fours	Twos	Ones
Positional value	4	2	1
Positional value as a power of the base (2)	2^2	2^1	2^0

Fig. D.5 Positional values in the binary number system.

Positional values in the octal number system

Decimal digit	4	2	5
Position name	Sixty-fours	Eights	Ones
Positional value	64	8	1
Positional value as a power of the base (8)	8^2	8^1	8^0

Fig. D.6 Positional values in the octal number system.

Positional values in the hexadecimal number system			
Decimal digit	**3**	**D**	**A**
Position name	Two-hundred-and-fifty-sixes	Sixteens	Ones
Positional value	**256**	**16**	**1**
Positional value as a power of the base (16)	16^2	16^1	16^0

Fig. D.7 Positional values in the hexadecimal number system.

D.2 Abbreviating Binary Numbers as Octal Numbers and Hexadecimal Numbers

The main use for octal and hexadecimal numbers in computing is for abbreviating lengthy binary representations. Figure D.7 highlights the fact that lengthy binary numbers can be expressed concisely in number systems with higher bases than the binary number system.

Decimal number	Binary representation	Octal representation	Hexadecimal representation
0	0	0	0
1	1	1	1
2	10	2	2
3	11	3	3
4	100	4	4
5	101	5	5
6	110	6	6
7	111	7	7
8	1000	10	8
9	1001	11	9
10	1010	12	A
11	1011	13	B
12	1100	14	C
13	1101	15	D
14	1110	16	E
15	1111	17	F
16	10000	20	10

Fig. D.8 Decimal, binary, octal, and hexadecimal equivalents.

A particularly important relationship that both the octal number system and the hexadecimal number system have to the binary system is that the bases of octal and hexadecimal (8 and 16 respectively) are powers of the base of the binary number system (base 2). Consider the following 12-digit binary number and its octal and hexadecimal equivalents. See if you can determine how this relationship makes it convenient to abbreviate binary numbers in octal or hexadecimal. The answer follows the numbers.

Binary Number	Octal equivalent	Hexadecimal equivalent
`100011010001`	`4321`	`8D1`

To see how the binary number converts easily to octal, simply break the 12-digit binary number into groups of three consecutive bits each, and write those groups over the corresponding digits of the octal number as follows

```
100           011           010           001
4             3             2             1
```

Notice that the octal digit you have written under each group of thee bits corresponds precisely to the octal equivalent of that 3-digit binary number as shown in Fig. D.7.

The same kind of relationship may be observed in converting numbers from binary to hexadecimal. In particular, break the 12-digit binary number into groups of four consecutive bits each and write those groups over the corresponding digits of the hexadecimal number as follows

```
1000          1101          0001
8             D             1
```

Notice that the hexadecimal digit you wrote under each group of four bits corresponds precisely to the hexadecimal equivalent of that 4-digit binary number as shown in Fig. D.7.

D.3 Converting Octal Numbers and Hexadecimal Numbers to Binary Numbers

In the previous section, we saw how to convert binary numbers to their octal and hexadecimal equivalents by forming groups of binary digits and simply rewriting these groups as their equivalent octal digit values or hexadecimal digit values. This process may be used in reverse to produce the binary equivalent of a given octal or hexadecimal number.

For example, the octal number 653 is converted to binary simply by writing the 6 as its 3-digit binary equivalent 110, the 5 as its 3-digit binary equivalent 101, and the 3 as its 3-digit binary equivalent 011 to form the 9-digit binary number 110101011.

The hexadecimal number FAD5 is converted to binary simply by writing the F as its 4-digit binary equivalent 1111, the A as its 4-digit binary equivalent 1010, the D as its 4-digit binary equivalent 1101, and the 5 as its 4-digit binary equivalent 0101 to form the 16-digit 1111101011010101.

D.4 Converting from Binary, Octal, or Hexadecimal to Decimal

Because we are accustomed to working in decimal, it is often convenient to convert a binary, octal, or hexadecimal number to decimal to get a sense of what the number is "really" worth. Our diagrams in Section D.1 express the positional values in decimal. To convert a number to decimal from another base, multiply the decimal equivalent of each digit by its positional value, and sum these products. For example, the binary number 110101 is converted to decimal 53 as shown in Fig. D.8.

To convert octal 7614 to decimal 3980, we use the same technique, this time using appropriate octal positional values as shown in Fig. D.9.

To convert hexadecimal AD3B to decimal 44347, we use the same technique, this time using appropriate hexadecimal positional values as shown in Fig. D.10.

D.5 Converting from Decimal to Binary, Octal, or Hexadecimal

The conversions of the previous section follow naturally from the positional notation conventions. Converting from decimal to binary, octal, or hexadecimal also follows these conventions.

Suppose we wish to convert decimal 57 to binary. We begin by writing the positional values of the columns right to left until we reach a column whose positional value is greater than the decimal number. We do not need that column, so we discard it. Thus, we first write:

Positional values: `64 32 16 8 4 2 1`

Then we discard the column with positional value 64 leaving:

Positional values: `32 16 8 4 2 1`

Converting a binary number to decimal

Positional values:	32	16	8	4	2	1
Symbol values:	1	1	0	1	0	1
Products:	1*32=32	1*16=16	0*8=0	1*4=4	0*2=0	1*1=1
Sum:	= 32 + 16 + 0 + 4 + 0 + 1 = 53					

Fig. D.9 Converting a binary number to decimal.

Converting an octal number to decimal

Positional values:	512	64	8	1
Symbol values:	7	6	1	4
Products	7*512=3584	6*64=384	1*8=8	4*1=4
Sum:	= 3584 + 384 + 8 + 4 = 3980			

Fig. D.10 Converting an octal number to decimal.

Converting a hexadecimal number to decimal

Positional values:	4096	256	16	1
Symbol values:	A	D	3	B
Products	A*4096=40960	D*256=3328	3*16=48	B*1=11
Sum:	= 40960 + 3328 + 48 + 11 = 44347			

Fig. D.11 Converting a hexadecimal number to decimal.

Next we work from the leftmost column to the right. We divide 32 into 57 and observe that there is one 32 in 57 with a remainder of 25, so we write 1 in the 32 column. We divide 16 into 25 and observe that there is one 16 in 25 with a remainder of 9 and write 1 in the 16 column. We divide 8 into 9 and observe that there is one 8 in 9 with a remainder of 1. The next two columns each produce quotients of zero when their positional values are divided into 1 so we write 0s in the 4 and 2 columns. Finally, 1 into 1 is 1 so we write 1 in the 1 column. This yields:

Positional values:	**32**	**16**	**8**	**4**	**2**	**1**
Symbol values:	**1**	**1**	**1**	**0**	**0**	**1**

and thus decimal 57 is equivalent to binary 111001.

To convert decimal 103 to octal, we begin by writing the positional values of the columns until we reach a column whose positional value is greater than the decimal number. We do not need that column, so we discard it. Thus, we first write:

Positional values: **512 64 8 1**

Then we discard the column with positional value 512, yielding:

Positional values: **64 8 1**

Next we work from the leftmost column to the right. We divide 64 into 103 and observe that there is one 64 in 103 with a remainder of 39, so we write 1 in the 64 column. We divide 8 into 39 and observe that there are four 8s in 39 with a remainder of 7 and write 4 in the 8 column. Finally, we divide 1 into 7 and observe that there are seven 1s in 7 with no remainder so we write 7 in the 1 column. This yields:

Positional values:	**64**	**8**	**1**
Symbol values:	**1**	**4**	**7**

and thus decimal 103 is equivalent to octal 147.

To convert decimal 375 to hexadecimal, we begin by writing the positional values of the columns until we reach a column whose positional value is greater than the decimal number. We do not need that column, so we discard it. Thus, we first write

Positional values: **4096 256 16 1**

Then we discard the column with positional value 4096, yielding:

Positional values: **256 16 1**

Next we work from the leftmost column to the right. We divide 256 into 375 and observe that there is one 256 in 375 with a remainder of 119, so we write 1 in the 256 column. We divide 16 into 119 and observe that there are seven 16s in 119 with a remainder of 7 and write 7 in the 16 column. Finally, we divide 1 into 7 and observe that there are seven 1s in 7 with no remainder so we write 7 in the 1 column. This yields:

Positional values:	**256**	**16**	**1**
Symbol values:	**1**	**7**	**7**

and thus decimal 375 is equivalent to hexadecimal 177.

D.6 Negative Binary Numbers: Two's Complement Notation

The discussion in this appendix has been focussed on positive numbers. In this section, we explain how computers represent negative numbers using *two's complement notation*. First we explain how the two's complement of a binary number is formed, and then we show why it represents the negative value of the given binary number.

Consider a machine with 32-bit integers. Suppose

```
var value = 13;
```

The 32-bit representation of **value** is

```
00000000 00000000 00000000 00001101
```

To form the negative of **value** we first form its *one's complement* by applying JavaScript's bitwise complement operator (~), which is also called the *bitwise NOT operator*:

```
onesComplementOfValue = ~value;
```

Internally, **~value** is now **value** with each of its bits reversed—ones become zeros and zeros become ones as follows:

```
value:
00000000 00000000 00000000 00001101

~value (i.e., value's ones complement):
11111111 11111111 11111111 11110010
```

To form the two's complement of **value** we simply add one to **value**'s one's complement. Thus

```
Two's complement of value:
11111111 11111111 11111111 11110011
```

Now if this is in fact equal to -13, we should be able to add it to binary 13 and obtain a result of 0. Let us try this:

```
 00000000 00000000 00000000 00001101
+11111111 11111111 11111111 11110011
------------------------------------
 00000000 00000000 00000000 00000000
```

The carry bit coming out of the leftmost column is discarded and we indeed get zero as a result. If we add the one's complement of a number to the number, the result would be all 1s. The key to getting a result of all zeros is that the twos complement is 1 more than the one's complement. The addition of 1 causes each column to add to 0 with a carry of 1. The carry keeps moving leftward until it is discarded from the leftmost bit, and hence the resulting number is all zeros.

Computers actually perform a subtraction such as

```
x = a - value;
```

by adding the two's complement of **value** to **a** as follows:

```
x = a + (~value + 1);
```

Suppose **a** is 27 and **value** is 13 as before. If the two's complement of **value** is actually the negative of **value**, then adding the two's complement of value to a should produce the result 14. Let us try this:

```
a (i.e., 27)        00000000 00000000 00000000 00011011
+(~value + 1)      +11111111 11111111 11111111 11110011
                   ------------------------------------
                    00000000 00000000 00000000 00001110
```

which is indeed equal to 14.

SUMMARY

- When we write an integer such as 19 or 227 or -63 in a program, the number is automatically assumed to be in the decimal (base 10) number system. The digits in the decimal number system are 0, 1, 2, 3, 4, 5, 6, 7, 8, and 9. The lowest digit is 0 and the highest digit is 9—one less than the base of 10.
- Internally, computers use the binary (base 2) number system. The binary number system has only two digits, namely 0 and 1. Its lowest digit is 0 and its highest digit is 1—one less than the base of 2.
- The octal number system (base 8) and the hexadecimal number system (base 16) are popular primarily because they make it convenient to abbreviate binary numbers.
- The digits of the octal number system range from 0 to 7.
- The hexadecimal number system poses a problem because it requires sixteen digits—a lowest digit of 0 and a highest digit with a value equivalent to decimal 15 (one less than the base of 16). By convention, we use the letters A through F to represent the hexadecimal digits corresponding to decimal values 10 through 15.
- Each number system uses positional notation—each position in which a digit is written has a different positional value.
- A particularly important relationship that both the octal number system and the hexadecimal number system have to the binary system is that the bases of octal and hexadecimal (8 and 16 respectively) are powers of the base of the binary number system (base 2).
- To convert an octal number to a binary number, simply replace each octal digit with its three-digit binary equivalent.
- To convert a hexadecimal number to a binary number, simply replace each hexadecimal digit with its four-digit binary equivalent.
- Because we are accustomed to working in decimal, it is convenient to convert a binary, octal or hexadecimal number to decimal to get a sense of the number's "real" worth.
- To convert a number to decimal from another base, multiply the decimal equivalent of each digit by its positional value, and sum these products.
- Computers represent negative numbers using two's complement notation.
- To form the negative of a value in binary, first form its one's complement by applying JavaScript's bitwise complement operator (~). This reverses the bits of the value. To form the two's complement of a value, simply add one to the value's one's complement.

TERMINOLOGY

base
base 2 number system
base 8 number system
base 10 number system
base 16 number system
binary number system
bitwise complement operator (~)
conversions
decimal number system
digit
hexadecimal number system
negative value
octal number system
one's complement notation
positional notation
positional value
symbol value
two's complement notation

SELF-REVIEW EXERCISES

D.1 The bases of the decimal, binary, octal, and hexadecimal number systems are ________, ________, ________, and ________ respectively.

D.2 In general, the decimal, octal, and hexadecimal representations of a given binary number contain (more/fewer) digits than the binary number contains.

D.3 (True/False) A popular reason for using the decimal number system is that it forms a convenient notation for abbreviating binary numbers simply by substituting one decimal digit per group of four binary bits.

D.4 The (octal / hexadecimal / decimal) representation of a large binary value is the most concise (of the given alternatives).

D.5 (True/False) The highest digit in any base is one more than the base.

D.6 (True/False) The lowest digit in any base is one less than the base.

D.7 The positional value of the rightmost digit of any number in either binary, octal, decimal, or hexadecimal is always _________.

D.8 The positional value of the digit to the left of the rightmost digit of any number in binary, octal, decimal, or hexadecimal is always equal to _________.

D.9 Fill in the missing values in this chart of positional values for the rightmost four positions in each of the indicated number systems:

decimal	`1000`	`100`	`10`	`1`
hexadecimal	`...`	`256`	`...`	`...`
binary	`...`	`...`	`...`	`...`
octal	`512`	`...`	`8`	`...`

D.10 Convert binary **`110101011000`** to octal and to hexadecimal.

D.11 Convert hexadecimal **`FACE`** to binary.

D.12 Convert octal **`7316`** to binary.

D.13 Convert hexadecimal **`4FEC`** to octal. (Hint: First convert 4FEC to binary then convert that binary number to octal.)

D.14 Convert binary **`1101110`** to decimal.

D.15 Convert octal **`317`** to decimal.

D.16 Convert hexadecimal **`EFD4`** to decimal.

D.17 Convert decimal **`177`** to binary, to octal, and to hexadecimal.

D.18 Show the binary representation of decimal **`417`**. Then show the one's complement of **`417`**, and the two's complement of **`417`**.

D.19 What is the result when the one's complement of a number is added to itself?

SELF-REVIEW ANSWERS

D.1 **`10`**, **`2`**, **`8`**, **`16`**.

D.2 Fewer.

D.3 False.

D.4 Hexadecimal.

D.5 False. The highest digit in any base is one less than the base.

D.6 False. The lowest digit in any base is zero.

D.7 **`1`** (the base raised to the zero power).

D.8 The base of the number system.

D.9 Fill in the missing values in this chart of positional values for the rightmost four positions in each of the indicated number systems:

decimal		**1000**	**100**	**101**
hexadecimal	**4096**	**256**	**16**	**1**
binary		**8**	**4**	**2 1**
octal		**512**	**64**	**81**

D.10 Octal **6530**; Hexadecimal **D58**.

D.11 Binary **1111 1010 1100 1110**.

D.12 Binary **111 011 001 110**.

D.13 Binary **0 100 111 111 101 100; Octal 47754**.

D.14 Decimal **2+4+8+32+64=110**.

D.15 Decimal **7+1*8+3*64=7+8+192=207**.

D.16 Decimal **4+13*16+15*256+14*4096=61396**.

D.17 Decimal **177**
to binary:

```
256 128 64 32 16 8 4 2 1
128 64 32 16 8 4 2 1
(1*128)+(0*64)+(1*32)+(1*16)+(0*8)+(0*4)+(0*2)+(1*1)
10110001
```

to octal:

```
512 64 8 1
64 8 1
(2*64)+(6*8)+(1*1)
261
```

to hexadecimal:

```
256 16 1
16 1
(11*16)+(1*1)
(B*16)+(1*1)
B1
```

D.18 Binary:

```
512 256 128 64 32 16 8 4 2 1
256 128 64 32 16 8 4 2 1
(1*256)+(1*128)+(0*64)+(1*32)+(0*16)+(0*8)+(0*4)+(0*2)+
(1*1)
110100001
```

One's complement: **001011110**
Two's complement: **001011111**
Check: Original binary number + its two's complement

```
110100001
001011111
---------
000000000
```

D.19 Zero.

EXERCISES

D.20 Some people argue that many of our calculations would be easier in the base **12** number system because **12** is divisible by so many more numbers than **10** (for base **10**). What is the lowest digit in base **12**? What might the highest symbol for the digit in base **12** be? What are the positional values of the rightmost four positions of any number in the base **12** number system?

D.21 How is the highest symbol value in the number systems we discussed related to the positional value of the first digit to the left of the rightmost digit of any number in these number systems?

D.22 Complete the following chart of positional values for the rightmost four positions in each of the indicated number systems:

D.23

decimal	**1000**	**100**	**10**	**1**
base 6	...	...	**6**	...
base 13	...	**169**	...	...
base 3	**27**	...	...	...

D.24 Convert binary **100101111010** to octal and to hexadecimal.

D.25 Convert hexadecimal **3A7D** to binary.

D.26 Convert hexadecimal **765F** to octal. (Hint: First convert **765F** to binary, then convert that binary number to octal.)

D.27 Convert binary **1011110** to decimal.

D.28 Convert octal **426** to decimal.

D.29 Convert hexadecimal **FFFF** to decimal.

D.30 Convert decimal **299** to binary, to octal, and to hexadecimal.

D.31 Show the binary representation of decimal **779**. Then show the one's complement of **779**, and the two's complement of **779**.

D.32 What is the result when the two's complement of a number is added to itself?

D.33 Show the two's complement of integer value **-1** on a machine with 32-bit integers.

HTML Colors

Colors may be specified by using a standard name (such as **`aqua`**) or a hexadecimal RGB value (such as **`#00FFFF`** for aqua). Of the six hexadecimal digits in an RGB value, the first two represent the amount of red in the color, the middle two represent the amount of green in the color, and the last two represent the amount of blue in the color. For example, **`black`** is the absence of color and is defined by **`#000000`**, whereas **`white`** is the maximum amount of red, green and blue and is defined by **`#FFFFFF`**. Pure **`red`** is **`#FF0000`**, pure green (which the standard calls **`lime`**) is **`#00FF00`** and pure **`blue`** is **`#00FFFF`**. Note that **`green`** in the standard is defined as **`#008000`**. Figure E.1 contains the HTML standard color set. Figure E.2 contains the HTML extended color set.

Color name	Value	Color name	Value
`aqua`	`#00FFFF`	`navy`	`#000080`
`black`	`#000000`	`olive`	`#808000`
`blue`	`#0000FF`	`purple`	`#800080`
`fuchsia`	`#FF00FF`	`red`	`#FF0000`
`gray`	`#808080`	`silver`	`#C0C0C0`
`green`	`#008000`	`teal`	`#008080`
`lime`	`#00FF00`	`yellow`	`#FFFF00`
`maroon`	`#800000`	`white`	`#FFFFFF`

Fig. E.1 HTML standard colors and hexadecimal RGB values.

Color name	Value	Color name	Value
aliceblue	#F0F8FF	dodgerblue	#1E90FF
antiquewhite	#FAEBD7	firebrick	#B22222
aquamarine	#7FFFD4	floralwhite	#FFFAF0
azure	#F0FFFF	forestgreen	#228B22
beige	#F5F5DC	gainsboro	#DCDCDC
bisque	#FFE4C4	ghostwhite	#F8F8FF
blanchedalmond	#FFEBCD	gold	#FFD700
blueviolet	#8A2BE2	goldenrod	#DAA520
brown	#A52A2A	greenyellow	#ADFF2F
burlywood	#DEB887	honeydew	#F0FFF0
cadetblue	#5F9EA0	hotpink	#FF69B4
chartreuse	#7FFF00	indianred	#CD5C5C
chocolate	#D2691E	indigo	#4B0082
coral	#FF7F50	ivory	#FFFFF0
cornflowerblue	#6495ED	khaki	#F0E68C
cornsilk	#FFF8DC	lavender	#E6E6FA
crimson	#DC1436	lavenderblush	#FFF0F5
cyan	#00FFFF	lawngreen	#7CFC00
darkblue	#00008B	lemonchiffon	#FFFACD
darkcyan	#008B8B	lightblue	#ADD8E6
darkgoldenrod	#B8860B	lightcoral	#F08080
darkgray	#A9A9A9	lightcyan	#E0FFFF
darkgreen	#006400	lightgoldenrodyellow	#FAFAD2
darkkhaki	#BDB76B	lightgreen	#90EE90
darkmagenta	#8B008B	lightgrey	#D3D3D3
darkolivegreen	#556B2F	lightpink	#FFB6C1
darkorange	#FF8C00	lightsalmon	#FFA07A
darkorchid	#9932CC	lightseagreen	#20B2AA
darkred	#8B0000	lightskyblue	#87CEFA
darksalmon	#E9967A	lightslategray	#778899
darkseagreen	#8FBC8F	lightsteelblue	#B0C4DE
darkslateblue	#483D8B	lightyellow	#FFFFE0
darkslategray	#2F4F4F	limegreen	#32CD32
darkturquoise	#00CED1	linen	#FAF0E6
darkviolet	#9400D3	magenta	#FF00FF
deeppink	#FF1493	mediumaquamarine	#66CDAA
deepskyblue	#00BFFF	mediumblue	#0000CD
dimgray	#696969	mediumorchid	#BA55D3

Fig. E.2 HTML extended colors and hexadecimal RGB values (part 1 of 2).

Color name	Value	Color name	Value
mediumpurple	#9370DB	plum	#DDA0DD
mediumseagreen	#3CB371	powderblue	#B0E0E6
mediumslateblue	#7B68EE	rosybrown	#BC8F8F
mediumspringgreen	#00FA9A	royalblue	#4169E1
mediumturquoise	#48D1CC	saddlebrown	#8B4513
mediumvioletred	#C71585	salmon	#FA8072
midnightblue	#191970	sandybrown	#F4A460
mintcream	#F5FFFA	seagreen	#2E8B57
mistyrose	#FFE4E1	seashell	#FFF5EE
moccasin	#FFE4B5	sienna	#A0522D
navajowhite	#FFDEAD	skyblue	#87CEEB
oldlace	#FDF5E6	slateblue	#6A5ACD
olivedrab	#6B8E23	slategray	#708090
orange	#FFA500	snow	#FFFAFA
orangered	#FF4500	springgreen	#00FF7F
orchid	#DA70D6	steelblue	#4682B4
palegoldenrod	#EEE8AA	tan	#D2B48C
palegreen	#98FB98	thistle	#D8BFD8
paleturquoise	#AFEEEE	tomato	#FF6347
palevioletred	#DB7093	turquoise	#40E0D0
papayawhip	#FFEFD5	violet	#EE82EE
peachpuff	#FFDAB9	wheat	#F5DEB3
peru	#CD853F	whitesmoke	#F5F5F5
pink	#FFC0CB	yellowgreen	#9ACD32

Fig. E.2 HTML extended colors and hexadecimal RGB values (part 2 of 2).

Bibliography

(Al99) Allen, D. W., *Microsoft Internet Explorer 5 at a Glance,* Redmond, WA: Microsoft Press, 1999

(An99) Angel, J., "Video Servers Revisited," *Network Magazine,* September 1999, pp. 56-62

(Be99) Behr, A., "Dazzle 'Em Create your Own Digital Video For The Web," *InternetWeek,* August 2, 1999, pg. 36

(Bi99) Bickel, B., "Anatomy of an XML Server," *Web Techniques,* June 1999, pp. 59-64

(Bo99) Booker, E., "Databases Expand in to E-commerce," *InternetWeek,* April 12, 1999, pg. 9

(Br98) Braginski, L. and M. Powell, *Running Microsoft Internet Information Server,* Redmond, WA: Microsoft Press, 1998

(Bs99) Brust, A. J., "ADO 2.5 Embraces the Web," *Visual Basic Programmers Journal,* November 1999, pp. 105-110

(Bt98) Bouthillier, L., "Synchronized Multimedia on the Web," Web Techniques, September 1998, pp. 53-57

(Bu99) Burns, J., *JavaScript Goodies,* Indianapolis, IN: Macmillan Publishing, 1999.

(Ca99) Craig, R., "The Role of XML," *ENT,* May 5, 1999, pp. 38-40

(Cd99) Carr, D. F., "Web Architecture Without the Browser," *Internet World,* April 5, 1999 pg. 15

(Cf99) Coffee, Peter "XML Removes Last Bars To Online Data Archives," PC Week, January 25, 1999, pg. 38

(Ch99) Cohn, M., "An E-commerce E-primer For The E-perplexed," *ComputerWorld,* October 4, 1999, pg. 34

(Cm99) Campbell, B. and R. Darnell, *Teach Yourself Dynamic HTML In a Week,* Indianapolis, IN: Sams.net Publishing, 1999.

(Ct99) Catalano, C., "Networking Hardware," *ComputerWorld,* July 12, 1999, Pg. 66

(Cu99) Cusumano, M., "Mozilla Gambit Reveals Risks of Open Sourcing," *ComputerWorld,* October 18, 1999, pg. 34

(Cx99) Cox, J., T. Cox and E. Heydrick, *Quick Course in Microsoft Explorer 5,* Redmond, WA: Microsoft Press, 1999

(Da99) David, M., "SQL-Based XML Structure Data Access," *Web Techniques,* June 1999, pp. 67-72

(De99) Dell, T., *Dynamic HTML for Webmasters,* San Diego, CA: Academic Press, 1999.

(Di99) Disbrow, S., "Your Own Private Idaho," *Java Report,* April 1999, pp.66-69

(Ds98) De Soto, R., "Creating an Active Internet Presence: A New Alternative," *Telecommunications,* December 1998, pp. 73-75

(Du99) Duncan, A., "All The World's an Auction," *Business Week,* February 8, 1999, pp. 120-123

(Dw99) Dawson, F., "Internet Video Getting Up to Speed," *Inter@ctive Video,* September 6, 1999, pp. 44-48

(Ed98) Eddy, S. E., *XML in Plain English,* Foster City, CA: IDG Books Worldwide, Inc., 1998

(Fa98) Fan, M., J. Stallaert, and B. Whinston, "Creating Electronic Markets," *Dr. Dobb's Journal,* November 1998, pp. 52-56

(Fl98) Flanagan, D., *JavaScipt The Definitive Guide,* Sebastopol, CA: O'Reilly & Associates, Inc., 1998

(Fm98) Fomichev, M., "HTML Help in Distributed Environments," *Dr. Dobb's Journal,* October 1998, pg. 102

(Fo98) Floyd, M., "Extreme Markup," *Web Techniques,* July 1998, pp. 38-41

(Fu99) Fuchs, M., "Why is XML Meant For Java," *Web Techniques,* June 1999, pp. 42-48

(Ga99) Gaskin, J., "XML: user-Friendly Office Format," *Inter@ctive Week,* January 11, 1999

(Ge99) Gerber, C., "Transaction Servers," *ComputerWorld,* May 17, 1999, pg. 90

(Gi99) Gibbs, M., "Making Your Web Pages Active," *Network World,* April 12, 1999, pg. 36

(Gi99a) Gibbs, M., "Getting a Handle on RIFF Audio and Video Formats," *Network World,* August 2, 1999, pg. 32

(Gl98) Goldfarb, C. F. and P. Prescod, *The XML handbook, Upper Saddle River, NJ: Prentice Hall, 1998.*

(Go98a) Goodman, D., *JavaScript Bible*, Foster City, CA: IDG Books Worldwide, Inc., 1998

(Go98b) Goodman, D., *Dynamic HTML,* Sebastopol, CA: O'Reilly & Associates, Inc., 1998

(Gr98) Graham, I. S., *HTML Sourcebook a Complete Guide to HTML 4.0,* New York, NY: John Wiley and Sons, Inc., 1998.

(Ha98) Hall, M., *CORE Web Programming, Upper Saddle River, NJ: Prentice Hall, 1998.*

(Hf99) Hoffman, R., and R. Patt-Corner, "Control Freaks and Java junkies," *Network Computing,* May 17, 1999, pp. 124-126

(Ho98) Holzner, S., *XML Complete,* New York, NY: McGraw-Hill, 1998

(Hu98) Hunter J. and W. Crawford., *Java Servlet Programming,* Sebastopol, CA: O'Reilly & Associates, Inc., 1998

(Hy99) Hayes, F., "Distributed Component Object Model," *ComputerWorld,* February 12, 1999, pg. 73

(Hy99a) Hayes, F., "Common Gateway Interface," *ComputerWorld,* July 19, 1999, pg. 74

(Je98) Jelliffe, R., *The XML & SGML Cookbook, Upper Saddle River, NJ: Prentice Hall, 1998.*

(Ke99) Kepka, A., "Agent Secrets", *ComputerWorld,* January 4, 1999, pg. 23

(La99) Laurie B. and P. Laurie., *Apache The Definitive Guide,* Sebastopol, CA: O'Reilly & Associates, Inc., 1999

(Li99) Lindquist, C., "Personalization," *ComputerWorld,* March 22, 1999, pp. 74-75

(Lv98) Leventhal, M., D. Lewis and M. Fuchs, *Designing XML Internet Applications, Upper Saddle River, NJ: Prentice Hall, 1998*

(Ma98) Mansfield, R. and D. Revette, *Visual Interdev Bible,* Foster City, CA: IDG Books Wordwide, Inc., 1998

(Ma98) McGrath, S., *XML by Example, Upper Saddle River, NJ: Prentice Hall, 1998*

(Md98) Meade, J., Crowder D. and R. Crowder, *Microsoft Dynamic HTML,* Scottsdale, AZ: The Coriolis Group, Inc., 1998

(Me98) Megginson, D., *Structuring XML Documents, Upper Saddle River, NJ: Prentice Hall, 1998*

(Mf99) McFadden, M., "Internet Explorer 5.0: Trading Glitz for a Better UI," *ENT,* May 19, 1999, pg. 42

(Mg99) Morgan, C., "MP3," *ComputerWorld,* May 10, 1999, pg. 76

(Mi99) McCormick, G., "The Boston TV Party," *Mass High Tech Journal,* September 6-12, 1999, pp. 1, 20

(Mj99) Majer, A. and M. Dover., "License to Bill," *New Media,* January 1999, pg. 11

(Mk98) McKendrick, J., "XML Promises to Enrich the Data Experience," *ENT,* October 7, 1998

(Ml99) Mellen, S., "It's Future: Web, Web, More Web," *Mass High Tech Journal,* April 19-25, 1999 pg. 27

(Mn98) Morganthal, J. P., "Enterprise Messaging with XML," *Component Strategies,* May 1999, pp.54-70

(Mo98a) Morris, M. E. S. and J. E. Simpson, *HTML for Fun and Profit,* SunSoft Press, Upper Saddle River, NJ: Prentice Hall, 1998

(Mp99) Murphy, K., "Legislation Seeks to Spell Out Legality of Digital Signatures," *Internet World,* April 12, 1999, pp. 23-25

(Mr99) Murry, W. H. and C. H. Pappas, *JavaScript and HTML 4.0, Upper Saddle River, NJ: Prentice Hall, 1999.*

(Ms99) Moskowitz, R., "The Byways of Digital Certificates," *Network Computing,* May 17 1999, pp. 117-118

(Mu98) Musciano, C. and B. Kennedy, *HTML The Definitive Guide,* Sebastopol, CA: O'Reilly & Associates, Inc., 1998

(My98) Moody, J., "Scripting Your Way to Better Web Pages," *IT/IS BackOffice,* March 1998, pg. 68

(Oe99) Orenstein, D., "Active Server Pages Freed From Platform," *ComputerWorld,* May 24, 1999, pg. 64

(Ou99) Ouellette, T., "Spam," *ComputerWorld,* April 5, 1999, pg. 70

(Ou99a) Ouellette, T., "Digital Wrappers," *ComputerWorld,* April 26, 1999, pg. 79

(Pa99) Papa, J., M. Brown, C. Caison, P. Debatta and E. Wilson, *Professional ADO RDS Programming with ASP*, Birmingham, UK: Wrox Press Ltd., 1999

(Pf98) Pfaffenberger, B. and A. D. Gutzman, *HTML 4 Bible,* Foster City, CA: IDG Books Wordwide, Inc., 1998

(Pl98) Powell, T., L. Jones and D. Cutts, *Web Site Engineering, Upper Saddle River, NJ: Prentice Hall, 1998.*

(Po98) Powell, T. and D. Whitworth, *HTML Programmers Reference,* Berkley, CA: Osborn/ McGraw-Hill, 1998

(Ps99) Ploskina, B., "XML Builds Bridge for Object Developers," *ENT,* January 20, 1999, pg. 14

(Pw99) Powers, S., *Developing ASP Components,* Sebastopol, CA: O'Reilly & Associates, Inc., 1999

(Rt99) Rothman, M., "Public-Key Encryption for Dummies," *Network World,* May 17,1999, pg. 35

(Ru99) Rule, J, *Dynamic HTML the HTML Developer's Guide,* Reading, MA: Addison Wesley Longman, Inc., 1999

(Sa99) Sahu, M., "XML Development in Java," *Web Techniques,* June 1999, p. 51-55

(Sc98) Schwartz, R., "Making a Cookie Jar," *Web Techniques,* December 1998, pp. 28-31

(Sl99) Sliwa, C., "Secure Sockets Layer," *ComputerWorld,* May 31, 1999, pg. 69

(Sm98) Shmuller, J., *Dynamic HTML Master The Essentials,* Alameda, CA: Sybex Press, 1998

(Sp99) Spangler, T., "Racing Toward the Always On Internet," *Inter@ctive Week,* September 6, 1999, Pp. 7-12

(Su99) Sullivan, K., "Digital Certificates Grow Up," *PC Week,* March 1, 1999, pg. 143

(Ta99) Taylor, S., "Ready, Set, Script," *Application Development Trends,* January 1999, pp. 57-59

(Te98) Teague, S., *DHTML for the World Wide Web, Berkeley,* CA: Peachpit Press, 1998

(To99) Toub, S., "How to Design a Table of Contents," *Web Techniques,* February 1999, pp.16-21

(Tu99) Tucker, A., "Using Internet Explorer's HTML Parser," *Dr. Dobbs Journal,* August 1999, Pg. 82

(Vo99) Vonder Harr, S., "Music On the Web is About to Go Live," *Inter@ctive Week,* July 26 1999, pg. 37

(We99) Weissinger, A. K., *ASP in a Nutshell,* Sebastopol, CA: O'Reilly & Associates, Inc., 1999

(Wi98) Williams, A., Barber, K. and P. Newkirk., *Active Server Pages Black Book,* Scottsdale, AZ: The Coriolis Group, Inc., 1998

(Wi99) Witherspoon, C., *Microsoft Internet Explorer 5 Fast & Easy,* Rockilin,CA: Prima Tech Publishing, 1999

(Wn98) Weinman, L., "Fireworks vs. ImageReady," *Web Techniques,* September 1998, pp. 14-18

(Ze98) Zeichick, A., "Lesson 124: XML and XSL" *Network Magazine,* November 1998, pp. 23-24

(Ze99a) Zeichick, A. and L. O'Brien, "Are You Being Web Served?," *Internet Week,* April 12, 1999, pp. 36-42

Index

C

D

E

F

I

L

N

Q

R

S

T

U

V

W

X

Y

Z

End-User License Agreement for Microsoft Software

IMPORTANT-READ CAREFULLY: This Microsoft End-User License Agreement ("EULA") is a legal agreement between you (either an individual or a single entity) and Microsoft Corporation for the Microsoft software products included in this package, which includes computer software and may include associated media, printed materials, and "online" or electronic documentation ("SOFTWARE PRODUCT"). The SOFTWARE PRODUCT also includes any updates and supplements to the original SOFTWARE PRODUCT provided to you by Microsoft. By installing, copying, downloading, accessing or otherwise using the SOFTWARE PRODUCT, you agree to be bound by the terms of this EULA. If you do not agree to the terms of this EULA, do not install, copy, or otherwise use the SOFTWARE PRODUCT.

SOFTWARE PRODUCT LICENSE

The SOFTWARE PRODUCT is protected by copyright laws and international copyright treaties, as well as other intellectual property laws and treaties. The SOFTWARE PRODUCT is licensed, not sold.

1. GRANT OF LICENSE. This EULA grants you the following rights:

   1.1 License Grant. Microsoft grants to you as an individual, a personal nonexclusive license to make and use copies of the SOFTWARE PRODUCT for the sole purposes of evaluating and learning how to use the SOFTWARE PRODUCT, as may be instructed in accompanying publications or documentation. You may install the software on an unlimited number of computers provided that you are the only individual using the SOFTWARE PRODUCT.

   1.2 Academic Use. You must be a "Qualified Educational User" to use the SOFTWARE PRODUCT in the manner described in this section. To determine whether you are a Qualified Educational User, please contact the Microsoft Sales Information Center/One Microsoft Way/Redmond, WA 98052-6399 or the Microsoft subsidiary serving your country. If you are a Qualified Educational User, you may either:

(i) exercise the rights granted in Section 1.1, OR

(ii) if you intend to use the SOFTWARE PRODUCT solely for instructional purposes in connection with a class or other educational program, this EULA grants you the following alternative license models:

(A) Per Computer Model. For every valid license you have acquired for the SOFTWARE PRODUCT, you may install a single copy of the SOFTWARE PRODUCT on a single computer for access and use by an unlimited number of student end users at your educational institution, provided that all such end users comply with all other terms of this EULA, OR

(B) Per License Model. If you have multiple licenses for the SOFTWARE PRODUCT, then at any time you may have as many copies of the SOFTWARE PRODUCT in use as you have licenses, provided that such use is limited to student or faculty end users at your educational institution and provided that all such end users comply with all other terms of this EULA. For purposes of this subsection, the SOFTWARE PRODUCT is "in use" on a computer when it is loaded into the temporary memory (i.e., RAM) or installed into the permanent memory (e.g., hard disk, CD ROM, or other storage device) of that computer, except that a copy installed on a network server for the sole purpose of distribution to other computers is not "in use". If the anticipated number of users of the SOFTWARE PRODUCT will exceed the number of applicable licenses, then you must have a reasonable mechanism or process in place to ensure that the number of persons using the SOFTWARE PRODUCT concurrently does not exceed the number of licenses.

2. DESCRIPTION OF OTHER RIGHTS AND LIMITATIONS.

- Limitations on Reverse Engineering, Decompilation, and Disassembly. You may not reverse engineer, decompile, or disassemble the SOFTWARE PRODUCT, except and only to the extent that such activity is expressly permitted by applicable law notwithstanding this limitation.
- Separation of Components. The SOFTWARE PRODUCT is licensed as a single product. Its component parts may not be separated for use on more than one computer.
- Rental. You may not rent, lease or lend the SOFTWARE PRODUCT.
- Trademarks. This EULA does not grant you any rights in connection with any trademarks or service marks of Microsoft.
- Software Transfer. The initial user of the SOFTWARE PRODUCT may make a one-time permanent transfer of this EULA and SOFTWARE PRODUCT only directly to an end user. This transfer must include all of the SOFTWARE PRODUCT (including all component parts, the media and printed materials, any upgrades, this EULA, and, if applicable, the Certificate of Authenticity). Such transfer may not be by way of consignment or any other indirect transfer. The transferee of such one-time transfer must agree to comply with the terms of this EULA, including the obligation not to further transfer this EULA and SOFTWARE PRODUCT.

- No Support. Microsoft shall have no obligation to provide any product support for the SOFTWARE PRODUCT.
- Termination. Without prejudice to any other rights, Microsoft may terminate this EULA if you fail to comply with the terms and conditions of this EULA. In such event, you must destroy all copies of the SOFTWARE PRODUCT and all of its component parts.

3. COPYRIGHT. All title and intellectual property rights in and to the SOFTWARE PRODUCT (including but not limited to any images, photographs, animations, video, audio, music, text, and "applets" incorporated into the SOFTWARE PRODUCT), the accompanying printed materials, and any copies of the SOFTWARE PRODUCT are owned by Microsoft or its suppliers. All title and intellectual property rights in and to the content which may be accessed through use of the SOFTWARE PRODUCT is the property of the respective content owner and may be protected by applicable copyright or other intellectual property laws and treaties. This EULA grants you no rights to use such content. All rights not expressly granted are reserved by Microsoft.

4. BACKUP COPY. After installation of one copy of the SOFTWARE PRODUCT pursuant to this EULA, you may keep the original media on which the SOFTWARE PRODUCT was provided by Microsoft solely for backup or archival purposes. If the original media is required to use the SOFTWARE PRODUCT on the COMPUTER, you may make one copy of the SOFTWARE PRODUCT solely for backup or archival purposes. Except as expressly provided in this EULA, you may not otherwise make copies of the SOFTWARE PRODUCT or the printed materials accompanying the SOFTWARE PRODUCT.

5. U.S. GOVERNMENT RESTRICTED RIGHTS. The SOFTWARE PRODUCT and documentation are provided with RESTRICTED RIGHTS. Use, duplication, or disclosure by the Government is subject to restrictions as set forth in subparagraph (c)(1)(ii) of the Rights in Technical Data and Computer Software clause at DFARS 252.227-7013 or subparagraphs (c)(1) and (2) of the Commercial Computer Software-Restricted Rights at 48 CFR 52.227-19, as applicable. Manufacturer is Microsoft Corporation/One Microsoft Way/ Redmond, WA 98052-6399.

6. EXPORT RESTRICTIONS. You agree that you will not export or re-export the SOFTWARE PRODUCT, any part thereof, or any process or service that is the direct product of the SOFTWARE PRODUCT (the foregoing collectively referred to as the "Restricted Components"), to any country, person, entity or end user subject to U.S. export restrictions. You specifically agree not to export or re-export any of the Restricted Components (i) to any country to which the U.S. has embargoed or restricted the export of goods or services, which currently include, but are not necessarily limited to Cuba, Iran, Iraq, Libya, North Korea, Sudan and Syria, or to any national of any such country, wherever located, who intends to transmit or transport the Restricted Components back to such country; (ii) to any end-user who you know or have reason to know will utilize the Restricted Components in the design, development or

production of nuclear, chemical or biological weapons; or (iii) to any end-user who has been prohibited from participating in U.S. export transactions by any federal agency of the U.S. government. You warrant and represent that neither the BXA nor any other U.S. federal agency has suspended, revoked, or denied your export privileges.

7. NOTE ON JAVA SUPPORT. THE SOFTWARE PRODUCT MAY CONTAIN SUPPORT FOR PROGRAMS WRITTEN IN JAVA. JAVA TECHNOLOGY IS NOT FAULT TOLERANT AND IS NOT DESIGNED, MANUFACTURED, OR INTENDED FOR USE OR RESALE AS ON-LINE CONTROL EQUIPMENT IN HAZARDOUS ENVIRONMENTS REQUIRING FAIL-SAFE PERFORMANCE, SUCH AS IN THE OPERATION OF NUCLEAR FACILITIES, AIRCRAFT NAVIGATION OR COMMUNICATION SYSTEMS, AIR TRAFFIC CONTROL, DIRECT LIFE SUPPORT MACHINES, OR WEAPONS SYSTEMS, IN WHICH THE FAILURE OF JAVA TECHNOLOGY COULD LEAD DIRECTLY TO DEATH, PERSONAL INJURY, OR SEVERE PHYSICAL OR ENVIRONMENTAL DAMAGE.

MISCELLANEOUS

If you acquired this product in the United States, this EULA is governed by the laws of the State of Washington.

If you acquired this product in Canada, this EULA is governed by the laws of the Province of Ontario, Canada. Each of the parties hereto irrevocably attorns to the jurisdiction of the courts of the Province of Ontario and further agrees to commence any litigation which may arise hereunder in the courts located in the Judicial District of York, Province of Ontario.

If this product was acquired outside the United States, then local law may apply.

Should you have any questions concerning this EULA, or if you desire to contact Microsoft for any reason, please contact

Microsoft, or write: Microsoft Sales Information Center/One Microsoft Way/Redmond, WA 98052-6399.

LIMITED WARRANTY

LIMITED WARRANTY. Microsoft warrants that (a) the SOFTWARE PRODUCT will perform substantially in accordance with the accompanying written materials for a period of ninety (90) days from the date of receipt, and (b) any Support Services provided by Microsoft shall be substantially as described in applicable written materials provided to you by Microsoft, and Microsoft support engineers will make commercially reasonable efforts to solve any problem. To the extent allowed by applicable law, implied warranties on the SOFTWARE PRODUCT, if any, are limited to ninety (90) days. Some states/jurisdictions do not allow limitations on duration of an implied warranty, so the above limitation may not apply to you.

CUSTOMER REMEDIES. Microsoft's and its suppliers' entire liability and your exclusive remedy shall be, at Microsoft's option, either (a) return of the price paid, if any, or (b) repair or replacement of the SOFTWARE PRODUCT that does not meet Microsoft's Limited Warranty and that is returned to Microsoft with a copy of your receipt. This Limited Warranty is void if failure of the SOFTWARE PRODUCT has resulted from accident, abuse, or misapplication. Any replacement SOFTWARE PRODUCT will be warranted for the remainder of the original warranty period or thirty (30) days, whichever is longer. Outside the United States, neither these remedies nor any product support services offered by Microsoft are available without proof of purchase from an authorized international source.

NO OTHER WARRANTIES. TO THE MAXIMUM EXTENT PERMITTED BY APPLICABLE LAW, MICROSOFT AND ITS SUPPLIERS DISCLAIM ALL OTHER WARRANTIES AND CONDITIONS, EITHER EXPRESS OR IMPLIED, INCLUDING, BUT NOT LIMITED TO, IMPLIED WARRANTIES OR CONDITIONS OF MERCHANTABILITY, FITNESS FOR A PARTICULAR PURPOSE, TITLE AND NON-INFRINGEMENT, WITH REGARD TO THE SOFTWARE PRODUCT, AND THE PROVISION OF OR FAILURE TO PROVIDE SUPPORT SERVICES. THIS LIMITED WARRANTY GIVES YOU SPECIFIC LEGAL RIGHTS. YOU MAY HAVE OTHERS, WHICH VARY FROM STATE/JURISDICTION TO STATE/JURISDICTION.

LIMITATION OF LIABILITY. TO THE MAXIMUM EXTENT PERMITTED BY APPLICABLE LAW, IN NO EVENT SHALL MICROSOFT OR ITS SUPPLIERS BE LIABLE FOR ANY SPECIAL, INCIDENTAL, INDIRECT, OR CONSEQUENTIAL DAMAGES WHATSOEVER (INCLUDING, WITHOUT LIMITATION, DAMAGES FOR LOSS OF BUSINESS PROFITS, BUSINESS INTERRUPTION, LOSS OF BUSINESS INFORMATION, OR ANY OTHER PECUNIARY LOSS) ARISING OUT OF THE USE OF OR INABILITY TO USE THE SOFTWARE PRODUCT OR THE FAILURE TO PROVIDE SUPPORT SERVICES, EVEN IF MICROSOFT HAS BEEN ADVISED OF THE POSSIBILITY OF SUCH DAMAGES. IN ANY CASE, MICROSOFT'S ENTIRE LIABILITY UNDER ANY PROVISION OF THIS EULA SHALL BE LIMITED TO THE GREATER OF THE AMOUNT ACTUALLY PAID BY YOU FOR THE SOFTWARE PRODUCT OR U.S.$5.00; PROVIDED, HOWEVER, IF YOU HAVE ENTERED INTO A MICROSOFT SUPPORT SERVICES AGREEMENT, MICROSOFT'S ENTIRE LIABILITY REGARDING SUPPORT SERVICES SHALL BE GOVERNED BY THE TERMS OF THAT AGREEMENT. BECAUSE SOME STATES/JURISDICTIONS DO NOT ALLOW THE EXCLUSION OR LIMITATION OF LIABILITY, THE ABOVE LIMITATION MAY NOT APPLY TO YOU.

0495 Part No. 64358

Jasc End-User License Agreement

Links Disclaimer

The resources that can be accessed with links from jasc.com are not maintained by Jasc Software, Inc. Jasc Software, Inc. is not responsible for the contents of any such resources. The existence of a link should not be assumed as an endorsement by Jasc Software, Inc. of the content of the linked page.

What is an Evaluation Version?

Evaluation versions provide a way to obtain and evaluate software, giving users the opportunity to try a program on their own computer before buying it.

While evaluation versions are copyrighted, and the copyright holder retains all rights, the author specifically grants a user the right to freely evaluate and distribute the program, with limited exceptions.

After using an evaluation version for a defined trial period, the user must purchase a licensed copy or remove the evaluation version from their system.

Jasc Software Licenses, Warranties and Limitation of Warranties:

Jasc Software, Inc. provides the following End-User License Agreements with respect to the software it distributes. An End-User License Agreement is a legal agreement between you (either an individual or a single entity) and Jasc Software, Inc. for a Jasc software product. Such software product includes computer software and may include associated media, printed materials, and "online" or electronic documentation ("SOFTWARE PRODUCT"). By installing, copying, or otherwise using the SOFTWARE PRODUCT, you agree to be bound by the terms of the End-User License Agreement. If you do not agree to the terms of the agreement, do not install or use the SOFTWARE PRODUCT; you may, however, return it to your place of purchase for a full refund.

Evaluation Software

GRANT OF LICENSE. Jasc grants you the following rights with respect to Evaluation Software:

Installation and Use. You may install and use an unlimited number of copies of the SOFTWARE PRODUCT.

Reproduction and Distribution. You may reproduce and distribute an unlimited number of copies of the SOFTWARE PRODUCT; provided that each copy shall be a true and complete copy, including all copyright and trademark notices, and shall be accompanied by a copy of the End-User License Agreement which is provided with the SOFTWARE PRODUCT.

Term. Evaluation software has a term limited to a period of time specified in the documentation provided with the Evaluation software. At the expiration of such term, you no longer are licensed to use or possess the Evaluation Software.

OTHER TERMS. Demo Software is also subject to the rights and limitations listed below under the heading "Additional Terms and Conditions."

Additional Terms and Conditions

DESCRIPTION OF OTHER RIGHTS AND LIMITATIONS.

Limitations on Reverse Engineering, Decompilation, and Disassembly. You may not reverse engineer, decompile, or disassemble the SOFTWARE PRODUCT, except and only to the extent that such activity is expressly permitted by applicable law notwithstanding this limitation.

Separation of Components. The SOFTWARE PRODUCT is licensed as a single product. Its component parts may not be separated for use on more than one computer.

Support Services. Jasc may provide you with support services related to the SOFTWARE PRODUCT ("Support Services"). Use of Support is governed by the Jasc policies and programs described in the user manual, in "online" documentation, and/or in other Jasc-provided materials. Any supplemental software code provided to you as part of the Support Services shall be considered part of the SOFTWARE PRODUCT and subject to the terms and conditions of this End-User License Agreement. With respect to technical information you provide to Jasc as part of the Support Services, Jasc may use such information for its business purposes, including for product support and development. Jasc will not utilize such technical information in a form that personally identifies you.

Software Transfer. You may permanently transfer all of your rights under this End-User License Agreement, provided the recipient agrees to the terms of this End-User License Agreement.

Termination. Without prejudice to any other rights, Jasc may terminate this End-User License Agreement if you fail to comply with the terms and conditions of this End-User License Agreement. In such event, you must destroy all copies of the SOFTWARE PRODUCT and all of its component parts.

COPYRIGHT. All title and copyrights in and to the SOFTWARE PRODUCT (including but not limited to any images, photographs, animations, video, audio, music, text, and "applets" incorporated into the SOFTWARE PRODUCT), the accompanying printed materials, and any copies of the SOFTWARE PRODUCT are owned by Jasc or its suppliers. The SOFTWARE PRODUCT is protected by copyright laws and international treaty provisions. Therefore, you must treat the SOFTWARE PRODUCT like any other copyrighted material except that you may install the SOFTWARE PRODUCT on a single computer provided you keep the original solely for backup or archival purposes.

U.S. GOVERNMENT RESTRICTED RIGHTS. The SOFTWARE PRODUCT and documentation are provided with RESTRICTED RIGHTS. Use, duplication, or disclosure by the Government is subject to restrictions as set forth in subparagraph (c)(1)(ii) of the Rights in Technical Data and Computer Software clause at DFARS 252.227-7013 or subparagraphs (c)(1) and (2) of the Commercial Computer Software-Restricted Rights at 48 CFR 52.227-19, as applicable. Manufacturer is Jasc Software, Inc., PO Box 44997, Eden Prairie MN 55344.

The End-User License Agreement is governed by the laws of the State of Minnesota, USA.

Limited Warranty

NO WARRANTIES. Jasc expressly disclaims any warranty for the SOFTWARE PRODUCT. The SOFTWARE PRODUCT and any related documentation is provided "as is" without warranty of any kind, either express or implied, including, without limitation, the implied warranties or merchantability, fitness for a particular purpose, or noninfringement. The entire risk arising out of use or performance of the SOFTWARE PRODUCT remains with you.

NO LIABILITY FOR DAMAGES. In no event shall Jasc or its suppliers be liable for any damages whatsoever (including, without limitation, damages for loss of business profits, business interruption, loss of business information, or any other pecuniary loss) arising out of the use of or inability to use this Jasc product, even if Jasc has been advised of the possibility of such damages. Because some states/jurisdictions do not allow the exclusion or limitation of liability for consequential or incidental damages, the above limitation may not apply to you.

License Agreement and Limited Warranty

READ THE FOLLOWING TERMS AND CONDITIONS CAREFULLY BEFORE OPENING THIS SOFTWARE PACKAGE. THIS LEGAL DOCUMENT IS AN AGREEMENT BETWEEN YOU AND PRENTICE-HALL, INC. (THE "COMPANY"). BY OPENING THIS SEALED SOFTWARE PACKAGE, YOU ARE AGREEING TO BE BOUND BY THESE TERMS AND CONDITIONS. IF YOU DO NOT AGREE WITH THESE TERMS AND CONDITIONS, DO NOT OPEN THE SOFTWARE PACKAGE. PROMPTLY RETURN THE UNOPENED SOFTWARE PACKAGE AND ALL ACCOMPANYING ITEMS TO THE PLACE YOU OBTAINED THEM FOR A FULL REFUND OF ANY SUMS YOU HAVE PAID.

1. GRANT OF LICENSE: In consideration of your purchase of this book, and your agreement to abide by the terms and conditions of this Agreement, the Company grants to you a nonexclusive right to use and display the copy of the enclosed software program (hereinafter the "SOFTWARE") on a single computer (i.e., with a single CPU) at a single location so long as you comply with the terms of this Agreement. The Company reserves all rights not expressly granted to you under this Agreement.
2. OWNERSHIP OF SOFTWARE: You own only the magnetic or physical media (the enclosed media) on which the SOFTWARE is recorded or fixed, but the Company and the software developers retain all the rights, title, and ownership to the SOFTWARE recorded on the original media copy(ies) and all subsequent copies of the SOFTWARE, regardless of the form or media on which the original or other copies may exist. This license is not a sale of the original SOFTWARE or any copy to you.
3. COPY RESTRICTIONS: This SOFTWARE and the accompanying printed materials and user manual (the "Documentation") are the subject of copyright. The individual programs on the media are copyrighted by the authors of each program. Some of the programs on the media include separate licensing agreements. If you intend to use one of these programs, you must read and follow its accompanying license

agreement. You may not copy the Documentation or the SOFTWARE, except that you may make a single copy of the SOFTWARE for backup or archival purposes only. You may be held legally responsible for any copying or copyright infringement which is caused or encouraged by your failure to abide by the terms of this restriction.

4. USE RESTRICTIONS: You may not network the SOFTWARE or otherwise use it on more than one computer or computer terminal at the same time. You may physically transfer the SOFTWARE from one computer to another provided that the SOFTWARE is used on only one computer at a time. You may not distribute copies of the SOFTWARE or Documentation to others. You may not reverse engineer, disassemble, decompile, modify, adapt, translate, or create derivative works based on the SOFTWARE or the Documentation without the prior written consent of the Company.

5. TRANSFER RESTRICTIONS: The enclosed SOFTWARE is licensed only to you and may not be transferred to any one else without the prior written consent of the Company. Any unauthorized transfer of the SOFTWARE shall result in the immediate termination of this Agreement.

6. TERMINATION: This license is effective until terminated. This license will terminate automatically without notice from the Company and become null and void if you fail to comply with any provisions or limitations of this license. Upon termination, you shall destroy the Documentation and all copies of the SOFTWARE. All provisions of this Agreement as to warranties, limitation of liability, remedies or damages, and our ownership rights shall survive termination.

7. MISCELLANEOUS: This Agreement shall be construed in accordance with the laws of the United States of America and the State of New York and shall benefit the Company, its affiliates, and assignees.

8. LIMITED WARRANTY AND DISCLAIMER OF WARRANTY: The Company warrants that the SOFTWARE, when properly used in accordance with the Documentation, will operate in substantial conformity with the description of the SOFTWARE set forth in the Documentation. The Company does not warrant that the SOFTWARE will meet your requirements or that the operation of the SOFTWARE will be uninterrupted or error-free. The Company warrants that the media on which the SOFTWARE is delivered shall be free from defects in materials and workmanship under normal use for a period of thirty (30) days from the date of your purchase. Your only remedy and the Company's only obligation under these limited warranties is, at the Company's option, return of the warranted item for a refund of any amounts paid by you or replacement of the item. Any replacement of SOFTWARE or media under the warranties shall not extend the original warranty period. The limited warranty set forth above shall not apply to any SOFTWARE which the Company determines in good faith has been subject to misuse, neglect, improper installation, repair, alteration, or damage by you. EXCEPT FOR THE EXPRESSED WARRANTIES SET FORTH ABOVE, THE COMPANY DISCLAIMS ALL WARRANTIES, EXPRESS OR IMPLIED, INCLUDING WITHOUT LIMITATION, THE IMPLIED WARRANTIES OF MERCHANTABILITY AND FITNESS FOR A PARTICULAR PURPOSE. EXCEPT FOR THE EXPRESS WARRANTY SET

FORTH ABOVE, THE COMPANY DOES NOT WARRANT, GUARANTEE, OR MAKE ANY REPRESENTATION REGARDING THE USE OR THE RESULTS OF THE USE OF THE SOFTWARE IN TERMS OF ITS CORRECTNESS, ACCURACY, RELIABILITY, CURRENTNESS, OR OTHERWISE.

IN NO EVENT, SHALL THE COMPANY OR ITS EMPLOYEES, AGENTS, SUPPLIERS, OR CONTRACTORS BE LIABLE FOR ANY INCIDENTAL, INDIRECT, SPECIAL, OR CONSEQUENTIAL DAMAGES ARISING OUT OF OR IN CONNECTION WITH THE LICENSE GRANTED UNDER THIS AGREEMENT, OR FOR LOSS OF USE, LOSS OF DATA, LOSS OF INCOME OR PROFIT, OR OTHER LOSSES, SUSTAINED AS A RESULT OF INJURY TO ANY PERSON, OR LOSS OF OR DAMAGE TO PROPERTY, OR CLAIMS OF THIRD PARTIES, EVEN IF THE COMPANY OR AN AUTHORIZED REPRESENTATIVE OF THE COMPANY HAS BEEN ADVISED OF THE POSSIBILITY OF SUCH DAMAGES. IN NO EVENT SHALL LIABILITY OF THE COMPANY FOR DAMAGES WITH RESPECT TO THE SOFTWARE EXCEED THE AMOUNTS ACTUALLY PAID BY YOU, IF ANY, FOR THE SOFTWARE.

SOME JURISDICTIONS DO NOT ALLOW THE LIMITATION OF IMPLIED WARRANTIES OR LIABILITY FOR INCIDENTAL, INDIRECT, SPECIAL, OR CONSEQUENTIAL DAMAGES, SO THE ABOVE LIMITATIONS MAY NOT ALWAYS APPLY. THE WARRANTIES IN THIS AGREEMENT GIVE YOU SPECIFIC LEGAL RIGHTS AND YOU MAY ALSO HAVE OTHER RIGHTS WHICH VARY IN ACCORDANCE WITH LOCAL LAW.

ACKNOWLEDGMENT

YOU ACKNOWLEDGE THAT YOU HAVE READ THIS AGREEMENT, UNDERSTAND IT, AND AGREE TO BE BOUND BY ITS TERMS AND CONDITIONS. YOU ALSO AGREE THAT THIS AGREEMENT IS THE COMPLETE AND EXCLUSIVE STATEMENT OF THE AGREEMENT BETWEEN YOU AND THE COMPANY AND SUPERSEDES ALL PROPOSALS OR PRIOR AGREEMENTS, ORAL, OR WRITTEN, AND ANY OTHER COMMUNICATIONS BETWEEN YOU AND THE COMPANY OR ANY REPRESENTATIVE OF THE COMPANY RELATING TO THE SUBJECT MATTER OF THIS AGREEMENT.

Should you have any questions concerning this Agreement or if you wish to contact the Company for any reason, please contact in writing at the address below.

Robin Short
Prentice Hall PTR
One Lake Street
Upper Saddle River, New Jersey 07458

The DEITEL & DEITEL Suite of Products...

BOOKS

Visual Basic® 6 How to Program

BOOK / CD-ROM

©1999, 1015pp, Paper Bound w/CD-ROM, 0-13-456955-5

Visual Basic 6 is revolutionizing software development for conventional and Internet/ Intranet-based applications. This new volume in the Deitels' *How to Program* Series — the world's most widely used introductory/intermediate, college-level programming language textbook series — explains Visual Basic 6's extraordinary capabilities. Part of the Deitels' *Visual Studio* Series, this book uses the Deitel's "live-code" approach to cover Internet/ Intranet, World-Wide Web, VBScript, Active X, ADO, multimedia, animation, audio, video, files, database, networking, graphics, strings, data structures, collections, GUI, and control creation. The accompanying CD-ROM contains Microsoft's *Visual Basic 6 Working Model Edition* software, source code and hyperlinks to valuable Visual Basic resources.

Java How to Program Third Edition

BOOK / CD-ROM

©2000, 1200pp, Paper Bound w/CD-ROM, 0-13-012507-5

This edition incorporates Sun Microsystems' latest version of Java, the Java 2 Software Development Kit (J2SDK). The introduction of new functionality in this upgrade has made Java a friendlier and more accessible programming language. Reviewers of the book were unanimous in their praise that the Deitels have made the best use of these enhancements and written the introductory chapters in a very engaging and accessible style. Designed for beginning through intermediate courses, it uses the Deitels' proven "live-code" approach with hundreds of complete working programs, valuable programming tips, more than 16,000 lines of code, and over 1400 interesting and challenging exercises. The graphical user interface examples use Sun's new Swing GUI components. The authors have added significant coverage of JDBC, JavaBeans, RMI, Servlets, Java 2D, Java Media Framework, Collections, Serialization, Inner Classes, and other topics. Includes several examples and projects on multi-tier, client/server systems development.
The CD-ROM contains a complete Java Integrated Development Environment, source code for all examples in the text, and hyperlinks to valuable Java demos and resources on the Internet.

C++ How to Program Second Edition

©1998, 1130pp, Paper, 0-13-528910-6

The world's best-selling introductory/intermediate C++ text, this book focuses on the principles of good software engineering with C++, and stresses program clarity and teaching by example. Revised and updated to cover the latest enhancements to ANSI/ISO C++ and the Standard Template Library (STL), this second edition places a strong emphasis on pedagogy. It uses the Deitels' signature "live-code" approach, presenting every C++ object-oriented programming concept in the context of a complete, working C++ program followed by a screen capture showing the program's output. Includes a rich collection of exercises and valuable insights into common programming errors, as well as software engineering observations, portability tips, and debugging hints.

Internet and World Wide Web How to Program

BOOK / CD-ROM

©2000, 1200pp, Paper bound w/CD-ROM, 0-13-016143-8

The World Wide Web is exploding, and with it the deployment of a new breed of multi-tiered, Web-based applications. This innovative new book in the Deitels' *How to Program Series* presents traditional introductory programming concepts using the new scripting and markup languages of the Web. Now you can teach programming fundamentals "wrapped in the metaphor of the Web." Employing the Deitels' signature "live-code" approach, the book covers markup langauges (HTML, Dynamic HTML), client-side scripting (Javascript), and server-side scripting (VBscript, Active Server Pages). Advanced topics include XML and developing e-commerce applications. Updates are regularly posted to **`www.deitel.com`** and the book includes a CD-ROM with software tools, source code, and live links.

C How to Program Second Edition

©1994, 926pp, Paper, 0-13-226119-7

Among the pedagogical devices featured in this best-selling introductory C text are a thorough use of the structured programming methodology, complete programs and sample outputs to demonstrate key C concepts, objectives and an outline at the beginning of every chapter, and a substantial collection of self-review exercises and answers. *C How to Program* takes the Deitels' "live-code" approach featuring hundreds of complete working ANSI/ISO C programs with thousands of lines of code. The result is a rigorous treatment of both theory and practice, including helpful sections on good programming practices, performance tips, and software engineering observations, portability tips, and common programming errors.

Getting Started with Microsoft Visual C++™ 6 with an Introduction to MFC

©2000, 200pp, Paper, 0-13-016147-0

This exciting new book, developed in cooperation with Microsoft, is intended to be a companion to the ANSI/ISO standard C++ best-selling book, *C++ How to Program, Second Edition.* Learn how to use Microsoft's Visual Studio 6 integrated development environment (IDE) and Visual C++ 6 to create Windows programs using the Microsoft Foundation Classes (MFC). The book includes 17 "live-code" Visual C++/MFC programs with screen captures; dozens of tips; recommended practices and cautions; and exercises accompanying every chapter. Includes coverage of Win32 and console applications; online documentation and Web resources; GUI controls; dialog boxes; graphics; message handling; the resource definition language; and the debugger.

The Complete Java Training Course

Third Edition

BOXED SET

©2000, Boxed Set, 0-13-085247-3

This set includes the book *Java How to Program, Third Edition*, a complete Java Integrated development environment, and a fully interactive *Multimedia Cyber Classroom* CD-ROM that features:

- 200+ complete Java 2 programs with approximately 12,000 lines of fully-tested "live code"
- 1100+ questions and exercises over half of them with answers
- 400+ helpful hints and tips, marked with icons
- Over 8 hours of audio describing key Java concepts and programming techniques
- A browser-based display engine

Runs on Windows 95, 98, and NT 4.0 or higher

The Complete Visual Basic 6 Training Course

BOXED SET

©1999, Boxed Set, 0-13-082929-3

You get the worlds's #1 VB6 interactive *Multimedia Cyber Classroom* CD-ROM plus a worldwide best-selling VB6 book and Microsoft's *VB6 Working Model Software*—ideal for experienced VB5, C/C++ and Java programmers...as well as new programmers interested in VB6's latest features.

- 6+ hours of audio explaining key VB6 concepts
- Hundreds of VB6 programs with thousands of lines of fully-tested code
- Hundreds of interactive programming exercises
- Master ActiveX, objects, TCP/IP networking, VBScript, multimedia, GUIs, data structures, control creation, and more!

Runs on Windows 95, 98, and NT 4.0 or higher

Keep reading for more on Deitel & Associates!

Prentice Hall offers Multimedia Cyber Classroom CD-ROMs to accompany *Java How to Program, Third Edition, C++ How to Program, Second Edition, Internet and World Wide Web How To Program*, and *Visual Basic 6 How to Program*. If you have already purchased one of these books and would like to purchase a stand-alone copy of the corresponding *Multimedia Cyber Classroom* please call:

1-800-811-0912

For **Java Multimedia Cyber Classroom, 3/E**, ask for product number 0-13-014494-0

For **C++ Multimedia Cyber Classroom, 2/E**, ask for product number 0-13-095474-8

For **Internet and World Wide Web Cyber Classroom**, ask for product number 0-13-016842-4

For **Visual Basic 6 Multimedia Cyber Classroom** ask for product number 0-13-083116-6

International Customers: Please contact your local Prentice Hall office to order.

ORDER INFORMATION

SINGLE COPY SALES
Visa, Master Card, American Express, Checks, or Money Orders only
Tel: 515-284-6761 / Fax: 515-284-2607
Toll-Free: 800-811-0912

GOVERNMENT AGENCIES
Prentice Hall Customer Service (#GS-02F-8023A)
Toll-Free: 800-922-0579

COLLEGE PROFESSORS
Desk or Review Copies
Toll-Free: 800-526-0485

CORPORATE ACCOUNTS
Quantity, Bulk Orders totaling 10 or more books. Purchase orders only — No credit cards.
Tel: 201-236-7156 / Fax: 201-236-7141
Toll-Free: 800-382-3419

CANADA
Prentice Hall Canada, Inc.
Tel: 416-293-3621 / Fax: 416-299-2540 (Outside Toronto)
Toll-Free: 800-567-3800
Corp Sales Tel: 416-299-2514

LATIN AMERICA AND U.S. EXPORT SALES OFFICE
Simon & Schuster International
International Customer Service
200 Old Tappan Road
Old Tappan, NJ 07675 USA
Tel.: 201-767-5625 / Fax: 201-767-5625
Latin America Email: leonardo_martinez@prenhall.com
Export Sales Email: laura_rosenzweig@prenhall.com

UNITED KINGDOM, EUROPE, AFRICA & MIDDLE EAST
Pearson Education
128 Long Acre
London WC2E9AN
United Kingdom
Tel: 01-44-0171-447-2000
Fax: 01-44-0171-240-5771
Email: ibd_orders@prenhall.co.uk

JAPAN
Pearson Education
Nishi-Shinjuku, KF Building
8-14-24 Nishi-Shinjuku, Shinjuku-ku
Tokyo, Japan 160-0023
Tel: 81-3-3365-9224 / Fax: 81-3-3365-9225

ASIA—Singapore, Malaysia, Brunei, Indonesia, Thailand, Myanmar, Laos, Cambodia, Vietnam, Philippines, China, Hong Kong, Macau, Taiwan, Korea, India, Sri Lanka
Prentice-Hall (Singapore) Pte Ltd
317 Alexandra Road #04-01,
IKEA Building, Singapore 159965
Tel: 65-476-4688 / Fax: 65-378-0370
Cust Serv: 65-476-4788 / Fax: 65-378-0373
Email: asia@pearsoned.com.sg

AUSTRALIA & NEW ZEALAND
Prentice Hall Australia
Unit 4, Level 2, 14 Aquatic Drive
(Locked Bag 507)
Frenchs Forest NSW 2086 Australia
Tel: 02-9454-2200 / Fax: 02-9453-0117

SOUTH AFRICA
Prentice Hall South Africa Pty Ltd
P. O. Box 12122, Mill Street
8010 Cape Town, South Africa
Tel: 021-686-6356 / Fax: 021-686-4590
Email: prenhall@iafrica.com